This multivolume *History* marks a new beginning in the study of American literature. It embodies the work of a generation of Americanists who have redrawn the boundaries of the field and redefined the terms of its development. The extraordinary growth of the field has called for and here receives a more expansive, more flexible scholarly format. All previous histories of American literature have been either totalizing, offering the magisterial sweep of a single vision, or encyclopedic, composed of a multitude of terse accounts that come to seem just as totalizing and preclude the development of authorial voice. Here, American literary history unfolds through a polyphony of large-scale narratives. Each is ample enough in scope and detail to allow for the elaboration of distinctive views (premises, arguments, and analyses); each is persuasive by demonstration and authoritative in its own right; and each is related to the others through common themes and concerns.

The authors were selected for the excellence of their scholarship and for the significance of the critical communities informing their work. Together, they demonstrate the achievements of Americanist literary criticism over the past three decades. Their contributions to these volumes speak to continuities as well as disruptions between generations and give voice to the wide range of materials now subsumed under the heading of American literature and culture.

This volume is the fullest and richest account of the American renaissance available in any literary history. The narratives offer a fourfold perspective on literature: social, cultural, intellectual, and aesthetic. Michael Davitt Bell describes the social conditions of the literary vocation that shaped the growth of a professional literature in the United States. Eric J. Sundquist draws upon broad cultural patterns: his account of the writings of exploration, the frontier, and slavery is an interweaving of disparate voices, outlooks, and traditions. Barbara L. Packer's sources come largely from intellectual history: the theological and philosophical controversies that prepared the way for Transcendentalism. Jonathan Arac's categories are basically formalist: he sees the development of antebellum fiction as a dialectic of prose genres, the emergence of a literary mode out of the clash of national, local, and personal forms. Together, these four narratives constitute a basic reassessment of American prose writing between 1820 and 1865. It is an achievement that will remain authoritative for our time and that will set new directions for coming decades in American literary scholarship.

THE CAMBRIDGE HISTORY
OF AMERICAN LITERATURE

Volume 2
1820–1865

THE CAMBRIDGE
HISTORY OF
AMERICAN LITERATURE

Volume 2
1820–1865

General Editor

SACVAN BERCOVITCH
Harvard University

Associate Editor

CYRUS R. K. PATELL
New York University

CAMBRIDGE
UNIVERSITY PRESS

Published by the Press Syndicate of the University of Cambridge
The Pitt Building, Trumpington Street, Cambridge CB2 1RP
40 West 20th Street, New York, NY 10011-4211, USA
10 Stamford Road, Oakleigh, Melbourne 3166, Australia

First published 1995
Reprinted 1996

Printed in the United States of America

Library of Congress Cataloging-in-Publication Data is available.

A catalogue record for this book is available from the British Library.

ISBN 0-521-30106-8 hardback

CONTENTS

v

NARRATIVE FORMS   605
Jonathan Arac, University of Pittsburgh

ACKNOWLEDGMENTS

FROM THE GENERAL EDITOR

I would like to thank Harvard University for a grant that enabled the contributors to convene for three days of discussion and planning. I am grateful for the generous assistance of Andrew Brown, Julie Greenblatt, and T. Susan Chang of Cambridge University Press; for the steady support and advice of Daniel Aaron, Eytan Bercovitch, and Susan L. Mizruchi; and for the critical and clerical student help I received from Nancy Bentley, Michael Berthold, Lianna Farber, and Jessica Riskin. My special thanks to Margaret Reid, who helped at every stage.

Sacvan Bercovitch

FROM THE ASSOCIATE EDITOR

I wish to thank Jonathan Arac and David S. Shields for special assistance with the chronologies for volumes one and two; Pamela Bruton and Susan Greenberg for their meticulous copyediting; Katharita Lamoza for her patient and expert supervision of the production process; Julie Greenblatt and T. Susan Chang for their invaluable help through the various stages of this project; and Elizabeth Fowler for her constant moral support and good advice.

Cyrus R. K. Patell

CONDITIONS OF LITERARY VOCATION

I wish to thank the National Endowment for the Humanities for a 1986 Summer Stipend, and Williams College for a sabbatical leave in the fall of that year; their support freed up crucial time for researching and writing much of my contribution to this volume. I am also grateful to the staff of the Williams College Library for their rapid processing of interlibrary loan requests. I have tried to indicate my debts to other scholars in the body of my section and in my contributions to this volume's bibliography, but I am particularly indebted to Perry Miller, who first introduced me to many of the books and authors I discuss, and to the writings of William Charvat, particularly to the essays, finished and unfinished, collected posthumously as *The Profession of Authorship in America, 1800–1870.*

Michael Davitt Bell

THE LITERATURE OF EXPANSION AND RACE

I would like to acknowledge the assistance of a Humanities Research Fellowship provided by the University of California at Berkeley and the help of the staff at the Bancroft Library at Berkeley. For his advice on the whole I am grateful to Sacvan Bercovitch, and for comments on other portions of the manuscript I would like to thank Paula Gunn Allen, Richard Bridgman, Norman Grabo, and Kenneth Lincoln. In addition, I would like to acknowledge the indispensable help of Andrew Brown, Cyrus Patell, Julie Greenblatt, and T. Susan Chang.

I have benefited from numerous secondary sources, but I would like to single out the following: Henry Nash Smith, *Virgin Land: The American West as Symbol and Myth* (Cambridge, Mass.: Harvard University Press, 1950); Roy Harvey Pearce, *Savagism and Civilization: A Study of the Indian and the American Mind,* rev. ed. (Baltimore: The Johns Hopkins University Press, 1965); William H. Goetzmann, *Exploration and Empire: The Explorer and the Scientist in the Winning of the American West* (New York: Norton, 1966); Richard Slotkin, *Regeneration Through Violence: The Mythology of the American Frontier, 1600–1860* (Middletown, Conn.: Wesleyan University Press, 1973); Eugene D. Genovese, *Roll, Jordan, Roll: The World the Slaves Made* (New York: Pantheon, 1974); and Reginald Horsman, *Race and Manifest Destiny: The Origins of American Racial Anglo-Saxonism* (Cambridge, Mass.: Harvard University Press, 1981).

Parts of the material on African American slavery had their origin in a paper presented at the English Institute in 1983 and published as "Slavery, Revolution, and the American Renaissance," in Walter Benn Michaels and Donald Pease, eds., *The American Renaissance Reconsidered* (Baltimore: The Johns Hopkins University Press, 1985), pp. 1–33, and some passages have been incorporated into my book *To Wake the Nations: Race in the Making of American Literature* (Cambridge, Mass.: Harvard University Press, 1993). A section of the chapter on American Indians has appeared as "The Indian Gallery: Antebellum Literature and the Containment of the American Indian," Beverly Voloshin, ed., *American Literature, Culture, and Ideology: Essays in Memory of Henry Nash Smith* (New York: Peter Lang, 1990), pp. 37–64.

The quotation from Mariano Vallejo's *Recuerdos históricos y personales tocante a la Alta California* that opens the section on the literature of expansion is taken from the translation by Earl R. Hewitt held in the Bancroft Library.

The version of "El corrido de Gregorio Cortez" is taken from Américo Paredes, *With His Pistol in His Hand: A Border Ballad and Its Hero* (Austin: University of Texas Press, 1958). For quoted material in the section on American Indian oral tradition and oratory, I am indebted to a number of secondary works. Some quotations appear in more than one of the following sources, in varying translations, or in antebellum works cited in the text; the modern collections cited here reprint or adapt material from nineteenth- or early twentieth-century sources. The oratory of Red Jacket and Speckled Snake appears in Samuel G. Drake, *Biography and History of the Indians of North America* (Boston: B. B. Mussey, 1851); the account of White Antelope's lyric appears in George Bird Grinnell, *The Fighting Cheyenne* (1915; rpt., Norman: University of Oklahoma Press, 1956); the Pawnee creation story appears in Natalie Curtis Burlin, *The Indian's Book* (New York: Harper and Brothers, 1923); the song of the black bear, appearing first in Pliny Earle Goddard, *Navajo Texts: Anthropological Papers of the American Museum of Natural History* (vol. 34, New York, 1933), the song of the maize, appearing first in Francis LaFlésche, *The Osage Tribe: The Rite of Vigil* (39th Annual Report of the Bureau of American Ethnology, Washington, 1925), and the Mescalero Apache puberty song, appearing first in Pliny Earle Goddard, *Gotal: A Mescalero Apache Ceremony* (New York: Stechert, 1909), are included in Margot Astrov, ed., *The Winged Serpent* (New York: John Day, 1946; rpt. by Capricorn Books as *American Indian Prose and Poetry* in 1962 and again by Beacon Press as *The Winged Serpent: American Indian Prose and Poetry* in 1992); the oratory of Ten Bears, Petalesharo, Hinmaton Yalakit, and Little Crow appears in W. C. Vanderwerth, ed., *Indian Oratory* (Norman: University of Oklahoma Press, 1971); the oration of Seathl (Seattle) and the death song of Red Bird appear in Thomas E. Sanders and William E. Peek, eds., *Literature of the American Indian* (New York: Glencoe, 1973); and the Cherokee and Luiseno creation stories, as well as the Navajo night chant, appear in Gloria Levitas, Frank Vivelo, and Jaqueline Vivelo, eds., *American Indian Prose and Poetry: We Wait in the Darkness* (New York: G.P. Putnam's Sons, 1974).

Eric J. Sundquist

THE TRANSCENDENTALISTS

I should like to thank the Committee on Research of the UCLA Academic Senate for grants supporting this project. A fellowship year at the Center for Advanced Study in the Behavioral Sciences at Stanford gave me time to begin the work, and sabbatical leave from the University of California, Los Angeles, enabled me to complete it. I am grateful to Dean Grodzins, Gary Hall, and Robert Perrin for allowing me to read their unpublished studies of

Theodore Parker, Emerson, and Daniel Webster. Michael Colacurcio and
Dean Grodzins read parts of the manuscript and offered valuable advice.
Several talented research assistants – Sybil Brabner, Deanne Lundin, and
Mary Flory – helped me at different times during the writing of the chapter.
Three debts are especially great. My husband, Paul Sheats, gave me encouragement and intellectual companionship throughout the long process of
writing; my colleague Daniel Calder gave me invaluable assistance in getting
the project off the ground; and my patient editor at Cambridge University
Press, T. Susan Chang, gave a kind of support few editors are called upon to
give. Finally, I thank Sacvan Bercovitch for inviting me to participate in this
collective project and for offering wise advice at every stage of composition,
and Cyrus Patell, who offered fellowship as well as assistance with communications and bibliographies.

In attempting to construct a narrative account of Transcendentalist writings I have incurred more intellectual debts than I can hope to acknowledge
adequately. The list below is designed chiefly to direct readers to the sources
of the many quotations, facts, and interpretations that I have used or been
influenced by. Many books, particularly the biographies of individual Transcendentalists, have furnished material for more than one chapter, but they
are mentioned only the first time they are cited.

"Unitarian Beginnings" draws upon the work of scholars who have studied the
religious and philosophical debates that agitated New England in the early
decades of the nineteenth century and the foreign developments in criticism of
ancient literary and Biblical texts that were beginning to alter the very notion
of textual authority. These include Lewis P. Simpson, *The Federalist Literary
Mind: Selections from the "Monthly Anthology and Boston Review," 1803–11* (Baton
Rouge: Louisiana State University Press, 1962); James King Morse, *Jedediah
Morse: A Champion of New England Orthodoxy* (New York: Columbia University
Press, 1939); Conrad Wright, "The Election of Henry Ware: Two Contemporary Accounts, Edited with Commentary," *Harvard Library Bulletin* 17 (1969):
245–78; Andrew Delbanco, *William Ellery Channing: An Essay on the Liberal
Spirit in America* (Cambridge, Mass: Harvard University Press, 1981); Conrad
Wright, *The Beginnings of Unitarianism in America* (Boston: Starr King Press,
1955); *Three Prophets of Religious Liberalism: Channing, Parker, Emerson*, introduced by Conrad Wright (Boston: Beacon, 1961); Lilian Handlin, "*Babylon est
delenda* – the Young Andrews Norton," in *American Unitarianism 1805–1865*,
ed. Conrad Edick Wright (Boston: The Massachusetts Historical Society and
Northeastern University Press, 1989); Joseph Henry Allen, *Our Liberal Movement in Theology* (Boston: Roberts Brothers, 1882); John Locke, *Essay Concerning Human Understanding*, ed. Alexander Campbell Fraser (2 vols., 1894; rpt.

New York: Dover, 1959); John Locke, *The Reasonableness of Christianity, with A Discourse of Miracles, and Part of A Third Letter Concerning Toleration,* edited, abridged, and introduced by I.T. Ramsey (Stanford, Calif.: Stanford University Press, 1958); Paul Revere Frothingham, *Edward Everett, Orator and Statesman* (Boston: Houghton, Mifflin, 1925); Daniel Walker Howe, *The Unitarian Conscience: Harvard Moral Philosophy 1805–1861* (2nd. ed, rev., with a new intro., Middletown, Conn.: Wesleyan University Press, 1988); Daniel Walker Howe, "The Cambridge Platonists of Old England and the Cambridge Platonists of New England," in Wright, *American Unitarianism;* Merrell Davis, "Emerson's 'Reason' and the Scottish Philosophers," *New England Quarterly* 17 (1944): 209–28; David Fate Norton, *David Hume: Commonsense Moralist, Sceptical Metaphysician* (Princeton: Princeton University Press, 1982); Edgely Woodman Todd, "Philosophical Ideas at Harvard College, 1817–1837," *New England Quarterly* 16 (1943): 63–90; Linda Kerber, *Federalists in Dissent: Imagery and Ideology in Jeffersonian America* (Ithaca, N.Y.: Cornell University Press, 1970); Carl Diehl, *Americans and German Scholarship 1770–1870* (New Haven: Yale University Press, 1978); F.A. Wolf, *Prolegomena to Homer* (1795), trans., with an introduction and notes by Anthony Grafton, Glenn W. Most, and James E. G. Zetzel (Princeton: Princeton University Press, 1985); Lawrence Buell, "Joseph Stevens Buckminster: The Making of a New England Saint," *Canadian Review of American Studies* 10 (1979): 1–29; Jerry Wayne Brown, *The Rise of Biblical Criticism in America 1800–1870* (Middletown, Conn.: Wesleyan University Press, 1969); Elisabeth Hurth, "Sowing the Seeds of 'Subversion': Harvard's Early Göttingen Students," *Studies in the American Renaissance* (1992): 91–105; James Freeman Clarke, *Autobiography, Diary, and Correspondences,* ed. Edward Everett Hale (Boston and New York: Houghton, Mifflin, 1891).

"The Assault on Locke" examines American discontent with the tradition of empirical philosophy and the various routes by which news of Kantian and post-Kantian philosophy began to reach the United States. Sources for this section include Frederick Rudolph, *Curriculum: A History of the American Undergraduate Course of Study since 1636* (San Francisco: Jossey-Bass, 1989); Ronald Vale Wells, *Three Christian Transcendentalists* (New York: Columbia University Press, 1943); J. Christopher Herold, *Mistress to an Age: A Life of Madame de Stael* (New York: Harmony Books, 1979); John J. Duffy, ed., *Coleridge's American Disciples: The Selected Correspondence of James Marsh* (Amherst: University of Massachusetts Press, 1973); Joseph Torrey, ed., *The Remains of the Rev. James Marsh, D.D . . . with a Memoir of His Life* (Boston: Crocker and Brewster, 1843); John J. Duffy, "Problems in Publishing Coleridge: James Marsh's First American Edition of *Aids to Reflection,*" *New England Quarterly* 43 (1970): 193–208; John Clive, *Scotch Reviewers: The "Edin-*

burgh Review," 1802–1815 (Cambridge, Mass.: Harvard University Press,
1957); Joseph Henry Allen, *Sequel to "Our Liberal Movement"* (Boston: Roberts
Brothers, 1897); Lawrence Buell, *Literary Transcendentalism: Style and Vision
in the American Renaissance* (Ithaca, N.Y.: Cornell University Press, 1973);
Conrad Wright, "Rational Religion in 18th Century America," in *The Liberal
Christians: Essays on American Unitarian History* (Boston: Beacon, 1970);
Ralph L. Rusk, *The Life of Ralph Waldo Emerson* (New York: Columbia
University Press, 1949); Gay Wilson Allen, *Waldo Emerson: A Biography*
(New York: Viking, 1981).

"Carlyle and the Beginnings of American Transcendentalism" investigates
Carlyle's influence upon the young Boston intellectuals who read his anonymous but immediately recognizable articles in British periodicals of the
1820s and early 1830s. Sources for this section include Rene Wellek, "Carlyle and German Romanticism" and "The Minor Transcendentalists and German Philosophy," in *Confrontations: Studies in the Intellectual and Literary Relations between Germany, England, and the United States during the Nineteenth
Century* (Princeton: Princeton University Press, 1965); William Silas Vance,
"Carlyle in America Before Sartor Resartus," *American Literature* 7 (1936):
363–75; Joseph Slater, "George Ripley and Thomas Carlyle," *PMLA* 67
(1952): 341–9; James Freeman Clarke, *The Letters of James Freeman Clarke to
Margaret Fuller,* ed. John Wesley Thomas (Hamburg: Cram, de Gruyter,
1957); Mary C. Turpie, "A Quaker Source for Emerson's Sermon on the
Lord's Supper," *New England Quarterly* 17 (1944): 95–101; Karen Lynn
Kalinevitch, "Ralph Waldo Emerson's Older Brother: The Letters and Journal of William Emerson," Ph.D. dissertation, University of Tennessee, 1982;
Joseph Slater, ed., *The Correspondence of Emerson and Carlyle* (New York: Co-
lumbia University Press, 1964); Arthur S. Bolster, Jr., *James Freeman Clarke:
Disciple to Advancing Truth* (Boston: Beacon, 1954).

"Annus Mirabilis" surveys the outpouring of books, orations, and pamphlets in
the year of Transcendentalism's emergence into public prominence. It draws
upon the following sources: Perry Miller, *The Transcendentalists: An Anthology*
(Cambridge, Mass.: Harvard University Press, 1950); Octavius Brooks
Frothingham, *Boston Unitarianism 1820–1850* (New York: Putnam's, 1890);
Joel Myerson, "Convers Francis and Emerson," *American Literature* 50 (1978):
17–36; Joel Myerson, "A History of the Transcendental Club," *Emerson Society
Quarterly* 23 (1977): 27–35; Joel Myerson, "A Calendar of Transcendental
Club Meetings," *American Literature* 44 (1972): 197–207; Stephen Whicher,
Freedom and Fate: An Inner Life of Ralph Waldo Emerson (Philadelphia: University
of Pennsylvania Press, 1953); Sherman Paul, *Emerson's Angle of Vision* (Cam-

bridge, Mass.: Harvard University Press, 1952); Merton M. Sealts, Jr., "The Composition of *Nature*," in Merton M. Sealts and Alfred R. Ferguson, eds., *Emerson's "Nature": Origin, Growth, Meaning* (2nd. ed., enlarged, Carbondale: Southern Illinois University Press, 1979); Frederick C. Dahlstrand, *Amos Bronson Alcott: An Intellectual Biography* (East Brunswick, N.J.: Fairleigh Dickinson University Press, 1982); Arthur M. Schlesinger, Jr., *A Pilgrim's Progress: Orestes A. Brownson* (Boston: Little, Brown, 1966); Charles Crowe, *George Ripley: Transcendentalist and Utopian Socialist* (Athens: University of Georgia Press, 1967); William Hutchison, *The Transcendentalist Ministers: Church Reform in the New England Renaissance* (New Haven, Conn., Yale University Press, 1959); Nina Baym, "The Ann Sisters: Elizabeth Peabody's Millennial Historicism," *American Literary History* 3 (1991): 27–45; Josephine E. Roberts, "Elizabeth Peabody and the Temple School," New England Quarterly 15 (1942): 497–508; *The Letters of Elizabeth Palmer Peabody: American Renaissance Woman*, edited, with an introduction by Bruce A. Ronda (Middletown, Conn.: Wesleyan University Press, 1984).

"The Establishment and the Movement" traces the beginnings of the open war between the conservative forces within Unitarianism and the Transcendentalists, who were increasingly impatient with the slow pace of religious and political reform in a society weakened by economic depression. Sources for the section include William Charvat, "American Romanticism and the Depression of 1837," *Science and Society* 2 (1937): 67–82; Harriet Martineau, *Retrospect of Western Travel* (2 vols., London: Saunders & Otley, 1838); John Jay Chapman, *William Lloyd Garrison* (1913; 2nd ed., rev., Boston: Atlantic Monthly Press, 1921); Edwin Gittleman, *Jones Very: The Effective Years 1833–1840* (New York: Columbia University Press, 1967); Helen R. Deese, "The Peabody Family and the Jones Very 'Insanity': Two Letters of Mary Peabody," *Harvard Library Bulletin* 35 (1987): 218–29; Conrad Wright, "Emerson, Barzillai Frost, and 'The Divinity School Address,' " in *The Liberal Christians;* Gary Hall, "Emerson and the Bible: Transcendentalism as Scriptural Interpretation and Revision," Ph.D. dissertation, University of California, Los Angeles, 1989; Michael Colacurcio, "The Lucid Strife of Emerson's 'Address,' " *ESQ* 37 (1991): 141–212; Robert Habich, "Emerson's Reluctant Foe: Andrews Norton and the Transcendental Controversy," *New England Quarterly* 65 (1992): 208–37; Henry Steele Commager, "The Blasphemy of Abner Kneeland," *New England Quarterly* 8 (1935): 29–41; Roderick S. French, "Liberation from Man and God in Boston: Abner Kneeland's Freethought Campaign 1830–1839," *American Quarerly* 32 (1980): 202–21; Robert E. Burkholder, "Emerson, Kneeland, and the Divinity School Address," *American Literature* 58 (1986): 1–14; Clarence L. F. Gohdes, *The*

Periodicals of American Transcendentalism (Durham, N.C.: Duke University Press, 1931); Elizabeth R. McKinsey, *The Western Experiment: New England Transcendentalists in the Ohio Valley* (Cambridge, Mass.: Harvard University Press, 1973); Dean David Grodzins. "Theodore Parker and Transcendentalism," Ph.D. dissertation, Harvard University, 1993; John W. Rogerson, *W. M. L. de Wette, Founder of Modern Biblical Criticism: An Intellectual Biography* (Sheffield, U.K.: Journal for the Study of the Old Testament Press, 1992); Siegfied B. Puknat, "De Wette in New England," *Proceedings of the American Philosophical Society* 102 (1958): 376–95; Perry Miller, "Theodore Parker: Apostasy within Liberalism," *Harvard Theological Review* 54 (1961): 275–95; Philip F. Gura, "Theodore Parker and the South Boston Ordination: The Textual Tangle of a Discourse on the Transient and Permanent in Christianity," *Studies in the American Renaissance* (1988); 149–78; Dean Grodzins, "The Transient and Permanent in Theodore Parker's Christianity, 1832–1841," *Proceedings of the Unitarian Universalist Historical Society* 22, part 1 (1990–91): 1–18; James Martineau, "Strauss and Parker," *The Westminster and Foreign Quarterly Review* 47 (1847): 136–74.

"Letters and Social Aims" examines the growth of Transcendentalism from a church reform movement into a movement with wider ambitions. Desire to find places to publish without censorship led several of the Transcendentalists to found magazines of their own; these magazines in turn had important effects upon the development of Transcendentalist prose. Sources for the section include Joel Myerson, *The New England Transcendentalists and the "Dial": A History of the Magazine and its Contributors* (London: Associated University Presses, 1980); Charles Blackburn, "Some New Light on the *Western Messenger,*" *American Literature* 26 (1954): 320–36; David Robinson, "The Political Odyssey of William Henry Channing," *American Quarterly* 34 (1982): 165–84; Carl F. Strauch, "Hatred's Swift Repulsions: Emerson, Margaret Fuller, and Others," *Studies in Romanticism* 7 (1968): 65–103; Charles Capper, *Margaret Fuller: An American Romantic Life, Vol. 1: The Private Years* (New York: Oxford University Press, 1992); Julie Ellison, *Delicate Subjects: Romanticism, Gender, and the Ethics of Understanding* (Ithaca, N.Y., Cornell University Press, 1990); Joel Myerson, "Frederic Henry Hedge and the Failure of Transcendentalism," *Harvard Library Bulletin* 23 (1975): 396–410; Bernard Rosenthal, "*The Dial,* Transcendentalism, and Margaret Fuller," *English Language Notes* 8 (1970); 28–36; Helen Hennessey, "The *Dial:* Its Poetry and Poetic Criticism," *New England Quarterly* 31 (1958): 66–87; Robert Richardson, Jr., *Henry Thoreau: A Life of the Mind* (Berkeley and Los Angeles: University of California Press, 1986); Sherman Paul, *The Shores of America: Thoreau's Inward Exploration* (Urbana: University of Illinois Press,

1958); Richard Lebeaux, *Young Man Thoreau* (Amherst: University of Massachusetts Press, 1977); Walter Harding, *The Days of Henry Thoreau* (New York: Knopf, 1966); Raymond R. Borst, *The Thoreau Log: A Documentary Life of Henry David Thoreau 1817–1862* (New York: G.K. Hall, 1992); Robert Sattelmeyer, *Thoreau's Reading: A Study in Intellectual History with Bibliographical Catalogue* (Princeton: Princeton University Press, 1988); James McIntosh, *Thoreau as a Romantic Naturalist: His Shifting Stance toward Nature* (Ithaca, N.Y.: Cornell University Press, 1974); Robert Sattelmeyer, "Thoreau's Projected Work on the English Poets," *Studies in the American Renaissance* (1980): 239–57.

"The Hope of Reform" chronicles the aspirations and defeats of a group of Transcendentalists who were determined to put their theories about the just society into practice by founding associations designed to abolish misery and restore social harmony. Sources for this section include Ellen Tucker Emerson, *The Life of Lidian Jackson Emerson,* ed. Delores Bird Carpenter (Boston: Twayne Publishers, 1980); Carl J. Guarneri, *The Utopian Alternative: Fourierism in Nineteenth-Century America* (Ithaca, N.Y.: Cornell University Press, 1991); Octavius Brooks Frothingham, *George Ripley* (Boston: Houghton, Mifflin, 1882); Henry Sams, *Autobiography of Brook Farm,* (Englewood Cliffs, N.J.: Prentice-Hall, 1958); John McAleer, *Ralph Waldo Emerson: Days of Encounter* (Boston: Little, Brown, 1984); Maurice Gonnaud, *An Uneasy Solitude: Individual and Society in the Work of Ralph Waldo Emerson,* trans. Lawrence Rosenwald (Princeton: Princeton University Press, 1987); Richard Lee Francis, "Circumstances and Salvation: The Ideology of the Fruitlands Utopia," *American Quarterly* 25 (1975): 202–34; Horace Greeley, *Recollections of a Busy Life* (New York: J.B. Ford, 1868); Marianne Dwight Orvis, *Letters from Brook Farm 1844–1847,* ed. Amy L. Reed (Poughkeepsie, N.Y.: Vassar College, 1928); John Codman, *Brook Farm: Historic and Personal Memoirs* (Boston: Arena Publishing Company, 1894); Linck C. Johnson, "Reforming the Reformers: Emerson, Thoreau, and the Sunday Lectures at Amory Hall, Boston," *ESQ* 37 (1991): 235–89.

"Diaspora" follows the Transcendentalists as they diverge on paths of their own, some to become professional writers and lecturers, others to become social reformers or journalists, some to find new forms of church organization or to embrace new religions, some to become involved in foreign revolutions. Sources for the section include Guy R. Woodall, "Convers Francis, The Transcendentalists, and the Boston Association of Ministers," *Unitarian Universalist Historical Society Proceedings* 21 (1989): 41–8; Joel Myerson, "Convers Francis and Emerson," *American Literature* 50 (1978): 17–36; Guy R.

Woodall, "The Record of a Friendship: The Letters of Convers Francis to Frederic Henry Hedge in Bangor and Providence, 1835–1850," *Studies in the American Renaissance* (1991): 1–57; Larry Reynolds, *European Revolutions and the American Literary Renaissance* (New Haven, Conn.: Yale University Press, 1988); Richard Bridgman, *Dark Thoreau* (Lincoln: University of Nebraska Press, 1981); Linck C. Johnson, *Thoreau's Complex Weave: The Writing of "A Week on the Concord and Merrimack Rivers" with the text of the First Draft* (Charlottesville, Va.: University Press of Virginia, 1986); Carl F. Hovde, "Nature into Art: Thoreau's Use of His Journals in a Week," *American Literature* 30 (May 1958): 165–84; Lewis Perry, *Radical Abolitionism: Anarchy and the Government of God in Antislavery Thought* (Ithaca, N.Y.: Cornell University Press, 1973); James Brewer Stewart, *Wendell Phillips: Liberty's Hero* (Baton Rouge, La.: Lousiana State University Press, 1986); John C. Broderick, "Thoreau, Alcott, and the Poll Tax," *Studies in Philology* 53 (1956): 612–26; Raymond Adams, "Thoreau's Sources for 'Resistance to Civil Government,' " *Studies in Philology* 42 (1945): 640–53; Lawrence Buell, *New England Literary Culture: From Revolution through Renaissance* (Cambridge University Press, 1986); Stephen Fink, *Prophet in the Marketplace: Thoreau's Development as a Professional Writer* (Princeton, N.J.: Princeton University Press, 1992); Robert Sattelmeyer, " 'When He Became My Enemy': Emerson and Thoreau, 1848–49," *New England Quarterly* (1984): 187–204; Henry James, *William Wetmore Story and His Friends* (2 vols., Boston: Houghton, Mifflin, 1903); Ednah Dow Cheney, *Reminiscences of Ednah Dow Cheney* (Boston: Lee & Shepard, 1902); Robert Habich, "Margaret Fuller's Journal for October 1842," *Harvard Library Bulletin* 33 (1985): 280–91; Stephen Adams, "That Tidiness We Always Look for in Woman: Fuller's *Summer on the Lakes* and Romantic Aesthetics," *Studies in the American Renaissance* (1987): 247–64; Ann Douglas, "Margaret Fuller and the Search for History: A Biographical Study," *Women's Studies* 4 (1976): 37–86; Albert J. von Frank, "Life as Art in America: The Case of Margaret Fuller," *Studies in the American Renaissance* (1981):1–26; David Robinson, "Margaret Fuller and the Transcendental Ethos: *Woman in the Nineteenth Century*," *PMLA* 97 (1982): 83–98; Jeffrey Steele, *The Representation of the Self in the American Renaissance* (Chapel Hill: University of North Carolina Press, 1987); Paula Kopacs, "Feminist at the Tribune: Margaret Fuller as a Professional Writer," *Studies in the American Renaissance* (1991): 119–39; Bell Gale Chevigny, "To the Edges of Ideology: Margaret Fuller's Centrifugal Evolution," *American Quarterly* 38 (1986): 173–201; Joseph Jay Deiss, *The Roman Years of Margaret Fuller* (New York: Thomas Y. Crowell, 1969); Margaret Fuller, *"These Sad But Glorious Days"*; *Dispatches from Europe, 1846–1850,* ed. Larry J. Reynolds and Susan Belasco Smith (New Haven, Conn.: Yale University Press, 1991); Mary Caroline Crawford, *Romantic Days in Old Boston: The Story of the City and of Its People During the Nineteenth Century* (Boston: Little, Brown, 1910).

"The Antislavery Years" traces the growing involvement of the Transcendentalists in the antislavery movement in the years between the passage of the Fugitive Slave Law of 1850 and President Lincoln's Preliminary Emancipation Proclamation of 1862. Sources for this section include David M. Potter, *The Impending Crisis 1848–1861,* completed and edited by Don Fehrenbacher (New York: Harper and Row, 1976); Len Gougeon, *Virtue's Hero: Emerson, Antislavery, and Reform* (Athens: University of Georgia Press, 1990); Maurice G. Baxter, *One and Inseparable: Daniel Webster and the Union* (Cambridge, Mass.: Harvard University Press, 1984); Allan Nevins, *Ordeal of the Union* (New York: Scribner's, 1947); Robert Perrin, "Power and Probity: Emerson's Perceptions of Daniel Webster," M.A. thesis, University of California, Los Angeles, 1993; Samuel Shapiro, "The Rendition of Anthony Burns," *The Journal of Negro History* 44 (1959): 34–51; Thomas Wentworth Higginson, *Cheerful Yesterdays* (Boston: Houghton, Mifflin, 1898); Barry Kritzberg, "Thoreau, Slavery, and Resistance to Civil Government," *The Massachusetts Review* 30 (1989): 535–65; David Herbert Donald, *Charles Sumner and the Coming of the Civil War* (New York: Knopf, 1960); George H. Haynes, "A Know-Nothing Legislature," *Annual Report of the American Historical Association* 1 (1896): 177–197; David Robinson, *Emerson and the Conduct of Life: Pragmatism and Ethical Purpose in the Later Work* (Cambridge University Press, 1993); Philip Nicoloff, *Emerson on Race and History: An Examination of "English Traits"* (New York: Columbia University Press, 1961); Sharon Cameron, *Writing Nature: Henry Thoreau's Journal* (New York: Oxford University Press, 1985); J. Lyndon Shanley, *The Making of "Walden," with the text of the first version* (Chicago: University of Chicago Press, 1957); Leonard N. Neufeldt, *The Economist: Henry Thoreau and Enterprise* (New York: Oxford University Press, 1989); James Armstrong, "Thoreau, Chastity, and the Reformers," in *Thoreau's Psychology: Eight Essays,* ed. Raymond Gozzi (Lanham, Md.: University Press of America, 1983); Walter Harding, "A Check List of Thoreau's Lectures," *Bulletin of the New York Public Library* 52 (1948): 78–87; William L. Howarth, "Successor to *Walden?* Thoreau's 'Moonlight – An Intended Course of Lectures,' " *Proof* 2 (1972): 89–113; Bradley P. Dean, "Reconstruction of Thoreau's Early 'Life Without Principle' Lectures," *Studies in the American Renaissance* (1987): 285–364; Leonard Newfeldt, "The Severity of the Ideal: Emerson's 'Thoreau,' " *Emerson Society Quarterly* 58 (1970): 77–84; Joel Myerson, "Emerson's 'Thoreau': A New Edition from the Manuscript," *Studies in the American Renaissance* (1979): 17–92.

Barbara L. Packer

NARRATIVE FORMS

I am grateful for the support of the institutions I have served while working on this project: the University of Illinois at Chicago, Duke University, Columbia University, and the University of Pittsburgh. A Fellowship from the National Endowment for the Humanities in 1986–87 allowed necessary time for reading and starting to write. My initial work was greatly aided by the Library of America, which generously provided copies of the relevant volumes then available. Sacvan Bercovitch, Andrew Brown, and Cyrus Patell have done exemplary editorial work in founding, fostering, and carrying through this project, and in making occasions that allowed me to benefit from the responses of my fellow contributors Michael Bell, Barbara Packer, and Eric Sundquist. Friends and colleagues have been generous in critical dialogue over my work, especially those who have read all or most of the manuscript: Lauren Berlant, Paul Bové, Nancy Glazener, Carol Kay, Daniel O'Hara, Donald Pease, and Bruce Robbins.

Jonathan Arac

INTRODUCTION

THIS MULTIVOLUME *History* marks a new beginning in the study of American literature. The first *Cambridge History of American Literature* (1917) helped introduce a new branch of English writing. *The Literary History of the United States,* assembled thirty years later under the aegis of Robert E. Spiller, helped establish a new field of academic study. Our *History* embodies the work of a generation of Americanists who have redrawn the boundaries of the field and redefined the terms of its development. Trained in the 1960s and early 1970s, representing the broad spectrum of both new and established directions in all branches of American writing, these scholars and critics have shaped, and continue to shape, what has become a major area of modern literary scholarship.

Over the past three decades, Americanist literary criticism has expanded from a border province into a center of humanist studies. The vitality of the field is reflected in the rising interest in American literature everywhere, nationally and internationally, and at every level – in high schools and colleges, in graduate programs, in publications, conferences, and public events. It is expressed in the sheer scope of scholarly activity and in the polemical intensity of debate. Virtually every recent school of criticism has found not just its followers here but many of its leading exponents. And increasingly over the past three decades, American texts have provided the focus for inter- and cross-disciplinary investigation. Gender studies, ethnic studies, and popular-culture studies, among others, have penetrated to all corners of the profession, but their single largest base is American literature. The same is true with regard to controversies over multiculturalism and canon formation: the issues are transhistorical and transcultural, but the debates themselves have turned mainly on American books.

We need not endorse all of these movements, or any one of them entirely, to see in the activity they have generated the dynamics of intellectual growth. Nor need we obscure the hard facts of intellectual growth – startling disparities in quality, a proliferation of jargons, and the mixed blessings of the new, innovation and mere trendiness entwined – to recognize the benefits in this case for literary and cultural study. However we situate ourselves in current polemics, it seems clear that Americanist literary criticism has proved to be a forerunner of developments in other humanistic disciplines, precisely through its openness to diversity and debate. And for much the same reason, American literature has become something of a new-foundland for teaching and research. In addition to publishing massive new editions of the nation's literary classics, scholars have undertaken an unprecedented recovery of neglected and undervalued bodies of writing. We know far more than ever about what some have termed (in the plural) American literatures, a term grounded in the persistence in the United States of different traditions, different kinds of aesthetics, even different notions of the literary.

These developments have substantially enlarged the meanings as well as the materials of American literature. For this generation of critics and scholars, American literary history is no longer the history of a certain, agreed-upon group of American masterworks. Nor is it any longer based upon a certain, agreed-upon historical perspective on American writing. The quests for certainty and agreement continue, as they must, but they proceed now within a climate of critical decentralization – of controversy, competition, and, at best, dialogue among different frames of explanation.

This scene of conflict has been variously described in terms of liberal–democratic process, of the marketplace, and of professionalization. In any case it signals a shift in structures of academic authority. The practice of literary history hitherto, from its inception in the eighteenth century, has depended upon an established consensus about the essence or nature of its subject. Today the invocation of consensus sounds rather like an appeal for compromise, or like nostalgia. What used to be a relatively clear division between criticism and scholarship, aesthetic and historical analysis, has blurred and then subdivided over and over again (in various combinations) into a spectrum of special interests: special branches of expertise, special kinds of investment in the materials, and special modes of argument and strategies of persuasion.

In our times, in short, the study of American literary history defines itself in the plural, through volatile focal points of a multifaceted scholarly, critical, and pedagogic enterprise. Authority in this context is a function of different but connected bodies of knowledge. The authority of difference, if it may be so termed, resides in the critic's appeal to a particular constituency, in his or her command over a particular range of materials (with their distinctive set of authorities), and in the integrative force of his or her approach. The authority of connection lies in the capacity of a particular explanation or approach to engage with, challenge, or reinforce others – in its capacity, that is, to gain substance and depth in relation to other, sometimes complementary, sometimes conflicting modes of explanation.

This new *Cambridge History of American Literature* claims authority on both counts, individual and collaborative. In a sense, this makes it representative not only of the profession it speaks for but of the culture it describes. Our *History* is fundamentally pluralist: a federated histories of American literatures. And in part its representative quality lies in its *critical* bent. Our *History* is also an expression of ongoing debates within the profession about cultural patterns and values, including those of liberal pluralism. Accordingly, an adversarial thread runs through a number of these narratives, and it marks the *History*'s most traditional aspect. The high moral stance it assumes – literary analysis as the grounds for resistance, alternative vision, or relative detachment – is implicit in the very definition of art we have inherited from the Romantic era through the genteel critics. The earlier, consensual view of literature upheld the universality of ideals embodied in great books. By implication, therefore, and often by direct assault upon social norms and practices, it fostered a broad aesthetic oppositionalism – a celebration of literature (in Matthew Arnold's words) as the criticism of life, whether in formalist terms, as in the New Critics' assault on industrial society, or in the utopian forms of left-wing cultural critique.

What distinguishes our *History* in this respect is its variety of adversarial approaches and, more strikingly, the presence throughout of revisionary, nonoppositional ways of relating text and context. One result is the emphasis on nationality as a problem. "America" in these volumes designates the United States, or the territories that were to become part of the United States; and although several of our authors adopt a comparatist framework, by and large their concerns center upon the writing of English in this country – "American literature" as it is commonly understood here and abroad in its national implications. Nonetheless, the term "American" is neither a narrative premise in these volumes nor an objective background. Quite the reverse: it is the complex subject of a series of literary–historical inquiries. "America" is a historical entity, the United States of America. It is also a declaration of community, a people constituted and sustained by verbal fiat, a set of universal principles, a strategy of social cohesion, a summons to social protest, a prophecy, a dream, an aesthetic ideal, a trope of the modern ("progress," "opportunity," "the new"), a semiotics of inclusion ("melting pot," "patchwork quilt," "nation of nations"), and a semiotics of exclusion, closing out not only the Old World but all other countries of the Americas, north and south, as well as large groups within the United States. A nationality so conceived is a rhetorical battleground.

Precisely, then, by retaining the full range of its familiar meanings, these volumes make "America" intrinsic to the *literary* history of the United States. The matter of nationhood here becomes a focal point for exploring the two most vexed issues today in literary studies: the historicity of the text and the textuality of history.

Another result of narrative diversity is the emphasis on history as the vehicle of critical revision. This is the emphasis, too, not coincidentally, of our own cultural moment. At no time in literary studies has awareness of history – or more accurately, theorizing about history – been more acute and pervasive. It is hardly too much to say that what joins all the special interests in the field, all factions in our current critical dissensus, is an overriding interest in history: as the ground and texture of ideas, metaphors, and myths; as the substance of the texts we read and the spirit in which we interpret them. Even as we acknowledge that great books, a few configurations of language raised to an extraordinary pitch of intensity, transcend their time and place (and even if we believe that their enduring power offers a recurrent source of oppositionalism), it is evident upon reflection that concepts of aesthetic transcendence are themselves time-bound. Like other claims to the absolute, from ancient religion to modern science, the claims of aesthetics are shaped by history. We grasp their particular forms of transcendence (the aesthetics of divine inspiration, the aesthetics of ambiguity, subversion, and indeterminacy) through an identifiably historical consciousness.

The same recognition of contingency extends to the writing of history. Some histories are truer than others; a few histories are invested for a time with the grandeur of being "definitive" and "comprehensive"; but all are narratives conditioned by their historical moments. The claims for total description harden (because they conceal) the limitations of history: local biases, temporal assumptions, and vested interests that at once compel and circumscribe our search for absolutes. The interplay of narratives enables us to make use of such limitations in ways that open both literature and history to further and fuller inquiry. One way leads through the discovery of differ- ence: the interruptions and discontinuities through which literary history unfolds. Another way leads through the acknowledgment of connection: the shared anxieties, interests, and aspirations that underlie our perceptions of those conflicts and so impose a certain cohesion (professional, intellectual, and generational) upon difference itself.

These considerations have guided the choice of the particular format for this *History*. All previous histories of American literature have been either totalizing or encyclopedic. They have offered either the magisterial sweep of a single vision or a multitude of terse accounts that come to seem just as totalizing, if only because the genre of the brief, expert synthesis precludes the development of authorial voice. Here, in contrast, American literary history unfolds through a polyphony of large-scale narratives. Each of them is ample enough in scope and detail to allow for the elaboration of distinctive views (premises, arguments, analyses); each of them, therefore, is persuasive by demonstration (rather than by assertion) and hence authoritative in its own right; and each is related to the others through common themes and concerns.

The authors were selected first for the excellence of their scholarship and then for the significance of the critical communities informing their work. Together, they demonstrate the achievements of Americanist literary criticism over the past three decades. Their contributions to these volumes speak to continuities as well as disruptions between generations. They give voice to the wide range of materials now subsumed under the heading of American literature. They express the distinctive sorts of excitement and commitment that have led to the extraordinary expansion of the field. And they reflect the diversity of interests that constitutes literary studies in our time and that may be attributed in part to the ethnographic diversity (class background, ethnic group, and racial origin) that has come to characterize literature faculties since World War II, and especially since the 1960s.

The same qualities inform this *History*'s organizational principles. Its flexibility of structure is meant to accommodate the varieties of American literary history. Some major writers appear in more than one volume, because they belong to more than one age. Some texts are discussed in several narratives within a volume, because they are important to different realms of cultural experience. Sometimes the story of a certain movement is retold from different perspectives, because the story requires a plural focus: from the margins as well as from the mainstream, for example, or as being equally the culmination of one era and the beginning of another. In all such instances, overlap is a strategy of multivocal description. The diversity of perspectives this yields corresponds to, as it draws upon, the sheer plenitude of literary and historical materials. It also makes for a richer, more intricate account of particulars (writers, texts, movements) than that available in any previous history of American literature.

Every volume in this *History* displays these strengths in its own way. This volume is perhaps especially notable for the ways in which diversity, considered in its various forms — as complementarity, heterogeneity, contention, and conflict — becomes both subject and substance of the narrative. Each of the four authors has a distinctive focus. Michael Davitt Bell describes the social conditions of the literary vocation: the reciprocities among authorship, economic change, gender distinction, and regional interest that shaped the growth of a professional literature in the United States. Eric J. Sundquist draws upon broad cultural patterns. His account of the writings of exploration, the frontier, and slavery is an interweaving of disparate voices, out-

looks, and traditions. Barbara L. Packer's sources come largely from intellectual history: the theological and philosophical controversies that prepared the
way for Transcendentalism. Jonathan Arac's categories are basically formalist.
He sees the development of antebellum fiction as a dialectic of prose genres,
the emergence of a literary mode out of the clash of national, local, and
personal forms.

Together, then, these narratives offer a fourfold perspective on literature:
social, cultural, intellectual, and aesthetic. Bell surveys virtually the entire
spectrum of literary activity, from periodicals and the drama to the protean
forms of the novel. His account of the literary marketplace is remarkable not
only for its range and specificity – finances of publication, issues of copyright, systems of production and distribution – but also for the many links it
suggests between economic and aesthetic factors. His descriptions of different literary communities reveal dramatic contrasts in norms and values as
well as the relation between such contrasts and the perceived functions of art.
And he makes these connections concrete in the careers he details and the
texts he analyzes. Bell's approach blends traditional and revisionary methods.
He calls the canon into question, reevaluates the significance of regionalism,
and demonstrates the uses of gender-criticism, all while sustaining familiar
scholarly terms and techniques. This is an inside narrative of literature as
cultural work. Bell conveys with immediacy, from within the historical
moment, the processes by which literature first established itself professionally in the United States. Those processes, he demonstrates, were grounded
in patterns of social coherence and change; they involved a variety of enclaves,
networks, and institutions, corresponding to a variety of aesthetic standards;
and they resulted in several distinct "American renaissances."

Sundquist deals mainly with the texts of nonprofessional and paraprofes-
sional writers. His history brings together the multifarious strains of a culture
in formation: journals of explorers, ballads of border life, slave narratives,
anthropological treatises, sermons and orations, writings of abolitionists and
southern apologists, and records and legends of Native Americans. Nothing
more clearly shows the impact of the new American studies than the way that
these texts, more sumptuously displayed here than in any previous literary
history, come alive as literature. And nothing more clearly shows the author's
control over his materials than his success in letting them speak for themselves.
Sundquist's method is to juxtapose rather than conflate; not to subsume all
views under one concept, or all images under one metaphor, but to set them in
dialogue with one another. The story he tells is not of order and meaning
imposed from above but of meanings and possibilities generated by competing
ideologies, shifting realities, and the confrontation of cultures. His history is a
radical extension of the work of earlier scholars in its discussion of race, in its

negotiations between different modes of discourse, and in its representation of marginal, alternative, and oppositional literatures as central to the making of "America."

Sundquist's narrative turns on the ambiguities embedded in national myths; Packer's on the creative energies of debate. Her narrative traces the development of a great intellectual movement out of generational unrest and revolt. Transcendentalism, she shows, begins in a sweeping protest against the status quo; it develops through dissent in every sphere, religious and secular; and it issues in the doctrines of protest (nonconformity, self-reliance) that we have come to associate with Ralph Waldo Emerson. For Packer, too, Emerson is the major figure, as her extensive analysis of his work testifies. But she defines his importance in context. She explains the Transcendentalists by describing them in their time and place, through their interactions with each other, and as the New England heirs to a complex transatlantic legacy. The story she tells involves a tangle of abstruse beliefs and abstract issues: Calvinism versus Unitarianism, Locke versus Kant, Enlightenment versus Romantic aesthetics, the historical criticism of the Bible. Packer makes these and similar matters not only intelligible but compelling. She presents them with the sort of moral urgency they held for contemporaries, as part of the Trancendentalists' aggressive search for new ideas everywhere, their excitement about foreign literatures and cultures, their avid and open intellectual commerce with the world. In her account, the cultural, conceptual, and aesthetic dimensions fuse in the experiential, recasting the entire movement in a fresh light.

Arac takes literature itself as his subject. His narrative centers on the founding of a national literary tradition, and although he provides biographical information about each of the major prose writers he treats, his focus is upon the distinctive themes and structures they developed. The result is a genealogy of genres, and more specifically an analysis of the dynamics of narrative modes – national, local, personal, and literary – that eventuated in *Moby-Dick* and *The Scarlet Letter*. For Arac, such works of genius are also works mediated by the genius of literature and of culture, which is to say, by the exigencies of aesthetic form and the pressures of history. The story he tells concerns the triumph of an art programmatically freed from such pressures, released from history into some would-be autonomous realm of "Romance." It also demonstrates that that process of transcendence was itself shaped by profound reciprocities between politics and art. In effect, Arac's history of literary forms is an aesthetics of historical development. At every stage of his analysis, he accents individual differences within common patterns; at every stage he interprets the Americanness of those patterns within a comparatist framework; and at every stage the comparatist and formalist interpretation opens into a far-ranging commentary on the conflicted course of a nation intent simultaneously on unlimited expansion and civil war.

Considered separately or together, these four narratives constitute a basic reassessment of American prose writing between 1820 and 1865. Their diversity is a fit tribute to the achievement of a remarkable generation of Americanists. The problems they explore and the differences that emerge suggest new directions for American literary scholarship.

CONDITIONS OF LITERARY VOCATION

Michael Davitt Bell

BEGINNINGS OF PROFESSIONALISM

I N *American Renaissance: Art and Expression in the Age of Emerson and Whitman,* his seminal 1941 study of classic American writing, F. O. Matthiessen located the "renaissance" of his title in the 1850s, when Emerson, Whitman, Thoreau, Hawthorne, and Melville were all publishing major works. One might locate an earlier American renaissance (or "naissance") at the beginning of the 1820s, when three writers who would come to dominate American literature during the next two or three decades published their first important books. Washington Irving's *The Sketch Book of Geoffrey Crayon, Gent.* was issued in installments, by C. S. Van Winkle of New York City, beginning in June 1819 and running through September 1820. In September 1821, Hilliard and Metcalf, of Cambridge, Massachusetts, issued the first volume of *Poems* by William Cullen Bryant. Three months later, in New York City, Charles Wiley issued James Fenimore Cooper's *The Spy.* The earth did not, perhaps, shake at the time, but from the perspective of literary history the appearance of these three books within a little less than three years seems momentous. The careers of these writers would testify to a major change in the meaning of both literature and literary vocation in America — a change that affected almost all of their literary contemporaries.

Irving (1783–1859) was not exactly a new writer in 1819; he had been a celebrated fixture of the New York literary scene a decade earlier and was still known, for instance, as the author of *Diedrich Knickerbocker's History of New York* (1809). But he had been living in England and had been largely silent since 1815. Moreover, none of his earlier writings had achieved anything like the success of *The Sketch Book,* which was widely praised and widely purchased on both sides of the Atlantic. In England, where an edition appeared early in 1820, it was promoted by no less a lion than Sir Walter Scott, already a kind of mythological being to Americans; and Lord Byron, from Italy, declared that "Crayon is very good." *The Sketch Book* went through printing after printing in both England and America, suggesting what had previously seemed an impossibility: that international literary success could be attained by an American writer. Young Henry Longfellow, a student at Bowdoin College when he discovered Irving, was only one of many Americans enraptured by this new native celebrity. "Every reader," he would recall when Irving died in 1859, "has his first book . . . which in early youth first fascinates his imagination. . . . To me, this first book was *The Sketch Book* of Washington Irving."

The Spy was Cooper's (1789–1851) second fictional effort; its predecessor — a clumsy imitation of Jane Austen called *Precaution* (1820) — had fared poorly. The new book featured an American setting (Westchester during the American Revolution) and even a cameo appearance by George Washington, and like *The Sketch Book* it proved popular and profitable on both sides of the Atlantic. Here, it seemed, was the "American Scott," doing for American history and scenery what the author of *Waverley* had done for Scotland, and he was America's own. The success of *The Spy* set an attractive target for future striving, both for Cooper and for other would-be native authors. *The Spy* was followed by a torrent of American historical romances, often modeled on Scott but encouraged by Cooper's example to deal with native themes and settings. Cooper's own third novel, *The Pioneers,* is now valued because it introduced the character Natty Bumppo and thus inaugurated the series of five novels known as the Leatherstocking Tales. For the purposes of literary history, however, what may be more immediately important is the fact that when *The Pioneers* appeared on February 1, 1823, 3,500 copies were bought up in New York by noon. Cooper, like Irving, was a "star." During the 1820s the author of *The Spy* would earn from his writings an average of $6,500 a year, and in a single year, 1829, Irving's income from his writings would exceed $23,000. In America such professional literary success was wholly unprecedented.

Bryant's 1821 *Poems* produced no such immediate sensation. Before Longfellow in America, new poetry by native authors did not sell the way prose could sell, and publication in the Boston area, for reasons that we will turn to shortly, was also a liability. Although Bryant (1794–1878) would come to stand with Irving and Cooper as one of the foremost American writers of his generation, it would be more than a decade before he achieved such public stature, and this fame would come from the publishing centers of New York and Philadelphia, not from Boston. Of a first printing of 750 copies (compared, for instance, to 2,000 for the first number of Irving's *Sketch Book*) only 270 copies of Bryant's 1821 *Poems* had been sold by 1823. Still, the *Poems* brought their author a measure of *critical* recognition. Bryant had been encouraged by Bostonians R. H. Dana and E. T. Channing, and his *Poems* were reviewed favorably by Boston's *North American Review,* which Channing edited, and, through Dana's good offices, by the New York *American.* Even *Blackwood's Magazine* would declare from Scotland, in 1822, that "Bryant is no mean poet; . . . we should not be surprised at his assuming, one day or another, a high rank among English poets."

The Sketch Book, Bryant's *Poems,* and *The Spy* launched three enduring professional literary careers, and the simple fact of their endurance should not be
overlooked. There had been an outpouring of national literature a generation
earlier, spurred by the successful completion of the War of Independence – in
the work, for instance, of Philip Freneau, Hugh Henry Brackenridge, the
Connecticut Wits, and Charles Brockden Brown. But if this earlier outpouring
was a renaissance, it was a notably abortive one; none of these men, whatever
fame he achieved, succeeded as a professional author, or even devoted himself
primarily to literature. Brown is now probably the best-known writer of this
generation, but he in fact abandoned literature after a very brief trial. So
Irving, Cooper, and Bryant accomplished what these predecessors had found
beyond their reach. And this accomplishment owed at least as much to circumstances as to aesthetic considerations.

The most important of these circumstances was a transformation, or series
of transformations, in the means of producing and distributing literature in
America, a transformation that began to take place in the second and third
decades of the nineteenth century. Irving, Cooper, and Bryant participated
in, or at least responded to, the institutionalization and rationalization of
nonutilitarian writing as a market commodity. Irving and Cooper, if not
Bryant, were the first Americans to find something like commercial success
as literary professionals. These writers did not produce these changes; rather,
their careers were symptomatic of emerging innovations in the financing,
manufacture, and marketing of books and periodicals. The story of the
transformation of American literature in the 1820s and 1830s is among other
things a story of changes in literary production and distribution – of changes
in royalty arrangements, pricing, publishing, transportation, and the like. It
is also a story of changes in the social status and meaning of literary
vocation – of the identity, "writer" – from the ideal of the gentleman-
amateur (never in America much of a reality) to the actuality of the literary
professional. None of these changes was complete by the end of the 1820s, or
even by the end of the 1850s; what happened during the heyday of Irving,
Cooper and Bryant was part of a longer and larger process. Still, it is
important that we understand how this process affected the work and the
careers of these writers and of their American contemporaries.

BOOK PUBLISHING

At the beginning of the nineteenth century, the condition of American
book publishing was decidedly primitive and disorganized; there simply
were no literary publishers, in the modern sense of the term, in the United
States. By the 1850s things had changed dramatically; our present system

of publication — of capitalizing, manufacturing, advertising, and distributing literary property, and of rationalizing the different rights of author and publisher in this property — was not yet fully in place, but its outlines were clearly visible. This radical transformation of the American book-publishing industry in the first half of the nineteenth century has been ably described by a number of scholars — most perceptively by the late William Charvat, in *Literary Publishing in America, 1790–1850* (1959) and other works. The story will only be sketched in here.

The passage of the first American copyright law, in 1790, had made literature property and had therefore made authorship as a *profession* a possibility for American writers. Possibility did not immediately, of course, become actuality, for a number of reasons. First of all, no *international* copyright law would be negotiated until 1891, and the absence of such a law produced significant difficulties for native writers. Unless they could work out special arrangements abroad — as many in fact did, with varying degrees of success — American authors received no income from sales of their works in England. Moreover, they had to compete, in the United States, with cheap reprints of popular British works. Volumes of American poetry, fiction, or history, if their authors were to receive any significant income from them, were invariably more expensive than works by British writers who received no American royalties. Yet the effect of this situation was by no means wholly or even mainly negative. The wide circulation of inexpensive British books was a major factor in creating a taste and a market for literature in pre-Civil War America. Cheap editions of Scott and Byron and, later, of Dickens and Thackeray helped produce a reading public and a literary appetite to which American writers could seek to appeal. What may be more important, it was to a large extent the business of printing, advertising, and distributing British books that brought native publishing from infancy to the beginnings of maturity, and there had to be a mature and relatively stable publishing industry before a true "American literature" could come into existence.

American book production at the beginning of the century was largely dispersed or decentralized, except in the Philadelphia area. Elsewhere, local printers, who also functioned as booksellers, produced copies sufficient to meet the demands of the local audience, and authors often simply published where they lived. But as the century progressed, the manufacture and distribution of books concentrated increasingly in urban literary centers and in such major firms as Philadelphia's House of Carey, New York's House of Harper, and, later, New York's Wiley and Putnam and Boston's Ticknor and Fields — firms that often maintained offices in other centers as well. Between 1800 and 1810 nearly 50 percent of fiction by native authors was published outside New York, Philadelphia, and Boston. By the 1840s this figure had declined to 8 percent.

The major American literary centers were invariably seaport cities with access to important inland rivers, enabling publishers in these centers to distribute books at minimum expense to the interior market. Early in the period, New York, Philadelphia, and Baltimore were literary centers in this sense, and they came to dominate American publishing, with Philadelphia ultimately beating out Baltimore for control of the Susquehanna and the South. The eventual ascendancy of New York was guaranteed less by its indigenous literary culture than by the opening of the Erie Canal in the 1820s. Boston, with no important river, remained a provincial publishing center until the late 1830s and 1840s, when railroads began to supplement river shipping as a way of getting books to the crucial inland market. This partly accounts for the commercial failure of Bryant's 1821 *Poems,* printed in the Boston area, as contrasted with the successes of Irving's *Sketch Book* and Cooper's *The Spy,* both issued in New York.

Ambitious authors rapidly learned that success depended on access to the interior market. Bryant, in the 1830s, turned to New York, where the House of Harper brought out ten editions of his poems between 1836 and 1846, giving him the national circulation his first volume had failed to achieve, even though that volume had contained such future anthology pieces as "To a Waterfowl," "The Inscription for the Entrance to a Wood," "The Yellow Violet," and "Thanatopsis." Nor did authors identified with established literary centers necessarily publish in those centers. New Yorkers Irving and Cooper, in the 1820s, signed contracts with Philadelphia's House of Carey, which was able to offer excellent terms and a shrewd understanding of promotion and distribution; and both of them stayed with Carey well into the 1840s.

Access to the interior market was itself no guarantee of success; there were still basic problems in the business of publishing to be worked out. In the 1820s, for instance, most so-called publishers were both printers and booksellers, wholesalers and retailers, and inevitably there was conflict between these two functions. A firm's tendency as retailer to monopolize sales of its own titles restricted wholesale distribution of those titles; a popular book would often be available at only one store even in a large city. Early-nineteenth-century American publishers also operated with very little capital; indeed, books by native writers were frequently published at the expense of the author rather than the publisher, as was the case with both *The Sketch Book* and *The Spy.* This last arrangement, which was also common at the time in Britain, did not necessarily work to the author's disadvantage, at least if a book was successful. Since Irving and Cooper acted in effect as their own publishers, paying Van Winkle and Wiley royalties for distributing *The Sketch Book* and *The Spy,* they were able to keep a very high share of the profits on their books. But most native writers failed to achieve such sales, and even Irving and Cooper would soon choose to lease the rights to their works for set terms and fixed sums to regular publishers. The often ridiculously low capitalization of American publishing firms also produced extraordinary instability in the industry; failures were frequent, and were abetted, in the early 1840s, by cutthroat competition in cheap foreign reprints.

Yet order began to emerge from this chaos. Firms such as Carey in Philadelphia and Harper in New York soon acquired a sufficient financial base to take over the full functions of the literary publisher, including capitalization, and the most virulent forms of competition were brought under control by the mid-1840s. Moreover, the dominant publishers saw and remedied the problem of engaging in both wholesale and retail distribution. Harper, founded in 1817, restricted itself from the beginning to printing and publishing, and Carey abandoned retail bookselling in 1830. Business, in any case, expanded dramatically, spurred on not only by improvements in capitalization and distribution but by such technological innovations in book manufacturing as the introduction of cloth bindings and the cylinder press. The value of books manufactured and sold in the United States rose from $2.5 million in 1820 to $5.5 million in 1840, and then to $12.5 million in 1850.

By the 1840s, authors could begin to count on a market stability largely absent in 1820. Yet they paid a price for this stability. As publishers took over the capitalization of native works, they came to exert far more control over native writers. Publishers had good reason for trying to predict what would and would not sell (the ability to make such predictions was after all what made successful publishers successful), and they were necessarily inclined to pressure their authors to conform to their perception of the public taste. Whereas established authors might try to resist such pressure, newcomers had little choice but to accede, and even established authors ignored market considerations at their peril. A lasting result of the cutthroat competition of the early 1840s was a dramatic decline in the price of American books and hence a corresponding reduction in authors' returns from these books. At the same time, the percentage of even a popular author's effective royalty declined considerably, as publishers took over from authors the financial risk of publication. Thus by the 1840s successful professional authors like Irving and Cooper had to generate far more sales just to produce earnings equal to those they had received in the 1820s. William Charvat has calculated the specific effect of these changes on Cooper. In 1826 Cooper earned $5,000 from the sale of 5,750 copies of *The Last of the Mohicans* at $2.00 each. In

1842 *The Wing-and-Wing* sold 12,500 copies (more than twice as many as *The Last of the Mohicans* in 1826), but at only fifty cents each and at a significantly lower effective royalty percentage (20 percent versus 43 percent). Thus Cooper's earnings from *The Wing-and-Wing* were only $1,187.50, less than a quarter of his 1826 earnings from *Mohicans*.

Even disregarding pressure from publishers, then, writers had reasons of their own for catering literary production to the public taste. They also had reasons for producing as much writing as possible as fast as possible. Quantity, for an established writer, was far more important to sustaining earnings than was quality. Developments in book publishing from the 1820s to the 1840s made available to the native author a new and truly national audience and a relatively stable means of reaching this audience, but they did so, inevitably, by turning the literary work into a commodity. To say that the basis of literature was shifted from culture to commerce is perhaps to oversimplify; the meaning and authority of "high culture" in America had always been ambiguous. But by the early 1840s, market considerations had clearly become an inescapable component of the new American literary profession. For those who chose to engage in this profession, the expansion and consolidation of literary publishing presented a mixed and sometimes baffling blessing.

WASHINGTON IRVING

In an 1813 essay on the American poet Robert Treat Paine, in whose disastrous career he saw a vivid example of the dangers of literary vocation in America, Washington Irving described the general situation of the imaginative writer in the United States in notably bleak terms. "Unfitted for business," he wrote, "in a nation where every one is busy; devoted to literature, where literary leisure is confounded with idleness; the man of letters is almost an insulated being, with few to understand, less to value, and scarcely any to encourage his pursuits." The financial difficulties of the professional American writer at the beginning of the nineteenth century have already been suggested, but Irving's emphasis is on a deeper sort of difficulty, ultimately social and psychological. To be a professional writer was to be a kind of deviant – to be, in effect, un-American.

Literature itself had enormous prestige; it was taught in colleges, and its cultivation was a mark of social status. Fiction was for the most part an exception to this generalization, although Scott's *Waverley* novels would soon help make even fiction respectable. Still, the indulgence of imagination was anathema to orthodox opinion, and the popularity of fiction, particularly of sensational gothic novels and tales of seduction, cut it off from the official esteem accorded to "higher" forms of literature, especially to poetry and history. Yet the prestige of even these higher forms did not extend to those who produced them for a living. The writer was caught in a double bind. On the one hand, to devote oneself exclusively to literature rather than "business" was perceived as mere "idleness." Thus Hawthorne (1804–64), in his 1850 "Custom-House" preface to *The Scarlet Letter,* would imagine the hostile reaction of his Puritan ancestors to their descendant's literary vocation: "What is he? . . . A mere writer of story-books! What kind of a business in life . . . may that be? Why, the degenerate fellow might as well have been a fiddler!" On the other hand, to the extent that one pursued literature *as* a "business," one was betraying its true "gentlemanly" nature. Small wonder that Irving saw the American writer, in 1813, as an "insulated being."

The example of Irving's own career would suggest how the financial difficulties facing the American writer might be overcome and would help neutralize the American perception of the professional writer's social insulation. In 1835, Baltimore novelist John Pendleton Kennedy would thank the author of *The Sketch Book* for having "convinced the wise ones at home that a man may sometimes write a volume without losing his character." This effect was quite deliberate on Irving's part. Throughout his career he sustained his professional standing by carefully considering the shifting tastes of his audience; and, what may be more important, he carefully managed his image as a writer in order to mitigate public hostility or indifference to the man of letters. Irving ultimately managed the extraordinary feat of engaging in literature as a business enterprise (thus disarming public suspicion and perhaps his own guilt about "idleness") while at the same time maintaining the public pose of amateur (thus avoiding the appearance of debasing culture with commerce). He perceived that if literature was becoming a commodity, it was also inevitably a form of public relations, and he became a master of public relations.

Irving was born in 1783, six years before his namesake's inauguration as first president of the United States. His father was a New York merchant, and a number of the sons entered the family business, but Washington was trained for the law. Although he passed the bar exam in 1806, he never practiced very actively, gravitating instead toward the provincial literary world of New York, modeled – in its own perception anyway – on the literary society of eighteenth-century London. Literature for these young men, all of whom were engaged in business or professional activities, was primarily a social affair, a diversion, a provincial imitation or invention of British gentility. It might promise a release from the boredom of commercial responsibilities and access, in a bourgeois democracy, to something like aristocratic style, but it could hardly offer a living.

Yet Irving engaged in the activities of this world with unusual energy, perhaps out of frustration with his destined social role or out of guilt concerning his apparent inaptitude for this social role. In 1802 he began publishing his satirical *Letters of Jonathan Oldstyle, Gent.* in the *New York Morning Chronicle,* which his brother Peter edited. In 1807, together with brother William and brother-in-law James Kirke Paulding, he began publishing *Salmagundi; or the Whim-Whams and Opinions of Launcelot Langstaff, & Others* – another collection of essays, mainly satirical. Then in 1809 the death of his young fiancée, Matilda Hoffman, daughter of the judge who had offered him a legal partnership, drove him from even his desultory pursuit of the law. Instead he turned furiously to a literary project conceived the previous year: the burlesque *Diedrich Knickerbocker's History of New York,* an immediate success when it was published in 1809. His brothers, in order to give him more time for writing, made him an inactive partner in the family business.

Irving was by no means, yet, a successful professional author, or even a professional author at all. *Knickerbocker's History* was surprisingly successful (Irving made $3,000 on it), but it had no immediate successor except for a revised edition in 1812. In that year Irving became editor of a Philadelphia literary journal, the *Analectic Magazine,* which printed mostly extracts of British literature, but it folded in 1814. By this point Irving, now thirty-one, had come pretty much to the end of his rope; he had renounced business, more or less, but he was not really an author, whatever that might have meant in America at the time. So in 1815, at loose ends and with no plans, he sailed for England, where his brother Peter was running the Liverpool office of the family business.

At first, England was a disaster; Peter was ill, and Washington had to take over the Liverpool office, which was in trouble and which finally went bankrupt in 1818. Yet this disaster contained both an important lesson – that the "business" so touted by bourgeois orthodoxy was far from dependable – and an equally important imperative – that Irving, having seen the fragility of family support, would have to support himself. He had also, in 1817, met Sir Walter Scott, whose professional success was far more heartening than the literary dilettantism of New York, and who offered generous encouragement and advice. Irving set to work, first on a never-finished novel and then on the essays and tales that would become *The Sketch Book.*

He sent the first number of *The Sketch Book* to New York, to his brother Ebenezer, early in 1819. "My talents," he wrote in an accompanying letter, "are merely literary . . . If I ever get any solid credit with the public, it must be in the quiet and assiduous operations of my pen, under the mere guidance of fancy and feeling." The judgments in this statement are typical: although Irving did not publicly contest, and indeed openly shared, the conventional devaluation of literature (hence his "mere" and "merely"), he still held up literature as a *form* of "business," a means toward "solid credit." He would ingratiate himself with his audience, this is to say, by openly advertising his agreement with accepted opinions, even accepted opinions of his own vocation.

The Sketch Book itself was well calculated to turn mere idleness into profit. The alleged author, Geoffrey Crayon, was a professed idler, hardly one to challenge orthodoxy. Irving had used pseudonymous personae before (Jonathan Oldstyle, Launcelot Langstaff, Diedrich Knickerbocker), and he would use them repeatedly for the rest of his career. He thus protected himself (although everyone knew who actually wrote his sketches and satires) from overt personal identification with literature. Moreover, the "Gent." following "Geoffrey Crayon" in the title – like that following "Jonathan Oldstyle" seventeen years earlier – assured the reader that this work of literature, actually written by the son of a New York merchant, was the production of a gentleman-amateur. And gone now was the often acerbic or scatological satire of the earlier writings, replaced by a more gentle humor and a general suffusion of sentiment. There were sentimental tourist-sketches on such subjects as "Westminster Abbey" and "Rural Funerals," and there were the instant-classic short stories, attributed by Crayon to Diedrich Knickerbocker: "Rip Van Winkle" (which appeared in the first number) and "The Legend of Sleepy Hollow."

Irving has often been regarded as a mere imitator, a recycler of outworn British modes and styles, a charge already being lodged against him by contemporary detractors at the height of his greatest celebrity. It is certainly true that his works promote nostalgia, whether about old Britain or about old Dutch New York; such nostalgia was Irving's stock-in-trade. And he certainly drew on British models; he soon came to be known as the "American Goldsmith." All of this was no doubt deliberate. There was no reason to imagine that the American reading public wanted what they were not accustomed to, and what they were accustomed to was British writing. Still, Irving was also an important innovator, or at least profoundly influential. The pose of the idle lover of Europe and the picturesque, made famous by Geoffrey Crayon, established an important school of American writing, including much of the work of Nathaniel Parker Willis and of the early Longfellow. Irving might also lay claim to having invented the American short story; he was the only other American writer praised by Poe in the latter's laudatory 1842 review of Hawthorne's *Twice-told Tales.* The two Knickerbocker stories in *The Sketch Book,* "Rip Van Winkle" and "The Legend of Sleepy Hollow," turning the contrast between Dutch tradition and Yankee progress into a kind of elegiac allegory, might be cited as the source of the

American tradition of local-color fiction, which moved through Hawthorne's "Custom-House" and *House of the Seven Gables* (1851) into the outpouring of women's local-color writing in the 1880s and 1890s and, ultimately, in the twentieth century, into the fiction of Sherwood Anderson and William Faulkner. Moreover, without Irving's sentimental popularization of the British "Christmas" (another *Sketch Book* essay), Charles Dickens would hardly have had a tradition to draw on in *A Christmas Carol;* and Dickens, for all his social seriousness one of the great sentimentalists of the nineteenth century, was indebted to Irving in many other ways as well.

In any case, *The Sketch Book* was a resounding transatlantic success, a sensation. John Murray, who had first declined the work, published five British editions between 1820 and 1823. In the United States, Van Winkle produced the same number of editions between 1819 and 1826. In the next sixteen years there were nine more American reprints, and since he was living in England, Irving was able to reap returns from both American and British sales. He had indeed found "solid credit with the public," and he rapidly sought additional returns. *Bracebridge Hall,* also attributed to Geoffrey Crayon, appeared in 1822. Although it did not achieve the huge popularity of *The Sketch Book,* of which it was an obvious imitation, it came close, and Murray paid 1,200 guineas for the right to publish it in England.

In 1824 Irving issued his last effort to work the vein of *The Sketch Book* — *Tales of a Traveller, by Geoffrey Crayon, Gent.* — but here there were important differences. The influence of German gothic fiction, to which Scott had introduced Irving, was far more overt, and unlike *The Sketch Book* and *Bracebridge Hall, Tales of a Traveller* consisted entirely of short stories — works of fiction, generally considered the lowest of current literary modes. Irving apparently knew that he was taking a risk; many of the *Tales* deal quite self-consciously with the fictionality of fiction, and a quarter of the book, "Buckthorne and His Friends," takes the insubstantiality of the literary life as its subject. Irving's nervousness about fiction is also indicated by the fact that even Crayon, the alleged author of the *Tales,* himself attributes the stories to other invented tellers — a "nervous gentleman," Diedrich Knickerbocker once again, and others — thus placing the book's fiction at minimally two pseudonymous removes from the identity of Washington Irving.

Irving was right to be worried. Although Murray paid him 1,500 guineas for *Tales of a Traveller,* reviews on both sides of the Atlantic ranged from unfavorable to overtly hostile. To a considerable extent this reaction was justified; Irving was trying, a second time, to repeat an earlier success, and much of the writing in *Tales* is perfunctory. Yet some of the stories, in their humorous and sophisticated self-consciousness, are extraordinary, for instance, "The Adventure of the German Student"; and it was "The Story of the

Young Italian," from *Tales,* that Poe would single out for praise in 1842. Still, Irving had his eye on "credit with the public," and he took immediate instruction from the failure of the *Tales.* Never again would he devote an entire volume to fiction, let alone self-conscious fiction. The legacy of this phase of his career was in the future work of Poe, Hawthorne, and others. Irving himself turned to history.

Early in 1826 he went to Madrid, at the invitation of the American ambassador, Edward Everett. This visit, which lasted until 1829, was extremely fruitful. *The History of the Life and Voyages of Christopher Columbus,* a history published in four volumes in 1828, earned Irving more than $25,000. *A Chronicle of the Conquest of Granada* (attributed to a new pseudonymous persona, Fray Antonio Agapida) began appearing in August of the same year. Then, in 1829, Irving completed a sequel to *Columbus – The Voyages and Discoveries of the Companions of Columbus,* published in 1831 – and he began work on what came to be known as his "Spanish Sketch Book," *The Alhambra,* which was published in 1832 by Carey in Philadelphia and in London by Richard Bentley, who would thenceforth replace John Murray as Irving's British publisher.

Irving had hardly become a genuine historian. *The Alhambra* was a work of sentimental tourism, *The Conquest of Granada* mixed historical fact with fancy, and the *Columbus* volumes, although they were more conventionally historical, drew all their facts from a Spanish source that had appeared in 1825; indeed, the Columbus project had begun, at Everett's suggestion, as a translation of this source. Nevertheless, the *pose* of historian was of great importance to Irving in the management of his image following the debacle of *Tales of a Traveller.* Thus, he wrote to a friend, before the appearance of *Columbus,* with a mixture of apprehension and calculation: "If the work succeeds, it will be of immense service to me; if it fails it will be, most probably, what many have anticipated, who suppose, from my having dealt so much in fiction, it must be impossible for me to tell the truth with plausibility." *Columbus,* of course, did succeed, exploiting what Irving elsewhere called the "credence and dignity of history" in order to restore the author's "credit" with his public. An appointment as secretary of the American legation in London in 1829, secured through the patronage of Democrat Martin Van Buren, indicated the extent to which Irving had managed to neutralize the deviant implications of literary vocation and turn himself into a respectable and responsible public figure. A medal from the British Royal Society of Literature and an honorary degree from Oxford further secured his stature.

When Irving finally returned to America in 1832, he was a full-scale celebrity. That most of his writing had been concerned with Europe might have raised questions about his patriotism, but he set out, again quite deliberately, to make himself into a thoroughly "American" author. Indeed, even his return home, after an absence of seventeen years, was in part a move to cement the loyalty of his American readers. His first American-based work, *A Tour of the Prairies,* appeared in 1835; the tourist was still a tourist, but he had shifted his ground from England and Spain to that most "American" of American settings, the West. The year 1835 also saw the appearance of *The Crayon Miscellany,* another collection in the mode of *The Sketch Book;* Irving was playing all his cards. He then set to work on *Astoria; or Anecdotes of an Enterprise Beyond the Rocky Mountains* (1836), a work promoting John Jacob Astor and in fact commissioned by Astor. In Melville's "Bartleby the Scrivener" (1853), the narrator's obsequious deference to the good opinion of Astor may be an allusion to this arrangement. Melville's dig is in a sense unfair; Irving's "American" works have a genuine interest and an important place in the emerging literature of the West. Still, there can be no doubt of the calculation, even what we would now call the image management, in Irving's choice of subject.

The rest of Irving's career need not be described here in detail. In 1832 he had moved into Sunnyside, his home in Tarrytown, New York, and here he lived on as an American institution until his death in 1859 – except for the years from 1842 to 1846, when, having shifted his loyalties from the Democrats to the Whigs, he served as U.S. minister to the court of Spain. This American, who had originally turned from business and politics to literature, had by now, on the basis of his literary reputation, firmly entrenched himself *in* the worlds of business and politics. Although he still published fairly steadily, most of his "new" writings were culled from earlier manuscripts, and most of his literary earnings came from the republication of old books. Literature, for Irving, had become a wholly commercial enterprise. His literary income had fallen dramatically when book prices collapsed in the early 1840s, which is one of the reasons he disengaged himself from dependence on literature as a profession. Nevertheless, the income from republication could be impressive. Between 1848 and 1850 George Palmer Putnam, in New York, brought out a uniform edition of all of Irving's works to date. In an era of low book prices such recirculation of earlier titles was a shrewd way of maximizing earnings, far preferable to producing new works at the pace necessary, by the 1840s, to sustain an income comparable to the scale of the 1820s. And Putnam's "Author's Revised Edition" managed to sell almost 150,000 copies by 1853, netting Irving $22,000.

In the years immediately preceding his death, Irving produced his last work, the five-volume *The Life of George Washington,* (1855–9), another of what he called his "regular historical works." He was still a celebrity when he died, and his example had clearly inspired many other Americans to regard literature as a possible profession. From the perspective of literary history this may have been the most important legacy of his career. Yet there was an irony in this achievement all the same, in the use Irving made of his literary eminence; for what his professional success finally permitted him to do, during the last twenty years of his life, was to become in fact the kind of literary gentleman-amateur he had sought to pose as from the beginning. He had managed to become the image he created, and he would hardly be the last American writer to do so.

JAMES FENIMORE COOPER

Washington Irving and James Fenimore Cooper rose to literary eminence almost simultaneously, both were New Yorkers, and both signed long-term publishing contracts in the 1820s with Philadelphia's House of Carey. There, however, the similarity ended, or so Cooper, at least, would come to insist. At first he joined in the general praise for Irving, but his attitude soon hardened into a public scorn that embarrassed even his friends and that Irving, both publicly and privately, refused to reciprocate. Cooper's hostility to Irving owed at least something to professional rivalry and something, as well, to a clash of personalities and politics. Cooper, a loyal if often acerbic Democrat, was outraged by what he saw as Irving's opportunism – exemplified by his desertion of Democrat Martin Van Buren for the Whigs in 1840 (earning him the post of minister to Spain in 1842) and by his cozy relationship with wealthy Whig businessmen. "Columbus and John Jacob Astor!" Cooper fumed when he heard of the commission for *Astoria*. "I dare say Irving will make the latter the greatest man." Yet Cooper's public criticisms of Irving also grew out of sincere convictions about the proper role of the man of letters in the United States. Irving's "faults," he wrote in 1842, "were all meannesses, and I confess I can sooner pardon crimes, if they are manly ones." Irving, in Cooper's view, was "effeminately" deferential not only to his readers and to American plutocrats but to the standards of British literary taste. "This country," Cooper wrote, "must outgrow its adulation of foreigners, Englishmen in particular"; and Irving was not, he insisted, "a true American in feeling." Cooper sought, as a literary professional, to be both "manly" and "American" – terms often nearly synonymous for him, and synonymously vague.

In 1848, hearing the unfounded rumor that Irving had received a generous bequest in Astor's will, Cooper reacted with immediate credence and characteristic disgust: "What an instinct that man has for gold!" Yet Cooper's own instinct for gold, in spite of his public stance of "manly" independence from commerce, was hardly less intense than that of his rival. Cooper too succeeded as a writer, at least in the 1820s, by appealing to the public taste; the main difference is that he did not wish to appear to do so. Moreover, Cooper worked as a professional writer far more consistently than Irving, who was also a businessman, a politician, and a diplomat. Cooper was for his entire career mainly a professional author, and the only American author before 1850 to support himself wholly by earnings from his writings. His aloofness was in large part compensatory fantasy; he wished to see or present himself not simply as a professional supplier of market commodities (although on occasion he was willing to cultivate this pose) but as a national prophet, an instructor and castigator of the very public and marketplace he depended on for his income. The story of his career is a story of the conflict between these different visions of American literary vocation, a conflict further exacerbated by the need, in an era of falling book prices, for ever-expanding sales. Thus Cooper's unpleasant public denunciations of Irving (who was only one of many targets for such abuse among contemporary literary figures) may ultimately have expressed, and conveniently displaced, his sense of how his *own* "manliness" was simultaneously manifested and threatened by his status as literary professional.

Cooper, like Irving, pursued his involvement in literary commerce as a self-proclaimed "gentleman" – to the extent, after the first flush of celebrity in the 1820s, of willfully imperiling his popularity and antagonizing his market, often simply for *being* a market. Yet whereas Irving accentuated the "gentle," Cooper sought to accentuate the "man," and his equation of national loyalty and democratic principle with aggressive masculinity, making even hostility on the part of his reading public a badge of demonstrated integrity, set a pattern for later male American writers. For instance, Herman Melville (who in 1851 would describe Cooper's works as being "among the earliest I remember, as in my boyhood producing a vivid, and awakening power upon my mind") would proclaim literary nationalism in 1850 in the tones of his admired predecessor: "No American writer should write like an Englishman, or a Frenchman; let him write like a man, for then he will be sure to write like an American." Nevertheless, the question remained: what did it mean, exactly, to "write like a man" at a time when "writing" and "manhood" were considered to be fundamentally antithetical?

James Cooper (he himself would add the "Fenimore," his mother's maiden name, in 1826) was born in New Jersey in 1789. A year later he moved with his family to Cooperstown, on Lake Otsego in upstate New York, where his father, William, had bought a large parcel of land as a speculation in 1786. The speculation proved immensely successful; settlers bought tracts eagerly, and the future novelist's father presided over his community as the sort of gentleman the son would later idealize in his fiction. William Cooper was no landed aristocrat however; Cooperstown, for all its aura of a fiefdom, was still a commercial venture. The ambiguity of the son's status was foreshadowed in the ambiguous status of his father.

James was educated at the local academy, then sent to Albany. He entered Yale in 1803 but was dismissed for some sort of misconduct in 1805. He went to sea as a common sailor in 1806 and then enlisted in the U.S. Navy in 1808, serving for three and a half years on Lake Ontario, an experience that would help make him a future master of American sea fiction. Late in 1809, Judge William Cooper, an active Federalist, was physically assaulted by an opponent following a political meeting and died of his injuries. James inherited $50,000 and a share, with his brothers, of his father's estate. In 1811 he married Susan Augusta DeLancey, daughter of a prominent Westchester family, and ended up settling as a gentleman-farmer in Westchester. The violence of his father's death was hardly consonant with the life of genteel stability this death made possible, and the tension between aristocratic control and disruptive violence would animate much of Cooper's later fiction.

Cooper's family-based prosperity proved as fragile and short-lived as Washington Irving's. Between 1813 and 1819 all five of his brothers died, and James was confronted with their debts as well as with his own. By the early 1820s his father's estate was gone and Otsego Hall, the family mansion in Cooperstown, was sold. The gentleman-farmer had to look about him for a means to make a living, and it was at this point that he became an author, impelled first of all, like Irving, by financial considerations. Moreover, Cooper, unlike Irving, was a husband and father; his situation was truly desperate.

Cooper's literary career began with characteristic truculence. Reading a British domestic novel to his wife he proclaimed, so the story goes: "I could write you a better book than that myself." His wife challenged him to do so, and the result was *Precaution,* published in 1820. *The Spy,* whose commercial success has already been described, followed in 1821. Cooper had not, at least in his own mind, sacrificed the status of gentleman (whatever that title meant in the new America) for that of professional author; rather, his writing would *sustain* his status as gentleman. Yet *The Spy* itself suggests deep-seated anxieties about this status. The title character, Harvey Birch, is an American revolutionary patriot, disguised as a peddler, working for George Washington. But Birch's true identity, for reasons that are far from clear, can never be revealed. His manly patriotism remains a secret for the rest of his life, and it hardly seems farfetched to see in the plight of this figure Cooper's sense of his own situation as a patriot engaging, to his embarrassment, in commerce. Nevertheless, since *The Spy* proclaims what its title character can never himself reveal about the blamelessness of his own motives, the book perhaps also serves as a vindication of its author and his new vocation, defining authorship itself as a form not finally of commerce but of secret, manly heroism.

Similar anxieties lie beneath the surface of Cooper's next novel, *The Pioneers* (1823), and here they are located closer to home. The book's "Templeton," on the shores of Lake Otsego, is a thinly disguised version of Cooperstown, and the community's presiding founder, Judge Marmaduke Temple, is a thinly disguised, idealized version of Cooper's father, Judge William Cooper. Judge Temple stands for restraint and principle against the commercial greed and excess of the new settlers of Templeton, but the book's plot calls the legitimacy of his position into serious question. The War of Independence enabled him to buy out the share in Templeton of his original partner, Edward Effingham, who had fought on the Loyalist side, which would seem to implicate both Judge Temple and the American Revolution in the very greed and commercialism Temple denounces in others. And now, in 1793, Effingham and his son have returned to expose the judge's behavior. It turns out, though, that Temple has preserved the Effinghams' share in a secret trust, just as Harvey Birch, the peddler in *The Spy*, turned out to be a secret patriot. Judge Temple's claim to his property and status is thus transformed from a matter of corrupt business into a species of principled altruism, and when young Oliver Effingham marries the judge's daughter (Elizabeth), the book's potential conflict, linked to both commerce and revolutionary violence, is simply dissipated.

Another character in *The Pioneers*, however, presents a more profound challenge to the judge's authority and legitimacy. Natty Bumppo (later Cooper's famous "Leatherstocking"), a crusty old hunter loyal to the Effinghams, protests not simply against the judge's specific title to the land but against the whole idea of commercial civilization. All ownership, to Natty, is a form of unjust appropriation and excess. He therefore rejects the judge's distinction between his own principled conception of property and the greed of the self-interested settlers. Natty cannot remain in the community affirmed by the book's happy resolution but departs for the West, "the foremost of that band of pioneers who are opening the way for the march of the nation across the continent." As the irony of this final sentence indicates, even Natty's radical individualism is implicated in the spread of the civilization he seeks to flee: "the march of the nation across the continent." Yet he also suggests that Cooper was far from content with the reconciliation of gentlemanliness and commerce imaged in Judge Temple. Natty too is a projection of his author, who would revive him twice in the next four years, in *The Last of the Mohicans* (1826) and *The Prairie* (1827). Originally intended as a minor character, Leatherstocking would soon become Cooper's paradigmatic hero.

If Cooper was troubled, his doubts did not immediately upset his public reputation. The 1820s were for him a period of extraordinary success. In 1822 he moved his family to New York City, to be closer to his publisher, Charles Wiley. In 1823, along with *The Pioneers,* he published two stories, allegedly by "Jane Morgan," under the title *Tales for Fifteen. The Pilot* – Cooper's first sea novel, involving John Paul Jones and inspired by Cooper's contempt for Scott's supposed demonstration of nautical expertise in *The Pirate* – followed in 1823. Cooper then turned to a vast projected series, Legends of the Thirteen Republics, each volume to deal with the Revolution in a different colony, beginning with *Lionel Lincoln,* set in Boston and published in 1825. This was the only part of the series he ever wrote. In spite of heavy advance advertising, sales were not impressive; of a first printing of 6,000 copies, Wiley had sold only 4,500 by January 1826, and in that month Wiley himself, long in financial difficulty and poor health, died. So Cooper abandoned the Legends of the Thirteen Republics, turned to Philadelphia's Henry Carey, and returned to Natty Bumppo.

He had learned a lesson from *The Pioneers,* which in spite of an early triumph and high critical praise had ended up selling only moderately well, apparently because Cooper here neglected, as he had admitted to John Murray in 1822, "the present taste . . . for action and strong excitement." In *The Last of the Mohicans,* published in 1826, Cooper gave his readers what they apparently wanted, and confirmed his reputation in the United States and abroad as America's "national novelist." Natty Bumppo is here much younger, and his Indian friend Chingachgook (the drunken "Indian John" of *The Pioneers*) is now a vigorous warrior, accompanied by his warrior son, Uncas. These three – coming to the aid of two half sisters, Alice and Cora Munro, quite improbably wandering in the New York wilderness at the time of the French and Indian War – engage in an unrelenting sequence of "action and excitement." It is *A Midsummer Night's Dream* with weapons, and Cooper's readers loved it.

The Last of the Mohicans, for all its excesses and improbabilities, is in fact a masterpiece of mythic invention. What matters first of all, however, is that we recognize the calculation behind it, and behind most of Cooper's professional literary activity in the early 1820s. He would soon be denouncing Irving's "gold"-oriented obsequiousness, but the future patriot had first presented himself in *Precaution,* after all, as a British writer, assuming there was no market for native subjects. Cooper's turn to American materials in his second novel was a commercial gamble, one whose American success determined the course of his immediate future career. *The Pilot*'s open taunt to Scott mainly served to associate its author with the most popular British writer in America, while asserting, in the best tradition of what would later come to be known as public relations, the superiority of the advertised product. Assuming from the successes of *The Spy* and *The Pilot* the commercial value of the American Revolution, he began Legends of the Thirteen Republics, only to abandon it when *Lionel Lincoln* did not sell as well as he had apparently hoped. And in *Tales for Fifteen,* although he would later claim he did so only to aid his troubled publisher, "manly" Cooper was even happy to adopt the pseudonymous pose of sentimental woman author. The best of Cooper's writings from 1820 to 1826 reveal both a power beyond commercial speculation and a "gentlemanly" discomfort with dependence on commerce, a discomfort that would become his major political theme. Still, Cooper's conduct of his career in this period was thoroughly opportunistic, and not without reason. He had a family to support.

Following the publication of *The Last of the Mohicans,* Cooper moved himself and his family to Europe. In France he completed *The Prairie* – once again reviving a now older Natty Bumppo, who dies at the end of the book – and he published it first in England, in 1827, thus giving him (through a pattern already established by Irving) a greater assurance of income from British sales of the book. In America, however, sales were not impressive. *The Prairie* would sell steadily over time, but by the beginning of 1828, his American publisher, Carey and Lee, had not yet completely sold their first edition of 5,000 copies. Three more adventure stories followed, American books written in Europe: *The Red Rover* (1827), another sea tale, which sold 6,500 copies in America; *The Wept of Wish-ton-Wish* (1829), set in seventeenth-century New England at the time of King Phillip's War; and *The Water-Witch* (1829), a nautical romance set in New York Bay in the early eighteenth century. Cooper was working proven material, the wilderness and the sea, and he was maintaining his output, since 1823, of a book a year, for each of which Carey paid him $5,000. To this sum he added his more modest British earnings (Richard Bentley, to whom he had turned when relations with John Murray proved difficult, paid £250 for *The Prairie* and £400 for *The Red Rover*). He was also keeping journals of his European experiences and observations as material for travel books to be written when he returned to America. But one book produced early in this period was a departure from the pattern. *Notions of the Americans: Picked up by a Travelling Bachelor* (1828), supposedly written by a British visitor to the United States, was begun as an account of the Marquis de Lafayette's 1824–5 tour of the United States and was written at the request of the great French supporter of the American Revolution. Although the opinions expressed were almost wholly favorable to the democratic culture of the United States, the book did not do well; Carey, who thought it ill-advised, produced a first edition of only 2,500 copies. But Cooper had crossed a crucial bridge; he had become a spokesman, a role he would soon adopt in his own voice and with increasing vehemence.

In the early 1830s he embarked on a new venture, a trilogy of historical novels with European settings, concerned with serious political issues: *The Bravo* (1831), dealing with the corruption of democracy in Venice; *The Heidenmauer* (1832), casting a rather cold eye on the commercial underpinnings of the German Reformation; and *The Headsman* (1833), set in early-eighteenth-century Switzerland. This move was not immediately a disaster; Bentley paid £1,300, his highest payment ever to Cooper, for the right to publish *The Bravo* in England. Cooper's income from a particular book, however, had nothing to do with that book's sales; his publishers paid him a fixed fee in advance for the right to publish a book for a specific period of time, usually on the basis of only a description of the book's contents. His fee thus depended on the popularity of *earlier* works, and a commercial failure affected his earnings only as it inclined publishers to offer lower fees for subsequent productions, which is precisely what they became increasingly inclined to offer. They were proud to publish Cooper, but they wanted him to stick to his proven modes.

And there were ominous undercurrents in Cooper's European novels. The great patriotic but still expatriate novelist was apparently forsaking his native land as a subject. Even worse, to the extent that these books might be construed as being indirectly about America, neither *The Bravo's* depiction of democracy nor *The Heidenmauer's* portrayal of a revered revolution was flattering. Both books raise doubts about the legitimacy of democratic revolution similar to those implicit in the plot of *The Pioneers,* but here these doubts are not dissipated. Moreover, Cooper had embroiled himself, again out of friendship for Lafayette, in a French political controversy, which ended up pitting him against those Americans at home who were coalescing as a Whig party in opposition to Andrew Jackson's attack on the Bank of the United States. In 1832 an extraordinarily hostile review of *The Bravo* appeared in the Whig *New York American.* An enemy, for Cooper, was an enemy for life, and although he would have disliked the Whigs in any case, this review guaranteed the intensity of his future hostility toward American Whiggery.

Oddly or perversely enough, it was at this point, in November of 1833, that Cooper chose to return to America, purchasing and refurbishing Otsego Hall, his father's mansion, and settling in Cooperstown. The event was a far cry from Washington Irving's triumphant and calculated return a year earlier. First Cooper picked a quarrel with his fellow Americans. In *A Letter to His Countrymen* (1834) he attacked his treatment by the American press, castigated American political thinking, and announced his decision to retire from authorship. Then, this announcement notwithstanding, he immediately produced *The Monikins* (1835), its title sardonically echoing the "Mohicans" of his most celebrated success. This book, a nasty satire in which Britain and the United States are portrayed as two nations of monkeys, hardly advanced his public reputation. Btween 1836 and 1838 Cooper also published five volumes of travel writings and observations. The pace of publication was as furious as ever, even more so; in need of income, he had little choice. But he was failing to match his earlier earnings, and he even seemed to be defying his public to buy his books.

The hostility of his relations with American Whiggery was matched by his antagonism to his more immediate neighbors in Cooperstown. These neighbors had become accustomed to picnics on Three Mile Point, a Cooper family property on Lake Otsego, but in 1837 the returned proprietor of Otsego Hall asserted his own title to the land. The story got into the papers, and Cooper filed the first of many lawsuits, for libel, against the account in the Whig *Otsego Republican.* This and similar libel suits would occupy him for much of the rest of his life. Unlike Natty Bumppo, Cooper was more than willing to air his grievances before the bar. He also aired them in an extraordinary flurry of publications in 1838. *The American Democrat,* a rather Tocquevillian discussion of the cultural implications of democracy, was a genuine contribution to American political discourse, and small wonder: Cooper's predicament gave him a special sensitivity to one of the greatest issues of his time. How, he asked, was one to reconcile the ideals of personal legitimacy and distinction (ideals associated with the status of "gentleman") with the actualities of a commercial democracy? The Whigs were working their own compromise, but for this compromise, which he perhaps rightly regarded as mere commercial wealth masquerading in the sheep's clothing of democratic pretense, Cooper felt only contempt. And in any case the Whigs were turning against him and would soon be denouncing him as an "aristocrat" – a bitter irony, since Cooper was far more immediately dependent on commerce than such Whigs as, for instance, Boston's Lowells and Lawrences or Irving's patron Astor. In his own dilemma Cooper saw an image of his nation's, a time-honored American habit since the days of the Puritans. We can call his reaction principle or we can call it pique; it hardly matters. What does matter is that, for Cooper, the only imaginable way of asserting his integrity became, increasingly, to openly insult the tastes, values, and personalities of his public. He would not write an *Astoria* – not even if asked, and he hadn't been.

The American Democrat was followed in the same year by a pair of semiautobiographical novels; *Homeward Bound* and *Home as Found.* The first describes the voyage home from Europe of the Effingham family (descendants of Oliver and Elizabeth of *The Pioneers*). The second describes their experiences in New York City and their resettlement in Templeton, including a replay of the Three Mile Point controversy (which also appeared in *The Chronicles of Cooperstown,* another publication of 1838). Cooper gives the Effinghams' pushy

American antagonists – notably the democratic demagogue, Aristabulus Bragg – a genuine vitality, but this was hardly his intention, and the effect was lost on his enemies. The Whig journals, especially James Watson Webb's *Morning Courier and New York Enquirer* and William Leete Stone's *New York Commercial Advertiser,* leapt on the "Effingham Novels" with glee, and Cooper responded with more libel suits, simply supplying his antagonists with more material. In 1838 the erstwhile "American Scott" also chose to publish, in New York's *Knickerbocker Magazine,* a review of John Lockhart's *Life of Sir Walter Scott,* which took pains to attack the revered novelist's principles and character in terms similar to those in which Cooper was by now attacking Irving (with whom he more than once linked Scott). But insult and invective did not sell; they did not solve the problem of what a self-respecting professional author could write in order to support himself.

It is easy to describe Cooper's transformation in the 1830s as a movement from commerce to principle, from an ignoble to a noble understanding of democracy. This was basically his own view (although he would hardly have admitted to anything ignoble in his early success), and it is the way literary history has often chosen to regard this change. But the same literary history has always preferred the works he produced in the 1820s – notably *The Spy, The Pioneers, The Last of the Mohicans,* and *The Prairie* – to the more "principled" works of the 1830s. It is equally easy, on the other hand, to dismiss Cooper's professionally self-destructive behavior in the 1830s as a kind of personal aberration, which it surely was in part, but this is also far too easy. For one thing, Cooper's hostility to the growing ascendancy of the Whigs, who would win the national presidential election in 1840, was not simply an expression of personal resentment; it grew, as well, out of a serious belief in the potential of America's still-new political experiment, a potential Cooper felt the Whigs were betraying. In any case, Cooper's literary celebrity makes his behavior almost a litmus test of the conditions of literary vocation at the very time these conditions were first being established. Cooper, to his credit, was fully aware of what we might call his national-experimental status; if he was lashing about, even in unattractive ways, he had reasons for lashing about. He was admittedly nasty to Irving and others, but he was interested in asking questions Irving and others had chosen not to ask, even if he himself had no answers to these questions. This hardly makes him better as a person, or a better writer, but it does give him a special interest for the late twentieth-century literary historian interested in the very questions Cooper was agitating. What sort of literature *could* an American write – without, on the one hand, becoming simply commercial and without, on the other hand, simply losing his or her audience? This is the issue Cooper confronted in the

1840s. He did not resolve it, any more than any of his successors have; and the early 1840s, an era of collapsing book prices, may have been one of the worst times to try. Nevertheless, after the possibly self-inflicted fiasco of 1838, Cooper set out to restore his American literary reputation (he still had a family and a family mansion to support), and the results of his striving are at the very least instructive.

His first attempt to refashion his image involved the abandonment of both fiction and, so he hoped, controversy. Just as Irving had turned from fiction to history after the failure of *Tales of a Traveller* in 1824, so Cooper now turned from the Effinghams to *The History of the Navy of the United States of America,* published in 1839. He regarded this work as more important than his fiction and more likely to be lasting. Sales, however, were poor; in the next few years Bentley would cite his losses on *The History of the Navy* as grounds for arguing down Cooper's British fees for subsequent productions. In America the financial picture was better, but hardly what Cooper had hoped, and *The History of the Navy*'s impartial handling of the battle of Lake Erie embroiled its author in yet another controversy – this time between the family of Commodore Oliver Perry (all Whigs) and partisans of Jesse D. Elliott, a Jacksonian Democrat whom Perry had accused, some time after the famous battle, of neglect of duty. Cooper ignored these charges for plausibly good historical reasons, but in the era of "Tippecanoe and Tyler, Too," the Whigs could hardly resist another chance to abuse a prominent supporter of the Democrats – a supporter this party of wealth could accuse, as it had accused "King Andrew" Jackson, of "aristocratic" pretension.

It was at this point that Cooper once again revived Natty Bumppo, first in a work he described to Bentley in 1839 as "a nautico-lake-savage romance." The term is wonderful, foreshadowing the bravura with which modern advertising proclaims a combination of new, secret ingredients; in a single book Cooper would play all the cards that had proved so winning in the 1820s: nautical adventure (on Lake Ontario), the wilderness, and a Natty Bumppo now one or two years older than at the time of *The Last of the Mohicans*. *The Pathfinder* was published in 1840, and Natty was revived once more for *The Deerslayer* (1841), containing, as Cooper wrote to Bentley, "the *early* life of Leatherstocking – a period that is only wanting to fill up his career." The polemicist of the 1830s had apparently learned his lesson: he was returning to what his readers and publishers wanted. Indeed, in these last two Leatherstocking novels there are no Effinghams or even Temples; Natty is no longer an attendant or guide but a hero in his own right, failing at love (in *The Pathfinder*) or resisting it (in *The Deerslayer*). Yet the absence of genteel protagonists in these books is also ominous. For instance, in *The Deerslayer,* set on Lake Otsego well before the establishment of Cooperstown or Templeton, white civilization is represented only by Tom Hutter, a former pirate motivated entirely by naked greed, a grim parody of the Judge Temple of *The Pioneers*. Beneath the adventure tale of Natty's "First Warpath" lurks a somber and apocalyptic picture of the rise and fall of American civilization.

Still, one could simply read these books for the adventure. Bentley, for example, expressed his pleasure at Cooper's return in *The Pathfinder* to "the ground where you have earned for yourself such great reputation" and paid him £500 for the right to publish it (less £200 to help cover his own losses on *The History of the Navy*). In the United States, meanwhile, Lea and Blanchard (the current incarnation of the House of Carey) offered $3,600 for the right to publish 5,000 copies of *Pathfinder* and 2,000 more copies of *The History of the Navy*. Considering the state of the economy in general, and of the American publishing business in particular, these were impressive figures, and Cooper fully appreciated them. "Lea has sold near 4000 of Pathfinder," he wrote to his wife in May of 1840. "It has great success, in the worst of times — Indeed, it is the only thing that does sell." Critical reaction, after a decade of embattlement and still at the height of the libel suits, was equally gratifying. *The Pathfinder* was praised in Europe by no less a figure than Balzac, and it was also widely praised at home, its public supporters including Washington Irving. Even a negative notice by Park Benjamin, another of Cooper's Whig enemies, was able to find "one merit" in the work: "The book does *not* contain the mass of political, philosophical and philological ravings which have spoiled so many of the author's preceding works."

Nor were these Leatherstocking novels Cooper's only attempts to recover his reputation and his earning power. Between *The Pathfinder* and *The Deerslayer* he also published, in 1840, *Mercedes of Castille*, a tale drawing on the voyages of Columbus, which, to its author's surprise, did not sell. In 1842 he published two romances of naval warfare: *The Two Admirals* and *The Wing-and-Wing*. In 1843 appeared *Wyandotté*, set in the American wilderness during the Revolution; *Ned Myers, or A Life Before the Mast*, Cooper's rendition, as "editor," of the life of a sailor he had known at sea and recently rediscovered; and *The Autobiography of a Pocket-Handkerchief*, dealing with a French noblewoman reduced to menial labor after the July Revolution of 1830. This last book perhaps expressed Cooper's sense of his own situation, because he was now averaging two books a year and still failing to match his earnings from one book a year in the 1820s. And the pace continued. In 1844 Cooper published the two-part *Afloat and Ashore* and *Adventures of Miles Wallingford*. In 1845 and 1846 he produced a trilogy, the Littlepage Manuscripts (*Satanstoe, The Chainbearer*, and *The Redskins*), supporting the position of the Hudson Valley landowners in the current "Rent Wars."

Cooper had recovered from the debacle of the 1830s. Irving, facing the collapse of the economy in 1837 and of book prices in the early 1840s, had moved increasingly into other endeavors. In the parlance of modern business, he had "diversified." Cooper stuck with literature, but it was hardly clear that his renewed success in the 1840s was worth the price, or that it really *was* "success." In an 1846 letter to James Kirke Paulding, who had inquired about his publishing arrangements, Cooper summarized his situation in remarkably grim terms:

My pecuniary benefits, in this country amount to nothin worth naming. . . . The cheap literature has destroyed the value of nearly all literary property, and after five and twenty years of hard work, I find myself comparatively a poor man. Had I employed the same time in trade, or in travelling as an agent for a manufacturer of pins, I do not doubt I should have been better off, and my children independent. The fact is, this country is not sufficiently advanced for any thing intellectual, and the man who expects to rise by any such agency makes a capital mistake, unless he sells himself, soul and body, to a faction.

"If I were fifteen years younger," Cooper concludes, after noting that he expects to earn only $500 each from his three most recent books,

I would certainly go abroad, and never return. . . . You and I have committed the same error; have been American — whereas our cue was to be European, which would have given us success at home. The time was, when these things pained me, but every interest seems so much upside down, here, that another feeling has taken the place of even regret.

If Cooper saw his career as a kind of national experiment, it was to this, by 1846, that he thought the experiment had come.

By "cheap literature" Cooper probably did not mean sensational fiction aimed at a large, lower-class audience, although one of the first sensational American best-sellers, George Lippard's *Quaker City,* had appeared in 1844, just a year before the letter to Paulding. Rather, one guesses, Cooper was referring to the general collapse of book prices as a result of the competition of the early 1840s. *This* "cheap literature" consisted mainly of pirated European works, but Cooper's letter refers not to foreign competition, but to the pressure on *American* writers to "be European," and one suspects that, once again, he has Irving in mind. The irony, of course, is that Cooper's envy is here inflating Irving's "success at home," for in the 1840s Irving was no more able than Cooper to rely comfortably on the value of his "literary property."

Cooper continued writing for a living until his death in 1851, one day short of his sixty-second birthday. *The Crater* appeared in 1847, *Jack Tier* and *The Oak Openings* in 1848, *The Sea Lions* in 1849, *The Ways of the Hour* in 1850. Not all was the bleakness proclaimed in the letter to Paulding. With *The Sea Lions,* in 1849, Cooper moved to a new American publisher, New

York's George Palmer Putnam, who began issuing a uniform edition of his works (as he was also doing with Irving's). And in a review of *The Sea Lions,* a member of the new literary generation, Herman Melville, praised Cooper as "our national novelist." Yet for British rights to *The Ways of the Hour,* Richard Bentley was willing to offer, and Cooper was compelled to accept, only £100. Cooper's mood was increasingly revealed by the endorsement of aristocratic withdrawal in such works as the Littlepage Manuscripts, or by the apocalyptic energies of works like *Wyandotté* or *The Crater.* In the former, a settlement darkly modeled on the Templeton of *The Pioneers* is attacked by Indians at the time of the Revolution and its founder is killed. In the latter the founder is luckily absent when his Pacific island community, overrun with commercial excess, is destroyed in a volcanic eruption.

Cooper was indeed a "national novelist." Far more so than any of his American contemporaries, indeed virtually uniquely among these contemporaries, he had succeeded for over three decades in the new profession of literature. In his effort to reconcile "manliness" with the commercial requirements of this profession, however, he had in his own judgment failed. Cooper's ideal of manly integrity, expressed again and again in dramas (or melodramas) of beset manhood, was at least in part a response to the fragility of his own fortunes, a compensatory myth. This myth, embodied most purely in the nostalgic evocation of Natty Bumppo and of Indian life in the wilderness, is one of considerable power; it has become an enduring component of the ideology of "America." Still, it is important to recognize that even Cooper's great tragic theme of the destruction of Indian culture by the march of white commercial civilization is closely tied to his own personal and professional situation as he understood it. The major fear of his Native Americans, after all, is that someone – the whites, another tribe – may have "made women" out of them, and Natty Bumppo maintains his integrity, above all, by avoiding women.

Cooper, who distinguished Irving's supposed "meannesses" from manly (and therefore morally superior) "crimes," helped establish the equation of "America" with "masculinity," and the concomitant equation of commercial popularity with "feminization," that have lain at the heart of much nineteenth- and twentieth-century thinking about American literature. For instance, in Fanny Fern's *Ruth Hall* (1855), the heroine's effeminate brother is editor of a journal called the "Irving Magazine." The truth is that Cooper hardly knew what he wanted, which is why his ideas of manhood and America, so nearly synonymous in his thinking, are also so vague, so reactively negative. What matters, however, is that the equation of the American with the masculine (and with resistance to the feminine) has appealed to so many of Cooper's male American successors, successors faced with the same commercial predicament. As Irving helped create a taste and market for native tales and sketches, so Cooper suggested the possibilities of the novel, and both writers would have many American imitators. But their most important legacy, beyond demonstrating the possibility of professional literary success for Americans, lay in their promotion of contrasting and even antagonistic images of American literary vocation, of the writer's relationship to the public, and ultimately of the meaning of America and American identity. In effect, Cooper and Irving established, by their examples, contrasting schools or traditions of American literature. Twentieth-century literary historians have generally seen Cooper, rather than Irving, as the seminal American fiction writer, and not without reason. The myth or ideology of American identity and literary vocation to which he gave currency can be traced in the stances and careers of such later Americans as Melville, Mark Twain, and even Ernest Hemingway, and these male writers occupy central positions in the twentieth-century literary "canon." We should not, however, ignore Irving's legacy. Poe and Hawthorne, for instance, turned most consistently to the tale rather than the novel, and it was Irving, far more than Cooper, whose influence lay behind the most deliberately popular body of pre-Civil War American literature, especially the magazine writing that would signal in the 1840s and 1850s the real beginnings of mass literature.

NOVELS AND NOVELISTS IN THE 1820S

In 1820, according to Lyle H. Wright's *American Fiction, 1774–1850* (1948), five volumes of new prose fiction by native authors were published in the United States, only a marginal increase over the average of three and a half per year for the previous decade. The figure began to rise dramatically after 1820: to eighteen in 1825, to twenty-six in 1830, and to fifty-four in 1835. Severe economic conditions, both in the nation at large and in the publishing business, momentarily slowed the pace of expansion and even reduced the rate of production: to an average annual figure, from 1836 through 1842, of thirty-nine new titles. Then, with the national economy recovering and with the most virulent forms of competition in book publishing largely under control, production once again took off. In 1843, seventy-seven new titles entered the ranks of American fiction; in 1844, one hundred and two; in 1845, one hundred and fifty-eight. In quantitative terms at least, the period from 1820 through 1845 clearly marked the first major "renaissance" in American fiction.

More than a few of these new books were collections of tales and sketches, including the first and second series of Nathaniel Hawthorne's *Twice-told Tales* (1837 and 1842) and Edgar Allan Poe's *Tales of the Grotesque and*

Arabesque (1840). But most were novels, which almost always, then as now, sold far better than story collections. Although Irving's influence would spawn such blatant imitations as Henry Wadsworth Longfellow's *Outre-Mer* (1833) and Henry T. Tuckerman's *Italian Sketch Book* (1835), and although Irving's mode would receive wide currency in magazines, in the 1820s Cooper rather than Irving provided the model most imitated, and the immediate impact of Cooper's success as an incentive to emulation is revealed quite starkly by the figures. Between 1821 (when *The Spy* gained national and international acclaim) and 1822, the rate of publication of new native fiction rose impressively from five volumes a year to fifteen. Seldom does literary history find such precise quantitative evidence of at least crude influence – of new writers and publishers, in this case, trying to cash in on *The Spy*'s success.

Many of the new American novels published in the 1820s were, like *The Spy* and *The Pioneers,* works of historical fiction. What had worked for Scott and Cooper, these authors and their publishers apparently believed, might work for them. But only infrequently did such beliefs prove to be justified. For example, James McHenry (1785–1845), an Irish-born Philadelphian who produced six historical novels between 1823 and 1831, is now completely forgotten, and even during his lifetime he was better known for an 1822 verse collection, *The Pleasures of Friendship* (which had gone through seven editions by 1836), than for any of his hastily written historical fictions.

Several of the writers who turned to fiction in the 1820s did so only briefly and ultimately achieved professional success through other literary endeavors. Lydia Maria Child (1802–80) published three historical novels in the 1820s and 1830s: *Hobomok* (1824) deals with seventeenth-century Massachusetts; *The Rebels* (1825) with, as its subtitle puts it, "Boston before the Revolution"; *Philothea* (1836) with ancient Greece. These books sold well enough (new editions of *Philothea,* for instance, were issued in 1839, 1845, and 1849), but Child's most important efforts were not in fiction. In 1830 she published a manual of domestic advice, *The Frugal Housewife,* helping to establish one of the major genres of American women's literature. *The Mother's Book* followed in 1831, and from 1826 to 1834 Child edited a well-known children's magazine, Boston's *Juvenile Miscellany.* Her *Letters from New York* (1843, 1845), a collection of newspaper pieces written for the *Boston Courier,* went through eleven editions by 1850. And with her husband, David Lee Child, a founder of the New England Anti-Slavery Society, she was an active abolitionist, editing the *National Anti-Slavery Standard* from 1841 to 1849. Child was very much a successful literary professional, but fiction constituted a small and even incidental part of her professional activity. In this respect her career resembled that of Sarah Josepha Hale (1788–1879), who first made her mark with *Northwood* (1827), a New England local-color novel, and with a collection, *Sketches of American Character* (1829), but who thereafter devoted her energies mainly to magazines, especially as the influential editor of *Godey's Lady's Book* from 1837 to 1877.

The reputation of Timothy Flint (1780–1840) was also not mainly based on his works of fiction. His first historical romance, *Francis Berrian, or the Mexican Patriot,* (1826), was followed by other novels – *The Life and Adventures of Arthur Clenning* (1828), *George Mason, the Young Backswoodsman* (1829), *The Shoshonee Valley* (1830) – but he was better known as a magazine writer and editor, and his nonfictional works on the geography and history of the American West had a much wider circulation than did his novels. Born in Massachusetts and serving there as a minister from 1802 to 1814, Flint then traveled westward for the Missionary Society of Connecticut. His record of these travels, *Recollections of the Last Ten Years, Passed in Occasional Residences and Journeyings in the Valley of the Mississippi,* was published in 1826 and launched his literary career. From 1827 to 1830 he edited the *Western Monthly Review* in Cincinnati, where he also published such more-or-less factual volumes as *A Condensed Geography and History of the Western States* (1828, expanded in 1832 as *The History and Geography of the Mississippi Valley*) and *Indian Wars of the West* (1833). In 1834 Flint served briefly as editor of New York's new *Knickerbocker Magazine*. In 1833, meanwhile, he had published his *Biographical Memoir of Daniel Boone, the First Settler of Kentucky,* which went on, through fourteen editions, to become perhaps the most widely read account of the western frontier in the first half of the nineteenth century.

Not all of the new American fiction writers in the 1820s were new to literature. James Kirke Paulding (1778–1860) had been part of New York's literary culture since the beginning of the century. He was closely associated with Washington Irving: his sister had married Irving's brother William; he had collaborated with William and Washington on *Salmagundi* in 1807; and his *Diverting History of John Bull and Brother Jonathan,* a comic history published in 1812, was clearly inspired by the success of Washington's *Diedrich Knickerbocker's History of New York.* Paulding was apparently following his perception of the tastes of the American reading public, and two years after the success of Cooper's *The Spy,* he turned to historical fiction with *Koningsmarke* (1823), set in seventeenth-century Delaware. Two more historical novels followed in the early 1830s: *The Dutchman's Fireside* (1831), dealing with Dutch New York before the Revolution; and *Westward Ho!* (1832), set on the Kentucky frontier. By the standards of the time these books were quite successful; *The Dutchman's Fireside,* for example, went through six editions in the 1830s and 1840s.

In 1819–20 Paulding had published, without the collaboration of the

Irving brothers, a *Second Series* of *Salmagundi,* which included an essay on "National Literature." "By freeing himself from a habit of servile imitation," he proclaimed, the native writer "may and will in time destroy the ascendancy of foreign taste and opinions and elevate his own in the place of them." Although such literary nationalism, seventeen years before Emerson's "American Scholar," was already thoroughly conventional, Paulding was far from clear about what, exactly, would give the new "national literature" its "air and character of originality." For the most part his essay is an attack on the gothic marvels associated with the romances of Sir Walter Scott; it is a plea for what Paulding calls "Rational Fictions," based on "nature." Yet in spite of his attack on imitation, Paulding proposes a British novel, Fielding's *Tom Jones,* as the highest example of the sort of fiction most appropriate to America, and Fielding's influence is markedly evident in *Koningsmarke* and *The Dutchman's Fireside.*

Paulding played the role of American man of letters for three decades with energy, dedication, and considerable success, producing not only historical novels but short stories, verse, satire, literary criticism, essays, biographies, and plays (his *The Lion of the West,* a farce first produced in 1831, was long a popular favorite). He was also a successful man of affairs, serving as secretary of the navy under Martin Van Buren from 1838 to 1841. After this hiatus in his literary career he returned to historical fiction in the later 1840s with *The Old Continental* (1846), set in New York during the Revolution, and *The Puritan and His Daughter* (1849), which takes place in seventeenth-century New England and Virginia. Yet Paulding's very literary versatility – his cultivation of so many different modes, his following the leads first of Irving and then of Cooper, even while modeling himself on Fielding – is symptomatic of a general uncertainty in the 1820s and 1830s about just what sort of literature the American man of letters would or should produce.

The same uncertainty is clear in the more flamboyant career and writings of John Neal (1793–1876). Raised in poverty in Portland, Maine, Neal left school at the age of twelve and spent the next dozen years working in a series of mercantile establishments. Ending up in Baltimore in 1817, he began studying law and turned to literature in the hope that it might support him while he prepared for the bar. He was much enamored of Byron and wrote a hundred-and-fifty-page appreciation of the British poet for Baltimore's *Portico* magazine in four days, but he earned little money or reputation from his own literary works: a melodramatic novel, *Keep Cool* (1817); a long poem, *The Battle of Niagara* (1818); and a Byronic verse tragedy, *Otho* (1819). Undaunted, he produced four novels in 1822–3, following the success of Cooper's *Spy: Logan,* an overwrought historical romance involving an Englishman masquerading as a vengeful Indian chief; *Errata; or, the Works of Will. Adams,* a kind of melodramatized autobiography; *Randolph,* a novel risky both in its sexual concerns and in its often caustic sketches of Neal's contemporaries; and *Seventy-Six,* a historical novel of the American Revolution. In 1845 Nathaniel Hawthorne, who had been a student at Bowdoin when these books appeared, recalled "that wild fellow, John Neal, who almost turned my boyish brain with his romances," but these hastily written books hardly fulfilled their author's ambition of surpassing the reputations and commercial successes of Irving and Cooper.

Although Neal was an ardent nationalist, accusing both Irving and Cooper of being wanting on this score, it was oddly enough in England that he managed, briefly, to achieve notoriety as a representative American writer. Settling in London early in 1824, he began to place essays in Edinburgh's *Blackwood's Magazine,* most notably a series on "American Writers." Here, anonymously, he praised Brockden Brown and Paulding and criticized Irving's *Sketch Book* (in spite of its dashes of "bold poetry") for its "squeamish, puling, lady-like sentimentality"; Cooper was by no means the only American to equate Irving's popular appeal with effeminacy. Yet Neal was no kinder to the author of *The Spy,* whom he dismissed in a mere half column as "a man of sober talent – nothing more." Neal then went on to devote seventeen columns to his own work. These essays infuriated many of Neal's American contemporaries, but once the identity of their author became known, they did make him famous.

In his mixture of Byronic defiance and blatant self-promotion Neal anticipated, in different ways, Poe, Melville, and Whitman. The open preoccupation of his novels with sexual transgression and oedipal guilt makes him at least an interesting curiosity to the modern reader. And his fiction anticipates the sensational novels, aimed at a mass audience, that began appearing regularly in the 1840s. But Neal's contemporary vogue was very brief. William Blackwood brought out Neal's fifth novel, *Brother Jonathan,* in 1825, after requiring the excision of material he considered indecent, and when fewer than five hundred copies sold, out of a printing of two thousand, Blackwood's ardor for his American genius cooled almost instantly. Neal returned to America in 1827 and settled in provincial Portland, where he lived for the rest of his life. He continued publishing for a time, mostly works planned or written in England: *Rachel Dyer: A North American Story* (1828), *Authorship: A Tale* (1830), and *The Down-Easters* (1833). He produced new short stories for American periodicals and promoted such younger writers as Edgar Poe, but the fame, or infamy, of the 1820s gave way to growing obscurity. After recalling "that wild fellow, John Neal," in 1845, Hawthorne went on to surmise that "he surely has long been dead, else he never could keep himself so quiet." By the 1860s Neal was writing Western dime novels, on order and according to formula, simply for needed money. He died in 1876, after failing to interest Boston's J. R. Osgood in reissuing *Seventy-Six* to commemorate the centennial of American liberty.

Catharine Maria Sedgwick (1789–1867), although now almost as little known as Neal, was widely admired in the nineteenth century, and she was one of the most influential American fiction writers of her generation. Never marrying, she divided her time between Stockbridge, in western Massachusetts, and New York City. Her first literary effort, *A New England Tale* (1822), began as a tract crticizing the intolerance of New England's inherited Calvinism (Sedgwick herself converted to Unitarianism), but during composition it evolved into a genuine novel, chronicling the triumph over adversity of its orphan heroine, Jane Elton. *Redwood,* which followed in 1824, is the story of another exemplary young woman, Ellen Bruce. Then Sedgwick turned to historical fiction in 1827 with *Hope Leslie,* set in seventeenth-century Massachusetts. With these novels and their exemplary heroines Sedgwick established the basic formula that would lie behind such best-sellers of the 1850s as Susan Warner's *The Wide, Wide World* (1850) and Maria Cummin's *The Lamplighter* (1854), although Sedgwick's heroines are considerably more self-reliant than those of Warner and Cummins.

Although Sedgwick was a woman of independent means, with no need to support herself by her writings, and although she herself persistently deprecated her own literary abilities and ambitions, her books sold well. *Redwood* was translated into German, Swedish, Italian, and French; *Hope Leslie,* which was compared favorably to the work of Cooper and made its author the most celebrated American woman writer before Harriet Beecher Stowe, earned her $1,100 from the sale of an edition of two thousand copies; and in 1830 *Clarence,* a contemporary story with another strong heroine, earned her $1,200. Sedgwick was equally successful, and considerably more productive, in the 1830s. *The Linwoods,* a historical romance of the Revolution, appeared in 1835, but Sedgwick was turning increasingly to didactic fiction aimed at children or working-class readers. *Home* (1835) went through twenty editions by 1846; *The Poor Rich Man and the Rich Poor Man* (1836) went through sixteen; *Live and Let Live* (1837) went through twelve. From New York's House of Harper, which published *The Linwoods, The Poor Rich Man,* and *Live and Let Live,* Sedgwick earned more than $6,000 between 1835 and 1841. Her last novel, *Married or Single?* appeared in 1857.

It is more than a little difficult to generalize about the nature of American fiction or the status of the American fiction writer in the 1820s, and this difficulty of generalization is itself important. To writers as diverse as Lydia Child, Timothy Flint, James Paulding, John Neal, and Catharine Sedgwick, Cooper's success apparently suggested the possibility of fiction writing as an

American profession, but it suggested little else. Child and Flint soon abandoned fiction, and although Paulding and Neal were considerably more
dedicated, their very dedication reveals, in different ways, a good deal of
uncertainty about what, as American novelists, they were supposed to be
doing. Sedgwick's career came closest, in the 1820s and early 1830s, to the
professional consistency of Cooper's, but by the mid-1830s she, too, was
beginning to turn away from fiction. And unlike Cooper, even Sedgwick,
after the collapse of the literary marketplace at the end of the 1830s, did not
attempt to revive the experience of the 1820s.

A laudatory review of Sedgwick's *Hope Leslie* published in Boston's *North
American Review* in 1828 concludes by noting that "our authoress . . . , if the
truth must be told, appears to entertain a decided partiality for her own sex."
Exemplary, self-reliant heroines do dominate Sedgwick's fiction – Jane Elton
in *A New England Tale,* Ellen Bruce in *Redwood,* Hope Leslie in the novel that
bears her name – and yet Elizabeth Temple, for instance, in Cooper's *The
Pioneers* is no less self-reliant and no less willing to combat social injustice
than these young women. Cooper, who had begun his career with an inept
imitation of Jane Austen, was aware (or assumed) that women constituted the
bulk of his potential audience. It was only in the late 1820s and early
1830s – as Cooper increasingly shifted his interest to Natty Bumppo and
other isolated male figures, while such women as Child and Sedgwick gravi-
tated more and more toward children's fiction and advice manuals – that a
pronounced differentiation of "masculine" and "feminine" American fiction
began to emerge as perhaps the major fault line in the American literary
landscape.

There were clearly many reasons for this increasing division of the literary
marketplace. It coincided with the growing influence in the larger culture of
the so-called Cult of Domesticity, the doctrine of woman's separate "sphere,"
to which we will turn presently. There may also be reasons more directly
implicated in the professional careers of these writers. Cooper became more
aggressively "masculine" and more contemptuous of the "feminine" in response to anxieties about the commodification of his work, the commercial-
ization of his authorial identity. Male writers – at least writers like Cooper
who felt their masculinity imperiled – associated commercial success with
feminization long before women novelists had much actual market success. A
writer like Sedgwick, on the other hand, apparently felt no alienation from
her public; if her readers wanted didactic fiction and works for children, she
was content to supply this demand. But this differentiation of men's and
women's fictional traditions, never absolute in any case, took place later. In
1827 Sedgwick still found it perfectly natural to follow Cooper's example and
write a work of wilderness historical romance, complete with Indian massacre

and melodrama; and readers gratified by *The Last of the Mohicans* were happy to turn to *Hope Leslie*. This is hardly to say that the 1828 reviewer was incorrect about Sedgwick's "partiality to her own sex," but only that in the 1820s such partiality did not yet necessarily bear the nearly generic significance it would acquire by the 1850s.

DRAMA AND LITERARY VOCATION

In drama as in book publishing, the years from the 1820s through the 1840s witnessed extraordinary expansion. By the middle of the century there were more than fifty professional theatrical companies in the United States. Charleston, important for its theatrical productions in the eighteenth century, was on the decline, and activity centered in three northern coastal cities: Philadelphia, Boston (where the Massachusetts laws against theatrical exhibitions had been repealed as recently as 1792), and especially New York (already, by 1820, the dominant influence in American theater). But although these cities boasted the greatest number of theaters and new productions, they had no monopoly on American drama. Permanent and traveling companies appeared throughout the nation and across the frontier, and in the late 1840s two theaters even opened in California. The main attractions in American theaters were most often visiting British actors, but America was beginning to produce its own stars: for instance, Mary Ann Duff, Anna Cora Mowatt, Charlotte Cushman, and, above all, Edwin Forrest. Also, although most of the plays produced on the American stage were classics (especially plays by Shakespeare) or contemporary foreign works (for instance, melodramas by such popular playwrights as Edward Bulwer Lytton and August von Kotzebue), quite a few, including a number of major hits, were written by American playwrights.

Nevertheless, these developments in the American theater are at best incidental to the history of American literature and American literary vocation in the first half of the nineteenth century. Philip Hone, a wealthy businessman and devoted playgoer who would become a prominent New York Whig in the 1830s, expressed his hope in 1825, on the occasion of the laying of the cornerstone of New York's Bowery Theatre, that "at no distant period the latent talents of some native Bard may here be warmed into existence, who shall emulate the growing fame, acquired in other walks, by Irving and Cooper." But this hope, even though popular works by both Irving and Cooper were adapted for the stage, was disappointed. In part the problem was simply a matter of quality; none of the American plays produced before 1850, however great their interest as documents of popular culture, has survived as literature. The United States was hardly unique in its failure to produce an enduring dramatic literature at this time; it is equally true of England and Europe that the first half of the nineteenth century, from the perspective of the history of dramatic literature, is something of a black hole. There was a more basic reason for the failure of Hone's hopes, however. The careers of Irving and Cooper indicated that literature could be pursued in America as a profession. The years before the Civil War produced many important developments in *theater* as a profession, but they produced no comparable professionalizing of *playwriting*.

Professional American theaters were staffed by resident companies, whose members filled most of the parts in a remarkable (and taxing) variety of performances. Leading parts, however, were often filled by touring celebrities. On the positive side, this system meant that playgoers almost anywhere in the United States could eventually see the great actors of their day, that local actors could learn from these professionals, and that, since both star and company were most likely to have standard works in common, there was a built-in incentive for performing classic plays by Shakespeare and others. Other consequences were less salutary. The star system, together with the almost daily alternation of plays (at a time when even the largest urban populations could hardly support long runs), kept rehearsals to a minimum, at least rehearsals with the visiting star; and actors frequently forgot lines or even failed to appear for whole scenes. Unable to develop subtlety of dramatic interpretation, which was in any case not in much popular demand, American theaters tended to promote emotional and scenic spectacle, a development abetted by the shift from candles to gas lighting. The reliance on visiting stars encouraged the mounting (and commissioning) of plays dominated by single characters – often rather bombastic characters. Also, since a popular star could claim up to half a performance's total proceeds, *before* expenses, the star system further undermined the already precarious incomes of theater managers and especially of performers. Actors for the most part received only subsistence wages, supplemented, from time to time, by "benefit" performances, in which friends or supporters of a particular performer would buy tickets and the performer would receive all or some of the proceeds, *after* expenses.

A performer's abiding hope, or at least a young performer's abiding hope, was that this precarious situation might be only an apprenticeship, and a few American actors actually did rise to stardom. The most spectacular success in the years before 1850 was Edwin Forrest (1806–72). Born in Philadelphia, Forrest made his debut at Philadelphia's Walnut Street Theatre in 1820. He then embarked on his apprenticeship, first with a traveling company based in Pittsburgh and then with a resident company in New Orleans. In 1825 he landed a job in Albany, for $7.50 a week, and there he had the good luck to work with, and to learn from, the great British star Edmund Kean, playing Iago, for instance, to Kean's Othello. Then, in 1826, Forrest himself played Othello at New York City's Park Theatre and his reputation was made. New York's new Bowery Theatre signed him on for $800 a year, and the next year he was earning $200 *a night*. Forrest's success was no more typical than were the successes of Irving and Cooper, but he demonstrated that a professional American actor could not only succeed but make a fortune. No American playwright came even close to such a demonstration.

Forrest's acting style was "heroic," more physical than subtle, and his admirers were loyal and passionate, none more admiring or passionate than Forrest himself. He was fiercely nationalistic – a quality that expressed itself above all in public abuse of his British stage rivals, especially the British tragedian William Charles Macready. In May of 1849, during a Macready performance of *Macbeth* at New York's Astor Place Theatre, Forrest partisans in the house kept the play from proceeding. A public petition signed by leading New York citizens and literary figures (including Washington Irving and Herman Melville) apologized to Macready, and a repeat performance was arranged. That night the rowdies, forbidden entrance to the theater, rallied outside, some 10,000 to 15,000 strong, throwing stones through the windows, and it ultimately took three volleys from the rifles of the militia to disperse the mob.

The Astor Place Riot indicated both the passion that American audiences could feel for the theater and an apparently political dimension to Forrest's popularity. Whereas Macready's most ardent sponsors were Whig "gentlemen," Forrest's appeal in New York was especially to the so-called Bowery Boys, Democrats all. The day of the riot a poster challenged American "Workingmen" to come to the "English aristocratic opera house" and "Stand up to your lawful rights"; the same divisions would manifest themselves in the New York draft riots of 1863. On a deeper level, however, the incident suggests not so much the political seriousness of American theater as the potential of American politics for a dangerous theatricality. The Astor Place Riot – aroused not by any coherent political agenda but by the rivalry of dramatic stars, and resembling less the storming of the Bastille than the Rolling Stones' 1969 fiasco at Altamont – left twenty-two dead and thirty wounded.

Forrest's nationalism did have a more positive outlet. In 1828 he began his practice of offering prizes for works by American playwrights, and he was ultimately reported to have awarded a total of something like $20,000 to the winners of his many contests. Such munificence was hardly enough, however, to make playwriting a viable profession in the United States, and even those who produced hit plays were unable to support themselves, for a number of reasons. In the absence of an international copyright law, American theater managers could produce foreign works for free; what incentive did they have for paying more than token compensation to native authors? Even worse, there was no domestic copyright law protecting the performance (as distinguished from the publication) of plays. And there was no system of royalties governing the compensation of playwrights. Managers or star actors paid a flat fee for dramatic vehicles, which then became their property. Thus, a play running for decades was not necessarily worth any more to its author than a play that closed after its first performance. Some examples should clarify a situation that kept even hits from enriching (or, for that matter, from supporting) their authors.

The first American hit play of the 1820s was *The Forest Rose,* written by Samuel Woodworth (1785–1842) and first produced in New York in 1825. This "Pastoral Opera," as its subtitle described it, resembled what we would now call musical comedy, and its virtuous American farmers, its Yankee Jonathan, its villainous fop, its mixture of humor and melodrama, all led to enduring popularity over the next forty years. Both in the United States and in London it was performed more regularly than any other American play before 1850. Woodworth wrote many other plays and engaged in a variety of literary activities (for instance, he wrote the song "The Old Oaken Bucket"), but he received little compensation from the success of *The Forest Rose.* He abandoned literature in 1836 and died in poverty six years later.

The first of Forrest's prize competitions, in 1828, offered $500 plus half the proceeds from a benefit for a "tragedy, in five acts, of which the hero, or principal, shall be an aboriginal of this country." The winning play was *Metamora, or The Last of the Wampanoags,* by John Augustus Stone (1800–34), a professional actor. *Metamora* was loosely based on the seventeenth-century conflict known as King Philip's War but added such clichés of melodrama as a lascivious villain and the revelation of an orphan's true parentage. The play was first performed in New York in 1829 and was an instant sensation. It launched the American craze for Indian plays that would finally be lampooned by John Brougham in 1847 in *Metamora; or, The Last of the Pollywogs,* and it provided a dependable source of income for Edwin Forrest from 1829 to the end of his career. In 1853, for instance, it ran for six consecutive performances in Boston, an impressive run for the time, and brought in almost $4,000. But Stone, the author, earned nothing from *Metamora* beyond the original $500 and half the proceeds from the benefit. He wrote other plays but never again achieved a success on the order of *Metamora*'s; he committed suicide in 1834 in Philadelphia. In that same year, an audience for *Metamora* in Albany was so large the musicians in the orchestra had to give up their seats and retire to the wings to make room for more paying customers.

The American who came closest to establishing a viable career as a professional playwright before 1850 was Robert Montgomery Bird (1806–54). Trained to be a doctor, Bird soon abandoned medicine for literature, and in the early 1830s he won four of Forrest's prize competitions. *Pelopidas, or the Fall of the Polemarchs,* Bird's first winning entry, was never produced, but in the fall of 1831 Forrest did perform *The Gladiator* (Bird's version of the revolt of Spartacus) in New York, Philadelphia, and Boston. This play, like *Metamora,* became a staple of Forrest's repertory; between 1831 and 1854 he played the role of Spartacus at least a thousand times – an average, over twenty-three years, of almost forty-four performances per year. Bird followed *The Gladiator* with *Oralloossa, Son of the Incas* (1832) and *The Broker of Bogota* (1834), and although neither matched the success of *The Gladiator,* both received critical praise and continued to be performed by Forrest for some time. By the mid-1830s, Bird was clearly America's foremost dramatist, and his professional relationship with Forrest had warmed into friendship. Their friendship soon soured, however, not surprisingly over money. Forrest had paid Bird $1,000 each for *The Gladiator, Oralloossa,* and *The Broker of Bogota.* When the author, noting that Forrest was getting rich performing his plays, demanded a small share of the profits, Forrest refused, as he would later refuse Bird's son permission to publish his father's collected dramatic works. Bird asked for $6,000 in 1837; after Bird's death his widow estimated that Forrest must have made something like $100,000 performing *The Gladiator.* But Bird had no valid legal claim on any portion of these earnings; no wonder he abandoned drama, in the 1830s, for fiction. "What a fool I was to think of writing plays!" he wrote in his journal. "To be sure, they are much wanted. But these novels are much easier sorts of things and immortalize one's pocket much sooner."

The devaluation of playwriting in pre-Civil War America was not simply a fluke of the marketplace, or a consequence of inadequate copyright laws; it in fact represented public taste quite accurately. Anna Cora Mowatt (1819–70) was best known as an actress, but she also wrote a number of successful plays, most notably *Fashion,* a satire on American nouveaux riches first produced in 1845. Of this play Mowatt later wrote that "a *dramatic,* not a literary, success was what I desired to achieve." From our own perspective *Fashion* is a better play than much of its competition – including the inflated Forrest vehicles *Metamora* and *The Gladiator* – but Mowatt's distinction of the "dramatic" from the "literary" tells us a good deal about a theater with which, as both performer and playwright, she was intimately familiar. What succeeded were broad humor, melodrama, and spectacle. A play with Forrest was a good draw, but even better was a play with Forrest and real horses on the stage. Almost no one wanted literary subtlety, which would in any case have had to overcome both inept acting and, typically, a good deal of audible activity on the part of the audience.

A night at the theater in pre-1850 America did not simply involve seeing a single play performed; there were also curtain-raisers, songs and other entertainments during intermissions, and afterpieces (often farces). Thomas D. Rice introduced his famous blackface impersonation of "Jim Crow" as an afterpiece at New York's Bowery Theatre in 1830; by the 1840s the Virginia Minstrels and Christy's Minstrels had developed the full-fledged "minstrel show." Vaudeville and burlesque had similar origins. Such creations were hardly literature, but literature was not what most Americans went to the theater for – even, one gathers, when they went to see Shakespeare. The night of Macready's first performance at the Astor Place Theatre, in 1849, the rowdies in the crowd began hissing the local actor playing Duncan. They thought he was Macbeth.

Spectacle and crude entertainment ruled drama even when plays were allegedly moral in purpose; and didactic purpose, by disarming religious prejudice against theater, could help attract new customers. The first great success in this vein was *The Drunkard, or the Fallen Saved,* written by W. H. Smith (1808–72) and first performed in Boston in 1844. *The Drunkard* tells the story of the descent into alcoholism and the subsequent and astonishingly sudden recovery of one Edward Middleton. It ends with a wonderful tableau in which the cast, assembled in a "rural cottage," sings verse after verse of "Home, Sweet Home." The popularity of this confection was phenomenal; in New York, it played simultaneously at four different theaters for a time, and an 1850 production at P. T. Barnum's American Museum became the first play in the United States to run for one hundred consecutive performances. Although *The Drunkard* owed a good deal of its popularity to its temperance message (it was advertised as a "moral drama" or "moral lecture"), it inevitably converted this message into popular entertainment. On occasion the famous "delirium scene," in which Middleton, writhing on the floor, fights off imaginary snakes, was even performed on its own. This popular play did enrich its author, but only because W. H. Smith, a British actor who had emigrated to the United States in 1827, was manager of the Boston Museum, where *The Drunkard* had its first great success.

The same combination of didactic intention and popular spectacle lay behind the most extraordinary and long-lasting of all nineteenth-century theatrical phenomena: the many adaptations of Harriet Beecher Stowe's *Uncle Tom's Cabin* that swept the United States from 1852 until well into the twentieth century. The first version to succeed was commissioned by G. C. Howard, manager of the Troy, New York, Museum, who wanted to feature his four-year-old daughter, Cordelia (one is really not making this up), as Little Eva. Howard, who played Augustine St. Clare, and his wife, who played Topsy, had met while performing together in the original Boston production of *The Drunkard*. Their version of *Uncle Tom's Cabin* was written by George L. Aiken, Howard's cousin, who played the part of George Harris and who received forty dollars and a gold watch for his adaptation. This Troy production was apparently seen by 25,000 people (the total population of Troy was 30,000) before moving on to New York City, and the Howard family continued performing the play until 1887, when G. C. Howard died and when Cordelia, famous as Little Eva since the age of four, celebrated her thirty-fifth birthday.

Aiken's version of *Uncle Tom's Cabin*, which Stowe saw performed in Boston, is fairly faithful to the novel; indeed, much of the dialogue is simply lifted from the book. But Aiken included such bits of stage spectacle as Eliza crossing the Ohio on a moving block of ice, and subsequent dramatizations exploited spectacle on a much grander scale. Soon Eliza was crossing the ice pursued by real dogs, and Uncle Tom, at the close, was ascending skyward in a golden carriage, one that actually moved upstage (if the machinery was working), while the gates of heaven opened to reveal St. Clare and Eva, surrounded by angels, smiling down from golden clouds. Also, more and more elements from minstrel shows were entering into the performances and into the characterization of Tom, making the phrase "Uncle Tom" synonymous, as it had never been for Stowe, with obsequious black servility to whites. By the end of the century "Tom Shows" were available on a regular basis almost everywhere in the United States, but Stowe had never earned a penny from stage versions of her novel. Nor was her abolitionist message of much importance in the post-Reconstruction era, when "Jim Crow," first given currency by the stage, had become the label for the South's new set of repressive segregation laws. Message, as usual, had given way to crude entertainment.

Once again, none of this had much to do with literature, and no one claimed otherwise. After 1850, the efforts of such people as the actor–manager–playwright Dion Boucicault (1820–90) began to professionalize playwriting, but it would be a good deal longer before a play written by an American achieved anything close to literary distinction. The main importance of American drama for pre-Civil War American literature probably derives from its development and popularization of a number of stock characters, mainly comic stereotypes. There was the stage Yankee, who had first appeared as "Jonathan" in Royall Tyler's *The Contrast* in 1787. There was the Western boaster: for instance, Nimrod Wildfire in Paulding's *The Lion of the West* (1831). There were stage Irishmen and stage Germans and an urban variant of the rural yokel, named "Mose the Fireboy," who made his first appearance on the New York stage in 1848. There was the ubiquitous, racist stereotype of the shuffling, comic "darky," beginning with "Jim Crow" and minstrelsy but by no means confined to these formats.

It is harder to trace the influence of more "serious" pre-Civil War plays on American literature, since these plays are themselves so utterly derivative. But we might recall that a number of chapters in *Moby-Dick* are written in dramatic form and that the extraordinary impact of Shakespeare on Melville in the years immediately preceding *Moby-Dick* was undoubtedly at least partly mediated by performances of Shakespeare on the American stage, and by performances of such pseudo-Shakespearean "tragedies" as *Metamora* and *The Gladiator.* This is not to say that Melville's Ahab has very much in common with Stone's Metamora or Bird's Spartacus, beyond a love for ranting; unlike them he is a victim less of cruel external circumstance (white perfidy, Roman power) than of his own overweening conceptions of self and freedom. The deeper affinity is between Ahab and an actor like Edwin Forrest, between Ahab's monomania and the self-absorbed, "democratic" paranoia of the star who – as Metamora or Spartacus, as Macbeth or Lear – held American audiences in the palm of his hand. This is not to argue that Ahab was consciously based on Forrest but only that if the kind of magnetic power Forrest exercised over his audiences made its way anywhere into what we now regard as American literature, it was surely in Melville's portrayal of the charismatic captain of the *Pequod.*

MAGAZINES

American magazine publishing, like book publishing and theatrical production, expanded dramatically from the 1820s to the 1840s. At the beginning of this period the situation was much as it had been for the previous quarter century. In 1794 a new Postal Act had admitted magazines to the mails at a reduced rate ("when the mode of conveyance and the size of the mails will permit of it"), a privilege until then granted only to newspapers. The immediate result – as Frank Luther Mott describes it in his *History of American Magazines, 1741–1850* (1930), still the fullest account of this subject – was a flurry of new periodicals; seven were launched in 1795, and there were usually more than ten new entries a year thereafter. The number of magazines published in the United States rose from five in 1794 to almost one hundred by 1825.

The success of these ventures, however, was at best tenuous. The typical American magazine before 1825 failed in less than two years (often in considerably less than two years), and the reasons for this ephemerality are quite clear. Circulation was local, usually confined to the city in which a magazine was published, and it was extremely limited. Joseph Dennie's *Port Folio,* a weekly published in Philadelphia, was the most successful American periodical before the 1820s; in 1811 it became the first American magazine to survive for a decade. Yet it had only 2,000 subscribers in 1801 (each of them charged $5.00 a year), and at the time even a circulation of 2,000 was extraordinary. Closer to the norm were the sales of Boston's *Monthly Anthology* (440 subscribers in 1805) and of its successor, the *North American Review* (between 500 and 600 subscribers in 1820). There were no literary magazines aimed at mass or lower-class audiences. Moreover, subscribers were chronically delinquent in their payments. Thus neither editors nor authors could expect much remuneration for their efforts. The income of editors was usually tied to prospects of commercial success, which were seldom if ever realized, and it was not until 1819 that an American magazine (New Haven's *Christian Spectator*) proposed to pay contributors (at the rate of $1.00 per printed page).

Nevertheless, new literary magazines *were* launched in increasing numbers between 1795 and 1825, often to provide an outlet for local pride or talent — as in the case, for instance, of Baltimore's short-lived *Portico* magazine (1816–18), in which John Neal got his start. There was also the oft-expressed desire to counter British aspersions, especially following the War of 1812, on the intellectual capacity of the new American nation (even as magazines proclaiming their nationalism relied heavily on reprinted selections from British and European journals). As time passed, magazines began to target specific audiences: religious groups, farmers, physicians, children, women (although the great age of "ladies' magazines" was still in the future). The contents of American literary periodicals also changed. Political controversy, often vicious and scurrilous, gave way gradually to belles lettres, as fiction, poetry, and literary reviews began to overtake the periodical essay as the dominant forms of magazine writing. Although literary periodicals were notoriously short-lived, they were continuously replaced, often with more or less the same personnel, and not all of them failed. Boston's *North American Review* — founded in 1815 in imitation of the great British quarterlies and drawing on the resources of Harvard and of a local elite seriously devoted to culture — became a truly national journal in the 1820s and remained influential, even with a limited circulation, throughout the nineteenth century.

The intellectual and cultural ambitions of the *North American Review* would become increasingly anomalous as America entered its first great age of popular magazines in the late 1820s. Far more characteristic of future trends was the *New York Mirror*, a weekly founded in 1823 by George Pope Morris and Samuel Woodworth (the latter of whom would achieve fame, but not fortune, as author of the popular stage musical *The Forest Rose*). Woodworth soon dropped out of the business, leaving Morris to run the *Mirror*, in various incarnations, for twenty-one years, assisted in his editorial efforts by such writers as Theodore Sedgwick Fay and especially Nathaniel Parker Willis. The *Mirror* avoided overt discussion of politics, idolized Sir Walter Scott, cultivated gentle humor and sentiment in the manner of Washington Irving, and announced in its first number its ambition to appeal "to the LADIES, in particular." In fact from 1823 to 1831 it was subtitled, in part, the *Ladies' Literary Gazette,* and it featured both works by women writers and articles on such "feminine" topics as fashion and female education. Also, as early as 1824 Morris was using prize competitions to attract contributors, an innovation soon widely imitated. Boston's *North American Review,* holding to the intellectual seriousness of the early 1800s, survived, and its example helped spawn such later quarterlies as Philadelphia's *American Quarterly Review* (1827–37) and the *New York Review* (1837–42). But the *Mirror,* launched in New York in the 1820s with the intention of expanding circulation by *entertaining* its readers, was the truer harbinger of things to come.

Between 1825 and 1850, according to Mott's estimate, the number of magazines published in the United States rose from less than one hundred to something like six hundred; and although failure remained the norm, a growing number of these ventures achieved enduring commercial success and circulations unheard of earlier. Subscriber delinquency was still notorious; when, for example, Timothy Flint's *Western Monthly Review* (founded in 1827) failed in 1830, it was owed about some $3,000 in back payments. Nor were other problems immediately solved. A new regulation of 1825 fixed postal rates for magazines at one and a half to two and a half cents per sheet – well above the rate for newspapers (one to one and a half per *issue*). As a result, editors sought alternative means of shipping their products or sought to present these products as newspapers in order to reduce postal costs. On the positive side, inland transportation was improving rapidly – in 1825, for instance, the Erie Canal was completed – and, what may be most important, an increasing number of native writers were available to produce magazine material. The contents of a typical magazine at the beginning of the century were written mainly by the editor or his friends or reprinted from British journals. By the 1830s a growing group of known and unknown Americans was eager to appear in print, and in the 1840s some magazines began to stimulate productivity by offering liberal compensation, at least to writers with bankable public reputations. Readers were further enticed with woodcut and copperplate illustrations. The practice of using advertising for income, fundamental to modern magazine publishing, was still in its infancy.

Some of the most important literary "magazinists" (as they came to be called) got their starts in Boston. In 1829 Nathaniel Parker Willis founded the *American Monthly Magazine,* which launched the magazine career of Park Benjamin. Two years later Joseph T. Buckingham (editor of a Whig newspaper, the *Boston Courier*) founded the *New-England Magazine,* whose contents (compensated at the handsome rate, for 1831, of $1.00 a page) included works by Henry Wadsworth Longfellow, Oliver Wendell Holmes, John Greenleaf Whittier, and Nathaniel Hawthorne (who placed fifteen stories in this journal). Neither of these periodicals lasted long however. Boston literary society was not amused by Willis's flippant irreverence (or by the dandified personal style he affected), and in 1831, having failed to achieve the success he sought, Willis sold his subscription list to George Pope Morris, moved to New York to serve as assistant editor of Morris's *Mirror,* and went on to become one of the most popular writers of the age. The *New-England Magazine* survived only until 1835, and Park Benjamin, after a stint as its editor in 1835, followed Willis and the action to New York, joining the *American Monthly Magazine* (which soon absorbed the *New-England Magazine*).

Later Boston literary magazines were for the most part equally short-lived. The Transcendentalists' *Dial,* founded in 1840 and edited first by Margaret Fuller and then by Ralph Waldo Emerson, collapsed in 1844, and its circulation never exceeded three hundred. James Russell Lowell's *Pioneer,* founded in 1843 and including contributions of high quality (Hawthorne's "The Birthmark," for example), failed after only three issues. Boston's oldest equivalent to an enduring popular magazine was a giftbook, or "keepsake," called *The Token,* an annual collection of tales, verse, and illustrations aimed quite overtly at women readers, founded in 1827 and edited by Samuel Goodrich. There were many such annuals in America, forerunners of the popular "ladies' magazines." Perhaps the principal interest of *The Token* now is that it published many tales by Nathaniel Hawthorne (always anonymously) in the early 1830s. It was not until 1857, with the founding of the *Atlantic Monthly,* that Boston acquired an important and enduring popular literary magazine; until then, ambitious New England magazinists had to seek their success elsewhere.

Two of the most successful literary magazines of the 1840s were published in Philadelphia. One of these had its beginnings in 1826 when Samuel C. Atkinson and Charles Alexander (also founders of the *Saturday Evening Post* in 1821) launched the *Casket: Flowers of Literature, Wit and Sentiment.* The *Casket* was bought by George R. Graham in 1839, who merged it with *Burton's Gentleman's Magazine* a year later to form *Graham's Magazine.* Short fiction, poetry, essays, biography, travel sketches, and literary reviews were solicited from a list of contributors including William Bryant, James Cooper, James Paulding, James Lowell, Lydia Sigourney (the widely popular "Sweet Singer of Hartford"), Henry Longfellow, Nathaniel Willis, and Edgar Allan Poe. Poe served as literary editor for fifteen months in 1841 and 1842. He was succeeded by Rufus Wilmot Griswold, another transplanted New Englander, now infamous as Poe's hostile literary executor and biographer and throughout the period as an influential literary editor. In 1842 Graham launched his policy (which he took pains to publicize) of offering liberal payments to well-known authors: up to $50 a poem to Longfellow, $11 a page to Willis and $1,000 to Cooper for a series of biographies of naval commanders. Poe, less of a draw, received from $4 to $5 a page, and in 1842, Hawthorne was offered $5 a page. Griswold was paid $1,000 a year for his editorial services. In the late 1840s Graham encountered serious financial difficulties, brought on by bad outside investments, and he was forced to sell out his interest in 1853. *Graham's Magazine* had by then in any case lost much of its original popularity, but in the early 1840s its success was nothing short of astonishing. In its first year circulation increased from 5,500 to 25,000 (at a standard subscription rate of $3 a year), and Graham was soon able to claim 40,000 subscribers. The *North American Review,* in the same period, had managed to achieve a fairly stable circulation of 3,000.

Graham's most successful Philadelphia rival was Louis A. Godey. During the Panic of 1837 Godey purchased the *Ladies' Magazine,* founded in Boston in 1828 by Sarah Josepha Hale, and hired Hale as literary editor of its Philadelphia successor, *Godey's Lady's Book. Godey's* contents consisted mainly of verse, short fiction, travel sketches, and book reviews (but no discussions of politics) by such writers as Sigourney, Catharine Sedgwick, Willis, Harriet Stowe, Paulding, Ralph Emerson, Longfellow, Oliver Holmes, Hawthorne, and Poe. But the hallmarks of the magazine were fashion plates, watercolored by hand, and copperplate engravings of famous or original works of art, and it included recipes, essays on fashion, domestic advice, and other "women's" features. Godey also soon adopted Graham's policy of paying top rates to the most popular writers (but nothing to unknowns), and his successes more than matched Graham's. By 1839 he was predicting a circulation of 25,000 (also at $3 a year). By 1850 he had amassed a list of 50,000 subscribers, and the figure rose to 150,000 before the Civil War. The success of *Godey's* spawned a host of imitators — most notably *Peterson's Lady's Magazine,* founded in Philadelphia in 1842 — and it also had a pronounced influence on the content and format of many more general literary magazines, for whom it identified both a large audience and a set of strategies for winning and holding this audience's allegiance.

New York, in the meantime, was making its own innovations in the business of magazine publication. These innovations involved not the promotion of native writers but the blatant piracy of their British contemporaries. Such piracy had always been a staple of American magazines. In 1836 Horace Greeley, who would found the *New York Tribune* in 1841, started the *New-Yorker,* whose contents consisted mainly of reprinted (and uncompensated) foreign literature, and the title of Willis's *Corsair* (1839–40) revealed his purposes quite clearly; in fact he originally planned to call it, even more frankly, the *Pirate.* In New York in the late 1830s and early 1840s, literary piracy was undertaken on a new scale – a scale that briefly threatened to bring the fledgling book-publishing industry to its knees.

The story begins in 1839, when Park Benjamin and Rufus Griswold founded *Brother Jonathan.* They called it a newspaper to secure low postal rates, and its large-page format aided the deception, but its contents consisted almost entirely of serials of pirated British novels. When Benjamin and Griswold lost control of *Brother Jonathan* in 1840, they immediately founded a nearly-identical rival, the *New World.* These journals and their imitators were soon dubbed "Mammoth Weeklies." There was still the problem, however, that full copies of the novels these Mammoths were pirating were available from book publishers long before the serials had run their courses, and readers were willing to pay the higher book price for a full novel. So in 1841 the *New World* inaugurated a new technique: it began issuing complete novels as "extras" – still in large-page, multicolumn format, still distributed as newspapers, and selling for fifty cents an issue. *Brother Jonathan* and others immediately followed suit, competition rapidly drove the price down as low as six cents, and book publishers were forced to slash their own prices. By 1843 the market was becoming glutted; even the *New World* and *Brother Jonathan* were feeling the pinch of low prices. Then, in April, the Post Office ruled that the Mammoths could no longer enter the mails at newspaper rates, bringing this curious episode to a close. *Brother Jonathan* sold out to the *New World* early in 1844, and the *New World* itself folded a year later, but the effects of the episode were long-lasting. Although competition and price-cutting were brought under control, the standard price charged by book publishers for a novel, previously one to two dollars, now stabilized at fifty cents. It was this change, as has already been noted, that forced Cooper and others into overproduction in the 1840s.

New York also had its share of more conventional literary magazines. Foremost among them (along with the *Mirror,* which continued to appear throughout the period) was the *Knickerbocker Magazine,* founded in 1833. It was edited, in brief succession, by Charles Fenno Hoffman, S. D. Langtree, and Timothy Flint, but it achieved stability only in 1834, when it was purchased by Clement Edson and Lewis Gaylord Clark, with Clark serving as editor through the 1850s. The magazine's affection for Irving was indicated frankly by its title, and from 1839 to 1841 Irving himself served as a regular contributor at a munificent salary of $2,000 a year. Other contributors included Cooper, Bryant, Paulding, Hoffman, Willis, Benjamin, Longfellow, Whittier, Holmes, and Hawthorne. What distinguished the magazine, however, were its self-styled Rabelaisian humor and Clark's opinionated "Editor's Table," a standard feature of every issue. By 1837 circulation had increased (at a subscription rate of $5 a year) from something like 500 to more than 5,000.

The *Knickerbocker* never approached the commercial success of *Graham's* or *Godey's,* but it was influential nonetheless, and it came to play an important part in the so-called literary wars that erupted in New York in the 1840s. On one side were Clark's *Knickerbocker* and Morris's *Mirror,* which were Whig in politics and urbane and cosmopolitan (which is to say generally Anglophile) in their literary sentiments; it was not irrelevant that the *Knickerbocker* took its name from Irving. On the other side was a group of writers and editors loosely allied under the rubric Young America, including such figures as Cornelius Mathews, William A. Jones, and the brothers Evert and George Duyckinck — and, more peripherally or briefly, William Gilmore Simms, Edgar Allan Poe, and Herman Melville. Young America was generally Democratic in politics, nationalistic in literature, and committed among other things to the search for an original "American Genius" (which Clark and his circle ridiculed) and the battle for an international copyright law (which Clark and his circle opposed).

More will be said shortly about these literary wars of the 1840s; what needs to be noted here is that Young America also conducted its campaigns in magazines. Mathews and Evert Duyckinck edited *Arcturus* from 1840 until it failed in 1842, this failure resulting largely from their serialization of Mathews's incoherent satirical novel *The Career of Puffer Hopkins,* which Clark lambasted with gusto in the *Knickerbocker. Arcturus* also printed contributions from such writers as Hawthorne, Longfellow, and Lowell. Young America received some support (and space) in John Louis O'Sullivan's *United States Magazine and Democratic Review,* founded in Washington in 1837 and moved to New York in 1840 when the Whigs won the national election. O'Sullivan was a close friend of Hawthorne (he was the godfather of the Hawthornes' first daughter, Una), and many of Hawthorne's tales appeared in the *Democratic Review.* Charles Frederick Briggs, the founder of the *Broadway Journal* in 1845, was a Whig, but Poe soon forced Briggs out and devoted the *Broadway Journal* to his ongoing attacks on Longfellow's alleged plagiarisms and more generally on the supposed imitative Britishism of literary Boston. From 1847 to 1853, the *Literary World* provided another outlet for Young America's literary opinions (and its attacks on Clark and the *Knickerbocker*), especially after 1848, when the magazine was purchased by Evert and George Duyckinck. Evert Duyckinck was among Melville's first literary mentors, until *Moby-Dick* cooled his enthusiasm. Melville's nationalistic appreciation of Hawthorne, "Hawthorne and His *Mosses*" (1850), was published in the *Literary World*.

There were also influential literary magazines in other centers, in the South and West. The most notable was the *Southern Literary Messenger*, founded in Richmond, Virginia, in 1834 by Thomas W. White and now best known because Edgar Allan Poe was a frequent contributor and served as assistant editor from 1835 to 1837 (at a salary of $15 a week). Other journals sought like the *Messenger* to tap the cultural pride of specific regions, but northern cities – Boston and especially New York and Philadelphia – clearly dominated magazine publishing in the 1830s and 1840s. Even within the southern market, for instance, the *Messenger* never matched the sales of its northern rivals, and its total circulation never greatly exceeded 4,000 (at a subscription rate of $5 a year). In any case, major magazines did not, for the most part, confine themselves to local contributors, or even to local editors. The same names kept appearing in the contents pages of magazines from Boston, New York, Philadelphia, Richmond, and elsewhere: such figures as Bryant, Sedgwick, Hawthorne, Lowell, Longfellow, and, above all, N. P. Willis and Lydia Sigourney, the last claiming to have placed her work in as many as three hundred American journals.

Boston may have had no enduring popular literary magazine before 1857, but contributions by Boston authors had by the 1840s become staples of the magazines published elsewhere, and a significant number of the period's most influential magazinists (Sarah Hale and Willis, for example) had emigrated from Boston. Among editors, some had decidedly local identities (for instance, Lewis Gaylord Clark), but more had strikingly peripatetic careers. Poe edited magazines in Richmond, Philadelphia, and New York, and Griswold was active in both New York and Philadelphia. The homogeneity of American literary magazines is not surprising. These magazines were competing for the same national reading public – still not so much a "mass" readership as an audience of educated, middle-class readers, often women – wherever they lived in the United States. Editors inevitably sought to woo this audience with the kinds of writing that had brought success to other magazines, more often than not with the same writers.

The influence of the rise of magazines on the development of American literature in the second quarter of the nineteenth century can scarcely be exaggerated. Cooper and Irving achieved fame in the 1820s as authors of books, but by the 1840s new native writers were far more likely to appear first in magazines. Such magazines as *Graham's* and *Godey's,* with circulations of 40,000 to 50,000, reached a far broader public than Irving and Cooper could have dreamed of only two decades earlier. It would not be until the late 1840s and early 1850s that publishers of books by native authors would begin to capture this audience. In the meantime the most popular and successful American books of fiction tended increasingly to be works by writers who had won their fame in the magazines, and more than a few of these books simply reprinted material that had already appeared in magazines. More and more the tastes of magazine readers – for gentle humor, sentiment, and light entertainment – were coming to determine the kinds of literature that appeared in books, and many of the most successful magazine writers seldom even bothered to reissue their writings in book form. The Mammoth Weeklies had generated sales of up to 30,000 copies by reprinting book-length novels, but the most significant trend of the 1840s was in precisely the opposite direction. Writers of novels and story collections were imitating the literature of the magazines, where the most successful of these writers, in an era of fallen book prices, were earning the bulk of their literary incomes.

FICTION IN THE 1830S AND 1840S

Magazines, Mammoth Weeklies, and the aftermath of the Panic of 1837 radically transformed both the American literary marketplace and the nature of American fiction in the 1840s. In the 1830s there were some indications of the coming changes, but the decade's most obvious trends were not transitional but conservative, even reactionary. This is especially true of the emergence in the 1830s of what one might call the "school of Cooper," as American novelists and publishers, encouraged by Cooper's success, attempted to exploit the presumed market for regional historical novels. By the mid-1830s, the most prolific American historical novelists were almost exclusively male, and they were supported by the most influential publishing houses. American historical fiction was only a decade old, but new writers and established publishers seemed to assume that the mode of Cooper was the appropriate, even the inevitable, fictional expression of national character and serious literary vocation.

The most important and professionally consistent of these new writers was William Gilmore Simms of South Carolina, but Simms had a good deal of literary company. Henry William Herbert (1807–58), a British-born writer who would achieve his greatest fame writing on field sports under the pseudonym Frank Forrester, published the first of his many historical romances, *The Brothers, a Tale of the Fronde,* in 1835. Boston's John Lothrop Motley

(1814–77), who would become famous as a historian in 1856 with *The Rise of the Dutch Republic,* wrote two New England historical romances in the late 1830s: *Morton's Hope* (1839) and *Merry-Mount* (which was not published until 1849). New Yorker Charles Fenno Hoffman (1806–84), the brother of Washington Irving's fiancée Matilda, achieved considerable success in 1840 with *Greyslaer: A Romance of the Mohawk,* but his literary activities, like Paulding's, were rather miscellaneous (including satire, travel letters, verse, and the editing of newspapers and magazines in New York), and they were cut short by the onset of mental illness in 1849. Vermont's history entered American literature in 1839 when Daniel Pierce Thompson (1795–1868) published *The Green Mountain Boys,* which had gone through fifty editions by 1860. Although Thompson continued to produce works of historical fiction, he never again matched this initial success.

Robert Montgomery Bird (1806–54) turned from drama to historical fiction when Edwin Forrest refused to share the enormous profits he was making from performances of *The Gladiator* (1831). Bird's first historical novel, *Calavar,* deals with Cortéz's sixteenth-century exploitation of Mexico; it was published in 1834 by Philadelphia's House of Carey (doing well, at the time, with Cooper's historical fiction), and it was still being reprinted in the 1840s. In 1835 Bird published *The Infidel,* another Mexican historical romance, and *The Hawks of Hawk-Hollow,* set in the Delaware Valley of Pennsylvania at the end of the American Revolution. Bird's most interesting historical novel, *Nick of the Woods; or, the Jibbenainosay. A Tale of Kentucky,* was published in 1837 (still by Carey). Overtly dissenting from Cooper's vision of the nobility of American Indians (and perhaps more personally from Forrest's endless successes with John A. Stone's *Metamora*), *Nick of the Woods* is dominated by the character Nathan Slaughter, a mild Quaker by day who secretly and brutally kills Indians by night, more or less at random, to avenge the family he lost to an Indian massacre. This novel achieved considerable success, and Bird published two more books (a collection of Mississippi River sketches and a picaresque novel) in 1838 and 1839, but his health collapsed in 1840, prematurely ending his literary career.

The 1830s also saw the belated entry of the South into the annals of American historical fiction. William Alexander Caruthers (1802–46) (whose contemporary epistolary novel *The Kentuckian in New York* had appeared in 1834) published *The Cavaliers of Virginia,* a historical novel about Bacon's Rebellion, in 1835, and a second historical work, *The Knights of the Horseshoe,* in 1845. Nathaniel Beverly Tucker (1784–1851) published both *George Balcombe* and *The Partisan Leader: A Tale of the Future* in 1836. The first of these, a regular historical romance, was issued by the Harpers in New York. The second, a fantasy of the future of the South, supposedly from the vantage point of 1856, was published in Washington; it was clearly not aimed at a national audience. A third Tucker novel, *Gertrude,* was serialized in the *Southern Literary Messenger* in 1844–5. But the most important of the new southern historical novelists were John Pendleton Kennedy and especially William Gilmore Simms.

That this first literary "southern renaissance" was belated is hardly surprising; the South had no publishing centers on the scale of New York or Philadelphia. And it may be a bit misleading to describe this belated outpouring of historical fiction as a southern renaissance at all. There can be no doubt that the economic, political, cultural, and intellectual traditions of the South were significantly different from those of the North, but (with the exception of purely sectional works like Tucker's *Partisan Leader*) these differences did not manifest themselves all that notably in the production and distribution of southern historical fiction in the 1830s. Even in the South, we recall, the circulation of regular literary magazines was far surpassed by national journals produced in the North, and Simms and Kennedy more or less automatically turned to northern book publishers in their pursuit of a national audience.

What matters here is not simply that the South did not control its own literary market, although this does matter; more important is the fact that southerners like Simms and Kennedy conceived of their audience in national, not regional, terms. Although their novels deal with the customs and history of the South, such regionalism was after all the dominant quality of most historical fiction in the 1830s – at least the fiction inspired by the example of Cooper. The careers of Simms and Kennedy were in any case by no means harbingers of secession, of southern cultural separatism; they were, rather, expressions of a nationalism (at once political and literary) that fell apart in the 1840s as sectional conflict loomed larger and as the example of Cooper became increasingly irrelevant to the realities of the literary marketplace. Kennedy and Simms ended up taking different sides on the issue of secession, but the approach of civil war affected both of them in much the same way. It destroyed the assumptions upon which they, and many of their southern contemporaries, had undertaken the vocation of literature.

John Pendleton Kennedy (1795–1870), the son of a prominent Baltimore merchant who moved his family to Virginia when his business failed, began practicing law in Baltimore in 1816, but he gradually turned to literature and politics. *Swallow Barn,* a volume of fond sketches of Virginia life published (as were all of Kennedy's works) by the House of Carey, appeared in 1832. *Horse-Shoe Robinson,* a historical romance of the Revolution in Virginia and the Carolinas, appeared in 1835 and was compared favorably to the work of Cooper. *Rob of the Bowl* (1838), set in colonial Maryland, was less popular; the Panic of 1837 was having its effect on literary sales. In any case, Kennedy, who was elected to Congress in 1838, was becoming increasingly involved in Whig politics. *Rob of the Bowl* was his last work of historical fiction; his subsequent writings were mainly political and polemical. Moreover, as Simms's career would demonstrate more clearly, the growing crisis over slavery was beginning to make untenable the position of the white southern writer who wished to appeal to a national audience through northern publishing centers while remaining loyal to his or her native region. In the 1850s Kennedy, whose ideals in both literature and politics had always been national, took the Union side in the sectional conflict; he opposed secession in 1860 and voted for Lincoln in 1864. After the war, however, he advocated conciliatory treatment of the South by the North. He died in Newport, Rhode Island, in 1870 and was buried in Baltimore.

Cooper's most successful rival among his American contemporaries was also the most successful southern writer before the Civil War. William Gilmore Simms (1806–70) was widely read and widely praised. For example, in 1844, Poe declared that although "Mr. Simms has abundant faults. . . . Nevertheless, leaving out of question Brockden Brown and Hawthorne, (who are each a *genus* [*sic*],) he is immeasurably the best writer of fiction in America. He has more vigor, more imagination, more movement and more general capacity than all our novelists (save Cooper,) combined." Simms was also, as the conditions of the literary marketplace increasingly demanded, extraordinarily productive. During his long career he published eighty-two volumes of poetry, fiction, and nonfiction, including thirty-four novels or story collections. At the same time he contributed regularly to periodicals, was actively involved in politics, and edited a number of newspapers and magazines.

Although it has become a commonplace of literary history that Simms turned to writing to overcome his supposed exclusion as an impoverished outsider from the patrician society of Charleston, South Carolina, there is abundant evidence that Simms was in fact, and not just in aspiration, at home in the plantation-based aristocracy of his native region. In any case, insider or outsider, his early years were clearly traumatic enough to help explain the single-mindedness of his later dedication to literature. When he was only two years old, his mother died in childbirth and his distraught father departed for the Southwest, leaving Simms in the care of his maternal grandmother. Eight years later his father's attempt to regain custody ended up in the courts, and when the decision was left to the ten-year-old boy, he chose (and one assumes the choice was painful) to stay with his grandmother. Simms would later recall his childhood as a time of mourning and isolation, which he relieved as best he could through voracious reading. By the age of sixteen he was publishing verse in the Charleston papers, and in 1825, after a year traveling with his father on the Southwest frontier of Mississippi, Alabama, and Louisiana, he returned to Charleston to combine literary activities with the study of law. He was married in 1826, at the age of twenty, and admitted to the bar a year later.

Literature, however, soon won out over the law. Simms published five volumes of poetry in Charleston, was coeditor of the *Southern Literary Gazette* in 1828–9, and in 1830 purchased a Jacksonian daily newspaper, the *Charleston City Gazette,* in whose pages he vigorously supported the Union side in the virulent Nullification controversy. This stand cost him subscribers, and in 1832, after the death of his wife (leaving Simms with the care of their daughter), he sold the paper at a loss and left Charleston with a packet of unpublished literary manuscripts to seek his literary fortunes in the North, ending up in New York. Here his *Atlantis: A Story of the Sea,* a long poem published in 1832 by the Harpers, was a great success. He was back in New York in the summer of 1833, and from then on, until the Civil War intervened, he normally spent his summers in the North, where he was very much a part of the New York literary scene, and the rest of the year in the South.

The Harpers brought out *Martin Faber,* a crime novella and Simms's first published volume of fiction, in 1833, and the edition was exhausted in four days. *Guy Rivers,* set on the Georgia frontier, appeared in 1834 and was hugely successful; a second edition was required by the end of the year, the book was reprinted in London in 1835, and reviews were almost universally favorable. Although his subject matter was southern, Simms was by now in every other respect a national writer. In 1835, at what would turn out to have been the peak of his career, he published two historical romances. *The Yemassee: A Romance of Carolina* dealing with the destruction of an Indian tribe by white civilization in the early eighteenth century and was a literary sensation. The first edition of 2,500 copies were sold in three days, there were two more editions in 1835, and the book was reprinted and praised in England. American reviews were laudatory, and in the *New-England Magazine,* Park Benjamin, himself on the point of departing for New York, went so far as to declare that "the Yemassee is superior, in plot, style, and execution, to the Last of the Mohicans." In the fall of the same year Simms published *The Partisan* – the first of a series of seven romances of the Revolution on the Carolina frontier that would ultimately come to include *Mellichampe* (1836), *The Kinsmen* (1841, later renamed *The Scout*), *Katharine Walton* (1851), *The Sword and the Distaff* (1852, later renamed *Woodcraft*), *The Forayers* (1855), and *Eutaw* (1856). In 1835 Simms's earnings from his writing amounted to about $6,000, a figure nearly equal to Cooper's average of $6,500 a year in the heyday of the 1820s.

After 1835 Simms's productivity seldom slackened (and hurried composition left its mark on all his works), but circumstances were becoming more complex and less auspicious. The Harpers were especially hard hit by the Panic of 1837; they were reluctant to risk new ventures and even had difficulty paying Simms any of the $1,300 he was owed on account. So in 1838, with *Richard Hurdis; or the Avenger of Blood,* Simms moved to Philadelphia's House of Carey, which – with Cooper, Bird, Kennedy, and now Simms on its list of native novelists – was gaining clear dominance in American fiction. Still, the economic instability of the literary marketplace continued, and the drop in prices fueled by competition and the Mammoth Weeklies drove even Simms, for a time, from the novel. In the 1840s he turned to biography, criticism, and tales for magazines and annuals. This move did not necessarily indicate a decline in popularity – in terms of sales the most popular of all his works was a biography of the Carolina revolutionary hero Francis Marion, published in 1844 – but increased sales, as we have already seen, no longer translated into increased earnings or even sustained earnings. "My income from Literature," Simms lamented in 1847, "which in 1835 was $6000 per annum, is scarce $1500 now, owing to the operation of cheap reprints which pay publishers and printers profits only & yield the author little or nothing."

Cheap reprints were hardly Simms's only problem. In New York he became embroiled in the literary wars between Young America and the Whig writers gathered around Lewis Gaylord Clark's *Knickerbocker* magazine and George Pope Morris and N. P. Willis's *Mirror.* In the late 1830s, for reasons now somewhat obscure, Simms and Clark became enemies, and Simms's Democratic politics and his nationalistic stance in his critical writings – some of which were later collected as *Views and Reviews in American Literature, History and Fiction* (1846, 1847) – naturally allied him with Young America. The members and allies of this group defended him, hence Poe's lavish praise in 1844, in John Louis O'Sullivan's *United States Magazine and Democratic Review.* But from 1838 on, the attacks in Whig papers and journals became increasingly vicious.

In 1836 Simms married again and thenceforth made his southern home at Woodlands, his father-in-law's plantation seventy miles inland from Charleston. By the late 1840s, with sectional controversy on the rise and Young America in growing disarray, he was identifying himself more and more as a specifically southern writer, in opposition to the politics and literary culture of the North. In the presidential election of 1848 he broke with the Democratic Party to support the Whig candidate, Mexican War hero General Zachary Taylor, a slaveowner from Louisiana. He returned to historical fiction in 1850, when *Katharine Walton* (published in book form in 1851) was serialized, but by the 1850s the old Scott-derived formulas of historical romance – placing a genteel love story against the backdrop of historical events and legends – had become something of an anachronism. In any event, the intersection of regional and national interests that had made Simms's success possible in the 1830s had long since collapsed under the weight of political and literary controversy. His historical fiction was no longer a regional component of a national enterprise; it was rather a partisan defense of his native land against its enemies. Although Simms was still visiting New York in 1856, he was now there to lecture in defense of slavery, and he vigorously supported secession in 1860. In 1866, when he returned to New York in the aftermath of the war, he was welcomed by his friends, but his efforts to revive his northern publishing connections proved unsuccessful. He died four years later in Charleston.

Although serious historical and regional fiction in the mode of Scott and Cooper dominated American book publishing in the 1830s, its dominance was by no means uncontested. For instance, a few women writers were following the example of Catharine Sedgwick's domestic fiction – and in the process laying the groundwork for the extraordinary outpouring of best-sellers written by and for women that would distinguish the early 1850s. These women wrote in the context of the reigning ideology now referred to as the Cult of True Womanhood or the Cult of Domesticity. A woman, for instance, was not to concern herself with politics; "woman's sphere" (to use a phrase in wide circulation during this period) was the home, and a woman was to work through loving and submissive influence, not worldly ambition. The Cult of Domesticity confronted aspiring women authors with a profound and potentially unsettling problem, for was not the pursuit of literary fame a form of "unfeminine" ambition? "There is a delicacy . . . ," wrote Nathaniel Hawthorne in an 1830 discussion of women writers, "that perceives, or fancies, a sort of impropriety in the display of woman's natal mind to the gaze of the world . . . ; and woman, when she feels the impulse of genius like a command of Heaven within her, should be aware that she is relinquishing a part of the loveliness of her sex, and obey the inward voice with sorrowing reluctance."

Hawthorne had obvious reasons for wishing to discourage authors with whom he was in direct competition, but what matters is that in pre-Civil War America such sentiments were widely shared, even and perhaps especially by literary women. Sarah Josepha Hale, soon to become one of the most influential literary women of her era, insisted in 1829 that "the path of poetry, like every other path in life, is to the tread of woman, exceedingly circumscribed. She may not revel in the luxuriance of fancies, images and thoughts, or indulge in the license of choosing themes at will, like the Lords of creation." Few women writers openly or even privately contested this assumption. Catharine Sedgwick wrote in her journal in 1835, at the height of her fame, that her *"author's* existence always seemed something accidental."* Thus could a successful woman neutralize guilt about inappropriate ambition by denying ambition altogether (even overt literary intention), and many women writers adopted this rationale. Many also published anonymously or adopted euphonious pseudonyms. Moreover, many women turned to literature as a profession only when their husbands or fathers died or became incapable of providing necessary support. Such women were not forsaking but fulfilling their domestic duties by writing; they had to feed their families. And if woman's proper sphere was the home, women writers could make the home, the domestic lives of women, their subject. After all, this subject was the familiar experience of the great majority of the American reading public for fiction, women to whom Natty Bumppo and Chingachgook were bound eventually to become a bit tiresome. In any case, the body of assumptions underlying the Cult of True Womanhood determined both the public stance of many American women writers and the subject of much of the fiction they produced.

The phenomenon of best-selling domestic novels still lay in the future, but works by two writers of the 1830s – Hannah Farnham Lee (1780–1865) and Emma Catherine Embury (1806–63) – foreshadow the concerns of such later best-sellers as Susan Warner's *The Wide, Wide World* (1850) and Maria Cummins's *The Lamplighter* (1854). The death of Hannah Lee's husband in 1816 left her a widow at age thirty-six, with three daughters to support. It was presumably financial necessity that led her to take up the pen in 1830, and by 1854 she had published more than twenty novels, all anonymously. She scored her first great success with *Three Experiments in Living* in 1837, chronicling the financial and spiritual hardships of the once-prosperous Fulton family, hardships brought on by living beyond their means. The book was reprinted at least thirty times in America and England and was immediately followed by a sequel, *Elinor Fulton,* in which a strong-willed Fulton daughter assumes the moral leadership of her mother and siblings, teaching them to accept the error of their former extravagance while the father seeks the basis of a new living in the West. If Elinor recalls Catharine Sedgwick's exemplary heroines, she also anticipates Susan Warner's Ellen Montgomery and Maria Cummins's Gertrude Flint.

The same sort of exemplary female success story underlies Emma Embury's most popular work of fiction. Embury (1806–63) grew up in New York, married the president of a Brooklyn bank, and made her home a literary salon frequented by Poe and other New York literati. Her first publication was a poetry collection issued in 1828, but she was most widely known for her fiction, especially for *Constance Latimer; or, the Blind Girl, With Other Tales,* a collection published by the Harpers in 1838. Like Lee's Fultons, the Latimers of Embury's title story fall suddenly from prosperity; scarlet fever kills their son and blinds their daughter, Constance, and then they lose their fortune in the Panic of 1837. But Constance, in spite of her blindness, provides the moral example and the financial assistance that rescue her family from the destitution her father could not evade. In the works of Lee and Embury – and of Catharine Sedgwick, who was still the best-known American woman fiction writer in the 1830s – a tradition of women's fiction was indeed beginning to emerge, domestic in subject matter, didactic in intention, and demonstrating again and again the power of an exemplary (but neither bitter nor defiant) heroine to triumph over the evils of both immoral extravagance and family hardship. Embury continued to produce tales and collections until she was permanently disabled by illness in 1848.

The 1830s and early 1840s also saw the emergence in print of the vernacular American humor that would culminate in Mark Twain's *Adventures of Huckleberry Finn* (1884). In Maine, in 1830, Seba Smith (1792–1868) began publishing humorous Yankee-dialect letters attributed to "Major Jack Dowling"; collected in 1833 as *The Life and Writings of Major Jack Downing of Downingville,* they went through nine editions in two years. In 1835, in Augusta, Georgia, Augustus Baldwin Longstreet (1790–1870) published a collection of sketches called *Georgia Scenes, Characters, Incidents, &c., in the first Half Century of the Republic.* It was picked up by the Harpers in 1840 and regularly reprinted during the next decade, establishing the vogue of what came to be known as Southwestern Humor. This vein was also worked successfully by Longstreet's friend William Tappan Thompson (1812–82), whose *Major Jones's Courtship,* first published in 1843, was reprinted (in an expanded version) by Philadelphia's Carey and Hart in 1844 and was followed by *Chronicles of Pineville* (1845) and *Major Jones's Sketches of Travel* (1848). The ranks of the Southwestern Humorists also included such writers as George Washington Harris (1814–69), creator of "Sut Lovingood"; Johnson Jones Hooper (1815–62), creator of "Simon Suggs"; and Thomas Bangs Thorpe (1815–75), now best known for his short story "The Big Bear of Arkansas" (first publlished in 1841). American historical romances, usually running to three volumes, were conceived and published as *books.* In the case of southwestern humor, book publishers like the Harpers and Carey and Hart were turning to a mode conceived and produced, first of all, for newspapers and magazines – notably, in the 1840s, for William Trotter Porter's *The Spirit of the Times,* published in New York.

More and more of the new fiction in the 1830s and early 1840s was magazine fiction, and many writers, including Poe and Hawthorne, pursued their vocations primarily in and for magazines. Magazines were particularly hospitable to literary women. For instance, Eliza Leslie (1787–1858) was for two decades an active magazinist in Philadelphia, both as popular contributor and as editor, including *Miss Leslie's Magazine* in 1843. She had made her first success with a cookbook, published in 1827 and consistently reissued and expanded thereafter. Leslie also wrote children's literature and etiquette books and formally entered the Philadelphia literary world in 1832 when her story "Mrs. Washington Potts" won a prize from *Godey's*. She produced only one novel, *Amelia; or, a Young Lady's Vicissitudes* (1848), but issued a number of collections, including three volumes of *Pencil Sketches; or, Outlines of Characters and Manners,* published by Carey, Lea, and Blanchard in 1833, 1835, and 1837. It is important to recognize how different Leslie's career was from the careers of such male writers, also published by the House of Carey, as Simms, Bird, and Kennedy.

Caroline Howard Gilman (1794–1888) moved from Boston to Charleston, South Carolina, when she married in 1819 and turned to literature to supplement the meager income of her husband, a Unitarian minister. She founded a children's magazine, the *Rose-Bud,* in 1832, for which she wrote much of the material. It became the *Southern Rose-Bud* in 1833 and then the *Southern Rose* in 1835, by which time it had evolved from a juvenile miscellany into a general family magazine. Gilman edited it until it failed in 1839, a belated victim of the Panic of 1837. In 1834 the Harpers, in New York, published her first popular book, *Recollections of a Housekeeper* (later *Recollections of a New England Housekeeper*), in which the wife of an ambitious Boston lawyer describes her domestic duties and frustrations, the latter having mainly to do with servants. This was followed in 1838 by *Recollections of a Southern Matron,* which was more nearly a novel or story but still basically a plantation version of its predecessor and included an argument for the beneficence of slavery. Gilman's third novel, *Love's Progress,* appeared in 1840. Although both volumes of *Recollections* were quite popular, their author earned surprisingly little money from their success. The Harpers paid her a mere $50 for *Recollections of a Housekeeper* in 1834, and a sale of 2,000 copies of *Recollections of a Southern Matron* in six months in the post-Panic year of 1838 netted Gilman only $200. For the most part she was compelled to rely on the magazines, in which she published not only fiction but poetry and essays.

Caroline Kirkland (1801–64) did not begin as a magazine writer. Born and raised in New York City, she moved with her husband to Detroit in 1835. Her *A New Home – Who'll Follow? Or Glimpses of Western Life* was published in New York in 1839. A vaguely fictionalized collection of essays and sketches on the life of the western frontier, it had gone through four editions by 1850. *Forest Life,* a semifictional account of a tour of Michigan, followed in 1842, and *Western Clearings,* in which Kirkland was turning increasingly to the short story, appeared in 1845. A year later Edgar Poe described Kirkland as "unquestionably . . . one of our best writers" and singled out her *"freshness* of style" and "verisimilitude" for special praise. Meanwhile, the Kirklands had returned to the East in 1843. When William Kirkland died three years later, leaving his widow with four children, she supported them by editing and writing for magazines in New York City.

The New York literary scene in the 1830s and early 1840s was dominated by magazines and magazinists and by their public feuds, especially by the literary wars between the Anglophiles of the *Knickerbocker* group and the literary nationalists of Young America. This feud was reflected in the fiction produced by both camps. Nathaniel Parker Willis (1806–67), popular magazinist and foe of Young America, perfected his Irvingesque stance during a five-year sojourn in Europe and produced such Crayon-like collections as *Inklings of Adventure* (1836), *Loiterings of Travel* (1840), and *Dashes at Life with a Free Pencil* (1845). Also for a time coeditor of the *Mirror* was Theodore Sedgwick Fay (1807–98), a collection of whose early *Mirror* pieces was issued in 1832 with the Irvingesque title *Dreams and Reveries of a Quiet Man.* Fay's subsequent travels in Italy inspired a highly melodramatic novel, *Norman Leslie: A Tale of the Present Times,* published by the Harpers in 1835; a second edition was soon required, a stage adaptation had some success in New York, and the book continued to be reprinted during the next half-dozen years.

Norman Leslie's concern with American characters in a gothically mysterious Italy might be seen as foreshadowing Hawthorne's *Marble Faun* (1860), but the book's most immediate impact grew out of the extraordinarily hostile mockery it elicited from Edgar Poe in the *Southern Literary Messenger.* "The plot," Poe wrote, after summarizing it in cruel and hilarious detail, " . . . is a monstrous piece of absurdity and incongruity." Attacking Fay, Poe was attacking the whole Whig literary circle gathered around the *Mirror,* and he knew it: his review repeatedly mentions that the author of *Norman Leslie* is an "Editor of the New York Mirror"; it speaks of the title character's decision "to go a-Willising in foreign countries"; it remarks that even this character, "goose as the young gentleman is," is not "silly enough to turn travelling correspondent to any weekly paper"; and it finally explains the book's stylistic infelicities (after providing copious examples) by speculating that Fay himself has been abroad "so long as to have forgotten his vernacular language." Poe patched up his quarrel with Willis, who in any case well understood the importance of sensationalism and controversy to the self-publicizing world of magazines and who may have appreciated the humor of the performance from the beginning. But other members of the Whig literary circle, particularly Lewis Gaylord Clark, were permanently alienated. The *Norman Leslie* review began the process that eventually made Poe, if only by default, an ally of Young America.

Other members of the New York literary scene were seeking to produce an American fiction outside the traditions of both Irving and Cooper. Charles Frederick Briggs (1804–77) – an independent-minded ally of the Whigs, who would found the *Broadway Journal* in 1845 and then be forced out a year later by his coeditor, Poe – published *The Adventures of Harry Franco: A Tale of the Great Panic* in 1839. The book was popular and was followed by *The Haunted Merchant* in 1843 (the first and only number of a projected series of *Bankrupt Stories*) and by *Working a Passage; or, Life in a Liner* in 1844. In 1846, in the *Mirror,* Briggs began serializing *The Trippings of Tom Pepper,* a Dickensian picaresque novel set in New York including thinly disguised caricatures of various New York literary figures. The first volume was published in book form a year later, but the story was not completed until a second volume appeared in 1850, and this was Briggs's last novel. In 1853 he became an editor of *Putnam's Monthly Magazine.*

One of the principal targets of the satire of *Tom Pepper* (in which he appears as "Mr. Ferocious") is Cornelius Matthews (1817–89), who in the 1840s was disastrously promoted by Young America (particularly by Evert Duyckinck) as its great hope for a new, original "American Genius." Matthews's first novel, *Behemoth: A Legend of the Mound-Builders* (1839), is set in the prehistoric Mississippi Valley. It was followed by *The Career of Puffer Hopkins* (1842), an incoherent tale of contemporary New York City, and by *Big Abel and the Little Manhattan* (1845), an allegorical fantasy in which a white man and a descendant of the Indian chief who sold Manhattan to the Dutch wander around New York. In one sense Matthews fulfilled the hopes of his supporters: he was certainly new and original, in something like the flamboyant, self-promoting manner of John Neal two decades earlier. That his literary hodgepodges were works of genius was far less evident. His main importance to literary history may be that the efforts of Duyckinck and others to deny his inadequacies helped accelerate Young America's disintegration.

What was finally at stake in the New York literary wars of the 1830s and early 1840s was Young America's creation or discovery of an American fiction free of the oppressive influence of both Irving and Cooper. Many literary historians have seen the works of Poe, Hawthorne, and Melville as the ultimate outcome of this struggle. All three writers had ties to Young America and had works published in the "Library of American Books" Duyckinck edited for New York's Wiley and Putnam: Poe's *Tales* and *The Raven and Other Poems* in 1845 and Hawthorne's *Mosses from an Old Manse* and Melville's *Typee* in 1846. But in 1845 – with Poe's *Tales* selling only about 1,500 copies, with Hawthorne still regarded in most quarters as a writer of minor stories and sketches, and with Melville as yet unpublished – such an outcome for the ambitions of Young America was far from clear. Nor, for that matter, was this outcome any clearer a decade later, when Hawthorne, though far better known, was still by no means a best-seller, when Melville, after brief fame, was on his way back to obscurity, and when Poe, like Young America itself, was long since dead. We should be careful about reading our own ideas of literary value and the literary canon back into the pattern of literary history; in 1845, it would seem, the nature and future of American fiction were as unclear as they had been in 1830.

If there were significant trends emerging in the profession of fiction writing by 1845, they had rather little to do with Poe, Hawthorne, and Melville — or even with Simms and Cooper or with Fay, Briggs, and Matthews. The most obvious developments were taking place elsewhere. In 1844, for example, George Lippard (1822 – 54) began issuing as a series of pamphlets *The Monks of Monk Hall* (later called *Quaker City*), which he described as "an illustration of the life, mystery, and crime of Philadelphia." For all its lurid sensationalism and stylistic sloppiness, *Quaker City* is a fascinating picture of urban depravity, and Lippard was quite sincere in his horror at the exploitation of the lower classes in supposedly democratic America. But the book's appeal clearly derived from its sensationalism, and what makes it matter most immediately to the literary historian is its astonishing commercial success. When the first two-thirds of the pamphlets were bound together as a "book," 48,000 copies were sold in six months; an edition of the whole book sold 60,000 copies in 1845; and by 1850 Lippard had issued twenty-seven more editions, running from 1,000 to 4,000 copies each. One should recall that Simms's *The Yemassee,* only ten years earlier, had become a sensation by selling out a first edition of 2,500 copies in three days. In 1845, with the phenomenal success of *Quaker City,* the age of the American best-seller was on its way.

Lippard was not the only American in the 1840s to write sensational pamphlet-novels aimed at a large, mainly lower-class audience. Such cheap mass fiction soon came to constitute almost a separate industry. Oddly enough, given our current notion of the literary tone of New England, much of this cheap literature was published in Boston. A writer named George Thompson produced such works as *City Crimes; or, Life in New York and Boston* and *Venus in Boston: A Romance of City Life* (both in 1849). Joseph Holt Ingraham (1809–60), who had tried out various fictional modes in the 1830s, turned himself into a kind of fiction factory in the 1840s, publishing rapidly written "novels" of fifty to a hundred pages; in 1846 he boasted to Longfellow that he had produced twenty such works in the previous year, earning $3,000. Timothy Shay Arthur (1809–85) — magazinist, editor, and temperance writer — was equally prolific. His *Ten Nights in a Bar Room* (1854) would become one of the great American best-sellers of the 1850s, its sales surpassed only by those of *Uncle Tom's Cabin*. Arthur had no comparable success in the 1840s, but it is worth noting that in 1843 he published thirteen separate volumes of fiction. When Cooper and Simms complained about "cheap" competition in the 1840s, they were talking about pirated editions of foreign novels. What the successes of Lippard's *Quaker City* indicated was that the "cheap" fiction of the 1850s might be more likely to be of domestic manufacture. A distinctively American mode in fiction was perhaps emerging, but such market-oriented mass production was hardly what the nationalists of Young America had in mind.

At the end of the 1840s, both American fiction and the conditions of professional literary vocation in America were approaching a watershed. Cooper, through his own works and by influence and example, had held sway over the previous three decades. But Cooper, who would die in 1851, was at the end of his career, and Scott-derived historical fiction was on the wane, as Simms's attempt to revive the mode in the 1850s would demonstrate. Poe, whose book sales had never been impressive, died in 1849. But Melville was at the height of his fame at the end of the 1840s, as the author of *Typee* (1846), *Omoo* (1847), and *Redburn* (1849). And Hawthorne's most productive years were immediately ahead of him; between 1850 and 1853 he would publish *The Scarlet Letter, The House of the Seven Gables,* and *The Blithedale Romance,* as well as three books for children, two collections of stories (one a new edition of an earlier collection), and a campaign biography of Franklin Pierce. Melville, in the same period, would produce three more novels, including his masterpiece, *Moby-Dick* (1851). What lay ahead, this is to say, was the first *true* American renaissance. This is the literary history to which we have long been accustomed, for good reasons.

From the point of view of the literary marketplace, however, the story looks a bit different, in terms both of significant trends and of major players. Hawthorne's extraordinary literary activity in the early 1850s did not produce a great deal in the way of earnings; his total *lifetime* income from American sales of *The Scarlet Letter,* for instance, amounted to a mere $1,500. And Melville, of course, would fail as a professional author; at the end of the 1840s *Mardi* (1849) was already providing a taste of the inclinations that would soon cost him his audience, and our sense that *Moby-Dick* is a masterpiece was not shared by many of Melville's contemporaries. So from the point of view of the marketplace the most significant portents of future developments may not have been the prospects of writers like Hawthorne and Melville but such things as the rise of authorial mass production on the part of such writers as Joseph Ingraham and Timothy Arthur, the emergence of an increasingly distinct "women's fiction" in the work of such writers as Catharine Sedgwick, Hannah Lee, and Emma Embury, and the phenomenal sales of George Lippard's *Quaker City*. Developments in the late 1840s were beginning to suggest the existence of two potentially large and quite different audiences for fiction. There was a mostly urban, lower-class audience, presumably the main consumers of sensational pamphlet fiction. And there was a national, middle-class audience, apparently consisting mainly of women, the principal readers of literary magazines. This second audience was to prove the most important for the early 1850s, producing a renaissance in American fiction quite different from the one represented by Hawthorne and Melville. It is to this renaissance that we now turn.

2

WOMEN'S FICTION AND THE LITERARY MARKETPLACE IN THE 1850S

L ET US BEGIN our consideration of the 1850s by returning to F. O. Matthiessen's classic 1941 study, *American Renaissance: Art and Expression in the Age of Emerson and Whitman*. Matthiessen commences by observing "how great a number of our past masterpieces were produced in one extraordinarily concentrated moment of literary expression" in the first half of the 1850s. For Matthiessen the literary masters of this American renaissance are Emerson, Hawthorne, Melville, Thoreau, and Whitman. Noting that "the half-decade of 1850–55" saw the appearance of *Representative Men* (1850), *The Scarlet Letter* (1850), *The House of the Seven Gables* (1851), *Moby-Dick* (1851), *Pierre* (1852), *Walden* (1854), and *Leaves of Grass* (1855), he goes on to declare, "You might search all the rest of American literature without being able to collect a group of books equal to these in imaginative vitality."

In 1940, a year before *American Renaissance*, Fred Lewis Pattee published a quite different account of American literature in the years just before the Civil War, called *The Feminine Fifties*. Emerson, Hawthorne, Melville, Thoreau, and Whitman play a part in Pattee's version of midcentury American literature, but it is a notably subordinate part. Far more important are such writers as Susan B. Warner, Anna Warner, Timothy Shay Arthur, Fanny Fern (the pen name of Sara Payson Willis), Caroline Lee Hentz, Mrs. E. D. E. N. Southworth, Ann Sophia Stephens, Henry Wadsworth Longfellow, Sylvanus Cobb, Jr., Ik Marvel (Donald Grant Mitchell), Grace Greenwood (Sara Jane Clarke), and Fanny Forrester (Emily Chubbuck). What distinguishes Pattee's 1850s from Matthiessen's is his emphasis on writers who were widely popular and commercially successful in a decade when Melville was losing the audience he had won briefly in the late 1840s, when Thoreau and Whitman attracted only very limited circles of readers, and when even Hawthorne's novels fell far short of best-seller status. It is also notable that whereas Matthiessen's writers are all men (he considered calling his book "Man in the Open Air"), the majority of Pattee's are women (hence, in part, the "Feminine" of his title).

Matthiessen admits in his introduction that his "choice of authors" might

74

be considered "arbitrary," that none of their works achieved the popular success of Longfellow's *Hiawatha* (1855), T. S. Arthur's *Ten Nights in a Bar Room* (1854), or Willis's *Fern Leaves from Fanny's Portfolio* (1853). (Oddly enough, Matthiessen's introduction does not mention the most famous best-seller of the 1850s, Harriet Beecher Stowe's *Uncle Tom's Cabin,* which is acknowledged only once in *American Renaissance* – as having reached a wider audience than Emerson.) The popular "feminine" literature of the 1850s, Matthiessen writes in his introduction,

> still offers a fertile field for the sociologist and for the historian of our taste. But I agree with Thoreau: "Read the best books first, or you may not have a chance to read them at all." And during the century that has ensued, the successive generations of common readers, who make the decisions, would seem finally to have agreed that the authors of the pre-Civil War era who bulk largest in stature are the five who are my subject.

Matthiessen's standards for determining and canonizing literary excellence are a bit curious. The "best" writers are apparently the biggest, those "who bulk largest in stature," yet the power implied by this image hardly seems consonant with the fact that, in market terms at least, Matthiessen's five masters were by no obvious quantitative standard among the "biggest" writers of the 1850s. And if the "one common denominator" linking these five writers was, as Matthiessen writes, "their devotion to the possibilities of democracy," it seems somewhat paradoxical to dismiss other writers because they were widely popular. Moreover, Matthiessen seems here to argue, again rather paradoxically, that whereas popular writers failed of greatness because they only reflected public "taste," it is nevertheless precisely the taste of "generations of common readers" that guarantees or legitimizes *his* canon. If readers' taste is in both cases the standard, it is more than a little difficult to understand why *contemporary* popularity should be an index of literary inferiority.

One should note that Pattee, for all the difference of his emphasis, does not finally disagree with Matthiessen's devaluation of popular American writing in the 1850s. He intends the "Feminine" of his title mainly as a pejorative epithet – synonymous, as he puts it, with "*fervid, fevered, furious, fatuous, fertile, feeling, florid, furbelowed, fighting, funny.*" He presents himself, in Matthiessen's phrase, as a "historian of our taste," a taste that he considers to be (like the "feminine") cute but inferior. And in any case, whatever disagreement there is between Matthiessen and Pattee about the midcentury literary canon, it would seem to have been settled very much in Matthiessen's favor. *The Feminine Fifties* has long been out of print, but *American Renaissance* has been bought, read, and admired consistently since 1941. Matthiessen gave the literary 1850s a name still in use, the "American renaissance," and his canon is still, for the most part, our canon – although we have, in recent years, been adding to it.

Matthiessen's influence is understandable; his interpretations of his five authors are brilliant, and these authors produced a kind of writing that literary "modernism," especially in academic circles, had by 1941 legitimized as central and valuable: complex, ironic, often self-reflexive, and concerned with national political issues and questions of American identity, of empire, and abuse of empire. Except for *Uncle Tom's Cabin,* fiction by women in the 1850s seldom touched on political questions, and self-reflexive complexity, then as now, was an unlikely ingredient of successful popular writing. There is surely nothing wrong with devoting attention to writers only modestly popular or even unknown among their contemporaries; one would hardly wish to dismiss Emily Dickinson, for instance, because her works came to the attention of the public only after her death. But to suppress a large body of popular literature in order to assert the "stature" of five male writers is to suppress what may be *the* crucial fact about American literature in the 1850s. Not only were most *readers* women (who cared not at all for Melville and Whitman, and whose enthusiasm for Hawthorne was, in commercial terms, rather moderate); the most successful *writers,* especially of fiction, were also by and large women, women now mostly forgotten. More recent critics – for instance, Ann Douglas in *The Feminization of American Culture* (1977), Nina Baym in *Women's Fiction* (1978), Mary Kelley in *Private Woman, Public Stage* (1984), and Jane Tompkins in *Sensational Designs* (1985) – have begun the essential task of rediscovering these "lost" writers. Responsible literary history, whether feminist or not, should no longer conspire to ignore them.

The point of this rediscovery is not to determine which group of writers is "better." Indeed, one benefit of the debate over the midcentury American literary canon has been to make us more aware of the political and gender biases, the usually unspoken ideological assumptions, underlying many determinations of literary "value." Faced with assertions that particular works or writers are "good," we have learned to ask what they are "good" *for.* Nor does one turn to the popular literature of the 1850s in order to substitute it for the current canon. The point, rather, is to recognize the simultaneous existence of *two* literary traditions in the 1850s – and, what may be more important, to recognize their interconnectedness.

All of these writers – women and men, popular and unpopular – were competing in the same literary marketplace, and their awareness of this competition is clear in many of the texts they produced, particularly in the texts produced by Matthiessen's "masters." In fact Matthiessen's impulse to suppress the "feminine fifties" might be traced to a similar impulse in the writers he canonizes. Male writers, threatened (successfully) by the market power of women readers and writers, had every reason to try to marginalize them, to advertise their supposed inconsequence. We should also recognize that these competing traditions, for all their apparent differences (man in the open air, woman in the home), shared a good deal of common ground. Both the open air and the home were above all refuges from a nineteenth-century present viewed as increasingly complex, unmanageable, and incomprehensible. It is in this sense that both literary traditions of the 1850s are allied with the intellectual movement we now call Romanticism. But to understand either tradition, we need first to attend to the context in which both had their being: the expanding market for literature in the 1850s.

THE MARKETPLACE IN THE 1850s

The growth of American book and magazine publishing from the 1820s through the 1840s has already been described. Book publishing, by the 1840s, had consolidated in dominant firms in major cities, notably the House of Carey in Philadelphia and the House of Harper in New York, and increased capitalization and efficiencies of production and distribution had made an increasingly national market available to native writers. By the late 1840s two new firms were contesting the hegemony of Carey and Harper. In New York, in 1840, George Putnam became a partner of John Wiley; he began publishing on his own in 1847, his ventures including highly successful uniform editions of Carlyle, Irving, and Cooper. And in Boston, James T. Fields turned the business of William D. Ticknor (in which he became a partner in 1843) into New England's first major literary publishing house; they published Tennyson, Longfellow, Holmes, and Whittier, and their list of New England writers would be joined by Hawthorne in 1850, when Ticknor and Fields issued *The Scarlet Letter*. Meanwhile, a large national reading public, consisting mainly of women, had been developed by the most successful literary magazines, notably *Graham's Magazine* and *Godey's Lady's Book* in Philadelphia. By the end of the 1840s, the magazine writer had become perhaps the most characteristic American literary figure, and the tastes of magazine readers were coming to determine the most characteristic modes of American literature.

Not all was prosperity for American literary magazines in the 1850s. The Panic of 1857 wiped out a number of ventures, and at the end of the decade the onset of the Civil War not only raised costs for ink and paper but deprived national, northern magazines of their southern readers. Indeed, the 1850s saw the demise of several of the most influential magazines of the 1840s, including

Graham's, O'Sullivan's *United States Magazine and Democratic Review,* and Morris and Willis's *New York Mirror.* Among the dominant literary periodicals of the 1840s, only *Godey's Lady's Book* retained its position through the 1850s. Still, a new postal regulation of 1852, reducing magazine rates and for the first time allowing the publisher rather than the recipient to pay postage, created a more favorable commercial climate, and new popular magazines soon replaced or surpassed their declining predecessors.

In 1850, for example, New York's House of Harper launched *Harper's New Monthly Magazine,* whose contents consisted mainly of reprints from British periodicals and serialized British novels (including Dickens's *Bleak House* and *Little Dorrit* and Thackeray's *The Newcomes* and *The Virginians*). Although some American materials were included — for instance, short stories by such writers as Caroline Cheesebrough, Herman Melville, Elizabeth Stuart Phelps, and Rose Terry — the emphasis was always on reprinted British literature, and this emphasis paid off. In the magazine's first six months, circulation (at $3 a year) rose from 7,500 to 50,000; by 1860 it had reached 200,000. Detractors could question the Harpers' patriotism but hardly their success. In 1853, in part as a direct challenge to *Harper's,* George Palmer Putnam founded *Putnam's Monthly Magazine,* edited by Charles F. Briggs (with George William Curtis and Parke Godwin) and dedicated to the publication of works by American writers. Contributors included Longfellow, Cooper, Lowell, Thoreau, and Melville — the last contributing a number of stories and the novel *Israel Potter* as a serial. *Putnam's* published many of the writers now in the literary canon, and it is worth noting that this strategy did not at the time prove successful. Circulation, which started in 1853 at 20,000, declined steadily from that figure, and Putnam sold the magazine to another publisher in 1855. It failed two years later, in the Panic of 1857, although it was revived after the Civil War.

The year of the Panic also saw the founding of an important and enduring new literary magazine: Boston's *Atlantic Monthly,* published by Moses Phillips and edited by James Russell Lowell. When Phillips died in 1859, the magazine was purchased by Ticknor and Fields, and Fields succeeded Lowell as editor in 1861. The *Atlantic* rapidly became an influential vehicle for New England writers, many of them veterans of *Putnam's;* the first issue included contributions from, among others, Emerson, Longfellow, Holmes, Lowell, John Lothrop Motley, Rose Terry, and Harriet Beecher Stowe, and the New England focus remained dominant, sometimes to the irritation of writers in other regions. Moreover, Lowell's strong antislavery position (as contrasted with the avoidance of politics in *Harper's*) alienated potential southern readers. The new magazine nevertheless survived; following the Civil War, under the editorship of William Dean Howells, it was to become extraordinarily influential. Yet the *Atlantic* was hardly a typical popular literary magazine of the

1850s. *Godey's* – still edited by Sarah Josepha Hale and still featuring engraved fashion plates, domestic advice, and sentimental fiction and verse – remained far more popular, with growing competition for the "ladies" market from its Philadelphia imitator, *Peterson's Lady's Magazine*. The same market was tapped from New York by *Frank Leslie's Illustrated Newspaper*, a weekly containing both news and light literature (with copious illustrations) founded in 1855 by Henry Carter. By 1858 *Leslie's* was claiming a circulation of 100,000, and by 1860 more than 160,000.

But the most spectacular and sensational success of the 1850s was the *New York Ledger*, edited and published by an enterprising Irish-born New Yorker named Robert Bonner. In 1850 Bonner, a printer, invested his meager savings in a commercial journal, the *Merchant's Ledger and Statistical Record*, which he gradually made over into a literary weekly. In 1853, for instance, he began including verse by Lydia Sigourney, and in 1855 he transformed the magazine dramatically – dropping the commercial features, changing the title to the *New York Ledger*, and hiring newly famous "Fanny Fern" (Sara Payson Willis) at the extraordinary rate of $100 a week for a regular column. Bonner promoted the *Ledger* by advertising lavishly, by publishing early portions of serials in other magazines and newspapers (only to announce at the end of a suspenseful installment that the story would be continued exclusively in the *Ledger*), and above all by paying high rates to secure the contributions of popular or famous writers. Fanny Fern ended up earning $5,000 a year for her contributions, and Mrs. E. D. E. N. (Emma Dorothy Eliza Nevitte) Southworth, who became an exclusive *Ledger* author in 1857, came to earn at least that amount. Bonner also managed to secure a year's worth of weekly columns from Boston's Edward Everett, hardly one to succumb to pecuniary enticement, by offering to donate $10,000 to Everett's pet project, the Mount Vernon Association. Everett, Bryant, Longfellow, and Tennyson gave the *Ledger* an aura of culture, but its staple remained serialized popular fiction, especially works by Southworth and Sylvanus Cobb, Jr., who was signed on in 1856 and whose contributions to the *Ledger* would ultimately include about one hundred and thirty serial novels (notably, in 1859, the widely popular *Gunmaker of Moscow*). Bonner's promotional strategies were highly successful; by 1860 the *Ledger* had achieved a circulation (at $2 a year) of 400,000, a figure unmatched by any other American literary magazine of the time.

The *Ledger's* 1860 circulation had already been matched and surpassed, however, in book publishing as America entered its first great "age of best-sellers." The story of this age begins in 1850, when an unknown author submitted a novel manuscript to George Palmer Putnam. The author, Susan

B. Warner, was the daughter of a New York lawyer who had lost his fortune in the Panic of 1837. The burden of supporting the family had fallen on Warner and her sister, and she had turned to literature out of financial necessity. Her manuscript had already been turned down by a number of New York publishers (the Harpers, for example, had dismissed it as "Fudge") and Putnam was not initially inclined any more favorably. But he took it home and gave it to his mother, asking if she thought it worth publishing. "If you never publish another book, George," she responded after reading Warner's novel and being moved to tears, "publish this." "Providence," she later insisted, "will aid its sale." The book appeared in December under the pseudonym Elizabeth Wetherell, and Mrs. Putnam's prophecy was soon fulfilled. *The Wide, Wide World,* chronicling the trials and triumphs of an orphan named Ellen Montgomery, went through thirteen editions in the next two years, outselling any previous novel by an American author and ultimately selling more than half a million copies in the United States. It was also widely popular in England.

The Wide, Wide World inaugurated an extraordinary decade in American book publishing. In 1851, Harriet Beecher Stowe began serializing *Uncle Tom's Cabin* in Washington's *National Era* magazine. Readers were enthralled, and Boston's John P. Jewett offered Stowe a contract for book publication. The book appeared in two volumes in March of 1852 and sales were spectacular: 20,000 copies in the first three weeks, 75,000 in the first three months, 305,000 in the first year. By 1857 *Uncle Tom's Cabin* had sold 500,000 copies and was still being bought at the rate of 1,000 copies a week. No other American writer matched Stowe's success in the 1850s, but several came close. Sara Payson Willis's collection of sketches *Fern Leaves from Fanny's Portfolio* (1853) sold 70,000 copies in its first year; a collection of sketches for juveniles and a sequel to *Fern Leaves* (both also attributed to Fanny Fern) appeared in 1853 and 1854, and combined sales of the three volumes in the United States and England reached 180,000. In the same year Maria Cummins's *The Lamplighter* created another sensation, selling 40,000 copies in eight weeks and 70,000 in its first year. Other women – for instance, Augusta Evans Wilson, Mrs. Southworth, and Ann Sophia Stephens – were soon to join the ranks of best-selling authors.

Not all the best-selling writers of the 1850s were women. The most popular book in the 1850s after *Uncle Tom's Cabin* was *Ten Nights in a Bar Room* (1854), a temperance tract by Philadelphia author and magazine editor Timothy Shay Arthur. *Reveries of a Bachelor* (1850), a collection of sentimental sketches written by Donald Grant Mitchell under the pseudonym Ik Marvel, sold 14,000 copies in its first year and continued to sell for decades. In 1855, while the first edition of Whitman's *Leaves of Grass* remained largely unread,

Longfellow's *Song of Hiawatha* sold 11,000 copies in its first month and 30,000 in its first five months; in 1860 it was still being bought at the rate of 2,000 copies a year. Nevertheless, a clear majority of the most successful writers were women – as were the overwhelming majority of readers, the readers who made Arthur, Mitchell, and Longfellow (along with Warner, Stowe, Fern, and Cummins) successful. For instance, in 1852, Ik Marvel's *Reveries of a Bachelor* was devoured eagerly in Amherst by Emily Dickinson, who would write of Whitman ten years later, "I have never read his book, but was told that it was disgraceful." Longfellow became a best-seller by tailoring his poetry to the tastes of the largely feminine reading public. Thus both as writers and as readers women were at the center of the phenomenal growth in book sales in the 1850s. And of the popular American writing of the 1850s, the most interesting is the fiction written by women for women.

FICTION BY WOMEN

The success of the best-selling American women novelists in the 1850s was unprecedented. Susan Warner's *The Wide, Wide World* sent a signal to women writers and male publishers in 1850 analogous to the signal sent in 1821 by the success of Cooper's *The Spy*. And the new signal was considerably more precise, identifying not only a specific subject (women's domestic experience) but a specific (and large) audience. Moreover, novels like *The Wide, Wide World*, *Uncle Tom's Cabin,* and *The Lamplighter* achieved sales far beyond what Cooper, in his prime, could even have dreamed of. Nevertheless, the women novelists of the 1850s, their commercial success notwithstanding, were as deeply influenced as their predecessors had been in the 1830s and 1840s by nineteenth-century assumptions about woman's proper sphere – by the Cult of Domesticity, or Cult of True Womanhood.

Women writers, however successful, were never to proclaim worldly ambition, or even admit it to themselves, and the popular women novelists of the 1850s all disclaimed such ambition. Woman's place, they agreed, was in the home rather than the marketplace, and although commercial success seemed therefore by definition "unfeminine" (as many a male novelist protested), several factors served to exonerate these women writers in their own eyes and in the eyes of others. They were writing to support their families or children (often after the death or bankruptcy of a father or husband); they were thus not competing with men but fulfilling their "feminine" duties. Nor were they flaunting their success as a form of personal self-assertion; many went so far as to insist that their books virtually wrote themselves (or at least were not produced with conscious deliberation). Most also protected personal privacy and "feminine" delicacy by assuming pseudonyms or by publishing anonymously. Finally, if woman's place was in the home, the home — the domestic life of women — was the great subject of these writers, and the values rewarded in their novels are almost uniformly "feminine" and "domestic." *Uncle Tom's Cabin* might seem an exception to the assumption that women were not to concern themselves with politics (exclusively, it was generally agreed, a province of *man's* sphere), but from her title to the final scene of her novel, Stowe deals with politics very much under the guise of domesticity.

Both in their public stances as authors and in their novels, then, these writers in different ways advertised their conformity to contemporary ideas of woman's proper sphere, and it may well have been this very forswearing of ambition and the masculine world that guaranteed their success in the supposedly masculine competition of the marketplace. The primary consumers in this marketplace, after all, were also women. For them the home *was*, by definition, the world, a world with which only other women could claim full familiarity — hence the rising vogue of "ladies' magazines" in the 1830s and 1840s. The Cult of Domesticity did not, then, only or even mainly constrict the novelists who embraced it, at least in commercial terms. It made these novelists, writing out of their own experience, particularly well situated to appeal to the experience of their readers.

The outpouring of women's fiction in America in the 1850s is impressive not only because of the huge sales of particular best-sellers but also because of the growing number of women producing best-sellers, in some cases long series of best-sellers. One could devote many pages simply to chronicling these women and the novels they produced — from Susan Warner's *The Wide, Wide World* in 1850 through Mrs. Southworth's *The Curse of Clifton* (1852) and *The Hidden Hand* (1859) and Augusta Evans Wilson's *Beulah* (1859) and, to look beyond 1860, her extraordinarily popular *St. Elmo* (1867), whose publisher, only four months after the book was issued, claimed that it had been enjoyed by one million readers. It seems wiser, however, to concentrate in more detail on three of these writers and their most popular novels: on Susan Warner and *The Wide, Wide World,* on Maria Cummins and *The Lamplighter,* and on Fanny Fern and *Ruth Hall.* The career and writings of Harriet Beecher Stowe are the subjects of a separate section.

Susan Warner (1819–85) was born in the same year as Walt Whitman, Herman Melville, George Eliot, and John Ruskin. Her father, Henry Warner, was a successful New York lawyer. Susan was raised in something approaching luxury and educated by her father and by private tutors in a wide range of subjects. When Susan's mother died in 1827, Henry Warner's unmarried sister, "Aunt Fanny," moved in to take charge of the house and children. Susan's young sister, Anna, who would also turn to fiction writing in the 1850s, later recalled in Susan "a strong temper, an impervious will, a masterful love of power that very ill brooked curbing," but the personal journal Susan began keeping at the age of twelve reveals an equally strong current of self-doubt, of guilty dedication to possibly irrelevant duties. An elite young woman in America in the 1820s and 1830s had few if any outlets for "impervious will" and "love of power."

In the spring of 1837, when Susan was seventeen, the Warners' privileged status collapsed. Bad investments forced Henry to sell much of his property, including his New York town house, and the family retired to a farmhouse on Constitution Island, near West Point on the Hudson River, where they had planned to build a country estate and where they now eked out a precarious living in growing poverty and almost total isolation. "It has been a long time," Susan confided to her journal in 1839, "since we were used to seeing many people." Whatever her education had been preparing her for was now no longer a possibility. Moreover, her father's inept efforts to improve the family's condition through further speculation only made things worse, and Susan turned more and more to reading for consolation. But the need for money became increasingly acute; there were repeated threats of eviction, and the family lived at times without furniture. The daughters would have to compensate somehow for the father's failures.

Late in 1846 Anna designed and sold a "Natural History" card game to help make ends meet, and then Aunt Fanny announced to the older sister: "Sue, I believe if you would try, you could write a story." "Whether she added 'that would sell,' " Anna wrote later, "I am not sure; but of course that is what she meant." The result of this urging was *The Wide, Wide World*, attributed to "Elizabeth Wetherell." Its success, once it finally found a publisher, has already been described. It was followed in 1852 by *Queechy*, nearly as popular, and by Anna's *Dollars and Cents* (attributed to "Amy Lothrop"), and Elizabeth Wetherell and Amy Lothrop would ultimately produce, separately or in collaboration, a total of twenty-one novels, along with books of domestic advice and religious instruction. This furious literary activity never restored the family's affluence; much of what Susan and Anna earned went to pay their father's debts and legal costs, and the need for ready money forced the sisters to sell most of their copyrights rather than wait for royalties on sales. Still, from 1851 on, Susan and Anna were supporting the family, and in six months in 1853, *The Wide, Wide World*, whose copyright Susan had not sold, earned royalties of $4,500.

The Wide, Wide World also, of course, brought fame, but Susan Warner took pains to hide herself behind her pseudonym. To a male editor who had discovered her identity and asked permission to reveal it to the public, she replied in 1851: "I had no mind in the first place to have my real name known at all, and though that is now beyond my control, I do certainly never wish to see it in print." "Mere personal fame," she explained, "seems to me a very empty thing to work for." Later in the same year she was a bit clearer in her journal about the reasons for her privacy: "fame," she wrote, "never was a woman's Paradise, yet." Although Elizabeth Wetherell's real name was soon revealed anyway, Susan Warner continued to live in personal seclusion. She remained loyal to the doctrine of woman's circumscribed sphere, even minimizing her own agency in producing her best-selling novels. "I do not deserve your commendations, – not in anywise," she wrote in 1852 to Dorothea Dix, who had praised *The Wide, Wide World*. "You say 'God bless me' for what I have done, – nay but say 'Thank him for it,' and I wash my hands of all desert in the matter." Such self-effacement was typical of the best-selling American women writers of the 1850s, and self-effacement and the acceptance of women's limited roles also lie at the heart of Warner's first and most popular novel.

The Wide, Wide World is explicit enough about the powerlessness of women and even about the cruelty that often exploits and sustains this powerlessness. At the outset, ten-year-old Ellen Montgomery learns that she is about to be separated from her invalid mother. Her father, Captain Morgan Montgomery, has imperiled his fortune (like Warner's father) through obscure business dealings. He must relocate from New York to Europe, and his wife must accompany him, supposedly for her health. He insists, however, that he cannot afford to take Ellen along; she is to live in the country with his unmarried half sister, Fortune Emerson. This opening suggests an intriguing set of subterranean connections. It is as if the mother's illness were somehow caused by the father's inept financial dealings, or even as if he had designed it all to break up the intense relationship between Ellen and her mother. In any case, his overt cruelty and insensitivity are quite clear: he is almost never at home with his wife and daughter, he refuses to pay for his wife's parting presents for Ellen (instead, she sells a gold ring given her by her own mother to raise the money), and, when arrangements have finally been made for Ellen's trip to her Aunt Fortune's, he prevents his wife from waking her early, thus denying them their last moments together. Ellen is quite conscious of Captain Montgomery's meanness; her sorrow at parting from her mother, we are told, was "perhaps . . . sharpened by a sense of wrong and a feeling of indignation at her father's cruelty." For all her sorrow, however, she does go. She has no choice, and neither does her mother; they are both male property.

For the rest of her story Ellen is victimized, more or less, by various people chosen by her absent father to serve as her legal guardians. The snobbish family with whom she travels to her Aunt Fortune's home neglects and humiliates her. Aunt Fortune herself provides food and shelter but no love, and she delights in such petty torments as dyeing Ellen's white stockings gray-brown and withholding letters to Ellen from her mother. The girl nevertheless finds warm friends and supporters: the farmer who works for Aunt Fortune, a well-educated young woman named Alice Humphreys, Alice's clergyman brother, John, and others. Alice and John provide comfort when the news arrives that Mrs. Montgomery has died abroad, and they lovingly see to the education Aunt Fortune has neglected. When Alice reveals that she too, like Ellen's mother, is dying, Ellen moves in with her, and she stays on to care for Alice's bereaved father and brother. This arrangement seems fairly stable, because news had arrived a year earlier that Captain Montgomery had been lost at sea. Alice and John have claimed Ellen as their "little sister," but this adoption unfortunately has no standing in law; in *The Wide, Wide World* legal relationships are rigorously distinguished from those based on love and communal feeling.

After a year at the Humphreys' Ellen discovers that Aunt Fortune has been concealing a letter written by her father before his death and announcing that her mother's wealthy family, the Lindsays, are living in Edinburgh, that they wish to take Ellen in, and that he has placed her in their custody. So Ellen goes to Scotland to become the property of yet another set of legal guardians. Her uncle Lindsay insists that she forget America and the Humphreys, that she call him "father," that she call herself Ellen Lindsay. He is loving on his own terms, but these terms are, to say the least, peremptory. Although Ellen is only fourteen when she arrives in Edinburgh, one detects in her relationship with this guardian/uncle, who changes her name to his, Warner's figuration of the conditions of nineteenth-century marriage. "When Mr. Lindsay clasped her to his bosom," we are told, "Ellen felt it was as *his own* . . . ; in his whole manner love was mingled with as much authority." "It was singularly pleasant," Ellen reflects on her life in Scotland; "she could not help but enjoy it all very much; and yet it seemed to her as if she were caught in a net from which she had no power to get free." This picture of Ellen's status as pampered property could scarcely be more stark. No doubt many a reader of *The Wide, Wide World* responded in sympathy, and no historian should ignore the profound social significance of Mrs. Putnam's tears — or of the novel's extraordinary sales.

The book's brief and rather perfunctory conclusion — in which John Humphreys appears at the Lindsays', impresses them with the strength of his character, and reestablishes his relationship with Ellen — only barely overcomes the stark picture of her condition. One assumes that Ellen will return to America eventually and marry John (she is now almost sixteen), but marriage somehow does not seem a fully adequate solution to her predicament. Ellen has earlier reflected, contrasting Mr. Lindsay's love with John's, that John's was not only "a higher style of kindness" but also "a higher style of authority." Her best possible conception of freedom is based on the assumption that she must in any event be governed, owned. This assumption, it should be noted, inevitably controlled the lives of Susan Warner and of most of her readers.

The Wide, Wide World has often been dismissed, at least by modern readers, as sentimental or melodramatic. "Melodramatic," according to Webster's, refers to literature that is "sensational, violent, and extravagantly emotional"; the label also tends to get applied to works in which character is radically simplified along moral lines, to works populated mainly by paragons of virtue and monsters of vice. "Sentimental" is the term more often used to denigrate The Wide, Wide World and other works of American women's fiction. Among Webster's definitions of the term the most pertinent in this context would seem to be "influenced more by emotion than reason; acting from feeling rather than from practical and utilitarian motives," and the values of many popular women novelists of the 1850s (and of many of the writers we now call Romantics) would indeed seem to be "sentimental" in this sense. But modernist standards of taste have made "sentimental" a pejorative, and not simply a descriptive, term. To be "sentimental," we have been assured through much of the twentieth century, is to be insincere and unrealistic. The only genuine emotion is that which remains unexpressed, or at least understated, and the emotion in "sentimental" literature is therefore false and excessive. Or so we have been led to believe.

Why, then, is The Wide, Wide World now generally dismissed as "sentimental" or "melodramatic"? Nothing could be more "realistic" than Ellen Montgomery's sense of the limitations on her freedom, and much of the charm of her story grows out of Warner's "realistic" notation of country customs and domestic routines. Moreover, compared, for instance, to Charlotte Brontë's Jane Eyre, which had appeared in 1847, The Wide, Wide World is relatively unmelodramatic. In Ellen Montgomery's world there are no gothic mysteries, and those who claim to own her are by no means the villains of melodrama. Mr. Lindsay and Aunt Fortune behave decently enough on their own terms — they are a far cry from Brontë's Reed family — and Ellen, unlike Jane Eyre, is always able to find friends. Modern readers have complained about Ellen's frequent fits of crying, of which there are a great many, but tears are clearly her only permissible means for expressing her unhappiness, and she soon learns to cry in private. Nor is Warner's novel notably damper, in this respect, than much of Dickens.

The deepest problem for modern readers of The Wide, Wide World is Ellen Montgomery's *response* to her constricted situation: her rejection of rebellion for Christian submission. "Her passions," we are told early on, "were by nature very strong, and by education very imperfectly controlled." What happens in *The Wide, Wide World* is that Ellen learns to control these passions. "Remember, my darling," her mother tells her while explaining that they must soon part, "who it is that brings this sorrow upon us – though we *must* sorrow, we must not rebel." She is referring not to Captain Montgomery but to God. Again and again Ellen's mentors – Alice Humphreys, John Humphreys, and others – insist that Ellen recognize God's love in her own sorrows. She is to be weaned from earthly affections – parted from her mother, from Alice, from John – so that she may recognize the superior love of Christ. In short, she must learn to submit, and to the modern reader (to whom it seems clearly to be Captain Montgomery who "brings this sorrow upon us") such submission may well seem offensive. To some contemporary feminist critics, novels like *The Wide, Wide World* simply seem to urge women to conspire in their own subjection.

Others reply that Warner, whatever her message, nonetheless does present a stark and potentially subversive picture of Ellen's situation. Yet Ellen's mentors repeatedly warn her against the implications of even this sort of subversive "realism," and Warner provides no hint whatsoever that their admonitions are to be regarded ironically. "Take care, dear Ellen," Alice Humphreys cautions her, "don't take up the trade of suspecting evil; you could not take up a worse; and even when it is forced upon you, see as little of it as you can; and forget as soon as you can what you see." This is precisely what Ellen learns to do, and her self-effacement is presented as an admirable achievement. Readers who prefer Ahab's defiance in Melville's *Moby-Dick* can only be annoyed; but then these readers, who are not sailing on the *Pequod*, are not obliged to bear the consequences of their preference. Warner and her enthusiastic audience knew well the conditions of their own voyage, and to object to their accommodation, to their desire to discover the possible pleasures of their circumscribed condition, smacks of something very close to easy condescension.

The Wide, Wide World certainly has its faults, especially in plotting. For instance, an "old gentleman" who befriends Ellen in New York and then sends a barrage of gifts to her mother and whose identity is kept shrouded in tantalizing secrecy is never identified. (It might be noted that *Moby-Dick*, in which the sailor Bulkington simply disappears after a spectacular introduction, fares little better on this score.) But those who deplore Susan Warner's response to Ellen Montgomery's situation should at least recognize that Warner fully understands the limits of this situation. They should also attend to the gifts given to Ellen by her mother during a joint shopping expedition before their separation. First of all, Ellen chooses a Bible from an elaborate display of possibilities. "Such beautiful Bibles," we are told, "she had never seen; she pored in ecstasy over their varieties of type and binding, and was very evidently in love with them all." Warner here seems oddly enough to propose a kind of spiritual consumerism as an antidote to woman's status as male property, and it is certainly disconcerting to have a display of Bibles described as "so many tempting objects." But this dissonant note is not sustained; what finally matters about the Bible given to Ellen by her mother is that it helps her – like a hymnal given her by a kind stranger and a copy of *Pilgrim's Progress* presented by John Humphreys – to learn the discipline and gratification of Christian submission.

It is also significant that these lessons come from books and that Mrs. Montgomery's second gift to her daughter, again elaborately chosen, is a writing desk complete with paper, envelopes, pens, and ink. *The Wide, Wide World* is filled with warnings against the dangers of fiction, and Warner was disturbed when the book was described as a "novel"; she herself preferred to call it a "story." Still, many of the most important relationships in *The Wide, Wide World* are sustained by reading and writing, and the cruelty of Ellen's legal guardians often takes the form of interfering with these relationships. Thus Aunt Fortune withholds letters to Ellen from her dying mother, and her uncle Lindsay seizes and hides her copy of *Pilgrim's Progress*. Alice and John Humphreys, by contrast, encourage Ellen's literary development; in fact ten-year-old Ellen first speaks to John, at a Christmas house party, to request his assistance with a piece of writing. Finally, the point of John's successful intervention with the Lindsays, at the close of the novel, is to secure permission for him to correspond with Ellen from America. Reading and writing, books and private correspondence, may not seem much of a response to a legal system that defines women as male property, but one should recall that Susan Warner began a private journal when she was twelve, that she turned more and more to reading after the collapse of her father's fortune, and that writing ultimately rescued her family from poverty. One should recall, too, the extraordinary circulation of *The Wide, Wide World* in nineteenth-century America. If reading and writing about shared experience testified to a community that transcended or at least helped compensate for the strictures of legal subjugation, Susan Warner's novel revealed that this community was very large indeed – and potentially very powerful, at least in its own sphere.

If the labels "sentimental" and "melodramatic" seem finally inappropriate to *The Wide, Wide World,* they are rather more justly applied to *The Lamplighter,* published in 1854. In fact, it was this first and most popular of Maria

Cummins's novels that inspired Nathaniel Hawthorne's famous declaration, in an 1855 letter to his publisher William Ticknor, that "America is now wholly given over to a d——d mob of scribbling women." "I should have no chance of success," Hawthorne complained, "while the public taste is occupied with their trash — and should be ashamed of myself if I did succeed. What is the mystery of these innumerable editions of the Lamplighter, and other books neither better nor worse? — worse they could not be, and better they need not be, when they sell by the 100,000." Behind Hawthorne's exasperation one detects clear envy. In the same letter he estimates the total value of his copyrights on all the books he had published since 1837, together with his Concord real estate, at $5,000. By the end of 1854, sales of *The Lamplighter* had earned Maria Cummins something like $7,000. Whatever the "mystery" was, Hawthorne could not understand it, and by 1855, two years into his political appointment as American consul at Liverpool, he had at least temporarily given up writing fiction.

Unlike most of the popular American women novelists of the 1850s, Maria Susanna Cummins (1827–66) did not write out of financial necessity. Her father, David Cummins, whose antecedents went back to colonial Ipswich, was a successful lawyer who ultimately became judge of the Court of Common Pleas of Norfolk County, Massachusetts. Maria was born in Salem, the first of four children by David Cummins's third wife, Mehitable Cave Cummins (there were four older children from his first two marriages). The family moved to Springfield and then to a comfortable home in Dorchester, where Maria, who never married, would live until her early death at the age of thirty-nine. David Cummins provided his daughter with a solid education at home and then sent her to the Young School in Lenox, Massachusetts. This school was run by Mrs. Charles Sedgwick, sister-in-law of the famous novelist Catharine Maria Sedgwick, who lived nearby and visited frequently.

All of Maria Cummins's novels were published anonymously. Like Susan Warner, she carefully insulated her personal privacy from her public fame, and in Dorchester she was less a literary celebrity than an exemplary citizen, admired for her devotion to the Unitarian church. Nevertheless, she did keep writing: *The Lamplighter* was followed in 1857 by *Mabel Vaughan;* then came *El Fureidis* in 1860 and *Haunted Hearts* in 1864. Cummins's value to her publishers, as indicated by the royalties they paid her, rose steadily. Boston's John P. Jewett, also the publisher of *Uncle Tom's Cabin,* paid a royalty of 10 percent on her first two novels, but overexpansion to handle the sales of Stowe's and Cummins's best-sellers weakened his business, and it failed in the Panic of 1857. Cummins took *El Fureidis* to Ticknor and Fields, who offered a royalty of 15 percent. For *Haunted Hearts,* finally, J. E. Tilton paid a royalty of thirty cents a copy. Still, none of the later novels matched the sensational success of *The Lamplighter,* which provides the clearest index of the "mystery" that so baffled Hawthorne.

At the beginning of *The Lamplighter,* its eight-year-old heroine, an orphan named Gerty, is living in poverty in Boston. The unsympathetic woman, Nan Grant, with whom she was left at the age of three when her mother died and with whom she still lives has not revealed the mother's identity or even Gerty's last name. Gerty's situation recalls that of Warner's Ellen Montgomery, living with her unsympathetic Aunt Fortune, and *The Lamplighter* is indebted in many ways to *The Wide, Wide World,* but here at the opening, as everywhere else, Cummins is far more melodramatic than Warner. When Gerty spills a pail of milk, she is "scolded, beaten, deprived of the crust which she usually got for her supper, and shut up in her dark attic for the night." She is befriended by the lamplighter of the title, an old man significantly named Trueman Flint, who gives her a kitten. When Nan discovers the kitten, she throws it into a large pot of boiling water, where it dies in agony, and Gerty, when she reacts violently, is thrown into the street. Rejected by Nan, Gerty is taken in by the lamplighter, who says of what he can offer her: " 't ain't much . . . ; but it's a *home* – yes, a *home;* and that's a great thing to her that never had one." Gerty is also befriended by True's neighbors, Mrs. Sullivan and her son Willie, and by an exemplary and wealthy young blind woman named Emily Graham, and with the benefit of these "home" influences she prospers.

Part of what happens to Gerty in the course of her story is that, like Ellen Montgomery, she learns Christian forbearance; she learns to suppress "her ungoverned and easily roused nature." "Who can be happy?" she asks Emily. "Those only, my child," Emily replies, "who have learned submission; those who, in the severest afflictions, see the hand of a loving Father." But the truer significance of Gerty's growth lies elsewhere. "I an't good," she complains to Emily; "I'm real bad!" "But you *can be good,*" Emily assures her, "and then everybody will love you." Emily's assurance effectively summarizes the story of *The Lamplighter:* Gerty's goodness does bring her love and glowing admiration. When her "Uncle True" suffers a stroke, she cares for him and nurses him, earning almost universal public admiration. After True's death, Emily becomes her guardian. At the Graham house, Gertrude (as she is now called) is persecuted by the housekeeper, but she resists the impulse to anger and leaves the housekeeper with "a stinging consciousness of the fact that [the girl] had shown a superiority to herself." Gertrude has done nothing deliberately to call attention to this superiority, and although she never mentions the housekeeper's behavior to Emily, Emily learns of it anyway, so that her protégée's self-effacing reticence has the effect of producing an even more perfect self-promotion. Willie Sullivan, meanwhile, has left for India to pursue his fortune – not for himself but so that he can support his mother and his grandfather, Mr. Cooper. Gertrude, by now fourteen, has promised to care for Mrs. Sullivan and Mr. Cooper in Willie's absence.

Four years later Gertrude leaves the Grahams' suburban summer home for Boston to fulfill her promise to Willie (whose mother and grandfather are now ill) and to support herself by teaching. Emily's father objects, insisting that Gertrude is now in his power, but Gertrude defies him – not, of course, out of self-assertion but out of duty. "I see in the sacrifice you are making of yourself," declares an admiring Emily, "one of the noblest and most important traits of character a woman can possess." For Gertrude, as is far from the case with Ellen Montgomery, "feminine" self-sacrifice is thus rather directly transmuted into a form of personal power, even autonomy and freedom, the trick being that this transmutation is never intentional. In Boston, Gertrude nurses Mr. Cooper and Mrs. Sullivan until they die and also provides for Nan Grant, who has rather miraculously reappeared, until *she* dies. And the more she is good, as Emily prophesied, the more others come to love and admire her.

At this point, less than halfway through *The Lamplighter,* all the conflicts involved in the story of Gertrude's growth have pretty much been resolved. She has learned to control her early rebelliousness, and through her self-sacrificing benevolence she has overcome the stigma associated with her early poverty and obscure origins. The rest of the novel defies summary. There are excursions into the terrain of Dickens: an eccentric old woman named Patty Pace, whose outlandish clothes are matched by her orotund diction; a mysterious Byronic stranger named Mr. Phillips, who seems wracked by melancholy remorse and who follows Gertrude and Emily on their travels. There are excursions, too, into the realm of Jane Austen: for instance, a love triangle in which an idle young man forces his attentions on a young woman named Kitty Ray in order, as he supposes, to arouse Gertrude's jealousy. There is also considerable cultivation of one of the favorite themes of Catharine Sedgwick and other American women writers of the 1830s and 1840s: the contrast between the frivolous life of fashion and the solid virtues of domestic competence.

Through all of this Gertrude marches triumphantly. She returns to the Grahams to care for Emily. On a burning Hudson River steamboat, she risks her own life to save that of an idle young woman of fashion whom she supposes to be her rival for the love of Willie Sullivan (now returned from India). She learns that Mr. Phillips is in fact Phillip Amory – and that he is both Emily's former beloved and Gertrude's own father! She then learns, of course, that Willie has loved her all along. "What is there," he has already exclaimed to Phillip Amory, whom he turns out to have rescued from Bedouins years before in the deserts of Arabia,

in the wearisome and foolish walks of Fashion, the glitter and show of wealth, the homage of an idle crowd, that could so fill my heart, elevate my spirit, and inspire my exertions, as the thought of a peaceful, happy home, blessed by a presiding spirit so formed for confidence, love, and a communion that time can never dissolve, and eternity can but render more serene and unbroken?

Gertrude and Willie finally come to an understanding in a rural cemetery, over the graves of Willie's family and Gertrude's lamplighter. At the conclusion they are married – as are Emily and Phillip Amory, the latter now cured of his Byronic despair. "Through the power of a living faith," we are told on the final page, "he has laid hold on eternal life."

Although *The Lamplighter* is clearly something of a hodgepodge, especially following the deaths of Trueman Flint, Nan Grant, and Willie Sullivan's family, the reasons for its appeal to contemporary readers are also clear. It advertises the virtues of domesticity, of what Willie calls the "peaceful, happy home," far more consistently and extravagantly than does *The Wide, Wide World.* And it persistently turns submission and self-sacrifice into unconscious triumph. Gertrude never *intends* to triumph, and she never calls attention to her own virtue or to her mistreatment by others, but both the reader and the characters, compelled alike into the role of admiring spectators, are repeatedly reminded of her superiority. This superiority is singularly uncomplicated. As has been noted, Cummins draws for much of the plot of the later portions of *The Lamplighter* on the kinds of romantic misunderstanding central to the plots of Jane Austen, yet Gertrude (unlike, for instance, Austen's Emma) is never in the wrong. Moreover, Gertrude's superiority, unlike that of Warner's Ellen Montgomery, is relentlessly rewarded.

The basic messages of *The Lamplighter* must have been clear to the novel's many readers and must have been consoling. Domesticity is not confinement to the home but liberation from the idle extravagance of fashion. Self-sacrifice and adherence to duty lead not to suffering but to happiness, including worldly happiness. All of this is a far cry from the abiding sense of at least worldly constriction and limitation one encounters in *The Wide, Wide World,* even in its conclusion. In *The Lamplighter,* in other words, *The Wide, Wide World*'s sense of Christian self-sacrifice gets secularized. If Ellen Montgomery's story seems meant to recast the progress of Bunyan's pilgrim Christian in "feminine" terms, Gertrude's story seems more nearly a "feminine" foreshadowing of the progress from rags to riches of the heroes of Horatio Alger.

On a deeper level, though, what is most interesting about these two books is what they have in common. Like so many nineteenth-century novels, both tell the stories of orphans, and yet there is in them little abiding sense of the alienation and guilt associated with orphanhood in the works of Dickens or the Brontës or in Melville's *Redburn* and *Moby-Dick*. Ellen, and especially Gertrude, learn rather rapidly to suppress their antisocial anger and to find ideal substitute families; neither blames society in general for her own situation, so that orphanhood is for them less a general symbol than an unfortunate personal condition. They welcome love when they get it, and they both do get it; love is their sure reward for "feminine" virtue and forbearance.

In both novels, too, love is so fully subsumed into the home, so thoroughly equated with domestic relationships, that all true relationships become in effect family relationships — between ideal pseudoparents and pseudochildren or between ideal pseudosiblings — and it is often difficult to distinguish parent–child relationships from sibling–sibling relationships or to distinguish either from sexual, or "romantic," relationships. Gertrude's extended adoptive family consists of her "Uncle" True, Mrs. Sullivan (who functions as her mother), Willie (her adoptive brother), and Emily Graham (her adoptive older sister, a role assumed by Alice Humphreys for Ellen Montgomery). But these relationships are far from stable. After True's stroke we are told that "the cases are quite reversed"; the "robust man" who had been to little Gerty both "a father and a mother" is now "feeble as a child," and Gerty, "with the stature of a child, but a woman's capacity," becomes *his* mother. As Emily comes to depend on Gertrude, their relationship also tends to get reversed, as Gertrude comes to function as *Emily's* mother, and the introduction of the mysterious Mr. Phillips abets the confusion. His indeterminate age (he looks like a young man with prematurely gray hair) and his increasingly fervent attentions to Gertrude lead us to believe that he is her suitor, and the revelation that he is actually her father and Emily's former beloved scarcely diminishes the oddity of the family romance implicit in *The Lamplighter*, especially since Phillip Amory was originally Emily's stepbrother, and they were raised (like Willie and Gerty) as brother and sister. It is as if Gertrude's and Emily's ties to this father/brother/suitor were both displacements of some deeper tie, an implication reinforced at the close when Gertrude, having proved her virtue by playing "mother" to most of the characters in the book, marries *her* "brother" Willie.

The symbolic family situation in *The Wide, Wide World* is not quite so complicated as in *The Lamplighter*, but its deepest implications are significantly similar. Alice and John Humphreys adopt Ellen Montgomery as their "little sister." When Alice learns that she is dying, she says to Ellen: "You must come here and take my place, and take care of those I leave behind." That this charge should lead, as the book's conclusion strongly hints, to

Ellen's eventual marriage to her "brother" John should not seem entirely surprising; in fact, the tie between John and Alice has all along seemed more like the passion of lovers than the affection of siblings. When John is absent at seminary, Alice pines for him with the melancholy of the Romantic heroine, and when he returns home just in time for her death, they embrace passionately. "Are you happy, Alice?" he asks. "Perfectly," she replies. "This was all I wanted. Kiss me, dear John." "As he did so," the narrator continues, "again and again, she felt his tears on her cheek, and put up her hands to his face to wipe them away; kissed him then, and then once again laid her head on his breast." In this embrace Alice dies, and the intensity of the scene suggests what it might mean for Ellen to fully take her place.

One does not necessarily wish to argue that there is some sort of secret incest theme in *The Wide, Wide World* and *The Lamplighter.* There may well be, but what matters most is that we recognize how something like incest, however displaced or confused, may be the inevitable result of setting up the home and its web of domestic relationships as the alternative to a world dominated by masculine power, including masculine sexual power. Paradoxically enough, if the family or ideal pseudofamily is divorced from the realm of sex and is presented as a refuge from the realm of sex, then sexual relationships or their equivalents can take place only within the family. And we should recognize in any case that intimacy and sexual attraction are largely missing from these books, especially from *The Lamplighter.* As virtue becomes exemplary, relationships become spectatorial, based not on private intimacy but on the public demonstration and appreciation of right conduct. Such conduct makes no direct claim to power; it works indirectly, through the "influence" that was the hallmark of the Cult of Domesticity: the influence of the ideal mother.

The most passionate image of this influence, in either novel, may be Mrs. Sullivan's dream, shortly before her death, of flying across the ocean to lift her absent Willie from the sexual temptations of the world of fashion. "As we rose in the air," she tells Gertrude,

my manly son became in my encircling arms a child again, and there rested on my bosom the same little head, with its soft, silken curls, that had nestled there in infancy. Back we flew, over sea and land, and paused not until on a soft, grassy slope, under the shade of green trees, I thought I saw my darling Gerty, and was flying to lay my precious boy at her feet, when I awoke, pronouncing your name.

Gerty's marriage to her "brother" is thus not so much a displaced violation of sexual taboo as a regression into an ideal childhood (quite different from the one she actually had), in which she can be at once admiring sister and admired mother. Willie later reveals that he *was* saved from temptation and

preserved pure for Gerty by "the recollection of my pure-minded and watch-
ful mother," by "the consciousness of her gentle spirit, ever hovering around
my path, saddened by my conflicts, rejoicing in my triumphs." Even in the
world of spirits, this is to say, virtue is exemplary, and relationships are
spectatorial. At the beginning of *The Lamplighter,* little Gerty is discovered at
her window, gazing out in wonder as Trueman Flint lights the lamps along
her street. At the close, Gertrude and Willie are gazing out another window,
the window of their new home, as the gas-man lights the lamps of a modern-
ized and efficient Boston. "Dear Uncle True!" Gertrude sighs, "his lamp still
burns brightly in heaven, Willie; and its light is not yet gone out on earth."

In 1855, a month after complaining to William Ticknor about "these innumerable editions of the Lamplighter, and other books neither better nor
worse," Nathaniel Hawthorne sent another letter to his publisher, announcing an exception to the "vituperation" he had bestowed "on female authors."
"I have since been reading 'Ruth Hall,' " he wrote, "and I must say I enjoyed
it a good deal. The woman writes as if the devil was in her. . . . Can you tell
me anything about this Fanny Fern? If you meet her, I wish you would let her
know how much I admire her." Although few other contemporary male
readers were inclined to admire a woman for writing "as if the devil was in
her," it was clear to all that *Ruth Hall* (1854) was markedly different from
such books as *The Wide, Wide World* and *The Lamplighter.* And the life of the
author of *Ruth Hall* – which by 1855 had included two marriages, with the
second ending in divorce, and which would lead to another marriage in
1856, to James Parton – had been equally different from the lives of Susan
Warner and Maria Cummins. Yet in at least one significant respect the career
of Sara Payson Willis Eldredge Farrington Parton (1811–72) resembled that
of Susan Warner and most other American women writers of the 1850s. She
had turned to literature as a profession only rather late in her life (at the age
of forty) and only under the pressure of acute financial hardship.

Sara Payson Willis was born in 1811, in Portland, Maine, the fifth of nine
children. The family soon moved to Boston, where Sara's father, "Deacon"
Nathaniel Willis of Boston's Park Street Church, founded *The Recorder,* a
religious weekly, in 1816 and *The Youth's Companion,* a children's weekly that
he would edit for thirty years, in 1827. Three of his sons, most notably
Nathaniel Parker Willis, would follow him into the world of magazines. Even
as a girl of twelve, Sara helped with the *Youth's Companion,* although she was of
course not encouraged to contemplate a literary career. She was well-educated
nonetheless, attending, among other institutions, Catharine Beecher's Hartford Female Seminary. Harriet Beecher, who at the time was both a student and
a teacher at her sister's school, would later recall Sara Willis as a "laughing

witch of a half saint half sinner." Sara returned to Boston at eighteen, and eight years later, in the Panic year of 1837, she married Charles Eldredge (known as "Handsome Charlie").

The marriage was apparently happy and produced three daughters, but in the mid-1840s the happiness turned sour. In 1844 Sara Eldredge's mother, whose influence Sara would later credit for her own poetic inclinations, died, and in 1845 Sara's oldest daughter, Mary, died. Then, in 1846 Charles Eldredge died, and the claims of his creditors left nothing to support his widow and her two surviving children. She received only minimal and grudging support from her father and parents-in-law, and early in 1849 she was more or less forced into a disastrous second marriage with a widower named Samuel Farrington. Two years later she left him, and they were subsequently divorced. Her first husband's parents had taken responsibility for her older surviving daughter, Grace, but only on the terms that the mother have no control over her, and both her father and the Eldredges used the scandal of her separation as an excuse for refusing Sara further support. Left completely on her own, she sought to support herself by teaching (she passed the Boston teachers' examination but was unable to get a teaching job) and then by sewing (never earning more than seventy-five cents a week).

It was at this point that Sara Willis Eldredge Farrington turned to writing for a living. In June of 1851 she published, pseudonymously, her first piece in Boston's *Olive Branch,* and she was soon producing five to ten pieces a week (for a total of only six dollars) for the *Olive Branch* and for Boston's *True Flag.* In September she settled on the pseudonym Fanny Fern. She had sought help from her influential brother Nathaniel, but he had refused her contribution to the *Home Journal* (where he was advancing the careers of other women writers), he had ridiculed her writing, and he later even refused to allow his editor, James Parton, to reprint pieces by her that had appeared elsewhere. Parton, incensed, resigned. Meanwhile, in 1852, another New York magazinist, Oliver Dyer, solicited her contributions for his *Musical World and Times,* doubling the fee she was receiving in Boston. "Fanny Fern," in spite of the hostility of her famous brother (whose relationship to her was in any case not publicly known), was becoming popular, and in 1853 New York publisher James Derby brought out the first collection of her newspaper sketches, *Fern Leaves from Fanny's Portfolio,* whose instant success has already been described. *Fern Leaves* also demonstrated its author's growing business acumen. Offered the choice of a flat fee of something like $1,000 or a royalty of ten cents a copy, she chose the latter; as a result, sales earned her close to $10,000 in less than a year, and she was soon earning even more from *Little Ferns for Fanny's Little Friends* (1853) and from a second series of *Fern Leaves* (1854). By the summer of 1853 she was doing well enough to move to New York and to reclaim her daughter Grace.

In 1856 she married James Parton, eleven years her junior; their marriage agreement guaranteed her control of her own property and income. In the same year she began her career as an exclusive columnist in Robert Bonner's *New York Ledger,* to which she would contribute faithfully until her death from cancer in 1872. Bonner originally offered her $25 for each weekly column; she held out for $100, a fee Bonner then proceeded to advertise widely. By the mid-1850s the former Sara Willis was known as Fanny even to her friends and to her husband. As Fanny Fern, author of sometimes sentimental but far more often colloquial, humorous, and satirical newspaper sketches, she had become a nationally known celebrity, a star, and her literary earnings enabled her to buy comfortable homes first in Brooklyn and later in Manhattan.

Although Fanny Fern was by 1854 already a best-selling writer, her ultimate celebrity was to some extent a result of the scandal produced by the publication of *Ruth Hall* at the end of that year. Thinking herself protected by her pseudonym, she produced in her first novel (*Rose Clark* followed in 1856) a very thinly veiled version of her mistreatment by the world and by members of her own family — a version that included a clearly recognizable and devastating portrait of her famous brother as an insensitive and affected dandy named "Hyacinth Ellet," editor of the "Irving Magazine." The true identity of the author of *Ruth Hall* was revealed in print shortly after the book appeared, and she was widely condemned for "unfeminine" indelicacy and vindictiveness. Although this public exposure was deeply embarrassing, the scandal only helped sales, which soon reached 70,000; and to Fanny Fern, who had turned to literature for support only after her family had refused to help her, such sales must have been doubly satisfying. The Christian submission and "feminine" self-sacrifice advertised pseudonymously or anonymously by such writers as Susan Warner and Maria Cummins were not central to the repertoire of Deacon Willis's daughter, and the story of *Ruth Hall* is the story of a woman who, rather than accepting her circumstances, overcomes them to achieve economic and psychological autonomy — albeit, still, in order to fulfill her duties as a mother.

The book opens on the eve of Ruth Ellet's marriage to Harry Hall. Unlike Sara Willis, who married at the age of twenty-six, Ruth is only eighteen when she marries, and just returned from the boarding school where she had been sent following her mother's death. She is now glad to be leaving "her father's roof, (for her childhood had been anything but happy,)," but she wonders apprehensively if "that craving heart of her's [had] at length found its ark of refuge?" That is, she is not seeking freedom but only a more benign dependency, to be guaranteed by the "love" she never received as a child. Although Harry gives her this love, her worries turn out to have been well-founded. Her parents-in-law, with whom the newlyweds at first live, subject Ruth to an unending series of petty cruelties and humiliations. When Ruth and Harry move to their own house in the country, following the birth of their daughter Daisy, Dr. and Mrs. Hall move into a house nearby ("for Harry's sake," as his jealous mother puts it), and they continue to torment their daughter-in-law. Then little Daisy dies of croup, and Dr. Hall comments to a neighbor on Ruth's sorrow: "Now that proves she didn't make a sanctifying use of her trouble. It's no use trying to dodge what the Lord sends." This sounds very much like the advice Alice Humphreys gives Ellen Montgomery in *The Wide, Wide World* when Ellen learns of her mother's death, but in *Ruth Hall* such declarations are motivated mainly by self-centered hypocrisy.

Eight years later Ruth and Harry are staying at a seaside hotel, with two new daughters, Katy and Nettie. There Harry dies of typhoid fever (the disease that killed Charles Eldredge) and Ruth's real troubles begin. Although both the Halls and Mr. Ellet have money to spare, they provide Ruth with less than she needs for subsistence, and she and her children end up living on a meager diet of bread and milk in a shabby urban boardinghouse where Ruth sews late into the night to try to support them. Her wealthy cousins, the Millets, find her poverty so embarrassing that they ask her to keep Katy and Nettie from acknowledging them in public. Mr. Millet also votes against her when she applies for a teaching job at a school on whose board he sits. Eventually, Mrs. Hall even gets Katy away from her and subjects the child to treatment that recalls Ellen Montgomery's life with Aunt Fortune.

In her preface to *Ruth Hall*, Fanny Fern insists that she does not dignify her "story . . . by the name of 'A novel.' " "There is no intricate plot," she explains, "there are no startling developments, no hair-breadth escapes." All of this is clearly true. Unlike *The Lamplighter*, for instance, *Ruth Hall* makes no use of tantalizing mystery and surprising discovery, and there are no reunions with lost relations at the close; after all, Ruth's relations are precisely her problem. The account of Ruth's troubles might be called melodramatic; it is certainly the case that there is almost no form of petty nastiness that her persecutors do not commit. But these persecutors are less villains than comic buffoons, and the tone with which they are treated has less in common with melodrama than with satire. For instance, Ruth's brother Hyacinth, at Harry's deathbed, is concerned only with Ruth's unattractive appearance (she has fainted). "Somebody ought to tell her, when she comes to," he comments, "that her hair is parted unevenly and needs brushing sadly." And the point of the accounts of Mr. Ellet's stingy and unloving meanness to his daughter is mainly to satirize the hypocrisy of those for whom religion consists only of maintaining "correct" doctrine and a "Christian" reputation.

The first half of *Ruth Hall* might be described as sentimental, although this term also distorts the actual effect. The book proceeds by brief chapters, many running to little more than a page; we shift from scene to scene, with little narrative comment or expository connection. On occasion the narrator does intrude with the full, flowery language of "sentiment." For example, while Ruth, newly married, suffers in silence at the home of the Halls, the narrator exclaims: "Oh, love! that thy silken reins could so curb the spirit and bridle the tongue, that thy uplifted finger of warning could calm that bounding pulse, still that throbbing heart, and send those rebellious tears, unnoticed, back to their source." In the next paragraph, however, the tone shifts from indulgence to indictment: "Ah! could we lay bare the secret history of many a wife's heart, what martyrs would be found, over whose uncomplaining lips the grave sets its unbroken seal of silence." Although the language in this second paragraph is equally "sentimental" (and the parallelism is clearly deliberate), the effect is now to parody the rhetoric of "feminine" submission by revealing the actual conditions it masks.

There is also an ecstatic narrative effusion on the birth of little Daisy: "Joy to thee, Ruth! Another outlet for thy womanly heart; a mirror, in which thy smiles and tears shall be reflected back; a fair page, on which thou, God-commissioned, mayst write what thou wilt; a heart that will throb back to thine, love for love." But we are then immediately informed (with no comment on the irony of the juxtaposition) that "Ruth thinks not of all this now, as she lies pale and motionless upon the pillow." She has passed out from the pain of childbirth. Fanny Fern hardly dismisses the "joy" of motherhood, but throughout *Ruth Hall* the conventional langauge of sentiment is deftly balanced and qualified by an ironic sense of actual circumstance.

Eight years after little Daisy's death, we discover Ruth in her room, weeping over cherished tokens of her departed daughter: a little shoe and a lock of Daisy's golden hair — the latter, surely, a reference to the famous scene in *Uncle Tom's Cabin* during which little Eva, dying, dispenses countless locks of *her* golden hair to those she will be leaving behind. Little Katy Hall interrupts her mother's sentimental reverie. "Daisy's in heaven," she comments. "Why do you cry, mamma? Don't you like to have God keep her for you?" Then she adds: "*I* should like to die, and have you love *my* curls as you do Daisy's, mother." This declaration startles Ruth out of her self-absorbed reverie. Recognizing both the excesses and the potential cruelty of her sentimental indulgence, she cuts a lock of Katy's brown hair and places it next to Daisy's. Then Katy, in a wonderful touch on Fanny Fern's part, gives her mother one of her own shoes. This is a "sentimental" moment, to be sure, but the sentiment is fully human, and not without humor.

Ultimately, Ruth responds to her predicament with neither "feminine" self-sacrifice nor sentimental self-indulgence; instead, she asserts her own power to compete, and succeed, in the marketplace that has made no provision for her. She comes to no overt recognition of the political conditions that have made her predicament possible, but a series of increasingly surreal scenes and interpolated stories expresses her growing understanding – her disillusionment with the "love" on which she has been taught to depend. There is the comic story of her landlady, Mrs. Skiddy, and her henpecked husband, who is obsessed with the dream of escaping to California. These characters are drawn from Dickens (who is mentioned twice in the course of their story), but the outcome enforces a very un-Dickensian point. Mr. Skiddy finally makes his escape and our sympathies are with him, even when he writes back to say that California has been a failure and to request passage money to return home. Then both sympathy and valuation are suddenly reversed. "Drawing from her pocket a purse well filled with her own honest earnings," Mrs. Skiddy "chinked its contents at some phantom shape discernible to her eyes alone; while through her set teeth hissed out, like ten thousand serpents, the word 'N – e – v – e – r!' "

Then, with Katy (not yet captured by Mrs. Hall), Ruth visits a hospital for the insane. "There," we are told, "was the fragile wife, to whom *love* was breath – being! – forgotten by the world and him in whose service her bloom had withered, insane – only in that her love had outlived his patience." Ruth sees a woman, chained in a cell, whose husband has left her and, with full support of the law, has taken their child with him. Then Ruth views the body of a former friend, Mary Leon, confined in the hospital by her husband with the full connivance of his close friend, the hospital's male superintendent. Mary has left a note for her: "I am not crazy, Ruth, no, no – but I shall be; the air of this place stifles me; I grow weaker – weaker. I cannot die here; for the love of heaven, dear Ruth, come and take me away." Her last words, Ruth learns, were, "I want to be alone." The asylum visit, by 1854, had long been a staple of sentimental fiction, in both America and England, but here the visit is not an occasion for the indulgence of feeling (Ruth's reaction is scarcely reported) but a surreal image of the imprisonment of women not only by masculine power but by the compensatory rhetoric of "love."

Ruth, in any case, turns to writing for the newspapers, and the story of her eventual triumph (closely paralleling the life of her author) dominates the final chapters of *Ruth Hall,* which carefully detail the consequent humiliation of the relatives, who now try, unsuccessfully, to take credit for the triumph of "Floy" (Ruth's nom de plume). One of her Millet cousins complains, in a letter to his parents: "How could *I* tell she was going to be so famous, when I requested her not to allow her children to call me 'cousin John' in the street?" Ruth's brother Hyacinth has taken pains to impede her advancement, but, as before, the point is not so much to accentuate his melodramatic villainy as to score satiric points — in this case on the corruption of the world of American literary magazines. For instance, Hyacinth's subeditor Horace Gates (based on Fanny Fern's future husband, James Parton) remembers Hyacinth's insistence that the "Irving Magazine" provide only a neutral "notice" of "Uncle Sam's Log House" (i.e., *Uncle Tom's Cabin*) "for fear of offending southern subscribers." What matters most, however, is that Ruth does triumph; her first collection, "Life Sketches" (i.e., *Fern Leaves*), is a tremendous financial success and enables her to rescue Katy from the Halls and to move to another city (i.e., New York) and live in welcome comfort and independence. And the accent is very much on independence; the conventional "happy marriage" plays no part in the happy ending of *Ruth Hall*.

What saves all this from the charge of "unfeminine" egotism (a charge Fanny Fern obviously knew she was risking) is that Ruth triumphs not for herself but for her children. She masters the business of writing and publishing and then beats her various male oppressors at their own game in order to feed Nettie and recover custody of Katy. " 'Floy' scribbled on," we are told, "thinking only of bread for her children." Moreover, it is not Ruth but John Walter, a male editor who befriends her, who explicitly denounces the way she has been treated. Ruth herself never boasts of her achievements. When she reads one of her stories to little Nettie, her daughter asks, "when I get to be a woman shall I write books, mamma?" "God forbid," Ruth replies, to herself; "no happy woman ever writes. From Harry's grave sprang 'Floy.' " Even Ruth's apparent ambition, this is to say, is really a fulfillment of her duties as wife and mother. When a correspondent requests a portrait bust of "Floy" for a young lady's parlor, Ruth says to herself: "No, no, . . . better reserve the niche destined for 'Floy' for some writer to whom ambition is not the hollow thing it is to me." Instead, she focuses her attention on another letter, expressing gratitude for the effects of her moral influence.

Nevertheless, Ruth Hall clearly (and justly) glories in the fruits of her labors, both financial and psychological. When Nettie expresses her unwillingness to forgive Grandmother Hall, Ruth responds with the appropriate Christian message, but with a special twist. "She has punished herself worse than anybody else could punish her," she explains. "She *might* have made us all love her, and help to make her old age cheerful; but now, unless she repents, she will live miserably, and die forsaken, for nobody can love her with such a temper." Human vengeance is unnecessary because the Lord, apparently, will work his own vengeance in the here and now, and we never learn that Mrs. Hall or any of Ruth's persecutors *have* repented. On the morning she decides to try writing for the newspapers, Ruth recognizes that she will face long and difficult struggles. "*Pride,*" she tells herself, "must sleep!" "But," she continues, glancing at her sleeping children, "it shall be *done.* They shall be proud of their mother." "Pride," in other words, will not sleep forever; it must only be deferred in order to be perfected. In the next-to-last chapter of the novel, John Walter presents Ruth with a certificate for one hundred shares of bank stock, her first investment of the surplus earnings from "Life Sketches." "Now confess," he urges, "that you are proud of your-self." Ruth remains modestly silent, but Nettie chimes in, "We are proud of her, . . . if she is not proud of herself."

It is not easy to name Fanny Fern's literary descendants. One perhaps finds traces of her irony and humor in the work of Dorothy Parker, in the twenti-eth century, but Fanny Fern exhibits none of Parker's self-destructiveness. *Ruth Hall*'s reliance on brief scenes and ironic contrast rather than authorial exposition and her often parodic use of the language of sentiment foreshadow similar qualities in the work of Stephen Crane, another writer who would have his beginnings in the mode of the newspaper sketch. One might also see affinities between *Ruth Hall* and Kate Chopin's *The Awakening* (1899), which also portrays the condition of women and the ideology of "feminine" submis-sion with telling irony. Nevertheless, *Ruth Hall* is finally a singular book. For all its overt adherence at least to the letter of the Cult of Domesticity, it is mainly an anomaly among the best-selling works of American women's fiction in the 1850s.

HARRIET BEECHER STOWE

Uncle Tom's Cabin, published in book form in 1852, made Harriet Beecher Stowe (1811–96) a national and international celebrity, the most famous American novelist of the 1850s and perhaps the most famous American woman of the nineteenth century. The book's phenomenal sales, described earlier, provide only a limited sense of its full impact. There was wide-spread praise and also condemnation, especially from the South, including counternovels portraying slavery and plantation life as wholly beneficent. To an astonishing extent, between 1852 and 1860, the national debate over slavery became a debate over the truth or falsity of Stowe's fictional picture of life in the South. And in the years following the Civil War, Stowe's story, increasingly drained of its abolitionist message, became a staple of American popular culture, in songs, giftbooks, card games, souve-

nir plates, and above all in plays, theatrical spectacles, and even in traveling minstrel shows.

Stowe's personal celebrity set her apart even from such widely popular
women writers as Susan Warner and Maria Cummins. For one thing, although Stowe's "literary" merit has often been questioned, she has never been
forgotten; *Uncle Tom's Cabin* has remained in print consistently since it was
published in 1852, and it is now quite solidly entrenched in "American
literature" as that literature is defined by the academic curriculum. Moreover, in her own time Stowe departed in a number of significant ways from
the postures and practices of contemporary American women writers. With
Uncle Tom's Cabin she directly confronted the principal political controversy of
her day, and in the wake of that novel's success she embraced the role of
public figure with relish. She toured Scotland and England in 1853 as a
celebrity, expressed her strong opinions on such political matters as the
struggle over "Bloody Kansas" in a weekly newspaper column, and even, in
the early years of the Civil War, took public issue with the policies of
President Lincoln.

This penchant or compulsion for outspokenness would eventually lead to a
major scandal. In 1869, responding to an attack on Lord Byron's widow
(with whom she was acquainted), Stowe came to the woman's defense with
"The True Story of Lady Byron's Life." Here she made public the story that
Byron had committed incest with his sister. Both Calvin Stowe (her husband)
and Stowe's publisher, James R. Osgood, protested, but a writer of Stowe's
reputation and determination was not easily opposed, and the piece appeared
in the *Atlantic Monthly* in Boston and in *Macmillan's* in England. Public
discussion of slavery was one thing; discussion, especially by a woman, of
incest was quite another; and the reaction to this scandalous violation of the
Cult of Domesticity – and to the book-length version, *Lady Byron Vindicated,*
that followed in 1870 – was swift and overwhelming. *Atlantic Monthly* readers canceled their subscriptions in droves, Stowe was repeatedly attacked in
public, and the incident ended up undermining much of her undisputed
eminence.

Nevertheless, Stowe's departure from the Cult of Domesticity was not
quite as complete as this evidence might suggest, at least not in the case of
Uncle Tom's Cabin. Stowe indirectly acknowledged the possibly "unfeminine"
implications of her plan to write a story protesting the evils of slavery when
she wrote to the editor of the *National Era* in 1851: "Up to this year I have
always felt that I had no particular call to meddle with this subject, and I
dreaded to expose even my own mind to the full force of its exciting power.
But I feel now that the time is come when even a woman or a child who can
speak a word for freedom and humanity is bound to speak." Only the

intensity of the moral crisis, that is, could lead her to transgress the boundaries of "woman's sphere." Nor did Stowe present herself as contending with men in the realm of *artistic* endeavor. Looking back on *Uncle Tom's Cabin,* after it had made her famous, she declared that she "no more thought of style or literary excellence than the mother who rushes into the street and cries for help to save her children from a burning house, thinks of the teachings of the rhetorician or the elocutionist." There is a dig here, to be sure, at the political or moral irrelevance of those who concern themselves with "literary excellence," but in forswearing all "thought of style," Stowe was conforming rather precisely to the standard rationale adopted by most American women writers of the 1850s, and it is surely significant that ambition is here transmuted into a manifestation of maternal duty – domesticity animated to action only by a child-threatening emergency. Equally conventional, and equally "feminine," was Stowe's famous and oft-repeated declaration that it was not she, but God, who wrote *Uncle Tom's Cabin.* It should also be recognized that Stowe's controversial political writing of the 1850s, although it accounts for her widespread fame, represents only an episode in the story of her full career as a highly successful professional writer. *Uncle Tom's Cabin,* although it is a clear and sincere expression of Stowe's character and beliefs, is by no means representative of her full oeuvre.

Harriet Esther Beecher was born in 1811 in Litchfield, Connecticut, into an extraordinary family. Her father, Lyman, was a Presbyterian minister and was one of the most famous preachers in America and a dominant influence on his children. His seven sons all followed him into the ministry, and one of them, Henry Ward (1813–87), would become at least as famous as his father. Daughters, of course, could not enter the ministry, but Harriet's older sister (and oldest sibling), Catharine, would become an influential proponent of education for American women. For many years, Harriet Beecher hardly seemed the most likely candidate for ultimate distinction in this distinguished family. By the age of eleven she had become shy and retiring, with a passion for solitary reading. At the age of thirteen she was enrolled in the Hartford Female Seminary, established by sister Catharine. When Catharine discovered that Harriet was secretly writing a long verse tragedy, Stowe later recalled, she "pounced down upon me and said that I must not waste my time writing poetry." More serious writing, however, was by no means forbidden. Harriet had already earned her father's praise in Litchfield for a prize-winning school essay entitled "Can the Immortality of the Soul Be Proved by the Light of Nature?"

In 1832, Lyman Beecher accepted an offer to become president of Lane Theological Seminary, a new Calvinist divinity school in Cincinnati, and

Catharine and Harriet both joined the family crusade to spread the Gospel in the West. In Cincinnati Catharine established a new school, the Western Female Institute, where Harriet also taught, and here, in a somewhat desultory fashion, Harriet Beecher launched her literary career. In 1834 she began publishing stories in Judge James Hall's *Western Monthly Magazine,* and one of these stories won a prize of $50, teaching its author the important lesson that literature could provide a source of at least supplemental income. The need for such income would soon become pressing. In 1836 Harriet Beecher married Calvin Ellis Stowe, a widower and Lane professor whose circumstances were far from prosperous. "I was married when I was twenty-five years old," she wrote in 1853, "to a man rich in Greek and Hebrew, Latin and Arabic, and, alas!, rich in nothing else." It was impossible to support their growing family, eventually including seven children, on his professor's salary, so that whatever Harriet Beecher Stowe could earn from her writing was not only welcome but essential, and she pursued literature with a solid professional sense. In 1842, when she had written enough sketches to constitute a collected volume, she traveled to New York to negotiate with the House of Harper; she clearly knew where to look for national distribution. "On the whole, my dear," she wrote to Calvin from New York, "if I choose to be a literary lady, I have, I think, as good a chance of making profit by it as any one I know of." "My dear," Calvin replied, "you must be a literary woman." "If I am to write," his wife responded, "I must have a room to myself, which shall be *my* room."

The result of this mutual enthusiasm was *The Mayflower,* published by the Harpers in 1843, but its impact was far from sensational, and it is not recorded whether Harriet Beecher Stowe, at this time, actually got a room of her own. In any case, she hardly had the time or physical well-being to pursue a serious literary career. Between 1836 and 1850 she gave birth to seven children, she suffered at least two miscarriages, she was frequently prostrated by her pregnancies and recoveries, and when she was well enough to write, there was a growing family to care for. "I am but a mere drudge," she wrote to a friend in 1838, "with few ideas beyond babies and housekeeping," and in 1838 the press of duty and illness had hardly reached its peak. "I am determined," she wrote in 1839, explaining her need for literary income, "not to be a mere domestic slave, without even the leisure to excel in my duties." All of this climaxed in 1846–7, in a year of isolation and hydrotherapy in Brattleboro, Vermont.

Other circumstances were filling in the background of *Uncle Tom's Cabin.* In 1836, in Cincinnati, antiabolition mobs had threatened the office of James G. Birney, editor of the abolitionist *Philanthropist.* "I wish he would man it with armed men," Stowe wrote to her husband, who was in Europe buying books for the Lane library, "and see what can be done. If I were a man, I would go, for one, and take good care of at least one window." The mob prevailed, and Birney left Cincinnati, but the incident had its effect on Stowe and on her younger brother Henry Ward Beecher, now also in Cincinnati. Thirteen years later, in 1849, a virulent cholera epidemic killed one-year-old Samuel Charles Stowe. In 1853 his mother wrote:

It was at his dying bed that I learned what a poor slave mother may feel when her child is torn away from her. In those depths of sorrow which seemed to me immeasurable, it was my only prayer to God that such anguish might not be suffered in vain. . . . I felt that I could never be consoled for it unless this crushing of my own heart might enable me to work out some great goods to others.

The tension between the sense that domesticity was "duty" and the sense that it was "slavery" was beginning to crystallize into the complex metaphor that would enable Harriet Beecher Stowe to transform the Cult of Domesticity into a political weapon.

In 1849 Calvin Stowe was offered an appointment at Bowdoin College, and in 1850 the Stowes moved from Cincinnati to Brunswick, Maine. But this liberation also entailed an obligation. Calvin was to be paid a salary of only $1,000 a year at Bowdoin; Harriet Beecher Stowe would need to make more money from her writing. She became a regular contributor to the *National Era,* an abolitionist journal that had been founded in Washington in 1847 by Gamaliel Bailey, who had succeeded James G. Birney in 1836 as editor of Cincinnati's *Philanthropist.* Meanwhile, the new federal Fugitive Slave Law, part of the legislative package known as the Compromise of 1850, aroused strong protest and resistance in the North. "Hattie," Stowe's sister-in-law wrote to her, "if I could use a pen as you can, I would write something that will make this whole nation feel what an accursed thing slavery is." Stowe, after reading the letter aloud to her children, declared: "I *will* write something. I will if I live." Then, in February of the following year, while taking communion, she had a vision of a slave being flogged to death on the orders of his vicious master and forgiving his persecutors as he died – a vision that would become Chapter 40 of *Uncle Tom's Cabin.* When Stowe insisted that "the Lord himself wrote" *Uncle Tom's Cabin,* that she "was but an instrument in His hand," she was being perfectly sincere. She now knew where her story would end, and she had only to imagine the events leading up to this climax. Her story began appearing in the *National Era* as a serial in June, its length ultimately far exceeding anything Stowe had had in mind when she started.

When Stowe visited the White House in 1862, President Lincoln is supposed to have said: "So this is the little lady who made this big war?"

Whatever effect *Uncle Tom's Cabin* may have had on American politics, it soon made its author a major spokeswoman for antislavery opinion, and it transformed the finances of the Stowe household. In July 1852 the Stowes moved to Andover, Massachusetts, where Calvin joined the faculty of Andover Theological Seminary. In the same month Harriet received her first royalty check from John P. Jewett — for $10,300 (more than ten times the annual salary Calvin had been paid at Bowdoin). From now on she was not just supplementing family income; she was the principal source of family income, and she also took charge of financial decision making. She and her family could now live in comfort. In 1863, content to live on his wife's ample income, Calvin retired, and the Stowes moved from Andover to Hartford. There were still domestic trials. In 1857 the Stowes' son Henry, a freshman at Dartmouth, drowned while swimming in the Connecticut River. Another son, Fred, enlisted in the Union army, was wounded at Gettysburg, and emerged from the war an incurable alcoholic; in 1870 he would flee to California and disappear. But from 1852 on, Harriet Beecher Stowe's days of poverty and domestic drudgery were over. Magazine editors and book publishers now competed for her writings, whatever the subject, and it has been estimated that her literary income, for at least the next two decades (i.e., until the Byron scandal of 1870), average something like $10,000 a year.

Stowe did not immediately return to fiction. Her next book, *A Key to Uncle Tom's Cabin* (1853), was an effort to demonstrate the factual accuracy of her best-seller, and in the midst of the controversy over *Uncle Tom's Cabin* it sold 90,000 copies in its first month. *Sunny Memories of Foreign Lands* (1854) described Stowe's European tour of 1853. There were newspaper and magazine articles, an abridged version of *Uncle Tom's Cabin* for children, and a reissue of the 1843 collection of stories and sketches. Stowe's second abolition novel, *Dred: A Tale of the Great Dismal Swamp,* did not appear until 1856. This time, to guarantee British royalties, Stowe traveled to England to publish the book there before it was issued in the United States. Although reviews were disappointing, the novel did well commercially, selling about 165,000 copies in England and about 150,000 in America in its first year.

Dred is considerably more violent — or, we might say, more "militant" — than its predecessor, and it is also a good deal less coherent. It is, in fact, a bit of a mess. The title character, supposedly a son of Denmark Vesey, lives in hiding with a band of followers, where he advocates not Christian submission, like Uncle Tom, but violent rebellion. Yet Dred never leads his uprising, he is finally rather pointlessly killed, and at the end of the book even the few good white southerners, those who free their slaves, are compelled to flee to Canada along with the black fugitives. One can hardly blame Stowe for her inability to produce a successful abolition novel in 1856, and one suspects that the violence and incoherence of *Dred* owe something to her recognition that *Uncle Tom's Cabin*, although it had brought her fame and professional success, had done very little to advance the prospects of abolition and sectional understanding.

Dred has much more in common with the popular American women's fiction of the 1850s than *Uncle Tom's Cabin* did. The novel begins by introducing Nina Gordon, a seventeen-year-old orphan—heiress just returned to her family's plantation from a northern boarding school. As the book proceeds, we follow Nina's conversion from frivolous coquetry to Christian charity, self-sacrifice, and submission. Nina proves herself worthy of her noble and Byronic suitor, Edward Clayton, who is trying to overcome the evils of slavery on his own plantation. In *Dred*, then, Stowe is attempting to adapt the story of the exemplary orphan, or of the orphan who learns to be exemplary, to *structure* an abolition novel. Two-thirds of the way through the book, however, this attempt is rather summarily abandoned. Nina, who has perhaps been reminding us of Susan Warner's Ellen Montgomery or even of Maria Cummins's Gerty, suddenly turns into little Eva and dies in a cholera epidemic, and it is at this point that what little coherence the novel has had is more or less completely dissipated. Nor does Nina's death have much to do with *Dred*'s message. Although Eva is killed pretty much directly by the evils of slavery, which shock her sensitive nature, Nina seems to die mainly because her author cannot figure out what else to do with her. Still, Stowe is here drawing, in a way she was not in *Uncle Tom's Cabin*, on the central formula of popular American women's fiction, and the story of the exemplary heroine, in one form or another, would continue to be important as a structural device in her novels.

Thus *The Minister's Wooing*, set in Newport toward the end of the eighteenth century, focuses on the trials and ultimate triumph of a young woman named Mary Scudder. This novel, first serialized in Boston's new *Atlantic Monthly*, appeared in book form first in England and then in the United States, in 1859. Unlike *The Wide, Wide World* or *The Lamplighter*, *The Minister's Wooing* is a historical novel; it is concerned with the amelioration of the Calvinism of Jonathan Edwards and even features an appearance by Edwards's famous grandson, Aaron Burr. At the center of the book, however, is the exhibition of Mary Scudder's exemplary piety and virtue. She loves her cousin, James Marvyn, who goes to sea (like Willie Sullivan in *The Lamplighter*). When James is reported drowned, with no evidence that he was converted beforehand, his mother collapses, but Mary is reconciled. She even agrees, out of a sense of duty, to become engaged to the Calvinist minister, Dr. Samuel Hopkins (another historical character). Then, when James reappears, not only undrowned and prosperous but also converted, Mary chooses duty over love. But she is spared the consequences of her choice when a local gossip, Miss Prissy Diamond, explains the situation to Hopkins, who renounces his claim to Mary and frees her to marry her cousin.

We are told that Dr. Hopkins "scarce ever allowed a flower of sacred emotion to spring in his soul without picking it to pieces to see if its genera and species were correct," whereas Mary, by contrast, "had the blessed gift of womanhood — that vivid life in the soul and sentiment which resists the chills of analysis, as a healthful human heart resists cold." Yet Mary is no mere advocate of feeling and the heart; a true daughter of the Puritans, she saves her French friend, Virginie de Frontignac, from the wiles of Aaron Burr, and in the moment of crisis she is willing to submit her own desires to what she sees as her Christian duty. What perhaps distinguishes Stowe from such writers as Susan Warner and Maria Cummins is that she to some extent criticizes Mary's submissive self-denial. But Mary herself never acts on such a criticism; it takes the common sense of Miss Prissy to save her from her potential fanaticism. In the end Mary is as lavishly rewarded for her virtue as was Cummin's Gerty: by marriage, wealth, and family.

Stowe's expenditures rose at least as rapidly as her literary income, forcing her to take on more and more literary tasks to keep up with her obligations, and in 1861 she was publishing two novels as serials: *Agnes of Sorrento* in monthly installments in Boston's *Atlantic Monthly* and *The Pearl of Orr's Island* as a weekly in the New York *Independent*. Both were published as books, by Ticknor and Fields, in 1862. Stowe had a high opinion of *Agnes,* set in Italy, but most readers (including James T. Fields, who published it rather reluctantly in the *Atlantic*) have disagreed, preferring *The Pearl of Orr's Island.*

In one sense the story of Mara Lincoln, the "Pearl" of the title, is as sentimental and melodramatic as anything Stowe wrote. Mara is orphaned at birth and, in what may be a reference to one of Lydia Sigourney's better-known poems, baptized at the double funeral of her parents. She is raised by her grandparents on the Maine coast, and there, when Mara is three, a storm washes up a dead woman holding a live male child. This child is named Moses and is also raised by Mara's grandparents. There are mysteries and secrets: for instance, the local minister, Theophilus Sewell, recognizes Moses' dead mother, whom he loved and lost years earlier. But the main story turns on the relationship between Mara and Moses. She is devoted, he is selfish, yet finally, years later, they are engaged, just before Moses sails for the first time as master of his own ship. Mara then becomes ill, as suddenly as Nina Gordon before her, and Stowe intrudes quite overtly to answer the complaint of readers who "want to read only stories which end in joy and prosperity." "We wished in this history," she replies, "to speak of a class of lives formed on the model of Christ, . . . which . . . have this preciousness and value that the dear saints who live them comes nearest in their mission to the mission of

Jesus." Mara dies, but not before her "mission" is accomplished. She brings her careless neighbor, Sally Kittridge, to Christ, and Moses, who returns shortly before her death, is also ultimately converted by her example. Four years later, we are told, Moses and Sally are married.

Such a summary, however, provides little sense of the flavor of this book, which depends less on plot or story than on descriptions and evocations of country customs and dialect. Already in *The Minister's Wooing* the first four chapters were devoted to the conversation and behavior at a country tea party, and the final wedding was described in a long dialect letter from Miss Prissy Diamond to her sister, "Lizabeth," in Boston. In *The Pearl of Orr's Island,* Miss Prissy is replaced by a pair of old, unmarried sisters, Roxy and Ruey Toothacre, who function far less for comic relief than as guardians or avatars of folk wisdom and of the communal spirit. They are constantly telling dialect stories, as is Captain Kittridge, Sally's father. For long stretches the novel's plot functions mainly as a framework for description and anecdote so that, oddly enough, this tale of Mara's Christ-like renunciation of the world ends up being most memorable for evoking the very world Mara renounces.

Stowe's growing emphasis on community came to fruition in the last novel she published before the Byron scandal. *Oldtown Folks* (1869) is not, however, without clichéd and melodramatic plot devices. We have a pair of mysterious orphans (Harry and Tina Percival), who come into their rightful fortune at the close; we have a haunted mansion with a secret chamber, and an elegant rake named Ellery Davenport (like Aaron Burr, a grandson of Jonathan Edwards). The main character and narrator, Horace Holyoke, is male rather than female, but Tina Percival (whose first name recalls that of Nina Gordon in *Dred*) goes through a number of the stages of the standard career of the exemplary heroine. When Tina is forced, early on, to live with a strict and unsympathetic old woman, Stowe is fairly clearly drawing on the Aunt Fortune episode of *The Wide, Wide World,* and by the end Tina's charity is in full flower, setting all problems aright.

These devices do little more, however, than provide a loose structure around which Stowe arranges descriptions of "Oldtown" (Natick, Massachusetts, where Calvin Stowe had grown up) at the end of the eighteenth century, with brief excursions to Boston and to "Cloudland" (Stowe's native town of Litchfield, Connecticut). There are loving descriptions of funerals, of small-town Sundays, of religious controversies, of New England Thanksgivings, and so on. Above all, there are dialect stories told by the town gossip, Sam Lawson, stories Stowe had learned from her husband. His object in writing, Stowe's narrator explains, is "to show how the peculiar life of old Massachusetts worked upon us [i.e., upon himself, Harry, and Tina], and determined our growth and character and destinies." But these "destinies" for the most part take a back seat to "the peculiar life of old Massachusetts." Toward the end of the book, for instance, when Horace tells of having learned that his beloved Tina was planning to marry Ellery Davenport, we might expect a detailed account of his sorrow; instead, we get a long chapter in which Ellery, in company, draws out the loquacious Sam Lawson. And at the beginning of the next-to-last chapter, after apologizing for the "minuteness" of the narrative thus far, Horace simply begins summing up the final twelve years of his story, devoting only one short paragraph to his own eventual marriage to Tina.

The Byron scandal severely damaged Stowe's reputation, but it hardly ended her career as a professional writer. She continued to write and publish, her works coming to include two more volumes of New England fiction, *Sam Lawson's Oldtown Fireside Stories* (1872) and *Poganuc People* (1878). She continued to earn royalties from earlier works. And she was a significant influence on younger women writers, most notably, perhaps, Sarah Orne Jewett. "You must throw everything and everybody aside at times," Jewett wrote in 1899, three years after Stowe's death, "but a woman made like Mrs. Stowe cannot bring herself to that cold selfishness of the moment for one's work's sake, and the recompense for her loss is a divine touch here and there in an incomplete piece of work." Yet Jewett learned a great deal from Stowe all the same, and Stowe's most immediate importance to the development of American literature in the nineteenth century, beyond the sheer magnitude of her accomplishment as a successful professional writer, probably lay in her cultivation or invention of the New England "local-color" writing that Jewett, Mary Wilkins Freeman, and others would develop, perhaps more completely, in the 1880s and 1890s.

However atypical it may be of her writing as a whole, *Uncle Tom's Cabin* remains Stowe's masterpiece – and an American classic. It has been charged with plenty of faults, and although these charges usually involve applying contemporary standards of taste retroactively, they do identify significant qualities in the book. With its overt and frequent appeals to feeling, including the closing declaration that what "every individual can do" about slavery is "see to it that *they feel right,*" *Uncle Tom's Cabin* is clearly sentimental, in the most literal sense. Complaints that Stowe relies too much on melodrama seem less persuasive. Few of the novel's characters, Eva and Simon Legree being the most obvious exceptions, are wholly virtuous or vicious, and the rest are rather notably mixed. There are moments of high excitement, such as Eliza's famous crossing of the ice, but for the most part readers who complain about the melodrama of *Uncle Tom's Cabin* are really complaining about the melodramatic violence of slavery, which is of course just what Stowe wished them to object to.

Uncle Tom's Cabin clearly perpetuates a number of sexist and racist character stereotypes. Stowe's good women rely on "feeling," and most of her men are misled by "judgment." Men are naturally forceful and energetic, and women are naturally submissive. As for blacks, we are told that they have "naturally fine voices," that cooking is "an indigenous talent of the African race," that "the negro mind" is innately "impassioned and imaginative," and that "there is no more use in making believe to be angry with a negro than with a child." And this is only a very selective catalogue. Stowe's sexist and racist stereotypes are in fact fairly identical: that is, the "masculine" characteristics of white males are consistently contrasted with the "feminine" qualities not only of white and black women but of black men. Thus Uncle Tom possesses "the gentle, domestic heart" that, we are told, "has been a peculiar characteristic of his unhappy race," and we are told that blacks, again like women, "are not naturally daring and enterprising, but home-loving and affectionate." George Harris, a slave who openly defies slavery, might seem an exception to this stereotype, but Stowe's explanation only confirms her racism: George has inherited his "European features" and his "high, indomitable spirit" from his white father.

These sexist and racist stereotypes are by no means incidental to Stowe's novel; they are quite central to its meaning. The story begins at the Shelby plantation in Kentucky, with a marriage characterized principally by the contrast between husband and wife. "Feel too much!" Emily Shelby responds to her husband, who is in the process of selling Tom and Eliza's son Harry in order to cover his debts. "Am I not a woman, – a mother?" Yet Emily Shelby does not defy her husband's corrupt authority; the contrast between masculine power and feminine feeling does not emerge as open conflict. Rather, what happens in *Uncle Tom's Cabin* is that we move through a succession of homes that present different aspects of this opening domestic situation, variations on the contrast between men who dominate and women who "feel" while submitting. As we move north, with Eliza and then with Eliza and George, each variation is an improvement on its predecessor. Senator and Mrs. Bird, to whose house Eliza first goes once she gets across the Ohio River, are similar to the Shelbys; he is a man of the world and she exerts her influence only in the home. But Senator Bird, unlike Mr. Shelby, is susceptible to such influence, which leads him to help Eliza escape. He allows himself to become, in effect, partly "feminized," and this process of feminization is more or less completed in the next northern variation on the Shelby plantation, the Quaker settlement where Eliza is reunited with George. This settlement is a kind of symbolic domestic, feminine utopia. Its center is Rachel Halliday's immaculate kitchen, from which she presides over community affairs. Her matriarchal authority works effortlessly through "influence," and she is never challenged by any of the Quaker men. Thus to move to the North, for Stowe, is not just to move toward freedom; it is also to move from public to private, from masculine power to feminine influence. And this movement finally brings about the conversion of George Harris from the "high, indomitable spirit" of his white father to the feminine virtues of Eliza and his own black mother.

The movement south, with Uncle Tom, is both more ominous and more strange. The New Orleans home of Augustine and Marie St. Clare is Stowe's most unusual variation on the domestic situation at the Shelby plantation. The length of the St. Clare episode far exceeds any obvious contribution it makes to the plot of *Uncle Tom's Cabin,* and Uncle Tom, in the affairs of this family, is a rather subordinate character. What matters here is that gender roles have gotten reversed: Augustine is sensitive, Marie is selfish. Or, to speak more precisely, gender roles have gotten confused in complex and interesting ways. Marie manipulates the ideas and values by which Emily Shelby sincerely lives. Augustine hides his "feminine" nature – which he has apparently inherited directly from his mother and which he seems to pass on, undiluted, to his daughter, Eva – beneath a veneer of "masculine" rationality and sarcasm. There are other variations on the feminine here: for instance, Eva's world-renouncing sensitivity and Topsy's insubordination. The portrayal of Topsy is likely to seem especially racist and offensive, but we should pay close attention to the precise nature of her misbehavior. We are told that she learns reading rapidly but that "the confinement of sewing was her abomination." Topsy, that is, seems to rebel mainly against "women's work."

Beneath Stowe's overt attack on slavery, then, and implicit in the metaphorical identification of black and female stereotypes lurks a more covert protest against what Stowe called, in 1839, "domestic slavery." This protest comes closer to the surface in the book's final episode, at the plantation of Simon Legree. In the figure of Cassy, at once Legree's mistress and his property, the analogy between marriage and slavery is made quite explicit, and here, finally, the contrast between masculine domination and feminine submission is engaged as conflict. Cassy does not rebel directly; Uncle Tom talks her out of her plan to kill Legree. And Tom's Christian triumph, the scene toward which Stowe had been working all along, seems not to have much effect on Legree. Rather, what brings Legree down is a subversive power at the heart of feminine submission – a power acting through a lock of Eva's hair, through Legree's memory of his mother, through Cassy's manipulation of Legree's superstition. Cassy – like Emily Shelby, Mrs. Bird, and

Rachel Halliday — works through "influence," and she maintains it by playing on Legree's guilt. This guilt turns even "things sweetest and holiest," such as the memory of his mother's "dying prayers, her forgiving love," into "phantoms of horror and affright." Thus, "to the soul resolved in evil, perfect love is the most fearful torture, the seal and sentence of the direst despair." What happens at the end of *Uncle Tom's Cabin* is that the Cult of Domesticity becomes a secret weapon, a weapon that need not even be used consciously. The "dying prayers" and "forgiving love" of Legree's mother were perfectly sincere; it is not her fault that they drive her son crazy and, incidentally, permit Cassy to escape with Emmeline.

Although Legree's plantation is in one sense the antithesis of the Shelby plantation, in a deeper sense it reveals the fundamental domestic economy at work from the beginning of the book. Legree is clearly meant to dramatize the true nature, the essential brutality, of slavery as an institution, to reveal what was really going on even at the Shelbys'. And Legree's relationship with Cassy may dramatize the true nature of even the Shelbys' marriage. It is worth noting, in any case, that it is only well into the Legree episode that we learn of Mr. Shelby's death, as if there were some sort of subterranean connection between the fates of the two men. Emily Shelby has not rebelled, but she has triumphed, and when she takes over the plantation, she also proceeds to demonstrate her husband's previous incompetence through her own successful and prudent management. None of this, of course, is as clear as Stowe's attack on slavery, and *Uncle Tom's Cabin* is not a "woman's novel" in the same sense that it is an abolition novel — specifically, a Christian abolition novel. But from first to last, and not surprisingly, Stowe's vision of slavery grows out of her experience and understanding of the constricted role of women in mid-nineteenth-century America — just as the cause of abolition allows her to insinuate a vision of women's experience she could hardly have expressed directly. The story of *Uncle Tom's Cabin* has little in common with the stories of Ellen Montgomery, Gertrude Sullivan, or Ruth Hall. But it does share with the works of Warner, Cummins, Fern, and other women novelists of the 1850s a more general subject: a world in which men dominate, often cruelly, and in which women, domestic slaves, have only domesticity itself to protect their severely limited moral autonomy.

CONFLICTS AND CONNECTIONS

Man in the open air, woman in the home: so might we distinguish the main male and female traditions of American writing in the 1850s. The simplicity of this formulation is quite attractive, but it masks a more complex and messy reality. We might, for instance, understand the distinction between popular women's fiction and the male canon in terms of genre, and with considerable justification. It has long been recognized that the pre-Civil War American fiction writers most often canonized in the twentieth century — Cooper, Poe, Hawthorne, and Melville, all of them men — were more deeply influenced by the tradition of gothic fiction than were most of their British contemporaries (at least, those British writers also canonized in the twentieth century). So we could distinguish between a masculine *gothic* tradition of American fiction and a *domestic* tradition established by American women novelists.

The first complication lurking in this view of things is that gothic fiction in England, first popularized by Ann Radcliffe in the 1790s, was very much a woman's mode, again and again sending a sensitive protagonist (usually a young woman) into an apparently haunted domain (usually a mansion or castle presided over by a threatening male figure). So a major component of the "masculine" American canon grows out of a British *women's* tradition. Moreover, gothic conventions play almost no role in the most popular novels by *American* women in the early 1850s, and the absence of these conventions is a bit curious. In *The Madwoman in the Attic* (1979), Sandra Gilbert and Susan Gubar describe a subversive feminist tradition in nineteenth-century literature by women, mainly British women. Their title refers to Bertha Rochester in Charlotte Brontë's *Jane Eyre,* whose madness indirectly or unconsciously expresses Jane's own rebellion against domesticity and masculine domination. Brontë, this is to say, exploited a useful strategy of women novelists: could not gothic terrors serve as agents of a subversive women's power, a power lurking beneath the pose of submissive self-denial, beneath the Cult of Domesticity? For the most part, however, the American answer to this hypothetical question was no. Best-selling American novelists like Warner, Cummins, and Fern made little or no use of the gothic, even though *Jane Eyre,* adapting gothic for the purposes of the female bildungsroman, had been published in England and America in 1847, just three years before *The Wide, Wide World* made the female bildungsroman one of the most popular fictional modes in America.

One can speculate about the reasons for the divergence of Warner, Cummins, and Fern from the example of Charlotte Brontë. We remember that Warner called her works "stories" rather than "novels"; "novels," for such Christian writers as Warner and Cummins, were immoral and dangerous, and few kinds of fiction were more symptomatic of these dangers than gothic. There is also a crucial difference between Jane Eyre, on the one hand, and Ellen Montgomery or Gertrude Flint, on the other. Whereas Brontë's heroine alternates between self-assertion and submission, Warner's and Cummins's heroines simply submit, eradicating every vestige of private self.

There is nothing, in their cases, for a symbolic madwoman to symbolize. Finally, the mystery and secrecy of gothic are antithetical to the kind of exemplary power Ellen and Gertrude achieve, a power that depends absolutely on public performance and public appreciation. One episode in *Ruth Hall* – Ruth's visit to the "insane Hospital," where madness is induced in women by agents of their husbands – comes closer to the conventions of gothic fiction. Indeed, the story of Ruth's friend Mary Leon, who is imprisoned in the hospital and who dies after writing "I am not crazy, Ruth, no, no – but I shall be," anticipates the gothic feminism of Charlotte Perkins Gilman's "The Yellow Wallpaper" (1892). But this episode is hardly typical of *Ruth Hall* as a whole, nor is it particularly relevant to the meaning of Ruth's story. Even here Fanny Fern is far more interested in social criticism than in inspiring terror, and once Ruth has achieved genuine power and autonomy, as the author "Floy," she has no need to impersonate madwomen, or even to visit them. The subversive power of gothic fiction has little to do with royalty checks and stock certificates.

Thus, three of the most popular American domestic novelists of the early 1850s did not exploit the potential intersection of the domestic and gothic modes. This fact sets them apart not only from the gothic tradition of Poe and Hawthorne but equally from the subversive feminist tradition described by Sandra Gilbert and Susan Gubar. Yet one still might be a bit nervous about any rigid generic distinction between gothic and domestic fiction. In both genres, after all, the defining symbolic setting is a house. In domestic fiction we have a "home," ideally protected and presided over by a beneficent maternal influence. In gothic fiction the connotations of the setting are quite different – it is not beneficent but haunted, by some sort of mysterious menace – but the setting is still, usually, some sort of house. And the simultaneous prominence of these two modes in pre-Civil War America created the potential for a kind of generic instability or ambiguity. To know whether one was safe or at risk, protected by domestic influence or menaced by gothic horror, one had to determine what kind of house, what kind of fiction, one was in. One had to determine who was in charge: mother or monster.

In America – at least in the works of such canonized writers as Cooper, Poe, Hawthorne, and Melville – the British gothic formula was modified in significant ways. Since native castles were in short supply, their place was often taken by the terrors of the wilderness. What this means, however, is not so much that men opened up the gothic as that the "open air" of nineteenth-century American fiction often *functions* as a constricted, mysterious, interior space. Also, in the hands of male American writers, the gender implications of gothic (implications that grew directly out of the conventions of the mid-eighteenth-century seduction novel) get inverted. In so-called classic *American* gothic fiction, the sensitive protagonist is more often male than female, and the terrors that confront him are tied not to masculine rapacity but to female sexuality, or to guilty masculine fantasies of female sexuality.

Thus in Hawthorne's "Young Goodman Brown" (1835) the title character heads for a witches' sabbath in the woods shortly after his marriage, the Devil's list of sins prominently features sexual evils (seductions, husband-murders, abortions committed by unmarried young women), and Brown's ultimate revulsion stems from his discovery that his wife, Faith, is present at the midnight ceremony. Similarly, in story after story, Poe's sensitive male protagonists are beset by innocent but nonetheless obscurely terrifying women: Berenice, Morella, Ligeia, Madeline Usher. Indeed, what happens in "The Fall of the House of Usher" (1839), most essentially, is that a nightmare version of female "influence" triumphs over male domination, both literally and symbolically. After Madeline falls upon her catatonic brother, a widening "fissure" opens in the erect, masculine tower, revealing a "blood-red moon"; and then all collapses into "the deep and dank tarn." In mid-nineteenth-century American gothic fiction — as also, much later, in Alfred Hitchcock's gothic film *Psycho* (1960) — the mother, or the son's fearful and guilty fantasy of the mother, *is* the monster.

All of which is to say that the symbolic haunted house of American gothic fiction and the home of the domestic novel are in effect doubles, or mirror images, of one another; in both, the symbolic inner space is suffused with feminine influences. The main difference is that this influence, terrifying in gothic fiction, is beneficent in domestic, so that to move from one mode to the other is to redefine the essential meaning of the house. This sort of redefinition lies at the heart of what happens at the end of Hawthorne's *House of the Seven Gables*. At the outset the house of the title seems rather conventionally gothic, symbolizing masculine power and a masculine curse on that power. At the close, following the death of Judge Pyncheon, all of this gets explained away in the fashion of Radcliffean, or "rational," gothic: "Maule's Curse" on the male Pyncheons was simply a hereditary propensity for apoplexy. But the death of Judge Pyncheon transforms the meaning of the house in a more fundamental way. Suddenly the posies, whose seeds were brought from Italy by Alice Pyncheon, bloom on the roof — suggestively, in the angle between the two front gables. Then Phoebe returns, with "the quiet flow of natural sunshine over her," and two symbolic transformations, from masculine to feminine and from gothic to domestic, are brought to completion. Thus, one could describe the ending of *The House of the Seven Gables* as a domestic revision of the ending of "The Fall of the House of Usher."

In the years following the Civil War, we have been told again and again, a tradition of "romance" in American fiction (the tradition of Cooper, Poe, Hawthorne, and Melville) gave way to a tradition of "realism." These terms and this generalization are inevitably problematic. Nevertheless, one might describe Warner, Cummins, and Fern, in that they ignore the gothic to elaborate the domestic realities of women's lives, as harbingers of this development. This description is least plausible in the case of Cummins; whatever realism there is at the beginning of *The Lamplighter* rapidly gives way to fantasy. But both *The Wide, Wide World* and *Ruth Hall* are, in different ways, significantly "realistic." Many of Harriet Beecher Stowe's works, especially her New England novels of the 1860s, also anticipate later works of so-called American realism, and not surprisingly. Stowe was an *Atlantic Monthly* author, and William Dean Howells, who would lead the battle for realism in the 1880s, got his start on the *Atlantic* in the 1860s.

In the final episode of *Uncle Tom's Cabin,* however, Stowe *does* exploit the gothic possibilities of domestic fiction, or, to speak more precisely, the possibilities of confusing and combining the gothic and the domestic. She draws on something like "romance," and for clearly subversive purposes. Cassy and Emmeline hide in a supposedly haunted room in the attic of Legree's mansion while Legree searches the swamps. At night, dressed in a sheet, Cassy visits Legree downstairs to sustain his superstitious fear of the attic chamber. Eventually, the two women make their escape. Although Cassy's attic hideout suggests that Stowe has Brontë's madwoman, Bertha Rochester, very much in mind, the effect seems to be quite different, since Cassy only pretends to be a ghost. Brontë's true psychological gothic seems to give way, in Stowe, to gothic hoax, in the manner of Washington Irving's "Legend of Sleepy Hollow" (1820). Just as Brom Bones impersonates the Headless Horseman in order to frighten Ichabod Crane (and win the hand of Katrina Van Tassel), so Cassy impersonates a ghost in order to frighten Legree (and escape with Emmeline).

In another sense, however, Cassy's masquerade reveals an authentic rebellious power beneath the doctrine of domestic submission and feminine influence. Legree is Cassy's "owner, her tyrant and tormentor . . . ; and yet so it is, that the most brutal man cannot live in constant association with a strong female influence and not be greatly controlled by it." Thus, Legree alternately tyrannizes Cassy and dreads her. As "influence" becomes a cause of "creeping horror," even little Eva gets turned, briefly but quite literally, into a kind of Madeline Usher. When Legree takes hold of the lock of hair Eva gave to Uncle Tom, it twines itself suggestively around his fingers, "as if it burned him," and we learn that a lock of his mother's hair accompanied the letter in which, "dying, she blest and forgave him." Then come nightmares, in which the veiled figure of his mother appears to Legree, and he feels *"that hair* twining round his fingers; and then . . . round his neck." We also learn that the attic room in which Cassy and Emmeline hide is one in which, years earlier, Legree had confined, tortured, and killed a female slave, presumably a prior mistress. So, although Cassy's masquerade may be a hoax, Legree's guilty reaction to it is quite genuine. Cassy acts, in effect, as an avenging angel for all the women Legree has wronged, and her masquerade ultimately kills him.

Legree's death is a kind of gothic inversion of Augustine St. Clare's domestic triumph. "His mind is wandering," says the doctor as St. Clare lies dying. "No!" St. Clare interrupts, "it is coming *home,* at last!" "Just before the spirit parted, he opened his eyes, with a sudden light, as of joy and recognition, and said *'Mother!'* and then he was gone." Legree, too, has dying visions of his mother, but they are less joyful: "a cold hand touched his; a voice said, three times, in a low, fearful whisper, 'Come! come! come!' And, while he lay sweating with terror, he knew not when or how, the thing was gone." Legree begins drinking "imprudently and recklessly"; "and, at his dying bed," we are told, "stood a stern, white, inexorable figure, saying 'Come! come! come!' " That this figure turns out to be Cassy in disguise scarcely lessens the significance of what is happening here, for it is Legree's own guilt that turns domestic bliss into gothic terror, "perfect love," as the narrator puts it, into "the most fearful torture."

Uncle Tom's Cabin is, most fundamentally, a Christian novel, and this fact suggests a link between Stowe and such contemporaries as Warner and Cummins. But Stowe is a very different kind of Christian novelist from Warner and Cummins. Christian submission does not, for her, lead to public approbation and worldly success; for example, her two most exemplary Christian characters, Eva and Tom, die. Also, *Uncle Tom's Cabin,* unlike *The Wide, Wide World* and *The Lamplighter,* follows Christian belief into overt protest. Stowe attacks slavery as a *sin,* and the form her novel takes, with all its direct authorial interjections, is finally the form of a sermon. Stowe's Christianity would seem to distinguish her even more clearly from writers like Poe, Hawthorne, and Melville. There is certainly nothing like Tom's "Victory," the climactic event of *Uncle Tom's Cabin,* in the works of any of these men. For Poe, presumably, Tom's death would have mattered mainly as an example of what he called "the human thirst for self-torture," and if we think of the death of Arthur Dimmesdale on the scaffold at the end of *The Scarlet Letter* or of the death of Melville's Billy Budd, we see part of what is distinctive about Stowe: she regards Tom's triumph without any irony whatever.

"Do the worst you can," Tom says to Legree before he is killed, "my troubles'll be over soon; but if ye don't repent, yours won't *never* end!"

Modern readers, at least those who do not share Tom's belief in salvation and eternal damnation, may have trouble accepting Tom's (and Stowe's) certainty. Twentieth-century readers are more likely to believe in the reality of unending *psychological* torments, which is one reason the twentieth century has canonized Poe, Hawthorne, and Melville. These writers, in the phrase Henry James applied to Hawthorne, "cared for the deeper psychology," and all three adapted gothic conventions to probe this "deeper psychology." There is nothing like this in Stowe's account of Uncle Tom's triumph. But what happens in the story of *Cassy's* triumph over Legree, the climactic event of the novel's protest against "*domestic* slavery," is that the religious terms of Tom's story get, we might say, gothicized and psychologized. Cassy does not have to wait for divine judgment; her "influence" torments Legree in the here and now. Even Cassy, at the close, is converted and domesticated; the "despairing, haggard expression of her face" gives way to "one of gentle trust" and, secure in "the bosom of the family," she becomes "a devout and tender Christian." Of course, she has no more need to act the madwoman; she and Emmeline are free and, what may be more important, Legree is dead.

In the context of the literary marketplace in the 1850s, the distinction between women's and men's traditions may be even less clear than the generic distinction between domestic and gothic fiction. One thing certainly is clear: Poe, Hawthorne, and Melville never came close to matching the sales achieved by Warner, Stowe, Cummins, and Fern. But sales figures do not necessarily, of themselves, constitute traditions. We should recognize, for instance, that works representing the supposedly distinct traditions of women's and men's writing usually appeared in the same or in similar magazines and were issued by the same book publishers. Between 1853, when it was founded, and 1855, when it was sold, *Putnam's Monthly Magazine* published a number of writers now canonized, including Cooper, Thoreau, and Melville. But George Palmer Putnam had also published Warner's *The Wide, Wide World* in 1850. Boston's *Atlantic Monthly,* founded in 1857, came to publish a number of *Putnam's* authors, and the firm of Ticknor and Fields, which acquired the *Atlantic* in 1859, had been Hawthorne's publisher since *The Scarlet Letter* in 1850. But Hawthorne, like Poe, had published much of his early work in giftbooks and ladies' magazines. Also, when the *Atlantic* was founded, it prided itself on listing Stowe prominently among its contributors, and when John P. Jewett failed in 1857, Stowe moved to Ticknor and Fields. In fact, James T. Fields numbered both Hawthorne and Stowe among his friends. Fern, like Mrs. Southworth, came to publish exclusively in Robert Bonner's *New York Ledger,* a magazine calculated for wide popularity, but Bonner also paid top dollar for works by such writers as

Edward Everett, Bryant, Longfellow, and Tennyson. For the most part, then, the people who read Hawthorne and Melville were the same people (or a subset of the same people) who read Warner and Cummins.

We should also recognize that if there was anxiety or antagonism between these male and female "traditions," it flowed almost exclusively in one direction. Writers like Hawthorne and Melville aroused little professional anxiety in popular women writers, and no wonder; neither, after all, had very much of what we would now call market share – not, at least, compared with women like Warner, Stowe, Cummins, and Fern. The male writers who mattered to these women were such popular (mainly British) novelists as, most notably, Charles Dickens. Yet Hawthorne and Melville were clearly threatened by the authors the former called a "d——d mob of scribbling women." Both Hawthorne and Melville discovered their full powers at precisely the time of the rise of the best-selling women writers of the early 1850s, and they were both soon compelled to exercise their powers in the context created or revealed by these best-sellers. Both men tried in the 1850s to appropriate some of the themes (and some of the readers) of popular women's fiction, even as they sometimes subverted or burlesqued the conventions and values of this fiction. And by the end of the decade both men had pretty much abandoned fiction writing.

There is a considerable tradition of what we might call antidomestic American literature, and this tradition is abundantly represented in the version of "American literature" often canonized in the twentieth century. One thinks, for example, of Mark Twain or Ernest Hemingway; Huck Finn and Nick Adams keep running away from precisely the sorts of female-dominated homes and the kinds of feminine "influence" that Stowe idealizes. But Hawthorne, for one, did not respond to female competition by attacking domesticity; quite the contrary. *The House of the Seven Gables* (1851) is as domestic in its setting as in its title; its author was quite deliberately trying – in this, his second novel – to escape from what he called the "gloom" of *The Scarlet Letter,* and he was also clearly seeking to appeal to female readers, with considerable success. After her husband read her the story aloud (a practice that tells us a great deal about his sense of his audience), Sophia Hawthorne praised the "dear home-loveliness and satisfaction" of the conclusion. Phoebe Pyncheon of *Seven Gables* was, for the author of "Rappaccini's Daughter" and *The Scarlet Letter,* a rather new sort of heroine, and this heroine reappeared, in increasingly exemplary forms, as Priscilla in *The Blithedale Romance* (1852) and as Hilda in *The Marble Faun* (1860). Priscilla's curiously self-serving submissiveness suggests an ironic attitude toward the exemplary heroine, but many readers, including quite a few in the twentieth century, have read Priscilla without irony, as the unambiguous moral center of *The Blithedale Romance.* And it is rather difficult to read Phoebe and Hilda, and their affirmations of domestic ideals, in any other way. "Forgive me, Hilda!" pleads the hero, Kenyon, at the end of *The Marble Faun,* after Hilda has expressed "horror" at his speculation on the possibly beneficial effects of sin, "I never did believe it! . . . Oh, Hilda, guide me home!"

It makes more sense to identify Melville with an antidomestic American tradition. After all, such books as *Redburn* (1849), *White-Jacket* (1850), and *Moby-Dick* (1851) avoid women and domesticity almost entirely, and *Pierre* (1852) becomes, among other things, an all-out attack on the domestic. Yet *Pierre* was apparently begun as an effort to court the very audience it ended up alienating. Melville told Sophia Hawthorne in 1852 that the successor to *Moby-Dick* would be "a rural bowl of milk," and he assured his British publisher that *Pierre* would be "very much more calculated for popularity than anything you have yet published of mine." In the event, of course, this prediction proved wrong, even perverse. *Pierre,* however, did not immediately end its author's professional literary career, and the last stage of that career suggests the complexity of Melville's relation to domesticity. In spite of the hostile critical reaction to *Pierre,* and despite the book's dismal sales, *Putnam's* in 1852 asked Melville to contribute to their new monthly, where "Bartleby, the Scrivener" appeared late in 1853. Between 1853 and 1856 Melville placed five more stories and the serialization of *Israel Potter* in *Putnam's* and eight stories in *Harper's.* When he turned to domestic themes in these stories — for instance, in "I and My Chimney" and "The Apple-Tree Table" (1856) — his aggressions were considerably more under control than they had been in *Pierre.* It is also worth noting the dominant influence on many of Melville's magazine stories of the widely popular and far from antidomestic Dickens, whose *Bleak House* had been serialized in *Harper's* in 1852 and 1853.

We should not attribute all concern with the domestic in works by non-canonized male writers to the effort to cash in on or attack the values of women writers and readers. It is hard to imagine a book more sincerely domestic, both in its values and in its details, than Thoreau's *Walden.* Similarly, when Huck Finn and Hemingway's Nick Adams flee civilization, they do so ultimately in order to set up "homes" of their own, on the Mississippi raft or on the banks of the Big Two-Hearted River. In much canonized American literature, men who see themselves as fleeing the domestic or sentimental are often simply running away from women to indulge their own versions of domesticity and sentiment. There is nothing domestic about Ahab's pursuit of the White Whale, but on two major occasions toward the end of *Moby-Dick* a cluster of values we might call both domestic and sentimental emerges in opposition to Ahab's suicidal monomania. First, Ahab invites Pip to share the protection of his cabin, his home — as Uncle True, in *The Lamplighter* (published, of course, three years after *Moby-Dick*), takes in the abandoned Gerty. Then, just before the chase begins, Ahab stares into the "magic glass" of Starbuck's "human eye," where he sees "the green land," "the bright hearth-stone," "my wife and child"; and Starbuck exhorts him to abandon his quest. These domestic impulses are rapidly rejected. Unlike, say, Stowe's George Harris, Ahab will not be feminized or domesticated. Yet these are moments of genuine power; they do not mock the emotion they evoke. Of course, one would still never confuse *Moby-Dick* with *The Wide, Wide World* or *Uncle Tom's Cabin;* here there surely *is* a difference between man in the open air and woman in the home. But we should be careful about applying this distinction too generally and too rigidly to American literature in the 1850s; the reality of this literature is more complicated. Even Ahab, as Captain Peleg puts it, "has his humanities," and Ishmael is saved, at the close, by *"the devious-cruising Rachel, that in her retracing search after her missing children, only found another orphan."*

THE LITERATURE OF EXPANSION AND RACE

Eric J. Sundquist

EXPLORATION AND EMPIRE

LOOKING BACK on the years following the U.S. conquest of the territories of northern Mexico in 1848, the former Mexican military commander Mariano Vallejo concluded his five-volume *Recuerdos históricos y personales tocante a la Alta California,* completed in 1875, with an illuminating but unusual critique. Despite the Treaty of Guadalupe Hidalgo, he wrote,

the Americans have treated the Californians as a conquered people and not as citizens who willingly became part of that great family which, under the protection of that glorious flag that proudly waved at Bunker Hill, defied the attacks of European monarchs, those who, seated upon their tottering thrones, were casting envious eyes toward California and the other regions embraced within the great federation of the sons of liberty.

Vallejo's assessment, marked as it is by his consent to the ideology of American empire, has to be read in the context of his own highly nationalistic narrative, and his views were by no means representative of the newly colonized Mexican people of the Southwest and California. Yet his memoir sums up the important paradoxes generated during nineteenth-century American expansion by the clash between the liberating ideals of democracy and the contrary drive to territorial acquisition, just as his own life symbolically reflected the ambiguities of national allegiance and power in the contested lands of the American continent.

Vallejo's career, in fact, followed a pattern not entirely unlike that of leading Anglo-American political leaders or advocates of western expansion such as Andrew Jackson. By the time of Mexico's war with the United States, Vallejo was an eminent figure in California history. He had led Mexican troops in a bloody battle against an 1829 uprising of Indians at Mission San José; had commanded the northern frontier of California against the fear of Russian and European encroachment and in warfare against other American Indian tribes; had created for his family a vast feudal barony in the area north of San Francisco Bay; had, with his nephew Governor Juan Batista Alvarado, briefly proclaimed an independent state of California in 1836; and had gradually become a proponent of the annexation of California by the United States, which he thought preferable to the disorganization of local governments and distant Mexican rule. Whatever the importance of Vallejo's adopted patriotism, his view that the Mexican War was fought primarily to protect America's national interests from foreign threat and to rescue a willing native population from despotic rule was clearly not accepted by many Mexicans, or even by all Anglo-Americans, in 1848. But his remarks drew upon long-standing arguments about the destined expansion of America as a democratic nation free from tyranny – arguments that, since the outset of colonial settlement, had typically remained untroubled by the fact that the economic and political greatness of the United States would be achieved at the expense of American Indians and other nonwhite groups. Vallejo's own appropriation of the rhetoric of the American Revolution, as crucial to the U.S. war against Mexico as it was in the sectional conflict over African American slavery that led to the Civil War, indicates the confluence of ideological forces that gave complex meaning to the territory coveted by the "sons of liberty."

To extend America's "area of freedom," as Andrew Jackson called it, necessitated the absorption or the subjugation of American Indian tribes and Mexicans. In this respect, however, American expansion in the nineteenth century was not unique. A common argument closely linked to Enlightenment ideas of progress based on scientific inquiry was that the exploration of unknown lands and the conversion of alien peoples through political and economic expansion took place according to organic laws of growth. Throughout the world, the nineteenth century was a great age for exploration, as the limits of the seas from pole to pole were probed, and the interiors of previously uncharted continents in both hemispheres revealed. Although American explorers and settlers, like their European counterparts, usually believed their quests to be scientifically progressive and culturally beneficial, they frequently remained blind to the integrity and achievements of the peoples they encountered. While European powers established colonies in Africa, Asia, and Latin America, the United States in the four decades before the Civil War enveloped an enormous contiguous territory between the eastern seaboard and the Pacific coast. Roughly twice the size of the former U.S. holdings, this territory might also be thought of as "colonial" in that it was originally occupied by politically and militarily less powerful peoples. Its literature is the narrative of a relentless conquest in which the march of one civilization destroyed or utterly changed many others through dispossession and absorption.

Treaties with Great Britain in 1818 and 1846 gave the United States the

upper Great Plains and the Pacific Northwest to the Forty-ninth Parallel; the
Mexican cession of 1848 and the Gadsden Purchase of 1853 established the
southern border along the Rio Grande in Texas, then west through the New
Mexican territory and southern California to the Pacific. The literal mapping
of the United States was accompanied by a vast written record that established the psychological and political boundaries of the nation – a territory
that existed as an act of prophetic vision even before poets and novelists
expanded its horizons. Written in the form of diaries, journals, formal reports, travel narratives, and fiction, and composed by trappers, adventurers,
scientists, common pioneers, soldiers, and professional writers, the literature
detailing the exploration of the territories opened to conquest by the American Revolution and the Louisiana Purchase, and later by treaty and war with
Great Britain and Mexico, may claim to be the new republic's first national
literature. The writing about actual exploration often borrowed the imperial
rhetoric of expansionism produced by politicians and journalists who had
little contact with the vast wilderness but who foresaw its economic and
social significance and coveted its wealth of natural resources. The prevailing
idea of America's "manifest destiny" – its mission to conquer and regenerate
the North American continent, the Western Hemisphere, or even the entire
world – picked up strains of perfectionism from Puritan discourse and,
guided by the imagined fulfillment of America's democratic promise unleashed by the Age of Revolution, made the mapping of the United States
coincident with an eschatological idealism. The extension of American
boundaries, it was argued, would mean the extension of democracy; the
opening of a "virgin land" to settlement would release boundless energies of
creativity and industry; the discovery and cultivation of material abundance
would benefit the entire world by giving America the means to make itself an
asylum for the oppressed of foreign nations.

Throughout the antebellum period poetic and political visions often
shared the belief that the civilizations of the past were to be telescoped into
the future of America and made a function of its limitless vistas of space. A
number of important American writers of the antebellum period – James
Fenimore Cooper, William Cullen Bryant, Mary Jemison, Washington Irving, Herman Melville, Henry David Thoreau, Francis Parkman, Black
Hawk, Frederick Douglass, and Edgar Allan Poe among them – explored
the theme of expansion. The issue found perhaps its most representative voice
in Walt Whitman, who wrote in "Starting From Paumanok" (1860):

See revolving the globe,
The ancestor-continents away group'd together,
The present and future continents north and south, with the isthmus between.

See, vast trackless spaces,
As in a dream they change, they swiftly fill,
Countless masses debouch upon them,
They are now cover'd with the foremost people, arts, institutions, known. . . .

Americanos! conquerors! marches humanitarian!
Foremost! century marches! Libertad! masses!
For you a programme of chants.

Whitman's use of the Indian name for Long Island (Paumanok) and the Spanish word for "liberty" suggest the ironies latent in American expansion. American Indians seldom belonged, except symbolically, to the envisioned greatness of American futurity, at best offering a special problem of assimilation for the "nation of nations." In addition, the settlement of the Southwest and the Mexican War were justified by many on the principle that the United States would democratically "regenerate" backward and slavish Mexicans. Moreover, only civil war, not a "programme of chants," brought the semblance of freedom to black American slaves. Although the question of slavery's extension was important to settlement and boundary questions in the Plains and southwestern territories, it sometimes seemed to have little effect on inspired proclamations of America's destiny. Like other social problems, slavery appeared to many to be an example of human tyranny that would be eradicated upon the realization of democratic perfection. Class, racial, and sexual inequities, claimed important proponents of American expansion, would disappear if only the highest ideals were kept in view. Catharine Beecher, for example, writing on the role of women and the necessity of a domestic model to the realization of democratic ideals in her *Treatise on Domestic Economy* (1841), placed herself securely in the tradition of America's millennial evolution. Women engaged in "renovat[ing] degraded man," she argued, "are agents in accomplishing the greatest work that was ever committed to human responsibility. It is the building of a glorious temple, whose base shall be co-extensive with the bounds of the earth, whose summit shall pierce the skies, whose splendor shall beam on all lands."

Conceived of as organic, predestined, or necessitated by the claims of political morality, expansion was authorized on a variety of grounds: territorial security; the development of resources, navigation, and trade; the guarantee of individual liberty and self-sufficiency; and notions of predestination and futurity. Nonetheless, the notion of America's exceptional mission was so clearly a function of the great wealth of new territories open for exploration, marketing, and development that the notion of millennial destiny explains less than some of its most vocal advocates thought. The "passage to India," whether overland, upriver, or by transcontinental railroad, was possible only because the land was there to be opened to Euro-American progress. However culpable the United

States might come to seem in its treatment of American Indians and Mexicans over the next century and beyond, nineteenth-century observers argued that the social organization and land use of the two groups were a hindrance to progress as it was defined according to the standards of Euro-American civilization. The literature of exploration, like the claims of manifest destiny, played a significant role in the construction of the frontier ideology by which both Indians and Mexicans were categorized in the white mind. Many accounts by explorers and settlers were very sympathetic to native inhabitants, but much of the writing was imbued with fatalistic notions of the inevitable demise of "savage" life or the corruption and degeneration of Hispanic culture.

The concept of the primitive (or the savage) split off in several directions that were important for ideas about the western expansion. The wilderness could be portrayed as an Edenic abode for the realization of man's true primordial instincts (suppressed in complex society); it could seem the refuge of renegades and "mountain men" who sought an arena for dissipation; or it could be imagined as a source of sublime inspiration, which would liberate the American mind from its enslavement to corrupting or decaying Old World ideas and institutions. Until well into the 1850s, moreover, "the West" could refer to virtually any territory beyond the Allegheny Mountains. The argument between Old World antiquity and New World virginity, central to rising calls for a nationalistic culture and literature from the 1820s on through the 1860s, was thus played out in successive stages in America's westward development. The differentiations provided by narratives of exploration did not so much modify claims of national destiny as give them an ever more magnificent national stage setting.

America's vast and complex geography prompted a multitude of political and literary responses ranging from ecstatic celebrations of its sublime beauty to utilitarian proposals for its industrial and agricultural use, all of them grounded in a sense of America's special destiny among the nations of the world. The vast American West imposed upon the Euro-American mind a landscape that was alternately beautiful, sublime, terrifying, and anarchic precisely because it seemed as yet uncontaminated by extensive human presence. What are "the towers in which feudal oppression has fortified itself," with its "despotic superstitions," asked Charles F. Hoffman (1806–84) in *A Winter in the West* (1835), compared "to the deep forests which the eye of God has alone pervaded, and where Nature, in her unviolated sanctuary, has for ages laid her fruits and flowers on His altar!" Similarly, journalist and man of letters Nathaniel Parker Willis (1806–67), in an Emersonian moment, wrote in *American Scenery* (1840) that Americans look "upon all external objects as exponents of [their own] future." Instead of finding himself surrounded by unchanging names, landmarks, and modes of culture, as in Europe, the American's first thought when looking over an untouched valley "is of the villages that will soon sparkle on the hill-sides, the axes that will ring from the woodlands, and the mills, bridges, canals, and railroads that will span and border the streams that now rush through sedges and wild flowers."

Writing about the West, whether documentary or fictional, fed the enthusiasm for Romantic primitivism that permeated much American literature in the antebellum period and that provoked echoes of revolutionary rhetoric about breaking the constraints of British and European custom. A writer for the *United States Magazine and Democratic Review,* for example, offered a strong challenge in 1841:

We look to see yet in the West a bolder and manlier action of the American mind, which will scorn that emasculate imitativeness of England and English things that yet holds us in an unworthy thraldom, which will surrender itself more freely to the guidance of the genius of American democracy, and will find an inspiration stimulating it to achievements worthy of itself, in all those vast sublimities of nature, ever young in her most hoary age, that are there spread out before it as though for this very purpose.

The ideas of liberty, originality, wilderness, moral health, and national mission became intertwined, not always exactly equivalent but nonetheless provoking constant associations with one another. Reflected in various writings about the West, as well as in the grand landscapes of nineteenth-century American painters, the sublime in America became at once an aesthetic, a metaphysical, and a political force at the heart of the country's new spirit of nationalism – a spirit that deliberately conceived of the "heart" of America as its interior or western regions.

As early as 1815, Daniel Drake, writing of Ohio, had declared that the inhabitants of the West, secluded from inordinate contact with "foreign luxuries," were "destined to an unrivaled excellence in agriculture, manufactures, and internal commerce; in literature and the arts; in public virtue; and in national strength." Perhaps the fullest early expression of the western promise appeared in Edward Everett's 1824 Phi Beta Kappa oration, "The Circumstances Favorable to the Progress of Literature in America." In Everett's conception, the democratic institutions of the United States, its apparently limitless space, and its rapidity of development had combined to create a remarkable commonality of governmental purpose and linguistic energy. In terms that were soon used by others to describe the land beyond the Rocky Mountains, Everett argued that Providence had provided America as a "last refuge" to men "flying westward from civil and religious thraldom." Quoting with admiration Bishop Berkeley's famous stanza beginning "Westward the course of Empire takes its way," Everett called upon patriots and scholars alike to realize the ancient prophecies of "a land of equal laws and happy men," a Golden Age in the West:

We are summoned to new energy and zeal, by the high nature of the experiment we are appointed [by] providence to make, and the grandeur of the theatre on which it is to be performed. . . . Here must these bright fancies [of a Golden Age] be turned to truth; here must these high visions be realized, in which the seers and sages of the elder world took refuge from the calamities of the days in which they lived. There are no more continents to be revealed; Atlantis hath arisen from the ocean; the farthest Thule is reached; there are no more retreats beyond the sea, no more discoveries, no more hopes.

The rhetoric of Drake and Everett became commonplace in arguments for expansion during the first half of the nineteenth century. As Whitman wrote in his final preface to *Leaves of Grass*, America and its poets were to have leading parts in the unfolding of history, "as if in some colossal drama, acted again like those of old, under the open sun, the Nations of our time, and all the characteristics of Civilization, seem hurrying, stalking across, flitting from wing to wing, gathering, closing up, toward some long-prepared, most tremendous, denouement." The American geography was to embody the destiny of a new democratic nation that now more than ever imagined itself as a "city upon a hill," a moral example for the rest of the world. John L. O'Sullivan (1813–95), editor of the *New York Morning News* and the *Democratic Review,* would become famous for coining the term "manifest destiny" in an 1845 essay calling for the admission of Texas into the Union. But the concept was hardly new, and O'Sullivan himself had used a variation of the idea in an 1838 essay entitled "The Great Nation of Futurity," which expressed the prevailing view of America's "boundless future":

In its magnificent domain of space and time, that nation of many nations is destined to manifest to mankind the excellence of divine principles; to establish on earth the noblest temple ever dedicated to the worship of the Most High – the Sacred and the True. Its floor shall be a hemisphere – its roof the firmament of the star-studded heavens, and its congregation an Union of many Republics, comprising hundreds of happy millions, calling, owning no man master, but governed by God's natural and moral law of equality.

The secular literature of exploration and expansion was in this sense a natural continuation of the colonial literature of Christian self-examination and prophecy. The Puritan goal of inspiring religious freedom in Europe was transfigured into the postrevolutionary purpose of inspiring further democratic revolutions in Europe. As Catharine Beecher's father, Lyman Beecher (1775–1863), wrote in *A Plea for the West* (1835), the example of the American West should rouse "from the sleep of ages and the apathy of despair" the oppressed of Europe, throwing the light of freedom into "their dark prison house" and "sending [an] earthquake under the foundations of their [rulers'] thrones." Even before it was inhabited or adequately explored, the West acted, paradoxically, as a line of division between the New World and the Old, less a geographical area than an imagined sphere collapsing present time and future space. As Thoreau would write in his late essay "Walking" (1862):

> We go eastward to realize history and study the works of art and literature, retracing the steps of the race; we go westward as into the future, with a spirit of enterprise and adventure. The Atlantic is a Lethean stream, in our passage over which we have had an opportunity to forget the Old World and its institutions. . . . The West of which I speak is but another name for the Wild; and what I have been preparing to say is, that in Wildness is the preservation of the World. Every tree sends its fibres forth in search of the Wild. The cities support it at any price. Men plow and sail for it. . . . The West is preparing to add its fables to those of the East. The valleys of the Ganges, the Nile, and the Rhine having yielded their crop, it remains to be seen what the valleys of the Amazon, the Platte, the Orinoco, the St. Lawrence, and the Mississippi will produce. Perchance, when, in the course of ages, American liberty has become a fiction of the past – as it is to some extent a fiction of the present – the poets of the world will be inspired by American mythology.

More frequently than Thoreau, Melville tempered his view of the western frontier, the terrain of the future, with skepticism about such fictive promises of American liberty. In *Moby-Dick* (1851), to cite the most famous example, the symbolic white whale is "a most imperial and archangelical apparition of the unfallen western world," an American emblem of "those primeval times when Adam walked majestic as a god, bluff-bowed and fearless." It is also a sign of annihilation and atheism, the abundance of nature painted "like a harlot, whose allurements cover nothing but the charnel-house within." The duplicitous mirage of the West in *Moby-Dick,* in pursuit of which the mad captain Ahab sacrifices his entire ship of state, is a territory not of promise but of alienation and destruction. In fact, the American West frequently united Edenic possibility and demonic desire; its mythology, created largely in advance of its history, provided a simultaneously geographical and psychological stage on which Americans' dreams of liberty, prosperity, and world leadership could be enacted.

In the aftermath of Lewis and Clark's achievement of a Northwest Passage in their journey of 1804–6 (made famous in Nicholas Biddle's 1814 *History of the Expedition Under the Command of Captains Lewis and Clark to the Sources of the Missouri, Thence Across the Rocky Mountains and Down the River Columbia to the Pacific Ocean*) and Zebulon Pike's survey of the southern Rocky Mountains and northern New Mexico in 1805–7 (recounted in his 1810 volume *Account of Expeditions to the Sources of the Mississippi and Through the Western Parts of*

Louisiana), the future shape of the United States had begun to be defined. The overland route out of St. Louis and up the Missouri River to Oregon and northern California, and the Santa Fe Trail into the Southwest, became the most traveled in the country. The two expeditions served to frame the penetration of the West, in both cases because they detailed not only the geographical features of their respective regions but also the prospects for establishing trading posts and routes. Commerce and scientific or military inquiry were tied together in the expeditions, as they would be in all the important surveys of the West and the narratives of its settlement. Capped by the Gold Rush of the late 1840s and early 1850s, the advances of Euro-American explorers and pioneers alike in the decades following the 1820s usually had in view several goals: freedom from social and political constraint, the discovery of untrammeled landscape, the cultivation of fresh agricultural or mineral resources, and the means of marketing in the East the new wealth of the West. The trade routes to the Southwest, the Northwest, into the Rocky Mountains, and finally across the Sierra Nevada were the weblike lines of America's immense expansion, later echoed in roads and railroads, and the narratives that accompany them told the story of nationalism so fervently advocated by politicians and literary intellectuals in the already established states of the Union. Although the vast majority of settlers and explorers left no lasting record of their journeys, those who did write their stories composed in effect the nation's first and most influential nationalistic literature.

The 1820s were an especially important period for the establishment of an American empire. In the aftermath of the War of 1812, penetration south by the British fur trade declined and American activity haltingly accelerated; in the Southwest, the Mexican Revolution of 1821 left the territory of New Mexico much more vulnerable to incursion and settlement. The euphoric sense of national security that followed the War of 1812 was driven by technological developments in transportation and industrial and agricultural machinery which augmented the spiritual and material romance of America. In the postrevolutionary period and especially after 1815, exploration of the continental territory implied profitable contact with territories beyond. Missouri senator Thomas Hart Benton, a vocal expansionist throughout the coming decades, predicted in an editorial of 1818 that significant trade with Asia would be opened by settlement of Oregon: "In a few years, the Rocky Mountains will be passed, and the 'children of Adam' will have completed the circumambulation of the globe, by marching to the west until they arrive at the Pacific ocean, in sight of the eastern shore of that Asia in which their parents were originally planted." Elaborated by Thoreau and Whitman, among others, the idea that the destiny of the "children of Adam" lay in Asia capitalized upon an existing trade with China that would be dramatically increased by the development of efficient overland routes to the Pacific. The route East by way of the West aroused conflict on all sides. The contest with Great Britain over Oregon would not be resolved until the treaty of 1846, which divided the United States and Canada at the Forty-ninth Parallel and was signed by President Polk on the eve of war with Mexico over territory in the Southwest and California. By then, however, the success of Lewis and Clark had long since opened the way to traders and, more important, to agricultural pioneers.

Although Manuel Lisa, George Drouillard, and John Colter preceded him in the Euro-American exploration of the upper Missouri and Yellowstone, it was John Jacob Astor who was most responsible for opening the Northwest to trade. A German immigrant who organized the Pacific Fur Company to compete with existing outfits such as the Hudson's Bay Company, Astor sent a ship around Cape Horn to build Fort Astoria on the Columbia River and at the same time launched overland expeditions in 1811 led by Wilson Price Hunt and Robert Stuart. Fort Astoria and Astor's trading company fell victim to the War of 1812, but the Hunt and Stuart expeditions established the main lines of what would come to be known as the Oregon Trail. Both wrote diaries that record their daily hardships; yet the major literary record of the Astor enterprise would have to wait more than two decades until Washington Irving (1783–1859) was persuaded by Astor to set down the story in *Astoria; or, Anecdotes of an Enterprise Beyond the Rocky Mountains* (1836). In the period between the explorations sponsored by Astor and Irving's account, a great deal of territory had been opened and written about, often in documents less popular but more reliable than Irving's.

The "Yellowstone Expedition" of Stephen Long, which set out in 1819 on a military and scientific survey, never reached the upper Missouri (the unique assault by steamboat failed), and the intention of finding a suitable location for the military outpost desired by Secretary of War John Calhoun therefore came to naught. Ordered to turn south, Long's group proceeded along the east range of the Rocky Mountains (where they were the first to climb Pike's Peak), then split into two groups that followed river routes back to Arkansas. The expedition itself was not a striking success: Long was stigmatized with having mapped and immortalized the seemingly useless "Great American Desert" of the southwestern Plains and having wasted the technological resources of his topographical engineers. Yet the main source of information about the expedition, botanist Edwin James's *Account of an Expedition from Pittsburgh to the Rocky Mountains* (1823), is a significant report on the country's flora and geological formations, the ethnology of the Kansas and Omaha tribes (with, typically, particular attention to intertribal warfare), and the vast, mysterious region of the Plains. James (1797–1861) echoed Long's own report to Calhoun, which declared that the region was "almost wholly unfit for cultivation, and of course uninhabitable by a people dependent upon agriculture for their subsistence." James's volume foreshadowed the tremendous influence of later reports by topographical engineers attached to military and mercantile expeditions, and it established a paradigm for Euro-American frontier attitudes and character when little was known of the middle Plains. The *Account* was a primary source, for example, for James Fenimore Cooper's conception of the landscape in *The Prairie* (1827), and the popularization of the theory that the central Plains regions were uninhabitable was instrumental in President Monroe's advocacy of a policy of Indian Removal.

The failure of the Long expedition to penetrate the Northwest did not deter William Henry Ashley from placing a famous advertisement in a St. Louis newspaper in 1822 calling for "Enterprising Young Men" to spend several years developing routes to the Pacific. Like the most successful of the "mountain men" who would follow after him, Ashley, the lieutenant governor of Missouri, was both a businessman and an adventurer, and his establishment of a fur trade on the upper Missouri took precedence over the romance of exploration. His initial company nevertheless included some of the men who would become best known as western explorers: Jedediah Smith, William Sublette, James Clyman, and James Beckwourth. Their several expeditions from 1822 through 1826, followed by further advances into the Far West by Smith over the next few years, opened the entire central Rockies to the fur trade and established the South Pass as the key feature of the route followed by future settlers along the Oregon Trail into the Northwest. The journals and diaries of Ashley, Clyman, and Smith, like those of many other mountain men, have been published in the twentieth century. Smith, however, became a particularly popular figure in his own day. His forays beyond the Green River and the Great Salt Lake on into California by way of the Mohave Desert were signs of a country opened not just to fur trading but to immigration, and his map of the western Rockies, partially incorporated into Albert Gallatin's *Map of the Indian Tribes of North America* (1836), remained the standard ethnographic map until the 1850s. Maps, like the taxonomy of natural phenomena and Indian tribes, were classifying representations of the West that codified the superimposition of an inherently imperialistic scientific paradigm upon the Romantic literary imagination.

As Edwin James's account of the Long expedition indicated, the opening of the Far West coincided with two related phenomena: an increase in the sophistication of scientific investigations of western lands and a growing pressure for exploration that would eventually reach beyond the territory of North America. Both the new interest in minerological and biological infor-

mation about the country and the quest into unknown regions at the far ends
of the hemisphere promoted the energies of manifest destiny and signaled the
beginning of an imperial drive that would soon bring Texas, the New Mexican Southwest, and California into the U.S. orbit. In 1838 the government
made the Army Corps of Topographical Engineers a separate branch of the
military under the command of Colonel John James Abert. Its express purpose was to explore and develop the West for settlement, transportation, and
production. Some of the most important writing to come from nineteenth-
century expeditions was done by talented scientists, whether in private enterprise or employed by the Army Corps. Long's expedition produced not only
Edwin James's famous account but also the collections and observations that
would appear in Thomas Say's *American Entomology* (1824–8). The Bostonian
Nathaniel Wyeth's second expedition to Oregon included the botanist
Thomas Nuttall and the zoologist and ornithologist John Kirk Townsend,
who provided a full account of the trip in his dramatic and well-written
Narrative of a Journey Across the Rocky Mountains to the Columbia River (1839).
The enormous wealth of scientific materials collected by those who accompanied the explorations of the West, rendered in volumes such as John James
Audubon's famous *The Birds of America* (1840–4), coincided with the similarly staggering wealth of data about American Indians collected by ethnologists like Henry Rowe Schoolcraft, Thomas McKenney, and George Catlin.
The classifying of vast quantities of both natural phenomena and alien
human customs thus often tended to blur into a combined scientific, diplomatic, and economic enterprise that worked in service of political and cultural hegemony. For example, Samuel Morton's influential study of racial
traits based on skull size and other physiological data, *Crania Americana*
(1839), was modeled on Alexander Wilson's nine-volume *American Ornithology* (1808–14). On the Long expedition, Say investigated the racist hypothesis that Indians, blacks, and simian animals were related species but found
he could not place American Indians in a workable zoological context. As
ethnology and zoological classification became more and more entangled,
white people's propensity to view Indians as part of "savage nature" was
increased and the ease of linking political conquest to scientific progress
heightened. Whereas personal journals often recorded the mundane, frequently harsh details of the journey west, public documents, typically uniting scientific observation and imaginative projection, better revealed national identity.

The figure of the explorer as hero, derived from Biddle's account of Lewis
and Clark and given new significance by the expeditions of Long, Ashley, and
others served a variety of nationalistic purposes that were well established
before Irving published *Astoria* in 1836. Because of his fame as an expatriate

interpreter of America and a historian of world events, Irving's authorship of western narratives was itself symbolic of the new penchant for national literature sweeping the United States. Upon his return from residence in Europe to the United States, Irving undertook a trip into Oklahoma with a military company that resulted in a very popular narrative of camp scenes, hunting, and Indian life entitled *A Tour of the Prairies,* part of *The Crayon Miscellany* (1835). Given the significant volumes of history Irving had already produced up to this point in his career — for example, *The History of the Life and Voyages of Christopher Columbus* (1828), *A Chronicle of the Conquest of Granada* (1828–9), and even the burlesque *History of New York* (1809) — it is no surprise that he turned again to his native country and portrayed it in terms that placed it on the same stage with great epic events of world history. Allusions and comparisons to Europe appear throughout *A Tour of the Prairies,* but the volume also advocates the pastoral reflection that such a tour made possible for the member of a democratic society: "We send our youth abroad to grow luxurious and effeminate in Europe; it appears to me that a previous tour on the prairies would be more likely to produce that manliness, simplicity, and self-dependence, most in union with our political institutions."

Astoria was an even more pronounced instance of such nationalistic intentions. Although some historians have criticized the book's authenticity, it was based on the diaries of Hunt and Stuart, the letters and reports of Astor, and a variety of other primary materials, and it is an important expression of the American enthusiasm for expansion in the decades after Astor's initial expedition. The biographical sections devoted to Astor and his fur trade minimize the economic failure of the enterprise not only in order to glorify Astor himself as an exponent of Jacksonian capitalist energy but also to signal the coming American dominion over the continent. In the context of Irving's works, the portrait of Astor links him to other heroic figures like George Washington and Andrew Jackson, men in whom Irving located the masculine power necessary to open and command the American wilderness. The hero thus imagined had to combine traits of unharnessed energy and clear-sighted organization. Irving joined commonplace conceptions of frontiersmen as rugged outlaws to the theory that the central plains were uninhabitable – a "Great American Desert," in the image first elaborated by Zebulon Pike – and predicted the rise there of "new and mongrel races, like new formations in geology, the amalgamation of the 'debris' and 'abrasions' of former races . . . [the descendants of] deperadoes of every class and country yearly ejected from the bosom of society into the wilderness." At the same time, however, he was confident that the course of American economic destiny, and thus its political interests, lay in the West. The volume concludes with Irving's regret that the federal government had not seized the disputed Oregon territory, which was now so clearly within its necessary sphere: "As one wave of emigration after another rolls into the vast regions of the west, and our settlements stretch towards the Rocky Mountains, the eager eyes of our pioneers will pry beyond, and they will become impatient of any barrier or impediment in the way of what they consider a grand outlet of our empire."

Astoria supports Irving's claims of empire with an enormous variety of material, including Astor's representative life, a detailed story of the expeditions, accounts of the Indian tribes of the Missouri River and Northwest, and brilliantly drawn landcapes that pictured for readers, usually for the first time, the immense spaces of their country's future. Irving helped popularize the idea that a vast part of the central Plains was a virtual wasteland, but his sublime descriptions sometimes betrayed a corresponding fascination with the empty terrain and its wildlife, as in his account of the Stuart party's return along the Missouri and Platte rivers:

They continued on for upwards of a hundred miles; with vast prairies extending before them as they advanced; sometimes diversified by undulating hills, but destitute of trees. In one place they saw a gang of sixty five wild horses, but as to the buffalos they seemed absolutely to cover the country. Wild geese abounded, and they passed extensive swamps that were alive with innumerable flocks of water fowl, among which were a few swans, but an endless variety of ducks.

The river continued a widening course to the east northeast, nearly a mile in width, but too shallow to float even an empty canoe.

The country spread out into a vast level plain, bounded by the horizon alone, excepting to the north, where a line of hills seemed like a long promontory stretching into the bosom of the ocean. The dreary sameness of the prairie wastes began to grow extremely irksome. The travellers longed for the sight of a forest, or grove, or single tree to break the level uniformity and began to notice every object that gave reason to hope they were drawing towards the end of this weary wilderness. . . . Thus they went on, like sailors at sea, who perceive in every floating weed and wandering bird, harbingers of the wished for land.

Irving's description of the prairie, like other renderings of landscape in the volume, outlines the human drama of exploration at the same time it indicates the Euro-American conception of the West's unrealized potential. The enterprise of Astor and his explorers can be conceived of in both physical and unintentionally self-reflexive psychological terms, as they penetrate "to the heart of savage continents: laying open the hidden secrets of the wilderness."

Irving's next volume on the American West, *The Adventures of Captain Bonneville in the Rocky Mountains and Far West* (1837), extended his celebration of the pioneer spirit to embrace a larger territory and the larger group of mountain men and fur traders who followed in the wake of William Ashley and Jedediah Smith. One of them, Benjamin Bonneville, in 1832 headed an expedition less important for his own accomplishments than for those of his subordinate, Joseph Walker, who led a reconnaissance of the western shores of the Great Salt Lake and then made his way into California, down the Humboldt River, and eventually to Monterey. Bonneville himself turned north to follow the Astorian route to Oregon. Information about the territory recorded in his journals would appear first in Irving's *Astoria* and then in *Captain Bonneville,* along with maps of the Rocky Mountain West and Great Basin region by Bonneville that were the most detailed of the day. Irving's treatment of Bonneville as hero is less inspired than his account of the explorers in *Astoria,* and his theorizing about the literary value of his material became self-consciously intrusive: "all this romance of savage life," he notes, will soon "seem like the fictions of chivalry or fairy tale." But his portrait of the heroic age of mountain fur trappers is valuable in its own right and as an indication that the work of exploration had reached a point where it could be romanticized and its gradual displacement by more permanent settlement foreseen.

As Irving's volumes proved, the exploration of the American West brought forth rugged individuals whose achievements were easily shaped into myth. The mountain men were significant not just for their role in the fur trade but also for their popular fame as rough men of opportunity willing to strike out into a dangerous life in the hope of wealth and exotic adventure. As one of them, George Ruxton, wrote in his *Adventures in Mexico and the Rocky Mountains* (1847), there is "not a hole or corner [that has not] been ransacked by these hardy men. From the Mississippi to the mouth of the Colorado of the West, from the frozen regions of the north to the Gila in Mexico, the beaver-hunter has set his traps in every creek and stream. All this vast country, but for the daring and enterprise of these men, would be even now a *terra incognita* to geographers." Responsible for the earliest and often the most reliable maps, the mountain men also produced some of the best literary accounts of the Euro-American exploration of the West. Joseph Walker's pioneering 1834 penetration of the Sierra Nevada to San Francisco Bay, down through San Joaquin Valley, and back across the Sierra through Walker's Pass (which would become a popular route to California) was recorded in his own report on the journey, in a later narrative dictated to George Nidever, and most famously in Zenas Leonard's *Narrative of the Adventures of Zenas Leonard, Fur Trader* (1839).

Leonard's exhilarating account, which covers his trapping career from 1831 to 1835, offered a model later followed by Alexander Ross, Warren Ferris, James Beckwourth, and others. Leonard gave a more authentic view of Walker's expedition than that found in Irving's *Captain Bonneville* and, like other advocates of expansion, he praised the economic potential of the West. More important, he saw the issue of the West in terms of the conjunction of domestic and foreign policy and warned of inroads being made by the Spanish, British, and the Russians in the valuable West:

Even in this remote part of the Great West before many years will these hills and valleys be greeted with the enlivening sound of the workman's hammer, and the merry whistle of the ploughboy. . . . Our government should be vigilant. She should assert her claim by taking possession of the whole territory as soon as possible – for we have good reason to suppose that the territory *west* of the mountains will some day be equally as important to the nation as that [to] the east.

James Beckwourth's *Life and Adventures* (1856) is notable for its material on the fur trade, its western tall tales, and its unorthodox account of Beckwourth's life among the Crow, with whom he lived intimately but continued to reject as barbaric people who might best be expeditiously exterminated. Narratives such as Beckwourth's suggest that the factual account of exploration and the frontier novel of Indian conflict were equally responsible for creating the mythic image of the mountain man as a figure who lived among "savages" without succumbing to savage life. David Coyner's *The Lost Trappers* (1847) crossed fact and fiction in that its largely fabricated account of life in the fur trade was supposedly based on the journal of Ezekial Williams, a member of the first trapping expedition after Lewis and Clark. Like Beckwourth, Coyner wrote at a time when the continent was mapped and its history could be written with the expectation that the increasing emigration to California in the 1840s would lead to complete possession. Caught in the same irony as James Fenimore Cooper, who respected the advance of "enlightened" society but created its most magnificent outcast in Natty Bumppo, Coyner advocated the destined rise of American civilization on the shores of the Pacific even as he celebrated the trapper as a man who "despises the dull uniformity and monotony of civilized life" and rejects "the galling restrictions of organized society." Closest among living figures to Cooper's mythic hero was the trapper, scout, and Indian agent Christopher ("Kit") Carson, the best known of mountain men. His autobiography, published in the next century, showed a frontier hero somewhat less flamboyant and isolated than the one who had appeared in the popular volumes *Life and Adventures of Kit Carson,* by DeWitt C. Peters (1858), *Life of Kit Carson: The Great Western Hunter and Guide* (1862), by Charles Burdett, and the earlier novel by Charles Averill, *Kit Carson, The Prince of the Gold Hunters* (1849). The Kit Carson of popular literature overshadowed the real man and accentuated all those characteristics the mountain men claimed for themselves and which their mythologizers assigned them in any event: extraordinary courage, melodramatic skills in woodcraft and combat, and a visionary belief in American destiny. Because Carson's fame rested in large part on his role in John Frémont's western explorations and the events of the Mexican War, he additionally gave expression to those characteristics of the popular masculine dream of western empire – virility, independence, and daring – that were implicit in the heroes created by Cooper and Irving, as well as in the lives of the mountain men themselves.

Even though he did not qualify as a mountain man and his journey into the Rocky Mountain West took him by steamboat and horseback only as far as Fort Laramie, Wyoming, the historian Francis Parkman (1823–93) wrote one of the most popular nineteenth-century narratives of western life. First serialized in the *Knickerbocker Magazine* in 1847, *The California and Oregon Trail* (1849) recorded brilliantly detailed, often breathtaking depictions of the region and of the Sioux and Pawnee hunting culture of the Platte River. Parkman's reflections on Indian life, more so than those found in the journals of more experienced trappers and explorers, were marked by both tendentious romanticism and racialist notions of savagism, and his observations of life along the emigrant trail paradoxically offered little aid for the many emigrants by then eagerly seeking a route west. Even so, Parkman in some passages ranks with Melville in his ability to capture the turbulence of man's appropriation of the natural world – perhaps most eloquently in his many descriptions of the decimation of buffalo herds, which were also implicitly descriptions of the demise of the western Indian tribes:

While we were charging on one side, our companions attacked the bewildered and panic-stricken herd on the other. The uproar and confusion lasted but a moment. The dust cleared away, and the buffalo could be seen scattering as from a common centre, flying over the plain singly, or in long files and small compact bodies, while behind them followed the Indians, riding at furious speed, and yelling as they launched arrow after arrow into their sides. The carcasses were strewn thickly over the ground. Here and there stood wounded buffalo, their bleeding sides feathered with arrows; and as I rode by them their eyes would glare, they would bristle like gigantic cats, and feebly attempt to rush up and gore my horse.

Like his later classic statement of the "doom" of the American Indian in *The Conspiracy of Pontiac* (1851), Parkman's account of life on the Plains elevates into a metaphoric, elegiac vision comparable to Melville's in *Moby-Dick* his own essential understanding of the irreversible course of American empire. Indeed, the book's significance as a literary treatment of frontier life was best described by Parkman himself when he reflected on the change in the American West in a preface to *The California and Oregon Trail* written in 1892: "The buffalo is gone, and of all his millions nothing is left but bones. Tame cattle and barbed wire have supplanted his vast herds and boundless grazing lands. . . . The slow cavalcade of horsemen armed to the teeth has disappeared before parlor cars and the effeminate comforts of modern travel."

The transfiguration of the West witnessed by Parkman, however, did not have to wait until the end of the century. The advance of the agricultural frontier across the Midwest from the 1820s through the 1860s, accelerated by innovations in production and transportation, quickly modified conceptions of western territory even as it destroyed American Indian cultures and drove the mountain men toward the Pacific. Space became functional and commercial before its mythic allure had fully dissipated. Emerson's 1844 essay on expansion, "The Young American," asserted that the mystic power of the land would have an "Americanizing influence, which promises to disclose new virtues for ages to come." Americans, he added, who "have grown up in the bowers of a paradise," in "the country of the Future," must therefore be educated in the arts of engineering, architecture, scientific agriculture, and minerology. Like Melville's Ahab, he envisioned the paradisal garden of America vitalized by mechanical technology: "Railroad iron is a magician's rod, in its power to evoke the sleeping energies of land and water."

Emerson's characteristic location of the idealistic abstraction within the realm of commerce philosophically broke down distinctions between mind and nature. Much commonplace literature of the western landscape did so pragmatically, and none more so than the emigrant guide, which by 1840 had become a literary genre in its own right. In the emigrant guide, factual information dramatized stories, and autobiographic reflection were often combined. Space, the promise of a boundless future, was translated into time, supplies, profit and loss and was set in a moral framework in which self-discovery and national character were synonymous. A staunch advocate for the West who ranks with Ashley as a promoter of expansion, the New England merchant Hall J. Kelley issued pamphlets such as "A General Circular to All Persons of Good Character Who Wish to Emigrate to the Oregon Territory" (1831), which helped to set in motion the settlement of Oregon and California. In a variety of publications and petitions to Congress, Kelley called for the swift American colonization of the Pacific Northwest. One of his followers was Nathaniel Wyeth, a Boston ice merchant whose enterprises were later alluded to in *Walden* when Thoreau contemplated the way in which the waters of Walden Pond become mingled with those of the Ganges River. Wyeth organized his own expeditions to Oregon in the 1830s, which included Christian missionaries, a distinguished array of scientists, and veteran mountain men like William Sublette, who discovered that more money was to be made in outfitting and guiding western caravans than in fur trading. The most important emigrant guides were documents that not only offered practical advice but also carefully endorsed prevailing conceptions of manifest destiny. One of the most influential handbooks of the day, Lansford

Hastings's *The Emigrant's Guide to Oregon and California* (1845), celebrated the rich resources of the area and their potential for economic development while characteristically playing upon anti-Mexican, anti-Indian, and anti-Catholic sentiments to glorify faith in Anglo-American progress and "promote the unbounded happiness and prosperity, of civilized and enlightened man." The eschatological character of the emigrant guides would reach a new pitch once the Mexican War had opened California to Anglo-American settlement. In journalist Charles Dana's *The Garden of the World; Or, the Great West* (1856), the several hundred pages of information on all the middle and western territories were preceded by introductory passages demonstrating the continuity between Puritan thought and the ideals of manifest destiny:

The *Land of Promise,* and the *Canaan* of our time, is the region which, commencing on the slope of the Alleghenies, broadens grandly over the vast prairies and mighty rivers, over queenly lakes and lofty mountains, until the ebb and flow of the Pacific tide kisses the golden shores of the El Dorado. . . . O, the soul kindles at the thought of what a magnificent empire the West is but the germ, which, blessed with liberty and guaranteeing equal rights to all, shall go on conquering and to conquer, until the whole earth shall resound with its fame and glory.

Although they followed Hastings's model in offering the wisdom of their own experiences to would-be emigrants to the Northwest, both Overton Johnson, in *Route Across the Rocky Mountains* (1846), and Joel Palmer (1810–81), in *Journal of Travels Over the Rocky Mountains* (1847), presented the territory not as a magic Eden but as a place where hard work and a difficult life could lead to independence and success. Similarly pragmatic in their assessments were Rufus B. Sage, whose *Scenes in the Rocky Mountains* (1846) provided a wide range of detailed information on territories from Texas to Oregon to a public agitating for expansion, and the German immigrant F. A. Wislezenus (1810–89), whose *Journey to the Rocky Mountains in the Year 1839* (1840) employed a common metaphor (one that reached its apotheosis in Frederick Jackson Turner's work at the end of the century) in speaking of the "waves of civilization" that now "cast their spray on the feet of the Rockies." The rush to capitalize upon the West could be so powerful that pretense alone would serve: thus the journalist and poet Edmund Flagg (1815–90) published a work entitled *The Far West: Or, A Tour Beyond the Rocky Mountains* (1838), which is in fact concerned almost exclusively with Ohio, Illinois, and the Mississippi Valley.

At the extremity of speculative depictions of the West is Edgar Allan Poe's fictional work *The Journal of Julius Rodman, Being an Account of the First Passage Across the Rocky Mountains of North America Ever Achieved by Civilized Man* (1840), which illuminated the lure of the fantastic latent in most exploration narratives. Based on his readings in Biddle's volume on Lewis and Clark, as well as in Irving, Flagg, Robert Townsend, Samuel Parker, and others, Poe's uncompleted farce, as its title suggests, claimed in setting its action in the 1790s to record an adventure in the Far West that preceded all others, a tactic he had already pursued much more successfully in *The Narrative of Arthur Gordon Pym of Nantucket* (1838). Poe's temporal dislocation of the narrative of Julius Rodman into the past has a multiple significance. In addition to burlesquing its genre and the frequently exaggerated claims made by explorers, it corresponded to contemporary efforts by Parkman and others to displace the conquest of the continent and the "doom" of the American Indian into an earlier century. At the same time, it accentuated Poe's own obsession with America's futurity as expressed in his short science fiction tales or in the philosophical dream tract *Eureka* (1848), in which boundless cosmic space appears in part as a figure for the unfolding destiny of the nation. Along with Emerson in *Nature* (1836) and Whitman in numerous poems and prose works, Poe pushed the vision of hemispheric conquest and the establishment of a limitless new Canaan past literal geographical boundaries.

Against the backdrop of American political opinion, however, Poe's vision was not illegitimate. American horizons appeared capable of expanding far beyond what would later come to be the nation's borders. James G. Bennett, the editor of the *New York Herald*, wrote a column in 1845 that hardly seemed extravagant at the time. No longer bounded by the limits that restrained the last generation, "the pioneers of Anglo-Saxon civilization and Anglo-Saxon free institutions now seek distant territories, stretching even to the shores of the Pacific; and the arms of the republic, it is clear to all men of sober discernment, must soon embrace the whole hemisphere, from the icy wilderness of the North to the most prolific regions of the smiling and prolific South." The idea of America's mission in the hemisphere became crystallized during the Mexican War, but terms as comprehensive as Bennett's were plausible in part because of the extracontinental exploration that had taken place in the previous decades. The possibility of America's eventual extension into the far corners of the hemisphere grew from an idealistic belief that the United States would soon be in a position to bring Christianity, republican government, and commercial trade to an enormous part of the globe, after first claiming as wide a territorial base as possible. Bennett's projection aside, the drive toward the Arctic would not take place for several years, and the British and the Russians dominated the early exploration of the North Pole. Although the United States launched few important ventures to this area in the 1850s and 1860s (interest in the Arctic increased after Secretary of State William Seward, foreseeing geological wealth and a possible gateway to American control of Canada and parts of Asia, negotiated the purchase of Alaska from Russia in 1867), a handful of significant volumes on the region appeared: William Snelling's early *The Polar Regions* (1831), firsthand reports such as Elisha Kane's *The U.S. Grinnell Expedition in Search of Sir John Franklin* (1854) and his extremely popular *Arctic Explorations* (1856), Charles Francis Hall's *Arctic Researches* and *Life with the Esquimaux* (both 1864), and the Eskimo Hans Hendrik's *Memoirs,* translated in 1878 at a time of heightened interest in polar exploration.

In the era of manifest destiny, however, the South Pole commanded the most attention in the United States because of interest in Latin America and sea routes to the Pacific. The most significant chapter in this part of antebellum history was a venture that encompassed all of these interests, the United States Exploring Expedition of 1838–42, commanded by Charles Wilkes (1798–1877) and recorded in great detail in the massive five-volume *Narrative of the United States Exploring Expedition* (1845). Conceived by Jeremiah Reynolds, the author of "Mocha-Dick" (1839), one source of Melville's *Moby-Dick,* the expedition originated with his desire to explore the landmass of the Antarctic and the islands of the South Pacific but eventually was extended to include a survey of the Oregon coast. One of Reynolds's inspirations was the theory, propounded by John Symmes (1780–1829), that the earth was hollow and could be entered through vortices at the poles. The theory had received fanciful treatment in a novel by Adam Seaborn (Symmes's pseudonym) entitled *Symzonia: Voyage of Discovery* (1820), which imagined the discovery of a perfectly rational race living in tropical comfort inside the South Pole. Because the Symzonians rejected all appetites and desires as gross and depraved and possessed perfect white features, along with a disgust for darker peoples, the book implicitly argued for a conjunction of white racial superiority and rational perfection, just the features that often underlay the analogy between scientific progress and manifest destiny. These theories, brought to public attention by the Wilkes expedition, offered a great opportunity for the master of hoax Poe, whose *Narrative of Arthur Gordon Pym* described a voyage to the South Pole occurring in 1828 (thus, as in Poe's narrative of Julius Rodman, antedating the actual expedition, which had just begun) and featured wild, parodic flights of fantasy, episodes of cannibalism, the total breakdown of rationality, and a ferocious antagonism between white and darker races. Poe's strikingly imagined narrative superimposed nightmares about southern slavery and slave rebellion upon the public fascination with exotic exploration to burlesque both and caricature the Wilkes expedition before its own reports could be brought in.

In the event, Poe's version was not quite as absurd as it appeared. For one thing, his interest in the expedition was genuine. In his 1837 essay on Reynolds's belief in a hollow earth — one of several essays by Poe devoted to Lewis and Clark, Irving's *Astoria,* and other accounts of American exploration — he applauded the seamen of the United States who aspired to circle the globe and reach the Pole so as "to cast anchor on that point where all the meridians terminate, where our eagle and star-spangled banner may be unfurled and planted, and left to wave on the axis of the earth itself!" His burlesque in the *Narrative of Arthur Gordon Pym* did not so much undermine this apparently genuine patriotic view as it comprehended the contradictory impulses and near chaos of intelligent energies that motivated an expedition as grand as that led by Wilkes. Indeed, Wilkes's *Narrative* itself was a massive, often bizarre report on the geography and ethnology of South American countries, South Pacific islands, Australia, Hawaii (the Sandwich Islands), Asia, and the western coast of North America. Altogether, the work by 1874 ran to twenty-three volumes written by various hands (including, e.g., Titian Peale's *Mammology and Ornithology,* based on hundreds of collected specimens; Charles Pickering's *Races of Man,* a taxonomy of human species; and Horatio Hale's *Ethnography and Philology,* a study of Polynesian and Northwest American Indian languages). Besides recording a great quantity of data relevant to nautical routes, trading practices, and foreign customs and terrain, the narrative also promoted reforms in the whaling trade, in the treatment of both crew and natives, in order to "promote the great cause of morality, religion, and temperance" abroad. Wilkes's *Narrative* verified the existence of the Antarctic landmass and rendered enchanting descriptions of its wildlife and ice fields, some echoing Poe's invented landscapes ("blindfolded as it were by an impenetrable fog"). And in discussing the cannibalism of the Fiji Islanders, Wilkes outdid Poe's demonizing romanticism: he reports that one crew member negotiated with the natives to purchase a "skull yet warm from the fire, much scorched, and marked with the teeth of those who had eaten of it," from which the brain had just been devoured and from which a remaining eye had to be eaten before it could be traded.

The Pacific had become a magnetic territory both because of the many commercial and missionary enterprises that had spread throughout the islands by the 1830s and because it was a logical extension of the drive toward Asia, the "passage to India." Jeremiah Reynolds, for example, had written an exploration narrative and brief for a strong navy in *Voyage of the U.S. Frigate Potomac* (1835); Edmund Fanning's *Voyages to the South Seas* (1833), an account of nineteenth-century expeditions, was in its fifth edition by 1838, the year Wilkes set out; and there appeared such narratives of whaling adventure as Owen Chase's *Narrative of the Most Extraordinary and Distressing Shipwreck of the Whale-Ship Essex* (1821) — another source of *Moby-Dick* — and Francis A. Olmsted's *Incidents of a Whaling Voyage* (1841), before Melville's work one of the best accounts of whaling and the South Pacific available. Officially sanctioned trade with China was begun in 1844 (American ships had actually traded with China since the late eighteenth century), and the popular travel writer Bayard Taylor (1825–78), among others, recorded his trans-Pacific journey in *A Visit to India, China, and Japan in 1853* (1855). But the most significant such volume about Asia in historical, if not literary, terms may be Francis Hawks's *Narrative of the Expedition of an American Squadron to the China Seas and Japan* (1856), which gives an account of the expedition under Matthew Perry in 1852–4 to open Japan by force to American trade. Hawks (1798–1866) used much of Perry's correspondence and journals verbatim; and although two of the three volumes are given over to reports by the crew on scientific materials brought back, maps, nautical charts, and astronomical phenomena, one illustrated volume brought Asia dramatically into American consciousness in its detailed descriptions of Japanese history, religion, geography, ethnology, trading information, and artistic and scientific achievements.

It was not the Asian continent, however, but the islands of the Pacific that most clearly represented the imperial achievement of America's westward drive in the antebellum years. Calls throughout the period for the annexation of Hawaii were based on the strategic importance of the islands in the routes to Asia, and the islands were written about in volumes such as William Ellis's *A Journal of a Tour Around Hawaii* (1825) and the Reverend Hiram Bingham's *A Residence of Twenty-One Years in the Sandwich Islands* (1847). James Jarves's *History of the Hawaiian Islands* (1847) had a large audience, as did his *Kiana: A Tradition of Hawaii* (1857), which was based on the legend that during Cortés's journey to California a Spanish vessel was wrecked on the islands, stranding a white priest and a white woman, through whom the mitigating effects of Christianity and civilization on the islanders' purported superstition and savagery were first felt. In two volumes devoted to his mission to Hawaii – *A Residence in the Sandwich Islands* (1828) and *A Visit to the South Seas* (1831) – the Reverend Charles Stewart espoused the millennial theory that the advance of Christian civilization would "scatter the spiritual darkness resting on the land, like the vapors of the morning before the rising sun." To many writers, the Pacific islands and Hawaii were at once a realization of the promised American Eden and the site where the clash between American technology and native primitivism would be engaged. Early in the century, David Porter's *Journal of a Cruise Made to the Pacific Ocean* (1815) – a military venture to protect American whalers – recounted his forceful establishment of a new social order on the Marquesas island of Nuku Hiva (Nukuheva, the locale of Melville's *Typee*) but left a melancholy description of his march through the Typee valley, where "a long line of smoking ruins now marked our traces from one end to the other."

One of the most penetrating treatments of Hawaii and Tahiti under American imperial incurison, Edward T. Perkins's *Na Motu: Or, Reef-Rovings in the*

South Seas (1854), attacked European colonialism but praised the prosperity brought about by American advances in the region. "To kingdoms and tribes we have bequeathed indelible impressions of our national worth and distinterested philanthropy," Perkins argued. With less withering irony than one finds in Melville's *Typee* (1846), Perkins's volume highlighted the analogy between Polynesian Islanders and American Indians in the Euro-American mind, both of them subject to idealistic, if deluded, claims of salvation and disinterested benevolence. Hawaii was a virtual emblem of the New World unencumbered by Old World antiquities: "Though we discover no hieroglyphics of mystic import to conjure up gloomy reveries, we are ever opening a new page in the Book of Nature, fresh and glowing with the intelligible symbols of beauty and sublimity." Popularly uniting Romantic contemplation with America's own imperial design, Perkins's *Na Motu* perfectly represents the expansionist vision whose potentially corrosive internal mechanisms Poe and Melville had already attempted to expose to view, but whose cultural politics were destined to prevail for decades to come.

Analogous problems of cultural interpretation were played out at the same time in the U.S. expansion into regions of Latin America. Just as the literature of the American frontier can only be understood in counterpoint to Native American culture and traditions, however, the U.S. empire in the greater Southwest and Latin America requires one to see the Anglo-American literature of that region in relation to the rise of a Mexican American literature, written mostly in Spanish but sometimes in English, which would form the groundwork for modern Latino and Chicano cultural identity. As in the case of American Indians, Mexicans in the colonized regions of the Southwest and California were not simply assimilated into the dominant culture but also preserved autonomous cultural forms that were transfigured but by no means destroyed by the Anglo-American conquest.

Most of the numerous travel accounts of Mexico more properly belong to the border literature of the New Mexican Southwest and the Mexican War, but South and Central America were also of crucial importance to U.S. nationalism from the 1840s through the 1860s. James Jarves, for example, had turned to Hawaii only after publishing his *Scenes and Scenery in the Sandwich Islands and a Trip Through Central America* (1844). Irving's friend George Washington Montgomery translated his *Granada* into Spanish and wrote *Narrative of a Journey to Guatemala* (1839); E. G. Squier published *Nicaragua* (1856) and *The States of Central America* (1858); and works on the Panama route to California included Joesph W. Fabens's *A Story of Life on the Isthmus* (1853) and the western writer Theodore Winthrop's *Isthmiana* (1863). Among the most influential American travel books of the period were John Lloyd Stephens's *Incidents of Travel in Central America, Chiapas, and Yucatan* (1841) and *Incidents of Travel in the Yucatan* (1843), accounts of his explorations during 1839–43 of the magnificent ruins that would later be established as Mayan. Stephens's descriptions of the ruins, idols, artwork, hieroglyphs, and geography, accompanied by Frederick Catherwood's excellent illustrations of the antiquities and the Mayan communities, gained the volumes a wide audience in a country often paradoxically eager to discover its own antiquity even as it insisted that it was unmarred by Old World burdens. As will be noted below, however, Stephens's monumental works cannot be disconnected from the imperial vision that put historical research in the service of contemporary political power.

Equally popular and, like Wilkes's *Narrative* and others, intertwined with the politics of empire, William Louis Herndon's *Exploration of the Valley of the Amazon* (1854) records the first Anglo-American descent of the Amazon from Peru to its mouth in 1851 in a compelling narrative. Set in motion by Lieutenant Matthew Maury, a pioneer in oceanography at the United States Naval Observatory, Herndon's trip sprang from a desire to open the Amazon to navigation and trade (not achieved until 1867). More important, it sprang from Maury's plan, after the Compromise of 1850 had blocked the continental expansion of slavery, to open the territory for the importation of American slaves, a project Maury outlined in *The Amazon and the Atlantic Slopes of South America* (1853). Because the potential for establishing a slave empire in Latin America appealed to many southerners, the Caribbean, Yucatan, and Central America became the focus of dreams of a "Golden Circle" of commerce centered on the Gulf of Mexico and sustained by slave labor. The most volatile pronouncement of slaveholding expansionism appeared in *The War in Nicaragua* (1860) by the adventurer William Walker, who led a renegade guerrilla band first in Mexico and then in a brief conquest of Nicaragua. His narrative offers a complete account of his filibustering activities and a rationale for the extension of slavery based on the white man's supposedly benevolent improvement of the degraded African's lot: "Africa [was] permitted to lie idle until America [was] discovered, in order that she [might] conduce to the formation of a new society in the New World. [Therefore] the true field for the exertion of slavery is in tropical America; there it finds its natural seat of empire and thither it can spread if it will but make the effort."

As Walker's argument indicates, the heart of the American West, if one shared the widespread conception of the West as an arena of Anglo-American triumph, could lie entirely outside the present latitudes of the Union and could involve an even more complex and extensive version of conquest and race mastery. The wealth of the West itself was considered fuel for the engine of American expansion. California gold, the most potent symbol of expansion after 1848, would soon so enrich the nation, claimed *De Bow's Review* in 1854, that no possible investment would be equal to it but the cultivation of the entire Western Hemisphere. Lying between the two great valleys of the world, the Mississippi and the Amazon, the Gulf of Mexico would link the most productive regions of the earth and, by unlocking trading access to the wealth of the Pacific Basin, make the Atlantic in the modern world what the Mediterranean had been "under the reign of the Antonies in Rome." Given the continued dissolution of European political power, combined with possession of Cuba, Santo Domingo, and Haiti, the United States might control the Gulf and through it the world: "Guided by our genius and enterprise, a new world would rise there, as it did before under the genius of Columbus." But this new Columbian vision had a price. As the author argued, "slavery and war have [always] been the two great forerunners of civilization."

American expansion into Central or South America only made sense if the territories that are now the southwestern United States and Mexico could be brought under American dominion. In the 1830s and 1840s such an extension of democracy's "area of freedom" (in Andrew Jackson's phrase) was often advocated. The annexation of the Republic of Texas in 1845 and victory in the Mexican War, by which the New Mexican territory and California were acquired, proved, however, to draw the limits of the Anglo-American march. Further calls to take possession of "All Mexico" were sounded for another twenty years, but with the exception of the Gadsden Purchase of 1853, which added a strip of land in southern Arizona, the southwestern United States was now complete. Although much of its land was less suited to settlement and sustained cultivation than that of the Northwest, early in the century New Mexico and the southern deserts were recognized as important areas of trade and avenues to the rich lands of California. Many accounts, especially popular ones such as Richard Henry Dana's *Two Years Before the Mast* (1840), viewed Spanish California as the most important object of American destiny, and the narratives of a number of explorers (e.g., those of Jedediah Smith, Zenas Leonard, George Ruxton, and James Pattie) recount expeditions that embraced almost the whole of the Far West, from Arkansas to the central and southern Rockies to the Pacific coast. Central to all the major narratives are the meaning of Mexico's holdings and the question of America's moral or political right to settle and cultivate what was for the most part a commercially undeveloped, but hardly an uninhabited, territory.

Not only did Native Americans precede white settlers in these areas, but Mexican settlements and Mexican culture had long been established. The modern period witnessed the wide settlement of Nueva México, a process documented in ways that have yet to be studied in requisite detail. In 1776, for example, while American colonists were revolting against British rule,

Juan Bautista de Anza established a Spanish colony on San Francisco Bay. In the same year a Spanish sea captain reached the mouth of the Columbia River, and Francisco Silvestre Vélez de Escalante set out from Santa Fe to explore Colorado, the Green River, and the Great Basin, territory that Anglo-Americans would not begin to chart for another forty years. Santa Fe itself had been settled in 1609, and by the end of the eighteenth century missions and presidios ran from Texas across New Mexico and Arizona through much of California, principally as a line of defense against the encroachment of France, Russia, and Great Britain upon Spain's control of Latin American commerce and maritime trade. The revolt against Spain and the establishment of the Republic of Mexico in 1821 were followed in the northern provinces of New Mexico and California by intermittent local rebellions and dissatisfaction with national Mexican government. For the most part, however, life in the territories soon to be engulfed by American pioneers was independent of governmental control and comparatively tranquil. The liberal Mexican Colonization Act of 1824 and the secularization of mission lands in 1831 led to easy and widespread ownership of large ranchos, especially in California, most of which continued to be worked by Indian laborers who were often virtual slaves. In the province of New Mexico, however, corruption and a stagnant economy were greater problems and led the government to acquiesce to American settlement in Texas and to open the region to American trade in 1822. By 1830, "Texas fever" had created a large American colony that would become the wedge opening the entire region to eventual American domination and military conquest.

By the time Mexico opened its territories to trade, the expeditions of Zebulon Pike, Stephen Long, and others had penetrated New Mexico. Within a few years a regular trade between Santa Fe and the Mississippi Valley had grown up, and the Santa Fe Trail from Independence, Missouri, to Santa Fe (advocated by Senator Thomas Hart Benton and authorized by President Monroe) was established by 1827. Both Americans and some Mexicans in the region argued that the extension of U.S. dominion was in many ways preferable to the distant and often inadequate legal and military protection offered by the Mexican government. The increasing flow of immigrants followed the lead of pioneer explorer–traders such as William Becknell, Thomas James, and Jacob Fowler, who had set out on expeditions to Santa Fe in 1821. James and Fowler left journals of their ventures and residence in Mexico — respectively, *Three Years Among the Indians and Mexicans* (1846) and *Journal of Jacob Fowler* (1898) — as did Susan Shelley Magoffin, the wife of a trader (and secret agent) who kept an excellent diary during the 1840s that was later published under the title *Down the Santa Fe and Into Mexico* (1926). She reported her views of American military victories in the war but gave more attention to the mechanisms of trade and to the political and domestic life of New Mexico. A comparable autobiographical work by David Meriwether, governor of New Mexico in the 1850s, was discovered and published in the next century as *My Life on the Mountains and on the Plains* (1965).

Easily the most impressive narrative of early southwestern exploration belongs to James O. Pattie (1804?–50?), who with his father and others surveyed an incredible territory in New Mexico, southern California (he was preceded among Anglo-American explorers to Los Angeles only by Jedediah Smith), and the central Rockies in several nearly catastrophic years before he reached the age of twenty-six. His *Personal Narrative,* dictated to Timothy Flint and published in 1831, often verges on a tall tale, but much of it has been authenticated. As Flint's introduction points out, however, its value lies in the "moral sublimity [found] in the contemplation of the adventures and daring of such men" as Pattie – even though such moral sublimity was often purchased by obliviousness to existing Native American and Mexican culture or a denial of the racist foundations of America's new empire. More reliable and surpassing Pattie's narrative as a statement of growing American interest in the acquisition of Mexican territory is the account by Josiah Gregg (1806–50) of several trading caravans to Santa Fe between 1831 and 1840. *Commerce of the Prairies; or, The Journal of a Santa Fé Trader* (1844) provides a superior history of the trail and the development of trade; despite its own characteristic denigration of many aspects of Indian and New Mexican life, it offers a picture of Gregg's own career and character somewhat at odds with the implied mercenary designs on Mexico. His "passion for Prairie life," he says, created in him a need for solitude and wildness. He had no greater desire than "to spread my bed with the mustang and the buffalo, under the broad canopy of heaven – there to seek to maintain undisturbed my confidence in men, by fraternizing with the little prairie dogs and wild colts, and the still wilder Indians – the *unconquered Sabaeans* of the Great American Deserts." What the successes of Gregg and others proved, however, was that neither the so-called Great American Desert nor the Indian territories of Oklahoma and Arkansas would stand in the way of American prosperity in Texas and New Mexico. The mountain man's solitude had poetic value, yet in practical terms it symbolized but a phase in the absorption of one people and their land by another more commercially and militarily powerful.

Before the era of the Mexican War, the question of Texas, the trial ground for the eventual victory of the United States over Mexico, brought forth several significant documents that expressed that colony's own nationalistic ambitions. The first book published in Texas, Stephen Austin's *Establishing Austin's Colony* (1829), was a brief chronicle of colonization and a compendium of Mexican laws relevant to new settlers. Austin's cousin, Mary Austin

Holley, soon after wrote a historical survey, including domestic advice for prospective middle-class settlers on the prairie, entitled *Texas: Observations, Historical, Geographical, and Descriptive* (1833). The rhetoric of the two books suggests how clear was the assumption that Texas, whether by independence, annexation, or both, would eventually enter the U.S. orbit. Joseph Field's *Three Years in Texas* (1836) offers a firsthand view of the "Texas Revolution" for independence in 1836. Some of Sam Houston's voluminous letters, speeches, and proclamations appeared in Charles Edwards Lester's popular *Life of Sam Houston* (1855); but a full picture of Houston's epic life as the heroic antagonist of Santa Anna in the battle of San Jacinto, as president of the Republic of Texas, and as governor and senator following statehood in 1845 would have to await modern scholars. Popular views of Texas history generally were in accord with the image of pioneering heroics that Houston projected. Dedicated to Houston, Anthony Ganilh's novel *Mexico Versus Texas* (1838) followed the argument of many politicians in forecasting the "regeneration" of Mexico. Comparing the country to a prisoner released from a dungeon into sunlight, Ganilh wrote that "Mexico, emerging from the darkness into which the policy of Spain had plunged her, as yet supports with difficulty the brilliancy of modern civilization." Likewise, James W. Dallam contended in his novel *The Lone Star* (1845) that Texas, by the time it joined the Union, had come to seem the nation's newest "city upon a hill." It was "the outpost, the resting place, of Freedom, on its march, and, as such, the gaze of the civilized world is fastened, anxiously and inquiringly, upon her."

The numerous accounts of expeditions and settlement in New Mexico and California that survive from the 1840s and later can be divided generally into three groups: those appearing before the outbreak of war (and thus in some cases contributing to it); those written by Americans as a result of their experiences in the war; and those published in following years from the perspective of pride taken in victory and the magnificent abundance of resources now opened to American use. Of the central works that molded Anglo-American perceptions of California and its Mexican population, none is as important as Richard Henry Dana's *Two Years Before the Mast* (1840). Later known as a prominent Boston attorney and advocate on behalf of American slaves, Dana (1815–82) left Harvard in 1834 to undertake a sea voyage that was to restore his failing eyesight. The volume that described his voyage around the Cape and his work as a hide gatherer on the California coast was extremely popular and fixed in the mind of the eastern public an image of California as a land of potential abundance going to waste because of what was portrayed as Mexican indolence. *Two Years Before the Mast* is neither a work of deep philosophical reflection like *Walden* nor one of complex allegory like *Moby-Dick;* but its detailed treatment of Mexican California's history and customs, along with the superb rendering of Dana's hazardous and grueling life as a sailor, makes it an indispensable work of the period. Like Dana's next volume, *The Seaman's Friend* (1841), a handbook on sailors' rights, the continual meditation in *Two Years Before the Mast* on the questions of labor and individual rights, either aboard ship or on shore, anticipates Melville's *White-Jacket* (1850) in its concern with the role of workers in an industrialized but republican society. The values of Dana's New England are set against the rigidity of ship discipline on the one hand and the carefree luxury of California life on the other. In the wake of independence, Mexican California, in Dana's presentation, is burdened by corruption, arbitrary justice, constant revolution, and domestic immorality, despite the fact that the people inhabit a land with extraordinary natural riches and a five-hundred-mile coastline with excellent harbors. At the same time, Dana's skepticism about the rigidities of Protestant New England often makes his depiction of California a foil for his criticism of the materialist, expansionist spirit of his own culture. "In the hands of an enterprising people," Dana argues with double-edged language, "what a country this might be!" The book's complex treatment of the question of labor is thus linked to the growing myth of the golden possibilities of the American West and, underlined by Dana's irony, to Protestant America's contempt for purported Mexican inefficiency and superstition: "There's no danger of Catholicism's spreading in New England; Yankees can't afford the time to be Catholics."

Because it superimposed the clash between a rising technological society in need of labor and a Romantic vision of "natural" independence upon the era's representative genre, the western travel narrative, *Two Years Before the Mast* signaled a new direction in the ideology of western adventure. Within a matter of years it was joined by a flood of volumes devoted to California and the methods to be employed in getting there. Lansford Hasting's 1845 *Emigrant's Guide*, mentioned above, was preceded by Alexander Forbes's *California* (1839), John Bidwell's *A Journey to California* (1843), and Thomas Jefferson Farnham's *Travels in the Great Western Prairies* (1841) and *Life and Adventures in California* (1844), the last of which appeared in several editions and detailed Farnham's wagon train to Oregon and his travels to Hawaii, California, and Mexico. Although he warned of the hardships to be encountered in the West, Farnham also maintained without irony that California, as its history of Spanish settlement proved, was an "incomparable wilderness" as yet undeveloped by a race driven by the "love of wealth, power, and faith." Alfred Robinson, employed like Dana in the California hide and tallow trade, provided one of the best descriptive histories and geographies of the region during the period before the Gold Rush in *Life in California* (1846), in which he took note of the people's readiness to break with the Mexican government and predicted an imminent American conquest. It is no surprise, then, that one of the most widely read narratives of all was Edwin Bryant's *What I Saw in California* (1848), which included an account of his participation in Frémont's Bear Flag Revolt and forecast the day when San Francisco would be "one of the largest and most opulent commercial cities in the world." The books by Robinson and Bryant were in harmony with the impulses of the U.S. government under Polk and the general mood of America's perceived destiny to liberate the Mexicans from "the profound darkness of their vassal existence," as an 1847 editorial put it. A writer for the *Boston Times* in the same year could not characterize the war with Mexico as a matter of conquest, because in this case it "must necessarily be a great blessing to the conquered. It is a work worthy of a great people who are about to regenerate the world by asserting the supremacy of humanity over the accidents of birth and fortune."

Given the mood and circumstances of the 1840s, John Frémont (1813–90), explorer, soldier, and politician, was a likely hero. Frémont's exact mission in California remains mysterious. Was he instructed, on secret orders from Polk, to initiate a revolt, or did he simply decide to take on the role of Sam Houston in California? The son-in-law of Senator Thomas Hart Benton, a staunch advocate of western advance, Frémont was on his third official exploring expedition in 1845 when he led the Bear Flag Revolt, which culminated in his capture of northern California for the United States, with southern California falling to regular military forces following outbreak of the Mexican War. His trial for mutiny (after he refused to recognize the authority of Brigadier General Stephen Kearny in California), his success in the Gold Rush, and his later political and military careers made him one of the most popular and controversial western figures in the decades before and after the Civil War. His official *Reports* on the expeditions, published in 1843 and 1845, and his unfinished *Memoirs of My Life* (1887) give a wealth of detail about the western territories he explored on surveys whose primary public purpose was to encourage overland emigration. Recalling Irving's depiction of Astor as the incipient hero of capitalist energy, Frémont's writings, widely read by politicians and common emigrants alike, portray him as a model expansionist who was the first to recognize and articulate California's great agricultural value.

War with Mexico in 1846 was rationalized on several premises: the actual desire of some inhabitants of both New Mexico and California to be annexed, grievances over violence against Americans (often provoked by aggressive, unlawful American settlers), the Mexican government's impediments to open trade, and simple land hunger among American pioneers and their official representatives in Washington. The volatile question of slavery also played an

immense part in the controversy. In the speeches of political leaders like
Thomas Hart Benton and Daniel Webster, the orations of abolitionists such
as Theodore Parker, and the fiction of writers like Melville and Martin
Delany, slavery determined the nature of the rhetoric and the shape of the
debate over Mexico and the Southwest by linking the issue to widespread
anti-Catholicism (as when antislavery polemicists depicted Catholicism as a
religion of bondage and feudal subjugation) and to the commercial order of
the Caribbean and Latin America.

Journalistic and political expressions of America's manifest destiny in
Mexico, as evidenced in editorials and proclamations, were supported as well
by the Anglo-American travel narratives and fiction devoted more specifically to the Southwest and to the politics of the war. Much interest in the
conquest of Mexico was aroused by George Wilkins Kendall's *Narrative of the
Texas Santa Fe Expedition* (1844), an account of the ill-fated attempt of a
group of Texans to capture Santa Fe. The Santa Fe Trail itself continued to be
the primary route of the mountain men and adventurers, but their writings
increasingly voiced anti-Mexican sentiments and invited political and military action on behalf of resident Americans. One of the best writers among
southwestern travelers, the British adventurer George F. Ruxton (1820–48),
occupied a middle ground on the question of American conquest. Although
he maintained that an American attack was not justified, his *Adventures in
Mexico and the Rocky Mountains* (1847) nevertheless portrayed the Mexicans as
degraded and incapable of advanced civilization. Waddy Thompson's *Recollections of Mexico* (1846) gave a full portrait of the history, geography, and
resources of Mexico but argued that whereas the comparatively sterile environment of Massachusetts had produced prosperity, the rich landscape of Mexico
appeared to have been wasted. If Mexico was not ready to be a republic, he
maintained, it ought to be sheltered by American occupation from the
constant revolutionary tumult in which it now existed. Because its sketches
of life along the Santa Fe Trail emphasized that men and women in nature
were "stripped of the disguises of civilized life" and existed without "the
protection of the social state," Benjamin Taylor's *Short Ravelings From a Long
Yarn* (1847) could likewise be seen to promote annexation, whereby a chaotic
Hobbesian world would be redeemed by the ordering principles of democracy. Post-Mexican War travel works written amid further calls for expansion
into Mexican territory – among them Asa B. Clarke's *Travels in Mexico and
California* (1852) and Robert A. Wilson's *Mexico: Its Peasants and Priests*
(1856) – continued to reflect patterns of race prejudice and cultural domination that have lasted into the twentieth century.

The portrayal of Mexico and Mexicans in the antebellum years thus frequently depended upon racism and religious bigotry, and elements of tenden-

tious rhetoric were common to travelogues, to fiction, and to historiography devoted to all of Hispanic America. In the Anglo-American novel the merger of domestic romance with the ideology of manifest destiny was underpinned by the novelists' employment of historical frameworks and allusions to the violent and pagan past of Mexico. Before William Prescott's histories of the region were available, Robert Montgomery Bird, for example, had written *Oralloossa* (1832), a play about the killing of a Peruvian Inca prince by Pizarro, and had popularized Cortés's conquest and the decline of the Aztec Empire in novels like *Calavar; Or, the Knight of the Conquest* (1834) and *The Infidel; Or, The Fall of Mexico* (1835). John Stephens's popular travel works, cited above, had benefited from the vogue for works of exoticism such as Timothy Savage's Peruvian travel fantasy *The Amazonian Republic* (1842), Edward Maturin's *Montezuma; The Last of the Aztecs* (1845), Joseph Holt Ingraham's *Montezuma, the Serf* (1845), and Charles Averill's *Aztec Revelations* (1849), fictions of American empire that were built upon barely concealed racist constructions and theories of savagism. A strikingly unusual work combining diverse themes of the western conquest was Lewis Garrand's *Wah-To-Wah, and the Taos Trail; or, Prairies Travel and Scalp Dances, with a Look at Los Rancheros from Muleback and the Rocky Mountain Campfire* (1850), a semi-autobiographical work of mountain life that included an account of the 1847 "Taos Massacre," a brief uprising against the Americans newly in military occupation by Pueblo Indians and Mexicans. In language that might later have been turned against the U.S. theory of manifest destiny by Mexico itself, Garrand characterized the triumph of American power as the codification of progressive history: "the extreme degradation into which [the Mexicans] are fallen seems a fearful retribution upon the destroyers of [the] Aztec Empire."

The romance of ancient Latin American history, however, was most vividly exemplified by William H. Prescott's three-volume *History of the Conquest of Mexico* (1843), one of the most internationally admired histories of its day and the greatest example of the progressive historicism adopted by Garrand, Bird, Stephens, and others. In a masterpiece of Romantic style, Prescott (1796–1859) portrayed the conquest of the Aztecs by Cortés as a prefiguring of the rise to supremacy of the United States. In Prescott's epic account, Aztec barbarism, made especially melodramatic in Prescott's depictions of sacrificial rites, was balanced by a clear portrayal of Spanish greed and plundering – notably in the Poe-like grotesquerie of the city of Tenochtitlán, a virtual charnel house after Cortés's final assault – thus implying an unsettling parallel in the United States' own conquest of North American Indians and Mexicans. But the more powerful implied analogy for most readers in the United States was between the failure and fall of Aztec civilization and that of the contemporary Mexican government. "We cannot regret the fall of an empire, which did so little to promote the . . . real interests of humanity," Prescott wrote.

Its fate may serve as a striking proof, that a government, which does not rest on the sympathies of its subjects, cannot long abide; that human institutions, when not connected to humanity and progress, must fall — if not before the increasing light of civilization, by the hand of violence; by violence from within, if not from without. And who shall lament their fall?

Whatever reflection upon America's own destiny could be read into Prescott's masterwork, the advent of actual war reduced irony to a minimum and brought forth vigorous reassertions of America's millennial promise. Readers relied on Gregg's *Commerce on the Prairies* and Prescott's *History of the Conquest of Mexico* for information about the region; but they took their main view of the war from journalists, soldiers, and fiction writers. Accounts of the military campaign, especially the famous expedition of Alexander Doniphan, were written by a number of participants. F. A. Wislizenus, the German explorer, was on a scientific expedition in the Southwest when he was swept up in the war and made a medical officer with Doniphan, experiences recounted in *Memoir of a Tour to Northern Mexico* (1848). Thomas B. Thorpe (1815–75), better known as the author of "The Big Bear of Arkansas" and other tall tales collected in such volumes as *The Mysteries of the Backwoods* (1846), also described his view of the war in *Our Army on the Rio Grande* (1846) and *Our Army at Monterey* (1847). A significant number of soldiers acted as newspaper correspondents, providing the first significant coverage of an American war and helping to magnify the patriotic outpouring of sentiment that accompanied it. To many, the war seemed a fulfillment of the promises of the American Revolution, which had recently been reawakened in a number of popular histories by Benjamin Lossing, Jared Sparks, George Bancroft, and others. "Yankee Doodle" was the most famous song in the field and at home, and Zachary Taylor replaced Andrew Jackson, who died in 1845, as the nation's favorite soldier–statesman. While Thoreau and Emerson took exception to the war and James Russell Lowell (1819–91) employed the satiric poetry of *The Biglow Papers* (1848) to attack the war as an imperialistic blunder of corrupt politicians, the majority of poets and essayists celebrated American victories and heroism in an orgy of romantic and chivalric images. A compendium of the jingoistic literature of the war was edited early on by William McCarty in *National Songs, Ballads, and Other Patriotic Poetry, Chiefly Relating to the War of 1846* (1846). As a contemporary journalist wrote in his account of Doniphan's campaign, "the American eagle seemed to spread his broad pinions and westward bear the principles of republican government."

The simultaneously invigorating and enervating spirit of manifest destiny is nowhere more clear than in the fiction the Mexican War produced. The stage for such works, however, had been set by fictional portraits of Mexico before the war. Timothy Flint's *Francis Berrian, or the Mexican Patriot* (1826) dramatized Mexico's 1821 revolution in terms of its New England hero's image of the American Revolution — with the irony that by the time of the Mexican War the spirit of the American Revolution would justify war *against* Mexico. Justin Jones's somewhat later portrayal of Mexico's postrevolutionary period, *The Rival Chieftains* (1845), exemplified an increasingly widespread view that the chaos and exoticism of Mexico, "the El Dorado of the New World," made it the perfect scene for romance and novelistic enchantment. The first fiction of New Mexico by an Anglo-American who had actually been there, Albert Pike's *Prose Sketches and Poems* (1834), divides its attention between the beauty and desolate terror of the prairies and sketches of the Mexicans as colorful but at the same time crude and villainous.

Such portraits of Mexicans reached a climax in the imaginative writing about the war itself. For example, the extravagant nationalistic rhetoric that accompanied the portrait of the American Revolution in George Lippard's *Washington and His Generals* (1847) appeared in a slightly revised form in his very popular *Legends of Mexico* (1847). Lippard (1822–54), the author of a variety of gothic tales in other settings, created a commanding paradigm for much of the subsequent fiction about the war by relying on exotic and terrifying scenes, the rescue of endangered maidens or innocent people from dark-skinned ogres, and attacks on the corrupt, even perverse, superstitions of Catholicism. The war, in Lippard's view, was the "Crusade of a civilized People, against a semi-barbarous horde of slaves." As the fulfillment of the nation's destiny initiated by the American Revolution, moreover, the conquest of Mexico would prove the supremacy of Anglo-American blood, spilled and purified in contest with the doomed American Indian, and the legitimacy of democratic principles, forged by revolution and sustained by a Puritan God:

A vigorous People, rugged as the rocks of the wilderness which sheltered them, free as the forest which gave them shade, bold as the red Indian who forced them to purchase every inch of ground, with the blood of human hearts. To this hardy People — this people created from the pilgrims and wanderers of all nations — this People nursed into full vigor, by long and bloody Indian wars and hardened into iron, by the longest and bloodiest war of all, the Revolution, to his People of Northern America, God Almighty has given the destiny of the entire American Continent. . . . As the Aztec people, crumbled before the Spaniard, so will the mongrel race, moulded of Indian and Spanish blood, melt into, and be ruled by, the Iron Race of the North.

The arc of liberty connecting the Revolution to the Mexican War and symbolizing the march of the United States across the continent is perfectly contained in Lippard's concluding image: "THE unsheathed sword of WASHINGTON resting upon the map of the NEW WORLD."

Lippard's prediction that the Americans would absorb the Mexicans points to a quandary that would confront those who advocated the conquest of "All Mexico" in coming years: would the inevitable amalgamation of the races save the Mexicans or destroy the Anglo-Americans? Even during the debate over annexation of New Mexico and California, John Calhoun and others who opposed President Polk's militaristic designs argued that Mexico was unassimilable. The war fiction itself, because it turned so often to the categories of gothic romance in which a Mexican maiden was rescued from villainous brutes or corrupt Catholic priests to become the bride of an American hero, appeared to endorse absorption. The large number of novels and novelettes the war produced played constantly with variations on the theme of rescue and romance. As in the fiction of Indian captivity and the urban gothic novel (itself often violently anti-Catholic), romance in its sexual dimensions – capture, the threat of assault, rescue, and marriage – structured the military exploits recounted in numerous tales, including Arthur Armstrong's *The Mariner of the Mines: Or, the Maid of the Monastery* (1850), William L. Tidball's *The Mexican Bride; Or, the Ranger's Revenge* (c. 1858), George Lippard's *'Bel of Prairie Eden: A Romance of Mexico* (1848), Lorry Luff's *Antonita, The Female Contrabandista* (1848), Justin Jones's *Inez, the Beautiful: Or, Love on the Rio Grande* (1846) and *The Volunteer: Or, the Maid of Monterey* (1847), Harry Halyard's *The Chieftain of the Churubusco, or, the Spectre of the Cathedral* (1848), Robert Greeley's *Arthur Woodleigh: A Romance of the Battle Field of Mexico* (1847), Charles Averill's *The Mexican Ranchero; Or the Maid of the Chapparal* (1847), and Eliza Ann Billings's *The Female Volunteer* (1851). To cite two typical examples: in Newton Curtis's *The Hunted Chief; Or, the Female Ranchero* (1847), the American hero at the fall of Monterey weds the Mexican woman who has fought throughout disguised as a male ranchero; and in Averill's *The Secret Service Ship* (1848) the marriage of the white hero and the Mexican woman symbolizes the triumph of American strength over Mexican weakness, or "femininity," as well as the resulting union of the two nations ("rapid and brilliant is the conquest of Peace by the glorious, ever victorious Flag of our Union"). Figuring territorial acquisition as sexual conquest and conjugal union, the fiction of the Mexican War thus projected the fulfillment of American destiny in expansion and in the absorption of a West that simultaneously included the geography and the customs and identity of the Mexican people.

The Mexican War continued to attract periodic romantic assessment for several decades, but its great contemporary interest was soon engulfed by the crisis over slavery and sectionalism. A number of soldiers who got their training in Mexico went on to significant careers in America's own internal cataclysm, and the question of African American slavery, which had played a significant role in arguments over the value of Mexican lands, would be resolved as a consequence of the Civil War. By the 1860s, however, the future geographical shape of the continental United States was complete. In the previous decade, a wealth of land and resources, with numerous potential transcontinental routes, had been made available to expansion by force of arms and helped give rise to the very conflicts that appeared to make civil war inevitable. With the American victory in the Mexican War, the questions of manifest destiny, the "Indian problem," and slavery became bound together even more tightly, as did the literatures those questions produced.

The American victory in the war against Mexico dramatically changed the course of American cultural history, making the West a region of even greater economic and political importance while at the same time ensuring that it would remain contested territory. Much of the region's literature, in both oral and written forms, appeared predominantly in Spanish until the twentieth century, when Mexican culture gave way, at least by political definition, to Mexican American culture. Parts of the territories of Texas, New Mexico, Arizona, and California could be defined as "border" regions even before 1848, however, and any account of the literature of the newly conquered territory must include recognition of its historical sources and of the suppression of Mexican cultural voices by Anglo-American domination. The difficulty in assessing the region's native Mexican literature is tied in turn to the ignorance and hostility with which it was treated by Anglo-Americans for the next hundred years. Because there remains a vast amount of as yet unstudied historical, journalistic, autobiographical, and literary material in libraries and archives of California, Texas, the Southwest, and Mexico, it is only at the end of the twentieth century becoming possible to give an adequate account of the literary history of the region. Even so, there were a number of significant *Mexican* works written in or about the greater Southwest before, during, and soon after the antebellum period which may be said to constitute the backgrounds (and in some instances what some scholars might identify as the beginnings or sources) of modern Chicano literature.

Even with the inclusion of very early narratives of the Spanish conquest, the currently documented literary record of the region is very scattered before the nineteenth century. The known story begins with Alvar Núñez Cabeza de Vaca, who was one of the few survivors of a failed Spanish conquistadorial expedition to Florida and endured an excruciating overland trek along the

Gulf of Mexico. His *Relación,* composed in 1542, appears to be the first authentic written account of the Southwest and its native tribes as seen by an outsider. The most significant exploration of New Spain, Coronado's expedition up the Colorado River and across the central Great Plains in 1540, was recounted by a number of the participants, but the most important chronicle is Pedro de Nágera de Castañeda's *Relación de la jornada a Cíbola* (c. 1565), which is marked by evocations of the marvelous similar to those appearing in Spanish literature of the same period by Miguel de Cervantes Saavedra and others. The Spanish search for the "golden lands" of the North, in some instances linked to a quest for Aztlán, the Aztec land of origin, worked its way into several imperial texts and histories of the period. Fray Diego Durán's *Historia de las Indias de Nueva España* (1579–81) and the anonymous *Códice Ramírez* (1853–7) based the myth of an Edenic Aztlán on the legends of native informants, whereas *Crónica Mexicáyotl* (1610), originally written in Nahuatl by Alvarado Tezozomac, and *Crónica miscelánea* (1652), by Fray Antonio Tello, tentatively identified Aztlán with the Pueblos of the Southwest. Later historical works, such as Manuel Orozoco y Berra's *Historia antigua y de la conquista de México* (1880) and Alfredo Chavero's volume of the same name published in 1887, argued for yet other geographical locations of Aztlán, and in 1885 William G. Ritch, the secretary of the Territory of New Mexico and president of the New Mexico Bureau of Immigration, published a highly commercial work intended to promote immigration to the region entitled *Aztlán: The History, Resources and Attractions of New Mexico* (also issued under the title *Illustrated New Mexico*). More important than attempts to pinpoint a geographical Aztlán, which remained a matter of historical debate and diverse appropriation on into the twentieth century, are the ways in which Aztlán came to be embraced by some modern Mexican Americans, particularly those identifying with the movement for Chicano nationalism, as their spiritual homeland. A history of the region, in the form of an epic poem dedicated to Phillip III, survives in Gaspar Pérez de Villagrá's *Historia de la Nueva México* (1610), which celebrated Juan de Oñate's crossing of the Rio Grande to colonize New Mexico and appeared fourteen years before Captain John Smith's *General History of Virginia.* Composed in thirty-four cantos, Villagrá's *Historia* traces the history of New Mexico from Mexico's Aztec origins through the period of exploration that led up to Oñate's venture. In its account of the battle between the Spanish and the Acomas, its detailed portrait of the landscape and the working lives of the explorers and vaqueros, and its reflections on the cultural conflict entailed in colonial conquest, Villagrá's epic may be said to have provided the early groundwork for subsequent Mexican American literature.

A few other narratives, by both explorers and priests, appeared during the next two centuries, but the most significant firsthand accounts of the modern period date from the late eighteenth and early nineteenth centuries in the journals of explorers, missionaries, and political leaders, among them Fray Junípero Serra, Gaspar de Portolá, Miguel Costansó, Juan Bautista de Anza, Fray Juan Díaz, and Fray Francisco Gracés. Many such texts had very little circulation until their study by modern scholars; but Fray Geronimo Boscana, at the mission of San Juan Capistrano, recorded traditional Native American legends and creation myths in *Chinigchinich* (1831), which became widely known later when it appeared as an appendix to Alfred Robinson's *Life in California* (1846). Even though New Mexican religious poetry, folk songs, and religious drama such as Corpus Christi plays are documented from the sixteenth century forward, it is only near the period of independence that extensive examples of such literature began to be recorded by contemporaries. The late-eighteenth-century *Los comanches,* a heroic folk drama in verse, recounts the war between the conquistadores and the Comanche chief Cuerno Verde in 1774, though the drama takes one of its central features, the abduction of Christian children by infidels, from earlier Spanish versions of the drama (in which Moors took the place of Comanches) and belongs to a larger genre of such folk works portraying the contest between Christianity and "barbarism" known in both Spain and America as *moros y cristianos.* A play from the early 1840s, *Los tejanos,* depicted the 1841 defeat of the invading Texas Santa Fe expedition by the forces of General Manuel Armijo and offered a form of nationalistic commemoration and political satire that promoted New Mexican territorial integrity even as it adumbrated future threats against it.

The most important literary genre of the region, which would form the basis for much modern Chicano poetic literature, is the corrido, a narrative ballad sung or spoken with musical accompaniment. In addition to documenting the rise of borderland political and economic conflicts, which would remain integral to much Mexican American literature and to Chicano cultural nationalism, the corridos afford the most important of the oral, folkloric roots of modern Chicano literature. Descended in part from Spanish ballad forms and widespread in Mexico, the corridos flourished in the Mexican–American border area, especially in Texas, from the 1830s to the 1930s, and have continued to be performed and recorded through the twentieth century. In addition to having an important place in Spanish-speaking theater, which was well established in San Antonio, San Francisco, and Los Angeles by the 1860s, corridos were printed along with other folktales, *decimás,* and canciones in Spanish-language newspapers and in bilingual newspapers such as the *New Mexican,* founded in 1849. Although only a few printed fragments from the pre-1848 years have been recovered, the majority of the nineteenth-century corridos were devoted to episodes and legends of Indian warfare, to love affairs, to cattle drives, and, especially, to the extensive civil conflict along the Rio Grande. Even when the cultural conflict depicted is nonviolent or comic, the corrido in its early forms, highlights the uneasy truce of the newly colonized region. "El corrido de Kiansis," for example, portrays the professional rivalry between Mexican vaqueros and Anglo cowboys, with the latter made out to be less than competent hands on the cattle drive.

The most famous of the corridos would appear several decades later, but its construction and its themes illuminate an oral tradition that began much earlier. "El corrido de Gregorio Cortez" concerns the legend of the best known of several rebel figures whose resistance to Anglo-American rule (or, as in the case of Cortez, the Anglos' overt lawlessness and racism) is commemorated by folk ballads. Hunted down and imprisoned along with his wife, Leonor Diaz Cortez, after his 1901 killing of an Anglo sheriff who was attempting to make an illegal arrest, Gregorio Cortez was later pardoned, but not before he had been immortalized as defending his rights *"con su pistola en la mano"* (with a pistol in his hand). Throughout the variants of this corrido, Cortez, though he is represented as a single man pressured into revolt by political injustice, is an individual whose actions express the will of the larger Mexican–American border community, which finds its greater cultural struggle epitomized by his rebellion. In many versions of the Cortez corrido, the hero's violent acts and subsequent legal prosecution are diminished in favor of a focus on his symbolic resistance to the massed authority of the dominant Anglo-American world. The last half of one variant recorded and translated by Américo Paredes reads:

> En el condado de Kiancer
> lo llegaron a alcanzar,
> a poco más de trescientos
> y allí les brincó el corral.
>
> Decía el Cherife Mayor
> como queriendo llorar:
> —Cortez, entrega tus armas
> no te vamos a matar.
>
> Decía Gregorio Cortez
> con su pistola en la mano:
> — Ah, cuánto rinche montado
> para un solo mexicano!
>
> Ya con ésta me despido
> a la sombra de un ciprés
> aquí se acaba el corrido
> de don Gregorio Cortez.

(And in the county of Kansas
They cornered him after all;
Though they were more than three hundred
He leaped out of their corral.

Then the Major Sheriff said,
As if he was going to cry,
"Cortez, hand over your weapons;
We want to take you alive."

Then said Gregorio Cortez,
With his pistol in his hand,
"Ah, so many mounted Rangers
Against one lone Mexican!"

Now with this I say farewell
In the shade of a cypress tree,
This is the end of the ballad
Of Don Gregorio Cortez.)

"El corrido de Gregorio Cortez," though written about events half a century after the Mexican War, reflects the scattered evidence of comparable motifs in the earlier corridos. Juan Nepomuceno Cortina, who organized a guerrilla band to occupy Brownsville, Texas, to protest Anglo abuse in the 1850s, is the subject of surviving ballad fragments that anticipate the corridos devoted to Cortez. Likewise, Ignacio Zaragoza, the hero of the battle at Puebla (in which Mexico's victory over invading French forces on May 5, 1862, gave birth to the national holiday Cinco de Mayo), became the subject of an 1867 corrido that is technically Mexican in origin but, like other such works infused with nationalistic consciousness, is equally significant for an understanding of the origins of Mexican American culture.

Especially in the border area between Mexico and the United States, where the problem of national identity would remain acute on through the twentieth century, the corridos thus put political sentiment in a popular form and directly reflected the experiences of Mexican men and women, whose lives were shaped by conflicting ideological forces and often marked by violent racism. The period between 1821 and 1848 in particular necessitated wrenching decisions about national loyalty for some Mexicans in the Southwest. For example, Lorenzo de Zavala wrote a group of important essays about Mexico's independence from Spain, entitled *Ensayos históricos de las revoluciones de México* (1831); but when he advocated independence for Texas in an anti-Mexican, pro-American travel narrative entitled *Viaje a los Estados Unidas del Norte de America* (1834), he lost his Mexican citizenship. Of particular interest as a counterview of the Mexican War is Ramón Alcaraz's *Apuntes para la historia de la guerra entre México y los Estados-Unidos* (1848), translated in 1850 as *The*

Other Side, which provides excellent detail about key battles and Mexican military leaders and is a useful corrective to the chauvinistic American versions of the war. Contemporary histories of the New Mexico region by its residents include Don Pedro Bautista Pino's *Exposición sucinta y sensilla de la provincia del Nuevo México* (1812); Antonio Barreiro's *Ojeada sobre Nuevo-México* (1832), a work that supported a more vigorous imperial trade policy toward New Mexico and warned Mexico of the territory's vulnerability to U.S. invasion; and José Agustín de Escudero's *Noticias históricas y estadísticas de la antigua provincia del Nuevo-México* (1849), a volume that essentially combined the texts of Pino and Barreiro. From the other side of the cultural divide came *El Gringo; or, New Mexico and Her People* (1857), by William W. H. Davis, U.S. attorney for the Territory of New Mexico from 1853 to 1856, and the letters of Madame Calderón de la Barca, the English wife of a Spanish minister to colonial Mexico, which were published in 1931 as *Life in Mexico* and offer an impressive if often Eurocentric portrait of the social world and the role of women in New Mexico in the years 1839–40.

The most comprehensive contemporary account of the region's history from the Mexican American point of view would not appear until 1875, in Mariano Vallejo's five-volume *Recuerdos históricos y personales tocante á la Alta California,* cited at the outset of this chapter. Military commander of Alta California from 1836 to 1842, Vallejo surveyed the entire history of Mexican–Anglo relations in California in his often autobiographical study. Aware that much of his own cultural heritage, as well as the political and property rights of many *californios,* had been abrogated by the annexation of California by the United States, Vallejo nonetheless tempered his criticism with a patriotic view of the nation of which he had become a prominent citizen. In a forward to his monumental work that combined familiar American revolutionary rhetoric with an equally familiar belief in the progress of empires, he wrote (in Spanish) that he considered himself

an eyewitness to the efforts of self-sacrificing military men and missionaries who, by dint of trials, sleepless nights, privations, and incredible perseverance, succeeded in wrestling from the control of savage Indians this beautiful land, which, redeemed from the bloody grasp of idolatry and raised by its sons to the heights of prosperity, stretches forth its loving arms to the oppressed of monarchical Europe and offers them the shelter of its fertile countryside, a fountain of wealth and prosperity.

That Vallejo wrote in Spanish, however, was but one index of the ambivalence that marked the range of early Mexican American literature. Both the pressure of acculturation and resistance to it were embedded in the bilingualism of much southwestern and California culture, a fact later captured by Jesús María H. Alarid in an 1889 poem entitled "El idioma," in which the author affirmed that English would be the national language of Mexican Americans but that they must never cease to speak and write in Spanish as well. Like the first histories and autobiographical narratives in California and the Southwest, the first Mexican-American novels, Eusebio Chacón's *El hijo de la tempestad* (Son of the Storm) and *Tras la tormenta la calma* (Calmness after the Storm), both published in 1892, were written in Spanish. But neither the language nor the border literature of Mexican America belonged in fact to the United States on the one hand or to Spain's colonial world on the other. Both were Mexican in origin and essence; and although the cultural traditions and literature of the region would, over time, become partially merged with the dominant ideological forms of Anglo America, they would maintain their own voices and historical particularity, rooted in the folk traditions passed down and recorded in such modern collections as Juan B. Rael's *Cuentos españoles de Colorado y Nuevo Mexico* (*Spanish Tales from Colorado and New Mexico*, 1977) and Elaine Miller's *Mexican Folk Narrative from the Los Angeles Area* (1973), as well as in pre-1848 historical and autobiographical narratives. Marked by colonialism but also by a wealth of indigenous traditions, the literature that pointed toward artistic expressions of Chicano and Latino nationalism in the twentieth century remains to be adequately interpreted both in its own terms and as an essential part of early American literary history.

By the end of the 1840s the opening of transmontane routes to the West, the U.S. victory in the Mexican War, and the discovery of gold in California released a wave of Euro-American pioneer emigrants that rapidly moved toward the coast and began to settle throughout sizable areas of the Great Plains and the Rocky Mountain West. The myth of the Great American Desert popularized by Pike, Long, Irving, Parkman, Gregg, Farnham, and others was disputed and disproved. As theories that free land in the West would accommodate surplus labor from the East emerged, and as Free Soil politics arose in opposition to the extension of slavery, a national vision of a western agrarian utopia of yeoman farmers served to reanimate the image of America as the "garden of the world." Drawing on conceptions of natural rights expounded by Locke and Jefferson, the agrarianist theory that resulted in the Preemption Act of 1841 and the Homestead Act of 1862 was based on independence, the right to private property, and the discipline of work. The various crusades for a transcontinental railroad by Asa Whitney, Thomas Hart Benton, and Stephen Douglas, among others, represented conflicting ideological interests but shared a vision of the American continent in which the mapping of the western garden would reveal the material value latent in a transcendent myth. The relative ease of acquisition and settlement of rich, abundant land on inland and coastal plains and the lure of mineral wealth in the Rockies and Sierra Nevada sparked a sudden, massive migration (and an often violent displacement of American Indians) that dramatically changed the character of the United States within a matter of decades.

Between the Mexican War and the Civil War, the primary Euro-American documents of the far frontier (besides the many scientific reports of the Army Corps of Topographical Engineers and others employed in the reconnaissance of transcontinental rail routes, mineralogical deposits and geographical formations, and Indian encampments) were devoted to promoting settlement in the West. Among the significant travel and emigration guides are Andrew Child's *Overland Route to California* (1852); two publications that warned explicitly against a utopian vision of gold wealth, James Abbey's *California, A Trip Across the Plains* (1850) and J. S. Shepherd's *Journal of Travel Across the Plains to California and Guide to the Future Emigrant* (1851); Charles Dana's *The Garden of the World,* cited above; and Joseph Colton's *Colton's Traveler and Tourist's Guide-Book Through the Western States and Territories* (1856), which was probably the most popular as a celebration of American industry and progress, featuring mileage, maps, and detailed information about the Mississippi Valley and the Great Plains regions. As Colton's guide suggests, the "West" continued to mean virtually all the territory beyond the Mississippi River. Yet the growing literary treatment of the frontier Middle West in personal narratives and frontier fiction was a sign in its own right that settlements would soon crowd out those seeking an unrestricted life in the wilderness or on the prairie.

If the desire for land and later for gold drove most men and women toward the Pacific, other forces as well governed the promise of frontier liberty. Reenacting the original Puritan settlement of America in new terms, for example, the Mormons wanted freedom from religious persecution. A Christian sect that grew to have an enormous following in the twentieth century, the Mormons orginated under the leadership of Joseph Smith, who transcribed and published several sacred works, including *The Book of Mormon* (1830), purportedly the text of a fifth-century prophet who forecast a New Jerusalem and millennial salvation in America. The Mormons were driven ever westward from their original church home in New York State, and after Smith was murdered by a mob in Illinois, they set out for Utah under Brigham Young. Guided by writings on the West by Lansford Hastings and John Frémont, Young established a new colony at Salt Lake in 1847. Both members and visitors wrote a variety of commentaries on the colony. Accounts of the migration are recorded, for example, in *Memoirs of John R. Young, Utah Pioneer of 1847* (1920) and *William Clayton's Journal* (1921), whereas the Mormons' early political and social organization is described in J.

Howard Stansbury, *An Expedition to the Valley of the Great Salt Lake of Utah* (1852), James Linforth, *Route from Liverpool to Great Salt Lake Valley* (1855), and Thomas B. H. Stenhouse, *The Rocky Mountain Saints* (1873). In addition to condemnations of the kind that drove them from the East, the Mormons became increasingly the object of satire and exposé in popular fiction. Like the anti-Catholicism of gothic fiction, anti-Mormonism in the novel focused on sexual immorality, in particular the Mormon's advocacy of polygamy. Revelations of what were declared to be the bondage and perversions of Mormon marital life appeared in domestic melodramas such as Metta Victor's *Mormon Wives* (1854), Maria Ward's *Female Life Among the Mormons* (1855), and Ann Eliza Young's *Wife No. 19: or, the Story of a Life in Bondage* (1875), the supposed confessions of a former wife of Brigham Young. Despite these and other attacks on Mormon faith and enterprise, the Mormon migration, which resulted in one of the most stable and economically successful religious communities in American history, embodied in microcosm the revolutionary advent and popular pursuit of the ideal symbolized by the American West.

Nothing more completely summarized the often dreamlike meaning of the West than California during the Gold Rush. The narratives of exploration and the emigrant guides had already proclaimed California the land of America's future; after the Mexican War and the discovery of gold in 1848, the region became, like Ahab's gold doubloon in *Moby-Dick,* which alluded to it, a mirror of each pioneer's dreams. The symbolic significance of California was pinpointed by popular writer Bayard Taylor in the very title of the travel report he filed for Horace Greeley's *New York Tribune: Eldorado; or, Adventures in the Path of Empire* (1850). Completing and capping America's drive toward empire, California, according to Taylor, proved that the essence of America was hard work, risk, and a democratic leveling that made labor respectable and prosperity across the classes acceptable.

Various journals and emigrant guides to the gold country appeared immediately, including Henry Simpson's *Three Weeks in the Gold Mines* (1848), William Kelley's *A Stroll through the Diggings of California* (1852), the future California Supreme Court justice Lorenzo Sawyer's *Way Sketches* (1850), and Alonzo Delano's fine geological study, *Life on the Plains and Among the Diggings* (1854). The Australian William Shaw warned of the demoralizing effects of "gold mania" in *Golden Dreams and Waking Realities* (1851), and the Scottish writer John D. Borthwick argued in *Three Years in California* (1857) that the "Golden Legend," "one of the most wondrous episodes in the history of mankind," would momentously transfigure world trade. Life in the mines themselves – with its wild mix of races, rough frontier justice, and kaleidoscope of fulfilled and shattered dreams – was quickly recorded as history by J. Quinn Thornton in *Oregon and California in 1848* (1849) and in sketches such as Leonard Kip's *California Sketches With Recollections of the Gold Mines* (1850). Most famous of all were Louise Amelia Knapp Smith Clappe's *Dame Shirley Letters,* which first appeared in the San Francisco *Pioneer Magazine* in 1854–5. Based on her own experiences in the mining country in 1851–2 and written under the name Dame Shirley, these letters ostensibly to her sister in Boston recorded in magnificent detail the danger, profanity, and gamble of mining life, conveying at the same time a perfect sense of what Tocqueville had diagnosed as the dreamy restlessness of Americans, who seemed never content but always in search of new wealth or greater freedom and adventure.

Most of the fiction devoted to the Gold Rush was cheap melodrama like George Payson's *Golden Dreams and Leaden Realities* (1853) and *The New Age of Gold* (1856); gothic romance like the anonymous *Amelia Sherwood; or, Bloody Scenes at the California Gold Mines* (1849); or travel fantasy like Fanny Foley's *Romance of the Ocean: A Narrative of the Voyage of the Wildfire to California* (1850). The only fiction to raise more complicated issues were the legendary 1854 treatment of the bandit Joaquin Murieta by the Cherokee writer Yellow Bird (John Rollin Ridge) and Charles Averill's *Kit Carson: The Prince of the Gold Hunters* (1849) and its sequel *Life in California, or, The Treasure Seeker's Expedition* (1849), rambunctious adventure stories that presaged Frank Norris's *McTeague* in probing the "boundless power of unbridled lust for gold."

In the best writing about California in the 1850s, however, gold was not a rigid symbol but a metaphor evocative of the apparent triumph of American destiny. In the events transpiring within just three years, the Reverend Walter Colton wrote in *The Land of Gold; or, Three Years in California* (1850), the region "has sprung at once from the shackles of colonial servitude to all the advantages and dignities of a sovereign state." Although Colton noted that the miners were still in need of women, whose "smiles garland the domestic hearth," he considered the acquisition of California and the discovery of gold an omen of future greatness and issued an evangelical appeal to emigrants to settle and purify the region as a prelude to universal conquest:

Our globe was invested with no claims of utility till it had emerged from chaos; then verdure clothed its hills and vales; then flowing streams made vocal the forest aisles; then rolled the anthem of the morning star. . . . The tide of Anglo-Saxon blood stops not here; it is to circulate on other shores, continents, and isles; its progress is blent with the steady triumphs of commerce, art, civilization, and religion. It will yet flow the globe round, and beat in every nation's pulse.

The moral redemption to be accomplished by California needed to begin in California itself, claimed Eliza Farnham, wife of the travel writer Thomas Jefferson Farnham and author of a volume on midwestern emigration entitled *Life in the Prairie Land* (1846). Her *California, In-doors and Out* (1856) agreed with Colton and with a number of frontier novelists in arguing that women and the transforming powers of homemaking would be the key to California's success, notably because the domestic ideal was an emblem of democratic powers at work: "the loyalty that other nations pay to kings and queens, to old institutions, and to the superiority of caste, is paid by [men in America] to women." Without wives and mothers in a world of violent greed and vigilant justice, said Farnham, adopting a metaphor from mining geology, the "beautiful proportions of the moral nature will be gradually broken down, as the surface of the stone is hollowed, and its original form in part destroyed by the unceasing friction."

Easily the most dramatic prophecy to grow from the acquisition of California and the military and scientific conquest of the Rocky Mountain West appeared in a work by explorer, writer, and later governor of the Colorado Territory William Gilpin (1813–94). In a series of addresses collected as *The Central Gold Region. The Grain, Pastoral and Gold Regions of North America* (1860), he argued that the heart of this region, from the Great Plains to California, lay in the hemispheric band, postulated by Alexander von Humboldt, known as the isothermal zodiac. Falling in the path that had previously produced the empires of China, India, Greece, Rome, Spain, and Britain, the regions of the American West were thus set to usher in the great empire of North America. By means of an emigration "resembling the undulation of the sea, which accompanies the great tide-wave," a pastoral, Anglo-American empire, operating according to the "universal instincts of peace" and having at its command enough gold to accomplish the "*industrial* conquest of the world," would soon arise. With "moral grandeur" distinct from that of Europe, it would represent the fruition of the American Revolution; its "*untransacted destiny*" would be to "unite the world in one social family — to dissolve the spell of tyranny and exalt charity — to absolve the curse that weighs down humanity, and to shed blessings around the world." The pioneer heroes would lead the way in this millennial project, and a transcontinental railroad would be the material sign of its fulfillment. Gilpin's essentially Whitmanian prophecy appeared in a variety of forms on the eve of the Civil War, not least in the arguments of proslavery southerners, who saw the question of empire from a different angle of vision and asserted that the benevolent employment of slave labor could make possible the cultivation of the entire Western Hemisphere and open limitless trade across the Pacific.

The two views of empire shared an assumption that America's destiny in the 1850s had reached a climactic point and that the true passage to Asia would at last be achieved. Momentarily setting aside the explosive civil war that he saw on the horizon, in 1850 then Senator William Seward contemplated what the Treaty of Guadalupe Hidalgo and settlement of the Pacific Coast appeared to promise:

If, then, the American people shall remain an undivided nation, the ripening civilization of the West, after a separation growing wider and wider for four thousand years,
will in its circuit of the world, meet again, and mingle with the declining civilization of the East on our own free soil, and a new and more perfect civilization will
arise to bless the earth, under the sway of our own cherished and beneficent democratic institutions.

Both in geographical terms and with respect to the conflict over slave labor
and sectional power, a crisis was inevitable. The full development of the
West, and with it the further decimation of American Indian cultures, would
follow the Civil War, but America's modern shape and meaning, recorded in
a variety of forms and prophetic detail, were already powerfully clear in the
antebellum era's literature of exploration and empire.

THE FRONTIER AND
AMERICAN INDIANS

IN 1879, Hinmaton Yalakit (Thunder Rolling in the Heights), a Nez
Percé leader known to whites as Chief Joseph, delivered an oration in
Washington, D.C. His words summed up an escalating history of betray-
als by settlers and government officials:

The earth is the mother of all people, and all people should have equal rights upon it.
You may as well expect the rivers to run backward as that any man who was born a
free man should be contented when penned up and denied liberty to go where he
pleases. If you tie a horse to a stake, do you expect that he will grow fat? If you pen
an Indian up on a small spot of earth, and compel him to stay there, he will not be
contented, nor will he grow and prosper. I have asked some of the great white chiefs
where they get their authority to say to the Indian that he shall stay in one place,
while he sees the white men going where they please. They cannot tell me. . . .
Whenever the white man treats an Indian as they treat each other, then we will have
no more wars. . . . Then the Great Spirit Chief who rules above will smile upon this
land, and send rain to wash out the bloody spots made by brothers' hands across the
face of the earth. For this time the Indian race are waiting and praying.

American Indians would wait in vain. Chief Joseph's oration, one of many
such protests, which form a powerful genre of resistance literature, looked
both backward and forward from the historical midpoint in the long process
of Indian Removal and the destruction of tribal integrity that was a consequence of the Euro-American conquest of the West. His words in the nation's
capital are a simple reminder that American literature of the frontier was
always a literature of political and cultural conflict, one in which language
itself was a weapon of subjugation and an agent of transformation.

The acceleration of the U.S. westward expansion following the American
Revolution put sudden, overwhelming pressure on resident Native American
tribes, especially those east of the Mississippi River. The origins of the warfare
waged against most tribes during the nineteenth century lay in the colonial
period, but the several decades before and after America's own struggle for
independence were crucial to the long-term imperial thrust. During the first
half of the nineteenth century, the French and Indian Wars were central to
American development and the progress of settlement across the continent.

France's enormous cession of Indian land to Britain, the Indians' loss of allies, and the lessening of colonial reliance on Britain for protection created the conditions for the American Revolution and expansion east of the Mississippi. The Louisiana Purchase in 1803 gave the United States presumptive control over Indian territory west of the Mississippi and made possible the creation of a formal policy of Indian Removal. Prompted by a national ideology whose expressed intentions ranged from benevolent paternalism to virtual genocide, treaties negotiated between Indian tribes and the United States or state governments were often violated by American officials themselves and more often by the frontiersmen who wanted new land.

The War of 1812 marked important defeats for American Indians in both the North and the Southeast and elevated to national fame General William Henry Harrison and General Andrew Jackson. Both were vociferous on the subject of removing Indians from territories coveted by whites. Harrison asked: "Is one of the fairest portions of the globe to remain in a state of nature, the haunt of a few wretched savages, when it seems destined by the Creator to give support to a large population and to be the seat of civilization?" Although they sometimes took the ideas of Indian life from the Romantic philosophy and literary archetypes of natural life promulgated by those followers of Rousseau who valued the "state of nature" over the promised advance of Euro-American "civilization," most Euro-Americans accepted the verdict rendered by the essayist and novelist Hugh Henry Brackenridge in 1793: "I consider [that] men who are unacquainted with the savages, like young women who have read romances, have as improper an idea of the Indian character in the one case, as the female mind has of real life in the other." The "virtue" of primitive life, Brackenridge maintained, was an illusion of Enlightenment thought; true knowledge of Indian life proved that tribes standing in the path of white settlement would have to be assimilated, removed, or vanquished. Settlers and governmental officials agreed.

Advanced with differing degrees of urgency by Jefferson, Monroe, and John Quincy Adams as the best solution to the certain conflict and warfare over land, the government's policy of Indian Removal was solemn doctrine for Jackson, who became known among many Indians as Sharp Knife. Although it was preceded by a good deal of public and congressional debate (which often had more to do with the future use of the lands than with tribal rights), the practice of Removal, begun in the 1820s, technically "allowed" — but in point of fact forced — Indians to exchange their tribal lands for territory west of the Mississippi. The policy became official with the passages of the Removal Bill in 1830 and with Jackson's refusal to abide by two Supreme Court decisions, *Cherokee Nation v. Georgia* (1831) and *Worcester v. Georgia* (1832), which held that the laws of the state of Georgia were subordinate to federal jurisdiction over the Cherokees. Although Georgia could therefore not permit the seizures of Cherokee lands by white settlers, the Cherokees were defined by the court as "domestic dependent nations" – in effect, a foreign country and people within the United States – and placed legally in a position of paternalistic dependence upon the federal government for protection and redress. Jackson simply ignored the continued illegal actions of the state of Georgia, and by 1838 most members of the "Five Civilized Tribes" (the Cherokee, Creek, Seminole, Chickasaw, and Choctaw) had been forced to follow what they came to call the Trail of Tears into newly created Indian Territory west of the Mississippi.

However indefensible Jackson's policy and his flouting of the Supreme Court, it is unlikely that federal interference could have halted the Euro-American drive on the frontier and the consequent challenge to Indian rights in territory farther and farther west. Jackson was not alone in believing that the expansion of white civilization was foreordained and that Removal was therefore not only expedient but also a humane alternative to certain warfare and slaughter. Whatever the good intentions of some of its advocates, however, Removal was a process whose practical effects amounted to extermination. The burden of Jackson's views, summed up in 1830 in his Second Annual Message, demonstrated this clearly enough:

To follow to the tomb the last of his [the Indian's] race and to tread on the graves of extinct nations excite melancholy reflections. But true philanthropy reconciles the mind to these vicissitudes as it does to the extinction of one generation to make room for another. . . . Philanthropy could not wish to see this continent restored to the condition in which it was found by our forefathers. What good man would prefer a country covered with forests and ranged by a few thousand savages to our extensive Republic, studded with cities, towns, and properous farms, embellished with all the improvements which art can devise or industry execute, occupied by more than 12,000,000 happy people, and filled with the blessings of liberty, civilization, and religion?

In the context of Jackson's era, which boasted few defenders of an egalitarian society without regard to what were assumed to be inherent racial or national characteristics, his rationale for Removal was not in the least radical. Nevertheless, the ultimate result of the policy, degradation and extinction, was not difficult to forecast. Speckled Snake, a Cherokee, predicted as much in his answer to Jackson's advocacy of Removal through a policy of benevolent paternalism:

Brothers! We have heard the talk of our great father; it is very kind. He says he loves his red children. Brothers! When the white man first came to these shores, the Muscogees gave him land, and kindled him a fire to make him comfortable. . . . But when the white man warmed himself before the Indian's fire and filled himself with the Indian's hominy, he became very large; he stopped not for the mountain tops, and his feet covered the plains and the valleys. His hands grasped the eastern and the western sea. Then he became our great father. He loved his red children; but said, "You must move a little farther, lest I should, by accident, tread on you." With one foot he pushed the red man over the Oconee, and with the other he trampled down the graves of his fathers. . . . I have heard a great many talks from our great father, and they all began and ended the same.

By the policy of Removal, the population of American Indians east of the Mississippi was reduced from the 1820s through the 1840s to a quarter of its original size. In the case of the Cherokees alone, about four thousand out of twenty thousand died from disease and starvation in the journey from Georgia to Oklahoma. The Sauks and Foxes, the Winnebagos, and the Ojibwa (Chippewa), along with the southeastern tribes, were among those forced to cede or sell land and move west, where they were thrust into conflict with resident tribes of Sioux, Blackfeet, Osages, Pawnees, Comanches, Arapahos, and others. The policy of Removal, because it sought to provide a homeland for dispossessed tribes, was considered by most to be in many respects *more benevolent* than forcing Indians to adopt a culture not their own. But such programs as the government's appropriation of $10,000 a year starting in 1819 for a Civilization Fund to educate and Christianize Indians, although mildly successful with some tribes, were a meager form of benevolence. As Alexis de Tocqueville wrote in *Democracy in America* of the forced migration of Creeks, Cherokees, and Choctaws, "it is impossible to destroy men with more respect [for] the laws of humanity."

Yet Tocqueville too considered Native Americans to be resistant to "natural laws" of progress. In this he shared the views of Lewis Cass, governor of the Michigan Territory from 1813 to 1831 and secretary of war under Andrew Jackson. Along with Jackson, Cass was a primary architect of the policy of Removal, arguing in several influential essays in the *North American Review* in the late 1820s that the Indian, unlike the Euro-American, was indolent and "stationary," content to live in the same circular routines as the bear, the deer, and the buffalo: "He never looks around him with a spirit of emulation, to compare his situation with that of others, and to resolve upon improving it." Or as the more expressive metaphor of Francis Parkman (1823–93) later put it: "[T]he Indian is hewn out of rock. You can rarely change the form without the destruction of the substance. . . . He will not learn the arts of civilization, and he and his forest must perish together." Parkman's comments appear in his *The Conspiracy of Pontiac* (1851), which played a large role in fixing the idea of Indian "doom" as part of American's prevailing mythology for the rest of the century. His careful identification of Indians with the natural world – both doomed to defeat and cultivation by a greater race – is representative of white conceptions of the Indian's quasi-human form, as is his equally careful paternalistic imagery: "We look with deep interest on the fate of this irreclaimable son of the wilderness, the child who will not be weaned from the breast of his rugged mother." Widespread cultural perceptions of the American Indian as a "child" of nature – both innocent and given to uncontrolled violence – reenforced the policy of Jackson and others who developed a paternalistic structure of care and discipline to promote Removal. The natural metaphors employed by Cass and Parkman would proliferate in the nineteenth-century depictions of American Indians. In both political and psychological terms they perform a crucial role in situating Euro-American conquest within an epic pattern that was claimed to be at once providential and natural, unfolding according to observable laws of national purpose.

As the new nation was mapped and settled by white pioneers, Native American tribes occupied smaller and more remote areas of the map, in many cases even more distant from their ancestral lands, while at the same time they became increasingly popular as subjects of American cultural expression and academic research. The absorption of the figure of the Indian into America's mythic consciousness, a process begun with the narratives of captivity and Indian warfare in the colonial period, was accelerated in the nineteenth century. Indian chiefs or heroes could become celebrities once they were no longer threatening as warriors, and whole tribes could be portrayed as virtuous and tragic to a public that had already been assured of final white triumph and saw battle and captivity as part of the ordained mission of America in the New World. A spirit of nationalism, prevailing attitudes toward "primitive" or "savage" life, and land hunger combined to create the conditions for a literature that largely supported the policy of Indian Removal even if it scorned the often violent or dishonest methods by which it was accomplished. During the period from the government's first official policy of Indian Removal through the completion of pioneering routes west across the plains and mountains to the Pacific coast (roughly from the mid-1820s through the 1850s) novelists like James Fenimore Cooper, ethnographers like Henry Rowe Schoolcraft, historians like Thomas McKenney, and poets like Henry Wadsworth Longfellow dramatized American Indians as a people who belonged to a passing phase of human development, destined to die out if they remained unable to accept acculturation into the new nation. The policy of Removal, not always sinister but nonetheless tragic, gave direction to the representation of American Indians in the cultural documents of Euro-Americans and, at times, to the self-representation by Indians themselves.

Not surprisingly, the lives and voices of American Indians were often distorted in the texts that tried to portray them. Relatively few documents written by, or recorded from, Indians in the pre-Civil War period survive, and those that do are suspect either because they reflect less their native traditions than the expectations of the white audience to whom they were presented or because of problems in translation. Even so, there are a number of Indian texts written in English and a far larger number of traditional stories and legends recorded and translated by researchers like Schoolcraft and George Catlin, that to some degree counter the denigrating or misguided views of Indian life depicted in popular Euro-American fiction and poetry. Native American cultural expression, largely nonliterate until the twentieth century, is difficult to conceptualize according to the chronological divisions and interpretive traditions of Euro-American literary history. Moreover, the isolation of Indian culture into an American "antebellum" period or even under the heading of either "American Indian" or "Native American," which falsely universalizes the traditions of hundreds of diverse tribes, imposes artificial definitions that are at times as inadequate and restricting as the Anglo-American penchant for speaking metonymically of "the Indian." Nonetheless, traditional native culture not only remained powerful during the exterminating wars of the nineteenth century but also began to be systematically recorded in written Euro-American forms for the first time. Because the history of American Indian literature in the antebellum period is inevitably a history of cultural appropriation and conflict – but one in which Native American culture does survive, under overwhelming and violent pressures – the language, ideology, and analytic methods of the dominant white world often ironically provide one of the primary means by which Indian cultural expression was preserved.

In the literature of western expansion, even those documents that did not focus on American Indians often took for granted that the "Indian problem" was in the process of being solved. Because Indian tribes seemed destined to recede or vanish in the face of advances by white pioneers, however, the Indian often became for white writers a nostalgically or ironically charged symbol, capable of representing a variety of ideas: the loss of innocence that progress entails; a mythic age that would give historical scope to an America eager to assert its nationalism; or a primitivistic stage of social organization preferable to an increasingly urban, industrial world. Most of all, perhaps, the Indian could be figured as a noble hero, tragic in defeat but in pride and stoicism also a mask – at times a mirror – for white anxiety over the destruction of Native American tribal life.

A representative measure of prevailing cultural and political attitudes toward Indians at midcentury can again be found in Parkman's *The Conspiracy of Pontiac,* which differs little in outlook from the work of other historians and ethnologists but stands out for its lyrical view of the continent's swift transfiguration. It is also a good example in popular literature, not so much of the cultural "removal" of Indians from the American landscape, but of their containment within a carefully circumscribed area of thought. Just a few years earlier in *The California and Oregon Trail* (1849) Parkman had presciently depicted the escalating slaughter of buffalo as though their death were coincident with that of the Indians who relied on hunting them, both destined to die out by what Parkman represented as a natural process. In the *Conspiracy of Pontiac,* a work comparable to *Moby-Dick* it its epic sweep at a climactic moment of mid-nineteenth-century history, Parkman locates the American Indian's vanquishing and death in the past by making the French and Indian Wars and Pontiac's uprising the last obstacle to white supremacy on the continent. As Melville's *Pequod* sinks into the maelstrom after its captain's monomaniacal pursuit of Moby Dick, a hammer wielded by the Indian Tashtego pins a screaming sky hawk against the mainmast. Parkman did not share Melville's tragic vision of America's western expansion, but his epic account of Pontiac likewise symbolized the meaning of that expansion by portraying the "American forest and the American Indian at the period when both received their final doom." Like Cooper and other novelists who set their accounts of Indian warfare in the past, Parkman displaced anxiety over contemporary violence and Removal into another era, rendering Native Americans fatalistically "lost" – already part of a mythic past – and thereby generating a powerful historical depth for America's ideological identity. A portrait of the defeated Pontiac, musing upon Lake Erie in 1766, reveals the scope of Parkman's own vision:

Little could he have dreamed . . . that within the space of a single human life, that lonely lake would be studded with the sails of commerce; that cities and villages would rise upon the ruins of the forest; and that the poor momentoes of his lost race – the wampum beads, the rusty tomahawk, the arrowhead of stone, turned up by the ploughshare – would become the wonder of school-boys, and the prized relics of the antiquary's cabinet.

Along with national artworks, like Horatio Greenough's sculpture *Rescue Group,* erected at the Capitol in 1853, and mundane artifacts of cultural and economic policy, like the Indian-head penny, first minted in 1859, Parkman's 1851 rendering of Pontiac indicated that one phase of American history, that encompassing the first decades of Removal, was reaching a close. In a journal entry of 1859, Thoreau, long a philosophical student of Native American relics and names, could declare that the arrowhead was a kind of "stone fruit" or a seed, slow to germinate, that would "bear crops of philosophers and poets." In fact, however, the poetic appropriation of Indians as a primary element in American mythology had begun long before. Because few writers had direct knowledge of Native American life, most relied on romantic clichés and frontier tales of savage violence. As Washington Irving remarked in an 1848 essay, "Traits of Indian Character," Indians were likely to have been doubly mistreated: "The colonist often treated them like beasts of the forest; and the author has endeavoured to justify him [the colonist] in his outrages." Hardly immune to romanticism himself, Irving found that the "proud independence, which formed the main pillar of savage virtue, has been shaken down, and the whole moral fabric lies in ruins." Turned into a "ruin" in both aesthetic and moral terms, American Indians were just as significant a problem for the intellectual as they were for the government official. For both, the disappearance of the present tribes could be understood as part of the same geohistorical process that was sweeping forward the Euro-American race. The ideology of Removal was required to perform a double function. On the one hand, it had to provide a philosophy to justify purging the continent of "alien" and potentially deadly people. On the other hand, it had to create a political and cultural medium in which conquest could be naturalized or set within a panoramic elaboration of predestined history, as in Cornelius Matthews's novel *Behemoth: A Legend of the Mound-Builders* (1839), which treats the remains of the prehistoric forerunners of contemporary American Indians as the North American equivalent of Greek antiquities. "A decaying bone, an old helmet, a mouldering fragment of wall," Matthews wrote, can make us feel our "kindred with generations buried long ago."

Irving, for one, was not sanguine about the survival of American Indians in actuality or in his dignified remembrance in the national myths of America:

If, perchance, some dubious memorial of them should survive, it may be in the romantic dreams of the poet, to people in imagination his glades and groves, like the fauns and satyrs and sylvan deities of antiquity. But should he venture upon the dark story of their wrongs and wretchedness; should he tell how they were invaded, corrupted, and despoiled, driven from their native abodes and the sepulchres of their fathers, hunted like wild beasts about the earth, and sent down with violence and butchery to the grave, posterity will either turn with horror or incredulity from the tale, or blush with indignation at the inhumanity of their forefathers.

The "dark story" would get told only with difficulty, and even the most generous accounts struggled against ingrained notions of savagism and the tendency to romanticize Native American life in compensation for its destruction. With some irony, the Indians' own words and stories, whether preserved in oral tradition or by sympathetic travelers, would become literary artifacts, not unlike the stone and clay relics that pioneer farmers (and natural philosophers like Thoreau) would find for generations. An anthropological or archeological attitude toward Indians thus preceded actual fieldwork; Indians were memorialized in the very moment they were doomed, celebrated as part of America's innocent, mythic past even as they were pushed ever westward and declared to be savages beyond the bounds of civilized life.

In the Euro-American literature devoted to American Indians, as in that devoted to slavery, official speeches and documents, ethnographic materials, and historical commentary are equal in importance and often in literary quality to the work of novelists, dramatists, and poets. Moreover, the questions of African American slavery and Indian Removal were not unrelated but together belonged to the central dilemma of race in its relation to the promise of the American Revolution. The Declaration of Independence spoke with alarm of the "merciless Indian savages," who threatened colonial life, and Washington, Jefferson, Adams, and others of the early national generation were often less than sympathetic to the Indians' plight as long as they were perceived to be military enemies. Yet black slaves and American Indians, however they might both be ranked below whites in the hierarchy of "nature" (as would Mexicans by the 1830s), hardly constituted a single issue. In fact, as Tocqueville noted in *Democracy in America,* their situations could be seen as nearly opposite: "the Negro has reached the ultimate limits of slavery, whereas the Indian lives on the extreme edge of freedom" and enjoys a kind of "barbarous independence." Tocqueville's portrait of the American Indian was sympathetic – if nonetheless informed by an ineradicable belief in savagism – but his theory of the Indian's "freedom" bears notice because it defines the double attitude American culture would hold more and more rigidly as the century passed and Indian tribes perished. In this prevailing theory, Indians were noble, courageous, and independent; but they were also improvident, childlike, superstitious, vengeful, and thus a threat to stable and complex social order.

Both official policy and popular literature promulgated this double attitude, as did some Native Americans who converted to Christianity and accepted white social and economic culture. The result was an image of the American Indian often placed in polar opposition to the advancing Euro-American society: primitivism versus civilization, demonic revenge versus Christian charity, or nomadic hunting life versus property rights and agricultural development. The defining characteristics of "savage" life advanced by politicians, historians, and imaginative authors alike included Indians' propensity to fight by guerrilla methods and to indulge in scalping and other brutalities; their lack of Christian forgiveness and idealization of vengeance; their weak family structure and immature sense of organized society; and their stoic willingness to endure intense pain and hardship. That the same savage traits were also assigned to white pioneers who chose a wild frontier life over the confinement of society only underlines the fact that the idea of the Indian and the idea of the frontier were often inseparable in both geographical and psychological terms. As Thoreau said he might devour a woodchuck raw in order to incorporate its "wildness," so Indians and their ways might be sought out by the frontiersman, the renegade from society, or writers determined to place their work at the borders of a developing frontier tradition. Yet Indians, like their land and its riches, would likewise be devoured in the process – either literally exterminated or else absorbed into the nation's culture, subtly changing it perhaps but submitting at last to its dominating myths. In any event, official policy would remain divided between the advocates of virtual annihilation and those like Jedediah Morse, who in his *Report to the Secretary of War . . . on Indian Affairs* (1822) predicted both the necessity and the enormous difficulty of the "godlike work" of education and acculturation.

Some portraits were legitimately sympathetic to the Indians' plight; others simply took advantage of the popular rage for melodrama and sentiment on stage and in prose fiction. On occasion a virtual catalogue of major ideas appeared in a single work, as in James S. French's novel about General William Henry Harrison's campaign against the Shawnee chief Tecumseh, *Elkswatawa; or, the Prophet of the West* (1836). Both the novel and its subject are instructive examples of the mythologizing process at work, and *Elkswatawa* is best seen in the context of other treatments of its events and ideas that demonstrate how fiction and drama overlapped with historiography and Indian narrative to create a multidimensional artifact of composed American Indian life.

In the face of relentless advances of white settlers, Tecumseh had set out in 1811 to organize the tribes of the entire Mississippi Valley in an alliance. Along with his brother Elkswatawa, known as the Prophet, Tecumseh espoused a form of Indian nationalism that rejected all corrupting influences of Euro-American life. Defeated by Harrison at the battle of Tippecanoe, an event that helped precipitate the War of 1812, Tecumseh's forces fell into disarray and his powerful leadership was dissipated. Yet over the next several decades, as the conclusion of the war and the advent of Indian Removal opened the Mississippi Valley to unimpeded white pioneer expansion, Tecumseh was readily incorporated into a national myth, as though his defeat necessitated ritual internalization. For example, whereas William R. Wallace's *The Battle of Tippecanoe* (1835) made Tecumseh's enemy, General Harrison, the hero in an ornate patriotic epic, George H. Colton's heroic poem *Tecumseh; Or the West Thirty Years Since* (1842) depicted the Shawnee chief as a savage hero, destined to fall to a greater force. Colton memorialized that fall by providing Tecumseh with a pseudoglorious "War Song" to mark his passing:

> I smell the carnage of the battle!
> Terrible is the strife,
> Where gushes the tide of life!
> But 'tis joy, as we sink,
> Of the red stream to drink,
> That warms from a foeman our hatchet and knife!

Even poems with opposing heroes, that is to say, could accomplish much the same cultural work. In a more critical vein, Benjamin Drake's *Life of Tecumseh* (1841) portrayed Tecumseh as brave and humane, even a military genius (Drake quotes James Hall, who called the Shawnee chief a "Napoleon of the West"), whereas the white advance was seen to be the result of "insatiable cupidity and a wanton disregard of justice." The less sympathetic portrait in Benjamin B. Thatcher's *Indian Biography* (1832), though it made Tecumseh a great statesman and patriot, recognized a fatality in the fact that he used his great genius in fighting "only for wild lands and wild liberty." What were claimed to be Tecumseh's own words, quoted in a variety of texts, became ironic evidence of Euro-American destiny – for example, this 1811 speech, advocating the unity of all Indians and invoking aid from the British, which was recorded in a popular captivity narrative, John Dunn Hunter's *Memoirs of a Captivity Among the Indians of North America* (1824):

> Brothers. – Who are the white people that we should fear them? They cannot run fast, and are good marks to shoot at: they are only men; our fathers have killed many of them: we are not squaws, and we will stain the earth red with their blood.
> Brothers. – The Great Spirit is angry with our enemies; he speaks in thunder, and the earth swallows up villages, and drinks up the Mississippi. The great waters will cover their lowlands; their corn cannot grow; and the Great Spirit will sweep those who escape to the hills from the earth with his terrible breath.

It is in this context that both Tecumseh's famous oration and a representative novel like French's ought to be read. Speeches by both Tecumseh and General Harrison are quoted in *Elkswatawa,* and Tecumseh appears as a brave, almost magnificent figure; but these elements are subordinated to the archetypal story of the rescue of a white heroine from captivity. Because it converges with the battle of Tippecanoe, the rescue becomes emblematic of the justification for warfare often urged by politicians and military leaders: that frontier settlers had to be "rescued" from marauding Indians. The white Indian hater, evocatively named Earth, returns to a peaceful life in civilized society at the end of *Elkswatawa,* suggesting that the killing of savage Indians is only a temporary and practical phase of American progress, which must itself momentarily employ savage methods in order to triumph. Tecumseh's humanity and courage, and the idealism of his brother, the

Prophet Elkswatawa, whose vision of a pristine, communal native existence is tragically betrayed, are thus traits to admire but ones that, significantly, now belong to a past subject to the generic laws of romantic historical fiction. Tecumseh, one could say, is deliberately staged as both a historical and political icon within these texts, a figure whose sacrificial role translates imperial warfare into naturalized destiny.

The generic expectations of Romantic historical fiction shaped most novelistic treatments of American Indians, and in some cases their rationale became an explicit part of the author's concerns. James Fenimore Cooper, William Gilmore Simms, and Nathaniel Hawthorne are only the most famous of the many authors who sought to develop a theory of the Romance suitable to an American setting. Like Hawthorne's preface to *The Scarlet Letter,* such theories exploited the possibilities of American exceptionalism but at the same time worked to discover the historical depth and resonance of the country that critics, both foreign and domestic, claimed America lacked. In the case of American Indians, the Romance thus joined forces with ethnography, and for imaginative writers such as Irving and Thoreau, and historians such as McKenney and Schoolcraft, the Indian's demise became perfectly representative of America's potential antiquity even as it authorized a progressive futurity.

Although most writing by whites about American Indians in the period from 1820 through 1865 at least implicitly reflected such a dual vision, it is especially prominent in the major historical and ethnographical work that preserved in written form a large body of Native American history and legends while attempting to give a coherent, if inevitably distorted, account of it in Euro-American terms. The histories produced in the antebellum period, because they were usually governed by nationalistic assumptions about the superiority of the new American government and its people, constitute a significant statement of the "Indian problem." Although most historians took for granted the Indian's eventual displacement, several accounts that were not prominently ethnological in character sought to provide reliable and sympathetic information about Native American life before it disappeared. Among these are Henry Trumbull's *History of the Indian Wars* (1811; revised, 1841), John G. Heckewelder's *History, Manners, and Customs of the Indian Nations* (1818), Benjamin B. Thatcher's *Indian Biography* (1832), Harvey Newcomb's *The North American Indians* (1835), John Frost's *Indian Wars of the United States* (1840), and Samuel Goodrich's *Lives of Celebrated American Indians* (1843). One of the best-known works, Samuel Drake's *Biography and History of the Indians of North America* (1832), although not as comprehensive or informed as the later works of McKenney, Schoolcraft, and Catlin, is especially important as a compendium of history, biography, captivity narratives, and Native American oratory. In addition to Drake's own critique of the methods of white progress, his reliance on primary (but translated) Indian documents, such as Speckled Snake's reply to Jackson, noted above, gives his work a dimension of strongly counterpointed voices.

This was not always true of more prominent work. The period's leading national history, George Bancroft's *A History of the United States* (1834–75), depicted Native American culture as politically dignified but socially primitive – a combination of simplicity, immorality, and irrationality. In his sections on "The Red Men East of the Mississippi," for example, Bancroft noted that "the American savage has tongue and palate and lips and throat; the power to utter flowing sounds, the power to hiss"; but before contact with Europeans, none of the eastern tribes "had discriminated the sounds which [they] articulated" and formed an alphabet, "and the only mode of writing was by rude imitations and symbols." The savage's "system of morals" was but a "license to gratify his animal instincts," and even if the red men carried the federal form of government to a perfection rivaling the ancient Hellenic councils, they were still "deficient in the power of imagination and abstraction" and "inferior in reason and in ethics."

Bancroft's chapter is a good index of the ways in which historical and ethnological writing about Indians overlapped. Both assumed that writing was the primary technology that distinguished whites from Indians; by the same token, writing, along with the collecting of legends and artifacts, was seen to be the primary means by which Indians would be preserved, since in actuality expectations for the survival of tribal life were slim. The force of this assumption was codified when Albert Gallatin founded the Bureau of American Ethnology in 1842, centralizing the enormous labor to catalogue Indian languages and customs that took place over the nineteenth century, an effort according to prevailing standards of inquiry, that constituted one of the first large-scale scientific projects in the United States. The foremost American ethnologist of the nineteenth century, Lewis Henry Morgan (1818–81), created over his career a paradigmatic anthropological picture of American Indians as sublime but simple, the noble victims of white rapaciousness yet destined to wither under the powerful advance of a superior culture. Morgan's most influential work appeared in the 1870s, and by then he spoke straightforwardly of the preservation of Indian life within the structures of anthropological museum work. In an essay entitled "Montezuma's Dinner," which appeared in 1876, he remarked: "The question is still before us as a nation, whether we will undertake the work of furnishing to the world a scientific exposition of Indian society, or leave it as it now appears, crude, unmeaning, unintelligible, a chaos of contradictions and puerile absurdities." If persons willing to undertake such work could be found, Morgan insisted, "it will be necessary for them to do as Herodotus did in Asia and Africa, to visit the native tribes at their villages and encampments, and study their institutions as living organisms, their condition, and their plan of life."

Morgan's own research began many years earlier, however, and his *Ancient Society* (1877), which put forward a theory of the social evolution of all world races from a common origin, grew out of earlier studies among Native Americans, in particular the Iroquois. His later work was less prone to the condemnations of "savage" traits that are scattered throughout his first important study, *League of the Ho-de-no-sau-nee, or Iroquois* (1851). The *League* appeared in the same year of Parkman's *Conspiracy of Pontiac* and the first volume of Schoolcraft's monumental *Historical and Statistical Information,* and the three works all represented in their different ways the common belief that the Indians' reign was finished, suitable now only for historical and ethnological evaluation. Based on his famous "Letters on the Iroquois" in the *American Review* in 1847, Morgan's *League* offers a detailed account of tribal government, numerous renderings of tales and mythic beliefs, and descriptions of family life and customs. As a people without sophisticated literacy or industrial arts, however, the Iroquois are depicted by Morgan as tapped in the hunter state, referred to as "the zero of human society." The Iroquois are united with the phenomena of the natural world, but they pay the price by falling "under the giant embrace of civilization, victims of the successful warfare of intelligent social life upon the rugged obstacles of nature." Morgan's arguments on behalf of Indian land rights and his detailed, ostensibly objective record of Iroquois culture thus remain in conflict with his view that the Iroquois are themselves an aspect of "rugged nature" and his consequent belief in the superiority of the Euro-American community.

Equally important in establishing American Indians as a subject of study was the painter and writer George Catlin (1796–1872). Some of his work, like the notorious accounts of a painful Mandan initiation ceremony, recorded in most detail in *O-kee-pa: A Religious Ceremony and Other Customs of the Mandans* (1867), was attacked by Schoolcraft; but Catlin's description of the Mandan ceremony was defended by Morgan and corroborated by later researchers. If Catlin's work is less professedly scientific than Morgan's, his descriptive observations, if not his romantic racial speculations, are comparatively reliable. He grew up in frontier Pennsylvania and, like Morgan, was trained for a legal career, but he abandoned law for portrait painting and seized upon American Indians as his life's work. In 1832 Catlin began an eight-year journey among the western and southern Indians, visiting some forty-eight different tribes and producing over five hundred portraits, landscapes, and paintings of artifacts. Setting out by steamboat up the Missouri, Catlin wrote to his publisher that he was intent on the Indians' rescue – the rescue "not of their lives or their race (for they are 'doomed' and must perish)" but rather "of their looks and their modes," so that "phoenix-like, they may rise from a 'stain on a painter's palette,' and live again upon canvass, and stand forth for centuries yet to come, the living monuments of a noble race." The record of the Indian's image, then, the resurrection from his dying body of a mythic presence in the monumental form of hundreds of canvases, was all Catlin could hope to achieve. Artistic and literary representation would take the place of tribal survival (as Cooper had already begun to prove in his Leatherstocking Tales) and would fix an artistically objectified figure of the American Indian at a moment of tragic heroism outside the progressive flow of historical time.

Recorded in *Letters and Notes on the Manners, Customs, and Condition of the North American Indians* (1841), Catlin's trip ranks among the most significant Euro-American imperial explorations of the century. It gave him the means to set down in pictures and words "the living manners, customs, and character of an interesting race of people who are rapidly passing away from the face of the earth – lending a hand to a dying nation, who have no historians or biographers of their own to portray with fidelity their native looks and history." Catlin also organized a popular show of his paintings and artifacts and staged dances and ritual performances by actual Indians in the United States, England, and France in the 1840s. From 1852 to 1857 he undertook another long exploring trip through Central and South America and the Far West, which he recorded in several volumes, including *Last Rambles Amongst the Indians of the Rocky Mountains and the Andes* (1867). These travels reinforced his impression that increasingly Indians could be seen on the frontiers only "as a basket of *dead game* – harassed, chased, bleeding, and dead." Catlin abhored the general misuse of the term "savage" and responded to the tribes he visited in respecful terms. Yet he also perpetuated the naive hypothesis that Native Americans untouched by white life – those beyond the frontier – remained nobly pure, whereas contact with white traders and pioneers inevitably degraded the native tribes. For Catlin, a perfect exponent of the parodox of ethnography, civilization was certain "to obliterate the grace and beauty of Nature." His extensive painted catalogue of Indian customs, utensils, clothing, houses, and faces was intended to preserve from extinction a race who, like the buffalo, had "taken up their *last abode.*"

Despite their devotion to Indian study, neither Catlin nor Morgan worked from within the governmental structure that was responsible for administering American law on the frontier. Thomas McKenney, author with James Hall of the three-volume *History of the Indian Tribes of North American* (1836–44), labored diligently within the government to preserve a record of Native American life even as he may be said to have overseen its vanquishing. As superintendent of Indian trade, an office in the War Department, McKenney (1785–1859) administered the system of government trading posts, and as head of the Bureau of Indian Affairs, created in 1824, he became a strong advocate of philanthropic reform among Indian tribes. On several occasions McKenney helped to negotiate treaties in the field with Indians of the North and the Southeast. Although he was thrown out of office by Jackson in 1830, McKenney fundamentally believed, along with the president, that Removal was the only way to save the Indians – *and* to make their lands available for cultivation. McKenney come to office largely ignorant of actual Indian life, and his early volume *Sketches of a Tour to the Lake* (1827), which covers the trip with Lewis Cass to negotiate with the Ojibwa, is sometimes mistaken in its facts. Later works such as *On the Wrongs and Rights of the Indians* (1846) and his *Memoirs* (1846) continue to lament Indian vengefulness and improvidence, and McKenney always endorsed conversion to white values of agriculture, education, and Christianity. His major work, the *History* written with Hall, contains reproductions of numerous portraits of Indian chiefs and leaders by Charles Bird King and James Otto that McKenney had assembled in an "Indian Gallery" of the War Department. The reproductions accompany biographical and historical chapters on many tribes and about a hundred and fifty individuals, among them Red Jacket, Kiontwogky (Cornplanter), Sequoyah, Osceola, Black Hawk, and Major Ridge. Most of the biographical text has been attributed to McKenney, but a separate essay signed by Hall outlined a recognizable theory of savagism. Nomadic, improvident, and lacking a "code of empires" that could be integrated into international law, the Indian tribes of America are in essence depicted as part of the kingdom of animals. "Lost in the most degrading superstition," Hall remarks, "they look upon Nature with a vacant eye, never inquiring into the causes, or the consequences of the great revolutions of Nature, or into the structure or operations of their own minds." McKenney's view was less pessimistic. Like Catlin, he had a genuine humanitarian interest in Indian reform – certainly preferable, he thought, to genocide – but his great work also turned into a virtual museum of antiquities in his own lifetime. His Indian Gallery became part of the Smithsonian in 1858 (most of the portraits were destroyed in an 1865 fire). It effectively marked the absorption or elimination of many Native American tribes in the eastern United States, and it is strikingly emblematic of their cultural containment by Euro-American writers and politicians in the antebellum period.

Easily the most important Euro-American work of ethnographic preservation of Native American culture was done by Henry Rowe Schoolcraft (1793–1864). A geologist and Indian agent from 1822 to 1841 in the Great Lakes region, Schoolcraft married an Indian, lived with various tribes and studied their languages (especially the Ojibwa, Ottawa, and Lakota), and attempted both to catalogue every fact of Native American civilization he uncovered and at the same time to justify its displacement by a superior culture. He accompanied McKenney and Cass on a treaty expedition in 1820 and recorded the event in *Narrative Journal of Travels Through the Northwestern Regions of the United States* (1821). His explorations of the valley and sources of the Mississippi are detailed in *Travels in the Central Portions of the Mississippi Valley* (1825) and *Narrative of an Expedition through the Upper Mississippi* (1834). These works, along with the earlier *A View of the Lead Mines of Missouri* (1819) and a poem about the Mississippi River entitled *The Rise of the West* (1830), demonstrate Schoolcraft's ability to combine precise geological and geographical observation with a theory of U.S. expansion. Like other trappers, miners, and explorers, Schoolcraft saw the land with double vision: on the one hand, he valued aesthetically its pristine beauty; on the other, he was aware of its speculative value in land and mineral rights. Because he saw Indians the same way, Schoolcraft's work of recording Native American customs and history, which occupied the last half of his life, fails to make clear sense of a great wealth of data.

Before his six-volume *Historical and Statistical Information Respecting the History, Condition, and Prospects of the Indian Tribes of the United States* (1851–7), Schoolcraft had already written several ethnological treatments of Indians and their literature, all of which were reprinted numerous times under various titles during the next several decades. *Algic Researches* (1839) collected a group of Ojibwa and Ottawa legends and myths. Reprinted in expanded form in 1856 as *The Myth of Hiawatha,* the volume capitalized on the fact that Longfellow had relied heavily on Schoolcraft's tale of Manibozho, an Ojibwa trickster figure, for his famous poem *The Song of Hiawatha.* (Whittier, Lowell, and other writers would also be inspired by Schoolcraft's materials.) He used the legend of Manibozho and the rest of the volume's tales to corroborate his theory that the apparent ambiguities and monstrosities in the tales are a result of Indian "barbarism." *Onéota* (1844–5), a collection of primary materials and essays by various hands, and *Notes on the Iroquois* (1846), a report to the federal government on the prospects for converting the tribe to market agriculture, reached a similar conclusion. The Indian's supposedly barbaric state, they argue, makes white reform difficult, even for the agent, like Schoolcraft, who attempts to be as faithful as possible to the language and forms of Native American culture.

Schoolcraft, by then superintendent of Indian affairs was commissioned by the secretary of war in 1847 to collect statistics and cultural material illustrating the present condition and future prospects of all Native American tribes. He gathered information from a variety of sources, including his own previous writings, and within several years began to publish his massive *Historical and Statistical Information*. As in earlier works, he approached his material with a combination of sympathy and perplexity, if not contempt. His point of view is without question that of the superior who acknowledges certain strong and admirable personal traits in Indians but finds them culturally weak, socially uncouth, and morally degenerate. His purpose, he remarks, is to furnish a basis in both political and philosophical terms, for the government's Indian policy. Indians for Schoolcraft are "fallen," in a state of decline; they worship nature, not God, and they hunt instead of raising grain and developing industrial arts (on these factual points alone, Schoolcraft, like many other Euro-American observers, was often simply wrong). Schoolcraft is committed to the theory that the Indian's degradation is a result of neglecting "higher and sublime principles." At times he seems almost impulsively unable to interpret properly the fascinating abundance of material he collects, and his volumes are often a chaos of evidence. And yet Schoolcraft's governing myth continually serves to organize potentially intractable native material. For example, his account of the importance of the Oneida Stone as a symbol of that tribe's collective nationality intersects with his minerological interest in the formation, which then becomes indicative of the primacy of "scientific" over "primitive" thought. Strategically extending his mischaracterization of the Oneida as a hunting society, Schoolcraft writes that no observer witnessing the vista of farms and villages visible from the top of the stone can "view this rich scene of industrial opulence, without calling to mind that once proud and indomitable race of hunters and warriors, whose name the country bears." That tribe, however, was "destined to fall before the footsteps of civilization," and today its people are dead, scattered, or subjugated to the "social liberality" of "the school, the church, the farm, and the workshop." The scientifically based ideal of market production – central to the collective "tribal" life of Euro-American progress – is thus derived from the totemic stone in such a way that the now-vanquished tribe becomes a symbolic father race to the new American.

The volumes of Schoolcraft's *Historical and Statistical Information* vary in their contents and organization, but each typically contains historical accounts of various tribes, etymological and mythological studies of their languages, histories of migrations and warfare, and sections on geography, mineralogy, antiquities, medicine, totems, demonology, and graphic arts, all held together by Schoolcraft's theories of savage decline. They are illustrated by the brilliant plates of Seth Eastman, a military officer who, while stationed at Fort Snelling, Minnesota, studied and sketched Ojibwa and Sioux scenes that he hoped to assemble in an Indian Gallery. When Catlin turned down Schoolcraft's request for illustrations (because the government had refused to purchase his paintings), Eastman prepared hundreds of plates, which appeared in *Historical and Statistical Information* as well as in two 1853 volumes: *The Romance of Indian Life* and *The American Aboriginal Portfolio*, coauthored with his wife, Mary Eastman. The very concept of an "aboriginal portfolio" suggests the contradictory imposition of the artifice of representation upon the artifacts of native culture and Native Americans themselves. The Eastmans' volumes demonstrated with visual clarity that the two decades following the initiation of Removal in 1830 coincided with the escalating white appropriation of the Indian's world as the territory of romance. Their earlier volume, *Dahcotah; or, Life and Legends of the Sioux* (1849), was a rambling compilation of anecdotes and ethnographic materials, most valuable for its brief sketches centering on the lives of frontier women. But its preface by Caroline Kirkland succinctly incorporates the mythologized imperial portrait of the American Indian generated by a frontier ideology. "The study of Indian character is the study of the unregenerate human heart," and only determined benevolence can rescue the savage from his enslaving traits of envy and revenge. By the same token, the Indians virtually "live" poetry, and we should "write it out for them." Their great poetic value lies in their "aboriginality," in their role as "our" lost past which can serve as the basis for a nationalistic literature: "nothing is wanting but a Homer to build this Iliad material into 'lofty rhyme,' or a Scott to weave it into border romance." The models were thus still foreign for Kirkland and Eastman, as they were for Cooper, Morgan, and Schoolcraft, but the material was purely "American," not least because it was by then so fully enveloped in the shroud of fantastic legend. The picture frame, like the book of Indian life, became a domain of distorting ethnographic appropriation at just the historical moment American novelists like Hawthorne, Cooper, and Melville were most concerned to define the fictive territory of American Romance.

Schoolcraft's masterwork, appearing at the midpoint of the period later known as the American Renaissance, participates in the triumph of a mythology of American mission and savage decline that animates some of the most important imaginative works of the antebellum years. That is not to say, however, that *Historical and Statistical Information* is itself pure fabrication. If it fails to meet modern anthropological standards and systematically imposes an alien ideology on the materials it surveys, it nonetheless remains a powerful study, both as an expression of Schoolcraft's own representative mind and as a collection of primary Native American material, including pre-Columbian antiquities, detailed linguistic studies, portraits and illustrations of contemporary artifacts, speeches and biographies of famous chiefs, and delineations of Indian dream theory. All of this is juxtaposed to countervailing documents such as cranial measurement statistics, President Monroe's 1825 speech on Removal, and bloody captivity narratives. There are also apocryphal reports of atrocities in warfare, such as the passage quoted from Jonathan Carver's 1788 volume *Travels through the Interior Parts of North America* (later echoed in the famous scene in Cooper's *The Last of the Mohicans*), which described the 1757 massacre of British troops and civilians at Fort William Henry: "Many of these savages drank the blood of their victims, as it flowed warm from the fatal wound." By containing a mixture of contrary impulses originating in observed American Indian culture and in the often demonized mythology of Euro-American cultural production, Schoolcraft's *Historical and Statistical Information* is a comprehensive expression of antebellum frontier ideology. The encyclopedia character of the work — its incorporation of myth, technical lore, scientific speculation, and political judgment — along with its habit of symbolic self-constitution parallels other contemporary epic expressions of the American imperial imagination, such as Thoreau's journals, Whitman's poetry, and Melville's fiction.

From the standpoint of literature, however, Schoolcraft's work is most valuable for recording numerous Native American tales, songs, orations, and legends in paraphrase or in translation. Imagining the wilderness to be a storehouse of symbolic language corresponding to primitive consciousness, Schoolcraft, like many of his contemporaries, saw the Native American mind as inherently "poetic" and spiritual, yet he paradoxically refused to admit that Indian traditions or oral expressions could constitute a proper literature. In particular, Schoolcraft found pictographic material to be "the literature of the Indian" written in the "language of idolatry," evidence of an elaborate craft but one that showed the Indian to be unchanged since pre-Columbian times. Besides recording events of warfare, religion, love, prophecy, cosmology, hunting, and the like, pictography could also become an ironic emblem of its own limitations. Thus, when Schoolcraft reproduces a complicated Ojibwa pictographic petition to President Taylor in 1849 asking for retrocession of lost land, its ethnological value is dwarfed by its practical futility. Similarly, the legends often point apocalyptically to the ultimate results of white conquest, as in the case of Manibozho, the trickster–warrior said to be living in the ice of the Arctic Ocean: "We fear the white race will some day discover his retreat and drive him off. Then the end of the world is at hand, for as soon as he puts his foot on the earth again, it will take fire, and every living creature will perish in the flames." Like some other Native American stories of the period, this legend appears to displace onto whites the annihilation suffered by Indians; but in any case it is a more accurate rendition of Native American thought than Longfellow's appropriation of the legend in *Hiawatha*. Schoolcraft wrote that his aim in the massive research he conducted was "to furnish a true basis for the governmental policy to be pursued with [the Indians] as tribes and nations, and for the pursuit of the momentous object of their reclamation and salvation as men." What he did not recognize (or chose not to articulate) was that the twin projects of removal and salvation, although they were often announced in the same language, were built on a contradiction as fundamental as that between progress and genocide.

Schoolcraft's achievement in fieldwork and analysis is a telling combination of fine perception and cultural misunderstanding. As a result, there is the risk that his tales and artifacts will be ignored altogether or will appear as unrevealing as the arrowhead of which Thoreau wrote in his journal, "it is no digusting mummy, but a clean stone, the best symbol or letter that could have been transmitted to me . . . no single inscription on a particular rock, but a footprint − rather a mindprint − left everywhere, and altogether illegible." Whatever the ethnocentric limitations of Schoolcraft's work or that of other nineteenth-century white writers, however, the period's imperial ethnography remains a valuable resource on Native Americans. Modern readers, for example, have made important use of Schoolcraft's collected legends, the pictographic poetry and political orations, and the vast number of verses and songs, such as these Ojibwa war songs recorded in 1824:

> Todotobi penaise
> Ka dow wiawiaun.
>
> I wish to have the body of the fiercest bird,
> As swift − as cruel − as strong.
>
> Ne wawaibena, neowai
> Kagait ne minwaindum
> Nebunaikumig tshebaibewishenaun.
>
> I cast away my body to the chance of battle.
> Full happy am I to lie on the field −
> On the field over the enemy's line.

More than anything else, perhaps, Schoolcrafts's project commandingly represents the Euro-American perspective on the great diversity of Indian cultural expression. Little appreciated even by some current interpretations of Native American life is his early recognition that the dimensions of Native American "literature" would have to include not just songs, chants, and oral legends but also pictography on animal skins or walls, totem poles, ornate pottery or weaving, inscriptions on bark, pipes, or other ceremonial objects, beaded belts or bands, and other forms of expression in signs and artifacts central to Native American traditions.

The records made by Schoolcraft and others in the antebellum period highlight the ironic fact that American Indian texts (i.e., written documents) were seldom produced or transcribed until the 1830s, coincident with the acceleration of Removal policies. Moreover, the primary collected examples of the Indian's voices – their war rhetoric and their protests against violated promises and treaties – were typically framed by an alien ideology by the time they reached the American public. Virtually all examples of recorded Native American literature prior to the twentieth century were a combination of transcription and translation, with the attendant potential for mirsrepresentation, intentional or not, that those processes imply. Much of the collected written literature, even that from decades or centuries earlier, was compiled under the auspices of the Bureau of American Ethnography and published in their bulletins beginning in the 1880s, the point of final military defeat for most western tribes. Especially in the case of tales, songs, and poems, Native American literature is traditional and communal. With the exception of specific autobiographical works written in English by Indians, no single author can or in many cases should be identified, and the date of a work's origin is difficult to ascertain. In many instances, too, the work was originally performed in song, dance, chant, or ritual drama, and however precise the descriptions by Schoolcraft, Catlin, or others, these components can seldom be reconstructed with complete authenticity.

From the pre-Civil War period, the preserved written literature of American Indians is generally of three kinds: myths, tales, and songs transcribed by ethnologists; war or treaty orations recorded by witnesses; and autobiographical works, essays, and some prose fiction by Indians or their amanuenses. Although ethnological transcription of Indian literature has taken place primarily since the beginning of the twentieth century, scholars and writers in the early nineteenth century often recognized the vital significance of the oral tradition of Native Americans. Writing in the *North American Review* in 1815, for example, Walter Channing called upon that tradition as one means of establishing a national American literature. Sounding a common theme, Channing remarked that the United States as yet had no national character and doubted, therefore, that it could be said to have a national literature. Even though circumstances in colonial and postrevolutionary America had been "peculiarly opposed to literary originality," however, Channing argued that the oral traditions of America's "aborigines" could be said to constitute the nation's proper native literature. Channing joined other commentators – missionaries, ethnologists, and novelists like Cooper – in pointing to the unique sounds and metaphoric figures of Native American language:

The language of the Indian . . . was made to express his emotions during his observance of nature, and these emotions were taught him at a school, in which the master was nature, and a most unsophisticated heart the scholar. Hence it is as bold as his own unshackled conceptions, and as rapid as his own step. It is now as rich as the soil on which he was nurtured, and ornamented with every blossom that blows in his path. It is now elevated and soaring, for his image is the eagle, and now precipitous and hoarse as the cataract among whose mists he is descanting. In the oral literature of the Indian, even when rendered in a language enfeebled by excessive cultivation, every one has found genuine originality.

Channing's assessment, despite its fanciful and stilted language, points to those features of American Indian literature that modern scholars and poets have continued to recognize as central to its traditional forms. Although it is very difficult to generalize about a literature produced by hundreds of diverse tribes speaking as many languages and dialects, there is a pervasive emphasis in Indian literature on a consonance between expressed form and natural or physiological process. Native American literature is grounded in the rhythms of nature and the body; it often employs repetition and stylized ceremonial forms to create on organic compact with the surrounding visual and aural world. Frequently, commonplace events or daily actions are infused with mystic or spiritual elements, and a dreamlife or sense of other dimensions of the universe pervades the basic forms of linguistic or sign expression. Harmonious wholeness with the universe is the subject of much ceremonial material, whose chants and songs function to restore unnatural divisions between self, spirit, community, and the natural world. For example, a widely translated Navajo night chant designed to heal the rift of spiritual being fuses the separated self with a world at once natural and cosmic. As a small portion of the chant indicates, the calling forth of the divinity of rain links the spiritual journey of regeneration to the earth's cycles of growth and production:

With the rainbow landing high on the ends of your wings, come to us soaring.
With the near darkness made of the dark cloud, of the he-rain, of the dark mist,
                              and of the she-rain, come to us.
With the darkness on earth, come to us.
With these I wish the foam floating on the flowing water over the roots of the
                              great corn.
I have made your sacrifice.
I have prepared a smoke for you. . . .
Happily I recover.
Happily my interior becomes cool.
Happily my limbs regain their power. . . .
Happily abundant passing showers I desire.
Happily an abundance of vegetation I desire.
Happily an abundance of pollen I desire. . . .

Happily may fair white corn, to the ends of the earth, come with you.
Happily may fair yellow corn, to the ends of the earth, come with you.
Happily may fair blue corn, to the ends of the earth, come with you. . . .

Native American oral literature is thus inherently tribal and communal, inspired by and focused on links across generations and geographically diverse communities rather than on aesthetic distinction or individual self-expression. Ceremonial expression — composed of song, chant, story, and dance — serves to integrate private emotion into a cosmic network of experience that unites men and women with the processes of the earth; and this multi-dimensional language itself becomes a conduit of shared tribal knowledge. Mysticism is thus not the province of special study or of a select priestly order but is instead an essential component of the holistic consciousness all share in the experience of a living, traditional culture.

In most cases the traditional legends and songs cannot be said with certainty to belong to a particular period, and it is therefore difficult or counterproductive to interpret American Indian literature according to the chronological divisions of Euro-American literary history. Many important tales and songs concern the creation of the earth or of a particular tribe, often when a hero leads his or her people forth from a cave, lake, or underground world. As in other literary traditions, flood myths, stories of regeneration after natural catastrophe, and accounts of the creation or spiritual dimensions of the world's phenomena predominate. Native American sacred myths often emphasize a complete integrity of body and spirit and an intersection of human belief and action with the natural world of mineral, plants, animals, weather, and the astronomical heavens. For example, the beginning of a Pawnee creation myth personifies divine beings above as stars but humanizes the creation of the earth as a story of courtship and consummation:

Over all is Tirawa, the One Above, changeless and supreme. From Tirawa come all things: Tirawa made the heavens and the stars.
The Pathway of Departed Spirits [the Milky Way] parts the heavens. In the beginning, east of the path was Man: west of the path was Woman. In the east was creation planned: in the west was creation fulfilled. All that the stars did in the heavens foretold what would befall upon the earth, for as yet was the earth not made.
In the west dwelt the White Star Woman, the Evening Star, who must be sought and overcome that creation might be achieved. From the east went forth the Great Star, the Morning Star, to find and overcome the Evening Star, that creation might be achieved. . . .

A Cherokee creation myth combines poetic vision of elemental creative powers lodged in godlike animals with an apprehension of the primordial processes of geological and biological formation:

The earth is a great island floating in a sea of water, and suspended at each of the four cardinal points by a cord hanging down from the sky vault, which is of solid rock. When the world grows old and worn out, the people will die and the cords will break and let the earth sink down into the ocean, and all will be water again. . . . At first the earth was flat and very soft and wet. The animals were anxious to get down, and sent out . . . the Great Buzzard, the father of all the buzzards we see now. He flew all over the earth, low down near the ground, and it was still soft. When he reached Cherokee country, he was very tired, and his wings began to flap and strike the ground, and wherever they struck the earth there was a valley, and where they turned up again there was a mountain. . . . Men came after the animals and plants. At first there were only a brother and a sister until he struck her with a fish and told her to multiply, and so it was. In seven days a child was born to her, and thereafter every seven days another, and they increased very fast until there was danger that the world could not keep them. Then it was made that a woman should have only one child a year, and it has been so ever since. . . .

Native American creation theory is less a part of systematic religious worship in the Euro-American sense than it is the basis for an integrated moral philosophy and epistemology that includes all human interaction with nature. In counterpoint to traditional beliefs whose figures are firmly grounded in the physical world, a substantial portion of Native American thought is highly abstract. The account given by the California Luiseno tribe of the origin of the world begins with a remarkable combination of subtle abstraction and metaphoric juxtaposition of ideas about sexual division and the engendering of the world:

The first [things] were *Kyuvish,* "vacant," and *Atahvish,* "empty," male and female, brother and sister. Successively, these called themselves and became *Omai,* "not alive," and *Yamai,* "not in existence"; *Whaikut Piwkut,* "white pale," the Milky Way, and *Harurai Chatutai,* "boring lowering"; *Tukomit,* "night," with the implication of "sky," and *Tamayowut,* "earth." She lay with her feet to the north; he sat by her right side; and she spoke: "I am stretched, I am extended. I shake, I resound. I am diminished, I am earthquake. I revolve, I roll. I disappear." Then he answered: "I am night, I am inverted (the arch of the heavens). I cover, I rise, I ascend. I devour, I drain (as death). I seize, I send away (the souls of men). I cut, I sever (life)."

These attributes were not yet; but they would be. The four double existences were not successive generations: they were transitions, manifestations of continuing beings.

Then as the brother took hold of her and questioned, she named each part of her body, until they were united. He assisted the births with the sacred *pavuit* stick, and the following came forth singly or in pairs, ceremonial objects, religious acts, and avenging animals:

Hair (symbolic of the spirit).
Rush basket and throwing stick.
Paint of rust from springs and paint of pond scum.
Water and mud.
Rose and blackberry, which sting for Chungichnish.

Tussock grass and sedge, with which the sacred pits for girls were lined.
Salt grass.
Bleeding and first periods.
These were human; and so were the next born, the mountains and rocks and things of
   wood now on earth. . . .

Despite the unique description of the first things created by the mystic
incestuous union – a relatively common element in Native American natural
theology – the Luiseno story is conceptually closer to modern scientific
theory than are most accounts of the origin of the universe in either Western
or Indian traditions.

As many creation myths suggest, animal figures, usually treated with the
respect due those possessed of divine or magic powers, are central to Native
American oral tradition. Numerous tales concern trickster figures, who can
change into other persons or into inanimate objects, but most often into
animal forms. Like folktales from many traditions, the trickster tale usually
points out a good or bad moral model for the community, and in some cases
challenges or satirizes institutional powers: the tribal leadership, the wisdom
of ancestors, the magic of religion or medicine, or dealings with enemy tribes
or Euro-Americans. Often the trickster is at the center of erotic or crude
stories and jokes, but he may also take part in legends of heroism or romance
central to the tribe's self-conception. Manibozho (Schoolcraft's and Longfellow's Hiawatha) is the hero of numerous Ojibwa and Menomini trickster
tales. Especially prevalent are tales of Coyote, a cunning and deceitful but
also often foolish figure, who is sometimes represented as responsible for the
advent of much of the world's evil. Yet he is likewise a figure of comic or
ironic power, evanescent and fluid, embodying a primal force that bears
responsibility for the conflicts between hardship and triumph that constitute
the destiny of tribal peoples. In a Caddo myth set before the origin of death,
for example, the tribe decides that because the world is getting too crowded,
people should die for a period before returning to earth; Coyote, however,
wants people to die forever. The medicine men build a grass house where the
dead are to come to be restored to life, but when the first one comes, in the
form of a spirit that inhabits a whirlwind circling the grass house, Coyote
closes the door and prevents the whirlwind from entering. Grief is thus
introduced into the world, the legend says, and ever since, the spirits of the
dead have wandered the earth in whirlwinds until they find the road to the
Spirit Land.

Both myths and trickster tales have been transcribed in verse form as well,
suggesting the vocal lyricism of Native American oral tradition. Although
the use of dance, chanting, and drums and other instruments change the
nature of transcribed songs and poems, many works on such topics as love,

illness, death, hunting, war, thanksgiving, birth, fertility, and dreams have been set down to resemble traditional English lyrics. A number of tales or verses, such as this Osage song of the maize, incorporate into the divine cycle of planting and cultivation the spirits of the dead, whose voices here bring the corn crop to maturity:

> Amid the earth, renewed in verdure,
> Amid the rising smoke, my grandfather's footprints
> I see, as from place to place I wander,
> The rising smoke I see as I wander. . . .
>
> Amid all forms visible, the little hills in rows
> I see, as I move from place to place.
>
> Amid all forms visible, the spreading blades
> I see, as I move from place to place. . . .

Some transcribed texts depict visionary quests, often undertaken in connection with puberty or death rites, while others, drawing on the widespread belief in the existence of animal souls and even in the spirits of inanimate objects, concern ceremonies or taboos related to food or the handling of certain objects. A portion of an elaborate Mescalero Apache song cycle devoted to the rites of adolescence for young girls links the beginning of womanhood to the creative power latent in the arrival of dawn:

> The sunbeams stream forward, dawn boys, with shimmering shoes of yellow.
> On top of the sunbeams that stream toward us they are dancing.
> At the east the rainbow moves forward, dawn maidens, with shimmering shoes
> and shirts of yellow, dance over us.
> Beautifully over us it is dawning . . .
> Above us among the mountains, with shoes of yellow I go around the fruits and
> the herbs that shimmer.
> Above us among the mountains, the shimmering fruits with shoes and shirts of
> yellow are bent toward him.
> On the beautiful mountains above it is daylight.

That the imagistic symbolism of dreams, or the spirit world, is highly respected is evident in the significance accorded encounters with animal totems or ancestors, prophetic indications of success in coming hunts, travels, and wars, and transhistoric visions of tribal regeneration of the kind recorded in John G. Neihardt's classic text, *Black Elk Speaks* (1932). Dream sons are a particularly important aspect of American Indian tradition in that they typically have a powerful mystic significance for each person, directing the individual to a closer spiritual communion with the natural world. The Iroquois in particular created a sophisticated dream theory, which held that the deepest expression of the soul could be communicated in dreams, in what would later be understood to be the symbolic language of the unconscious. The poetic materials in which Schoolcraft saw superstition and idolatry were in fact a source of complex beauty and long, carefully articulated traditions and philosophies. Ritual song, dense metaphoric patterns, and a spiritual animation of the natural world therefore frequently intersect in the Native American text. In the Navajo song of the Black Bear, for example, the attributes of divine power ascribed to the bear also represent an extension of his intimate relationship to the tribe. The kinetic figures of the song are drawn at once from the human and from the inanimate world; repetition and catalogue (in some respects not unlike that of Whitman's poetry) create a ceremonial voice and motion for the surrogate tribal singer who takes on the bear's role in performance:

> My moccasins are black obsidian,
> My leggings are black obsidian,
> My shirt is black obsidian.
> I am girded with a black arrowsnake.
> Black snakes go up from my head.
> With zigzag lightning darting from the ends of my feet I step,
> With zigzag lightning streaming out from my knees I step,
> With zigzag lightning streaming from the tip of my tongue I speak.
> Now a disk of pollen rests on the crown of my head.
> Gray arrowsnakes and rattlesnakes eat it.
> Black obsidian and zigzag lighting stream out from me in four ways.
> Where they strike the earth, bad things, bad talk does not like it.
> It causes the missiles to spread out.
> Long Life, something frightful I am.
> Now I am.
>
> There is danger where I move my feet.
> I am whirlwind.
> There is danger when I move my feet.
> I am a gray bear.
> When I walk, where I step, lightning flies from me.
> Where I walk, one to be feared I am.
> Where I walk, Long Life.
> One to be feared I am.
> There is danger where I walk.

Some of the most important and most frequently recorded American Indian literature appears in the form of war songs or oratory connected with battle and with treaties or their violation. That such material is among the most often transcribed attests both to the prevailing Euro-American portrait of Indians as noble, doomed warriors and to the underlying need, within the ideology of imperial advance, to depict Indian tribes as inherently belligerent. Because the translated records are almost always open to question,

Indian oration of necessity belongs to a world defined in part by dramatic invention. In fact, the treaties themselves, beginning in the colonial period, have been treated by some historians of culture as the earliest American drama. Benjamin Franklin, among others, thought them important enough to print for a general reading public. Unfolding somewhat in the form of chronicle plays rich in symbolic and performative oratory, the treaty records often dramatized ritual exchanges of words and gifts between Indians and whites. The roles of agents and interpreters were critical to the ceremony, the place was often chosen for its symbolic significance (marking a frontier, a sacred meeting place, or the confluence of paths or territories), and dances or chants sometimes formed a necessary part of the compact. The history of treaties, however, was one of disappointment and betrayal for American Indians, and the transcribed literary record of orations and songs takes its principal power from the language of tragedy and protest. The Winnebago chief Red Bird sang the following death song in 1827 upon surrendering to the U.S. troops after a bitter series of raids prompted by white violations of Winnebago property:

> I am ready.
> I do not want to be put in chains.
> Let me be free.
> I have given away my life –
> (*Stooping, he picked up a pinch*
> *of dust and blew it away.*)
> – it is gone like that!
> I would not take it back.
> It is gone.

Another brief lyric that speaks all the more powerfully for its condensed, imagistic form was recorded by the Cheyenne George Bent, a witness to the 1864 massacre of hundreds of Arapaho and Cheyenne, including women and children, at Sand Creek, Colorado:

At the beginning of the attack Black Kettle, with his wife and White Antelope, took their position before Black Kettle's lodge and remained there after all others had left the camp. At last Black Kettle, seeing that it was useless to stay longer, started to run, calling out to White Antelope to follow him, but White Antelope refused and stood there ready to die, with arms folded, singing his death song:

> *Nothing lives long,*
> *Except the earth and the mountains,*

until he was shot down by the soldiers.

A much more extensive record of oratory connected with contention over tribal land, or more specifically with treaties and their violation, survives from the antebellum period, and the conceptions expressed often starkly contrast with prevailing Euro-American views of the progress of civilization on the frontier. At the heart of many such speeches by Indians is a radically different understanding of the interaction between the human and natural worlds, one more closely tied to seasons, migratory patterns, and the open spaces of the prairies than to property rights and physical or legal enclosures. The Comanche chief Ten Bears asked the white peace commissioners who joined the prestigious group of Indian leaders assembled at the Medicine Lodge council in 1867, "[W]hy do you ask us to leave the rivers, and the sun, and the wind, and live in houses? Do not ask us to give up the buffalo for the sheep." Remarking that he was born on the prairie, "where the wind blew free, and there was nothing to break the light of the sun . . . where there were no enclosures, and where everything drew a free breath," Ten Bears said he wanted to die there, and "not within walls."

In the decades following the Civil War the American government system-atically imposed an alien notion of property rights on plains Indians by deliberately slaughtering buffalo in order to destroy the migratory patterns of western tribes and force them onto reservations. This strategic decimation of Indian and animal life was implicit at the outset of Removal, however, as Parkman recognized in the analogy, noted earlier, that he drew in *The California and Oregon Trail* between the killing of buffalo and the demise of American Indians. That is to say, not just war but killing itself became part of a "natural" process. Some four decades earlier the Pawnee chief Petalesharo anticipated such a result in the rapidity of white settlement. Attending a conference with President Monroe in 1822, Petalesharo (Man Chief) spoke with dignity of an Indian view of natural resources that stood in opposition to the market and labor values of the whites:

Let me enjoy my country, and pursue the buffalo and the beaver, and the other wild animals of our country, and I will trade their skins with your people. I have grown up and lived thus long without work – I am in hopes you will suffer me to die without it. We have plenty of buffalo, beaver, deer and other wild animals – we have also an abundance of horses – we have everything we want – we have plenty of land, if you will keep your people off it. . . . Let us exhaust our present resources before you make us toil and interrupt our happiness. . . . Before our intercourse with the whites (who have caused such a destruction in our game), we could lie down and sleep, and when we awoke we would find the buffalo feeding around our camp – but now we are killing them for their skins, and feeding the wolves with their flesh, to make our children cry over their bones. . . . I know that the robes, leggings, mockasins, bear claws, etc. [presented as gifts] are of little value to you, but we wish you to have them deposited and preserved in some conspicuous part of your lodge, so that when we are gone and the sod turned over our bones, if our children should visit this place, as we do now, they may see and recognize with pleasure the deposits of their fathers, and reflect on the times that are past.

The intimate relationship with the animal world observed by most Native Americans thus grew from practical events of daily life that were not to be separated from the ceremonial significance of tribal memory. Little Crow, a Santee Sioux, echoed Parkman's analogy in a figurative address to a Minnesota war council in 1862 that was prophetic:

We are only little herds of buffalo left scattered; the great herds that once covered the prairies are no more. See! – the white men are like locusts when they fly so thick that the whole sky is a snowstorm. You may kill one – two – ten; yes, as many as the leaves in the forest yonder, and their brothers will not miss them. Kill one – two – ten, and ten times as many will come to kill you. Count your fingers all day long and white men with guns in their hands will come faster than you can count.

Although he converted to Catholicism and cooperated with whites fully enough to have the city of Seattle named after him in 1854, Seathl (Dwamish) responded to the honor after the organization of the Washington Territory in a forceful, unsettling oration:

There was a time when our people covered the land as the waves of a wind-ruffled sea cover its shell-paved floor, but that time long since passed away with the greatness of tribes that are now but a mournful memory. I will not dwell on, nor mourn over, our untimely decay, nor reproach my paleface brothers with hastening it as we too may have been somewhat to blame. . . . It matters little where we pass the remnant of our days. They will not be many. The Indian's night promises to be dark. Not a single star of hope hovers above his horizon. Sad-voiced winds moan in the distance. . . . Ane [yet] when the last Red Man shall have perished, and the memory of my tribe shall have become a myth among the White Men, these shores will swarm with the invisible dead of my tribe, and when your children's children think themselves alone in the field, the store, the shop, along the highway, or in the silence of the pathless woods, they will not be alone. In all the earth there is no place dedicated to solitude. At night when the streets of your cities and villages are silent and you think them deserted, they will throng with the returning hosts that once filled them and still love this beautiful land. The White Man will never be alone.

Because Seathl's moving oration, it is now known, was embellished by a journalist far beyond its original scope, it also offers an object lesson in the problem of textual authenticity. In the twentieth century, however, a letter reportedly sent from Seathl to President Pierce in 1855 was also discovered. It reiterates some of the same themes of the oration and sums up the contrasting conceptions of life that inevitably pitted Euro-American settlers against the native inhabitants, all the more remarkably in that it also obliquely links its ecological attack on white development to a common antebellum critique of Jacksonian mobility and disinterest in ancestral authority:

The earth is not [the white man's] brother, but his enemy, and when he has conquered it, he moves on. He leaves his father's graves, and his children's birthright is
forgotten. . . . There is no quiet place in the white man's cities. No place to hear the
leaves of spring or the rustle of insect's wings. . . . The Indian prefers the soft sound
of the wind darting over the face of the pond, the smell of the wind itself cleansed by
a mid-day rain, or scented with a piñon pine. The air is precious to the red man. For
all things share the same breath – the beasts, the trees, the man. . . . What is man
without the beasts? If all the beasts were gone, men would die from great loneliness
of spirit, for whatever happens to the beast also happens to man. All things are
connected. Whatever befalls the earth befalls the sons of the earth.

The most famous and frequently reprinted orations, which revealed much
about both the speakers and the Euro-Americans who made use of the orations, belonged to the most notorious warriors, such as Tecumseh and Black
Hawk. Their lives and symbolic fame, like that of the earlier imposing
figures of King Philip and Pontiac, were the subject of white writers in a
variety of genres and became entangled in white frontier mythology and its
burgeoning literature of conquest. In all cases – whether in Drake's record of
Tecumseh's challenge to Harrison, the treaty orations collected by Schoolcraft
and others, or Black Hawk's edited and translated autobiography – the appropriation of the Indian's words by the languages of ethnology and literary
production inevitably raises problems of accuracy. Of special importance
during the age of Euro-American conquest is the appearance of the first major
documents composed in English by Native Americans, in which the problem
of translation gives way to a more comprehensive question about the assimilation of one culture to another. Inevitably, written English was for Indians
both a means of wider communication and a sign of cultural fragmentation
and loss.

The first such written histories appeared in the antebellum period alongside the first significant histories of the Indian nations by whites. William
Warren completed his *History of the Ojibways* in 1853 (although it went
unpublished until 1885), but it followed by several decades *Sketches of Ancient
History of the Six Nations* (1827) by David Cusick (Tuscarora), which begins
with historical–mythological tales of creation, migration, and warfare, and
follows the history of the Iroquois through the establishment of the League.
Among the most important works of literature written in English by American Indians in the antebellum period were autobiographical conversion narratives, which were themselves a form of history writing firmly set in the
Protestant tradition of spiritual autobiography. Although some of the narratives, such as *A Memoir of Catherine Brown, A Christian Indian of the Cherokee
Nation* (1825), were probably transcribed into English by missionaries, a few
important autobiographies composed in English were published during the

decades of Removal. They typically display little of the keenness of vision or richness of figurative language evident in the transcribed orations of Seathl or Tecumseh. Indeed, they must be measured against the far stronger assertions of resistance to the Christian mission evident in some orations. A good index of such Indian counterargument appears in the reply of the Iroquois chief Sagoyewatha (He Who Causes Them To Be Awake), known to whites as Red Jacket, to a representative of the Boston Missionary Society in 1805. Sagoyewatha ironically subverted some of the missionary's central tenets while focusing on a contrast between the written and oral tradition that Cooper and other white writers would appropriate in distinguishing between the language of civilization and the "book of nature":

> You say that you are sent to instruct us how to worship the Great Spirit agreeably to his mind; and if we do not take hold of the religion which you white people teach, we shall be unhappy hereafter. You say that you are right and we are lost. . . . We understand that your religion is written in a book. If it was intended for us as well as for you, why has not the Great Spirit given it to us; and not only to us, but why did he not give to our forefathers the knowledge of the book, with the means of understanding it rightly? . . . How shall we know when to believe, being so often deceived by the white people?

Sagoyewatha's oration destroys the logic of Euro-American missionary work, which lay at the heart of arguments about manifest destiny and the regeneration of America's savages through conquest. It also casts an important light on the historical accuracy and ideological motivations of conversion documents ascribed to or written by American Indians. By internalizing the national myth of Christian mission, the autobiographical conversion narratives express clearly the power of political containment, which could operate as effectively in language as in arms.

The first American Indian to write extensively in English was the Pequot William Apess (1798–1839). His autobiography, *A Son of the Forest. The Experience of William Apes, a Native of the Forest* (1829), is a conversion narrative that plays on his transformation from what is represented as native, natural ignorance to the educated light of Christian grace. He notes at the outset that he is descended from King Philip but, shrewdly playing on the rhetorical value of this genealogy, undermines his distinctive character by noting that we are all – white and Indian alike – "descended from *Adam*." Converted to Methodism at age fifteen, Apess was raised among whites (he was one quarter white) after a brutal childhood among separated parents and violent, alcoholic grandparents. Despite lapses of faith and service in the army in the War of 1812, he eventually became a missionary, a living "monument of [God's] unfailing goodness." *A Son of the Forest* is less interesting as autobiography than as a text that mirrors Christianity's uneasy complicity in the process of conquest. Apess's appendix to the volume attacks the notion of savagism and follows a rather common evangelical argument that Indians are descendants of ancient Israelites; but it also reproduces a doggerel "Indian Hymn" that makes the Indian into a crude minstrel figure:

> God lub poo Indian in da wood
> So me lub God, and dat be good.

Nonetheless, Apess's subsequent writings were increasingly articulate on behalf of Native American rights. *Experience of Five Christian Indians of the Pequot Tribes* (1833) is more critical of white aggression and treaty violations; and *Indian Nullification of the Unconstitutional Laws of Massachusetts Relative to the Marshpee Tribe* (1833) contains a strong attack on the state's illegal acts against tribal property and a brief for tribal self-government. Apess's critique of Euro-American conquest reaches a peak in his *Eulogy on King Philip* (1836), a fiery pamphlet that depicts his ancestor Philip to be a hero as glorious as those of the American Revolution – a "noble" figure, made by the "God of Nature," but no savage. The *Eulogy* ridicules Puritan piety and the "hideous blasphemy" of their wars. Increase Mather's famous account of the war, says Apess, relies on prayers that are but "the foundation of all the slavery and degradation in the American Colonies, towards colored people." The pamphlet borrows from the tradition of the jeremiad in advocating Euro-American reform *and* Christian conversion among the Indians, but its most memorable passages belong to the rhetoric of tragic lamentation. Would the Euro-Americans, Apess rhetorically asks, like to see *their* wives and children "slain and laid in heaps, and their bodies devoured by the vultures and wild beasts of prey? and their bones bleaching in the sun and air, till they moulder away, or were covered by the falling leaves of the forest?" Like Euro-American writers such as Parkman and Cooper, whose works were often set in the colonial period but acted out anxieties coincident with the destruction of Indian tribes, Apess casts back to the seventeenth century for genocidal scenes prophetic of tragedies that were occurring as he wrote.

Less starkly eloquent but at once more complex and more popular than Apess's autobiography was George Copway's *The Life, History, and Travels of Ka-ge-ga-gah-bowh* (1847), which immediately went through six editions and was issued in revised forms for a number of years. Copway (1818–69), a Canadian Ojibwa who became a Methodist missionary before moving to the United States in 1846, benefited from the vogue of ethnological work in the 1840s. His *Life* included romanticized yet detailed accounts of Ojibwa tribal life along with the dominant story of his own conversion; its combination of native exoticism and alien subjugation by the ideology of mission was thus perfectly suited to public reading tastes. Copway's second important work, *Traditional History and Characteristic Sketches of the Ojibway Nation* (1850), was more critical of Euro-American practices but focused primarily on geography, tribal history, ethnographic material, and the transmission of Ojibwa oral legends. The same year, he wrote *The Ojibway Conquest,* a narrative poem about the Ojibwa defeat of the Sioux in the Great Lakes region, and dedicated it to Thomas McKenney. Copway lectured extensively in America and Europe, briefly edited a jounal entitled *Copway's American Indian,* and wrote futilely in favor of a separate Indian state east of the Missouri River. He enjoyed the admiration of Irving, Cooper, Longfellow, and Parkman, perhaps the surest sign that his message was largely consistent with their own in its adherence to the archetypes of savagism combined with a mild liberal critique of the rapacity of civilized progress. Throughout most of his work American Indian life is viewed nostalgically, doomed in direct ratio to Copway's own proselytizing for Christianity and the ideals of white culture.

Two other Ojibwa missionaries wrote autobiographical accounts of their tribal lives and personal conversions: Peter Jacobs, *Journal of the Reverend Peter Jacobs* (1857); and Peter Jones, *History of the Ojibway Indians* (1861), which departs from type in condemning the white man as an agent of Satan and includes a good deal of ethnographic material in the vein of Schoolcraft. However, neither surpasses Copway in celebrating education, cultivation, and refinement – in particular the *written* English language, which Copway believed would allow him to live beyond his mortal life. Written English is thus allied to Christian salvation, both aspects of the civilizing process that were said to distinguish the "reclaimed" savage from his or her illiterate and heathen people. Renouncing the savage life of hunting and warfare, says Copway, "I now take the goose quil[l] for my *bow,* and its point for my *arrow."* Despite the often absorbing record of Ojibwa culture contained in the *Life,* and despite its impassioned attacks on alcoholism, land greed, and Removal, it is Copway's faith in the "arts of civilized life," which he thought would overcome the Indian's benighted ignorance and lead to "intelligence and virtue," that dominates the volume and established its great popularity with his white audience. Although his autobiography is more interesting and historically valuable than that of Apess, Copway over the course of his career was more thoroughly assimilated by the very society that defined for him the paradoxical taint of "noble savagery" he might conceal but could never completely escape.

Two of the most important Native American writers of the early nineteenth century were Cherokee, Elias Boudinot and John Rollin Ridge, whose importance stemmed in part from the unique features of Cherokee culture. The Cherokees stood alone among Native Americans in what was judged to be the sophistication of their agricultural and educational systems according to Euro-American models by the 1820s. With Sequoyah's invention in 1821 of an eighty-six-character syllabary, referred to as his "talking leaves," the Cherokees developed a European form of literacy and initiated a bilingual newspaper, the *Cherokee Phoenix,* edited by Boudinot from 1827 to 1832. Interested less in Cherokee improvement and self-government than in the cession of their lands, however, the state of Georgia abolished Cherokee national government. As noted above, an 1832 Supreme Court decision upholding Cherokee rights was ignored by the state and ridiculed by President Jackson, with the result that in 1835 the Cherokees were forced to sign the Treaty of Echota, authorizing their removal to western lands. Precisely because of their advances in industry and learning, it was argued by both whites and some influential Cherokee leaders that the tribe would be better off with apparent political independence in a new sovereign territory. John Ridge (the father of John Rollin Ridge) thus argued for resettlement as a form of cultural preservation, but his view of "civilization" was infused with a classic doubleness. In an 1826 letter to Albert Gallatin, Ridge outlined the Cherokee Nation's political, economic, and cultural structure, but he concluded with an ambivalent assertion of Cherokee destiny:

Mutability is stamped on everything that walks on the Earth. Even now we are forced by natural causes to a Channel that will mingle the blood of our race with the white. In the lapse of half a Century if Cherokee blood is not destroyed it will run its courses in the veins of fair complexions who will read that their Ancestors under the Stars of adversity, and curses of their enemies became a civilized Nation.

In 1839 John Ridge, his father (Major Ridge), and Elias Boudinot were executed by other Cherokees in accordance with an 1829 Cherokee law that made the cession of tribal land a capital offense.

Educated at a Moravian mission school and then in Connecticut, Boudinot (1804–39) took the name of his benefactor, the revolutionary statesman and president of the American Bible Society Elias Boudinot. The elder Boudinot was the author of the widely cited *Stars in the West* (1816), which argued that Native Americans were descended from ancient Hebrews and would thus, when converted, augur a new millennium. (The theory, dating from both the Spanish conquests in Mexico and colonial New England writing, appeared in a variety of forms in legitimate histories of the Indian tribes, works of religious inspiration such as *The Book of Mormon,* and in popularizations of the idea such as Ethan Smith's 1823 volume *Views of the Hebrews.*) The Cherokee Boudinot gave up complete assimilation after a furor over his interracial marriage, but he argued ardently as a teacher, a missionary, and a writer and translator for the civilizing of his tribe. The weekly *Cherokee Phoenix* was a compendium of news, cultural notices, laws, and advertisements for material goods – a catalogue, Boudinot thought, of the civilizing process at work. He supported Removal because he had faith in territorial integrity and believed that the fate of the Cherokee Nation in Georgia would be "servitude and degradation." In numerous public letters and pamphlets such as "An Address to the Whites" (1826) and "Letters and Other Papers Relating to Cherokee Affairs" (1837) and in a fictional tract entitled *Poor Sarah; or, The Indian Woman* (1833), he outlined his fear that the Cherokee Nation, if it failed to accept the Removal treaty, would become the "relics of a brave and noble race." His execution only highlighted the ironic pressures of his role as both an apologist for Removal and a staunch advocate of Indian rights and national sovereignty.

John Rollin Ridge (1827–67), known also by his chosen name of Yellow Bird, was only twelve years old when he witnessed the killing of his father and grandfather in Oklahoma. After a brief eastern education in Massachusetts and a marriage in Arkansas, he followed the Gold Rush to California, where he became a journalist and poet. His *Poems,* published posthumously in 1868, are largely light verse combined with nationalistic celebrations of American progress and the grandeur of the West. Much of the poetry, in fact, appears to justify Euro-American supremacy in the hemisphere. Yet his jounalistic writings on the Indian's condition, later collected in *A Trumpet of One's Own* (1981), have a more independent cast, indicating his advocacy of a separate Cherokee state as part of the Union, criticizing the gold miners' brutality toward "Digger" Indians, and calling for continued belief in Indian spiritual practices instead of the adoption of a sterile and impractical Christianity. Yellow Bird's most important work, however, was the double-edged novel *The Life and Adventures of Joaquin Murieta* (1854), which posed as the true story of a legendary California bandit and may have been based on the exploits of one or more contemporary figures. Half Mexican and half Indian, Murieta as drawn by Yellow Bird incarnates the urge for vengeance brought about by anti-Mexican prejudice in the gold fields. In addition to being a popular mythic model for future western outlaws in American literature, the figure of Murieta may be understood to be Yellow Bird's own indirect statement about the justification for revenge against whites felt by American Indians, whether in California, Georgia, or Oklahoma. Although his father and grandfather were killed by other Cherokees, it seems likely that Ridge saw their deaths in the same light as the legend's story of the rape of Murieta's mistress, the murder of his brother, and the theft of his land. The fictional bandit, that is, unleashes the vengeance that neither the Mexicans nor the Cherokees could act out on any scale comparable to the violent force exercised in their conquest.

The contradictions of assimilation evident in the educated Boudinot and the acculturated Cherokees is even harsher in the case of Black Hawk (1767–1838), chief of the Sauks, who led a bitter Illinois frontier war in 1832 rather than submit to the resettlement required by a treaty of 1804. Black Hawk's 1833 *Autobiography,* also published as the *Life of Ma-Ka-Tai-Me-She-Kia-Kiak,* records this more radical struggle. Its voice of resistance would not prevail, but the autobiographical act, fully expressing the paradox of white conquest and Indian assimilation, gave greater permanence to the oratorical powers Black Hawk had used in 1832 to set the stage for warfare with the whites and to prophesy the course of nineteenth-century American empire:

The Great Spirit created this country for the use and benefit of his red children, and placed them in full possession of it, and we were happy and contented. Why did he send the palefaces across the great ocean to take it from us? . . . Little did our fathers then think they were taking to their bosoms, and warming them to life, a lot of torpid, half-frozen and starving vipers, which in a few winters would fix their deadly fangs upon the very bosoms that had nursed and cared for them when they needed help.

From the day when the palefaces landed upon our shores, they have been robbing us of our inheritance, and slowly, but surely, driving us back, back, back towards the setting sun, burning our villages, destroying our growing crops, ravishing our wives and daughters. . . . They are now running their plows through our graveyards, turning up the bones and ashes of our sacred dead, whose spirits are calling to us from the land of dreams for vengeance on the despoilers.

The same sentiments are recorded in the *Autobiography,* though with somewhat different effect. As in the case of the oration, the composition of Black Hawk's story by a white translator (Antoine LeClaire) and a white editor (J. B. Patterson) reflects the American Indian's submission to an alien language, but the autobiography places the Indian's language in a more elaborate and controlled system of cultural expression. Black Hawk's text borrows elements from the conversion narrative but can more profitably be compared to the *Confessions* of the slave rebel Nat Turner, which were recorded and printed in similar circumstances at about the same time. The voices of both Black Hawk and Nat Turner were thus allowed to speak – even to protest the destruction or enslavement of their people and to justify their countering acts of violence – but at the same time their transcribed words were contained within structures of confession and capitulation, and further screened by the commercial process of publication and sale. Whereas Nat Turner was executed, however, Black Hawk became a popular public figure, a distinction that symbolizes the fact that the African American rebel remained a specter of terror whereas the Indian rebel by then could more easily be absorbed into the narrative of Romantic nationalism.

Captured and jailed in 1833, Black Hawk was taken east to meet the man his story designates our "great Father" and the "great brave" – President Jackson – and to tour several cities. He came away understandably impressed with the technological power and sheer size of white civilization, ready to voice the subjugation recorded at the end of his text: "The tomahawk is buried forever! We will forget what has past – and may the watchword between the Americans and the Sacs and Foxes, ever be – '*Friendship!*' " Whether or not this ending is an honest expression of Black Hawk's sentiments (it accords with his public statements), the autobiography is factually reliable and, if ornate, clear evidence of his general distrust of white society. The account of his early life, including warfare against the Ojibwa and Osage and service with the British in the War of 1812, describes the increasing deceit and incursions by white frontiersmen into tribal territory. The war resulting from the seeming betrayal of Black Hawk's rival Keokuk is reduced to the question of land, stated simply by Black Hawk:

My reason teaches me that land *cannot be sold.* The Great Spirit gave it to his children to live upon, and cultivate, as far as is necessary for their subsistence; and so long as they occupy and cultivate it, they have the right to the soil – but if they voluntarily leave it, then any other people have a right to settle upon it. Nothing can be sold, but such things as can be carried away. . . . I told [Governor Cole and James Hall] that the white people had already entered our village, *burnt our lodges, destroyed our fences, ploughed up our corn, and beat our people:* that they had brought *whiskey* into our country, *made our people drunk,* and taken from them their *horses, guns,* and *traps;* and that I had borne all this injury, without suffering any of my braves to raise a hand against the whites. . . . I had appealed in vain, time after time, to our agent, who regularly represented our situation to the great chief at St. Louis, whose duty it was to call upon our Great Father to have justice done to us; but instead of this, we are told *that the white people want our country, and we must leave it to them.*

Black Hawk's defeat left him spiritually dignified but a broken man, nursing the illusion that the Mississippi River would successfully protect his tribe from further advances of Euro-American settlement. His eastern tour, anticipating later appropriations of native figures for commercial enterprise, made him a momentary celebrity. He was interviewed by McKenney for his *History of the Indian Tribes of North America,* and his activities were portrayed in gossip columns of the day and later in a number of histories of Indian affairs, as well as in individual volumes like Benjamin Drake's sympathetic *The Life and Adventures of Black Hawk* (1838) and Elbert Smith's epic poem, *Ma-Ka-Tai-Me-She-Kia-Kiak; or, Black Hawk and Scenes in the West* (1848). Smith's further subtitle, *A National Poem,* suggests the dual purpose that Black Hawk, like other heroic Indian figures, served: at once a noble warrior defying the superior might of white technology and still virtually an extension of the richly described western landscape waiting to be subordinated:

> The red man of the wood, like morning dew,
> Has disappeared, except a harmless few.

If Black Hawk thought the land could never be sold, his adversaries thought it could never resist the superior force of cultivation and market improvement. Although he retained less control of his own story than other Native American autobiographers, such as Apess and Copway, Black Hawk produced a life story in many ways more alive to the contradictions of military and governmental paternalism and more aware of the costs of compromise with Euro-American values.

Although the Euro-American fiction devoted to the frontier and the figure of the Indian is superior in both quality and scope, contemporary poetry and drama often combine the vanquishing of Indians with a rhetoric of nationalism. Longfellow's *The Song of Hiawatha* (1855) was only the most famous of these productions. In the period between the American Revolution and the War of 1812, a number of poets and dramatists, adopting the same archetypes of sentimental romance and tragic vanquishing found in the novel, had begun to fix in stylized forms the elegiac images of the Indian that would come to prominence during the decades of Removal. Three decades before Longfellow's poem appeared, Lydia Sigourney's epic poem *Traits of the Aborigines of America* (1822) had already provided a sweeping history of American Indians, complete with a plethora of biblical and classical allusions.

Less grandiose and more typical in its ranges of concerns was William Cullen Bryant's poetry. "The Indian Girl's Lament" is a romantic song for a slain lover, for example, and in "An Indian Story" a brave rescues his captive maiden. Bryant's popular poem "The Prairie" is an excellent index of the Euro-American naturalization of conquest, moving from a tone of melancholy doom to one celebratory of the triumph of civilization. The laws of nature ensure that one society always succeeds another, just as the American Indians once conquered the Mound Builders:

> The red-man came –
> The roaming hunter-tribes, warlike and fierce,
> And the mound-builders vanished from the earth. . . .
> The strongholds of the plain were forced, and heaped
> With corpses. The brown vultures of the wood
> Flocked to those vast uncovered sepulchres . . .
> Thus change the forms of being. Thus arise
> Races of living things, glorious in strength,
> And perish, as the quickening breath of God
> Fills them, or is withdrawn. The red-man, too,
> Has left the blooming wilds he ranged so long. . . .

The process of conquest and expansion is thus demonstrated to be part of an unfolding national drama, directed by God's intercession, in whose most recent scenes the Indian has "left," first the eastern woodlands and now the midwestern prairies. Reflecting the same fascination with commanding leaders and biography contained in the histories of American Indian tribes and warfare (as well as in nineteenth-century American historiography in general), popular poems on Indians were often devoted to single heroic figures. The heroic Indian was often depicted as a magnificent outcropping of the natural landscape that resisted settlement but could not prevent it; in him were summed up the noble traits ascribed to Indians resolutely facing the superior force of white soldiers and pioneers. At times, however, the Indian's lament had a philosophical acuteness that was not entirely the result of the myth of American mission. James W. Eastburn's *Yamoyden, A Tale of the Wars of King Philip* (1820), for example, furnished epigraphs for a number of novels. Its conventional romantic adventure set against the backdrop of King Philip's War rendered a melancholy lesson for the powerful:

> Tis good to muse on nations passed away,
> For ever, from the land we call our own;
> Nations, as proud and mighty in their day,
> Who deemed that everlasting was their throne.

Longfellow's *The Song of Hiawatha* capitalized on the twin vogues for heroic representation of defeated Indians and for ethnographic detail of the kind available in Schoolcraft. The poem's unusual meter derived from the Finnish epic *Kalevala,* and the story borrowed from the Native American legends in Schoolcraft, Catlin, and Heckewelder. Like Daniel Bryan's 1813 epic about Daniel Boone, *The Mountain Muse,* Longfellow's *Hiawatha* acts out in cultural form the conquest of native life with the native's own complicity. By combining European and Native American mythologies and yoking Native American mysticism to the principles of Christianity, Longfellow creates a god-hero whose exploits belong to legend but whose purpose is to sanctify the rise of a Western, Christian, agricultural empire in the United States. The sensual, earthy elements of the legendary materials are made genteel for Longfellow's audience; and Hiawatha appears not as the devious trickster figure of the Manibozho legend but as a classical hero who bestows order upon his nation and prepares the way for the Euro-American arrival. After Hiawatha commands his people to heed the Christians' "words of wisdom" ("For the Master of Life has sent them / From the land of light and morning!"), the poem's conclusion links the hero's departure and death to an image of the evening West:

And the evening sun descending
Set the clouds on fire with redness,
Burned the broad sky, like a prairie,
Left upon the level water
One long track and trail of splendor,
Down whose stream, as down a river,
Westward, westward Hiawatha
Sailed into the fiery sunset,
Sailed into the purple vapors,
Sailed into the dusk of evening.

Hiawatha's message ameliorates white conquest, and in his death and disappearance he, like the Indians of America, is symbolically absorbed by the West – the Christian eternity, the temporary home of removed Indians, and the ultimate goal of Euro-American manifest destiny.

The artifice of Hiawatha's character was acceptable to an audience conditioned by fiction and drama – and even by the ethnological writing that burgeoned by the middle of the century – to imagine Indians as romantic, domesticated stage figures. The drama in particular heightened this distorted expectation. From one point of view, as noted above, the historical record of legal interchange and treaties between whites and Indians constituted a version of American drama, a series of chronicle plays structured by symbolic action and oratory. Nonetheless, the Indian plays that gained a popular audience by the 1820s and evolved over the course of the century into the circuslike melodrama epitomized by Buffalo Bill Cody's famous "Wild West Exhibition" were fantasy representations of Indian life and Euro-American benevolence. Stage versions of Cooper's *The Last of the Mohicans* and Bird's *Nick of the Woods* were particularly well received, no doubt because the distinction between stage melodrama and dramatic narrative was already a rather fine one in the books themselves. Perhaps the earliest dramatization of Indian relations, Robert Rogers's *Ponteach* (1766) was unique in its critical treatment of the white colonists' betrayal and cheating of Pontiac. Following the lead of Indian biographies, later battle plays such as Richard Emmons's *Tecumseh; or, The Battle of the Thames* (1836) and Alexander Macomb's *Pontiac; or The Siege of Detroit* (1838) glorified white victory over strong, noble enemies. In those stage works, as in the proliferation of warrior songs and legends, Indian nobility in action and in speech was deliberately detached from the real world of armed conflict and dispossession and frozen in the timeless world of performance. Long after the events that prompted it, the famous speech of Logan justifying his revenge for the destruction of his family, included in Jefferson's *Notes on the State of Virginia,* became a rhetorical set piece in nineteenth-century primers and was made the concluding oration of Joseph Doddridge's *Logan: The Last of the Race of Shikellemus, Chief of the Cayuga Nation* (1823). Even more markedly than the reprinting of Indian oratory in histories, ethnological collections, or autobiographical narratives like that of Black Hawk, the drama at once highlighted the stoic dignity of American Indians and imprisoned their voices in a form of ceremonial utterance almost entirely at odds with their own native cultures.

The most popular and now notorious among dramatizations of Native-American life were those devoted to the story of Pocahontas. As its title suggests, James Nelson Barker's operatic *The Indian Princess; or La Belle Sauvage* (1808) anticipated much literary treatment of American natives in portraying the famous daughter of Powhatan as an exotic but ideologically astute heroine and in providing its hero, Captain John Smith, an opportunity to praise the new American nation:

> Oh, enviable country! thus disjoined
> From old licentious Europe! may'st thou rise,
> Free from those bonds which fraud and superstition
> In barbarous ages have enchain'd *her* with; –
> Bidding the antique world with wonder view
> A great, yet virtuous empire in the west!

Other plays casting Pocahontas as the archetypal melodramatic heroine include Robert Dale Owen's *Pocahontas* (1838), Charlotte Barnes Conner's *Forest Princess* (1848), and George Washington Custis's *Pocahontas; or, the Settlers of Virginia* (1827), the last distinguished for its placing of Pocahontas's rescue of Smith at the end of the action, thus heightening the symbolic import of her marriage to John Rolfe and Powhatan's final benediction: "Let their union be a pledge of the future union between England and Virginia . . . looking thro' a long vista of futurity, to the time when these wild regions shall become the ancient and honour'd part of a great and glorious American Empire." Despite the unavoidable fact of Pocahontas's marriage to Rolfe, the Indian plays were pervaded by problems of courtship and marriage but seldom suggest the possibility of mixed marriage or miscegenation. Rather, they displace problems of government and military paternalism, often enforced by policies of starvation and violence, to the stage drama of domesticity. When physical union between races was represented by Custis and others, anticipating the apparently more acceptable union of white soldiers and Mexican women portrayed in numerous novels after the Mexican War, it took on a ritual, symbolic character. The representation of Pocahontas's life and marriage thus became a sacrament of absorption authorizing the empire being brought to fruition at the time Custis and his contemporaries were writing. It violated the prohibition of racial mixing established in *The Last of the Mohicans;* but it did so in a far more distant past and in the name of generating out of an erotic union between Indian nature and English property an imperial vision of America that would restrict the dangerous potential for contamination in frontier life.

The most popular of all Indian plays, John Augustus Stone's *Metamora; or The Last of the Wampanoags* (1829), was written for the famous actor Edwin Forrest, who portrayed Metamora (King Philip) as an honorable and unrepentant hero who dies with a curse of the white race on his lips. Because the Indian drama relied so heavily on simplistic characterizations of warfare, treaty, and Indian life, it was best known even in the decades of its greatest popularity more for its rhetorical fireworks than for its power to reveal the significance of the Indian's demise. Stone's play was parodied in John Brougham's *Metamora; or, The Last of the Polywogs* (1847), whose later companion piece *Po-Ca-Hon-Tas; or, The Gentle Savage* (1855) anachronistically mixed in lampoons of various ethnic groups and contemporary political events in order to ridicule the artificiality of the literary use of Native American language, the stage gimmicks of the Pocahontas plays, and the public rage for Longfellow's *Hiawatha.* Such satire brought to the surface tendencies that were implicit in most of the drama devoted to the Indian question: a willingness to distort historical circumstance in the interest of national mythology and a psychological need to envision the destruction of native culture in melodramatic forms that would make conquest appear glorious and cathartically burn off in faked tragedy any doubts the audience might entertain about the wisdom and justice of western expansion.

The drama often played on two themes that were intimately related: the idea of the noble Indian hero and the ordeal of white captivity. Likewise, these themes are often dominant in the fiction devoted to American Indians, which in large part reflected the prevalent characteristics of the era's domestic fiction. The cultural power of the novel as a form therefore lay to a great extent in its use of the sentiment generated by familial violence and captivity, an ideological argument to which standard histories and biographies also resorted. However sympathetic the fictional portrait of Indian life or of such Indian heroes as Pontiac, King Philip, and Black Hawk, the novel's stock use of melodramatic plots, its tendency to celebrate the epic conquest of a "virgin land," its fascination with the exotic, and its easy sentimentalizing of dead or dying Indians made it inherently incapable of treating Native American culture with accuracy or objectivity. One direct source of these distortions was the long-standing popularity of captivity narratives, whether actual or fictional, which had in essence been the colonies' first imaginative literature and which remained through the nineteenth century a widely read and influential genre. The colonial captivity narrative, such as Mary Rowlandson's, made its heroines or heroes representative of a larger community whose resolve was being tested be the satanic forces of the wilderness. Outside God's community all was primitive, demonic. White aggression was converted into victimization, and the rescue or return of the captive often appeared as a sign of grace. The captive's gravest risk was not death but rather the temptation to identify with the alien way of life and become a savage. As a literature organized along psychogeographical boundaries that justified Euro-American advance while also revealing deep anxieties about it, the captivity narratives were often sensational, even incredible, at the same time that they posed as factual accounts of life beyond the frontier.

By the end of the eighteenth century, the captivity narrative had begun to merge with sentimental fiction, so that a popular work like Ann E. Bleecker's *History of Maria Kettle* (1793) resembled less a historically valid captivity narrative than it did a gothic melodrama. The rise of the novel and the accelerating process of western expansion and Indian Removal were coincident in America, and episodes of captivity played an important part in novels treating frontier life as a symbolic moment in the drama of American historical development. Because they were based on dubious evidence or conformed to the dictates of popular fiction and national ideology, many of the dozens of captivity narratives printed and reprinted throughout the antebellum period are spurious or, at the least, factually unreliable. Set in a liminal realm of the national imagination, at a moment of critical political redefinition, the post-Revolution captivity narrative mixed explorations of anxiety about the revolt against paternal order and authority with evocations of the loss of moral structure and social coherence possible on the frontier. The relatively widespread use of captivity narratives in the work of historians and ethnologists of the day tended not to contradict the elements of the gothic present in the fiction but instead to corroborate them within an apparently scientific context. The historian John Frost, author of a number of works on warfare with American Indians and frontier life, recorded a series of sketches of pioneer women under attack or in captivity in *Heroic Women of the West* (1854). Schoolcraft employed the narratives in his massive *Historical and Statistical Information,* and Drake included them in his *Biography and History of the Indians of North America* (1832) and also issued scholarly collections of them. In such volumes as *Indian Captivities* (1839) and *Tragedies in the Wilderness* (1841), he claimed historical accuracy but implicitly developed a theory of savagism consistent with his focus on "barbarous rites and ceremonies."

Especially as it was transfused into fiction, captivity thus justified white violence as a means of rescuing the besieged frontier community and, by linking violence to the notion of a vulnerable family, played upon the popular stereotypes of seduction fiction. Actual tragedies in the wilderness merged with hypothetical or fantastic violence and suffering. For example, the *Narrative of the Captivity and Sufferings of Mrs. Mary Smith* (1818) not only plagiarizes previous narratives but serves an explicit ideological purpose by reveling in the supposed cannibalistic torture and sexual abuse of young virgins during the Creek Wars of 1813–14, with the heroine eventually rescued by a brave soldier of Andrew Jackson's troop. Similarly, the *Narrative of the Capture and Providential Escape of Misses Frances and Almira Hall* (1832), although based on actual captivities, is transmuted into straightforward propaganda against Black Hawk by its focus on the Indian's butchering of white settlers. In the *Narrative of the Massacre, by the Savages, of the Wife and Children of Thomas Baldwin* (1836), two children are burned at the stake, thus setting the stage for the hero's transformation into an archetypal hermit and Indian hater. One of the most striking narratives, corresponding to a later phase of warfare against western tribes, is Royal B. Stratton's *The Captivity of the Oatman Girls* (1857), which recounts the stories of several family members held by Apaches and Mohaves in New Mexico in order to predict the coming achievement of manifest destiny:

But this unpierced heathenism that thus stretches its wing of night upon these swarming mountains and vales, is not long to have dominion so wild, nor possess victims so numerous. Its territoy is already begirt with the light of a higher life; and now the footfall of the pioneering, brave Anglo-Saxon is heard upon the heel of the savage, and breaks the silence upon his winding trail.

Although the majority of captivity narratives and captivity fictions relied on a theory of savagism to authorize the destruction of American Indians, a few narratives, such as John Dunn Hunter's *Manners and Customs of Several Indian Tribes Located West of the Mississippi* (1823) and *Memoirs of a Captivity Among the Indians of North America* (1824), which recorded his captivity since childhood among the Kansas and Osage, were decidedly more sympathetic and accurate in their accounts of Native-American culture. One of the most remarkable of such narratives concerned the life of John Tanner (1780?–1847), who was captured at age nine and lived for about thirty years among the Ojibwa. After marrying within the tribe and raising a family, he found it impossible to return to white society. Set down by Edwin James in *A Narrative of the Captivity and Adventures of John Tanner* (1830), his story offers a detailed account of Native American life, including hunts, marriage, warfare, and ritual ceremony. The narrative is an important ethnological source as well, for it records a variety of songs and reproduces a number of pictographs with transliteration, translation, and commentary. Even as he lamented the Euro-American destruction of Native American culture, however, Tanner (at least by James's account) accepted that destruction as the certain result of Euro-American military and material strength. Moreover, that technological superiority was not unrelated to what Tanner designated as the limits of native cultural development. The oratory and music of American Indians are vehement and repetitive rather than refined, Tanner argues, and their lack of a useful documentary language symbolically marks their relation to the conquerors: "without literature to give perpetuity to the creation of genius, or to bear to succeeding times the record of remarkable events, the [Native] Americans have no store house of ancient learning to open to the curiosity of the European race." Not only the wealth of oral and material culture that had survived through centuries of transmission but the evidence of Tanner's own text partially contradicted this assertion of inferiority. Yet his recognition of the power of European culture, combined with his personal preference for life among the Ojibwa, left him stranded between two worlds, his text a sign of the frontier that divided them.

Perhaps only the life of Mary Jemison bears comparison to that of John Tanner for the cultural paradoxes it contains. In her case, the issue of gender further increased the difficulty she faced in a life split between two worlds. In captivity narratives based on actual events, as in the novels built around episodes of bondage, women are often central figures. This fact is most clearly reflected in the great popularity of such novels as Cooper's *The Last of the Mohicans* and in Bancroft's dramatic rendering of Jane McCrea's captivity in his *History* (1834), which capitalized on one of the best-known American paintings of the era, John Vanderlyn's *Death of Jane McCrea* (1804), a work depicting the imminent slaughter of McCrea by two Indians, with implicit suggestions that the violence is a form of sexual violation. Although women thus occupied a symbolic role of vulnerability in the bulk of the narratives and fiction, a stunning exception is James E. Seaver's *A Narrative of the Life of Mary Jemison* (1824), which was an immediate best-seller and went through a number of editions during the nineteenth century. Mary Jemison's captivity, after the killing of her family in the French and Indian Wars, led her to live the rest of her life among Indians. She married first a Delaware, then a Seneca, and finally lived alone with half-blood children who could not easily return to white society. Her story thus went beyond melodrama. Its realistic account of life "as an Indian" gave witness to the decline and subjugation of two tribes during her lifetime, and her own "savage" acculturation can be seen as a kind of atonement for the policy of Removal. Most important, however, the narrative tells in detail the story of a woman's daily life on the frontier, her management of house and land, and makes her in effect the female equivalent of Daniel Boone, not only surviving but prospering in the wilderness.

Measured against other captivity narratives, Mary Jemison's story was quite atypical in the strength and independence accorded her. However, if the heroine of the frontier was more often drawn with significant characteristics corresponding to the sentimental pattern of domestic romance, she could nevertheless be shown to have achieved a kind of freedom and individual identity more available on the frontier than in eastern society. Several women writers found particular success in the genre of frontier fiction by rendering the transition from scenes of violence and captivity to a life of agrarian settlement and domestic labor. Catharine Sedgwick's *Live and Let Live* (1837), Marian Susanna Cummins's *Mabel Vaughan* (1857), Caroline Soule's *Little Alice; or, The Pet of the Settlement* (1863), and Metta Victor's dime novels *Alice Wilde, the Raftsman's Daughter* (1860) and *The Backwoods Bride* (1860) use novelistic accounts of family life to portray an agricultural West in which the domesticated community tended to break down, if not erase, class distinctions and promote an idealized vision of labor on the land, one that was at times more in accord with Native American social practice, with its frequent reliance on matrilineal rule and agricultural economy. At the same time, some important fiction by women anticipated later populist writing in challenging the idyll of the agricultural West. Elizabeth Fries Ellet's historical work *Pioneer Women of the West* (1852) and Eliza Hopkins's novel *Ella Lincoln; or, Western Prairie Life* (1857) presented reliable versions of the woman pioneer's experience, the latter undermining the sentimentality of marriage by portraying clearly the "homely faces and undraped outlines" of women on the prairie. Similarly, Alice Cary, the author of *Clovernook* (1852–3), two volumes depicting the transformation of frontier Ohio from a pastoral to an industrial economy, and the less valuable *Married, Not Mated* (1856), concentrated on the somber and melancholy side of family life: "Poverty is the pioneer about whose glowing forges and crashing forests burns and rings half the poetry that has filled the world."

As noted in the previous chapter, on exploration, pioneer journals, most of them published years later, and emigrant guides provide some of the most exceptional writing by frontier women. Likewise, a British emigrant, Rebecca Burlend, recorded her family's journey to an Illinois farm in *A True Picture of Emigration* (1848). The most important observer of midwestern frontier life was Michigan author Caroline Kirkland (mother of the realist writer Joseph Kirkland), whose several volumes on emigrant life are a full account of its hardships and rewards. Kirkland (1801–64) was inspired by Tocqueville, and her work often matches his precision and insight, whether discussing the philosophical question of liberty on the frontier or weather and natural resources. *A New Home – Who'll Follow?* (1839) and *Forest Life* (1842) were specifically composed as emigrant guides to the new territory, but Kirkland's strength lies particularly in her presentation, through fine details of domestic life, of the harsh but sometimes liberating life discovered by frontier women. In *Western Clearings* (1845) she looks back on the land fever of the mid-1830s and the resultant growth of social classes and diversity in labor, thus adding a political–economic dimension to her personal portrait of the garden world of the West.

Because the roles of women were in part determined by an ideology common to the domestic novel and the captivity narrative, the frontier romance often added to the captivity narrative's basic plot of capture and rescue elements of repetition, temptation, seduction, white villainy, and national purpose. Captivity became a stock device in the novels of Cooper, Simms, Timothy Flint, Catharine Sedgwick, and others, for whom the ritual of the frontier passage was the essence of expansionist spirit. A number of the most successful captivity novels set their action in the seventeenth century, thus establishing historical depth for America's national ideology. Like Parkman's *Conspiracy of Pontiac* and the better-known novels of Cooper and Simms, they thus displaced the violence of contemporary warfare and Indian Removal into a previous era and so legitimized the inevitability of the vanquishing of the Indians. Lydia Maria Child's *Hobomok* (1824) concerns a noble tribal chief who marries an apparently widowed Puritan woman but gives her up along with their half-blood son when the former husband unexpectedly returns. White savagism is thus averted, and the half-blood child, who goes off to England for his education, is a symbol of what the Native American should become: an Anglicized, obedient child. Catharine Sedgwick's *Hope Leslie* (1827), Eliza Cushing's *Saratoga* (1824), Joseph Hart's *Miriam Coffin* (1834), John T. Irving's *The Hawk Chief* (1837), Anna Snelling's *Kabaosa* (1842), and Eastburn's poem *Yamoyden* all similarly employ captivity as a means to represent the final absorption of American Indian life by the Euro-American world and to release anxiety generated by the energy of national conquest. Featuring elements central to most literatures of empire, they employ stock dramatic devices as a means of testing the nation's paradoxical capacity to decimate native cultures in the name of expanding the Jacksonian area of freedom. Anchoring this strategy in the age of the American Revolution, Josiah Priest's *Stories of the Revolution* (1836) and *A History of the Early Adventures of Washington Among the Indians of the West* (1841) borrowed from strategies current in the Indian drama in mixing captivity narratives with glorification of America's founding heroes. If he is not a brutal devourer of women and children, the Indian hero can in this way sometimes be elevated and partially cleansed by his alliance with white national figures or, as in *Hobomok*, by his contact with white family life. Yet even in those cases where life among Indians is depicted as in some ways preferable to white colonial life (e.g., *Hope Leslie*, *Yamoyden*, or John H. Robinson's *Kosato;*

The Blackfoot Renegade [1850]), the ultimate purpose of the test is to explain the demise of the Indian tribes. Edward S. Ellis's *Seth Jones; or, The Captive of the Frontier* (1860), one of the first dime novels, reduces the action of countless examples of the genre to a simple formula: "When the Anglo-Saxon's body is pitted against that of the North American Indian, it sometimes yields; but when his mind takes the place of contestant, it *never* loses."

The Euro-American body might fail or become contaminated by savagery, but the mind would prevail – this message permeates American frontier literature. Underlying the portrayal of women and families at risk from savagery is a pervasive fear of miscegenation, which is latent in the Pocahontas stories and elsewhere but has its full articulation in *The Last of the Mohicans*. These texts are typically less vile than the antimiscegenation literature directed against blacks and abolitionists in the period, but they are nonetheless revealing of the relationship between popular melodrama and racial fears. In John Neal's witchcraft novel, *Rachel Dyer* (1828), the half blood is a gothic hero representing a psychic and social struggle between Puritan "light" and demonic "darkness." The half-blood hero of Ann Stephens's *Malaeska; the Indian Wife of the White Hunter* (1839), an Indian hater unaware of his own heritage, is prevented from contaminating a white woman in marriage by the last-minute discovery that his mother is an Indian; the mother and son, victims of unnatural amalgamation, then commit suicide. By contrast, the Indian hero of John S. Robb's *Kaam; or Daylight, The Arapahoe Half Breed* (1847) becomes a white hater and assumes the name of "Night." Poe's Dirk Peters, in *The Narrative of Arthur Gordon Pym* (1838), is a deformed Hobbesian creature who probably inspired the similar depiction of a "monkey-like" half-blood monster in John Esten Cooke's *Lord Fairfax* (1868), which employs specific parallels to *The Tempest* in order to suggest that the half blood's brutality can be tamed by the beauty of a white woman.

Like the theme of captivity, the theme of mixed blood became a mechanical device, a means of generating the horror of transgressed or collapsed boundaries in the body comparable to boundaries violated and crossed by actual Indian warfare and Removal. The numerous popular novels turned out by hack writers like Osgood Bradbury and Emerson Bennett, and later by the dime novelists, used the two themes in tandem. In Bradbury's *Larooka: The Belle of the Penobscots* (1846), the mixed-blood heroine's exotic sensuality almost leads to incest with her brother; in *Lucelle; or, The Young Iroquois* (1845), the heroine's virtue supports Bradbury's manifesto in favor of intermarriage as a way to "purify" the Native American "stock"; whereas in *Pontiac; or, The Last Battle of the Ottawa Chief* (1848), the French and Indians must twice rescue Pontiac's half-blood daughter from the British so that she can finally marry a French soldier and become – as the "Italian beauty" – the toast of Paris society. Bennett, far from praising miscegenation, saw it as savage evidence of degradation. The captured heroine of *The Forest Rose; A Tale of the Frontier* (1850) is barely prevented from becoming a fierce woman warrior, the final loss of her social role: "By a righteous law of nature, man loves what he can foster and protect: woman, what can cherish and protect her." In *The Prairie Flower; or, Adventures in the Far West* (1849) Bennett's characters are protected from both natives and dangerous mountain men along the Oregon Trail by Kit Carson, and in *Kate Clarendon; or, Necromancy in the Wilderness* (1848), the angelic heroine must be rescued from a rejected suitor, who has joined the other serpents and "swarthy savages" crawling about in the Ohio woods.

As it converged with the standard gothic romance, then, the captivity story, on stage and in fiction, superimposed an ideology of racial superiority upon the stereotypes of popular culture, the two working together to ward off the threat of contamination. Woman's symbolic role as besieged maiden in the gothic novel assumed nationalistic purpose in the captivity novel, where she appeared as the sacred embodiment of racial purity and the vessel of future generations destined to sweep across the opened western territories. Over that destiny, however, loomed the shadow of other races. The apocalyptic threat of miscegenation, anticipating the hysteria of later periods of American and European racial conflict, was voiced in James Kirke Paulding's *Konnigsmarke* (1823) by a black slave figured by Paulding as a witch: "the time shall surely come, when the pile of oppression ye [whites] have reared to the clouds shall fall, and crush your heads. Black men and red men, all colours, shall combine against your pale, white race; and the children of the masters shall become the bondsmen of the posterity of the slave." Paulding's passage was prophetic of later reactions to racist ideology by non-Western peoples; but even in the decade before the official policy of Indian Removal was adopted, it revealed volatile fears hidden within the literature devoted to the passing of the noble American savage and the heroic redemption of innocent white captives.

The portrayal of American Indians in both history and literature, and the special power of the captivity narrative and its fictional derivatives in post-revolutionary "family romance," can be fully understood only as developments parallel to the rise of the American frontier hero, the subject of much of the most significant and influential American writing of the period. Indeed, the Euro-American hero and the Native American hero in white literature were in many respects mirror images of one another. The hero of the captivity narrative, as the genre assumed a more novelistic form in the early nineteenth century, was as likely to be a rough frontiersman as a soldier or community leader. Often he was a husband, father, or son driven to vengeful madness by the slaughter or abduction of his family, a paradigm repeated on through twentieth-century popular culture. Whatever shape he took, however, his portrayal was likely to be influenced by the central myth of Daniel Boone (1734–1820), the famous eighteenth-century land agent, pioneer, and patriarch of Kentucky. First immortalized in an appendix to John Filson's *The Discovery, Settlement, and Present State of Kentucky* (1784), Boone became the inspiration for numerous frontier heroes and the subject of many versions of his own exploits. Filson's Boone is celebrated as the founder of a new republic, a hero destined by Providence and by the laws of nature to journey through a dark wilderness and lead his people into a promised land of rich, pristine territory. A true Enlightenment hero, Boone is tempted by the forces of primitivism but remains a harbinger of progress, in particular the agricultural regeneration of the wilderness. Daniel Bryan's epic poem *The Mountain Muse* (1813) portrays Boone as the incarnation of a national aristocratic force that will subjugate the chaos figured both in the sublime but wild landscape and in the undisciplined ferocity of the American Indian.

Boone appeared as a character in a number of histories, plays, poems, and novels, but none as popular or influential as Timothy Flint's *Biographical Memoir of Daniel Boone* (1833), also published as *Life and Adventures of Colonel Daniel Boone*. Flint relied on newspapers, interviews, and folktales in constructing a hero great enough to embody the mythology of a whole nation. This Boone is, among other things, a representative "westerner" – the new type of rough, independent, stoic American man that only frontier life can produce. His necessary identification with the Indian, as part of his immersion in the wilderness, is more emphatic in Flint's version, and his role as a hunter is made prominent (as a young boy, Flint writes, Boone "waged a war of extermination" against animals, in anticipation of his role as an Indian fighter). Flint notes that Boone was surely one model for Cooper's Leatherstocking. But it is clear that the influence went both ways, for Flint's Boone, like Natty Bumppo, is a crack hunter, a tracker with perfect "instinct," and a natural but unlettered Christian: the "woods were his books and his temple." The stories of Boone's own captivity and that of his daughter, like the notorious courtship scene, in which the deer Boone is tracking leads him to his future wife, Rebecca, tend toward the fantastic in Flint's account. Like the novelistic version of captivity narratives, the domestic drama highlights the ideological function of the primary myth of Boone's leadership, which is evidence that a new "garden of earth" "had been won from the domination of the savage tribes, and opened as an asylum for the oppressed, the enterprising, and the free of every land."

Boone, of course, is driven farther west by the arrival of the very civilization he has made possible. His stoic isolation, like that of Leatherstocking, serves in part to keep him from the corruptions of society, but it may also be seen as an expression of his sacrificial character. As his exploits became more and more mythic, Boone's singularity could also be made to bear the burden of anxiety over violations of the wilderness and decimation of its native inhabitants. Something of this contradictory vision about its heroes is surely present as well in the public's enthusiastic response to the legends of the idiosyncratic frontier figure recorded in *Narrative of the Life of David Crockett* (1834). A Tennessee state legislator and U.S. congressman, Crockett (1786–1836) was best known as the tall-tale hero of the folklore created to advance his minor political career. Exaggerated stories of his bear hunting and Indian killing, narrated and parodied in backwoods slang, made stories about him, including his own dubious *Life,* very popular. He broke with fellow Tennessean Andrew Jackson over land rights and the president's policy of Indian Removal; his career ended, he went to Texas and became immortalized as a slain hero in the battle of the Alamo. As the model for the Indian-killer Earth in *Elkswatawa,* burlesqued by Paulding as the character Nimrod Wildfire in his play *The Lion of the West* (1830), and the subject of numerous frontier rags-to-riches stories and editorials, Crockett nearly became a living caricature of the frontiersman myth, a comic Boone whose braggadocio heightened the illusion of masculine virility even as it exposed its tall-tale character. Along with Sam Houston, whose autobiography told the story of his life among the Cherokees and as the father of Texas, Crockett (at least in his own myth) inhabited two overlapping worlds: a powerful world of social and political order, sustained in its drive west by another world of isolated, rugged, outlaw heroes prone to daredevil risk and comic outburst.

As the examples of Boone and especially Crockett made clear, the proliferation of violence and the propensity for tall tales on the frontier often transcended attitudes toward Indian savagery. For example, Indiana minister Bayard Rush Hall's *The New Purchase; or, Seven and a Half Years in the Far West* (1843), written under the pen name of Robert Carlton, is one of the most bizarre works about frontier life. The novel combines strong pleas on behalf of violated Indian rights with wild burlesques of hunting, boating, preaching, and "savage" life. Hall's style is an anarchic mix of pathos, bombast, and farce, less successfully realized in a sequel entitled *Something for Everybody* (1846). Also unique in the frontier genre, and notable for both its careful observation and its sense of justice across racial and cultural lines, is the work of the German emigrant Karl Postle (1793–1864). Postle traveled widely in the western United States and Mexico and, writing under the pseudonym of Charles Sealsfield, became an important advocate for Native Americans. His novel *Tokeah; or, The White Rose* (1829) was the first in a series of internationally popular books on frontier life and American pioneers, among them *The Cabin Book; or, Sketches of Life in Texas* (1844), *Life in the New World* (1844), and *Frontier Life* (1856).

More typical of the western fiction that began to appear in cheap periodicals in the 1850s and flowered in the dime novel of the post-Civil War years were melodramas such as E. C. Judson's ("Ned Buntline") *Norwood; or, Life on the Prairie* (1850) and David Belisle's *The American Family Robinson . . . Lost in the Great Desert of the West* (1854), a captivity and survival tale that concludes with settlement in California, where "in giant strides science and art triumph over the rough barriers, and open avenues for the advancement of moral reform." In the dime novel and its predecessors, the author often examined characters who, whether out of a sense of justice, a desire for outlaw life, or sheer perversion, not only fled to the frontier but became "white Indians" and often turned their violence back against other white frontiersmen. Charles Webber's *Old Hicks the Guide* (1848), John Richardson's *Wacousta; or, The Prophecy* (1851), Emerson Bennett's *The Renegade* (1848), and H. R. Howard's *The Life and Adventures of John A. Murrell, the Great Western Land Pirate* (1847) contain notable antebellum examples of such renegades. Implicit in the dime novels, as in the Indian drama, was a fantasy enactment of the process of Removal. Judson, for example, would go on to write a series of Buffalo Bill dime novels, later staged as part of Cody's traveling show. Common to virtually all fiction set on the frontier was a sense of the inevitable vanquishing of the Indians and the gradual establishment of social and economic order in an outlaw environment. The lesson of the novel was that both the untamed Indian and the white renegade would be replaced by pastoral and, later, industrial life.

This, too, was the lesson of the fictional character who was to become the most famous of frontier heroes trapped between two worlds. Even the mythological versions of Boone's life were no match for the frontiersman Leatherstocking, created by James Fenimore Cooper (1789–1851) in five novels that depict the hero's life from early years to his death on the far western plains: *The Deerslayer* (1841), *The Last of the Mohicans* (1826), *The Pathfinder* (1840), *The Pioneers* (1823), and *The Prairie* (1827). Because the novel dealing with Leatherstocking's youth in the 1740s, *The Deerslayer,* was written last, it represents in part Cooper's self-conscious return to an earlier, socially less complex phase of American history. Revolving around several episodes of captivity (as do all the novels except *The Pioneers*), *The Deerslayer* depicts the formation of Leatherstocking's frontier character against the background of a now faded, mythic Indian world that has been conquered and reordered by "paleface" names and customs. Born Natty Bumppo, the hero regresses from white life, acquiring the names Deerslayer and Hawkeye for his prowess in killing first an animal, then a man. Like Boone, he is an isolated, stoic figure, in this novel rejecting the love of Judith Hutter for the comradeship of his lifelong Delaware companion Chingachgook. But from Judith he receives his mythic gun, "Killdeer," which symbolizes the male fertility channeled away from family into ascetic wilderness life and which (at the time Cooper is writing in 1841, after over a decade of Removal) may also be taken to represent the increased propensity for violence and Indian-hating Cooper's young hero displays.

In all the novels Leatherstocking is a man torn between two worlds. He shares the "gifts" of the Indian, fine instincts and often incredible skills in woodcraft, but he has "white" sympathies, relying on a "natural" sense of justice and implicitly Christian forgiveness, while continually condemning the purported Indian ideal of violent revenge and the practice of scalping (although he argues that both belong to the American Indian's particular "gifts"). Leatherstocking had become a national hero by the time Cooper, after a pause of thirteen years, returned to him in *The Pathfinder* and *The Deerslayer*. In the former, it is Natty who falls in love but must, fortunately for his myth, be rejected by the white heroine. Set amid 1759 battles between the British and the Iroquois near Lake Ontario, *The Pathfinder,* along with the earlier *The Last of the Mohicans,* depicts Leatherstocking as a mature scout and warrior. By placing his exploits in the context of the French and Indian Wars, Cooper called attention to the war's instrumental role in forming the United States and thus preparing the way for Euro-American conquest of Indian tribes and territories. Cooper's saga encompasses that expansion, at once deploring the tragic alienation of the frontier hero Leatherstocking and mourning the "destined"demise of Indians, yet carefully detailing the social and economic necessity of the land's transfiguration into property and capital.

In the first of the novels, *The Pioneers,* the forces of law, property, and social order (represented by Judge Temple, modeled in part on Cooper's father) are in conflict with Leatherstocking's belief in his natural right to the land and its bounty. A figure of romantic dispossession, Leatherstocking is driven out of the community at the book's conclusion, and the marriage of Temple's young heirs underscores Cooper's belief in the value of lawfully transmitted property. By the time of *The Prairie,* set on the western plains in 1804, just after the Lousiana Purchase, the old man Natty Bumppo is virtually the last of a race of individualistic frontiersmen (even though Cooper was in fact writing at the height of the "mountain man" era). Entangled in a new series of captivities and skirmishes by a dissolute group of squatters, Leatherstocking once again proves his physical prowess and his preference for Indian life over white society before succumbing to a death that seems already coincident with the closing of the initial phase of America's postrevolutionary expansion: "The trapper had remained nearly motionless for an hour. His eyes alone had occasionally opened and shut. When opened, his gaze seemed fastened on the clouds which hung around the western horizon, reflecting the bright colors, and giving form and loveliness to the glorious tints of an American sunset. The hour – the calm beauty of the season – the occasion, all conspired to fill the spectators with solemn awe." Conquest has here become a carefully composed landscape portrait, with the dying scout a memorial witness to the necessary human cast of the nation's future.

The period between *The Prairie*'s setting and its composition in 1827 allowed Cooper to see clearly the destiny of the western territories and their inhabitants. Like Lewis and Clark, Leatherstocking, the tragic harbinger of white settlement, had traversed the continent; the mountains and plains were being settled; and Monroe had formulated the policy of Removal, which would accelerate under Jackson. Thus, Cooper in 1826 could speak with symbolic accuracy of the "last" of the Mohicans. In the novel of that name, the young Delaware chief Uncas is the last of his distinguished line; but his father, Chingachgook, who outlives him only to die in a forest fire (by virtual suicide) in *The Pioneers,* might also be considered the "last" of the Mohicans. Even though Hawkeye and Chingachgook triumph over the enemy Indians and rescue the white heroines from captivity, it is "white blood" that prevails in the novel. In Cooper's deepest meditation on the question of miscegenation (which he projected to be the ultimate result of any actual assimilation), the Euro-American Cora, marked by the black blood of her West Indian slave mother, and Uncas, the Indian who loves her, are sacrificed, while her sister Alice, a submissive woman who has no place on the frontier, is saved for marriage to the soldier Duncan Heyward. Cooper draws the "evil" Magua with something of the enchanting power of Milton's Satan, but though Magua was clearly wronged by whites and justly seeks revenge, he is also destroyed.

The action of *The Last of the Mohicans,* divided into two captivity sequences, pivots around the historical 1757 massacre of the British by French-allied Hurons at Fort William Henry. Cooper's significant enactment of the massacre resembles many of his battle scenes in its stylized caricature of combat, but it is especially important insofar as it turns the image of an Indian attack upon a woman and child, already a widespread literary and political cliché, into the spark initiating a ferocious loss of control:

The savage spurned the worthless rags [of offered clothing], and perceiving that the shawl had already become a prize to another, his bantering but sullen smile changing to a gleam of ferocity, he dashed the head of the infant against a rock, and cast its quivering remains to her very feet. For an instant, the mother stood like a statue of despair, looking wildly down at the unseemly object, which had so lately nestled in her bosom and smiled in her face; and then she raised her eyes and her countenance toward heaven, as if calling on God to curse the perpetrator of the foul deed. She was spared the sin of such a prayer; for, maddened at his disappointment, and excited at the sight of blood, the Huron mercifully drove his tomahawk into her own brain. The mother sank under the blow, and fell, grasping at her child, in death, with the same engrossing love that had caused her to cherish it when living.

At that dangerous moment Magua placed his hands to his mouth, and raised the fatal and appalling whoop. . . . Death was everywhere, and in his most terrible and disgusting aspects. Resistance only served to inflame the murderers, who inflicted their furious blows long after their victims were beyond the power of their resentment. The flow of blood might be likened to the outbreaking of a torrent; and as the natives became heated and maddened by the sight, many among them even kneeled to the earth, and drank freely, exultingly, hellishly, of the crimson tide.

The violence of the Hurons, who are allied with the French and led by the vengeful Magua, dominates the book, and Hawkeye's exploits are all in answer to it. Although French and British incursions have destroyed the existing "harmony of warfare" among Indian nations, turning them unnaturally against one another and corrupting or humiliating their leaders (as in the case of Magua, debased by white alcohol and whipped in public by the father of Cora and Alice), Cooper's novel inevitably links the doom of the "noble" Indians to the savage violence of the "bad" Indians. Projecting into a past war the exterminating violence that his own generation both feared and set in motion, Cooper authorized the destiny envisioned at the book's end by Tamenund, the ancient chief of the Delaware: "The palefaces are masters of the earth, and the time of the Red Man has not yet come again."

The Last of the Mohicans may lack the freshness of adventure and clear delineation of Hawkeye's character found in *The Deerslayer,* the broad mythic scope of *The Prairie,* and the complex interaction of individual freedom with laws and social obligations seen in *The Pioneers,* but it is nevertheless Cooper's most complete examination of the Indian question as it was defined by the ideology of Removal. Hawkeye's fanatic insistence throughout the book that he is a "man without a cross" (i.e., a man with pure white, uncrossed blood) suggests the double bind that made him for Cooper such a powerful hero: he must reject white society because of its constraints, corruption, and hypocrisy, but his innate, if unlettered Christian sensibility and loathing of what he defines as the cruelty of true Indian customs leave him monastically isolated, a patriarch without a dynasty. When Parkman reviewed Cooper's collected novels in 1852, he recognized Leatherstocking as an "epitome of American history" in the era of exploration and settlement, a "hybrid offspring of civilization and barbarism," but saw him too in essence as a renegade, emblematic of the savage life by then passing away.

In Cooper's conception, however, Natty Bumppo is also the tragic, sacrificial figure who both forecasts and atones for Euro-American conquest as, indeed, does the body of Cooper's work itself. His other Indian novels are less successful than the Leatherstocking Tales. In *Wyandotté* (1843), set during the American Revolution, the title character rises from his degraded role as a servant to kill his white master. *The Oak Openings* (1848) makes its western hero a more refined, less violent bee hunter who survives the Indian wars in Michigan to become a farmer and politician and portrays the high potential for Christian conversion among the Indians. Indians have a minor role in Cooper's Littlepage novels. In *The Redskins* (1846), for example, real Indians drive off the "Injins," an anti-rent mob who adopt Indian disguises as a sign of rebellion and defiance of the law. Only in the earlier *The Wept of Wish-ton-Wish* (1829) does Cooper achieve the complex force of the Leatherstocking series. Set against successive generations of a Puritan community, the novel employs King Philip's War, the themes of witchcraft and regicide, episodes of captivity, and the threat of miscegenation to chart the rise of New England as a securely held Euro-American territory. With any of these novels Cooper might have secured a place for himself as an important white writer about American Indians. Yet it is his panoramic Leatherstocking Tales, which unite the era's central myth of frontier individualism with a grand dramatization of the military defeat and cultural dispossession of Native Americans, that elevated Cooper above his contemporaries and made him widely read by Europeans, for whom the American frontier was the height of the exotic, and by succeeding generations of Americans, who were eager to discover, as in a mirror, the mythical heroic traits, bloody and disturbing as they may be, of their own national character.

The years from the 1820s through the 1840s, during which the necessity for Indian Removal fully entered public consciousness, saw the most significant production of fiction that made its noble native heroes the "last" of their tribes or families or simply the last to resist absorption or dispersal to western lands and eventually to reservations. Among novels of the period that display the search for a theory of conquest, Nicholas Hentz's *Tadeuskind, the King of the Lenape* (1825) anticipated Cooper's characterization of Uncas by comparing its real, historical chief to the "Torso of Hercules," in effect relegating him to antiquity. Likewise, Charles F. Hoffman's revolutionary novel *Greyslaer: A Romance of the Mohawk* (1840) made Chief Joseph Brant one of nature's doomed "children," and Daniel P. Thompson's later *The Doomed Chief* (1860) celebrated King Philip in the title role but concluded with the graceful suicide of the Native American heroine and a familiar message: "all was lost, forever lost, to the red man." James B. Ransom's *Osceola: a Tale of the Seminole Wars* (1838) depicts an idyllic tribal state contaminated by white contact and throws into relief the emblematic melancholy wasting of

Osceola, whose "majestic form soon dwindled to a mere shadow." Like the various portraits of Tecumseh's and Black Hawk's doom, Robert Strange's *Eoneguski; or, The Cherokee Chief* (1839) justifies Removal by making its Indian hero a subordinate soldier in Andrew Jackson's 1812 army who fails to fulfill his dying father's command of revenge and in the end chooses a pacific agricultural life in North Carolina.

Employing a strategy of retrospection that he would repeat in his best-known novels of the South, William Gilmore Simms, (1806–70) depicted the emergence of a gentry and a frontier middle-class structure in South Carolina after the extermination of Yemassee Indians in *The Yemassee* (1835). Based on warfare that took place in 1715, the novel confidently asserted the doctrine of Removal, which by then was fully incorporated in the public mind through the southern states' forcible eviction of the Five Civilized Tribes: "Conquest and sway are the great leading principles of [civilization's] existence, and the savage must join in her train, or she rides over him relentlessly in her onward progress." Like Tamenund in *The Last of the Mohicans,* the Yemassee chief Sanutee foresees the death of his tribe. Corrupted by alcohol and white customs, his son Occonestoga is eventually expelled from the tribe and killed by his mother to prevent a ceremonial humiliation. Like Cooper, Simms in his preface depicted the Romance as a combination of novelistic and epic features, and the Indian as a fit subject for "the natural romance of our country." He thought assimilation impossible and had no qualms about inventing Native American mythology in order to create for them an antiquity comparable in his eyes to that of Greeks or Saxons, presumably to assert the historical depth of America and at the same time to answer white compunctions about the natives' demise. His essays on Boone, "The First Hunter of Kentucky" (1845), and on "Literature and Art Among the American Aborigines" (a review of Schoolcraft's works published in 1845) supported his contention that the "North American Indian was as noble a specimen of crude humanity as we can find" – that is, a specimen like one of those featured in McKenney's Indian Gallery, belonging now to the past but nonetheless deserving of archeological study: "We are apt to think him no more than a surly savage, capable of showing nothing better than his teeth. . . . We are unwilling to read his past as we are unable to control his future; – refuse to recognize his sensibilities, and reject with scorn the evidence of any more genial attributes." Within a matter of two decades after the official proclamation of Removal, the novel had adapted itself almost seamlessly to an ethnological attitude toward the Native American. The preservation of Uncas and similar native heroes as though in stone monuments was mirrored by the elevation into myth of their closely matched but finally superior white antagonists.

Boone, Crockett, Jackson, and Cooper's Leatherstocking became heroes at the moment the "West" became a definitive aspect of American thought and life. The violent displacement and subjugation of Native Americans were thus an integral part of the process by which both white and Indian archetypal heroes would become permanent elements of American cultural thought. Two authors who had an equally large share in establishing the West as a subject for literature and, in fact, as the distinguishing feature of America's nationalistic culture were Timothy Flint (1780–1840) and James Hall (1793–1868). Flint, a Massachusetts missionary, first wrote an account of his travels in the Mississippi Valley, *Recollections of the Last Ten Years* (1826), before turning to history and fiction. His *History and Geography of the Mississippi Valley* (1827) is one of the best studies of the region; and *Indian Wars of the West* (1833) contains the central materials of the Boone legend he expanded into the *Memoir* that same year. *Indian Wars* not only gives a partisan rendering of exploration and settlement but also argues for the historical depth and importance of the New World indicated by recent archeological finds. Establishing the American West as a legitimate ground for ideology and for fiction was one of Flint's special goals, reflected, for example, in *George Mason, the Young Backwoodsman* (1829), a novel about the children of a New England minister who moves his family to the Mississippi Valley. "I feel as much interest in the march of these barefooted boys along the deep forest," Flint wrote, "as I do in reading about the adventures and ridiculous distresses of fine dressed lords and ladies." This theme runs through most of Flint's fiction, despite its very diverse settings. In *Francis Berrian, or the Mexican Patriot* (1826), a New Englander brings the spirit of the American Revolution to the 1822 rebellion in Mexico. *The Life and Adventures of Arthur Clenning* (1828) concerns South Seas castaways who live as "Adam and Eve," adopt a native girl (named "Rescue") and teach her English and Christianity, then return to the Illinois frontier and marry her to a Pottawatomie chief before giving up their landed estate in England for frontier life in America. Both Poe's *Narrative of Arthur Gordon Pym* and Melville's *Typee* seem indebted to Flint's *Arthur Clenning,* particularly to the extent that they equate South Seas natives with Native Americans as similarly alien groups. Flint's best-known novel, *The Shoshonee Valley* (1830), is a complex story of a white man and his Chinese wife living in the ethnically diverse Oregon Territory among mountain men, Native Americans of various tribes, Spaniards, Russians, and Asians. A tragic love story, with episodes of captivity, rescue, and warfare, is here balanced by Flint's attempts at anthropological realism, whereby the civilization of the Shoshone appears as a Rousseauistic state that slowly succumbs to the fatal effects of white money, alcohol, and debauchery.

James Hall is best remembered now as the source of Melville's chapter in

The Confidence-Man (1857) entitled "The Metaphysics of Indian-Hating," an ironic meditation on the "Indian problem" derived from Hall's story of Colonel John Moredock in *Sketches of History, Life, and Manners in the West* (1834). After his family was massacred, Moredock became a classic Indian hater – a "Leatherstocking Nemesis," in Melville's words, dedicated to "a calm, cloistered scheme of strategical, implacable, and lonesome vengeance." Decent and generous in polite society, but driven by violent longings for revenge on the frontier, the figure of Moredock epitomized the cycle of vengeance that expansion brought to the surface of individual and national character. Grim violence permeates Hall's sketches and stories, and revenge preoccupies everyone in his frontier world. In his only novel, *The Harpe's Head, A Legend of Kentucky* (1833), a love story holds together a similar (and in this case authentic) tale of two brothers who unaccountably became mad killers. If the theory of savagism articulated in his contribution to McKenney's *History of the Indian Tribes of North America* was based on a perceived antagonism between native savagery and superior white culture, *The Harpe's Head* portrayed an indulgence in violence, especially among national leaders and chiefs, to be universal. From Nimrod to Black Hawk, Hall writes, "the magnates of the earth have ever taken great delight in killing animals, and cutting the throats of their fellow men."

Besides working as a lawyer and a judge, Hall edited the *Illinois Gazette* (1820–2) and the *Illinois Intelligencer* (1829–32) and was founding editor of the *Illinois Monthly Magazine* (later called the *Western Monthly Magazine*), the first literary periodical in the West. His stories and sketches appeared in a number of volumes with different titles and arrangements, beginning with *Letters from the West* (1828), which sought to establish the West as a legitimate literary subject and attacked European observers who had ridiculed American manners. His work offered credible descriptions of frontier life and developing cities such as Pittsburgh, Wheeling, and Cincinnati. Yet his dominant theme was the one Melville picked out for scrutiny: the sources and practice of Indian-hating in American history and myth. In "The Pioneer," from *Tales of the Border* (1835), the hero's desire for revenge against Indians – his "insatiable thirst for the blood of the savage" – is only overcome when he nearly murders his own captive sister, now living with an Indian husband and children. "The Indian-Hater," collected in *Legends of the West* (1832), portrays a man whom the mere sight of an Indian in a store can drive into frenzy: "His eyes rolled wildly, as if he had been suddenly stung to madness, gleaming with a strange fierceness; a supernatural lustre, like that which flashes from the eye-balls of the panther, when crouched in a dark covert, and ready to dart upon his prey."

By the time Melville explored the theme of Indian-hating, it was thus a fundamental part of literary ideology. Projecting violence onto the mirror of the Indian, the pioneer and the novelist alike risked a reversal of savagism, a containment of Indian violence by its inversion to the white imperial self. As Parkman wrote in *The Conspiracy of Pontiac,* "the chronicles of the American borders are filled with the deeds of men, who, having lost all by the merciless tomahawk, have lived for vengeance alone; and such men will never cease to exist so long as a hostile tribe remains within striking distance of an American settlement." The revenge of the Indian hater is central, for example, to Bennett's *The Forest Rose,* Samuel Young's *Tom Hanson, the Avenger* (1847), Samuel B. Hanson's *Tom Quick, the Indian Slayer* (1851), and James McHenry's historical narratives *The Wilderness; or, Braddock's Times* (1823) and *The Spectre of the Forest* (1823). In James Kirke Paulding's *The Dutchman's Fireside* (1831), Indian-hating forms part of the material that Paulding argues should constitute our national literature; and in his *Western Ho!* (1832), a novel based on Flint's work, the hunter Ambrose Bushfield is a Boone-like isolato whose experience has made him of one mind on Indians: "When [pioneers] plough their fields, they every day turn up the bones of their own colour and kin who have been scalped, and tortured, and whipped, and starved by these varmints, that are ten thousand times more bloodthirsty than tigers, and as cunning as 'possums." Bushfield's lament simply reverses the more common, and more accurate, Native American assertion that Euro-American plows were turning up the sacred bones and relics of *their* ancestors.

Easily the most famous fiction of Indian-hating was written by Robert Montgomery Bird (1806–54). Trained as a physician, Bird wrote several historical dramas before turning to novels, such as *The Infidel; or, the Fall of Mexico* (1835) and *The Hawks of Hawk-Hollow* (1835), a revolutionary romance. But it is *Nick of the Woods; or, the Jibbenainosay* (1837), dramatized by Louisa Medina the following year, that fixed the bloodstained Indian hater in western mythology. Attacking the "dreams of poets and sentimentalists" who saw the Indian as a noble figure, Bird's novel took Boone as a model for the Janus-faced Nathan Slaughter, a Quaker who, once his family is massacred, leads a double life as pacifist and Indian-hunter. His vengeance never fully satisfied, he mutilates and scalps his victims, as he himself was once scalped. Considered a madman by other pioneers, Nick's revenge seems indeed to exacerbate his insanity:

The bundle of scalps in his hand, the single one, yet reeking with blood, at his belt, and the axe of Wenonga, gory to the helve, and grasped with a hand not less bloodstained, were not more remarkable evidences of transformation than were manifested in his countenance, deportment, and expression. His eye beamed with a wild excitement, with exultation mingled with fury; his step was fierce, active, firm, and elastic, like that of a warrior leaping through the measures of the war-dance.

Nathan Slaughter's madness, like Bushfield's psychological reversal of the Indian's grievance, suggests that the celebration of revenge could reveal an undercurrent of white guilt, a paradoxical imbalance of emotions brought on by the ideology of conquest that harbored a powerful identification with that which was being destroyed. Because the literature of Indian-hating was an extreme case of the process of inversion by which white writers exchanged attributes, both heroic and savage, with those they identified as enemies, the hero often remained trapped in a self-reflexive theory of savagism.

By midcentury, the time of Parkman's seminal *Conspiracy of Pontiac,* the rhetoric of Indian-hating and the romantic incorporation of the American Indian hero had merged. The annexation of Texas and Mexican territories at midcentury extended the official frontier, accelerated Removal, and increased warfare with the numerous tribes of the West. Proposals to treat with the Plains Indian tribes with a view to creating reservations for them date from 1849, following the creation of a new Department of the Interior, which oversaw the Indian Bureau. In 1850, Commissioner of Indian Affairs Orlando Brown recommended a policy of "concentration – the creation for each tribe of a reservation consisting of "a country adapted to agriculture, of limited extent and well-defined boundaries; within which all, with occasional exceptions, should be compelled constantly to remain until such time as their general improvement and good conduct may supercede the necessity of such restrictions." What would constitute such conduct and improvement was never self-evident, and the advance of the white agricultural frontier, fueled by the rapid construction of roads and railroads and important mineral discoveries in California, Colorado, and other interior areas, soon flooded the region with frontiersmen who had little respect for the fragile bargains struck between the federal government and tribal chiefs. The creation of reservations, with all its implications for the course of Native American culture and literature on into the twentieth century, was the logical outcome of the policy of Removal as the tragic experience of eastern tribes was repeated on the Plains and in the transmontane West.

By the 1850s the Euro-American cultural response to Native Americans was firmly in place. One can trace it clearly in the major historical and ethnological works of the period, or perhaps more effectively in the now less well known novels that nonetheless display the infusion of archetypal thought into popular culture. Two examples that superimpose past upon present, the originating configurations of myth upon currently volatile issues, serve to sum up the status of American Indians in the white mind in the decade before the Civil War. In *Mount Hope; or, Philip, King of the Wampanoags* (1850), Gideon Hollister sets out "to retrace some of the faded and now scarcely-visible features of those exterminating wars" of early settlement and to delineate historical figures who are now "almost as fabulous as the fictions of poets or the creations of an early mythology." Philip is compared to Caesar and Hannibal, but more conspicuously – in a figure of striking duality – to an eagle that never faltered "in its flight till it was quenched in the radiance of the orb of civilization, which it sought in vain to blot from the heavens." Hollister's imperial poetic style is everywhere driven by a concept of manifest destiny that by midcentury gave a new force to the incorporation of the Native American into national ideology. Similarly, in M. C. Hodge's *The Mestico; or, the Warpath and Its Incidents* (1850), the Creek Wars of 1836 are the backdrop for a simultaneous meditation on mixing and miscegenation, Removal, and the metaphoric value of the Native American. Hodge typically finds the Indian's pristine state romantically noble but sees his bad traits exaggerated and "swelled into fearful controlling influence" by white contact. Indians become vile, drunken, and rapacious when "artificial desires" are "grafted into the parent stem" by contact or interbreeding. A standard melodrama of native attacks and the captivity of a white heroine fuels the claim that "poetry and romance have given a charm to Indian character which stubborn facts, instead of enhancing, will dispel." The migrants crowding into Creek territory simply act out a natural process, just as the heroine's rescue and concluding marriage symbolize the land's restoration to peace and fecundity: "the fertile land that was wasting under their [the Creeks'] tillage now blooms under the industry of the whites." As much a minor and forgotten novel as Hollister's *Mount Hope*, Hodge's *The Mestico* contains in brief the multitude of themes that Euro-American literature derived from, and imposed upon, the events of Indian Removal.

Such novels overlapped the popular ethnographic material produced in abundance at midcentury by Schoolcraft and Catlin, among others, and they tended to mirror the fixed attitudes of conquest and Euro-American progress that almost every account of western exploration and development conveyed. The Mexican War, the Gold Rush, and the gradual demise of the theory of the Great American Desert opened for white settlement an enormous new territory and undermined the futile theory that removal of Native American tribes to the west of the Mississippi would protect them and halt border warfare. The increasingly complex but also ideologically paradigmatic view of American Indians found in historical documents and fiction by the 1850s testifies to the triumph of a psychopoetic image over a more disturbing and often brutal reality, to the need to contain in carefully controlled forms of discourse the dangerous energy of the imperial mind.

3

THE LITERATURE OF SLAVERY AND
AFRICAN AMERICAN CULTURE

O
N THE FIRST ANNIVERSARY of the founding of his famous antislavery magazine, the *Liberator,* William Lloyd Garrison invoked the
"Spirit of Liberty" that was "thundering at castle-gates and prison-
doors" throughout the world. Rather than celebrate the fires of democratic
revolution that had spread from America in 1776 to revolutions in a number
of European countries by the early 1830s, however, Garrison dwelt on the
significant failure of the American Revolution – the problem of slavery.
When liberty "gets the mastery over its enemy," Garrison inquired rhetorically, "will not its retaliation be terrible?" Only "timely repentance" could
save the American nation's "blind, unrelenting, haughty, cruel, heaven-
daring oppressors" from the fate of foreign despots and aristocracies. Because
repentance on a national scale did not seem likely in the 1830s, Garrison put
forth a paradoxical proposition: in order to avoid having to join in defending
the South against slave insurrection, the North ought to dissolve the Union.
Were this threat to "break the chain which binds [the South] to the Union"
carried out, however, Garrison predicted that "the scenes of St. Domingo
would be witnessed throughout her borders."

Garrison was no doubt thinking of Nat Turner's slave rebellion in Southampton, Virginia, the previous year. The most successful slave uprising in
American history, Turner's rebellion caused alarm in the South about a
repetition of the massive democratic rebellion of slaves in San Domingo
(Haiti) at the end of the eighteenth century and quickly became a touchstone
of both antislavery and proslavery sentiment. But Garrison may also have had
in mind the black abolitionist David Walker's fiery pamphlet, *Appeal . . . to
the Coloured Citizens of the World,* which had appeared in 1828 and which some
had held responsible for Turner's rebellion. Like many writers of his generation, Walker invoked the central paradox of American democracy that lay at
the core of arguments over slavery:

Man, in all ages and all nations of the earth, is the same. Man is a peculiar creature – he
is the image of God, though he may be subjected to the most wretched conditions upon
earth, yet the spirit and feeling which constitute the creature, man, can never be
entirely erased from his breast, because God who made him after his own image,

planted it in his heart; he cannot get rid of it. The whites knowing this, they do not
know what to do; they know that they have done us so much injury, they are afraid that
we, being men, and not brutes, will retaliate, and woe will be to them; therefore, that
dreadful fear, together with an avaricious spirit, and the natural love in them, to be
called masters . . . bring them to the resolve that they will keep us in ignorance and
wretchedness, as long as they possibly can, and make the best of their time, while it
lasts.

Fearful of violent slave rebellion, the pacifist Garrison drew back from advocating outright "treachery to the people of the south," and the more radical
Walker perceptively underlined the mechanisms of suppression that would
keep slavery in place for another generation and racism long after. Still, the
prediction of a "double rebellion," as Garrison called it, which both writers
found stirring – the rebellion of the South against the U.S. government and
of slaves against masters – was at least partially fulfilled. African American
slaves did not rise in large-scale revolt against their masters, as had the slaves
in San Domingo, but individually they did rebel, and the slave narratives are
filled with instances of small-scale resistance and plots of escape, with impassioned orations about freedom, and with folktales and religious songs of
resistance. Many blacks, moreover, joined both the abolitionist movement
against southern slaveholding and the Union ranks in the Civil War. Ultimately it was the South that revolted against the Union, and the Civil War
was officially designated "the War of the Rebellion." That very fact, however, made evident how closely allied had been the North and the South in
maintaining the immoral institution of slavery in the name of preserving the
political integrity of the new nation. The price of union was named by
Garrison in 1844 when he announced the American Anti-Slavery Society's
policy of "No Union with Slaveholders" and declared that "the Union which
grinds [slaves] to the dust rests upon us" as well, that "their shackles are
fastened to our limbs."

  Although he dissented from orthodoxy in calling for the dissolution of the
Union at a time when most American writers and politicians were searching
anxiously for ways to preserve it, Garrison's nonviolence was symbolic of the
reluctance many white Americans felt about acting resolutely against the
institution of slavery, which seemed to have the blessing of the founders and
the protection of the Constitution, and which both augmented and concealed
within the protection of law deeper forms of racism. On this issue, as on
many others, the new generations, including free blacks and ex-slaves, were
ambivalent about the meaning and the heroes of the Revolution. Whereas
David Walker called for strenuous, violent resistance to bondage, Frederick
Douglass, despite his own experience of slavery, would not espouse violence
until the early 1850s, and even then he would remain a proponent of tradi-

tional American revolutionary idealism. The Revolution itself became in many instances a conservative constraint on reform impulses; in the case of slavery, defenders of the institution identified potential slave rebellion not with the achievement of liberty in the American Revolution but with the forces of license, madness, and primitive energy often attributed to the French Revolution. In defining their relationship to the past, the descendants of the Revolution thus embraced conflicting impulses and contradictions, which also mark the literature of the period. Just as the political and social documents of the antebellum period constitute some of its greatest and most imaginative writing, so the literary work in its most powerful forms is infused with directly engaged social and political issues – the greatest of all being the problem of African American enslavement, which produced a national ideology riddled with tension and ambiguities.

The "renaissance" that classic American literature of the mid-nineteenth century is often said to constitute occurred in an era (from the 1830s through the Civil War) in which the authority of the Founding Fathers was in question and the issue of slavery had compelled a return to the fraternally divisive energies of the revolutionary period. The Civil War restored union and may therefore be seen as essentially conservative and redemptive, just as the American Revolution itself came in a later generation to seem a return – a *revolution* rather than a *rebellion* – to freedoms suppressed in 1776 or betrayed early on in American colonial history by the trade in the "black cargo" of African slaves initiated soon after the Columbian voyages. Indeed, the rise of the ideal of liberty and the rise of slavery in America took place simultaneously from the seventeenth to the nineteenth century. In Virginia especially, slavery made free, white society more homogeneous, allowed the flourishing of commonwealth ideas about taxation, property, and representation, and thus brought Virginians into the political tradition of New England. As Nathaniel Hawthorne wrote in one of his few allusions to the problem of slavery, appearing in an essay entitled "Chiefly About War Matters" (1862), "the children of the Puritans" were connected to the Africans of Virginia in a singular way, since the "fated womb" of the Mayflower "sent forth a brood of Pilgrims on Plymouth Rock" in her first voyage and in a subsequent one "spawned slaves upon the Southern soil." First as colonies, later as an independent nation, America found its political freedom and economic prosperity entangled with the unpaid labor, and often the deaths, of millions of African slaves over the course of three centuries.

The links between liberty and slavery were all the more complicated in view of the rhetoric of enslavement that American colonists employed during the Revolution. A famous suppressed clause of the Declaration of Independence charged George III with "violating the most sacred rights of life and liberty" in the practice of the slave trade and, moreover, with instigating rebellion among American slaves, "thus paying off former crimes committed against the *liberties* of one people, with crimes he urges them to commit against the *lives* of another." Revolutionary pamphlets often cast Americans as slaves of king and Parliament, suggesting at times that chattel slavery was but an extreme form of a more pervasive political oppression. As attempts to abolish slavery after the Revolution foundered upon questions of (human) property rights, vital economy, fear of insurrection and miscegenation, and the legacy of the founders, the tentative identification between colonists and slaves collapsed. Yet the irony of the comparison remained intact. Fixing on the more important dimension, that of American tyranny over slaves, Charles Ball's 1836 narrative *Slavery in the United States: A Narrative of the Life and Adventures of Charles Ball, a Black Man* (composed by Isaac Fisher) introduced the former slave's story with a trenchant observation:

Despotism within the confines of a plantation, is more absolute and irresistible than any that was ever wielded by a Roman emperor. The power of the latter, when no longer supportable, was terminated by revolt or personal violence, and often with impunity. But to the despotism of the master, there is scarcely any conceivable limit, and from its cruelty there is no refuge. His plantation is his empire, his labourers are his subjects, and revolt and violence, instead of abridging his power, are followed by inevitable and horrible punishment.

The very fact that some of the most influential Founding Fathers – among them Thomas Jefferson and George Washington – were slaveholders enhanced the doubleness at the heart of the American experiment and in the long run invited the two-edged sarcasm of Theodore Parker in his great speech on "The Nebraska Question" (1854). "The most valuable export of Virginia is her Slaves," Parker wrote, "enriched by 'the best blood of the old dominion;' the 'Mother of Presidents' is also the great Slave Breeder of America. Since she ceased to import bondsmen from Africa, her Slaves [have] become continually paler in the face; it is the 'effect of the climate' – and Democratic Institutions."

Parker's attack on the internal slave trade, on miscegenation, and on the irony of Virgina's revolutionary heritage highlights issues that had produced a political crisis by the 1850s. By then, both proslavery and antislavery sentiment had hardened into recalcitrant forms: the Compromise of 1850 (which seemed to many in the North a victory for the slaveholding South) and contention over the extension of slavery into western territories signaled a further crisis in the Union that was implicit in the flawed design of the revolutionary era but only became clear as the nation expanded. The 1830s, while the country was still transported by the enthusiastic nationalism of the previous decade, witnessed a surge in America's sense of democratic mission and the belief in its "manifest destiny" to settle the territory of the continent if not the entire hemisphere. But it remained to be seen whether the newly acquired territories would allow the extension of slavery and at what price, then, the Union could be preserved. Celebrating the centennial of Washington's birth in 1832, Senator Daniel Webster of Massachusetts reminded his audience that nothing was of greater importance than the "integrity of the Union" and warned that "disunion and dismemberment" would "sweep away, not only what we possess, but all our powers of regaining lost, or acquiring new possessions." The following year, the novelist and social activist Lydia Maria Child, taking a different point of view, argued in *An Appeal in Favor of that Class of Americans Called Africans* that Washington's farewell advice about the necessity of union no longer "operated like a spell upon the hearts and consciences of his countrymen." Although she was thankful that Mexico, at that point, prevented the annexation of Texas by the United States, she was nonetheless fearful that southern threats of secession had so eroded public reverence for union that all restraints upon the spread of slavery would soon be lost. Once Texas was acquired in 1845 and the cession of Mexican territory accomplished following war in 1848, the risk to the Union became all the greater.

Yet the South, like the North, claimed that its interests were authorized by the legacy of the Revolution. The spirit of American mission that legitimized war with Mexico and prompted self-congratulation that 1776 was the source of contemporary democratic revolutions in Europe also prompted patriotic defenses of moderation, and sometimes even "fire-eating" extremism, on the question of slavery. In his inaugural speech as president of the Confederacy, on Washington's birthday of 1862, Jefferson Davis underlined the symbolic difference of the date by attacking the *North* for its deviation from the rights and principles authorized by the founders and by calling upon divine Providence to guide the South in its quest to preserve liberty without union: "The experiment instituted by our Revolutionary fathers, of a voluntary union of sovereign States for the purposes specified in a solemn compact, [has] been perverted by those who, feeling power and forgetting right, [are] determined to respect no law but their own will. The Government [has] ceased to answer the ends for which it was ordained and established. . . . To show ourselves worthy of the inheritance bequeathed to us by the patriots of the Revolution," Davis concluded, the South "must emulate that heroic devotion" and be itself tested in "the crucible in which their patriotism was refined."

A belief in the divine mission of America could sanction antislavery ideology, then, but it could just as easily compel a devotion to union based on the preservation and expansion of slaveholding rights. The vexed relationship

between the revolutionary tradition and slavery animated almost every significant political and cultural issue of the antebellum years, often in fact providing
the grounds on which politics and literature met. For example, Nathaniel
Hawthorne, in his presidential campaign biography of his college friend Franklin Pierce, celebrated Pierce's descent from a renowned revolutionary father
and took note of his distinguished service in the Mexican War, which "struck
an hereditary root in his breast" and linked him to the heroic past. He argued
that Pierce's support of the Compromise of 1850 indicated his understanding
that slavery could not be stopped without "tearing to pieces the Constitution . . . and severing into distracted fragments that common country which
Providence brought into one nation, through a continued miracle of almost
two hundred years, from the first settlement of the American wilderness until
the Revolution." Hawthorne's *Life of Franklin Pierce* (1852) thus ties together
union and slavery, sentimental politics and expansion, much as Pierce himself,
in making his 1853 inauguration speech "within reach of the tomb of Washington," would invoke the providential guidance of "our fathers" and call for the
protection of slavery and the acquisition of Cuba.

The American Revolution and its legacy in this way gave rise to strong
sentiments both for and against slavery and to political clashes that not only
divided the nation but also divided partisans of each section. Sociological and
political writing became intertwined with literature on both sides of the
question, and the writings produced by the two sections sometimes fed off
each other, as extremists imagined conspiracies of abolitionist fanaticism or
slave power directed against them. That such conspiracies were more often
rhetorical than real did not mitigate their influence or their ability to crystallize the most deeply rooted doubts about the just course of American
democracy in both the political and the cultural spheres.

The abolitionist Thomas Wentworth Higginson wrote in an 1861 *Atlantic
Monthly* essay that Nat Turner's rebellion became "a memory of terror, a
symbol of wild retribution" in the South. Even though the rebellion was
minor (about 60 whites were killed, but twice as many blacks, including the
rebels, died in violent response) compared to much larger uprisings in Latin
America and the Caribbean, it provoked fears that the terror of the Haitian
revolution would spread to the United States. Following the flight of terrified
planter refugees to America in the 1790s, San Domingo was often summoned
up in arguments over the possibility of slave or free black insurrection, and it
eventually became central to literary treatments of revolt such as Herman
Melville's *Benito Cereno* and Martin Delany's *Blake*. It led to the demise of
French power in the New World and thus provoked the Louisiana Purchase,
which in turn resulted in the period's central question about the territorial

expansion of slavery. Like a prism, therefore, San Domingo reflected all sides of the issue of slavery, as would Turner's revolt, with which it became inevitably linked.

In the wake of Turner's rebellion at Southampton, the Virginia House of Delegates undertook the most serious debate in its history on the question of slave emancipation. The delegates were almost evenly divided on the possibility of abolishing slavery in its American place of birth, with a significant number arguing that the bloody Turner rebellion was a sign of the need to dismantle the "peculiar institution" and a portent of larger revolts. At the same time, however, the proslavery side contended that emancipation would lead neither to the tranquil assimilation of freed slaves nor to the easy dispersal of them to the North or outside the borders of the United States. Instead, they feared widespread crime, economic and political dependency, and even a race war. Moreover, emancipation would be financially ruinous for many southerners. The defeat of abolition legislation coincided with the revival of the state's economy after a depression and the rapid increase throughout the South in the cultivation of cotton. The spread of the Cotton Kingdom into the Deep South during the 1820s to 1850s (resulting in a tenfold increase in production, to a peak of nearly five million bales per year, three-fourths of the world's cotton, by the outbreak of the Civil War) guaranteed the survival and expansion of slavery. Sentiment in favor of emancipation was submerged by the economic growth of a complex market that benefited large aristocratic planters, small frontiersmen, and northern manufacturers alike.

Within this context, the representation of Nat Turner's rebellion as an isolated act of fanaticism, instead of a legitimate if futile quest for freedom, can be seen as a strategic necessity. The publicity that surrounded the trial and execution of Turner, as well as his purported *Confessions* (1831), recorded by the attorney Thomas Gray, suggested a black viciousness that had to be held in check by the careful use of force by slaveholders. The legalistic form of the account of Turner's confessions, half autobiographical narrative and half court document, ambiguously participates in the suppression of ideas of rebellion and freedom. The emphasis lies, in Turner's recorded words, on his messianic and apocalyptic visions and, in Gray's editorial commentary, on the derangement of Turner and his "dreadful conspiracy" of "diabolical actors." By staging Turner as a "gloomy fanatic" lost "in the recesses of his own dark, bewildered, and overwrought mind" as he plotted and carried out his revolt in methodical, cold-blooded fashion, Gray attempted to reduce Turner's revolt to a unique example of deviation from the normally goodwilled, safe relationship of master and slave. But because the *Confessions* embodied the central paradox of southern representations of slaveholding – that the institution was one of affectionate paternalism *but* that bloody insurrection could break forth at the least relaxation of vigilance – they served both to sound an alarm and to suppress the justness of Turner's plot. Although Gray's text situates him within a tradition of revolutionary archetypes and romantic artifice, there is little doubt that Turner was a legitimate millenarian visionary, and careful attention to the *Confessions* reveals how his voice controls its replication of the revolt in the realm of polemical resistance. The fact that Turner quickly became a heroic figure in black folk history underlines the degree to which his recorded words, despite Gray's legalistic framework, establish a vital link between African American religious practice and a formative tradition of revolutionary thought. That this was not lost on the slaveholding South is registered, among other places, in the account of the Turner aftermath given by Harriet Jacobs in her *Incidents in the Life of a Slave Girl* (1861). After Turner's capture had somewhat reduced anxiety among Virginia's slaveholders, Jacobs writes that

the slaves begged the privilege of again meeting at their little church in the woods, with their burying ground around it. It was built by the colored people, and they had no higher happiness than to meet there and sing hymns together, and pour out their hearts in spontaneous prayer. Their request was denied, and the church was demolished. They were permitted to attend the white churches, a certain portion of the galleries being appropriated to their use. . . . The slaveholders came to the conclusion that it would be well to give the slaves enough of religious instruction to keep them from murdering their masters.

The increasing rigidity of southern opinion that came to prevail in succeeding decades was characterized with fierce precision by the professor of political law (and later president) at the College of William and Mary, Thomas R. Dew (1802–46), who likewise invoked the archetypes of revolutionary fanaticism in describing the grave risks of slave emancipation. Drawing on the example of Turner's rebellion, Dew's classic 1832 essay "Abolition of Negro Slavery" (expanded as *Review of the Debate in the Virginia Legislature of 1831–2*), argued against both emancipation and the colonization of freed slaves in Africa or other foreign territories. Pointing to the example of Haiti and comparing potentially freed slaves to a Frankenstein monster incapable of coping with liberty, Dew belittled analogies between the cause of American slaves and current revolutions in Poland and France. He contended that, incited by abolitionist propaganda which is "subversive of the rights of property and the order and tranquillity of society," emancipated blacks would become "*parricides* instead of *patriots.*" The "right of revolution" cannot exist for persons "totally unfit for freedom and self-government," Dew argued. In this case, revolution was certain to bring "relentless carnage and massacre" upon their former benefactors. If slaves were freed, "the melancholy tale of

Southampton would not alone blacken the page of our history, and make the tender mother shed the tear of horror over her babe as she clasped it to her bosom; others of a deeper die would thicken upon us; those regions where the brightness of polished life has dawned and brightened into full day, would relapse into darkness, thick and full of horrors." Like Garrison on the antislavery side, Dew defined the most extreme form of southern polemics for the next thirty years. His gothic figures indicate a central strain in much proslavery and later racist thought: slavery was justified on the grounds that blacks were infants or beasts who could not cope with liberty and would, if set free, give vent to murderous animalistic passions.

The fear and abhorrence of blackness and blacks that lurked beneath the plantation myth were brought quickly to the surface in the racist tracts and fiction of the postwar era; but their appearance throughout the antebellum period suggests the ways in which the devices of the gothic novel, used by the North to expose the sufferings of slaves, could in contrast express anxieties about the mixing of races. More often, such devices revealed less a corrosive racism than the rationalization of a profitable labor system. A clear example is the long didactic poem *The Hireling and the Slave* (1856), by William J. Grayson (1788–1863), one of the most famous replies to *Uncle Tom's Cabin*. Grayson's poem includes a representation of the American slave's escape from the darkness of African superstition and primitivism that had become increasingly commonplace in proslavery argument in the decades before the war:

> In this new home, whate'er the negro's fate —
> More blessed his life than in his native state!
> No mummeries dupe, no Fetich charms affright,
> No rites obscene diffuse their moral blight;
> Idolatries, more hateful than the grave,
> With human sacrifice, no more enslave;
> No savage rule its hecatomb supplies
> Of slaves fore slaughter when a master dies:
> In sloth and error sunk for countless years
> His race has lived, but light at last appears —
> Celestial light: religion undefiled
> Dawns in the heart of Congo's simple child.

The contradiction between infantilization ("simple child") and demonization ("human sacrifice") in views of Africans is characteristic of much proslavery theory. Grayson portrays Harriet Beecher Stowe as a literary scavenger who

> Snuffs up pollution with a pious air,
> Collects a rumor here, a slander there;

> With hatred's ardor gathers Newgate spoils,
> And trades for gold the garbage of her toils.

This appropriately classes Stowe with the Victorian urban novelists, since Grayson's main line of attack was to suggest, as did many of his southern colleagues, that wage labor in England and the North was more vicious than slavery:

> No mobs of factious workmen gather here,
> No strikes we dread, no lawless riots fear . . .
> In useful tasks engaged, employed their time,
> Untempted by the demagogue to crime,
> Secure they toil, uncursed their peaceful life,
> With labor's hungry broils and wasteful strife.
> No want to goad, no faction to deplore,
> The slave escapes the perils of the poor.

A journalist and congressman, Grayson also defended slavery in *Letters of Curtius* (1851), but he opposed secession in *Letter to Governor Seabrook* (1850), arguing that it would be economically disastrous and would only advance the cause of abolitionism.

In his thought and in his poem Grayson represents those arguments in political and social theory that emerged along with a distinctive southern literary culture and constituted what was in many respects the most significant southern writing on this question. The most famous congressional orators like Henry Clay, Robert Hayne, and John Calhoun produced speeches that argued with ornate eloquence that slavery was a benign labor system and a just social arrangement. In his efforts as secretary of war and of state, as vice-president, and as senator, in his secretly authored brief for the doctrine of Nullification, *South Carolina Exposition and Protest* (1828), and in his posthumous volumes *Disquisition on Government* and *Discussion on the Constitution and Government of the United States* (1851), Calhoun (1782–1850) in particular argued from a strong states' rights position and proposed various measures that would safeguard the vital interests of the southern minority from the despotic will of the majority and ensure that slavery could be extended to newly acquired territories. Running through Calhoun's thought is a correlation between liberty and order that is characteristic of proslavery thought in both the literary and the political arenas. Freedom, as Calhoun understood it, was only possible in a carefully regulated society that recognized some persons to be more suited to it than others, a society that "enlarges and secures the sphere of liberty to the greatest extent which the condition of the community will admit." Antislavery argument, in Calhoun's view, because it pressed governmental power beyond its proper limit, belonged to that illicit expansion of federal reach that "exposes liberty to danger and renders it insecure." For Calhoun, as for many of his white contemporaries, South and North, the institution of slavery did not contradict liberty but instead supported it.

Even though clearly articulated proslavery theory can be found among the political records of the South in the early decades of the century, Calhoun's work and Dew's "Abolition of Negro Slavery," following just a few years after the Nullification crisis, marked a point of departure for a surge of writing that eventually led to two important collections of documents: *The Pro-Slavery Argument* (1852) and *Cotton is King and Pro-Slavery Arguments,* edited by E. N. Elliott (1860). As these collections proved, the defense of slavery could take a variety of forms. In the book that gave Elliott's collection its name, *Cotton is King* (1855), the Cincinnati journalist David Christy argued that the markets and labor forces of the South, North, and Europe were bound together by King Cotton and that, despite the evils of slavery, little was to be gained and much to be lost by allowing abolitionist "quacks" to destroy the system: "KING COTTON is a profound statesman, and knows what measures best sustain his throne. He is an acute mental philosopher, acquainted with the secret springs of human action, and accurately perceives who will best promote his aims." Christy's remark is an excellent delineation of the strength of proslavery argument, which effectively kept most of the North, even through much of the Civil War, skeptical about emancipation.

The most sophisticated arguments for slavery, like those against it, tended to be economic and political in character and were advanced in the immense southern periodical literature by men like George Fitzhugh, William Harper, Hugh Swinton Legare, and James D. B. De Bow. But the most visceral proclamations appropriated the received scriptural truths of religion and tendentious theories of science. The elaborate biblical defense of slavery rested principally on three claims: that blacks were descended from Canaan, the son of Ham, whose father cursed him by saying "a servant unto servants shall he be to his brethren"; that Mosaic law authorized slavery; and that in the New Testament Paul commanded servants to obey their masters, and Christ himself uttered no specific condemnation of slavery. Representative of the many who argued that the Bible condoned slavery and offered no commanding proscription against it, the Virginian Baptist minister Thornton Stringfellow (1788–1869) contended in such works as *Scriptural and Statistical Views in Favor of Slavery* (1856) and *Slavery: Its Origin, Nature and History* (1860) that the South's guardianship of the black race in slavery was a moral obligation, as could be demonstrated by numerous scriptural passages on the subject. His best-known work, *A Brief Examination of Scripture Testimony on the Insitution of Slavery* (1841; reprint, 1850), later included in Elliott's *Cotton Is*

King, added the humanitarian argument that slavery had throughout history often rescued men from certain death after capture in battle:

> The same is true in the history of Africa, as far back as we can trace it. It is only sober truth to say, that the institution of slavery has saved from the sword more lives, including their increase, than all the souls who now inhabit this globe.
>
> The souls thus conquered and subjected to masters, who feared not God nor regarded men, in the days of Abraham, Job, and the Patriarchs, were surely brought under great obligations to the mercy of God, in allowing such men as these to purchase them, and keep them in their families.

Stringfellow in this way combined the scriptural defense of slavery with the equally widespread claim that the history of conquest had always included the humanitarian practice of enslavement, thus making it a cornerstone of all the great world civilizations.

The scientific argument for slavery on the basis of race, often more rigorous but no less dependent upon flights of faith grounded in racism, reached a climax of offensive theorizing in *The Moral and Intellectual Diversity of Races* (published in the United States in 1856) by the European writer Joseph Arthur de Gobineau (1816–82). Some years earlier, similar arguments were advanced by the Alabama physician Josiah Nott (1804–73). Building on the scientific ethnology of Samuel Morton's influential *Crania Americana* (1839) and *Crania Aegyptiaca* (1844) – two works that distinguished supposed mental capacities on the basis of such physiological differences as skull size and shape but that were not themselves so blatantly racist in the conclusions derived from their data – Nott in turn promoted the polygenetic theory that the races of humankind had different origins and, because they are therefore predisposed to different laws of development, could be subjected to different ethical and political rules. In the massive *Types of Mankind* (1854), written in collaboration with the Egyptologist George R. Glidden, and in other volumes such as *Two Lectures on the Natural History of the Caucasian and Negro Races* (1844), Nott drew on a wide range of biblical, archeological, statistical, and ethnographic evidence to argue that blacks belonged to a separate species created by God at the beginning of time. Joining an old argument (appearing provisionally, for example, in the thought of Thomas Jefferson) that would be revived periodically by racists on into the twentieth century, Nott concluded that Negroes stood between Caucasians and apes in the hierarchy of nature and that the popular theory of "savagism" could be scientifically proved:

> The difference to an Anatomist, between the Bushman or Negro and the Caucasian, is greater than the difference in the skeletons of the Wolf, Dog, and Hyena, which are allowed to be distinct species. . . . Now can all these deep, radical and enduring differences [between races] be produced by climate and other causes as-

signed? It is incumbent upon those who contend for such an opinion, to show that some changes either *have* taken place, or that similar changes in the *human race* are *now in progress*. . . .

We can carry back the history of the Negro (though imperfectly) for 4,000 years: we know that he had all the physical characteristics then which he has now, and we have good grounds for believing that he was morally and intellectually the same then as now. . . . Can any reasoning mind believe that the Negro and Indian have always been the victim of circumstances? No, nature has endowed them with an inferior organization, and all the powers of earth cannot elevate them above their destiny.

Imperfect as the civilization of St. Domingo now is, if you were to abstract the white blood which exists amongst them they would sink at once into savagism.

Accompanied by an essay written by the famous Harvard zoologist Louis Agassiz, who had emigrated to the United States in 1846, *Types of Mankind* sold 3,500 in several months and went through ten editions by 1871. Subjecting blacks to the same scrutiny as Native Americans, Latinos, and Polynesians, Nott and Glidden, among other ethnologists, deduced from the theory of polygenesis a belief in the decline of racially inferior races and the missionary triumph of Anglo-Americans. Appearing in both books and in a voluminous northern and southern periodical literature from the 1820s through the post-Civil War period, proslavery argument and commentary on the "doom" of American Indian tribes joined hands with the search for humanity's origins in etymological evidence, Egyptian artifacts, Indian pictographs, and African and South Sea tribal practices – and even in the occasional fictive extravaganza uniting them all, such as Edgar Allan Poe's *The Narrative of Arthur Gordon Pym of Nantucket* (1838).

Nott's characterization of Haitian savagery corresponded to the rather paradoxical prevailing view of that country's slave revolution and subsequent independence. His contention that miscegenation created a "hybrid" race–species also accorded with the opinion of many that mixing the races would degrade the white race, perhaps eventually exterminating it. From the antebellum period until well into the next century, physiological expressions of racism made miscegenation a central theme. The most eloquent refutation of the theory that miscegenation would elevate the black race without harming the white came from New York physician John H. Van Evrie in *Negroes and Negro "Slavery"* (1861), which pointed out that the abolition of slavery would only increase the "awful perversion of the instincts of reproduction" that slaveholding miscegenation had already set loose. Uncertain that the South, or the nation, could ever "recover from the foul and horrible contamination of admixture with the blood of the negro," Van Evrie attacked what he characterized as the North's sentimental fascination with mulattoes, while lamenting the fact that the North ignored the degradation in poverty and prostitution of its own white women. Echoing the savage campaigns against Lincoln as a supporter of miscegenation, Van Evrie prophesied a near holocaust for the white race. Because he wrote in large part for a northern audience, his additional attack on all aristocratic class-based distinctions among whites, in both Europe and America, had a Jacksonian appeal that probably strengthened rather than contradicted his argument for the complete subjugation of blacks on the basis of their race. Reissued as *White Supremacy and Negro Subordination* after the war (1868), his book anticipated the vast racist literature to come in arguing, for example, that because the sentiment of family is not "natural" to the African, the slave mother ceases to care for her offspring once it is old enough to survive alone and soon "forgets it altogether," since in the "affections corresponding with her intellectual nature, there is no basis, or material, or space for such things."

Van Evrie's perverse but influential combination of liberal egalitarianism and racism had elements in common with Free Soil doctrine, which sought to protect labor and western territory from competition by both slavery and free black labor. He appealed to those in both sections who believed not only that blacks were inferior to whites but also that slavery (and here he produced a less sophisticated version of Calhoun's arguments) had permitted the flourishing of democracy among *"all those whom the almighty creator has himself made equal."* Van Evrie's claims corresponded as well to the famous metaphor of the "mud-sill" advanced by South Carolina senator James Henry Hammond in an 1858 speech to describe the necessity of a menial class on which to build a social order – a "mud-sill" the South conveniently found among its slaves: a "race inferior to her own, but eminently qualified in temper, vigor, in docility, in capacity to stand the climate, to answer all her purposes. . . . We found them slaves by the common 'consent of mankind,' which, according to Cicero, *'lex naturae est.'* The highest proof of what is Nature's law."

So much does the idea of order and nature's supposedly self-evident "law" permeate southern thought that one reviewer of *Uncle Tom's Cabin* quite correctly apprehended that its critique of social evil might reach beyond chattel slavery. Requested by the editor of the *Southern Literary Messenger* to write a review "as hot as hell fire, blasting and searing the reputation of the vile wretch in petticoats who could write such a volume," George Frederick Holmes responded:

If it was capable of proving anything at all, it would prove too much. It would demonstrate that all order, law, government, society was a flagrant and unjustifiable violation of the rights and mockery of the feelings of man. . . . The fundamental position, then, of these dangerous and dirty little volumes is a deadly blow to all the interests and duties of humanity, and is utterly impotent to show any inherent vice in the institution of slavery which does not also appertain to all other existing institutions whatever.

It was a matter, argued William Harper along the same lines, of choosing between the comparative evils of different systems of labor and hierarchical arrangement: "To say that there is evil in any institution, is only to say that it is human." Judge, senator, and state chancellor of Missouri and South Carolina, Harper (1790–1847) examined not just southern slaveholding but the institution of human bondage, "deeply founded in the nature of man," in his *Memoir on Slavery* (1838). He concluded that "the relation of Master and Slave, when there is no mischievous interference between them, is as the experience of all the world declares, naturally one of kindness." He asked, "is it not natural that a man should be attached to that which is *his own,* and which has contributed to his convenience, his enjoyment, or his vanity?" Harper followed Dew in believing that the denial of liberty to slaves means simply that they are relieved of the burdens "of self-government, and the evils springing from their own perverse wills." In this they participate, at the mud-sill, in the general hierarchy of social dependence that also includes, for example, women and children. "The virtues of a freeman would be the vices of slaves," Harper suggested. "To submit to a blow, would be degrading to a freeman, because he is the protector of himself. It is not degrading to a slave – neither is it to a priest or woman."

In demanding analogically whether one would "do a benefit to the horse or ox, by giving him a cultivated understanding or fine feelings," Harper anticipated Henry Hughes's *Treatise on Sociology* (1854), James D. B. De Bow's *The Interest in Slavery of the Southern Non-Slaveholder* (1860), and the most elaborate of all southern defenses of slavery, George Fitzhugh's *Cannibals All! or Slaves Without Masters* (1857), which carefully argued that the labor system and resulting social life of northern capitalism was less free and more inhumane than southern slavery. "It invades every recess of domestic life, infects its food, its clothing, its drink, its very atmosphere, and pursues the hireling, from the hovel to the poor-house, the prison and the grave." In this volume, in others such as *Sociology for the South; or the Failure of Free Society* (1854), and in frequent articles in the prominent proslavery journal *De Bow's Review,* Fitzhugh (1806–81) contended that, far from eliminating slavery, the modern world ought to extend it to certain classes of whites as well, thus eliminating the economic anarchy of Jeffersonian liberalism and protecting the lower classes from poverty and competitive exploitation. Liberty, he also argued, was in fact antagonistic to democracy, which proposes, "so far as is possible, to equalize advantages, by fairly dividing the burdens of life and rigidly enforcing the performance of every social duty by every member of society, according to his capacity and ability." Within the bounds of liberty authorized by Fitzhugh's construct, "the slave, when capable to do so, must work for the master; but the master, at all times, must provide for the slave. . . . The protection or support to which the

slave is entitled [is] an ample consideration of itself for the sale of his liberty" –
a larger consideration, Fitzhugh maintained, than that provided by capitalists
of Europe and the North, who rightly "say that free labor is cheapest." Citing
the fact that God had authorized slavery and that "human law cannot beget
benevolence, affection, [or] maternal and paternal love," Fitzhugh summed up
the hierarchical principles that supported slaveholding paternalism and distinguished it from the capitalistic struggle for survival:

> Within the family circle, the law of love prevails, not that of selfishness.
> But, besides wife and children, brothers and sisters, dogs, horses, birds and
> flowers – slaves, also, belong to the family circle. Does their common humanity,
> their abject weakness and dependence, their great value, their ministering to our
> wants in childhood, manhood, sickness, and old age, cut them off from that affection
> which everything else in the family elicits? No; the interests of master and slave are
> bound up together, and each in his appropriate sphere naturally endeavors to pro-
> mote the happiness of the other.
> The humble and obedient slave exercises more or less control over the most brutal
> and hard-hearted master. It is an invariable law of nature, that weakness and depen-
> dence are elements of strength, and generally sufficiently limit that universal despo-
> tism, observable throughout human and animal nature.

Built on the argument that free-market competition left many laborers with
miserable lives, Fitzhugh's utopian vision of a "familial" slavery in which the
slave's power over the master is exceeded only by the master's affection for the
slave won the consent of none but those already converted to the proslavery
view. Nonetheless, it served in a forceful way to borrow the abolitionists'
central claims of morally superior benevolence and domestic affection.

As Fitzhugh proved, the paternalistic ideal espoused by so many southern
novelists would have to be contradicted by more than sentimental fiction.
Although their voices were seldom heard, however, there were those within
the South who vigorously opposed the corruptions of slaveholding paternalism, none more eloquently perhaps than Mary Boykin Chesnut (1823–86),
wife of a planter and Confederate official. In her diary of the years 1861–5,
which was not written in full until the 1880s and was first published in
1905, Chesnut created a remarkable counterstatement to the image of the
family advanced by slavery's apologists. Based on journals kept during
different portions of her life and on her memory of the war years, the *Diary*
is a fascinating personal account of plantation life, with astute observations
on the politics of the day, the lives of slaves, and most particularly the
effects on the family of the slaveholder of the brutal and morally corrupt
institution of bondage and slave sexual abuse. A similar critique, describing
the slaveholding South as tied to "the dominion of Satan," may be found in
Charles W. Andrews's *Memoir of Mrs. Anne R. Page* (1844).

Among other such personal records of plantation life, Chesnut's is matched only by the detailed account of Edmund Ruffin's life and theories of southern society found in his *Diary,* unpublished until 1972. A successful agricultural scientist and staunch defender of slavery who personally fired the first shell against Fort Sumter, Ruffin (1794–1865) was also well known for his essays and his *Political Economy of Slavery* (1853), but he is best remembered for an avowed hatred of "the perfidious, malignant and vile Yankee race," whose victory prompted him to immediate suicide. Such extraordinary animus against the North was not widespread among prewar southerners, of course, but Ruffin's views represented a definite intensification in proslavery's embattled defense that accompanied renewed calls in the 1850s for the expansion of slavery. The more radical views of Van Evrie and Fitzhugh were developed within a context of southern thought that envisioned not just the survival of King Cotton but its extension to western territories or to lands beyond the continental borders. Whereas some southerners had imagined that the leveling forces of westward expansion would lead eventually to the demise of slavery, a different interpretation of expansion, which foresaw the Gulf of Mexico as the heart of a slaveholding region stretching across the Americas, continued in force during the same period and was buttressed by calls to reopen the legal African slave trade.

The southern dream of a Caribbean empire antedated the Mexican War, but the bounteous acquisition of land in the war, combined with longstanding designs on Cuba, Haiti, and other Latin American territories, served to inflame slaveholding interest once again during the 1850s. The proslavery colony established in Nicaragua in 1856–7 by the filibustering ideologue William Walker (1824–60) was only the most extreme realization of this vision. Although Walker claimed to be building a new nation according to principles of the American Revolution, the engine of his colony was to be black chattel slavery. In a variation of Fitzhugh's theories, Walker believed that the victory of a wage labor society in the United States (or in the Americas generally) would lead to a repetition of European political tyranny and economic failure; only a slave-based society, he wrote in *The War in Nicaragua* (1860), could give capital a firm basis and enable "the intellect of society to push boldly forward in the pursuit of new forms of civilization." The failure of Walker's venture (he was overthrown in 1857) did not diminish the appeal of his argument that slavery was justified both on the grounds of political economy and by reason of the fact that the whites, in enslaving Africans and bringing them to the New World, were teaching them "the arts of life" and bestowing upon them "the ineffable blessings of a true religion. Then only do the wisdom and excellence of the divine economy in the creation of the black race begin to appear with their full lustre."

Until the conclusion of the Civil War, proslavery groups such as the Knights of the Golden Circle continued to predict an American slave empire surrounding the Gulf of Mexico. Edward Pollard's *Black Diamonds Gathered in the Darkey Homes of the South* (1861), for example, claimed that southern expansion was not a sectional issue but one involving "the world's progress, and who shall be the founders of its greatest empire of industry." Eventually, he maintained, the seat of the southern empire would be in Central America; control of the West Indies, the isthmuses of Central America, and the production of the world's cotton and sugar would complete America's destiny:

What a splendid vision of empire! How sublime in its associations! How noble and inspiriting the idea, that upon the strange theater of tropical America, once, if we may believe the dimmer facts of history, crowned with magnificent empires and flashing cities and great temples, now covered with mute ruins, and trampled over by half-savages, the destiny of Southern civilization is to be consummated in a glory brighter even than that of old, the glory of an empire, controlling the commerce of the world, impregnable in its position, and representing in its internal structure the most harmonious of all systems of modern civilization.

At the same moment, however, the South was also capable of producing an intellectual point of view entirely inimical to an empire based on black slavery. Likely to have been ranked among the most important abolitionist writers except for the fact that he was a violent racist and thus gained little sympathy among social reformers, North Carolina author Hinton Rowan Helper (1829–1909) published a firsthand account of the California Gold Rush, *Land of Gold: Reality Versus Fiction* (1855), before returning to the South. Following lines of argument advanced by Daniel Reeves Goodloe (1814–1902) in *Inquiry into the Causes Which Have Retarded the Accumulation of Wealth and Increase of Population in the Southern States* (1844), Helper's major work, *The Impending Crisis of the South: How to Meet It* (1857), proved by statistical evidence that slavery retarded economic growth, but he proposed unfeasible means to abolish it that involved economically pitting nonslaveholders and planters against one another. Helper concluded with a brief account of southern literature – one more casualty of slavery's degrading effect, in his view – that represented at large the consequences of the peculiar institution: "The truth is, slavery destroys, or vitiates, or pollutes, whatever it touches. No interest of society escapes the influence of its clinging curse. It makes Southern religion a stench in the nostrils of Christendom – it makes Southern politics a libel upon all the principles of Republicanism – it makes Southern literature a travesty upon the honorable profession of letters." Helper overestimated the destructive effects of slavery on white southern culture. In addition, his own theories of abolition were tainted by his insistence that blacks be deported, since in his view they could not – and should not – find a place in U.S. society and economy. His views became even more extreme in the postwar years; he then joined the ranks of major Reconstruction racists with such works as *Negroes in Negroland* (1868) and *Nojoque; A Question for a Continent* (1867), in which he states that his object is "to write the negro out of America, and . . . to write him (and manifold millions of other black and bi-colored caitiffs, little better than himself), out of existence." His anthropological account of inequality led Helper to predict an ultimate choice between "deportation and fossilization." Although he received a political appointment as consul to Buenos Aires under Lincoln (after Horace Greeley successfully brought out *The Impending Crisis* in the form of a Republican campaign document), the president was resistant to Harper's fanaticism. However distorted its reasoning, his argument against slavery was still the strongest to come from the South. If it was burdened by racism, it only expressed in an ultimate form the ambivalent views held by a significant number of northern abolitionists as well – a fact corroborated by the rise of proscriptions against black political, social, and economic freedom after the collapse of Reconstruction.

Despite the new stridency of its argument from the 1830s through the Civil War, the defense of southern slavery was not limited to political theorists or even, for that matter, to southerners. Figures whose work was primarily literary played an enormous role in the idealization of southern plantation life and the justification of slavery. One could even assert that the defense of human slavery was first and foremost an act of the imagination, since the portraits upon which it depended were often contrary to brutally evident realities. In a few cases, those who contributed significantly to the literary defense of the slaveholding South were distant from its daily life. Aside from those northerners who wanted first to protect the Union, many other literary and political figures were actively sympathetic to the southern cause. A central example is James Kirke Paulding (1778–1860) of New York, who had a varied career as a man of letters and in governmental service. His novel *Westward Ho!* (1832), which follows the migration of a Virginia planter to frontier Kentucky, depicts the disintegration of the planter ethic in a western setting. *Letters from the South* (1817; revised edition, 1835) collects a group of Paulding's travel sketches that picture an independent and romantic country life in Virginia distrustful of the industrial progress of the North but that seek to remind his northern audience that "we are a nation of brothers." In his major defense of slavery, *Slavery in the United States* (1836), Paulding voiced the increasingly common argument that the abolition of slavery was not worth the sacrifice of the Union. The slaves, he maintained, were better off than their "savage" brothers in Africa or the working peasantry of Europe; moreover, Paulding contended, they were accustomed to, and content in, their ceaseless "round of labor and relaxation." If slavery "be an evil, let those who cherish [it] bear it," he wrote, "but let not us, their kindred, neighbors, and countrymen, become instruments to scatter the firebrands of fanaticism among them, and lend a helping hand to insurrection and massacre." Like most northern moderates, Paulding framed an issue in terms that predicted dangers to the American democratic experiment: those who interfered with slavery were "laying the axe to the root of the fairest plant of freedom that adorns the New or the Old World."

The argument for slavery's compatibility with democratic ideals, as indicated above, was not in the least uncommon in the South, for proslavery thought erected elaborate philosophical and "scientific" demonstrations of the inferiority of blacks to justify their exclusion from democratic life. Nevertheless, the plantation myth generated by much southern literature (both before the Civil War and even more prominently in the later nineteenth century in the work of writers such as Thomas Nelson Page) often exploited aristocratic and feudal elements as the basis for Confederate tradition. Although the "cult of chivalry" that modern observers have sometimes identified as the essence of the Old South stems more from the conceptions of postwar writers and historians than from antebellum realities, it is still the case that the culture of the slave South was preoccupied with the value of tradition and ideals of personal and communal honor. The novels of Walter Scott were popular and influential even if the romantic feudal world they described – and which some planters imagined could be re-created in the Cotton Kingdom – was economically within reach of only a small fraction of the South's landowners. The spread of Jacksonian democracy after the 1830s eroded aristocratic privilege in the South as well as the North, a fact generally misunderstood and misrepresented by both radical abolitionists and more moderate northern writers, who sometimes portrayed the feudal planter with hundreds of slaves as the southern norm. "The Southern States of the Union," the historian Richard Hildreth remarked in *Despotism in America* (1854), "though certain democratic principles are to be found in their constitutions and their laws, are in no modern sense of the word entitled to the appellation of Democracies: They are Aristocracies; and aristocracies of the sternest and most odious kind." If anything, the myth of the aristocratic plantation was in part a self-generated representation of idealized political order under threat by periodic economic depression and seemingly anarchic pressures of expansion, and in part the fantasy or the rhetorical ploy of antislavery forces.

The South's agrarian bias against the North, although it was not by any means univocal, grew in proportion to the attack upon it, and abolitionist oratory sometimes obscured the legitimate arguments the South made against the development of northern industry and wage labor. In addition to charting the decline of aristocratic tendencies in the South (rather than their increase), many southern writers advocated a closer economic and social relationship between the two sections. Others sought greater independence for the South but were certain it would come from a realistic combination of modernization and conservatism. In a long and diverse writing career, the economist, historical novelist, and University of Virginia professor George Tucker (1775–1861) argued in books such as *Political Economy for the People* (1859) that slavery was inefficient and discouraged the development of manufacturing, thus making the South more and more dependent upon the North. Although his *History of the United States* (1856–7) strongly favored states' rights, Tucker's *Letters From Virginia* (1816) criticized the Virginian aristocracy, and his *Life of Thomas Jefferson* (1837) portrayed Jefferson as a man of democratic national principles. His best novel, *The Valley of the Shenandoah* (1824), is a domestic seduction tale set against the self-destructive decline of a prosperous Tidewater planter family. As in numerous northern novels of the period devoted to the reformation of industrial labor, the family in Tucker's novel, as in his political thought, was a figure for the economic health and independence of the South.

Also suspicious of the South's ability to sustain itself in aristocratic seclusion was the physician William Alexander Caruthers (1802–46), whose historical novels portray the South as a central, but not the only, contributor to American national character. *The Kentuckian in New York* (1834), an epistolary romance, sought to join the sections by criticizing both the North's moral and financial corruption and the South's degradation in slavery and self-indulgence. In *The Cavaliers of Virginia* (1835), a novel of Bacon's Rebellion, Caruthers's advocacy of western expansionism, which he believed owed much to the strength of Virginian Cavalier character, responds as much to contemporary concerns about manifest destiny as to the dramatized historical incident. Likewise, his romance based on the career of Virginia's Governor Spotswood, *The Knights of the Horseshoe* (1845), was influenced by the legend of Daniel Boone. It predicts a westward "march which would be renewed generation to generation, until in the course of a single century it would transcend the Rio del Norte, and which, perhaps, in half that time may traverse the utmost boundaries of Mexico." Because in Caruthers's view the harshness of slavery was determined largely by the region and class of the slaveholder (the Virginia planter might be benevolent but his South Carolina counterpart a crude tyrant), both western expansion and the leveling effects of Jacksonian forces entailed the eventual eradication of chattel slavery as the nation's various factions and characteristics merged in a single destiny.

John Pendleton Kennedy (1795–1870) denounced secession and wrote a volume supporting the Union in the Civil War entitled *Mr. Ambrose's Letters on the Rebellion* (1863). Earlier in his life, however, he wrote one of the most influential literary defenses of the South, a series of sketches of Virginia life entitled *Swallow Barn* (1832). Trained in law and politics, Kennedy served several terms in Congress and, as secretary of the navy under President Fillmore, was responsible for sending Matthew Perry to Japan. His political works include the *Memoirs of the Life of William Wirt* (1849), a biography of the famous Virginia statesman and writer; *A Defense of the Whigs* (1842); and *Quodlibet* (1840), a Whig satire of Jacksonian political demogoguery. Kennedy assisted Poe by helping him obtain a position with the *Southern Literary Messenger* and by awarding a prize to "MS. Found in a Bottle." His activity in important literary circles also brought him into contact with William Makepeace Thackeray, to whom he gave material the British writer would use in *The Virginians*. Kennedy's other works include two important historical novels. *Rob of the Bowl* (1838) chronicles the conflicts between Catholics and Protestants in colonial Maryland; *Horse-Shoe Robinson* (1835), a backwoods southern Revolutionary War romance reminiscent of Cooper's *The Spy* and other similar fiction of the 1820s and 1830s, depicts a colonial family fractured by the divided national and sectional loyalties unleashed by the Revolution. It was the fictional essays of *Swallow Barn,* however, on which Kennedy's reputation as a writer rested. Influenced by the sketches of Irving and by Wirt's popular *Letters of the British Spy* (1803), a group of essays on southern life, Kennedy's volume employs the standard ruse of a northerner visiting the South who writes with mixed sympathy and mild satire in portraying the planter as an aristocratic country squire. *Swallow Barn* includes a few minor portraits of slave life, and Kennedy's general support of states' rights and the benevolent paternalism of the peculiar institution coincides with his contention that the abolition of slavery must come from within the South itself. Appearing in the wake of Nat Turner's uprising, the book was designed to restore calm and to reassure the South, as well as the North, that the great majority of Virginia's blacks, as in this description of slave children, were pacific and content: "Their predominant love of sunshine, and their lazy, listless, postures . . . might well afford a comparison to a set of terrapins luxuriating in the genial warmth of summer, on the logs of a mill-pond."

Unambiguous literary defense of the South and slavery is perhaps best reflected in the work of William Gilmore Simms, but the representatives of two distinct generations, Nathaniel Beverly Tucker (1784–1851) and John Esten Cooke (1830–86), prominently frame the argument for the southern Cavalier tradition. Son of the legal theorist St. George Tucker, whose *Dissertation on Slavery* (1796) outlined a plan for eventual emancipation, Tucker was himself a professor of law but also an early supporter of secession. His *Series of Lectures on the Science of Government* (1845), along with various essays in southern periodicals, prescribed a reactionary line. His first novel, *George Balcombe* (1836), an adventure and mystery story set in Virginia and Missouri, was thought by Poe to be one of the best American novels. But more important was *The Partisan Leader* (1836), a futuristic novel set in 1849, when Martin Van Buren has become a tyrannical dictator; the novel was reissued during the Civil War, and its prophecy of secession and sectional violence was viewed as uncanny. Cooke's career spanned the war and its aftermath, so that he participated in the cultural nostalgia for the Confederacy that flourished in the 1880s, but even in his youthful work he appears to be a prophet of the "Lost Cause." Brother of the poet and critic Philip Pendleton Cooke, he served as a staff officer for J. E. B. Stuart in the Confederate army and wrote important military biographies of Stonewall Jackson (1863) and Robert E. Lee (1871) and a number of war romances, such as *Surry of Eagle's Nest* (1866), *Hilt to Hilt* (1869), and *Hammer and Rapier* (1871). Although he continued to write fiction for several decades after the Civil War, his best-known fictional work remains the group of novels set in colonial Virginia written in the decade before the war began: *Leather Stocking and Silk* (1854), *The Virginia Comedians* (1854), and *Henry St. John, Gentleman* (1859). In all cases, the stories of romance and adventure are set against a backdrop of landholding gentility and slaveholding paternalism in which sectional differences are at once historical and resonant with contemporary tensions.

It is in the work of William Gilmore Simms (1806–70) that the use of the historical novel in defense of the South reaches full maturity. Just as *The Yemassee* (1835) depicted colonial South Carolina warfare against Indians but illuminated contemporary questions of Indian Removal, so Simms's series of Revolutionary War novels from *The Partisan* (1835) through *Eutaw* (1856) dramatized divided national and familial loyalties in ways that referred simultaneously to the history of American independence and the possibility of southern conflict with, or secession from, the Union. Along with other advocates of the Young America movement, Simms in the 1840s vigorously supported American expansionism and viewed democratic revolutions in Europe as an expression of the same ideals of liberty that gave the United States a moral right to territorial destiny in the New World. The Revolution was for Simms therefore a sign not just of America's strength but of the nation's necessary resolve to resist internal destruction. Liberty in this view became more and more clearly identified with white, Anglo-Saxon, southern ideals, and slavery was explained as a benevolent alternative to the degraded wage slavery of northern industrialism. Simms's varied and energetic career as a man of letters gave him considerable fame and made him an ardent spokesman for the South on the lecture platform and in numerous editorials and essays. His political theory stressed a stable, class-structured society in which democracy was not an invitation to mobility and disorder but a principle of coherence and control. In answer to the English writer Harriet Martineau's attack on slavery in *Society in America* (1837), Simms wrote in a much-cited essay in the *Southern Literary Messenger* (later reprinted in an 1838 pamphlet entitled *Slavery in America* and then again in the collection *The Pro-Slavery Argument*):

Democracy is not levelling – it is, properly defined, the harmony of the moral world. It insists upon inequalities, as its law declares, that all men should hold the place to which they are properly entitled. The definition of true liberty is, the undisturbed possession of that place in society to which our moral and intellectual merits entitle us. *He is a freeman, whatever his condition, who fills his proper place. He is a slave only, who is forced into a position in society below the claims of his intellect.*

To Simms, as to many of his contemporaries, South and North, such a theory of liberty and of intellect (however presumptively based on color) was not implausible. Harmony and hierarchical order – in terms of both class and race – were tied together, and the underlying pessimism about the final progress of humanity was subjugated to a view of permanent vertical rule within a democratic structure. The main question for Simms was whether, given the chaotic pressures of Jacksonian America, such a society could be made to work without at the same time destroying the democratic ideals that supported it.

The answer was that it could not. By the 1850s, moreover, the attack on the South was not simply one of political theory or of abolitionist lecturing but came in the form of Harriet Beecher Stowe's widely popular *Uncle Tom's Cabin,* which raised a fury of fictional replies in the South. Among them was one of Simms's important novels, *The Sword and the Distaff* (1853), later revised as *Woodcraft* (1854). Set at the conclusion of the Revolution, the novel concerns the restoration to order of Captain Porgy's plantation after the destructive "civil war" between patriots and Loyalists. Among other incidents, the scenes depicting the relationship between Porgy and his trusted slave Tom are calculated defenses of slaveholding benevolence and, more particularly, answers to what Simms took to be the fabricated sufferings of Stowe's own Tom. Porgy says he will shoot Tom "in order to save him" from the hostile enemy (in allegorical terms, "abolitionist") forces that would carry him off, and he even tells Tom to kill himself to prevent capture. Likewise, Tom says to Porgy: "Ef I doesn't b'long to *you, you* b'longs to *me!* . . . so, maussa, don't you bodder me wid dis nonsense t'ing 'bout free paper any more. I's well off whar' I is I tell you." The purported "nonsense" of freedom, of course, speaks more pointedly to the 1850s than to the 1780s, and the ruin of the southern landscape, even in victory, appears to anticipate a new civil war on the horizon. In 1856 Simms, speaking before a Buffalo audience in a speech about slavery in Kansas and alluding to Charles Sumner's notorious attack on South Carolina, foresaw the collapse of the Union but predicted the battered, ambiguous triumph of his home state, "a monument, more significant of ruin than all the wreck which grows around her – the trophy of a moral desolation." Simms's own South Carolina home would be burned twice (and his extensive personal library destroyed) during the war, once by accident and once by design during Sherman's march. With the deaths of his wife and two of his children, the war's toll on Simms was thus so heavy that it is remarkable that he continued to write in its aftermath, producing such volumes as *War Poetry of the South* (1866) and his eyewitness account of the destruction of Columbia, South Carolina. The prophetic character of *Woodcraft* was marred only by the fact that the North won the war, leaving the illusion of the paternalistic relationship of master and slave, which Simms thought of as an expression of democratic order held in place by the revolutionary heritage of the South, once and for all destroyed. It remained in memory and in myth, however, not least because of the effort of Simms over the course of his intellectual career to define a proslavery America free from the capricious and cruel behavior of bad masters and the inefficient political economy of a divided South.

Simms, Kennedy, Caruthers, the two Tuckers, and Cooke all worked in the context of the increasingly strident proslavery writing that appeared after the early 1830s. The same can be said of the southerner Poe, who was decidedly reactionary in his domestic political views and whose *Narrative of Arthur Gordon Pym* and short stories such as "Murders in the Rue Morgue" and "The System of Doctor Tarr and Professor Fether" hid fears of black rebellion and race contamination within baroque allegorical tales. Working in a similar vein of the grotesque, Oliver Bolokitten produced a futuristic, scatological burlesque of an America plunged into miscegenation, *A Sojourn in the City of Amalgamation* (1835). Set in an unspecified year of the twentieth century, the book's new republic affords its citizens an industrial amalgamating process by which all men, women, and animals must be mentally and bodily purged of prejudice, and the wars of various colored particles of their physiologies brought under control. Like Poe's work, the novel was most effective because its attack on liberal, romantic ideals of race harmony exposed the sobering fears and hatreds that underlay both sides of the argument over racial equality and the correct means to achieve it. Among southern local-color and frontier sketches – such as Mexican War journalist and politician Thomas B. Thorpe's *The Mysteries of the Backwoods* (1843) and *The Hive and the Hunter* (1854), Joseph G. Baldwin's satire *The Flush Times of Alabama and Mississippi* (1853), and George Washington Harris's tall tales in *Sut Lovingood Yarns* (1867) – there is little mention of slavery as an institution. However, their depiction of southern characters prone to violent outburst and comic extravagance echoes the work of Simms and Caruthers (and adumbrates that of Twain and Faulkner) in showing that the aristocratic veneer of the South covered a wilder, often crude interior that thrived in a frontier environment economically energized and socially structured by slavery.

Although the great outpouring of southern domestic novels in support of slavery, many by women, did not begin until the 1850s, significant titles appeared earlier. Caroline Gilman's *Recollections of a Southern Matron* (1838) and the anonymous *Lionel Granby* (1835) depict the harmonious, comfortable life of slaves and masters; and the northerner Sarah J. Hale, later famous as the editor of *Godey's Lady's Book,* produced a book that would remain one of the most popular domestic defenses of plantation life, *Northwood; A Tale of New England* (1827). The cross-sectional romance of Hale's novel supports her view that the family is a model of social order and stability and the South an arena of benevolence and cultivated leisure that can moderate the North's contemplative greed and harshness of character. Reissued in 1852 with a preface condemning the abolitionist forces of disunion, *Northwood* argues that both the Bible and the Constitution regulate slavery (even if they did not specifically establish it), and that it is not "the tearing up of the whole system of slavery, as it were, by the roots, that will make the bondman free." Only careful religious instruction and gradual colonization can give freedom and a home to American slaves and at the same time rescue African blacks from degraded savagery. "The mission of American slavery is to Christianize Africa," she writes, a view elaborated at length in her novel devoted to the most extensive effort at African resettlement, *Liberia; or, Mr. Peyton's Experiment* (1853). In both novels, Hale joins the argument over women's role in the slavery question, strongly advocating the domestic ideology her magazine made famous: " 'Constitutions' and 'compromises' are the appropriate work of men: women are conservators of moral power, which, eventually, as it is directed, preserves or destroys the work of the warrior, the statesman, and the patriot."

To the extent that they answer Harriet Beecher Stowe's representation of the slaveholding South, Hale's novels of the 1850s and Simms's *Woodcraft* belong to a large group of novels appearing in the decade after *Uncle Tom's Cabin* that raise strident, and often incredible, voices in defense of the plantation myth. The numerous direct replies to Stowe's novel (a number of them written by northerners sympathetic to the South) claimed that she had misconceived the benevolent paternalism of southern slaveholding, and they pointed out that Simon Legree was a northerner and thus an exception to the norm of kind southern masters. Like the proslavery essayists, the novelists also traded on the common argument that northern wage labor was far more vicious than chattel slavery. In Robert Criswell's *Uncle Tom's Cabin Contrasted with Buckingham Hall* (1852), the sedition of abolitionism is countered by the romanticized life of the decent planter, whereas northern labor and Jim Crow laws are exposed as corrupt and demeaning. Likewise, in John W. Page's *Uncle Robin, in His Cabin in Virginia, and Tom without One in Boston* (1853), it is argued that the miseries that this Tom encounters as a freeman in Boston would be multiplied exponentially if slavery were abolished; and in W. L. G. Smith's *Life at the South; or, "Uncle Tom's Cabin" As It Is* (1852), the escaped slave hero, after suffering illness, poverty, and homelessness in the North returns home to the Virginia plantation, back to "his master, father, home." The conjunction or virtual equation of these three terms succinctly indicates the main rhetorical lines of the southern paternalistic argument for slavery penned in scores of essays and dramatized in other novels such as *Cabin and Parlor, or Slaves and Masters* (1852), by J. Thornton Randolph (pseudonym of Philadelphia magazine editor Charles Peterson); Caroline Lee Hentz's *The Planter's Northern Bride* (1854), which asserts, in the face of "the burning lava of anarchy and servile war" threatened by abolitionism, that slaves are "the happiest *laboring class* on the face of the globe"; Thomas B. Thorpe's *The Master's House, A Tale of Southern Life* (1854), a strikingly more realistic and balanced account that hopes for an arrest in the decline of the cultivated, paternalistic power of a southern landed gentry; and Mrs. G. M. Flanders's *The Ebony Idol* (1860), whose title is suggestive of its virulent satire of the supposed abolitionist "worship" of African American life and race mixing.

Like *Uncle Tom's Cabin* itself, however, the novels that were most popular and effective tempered realism with inflammatory melodrama. In Caroline Rush's *North and South; or, Slavery and Its Contrasts* (1852), the northern heroine, driven into poverty and prostitution by her family's bankruptcy, becomes a "white slave," and her tale of urban suffering is pointedly contrasted to "the pampered, well-fed lazy negro children of the South." Because the familial feelings of whites are more refined than those of blacks, Rush argues, "the bondage of poverty [that] forces a lady to give up her child to the care of strangers is worse in the North," and the novelist stands on moral high ground in addressing her genteel, sentimental audience: "We shall see whether 'the broad-chested, powerful Negro' [i.e., Uncle Tom], or the fragile, delicate girl, with her pure white face, is most entitled to your sympathy and tears." Similarly, in Mary H. Eastman's *Aunt Phillis's Cabin* (1852), the deathbed scene of the old slave Phillis shows her telling her master *not* to free her children, who are well cared for on the plantation and will suffer in the North or in Liberia. Because the tearful scene also forecasts a reunion of slave and master in heaven, where "the distinctions of this world will be forgotten," it testifies to the planters' need to rationalize slavery but at the same time to mitigate the sin they implicitly recognized to lie within it. The argument for Christian conversion and colonization often rested on a corresponding recognition of the domestic sin of slaveholding linked to a Calvinistic fear of blackness associated with the African and with the "barbarism" and purportedly satanic practices of African tribal life. Among the many theoretical and fictional critiques of African primitivism, Mrs. Henry Rowe Schoolcraft's tale of gothic sentimentality and vicious racism, *The Black Gauntlet* (1860), is thus both extreme and representative. The wife of the famous ethnologist of American Indians, Mrs. Schoolcraft joined a number of vocal opponents of what she called Lincoln's "Ethiopian equality party" in castigating the notion of amalgamation (the "reign of the Anglo-Africans approaches," she warned) and defining Anglo-American Christian work as an expunging of the mark of Cain placed on blacks by their cannibalistic ancestry. Taking a leaf from her husband's writing on Native Americans, she advised that whites should keep blacks "in bondage until *compulsory labor* [has] tamed their beastliness, and civilization and Christianity [have] prepared them to return as missionaries of progress to their benighted black brethren." If it was less sophisticated than political oratory and economic theorizing, the proslavery novel, South and North, used ignorance and racial fear as its equally effective weapons.

Abraham Lincoln's interest in colonization was fueled by Free Soil objection to competition from slavery and from free black labor, but it sprang from long-standing northern, as well as southern, sentiment in favor of deporting freed slaves to Africa or colonies in Latin America, a view that had been advanced by Thomas Jefferson among others. The rise of legal opposition to the slave trade, culminating in its prohibition by congress in 1808, the passage of the more far-reaching Anti-Slave Trade Act in 1819, and the establishment of the American Colonization Society in 1816, made colonization the most powerful antislavery movement until the 1830s. At that time, the South's reactionary turn (sparked by Turner's revolt and by profits in the burgeoning internal slave trade, which supported an expansion of the cotton economy in the lower South) and fierce condemnation of colonization by William Lloyd Garrison and other antislavery leaders crippled the movement. Goaded by the protests of those blacks who opposed colonization, abolitionists increasingly recognized that the American Colonization Society, whatever its intentions, worked primarily in the service of proslavery and racist interests. The society's journal, the *African Repository,* also made clear its ultimate prejudices by including such documents as one that declared that African Americans, no matter what their proportion of African "blood," were subject to "a degradation inevitable and incurable" and argued that white prejudice could never be overcome in America.

Although the idea of colonization continued to be revived by both black and white leaders until the Civil War was over, the British colony of Sierra Leone, established in 1787, and the American colony of Liberia, established in 1822, were the only significant results of the movement's efforts. The first group of Liberian settlers, and those who later joined them voluntarily, were not so much exiles as models of black independence. The emigrants' difficult but challenging experience in West Africa was recorded in annual reports throughout the rest of the century, in letters and stories in the *African Repository,* and in volumes such as James Hall's *An Address to the Free People of Color* (1819, 1835), Matthew Carey's *Letters on the Colonization Society* (1828), James Lugenbeel's *Sketches of Liberia* (1850), and in a modern edition of their letters entitled *Slaves No More* (ed. Bell I. Wiley, 1980). Paul Cuffee, an American black who led a group of colonists to Sierra Leone in 1815, wrote about the colony in *A Brief Account of the Settlement and Present Condition of the Colony of Sierra Leone in Africa* (1812). In a different vein, Frederick Freeman's widely read *Yaradee; A Plea for Africa* (1836) contended that blacks had been depraved both by nature and by enslavement and that prejudice against them could be removed by "nothing short of divine power." Perhaps the text of most interest to come from the early phase of colonization was Ralph R. Gurley's *Life of Jehudi Ashmun* (1835), the biography of a white minister and colonial agent in Liberia, which gave a detailed picture of the colony and included Ashmun's own diary accounts of his spiritual trials and growth.

Despite the moderate success of Liberia, however, forced colonization on a large scale remained both impractical and immoral. When ideas of colonization were revived in the 1850s by black nationalists and by whites anxious about the results of emancipation, the project was even less plausible than it had been thirty years earlier. Abolitionism often undermined legitimate attempts at colonization, but it did not stifle American interest in Africa, which reached its height later in the century when European imperialist exploration and settlement penetrated into the interior of the "dark continent" and when a significant number of historians, both black and white, began to recover Africa's past in detail. American travel and adventure writing set in Africa, which likewise flourished in the late nineteenth century, was also popular even in the antebellum period. One of the books with the greatest readership, reprinted until the 1850s, was James Riley's *Sufferings in Africa* (1817), an account of his shipwreck and enslavement by Arabs. Finally ransomed by the British in Morocco, Riley painted a vivid, if Anglocentric, picture of his wanderings and ordeal in North Africa. His account of life as a white slave, which Lincoln read, provoked sympathy that could be displaced to abolitionist sentiment: "we were obliged to keep up with the camels, running over the stones, which were nearly as sharp as gun flints, and cutting our feet to the bone at every step. It was here that my fortitude and my reason failed me. . . . I searched for a stone, intending if I could find a loose one sufficiently large, to knock out my own brains with it." A work with similar appeal, antislavery leader Charles Sumner's 1843 volume *White Slavery in the Barbary States,* was one of several historical works that treated the Islamic–Christian conflict and consequent enslavements predating those of the New World, and it thus added a historically resonant international context, for example, to Melville's treatment of slavery in *Benito Cereno.*

Voyages of trade and adventure, often with commentary on Liberia, appeared in W. F. W. Owen's *Narrative of Voyages to Explore the Shores of Africa, Arabia, and Madagascar* (1833), William B. Hodgson's *Notes on Northern Africa, the Sahara, and the Soudan* (1844), J. A. Carnes's *Journal of a Voyage from Boston to the West Coast of Africa* (1852), and Charles W. Thomas's *Adventures and Observations on the West Coast of Africa* (1855). Even though the most important works on African exploration and economic enterprise would not appear until the zenith of the imperial age, antebellum writing about Africa borrowed from the energy of mission and conquest that motivated the Euro-American drive into the continental West and the Pacific. In both cases, the voyages and the works that became their records were predicated upon an explicit racial hierarchy and the belief that white Americans – or, in the case of Africa, emancipated African Americans – could introduce Christian and democratic civilization into a primitive world. Here, as in the case of writings about the Pacific, military and mercantile literature overlapped with the representation of American nationalism and racial hierarchy. The U.S. naval operation against the slave trade was treated in Horatio Bridge's *Journal of an African Cruiser* (1845) and Andrew Hull Foote's *Africa and the American Flag* (1854); and the development of legitimate trade with Africa, which had existed alongside the trade in slaves, was recorded in such works as Edward Bold's *The Merchant's and Mariner's African Guide* (1823).

Perhaps the most revealing volume devoted to the United States and its relation to Africa was written by a former slave trader, Theophilus Conneau, who adopted the pen name Theodore Canot in publishing *Captain Canot; or, Twenty Years of an African Slaver* (1854). Conneau's work is finely detailed in its account of travel within Africa and the internal African slave trade, the perils and hardships of the middle passage, and the calculation of profit in human cargo transported illegally under the false flags of various ships. The record of his transport of slaves to the West Indies contains a highly personalized description of his successful career as a trader alongside events of mutiny and suicide. According to Conneau, his discipline was mild and his ship kept

comparatively clean, but the tenor of his prose alone signals the true cost of
trade in African slaves. Before shipping, newly purchased slaves were
branded, shaved, and stripped, since "perfect nudity, during the whole voyage, is the only means of securing cleanliness and health." The moral resonance of Conneau's text is entirely in harmony with its utilitarian purpose:

> In every well-conducted slaver, the captain, officers, and crew, are alert and vigilant
> to preserve the cargo. It is [in] their personal interest, as well as the interest of
> humanity, to do so. . . . At sundown, the process of stowing the slaves for the night
> is begun. The second mate and boatswain descend into the hold, whip in hand, and
> range the slaves in their regular places; those on the right side of the vessel facing
> forward, and lying in each other's lap, while those on the left are similarly stowed
> with their faces towards the stern. In this way each negro lies on his right side, which
> is considered preferable for the action of the heart. In allotting places, particular
> attention is paid to size, the taller being selected for the greatest breadth of the
> vessel, while the shorter and younger are lodged near the bows. When the cargo is
> large and the lower deck crammed, the super-numeraries are disposed of on deck,
> which is securely covered with boards to shield them from moisture. The *strict*
> discipline of nightly stowage is, of course, of the greatest importance in slavers, else
> every negro would accommodate himself as if he were a passenger.

Even though it was not written as an antislavery work, the effectiveness of
Conneau's volume lay to a degree in its revelation of a mind and spirit
hardened to suffering by an international economic web of legal and illegal
trade in human flesh.

The renewal of interest in colonization in the 1850s was prompted in part
by fears of emancipation and miscegenation that had been converted into
ideals of Christian mission by writers as different in their intentions as Mrs.
Henry Rowe Schoolcraft and Harriet Beecher Stowe. As in earlier decades,
those with antislavery sympathies sometimes argued even more ingenuously
for the benefits of colonization than did defenders of southern slavery. Like a
number of authors in the decade before the Civil War, Jacob Dewees employed his adventure narrative *The Great Future of America and Africa* (1854)
as a means to contend that colonization was the only path to black success
and redemption. David Christy, antiabolitionist author of *Cotton is King*,
rendered a complimentary picture of Liberia in *Ethiopia: Her Gloom and Glory*
(1857), arguing that American blacks returned there with civilized and
Christian principles to replace the brutishness and paganism of Africa. In
thus "securing to Africa the benefits of her own labor," Christy believed, the
new colonists both improved their ancestral land and recognized that "intellectually, morally, or politically, [blacks] can no more flourish in the midst of
whites, than the tender sprout from the bursting acorn can have a rapid
advance to maturity beneath the shade of the full-grown oak . . . its lordly
superior." So too, Thomas Jefferson Bowen, a Southern Baptist missionary

among the Yoruba who also wrote a grammar of their language, maintained in *Central Africa: Adventures and Missionary Labours in Several Countries in the Interior of Africa from 1849 to 1856* (1857) that God's evident purpose in allowing slavery had been to take the "millions of civilized negroes in America, better clothed and fed, and more virtuous and happy than the analogous classes of white people in some other countries," and use them to regenerate their homeland, "flowing back as a river of light and life upon the African continent."

From the beginning of the colonization movement, blacks as well as whites envisioned resettlement outside the borders of the United States, sometimes prophesying a millennial regeneration within the black community that would ultimately spread to the entire globe. J. Dennis Harris and James T. Holly, for example, pointed in the 1850s to the revolutionary success of Haiti as the forerunner of utopian Caribbean colonies. Holly's lecture, *A Vindication of the Capacity of the Negro Race for Self-Government and Civilized Progress, as Demonstrated by Historical Events of the Haytian Revolution* (1857), adopted a version of Bowen's argument in predicting that Haiti would become the "Eden of America, and the garden spot of the world": "Civilization and Christianity [are] passing from the East to the West . . . God, therefore in permitting the accursed slave traffic to transplant so many millions of the race, to the New World . . . indicates thereby, that we have a work now to do here in the Western World, which in his own good time shall shed its orient beams upon the Fatherland of the race [Africa]."

The providential view of slavery, which rested on a paradox inimical to modern liberalism, was thus hardly restricted to white intellectuals. In the more complex thought of Alexander Crummell, however, black American slavery was only the most obvious political dimension of a greater moral problem. Although his greatest fame and power as a spokesman for evangelical black nationalism would come later in the century, Crummell (1819–98) was second only to Frederick Douglass at midcentury in the breadth of his thought and influence. A black Episcopal priest and African missionary, Crummell believed that Africa was "the maimed and crippled arm of humanity" in need of regeneration by American blacks. He advanced his argument in such works as "The Relation and Duties of Free Colored Men in America to Africa" (1861) and *The Future of Africa* (1862), basing his call for black evangelism and the African commerce on the hope that such trade could be made to rival "the market value of the flesh and blood they [white traders] had been so eager to crowd beneath their hatches." Christianity and the market would redeem Africa, Crummell avowed, but not necessarily pacifically: "for the establishment of a strong black civilization in central Africa, a strong and bloody hand must be used." Crummell returned to the United

States in 1873 and became a leading figure in the conservative wing of the black nationalist movement, as well as one of the founders in 1897 of the American Negro Academy. Born free, he did not share the view of Douglass and other black leaders that slavery alone was responsible for black degradation but argued that the need for racial uplift stemmed in part from the rudimentary state of civilization in Africa. "Darkness covers the land," he wrote of Africa in 1861, "and gross darkness the people. Great devils universally prevail. Confidence and security are destroyed. Licentiousness abounds everywhere. Moloch rules and reigns throughout the whole continent, and by the ordeal of Sassywood, Fetiches, human sacrifices, and devil-worship, is devouring men, women, and little children." His estimate of Africa was sometimes hardly less scathing than that of European imperialists. Nevertheless, Crummell's call for evangelical colonization in the antebellum years was based on an idealized vision of African nationalism grounded in the recovery of an ancient racial "vigor," and throughout his career he espoused the need for a Pan-African territorial home and a mature role in world politics and economics for black people.

The increasing apprehension among blacks that they would never find freedom, much less equality, in America prompted calls for colonization that were not all missionary in spirit. The most prominent black political leaders in the antebellum period – Frederick Douglass, Martin Delany, and Henry Highland Garnet among them – held differing views on colonization at different points in their careers, though their sentiments in favor of it were usually based on a certain degree of Afrocentric nationalism. The shift in support for colonization from white missionaries (and proslavery advocates) to black nationalists that occurred from the 1820s to the 1850s is one index of the increasing frustration of abolitionists who thought that in condemning colonization they were striking an effective blow for the equality of freed African Americans.

William Lloyd Garrison's *Thoughts on African Colonization* (1832), which attacked colonization as futile and undemocratic, was a natural outgrowth of his embrace of more radical antislavery principles in the 1830s. Along with William Jay's *Inquiry into the Character and Tendency of the American Colonization Society* (1835), it worked to turn abolitionist sentiment away from colonization and toward the practical issue of freeing slaves to join the life of national democracy America was meant to offer. After working on the abolitionist newspaper *The Genius of Universal Emancipation,* edited by the Quaker and colonizationist Benjamin Lundy, Garrison (1805–79) launched his own more fiery journal, the *Liberator,* in 1831. His calls for "immediate emancipation" and eventually for disunion from the South made him the leader of the most extreme wing of antislavery, and his avowal of "perfectionism" (the religious social reform doctrine asserting that people could indeed be wholly freed from sin on earth) fixed slavery as the most degraded of evils infecting the world. However, his belief in the power of nonviolence and his general disregard of all institutional means of fighting slavery through the church, political campaigns, and social reform movements always threatened to leave him isolated from reality. Garrison's manipulation of the rhetoric of democratic liberty, noted at the outset of this chapter, was especially potent; for example, he entitled an 1860 collection of documents about violence and suppression in the South *The New "Reign of Terror" in the Slaveholding States*. His flair for melodramatic rhetoric fitted him for an age of oratory, and his excoriations of slavery appealed to humanitarian concerns bolstered by guilt. Speaking of the imminent abolition of slavery in British colonies in 1832, he thundered:

What heart can conceive, what pen or tongue describe, the happiness which must flow from the consummation of this act? That cruel lash, which has torn so many tender bodies, and is dripping with innocent blood; that lash, which has driven so many human victims, like beasts, to their unrequited toil; that lash, whose sounds are heard from the rising of the sun to its decline, mingled with the shrieks of bleeding sufferers; that lash is soon to be cast away, never again to wound the flesh, or degrade those who are made in the image of God. And those fetters of iron, which have bound so many in ignominious servitude, and wasted their bodies, and borne them down to an unlikely grave, shall be shivered in pieces, as the lightning rends the pine. . . . O, how transforming the change! In contemplating it, my imagination overpowers the serenity of my soul, and makes language seem poor and despicable.

Garrison's thought and language indicate two converging strains in antislavery ideology. On the one hand, Garrison voiced the romanticist drive of antislavery protest, a belief in the moral primacy of common people, especially those who are oppressed, and the consequent expressive power of sympathy; on the other, he underscored antislavery's evangelical nature, derived from the spirit of revivalism that swept many religious groups in the first third of the century and entered into the panoply of social reform causes that appeared from the 1820s to the 1860s.

The evangelistic spirit and the language of sympathy, in lectures as in fiction and poetry, lent a particular power to the antislavery crusade, for its egalitarian principles coincided with what were thought to be easily perceived moral truths. Its characteristic early texts were therefore expressions of direct experience and straightforward calls for action. For example, John Rankin, who developed the underground railroad in Ohio (and rescued the woman who became the model for Eliza in *Uncle Tom's Cabin*), made a direct appeal for citizen participation in *Letters on Slavery* (1826). Despite problems of factionalism, antislavery's success depended on its adherence to simple principles that were independent of the abstruse doctrines of organized churches, most of whose leaders were less than forthcoming in support of antislavery and as a result were severely criticized by Garrison, Stowe, Douglass, and others.

Even in the early decades of the movement, clear articulations of black rights and bold challenges for immediate emancipation, by means of insurrection if necessary, appeared in antislavery writing, especially in that by African Americans themselves. Although it counseled an ambiguous submission to suffering while awaiting deliverance at the hands of a coming savior, Robert Alexander Young's *Ethiopian Manifesto Issued in Defense of the Black Man's Rights in the Scale of Universal Freedom* (1829) is the first text of black nationalism produced by an African American. Far more striking and influential was the revolutionary pamphlet produced by the free black David Walker (1785?–1830). Entitled *Appeal . . . to the Coloured Citizens of the World,* Walker's 1828 pamphlet, cited earlier, was banned in the South because of its incendiary call for violent rebellion. In a carefully argued but blazing style, Walker replied directly to Thomas Jefferson's theory in *Notes on the State of Virginia* that the risk of miscegenation was a barrier to emancipation. Adopting the rhetoric of black messianism that runs through abolitionist and much later black nationalist thought, Walker attacked Christian doctrine that led blacks to submit to their bondage while prompting whites to ignore the certain judgment of the Almighty: "I call God – I call angels – I call men, to witness that your DESTRUCTION *is at hand,* and will be speedily consummated unless you REPENT." His important statement of black nationalist principles was not calculated to gain the favor of sympathetic whites, and it advocated an appropriation of principles of revolution that even Garrison would eschew:

But remember, Americans, that as miserable, wretched, degraded and abject as you have made us in [the] preceding, and in this generation, to support you and your families, that some of you [whites], on the continent of America, will yet curse the day that you were ever born. You want slaves, and want us for your slaves!!! My colour will yet, root some of you out of the very face of the earth!!!!! . . . I ask you candidly, [were] your sufferings under Great Britain, one hundredth part as cruel and tyrannical as you have rendered ours under you? Some of you, no doubt, believe that we will never throw off your murderous government. . . . If Satan has made you believe it, will he not deceive you?

Walker's *Appeal* anticipated the better-known jeremiads of black leaders like Douglass and Delany. Although Walker's fame was short-lived – he died two years after publication of his *Appeal* and was overshadowed by the figure of Garrison – his call increased black interest in antislavery even as it terrified slaveholders. As in the case of Garrison, radicalism here accomplished something short of its stated goals of violence and separatism, but its statement of principles and its ultimate effect on the consciousness of the nation were the true measure of its success.

More remarkable than Walker's rhetoric was that of Maria Stewart, a black evangelist from Boston whose *Productions of Mrs. Maria W. Stewart* (1835) included a group of meditations and public addresses directed especially at the "daughters of Africa." She placed herself squarely in the tradition of the jeremiad by invoking scripture and condemning the "foul and indelible" stain of American slavery for which the nation would be judged and punished:

Dark and dismal is the cloud that hangs over [America], for thy cruel wrongs and injuries to the fallen sons of Africa. The blood of her murdered ones cries to heaven for vengeance against thee. Thou art almost become drunken with the blood of her slain; thou hast enriched thyself through her toils and labours. . . . And thou hast caused the daughters of Africa to commit whoredoms and fornications. . . . O, ye great and mighty men of America, ye rich and powerful ones, many of you will call for the rocks and mountains to fall upon you, and to hide from the wrath of the Lamb, and from him that sitteth upon the throne; whilst many of the sable-skinned Africans you now despise, will shine in the kingdom of heaven as the stars forever and ever.

The "mighty men" of America were Stewart's particular target. Aligning slavery with a pervasive male dominance, Stewart told women that it was "no use for us to sit with our hands folded, hanging our heads like bulrushes, lamenting our wretched condition." Her message foreshadowed later black nationalist assertions of a separatist self-help ethic, but it did so in explicitly feminist terms: "How long shall the fair daughters of Africa be compelled to bury their minds and talents beneath a load of iron pots and kettles? . . . Shall [men] laugh us to scorn forever? Do you ask, what can we do? Unite and build a store of your own if you cannot procure a license. Fill one side with dry goods, and the other with groceries." Although white antislavery women like Stowe and Lydia Maria Child would receive more attention, Stewart's discourses are a significant chapter in antislavery writing and a striking early signpost in the literature of black feminism.

At the same time that Walker, Stewart, and Garrison embraced immediatism, more conservative religious and social groups, which typically advocated gradual measures and often maintained clearly hierarchical racial and sexual divisions, worked in a counterdirection. In the early years of relative harmony, the antislavery crusade gained numerous adherents, effectively petitioned politicians for action on civil rights, and drew on the energies of reform directed at the urban problems of prostitution, gambling, and temperance. It generated a number of important journals and newspapers, including the *Anti-Slavery Examiner,* the *Emancipator,* the *National Anti-Slavery Standard,* the *Liberty Almanac,* and the *Philanthropist.* It withstood the scorn of the South and of many northerners, who repeatedly attacked its offices and leading speakers in mobs. The more diffuse the movement became, however, the less coherent was its purpose. Moreover, Garrison's adoption of such extreme positions as religious perfectionism and the denunciation of all governmental authority and political processes, and his consequent attraction of eccentrics, tended to isolate him from the moderate majority. Men such as Lewis Tappan and Arthur Tappan, who had been instrumental in organizing and financing the American Anti-Slavery Society, were skeptical of, among other things, Garrison's support of women's direct participation in antislavery work, a controversy sparked by the 1837 lecture tour of Sarah Grimké and Angelina Grimké, southern Quaker sisters who had a great impact on the development of a feminist antislavery ethic. In 1840, a quarrel over Garrison's proposal to place a woman on the executive committee of the American Anti-Slavery Society created volatile dissension, which was exacerbated later in the year when the World Anti-Slavery Convention in London refused to admit women delegates from the United States. In the first case, Lewis Tappan split from Garrison and formed the American and Foreign Anti-Slavery Society; in the second, two of the delegates, Lucretia Mott and Elizabeth Cady Stanton, immediately resolved to launch a women's movement, and the 1848 Seneca Falls convention was the eventual result. The same resistance to their participation in the antislavery movement, ironically enough, was sometimes encountered by blacks in the North, who were more interested in action than in theory. Like women, blacks gradually gained an important place in the movement but at the expense of internecine fighting that retarded the effectiveness of the antislavery campaign.

Of particular interest in the shift of attitudes that spurred the alliance between revivalism and social reform, and in some respects provoked the convergence of the women's movement with antislavery, is the figure of Lyman Beecher (1775–1863), the father of Harriet Beecher Stowe. A New England Presbyterian minister who was instrumental in revivalist preaching, Beecher moved west to Cincinnati in 1832 to preside over the Lane Theological Seminary, which became a center for moderate antislavery thought and activity. In many of his sermons and essays, collected in his *Works* (1852), as well as in his influential volume entitled *A Plea for the West* (1835), Beecher mixed anti-Catholicism and a reformed Calvinist theology in calling for religious and political freedom in America, the alternative to the "prison house" and "slavery" of despotic Europe. With respect to the enslavement of American blacks, however, Beecher recommended moderation – moral suasion rather than violent activism – and looked to colonization of freed blacks as the best solution to the race problem. One of his sons, Henry Ward Beecher (1818–87), became the most famous minister of his day. Although Henry was best known for his urban reform activities and self-improvement writings such as *Seven Lectures to Young Men* (1844), for his writings on religion, and for a notorious adultery scandal in later years, his *Star Papers* (1855) and other works supported the antislavery cause and his New York church publicly aided escaped slaves. Another Beecher son, Edward (1830–95), was also an active opponent of slavery. In his *Narrative of Riots at Alton* (Illinois) (1838), an account of the murder of the prominent antislavery editor Elijah Lovejoy, he argued that the "nation" itself had been murdered and that a "deluge of anarchy and blood" would follow if peaceable abolitionism were not allowed its voice.

Because Lyman Beecher's beliefs were based upon the Calvinist theology of Jonathan Edwards, which held that humanity was depraved and dependent upon God's grace for salvation, he promoted gradualist methods for achieving salvation and combating slavery that came to seem too tentative to his children and most of all to his students, a large number of whom deserted Lane to follow the revivalist Charles Grandison Finney in establishing Oberlin in 1833. One of the Lane students who resigned after the antislavery controversy, Theodore Dwight Weld (1803–95), wrote the work that probably had the greatest influence on Stowe's conception of *Uncle Tom's Cabin* as a polemic. *American Slavery As It Is: Testimony of a Thousand Witnesses* appeared anonymously in 1839 with a terse, appropriate epigraph from Ezekiel: "Behold the abominations that they do!" From over 20,000 southern newspapers that Weld examined between 1837 and 1839 the volume drew myriad examples of the treatment and conditions of slaves in the South, along with other firsthand testimony and narratives, many from slaveholders, detailing the punishment, random violence, and day-to-day degradation inflicted upon blacks. Comparable to Weld's volume in popularity was the work of the Quaker John Greenleaf Whittier (1807–92), who wrote an American Anti-Slavery Society pamphlet entitled *Justice and Expediency* (1833) but was best known for his antislavery and reform poetry and for a quasi-fictional slave narrative he ghostwrote, *Narrative of James Williams* (1838). Working in the Garrisonian tradition of immediatism, Whittier called for the day when the Declaration of Independence would be honored, "when under one common sun of political liberty the slave-holding portions of our republic shall no longer sit, like the Egyptians of old, themselves mantled in thick darkness, while all around them is glowing with the blessed light of freedom and equality." His work as an editor of antislavery publications led to other important essays, "What is Slavery?" and "Thomas Carlyle and the Slavery Question" among them; and his poems, taking such titles as "The Hunters of

Men," "The Slave-Ships," and "To William Lloyd Garrison," reached a large popular audience. One of his most piercing, entitled "Ichabod," denounced Daniel Webster for his support of the Compromise of 1850:

> Of all we loved and honored, nought
>> Save power remains —
> A fallen angel's pride of thought,
>> Still strong in chains.

> All else is gone; from those great eyes
>> The soul has fled:
> When faith is lost, when honor dies,
>> The man is dead!

Throughout his poetry Whittier represents the South as an arena of cruelty and dissipation, its slaves driven by tyrants and its honorable character prostituted to greed and lust. As in much antislavery literature, of which *Uncle Tom's Cabin* is only the best-known example, the separation of families and the abuse of slave women are key features of the rhetoric of sentiment that ensured the popularity of Whittier's verse.

Daniel Webster's acquiescence in the Compromise of 1850 made him the symbol of New England's failure to actively resist the machinations of the "Slave Power" and brought into symbolic crisis the heritage of liberty, granted in the national Union by the Founding Fathers, that Webster had spent his political life celebrating. Other political figures who stood out in the antislavery fight include John Quincy Adams, whose impassioned campaign to repeal the gag rule that prevented antislavery petitions from being presented to Congress from 1836 to 1844 was ultimately victorious, and who successfully defended the rebel slaves from the *Amistad;* and Senator Charles Sumner, whose famous 1856 speech on "The Crime Against Kansas" resulted in his notorious assault on the Senate floor at the hands of Preston Brooks. But Webster (1782–1852) came to seem a tragic figure precisely because of his moderation and caution on the issue that, he correctly saw, might destroy the Union. Webster's obsession with the unity and "harmony" of the Union permeated his thought and speeches, notably in his 1830 reply to Robert Hayne's Senate speech on Nullification, in which Webster called on the memory of the founders to help suppress what he took to be southern divisiveness and factionalism.

But the issue that cast the most searching light on the paradoxes of union symbolized by Webster's career was the Compromise of 1850. Growing out of the crisis over slavery and the imbalance of sectional interests occasioned by the acquisition of western lands in the Mexican War and California's subsequent adoption of a free-state constitution, the Compromise was pivotal in the political and literary war over slavery. Not just the great political writing of the 1850s but also the central works of literature – *Moby-Dick, Uncle Tom's Cabin, Leaves of Grass,* and *My Bondage and My Freedom,* to name the most obvious – all reflected the fragile structure of the Compromise, its perilous balance of destructive national forces. The central provisions of the Compromise admitted California to the Union as a free state and abolished the slave trade in Washington, D.C., but at the same time organized the New Mexico and Utah territories without prohibiting slavery and enacted a new Fugitive Slave Law requiring northerners to aid in the return of escaped slaves to their masters. In words that linked his own feeble body to the body politic of the Union, the aged and dying John Calhoun rejected the proposals as destructive of the rights of the South: "The cry of 'Union, union, the glorious union!' can no more prevent disunion than the cry of 'Health, health, glorious health!' on the part of the physician, can save a patient lying dangerously ill." Webster's famous speech of March 7, 1850, in defense of Henry Clay's Compromise resolution invoked again the heritage of the revolutionary fathers that he had made his hallmark in speeches dedicating the Bunker Hill Monument, where he had advised his listeners standing "among the sepulchres of our fathers" to beware the day when "faction and dismemberment [would] obliterate for ever all hopes of the founders of our republic and the great inheritance of their children." Conciliating slave interests and calling for an end to antislavery agitation, Webster's reply glowed with optimism that Melville and others would quickly satirize. "Instead of dwelling in these caverns of darkness," Webster advised, "let us come out into the light of day; let us enjoy the fresh air of Liberty and Union. . . . Let us make our generation one of the strongest and brightest links in that golden chain which is destined, I fondly believe, to grapple the people of all the states to this Constitution for ages to come." The government of the United States, Webster proclaimed, had so far been entirely "beneficent" and had "trodden down no man's liberty" or "crushed no State." Antislavery writers, conscious of the suppressed liberties of African Americans, were quick to counter Webster's views with different interpretations of the revolutionary paradigm. Contemptuously alluding to Webster's "noble words" at his 1843 Bunker Hill speech, "the spot so reddened with the blood of our fathers," Theodore Parker answered Webster that "the question is, not if slavery is going to cease, and soon to cease, but shall it end as it ended in Massachusetts, in New Hampshire, in Pennsylvania, in New York, or shall it end as in St. Domingo? Follow the counsel of Mr. Webster – it will end in fire and blood."

Webster and others appealed to the Founding Fathers, whose views on slavery, embodied in the Constitution, were open to both proslavery and antislavery interpretation. Politicians in the North and South conceived of

America as a "family" presided over by benevolent paternal figures whose enormous achievement induced anxiety in the following generations and made them reluctant to contravene their inherited wisdom. By the same token, the vision of the Founding Fathers was open to antislavery exploitation. In courting the attacks of Parker and others, Webster made his own appeal to the Revolution ironic, even (as Emerson said of the Fugitive Slave Law) "suicidal." Conversely, William Gilmore Simms and others on the proslavery side feared the "suicide" of disunion and war that they thought abolitionism would bring on. Which course was most likely to destroy the fragile Union was the implied subject of every slavery debate. Although his views on slavery were close to those of Clay, and although it would take him the length of the Civil War to reconcile his attempted salvation of the Union with the destruction of slavery, Abraham Lincoln was finally not so paralyzed as Webster by the burden of the Founding Fathers. However, if Lincoln's warning in the famous Lyceum Address of 1838 that "as a nation of freemen we must live through all time or die by suicide" did not forecast abolition, it did adumbrate a crisis over slavery. Setting the context for his ostensible subject, "the perpetuation of our political institutions," Lincoln spoke against the kind of mob violence that took Elijah Lovejoy's life, and he chose as another example the lynching of "Negroes suspected of conspiring to raise an insurrection." Lincoln's address, often seen to desecrate the founders and to betray a monumental desire for personal power, marked his initial turn away from the mesmerizing influence of the revolutionary past, which he characterized as a "forest of giant oaks" now "despoiled of its verdure" and reduced to "mutilated limbs." Two decades later, in preserving the Union while abolishing slavery, Lincoln, not Webster, became the nation's tragic savior. In doing so, Lincoln carried the full weight of the revolutionary burden that had immobilized generation after generation on the issue of slavery, and he unified the contradictory symbolic sacrifices Stowe had portrayed in her 1851 antislavery sketch "The Two Altars, or, Two Pictures in One," which ironically compared the sacrifices of a family for the revolutionary cause at Valley Forge to the 1850 sacrifice of a fugitive slave on the "altar of liberty."

The crisis over the Union permeated the writing of Melville and Whitman, among others, but with the exceptions of Whittier, Stowe, and Douglass, the central literary figures of the antebellum period did not devote the greater part of their energies to antislavery writing as such. Among poets, Whitman (in *Drum-Taps*, 1865), Melville (in *Battle-Pieces*, 1866), and Dickinson in scattered allusive poems wrote of the war itself with great power, and Whitman's democratic poems of the 1850s contain a number of references to the tragedy of slaves in bondage, at auction, or as fugitives. In "Song of

Myself," for example, Whitman's searching phenomenological consciousness incorporates the experience of a pursued slave:

> I am the hounded slave, I wince at the bite of dogs,
> Hell and despair are upon me, crack and again crack the marksmen,
> I clutch the rails of the fence, my gore drips, thinn'd with the ooze of my skin,
> I fall on weeds and stones,
> The riders spur their unwilling horses, haul close,
> Taunt my dizzy ears and beat me violently over the head with whipstocks.

Most antislavery poetry was less distinguished, concerned primarily with the expression of outraged sentiment rather than with complex states of literary feeling. James Russell Lowell's *Biglow Papers,* the first series of which (1848) constituted a satiric poem on the Mexican War, implicitly castigated the wholesale extension of slavery that he contended the war would authorize, and he wrote a number of editorials for abolitionist newspapers. Lowell issued a second series of the *Biglow Papers* in 1867, devoted in part to the war, but his poems on the specific issue of slavery, like those of Holmes and most of all like the mass of antislavery verse appearing in reform periodicals, tended to rely on stylized rhetoric, as in "On the Capture of Fugitive Slaves Near Washington":

> Out from the land of bondage 't is decreed our slaves shall go,
> And signs to us are offered, as erst to Pharaoh;
> If we are blind, their exodus, like Israel's of yore,
> Through a Red Sea is doomed to be, whose surges are of gore.

Longfellow's *Poems on Slavery* (1842), collecting such poems as "The Slave's Dream," on freedom in Africa, "The Slave in the Dismal Swamp," and "The Quadroon Girl," was next to Whittier's work the most comprehensive poetic statement of antislavery. In "The Warning," for instance, Longfellow combines the theme of crisis over the meaning of the American Revolution with the possibility of a slave uprising that will destroy America itself:

> There is a poor, blind Samson in this land
>   Shorn of his strength and bound in bonds of steel,
> Who may, in some grim revel, raise his hand,
>   And shake the pillars of this Commonweal,
> Till the vast Temple of our liberties
> A shapeless mass of wreck and rubbish lies.

The most effective statements against slavery, however, came from essayists, not only maverick radicals like Garrison and feminists like the Grimké sisters but also writers associated with the literary and philosophical circles of New England Transcendentalism. The main figures of Transcendentalism, such as Emerson and Thoreau, remained on the periphery of the battle, however, contributing important statements but expressing here as elsewhere their deep skepticism of organized reform movements. Emerson circumspectly alluded to the issue of slavery in his early essays, and he gradually came to support the cause more openly, speaking out in such addresses as "Emancipation in the British West Indies" (1844) and "The Fugitive Slave Law" (1851). Thoreau attacked the Mexican War as a proslavery ruse in "Resistance to Civil Government" (1849; reprinted as "Civil Disobedience" in 1894), celebrated John Brown's assault on Harper's Ferry in "A Plea for Captain John Brown" (1859), and mockingly condemned Webster and the Compromise in "Slavery in Massachusetts" (1854):

I hear a good deal said about trampling this law under foot. Why, one need not go out of his way to do that. This law rises not to the level of the head or the reason; its natural habitat is in the dirt. It was born and bred, and has its life, only in the dust and mire, on a level with the feet; and he who walks with freedom, and does not with Hindoo mercy avoid treading on every venomous reptile, will inevitably tread on it, and so trample it under foot, – and Webster, its maker, with it, like the dirt-bug and its ball.

But slavery, like Indian Removal, often seemed for Thoreau to be a philosophical conundrum rather than an immediate political problem. Of greater importance were the writings of William Ellery Channing (1780–1842), the Boston Unitarian minister who had a significant influence on Emerson, Parker, and those instrumental in the formation of the Transcendentalist Club. The Unitarian emphasis on reason and the power of individual spirituality led Channing first to a gradualist doctrine in *Slavery* (1835), in which he chided abolitionists for their fanaticism. However, his *Remarks on the Slavery Question* (1839), a reply to Henry Clay on the question of the annexation of Texas, emphasized the "contamination" of the North by slavery. Our moral feeling is "palsied," he wrote, and our merchants, when they cast their eyes south, see "Cotton, Cotton, nothing but Cotton. This fills the horizon of the South. What care they for the poor human tools by which it is reared?" Channing also condemned the sexual abuse of slave women but at the same time accepted the thesis of African docility, which ensured that whites need fear no war of retribution if slaves were emancipated: "The iron has eaten into [the slave's] soul, and this is worse than eating into the flesh." In "Emancipation" (1840) and *Duty of the Free States* (1842), Channing approached the central views of Garrison in the 1840s, disunion and the individual's right to disavow connection to all abusive political authority: "There is a law of humanity more primitive and divine than the law of the land. [Man] has higher claims than those of the citizen. He has rights which date before all charters and communities; not conventional, not repeatable, but as eternal as the powers and laws of his being."

Channing's utopian belief in the power of the individual will, common enough among the Transcendentalists and Garrisonians but nonetheless impractical, is not unrelated to his conception of African American character. The racist belief in African simplicity and meekness (a critical issue in all the sentimental literature on slavery both before and after its great testament, *Uncle Tom's Cabin*) is earnestly laid out in *Slavery:* "The African is so affectionate, imitative, and docile that in favorable circumstances he catches much that is good; and accordingly the influence of a wise and kind master will be seen in the very countenance of his slaves." This, of course, is just what the leading proslavery thinkers pointed out in advocating benevolent paternalism as the only system under which African Americans could survive and prosper. It is also the view parodied in that most brilliant of all critiques both of slavery and of northern myopia about it: Melville's "Benito Cereno" (1855). Whereas Hawthorne's views can only be construed as moderately proslavery, and Poe's complex symbolic and psychological treatment of the issue erupted in racist trauma, and Stowe's great work perpetuated divisive conceptions of racial character, Melville continually drove right to the heart of America's crisis. In *Mardi* (1849), his allegorical assault on manifest destiny, Melville caricatured the slaveholding South and especially Calhoun as "a cadaverous, ghost-like man" named Nulli who wields a bloody whip and contends that although the ancestors of his slaves may have had souls, "their souls have been bred out of their descendents; as the instinct of scent is killed in pointers." At the same time, however, Melville was attuned to the extravagance and ineffectiveness of much antislavery rhetoric. In *Benito Cereno* he caricatured the northern romantic view, advanced by Channing and others, that masters were dissipated aristocrats and their slaves docile, imitative (but brutalized) creatures, yet he also played upon fears of slave rebellion spreading throughout the Americas.

Melville built his tale upon the actual story of Amasa Delano (recorded in his 1817 *Narrative of Voyages in the Northern and Southern Hemispheres*), a New England captain who in 1805 rescued the Spanish captain Benito Cereno's ship from a revolt by its cargo of slaves. In changing the name of Benito Cereno's ship from the *Tryal* to the *San Dominick,* Melville invoked the revolution in San Domingo, represented in the South as a still smoldering volcano of Jacobin horrors, and by an intricate web of allusions and historical references virtually recounted the history of New World slavery in his tale, including contemporary U.S. contention over annexation of potentially rich slave territories in Cuba and Latin America. The Spanish captain is mocked as the prototypical languid slaveholder, whereas Delano, unable until the last moments of the story to perceive the fact that a rebellion has occurred but has been hidden from his view by an intricate masquerade staged by the black slave leader, Babo, is ridiculed as a benevolent but complacent northerner, content to criticize slavery but shocked when it leads to violence and revolt. As a response to the Compromise, which in part defined American policy in the territory acquired in the Mexican War, *Benito Cereno* exploits the collision of domestic and international interests that had previously arisen in the cases of revolt aboard the slave ships the *Creole* and the *Amistad*. Instead of envisioning a civil war between North and South, it anticipates, as well it might have in 1855, a struggle among three forces: a Protestant, Puritan tradition of democratic liberty deriving from the American Revolution; a Hispanic, Catholic world of slaveholding and despotism based on the dying monarchical values of Europe; and a black world of rebellion driving a wedge between the others and threatening political upheaval throughout the slaveholding world.

During the first half of the nineteenth century, as was noted before, Haiti remained a touchstone for arguments about the consequence of slave liberation in the New World. Although the island republic had its defenders, the common opinion was that its record, like that of emancipated Jamaica, was largely one of economic sloth and political barbarism. *De Bow's Review*, the influential organ of southern interests, carried an essay in 1854 typical in its critique of Haitian commerce and government. For over thirty years, the essay claims, the "march of civilization" had been dead in Haiti, its social condition one of sustained indolence and immorality:

From its discovery by Columbus to the present reign of Solouque, the olive branch has withered under its pestilential breath; and when the atheistical philosophy of revolutionary France added fuel to the volcano of hellish passions which raged in its bosom, the horrors of the island became a narrative which frightened our childhood, and still curdles our blood to read. The triumphant negroes refined upon the tortures of the Inquisition in their treatment of prisoners taken in battle. They tore them with red-hot pincers — sawed them asunder between planks — roasted them by a slow fire — or tore out their eyes with red-hot corkscrews.

As in Melville's ambiguous antislavery tale, the conflation of Spanish and French rule, coupled with the allusion to the Inquisition, links anti-Catholic and anti-Jacobin sentiment. Indeed, the rhetoric of manifest destiny in the Caribbean was often a mix of the two, and *Benito Cereno* thus envisioned an explosive pattern of revolt that was interlocked with U.S. ambitions in the West and Mexico. The New England captain Amasa Delano, whose sunny optimism recalls Webster's embrace of the Compromise, confronts aboard the *San Dominick* the allegorical play of threats apparently offered to the United States by the New World at midcentury: Spanish misrule and deterioration combined with potential black insurrection and liberation dramatically realized in the subtle, heroic character of Babo.

Melville's imaginary transformation of Delano's true story undermined the romantic fantasy of African docility that Stowe and others promoted, and it was predicated on a conflict between Anglo-Americans and Spanish of the kind Theodore Parker had spoken of in his 1854 speech on "The Nebraska Question." As the "children of a decomposing State, time-worn and debauched," argued Parker, Spanish colonies in America were doomed to failure. Yet he thought that America's rabid claims of manifest destiny, often designed to conciliate slaveholding interests, were equally destructive of the ideals of liberty, which were not governed in America by monarchy and theocracy but by the "Almighty Dollar." A Boston Unitarian who took up the Transcendentalist cause but had few qualms about the use of violence, later supporting John Brown's attack on Harper's Ferry, Parker (1810–60) became a passionate spokesman for antislavery and other reform causes in the 1840s. He compared Webster to the traitor Benedict Arnold and lamented the "prostitution of [his] kingly power of thought," dramatizing him as a great tragic figure who had fallen from being "the hero of Bunker Hill" to become "a keeper of slavery's dogs." In "A Letter on Slavery" (1847), Parker stated succinctly the case against paternalism that Melville's tale of rebellion corroborated: "the relation of master and slave begins in violence; it must be sustained by violence, the systematic violence of general laws, or the irregular violence of individual caprice." The very idea of slavery, wrote Parker, echoing a common figure later to appear in Stowe's subtitle to *Uncle Tom's Cabin,* "is to use a man as a thing."

During the 1840s and 1850s, Parker and Garrison were rivaled in their attacks on slavery only by Frederick Douglass and, among whites, by Wendell Phillips (1811–84), one of the movement's most effective lecturers. Recruited by Garrison, Phillips nonetheless disregarded the former's idealistic advocacy of nonviolence and anti-institutionalism. He was particularly adept at creating an image of the South as a living hell, boiling over with punishment, sexual abuse, and misery, and he understood that masses of common people could be brought into agitated action more easily than recalcitrant institutions such as the church, the press, and political parties. His most famous address, *The Philosophy of the Abolition Movement* (1853), was a summary of the antislavery crusade, giving credit to eminent people and works, interspersed with fiery rhetoric of the kind that was echoed during the same years in the lectures and writings of Douglass:

The South is one great brothel, where half a million women are flogged to prostitution, or, worse still, are degraded to believe it honorable. The public squares of half our great cities echo to the wail of families torn asunder at the auction-block; [there is] no one of our rivers that has not closed over the negro seeking in death a refuge from a life too wretched to bear; thousands of fugitives skulk along our highways, afraid to tell their names, and trembling at the sight of a human being; free men are kidnapped in our streets to be plunged into the hell of slavery; and now and then one, as if by miracle, after long years, returns to make men aghast with his tale. The press says, "It is all right"; and the pulpit cries, "Amen." . . . The slave lifts up his imploring eyes, and sees in every face but ours the face of an enemy.

Phillips's allusion to the tale of the returned kidnapped slave was based on the fascinating narrative of Solomon Northup, and his piercing but clichéd rhetoric borrowed from countless short stories and magazine essays, as well as the kind of documentation collected in Weld's *Slavery As It Is*. Along with Weld and Phillips, William Goodell was similarly interested in exposing the codes and actual practices that lay behind the peculiar institution, and he did so in *Slavery and Anti-Slavery* (1852), a work dealing with both hemispheres, and a best-selling volume entitled *The American Slave Code* (1853), which was simply a compendium of laws governing slaveholding and manumission practices, which made brutal reading in their own right. Both the fugitive slaves and the New England lecturers frequently cited southern laws that for all practical purposes damned themselves.

The number of antislavery writers who could base their work on at least marginal experience of the South was great, given the popularity of travel writing in the period, but relatively few with direct experience produced work of high literary quality or accuracy. The unusual case of Hinton Rowan Helper, a southern abolitionist but also a virulent racist, has been discussed above. The antislavery Transcendentalist Moncure Conway (1832–1907) came from a prominent Virginia slaveholding family. His *Autobiography*, not published until 1904, reveals in retrospect his conversion to an abolitionist perspective; and his spiritual essay *The Rejected Stone* (1861) praised the Civil War as a providential and revolutionary action ensuring that "the kingdoms of this world shall become the Kingdom of Christ forever." But the testimony of converted southerners like Conway or the Grimké sisters was relatively rare. With the important exception of fugitive slaves, only several novelists and a handful of travelers gave reliable firsthand acccounts of the actual lives of slaves. Rather, the plantation itself was more often the subject. A typical travel work, C. G. Parsons's *Inside View of Slavery; Or, a Tour Among the Planters* (1855), with an introduction by Stowe, condemned the inefficiency of the slave economy and the brutal hardening of the master class. One of the most impressive works in its scope of observation and, at the time, the influence of its argument was the landscape architect Frederick Law Olmsted's *The Cotton Kingdom* (1861), a distillation of his three previous travel works, *A Journey in the Seaboard Slave States* (1856), *A Journey Through Texas* (1857), and *A Journey in the Back Country* (1860). Expressing the northern Free Soil sentiments of his day, Olmsted wrote with a keen eye for the details of plantation and more common life in the South. Yet he mistakenly portrayed slavery as a system in complete economic decay, with the majority of whites in the South nearly as degraded as the slaves of the few successful planters.

Some of the most trenchant commentary on slavery came from foreign visitors to the United States. The relative success of British abolitionism, which had played a part in the end of slavery in the British West Indies in 1833, gave force to the attacks by Harriet Martineau in *Society in America* (1837) and *The Martyr Age in the United States* (1840), by Charles Dickens in *American Notes* (1842), by Frances Trollope in *Domestic Manners of the Americans* (1832) and in her fictional slave narrative *Jonathan Jefferson Whitlaw* (1841), and by Fanny Kemble in *Journal of a Residence on a Georgia Plantation, 1838–39* (1863). Among French commentators, the famous tour of Gustave de Beaumont and Alexis de Tocqueville (who collaborated on a volume concerning the ostensible reason for their tour, *On the Penitentiary System in the United States*) resulted in the former's romantic novel of a tragic mulatto, *Marie, or Slavery in the United States* (1835), which appeared in the same year as the latter's monumental *Democracy in America*. Tocqueville's forecast of the inevitable end of slavery came with predictions of despair and race hatred on both sides, and his assessment of the meaning of modern slavery in the Western world, like so many of his observations, struck to the heart of the questions of liberty and democratic liberalism that Europe had faced and America had brought to a new crisis:

From the moment when the Europeans took their slaves from a race different from their own, which many of them considered inferior to all other human races, and assimilation with whom they regarded with horror, they assumed that slavery would be eternal, for there is no intermediate state that can be durable between the excessive inequality created by slavery and the complete equality which is the natural result of independence. . . . They first violated every right of humanity by their treatment of the Negro and then taught him the value and inviolability of those rights. They have opened their ranks to their slaves, but when they tried to come in, they drove them out again with ignominy. Wishing to have servitude, they have nevertheless been drawn against their will or unconsciously toward liberty, without the courage to be either completely wicked or entirely just.

Despite the careful portrayals of the slaveholding South by Olmsted and others, truth and the representations of sentimental fiction often merged in the pictures drawn by antislavery writers. Still, if they were romantically heightened, they were seldom completely distorted, a fact that explains the great success of *Uncle Tom's Cabin* (1851), which uncovered a moral truth transcending statistical data and full of emotive power. Born in Litchfield, Connecticut, the seventh of Lyman Beecher's nine children by his first wife,

Harriet Beecher Stowe aided her sister Catharine, a pioneer in women's education, at the Hartford Female Seminary from 1824 to 1832; she later contributed to several of Catharine's important textbooks when they taught together in Cincinnati. Influenced by the increasingly vocal antislavery activity of her brothers and the family's friendships with important abolitionists such as James G. Birney, Salmon Chase, and Gamaliel Bailey (later the editor of the *National Era,* where *Uncle Tom's Cabin* would be serialized from 1851 to 1852), Stowe too turned against the ineffective and often abstract views of her father and her husband, Calvin Stowe, a Lane professor of religion, whom she married in 1836. Although her direct experience of the slave South consisted of a brief visit to Kentucky in 1833, Stowe's family and friends had regular contact with men and women active in the underground railroad, and Cincinnati in the 1830s was a hotbed of antislavery activity and stories of escaped slaves, some of which found their way into Stowe's masterpiece. By the time she resettled in Maine, when Calvin took a job at Bowdoin College in 1850, Stowe had written several antislavery sketches (among other New England and midwestern stories), and she was poised to respond once the controversial Compromise of 1850, with its hated Fugitive Slave Law, was passed.

The literature of antislavery controversy into which Stowe entered so dramatically had in the previous twenty years produced a number of significant documents, though few of them reached an audience more than a fraction the size of Stowe's. The great speeches of Garrison and Phillips, for example, the congressional efforts of Adams, and even Whittier's popular poetry had made little impression. In addition to Weld's *American Slavery As It Is,* Stowe's sources were scripture, hymns, the sermons and religious readings of her family library, and probably a handful of antislavery fictions and slave narratives. In her *Key to Uncle Tom's Cabin* (1853), a documentary work put together by Stowe to prove that her novel had a basis in real events, she noted parallels to her work in the lives and slave stories of Henry Bibb, William Wells Brown, Solomon Northup, Frederick Douglass, Josiah Henson, and Lewis Clarke; indeed, the last two men built careers on the dubious claims that they were the models for the characters of Uncle Tom and George Harris. Among fictional works that may have influenced Stowe, the most famous were Whittier's ghostwritten *Narrative of James Williams,* noted above, which drew a picture of ruthless plantation cruelty that was condemned as spurious by southerners (the volume had been briefly promoted by the American Anti-Slavery Society as the preeminent slave narrative until it was revealed to have been largely fabricated by Williams); and Richard Hildreth's *The Slave; or, Memoirs of Archy Moore* (1836), which offered a number of potential parallels in plot and character that were, if anything, watered down and undermined by Stowe. The mixed-race Archy and his wife, Cassy, may lie behind Stowe's George and Eliza Harris, for example, but their lives end in tragic separation; and the black slave Tom, at first religious and obedient, becomes a fugitive rebel after witnessing the flogging death of his wife at the hands of an overseer. Tracked down by the overseer, Tom calmly murders him. Moreover, in Hildreth's novel, as in most authentic narratives, the Christianity and domesticity valued by Stowe are shown to be thoroughly corrupted by plantation life. What Stowe understood, however, was that her audience was less likely to be moved by the logic of violence than by sentimental stereotypes: "There is no arguing with *pictures*," she wrote her editor, "and everybody is impressed by them, whether they mean to be or not."

The stereotypes that would become famous – Eliza crossing the ice, Eva's melodramatic death, Tom's martyrdom at the hands of Legree – were scenes calculated, and driven by the book's great narrative powers, to demand the reader's sympathetic response. When it appeared in book form in 1852, 50,000 copies were sold within eight weeks, 300,000 within a year, and 1 million in America and England combined by early 1853. It added an entirely new dimension to a crusade that had often bogged down in petty quarrels and useless theorizing. By giving flesh-and-blood reality to the inhuman system for which the Fugitive Slave Law now required the North, as well as the South, to be responsible, it became a touchstone for popular sentiment, which was already reaching new heights in the North in response to the Mexican War and the Compromise (and soon to be heightened even further by passage of the Kansas–Nebraska Act). Stowe was hardly the first to call attention to slavery's destruction of both black and white families, but her novel perfectly combined sentimental fiction and the antislavery polemic. In scene after scene, the fragmentation of black households and its corrosive moral effect on white consciousness are her focal points. When the slave Lucy's child is sold by the unfeeling slave trader Haley, for example, Stowe writes bitterly: "You can get used to such things, too, my friend; and it is the great object of recent efforts to make our whole northern community used to them, for the glory of the Union."

Stowe's powerful use of families and familial metaphors drew not only on the notion of sentiment attached to "union" by Webster, Lincoln, and others but also on the more radical elements of domestic ideology that challenged the traditional patriarchal authority of society. According to some antislavery activists – for instance, the black feminist Maria Stewart, noted above – patriarchal dominance was epitomized by the degradations of slavery. The more moderate domestic tradition in fiction and in social thought declared women the moral superiors of men but at the same time attributed to them specific characteristics of sensitivity, docility, and weakness – the same qualities, in fact, that romantic racialists (Stowe among them) attributed to blacks. Drawing to itself the faltering powers of the clergy, the domestic tradition separated the "woman's sphere" of homemaking and the moral instruction of children from the masculine world of commerce and politics. However, it also risked providing a new rationale for the subordination of women which was recognized and resisted by the era's more ardent feminists. *Uncle Tom's Cabin* is split between these two kinds of power – domestic "influence" and public activism – for if it acts out patterns of bondage and rebellion that included for Stowe not just slavery and the Calvinist dogma of her father but also the bondage of women within the domestic ideal, the novel is in each case ambivalent about the limits and means of such rebellion.

From the 1820s through the 1840s the domestic ideal became an issue in various social reform causes; and as the split in ranks over female participation at the 1840 antislavery conventions suggests, not only men but women themselves were divided over the proper limits of their role. Catharine Beecher, for example, eschewed women's direct involvement in politics. In her *Essay on Slavery and Abolitionism* (1837), she denounced abolitionist societies for their public stridency; and carefully separating the duties of men from those of women, she warned that woman's deviation from the place she is "appointed to fill by the dispensations of heaven" would deprive children of their proper moral instruction and subvert the cause of reform: "For the more intelligent a woman becomes, the more she can appreciate the wisdom of that ordinance that appointed her subordinate station, and the more her taste will conform to the graceful and dignified retirement and submission it involves." Beecher's views were directed in particular at Sarah and Angelina Grimké, whose speaking tour of 1837 had aroused such controversy that the Congregational clergy of New England felt compelled to attack their inappropriate involvement in political affairs in a pastoral letter that argued that when woman "assumes the place and tone of man . . . she yields the power which God has given her for her own protection, and her character becomes unnatural." The "promiscuous conversation of females with regard to things which ought not to be named" (i.e., slavery and sexual abuse on the plantation) disturbs their modesty and opens the way "for degeneracy and ruin." In addition to their offensive lectures, Angelina had published *Appeal to the Christian Women of the South* (1836), which counseled women to study the Bible and seek ways to change the laws governing slavery. The attack of the clergy and Catharine Beecher's critique of feminist activism brought forth replies from both Sarah, in *Letters on the Condition of Women and the Equality of the Sexes* (1838), and Angelina, now the wife of Theodore Weld, in *Letters to Catharine E. Beecher* (1838). The latter volume, a group of essays first published in Garrison's *Liberator,* argued that a woman's rights are "an integral part of her moral being" and that "the mere circumstance of sex does not give to man higher rights and responsibilities than to women." Along with Lucretia Mott, Elizabeth Cady Stanton, and Susan B. Anthony, the Grimké sisters were instrumental in allying the forces of antislavery and feminism and defining women's public sphere of action as an outgrowth of larger movements of democratic social reform.

The appeal for feminist activism in *Uncle Tom's Cabin* stops short of the steps proposed by the Grimkés, Mott, and Stanton. The influence of its principal female characters is largely restricted to the "woman's sphere" of Christian example and moral instruction. But the book itself, however much it conforms to sentimental models, was an act of risk and of tentative rebellion, insofar as it attacked patriarchal society and likened the victimization of slaves to the suppression of women. The great emotive power of the novel arises from its capacity to equate the stations of the two groups, which are linked by children, a third supposedly oppressed group. In this respect, *Uncle Tom's Cabin* plays upon the potential conversion of sentiment into action adumbrated by another abolitionist, Lydia Maria Child. Both women and blacks, Child wrote, "are characterized by affection more than intellect; both have a strong development of the religious sentiment; both are exceedingly adhesive in their attachments; both, comparatively speaking, have a tendency to submission; and hence, both have been kept in subjection by physical force, and considered rather in the light of property, than as individuals." Child's characterization, advanced in letters and in *An Appeal in Favor of That Class of Americans Called Africans* (1836), is given further dimension in her story "Black Anglo Saxons," in which a group of slaves discusses the alternatives of flight or violent rebellion, with the mulattoes endorsing bloodshed and the blacks arguing for mercy and docility. Racial divisions here correspond to sexual divisions, with feminine, maternal submission and blackness ranged against masculine, paternal aggression and whiteness, as they are in Stowe's novel. If the ethical influence of mothers and wives were entirely to succeed in Stowe's novel, a host of problems attributable to male "lust" and patriarchal governance in politics and the family would disappear, and slavery – in which the abuse of women is taken to its extreme, as a number of northerners (like Wendell Phillips) and some southerners (like Mary Chesnut) suggested in characterizing the plantation as a brothel – would give way to a Christian democratic unity.

Stowe's use of the figure of the houschold, ranging from the maternal perfection of the Quakers to the degeneracy of Legree's house of sin, draws on the political rhetoric of union as a house threatened with division, a metaphor made famous in Lincoln's use of the New Testament phrase in his 1858 speech on the "House Divided" but in common use in the years before. In its gothic exploration of licentious behavior Stowe's novel diverges from the constrained role of influence advised by Catharine Beecher in her writings on abolitionism and in her handbook on homemaking, *Treatise on Domestic Economy* (1841). Although Stowe herself later contributed to a revised edition of the *Treatise,* it seems unlikely that she intended to endorse Beecher's argument that woman's role was to support Anglo-American manifest destiny by subordinating herself to man and contributing to the civil stability necessary to build "a glorious temple, whose base shall be coextensive with the bounds of the earth, whose summit shall pierce the skies, [and] whose splendor shall beam on all lands." Stowe's critique imagined the house not as a separate sphere but as a model of the political world, and her approach to moral influence more resembled Margaret Fuller's, who wrote in *Woman in the Nineteenth Century* (1845), "you see the men, how they are willing to sell shamelessly the happiness of countless generations of fellow-creatures, the honor of their country, and their immortal souls, for a money market and political power." In thus attacking the annexation of Texas and the extension of slavery it would promote, Fuller took a stance similar to Stowe's: "Do you not feel within you that which can reprove them, which can check, which can convince them? You would not speak in vain; whether each in her own home, or banded in unison. . . . Let not slip the occasion, but do something to lift off the curse incurred by Eve."

Bypassing the question of Original Sin and the Calvinist tradition of her father, Stowe embraced the New Testament and interpreted literally the saving power of Jesus, drawing out the feminine aspects of his character and depicting him, in essence, as a woman. Besides Tom, her central Christ figure is Eva: a child, a female, a typological figuring of Christ descended not from Adam but from Eve, and – as her full name Evangeline implies – the book's most powerful evangelist. In Eva are united the ministerial leader of evangelistic social reform and the prime actor of sentimental literature, the child. The proliferation of children in antislavery literature and in books and journals specifically directed at children, such as *The Child's Anti-Slavery Book* and *Anti-Slavery Alphabet,* assumed that, instead of needing moral instruction, children were perhaps best equipped to give it. Asexual and uncorrupted, the child, like Eva, was often imagined to be the "only true democrat." The antislavery tradition of "benevolence," which elevated feeling above reason and advocated the democratic extension of rights to the lowliest of society, sought to put into practice the radical doctrines of equality generated in the age of revolution by linking them to the evangelical power of conversion and portraying them in scenes of deliberately theatrical sentimentality. Eva's pious life and death are not simply ornamental melodrama. They construct a bridge between pathos and reform that is morally superior to the corruptions of the adult, masculine world – the world, Stowe suggests throughout, of organized religion, which has failed to speak and act against slavery. Subsuming the failed power of institutional religion into the realm of sentimental social reform, Eva's death belongs to the period's enormous literature of mourning and consolation but transcends its simple pieties as Stowe reconceives Christian man in the image of beatific child-woman.

In the character of Tom, which was to receive the greatest criticism of later generations of readers, Stowe sought to combine her ideals of feminine power and African meekness. A martyr but hardly a coward, Tom is murdered because he refuses to betray Cassy and Emmeline and to capitulate to Legree's demand that he renounce his religious beliefs. Yet the fate of Tom's character was to become, along with Eva's, the most frequently re-created figure of the popular minstrel and burlesque shows (which made *Uncle Tom's Cabin* even more famous than Stowe could) and to exemplify black humiliation in African American culture of the next century. Tom and the corrupt dramatic versions of the novel became indistinguishable to later audiences, but even in its own time the book produced a flood of imitation: drama, poetry, songs, engravings, and other consumable artifacts (card games, silverware, needle-point, and the like) that capitalized on its most saccharine scenes. The traveling "Tom troupes" purged any radical messages from the blackface drama (performed almost exclusively by whites until later in the nineteenth century) and made it conform to the degraded entertainment of the minstrel's song and dance. On stage, Topsy sang "Topsy's Song: I Am but a Little Nigger Gal"; the famous minstrel performer T. D. Rice "jumped Jim Crow" in the role of Uncle Tom; Tom and Eva were reunited in cardboard heavens; and abolitionism itself was attacked in such songs as "Happy Are We, Darkies So Gay." The further exploitation of the work onstage and in film continued into the twentieth century, destroying the integrity of Stowe's vision and accomplishment, which had made *Uncle Tom's Cabin* perhaps the most influential novel in the later nineteenth century for both white and black authors. By the modern era, the book's stereotypes had overwhelmed its moral intentions, inspiring one black writer, Richard Wright, to ironi-cally entitle his collection of stories about black life in the Jim Crow South *Uncle Tom's Children* (1940) and another, Ishmael Reed, to burlesque Stowe and the antislavery tradition in *Flight to Canada* (1976).

Even if one rescues Tom from history's manipulations, however, his char-acter as drawn by Stowe remains problematic. His conspicuous nonviolence — in contrast to the examples of San Domingo and Turner's Southampton rebel-lion, and in contrast to the calls for violence by Douglass and other antislavery leaders, black and white — stranded his power in the realm of sentiment, which might lead to direct antislavery action but might also produce only a cathartic release of tension. Stowe's next novel, *Dred: A Tale of the Great Dismal*

Swamp (1856), modeled its titular hero on Nat Turner (and even included a copy of his *Confessions* as an appendix) but concentrated on his religious delusions and failed to reenact his dangerous revolt. In *Uncle Tom's Cabin*, moreover, it is the mixed-race George Harris, goaded by his "white blood," who invokes the revolutionary fervor of the Founding Fathers and demands his rights. Even Garrison, the prime abolitionist voice of nonviolent tactics, who once nominated Jesus Christ for president, found in *Uncle Tom's Cabin* a reflection of his own confusion:

We are curious to know whether Mrs. Stowe is a believer in the duty of non-resistance for the white man, under all possible outrage and peril, as well as for the black man. . . . When [slaves] are spit upon and buffeted, outraged and oppressed, talk not then of a non-resisting Savior — it is fanaticism! . . . Talk not of servants being obedient to their masters — let the blood of the tyrants flow! How is this to be explained or reconciled? Is there one law of submission and non-resistance for the black man, and another law of rebellion and conflict for the white man? When it is the whites who are trodden in the dust, does Christ justify them in taking up arms to vindicate their rights? And when it is the blacks who are thus treated, does Christ require them to be patient, harmless, long-suffering, and forgiving? And are there two Christs?

Even as they support her argument on behalf of a feminized, maternal world vision, both Tom's martyrdom and George Harris's advocacy of a colonization movement that will found a millennial Christian nation in Africa indicate Stowe's grave anxieties about black rebellion and about the ultimate effects of emancipation.

Lincoln's own comparable hesitations about emancipation did not prevent him from being attacked by racists, and he often had to defend himself from charges that he favored miscegenation. In response to the Emancipation Proclamation, one southern pamphleteer wrote *Uncle Tom's Drama,* a play in which white maidens with "quivering limbs" and "snow-white bosoms, that ever throbbed in angelic purity," suffered "untold outrage, woe and wrong" at the hands of "Black Ourang-Outangs," who dragged them down in order to "gratify their brutal instincts." Northern apprehensions about miscegenation produced equally repellent racist prophecies; but more often the North, as John Van Evrie and others charged, romanticized the mulatto and made slaveholding miscegenation the epitome of domestic tragedy. Typical examples include Joseph Holt Ingraham's *The Quadroone; or, St. Michael's Day* (1841), a historical romance of creole New Orleans, and Lydia Maria Child's "The Quadroons," included in *Fact and Fiction* (1846), in which the illegitimate daughter of the mixed-blood heroine is seized and sold as a slave. Novels written in the wake of Stowe's capitalized on both the risk of miscegenation and the destruction of families. In Van Buren Denslow's *Owned and*

Disowned; or, the Chattel Child (1857), the planter's mulatto daughter, sold as a slave, is rescued and becomes an antislavery crusader; in Emily C. Pierson's *Jamie Parker, A Fugitive* (1851), the black hero is reunited with his family in the North; in Hezekiah Hosmer's *Adela, the Octoroon* (1860), the mulatto daughter of a benevolent planter is forced by an evil suitor to flee north; and in Mary H. [Langdon] Pike's *Ida May* (1854), a northern white girl is kidnapped and sold into slavery. Dion Boucicault's popular play *The Octoroon* (1859), based on Mayne Reid's novel *The Quadroon* (1856), ended in the heroine's tragic death but was inadvertently so farcical that it was easily parodied by the Christy Minstrels in *The Moctroon*. Among the more interesting antislavery novels written in the 1850s, are Elizabeth Roe's *Aunt Leanna* (1855), which follows a northern family to Kentucky, where they become slaveholders but work for emancipation and colonization (in order to stop the spread of black labor to Kansas and Nebraska); and Emily C. Pearson's *Cousin Franck's Household* (1853), which, although sympathetic to the South, dwells on the separation of slave families and their escapes to the North. Almost proslavery in his sympathies, Nehemiah Adams wrote in his novel *The Sable Cloud* (1861) that "a system which makes Uncle Toms out of African savages is not an unmixed evil." Adams's essays in *A South-Side View of Slavery* (1854) similarly adopted the racist view that under benevolent masters slaves were redeemed and blessed. Abolitionism, he maintained, was a hindrance to emancipation, espcially after being goaded on by *Uncle Tom's Cabin,* which "has entered like an alcoholic distillation into the veins and blood of very many people in the free States." Equally ambivalent, Bayard Rush Hall's *Frank Freeman's Barbershop* (1852) satirized both sides of the slavery controversy and ridiculed northern fascination with the mulatto theme: "Writers of *fiction kill off* the jet black − not knowing how to *work them* advantageously to the North."

Hall's complaint, its glib tone aside, was well founded, but he failed to grasp the importance of the mixed-race theme (given the sentimental expectations of the popular audience) and its power to expose the operation of northern prejudices that were often as destructive of black aspirations as slavery. Black writers' handling of the questions of slaveholding miscegenation and life in the North will be considered in more detail below in the context of the rise of the slave narrative and black abolitionism. In particular, these writers responded to *Uncle Tom's Cabin* by both incorporating and subverting Stowe's vision. Like Frederick Douglass, most of them sought the end of slavery through political action and the end of race hatred through education and integration. Stowe, on the other hand, for all the great power of her novel, conceived of colonization in Africa as the answer to inevitable contention over labor and social issues. Only with extraordinary caution, in the last pages of her novel, did she seek sanction for the violent overthrow of slavery in the suppressed Calvinistic vengeance of her father's religion: "This is an age of the world when . . . every nation that carries in its bosom great and unredressed injustice has in it the elements of [the] last convulsion. . . . Christians! every time you pray that the kingdom of Christ may come, can you forget that prophecy associates, in dread fellowship, the *day of vengeance* with the year of his redeemed?" The "wrath of Almighty God," however it might make itself known, was Stowe's solution; and when the war came, she wrote that it was "God's will that this nation – the North as well as the South – should deeply and terribly suffer for the sin of consenting to and encouraging the great oppressions of the South." Like Lincoln, she thought that "the blood of the poor slave, that had cried for so many years from the ground in vain, should be answered by the blood of the sons from the best hearthstones through all the free States." Although the war was almost a decade away when *Uncle Tom's Cabin* appeared, the work anticipated its rhetoric as it had summed up and brought into new focus, intentionally or not, the rhetorics of antislavery polemic, of sentimental domesticity, and even of the narratives of fugitive slaves. No work exceeded the novel in its impact on the public (though it can hardly be said to have caused the Civil War, as Abraham Lincoln is supposed to have remarked upon meeting Stowe), and only Frederick Douglass and Harriet Jacobs now challenge Stowe's position as the leading antislavery writer.

In iconographic stature, Abraham Lincoln was to become the nation's white embodiment of the spirit of emancipation, even if his views on abolition were less than clear. In his great speeches and in the symbolic role of sacrificial victim his assassination on Good Friday imposed, it was Lincoln who inadvertently gave credence to Stowe's vision. Wary of emancipation, fearful about miscegenation and free black labor, and uncertainly favoring colonization, Lincoln (1809–65) still abolished slavery and saved the Union, doing so as though in accordance with a divine plan. His eloquent conception of the war as an act of judgment in his second inaugural speech in 1865 gave shape to his own rebellion against the Founding Fathers and to the North's participation in the national sacrifice:

If we shall suppose that American slavery is one of those offenses which, in the providence of God, must needs come, but which, having continued through His appointed time, He now wills to remove, and that He now gives to both North and South this terrible war, as the woe due to those by whom the offense came, shall we discern therein any departure from those divine attributes which the believers in a living God always ascribe to Him? . . . if God wills that it continue until all the wealth piled by the bondsman's two hundred and fifty years of unrequited toil shall be sunk, and until every drop of blood drawn with the lash shall be paid by another drawn by the sword, as was said three thousand years ago, so still it must be said, "The judgments of the Lord are true and righteous altogether."

Like Stowe and others, Lincoln came to imagine the Civil War as a purifying redemption of America's great sin, accomplished only through violent purgation. The popularity of the view was best indicated in Julia Ward Howe's "The Battle Hymn of the Republic," first published in 1862, with its apocalyptic vision of God's judgment:

> Mine eyes have seen the glory of the coming of the Lord;
> He is trampling out the vintage where the grapes of wrath are stored;
> He hath loosed the fateful lightning of his terrible swift sword;
> His truth is marching on. . . .

Howe's hymn codified the New England Protestant interpretation of the war — a response appropriate to the psychological blockage and moral darkening that the conscious (or unconscious) contemplation of slavery could produce over a period of decades. Lincoln, it might be said, was a political version of that response. As noted above, his Lyceum Address of 1838 foreshadowed the role he would play in overcoming the ambivalence of the Founding Fathers on the question of slavery and grounding the politics of union *and* African American liberation in an American revolutionary tradition. Not only would the whole of his career seem in retrospect to lead to his own sacrificial greatness, but his magnificent orations, surpassing in their poetic beauty and expression of central American values all spoken words in the period, would seem to have moved toward the vision of war announced in his 1865 inaugural speech.

His debates with Stephen Douglas in 1858 and his Cooper Union speech of 1860, on the problem of slavery and the Constitution, show Lincoln at his political best. But his most significant speeches transcend the politics of the day even as they remain firmly rooted in them. Driven in part by the relative failures of his early political career, Lincoln developed a style of thought and speech that linked humility and an identification with common people to a lucid articulation of his own potential as a leader. The 1838 Lyceum speech, inviting comparison to Caesar or Napoleon, showed Lincoln imperfectly in control of his own ambitions: "Towering genius disdains a beaten path. It seeks regions hitherto unexplored. It sees no distinction to adding story to story upon the monuments of fame erected to the memory of others." The lull in his political fortunes before the 1850s seems to have tempered Lincoln's egotism with a degree of humor, melancholy, and poetry, and to have brought into focus the mature rhetorical brilliance that coincided with his rise to the role of providential savior of the Union.

The crisis over the Kansas–Nebraska Act in 1854 elevated Lincoln to a position of fresh power as he began to challenge the leadership of Senator Stephen Douglas; and his formal alliance with the Republican Party in 1856 set him on the road to immortality as the "great emancipator." Nonetheless, some of his most significant speeches are marked not by a forthright opposition to slavery or the South but by ambiguity and conciliation, an index of his foremost dedication not to the end of black bondage but to the preservation of the Union. For example, the famous House Divided speech, part of his debates with Douglas in the 1858 Senate race, borrowed a New Testament metaphor resonant with the nation's impending political splintering, yet it remained uncertain where Lincoln's analysis would lead. His detection of a proslavery conspiracy behind the Dred Scott decision did not clarify his central claim: "I believe this government cannot endure permanently half slave and half free. I do not expect the Union to be dissolved – I do not expect the house to fall – but I do expect it will cease to be divided. It will become all one thing, or all the other." Nevertheless, an earlier speech in reply to Douglas in 1857 attacked Douglas and, dwelling on the Dred Scott decision, argued that the position of both slaves and free blacks in America had deteriorated since the Revolution:

In those days, our Declaration of Independence was held sacred by all, and thought to include all; but now, to aid in making the bondage of the negro universal and eternal, it is assailed, and sneered at, and construed, and hawked at, and torn, till, if its framers could rise from their graves, they could not at all recognize it. All the powers of the earth seem rapidly combining against him [the Negro]. Mammon is after him; ambition follows, and philosophy follows, and the Theology of the day is fast joining the cry. They have him in his prison house; they have searched his person, and left no prying instrument with him. One after another they have closed the heavy iron doors upon him, and now they have him, as it were, bolted in with a lock of a hundred keys, which can never be unlocked without the concurrence of every key; the keys in the hands of a hundred different men, and they scattered to a hundred different and distant places.

Lincoln's wonderful elaboration of the metaphor of the locked prison house indicates a style in contrast with the brevity and precision of his more famous utterances such as the House Divided speech and the Gettysburg Address of 1863. In all cases, however, his remarkable use of repetition, subordination, and trope drives the moral truth of his argument with relentless and enchanting power. At the same time, his metaphors often revealed a moral tension within the concept of black freedom that was not peculiar to Lincoln alone but was indicative of northern ambivalence about social and economic forms of integration. In a further reply to Stephen Douglas (one that anticipated his later responses to false inflammatory charges that the Republican Party endorsed miscegenation), Lincoln remarked:

There is a natural disgust in the minds of nearly all white people at the idea of an indiscriminate amalgamation of the white and black races. . . . I protest against the counterfeit logic which concludes that, because I do not want a black woman for a slave I must necessarily want her as a wife. . . . In some respects she is certainly not my equal; but in her natural right to eat the bread she earns with her own hands without asking the leave of any one else, she is my equal, and the equal of all others.

Likewise, because he took the view that the founders had envisioned the "ultimate extinction" of slavery, he could adopt a moderate stand in the important Cooper Union speech of 1860:

Wrong as we think slavery is, we can yet afford to let it alone where it is, because that much is due to the necessity arising from its actual presence in the nation; but can we, while our votes will prevent it, allow it to spread into the national Territories, and to overrun us here in the free States? . . . Neither let us be slandered from our duty by false accusations against us, nor frightened from it by menaces of destruction to the government, nor of dungeons to ourselves. Let us have faith that right makes might, and in that faith let us to the end dare to do our duty as we understand it.

Both his ability to lead and his tragic stature were shored up by such conservative views, which withstood pressure from all sides at once. Dedication to the preservation of the Union at nearly any cost made Lincoln the complex figure he was and prompted his most moving and, at the same time, most troubled thoughts. His first inaugural speech in 1861 was perhaps the last moment (if one of false hopes) when he spoke both as the westerner and southerner he in fact was and as the northerner and easterner he had become, trying in vain to knit together the fragments of the now imperiled Union. Describing secession as anarchy, Lincoln appealed to the people of both sections not to "break our bonds of affection. The mystic chords of memory, stretching from every battlefield and patriot grave to every living heart and hearth-stone all over this broad land, will yet swell the chorus of the Union when again touched, as surely they will be, by the better angels of our nature." The speech is not necessarily one of Lincoln's greatest, but its concluding attempt to reconcile North and South presaged the practical statement of paradoxically unified sectional hopes he expressed in the second inaugural address: "Both [sides] read the same Bible, and pray to the same God; and each invokes His aid against the other. . . . The prayers of both could not be answered — that of neither has been answered fully."

Lincoln's assassination, foreseen in one of his own dreams, completed the role of tragic democratic king he had played. Whitman's poetic tribute to his death and the nation's mourning, "When Lilacs Last in the Dooryard Bloom'd," has remained the most famous literary response; but Emerson's

eulogy perhaps strikes a more fitting measure of simplicity: "He is the true
history of the American people in his time. Step by step he walked before
them; slow with their slowness, quickening his march by theirs, the true
representative of his continent; an entirely public man; father of his country,
the pulse of twenty millions throbbing in his heart, the thought of their
minds articulated by his tongue." Indeed, Lincoln's own eloquence might be
judged to be at its height of effectiveness on those occasions when what he
said was imbued most fully with his own flawed vision. His own hesitations
on the question of immediate freedom for African Americans have come over
time to seem more vexing; but the act of liberation, whatever the nuances of
Lincoln's motivations and however much military pragmatism overshadowed
idealism in his decision, remains a fact. One month before the final Emancipation Proclamation was issued on January 1, 1863, Lincoln spoke in his
annual message to Congress of the meaning of emancipation, choosing words
whose promise was made real by the course of the war itself – even though
true freedom for African Americans lay far in the future:

Fellow-citizens, *we* cannot escape history. We of this Congress and this administration will be remembered in spite of ourselves. No personal significance or insignifi-
cance can spare one or another of us. The fiery trial through which we pass will light
us down, in honor or dishonor, to the latest generation. We *say* we are for the Union.
The world will not forget that we say this. We know how to save the Union. The
world knows we do know how to save it. . . . In *giving* freedom to the *slave,* we *assure*
freedom to the *free* – honorable alike in what we give and what we preserve. We shall
nobly save or meanly lose the last, best hope on earth. Other means may succeed; this
could not fail. This way is plain, peaceful, generous, just – a way which, if followed,
the world will forever applaud, and God must forever bless.

Lincoln's dedication to saving the Union rested upon his perilous balance of
antagonistic sectional forces manifesting themselves throughout the major
thought and writing of the decade before the Civil War. The Compromise of
1850, not unlike the dreamlike oratorical embodiment given it by Webster or
the collusion of North and South to restrict the rights of blacks whether they
were slaves or free, or to deport them from the country that had put them in
bondage, represented a fragile consensus that could not hold. Exacerbated by
unstoppable western expansion, the sectional crisis reached new pitches of
danger with the passage of the Kansas–Nebraska Act in 1854 and the conflict
in "Bleeding Kansas" two years later. Within this volatile context, the Supreme Court reached a verdict in *Dred Scott v. Sandford* (1857) declaring that
Congress had no authority to prohibit slavery in federal territories (as it had in
the 1820 Missouri Compromise) and that blacks, free or not, had no rights as
citizens. Blacks, read Chief Justice Roger B. Taney's majority opinion, "were

not intended to be included under the word 'citizens' in the Constitution, and can, therefore, claim none of the rights and privileges which that instrument provides for and secures to citizens of the United States." Taney's reasoning, open to attack on a number of grounds, barely concealed a rising southern assault on antislavery and dramatically clarified the essence of African American enslavement. As Lincoln said, the Dred Scott decision imprisoned the slave "with a lock of a hundred keys . . . scattered to a hundred different and distant places." Frederick Douglass was even less temperate. "This infamous decision of the Slaveholding wing of the Supreme Court," he said in a speech before the American Anti-Slavery Society soon after the decision, "maintains that slaves are property in the same sense that horses, sheep, and swine are property [and] that slavery may go in safety anywhere under the star-spangled banner." The true threat of rebellion, Douglass recognized, lay neither with the antislavery movement nor with black slaves but with the South, which he considered in revolt against the Constitution:

The sun in the sky is not more palpable to the sight than man's right to liberty is to the moral vision. To decide against this in the person of Dred Scott, or the humblest and most whip-scarred bondman in the land, is to decide against God. It is an open rebellion against God's government. It is an attempt to undo what God has done, to blot out the broad distinction instituted by the *Allwise* between men and things, and to change the image and superscription of the everliving God into a speechless piece of merchandise.

The arguments over slavery between North and South, whether in political oration or imaginative literature, tended at times to become lost in cloudy theorizing and dry economic statistics or to lose sight of their principal subject – black Americans held in slavery. *Dred Scott* brought the subject back into focus by declaring that the founders had not intended to include blacks under the heading of "citizen" and that the slave, in the most essential way, was property. In the literature of slavery the testimony of both slaves and free blacks has a particular priority not simply because blacks were the institution's victims whose writings highlight the multiplicitous response slavery provoked but more important because they wrote in commanding proof of the fact that they were, or should be, citizens, not speechless objects of the nation's economy.

Lectures, essays, newspaper editorials, fiction, plays, songs and autobiographical narratives all compose the literature of slavery written by African Americans. As noted above, David Walker's *Appeal* in 1828 constituted one of the strongest antislavery statements of the early period, and its resolute defiance set the standard for the best polemical work that was to follow. A number of slave narrators responded to, or took issue with, Harriet Beecher Stowe, just as she had appropriated some of the materials of the slave narrative in her novel. More specifically, black novelists wrote from a wealth of experience that Stowe was compelled to invent, often producing works that effectively bridged the gap between fiction and truthful narrative. Just as the authenticity of slave narratives was often questioned (and was later disputed as reliable evidence by some historians), blacks who sought to tell their stories in fiction or in autobiography had to compete with fabricated texts such as the narrative of James Williams's life; the Briton Peter Nielson's *The Life and Adventures of Zamba, An African Negro King* (1850), which follows Zamba's life from Africa to a South Carolina plantation, with scathing attacks on slavery and America; and Mattie Griffiths's *Autobiography of a Female Slave* (1857), a work published anonymously that claimed it was "not a wild romance to beguile your tears and cheat your fancy" but that, on the other hand, was hardly a "truthful autobiography."

A striking example of the problems that have surrounded slave documents appears in Harriet Jacobs's *Incidents in the Life of a Slave Girl* (1861), which was "edited" by Lydia Maria Child and later taken to be substantially Child's work. Modern discovery of Jacobs's letters and other documents has revealed that she was born a slave in North Carolina around 1815 and that her narrative of her experiences as a slave and her life in the North following her escape is to a significant degree autobiographical. By 1849 she was active in the antislavery movement in Rochester, New York, and during the war she nursed black troops in Washington, D.C., where she remained until her death in 1897. Stowe refused a request from Jacobs to help compose her story, and Child's editing turned out to be only light stylistic work. Published under the pseudonym of Linda Brent, the main character, the story is Jacobs's own, and it testifies in moving detail to the sexual abuse of black women under slavery, supporting the abolitionist charge that slavery and sexual violation were inseparable, and the plantation an arena of erotic dissipation and male lust, a "cage of obscene birds" (in Jacobs's phrase) that scandalized the most intimate affections of the domestic ideal by revealing the painful hierarchy upon which it was built.

The sexual threats of her master drove Jacobs into hiding for nearly seven years in the hope that she would one day escape with her children. Aided by relatives and friends, some of them white, Jacobs lived confined in the tiny garret of her grandmother's house, imprisoned in a suffocating enclosure that resembled more than figuratively the excruciating middle passage of the slave trade:

The garret was only nine feet long and seven wide. The highest part was three feet high, and sloped down abruptly to the loose board floor. . . . The air was stifling; the darkness total. A bed had been spread on the floor. I could sleep quite comfortably on one side; but the slope was so sudden that I could not turn on the other without hitting the roof. The rats and mice ran over my bed; but I was weary, and I slept such sleep as the wretched may, when a tempest has passed over them. . . . It seemed horrible to sit or lie in a cramped position day after day, without one gleam of light. Yet I would have chosen this, rather than my lot as a slave, though white people considered it an easy one; and it was so compared with the fate of others.

From her ironic "loophole of retreat" (as she calls the garret once she has bored peepholes in the wall), Jacobs witnesses plantation life, including the lives of her children, from a concealed position that becomes a metaphor for her equally cunning position as narrator of her own story. As the passages about her long concealment suggest, Jacobs's narrative has the inventive power of a novel, employing a significant number of formal and plot elements common to gothic and sentimental fiction. Yet it is also marked constantly by the sharp edge of a personal polemic: "I can testify, from my own experience and observation, that slavery is a curse to the whites as well as the blacks. It makes the white fathers cruel and sensual; the sons violent and licentious; it contaminates the daughters, and makes the wives wretched." Gender allegiance sometimes overrides racial prejudice in *Incidents,* but Jacobs's only reliable help comes from black women, whereas her white mistress is shown to be a jealous accomplice in her husband's schemes to seduce the young slave girl. The text throughout weaves together a complex set of the central tropes of the literature of slavery – secrecy and concealment, writing and letters, violation and resistance – so as to draw together the lives of women on two opposing sides of the color line while at the same time keeping them firmly separated by the realities of the racial barrier. The realistic treatment of the lives of slaves and white women in the South is in part modulated by the narrative's awareness of its genteel northern audience, and her appeals to the conventions of domestic romance constantly move Jacobs's autobiography in a novelistic direction without for a moment undermining its credibility. The details of her life and the story's novelization operate in perfect conjunction, for her construction of an alternative social model for the life of the black female slave – necessitated by the fact, shocking to a middle-class audience, that she deliberately took a white lover and bore his illegitimate children in order to escape the harassment of her master – depends upon redefining the idea of home and women's political community according to the violence and racism that marked black life in the North as well as the South.

A comparable text whose full significance was only appreciated upon its rediscovery in the late twentieth century is Harriet E. Wilson's *Our Nig; or, Sketches from the Life of a Free Black* (1859), the first novel by an African-American woman. Because Wilson's novel focuses on the prejudice and poverty faced by free blacks in the North, it is likely that its obscurity for over a century after it was written grew in part from the fact that, like Harriet Jacobs's narrative, it directly challenged prevailing cultural codes. The northern literary audience was willing to accept tales of violence on the plantation but remained unresponsive to the facts of northern cruelty against blacks. Little is known of Wilson other than that she was born a free black in the North and lived primarily in New Hampshire and Massachusetts; it is likely, however, that the novel was based in part on her own experiences. As part of the book's long subtitle suggests – *Showing That Slavery's Shadows Fall Even There,* that is, in the North – its story transfers the cruelty of a heartless mistress (not unlike Stowe's Marie St. Clare) from the southern plantation to a New England household, where the servant–narrator, Frado, is a virtual slave. Daughter of a black laborer and a poor white woman, Frado also bears the burden of racial mixture. She is left pregnant and abandoned at the end by a black antislavery lecturer, and the story concludes without the happy marriage the sentimental plot of the novel might seem to call for. The novel thus fuses elements of northern domestic fiction with those of the slave narrative. By focusing on the plight of the lower class and free blacks in the North, it ironically reinforces the proslavery claim that northern laborers merited the sympathy of reformers as much as slaves did. Wilson, however, attacks the standard themes of the slavery argument in three ways: she overturns the proslavery arguments of Fitzhugh and others and exploits the racism that underlies Free Soil doctrine and daily life in the Jim Crow North; she overturns the tragic mulatto theme by erasing its exoticism and revealing the economic oppression it promotes; and she overturns the ideal of maternal domesticity by making the northern home a hell and its mother figure a relentless tyrant. Along with Jacobs's *Incidents,* Wilson's novel stands not so much as a reply to Stowe but a critique of Stowe's limitations and as a more scathing extension of the novel's political purpose.

Comparable in her literary achievement to Jacobs and Wilson, and far better known throughout the nineteenth century, was Frances Ellen Watkins Harper. Born free in Baltimore, Harper (1825–1911) would not write some of the poetry or the single novel for which she is best known, *Iola Leroy* (1892), until after the war; but in the antebellum period she was an active antislavery lecturer and the author of a popular book of *Poems* (1854) devoted to romantic but finely executed treatments of such topics as "Ethiopia," "The Fugitive's Wife," and, her most famous, "The Slave Auction":

> The sale began – young girls were there,
> Defenceless in their wretchedness,
> Whose stifled sobs of deep despair
> Revealed their anguish and distress.

> And mothers stood with streaming eyes,
> And saw their dearest children sold;
> Unheeded rose their bitter cries,
> While tyrants bartered them for gold. . . .

Standing between the autobiographical narratives, which recorded the flight from slavery into the promised land, and sentimental verse and fiction, which sometimes concealed racial protest behind a mask of maudlin style and theme, was Harper's long allegorical poem *Moses: A Story of the Nile* (1869). Seventy years before Zora Neale Hurston did so in prose, Harper rendered in typologically acute form a story of the black delivery from bondage – not in the valley of the Nile but the valley of the Mississippi. Her epic summed up the significance of an adopted biblical story that appears throughout African American culture and implicitly reminded her audience that some of the strongest models for the black Moses in the antislavery tradition were not men but women like Harriet Tubman and Sojourner Truth. The poem also spoke perceptively of the traces of slavery that would last decades beyond emancipation:

> If Slavery only laid its weight of chains
> Upon the weary, aching limbs, e'en then
> It were a curse; but when it frets through nerve
> And flesh and eats into the weary soul,
> Oh then it is a thing for every human
> Heart to loathe, and this was Israel's fate,
> For when the chains were shaken from their limbs,
> They failed to strike the impress from their souls.

The other fiction by African American writers in the period is less compelling or, like Delany's *Blake* (1859), is important most of all as political argument. Philadelphia author Frank J. Webb's novel *The Garies and Their Friends* (1857), published in England, is the story of mixed marriage and race prejudice in the North, particularly that between blacks and white immigrant groups. The best-known novel by a black man in the period was William Wells Brown's *Clotel: Or, the President's Daughter* (1853), which appeared in several subsequent revised editions. An escaped slave who went on to become one of the leading black abolitionists (later taking over Douglass's position in the Massachusetts Anti-Slavery Society and enjoying a very successful speaking tour of Europe), Brown (1816?–84) also wrote a narrative of his own life, a volume of poetry entitled *The Anti-Slavery Harp* (1848), and three minor plays that have not survived: *Miralda; or, The Beautiful Quadroon* (1855), a version of *Clotel; Experience; or, How to Give a Northern Man a Backbone* (1856); and *The Escape; or, A Leap for Freedom* (1858). As the titles of his literary works suggest, Brown frequently employed the theme of racial mixing, in particular the legend of Thomas Jefferson's slave children, as the central weapon in his attack on slavery. In his popular novel, Clotel is treated cruelly, used as a mistress, sold twice to harsh masters, separated from her daughter, jailed in the wake of Nat Turner's rebellion, and driven to suicide in the Potomac River: "Thus died Clotel, the daughter of Thomas Jefferson, a president of the United States; a man distinguished as the author of the Declaration of Independence, and one of the first statesmen of that country." The compromise with white ideals that the tragic mulatto theme necessitates is underscored in the words of one of the novel's minor nearly-white slave rebels, George (clearly modeled on Stowe's George Harris): "Did not the American revolutionists violate the laws when they struck for liberty?"

The comparison of rebel slaves to American patriots was commonplace in antislavery rhetoric, all the more effective because it could not be justly rebutted. As Brown wrote in 1855, in a published lecture on *St. Domingo: Its Revolutions and Its Patriots,* "the revolution that was commenced in 1776 would . . . be finished, and the glorious sentiment of the Declaration of Independence" realized, only when African-American slaves were liberated. Having "shed their [own] blood in the American Revolutionary war," Brown argued, slaves were now "only waiting the opportunity of wiping out their wrongs in the blood of their oppressors." "What to the American slave," asked Douglass in a famous 1852 address, "is your Fourth of July" – what but "a thin veil to cover up crimes which would disgrace a nation of savages." Surely, Brown and others suggested, there was a leader like Haiti's Toussaint L'Ouverture waiting to rise in revolt against the southern states, a "black Cromwell," as Theodore Parker wrote, ready to annihilate slavery just as theocracy, monarchy, and aristocracy had been (or were being) annihilated in Europe. Brown's historical works, *The Negro in the American Revolution* (1867) and *The Black Man: His Antecedents, His Genius, and His Achievements* (1863), argued for the place of blacks in the revolutionary and intellectual traditions that Euro-Americans considered their sole prerogative; and his lecture on San Domingo drew a withering comparison between the white father of American freedom and the black father of Haitian freedom:

Each was the leader of an oppressed and outraged people, each had a powerful enemy to contend with, and each succeeded in founding a government in the New World. Toussaint's government made liberty its watchword, incorporated it in its constitution, abolished the slave-trade, and made freedom universal amongst the people. Washington's government incorporated slavery and the slave-trade, and enacted laws by which chains were fastened upon the limbs of millions of people. Toussaint liberated his countrymen; Washington enslaved a portion of his, and aided in giving strength and vitality to an institution that will one day rend asunder the UNION that he helped to form. Already the slave in his chains in the rice fields of Carolina and the cotton fields of Mississippi burns for revenge.

With the exceptions of David Walker, noted above, and Frederick Douglass, Brown's only rival as spokesman for the ideal of black liberty was the minister Henry Highland Garnet (1815–82), who along with Martin Delany was an important early spokesman for black nationalism. Garnet's *Address to the Slaves* (1848), first delivered as a lecture to a convention of black abolitionists in Buffalo in 1843, called for violent revolt: "Brethren, arise, arise! Strike for your lives and liberties. . . . *Rather die freemen than live to be slaves.* Remember that you are FOUR MILLIONS." The call to revolution shocked most white abolitionists and many black leaders as well, among them at this point Frederick Douglass, who still followed the Garrisonian principles of nonviolence; but it gave new momentum to a rising tide of black separatism and renewed interest in emigration, which Garnet came to support during the next decade. Inspired by the independence of Liberia in 1848, Garnet and others began to look to it as a future empire for American blacks. Unlike Alexander Crummell, whose messianic view of Africa was predicated upon raising it from primitive barbarism to a civilized Christian standard of life and faith, Garnet depicted in *The Past and the Present Condition, and the Destiny, of the Colored Race* (1848) a proud tradition of black ancestors and issued a jeremiad on behalf of the nation's voiceless slaves, who, like all slaves of the New World, had been torn from their common African heritage:

We should have likewise, days of bitter bread, and tabernacle in the wilderness, in which to remember our griefworn brothers and sisters. They are now pleading with millions of tongues against those who have despoiled them. They cry from gory fields – from pestilential rice swamps – from cane breaks, and forests – from plantations of cotton and tobacco – from the dark holds of slave ships, and from countless acres where the sugar cane, nods to the sighing winds. They lift up their voices from all the land over which the flag of our country floats. From the banks of our silver streams, and broad rivers, from our valleys and sloping hills, and mountain tops.

The silence that reigns in the region where the pale nations of the earth slumber, is solemn, and awful. But what think ye, when you are told that every rood of land in this Union is the grave of a murdered man, and their epitaphs are written upon the monuments of the nation's wealth?

A decade later, when Garnet had founded the African Civilization Society, one of his first adherents was Martin Delany (1812–85), who immediately attempted to purge the society of all white influence. Delany's distrust of whites' motives and his belief that blacks would never receive freedom and fair treatment in the United States made him a strong emigrationist, a position forcefully argued in *The Condition, Elevation, Emigration, and Destiny*

of the Colored People of the United States (1852). The volume based its call for
political separatism on the assumption that only blacks could, and would,
correctly interpret their own historical experience and create a new moral
state in another country, perhaps in the Caribbean or Latin America, an
argument repeated in *Political Destiny of the Colored Race on the American
Continent* (1854). Born a free man, Delany worked for years as an editor and
lecturer in the antislavery cause and still found time to become a professional
physician (despite being forced out of Harvard Medical School when white
students protested his presence). Delany lived for a time in Canada, where in
1858 he discussed with John Brown the raid Brown would later undertake
against Harper's Ferry. Although Delany always rejected the type of colonization sponsored in Liberia, he and Robert Campbell explored the Niger Valley
in 1859 and published separate reports on their ventures as the basis of a
never-realized plan to settle a colony with a select group of black Canadian
emigrants. During the Civil War Delany was commissioned a major of black
troops, and he later worked for the Freedman's Bureau and was active in
Reconstruction politics in South Carolina.

Delany's most significant literary achievement, however, was not his writing on black nationalism but his novel, *Blake; or, The Huts of America,* which
was serialized in part in the *Anglo-African Magazine* in 1859 and probably in
full in the *Weekly Anglo-African* in 1861 (a complete text has not survived). In
accordance with Delany's view of the United States as a virtual prison for
blacks, his hero, Henry Blake combines the vision of Nat Turner with the
commanding intelligence and authority of Toussaint. Identifying divine deliverance with violent revolution and associating the plotted insurrections of
Gabriel Prosser, Denmark Vesey, and Turner with the spirit of the American
Revolution, Blake, a free man, spreads a plot for insurrection throughout the
South after his wife, a slave who rejects the attentions of her owner–father, is
sold to a planter in Cuba. Blake carries his plans for violent uprising to Cuba
(where the unresolved action of the novel ends), and this plot device plays
upon current contention over annexation of Cuba by the United States and
fears among southerners that a conspiracy between Britain and Spain to grant
freedom to slaves in Cuba (what was called the "Africanization of Cuba")
would lead to revolt and carnage in the United States. The same year that
Blake first appeared, for example, the *United States Magazine and Democratic
Review,* long a proslavery organ of manifest destiny, published a lead essay
promoting the acquisition of Cuba that implored the government to "rescue"
Cuba from European despotism and anticipated the continued onward movement of "the ark of the Democratic covenant."

More directly than Melville's *Benito Cereno,* Delany's *Blake* illuminates an
aspect of the slavery crisis that has been overshadowed by the civil conflagra-

tion that soon engulfed the United States. At the time, the Caribbean and Cuba in particular were at the center of arguments about expansion. New Spanish policies liberalizing slave laws, combined with the seizure in February 1854 of the American steamer *Black Warrior* on a violation of port regulations, accelerated both legal and extralegal maneuvering to obtain Cuba before it became, as a State Department agent wrote in March 1854, another "Black Empire" like Haiti, "whose example they would be prone to imitate" in destroying the wealth of the island and launching "a disastrous bloody war of the races." The height of imperialistic rhetoric came after the crisis had passed and attempts to force a purchase of Cuba had failed, in the notorious Ostend Manifesto of October 1854, which declared that Cuba belonged "naturally to that great family of States of which the Union is the providential nursery" and that the United States would be justified "in wresting it from Spain . . . upon the very same principle that would justify an individual in tearing down the burning house of his neighbor if there were no other means of preventing the flames from destroying his own home." The issue of Cuba, that is to say, was couched in the familial rhetoric that Lincoln would exploit, combining the domestic language of the revolutionary fathers and that of slaveholding paternalism.

The ironies of such patriotic designs upon Cuba are used to careful effect by Delany, who in his novel as in his essays connects the freedom of American slaves with black aspirations throughout the New World. Focusing on the same agony of sexual abuse and family separation that appears in the work of Stowe and Jacobs, for example, *Blake* answers the destruction of family not with tragedy and still less with sentiment but rather with an invocation of the suppressed power of the Age of Revolution. Delany borrows a number of polemical poems from James M. Whitfield's *America and Other Poems* (1853), and the novel throughout has the character of political theater enlivened by prophetic warning. *Blake* remains an unfinished novel in several senses; yet its vital amalgamation of contemporary events with a romantic plot of rescue and an anatomy of rebellion makes it one of the more astute political novels of the mid-nineteenth century. Along with Garnet and Brown, Delany defined in his work a tradition of black nationalism that would only in the following century stand out from under the imposing shadow of Frederick Douglass and achieve the recognition it deserved.

Delany did not share with Douglass or with the majority of the leading black abolitionists the experience of slavery or the intellectual initiation of the slave narrative, often the first important writing (or lecturing) undertaken by the escaped slave. As a group, the narratives are of enormous diversity, ranging from simple stories dictated to white sympathizers in the North to elaborately reported and richly detailed accounts of life in, and flight from, slavery. The authors variously employed the conventions of Euro-American sentimental fiction, political polemic, slave songs, the remnants of African folklore, and personal testimony in creating a unique and compelling genre of American literature. Only with the modern historical and literary recognition of the great richness of African American life, during slavery and after, did a more complete record and more complex theoretical interpretations of black cultural forms begin to appear. In the decades after the Civil War, published slave narratives of the earlier nineteenth century were complemented, and given a more reliable context, by projects in oral history, by the increasing collection of folktales and songs by ethnographers, and most important by black writers who began more assiduously to recover the culture of African American slavery, recognizing both its African sources and its unique American elements as they incorporated it into contemporary intellectual history, drama, fiction, and poetry. It is from that point forward that one can begin to see more clearly the continuity between antebellum black texts and African cultural survivals and the rise of black literature and arts on into the twentieth century.

African Americans were involved in most antislavery societies, but they were often expected to play subordinate roles or, like white women, to form auxiliaries to the main group. Black antislavery newspapers and magazines included the *Colored American*, the *Mirror of Liberty*, and *Freedom's Journal*, but the best known was Douglass's *North Star* (later renamed *Frederick Douglass's Paper*). As Douglass complained, however, blacks failed to support such journals with the same energy that they devoted to the underground railroad, where women like Harriet Tubman and men like David Ruggles (and whites like Levi Coffin) became legends for their heroic assistance to escaped slaves, a story recorded in great documentary detail by William Still in *The Underground Railroad* (1872). Tubman in particular was admired for her courage in returning to the South to aid in further escapes, and her anecdotal account of the underground railroad was recorded by Sarah H. Bradford in *Scenes in the Life of Harriet Tubman* (1869) and *Harriet Tubman: The Moses of Her People* (1886). Black writers also produced antislavery verse, the most notable being George M. Horton's volume *The Hope of Liberty* (1829), the first book of poetry by a black author since Phillis Wheatley. More important, African Americans were enormously effective as speakers on the antislavery circuit, though they often found themselves dominated and manipulated by white colleagues. By the 1840s Douglass, William Wells Brown, Tubman, William and Ellen Craft, and Sojourner Truth were among those lecturing in the North. Sojourner Truth's life story was transcribed by Olive Gilbert in 1850 in the *Narrative of Sojourner Truth*, but she gained lasting fame for a speech at an 1851 women's rights convention in Ohio in which she demanded:

Look at my arm! I have ploughed and planted and gathered into barns, and no man could head me – and ain't I a woman? I could work as much and eat as much as a man – when I could get it – and bear the lash as well! And ain't I a woman? I have born thirteen children, and seen most of 'em sold into slavery, and when I cried out with my mother's grief, none but Jesus heard me – and ain't I a woman?

Because of Sojourner Truth's effectiveness as a speaker, her words would have a celebrated life in the history of feminism. As Douglass would reveal in a famous episode of his autobiography, though, whatever his or her rhetorical power, the black speaker was likely to be subordinated to the white and was often expected to play the role of an exhibit or, at the most, to recount a saga of suffering on the plantation to audience after audience while leaving the discussion of politics and morality to Garrison, Phillips, or another white polemicist.

The fact that autobiography and antislavery rhetoric were often merged on the lecture platform accounts in part for the rhetorical form of many slave narratives. The centrality of the years immediately preceding and following the Civil War to the published record of slave narratives obscures the fact that important examples appeared before the antebellum period, among them *The Interesting Narrative of the Life of Olaudah Equiano, or Gustavus Vassa, the African* (1789) and *Narrative of the Life and Adventures of Venture, A Native of Africa* (1798). The majority, however, were published in the several decades after 1840, with many more being recorded later in the nineteenth century and in twentieth-century collections such as the enormous Federal Writers' Project compilation of oral remembrances, later edited by George Rawick and published as *The American Slave: A Composite Autobiography* (1972–8). In the years before the Civil War, the slave narratives sold well and were in large part responsible for the North's popular view of life under slavery, with the result noted before that autobiography and fiction in important cases came to resemble one another. With a few exceptions, the narratives were authentic, whether or not they carried the frequent caption "Written By Himself," and whether or not the writing was entirely the escaped slave's own. Some, like *Narrative of Lunsford Lane* (1842), reproduced fugitive slave ads or bills of sale for members of the slave family, for "such of my readers as are not accustomed to trade in human beings"; or like *Narrative of Moses Grandy* (1844), they mockingly recorded the prices of friends and relatives. Others enthralled their audiences (in print as on the lecture platform) with bizarre adventures of escape. The *Narrative of Henry "Box" Brown* (1851), in addition to its provocative attack on the cruelty of the plantation system, told the unusual story of the slave who had himself enclosed in a crate and shipped by railroad to freedom in the North. William and Ellen Craft, in *Running a Thousand Miles for Freedom* (1860), told the tale of their inventive 1848 escape from Georgia, she with her light skin posing as a young southern gentleman and he posing as her servant. Such intricate deceptions were less common than simple flight, but they revealed in magnified form a central fact of slave life the narratives bring forth – that the slaves were required for their own survival in some cases and for their sense of self-esteem and communal dignity in all cases to adopt roles and to wear masks that, however benevolent their white masters, were not often penetrated by those outside the African American community itself. The southern claims of slave contentment and the northern racist claims of African docility failed to take account of the fact, recognized easily on the evidence of the narratives and borne out by later historical research, that slaves had good reason to disguise their feelings, as well as their plans, and did so with great ingenuity. Questions of identity and voice are consequently of enormous importance in the slave narratives, and the best of the narratives are of special literary interest because they both preserve a sense of true black identity and communal life and at the same time reveal the protagonist's talents for fabrication, acting, and subtle deceit.

The narratives typically register the cruelty of slave masters in vivid detail (those who sought to escape were perhaps the most mistreated, but their narratives tell the story as well of the many who suffered even more brutality without chance of escape). The *Narrative of Adventures and Escape of Moses Roper, from American Slavery* (1839), for example, tells of an instance in which Roper's fingers were placed in a vise and his toes hammered on an anvil because he would not reveal the name of a slave who helped him remove his chains. John Brown's *Slave Life in Georgia* (1855) told of being subjected to sunstroke experiments, including blistering his skin to see how deep the "black" went. Both the narratives and documentary sources such as Weld's *American Slavery As It Is* and Stowe's *Key to Uncle Tom's Cabin* recount numerous instances of murder and brutality by slaveowners that pass without any legal sanction. The very popular *Slavery in the United States: A Narrative of the Life and Adventures of Charles Ball, a Black Man* (1836), which went through six editions by 1859 (the last entitled *Fifty Years in Chains*), told of Ball's separation from his parents, and later his wife and children, and included representative descriptions of whippings of himself and other slaves:

[Billy] shrank his body close to the trunk of the tree, around which his arms and his legs were lashed, drew his shoulders up to his head like a dying man, and trembled, or rather shivered, in all his members. The blood flowed from the commencement [of the whipping], and in a few minutes lay in small puddles at the root of the tree. I saw flakes of flesh as long as my finger fall out of the gashes in his back; and I believe he was insensible during all the time that he was receiving the last two hundred [out of five hundred] lashes. . . . The gentlemen who had done the whipping, eight or ten in number, being joined by their friends, then came under the tree and drank punch until their dinner was made ready, under a booth of green boughs at a short distance.

Such incidents appear in many of the narratives, giving rise to the suspicion that some of the popularity of the narratives derived from the white audience's voyeurism. Even so, whipping came to be the single defining emblem of southern slaveholding. Escaped slaves exhibited their scars on the lecture platform, and narrators like Douglass rhapsodized about the whip itself and its power to contaminate all, both white and black, with a corrupting lust for power: "Everybody, in the south, wants the privilege of whipping somebody else. . . . The whip is all in all."

The record of such cruelty became a stock device in the narratives without ever losing its powerful appeal or seeming fabricated. Whatever melodrama fired the episodes of rape, whipping, or humiliation, the slave narratives corroborated other evidence of violence and mistreatment and made the lives of their authors and protagonists representative of the thousands of stories that remained untold. Harriet Beecher Stowe's appropriation of slave narrative testimony was for good reason most effective in its revelation of violence against families, both physical and emotional. If the slave narratives generally lacked her stagecraft, though, they straightforwardly told of human pain. As he wrote in *Narrative of the Life and Adventures of Henry Bibb* (1849), Bibb "was compelled to stand and see my wife shamefully scourged and abused by her master," and his separation from his daughter, still in slavery, made him thankful that "she was the first and shall be the last slave that ever I will father, for chains and slavery on this earth." The protagonist of the *Narrative of Moses Grandy* (1844) was held at bay with a pistol while his wife was carried away; and William Grimes wrote in *Life of William Grimes, Runaway Slave* (1855) of the common situation in which blacks themselves were turned into brutal overseers and forced to whip their friends and family. Such degradation appears throughout the narratives, and it is all the more striking in the best narratives, like those of Ball, Douglass, Brown, and Northup, which portray it against a detailed backdrop of slave life and situate their polemics within a dramatic human context that ranges from gothic horror, inflicted at near random, to the orderly and efficient operation of the slave system. The general poverty of conditions – of food, clothing, shelter, medical care, and instruction – emerged clearly in the narratives. The multiple violations of slaves' lives by emotional and physical abuse, even if they were occasionally exaggerated by abolitionists, cast a damning light upon the proslavery claim that blacks were mere animals – the men beasts of burden unable to cope with freedom and the women vessels of lust and reproduction – who could be reduced to their bodily functions. When a slave accused of stealing meat is drowned in the *Narrative of William W. Brown, A Fugitive Slave* (1847), Brown remarks how the body is left to be picked up the next day: along came "a cart, which takes up the trash of our streets . . . and the body was thrown in, and in a few minutes more was covered over with dirt which they were removing from the streets." What the northern audience learned from the slave narratives – in contrast to the claims of southern essayists and accommodating northern travelers and novelists who portrayed the plantation in idyllic terms – was that the effect, if not the goal, of slavery was to reduce blacks to the least human dimension.

A few of the most successful narratives owed their popularity to the charismatic personalities or unusual careers of their protagonists. Elizabeth Keckley's *Behind the Scenes* (1868) told of her rise from slavery to become a White House dressmaker for Mary Todd Lincoln, and *A Sketch of the Life of Okah Tubbee* (1848) portrayed the life of a manumitted Natchez slave turned traveling musician who dressed in Indian clothing and claimed to be descended from Choctaw chiefs. Perhaps the best known of slave narrators until the twentieth century was Josiah Henson, a Methodist Episcopal minister whose own 1849 narrative (*Life of Josiah Henson,* written by Samuel A. Eliot) presented a simple but effective record of his conversion, his sufferings, and his family's escape to Canada, where he became the leader of Dawn, a successful black communal settlement. Henson's fame, however, came from his assertion, now discredited by scholarship, that he was the model for Stowe's Uncle Tom. By manipulation of, and acquiescence in, a legend that grew of its own accord (and eventually had Stowe's own participation), Henson made a career for himself by playing this part in subsequent versions of his autobiography, which appeared under titles such as *Truth Stranger than Fiction: Father Henson's Story of his Own Life* (1858). As with most other developments in the legend of Uncle Tom, however, Henson's posturing served mainly to drain Tom of his interest as a character as well as to obscure the significance of Henson's own life story.

Henson's narrative is one of many that are important as much for their portraits of life as freemen, whether North or South, as for their accounts of life under slavery. James W. C. Pennington's popular autobiography, *The Fugitive Blacksmith* (1849), recounts his escape, conversion, and the beginnings of his career as a minister, concluding with a letter to his former master begging him to release his slaves and be reconciled to God. Pennington's life is more notable, however, for the fact that he received an honorary doctorate from the University of Heidelberg but was denied admission to the classrooms of Yale, being permitted only to stand outside the doors to listen to lectures. Educated only after his escape from slavery, Pennington worked actively for antislavery and wrote a children's book entitled *A Text Book of the*

Origin and History of the Colored People (1841). Interestingly, Pennington maintained that in many respects mild slavery was the worst form, because of its subtle dehumanizing effects, and he condemned the institution most of all for forcing slaves to be deceitful and for denying them education, attitudes that were reinforced by his experience of prejudice against free blacks in the North. Again like Douglass, most escaped slaves not only feared constantly that they would be captured or kidnapped and returned to slavery but also faced Jim Crow laws and suspicion or hatred almost everywhere in the northern United States outside of antislavery circles (and in some cases certainly within them as well). The same was often true of those blacks born free. The *Life of James Mars* (1864) tells of a Connecticut man who, though born after the abolition of slavery in that state in 1788, had to remain in servitude under its terms until 1825. In his *Autobiography* (1984), written in the 1890s, James Thomas tells of his years among free blacks in Nashville, his life in Kansas and Missouri on the eve of the Civil War, and his eventual success as a businessman and property owner in St. Louis. Similarly, William Johnson, known as the "Barber of Natchez," wrote in a diary of 1835–51 (published in 1951) of his work as a farmer and a barber in a volatile Mississippi world of duels, romance, racism, and corrupt politics. One of the most famous antislavery orators, Samuel Ringgold Ward, escaped slavery to become a minister in the North, yet his *Autobiography of a Fugitive Negro* (1855) not only gives us a full picture of his abolitionist activities but is highly critical of the northern churches' complicity in slavery. After Austin Steward (1794–1860) moved to frontier New York with his master and eventually gained his freedom by hiring himself out, he became a successful grocer and an antislavery activist, and later organized the Canadian black settlement of Wilberforce. Like Benjamin Drew's *Northside View of Slavery* (1856), a collection of African-Canadian narratives that is structured by the irony that black Americans could only become free Americans by leaving the country altogether, Steward's volume, *Twenty-Two Years a Slave, and Forty Years a Freeman* (1857), takes its strength less from the fact than from the paradoxes of black American liberty. His story begins in slavery but dwells on prejudice against free blacks and the immoral implications of the Fugitive Slave Law for men and women of conscience in the North. If Steward's lot was not as grim as that of the heroine in *Our Nig,* the irony that Frederick Douglass pointed to in his treatment aboard a Massachusetts train (in *My Bondage and My Freedom*) was nevertheless typical of such black experience in the North: "At the same time that they excluded a free colored man from their cars, this same company allowed slaves, in company with their masters and mistresses, to ride unmolested."

Perhaps the most vicious irony of black life in antebellum America, however, fell upon those free blacks, like Solomon Northup, who were kidnapped and sold into slavery. Northup's *Twelve Years a Slave* (1853) describes his captivity and eventual redemption from a Louisiana plantation (when, after nine years, he finally obtains pen and ink to write North for help). The narrative includes some of the most remarkable and detailed writing about the daily routine of the slave, the elaborate marketing techniques that accompany the slave auction, and the slaves' development of an African American culture that separates them from the brutality of their masters. Stowe had included Northup's letter about his enslavement in her *Key to Uncle Tom's Cabin*, and he joined other blacks who wrote in the wake of her novel in both attacking proslavery apologists and implicitly criticizing the limits of understanding evident in the writings of men and women like Stowe:

Men may write fictions portraying lowly life as it is, or as it is not — may expatiate with owlish gravity upon the bliss of ignorance — discourse flippantly from arm chairs of the pleasures of slave life; but let them toil with him in the field — sleep with him in the cabin — feed with him on husks — let them behold him scourged, hunted, trampled on. . . . Let them know the *heart* of the poor slave — learn his secret thoughts — thoughts he dare not utter in the hearing of the white man . . . and they will find that ninety-nine out of every hundred are intelligent enough to understand their situation, and to cherish in their bosoms the love of freedom, as passionately as themselves.

Because Northup's narrative also takes advantage of his double perspective of a free man and a slave, it provides a special instance of the masking that slaves maintained was necessary to their daily survival and their development of a history, a consciousness, and an artistic culture of their own.

What also emerged from the slave narrative's bleak picture of plantation life or prejudice in the North, in fact, was a sense of the strength and independent spirit of survival, alongside forthright counteractions of slavery and racism, among a people who were building a world neither strictly American nor African but uniquely syncretic, a world destined to grow into its own distinct form and to have an important impact on American religion, art, social thought, and politics in coming years. The slave narratives in many cases provide not just a fragmentary record of early black culture but also form a bridge between the traditions of oral storytelling and the formal written narratives of Euro-American culture. In their creation of selves responsive to the demands of an often liminal existence between cultures — an existence that could depend on both spiritual strength and cunning — the narrators sometimes resemble the trickster figures of African American folklore, whose tales were increasingly collected by the turn of the century and later recorded in literary form, for example, by Joel Chandler Harris in his several volumes of Uncle Remus stories, by Charles Chesnutt in *The Conjure*

Woman, and by Zora Neale Hurston in *Mules and Men.* As in other forms of
self-expression and communication that flourished under slavery, the trickster tales of Brer Rabbit and Brer Fox, to name only the best-known of
animal tales, and the stories of Old Master and John could provide psychological relief or a realistic articulation of power in the hostile world of bondage.
Often, moreover, the tales became embellished in such a way as to extend
their allegorical commentary into the postwar period. For example, in one of
the Master–John tales recorded by Hurston, one among countless variations
on the widespread "Philly-Me-York" tale, Master pretends to leave town (on
a trip to "Philly-Me-York") but returns in disguise to catch John throwing a
dance for his fellow slaves in the "big house," drinking and eating Master's
stores, and killing his hogs. Master plans to hang John, but John tricks him
in turn by having a friend sit in the hanging tree with a box of matches when
John begins to pray to God for help. The tale concludes:

> "Now John," said Massa, "have you got any last words to say?"
> "Yes sir, Ah want to pray."
> "Pray and damn quick. I'm clean out of patience with you, John."
> So John knelt down. "O Lord, here Ah am at de foot of de persimmon tree. If
> you're gointer destroy Old Massa tonight, with his wife and chillun and everything
> he got, lemme see it lightnin'."
> Jack up the tree, struck a match. Old Massa caught hold of John and said: "John,
> don't pray no more."
> John said: "Oh yes, turn me loose so Ah can pray. O Lord, here Ah am tonight
> callin' on Thee and Thee alone. If you are gointer destroy Ole Massa tonight, his wife
> and chillun all he got, Ah want to see it lightnin' again."
> Jack struck another match and Ole Massa started to run. He give John his freedom
> and a heap of land and stock. He run so fast it took a express train running at the rate
> of ninety miles an hour and six months to bring him back, and that's how come
> [blacks] got they freedom today.

As this brief example suggests, layers of tall tale and grotesque irony are the
main operative mechanisms of the African American folktale. Inverting the
disguised roles of domination and submission so that the weak but cunning
"slave" figure, whether John or Brer Rabbit, gets the better of, or even
destroys, his "master," the folktales of slavery that would get set down in
countless variations in subsequent decades constitute one of the strongest
artistic legacies of African American slavery.

Perhaps the most important feature of antebellum black life in America – the
element that merged divergent geographical and chronological experiences,
linked slave to free black life, and became the central vehicle for the survival
and growth of distinctive African American cultural forms – was religion.
African-American religion united evangelical Protestantism with surviving

elements of African religion to create the African Methodist Episcopal Church, various formalized Baptist churches, and many noninstitutional worship groups. In the form of prayer, song, or worship, religion was an important part of slave life whether it was imposed as a means of control by the masters or developed in communal worship among the slaves. Religion was crucial to the narratives of both free blacks and slaves, in the latter case because the slave's escape often conformed to the biblical archetype of delivery from bondage. Frederick Douglass was only one of many narrators who recounted their experiences of religious conversion and periods of despair over the inability of religion, especially the Christian churches, to do anything about slavery. The *Narrative of the Life of Reverend Noah Davis* (1859), for example, gives a history of Davis's ministerial life in Baltimore and his frustrating attempts to purchase his children's freedom. In a representative pattern of the slave conversion narrative, the *Life of John Thompson, A Fugitive Slave* (1856) records a tale of family separation and escape, after which Thompson becomes literate and learns to read the Word of God before eventually departing for Africa. William Wells Brown dedicated his narrative to the Ohio man who aided him and from whom he took his name in words that drew an analogy between his experience and Christ's command to Christian duty: "Thirteen years ago, I came to your door, a weary fugitive from chains and stripes. I was a stranger, and you took me in. I was hungry, and you fed me. Naked was I, and you clothed me." Two free black women evangelists, Jarena Lee and Zilpha Elaw, recorded their stories before the Civil War; and several more, including Julia Foote and Amanda Smith, wrote autobiographies in later years. Smith's 1893 account of her career in the African Methodist Episcopal Church followed her evangelical activities in England and India; and her rise to deaconess, despite the pronounced opposition of male preachers, is all the more striking against the backdrop of her childhood experience of slavery. In the transport of her own conversion experience, the young Amanda Smith ran to a mirror to see whether her color had changed.

The Christian doctrine presented to slaves by their white masters typically emphasized a regime of submissiveness and docility derived from New Testament scripture. But the slaves' own worship and black preaching of the nineteenth century were more often centered on Old Testament stories of judgment and those passages from scripture that spoke of the liberation of enslaved peoples from bondage. Frances Harper's post-Civil War poem *Moses: A Story of the Nile,* noted above, is the clearest literary example of the archetype that would be repeated throughout African American culture well beyond slavery. The black minister was often a leading figure of the community not just for his ability to guide the community's faith or carry its spiritual burden but also to a degree for his role as an embodiment of surviving African customs or beliefs that remained hidden from, or misunderstood by, observing slaveholders or plantation visitors. The powerful preacher could unify African Americans who may have come from very different African traditions, and like storytellers or musicians, he could preserve cultural materials that might seem pagan or meaningless to Euro-Americans. Even though many plantations and white communities provided regular Sunday services for slaves, slave narrators and historians have shown that covert black services — often employing call and response, more emotive or rhythmically expressive music and dance, or aspects of African spiritualism — were crucial to the life of the slave community and the form of the black church beyond slavery. Black plantation music, for example, carried strong traces of African life in the practice of *juba* patting, or jubilee beating, a rhythmic inheritance of African drumming transferred to hands, voice, fiddle, or new percussive instruments. Partly through the medium of slave religion, African folktales — of animal spirits, trickster figures, powerful ancestors, and the like — survived in transfigured form, as did the complex rhythms of African music, which evolved into new folk practice and combined with the Christianity taught to slaves to form the music of the spiritual.

Black spirituals were a combination of white Protestant music, African influences, and indigenous creation by the slaves themselves, and have been praised worldwide as the foundation of America's most distinctive music. The songs of the slaves had a variety of modes and meanings, some of them encoded with fragmentary African folk forms and beliefs, but one primary theme was the longing for escape from slavery, both physical and spiritual. As Thomas Wentworth Higginson wrote in an 1867 essay on black spirtuals, slaves "could sing themselves, as had their fathers before them, out of the contemplation of their own low estate, into the sublime scenery of the Apocalypse." The first important collection was William Francis Allen's *Slave Songs of the United States* (1867), though over the course of the late nineteenth century, numerous collections of black spirituals appeared, the most famous based on the performances of black choral groups such as those at Fisk University and Hampton Institute. But it would remain for W. E. B. Du Bois, whose classic text *The Souls of Black Folks* (1903) folded the spirituals into the fabric of its argument on behalf of African American culture and civil rights, to make the strongest claim for the "sorrow songs": "The Negro folksong — the rhythmic cry of the slave — stands to-day not simply as the sole American music, but as the most beautiful expression of human experience born this side of the seas . . . the singular spiritual heritage of the nation and the greatest gift of the Negro people." The spirituals and the secular work songs of African American slaves (and the two forms often merged, as would gospel and blues in the next century) are in crucial respects the core of black oral culture. Marked by an inventiveness and improvisation that would remain characteristic of much black American music and literature, the songs celebrate a kind of individual performance that is most valuable in its contribution to a communal heritage constantly augmented as it is passed among groups and generations. Only in musical form can one feel the full power of the spirituals, especially those with the greatest melodic lines such as "Swing Low, Sweet Chariot," "Roll, Jordan, Roll," "Nobody Knows the Trouble I've Seen," and "Sometimes I Feel Like a Motherless Child." As in the case of the oral tradition of the folktales, both communal effort and improvisation are central to the legacy of the African American spirituals. Although the most common songs were those handed down and continually elaborated for the accompaniment of work – field hollers, boat songs, harvest songs, market cries, and songs for marching to work – the more intricate songs typically had a spiritual or allegorical character superimposed upon a narrative about the experience of slavery. For example, "My Lord, What a Mourning" also exists in variants that spell "mourning" as "morning," an index of both the metaphoric complexity and the moral ambivalence in the spirituals' adaptation of Christian eschatology to the circumstance of bondage:

> My Lord, what a mourning,
> My Lord, what a mourning,
> My Lord, what a mourning,
> When the stars begin to fall.
>
> You'll hear the trumpets sound
> To wake the nations underground,
> Looking to my God's right hand
> When the stars begin to fall.

One simple but powerful spiritual recorded by Allen and appearing in many variations thereafter, "Many Thousand Gone," was ascribed to the slaves' reaction to emancipation, yet its common theme of liberation (whether through death, escape, or emancipation), its iteration of slavery's round of labor and punishment, and its commemoration of those who have gone before suggest an earlier origin:

> No more auction block for me,
> No more, no more;
> No more auction block for me,
> Many thousand gone.
>
> No more peck of corn for me,
> No more, no more;
> No more peak of corn for me,
> Many thousand gone.

No more driver's lash for me,
No more, no more;
No more driver's lash for me,
Many thousand gone.

Sometimes the elements of secular work or activity were combined with religious themes, as in the drummer boy's song recorded by Higginson, who served with a black regiment during the war:

O! we're gwine to de Ferry,
   De bell done ringing;
Gwine to de landing,
   De bell done ringing;
Trust, believer,
   De bell done ringing;
Satan's behind me,
   De bell done ringing;
'Tis a misty morning,
   De bell done ringing;
O! de road am sandy,
   De bell done ringing!

Several of the narratives published in the antebellum period (and many collected in later oral testimony) include examples of the slave songs. William Wells Brown, for example, records a song sung by slaves about to be sold further south:

O, gracious Lord! when shall it be,
That we poor souls shall all be free;
Lord, break them slavery powers —
Will you go along with me?
Lord break them slavery powers,
Go sound the jubilee!

Dear Lord, dear Lord, when slavery'll cease,
Then we poor souls will have our peace; —
There's a better day a coming,
Will you go along with me?
There's a better day a coming,
Go sound the jubilee!

Slave songs often employed biblical imagery to prophesy spiritual or actual escape, and double meanings were an integral part of most songs. A British journalist who toured the southern states in 1856 preserved a chanted song, sung with extemporaneous variations, from a South Carolina prayer meeting:

In that morning, true believers,
                    In that morning,
      We will sit aside of Jesus
                    In that morning,

If you should go fore I go,
                    In that morning,
You will sit aside of Jesus
                    In that morning,
True believers, where your tickets
                    In that morning,
Master Jesus got your tickets
                    In that morning.

The most famous song to survive from the slave experience, "Go Down, Moses," reappeared in numerous versions and became an integral part of literary expressions of black life for writers from Frances Harper to William Faulkner. First printed in the *National Anti-Slavery Standard* in 1861, the hymn drew an explicit analogy between the bondage of the Israelites in Egypt and that of blacks in the South:

When Israel was in Egypt's land,
          O let my people go!
Oppressed so hard they could not stand,
          O let my people go!

O go down, Moses
          Away down to Egypt's land,
          And tell King Pharaoh
          To let my people go!

No more shall they in bondage toil,
          O let my people go!
Let them come out of Egypt's spoil,
          O let my people go!

"Go Down, Moses" and songs like it often had a widespread currency throughout the slave community before being written down, sometimes because of their potential to carry covert messages of subversion or resistance. Whether or not one can plausibly argue, as a later commentator would, that "Steal Away" was actually written by Nat Turner, it is an example of the coded call to flight — to freedom in the North or in Canada, or allegorically in a return to Africa — that is latent in a number of the spirituals:

Steal away, steal away,
Steal away to Jesus!
Steal away, steal away home,
I ain't got long to stay here.

My Lord, He calls me,
He calls me by the thunder,
The trumpet sounds within my soul,
I ain't got long to stay here.

Likewise, Sarah Bradford's narrative of Harriet Tubman reveals that she employed songs as coded messages, as in the stanza that was said to indicate to slaves that it was not then safe to attempt an escape:

> Moses go down in Egypt,
> Till ole Pharo' let me go;
> Hadn't been for Adam's fall,
> Shouldn't hab to die at all.

Along with slave narratives, antislavery publications, and magazine articles appearing on into the twentieth century, collections such as William Allen's *Slave Songs of the United States* and numerous subsequent volumes preserved these songs that would become the foundation of modern black culture. The survival of African elements in slave folklore and the creation of a distinct culture were a source of individual and family solace and an incipient form of nationalistic self-preservation that can be reflected in only fragmented ways in the written documents of the antebellum period. Such elements, especially in religious music, offered a means not only of expressing but also of combating the dehumanizing effects of slavery. Yet more than that, they were the first form of a rich and powerful African American artistic expression later to appear in black choral music, blues, and jazz and destined to have profound effects on America's intellectual life and performing arts.

According to Frederick Douglass, the slave songs had afforded him, as a boy, his "first glimmering conceptions of the dehumanizing character of slavery," because they revealed the pain beneath the superficial contentment of the slaves: "the songs of the slaves represent the sorrows, rather than the joys, of his heart; and he is relieved by them, only as an aching heart is relieved by tears." But the slave songs, whether spirituals, folk songs, or work songs, spoke at the same time of strength, dignity, and wit in the face of sorrow. They spoke too of protest, as in the example that Douglass himself offered as "not a bad summary of the palpable injustice and fraud of slavery":

> We raise de wheat,
> Dey gib us corn;
> We bake de bread,
> Dey gib us de cruss;
> We sif de meal,
> Dey gib us de huss;
> We peal de meat,
> Dey gib us de skin,
> And dat's de way
> Dey take us in.

We skim de pot,
Dey gib us the liquor,
And say dat's good enough for the nigger.

Particularly in the revised versions of his famous autobiography, Frederick Douglass (1817–95) offered one of the most various and comprehensive portraits of the lives of African American slaves and of the culture they created. Douglass's fame, however, derives primarily from his vigorous career as an antislavery lecturer and editor and from his continued importance as a spokesman for blacks in political and social matters after the Civil War, when his career included positions as marshal and recorder of deeds for the District of Columbia, as well as U.S. minister to Haiti.

Born into slavery on a large Maryland plantation, Douglass escaped in 1838 to Massachusetts, where he became a follower of William Lloyd Garrison and a brilliant public speaker. After publishing *Narrative of the Life of Frederick Douglass* in 1845, which exposed him as a fugitive, he spent several years as an extremely popular antislavery lecturer in England and Ireland before returning to buy his freedom from his former owner. Douglass broke with Garrison over a number of issues: his unwillingness to accept Garrison's argument that the Constitution was necessarily a proslavery document and that conventional political activities were useless in combating slavery; Garrison's opposition to Douglass's founding of his own antislavery newspaper, the *North Star,* in 1847; and Garrison's probable jealousy of Douglass's success as a speaker and a writer. As Douglass wrote in the revised version of his narrative, *My Bondage and My Freedom* (1855), he quickly had begun to resent the limited role that Garrison and others expected him to play at antislavery lectures: "I was generally introduced as a '*chattel*' – a '*thing*' – a piece of southern '*property*' – the chairman assuring the audience that *it* could speak." He was told to keep "a *little* of the plantation" in his speech and to tell his story without elaboration, leaving the philosophy to the white speakers like Garrison, who would then take Douglass as their "text" for commentary. As his writings imply, Douglass not only found this stifling but also considered it a new form of enslavement, in its own way as harsh as the physical abuse he had escaped in the South.

Despite Douglass's more forcefully articulated stance of independence in *My Bondage and My Freedom,* the central themes of his whole career are present in the 1845 *Narrative,* and some modern critics have found it to be the most authentic of Douglass's writings because it was the closest to his firsthand experience of slavery. Obvious from the outset is Douglass's splendid control of his language, in part a self-conscious reflection on the book's recurring idea of literacy as the key to freedom. Forbidden by his master to continue learning to read, for example, Douglass recalls: "It was a new and special revelation, explaining dark and mysterious things, with which my youthful understanding had struggled, but struggled in vain. I now understand what had been to me a most perplexing difficulty — to wit, the white man's power to enslave the black man. It was a grand achievement, and I prized it highly. From that moment, I understood the pathway from slavery to freedom." More so than many other slave narrators, Douglass was aware of his ability and his need to create a paradigmatic story. His narrative stands out above others because in addition to telling his own life story, it offers an almost mythic embodiment of the acts of speech and self-making denied by law to slaves. Douglass's *Narrative* sums up the purpose of testimony by former slaves, namely, to dramatize the spiritual survival of the black family and community within the cauldron of plantation slavery and to explore the means by which power and dehumanization were united in slavery to prohibit African Americans from gaining control of those cultural signs that lend full dignity to life. Although they indicate a degree of conflict between the oral tradition of black folk life and the dominant culture, speaking and writing are both modes of discovery in the *Narrative*. As avenues to "mastery" of himself, they allow him to fashion an "autobiography" in which the freed slave is in effect created as a man in the act of narration, whether before an audience or in print.

Even though it lacks some of the direct simplicity of the earlier *Narrative, My Bondage and My Freedom* bridges the two halves of Douglass's life, provides much more detail about his life in the North, and amplifies certain episodes in his life as a slave. It is not the simple story that his white advisers asked him to state on the lecture platform but an energetic, complex antislavery polemic that inquires deeply into the meaning of American freedom and the meaning of America for slaves and free blacks. The revisions constitute the first of several recastings of his life that appear in Douglass's thought and work, and they represent an extension of the lesson that lies at the heart of his life's story, as it does those of many of the escaped slaves — that literacy is the primary means to power. Just as the language of the "self-made man" comes to dominate his autobiographical writing in the postwar period, so in *My Bondage and My Freedom* the language of revolution and liberty is prominent. Both in the autobiography and in his 1853 short story "The Heroic Slave," which was based on a revolt aboard the slave ship *Creole* led by the slave Madison Washington, Douglass appropriated the ideals of democratic revolution to the cause of the black slave. As Madison Washington, the *black* Virginia patriot, says, "we have done that which you applaud your fathers for doing, and if we are murderers, *so were they*."

One of his most famous addresses, a speech on the meaning of the Fourth of July for blacks, invoked revolutionary rights but at the same time distanced the black man from the legacy of the white fathers. This is "the birthday of your National Independence, and of your political freedom," Douglass told his largely white Rochester audience in 1852. "This, to you, is what the Passover was to the emancipated people of God." For the American slave, Douglass charged, the Fourth of July was a sham and a mockery, "a thin veil to cover up crimes which would disgrace a nation of savages." Renouncing Garrisonian nonviolence, Douglass by the 1850s believed armed slave insurrection a just answer to black bondage. Whereas the proslavery arguments of Dew and others held that slaves would be "parricides" instead of "patriots," Douglass argued that they could be both at once. Or, as he wrote in *My Bondage and My Freedom,* the slaveholder every day violates the "just and inalienable rights of man" and thereby is "silently whetting the knife of vengeance for his own throat. He never lisps a syllable in commendation of the fathers of this republic, nor denounces any attempted oppression of himself, without inviting the knife to his own throat, and asserting the rights of rebellion for his own slaves."

Both "The Heroic Slave" and the reconceived argument for violent rebellion that came to mark Douglass's work in the 1850s can be understood, moreover, as a response to the widely popular example of Stowe's Uncle Tom. Douglass had from the outset of his career been skeptical of the church's commitment to abolitionism, and he wrote in a blistering appendix to the 1845 *Narrative:* "Revivals of religion and revivals in the slave-trade go hand in hand together. . . . The clanking of fetters and the rattling of chains in the prison, and the pious psalm and solemn prayer in church, may be heard at the same time. The dealers in the bodies and souls of men erect their stand in the presence of the pulpit, and they mutually help each other." After Douglass had renounced the pacifist principles of Garrison and called for violent resistance by slaves, the central incident in his own life as a slave, his fight with the slavebreaker Covey, was heightened in the revised autobiography in order to provide a contrast to Uncle Tom's capitulation to Legree:

I was a changed being after that fight. I was *nothing* before; I WAS A MAN NOW. It recalled to life my crushed self-respect and my self-confidence, and inspired me with renewed determination to be A FREEMAN. . . . He only can understand the effect of this combat on my spirit, who has himself incurred something, hazarded something, in repelling the unjust and cruel aggressions of a tyrant. . . . It was a resurrection from the dark and pestiferous tomb of slavery, to the heaven of comparative freedom. . . . I had reached the point where I was *not afraid to die.* This spirit made me a freeman in *fact,* while I remained a slave in *form.* When a slave cannot be flogged he is more than half free. . . . While slaves prefer their lives, with flogging, to instant death, they will always find Christians enough, like unto Covey, to accommodate that preference.

Douglass's response to Stowe can be judged as well in his recasting of his attack on the corruption of the family under slavery. When he remarks that "scenes of sacred tenderness, around the deathbed, never forgotten, and which often arrest the vicious and confirm the virtuous during life, must be looked for among the free," Douglass suggests the limitations of Stowe's vision even as he gives further ammunition to her attack on the destruction of the slave family. The issues of family and revolution are joined in Douglass's characteristic invocation of the revolutionary "fathers" that he must substitute for the white master—father he never knew and the unacceptable surrogates like his second master Hugh Auld or later Garrison. In Douglass's rhetoric the family was destroyed by slavery, but if reconstituted as part of the ideal democratic state, it could also become a weapon against slavery.

Douglass's lectures often burlesqued the purported paternalism of slavery and held up the slave codes themselves in counterpoint. He could do so all the more effectively because he knew, as his farewell speech in England had put it, that "the whip, the chain, the gag, the thumb-screw, the blood-hound, the stocks, and all the other bloody paraphernalia of the slave system are indispensably necessary to the relation of master and slave. The slave must be subjected, or he ceases to be a slave." In *My Bondage and My Freedom* the greater attention allotted to incidents of whipping is not simply a matter of gothic ornamentation but becomes a symbol of Douglass's more precisely characterized portrait of the institution of slavery. One need not consent to the much debated thesis that, in its dehumanization of slaves and inducement in them of an imitative pattern of behavioral bondage, the plantation resembled the concentration camp, the prison, or other "total institutions" in order to be struck by Douglass's new account of Colonel Lloyd's immense plantation in *My Bondage and My Freedom*. He not only gives a much fuller picture of slave life in the revised account, but the greater detail and the emphasis on the plantation's self-sufficient, dark seclusion, maintained by diverse labor and transbay trade on Lloyd's own vessels, create of this deceptively abundant, "Eden-like" garden world a veritable heart of darkness. Both the size of Lloyd's plantation and his prominent position as Maryland's three-time governor and two-time senator allow Douglass to expand his own story into a national archetype. In this era of reform movements and utopian communal projects, the plantation (in the proslavery argument) posed as a pastoral asylum in which state control and paternal coersion alike worked to the slave's benefit but did so by imprisoning him in a corrupt "family," one he might, like Douglass, belong to by blood but not by law.

Douglass's great success with the *North Star* (he changed its name to *Frederick Douglass's Paper* in 1851) was crucial to the expansion of his thought and of his capacity to reach a large audience. It made him to a great extent independent of Garrison and other white abolitionists and may be said to have created in him a Benjamin Franklin-like character of self-promotion and improvement, a side of his mature personality that is most evident in the later version of his autobiography, *Life and Times of Frederick Douglass* (published in 1881 and revised yet again in 1892). Douglass encouraged the participation of women in the antislavery movement and advocated their suffrage rights (the motto of *North Star* was "Right is of no sex — Truth is of no color"), and his campaign both before and after the war is perhaps more properly understood as one of human rights rather than simply black rights. His many volumes of speeches and editorial writings constitute probably the most complete social and political record left by any one individual of the struggle for black freedom in the nineteenth century. Lincoln sought Douglass's advice on several occasions, though the president moved more slowly on the issues of black troops and emancipation than Douglass would have liked. The distance between the two men, as well as the figurative status of blacks in the postwar period, is summed up in Douglass's remarks at the dedication of the Freedman's Lincoln Monument in 1876. Grant and his cabinet, the Supreme Court justices, and other dignitaries were in attendance as Douglass declared that "when the foul reproach of ingratitude is hurled at us, and it is attempted to scourge us beyond the range of human brotherhood, we may calmly point to the monument we have this day erected to the memory of Abraham Lincoln." But this concluding conciliatory apostrophe suspended a tone more critical of Lincoln's policies that marked much of his address. Truth compelled him to admit, he said, that Lincoln, in his habits and prejudices, "was a white man." "You," Douglass addressed his mostly white audience, "are the children of Abraham Lincoln. We are at best only his stepchildren; children by adoption, children by the forces of circumstance and necessity."

Douglass's public services as marshal for the District of Columbia and later as consul general to Haiti were in part political rewards for his allegiance to the Republican Party. But such roles indicated as well that Douglass was recognized beyond the circle of white antebellum figures whose paternalism he had found to be so binding. Although it recorded the failure of Reconstruction and the escalating degradation of black civil rights in the last decades of the century, his *Life and Times* emphasized black economic success and cultural achievement through "self-reliance, self-respect, industry, perseverance, and economy." Given this emphasis, it is hardly a surprise that Booker T. Washington would consider himself Douglass's logical heir. During these years of his life, as well as earlier, however, Douglass's autobiographical self-presentation does not tell the whole story. The 1892 *Life and Times* concluded by declaring that the consulship in Haiti and Douglass's subsequent appointment to represent Haiti at the World's Columbian Exposition of 1893 in Chicago were "the crowning honors to my long career and a fitting and happy close to my whole public life," but the true lesson of Douglass's appearance at the exposition must be found elsewhere. Except for exhibits devoted to African (not African American) life, blacks were excluded from any official role in the exposition. As Douglass wrote in his introduction to a pamphlet by black Americans protesting this cultural ignorance and injustice, "when it is asked why we are excluded from the World's Columbian Exposition, the answer is Slavery." Whereas Lincoln himself and his generation overcame the burden of the Founding Fathers and the problem of slavery, Douglass and his generation continued to face the harsh legacy of enslavement. Race prejudice and violence had not been destroyed, but neither had African American culture. By the end of Douglass's career, when the mantle of leadership had passed to Washington, Du Bois, Ida B. Wells, and others, black literature and art were on the verge of an extraordinary renaissance, one that remained rooted in the oral culture, poetry, fiction, song, and autobiography of antebellum African American slave life.

THE TRANSCENDENTALISTS

Barbara L. Packer

UNITARIAN BEGINNINGS

HEN RALPH WALDO EMERSON, in an introduction to a lecture series entitled "The Present Age" (1839–40), tried to explain the origins of the movement everyone was calling "transcendentalism," he found himself describing a cluster of discontents. The young people who form "the party of the Future" are, he admitted, "stiff, heady, and rebellious" and united only by the ferocity of their rejections: "They hate tolls, taxes, turnpikes, banks, hierarchies, governors, yea, almost laws. They have a neck of unspeakable tenderness; it winces at a hair." The belief that obsesses and propels them – *that the individual is the world* – "is such a sword as was never drawn before. It divides and detaches bone and marrow, soul and body, yea, almost the man from himself." Even the groups these young people join are devoted to the enlargement of the individual: "The association of the time is accidental and momentary; the detachment is intrinsic and progressive."

How had such insistence on the centrality of the individual arisen, and what were its effects? New Englanders had always been remarkable for the chilliness of their temperament, yet the New England Protestantism of an earlier age still vested its hopes in forms that were practically or imaginatively social: the family, the town meeting, the heavenly host, the City of God. And the young people Emerson spoke of yearn for love as much as they demand independence. In his 1841 lecture "The Transcendentalist," he describes them with sympathy: "These persons are not by nature melancholy, sour, and unsocial, – they have even more than others a great wish to be loved. Like the young Mozart, they are ready to cry ten times a day, 'But are you sure you love me?' "

Yet somehow their impulse to repel outweighs their impulse to associate. "They are lonely; the spirit of their writing and conversation is lonely; they repel influences; they shun general society; they incline to shut themselves in their chamber in the house, to live in the country rather than in town, and to find their tasks and amusements in solitude." Even so, Emerson refuses to dismiss his small brigade of self-tormentors as useless or pitiful. The very extravagance of the demand they make on human nature will yet lead their unthinking countrymen out of the wilderness of skepticism and greed in which all wander. "Their heart is the ark in which the fire is concealed, which shall burn in a broader and universal flame."

The contrast between this ardency and the amiable quiet of Bostonians thirty years earlier was striking. When Emerson looked over the writings left by his father, William Emerson (1769–1811), he found nothing beyond "candor & taste." His father's generation now seemed provincial and self-effacing in its literary ambitions. The literary society William Emerson had helped organize in 1805, the Anthology Club, was formed to publish a journal of American belles lettres. The *Monthly Anthology and Boston Review* contained a useful monthly catalogue of books published in America, and its reviews were vigorous. But the editors had difficulty finding enough original prose or poetry to fill the magazine or enough subscribers to keep it alive. It ceased publication a few months after William Emerson died in 1811.

As for his father's religion, the liberal wing of New England Congregationalism eventually known as Unitarianism, Emerson's dissatisfaction with it was slower to crystallize. During his boyhood, the men who led the revolt against the Calvinist doctrine of total depravity seemed brave to him. A Christ who ennobled through his example rather than atoned through his bloody sacrifice and a God who encouraged human striving after perfection rather than a humiliating dependence upon his inscrutable will were advances in the history of spirituality that marked Christianity's emergence from superstition. Unitarianism held out the promise of a Christianity enlightened enough to be tolerant and otherworldly enough to inspire and console. Even the civility of Unitarian discourse, which the younger generation eventually came to find wearying, had an ideological function in its own day, marking as it did a deliberate refusal to participate in the theological disputes that had split Congregationalism in the early decades of the century. The editors of the *Monthly Anthology* were firm in their warning to potential contributors: "No Religious controversy."

Visitors to Boston were bemused and at times exasperated by this parade of tolerance. A Presbyterian named Ashbel Green attended a meeting of the Boston Association of Ministers in 1791 and found a perfect jumble of theological opinions: He counted Calvinists, Arians, Arminians, and at least one Socinian. Partly because of this diversity very little religious discussion actually took place at the meeting, and Green thought it would be much healthier if the different parties were to go their separate ways. Yet he knew that his belief that the association ought to separate along doctrinal lines "would be esteemed by them as the effect of bigotry and narrowness of mind, and so they will meet and shake hands, and talk of politics and science, and laugh, and eat raisons and apples, and drink wine and tea, and go about their business."

Ten years later, the situation had hardly changed. Another visiting Presbyterian, Dr. Archibald Alexander, noted that "at that time all controversy was proscribed by the liberal party." Despite the variety of opinions and the growing gap between the most liberal and the most orthodox, there was as yet "no public line of demarcation among the clergy. One might learn with ease what each man believed, or rather did not believe, for few positive opinions were expressed by the liberal party." Alexander's comment suggests that the liberals were already distinguished more by what they denied than by what they believed — at least in the eyes of their opponents.

Alexander thought that he detected policy in this refusal to debate doctrinal differences. Under the banner of "tolerance" the liberals were gradually taking over the important offices of Harvard College, where "all the young men of talents" were liberal in sentiment and read with avidity the tracts and books that prominent liberal patrons presented to the library. This quiet liberal infiltration would soon be replaced by open war. When the Reverend David Tappan, a moderate Calvinist who occupied the important position of professor of divinity at Harvard, died in the fall of 1803, liberals saw an opportunity to confirm their growing domination of the college. President Joseph Willard, unable to find an orthodox candidate of sufficient stature to fill the position and unwilling to appoint the liberal candidate, Dr. Henry Ware, stalled for a year. Then Willard too suddenly died. Now the Fellows of the Harvard Corporation were faced with the task of choosing both a new president and a new Hollis Professor.

The six-member board was split more or less evenly between liberals and orthodox, but the stalemate that resulted was not entirely ideological. As in most academic disputes about appointments, vanity, resentment, and personal ambition also played a part in the forging of alliances. The Corporation met several times during the closing months of 1804 but was unable to agree on a candidate or accept a compromise. Finally, in February 1805, one of the orthodox Fellows switched his vote, and Henry Ware, the liberal candidate, was appointed. But Harvard's Board of Overseers still had to concur in the appointment. In the weeks between the Corporation meeting and the meeting of the Overseers one of the defeated orthodox Corporation Fellows, Eliphalet Pearson, prepared a highly colored account of the controversy in a last-ditch attempt to defeat Ware's appointment. Pearson's diatribe was never published — the meeting of the Overseers took place sooner than he expected, and they voted in favor of Ware — but the language of his account suggests the political terms in which the theological debate was conducted.

Harvard's theological liberals, like their orthodox opponents, were staunch Federalists, still smarting from their defeat at the hands of Jefferson's Democrats. But Pearson insinuated that the liberals, those "warmly attached to what they call *rational* Christianity, and flattering themselves that this part of the country was nearly ripe for a revolution in religion," were really Jeffersonian sympathizers in disguise, Jacobins in sheep's clothing. "Much is said about *liberality* & *charity*. Charming words, syren sounds, like *liberty* & *equality* on other tongues. God in mercy grant that they may not prove equally *delusive* & *fatal*." Pearson excoriated the liberals for engaging in just those political tactics that they had long professed to abhor. Even the liberals must agree that these tactics, when used in the recent federal elections, had "subverted the federal government." "Can Federalists then adopt a policy and make use of weapons in the cause of *religion*, which they so justly brand with infamy in the cause of politics? *O tempora! O mores!*"

It is doubtful that Pearson could have succeeded in getting his opponents to see themselves as Jacobins even if he had published his account before they voted. If anything, the theological liberals tended to be both wealthier and more conservative politically than the orthodox. Whereas few would have gone as far as the Harvard student Andrews Norton (1786–1853), who wrote his father that he would like to replace the assertion "All men are created equal" in the Declaration of Independence with "Most men are fit for nothing but to be governed," those Boston merchants and professionals who patronized the liberal clergy were in little danger of political radicalism. Indeed, when a similar dispute split the congregation in nearby Charlestown into old (orthodox) and new (liberal) churches, the members of "respectability, culture, and weight of influence in the town" were the ones who left the old church for the new. A candidate for the pulpit of the new church noted with satisfaction that his prospective congregation was "respectable in numbers and constantly increasing and in wealth is undoubtedly the first in the town." Indeed, at the recent Thanksgiving Day contribution for relief of the poor they had contributed one hundred and five dollars, whereas the orthodox had managed to collect only eighty-eight dollars.

This association between wealth and religious liberalism naturally invited the taunts of the orthodox and would later invite the scorn of the Transcendentalists. But the liberals could reply, and did reply, that their prosperity came from the same strenuous effort at self-culture that formed so large a part of their ethical system. To worship, as the orthodox did, a God who had predestined the greater part of the human race to eternal damnation by a decree promulgated before the foundation of the earth and to hope to be rescued from that damnation only by an influx of grace as unmerited as it was irresistible were beliefs seen by the liberals to be pernicious to the character and dangerous to the Republic. The great liberal preacher William Ellery Channing (1780–1842) argued that Calvinist doctrines of predestination all tend "strongly to pervert the moral faculty, to form a gloomy, forbidding, and servile religion, and lead men to substitute censoriousness, bitterness, and persecution, for a tender and impartial charity" ("Unitarian Christianity," 1819). In an 1820 essay entitled "The Moral Argument Against Calvinism," he was even blunter: "Calvinism owes its perpetuity to the influence of fear in palsying the moral nature."

The conflict between liberals and conservatives within New England Congregationalism, growing sharper throughout the eighteenth century, broke out into open warfare after the controversy at Harvard over Ware's appointment. The friendly custom Congregational ministers had of exchanging pulpits with one another (it relieved them of the duty of writing two sermons every Sunday and gave their parishioners a chance to hear a variety of opinions) began to break down as orthodox ministers refused to exchange with liberal ones. Parishioners naturally resented being deprived of something they regarded as their right, and in some cases they even went to court to force their ministers either to comply with the old custom or else to resign their parishes. Churches split, families quarreled, and one disgruntled member of Harvard's Board of Overseers became convinced that it was necessary to found an orthodox seminary (the Andover Theological Seminary) to serve as counterweight to the now hopelessly liberal Harvard. Things got so bad, Channing complained, that orthodox ministers denounced liberal Christianity as "the last and most perfect invention of Satan, the consummation of his blasphemies, the most cunning weapon ever forged in the fires of hell" ("Unitarian Christianity Most Favorable to Piety," 1826).

For a time the liberals tried to resist the term of opprobrium the orthodox fastened upon them – "Unitarian" – partly because they disliked doctrinal controversy and partly out of a hope that a final rupture within New England Congregationalism could be prevented and peace restored. As a French traveler to Boston in 1791 admiringly noted: "The ministers rarely speak dogmas: universal tolerance, the child of American independence, has banished the preaching of dogmas, which always leads to discussions and quarrels. . . . The ministers of different sects live in such harmony that they supply each other's places when any one is detained from his pulpit." But the orthodox were intransigent, and the liberals finally adopted "Unitarian," using the term with defiance and pride. Channing included the word in a whole series of sermon titles and magazine essays during the second decade of the nineteenth century. And in his famous sermon "Unitarian Christianity" (celebrating the ordination of Jared Sparks in Baltimore in 1819) Channing proclaimed Unitarianism the only form of Christianity adapted to the progressive improvement of mankind:

Our earnest prayer to God is, that he will overturn, and overturn, and overturn the strongholds of spiritual usurpation, until he shall come, whose right it is to rule the minds of men; that the conspiracy of ages against the liberty of Christians may be brought to an end; that the servile assent, so long yielded to human creeds, may give place to honest and devout inquiry into the Scriptures; and that Christianity, thus purified from error, may put forth its almighty energy, and prove itself, by its ennobling influence on the mind, to be indeed "the power of God unto salvation."

Channing's sermon so exhilarated Andrews Norton that he was inspired to write in his diary a threat as militant as anything that might be thundered by the Calvinists: "Orthodoxy must be broken down. *Babylon est delenda.*" Norton was admittedly the most pugnacious of the Unitarians, and it would be difficult to match his ferocious tone elsewhere in the liberal camp. Still, his exultation is an important clue to the spirit of the Unitarian movement. The Unitarians of Channing's generation saw themselves as heirs to the reforming zeal that had inspired the earliest Protestants; the "Babylon" they sought to destroy was the Calvinism that even as it decayed still tried to direct worship toward a God who tortured his own Son in order to ransom from punishment a tiny fraction of the souls he had created. In place of this "servile" religion, the Unitarians offered a "manly" reverence toward a Father who loved and a Son who came to save sinners from *sin* rather than from *punishment.* This benevolent deity offered men and women the chance to achieve salvation through a rigorous and continuous effort of self-culture. So pronounced was the Unitarian distrust of sudden conversion experiences that Channing declared himself unable to believe that the English poet John Milton had meant what he had said when he argued that the Holy Spirit gives us "immediate illumination" to read the Scriptures. Such hope for immediate insight "disparages and discourages our faculties, and produces inaction of mind," leading us to think we will receive in a "sudden flash from Heaven" the truths we should seek by the right use of our own powers ("Remarks on the Character and Writings of John Milton," 1826).

For preaching their faith the Unitarians had heard themselves vilified and had emerged triumphant, at least in their own eyes. If Unitarianism lacked the wide popular appeal of the evangelical movements, its influence during the 1820s seemed to be growing in the cities among the powerful and well-educated; congregations were formed in New York, Philadelphia, and Baltimore. Unitarians could feel proud that they had achieved their gains without appealing to either superstition or ignorant fears. In 1882 Joseph Henry Allen, a lecturer in ecclesiastical history at the Harvard Divinity School, reminded his Harvard audience that the two points most strongly marked in the history of the Unitarian movement were "first, that it was a movement of

Reason in sympathy with the scientific spirit; and second, that it was a movement of Right, in sympathy with the revolutionary spirit." Whether the Unitarians were really so friendly to either the scientific or the revolutionary spirit may perhaps be doubted, but they saw themselves in this way – as a vanguard, as a band bravely advancing on chaos and the dark.

Revolution and science, however, make uncomfortable bedfellows for a religion that wished to remain grounded in biblical revelation and, at the same time, loyal to an empiricism hostile to violations of natural law. How difficult it could be to keep revelation and reason together is suggested by a delicious remark Allen attributes to Channing: "He said we did not know enough about the nature of matter to criticise the story of the Ascension."

Channing's puzzlement about how the Ascension fit into a Newtonian universe and his willingness to suspend judgment in the face of scriptural authority resemble the modesty of the philosopher and biblical critic he revered, John Locke (1632–1704). In the *Essay Concerning Human Understanding* (1690) Locke carefully marks the limits of human knowledge. We can know intuitively only those truths that belong to deductive logic – the axioms of geometry, say, or the principle of noncontradiction in logic. All other propositions are based on information received through the senses, that is, from experience. Our assurance that iron will not float on water is essentially a form of probabilistic reasoning, which can produce only "confidence," not absolute certainty. Because we have never seen iron float in the past, we are justified in assuming that it will not float in the future.

When propositions concern things beyond the reach of the senses – the existence of angels, the resurrection of the dead – we can learn of them only through *revelation*. But we must not accept as divine revelation every testament promulgated by a visionary, "else we shall expose ourselves to all the extravagancy of enthusiasm, and the error of wrong principles" (*Essay* 4, 16.14). "To know that any revelation is from God, it is necessary to know that the messenger that delivers it is sent from God, and that cannot be known but by some credential given by God himself" (*A Discourse of Miracles*, 1702). The miracles of the Old and New Testaments constitute such credentials. They are events perceivable by the senses and hence verifiable by witnesses; at the same time, they are violations of the normal laws of nature and hence testify to a power superior to nature. Locke points out that it is no sign of skepticism to demand miraculous proofs. "Gideon was sent by an angel to deliver Israel from the Midianites, and yet he desired a sign to convince him that his commission was from God" (*Essay* 4, 19.15). Gideon is in fact Locke's exemplary reasoner. There is something patient and Newtonian about Gideon's experiments with the fleece in the sixth chapter of

Judges, where he asks God to give him a sign first by drenching with dew a fleece laid on the threshing floor while keeping the floor itself dry, and then, the next night, asks for a dry fleece and a wet floor.

Both in the *Essay* and in the later *Discourse of Miracles* Locke remains determined to deny the claims of religious "enthusiasts" who think they can perceive truth directly. He dismisses them contemptuously as partisans "of illumination without search, of certainty without proof." He argues that "light, true light, is or can be nothing but the evidence of the truth of any proposition; and if it be not a self-evident proposition, all the light it has, or can have, is from the clearness and validity of those proofs upon which it is received" (*Essay* 4, 19.13). He does not flinch from the obvious consequences of his opinions and goes out of his way in the *Discourse of Miracles* to consider a case in which violations of natural law were produced by sorcery:

The producing of serpents, blood, and frogs, by the Egyptian sorcerer and by Moses, could not to the spectators but appear equally miraculous, which of the pretenders then had their mission from God; and the truth on their side could not have been determined if the matter had rested there. But when Moses' serpent ate up theirs, when he produced lice which they could not, the decision was easy.

An empiricism so robust was difficult for most people to sustain without flinching, and many of Locke's contemporaries objected to the way he had in effect substituted an act of reasoning upon probabilities for true religious faith and limited our knowledge to the Jesus of history rather than the Jesus of faith. But Locke's experience of the bitter sectarian warfare that divided England during his lifetime had left him distrustful of anyone's claim to possess a truth not verifiable by the normal operations of intellect. To the fourth edition of the *Essay Concerning Human Understanding* (1700) he added a new chapter called "Enthusiasm." In this chapter he pauses to consider the "third ground of assent," which for some people takes the place of faith – "*enthusiasm:* which, laying by reason, would set up revelation without it."

Enthusiasm is a kind of shortcut by which people seek to avoid the laborious processes of reasoning or of judging the credibility of testimony.

In all ages, men in whom melancholy has mixed with devotion, or whose conceit of themselves has raised them into an opinion or a greater familiarity with God, and a nearer admittance to his favor than is afforded to others, have often flattered themselves with a persuasion of an immediate intercourse with the Deity, and frequent communications from the Divine Spirit. (*Essay* 4, 19.5)

These "conceits of a warmed or overweening brain," once indulged, are almost impossible to dislodge.

Reason is lost upon them, they are above it: they see the light infused into their understandings, and cannot be mistaken; it is clear and visible there, like the light of bright evidence: they feel the hand of God moving them within, and the impulses of the Spirit, and cannot be mistaken in what they feel. (*Essay* 4, 19.8)

This is the way of talking of these men; they are sure, because they are sure; and their persuasions are right, because they are strong in them. (*Essay* 4, 19.9)

To make the strength of one's persuasion the test of whether or not a revelation can claim to be divine leaves us reasoning in circles. Enthusiasts say, "*It is a revelation, because they firmly believe it; and they believe it, because it is a revelation.*" But if a firm persuasion of the truth of a doctrine guarantees its truth, "How come . . . the intractable zealots in different and opposite parties?" A lifetime of anger against the bigotry of enthusiasts is condensed into Locke's reminder that "St. Paul himself believed he did right well, and that he had a call to it, when he persecuted the Christians, whom he confidently thought in the wrong: but yet it was he, and not they, who were mistaken" (*Essay* 4, 19.11–12). Miracles provide us with an escape from the blindness of enthusiasm, for they mark with sensible proofs those few and simple doctrines God has deemed necessary for salvation.

The connection Locke establishes between empiricism, belief in biblical miracles, and freedom from religious fanaticism made his philosophy powerfully appealing to the liberal theologians of New England. They thought they could detect the dangerous spirit of "enthusiasm" in every crisis of New England's history, from the Antinomian Crisis of 1636–8 through the Great Awakening of the 1740s to the evangelical revivals of their own day. As an antidote to such excesses they offered the tolerant, rational patience of Locke, whose works formed a central part of the Harvard curriculum. In 1808 the precocious student Edward Everett (1794–1865) found that the easiest way for him to get through the required weekly recitations on Locke's *Essay* was to commit the whole text to memory.

I recollect particularly on one occasion of the review on Thursday afternoon that I was called upon to recite early and I went on repeating word for word, and paragraph after paragraph, and finally, not being stopped by our pleased tutor, page after page, till I finally went through in that way the greater part of the eleven recitations of the week.

Yet in the century since Locke's death his particular synthesis had come under attack from several directions, and the version of his philosophy that still dominated Harvard in the early nineteenth century bore the scars of the battles that had been waged to defend it. The most powerful challenge came from David Hume (1711–76). Whereas Locke argues that miraculous events testify to the truth of the doctrine they accompany, Hume points out that one cannot accept miracles as "credentials" before deciding whether the reports of the miracles are themselves credible. True, we must accept many facts on testimony, but our belief in testimony alters with our sense of the inherent probability of the events it relates. In the famous tenth section of his *Enquiry Concerning Human Understanding* (1748), entitled "Of Miracles," Hume subjects the very idea of belief upon testimony to withering scrutiny. "The reason why we place any credit in witnesses and historians, is not derived from any connexion, which we perceive *a priori*, between testimony and reality, but because we are accustomed to find a conformity between them." When the fact testified to is "such a one as has seldom fallen under our observation" what results is not conviction but mental strife:

The very same principle of experience, which give us a certain degree of assurance in the testimony of witnesses, gives us also, in this case, another degree of assurance against the fact, which they endeavor to establish; from which contradiction there necessarily arises a counterpoize, and mutual destruction of belief and authority.

Hume points out that we do not call an event "miraculous" unless it is "a violation of the laws of nature." But the laws of nature are drawn from uniform experience, which in itself constitutes "a direct and full *proof*, from the nature of the fact, against the existence of any miracle." This proof from uniform experience could only be destroyed by "an opposite proof, which is superior." But believers in miracles can offer only the testimony of witnesses against the strong proof of natural law, and testimony is a weak form of proof. The claim that a miraculous event has been witnessed must always be weighed against our suspicions that the testifiers are gullible, superstitious, or venal.

When anyone tells me, that he saw a dead man restored to life, I immediately consider with myself, whether it be more probable, that this man should either deceive or be deceived, or that the fact, which he relates, should really have happened. . . . If the falsehood of his testimony would be more miraculous, than the event which he relates; then, and not till then, can he pretend to command my belief or opinion.

The theologians who shaped New England Unitarianism argued against such skepticism in various ways (though Emerson was later to suspect that the repeated attempts to confute Hume proved only that Hume had never been confuted). Some, like Andrews Norton, devoted themselves to tipping the scales of probability in favor of testimony rather than experience, attempting to gather historical evidence that the Gospels were genuine in hopes of proving that the events narrated in them really happened as described. Others, like Channing, attacked Hume's dismissal of all miracle stories by arguing that the strikingly original character of Jesus and of the religion he preached testifies to the existence of the very supernatural order whose existence Hume was taken to have denied. "That a religion, carrying in itself such marks of divinity, and so inexplicable on human principles, should receive outward confirmations from Omnipotence, is not surprising. The extraordinary character of the religion accords with and seems to demand extraordinary interpositions in its behalf" ("The Evidences of Revealed Religion," 1821). An opponent might point out that Channing has slipped back into the circularity that Locke condemned in the enthusiasts: We recognize in Jesus' sayings a divinity that convinces us that the miracles ascribed to him could have happened.

How do we recognize the teachings of Jesus as divine in origin? Locke had refused to allow the fragmentation of reason into any subsidiary faculties; we must judge the truths of religion with the same faculty we use to sift any other kind of evidence, and all evidence is ultimately from the senses. But Locke's philosophy was not the only explanation available of the mechanisms of understanding. Two traditions in British philosophy, one older than Locke, one younger, had attempted to reestablish the objectivity of moral distinctions in a material universe that seemed to have no room for them. One group of seventeenth-century English theologians known as the Cambridge Platonists urged a return to an ontology that treated moral truths as objectively real. Ralph Cudworth (1617–88), a philosopher much admired by the New England Unitarians for his mixture of spiritual generosity and metaphysical intensity, argued that the principles by which we organize sense experience and recognize moral truths are innate, and that the laws they perceive in the moral and physical universes are immutable. God himself cannot violate the moral law, which is as much a part of the nature of things as is the law of gravitation. The study of nature penetrated through appearances to natural law, which was moral because the universe itself was moral throughout its structure.

Interest in the Cambridge Platonists was part of a general reassessment of seventeenth-century English culture taking place in Britain and America during the early decades of the nineteenth century. In his influential 1826 essay on the genius and character of Milton, Channing praised the stimulating difficulty of Milton's periodic prose; he dismissed Joseph Addison as "easy reading" in the same passage — a significant revolution in taste, because Addison's writing had always been admired in America as a model of perspicuity and grace. Samuel Taylor Coleridge's philosophical handbook *Aids to Reflection* (1825), which helped to spark the Transcendentalist movement when it was published in an American edition in 1829, included copious quotations from the "elder divines" of the English church, who were held up to admiration for both the spiritual intensity they express and the undisciplined richness of their prose.

The moral realism of the Cambridge Platonists was still wedded to an idealistic ontology that was difficult to sustain before the methodological revolution effected by Locke, a revolution as important to the Unitarians as was belief in the existence of moral absolutes. The problem was hardly trivial, for Unitarianism insisted that it was morally superior to the Calvinism it superseded. If all ideas are derived from sensation and reflection, it is difficult on the face to explain where we get our ideas of moral good and moral evil. Were such ideas (as skeptics like Thomas Hobbes and Bernard de Mandeville had argued) merely projections onto the sensible universe of our own fears and desires?

The philosopher Francis Hutcheson (1694–1746) attempted to find some way of grounding moral principles in human nature itself. His *Inquiry into the Original of Our Ideas of Beauty and Virtue* (1725) takes as its target Mandeville's attempt in *The Fable of the Bees* (1705) to unmask all moral virtues as hypocritical disguises for self-preservation or self-interest. Hutcheson's argument against such cynicism is that we all readily understand the difference between actions prompted by self-interest and those prompted by virtue. A "moral sense" must be therefore as much a part of our human equipment as the physical senses of sight and hearing.

Hutcheson points out that all imaginative literature implies the existence of a moral sense in the observers because self-interest could hardly prompt sympathy with a character known to be fictive. "If there is no moral Sense, which makes rational Actions appear Beautiful, or Deform'd; if all Approbation be from the Interest of the Approver, *What's* HECUBA *to us, or we to* HECUBA?" Even if we are made aware of this moral sense chiefly through the sentiments of approbation or distaste it provokes in us, the moral sense is more than an emotion. Its ultimate function is cognitive and, like the bodily senses, it operates more swiftly and surely to apprehend the moral qualities of actions than the reasoning process can. The same deity who has endowed us with bodily senses acute enough to preserve our lives has also instilled in us a moral sense whose operation – necessary for our survival – is as ineluctable as gravity, as trustworthy as the axioms of geometry.

Hutcheson's postulation of an innate moral *sense* differs from the Cambridge Platonists' belief in objective moral *law* by locating moral absolutes entirely within human nature; he never suggests that the law of gravitation is the same as purity of heart, or that the human spirit is one with the Divine Intelligence that informs the universe. Yet his humbler and more naturalistic explanation seemed to offer a way to retain belief in moral absolutes during an age of empiricism. For that reason it exercised a powerful attraction throughout the eighteenth century. Belief in the existence of a "moral sense" functioning intuitively to judge right and wrong offers us protection against the radical individualism of Hobbes and Mandeville, but it does more than that. It reinstalls within the self the social world that empirical philosophy threatens to obliterate. The swift reflexes of the moral sense, manifesting themselves in our consciousness as sentiments of approbation or disapprobation, link us in feeling to those other selves whose very existence empirical philosophy often has difficulty proving.

Another stay against radical skepticism came from a group of Scottish philosophers of the late eighteenth century. Refusing to accept Hume's skeptical deductions from Locke's principles, philosophers like Thomas Reid (1710–96) insisted that there were some things in the mind that were not before in the senses. These "intuitions," or "immediate beliefs," are "part of our constitution, and all the discoveries of reason are grounded upon them. They make up what is called *the common sense of mankind.*" Another Scottish philosopher, Dugald Stewart (1753–1828), gives examples of some common-sense propositions — "I exist, I am the same person to-day as I was yesterday; the material world has an existence independent of my mind; the general laws of nature will continue in future to operate uniformly as in time past" — and compares them to the *Elements* of Euclid, barren in themselves but necessary for reasoning about everything else.

This limited reaffirmation of the old doctrine of innate ideas was influential at Harvard during the early nineteenth century, where it was seen as a friendly corrective to Locke's radical empiricism. "Commonsense" propositions had to do with epistemology rather than ethics, but the conviction that there were intuitive principles in the mind that could be relied upon made the doctrine of the moral sense seem more plausible. Indeed, Stewart, whose *Elements of the Philosophy of the Human Mind* (Vol. 1, 1792) was an assigned text at Harvard, argued that the moral sense ought to be classed among the original and universal principles of the human mind, because its judgments appear in children in the very infancy of their reason, long before they are capable of forming abstract conceptions of right and wrong.

Stewart's arguments concerning the moral sense seemed persuasive to at least one reader who was not convinced that the Scottish school had succeeded in refuting the epistemological and religious skepticism of Hume. When Ralph Waldo Emerson (1803–82) submitted an essay, "The Present State of Ethical Philosophy," for the Bowdoin Prize at Harvard during his junior year in 1820, he admitted that Stewart's school had not quite managed to remove the "terror which attached to the name of Hume," but he expressed complete confidence in its postulation of a "moral faculty" which is an "original principle of our nature."

Humean skepticism was not, however, the only danger that Unitarian beliefs faced. Challenges from both natural science and biblical criticism were shaking the foundations upon which Christian faith had rested, and to these challenges the moral sense could supply no immediate answer. The science of geology was particularly unsettling. When geologists offered evidence that the earth was very much older than the Mosaic account of Creation suggested, orthodox ministers could simply denounce them. But Unitarians had always prided themselves on being hospitable to scientific inquiry and secure in their faith that no contradiction could exist between God's revealed Word and the truths inscribed in the Book of Nature. They were therefore faced with tasks of recuperative hermeneutics that grew more formidible all the time.

Even if the Mosaic chronology were quietly sacrificed to scientific enlightenment – something the Unitarians could more easily do because they believed in *progressive* illumination and were willing to regard Genesis as a fable suited to the childhood rather than to the maturity of the race – there remained the problem of the documents upon which Christianity itself was based. Unitarians firmly believed in the historical accuracy of the New Testament; they believed that Jesus of Nazareth lived, preached, performed miracles, died, and rose again and that the documents collected in the New Testament gave a faithful account of these events. Indeed, liberals were if anything more firmly wedded to the "historical Jesus" than their orthodox counterparts. Enthusiasts might need no more to confirm their faith than a firm persuasion of the spirit, but liberal Christians wanted to prove the divine origin of their religion by tracing it back to the moments when Divine Omnipotence could be proved to have altered the course of empirical events; they needed history to establish faith.

The growth of historical criticism in Germany during the last quarter of the eighteenth century seemed at first to promise to aid scholars seeking to make contact with distant historical reality. The philologians of Göttingen and Halle sought to understand ancient documents through more rigorous methods of textual criticism than had ever before been attempted, but they also insisted that the ancient documents could be deciphered only by placing them against the background of the culture from which they grew, a culture whose shape must be painstakingly reconstructed from surviving archaeological, literary, religious, and art-historical evidence. American scholars, eager to acquire this exciting new approach to classical and biblical authors, began to make pilgrimages to Germany to study with the great scholars of the day and to bring back their texts and methods to America.

Edward Everett and George Ticknor (1791–1871) both hastened upon their arrival in Germany in 1815 to study the most revolutionary of all philological manifestos, the *Prolegomena ad Homerum* (1795) of Friedrich August Wolf (1759–1824). Everett spent eighteen hours a day working through the Latin text by the scholar Ticknor called the "Ishmael of criticism," and when George Bancroft (1800–91) joined them a few years later he too became an initiate. "In Philology, Wolf & yet Wolf & yet Wolf," he grumbled in a letter to Andrews Norton (December 14, 1818). Wolf's hostility toward and contempt for all previous Homeric critics accounts in part for the nickname Ticknor gave him, but his monumental self-confidence also extended to the text of Homer itself, a text that it was the avowed aim of the *Prolegomena* to correct and restore. Wolf's method, as one modern scholar explains it, involved the location of discrepancies and anachronisms within the received text and the ruthless elimination of all explanations and rationalizations for them, as well as the substitution of new explanations supported by his extensive knowledge of Greek grammar and history.

Emerson would remember with some amusement Everett's attempt to graft the sophisticated techniques of German philology onto the rudimentary Harvard curriculum during Everett's tenure there as professor of Greek, which coincided with Emerson's own undergraduate days. But Emerson also remembered how exciting the discoveries seemed to the students. "It was all new learning, that wonderfully took and stimulated the young men," he wrote. And, Emerson continued:

Though nothing could be conceived beforehand less attractive or indeed less fit for green boys from Connecticut, New Hampshire, and Massachusetts, with their unripe Latin and Greek reading, than exegetical discourses in the style of Voss and Wolff and Ruhnken, on the Orphic and Ante-Homeric remains, – yet this learning instantly took the highest places to our imagination in our unoccupied American Parnassus.

Emerson once remarked that Wolf's thesis – that the written text of Homer was produced by a redactor who combined chants originally composed by an illiterate bard – inaugurated a new epoch in criticism. In the *Prolegomena* Wolf had asserted that we must give up the hope "that the original form of the Homeric Poems could ever be laid out save in our minds, and even there only in rough outlines." The scholar, laboring to dissolve and then recreate the text by rejecting all that is interpolated or corrupt, gives the great original poem of Western culture the only true shape it can have and effects on the textual level that transfer of the world into the mind that Emerson saw as the peculiar achievement of his age.

Yet Wolf himself confessed his indebtedness to an older tradition of textual scholarship. The great advances made by German biblical scholars during the eighteenth century in the understanding of ancient Near Eastern languages and the collation and correction of biblical texts had provided Wolf with a model for his own enterprise. His book was explicitly modeled on one of the most controversial works of biblical criticism, Johann Gottfried Eichhorn's

Einleitung in das Alte Testament (1780–3). Wolf's modern editors point out that Eichhorn (1752–1827) had ventured to treat the text of the Old Testament "as a historical and an anthropological document, the much-altered remnant of an early stage in the development of human culture."

More was at stake here than the reconstruction of the text itself: Eichhorn was proposing an entirely different way of *reading* the Old Testament, and the apologetic possibilities it offered were vast. Biblical scholars in England and America quickly saw in works like Eichhorn's a way of saving the Old Testament from on the one hand the ridicule of Deists and on the other the blind veneration of the believers in literal inspiration. The brilliant young Unitarian minister Joseph Stevens Buckminster (1784–1812) made sure he acquired Eichhorn's *Einleitung* during his tour of Europe. On that trip Buckminster spent a recent inheritance, amassing a library of three thousand volumes, including Johann Jakob Griesbach's Greek text of the New Testament (1796–1806) and many works of biblical criticism.

When Buckminster returned to New England in 1807 he began writing in the *Monthly Anthology* and its successor, the *General Repository and Review,* about Griesbach's achievement. In these pieces he explained the methods of the new textual criticism and urged the adoption of Griesbach's text, a one-volume edition of which Harvard had published in 1809 and adopted for use in its own classrooms. Although conservatives were shocked to hear someone assert that the received text of the Bible contained "corruptions," liberals were delighted to have Buckminster cast doubt upon the authenticity of scriptural texts that Trinitarians cited in support of their own theological position.

Buckminster was appointed to Harvard's newly created chair of biblical criticism, but he died at the early age of twenty-eight before he could assume the post. An auction held after his death offered the theological works he had amassed in Europe to bidders who were as eager to acquire the new books of criticism as he had been himself. A bidding war over the Eichhorn volumes erupted between Moses Stuart (1780–1852), the head of the recently founded Andover Theological Seminary, and Edward Everett. Shortly after the auction, Stuart (who had won the bidding war) invited Everett to Andover for an overnight visit during which he tried to interest Everett in translating another influential work of German biblical criticism, Johann Gottfried von Herder's *Vom geist der ebräischen poesie* (1782–3). Everett declined the translation task but borrowed the Eichhorn volumes and began immersing himself in them.

The friendship that sprang up between the liberal Everett and the orthodox Stuart is significant, for it suggests that the interest in the new methods of biblical criticism at this point transcended doctrinal divisions. Stuart even asked Everett to consider founding an "oriental club" at Cambridge where scholars could meet to discuss the new developments in the study of the scriptures. The club never materialized, but something of the ecumenical spirit that prompted the suggestion surfaced again when James Marsh (1794–1842), who had studied with Stuart at Andover, finally published a translation of Herder in 1833. The *Christian Examiner*, Boston's Unitarian quarterly, contained a series of essays devoted to Herder in 1834 and 1835, essays that would have a profound effect upon the way the young men and women who were beginning to be called Transcendentalists would interpret both Scripture and nature.

When Harvard appointed Everett professor of Greek in 1814 it took the unusual step of offering him a chance to study in Germany before he took up his duties at home; it even advanced him the money to pay for the enterprise. Everett had already begun to translate Eichhorn, and a five-hundred-page book he published in 1814 showed him becoming proficient enough in the new techniques of biblical interpretation to suggest innovations of his own. A disgruntled former minister had published a book examining the "grounds" of the Christian religion and finding them wanting. He argued that the writers of the Gospels had grotesquely twisted the meaning of Old Testament prophecies upon which they based their claims that Christ was the Messiah. Everett's *Defence of Christianity* replied that the Gospel writers were not misusing prophecies but rather employing them in a manner familiar to Jewish culture – employing them, in fact, just as the rabbis had in the Mishnah. Everett's book seemed promising. It suggested that the historical methods of German scholarship might support and defend Unitarian theology. His Harvard colleagues sent him to Germany hoping that he would bring home all that was most advanced in both the classical and biblical scholarship of the day.

Everett did become a brilliant student at Göttingen; in 1817 he became the first American to be awarded the Ph.D. But though he studied sacred criticism with Eichhorn himself he never taught the subject when he returned to Harvard. A few references in letters to doubts and anxieties that perplexed him shed some light on his refusal to teach at Harvard what he had learned in Germany. The letters suggest that Everett may have abandoned sacred criticism because he had begun to have fears that Eichhorn's latest conclusions were irreconcilable with even the most liberal interpretations of Scripture accepted by the Unitarian church.

Eichhorn by this time had turned his attention from the Old to the New Testament, and under his gaze the three synoptic Gospels dissolved into a set of redactions of a still more primitive gospel whose skeletal remains are visible beneath the concealing and elaborating flourishes of the canonical texts. In a rather truculent letter, Everett wrote to his brother Alexander that he planned to "trouble nobody's faith or peace" when he returned so long as he was left alone but that if he were not left alone he would "exhibit the subject of Christianity, which the modern historical and critical enquiries fully establish" (Everett to Alexander Everett, September 3, 1815). This way of putting matters makes German criticism sound much more like a threat than a promise. Several months later the whole enterprise seemed to weary him. Why should scholars waste such time and energy in their quest for the historical Jesus? Everett, who succeeded Buckminster for a brief but memorable pastorate in the pulpit of the Brattle Square Church before resigning to take up the Harvard professorship, confessed to his brother that he still felt a "strong attachment to the act of preaching." But he wished something could be done "to separate the public worship of God and the public teaching of duty, from all connection with arbitrary facts, supposed to have happened in distant nations and ages" (Everett to Alexander Everett, January 5, 1816). Everett's brusque dismissal of the crucifixion and resurrection of Jesus as "arbitrary facts" is probably, as has been suggested, a rephrasing of Gotthold Ephraim Lessing's assertion that accidental historical truths can never prove the necessary truths of reason. But it also hints at a restlessness always implicit in Unitarianism's exaltation of the moral sense. If the sense of duty is the inner divinity of which Jesus was only the most perfect exemplar, why do we need Jesus at all, let alone the miracles that prove his mission divine?

Whatever Everett's doubts, he did keep them to himself when he returned home, and the new scholarship from Germany continued to be discussed and studied by Unitarians. A steady stream of American students found its way to German universities; the latest books of sacred criticism were sent home from Europe and reviewed in American periodicals. Some English translations of prominent works of German scholarship – Bishop Herbert Marsh's 1802 translation of J. D. Michaelis's *Introduction to the New Testament* and Bishop Connop Thirlwall's 1825 translation of F. D. E. Schleiermacher's *Critical Essay upon the Gospel of St. Luke* – contained long historical essays by the translators surveying the development of biblical criticism and explaining the details of famous controversies. These accounts of progressive intellectual discovery in a subject so long characterized by bitter sectarian disputes suggested that theology too might finally begin to join the "progress" of intellect instead of merely opposing it.

True, the alleged impiety of the German critics and the skepticism inherent in every kind of textual criticism made some fear that (as Thirlwall put it) the new biblical criticism might "tend to destroy the reverence with which Christians are accustomed to regard these works as Holy Writ and containing the words of God." The trustees of the Andover Theological Seminary became worried enough in 1825 to warn that "the unrestrained cultivation of German studies has evidently tended to chill the ardor of piety," and at Harvard, Andrews Norton eventually became so convinced of the destabilizing effects of German criticism that he refused to let his son study the German language. To braver spirits, however, such anxieties only testified to the power of the new criticism. Watching the textual obscurities of centuries melt before the blast of the new historical criticism gave the young scholars of the era a confidence that, like the mysteries of nature, the mysteries of Scripture were soluble.

This sense of an imminent clarification, of a final destination for the progress of ethical philosophy and religious understanding, is Unitarianism's enduring legacy to the men and women who came to maturity in the first three decades of the nineteenth century. When the author and biographer Edward Everett Hale (1822–1909) looked back from the 1890s on the climate in Divinity Hall at Harvard in the late 1820s, he wished above all to communicate to his readers the sense of

a certain enthusiastic expectation which at the time quickened the lives of all young people in New England who had been trained in the freer schools of religion. The group of leaders who surrounded Dr. Channing had, with him, broken forever from the fetters of Calvinistic theology. These young people were trained to know that human nature is not totally depraved. They were taught that there is nothing of which it is not capable. From Dr. Channing down, every writer and preacher believed in the infinite power of education. In England the popular wave for the diffusion of useful knowledge had set in; and what was called the "March of Intellect" had begun. The great German authors swayed the minds of our young students with all their new power, and with the special seduction which accompanies a discovery, the study of German being wholly new. For students who did not read German, Coleridge was opening up the larger philosophy.

Hale mentions other signs of the times – the belief in the power of association and the organization of philanthropic societies:

For such reasons, and many more, the young New Englanders of liberal training rushed into life, certain that the next half century was to see a complete moral revolution in the world. . . . And no one rightly writes or reads the life of one of these young men or women, unless he fully appreciates the force of this enthusiastic hope.

2

THE ASSAULT ON LOCKE

OWARD THE END of the 1820s the philosophical synthesis that had supported Unitarianism throughout its period of expansion began to show signs of strain. Unresolved contradictions within it — the tension between sensationalism and idealism in its epistemology, the mingled attitude of desire and fear that marked its dealings with German biblical criticism — began to trouble new generations of students. Writings of the English and German Romantics kept arriving on American shores and finding enthusiasts among the young, despite their elders' contempt for the bathos of Wordsworth, the licentiousness of Goethe, the obscurity of Kant and of Coleridge. Reformers were beginning to demand that the churches leave their careful doctrine of individual self-culture and do something about the scandal of urban poverty or the greater scandal of slavery. By the end of the 1820s the discontents among the younger Unitarians had begun to find public expression.

The first sign of the trouble that would later be labeled "Transcendentalism" came with an attack on two fronts: on the philosophy of John Locke and on the educational system at Harvard. The two things were naturally allied in the minds of the young men who had been subjected to them simultaneously, and the connection was reinforced by the fact that Harvard's heavy reliance on drill seemed perfectly tailored to Locke's view of the mind's structure. If the mind is an empty tablet and if all ideas come from sensation and reflection, then memorization ought to be the foundation of all learning and recitation the proper medium for its display. Edward Everett's learning *The Essay on Human Understanding* by heart and reciting it day after day to his pleased tutor symbolizes perfectly what the old system valued.

Classes at Harvard (as at most American colleges) were "recitations" at which students were called upon to display their knowledge of the assigned materials. The students received an immediate score for their performance, and these scores were then used to determine rank in class and share of honors and privileges. How deadly, how infuriating, this system seemed to the young students (who often entered college when they were fifteen) can be seen in the anger that still animates the pages of the autobiography James

Freeman Clarke (1809–82) began a few months before his death. Clarke, a Unitarian minister and a Transcendentalist, recalled his dismay at finding that the Harvard system seemed designed to frustrate curiosity:

No attempt was made to interest us in our studies. We were expected to wade through Homer as though the Iliad were a bog, and it was our duty to get along at such a rate *per diem*. Nothing was said of the glory and grandeur, the tenderness and charm of this immortal epic. The melody of the hexameters was never suggested to us. Dr. Popkin, our Greek professor, would look over his spectacles at us, and, with pencil in hand, mark our recitation as good or bad, but never a word to help us over a difficulty, or to explain anything obscure, still less to excite our enthusiasm for the greatest poem of antiquity.

What intellectual excitement there was on campus was provided by the student-run literary societies. Campus literary societies had been fixtures of American college life since the eighteenth century – sponsoring debates, discussions, and oratorical displays; assembling libraries for the use of their members; encouraging original composition in verse and prose. They provided what one historian has called an "alternative curriculum" to the official one, an arena in which the students could find an outlet for the curiosity and love of literature that the classroom refused to acknowledge. The contrast between the grim, competitive atmosphere of the classroom and the freedom of the literary society only helped fuel undergraduate dissatisfaction with the college authorities. "When I recall what my classmates were interested in doing," Clarke remembered,

I find it was not college work, which might have given them rank, but pursuits outside of the curriculum. . . . We unearthed old tomes in the college library, and while our English professors were teaching us out of Blair's "Rhetoric," we were forming our taste by making copious extracts from Sir Thomas Browne, or Ben Jonson. Our real professors of rhetoric were Charles Lamb and Coleridge, Walter Scott and Wordsworth.

The appetite for Romantic literature Clarke and his classmates had developed in the "unofficial" Harvard curriculum received a powerful stimulus from another source of information about new developments in European thought, Madame de Staël's celebrated survey of German life and thought, *De l'Allemagne*. Anne-Louise-Germaine Necker, Baroness de Staël (1766–1817), exiled from France by the anger of Napoleon, had published an account of her travels through Germany in London in 1813. (An earlier, Paris edition had been confiscated and pulped on Napoleon's orders.) Her hostility to the French emperor, her admiration for British constitutional liberties, and her praise for the Scottish Common Sense philosophers all combined to win her the admiration not only of the British public but also of readers in New England.

De Staël's account of the development of European philosophy from Locke through the post-Kantians constitutes a sustained critique of the philosophical tradition that Harvard students had been taught to revere. De Staël excoriates the mocking, corrosive, godless skepticism of French Enlightenment culture and traces its lineage back not to Hume or Voltaire but to Locke himself. In de Staël's narrative of European intellectual history, Locke is the innocent originator of a mistake whose full implications were left to others to work out. De Staël argues that Locke's English piety and devotion to liberty prevented him from seeing that his sensationalist philosophy led inevitably to the tyrant worship of Thomas Hobbes and the skepticism of David Hume. The French followers of Locke had no such inherited defenses, and so they embraced without restraint a system that de Staël sums up as "materialism built upon sensation, and ethics founded upon interest."

Against the "scoffing scepticism" she sees as the product of a philosophy that derives ideas from sensations, de Staël opposes the inwardness and spirituality of the German tradition, beginning with Gottfried Wilhelm Leibniz (1646–1716) and culminating gloriously in Immanuel Kant (1724–1804). Leibniz had added to Locke's assertion that there is nothing in the intellect that was not previously in the senses this "sublime restriction" – *except the intellect itself.* Kant had then set himself the task of determining the laws that govern the intellect; he had asked himself, "What are the laws and sentiments which constitute the essence of the human soul, independently of all experience?"

Nothing less than absolute certainty would content Kant. He found this certainty in those "necessary notions," those laws of understanding, that determine the ways in which we can conceive of the world of the senses. He demonstrated that these notions – such as space, time, cause and effect, unity, plurality, possibility, and reality – are within us, and not the objects we contemplate; "in this respect, it is our understanding which gives laws to external nature, instead of receiving them from it."

Kant, according to de Staël, did not reject the world of experience; indeed, "nothing is more luminous than the line of demarcation which he traces between what comes to us by sensation and what belongs to the spontaneous action of our souls." He never attempted to move into the pure idealism of his successor, Johann Gottlieb Fichte, who, with "scientific strictness," made the whole universe "consist of the activity of mind." But in making our minds the active shapers of sense impressions instead of the passive recipients of them, Kant restored to the mind its centrality and dignity. This same dignity also informs Kant's ethical system, which makes conscience the "innate principle" of our moral existence: "The feeling of right and wrong is, according to his ideas, the primitive law of the heart, as space and time are of the understanding." Our inner assurance of moral liberty is the proof that we possess it, for neither moral liberty nor conscience can be the result of experience. Both are felt instead in that "power of reaction against circumstances, which springs from the bottom of the soul."

De Staël's great work of popularization made the young Bostonians aware of the massive changes that had taken place in Continental philosophy. Her vivid, epigrammatic style was a refreshing change from the dryness of metaphysical treatises, and the value she placed upon the dignity of the individual and upon moral liberty made her appealing to anyone raised in the tradition of Unitarian humanism. Emerson clearly loved de Staël; beginning in the early 1820s he fills his journals with maxims and anecdotes copied from *De l'Allemagne,* maxims to which he accorded an important place in his first book, *Nature* (1836). If he did not learn from de Staël any details of Kant's terminology (she disapproved of it), he did get the sense that answers to his pressing spiritual questions were likely to come from Germany or at least from those others who derived their ideas from that fertile source.

Samuel Taylor Coleridge was the most famous of these cultural mediators after de Staël, and the American publication of two of his prose works by James Marsh, the president of the University of Vermont, helped fan the fires of interest in German philosophy. Marsh was not a Unitarian. He had been a student of Moses Stuart's at Andover, but already during his years at the seminary he had become dissatisfied with both the prevailing methods of instruction at American institutions of higher learning and the philosophical system taught in them. He became convinced that Lockean empiricism and the Scottish Common Sense philosophy that came after it had entangled theology in a "metaphysical net" from which it could never break free. The fruitless doctrinal disputes among orthodox theologians led many faithful Christians either to abandon their faith altogether or to take refuge in unreflecting fideism. After Marsh left the seminary he began to search for something that would satisfy not only the intellect but also the emotions, not only the head but also "the heart in the head."

When Marsh stumbled across the works of Coleridge – first the *Biographia Literaria* (1817) and then *Aids to Reflection* (1825) – he became convinced that Coleridge's adaptation of Kant offered a way to rescue American theology from its marriage to a sensationalist philosophy inherently hostile to piety. He decided to publish an American edition of Coleridge's *Aids to Reflection.* This edition appeared in 1829, and Marsh prefaced it with a long "Preliminary Essay" in which he argued for the relevance of Coleridge's beliefs to the state of American theology. Marsh realized that his planned publication might be obnoxious to orthodox theologians; he also knew that he might have trouble getting the book reviewed in a country where literary magazines scrupulously avoided theological discussions and theological magazines were firmly committed to the doctrines of particular sects. He sent copies of his edition to prominent theologians at Andover and Princeton, hoping to enlist their support, only to find that they strongly objected to Coleridge's explanation of the Atonement as something that causes "subjective change" in us rather than as something that satisfies the legal demands of divine justice.

Meanwhile, Marsh's attack upon the prevailing system of metaphysics – "I mean the system, of which in modern times Locke is the reputed author" – was winning him converts among the very Unitarians he had made no effort to attract. The young Boston liberals had little interest in Marsh's attempt to place the doctrines of the Trinity or the Atonement upon firm metaphysical grounds. But they loved his attack upon the philosophical system they detested. Marsh described empirical philosophy as a system that by insisting that all knowledge is ultimately derived from sensation "tends inevitably to undermine our belief in the reality of any thing spiritual in the only proper sense of that word" and then "coldly and ambiguously" refers us for the support of our faith to "the *authority* of revelation."

In *Aids to Reflection* Coleridge makes a strong distinction between what is spiritual and what is natural and in so doing eliminates the need to reduce the one to the other. He argues that the faculties by which we perceive these different spheres of reality are as different as the spheres themselves, although these faculties somehow reside in a single human mind. The *Reason* is the supersensuous, intuitive power, at once the source of morality and of the highest kind of intellection; the *Understanding* is the humbler servant who works by combining and comparing ideas derived from sensation, who helps us reflect and generalize – the faculty Locke had mistaken for the whole of the mind, in other words.

The distinction between the Reason and the Understanding helps Coleridge dispose handily of a century's worth of Deist attacks upon the "unintelligible" doctrines of Christianity. *Of course* religious concepts like the Trinity, the Atonement, and Original Sin appear contradictory to the Understanding; they are spiritual doctrines rather than natural ones and must of necessity appear absurd to the faculty devoted to judging the natural world. The truths of Reason, in fact, can be expressed to the Understanding only as a paradox: "Before Abraham was, I am," or "God is a circle whose center is everywhere and his circumference nowhere." Locke's patient attempt to arrive at truth by comparing and analyzing sensory impressions can never succeed because the truth he was looking for resides elsewhere. "In Wonder all philosophy began; in Wonder it ends: and Admiration fills up the interspace."

Coleridge's distinction between the Reason and the Understanding seemed to offer Unitarians a way out of their spiritual dilemma – a way for them to satisfy the hunger for contact with the transcendent without abandoning the values of tolerance and rational enquiry. Clarke remembered how his discovery during his senior year at Harvard in 1829 of Coleridge's philosophy helped turn him toward the ministry: "Coleridge the poet I had known and loved. Coleridge the philosopher confirmed my longing for a higher philosophy than that of John Locke and David Hartley, the metaphysicians most in vogue with the earlier Unitarians down to the time of Channing." Like most of his friends Clarke had grown up among the ideas of sensationalist philosophy; he tells us that one of his earliest philosophical lessons had been Locke's polemic against innate ideas:

But something within me revolted at all such attempts to explain soul out of sense, deducing mind from matter, or tracing the origin of ideas to nerves, vibrations, and vibratiuncles. So I gave it up, until Coleridge showed me from Kant that though knowledge begins *with* experience it does not come *from* experience. Then I discovered that I was born a transcendentalist; and smiled when I afterwards read, in one of Jacobi's works, that he had gone through exactly the same experience.

As many people have noticed, Coleridge's terminology, though translated from Kant (*Vernunft* and *Verstand*), differs in significant ways from its source. For Kant, the Reason consists of all the categories of mental activity that make perception possible but cannot themselves be derived from it, the things Madame de Staël had called "necessary notions": space and time, causality, proportionality, relation, and so on. Kant's Reason is neither a repository of particular truths nor the faculty of intuitively apprehending them. But few of Coleridge's American readers knew *The Critique of Pure Reason* (1781), and most were happy to use Coleridge's terms as if they were Kant's.

"There is no delight like a new classification," Emerson would later observe. In the years following Marsh's edition of Coleridge, people rushed to apply the distinction between the Reason and the Understanding to every knotty problem that had perplexed them. Clarke noted how it had helped him when he came to the study of theology. It taught him to regard doctrinal differences as insignificant, as the product of the Understanding's attempt to formulate discursively the truths perceived immediately and intuitively by the Reason. Clarke thought that even the split between Unitarian and Trinitarian, apparently so wide, might simply be a different way of *expressing* the belief that Christ is "a visible manifestation of the invisible and eternal."

Emerson was quick to adopt the new classification too. Writing to his brother Edward in 1834 he asks whether Edward "draws the distinction of Milton Coleridge & the Germans between Reason and Understanding," a distinction he himself now regards as "a philosophy itself." "The manifold applications of the distinction to Literature to the Church to Life will show how good a key it is," he announces, and explains the difference to Edward in the shape of a little allegory. "Reason is the highest faculty of the soul — what we mean often by the soul itself; it never *reasons,* never proves, it simply perceives; it is vision. The Understanding toils all the time, compares, contrives, adds, argues, near sighted but strong-sighted, dwelling in the present the expedient the customary." So far the Understanding is merely the myopic servant of a visionary, but a little farther on the allegory darkens.

The thoughts of youth, & "first thoughts," are the revelations of Reason. . . . But understanding that wrinkled calculator the steward of our house to whom is committed to support of our animal life contradicts evermore these affirmations of Reason & points at Custom & Interest & persuades one man that the declarations of Reason are false & another that they are at least impracticable. Yet by & by after having denied our Master we come back to see at the end of years or of life that he was the Truth. (Emerson to Edward Emerson, May 31, 1834)

The Understanding now becomes a voice of wordly prudence, and the individual who listens to its promptings instead of to the Reason's is, like Peter in Gethsemane, denying the true Christ he will someday acknowledge again in tears and repentance. When Emerson heard an orthodox preacher say that "the carnal mind hates God continually," he could sit through the sermon without impatience because he could translate the preacher's words into his own new tongue: "I say, 'It is the instinct of the Understanding to contradict the Reason.' "

The hostility between the Reason and the Understanding explained a primal split in consciousness as well as the oscillations between uplift and collapse, nobility and timorousness, that plagued the aspiring. Even more, it offered to a class of people for whom the biblical history of the Fall and the redemption was losing intellectual authority the chance to interpret their inner life with the vividness of the faith once delivered to the Saints. The young Cambridge student of divinity who read his life as perpetual warfare between the holy promptings of the Reason and the worldly prudence of the Understanding had an inner life as complicated, as full of disheartening falls and miraculous recoveries, as any spiritual autobiographer of the seventeenth century.

How were the Reason and the Understanding related in the life history of the individual? Were they twin born, or siblings sometimes cooperative, sometimes bitterly hostile? The answer came this time not from philosophy, but from poetry, particularly from the poetry of Coleridge and William Wordsworth. Neither man had been very popular in the United States in the early decades of the century, when Lord Byron and the Irish poet Tom Moore were all the rage. Joseph Dennie (1768–1812) had reviewed some of Wordsworth's earlier lyrics with favor in his Philadelphia *Port Folio,* but Dennie had few imitators. Boston's *Monthly Anthology,* when it noticed Wordsworth at all, found his experiments politically dangerous and poetically ludicrous.

Suddenly, in the late 1820s, converts to Coleridge discovered that the verse they had once derided contained spiritual truths as profound as Kant's and equally as useful in the fight against sensationalism. Sampson Reed, a young Harvard graduate who had converted to Swedenborgianism in 1820, published in 1826 a small book entitled *The Growth of the Mind.* In it Reed argues against the reigning Lockean view of the mind's structure and suggests instead a model of mental development illustrated by the poetry of Wordsworth and other English Romantics. The mind, in this view, is not a passive receiver of stimuli, but a germ that grows and expands by assimilating things from its environment. In 1831 James Marsh issued the second of his Coleridgean publications, an American edition of Coleridge's periodical *The Friend* (1809–10), which contained extracts form Wordworth's unpublished autobiographical poem later titled *The Prelude.*

The young men and women around Cambridge who read these works delighted in a portrait of the individual mind and its relationship to nature that made ordinary perception seem revelatory and ordinary maturation Odyssean. It bothered no one that the Romanticism intoxicating Cambridge was decades old, and the Kantianism even older, or that the ideas being hailed as revolutionary were a jumble of bits and pieces torn from their contexts and served up by a haphazard collection of editors, translators, and book reviewers. If anything, this blurring of historical distinctions contributed to the sense of excitement. The fruits of a half-century of European progress in literature, philosophy, natural science, and sacred criticism all arrived on American shores more or less at once – Swedenborg and Schleiermacher, Herder and Strauss, Kant and Schelling, Goethe and Wordsworth, de Staël and Coleridge. Such opulence could hardly fail to suggest that the world was on the verge of a remarkable synthesis. The opening pages of Reed's *Growth of the Mind* (1826) give an idea of the mood:

The world is deriving vigor, not from that which is gone by, but from that which is coming; not from the unhealthy moisture of the evening, but from the nameless influences of morning. . . . Both mankind, and the laws and principles by which they are governed, seem about to be redeemed from slavery. . . . We appear to be approaching an age which will be the silent pause of merely physical force before the powers of the mind; the timid, subdued, awed condition of the brute, gazing on the erect and godlike form of man.

It seems curious to us that among the strong contributors to this sense of imminent apotheosis were the great British quarterly reviews, the *Edinburgh Review,* founded in 1802, and its Tory rival, the *Quarterly,* founded in 1808.

The lengthy review essays in these and similar periodicals were expected to do far more than offer opinions (though the opinions in the always anonymous reviews were famous for their frankness and malice). Reviews frequently offered surveys of entire fields. For instance, the December 1826 number of the *Edinburgh* contained a review of seven books and articles dealing with the work of Jean-François Champollion (decipherer of the Rosetta stone); it included an engraved fold-out chart giving a selection of phonetic hieroglyphics and their equivalents in demotic and Greek characters. Furthermore, a review of James Fenimore Cooper's *Notions of the Americans* and of a book by a British traveler in North America contained a survey of recent British–American political relations and a concise history of American literature going back as far as Jonathan Edwards.

This impression of intellectual mastery combined with vigorous expression of opinion gave the reviews an air of authority that could make each essay seem like an education in itself, a quality particularly valuable in the United States, where foreign books were difficult to obtain. The high caliber of the reviewers and their practice of quoting copiously from the books they reviewed gave readers a sense of contact with an intellectual world they might never otherwise approach. It may be true, as Sydney Smith, the editor of the *Edinburgh,* suggested, that every reader took up a review hoping to get wise at a cheap rate; but few periodicals ever made that hope seem capable of fulfillment as easily as his own.

Bostonians who read the British reviews quickly learned that their local idols were not always treated with reverence elsewhere. The *Edinburgh* reviewer of William Ellery Channing's essays on Fenelon, Milton, and Napoleon wrote in 1829: "We do not like to see a writer constantly trying to steal a march upon opinion without having his retreat cut off – full of pretensions, and void of offense." Channing

is always in advance of the line, in an amiable and imposing attitude, but never far from succour. He is an Unitarian; but then he disclaims all connexions with Dr. Priestly, as a materialist; he denounces Calvinism and the Church of England, but to show that this proceeds from no want of liberality, makes the *amende honorable* to Popery and Popish divines; – is an American Republican and a French Bourbonist; – . . . likes wit, provided it is serious – and is zealous for the propogation of the Gospel and the honour of religion, but thinks it should form a coalition with reason, and be surrounded with a halo of modern lights.

The writer of the review (who was in fact William Hazlitt) even suspected that Channing's want of moral daring may have been the product of that very democratic system of government whose "establishment of civil and religious liberty" was supposed to free opinion completely. But American democracy did not free opinion; it established a tyranny more onerous than ever. In a mixed government a dissident may appeal from one party to another, but when there is only one "body of opinion" in a country it is invincible. "There can be no reaction against it, and to remonstrate or resist, is not only a public outrage, but sounds like a personal insult to every individual in the community. It is differing from the company; you become a *black sheep in the flock.*" Hazlitt attributed to this subtle pressure "the too frequent cowardice, jesuitism, and sterility, produced by this republican discipline and drilling." So far from fostering individuality, republican government squelches it. "Whoever outstrips, or takes a separate path to himself, is considered as usurping an unnatural superiority over the whole. He is treated not with respect or indulgence, but with indignity." The criticism of Channing was particularly stinging because it could not be ascribed to programmatic anti-Americanism. The *Edinburgh,* though it loved ridiculing the faults of American literature as much as it loved ridiculing everything else, remained friendlier to the United States than did many other foreign periodicals. As another reviewer indulgently wrote: "Though the hussy ran away and married to disoblige us, she is a chip of the old block."

The style of the *Edinburgh* was infectious. Anyone who reads Frederic Henry Hedge's celebrated review of Coleridge's works for the *Christian Examiner* in 1833 can see just where Hedge is affecting the witty nonchalance of *Edinburgh*'s "invisible invincibles" in his study of Coleridge's career. Hedge (1805–90) was probably better qualified than anyone else in America to pull off such an imitation. Born in Boston and sent by his father, Levi Hedge (professor of logic at Harvard), to Germany when he was only thirteen, Hedge spent four years in German preparatory schools, an experience that made him fluent not only in academic German but also in German schoolboy slang. He remained in Germany until 1822, when he returned to Harvard to get his B.A. He entered the Divinity School in 1825 and upon his graduation in 1828 was ordained pastor of the West Cambridge Church. Hedge had read Kant's *Critiques;* he was also well-read in the various post-Kantian idealists who had influenced Coleridge. Already in Divinity School he had earned the reputation for intellectual fearlessness that led one eulogist to remark after his death, "He was not appalled by any result to which his thought might lead." He once mocked the kind of Christian who could be frightened by German biblical criticism. "What a sequel and summing up of the history of Christianity would that be, to say that 'God sent his Son into the World,' 'that the world through him might be saved,' but the Tübingen School and British 'Essays and Reviews' defeated that purpose and it had to be abandoned?"

When James Marsh's edition of *The Friend* appeared in 1831, Hedge seized the opportunity to review a good part of Coleridge's career: the *Poetical Works,* the *Biographia Literaria, Aids to Reflection,* and *The Friend.* Hedge praises the poetry, predicts that the *Biographia* will remain popular when the other prose works have faded, and commends the "depth of thought, clearness of judgment, sound reasoning, and forcible expression" to be found in *The Friend*. He thanks Marsh for the usefulness of his "Preliminary Essay" and ventures to hope that the talent for original philosophy that the "Essay" suggests will find fuller expression later. But distributing compliments is not really Hedge's main purpose in the review. The review's central portions tackle the thickly layered history of transcendental philosophy: first Kant himself, then the post-Kantian Idealists, then Coleridge, and finally Marsh's interpretation of Coleridge.

Hedge begins by warning his readers that unless they are willing to make the strenuous effort demanded by German metaphysicians they will never understand the sense of excitement the new methods create in their adherents. "The effect of such writing upon the uninitiated, is like being in the company of one who has inhaled an exhilarating gas. We witness the inspiration, and are astounded at the effects, but we can form no conception of the feeling until we ourselves have experienced it." The kind of philosopher who "contrives a theory of spirit, by nicknaming matter" and hopes to explain every phenomenon of consciousness by "reducing all things to impressions, ideas, and sensations" will never share in this mysterious exhilaration. Kant and his disciples "wrote for minds of quite another stamp," minds that seek with faith and hope a solution to questions that empirical philosophy declares are impossible to answer – "questions which relate to spirit and form, substance and life, free will and fate, God and eternity."

Hedge thinks that a preoccupation with such questions recurs periodically:

There are certain periods in the history of the society when, passing from a state of spontaneous production to a state of reflection, mankind are particularly disposed to inquire concerning themselves and their destination, the nature of their being, the evidence of their knowledge, and the grounds of their faith. Such a tendency is one of the characteristics of the present age, and the German philosophy is the strongest expression of that tendency; it is a striving after information on subjects which have been usually considered as beyond the reach of human intelligence, an attempt to penetrate into the most hidden mysteries of our being.

The transcendental system is, to be sure, not a *ratio essendi* but a *ratio cognoscendi*: "It seeks not to explain the existence of God and creation, objectively considered, but to explain our knowledge of their existence." In the strongest possible terms Hedge rejects the charge that the transcendental system is a skeptical philosophy: "It seeks not to overthrow, but to build up; it wars not with the common opinions and general experience of mankind, but aims to place these on a scientific basis, and to verify them by specific demonstrations."

Only toward the end of the review does Hedge turn his attention to *Aids to Reflection*. The Coleridgean distinction that had meant so much to his friends – between the Reason and the Understanding – Hedge mentions only in passing; he knows that the way Coleridge used the terms was un-Kantian. Indeed, the final pages of Hedge's review display contempt for Coleridge's pretensions as a religious thinker. "In this work he appears as a zealous Trinitarian, and a warm defender of the English church. We have no doubt of his sincerity; but unless we err greatly, he has either misunderstood his own views, or grossly misinterpreted the doctrines of his church." Coleridge's Trinity might pass equally well for the Godhead worshipped by a Unitarian. Nor do other traditional doctrines fare much better at Coleridge's hands. "His opinion of the atonement is far from Orthodox; the idea of vicarious suffering he rejects with disdain. The strong expressions of St. Paul in reference to this subject, he tells us are not intended to designate the *act* of redemption but are only figurative expressions descriptive of its effects." Any Christian doctrine Coleridge thinks unpalatable he simply pronounces to be a *mystery*. His project of recuperating traditional Christian doctrines through transcendental philosophy turns out to be an affair of language rather than of thought. "Every thing is first mystified into a sort of imposing indistinctness, and then pronounced to be genuine Orthodoxy."

Nevertheless, Hedge welcomes Coleridge's unconscious heterodoxy. He sees Coleridge as a valuable importer and disseminator of ideas that are quite easily separable from the husk of Anglican piety in which they are contained. He ends his review by quoting with approval Coleridge's own defense from the tenth chapter of the *Biographia Literaria*:

Would that the criterion of the scholar's utility were the number and moral value of the truths which he has been the means of throwing into the general circulation, or the number and value of the minds whom by his conversation or letters he has excited into activity, and supplied with the germs of their after-growth.

Judged by such standards, Coleridge's contribution to American intellectual life had been as great as he could have wished.

3

CARLYLE AND THE BEGINNINGS OF
AMERICAN TRANSCENDENTALISM

B Y THE TIME Frederic Henry Hedge had published his review of Coleridge's career in the *Christian Examiner* another writer had already begun to take Coleridge's place as supplier of excitations to the New World, a writer who was less interested in metaphysics than he was in the conduct of life. In the 1820s a remarkable series of review essays about German literature began to appear in the British quarterlies and attract the attention of the young Boston liberals. The style of these reviews – passionate, urgent, full of humor and outrage – marked them off immediately from the urbane acidities surrounding them. The reviews were written by Thomas Carlyle (1795–1881), who had been translating German literary works and writing essays about German literature in the 1820s and early 1830s. Carlyle's essay on the German writer known as Jean Paul (Jean Paul Friedrich Richter, 1763–1825) appeared in the *Edinburgh Review* in 1827, followed in the same year by an essay on "The State of German Literature." In 1828 Carlyle published two essays in the *Foreign Review:* an analysis of the "Helena" episode from the second part of Goethe's *Faust* and a later essay on Goethe's whole career. In 1828 and 1829 the *Edinburgh Review* published Carlyle's long biographical essays on the German classical scholar Christian Gottlob Heyne (1729–1812) and on the German poet and novelist Novalis (1772–1801). A London magazine, *Fraser's,* published Carlyle's review of the correspondence of Goethe and Schiller in 1831. In December 1831, Carlyle published in the *Edinburgh Review* his long and important essay "Characteristics," occasioned by the posthumous publication of Friedrich von Schlegel's *Philosophische Vorlesungen.*

A mere list of titles and subjects can scarcely explain why Carlyle's influence became so potent in America that (as O. B. Frothingham would later remember) "the dregs of his ink-bottle were welcomed as the precious sediment of the fountain of inspiration." Americans probably had fewer prejudices against German literature than the British readers whom Carlyle had tried to hector into admiration, but Americans were equally ignorant. Harvard University did not offer instruction in German until the mid-1820s, and even then the instructor had difficulty attracting students, because the courses were counted as electives. Furthermore, few German books were available in New England bookstores. Why should a group of essays giving biographies and critical accounts of German authors become the rage of intellectual Boston? By 1833 the mania for all things German had become so strong that James Freeman Clarke was almost ashamed to confess to his friend Margaret Fuller that he did not enjoy Goethe's poetry. "Those little *Lieder,* proverbs, etc., are darkness visible to me," he complains. "I really wish you would tell me why and how you like his poetry. Somehow I cannot rightly *auffassen* it" (Clarke to Fuller, September 9, 1833).

The appeal of Carlyle's essays came partly from their willingness to *auffassen,* or apprehend, everything from Goethe's lyrics to the various forms of transcendental philosophy whose ideas were agitating New England theology. In his review of Novalis's writings, Carlyle explains the necessity of giving some account of Fichte's *Wissenschaftlehre,* from which Novalis derived his own philosophical ideas; his summary of the wars between Idealists and empiricists takes the reader all the way from Pyrrho through Kant and the post-Kantian Idealists. Carlyle announces that under the new dispensation inaugurated by Kant – in which time and space are revealed not as external but as internal entities, as forms of the spirit – God's eternity and omnipresence are no longer mysteries. "Nay to the Transcendentalist, clearly enough, the whole question of the origin and existence of Nature must be greatly simplified: the old hostility of Matter is at an end, for matter is itself annihilated; and the black Spectre, Atheism, 'with all its sickly dews,' melts into nothingness forever."

Unlike Coleridge or James Marsh, who looked to German philosophy to solve theological problems, Carlyle gloried in the energy he discovered in German philosophy for its own sake. His essays resonate with contempt for established ideas and practices, and most of all for the complacent shallowness of the fashionable world. Carlyle dwells lovingly on Richter's simplicity, on Fichte's "cold, colossal, adamantine spirit," on Heyne's struggles to educate himself in the face of desperate poverty, and on Schlegel's lifelong efforts to forge a spiritual religion in the midst of denial and unbelief. In "The State of German Literature" (1827) Carlyle introduces his readers to Fichte's lofty conception of the role of the literary man.

According to Fichte, there is a 'Divine Idea' pervading the visible Universe; which visible Universe is indeed but its symbol and sensible manifestation, having in itself no meaning, or even true existence independent of it. To the mass of men this Divine Idea of the world lies hidden: yet to discern it, to seize it, and live wholly in it, is the condition of all genuine virtue, knowlege, freedom; and the end therefore of all spiritual effort in every age. Literary Men are the appointed interpreters of this Divine Idea; a perpetual priesthood, we might say, standing forth generation after generation, as the dispensers and living types of God's everlasting wisdom.

Nor can the literary man shun his obligations to his contemporaries. "For each age, by the law of its nature, is different from every other age, and demands a different representation of this Divine Idea, the essence of which is the same in all; so that the Literary Man of one century is only by mediation and re-interpretation applicable to the wants of another."

To New Englanders, who had scarcely outgrown their Federalist assumptions that a literary man was either a member of the clergy or a lawyer who dabbled in poetry and aimed to win converts to virtue by fictions in which virtue is pleasingly arrayed, such ideas were electrifying. Carlyle was proposing an alternative vocation, a vocation new to America. The literary man need adopt no particular profession; he need produce no poems or plays or essays. The literary life, if sincerely lived, would serve as well as literary works themselves to shadow forth the Divine Idea to the residents of this time and place.

And this time and place need such shadowing forth, for the present (as Carlyle reminds us in "Signs of the Times") is an age of mechanism, an age of soullessness, that believes only in "cause and effect" and no sooner hears of an example of nobility of spirit than it sets about "accounting for it." But if the present appears squalid, we must remember that "The poorest day that passes over us is the conflux of Two Eternities!" If we now "see nothing by direct vision; but only by reflection, and in anatomical dismemberment," we can heal our vision and reintegrate its objects. "Nay, after all, our spiritual maladies are but of Opinion; we are fettered by chains of our own forging, and which ourselves can rend asunder." The events convulsing the political world in recent history are not the signs of an approaching end but the birth pangs of a new world order. "There is a deep-lying struggle in the whole fabric of society; a boundless, grinding collision of the New with the old. The French Revolution, as is now visible enough, was not the parent of this mighty movement but its offspring."

Much that was comforting about the Old World necessarily perishes in this collision of new with old. In "Characteristics" (1831) Carlyle freely admits that the modern Age of Negation appears to offer only despair to the young man whose "whole nature cries aloud for Action" but who can find "nothing sacred under whose banner he can act." The task facing such seekers is as noble as it is daunting. "They have to realise a Worship for themselves, or live unworshipping. The Godlike has vanished from the world; and they, by the strong cry of their soul's agony, like true wonder-workers, must again evoke its presence." Still, though the present is bleak, Carlyle refuses to admit that it is hopeless. "Out of Evil comes Good; and no Good that is possible but shall one day be real," he says. "Nay, already as we look round, streaks of a dayspring are in the east: it is dawning; when the time shall be fulfilled, it will be day."

If Carlyle was right, the bewildering changes taking place in American society might simply be the grinding collision of the new with the old, the darkness that precedes the dawn. (Carlyle's 1829 article "Signs of the Times," after all, begins with a gently mocking rebuke of several British writers who feared that Catholic Emancipation presaged the end of the world. Could Andrew Jackson be worse than Catholic Emancipation?) And if young people were worrying about the disappearance of traditional avenues to power in a rapidly changing society, Carlyle suggested an intoxicating alternative: that their own spiritual struggle might itself *be* action of the most significant kind. They could render the greatest service to their communities simply by recording faithfully what they thought and felt. Such a call to action (O. B. Frothingham said) "kindled all honest hearts." Coleridge had offered philosophy, but what Carlyle offered was "better than philosophy. It was philosophy made vital with sentiment and purpose." Carlyle's new philosophy was the easier to assimilate because it resembled so closely the central Unitarian idea that spiritual life consisted in "self-culture," in the constant striving toward perfection that was every Christian's duty in this life of probation.

Nearly every one of the first-generation Transcendentalists confessed a debt to Carlyle, but Emerson, whose struggles with the problem of vocation were acute, was particularly moved by his words. Emerson's father William had been a theological liberal with an interest in *belles lettres* and had served on the editorial board of the *Monthly Anthology*. His death in 1811 left his widow, Ruth Haskins Emerson, obliged to run a boardinghouse to support her family of five surviving boys. The deprivations they faced, particularly during the difficult years of the War of 1812, left Emerson with a stinging memory of what poverty does to the spirit. But there were nourishing influences as well: the Boston Latin School, the intoxicating oratory of Edward Everett, the possibility of scholarships to Harvard.

Perhaps more important than any of these other influences was the mentorship of Mary Moody Emerson, William Emerson's sister, who lived with the family at various times during Waldo's youth and who kept up a vigorous correspondence with Waldo throughout her long life. Mary (1774–1863) was old enough to remember the earlier generations of family ministers, all of them believers in the doctrines advanced by Jonathan Edwards, convinced of the necessity of conversions and submission to the will of God. Her experience of the intensity of Puritan piety made her ridicule what her nephew later called the "poor, low, thin, unprofitable, unpoetical Humanitarians" of Boston's liberal religion. She kept a spiritual diary that spanned fifty years and ran to a thousand pages. While she lived with the Emerson family she supervised the education of the boys and wrote the family long prayers, which long after her death still echoed in Waldo's memory "with their prophetic and apocalyptic ejaculations." She was a voracious reader not only of theologians and philosophers (Plato, Plotinus, Spinoza, Cudworth, Butler, Clarke, Jonathan Edwards) but also of poets and prose writers (Akenside, Young, Byron, Wordsworth, de Staël). Even when she was not living with the Emerson family she superintended the boys' reading by letter and debated with them the meaning of what they had read. When Waldo entered Harvard in 1817 and made the unsettling acquaintance of the "Scotch Goliath," David Hume, he peppered her with letters containing Humean arguments in hopes that she might refute them. He often recorded her sayings in his journals and tended to adopt her oracular prose style whenever he strove after effects of elevation or spiritual intensity in his own writing.

Mary naturally wished to see the ministerial tradition of the family continued. At first the task fell to the eldest of the Emerson brothers, William (his father's namesake). After a period of schoolkeeping following his Harvard graduation in 1818 William had finally saved enough to pay for a trip to Göttingen to study theology — a course of study that was by now becoming familiar for Americans. He set sail for Europe in December 1823. At first William's letters home were enthusiastic. But gradually he found himself undergoing a crisis of faith similar to the one that seems to have afflicted Edward Everett ten years earlier. Unable to believe any longer in the historical veracity of everything in the Bible, and unable to reject the conclusions of the biblical criticism that had undermined his faith, William made a pilgrimage to Weimar to ask advice of Goethe, who had received earlier American students kindly. Goethe urged him not to abandon the ministry because he could not share all of his parishioners' beliefs. Even if William thought seriously of complying with this advice, he changed his mind during a rough voyage home, when a severe storm made him confront his conscience directly. He decided to give up the idea of becoming a minister, turning instead to the law.

Mary naturally was involved in the uproar that William's decision provoked in the family; to her, the whole episode testified to the "strange apathy of the skeptics of this period" who could bear to live without the presence of divinity. But William was not the only son in the family. Waldo, after spending several years battling ill health and keeping school to raise money for his mother and brothers, finally passed through Harvard Divinity School and in 1826 was approbated to preach. After a period spent "supplying" the pulpits of various country churches, he was asked by the Second Church in

Boston to replace its ailing pastor, Henry Ware, Jr. When continuing ill health forced Ware to resign his pastorate permanently, the church called Emerson to take his place.

The doubts that had bedeviled Emerson throughout the 1820s — stemming from Hume's arguments against miracles and the German critics' attack on the factuality of biblical narratives — had begun to fade before the new light of transcendental philosophy as filtered through de Staël, Coleridge, and Carlyle. If the Reason *is* God, then God is interior to the self, and the self has a principle of illumination no empiricism can menace. All the searches after "evidences," the quests for the historical Jesus or the historical Moses, are fruitless attempts to use the mechanics of the Understanding to discover a truth perceptible to the Reason; they are rendered superfluous by the discovery that the divine is present here and now, in individual human beings, and that it requires of individuals only that they not deny those truths they inwardly perceive. Indeed, submission to the kind of external authority that founds theological schools represents the only apostasy Emerson dreaded — the denial of what one believes to be true in the face of pressure to acquiesce in the beliefs of others.

Such rigorous fidelity to inner conviction would sooner or later cause friction in the life of any practicing minister, even in a denomination as indulgent as the Unitarian. Emerson loved the act of preaching. In the distinctive style of his sermons (over two hundred are still extant) the reader can see many intimations of the style and content of his later orations and essays. His pastoral duties, on the other hand, became increasingly irksome. But the issue on which he finally chose to resign his pulpit had to do with a ritual he had grown to hate celebrating, the Lord's Supper.

Admission to the communion table in Puritan congregations had been restricted to those full church members who could testify to an experience of conversion. It was both a privilege and a badge of spiritual distinction. But with the growth of liberal religion, the monthly communion rite had come to seem to many Unitarians to be at best the relic of an outmoded metaphysical system, at worst an activity slightly ghoulish. An article in the *Christian Examiner* for December 1832 suggests that Emerson was not alone in feeling uncomfortable with the Lord's Supper. According to the writer of this article, many sincere Christians try to live by the precepts of Jesus but cannot bring themselves to take communion because the *elements* of communion service — the bread and the wine — "bear an aspect of strangeness and mystery" that fills the minds of those who would approach them with "dreadful and discouraging impressions."

The writer of the article sees in this attitude the remnants of the superstition Protestantism has only partially expunged:

The peculiar awe, by which this ordinance is separated from every other ordinance of God's appointment; the habit of singling it out, and exalting it above every other mode of worship and means of grace; the singular dread, in the minds of many, of contracting some heinous and mysterious guilt by a wrong participation of it; . . . the very aspect, too, of many communicants, of constraint and almost of distress; the evident feeling which many of them have, that the *elements* are the solemn things in this commemoration, and that it becomes them to have a very special impression of their minds, at the moment when they take into their hands these elements, – all these things, are to our apprehension, proofs, that there is still on this subject a great deal of superstition among us.

The rite the Puritans had celebrated as a confirmation of membership in the society of the Saints had now become an occasion for guilty introspection and feelings of inadequacy or at least a sad reminder of the fervency that has disappeared. The minister, too, was implicated in this unhappiness, because the invitations he issued to attend the Lord's Supper were received by his congregation as occasions for dismay.

Some ministers nevertheless managed to overcome these scruples and revive enthusiasm for the rite in their congregations. Henry Ware, Jr., Emerson's predecessor at the Second Church, had given monthly lectures on the Lord's Supper that attracted large crowds of communicants. Ware's successful revival of the rite only made Emerson more acutely aware of his own discomfort when called on to celebrate it. "I cannot go habitually to an institution which they esteem holiest with indifference and dislike," he wrote. He proposed to the governing board of his church some revisions in the ceremony, including the removal of bread and wine; he wrote a letter to his parishioners explaining his feelings. And, on September 9, 1832, he preached a sermon, "The Lord's Supper," giving in fuller detail his reasons for believing that Jesus had not intended to institute a permanent ritual when he celebrated the Passover with his disciples and that, therefore, Christians are under no obligation to celebrate the Lord's Supper in any particular way.

Parts of Emerson's sermon recall Locke's reasonable arguments in the commentaries on the Epistles of St. Paul, as when Emerson points out that Jesus' injunction to "Do this in memory of me" applies as much to the washing of the feet as it does to the consumption of bread and wine, yet no New England church seriously proposes to have its members wash one another's feet. Other parts are clearly influenced by the historical criticism of the Bible as practiced in Germany (Emerson had asked his brother William for help in marshalling arguments against the authority of the rite). The example of the Quakers, who rejected the communion rite along with all other rituals of the established church, may have lent support to Emerson's decision; he was an admirer of George Fox and had recently read William Sewall's history of the Quakers.

The deciding argument for Emerson, however, was more personal than any of these. "This mode of commemorating Christ is not suitable to me. That is reason enough why I should abandon it." Even if Christ *had* intended to enjoin a permanent commemoration upon all Christians, "and yet on trial it was disagreeable to my own feelings, I should not adopt it. I should choose other ways which, as more effectual upon me, he would approve more." Such calm insistence upon the primacy of individual judgment is the end point of Protestant Christianity, the point at which even the historical Jesus can be discarded as an impediment to the spirit of the religion he founded. "Forms are as essential as bodies; but to exalt particular forms, to adhere to one form a moment after it is outgrown, is unreasonable, and it is alien to the spirit of Christ." What Emerson reveres in Christianity is "its reality, its boundless charity, its deep interior life, the rest it gives to mind, the echo it returns to my thoughts." Any form or rite that attempts to attract permanent devotion to itself should be rejected by the church, whose institutions "should be as flexible as the wants of men. That form out of which the life and suitableness have departed should be as worthless as the dead leaves that are falling around us." Two main themes of Emerson's mature work are already stated clearly in this sermon: the primacy of the individual and the superiority of the creating spirit to any forms it has generated.

Emerson's young wife, Ellen Tucker Emerson, had died of tuberculosis in 1831; his own health had been poor, and the strain of the crisis in his ministry had worsened it. Many of his parishioners were reluctant to part with Emerson and might have been willing to allow him to celebrate the Lord's Supper as a commemorative rite without bread and wine, but the proprietors of pews finally voted 30 to 24 to accept his resignation. He decided to travel to Europe in hopes of regaining his health and strength. On Christmas Day 1832 he set sail from Boston in the trading ship *Jasper,* arriving in Malta in February 1833. Like most American tourists in that distant age when American tourists were a curiosity, Emerson sought out his literary heroes wherever he could and was received by them. Many of these meetings were disappointing, sometimes comically so. Wordsworth almost made him laugh by suddenly offering to repeat some newly written sonnets for him, striking a pose in the garden walk like a schoolboy reciting. The anti-Unitarian harangue Coleridge delivered when his guest identified himself as a Bostonian sounded suspiciously as if it had been memorized. Only Thomas Carlyle gave Emerson the kind of expansive, exuberant conversation he had come to the Old World for, and the visit began a friendship and a correspondence that was to last (with some notable ruptures) for as long as both men lived.

Before he left for Europe Emerson had managed to find out the identity of the author of the *Edinburgh* articles that had excited him. He was determined to track Carlyle down – no easy task, because Carlyle and his wife Jane were then living in an isolated farmhouse at Craigenputtock in the countryside southwest of Glasgow. To get there Emerson had to hire a gig in the nearest town and travel sixteen miles through the hills. But his reception by the Carlyles was as warm as he could have wished. When he departed a day later after a torrent of talk he left behind an affection almost as great as the one he himself felt. *Sartor Resartus* was about to start appearing serially in *Fraser's,* and Carlyle promised to send Emerson a copy of the whole when publication was complete. *Fraser's* had printed copies of the episodes and stitched the pages together for Carlyle to distribute privately; he sent Emerson one copy for his own use and a few others for distribution to sympathetic friends.

For his part, Emerson elected to become Carlyle's unpaid literary agent in America. Because the United States had no copyright agreement with Great Britain publishers were free to pirate British works without paying royalties to the authors. By negotiating with publishers in the United States on behalf of Carlyle for rights to first American publication of his works, Emerson was able to ensure that his friend received royalties from the American editions of his books. He forwarded all profits from these editions to Carlyle. The bank drafts he sent to Carlyle over the course of their long relationship eventually added up to more than seven hundred pounds. (Carlyle, pleased but embarrassed by this generosity, did what he could to reciprocate by arranging the London publication of Emerson's *Essays* in 1841.)

Emerson's fascination with Carlyle was widely shared among the young Boston liberals. His cousin George Ripley (1802–80), a Unitarian minister in Boston, was so overwhelmed by reading one of the stitched-together copies of *Sartor* that he immediately drafted an effusive four-page letter to Carlyle proclaiming himself Carlyle's grateful disciple. But devotion to Carlyle involved more than feelings of exhilaration, as Ripley and others well understood. The closing paragraphs of "Characteristics" invoke Ecclesiastes: "Whatsoever thy hand findeth to do, do it with all thy might." The necessity of action is made even more explicit in *Sartor Resartus*. If Carlyle preached a new gospel, how were his American disciples to put it into practice?

Because most of Carlyle's Boston admirers were members of the clergy or theological students they naturally thought first of church reform when they sought occasions for principled action. If the Unitarians who had initially broken with orthodoxy at the turn of the century had carried the standard of liberal religion as far as they could, their successors would seize it and carry it the rest of the way – to a religion both enlightened and truly "spiritual." At the same time the reforming spirit began to bear fruit among those who were outside the ministerial class altogether. This wider participation was what gave more than one observer the feeling that some great transformation was about to take place in New England society.

The expansion of the literary universe was perhaps the first evidence of the transformation. Carlyle's essays on German authors moved many of the young people to try to learn what seemed an alien and menacing tongue. Harvard professors like George Ticknor and Edward Everett had brought back from Germany a high regard for the achievements of German scholarship and of German humanism generally; when the young German émigré Charles Follen joined the Harvard faculty in 1825, he too helped to bring German authors into notice. But the most aggressive study seems to have begun outside the academy.

Margaret Fuller (1810–50) was the brilliant and precocious daughter of a strong-willed New England congressman who chose to give his first-born child the kind of education usually reserved for boys. Timothy Fuller, who had graduated from Harvard in 1801 and who served in the United States House of Representatives from 1817 to 1825, appointed himself tutor to his daughter and supervised her reading carefully even when he was away in Washington. When she was eight years old she was already studying Latin and arithmetic and reading accounts of the warrior kings Charles XIII of Sweden and Phillip II of Spain in Valpy's *Chronology of Ancient and English History;* the next year she was reading and memorizing passages of Griesbach's Greek New Testament (the text used by Harvard undergraduates). When she was fifteen she passed on to chemistry, philosophy, and Lord Kames's *Elements of Criticism.* That same year (1825) she addressed a letter to General Lafayette, who had been the recipient of universal adulation when he visited Boston the previous year. She tells him of the "ardent sentiment of affection and enthusiastic admiration" that pervades her soul whenever she thinks of him and of the "noble ambition" the contemplation of his character arouses in her. An odd sentence follows. "Should we both live, and it is possible to a female, to whom the avenues of glory are seldom accessible, I will recal[l] my name to your recollection." What seems missing from the sentence is the hope too intense to be named: *if it is nevertheless possible for me to achieve glory.*

Such ambition seems to lurk behind Fuller's later approach to intellectual life. She treated new areas of study as if they were territories to occupy and did so with a speed that astonished her contemporaries. Her social life in Boston in the late 1820s brought her into contact with the Unitarian literati; she heard Emerson preach and struck up an intense friendship with James Freeman Clarke, then a student at the Harvard Divinity School. Fired with enthusiasm for German literature by Carlyle's essays, she began to study German with Clarke in 1832. He later remembered: "Within a year she had read Goethe's Faust, Tasso, Iphigenie, Hermann and Dorothea, Elective Affinities, and Memoirs; Tieck's William Lovell, Prince Zerbino, and other works; Körner, Novalis, and something of Richter; all of Schiller's principal dramas, and his lyric poetry." When Clarke listened to her talk confidently about German intellectual life he had a "very decided feeling of mental inferiority," as he confided to his journal in 1832. "I felt how she traced ideas through minds & works, how questions rose before her, how she carried the initiative idea everywhere. In other words how comprehensive & understanding is her intellect." In contrast, his own mind seemed "a sheet of white paper on which any one might write."

Yet self-culture was not the only area of interest to the emerging group of Transcendentalists. If the German philosophers were right about the mind's structure and relation to the world, then the prevailing system of education was hopelessly and radically wrong. Rote learning, drill, and coercion were all cruel and wasteful ways to teach children. True education should be a coaxing out or an unfolding of the mind's intuitions, not a cramming session in which unrelated facts are stuffed into empty and recalcitrant heads. In the late 1820s James Marsh had introduced a curriculum at the University of Vermont designed to replace recitation with lectures and discussions and to replace the haphazard curriculum of most American colleges with one in which the various subjects would be arranged to exhibit "a development and a growth" so that studying it "should be a growing and enlarging process to the mind of the student." In 1834 a largely self-taught educator named Amos Bronson Alcott (1799–1888) established a school in Boston where he could put into practice his conviction that children possessed an intuitive knowledge of truth and hence required rather to be "drawn out" than indoctrinated.

After a hardscrabble rural childhood in Connecticut and a series of unprofitable *wanderjahre* as a feckless Yankee peddler in the South, Alcott had turned to teaching in the common schools of Connecticut. Disliking the harsh methods and stultifying practices of the usual schools of the period, he replaced the backless wooden benches of the standard country classroom with comfortable desks and chairs he himself built. He decorated the walls with pictures and cypress boughs and left a bare space in the center of the classroom for pleasant activities like dancing, in hopes that the students would come to associate the classroom with pleasure and not with pain. He tried to engage the students' interest with teaching materials designed to awaken their curiosity and draw upon their own experiences. Although he was by no means a slack disciplinarian he insisted that students themselves judge infractions of rules in a student court; malefactors were not beaten but were instead required to make a public apology to the school.

While he taught he was also trying to work out a theory of education and child development, reading contemporary reformers like the Swiss educator Pestalozzi and studying philosophers from Plato through Kant. On the face of it, education seemed to be a Lockean enterprise, an inscribing on the blank tablet of the mind. Clearly, no child came to school knowing Latin or plane geometry. But if the Platonic, Neoplatonic, and Kantian Idealists Alcott had been reading or reading about were correct, the child's mind already contained within it the principles the teacher was trying to instill. How could one reconcile the contradiction? The problem was solved for Alcott when he read Marsh's edition of Coleridge's *Aids to Reflection*. This work became for Alcott, as it did for so many of his generation, a way of embracing the delights of Idealism without having to give up the solid good of the material world. Alcott now decided that the goal of education was *both* to draw out the spirit of the child and to store in the child's mind useful knowledge. And this goal was achievable because the world itself had been created by God and bore evidence of its divine origin. The world and the mind were hence reciprocal influences, "appulsive and impulsive," which a true pedagogy could unite. "The analogy between the mind and the outward world is the parent of thought," Alcott asserted.

His methods won Alcott the affection of the students, but parents accustomed to measuring their child's progress by the amount of material memorized were impatient with him and unwilling to pay the higher fees he asked or purchase the books and supplies he demanded for his classroom. Although his school in Connecticut received praise from visiting educational reformers, he lost pupils and had to close it. For the next seven years Alcott wandered from place to place — to Boston, then to Germantown, Pennsylvania, then to Philadelphia, and finally back to Boston again — opening and closing schools, experimenting with educational techniques, and reading voraciously in philosophy, theology, and the literature of reform. When his wife, Abby, gave birth to daughters, he determined to observe their behavior closely, convinced that an account of the mind's development from earliest infancy would give better insight into human nature than any explanation the philosophers could provide. A sentence from the manuscript of observations he made about his second child, Louisa May Alcott (born November 29, 1832), suggests how vast his view of his own profession had become. "Education, when duly regarded, is the preservation of the relations of the human being to the universe."

Unfortunately, Alcott's skill at preserving a child's relations to the uni-

verse rarely helped him to preserve his own family from want. He was so
dedicated an idealist that he reminded his friends of the ancient sages and so
impractical a provider that he repeatedly plunged his family into destitution.
Irrepressibly hopeful, opinionated, the strictest of vegetarians, he reminded
more than one observer of Don Quixote. When his Philadelphia school was
on the verge of collapse, one of Alcott's friends alerted William Ellery
Channing, who had been among Alcott's earlier Boston patrons, and Channing promised his assistance in securing patrons for Alcott in Boston. In this
project he was aided by the enthusiasm of Channing's admirer and secretary,
Elizabeth Peabody (1804–94).

Peabody had been so impressed by the journals written by Alcott's young
scholars and by Alcott's conversation when she met him ("He stayed and
talked like an embodiment of intellect," she wrote) that she helped engage
students for him. She also found a suitable room for the school in Boston's
Masonic Temple and donated some of her own furniture to furnish the room.
Most importantly, she agreed to serve Alcott as an assistant to teach those
academic subjects – Latin, arithmetic, and geography – he lacked the formal education to provide.

Peabody's response, like those of Fuller and Alcott, shows how people not
part of the traditional Boston–Cambridge educational system could be swept
up in the excitement of the new movements and contribute to their development. Born in Billerica, Massachusetts, in 1804, she received a thorough
education from her parents in history, rhetoric, and Latin before she began
teaching school. Hopeful of earning more money to help educate her brothers
by teaching school in either Boston or Cambridge she emigrated to the area
in the early 1820s. Peabody was immediately dazzled by the "brilliancy" of
Cambridge society. She heard Channing preach; she took Greek lessons from
Ralph Waldo Emerson and became friendly with James Freeman Clarke. She
wrote several history texts for schools (including studies of the Hebrews and
the Greeks) and held evening "conversations" on history for women who
would pay her ten dollars for a course of meetings on such subjects as "Some
articles on the Poetry &c of the Heroic ages from several sources; Herodotus'
History; – Schlegel on Dramatic literature as far as it is applicable to Greece
& the time of Socrates." Another course she planned would include "Herder's
exquisite book on the 'Spirit of Hebrew Poetry' – Parts of Michaelis upon the
Jewish law – The Old Testament history." Ability to converse upon such
subjects was a necessary accomplishment in a society where (as she had
written in one of her first letters home) "You seem to be moving all the time
for every thing about you is an a state of progressive improvement and if you
stand still – bye and bye they will forget you were ever 'one of them.' "

In 1833 Johann Gottfried van Herder's *Spirit of Hebrew Poetry* had just been published by James Marsh. The book by now was fifty years old; Moses Stuart had tried to interest Edward Everett in translating it as long ago as 1818, but the task remained unattempted until Marsh began publishing parts of his translation serially in the *Biblical Repertory* in 1826. Many changes had taken place in biblical criticism since Herder's book had originally appeared in 1782, and scholars in New England were already using the work of later and technically more accomplished scholars like Schleiermacher. Nevertheless, when Marsh completed his translation of *The Spirit of Hebrew Poetry* in 1833 and issued it from the same University of Vermont press that had published *Aids to Reflection* in 1829 and *The Friend* in 1831, it provoked considerable interest among the general reading public. Elizabeth Peabody wrote a series of articles prompted by Marsh's translation, for the *Christian Examiner* in 1833 and 1834 (until Andrews Norton, disturbed by the articles, stopped their publication). Herder's approach to the study of texts from "primitive" societies shaped Peabody's understanding of ancient cultures for the rest of her life.

Herder had become persuaded that (as one modern biblical scholar says) "poetry is in its origins no mere deliberate artifact, and language no mere signpost representing sense data and the substances for which they stand." Among primitive peoples poetry is a "spontaneous and natural expression" of feeling and perception: they speak in figures, and their narrative naturally assumes the shape of myth. "In the poetical vein of our native tongue," Peabody wrote, "we must find the key of interpretation to the language of the Old Testament, which is entirely primitive." God speaks to each generation in the language appropriate to it, and the truths about the outward Creation he gave to the ancient Hebrews "were conveyed, not with the logical precision in which they are now stated, but embodied in a narrative, brilliant, bold, glowing, full of imagery, calculated to take hold of the imagination and be amalgamated with the soul."

Obviously, Herder's *Spirit of Hebrew Poetry* offered weapons to anyone eager to attack the prevailing notion of biblical miracles as historical accounts of empirically verifiable violations of the natural order. But even more important, for the moment, was the secret stimulus given to creativity by Herder's glowing evocation of primitive poetry. If the Hebrews were not passive instruments of divine inspiration but rather were poets who perceived vividly and spoke faithfully of what they saw and heard, might not a similar adjustment in vision and a similar determination to be forthright produce a *modern* scripture? And might not a style "brilliant, bold, glowing, full of imagery" reawaken the piety that had animated those early men?

4

"ANNUS MIRABILIS"

I N THE SPRING OF 1836, the year that Perry Miller would call the *"Annus Mirabilis"* of the Transcendentalist movement, the American Unitarian Association issued a small pamphlet entitled *Christianity as a Purely Internal Principle.* Its author was a forty-year-old minister named Convers Francis (1795–1863), a genial man whom O. B. Frothingham called "a liberal scholar, in the best sense of the phrase; learned without pedantry; open to the light from every quarter; an enormous reader of books; a great student of German philosophy and divinity, as few at that time were." Francis had occupied the pulpit at Watertown, Massachusetts, since 1819, preaching a liberal Christianity that emphasized the human element in the Bible and publishing reviews in the *Christian Examiner* in which he affirmed his belief that the human soul was "a particle of the divine mind." In *Christianity as a Purely Internal Principle* Francis argues that Christianity's distinction lies in its having been "the first and only system, which professed to build its kingdom wholly within the soul of man." All attempts to derive religious feeling from something outward — whether the rituals of the Catholic church or the emotional conversion experiences of the evangelicals — are false to the spirit of Christianity's founder, who asked "for no province but the affections, principles, and motives of man, for no throne but his heart."

Francis's pamphlet, an eloquent expression of Unitarian piety, contained nothing radical, though its emphasis on Christianity as an inward principle of spiritual enlargement made it dear to the younger people whom he served as friend and mentor. Francis's slight reputation for daring came from his willingness to entertain ideas bolder than his own. But even that much openness was a welcome change from the cautious tone that marked the regularly scheduled meetings for Unitarian clergy. These gatherings were increasingly irksome to the younger clergy, who were reluctant to raise subjects their seniors disapproved of yet who felt frustrated at not being able to discuss freely the moral and theological issues that concerned them.

These younger clergy decided to form a club of their own. Frederic Henry Hedge, from his post in Bangor, Maine, had suggested the meeting in a letter to Emerson during the summer. "The plan is this, to have a meeting, annual or oftener if possible, of certain likeminded persons of our acquaintance for the free discussion of theological & moral subjects," Hedge wrote. Why was such an association necessary? Because the "lamentable want of courage" shown at regular conventions of Unitarian ministers and the diffidence of younger ministers in the presence of their "elders & betters" made candid discussion of theological issues impossible. Membership in this new society, which was to be by invitation, would be limited to Unitarian ministers like themselves (though Emerson insisted on being allowed to invite Bronson Alcott). The sole rule the members agreed to was that no one whose presence might prevent discussion of any particular subject could be invited to meetings. This club, which was to meet some thirty times in the next four years, was first called by Emerson "The Symposium"; he later called it by the less pretentious title "Hedge's Club," because it usually met when Hedge visited from Bangor. Most people simply called it the Transcendental Club, using the nickname they were beginning to apply to all members of the movement.

Hedge, Emerson, George Ripley, and Emerson's cousin George Putnam met in Cambridge on September 8, 1836, to plan the new club, which would hold its first official meeting at Ripley's house in Boston eleven days later. On September 9, 1836, a small book entitled *Nature* was published in Boston by James Monroe and Company. The author of the ninety-five-page book was anonymous, though area residents soon guessed that the author was Emerson. The book's title page bore an epigraph from Plotinus that spoke of nature as "but an image or imitation of wisdom, the last thing of the soul." Later in the book Emerson would say that this absolute Idealism can at one stroke transfer nature into the mind, leaving matter behind like an outcast corpse. In its calm assertiveness and refusal to descend into argument, this brief quotation from the third-century Egyptian philosopher reminds us of a time when poetry and philosophy were still (to use one of Emerson's favorite words in *Nature*) "coincident."

Yet the first words of *Nature's* "Introduction" come from a different stylistic universe altogether, one full of satire and scorn. "Our age is retrospective. It builds the sepulchres of the fathers." In two sentences Emerson seems to dismiss his own era as one in which piety to the dead has taken the place of fresh creation, and reverence is indistinguishable from morbidity. But then he proceeds to hold out hope, using the burly Saxon idiom Carlyle favored in his more encouraging moments. Why, after all, should we pay homage only to the dead? The whole lesson of nature is regeneration. "The sun shines today also. There is more wool and flax in the fields. There are new lands, new men, new thoughts. Let us demand our own works and laws and worship."

These two events — the publication of Emerson's *Nature* and the formation of the Transcendental Club — both suggest something important about Transcendentalism. We often think of the movement as an affair of isolated selves writing in lonely integrity, like Thoreau at Walden Pond. But Transcendentalism was also very much a coterie affair, and the strong emotions it evoked from its participants show how much fire lay beneath the native frost of the New England character. In 1836 few of the darker passions that might be generated by such elevated hopes and intense communing were yet visible. The Transcendentalists then felt confident that they were the conduits for a stream of revolutionary ideas from Europe intended to break up the last ice floes of provincial culture, that they were the renewers of spiritual life. Nowhere is the excitement more infectious than in Emerson's little book, which begins by inquiring "to what end is nature?" and (after carefully ascending a ladder of nature's "uses" to humanity) ends by offering a fable of apocalypse in which fallen man recognizes in the "great apparition" of external nature merely the form of the divine body he has alienated.

Unitarianism had always exalted the study of nature as a way of learning to admire God's infinitely wise design, and Emerson had from an early age filled his journals with facts gleaned from his scientific reading, convinced that "the axioms of physics translate the laws of ethics" (a maxim he borrowed from Madame de Staël's *De l'Allemagne*). His sermons were made vivid by his free use of these natural analogies. As he became increasingly dissatisfied with Christianity as a historical religion he longed to find its ethical truths inscribed elsewhere. Natural science provided one way of transforming the vast text of nature into legible truths; the Swedenborgian doctrine of "correspondence" seemed to offer another.

Emerson was strongly attracted to the system of beliefs that American admirers of the Swedish visionary Emanuel Swedenborg (1688–1772) were expounding in their periodical the *New Jerusalem Magazine.* The doctrine of "correspondence," or the belief that each object in the sensible world corresponds to some truth in the moral world, offered hope that nature itself might be a storehouse of meanings more coherent and more universally accessible than Scripture. Although Emerson rejected the rigid sectarianism of the Swedenborgians, he found the idea of correspondence intoxicating.

A simple translation of natural objects into meanings is one kind of "correspondence," but Emerson often uses the word to refer to a different kind of tallying, one that suggested itself to him when he visited the Jardin des Plantes in Paris during his European tour of 1833. As he stood before the specimens in the cabinet of natural history, he believed that he could see "the upheaving principle of life" suggested by the rows and rows of related specimens. "Not a form so grotesque, so savage, nor so beautiful but is an expression of some property in man the observer, — an occult relation between the very scorpions and man." This revelation caused him to announce, "I am moved by strange sympathies. I say continually, 'I will be a naturalist.' " Here the human being is at the center of the correspondential universe, and the natural world radiates out from him like a vast Unconscious; the task of the naturalist is to reverse the process (whatever it was) that alienated these human properties into the foreign shapes that constitute the vast allegory we behold as the universe.

Emerson's desire to explore these two kinds of "correspondence" received an unexpected stimulus from the new lyceum movement just gaining strength in the United States. When he returned home from Europe, Emerson discovered that this adult education movement (loosely modeled on the workingmen's colleges in England) and its appetite for trained lecturers gave him a handy pulpit from which to preach on any topic that appealed to him. Throughout the winter of 1834–5 Emerson delivered a number of lectures on natural history to different groups in Boston. Writing a course of lectures for a lyceum audience was very much like writing sermons, except that in Emerson's lectures nature had now become the sacred text to be expounded instead of merely the source from which illustrative metaphors could be drawn. "A fact is an epiphany of God."

Still, isolated facts, no matter how radiant with spiritual meaning, could never compose themselves into a new scripture without *theory*, an ordering principle emanating from the mind that arranges phenomena in such a way that they suggest the presence of an underlying *law* – as the phenomena of electricity suggest the more general law of *polarity* operating throughout nature. These terms are taken from Coleridge, whose "Essays on Method" in *The Friend* Emerson studied while he was working on *Nature*. By March 1836 Emerson had hit on a scheme that would allow him to arrange and classify the hundreds of observations about nature he had been collecting in his journals for years. Nature strives upward. It ministers to human needs, satisfies the love of beauty, furnishes us with language by providing sensible images for abstract thoughts. "Finally; Nature is a discipline, & points to the pupil & exists for the pupil. Her being is subordinate, his is superior. Man underlies ideas. Nature receives them as her god." But Idealism, though it seems at first like the goal toward which nature is tending, is quickly swallowed up in even vaster schemes for human glorification. As Emerson complains in "Spirit," the chapter that follows "Idealism," a theory of nature that only denies the existence of matter cannot "satisfy the demands of the spirit. It leaves God out of me."

Emerson means that final sentence quite literally. No religion or philosophical system that places God outside the self seems credible to him; it denies that primary experience of divinity that is exhilaration's gift to the soul. However impotent human beings seem when they compare themselves to the vast forces of the natural world, they still have sensations of omnipotence in those isolated moments when the "axis of vision" becomes coincident with the "axis of things." Records of such influxes of power are sprinkled throughout *Nature,* most notoriously in the "transparent eyeball" passage from its first chapter: "Standing on the bare ground, – my head bathed by the blithe air, and uplifted into infinite space, – all mean egotism vanishes. I become a transparent eye-ball; I am nothing; I see all; the currents of the Universal Being circulate through me; I am part or particle of God."

The *conviction* that nature is phenomenal and the *feeling* that we are divine combine to provide at last an answer to those venerable questions, "What is matter? Whence is it? and Whereto?" If we carefully attend to the truths that arise to us out of the recesses of consciousness we will learn that

spirit does not act upon us from without, that is, in space and time, but spiritually, or through ourselves; therefore, that spirit, that is, the Supreme Being, does not build up nature around us, but puts it forth through us, as the life of the tree puts forth new branches and leaves through the pores of the old.

The model for this curious extrusion theory of creation might have come from Fichte, whose ideas Emerson had found summarized in Carlyle's essay on Novalis, or from Alcott, who had cobbled together his own mythology from the Platonic and Neoplatonic philosophers he had read in Thomas Taylor's translations. Emerson had met Alcott when he visited the Temple School; the two had immediately become attracted to one another, and Alcott had visited Emerson in Concord and involved him in voluminous and gratifying conversation. But however Emerson came by his extrusion theory of creation, he finally dismisses it as inadequate. Though it reassures us that "the world proceeds from the same spirit as the body of man," it does not tell us how to make that world subject to our *will.* In the sexually charged language that dominates the closing chapters of *Nature,* Emerson complains, that "its serene order is inviolable by us."

"Prospects," the final chapter in *Nature,* does not offer advice about violating the serene order of nature, but it does explain how nature came to frustrate our desires in the first place. Emerson explains this not in discursive prose but in a fable, like the small fables embedded in Platonic dialogues or the *Märchen* contained in the German texts described by Carlyle. The fable in *Nature* describes man as a divine being who, fallen into division, is now the "dwarf of himself," timidly adoring a universe that is his forgotten emanation. The only divine power yet remaining in this dwarf is "instinct," a power not inferior but superior to man's will. Instinct is to the will what the Reason is to the intellect, and when we learn to work upon nature with all our might we will find that the "fallenness" of nature was an illusion created by the weakness of our wills. "The problem of restoring to the world original and eternal beauty, is solved by the redemption of the soul." When that restored world will come we cannot say, for it is, like the kingdom of heaven in the Bible, something that "cometh not with observation." But it will be beyond our present "dream of God."

Alcott was delighted with Emerson's little book, describing it in his journal as "the production of a spiritualist, subordinating the visible and outward to the inward and invisible." He was pleased to discover in it allusions to the vast manuscript on childhood development, entitled *Psyche*, he had left with Emerson the summer before. From England, Carlyle praised *Nature* as the "foundation and Ground-plan" on which he was sure Emerson would build his future achievement. In Boston a reform-minded Unitarian minister named Orestes Brownson (1803–76) reviewed *Nature* in the weekly paper he edited, the *Boston Reformer;* he hailed it as "an index to the spirit which is silently at work among us, as a proof that the mind is about to receive a new and more glorious manifestation." But Brownson's praise was tempered by dismay at Emerson's philosophical Idealism. To doubt the existence of the phenomenal world as Berkeley and Fichte had done seemed to Brownson to begin a process of questioning that would end by undermining the questioner. "He who denies the testimony of his senses, seems to have no ground for believing the apperceptions of consciousness; and to deny those is to set oneself afloat upon the ocean of universal scepticism."

Brownson differed in significant ways from most of his clerical colleagues. Orestes Brownson was born in 1803, the son of a poor Vermont farmer who died leaving his widow with six young children. She tried to keep the family together, but eventually she had to place Orestes and his twin sister, Daphne, with an elderly couple to raise. Strict Congregationalists, they gave him an appetite for religion that had him reading volumes of theology and arguing predestination while he was still a child. He early determined to become a minister, though his formal schooling had been limited to a brief stint in an academy in upstate New York, where his reunited family had moved when he was fourteen.

Brownson's spiritual life was restless, driven by a need for solace and a hunger for doctrinal consistency that sent him on a pilgrimage through various denominations. Moved by a Presbyterian sermon when he was about nineteen he joined the Presbyterian church, but he found himself repelled by its Calvinist theology. When he was subsequently stricken with a serious illness he had time to study the Universalist tracts a proselytizing aunt urged upon him and decided to join the Universalists. He liked the Universalist opposition to Calvinist preoccupation with sin and damnation as well as its reassurance that all men would be saved. When he had recovered from his illness he began a career as a Universalist minister.

His demands for logical consistency, however, soon made havoc of Brownson's second faith. He distressed his new colleagues by airing his doubts in the *Gospel Advocate and Universal Investigator,* a Universalist journal of which he had become editor. Perplexed by the problem of social evil here on earth, he went to hear the British radical Frances Wright lecture when she came to Utica, New York, and struck up a friendship with her. She led him to read the writings of the British social reformer Robert Owen, whose suggestions for solving the problems of poverty and degradation intrigued him, if they did not entirely convince him. He joined the Workingmen's party and briefly edited one of their newspapers, the New York *Free Enquirer.* By 1830, however, both his faith in the party and his faith in God were beginning to crumble. Labor seemed to him too weak ever to compete politically in the United States with capital; and the "natural theology" of moral philosophers like William Paley (1743–1805) seemed so unconvincing that reading them precipitated Brownson headlong into the skepticism of Hume.

After a few months of lingering in the bleak world to which his reason seemed to condemn him, his heart, that "witness within" whose testimony he found corroborated by the whole of external nature, recalled Brownson to faith. A friend read to him Channing's sermon "Likeness to God," and it so impressed him that he began to consider Channing his "spiritual father" and to think of himself as a Unitarian. He persuaded a Unitarian congregation in New Hampshire to offer him a position as its minister.

Gradually Brownson's vigorous preaching and lyceum lecturing attracted notice in Boston, where he often traveled. George Ripley befriended him and urged him to accept pulpits closer to Boston. He served for two years in Canton, Massachusetts, whose working-class population reawakened in him an interest in social issues which his contemporary reading in the works of Saint-Simon (1760–1825) helped to crystallize into a philosophy of reform. Brownson decided that Christianity was to be a social gospel: The "church of the future" he imagined would employ moral reform to make war against the personal selfishness that underlies systems of social inequality. Ripley had high hopes that Brownson's preaching might attract hearers among the working classes where Unitarianism's appeal was marginal and so help revitalize a denomination whose decorousness threatened to extinguish its life.

By the time Brownson had moved to Chelsea and started holding independent services in Boston during the early months of 1836 he had begun to speak out frankly against social inequality. On the last Sunday of May he preached a discourse, "The Wants of the Times," that warned of the conflict breaking out all over the world "between the many and the few, the privi-

leged and the underprivileged." He urged the formation of a Society for
Christian Union and Progress that would put into effect the principles of
Jesus, "the prophet of the workingmen."

Doubtless at Ripley's urging, Brownson was invited to the first full meeting of the Transcendental Club on September 19, 1836. He proved to be a
difficult companion — a brilliant talker fond of argument and impatient with
woolly reasoning, who chewed tobacco and pounded on the table when he
was angry. By the summer of 1837 the club's members appear to have
decided that Brownson had (as Hedge later put it) become unbearable, for his
name no longer appears on any lists of the members who attended meetings.
But in 1836 he still was publicly identified with the Transcendentalists, and
the book that he published on November 29 of that year was interpreted as
one of their manifestos.

New Views of Christianity, Society and the Church drew heavily on Brownson's
reading in French and German authors, particularly Victor Cousin, whose
philosophy of eclecticism was naturally appealing to a self-taught man. In
New Views Brownson unfolds a theory of history that portrays civilization as a
continual struggle between spiritualism and materialism. Jesus, as the God-
man, unites both spirit and matter (this is what is meant by "the atonement"); the "church of the future" must do so too. So far Brownson's doctrine
sounds innocuous enough, yet the historical interpretations he generates with
it are surprising. The "spiritual principle" is represented in history by Asia,
Egypt, Judea, and the Catholic church; the material principle, by Greece,
Rome, and Protestantism.

Protestantism (which was necessary to rescue the human race from the
excesses of the spiritual principle) as a material religion is friendly to civil and
political liberty and to industry; its exploits in recent history have been
nothing short of miraculous. It imagines for man "a new paradise . . .
inaccessible to the serpent, more delightful than that which Adam lost" and
tries to realize that paradise on earth. Protestantism reaches its ultimate
development in the American and French revolutions, particularly in the
latter. "God was converted into a symbol of the human reason, and man into
the Man-Machine; Spiritualism fell, and the Revolution marked the complete triumph of Materialism."

But the revolution failed, and men once again took "refuge in heaven."
The English discovered the mysticism of the East in the Hindu scriptures,
and the influence of the spiritual world is once again visible in European
literature, in Byron, Wordsworth, and the Schlegels. A new synthesis is now
possible. Unitarianism, as the "last word of Protestantism," clearly belongs
to the material order: "It vindicates the rights of the mind, accepts and uses
the reason, contends for civil freedom and is social, charitable, and humane."

Like all Protestant sects it lacks true spirituality; such piety as it has is merely a reminiscence of the beliefs of the medieval church. "It saves the Son of man, but sometimes loses the Son of God." Its contribution to progress up to now has been largely negative, "a work of destruction," clearing away the rubbish of the old church to make way for the future.

Unitarianism is the only sect that has "the requisite union of piety and mental freedom"; it alone can create a philosophy "which explains Humanity, determines its wants and the means of supplying them." Out of Unitarianism therefore shall come the "church of the future" and the salvation of the human race. Traditional Unitarians must have felt that such left-handed compliments to Unitarianism were almost worse than the abuse of the Calvinists; the more far-seeing among them might even have been able to predict that Brownson would end his spiritual quest in 1844 by converting to Roman Catholicism. But the radical theses he was propounding were largely overlooked amid the outbreak of hostilities in another controversy involving Brownson's friend George Ripley.

In March 1836 Ripley had published a long article entitled "Schleiermacher as a Theologian" in the *Christian Examiner.* In it he spoke favorably of Schleiermacher's attempt to formulate a "religion of the heart" based on intuition and a sense of communion with God. Later in the year Ripley reviewed the British Unitarian James Martineau's *Rationale of Religious Inquiry* (1836), which had attempted to apply inductive logic to questions of religious certainty and had placed great stress upon the miracles of Jesus as authenticating events. Ripley did not deny that the miracles had occurred and were important, but he argued that Jesus' moral teachings were self-evidently true and did not need to be confirmed by miraculous displays of power.

When Andrews Norton read Ripley's review he was furious enough to consider severing all connection with the *Christian Examiner,* of which he was an official "sponsor." Norton had retired from Harvard in 1830 to devote himself full time to his scholarship, but he had become increasingly distressed by the drift toward political and theological radicalism among the faculty and students of the Divinity School as well as by the refusal of the *Christian Examiner* to close its pages to writers Norton considered irresponsible. He had earlier tried and failed to convince the *Examiner*'s editor that the magazine was the "sole work in the world" in which intelligent Christians could express "correct views of religion"; allowing it to be polluted by the "crude thoughts" of undisciplined speculators was a betrayal of public trust (Norton to James Walker, December 7, 1835).

Norton finally decided to remain a sponsor of the *Examiner;* but he published a letter in the Boston *Daily Advertiser* on November 5, 1836, attacking Ripley and warning of the danger of doctrines that tend to destroy the only evidence upon which belief in the divine origin of Christianity can rest. Ripley replied in a dignified letter four days later that though he remembered with gratitude the instruction he had received from his former teacher, surely Norton of all people was scarcely in a position to brand doctrines as heretical or try to suppress their publication. Interest in the controversy was sufficiently great for the weekly *Christian Register* to print the exchange of letters in its November 12 issue; later correspondents continued the controversy.

Late November offered more material from the Transcendentalists to distress conservative Unitarians. On November 14 Emerson's childhood friend William Henry Furness (1802–96), now a Unitarian minister in Philadelphia, published his *Remarks on the Four Gospels*. In *Remarks* Furness attempts to replace the standard Unitarian interpretation of miracles as an interruption of the laws of nature (given by Channing in his famous Dudleian lecture, "The Evidences of Revealed Religion") with one that would see miracles as the "demonstrations of a supreme spiritual force, existing in the nature of things" and acting in harmony with the other agencies we witness every day. At about the same time, Ripley published a pamphlet, provocatively entitled *Discourses on the Philosophy of Religion Addressed to Doubters Who Wish to Believe,* which attempts to turn the tables on attackers like Norton by arguing that people who are afraid of free discussion are the real religious doubters – fearful that open inquiry will expose some rottenness at the core of their faith.

Ripley announces that he has no wish to discredit the Christian miracles; he says he believes in them and finds them holy and precious. But he refuses to believe that "human nature is so shackled and hemmed in, even in its present imperfect state, as to be confined to the objects made known by the eye of sense." Only the things which are unseen possess independent reality: "The material universe is the expression of an Invisible Wisdom and Power." To focus our attention exclusively upon that universe – the "dry husk and shell of matter" – in an attempt to verify faith is to "lose sight of the Infinite and Divine energy" from which matter draws its being. How much more pious it is to trust to the voice of the Reason within us, that Reason which is an "emanation from the mind of God" and a "partaker of the divine nature."

These opening squalls in the controversy over biblical miracles that would occupy so much of the next ten years were soon swallowed up by a much larger storm of public outrage. In the last week of December 1836, Bronson Alcott published the first volume of his *Conversations with Children on the Gospels,* a record of the conversations he had had with children in his Temple School. That school had opened its doors on September 22, 1834, with about thirty pupils, many of them from influential Boston families. For a time all seemed to be going well. Alcott's assistant, Elizabeth Peabody, had pub-

lished her one-volume *Record of a School* in 1835; it explained Alcott's methods and philosophy and had attracted favorable notices, though it did not
lead to the rush of new enrollments Alcott had hoped for. Educational
reformers from as far away as Germany began to visit the school and seek
Alcott's advice.

There were, however, also rumblings of discontent. Alcott's insistence on
relating every subject to the spirit began to alarm some of the parents.
Apparently, someone must have told Alcott that his teaching methods were
looked on with disfavor, for one day he asked the children if they would like
him to stop talking about conscience and spirit and begin teaching exclusively about rocks and trees and engines. In a letter Peabody described how
the children responded to Alcott's question: "One boy got up. – Oh *he is so
lazy* he cannot even play – said ever so many." Several more stalwarts braved
community disfavor and stood up to cast their votes for the material world,
but when Alcott warned them he could no longer read to them out of
Pilgrim's Progress or from Spenser (because these works involved the conscience), their opposition collapsed. "Well, said Mr. A. who had rather the
school would be as it is full of thoughts & feelings about conscience, God, the
mind, the soul – with all my punishments & all my disagreeable fault finding & the necessity of self-control & selfknowledge &c &c &c – They all rose
with acclamation" (Peabody to Elizabeth Davis Bliss, 1835).

Presumably Peabody meant only to suggest the children's love for Alcott
by this brief sketch, but his considerable talent for moral coercion emerges
from it as well. Her growing discomfort with this aspect of Alcott's pedagogy was one of the things that led her to resign from the school in the spring
of 1836. But by that time she had already completed a second book about the
school, recording a series of conversations about the gospels that Alcott had
begun in the school on Saturday, October 10, 1835. These "conversations"
were meant both to illustrate Alcott's teaching methods and to serve as
empirical proofs of the truths of Christianity. As Peabody pointed out in her
introduction to the two-volume record, "Mr. Alcott felt that what the children should freely say, would prove to be a new order of Christian Evidences,
by showing the affinity of their natures with that of Jesus." The spirit
incarnate will recognize the spirit inscribed, and the "juvenile commentary"
thus produced would serve, Alcott hoped, as "a revelation of Divinity in the
soul of childhood." With such living evidences in the souls of little children,
the elaborate structures of Unitarian historical scholarship – trying to trace
testimony back to the original witnessers of miracles – would be shown to be
unnecessary.

To provide the texts around which his conversations would be organized
Alcott selected and arranged passages from the Gospels in the manner of an

old gospel harmony to form a chronological account of the life of Jesus. He began with the opening chapters of John, then moved on to Luke for the Annunciation and Nativity stories, and continued until he reached the fiftieth conversation at the end of the second volume, which carried the children only as far as the twelfth chapter of Matthew and the third chapter of Mark. Alcott would read a biblical passage aloud to the children (who ranged in age from six to twelve) and then ask them what they liked or remembered about it. Sometimes he asked them to visualize the scene, oftener to speculate or comment upon matters discussed in the text. At the end of most conversations he asked them if they understood what the subject of the conversation had been.

Such methods sound innocent enough in themselves, but in Alcott's hands they had results that led Andrews Norton to judge the published book "one-third absurd, one-third blasphemous, and one-third obscene." Alcott's serene conviction that the souls of the children already contained the loftiest philosophical truths led him to try to coax abstract principles out of them by the Socratic method. The resulting dialogue (as the children adopted his terminology and tried with increasing desperation to guess what he was driving at) often sounds as if it had been written by a particularly relentless dramatist of the absurd.

Bostonians might have forgiven Alcott his unorthodox teaching methods, but they could not agree with him that such subjects as conception, childbirth, and circumcision should be discussed with the children as openly as angels, miracles, or the sayings of Jesus. The conversations that deal with these subjects are often sweet and funny (as when a chivalrous little boy suggests that the pain of childbirth ought to be given to men "since they are so much stronger"), and they seem so innocent to a modern reader that it takes an effort of historical imagination to understand how anyone could have thought them obscene. But Elizabeth Peabody had become worried enough about possible scandal by the summer of 1836 to beg Alcott by letter to excise certain things from her written transcription of the conversations before the book was published. She did not wish it known that she had even participated in the conversation about the Circumcision, and she thought that certain remarks — such as little Josiah Quincy's inspired guess that the infant's body was formed "out of the naughtiness of other people" — should be eliminated entirely. Alcott complied with her first request, but printed all the remarks she had marked out as possibly dangerous or offensive in footnotes with the heading "Restored by the Editor" — where, naturally, they caught the eye of critics more easily.

Alcott also adopted the book as his own, though in fact only an editor's preface and an introduction were written by him. The rest of the book is as much Peabody's as was *Record of a School*. The two title pages of the printed *Conversations* suggest as much. The first one reads "CONVERSATIONS / WITH / CHILDREN / ON / THE GOSPELS; / CONDUCTED AND EDITED / BY A. BRONSON ALCOTT." But beneath this page is another, similar in format: "RECORD / OF / CONVERSATIONS ON THE GOSPELS / HELD IN / MR. ALCOTT'S SCHOOL; / UNFOLDING / THE DOCTRINE AND DISCIPLINE / OF / HUMAN CULTURE."

This first volume of *Conversations* begins with a "Recorder's Preface" (by Peabody), an "Editor's Preface" (by Alcott) and an "Introduction" – "The Doctrine and Discipline of Human Culture," which Alcott had written and published separately as a pamphlet in the summer of 1836 and which he now reprinted as the clearest statement of his educational philosophy. The remainder of the long work is a fascinating case study in educational single-mindedness and the fluctuating strategies of the children who have to cope with it. They are sometimes charmed, frequently perplexed, and occasionally stoutly resistant to the things their peculiar teacher is trying to get them to say.

Peabody takes down the conversations but also participates in them (she appears in the text as Recorder); she becomes more and more willing to argue openly with Alcott as the book progresses, even taking him aside at some points to object strenuously to what he is doing. As the book proceeds we gradually become aware of her artistry. She arranges the conversations with an unerring sense of what makes them at once touching and funny. For Peabody is a keen ironist, as anyone who has read her letters can testify, and in presenting a series of the conversations between an innocent reformer and a roomful of children encouraged to be perfectly candid she finds rich possibilities for humor.

The children are all empiricists, as sturdy as Locke and as skeptical as Hume, and for the most part they stubbornly resist Alcott's attempt to tow them into the Unconditioned. Moreover, they are Bostonians, the children of the city's merchant and professional elite, and their view of the world reflects the values of their parents. One boy imagines the angel visiting Joseph in a "splendid" room. Peabody asks him how a poor carpenter in Nazareth could have a splendid room. The boy replies, "An angel would not come into a poor looking room. It would not be appropriate." After this Peabody adds a parenthetical note: "After some conversation, Edward seemed to think that such outward splendors were not particularly appropriate to angels, at least, upholstery." When Alcott asks if there are any students who worship money, two boys boldly stand up, prompting another to jeer and point out that one of them had wanted to know what became of the money when Jesus overturned the tables of the moneychangers in the Temple. When Alcott asks a boy about his mission in life the boy replies promptly, "I shall use my Soul in selling oil."

The conflict of wills grows stronger in those more important conversations dealing with matters such as miracles and the relationship of human nature to divinity. These were the conversations (even more than the ones about birth and circumcision) that provoked the real outrage against Alcott in the public press early in 1837, outrage that led to the vilification of Alcott and the collapse of the school. Ministers were furious at Alcott for trespassing on their territory; they were also horrified by what seemed like a caricature of certain tendencies that were always latent in Unitarianism – the belief in human perfectibility, for instance – but that Alcott insisted in carrying far beyond what Unitarians sanctioned.

The scandalized ministers and parents ought to have been cheered by what they read in the book when it treats of these subjects, for in fact the children are as resistant to attacks on miracles as they are to the idea of their own divinity. When Alcott asks whether the changing of water to wine at Cana was a miracle worked in the minds of the guests or upon the water, a boy named Augustine replies, "There must have been real wine made, for the governor of the feast tasted it." Alcott tries to nudge them into seeing the miracle as "emblematic," but when he asks them how many "think Jesus turned water into wine, literally and actually," all rise. When he asks them if they would have considered this a very great feat if Jesus had never performed another miracle, a boy named Welles candidly admits, "If he had not done any other miracle, I should have thought that Jesus brought the wine himself." So, too, when Alcott asks "Do any of you think, that if your bodies were taken away, you should be God?," he can get a girl named Emma to concede only that she might be "a part of God." Peabody takes him aside at this point and asks him angrily what he is driving at; he replies serenely that he is "ascertaining their views of the difference between the absolute and the derived, of God in man, and the idea of Absolute being typified in the Derivative." He returns to his questioning, but the children still refuse to be budged from the idea that they are *not* as good as or as powerful as God or Jesus, with or without their bodies.

Reading through the volumes of *Conversations with Children on the Gospels* one has the giddy feeling that the whole controversy that Emerson would touch off with his Divinity School Address the next summer is being previewed in Alcott's schoolroom, with Alcott playing Emerson and the children miniature versions of Emerson's conservative Unitarian critics. In the very last conversation of the second volume, a boy named Charles complains at always being forced to think of God as spirit and spirit as within. "I wish," he says, "that you would let me say that God is up in the sky; for I like to think of God up there, though I know he is in my thought and inspires it. For I like to have such a place; and that is so pure, so blue, and handsome, with such beautiful stars!" Alcott: "But there is a danger of mistaking the forms for the thoughts themselves." Charles: "Oh, I don't think I should ever go as far as that."

As a way of collecting a new set of Christian evidences, Alcott's pedagogy would seem to fail miserably, because the children can never be persuaded to adopt his beliefs and indeed argue back to him more and more as the conversations progress (as does the Recorder, Peabody, who ended her job as amanuensis by quitting the school). Yet Alcott seems as pleased with their resistance as with their concurrence. On the first page of the book itself is an illustration showing Alcott's classroom — Alcott at a desk, and the children ranged rather stiffly around in a semicircle at some distance from him. At the end of both volumes is another illustration, this time of the boy Jesus teaching the elders in the Temple. Between these two emblems occurs the education in self-reliance that finally comes to seem the real message of the book and gives it its power and its innocence.

Such subtleties were lost upon Alcott's reviewers. He had published the first volume of *Conversations with Children on the Gospels* in the last week of December 1836 and had sent review copies of the book to all the newspapers. They began to savage him as soon as the new year arrived. Alcott's good friend and brother-in-law, the minister Samuel May, had written to warn him that the Unitarian establishment would dislike the book because it expressed too plainly the end to which their doctrines led. May was right. Parents began to withdraw children from the school. By the summer of 1837 there were only eleven pupils left.

Margaret Fuller had taken over Elizabeth Peabody's job as assistant in the fall of 1836 (she taught French and Latin and took down the "conversations" that Alcott at that time planned to publish as a third volume in the series). She now found herself obliged to take up Alcott's defense. When her friend the British reformer Harriet Martineau sent her an inscribed copy of *Society in America* that summer — the book contained a violent attack on Alcott's school, which Martineau had never visited but had heard about from its detractors — Fuller rebuked her for her "intemperate tirade" and defended Alcott as a "true and noble man, a philanthropist, whom a true and noble woman, also a philanthropist, should have delighted to honor" (Fuller to Martineau, c. November 1837).

Nevertheless, the emotional support of his Transcendentalist friends could not save Alcott's school. It limped on for another year with five or six students. When it finally closed, Alcott accepted the offer of a job teaching poor children in Boston's South End. That school too collapsed when, with his characteristic fidelity to principle, Alcott refused to dismiss the only black student in the school despite protests by parents of the other children. Transcendentalism had generated several scriptures in 1836; in Alcott it had also managed to create a martyr. It was ready to mount an offensive.

5

THE ESTABLISHMENT AND THE
MOVEMENT

IN THE EARLY MONTHS OF 1837 the Transcendentalists began to
think of themselves as something more than a group of young clergy
eager to escape the circumspection of traditional Unitarian associations
for regions of freer speech. The manifestos of 1836 had given the writers a
collective visibility. Now, as conservatives began writing angry reviews and
warning against the errors of the "new school" of philosophy and religion, the
members of Hedge's Club suddenly found themselves elevated to the dignity
of rebels.

Bronson Alcott was the most savagely assaulted, but by the end of January
Emerson too found himself the target of conservative scorn. In the January
1837 issue of the *Christian Examiner* a young Harvard tutor named Francis
Bowen made a review of *Nature* the occasion for an attack upon the arrogance
and obscurantism of the whole Transcendentalist school. As a reviewer of
Nature itself Bowen was perceptive; he noticed that Emerson's love of Saxon-
isms and deliberate bathos were a kind of protest against "forced dignity and
unnatural elevation," and he declared himself bewildered by the sudden
change of direction in the second half of the book, when Emerson suddenly
aims a "back blow" at the universe he was teaching us to admire and love.

Yet Bowen's praise for the "beautiful writing and sound philosophy" he
found in the book quickly changed to blame when he considered a doctrine in
Nature that he found dangerous: its worship of intuition as the sole trustworthy guide in matters of the spirit. Bowen agrees that mathematical axioms
must be grasped intuitively, but he cannot leap with Emerson to the conclusion that intuition can grasp "the most abstruse and elevated propositions
respecting the being and destiny of man." The distinction is an important
one. Splitting the mind into two faculties incapable of communicating with
one another destroys the hope of a rational Christianity and leaves society
open to all the horrors of religious bigotry. Unless we are willing to agree that
"the argument for the existence of a God, or the immateriality of the soul, is
tested by the same power of mind that discovered and proved any proposition
in Euclid," we have no defense against dogmatism and intolerance. In fact,

Bowen says, the Transcendentalists already speak with the arrogance of religious sectaries:

From the heights of mystical speculation, they look down with a ludicrous self-complacency and pity on the mass of mankind, on the ignorant and the educated, the learners and the teachers, and should any question the grounds on which such feelings rest, they are forthwith branded with the most opprobrious epithets, which the English or the Transcendental language can supply.

Emerson's reply to this kind of criticism was a fierce reaffirmation of his original principles. In the tenth lecture of the "Philosophy of History" series he was then giving at the Masonic Temple in Boston, entitled "Ethics" (February 16, 1837), he reminded his audience that the self-trust he has been recommending to them as the fountainhead of all virtue is "not a faith in man's own whim or conceit, as if he were quite severed from all other beings and acted on his own private account, but a perception that the mind common to the Universe is disclosed to the individual through his own nature."

The very conditions under which Emerson now spoke seemed an allegory of the connectedness he believed in. Ever since his return from Europe in 1833 Emerson had been a popular lyceum speaker, delivering lectures to audiences who had paid a subscription fee to a local lyceum for a season ticket to a course of evening lectures on a variety of topics: natural history, biography, literature, history, travel. By 1836 the fees he received from lyceum lecturing almost equaled the income he received from "supply" preaching in Unitarian churches.

Emerson found lecturing exhilarating. He could speak on any topic that appealed to him and he could assume that his audiences (unlike church congregations) were brought there by desire rather than impelled by duty or custom. But a lyceum lecturer still had to await invitation from lyceum committees to speak and negotiate with the committees about fees and topics. An independent entrepreneur, on the other hand, might offer a course of lectures on his own — hire the hall, print and sell the tickets, write and deliver the lectures — and keep profits greater than the modest fees the lyceums offered. Such was the appetite for lectures in improvement-minded, amusement-starved Massachusetts that (as one historian of the lyceum movement puts it) "everyone from respectable Harvard professors to phrenologists or outright quacks could hire a hall, sell tickets, and hope to clear a profit." In the fall of 1836 Emerson had decided to try his hand at such independent lecturing. He announced a twelve-lecture series to begin in December entitled "The Philosophy of History," hired a room in the Masonic Temple, wrote his own advertising, and sold tickets (two dollars for the series) through a bookstore.

On the average, three hundred and fifty people attended each of Emerson's twelve lectures at the Masonic Temple during the winter of 1836–7. After paying his expenses he had three hundred and fifty dollars left – proof that the truths of the Reason he had been patiently depositing in his "savings bank" (as he called his journals) could be made to yield handsome dividends in the realm of the Understanding. Moreover, the lecture course, originally written for the Boston market, could be repeated in other cities or sold to lyceums in the smaller towns.

The lecturing was important to Emerson in more than financial ways. When he was twenty-one he had expressed his ambition to thrive in "eloquence," but up until now that eloquence had been mediated through institutions – the church, the lyceum, or the speaker's platform at some ceremonial occasion. In the Masonic Temple, Emerson for the first time found himself speaking to an audience whose only reason for coming was to hear *him* and whose only reason for staying was that they were interested in what they heard. It was a strangely thrilling experience for both speaker and listeners, as surviving accounts from the members of those early audiences make clear. And it offered empirical proof of a doctrine Emerson had held all his life: A speaker uttering private thoughts with perfect candor will speak universal truth.

Emerson was not the only member of the Transcendental Club to experience a surge of self-confidence at about this time. In the middle of January 1837, George Ripley wrote to Convers Francis that he had been thinking for some time of an ambitious plan to translate modern works of French and German philosophy, history, and theology. So long as Americans remained dependent upon British thinkers they could hardly escape from empiricism in philosophy and probabilistic reasoning in biblical interpretation. Making translations of important foreign books available in the United States would show that a world of thought existed outside of the Anglo-American tradition. The title Ripley chose for this vast project, which would eventually run to fourteen volumes, was *Specimens of Foreign Standard Literature* – "standard," because he wanted to drive home the point that what seemed outlandish to Americans was elsewhere solidly canonical.

But the mood of the country was about to shift. The United States had been enjoying a period of rapid expansion and financial growth, but the boom was about to end. President Andrew Jackson, alarmed at the way unchecked financial speculation was leading to a wild rise in the price of land, had announced the summer before that the government would accept only specie in payment for public lands. Speculators suddenly tried to exchange their paper money for specie, and the rapid deflation that followed triggerd a financial panic. By the time Jackson's successor, Martin Van Buren, took office in March 1837, banks and business had begun to collapse. In May the New York banks suspended payments in specie; many of the banks failed. Businesses and factories shut down. Wage laborers in the city faced starvation as the price of necessities doubled while their wages were cut nearly in half. Subsistence farmers or factory workers who had farms to return to could ride out the hard times by living on food they raised themselves, but wage laborers in the bigger cities suffered acutely.

The sight of this misery began to have profound effects on the two Transcendentalists whose ministries brought them into direct contact with the urban poor, Ripley and Orestes Brownson. Ripley's disenchantment with the current economic system would eventually lead him to resign his ministry and found Brook Farm, a community designed as an alternative to the self-destructive exploitation of unchecked capitalism. Brownson made the business collapse the occasion for a jeremiad. In May 1837 he preached to his congregation a sermon on the text "Babylon is falling, and the merchants of the earth shall weep and mourn over her; for no man buyeth their merchandise any more." Babylon he identified as the "spirit of gain" that drives the current system; its downfall is predicted in the current collapse. Capitalism, Brownson argues, produces nothing; it only robs others of what they have produced. The old Unitarian answer to the problems of the poor – encouraging them to "rise" in the world through education and industry – merely turns them from exploited to exploiters. As the wealth of the exploiting class increases, the misery of the poor grows; warfare between the classes is inevitable. "One party or the other must be exterminated before the war will end." But God has promised victory to the poor and dispossessed, and when the "system of universal fraud and injustice" is overthrown the *"people"* will see to it that justice reigns.

Emerson's response to the financial collapse was very different. When the Panic of 1837 began Emerson's instinctive sympathies were with the failing merchants rather than with the laborers idled by their ruin. His first reference in his journals to the crisis expresses a fear of violence from the kind of mob that had just burned down the New Orleans stock exchange. But soon a different note creeps into his voice as he surveys the financial wreckage of the cities from the relative security of Concord:

Behold the boasted world has come to nothing. Prudence itself is at her wits' end. Pride, and Thrift, and Expediency, who jeered and chirped and were so well pleased with themselves, and made merry with the dream, as they termed it, of Philosophy and Love, – behold they are all flat, and here is the Soul erect and unconquered still.

What fills Emerson with joy is the discovery that the world State Street warned him to treat with respect – the "solid" world of thrift, of prudence, of compromise and self-interest – had failed like an overextended bank. When Alcott asked Emerson to take his place as speaker at the opening of a new school in Providence, Rhode Island, Emerson delivered a speech, "Address on Education," that turned into an attack on the "immense hollowness" the financial collapse had revealed at the center of society. Like Brownson, Emerson identifies the "disease of which the world lies sick" as "desperate conservatism," but the struggle Emerson sees played out in the world around him is not the struggle between privileged and underprivileged classes but between the past and the future. Brownson looks at the current world and sees greed; Emerson sees fear – sees "that utter unbelief which is afraid of change, afraid of thought."

One may wonder whether by spiritualizing the conflict in this way Emerson is hiding from himself the hardheaded wisdom of an argument he had made in a lecture on "Politics" earlier that winter – that political power always grows out of *property*. If conservatives have been rendered desperate it is because the Panic threatens their property and the power it confers, not because it threatens their habits or their notions of the world. Replacing class antagonisms with temporal ones masks this hard fact and makes a hopeful outcome to the present conflict seem inevitable – for when has the past ever defeated the future? Emerson's refusal to conceive of historical conflict as a clash of irreconcilable interests makes it possible for him to achieve an elevation above the scene that feels like power. "Let me begin anew. Let me teach the finite to know its master. Let me ascend above my fate and work down upon the world."

He was to have his first opportunity very soon. Cornelius Felton, the professor of Greek at Harvard, wrote to Emerson at the end of June asking him to give the annual address to the Phi Beta Kappa Society during Harvard's August commencement week. The British author Harriet Martineau had attended the Phi Beta Kappa Society meeting two years earlier and had been shocked both by Harvard's air of indolence and privilege and by the Phi Beta Kappa address she heard then. She was startled, "among a people whose profession is social equality and whose rule of association is universal self-government," to hear "the contempt which the few express for the many, with as much assurance as if they lived in Russia or England." Granted, scholars in America formed their notions of virtue from the aristocratic literatures of Europe, but Martineau was still surprised that "within the bounds of a republic, the insolence should be so very complacent, the contempt of the majority so ludicrously decisive as it is."

Emerson's topic for the address – America's lack of an indigenous literary tradition – was by now a familiar one. Explanations for the nonexistence of American literature were so common in postrevolutionary America as to constitute a genre of their own. But "The American Scholar" derives its power from a confluence of forces more powerful than a sense of provincial inferiority. Emerson's memories of loneliness and boredom as a Harvard undergraduate, his anger at the way Alcott had been savaged by some members of the Cambridge establishment and abandoned by others, and the recent lashing he himself had gotten from Francis Bowen all made him eager to puncture the complacency of the college whose commencement ceremonies he had been invited to improve. At the same time, his pride in the success of his recent course of lectures and his barely suppressed glee when in the general financial collapse the businesses of State Street shattered all around him like towers of glass gave him a prophet's conviction that his reading of history was correct. Hence "The American Scholar," though written at a time of national crisis, is buoyed by an exhilaration almost continuous. In its conviction that nature and tradition can both be made transparent by the enlightened mind, Emerson's address gives us a sense of what an indigenous humanism on the German model might have been like had there been an academy capable of supporting it; and the shrewd advice Emerson includes for learning to tap the richness of past literary tradition without being bankrupted by a sense of inferiority to it marks the beginning of the modern phase of American literary history.

The address begins by conceding what foreign critics had delighted to assert – that there was in America no native intellectual tradition worth speaking of, that the "sluggard intellect" of this continent had as yet produced little more than "the exertions of mechanical skill." But this satirical view of American dullness quickly gives way to a vision of what the American scholar ought to be: *"Man Thinking."* This heroic figure confronts power incarnate in the circular processes of nature, and he matches it with a tyrannizing instinct to classify: piercing phenomena, reducing multiplicity to unity, inspired by the conviction that natural objects "have a law which is also a law of the human mind."

That same conviction should give the American scholar courage when he confronts a more intimidating incarnation of eternal law – "the mind of the Past." The books written by geniuses have a tendency to warp the reader out of his own orbit, making him "a satellite instead of a system." He must fight against this gravitational pull by becoming an inventor himself; he must use books only to inspire and seek in them only those words he had nearly said himself. In this way, he transforms masters into servants and makes someone else's words the key that will unlock his own thoughts and so acquaint him with himself. This is the "creative reading" without which there can be no "creative writing," the endlessly profitable trade that carries out wealth to bring wealth home. "When the mind is braced by labor and invention, the page of whatever book we read becomes luminous with manifold allusion." Such "self-trust," the only virtue Emerson ever really cared for, will cure literary imitativeness as it cures maladies far more dangerous, maladies whose effects were beginning to be visible everywhere.

Less than a month after Emerson delivered "The American Scholar," a series of events in a distant state seemed to offer a particularly vivid example of the heroism of self-trust. In Alton, Illinois, a mob stormed the offices of Elijah Lovejoy, editor of the *Alton Observer,* and smashed the press. Lovejoy had already lost presses to mobs who objected to his criticisms of slavery and of lynching; the press smashed on September 21 was his third. Undaunted, he ordered a fourth press. When the prominent men of Alton tried to persuade him to cease publishing and leave town, he replied that he feared God more than he feared man. The fourth press arrived by riverboat on November 6 and was spirited ashore at midnight to be guarded by Lovejoy's friends. But a mob the next evening attacked the newspaper offices. They were at first repulsed by Lovejoy's guard but returned hoping to set fire to the roof. During a lull in the firing Lovejoy himself stepped out to see where the attackers had gone. He was shot through the chest and killed.

According to the critic and historian John Jay Chapman (1862–1933), "nothing except John Brown's Raid ever sent such a shock across the continent, or so stirred the North to understand and resist the advance of slavery as Lovejoy's murder." A memorial service was held for Lovejoy a month later in Faneuil Hall, and, in the lecture "Heroism," Emerson went out of his way to praise "the brave Lovejoy" for his death in defense of free speech. Such willingness to honor defiance like Lovejoy's was one of the qualities that led James Freeman Clarke to praise Emerson's insistence upon "the *needed* truth" to Margaret Fuller. In a letter written to her from Louisville, Clarke said of Emerson: "He asserts the necessity of self-reliance in an age when imitation and sympathy predominate; he defends the individual man, when we all get melted together in masses" (Clarke to Fuller, March 29, 1838).

Orestes Brownson, however, remained unconvinced that free speech was all that an individual needed in this time of severe deprivation. Brownson took the shocking step (shocking to most of the Transcendentalists, anyway) of joining the Democratic party, and in the winter of 1837–8, he started his own journal, the *Boston Quarterly Review.* Brownson wanted an outlet for his overflowing energies, and the aggressiveness of printed polemical discourse suited his temperament as well as the lecture platform's alternating current of seduction and challenge suited Emerson's. In its first number Brownson frankly confessed that although no Unitarian journal had ever refused to print his work, the mere act of submitting his work for someone else's possible censoring involved a submissiveness he could no longer tolerate.

In one sense the *Boston Quarterly Review* stood as a shining illustration of Emerson's doctrine of self-trust. As Ripley later pointed out, "It was undertaken by a single individual, without the cooperation of friends, with no external patronage," and most of its pages were filled by Brownson himself. But Brownson's political education had carried him beyond the point where he thought that self-trust alone could solve the problems of the urban poor. He had already delivered a Fourth-of-July oration to a thousand people at a Democratic mass meeting on Bunker Hill. Now he publicly announced his sympathy for the Locofocos, the most radical members of the Democratic party, who advocated schemes for outlawing inherited property and for distributing government-owned lands free to needy immigrants. Henry David Thoreau, who had boarded with Brownson while he was teaching school in Canton, wrote to offer his praise for the *Boston Quarterly Review,* but some of the older members of the Transcendental Club were distressed at Brownson's affiliation with a political party whose contempt for high culture and willingness to use techniques of mass political appeal made it quite as distasteful to them as it was to their conservative Unitarian critics.

The stresses along this particular fault line were to be felt in tremors throughout the next few years. Transcendentalism placed absolute faith in the integrity of the soul's intuitions; when these intuitions were hostile to established institutions Transcendentalism appeared revolutionary. But in its relentless pursuit of spiritual gain and its corresponding contempt for the world of the Understanding, Transcendentalism was of little immediate use to reformers who wanted to feed the hungry or free the slave; indeed, the quietism the movement fostered and the self-absorption it encouraged favored existing institutions, even the ones that the Transcendentalists criticized. Moreover, the principle of association so necessary to effective political action was distasteful to the Transcendentalists because of the necessary loss of perfect sincerity involved in compromise and negotiation. Solitary heroes like Lovejoy (and later, John Brown) always appealed to Emerson's imagination; canvassers and founders of societies repelled him. He saw clearly enough that any kind of association was bound sooner or later to involve some degree of coercion or cant, and to coerce someone to obey the will of a reformer was only to replace vice with fear. Yet the earnest labors of the philanthropists troubled his conscience, and though he tried to shoo away doubts by describing himself as a man who "only loves like Cordelia after his duty," he admitted that the sense of shame he felt when reformers came calling was itself the best proof that the claims they had on him were real.

Emerson always insisted that he was a reformer too, though of a different kind, visiting souls in prison and bringing news of release. His words did indeed affect members of his chosen audience powerfully – particularly the generation of younger disciples that the original Transcendentalists were beginning to acquire. But the excitement they aroused was not always controllable, as the strange exaltation of a young Harvard tutor of Greek would shortly demonstrate. Jones Very (1813–80) – the son of a Salem sea captain and his wife, a freethinking and aggressive woman who did not scruple to express her doubts of God's existence – was in the spring of 1837 completing his first year at Harvard Divinity School. He was supporting himself during his theological studies by serving as Greek tutor to the freshmen of Harvard College, from which he himself had just graduated the year before.

Very was ten years younger than Emerson but had entered Harvard late, so that his Harvard class (1836) graduated a full fifteen years after Emerson's. But if Very belonged to a different generation, his college experiences followed a familiar pattern. He studied the required curriculum and at the same time immersed himself in poetry; he was intensely shy, studious, and ambitious of literary fame. An early fascination with Byron gave way to a reverence for Wordsworth, Coleridge, and "the Germans" – Goethe, Schiller, and Schegel. Victor Cousin introduced him to ideas derived from German Idealist philosophy. For his entry in the Bowdoin Prize competition his senior year in college he submitted a long essay (it won the prize) entitled "What Reasons Are There for Not Expecting Another Great Epic Poem?," in which he argued that the progress of human history and the advent of Christianity had made the epic impossible by making its traditional subjects unimportant. By "transferring the scene of action from the outward world to the world within," Christianity had made the consciousness of the individual the scene of all significant action. Far from lamenting the demise of traditional epic, Very hailed it as "the greatest proof of the progress of the soul – and of its approach to that state of being where its thought is action, its word power."

Very's own soul suffered intensely at times. Besides an instability of mood that made him subject to periodic depressions, he felt himself (he confessed much later) tormented by sexual desires that made him long for a spiritual regeneration in which his own will would be wholly lost in the will of God. After months of scarcely endurable distress he felt that he had experienced a "change of heart" that gave him great joy. Very's change of heart bore a close resemblance (as one of his classmates noticed) to the conversion of the Calvinists, in which a sense of election replaces an overpowering conviction of sinfulness. But the carnal man within him kept reasserting himself, despite Very's resolution to allow no occasion for sin. He took a vow not to speak to, or even look at, a woman – a decision he called his "sacrifice of Beauty."

Because thought was temptation and temptation sin, he resolved to banish thought and eliminate all traces of individual will.

By obliterating all traces of individual will Very may have hoped to find peace from his rebellious desires. Instead he propelled himself into an ecstatic sense of divinity. Signs of the change were already evident in the way Very marked up the copy of Emerson's *Nature* he read in the fall of 1836. Very's biographer points out that the chapter "Idealism" in *Nature,* which contained Emerson's insistence that the transference of nature into the mind leaves matter behind like an outcast corpse, interested Very the most. He sensed the apocalyptic impulse behind Emerson's Idealism and glossed the text with references to Revelation. Next to the Wordsworthian maxim – "Infancy is the perpetual Messiah" – Very wrote "R12," probably a reference to the twelfth chapter of Revelation, where a woman clothed with the sun gives birth to a male child who is later revealed to be the Christ. Next to Emerson's innocent remark that riding in a carriage or looking at the landscape upside down through one's legs affords a "pleasure mixed with awe" because it suggests that the world is only a spectacle while something in the self is stable, Very wrote "Rev XX:II," a verse that describes the fleeing of heaven and earth before the face of "a great white throne, and him that sat on it."

Throughout 1836 and 1837 Very pursued his theological studies and tutored his Harvard freshmen in Greek, making himself popular with them (and unpopular with the professors) by actually trying to interest them in the literature they were reading. He gained the reputation on campus of being the only teacher of classical languages who insisted on accurate translations. But he also tried to inspire students with a love of literature, speaking to them enthusiastically of Shakespeare and Milton and urging them to find moral instruction in the true representations of human nature given by all poets. News of his gifts for making literature attractive had spread sufficiently that by the winter of 1837 he was invited to speak on epic poetry at the lyceum in Salem, Massachusetts, where he caught the attention of Elizabeth Peabody (who had moved back there after the furor following the publication of *Conversations with Children on the Gospels* had ended her teaching career in Boston). She befriended Very and discovered that he was an "enthusiastic listener to Mr. Emerson" and wrote to urge Emerson to invite him to lecture at the Concord lyceum; she also introduced Very to Nathaniel Hawthorne, who liked him but found the intensity of his loneliness alarming.

On April 4, 1838, Very walked twenty miles from Salem to Concord to deliver his "Epic Poetry" lecture and to dine with the Emersons. Very poured out to Emerson all his theories about poetry and particularly about Shakespeare (with whom he had come to believe he had achieved a perfect identification); he asked Emerson to inscribe his copy of *Nature*. Emerson thought him remarkable. When Very came back to Concord a few days later with some Harvard friends, Emerson invited them all to dinner. Promise in young men was making Emerson feel hopeful again about the state of the country. Very's "Epic Poetry" was published in the *Christian Examiner* early in May 1838; in the same month Very came as Emerson's guest to the Transcendental Club, where the subject for discussion was "the question of Mysticism." Very explained the history of his own "change of heart," its partial success, and the continued effort he was making to eradicate his selfish will. Indeed, by the end of the school year in 1838 he began to be sensible of a change for the better in himself, a certain lightness and effortlessness in the performance of his duties, a great peace and contentment.

Emerson, on the other hand, was finishing a spring full of vexations, some of them self-inflicted. He had long wanted to get out of the position he still held as supply preacher to an East Lexington congregation, and he now began to take formal steps to find a replacement for himself. At the same time his dissatisfaction with organized Unitarianism reached new heights. At home he chafed under the wretched preaching of the Concord minister Barzillai Frost. Frost was a glaring example of what was wrong with theological instruction at Cambridge. When Emerson visited him at home and inspected his library, the works of historical criticism and proofs of the Christian religion from "internal and external evidences" ranged on his shelves made Emerson shiver. A year earlier Frost had preached the sermon when Emerson's son Waldo was christened: it had been a dismal performance delivered in a "ragged half screaming bass" that showed how thoroughly Frost had failed to learn the capital secret of the preacher's profession – "to convert life into truth."

Even the venerable Dr. Ripley, Emerson's step-grandfather and a man he usually venerated as a link with the Puritan past, now provoked Emerson's impatience. "This afternoon the foolishest preaching – which bayed at the moon. Go, hush, old man, whom the years have taught no truth." Dr. Ripley's confusion when he mislaid his glasses reminded Emerson of the stupid stare of squash bugs suddenly exposed to light under the rotten leaves of vines. Myopia seemed in fact the curse of the established churches, which clung to shreds of historical evidence, writing laborious volumes seeking to demonstrate that the Godhead had once dwelled on earth – when all around them its epiphanies were perpetual.

When Emerson received an invitation from the small senior class at the Harvard Divinity School to deliver an address at its graduating ceremonies in July he was at first reluctant. The young men of Cambridge were just setting out in the profession he had renounced. But the forces impelling him were greater than the forces restraining him. His old distaste for "historical Christianity" and the archaic epistemology upon which it was based, his anger at the bigotry that had quashed Alcott's innocent attempt to find new evidences of Christianity in his students' souls, his growing sense that the church was helpless to suggest any remedy for the recent sufferings of the poor or the chronic spiritual malaise of the educated classes, for whom the faith of the fathers had vanished as completely as melted snow, and most of all his sense that the traditionary preaching of the church was driving away entire congregations who desperately needed saving, all combined to provide enough indignation to fuel a jeremiad.

Yet the speech Emerson delivered at the Divinity School on July 15, 1838, also reflects the powerful sense of joy he was beginning to feel in his achievements as a lecturer and literary man and as father to a growing band of younger disciples. He had been disengaging himself gradually from the Unitarian ministry ever since 1832, when he resigned his pastorate. Giving up the East Lexington supply position completed this process of disengagement. In February 1838 he had written to ask his wife whether the step he was taking distressed her. His teasing letter suggests how strongly orthodox Christianity was becoming identified in his mind with something at once feminine and Oriental, with the archaic. "But does not the eastern Lidian my Palestine mourn to see the froward man cutting the last threads that bind him to the prized gown & band the symbols black & white of old & distant Judah?" His solicitude was greater for her loss than for his. He believed that the lecture platform was providing him with a more powerful and less encumbered pulpit than any that the church had offered, and the arrival of candidates for his influence and affection like Jones Very made him feel sure that his secular ministry could also promise a harvest of souls.

Emerson began his Divinity School Address by expressing adoration for the beauty of nature and the "more secret, sweet, and overpowering beauty" that appears to man when his heart and mind open to "the sentiment of virtue." Following the laws revealed by this sentiment brings us nearer to divinity; indeed, the man who is just at heart *is* God and dispenses "good to his goodness, and evil to his sin." To the man who beholds the sovereignty of law, "the worlds, time, space, eternity, do seem to break out into joy." The history of civilization is constituted by successive apprehensions of the moral sentiment, and the immense influence of Jesus upon the world stems from his fierce determination to speak for that sentiment without qualification or compromise. But "historical" Christianity has made a killing mistake. It deifies the *person* of Jesus and in so doing reduces itself to another ancient Near Eastern mystery religion, a "Mythus" whose stilted language represents Jesus as "a demigod, as the Orientals or the Greeks would describe Osiris or

Apollo." The Reason hears Jesus say "I am divine" and understands it as an exhortation to every soul to achieve spiritual perfection; the Understanding hears the same words and says, "This was Jehovah come down out of heaven. I will kill you, if you say he was a man."

So far Emerson has not really left behind traditional Unitarian accounts of the corruptions of Christianity, though in the violence of his language he sounds more like Carlyle than like Channing. But his declaration of independence from formal Unitarianism is more than stylistic, as he quickly makes clear. Perhaps most immediately wounding were his scathing attacks upon the dessication of the churches. Only thirteen years after the founding of the Unitarian association, every parish was feeling the loss of faith and the waning of piety. "Where shall I hear words such as in elder ages drew men to leave all and follow, – father and mother, house and land, wife and child?" The public worship now "has lost its grasp on the affection of the good and the fear of the bad." We inhabit our own religion like peasants stirring in the ruins of civilizations they did not create. "The prayers and even the dogmas of our church are like the zodiac of Denderah and the astronomical monuments of the Hindus, wholly insulated from anything now extant in the life and business of the people. They mark the height to which the waters once rose." The power a Congregationalist minister once commanded in his community has vanished. "In the street, what has he to say to the bold village blasphemer? The village blasphemer sees fear in the face, form, and gait of the minister."

This "bold village blasphemer" who intrudes into the Divinity School Address is more than a fiction. During March and early April 1838, the four-year-long judicial ordeal of an irrepressible freethinker named Abner Kneeland (1774–1844) was coming to a conclusion. The sixty-four-year-old Kneeland had begun as a Baptist, next had joined the Universalists and preached for twenty-five years there, and finally had become involved with Robert Owen and Frances Wright. In 1829 he announced in a New York lecture that he had rejected Christianity after what he said was a final review of its evidences (the book he then published on the subject went through six editions in ten years). In 1830 he moved from New York to Boston to take charge of Boston's First Society of Free Enquirers, where he was given the official title "Lecturer to the Free Enquirers." He also founded the *Boston Investigator,* a weekly journal of free thought, in 1830, and used it to campaign for rationalism, working-class rights, the abolition of slavery, racial equality, equal rights for women, and birth control.

In 1833 a particularly frank number of the *Boston Investigator* got Kneeland arrested for blasphemy (he had already spent time in jail for distributing his treatise on birth control). Challenged by one of his former Universalist colleagues to explain how he differed from them, Kneeland referred to God as "a chimera of the imagination," judged the story of Christ to be as much "a fable and a fiction as that of Prometheus," and denied the existence of miracles and the resurrection of the dead. Because an act passed July 3, 1782, had clearly made blasphemy an offense punishable by law, Kneeland was convicted in 1834. But appeals dragged the case out interminably, and there were many among Boston's leading liberal clergy who worried about the constitutionality of persecuting a man for exercising his rights of free speech, no matter how distasteful they might find Kneeland or his doctrines. The Lowell *Advertiser* called the case an "outrage upon *human* rights, upon *expediency,* upon the *freedom of the press,* and of *speech,* upon *mercy,* upon *truth,* upon *Christianity,* and upon the *Spirit of the Age.*"

Meanwhile Kneeland had soared to new heights of popularity; his Sunday services at the Federal Street Theater drew audiences of two thousand or more, and as many subscribed to the *Investigator.* Kneeland's alarming popularity was one reason that George Ripley had been so eager to bring Orestes Brownson to the Boston area, where Brownson's working-class background and familiarity with the free-thought movement might help him win back converts from those classes genteel Unitarians rarely could reach.

In April 1838 Kneeland's request to appeal his case to the U.S. Supreme Court was denied by the attorney general of Massachusetts; on June 18 he began serving his two-month sentence in the county jail, accompanied by throngs of supporters. The Reverend William Ellery Channing drew up a petition asking for Kneeland's pardon and circulated it among sympathetic clergy; Emerson was one of the signers. Channing's petition failed. Kneeland remained in his Boston cell until his release on August 17, 1838. While in jail he wrote an open letter reminding his fellow citizens that he was suffering imprisonment for the very liberty their fathers had fought to win.

Kneeland's case reminded everyone that congregationalism was losing its hold on congregations. "In the country, neighborhoods, half parishes are *signing off,* to use the local term," Emerson reminded his hearers when he spoke on that July evening at the Divinity School. "The Church seems to totter to its fall, almost all life extinct." Why? Why had the confidence of the Unitarians of 1805 or of 1815 given way so quickly to complacency and then to ossification? The Unitarians did not see that the "historical Christianity" whose empirical proofs they clung to as a defense against sectarian bigotry was fatal to the belief it was meant to protect. "Men have come to speak of the revelation as somewhat long ago given and done, as if God were dead. The injury to faith throttles the preacher; and the goodliest of institutions becomes an uncertain and inarticulate voice." Worshipping Christ as if he were a demigod means thinking of virtue and truth as already "foreclosed and monopolized." Worse still, we are encouraged to believe in the doctrines of Christianity by means insulting to our dignity as spiritual creatures — by the report of miracles. "To aim to convert a man by miracles is a profanation of the soul."

This last assertion turned out to be the one that generated the most explosive controversy, and it helps to remember just what was at stake. Traditional Unitarians looked on the miracles reported in the New Testament as the one place where the spiritual world erupted into the world of ordinary sense perceptions with effects the senses could perceive. Miracles were empirically verifiable and universally persuasive — a powerfully attractive combination in an age deriving its notions of rationality from empirical science and its notions of human nature from Enlightenment universalism. To dismiss miracles as either unverifiable or unimportant meant relegating faith to the wholly private world of the individual soul and its fitful "contact" with God — uncertain, unsteady, dangerous. Miracles were like Newton's laws, only better; they testified to a power above nature yet accessible through it, pores in the fabric of time and space through which eternal power once leaked down to men and women.

Emerson had read Hume's attack on the credibility of miracle testimony and found it irrefutable on its own terms. He felt that he had liberated himself from the need for such empirical proofs by his discovery that God was to be found within the self, here and now. He now was seeking to proclaim that happy news, preaching from the soul, not from the church. Emerson's *ecce homo* looks forward to a hero still unincarnated, not back to Jesus of Nazareth. "In the soul then let the redemption be sought. Wherever a man comes, there comes revolution. The old is for slaves. When a man comes, all books are legible, all things transparent, all religions are forms. He is religious. Man is the wonderworker. He is seen amid miracles." This new Teacher, when he comes, will preach moral law with a new authority, one not derived from miracles and prophecies and manuscripts and testimony, but rather one that flows from his power to see "the identity of the law of gravitation with purity of heart."

It is difficult to know from the surviving evidence whether Emerson knew his address to the Divinity School would prove to be as incendiary as it in fact was. His journals and letters written near the day of delivery betray no particular militancy; he seems far more preoccupied with the speech entitled "Literary Ethics" he was scheduled to deliver at Dartmouth College a few days later. When he returned from Dartmouth he found a letter waiting for him from Henry Ware, Jr., once his predecessor at the Second Church in Boston, now the professor of pulpit eloquence and pastoral care at the Divinity School. Ware (who had been in the audience when Emerson delivered the address and who had discussed it with him afterwards) found some of Emerson's ideas impossible to agree with.

Ware's mild strictures were nothing compared to the blast of fury that came from Andrews Norton when Emerson published the Divinity School Address on August 27. Norton could not wait for a quarterly like the *Christian Examiner* to appear; he published his review in the *Boston Daily Advertiser* (a newspaper that had recently applauded the sentencing of Abner Kneeland). Norton's diatribe, "The New School in Literature and Religion," blasts the arrogance and presumption of the whole Transcendentalist movement and its foreign progenitors, the "hasher up of German metaphysics," Cousin, and "that hyper-Germanized Englishman, Carlyle." Norton treats with raucous contempt the self-confidence of the Transcendentalist visionaries who announce a new future of glorious transformation but never tell us how it is to be achieved, who advance their intuitive convictions as indisputable, who barbarize language with neologisms and "coarse and violent" metaphors. But he reserves his special fury for Emerson and his Divinity School Address and for the graduating class who saw fit to invite him to insult religion in their presence. Any minister who agreed with Emerson was a menace to the Christianity he was hired to teach, a situation equally "disastrous and alarming."

Three days after Norton's article appeared in the *Advertiser*, Emerson attended the meeting of the same Phi Beta Kappa Society at whose festivities he had delivered "The American Scholar" the year before. That he found himself there the object of hostile curiosity can be inferred from the shaken tone of his journal entry the next day. "Yesterday at Phi Beta Kappa anniversary. Steady, steady. . . . The young people and the mature hint at odium, and aversion of faces to be presently encountered in society. I say, No: I fear it not." But he did fear it, and for obvious reasons. He had left the ministry for good in the spring of that year, and no Unitarian parish would have him now even if he wished to return. He now depended upon popular favor in the form of lecture tickets for at least half his income. The grim example of Alcott was there to remind him of what happened to people who offended popular taste. Would Emerson announce his winter lectures only to find the tickets unsellable? In his journal he gloomily recorded thoughts about economic self-sufficiency that look forward to Thoreau's experiment at Walden Pond: "It seems as if a man should learn to fish, to plant, or to hunt, that he might secure his subsistence if he were cast out from society and not be painful to his friends and fellow men."

In September Henry Ware, Jr., preached a sermon entitled "The Personality of the Deity" expressly designed to refute Emerson's chilly brand of impersonal theism by insisting that we must think of God as a Father if we are not to be cast into a loveless universe. Ware sent the sermon to Emerson asking for his comments and got in reply a letter full of calculated innocence. "I could not give account of myself if challenged," Emerson wrote.

I could not possibly give you one of the "arguments" on which, as you cruelly hint, any position of mine stands. For I do not know, I confess, what arguments mean in reference to any expression of a thought. I delight in telling what I think, but if you ask me how I dare say so or why it is so I am the most helpless of mortal men.

But Emerson's affectation of unconcern, almost indeed of dandyism, masked real anxieties, as his journals of the period make clear. "Steady, steady!" is an exhortation (from Emerson to himself) that recurs more than once.

Emerson nevertheless kept out of the controversy his Divinity School Address had generated, partly from principle, partly from a deep instinct for imaginative self-preservation. The minute an opponent can compel you to begin wasting your time in parrying and defense he has won, Emerson thought, because he has diverted your energies from promulgating the gospel you were sent to preach. Any temptations he might have had to enter the debate were quickly squelched by his second wife, Lidian (Lydia Jackson Emerson) – who, upon being told by her husband that he had things to say to his critics that were too good to be lost, replied, "then there is some merit in remaining silent."

Emerson did not lack defenders in this time of distress, though some of these were such allies as he probably could have spared. A disciple of Knee-land hailed Emerson as a fellow "free enquirer" in the pages of the *Boston Investigator,* and Kneeland himself later threw in a word of praise. In the October 1838 issue of the *Boston Quarterly Review* Brownson protested the abuse heaped on Emerson (though his criticism of the "Address" itself was almost more devastating than Norton's). Brownson then turned his attention to Norton's own summa, *The Evidences of the Genuineness of the Gospels,* savaging it by reducing it to absurdity. What do the postulates of Norton's "historical Christianity" amount to but a counsel of despair? Norton argues, in effect, that "religious truth never springs up spontaneously in the human mind; there is no revelation made from God to the human soul; we can know nothing of religion but what is taught us from abroad, by an individual raised up and specially endowed with widsom from on high to be our instructor." Norton believes that we cannot even recognize God's legitimate messengers unless they perform miracles, for without miracles we should not be able to tell whether the messenger comes from heaven or hell. The records describing those messengers thus become our only link with the divine, without which we should be "plunged into midnight darkness," left in gloom no light of reason or faith could illumine.

Meanwhile, Emerson was discovering, much to his relief, that the citizens of Boston and New York were willing "to allow much to the spirit of liberty" and to buy tickets to his winter lecture series despite his new fame as a heretic. He could be glad that at least he had not recanted in the face of opposition, and in the presence of nature's soothing influences he even managed to forget that he had been (and he underlined the word in his journal) "reviewed." But a disturbing drama beginning to play itself out during the fall of 1838 suggested to Emerson that conservatives who hated his philosophy might be far less menacing than disciples who embraced it with too much enthusiasm.

In September 1838 Jones Very began his third year of tutoring in Greek at Harvard. Very had always involved himself in the lives of his students, but now his spiritual advice became more urgent. He told his students to submit their wills wholly to God, then act as conscience prompted; God would then take up his abode in them. Such advice might not have sounded odd in an orthodox seminary like Andover, but at Harvard rumors began to circulate that Very had gone mad. On September 13 Very became sensible of a change in himself. His biographer reports that he felt he had completed the "identification with Christ" he had been urging on his students. And even though this sense of perfect identification wavered in its intensity, Very felt moved to proclaim that the coming of Christ was at hand.

Very called on Henry Ware, Jr., and announced that he had an interpretation of the twenty-fourth chapter of Matthew he had to give. When Ware tried to silence him, Very accused him of disobeying God and cried in frustration when Ware continued to oppose him. The next day in class, a student reported, Very declared to one of his Greek sections "that he was infallible: that he was a man of heaven, and superior to all the world around him" and then cried out a verse from the chapter of Matthew he had wanted to expound to Ware: "Flee to the mountains, for the end of all things is at hand." That evening he attended the Divinity School debating club and calmly announced that, because "the Holy Spirit was speaking in him," whatever he said was "eternal truth."

At this point the president of Harvard, Josiah Quincy, intervened, summoning Very's younger brother Washington (a Harvard freshman) to take Very home to Salem. Before Very left Harvard he mailed Emerson a recently completed essay on Shakespeare along with a letter calling on Emerson to rejoice and give thanks that the Father and Christ had taken him to themselves. "I feel that the day now is when 'the tabernackle of God is with men, and he will dwell with them, and they shall be his people.' " In Salem Very continued his proselytizing. He visited a startled Elizabeth Peabody, announcing that he was "the Second Coming" and offering to baptize her with fire; he visited several ministers, who were considerably less sympathetic than she had been. One angrily demanded to see Very perform some miracles to validate his mission; another threw him out of the house; a third − a good friend of Andrews Norton and an enemy of the Transcendentalists − vowed to have him committed by force to McLean Hospital for the Insane at Charlestown, a threat he in fact carried out.

Elizabeth Peabody offered a guess at the etiology of Very's insanity by supposing that it came from "overtaxing his brain in an attempt to look from the standpoint of Absolute Spirit." A modern clinician would be more likely to diagnose acute mania. Very's rapid transition from mild euphoria to exaltation, his immediate conviction of identity with the divine, his extreme lability of mood and sudden bursts of anger when frustrated, and the endless volubility he displayed both before and after he was committed to the asylum − these are all recognizable symptoms of mania. But the folio sheet of sonnets Very gave Peabody the day before he was hospitalized contains material very unlike the loosely associative or enigmatically discontinuous material produced by most writers in the manic state. On the contrary, the sonnets are highly organized and formally precise; in strictness of organization and in spiritual intensity they resemble the seventeenth-century English religious poetry the Transcendentalists admired.

After Very had been in the hospital for a month the doctor at McLean decided to dismiss him, judging him to be no danger to himself or others, though he still refused to renounce his beliefs. (The other patients are reported to have thanked Very as he left.) Very now determined to call on Emerson, whom he had wanted to see at the time of his removal from Harvard. His nearly week-long visit with Emerson at Concord was both intense and disturbing. Emerson at first found Very far less "mad" than he had expected; the things Very said about society, the church, and the college struck him as "perfectly just." When Very confronted the presiding preacher at a meeting of Sunday School teachers held in Emerson's house and "bid him wonder at the Love which suffered him to speak there in his chair, of things he knew nothing of," Emerson gleefully reported that Very "unhorsed" the desperate, dogmatizing minister "and tumbled him along the ground in utter dismay." It is not hard to see why Emerson should have enjoyed and even tacitly encouraged naked aggression by a younger and less inhibited self against the forces that were ranged against both of them. When he said goodbye to Very at the end of the visit Emerson felt − the words are revealing − as if he had "discharged an arrow into the heart of society."

Nevertheless, Emerson had to bear much abuse himself during the visit. Very accused Emerson of coldness, of being willing to receive the Truth but not to obey it. Emerson suddenly found himself playing Henry Ware to Very's Emerson, as he tried to argue with Very only to be met with flat refusals to engage in dispute. "It is the necessity of the spirit to speak with authority," Very said. Very could not have known it, but the problem of the source of spiritual authority had plagued Emerson throughout his own career in the ministry. Very's perfect sincerity and his passionate conviction gave him authority, and even if Emerson refused to become a convert he was moved to make an extraordinary confession nevertheless, and one that would return to haunt him.

I told J. V. that I had never suffered, & that I could scarce bring myself to feel a concern for the safety & life of my nearest friends that would satisfy them; that I saw clearly that if my wife, my child, my mother, should be taken from me, I should still remain whole with the same capacity of cheap enjoyment from all things.

After he had returned to Salem, Very sent Emerson some of his sonnets, and Emerson responded with interest and admiration. (Emerson published a volume of Very's poetry and essays in 1839.) Very continued to publish his sonnets in the Salem *Observer* and in James Freeman Clarke's *Western Messenger* and to circulate them in manuscript among the members of the Transcendental Club.

Clarke's periodical was coming to play an increasingly important role in the life of the Transcendentalists. The *Christian Examiner* was now closed to them, but the *Western Messenger* of St. Louis – nominally Unitarian but under the editorship of Clarke, and at safe distance away from the pressures of public opinion in Boston and Cambridge – could print what it chose. In November 1838 the *Western Messenger* devoted two articles to a survey of the controversy surrounding the Divinity School Address, pointing out that the Unitarian hierarchy was making itself a laughingstock by hurling at Emerson precisely those epithets the orthodox once delighted to hurl at the Unitarians. More importantly, it took the sneer "new school" over from Norton and turned it into a term of praise. The New School is made up of all those members of the clergy and laity who are "dissatisfied with the present state of religion, philosophy, and literature. The common principle which binds them together and makes them if you choose a school, is a desire for more of LIFE, soul, originality in these great departments of thought." Members of the New School are not any one person's disciples; they choose which doctrines and virtues to admire in their spokespersons. They agree only in their conviction "that life should not be a mechanical routine, but be filled with earnestness, soul, and spiritual energy." Early in 1839, Orestes Brownson continued his attack upon the conservative position by pointing out in the

Boston Quarterly Review that it was more truly "skeptical" to require sensory evidences before believing Jesus' teachings than to believe without such evidences. In this sense, Norton is the skeptic, Emerson the faithful believer.

Norton was not finished. A year after Emerson delivered his address, the newly formed "Association of the Alumni of the Divinity School" invited Norton to speak. His "Discourse on the Latest Form of Infidelity" attempts to present systematically the position he had argued the preceding year in his newspaper blast immediately following Emerson's address. Against those who argued that miracles were no necessary proof of the truth of revelation Norton pointed out that Jesus himself always referred to his miracles as attesting his divine mission, and that modern theologians who refuse to accept miracles as testamentary must therefore believe either that Jesus was lying or that he was deluded. Christianity, being a revelation from God, is inherently miraculous, and requires a miraculous confirmation of its doctrines.

Nothing is left that can be called Christianity, if its miraculous character be denied. Its essence is gone; its evidence is annihilated. Its truths, involving the highest interests of man, the facts which it makes known, and which are implied in its very existence as a divine revelation, rest no longer on the authority of God.

The intensity of Norton's language suggests how threatening he found the Transcendentalists' attempt to sever the link between truth and history and how repugnant he found their attempt to ground on "undefined and un-intellible feeings." Men who refuse to accept the indispensably evidentiary quality of miracles have no right to call themselves Christian teachers.

More than one spectator of the conflict must have been struck by its irony. Norton, the aggressive young iconoclast who had wanted to smash the strongholds of Calvinism and build new temples of liberal religion was now hurling charges of heresy at the younger members of his own sect. As John White Chadwick (author of a 1900 biography of Theodore Parker) noted:

The situation was a vivid reproduction of that which existed twenty years before, more irrational and less ethical than that, because the Calvinists of 1819 believed great truths to be in danger, – the Trinity, the Atonement, the Deity of Christ – while Mr. Norton and his friends had only to object that their great truths were not believed for their own particular reasons.

In attempting to insist that one must believe in miracles in order to be a Christian, Norton had let himself be pushed into arguing (as Chadwick put it) that "the unpardonable sin was belief in Christianity upon the grounds of its intrinsic excellence."

Yet what Norton was attempting to defend was not, after all, negligible. Miracles are important not just as sensible events but as historical events, as part of the many signs and wonders strewn through history to mark a series of covenants binding the people of God to God and assuring them of their eventual triumph. Getting rid of "historical Christianity" meant giving up a promise that history itself unfolded in the direction of fulfillment. How great a void this left became apparent every time the Transcendentalists tried to imagine the "church of the future." After a journey to New Hampshire in September 1839 Emerson wrote to Margaret Fuller confessing his weariness with existing denominations and his helplessness to come up with an alternative.

We heard in one place blue sulphureous preaching, in another the most ominous shaking of Unitarian husks & pods out of which all corn & peas had long fallen, the men were base the newspapers base & worse, the travellers did not find in themselves the means of redemption. I see movement, I hear aspirations, but I see not how the great God prepares to satisfy the heart in a new order of things. No church no state will form itself to the eye of desire & hope.

The oracle refuses to enlighten us as to the mode of our redemption. "A thousand negatives it utters clear & strong on all sides, but the sacred affirmative it hides in the deepest abyss" (Emerson to Fuller, September 6, 1839).

When Harrison Gray Otis Blake, one of the students who had been in the fateful graduating class at the Divinity School the previous year, wrote to express his doubts about continuing in the ministry, Emerson could only urge him to choose his path by the light of "a greater selfreliance – a thing to be spoken solemnly of & waited for as not one thing but all things, as the uprise & revelation of God." And he struggled to express his sense of the impermanence of all forms before the living soul. "Man seems to me the one fact; the forms of the church & of society – the framework which he creates & casts aside day by day. The whole of duty seems to consist in purging off these accidents & obeying the aboriginal truth" (Emerson to Blake, August 1, 1839). Blake can hardly be blamed for wondering how a practicing minister might implement such a program, particularly because in the Divinity School Address Emerson had warned that all attempts to contrive new systems of worship seemed to him as vain as the devotions to the Goddess of Reason introduced by the French revolutionaries – "today pasteboard and filigree, ending tomorrow in madness and murder." If the new forms are facticious and the old good for nothing but to be sloughed off, what kind of worship can be true?

Emerson was by this time too detached from the problems of the ministry to devote much time to considering the problem, and George Ripley, who waded into the battle with a series of thick pamphlets attacking Norton and replying to Norton's counterattacks, was also headed for separation from his ministry. His parish was poor to begin with and had continued to decline; the part he had played in the recent controversy had caused at least some of his parishioners distress. In a letter to them dated October 1, 1840, he looked back sadly over the excitement of the early days of the Unitarian controversy, when the liberal clergy "asserted the unlimited freedom of the human mind, and not only the right, but the duty of private judgment." Young people raised in such a heady atmosphere "had been taught that no system of divinity monopolized the truth, and they were no more willing to be bound by the prevailing creed of Boston or Cambridge, than their fathers had been by the prescription of Rome or Geneva." But now some clergy feared the forces of unlimited inquiry. "Liberal churches begin to fear liberality, and the most heretical sect in Christendom to bring the charge of being so against those who carried out its own principles." The suggestion by some of the church's proprietors that Ripley avoid all controversial topics in his sermons seemed to him depressing and embarrassing. "Unless a minister is expected to speak out on all subjects which are uppermost in his mind, with no fear of incurring the charge of heresy or compromising the interests of his congregation, he can never do justice to himself, to his people, or the truth which he is bound to declare." He offered his resignation to the proprietors of the church and preached his farewell sermon in March 1841.

Some Transcendentalist ministers, however, refused either to leave or to be driven out of the church. One of Ripley's close friends from the Transcendental Club was Theodore Parker (1810–60), a Unitarian minister who could trace his belief in intuitive religion back to his boyhood, when something in him rebelled at hearing a minister preach that the Resurrection of Jesus was the only proof we had of the immortality of the soul. He was unable at the time to explain to himself why he thought that a historical event could not prove a universal proposition, but some version of that problem was to recur in the work he did in his maturity.

Parker was the grandson of the captain who commanded the minutemen at the battle of Lexington in 1775. He was the youngest of eleven children. His father, a farmer, could not afford to send him to Harvard, but Parker applied for admission anyway and, once admitted, satisfied every requirement for the bachelor's degree except tuition and residency. (The university eventually granted him an honorary master's degree in 1840.)

Parker turned to schoolteaching in Watertown to earn enough money to enter the Harvard Divinity School, all the while pursuing an ambitious personal course of reading in literature, philosophy, and mathematics that kept him occupied ten or twelve hours a day besides the six hours that he spent in school. He had already begun to study Hebrew with a tutor and to borrow German books from his Watertown pastor, Convers Francis (1795–1863).

Francis was the oldest member of the Transcendental Club and the author of the suggestively named *Christianity as a Purely Internal Principle* (1836), which argued that Christianity was remarkable among religions chiefly for its independence of rituals and creeds. Francis was already well known for his extensive knowledge of German theological literature and for the size of his library; he would become a professor at the Divinity School in 1842.

Parker entered the Divinity School in 1834. At the time of his entrance his beliefs appear to have been unexceptionable by Unitarian standards, and he was chosen to help edit a magazine of biblical interpretation for the Unitarian faithful called the *Scriptural Interpreter*. But in the same year the teacher who had taught him Latin and Greek at the Lexington district school, Dr. George Noyes, published an article in the *Christian Examiner* questioning one of the traditional "evidences" of Christianity. Noyes argued that it was difficult to point out *any* predictions in the Old Testament that were fulfilled in the life of Jesus – an opinion deemed shocking enough by the attorney general of Massachusetts for him to demand Noyes's prosecution for blasphemy (proceedings were begun but the charges were later dropped).

Parker was inclined to agree with his old teacher. His labors for the *Scriptural Interpreter* had brought him into contact with modern critical investigators of the Bible. For the *Interpreter* he translated Jean Astruc's revolutionary *Conjectures* (1753) about the two sources of the book of Genesis (Parker's translation was published in two parts, in 1836 and 1837). But he also began to read the more recent German criticism; in fact, he was invited in 1835 to prepare a "Report on German Theology" for the Divinity School's student-run Philanthropic Club. Originally instituted to promote good works for prisoners and the poor, the club had become by the mid-1830s a forum for the discussion of ideas both intellectually and socially radical. Students would meet to hear reports and debate resolutions on everything from the Abner Kneeland case to antislavery and labor reform.

Parker immersed himself in German theology and biblical criticism for the report and began to discover what a truly critical approach to the Bible entailed. He became acquainted with the man whose work he was to spend so many years of his life translating, Wilhelm Martin Leberecht de Wette (1780–1849). De Wette's voluminous works include an *Introduction to the Old Testament* in which he argues, among other things, that Moses was not the author of the Pentateuch, which is itself not a single document but a collection of fragments with little connection to one another assembled many hundreds of years after Moses was supposed to have lived; that the books from Exodus through Numbers have more than one author; and that the account of the origin of Israelite ceremonial religion given in the book of Chronicles is wholly unreliable. In fact, the whole dream of the rationalist critics of the

Bible – which is to separate the truly "historical" elements in it from the supernatural – is doomed to failure, because the Bible is not a historical document at all but rather a poetic or mythological expression of the hopes and beliefs of the Jewish people at the time when the various fragments of the text were written.

Parker decided to translate this work of de Wette's, which one recent scholar has called the beginning of modern criticism of the Old Testament; the project, begun in 1836, was not brought to completion until 1843, when it was published in Ripley's *Specimens of Foreign Standard Literature* series. (Another work by de Wette, the autobiographical novel *Theodore; or, The Skeptic's Conversion,* was translated by James Freeman Clarke and published first serially in the *Western Messenger* and then in Ripley's series in 1841; it was particularly interesting to the Transcendentalists in giving an account of the hero's struggles to discover a satisfying faith as he leaves behind orthodoxy to pass successively under the influence of the ideas of Kant, Schelling, Fries, and Schleiermacher.) But the effects of Parker's study of German criticism were apparent long before the de Wette translation appeared.

Parker questioned the messianic interpretation of the fifty-second chapter of Isaiah in an article for the *Scriptural Interpreter,* to the great distress of one of its subscribers. When he was ordained and settled as a minister to a small congregation in West Roxbury, Massachusetts, he continued his heterodox researches. He wrote a long and detailed review of David Friedrich Strauss's *Das Leben Jesu* (1835) for publication in the *Christian Examiner* in 1840. The beginning of the review, which is taken up with a summary of Strauss's own introductory survey of the history of biblical interpretation since Origen, allows Parker the opportunity to explain how Strauss arrived at his radical argument. Strauss asserted that the New Testament did not merely contain mythological elements (like the Nativity story or the Ascension) but was itself fundamentally mythological in character. Most interpreters have rested their belief in the historicity of the Gospels upon the tradition that the Gospels were written by eyewitnesses, but Strauss "finds little reason for believing the genuineness or the authenticity of the Gospels," regarding them instead as "spurious productions of well-meaning men, who collected the traditions that were current in the part of the world, where they respectively lived."

Parker calls this the weakest part of Strauss's argument, but whether he really thought so is harder to determine. He wrote in his journal that he could not say all that he thought in the *Christian Examiner* review, but only what the readers of the journal would bear, and he wrote to Convers Francis to say that he was inclined to agree that Strauss might be right "in the main" when he calls the New Testament a "collection of Mythi" (Parker to Francis, March 22, 1839). In any case, Parker quickly proceeds in his review to give Strauss's definition of "myth" — it is not a history but "a fiction which has been produced by the state of mind of a certain community" — and to summarize with zest the main points of Strauss's attack upon the credibility of the Gospels, particularly the more than two hundred and fifty pages *Das Leben Jesu* devotes to the subject of miracles. By the end of Strauss's attack not a single miracle — not even the Resurrection itself — is left standing.

Does Parker accept Strauss's conclusions? At the end of his review he lists several deficiencies in the logic of *Das Leben Jesu:* first, that Strauss begs the miracles question by assuming from the outset that miracles are utterly impossible; next, that he refuses to believe that the Ideal can ever be incarnated in a single individual; next, that he assumes but never proves that the Gospels are not genuine and authentic; finally, that in his determination to find myths everywhere he makes the effect precede the cause. "He makes a belief in the resurrection and divinity of Christ spring up out of the community, take hold on the world, and produce a revolution in all human affairs perfectly unexampled; and all this without any adequate historical cause." Parker dismisses Strauss's attempt in his "Concluding Treatise" to save the "eternal truths" of Christian faith by seeing them as unconscious projections of the whole human race. "If there was not an historical Christ to idealize," Parker points out, "there could be no ideal Christ to seek in history."

Where in history do we then seek for Christ, if the tales about his life and resurrection are myths? Strauss leaves the authenticity of one element in the Gospels unchallenged. Parker quotes Strauss's contention that a comparison of the synoptic Gospels will show that "the granulary discourses of Jesus have not been dissolved and lost in the stream of oral tradition, but they have, not rarely, been loosened from their natural connexion, washed away from their original position, and like boulders rolled to places where they do not properly belong." One suspects that Parker was drawn to this sentence less for its critical than for its affirmative force: The discourses of Jesus, though granulary and dislocated, have survived the dissolving powers of time, oral transmission, and blundering apostolic redactors. On these small rocks Parker would found his mature faith.

When the miracles controversy broke out between the Transcendentalists and the traditional Unitarians, Parker naturally took part. He was by far the best linguist (he read some twenty languages, including Syriac and Coptic) and best biblical scholar among the Transcendentalists, and his familiarity with recent German criticism enabled him to meet the professional theologians on their own ground. His first contribution was a review in the *Christian Register* of a pamphlet edited and introduced by Andrews Norton.

The pamphlet was a reprinting of an attack by three Princeton scholars writing in the *Princeton Review* upon the Transcendentalists in general and Emerson's Divinity School Address in particular. They were particularly incensed by the assumption of the New School that

> the truths declared by Christ and his Apostles were from God only in the same sense in which all our own intuitions of truth are from God. The Koran is of equal authority with the Bible; all pretended revelations have one and the same authority, that is, the self-evidence of the truths which they contain. The Gospel of Christ is thus stripped of its high prerogative as a special message from God; and holy prophets and apostles, nay, our Saviour too, were deceived in supposing that they had any other kind of communication with God, than that which every man enjoys.

Andrews Norton had liked their argument so well that he reprinted their two essays as a pamphlet in Cambridge in 1840 and affixed a commendatory notice to it.

Parker attempts to crush this production with superior scholarship, showing that the Princeton scholars are shallow and dependent on secondary sources for knowledge of the philosophy and theology they attack. But his long piece sinks under the weight of its own learning and contains only one really memorable sentence: "Our countrymen are now wandering in the wilderness, parched with thirst, and pinched by hunger; we look longingly, – not back to the flesh-pots, and leeks and garlics of Locke, and the Egyptian bondage of sensualism, but forward to the promised land of Truth, Liberty, and Religion."

Parker's experience with theological niggling must have made him understand why Emerson refused to engage in it. In any case, he began to believe that the debate about miracles was fraying into squalid accusations and depressing occasions for self-display. In his journal he expressed his wish that someone would "move the previous question" – in other words, stop arguing about credentials and ask what everyone really wanted to know: *How does man attain to Religion?* He decided to attack Norton head-on in a pamphlet he published under the pseudonym of "Levi Blodgett." Blodgett presents himself as a plainspoken Yankee and addresses an open letter to the gentlemen of Cambridge asking them to explain what he cannot for the life of him understand – why a true Christian needs to be convinced of the truth of Jesus' doctrines by miracles. The truths of Jesus, being self-evident, are in no need of miraculous confirmation. To argue as Norton did that miracles constitute the sole proof that the relation between God and humanity is *real* makes us rest our "moral and religious faith" on "evidence too weak to be trusted in a trifling case that comes before a common court of justice." Besides, the Bible in which these miracle stories occur is frankly acknowledged by Unitarians to be full of fabulous material. Norton himself concluded in 1840 that the first two chapters of Matthew (the Davidic genealogy of Jesus and the story of the Annunciation) were spurious. How then can perfect historical accuracy be claimed for any part of a document so riddled with interpolations and embellished with myth?

This was bad enough, but Parker's real heresy lay less in the critical weapons he turned against Scripture or the logical ones he turned against testimony than in the quiet relinquishing of Christianity's claim to exclusive possession of truth. "All religions are fundamentally the same," Christianity being only "one religion among many, though it is the highest." Hence all religions must appeal to the "primary essential truths of religion, which are innate with man." Religious geniuses like Jesus appeal to these innate truths, and their utterances become the scriptures of nations.

These principles were already implicit in the Divinity School Address, but in his pamphlet Parker was willing to state them with particular frankness and in so doing reveal what the underlying quarrel concerning "miracles" had really been about all along. What miracles offer us is proof that our revelation is *the* revelation, that we are not merely children of God but inheritors of his blessing – Jacobs rather than Esaus. Remove miraculous confirmation from the teachings of Jesus and Christianity becomes merely "one religion among many." Trinitarians had always warned that denying divinity to Jesus would end in this diffuse sort of Theism anyway, and they naturally were quick to point out that the Transcendentalists had taken the final step beyond Christianity that the Unitarians had initiated.

Despite his attempt at anonymity Parker soon found himself the object of hostile speculation. His defense of the Transcendentalists in the *Christian Register* and similarly disturbing articles in *The Dial* attracted the hostile attention of his clerical colleagues. At an annual meeting of Unitarian ministers in May 1840 Parker discovered that the question to be debated was "Ought differences of opinion on the value and authority of miracles to exclude men from Christian fellowship and sympathy with one another?" Parker held his peace at this meeting, where older liberals like Frederic Henry Hedge and George Ripley defended the Unitarian tradition of allowing the widest possible latitude of opinion. But Parker went home and confided to his journal his outrage that such a question should be raised. "This is the nineteenth century! This is Boston! This among the Unitarians!" And he added, "For my own part, I intend in the coming year to let out all the force of transcendentalism that is in me, come what will come." By the end of the year he had already started to suffer that polite freezing out that was Boston's only form of excommunication: his colleagues in the ministry began refusing to exchange pulpits with him.

Whether Parker was sufficiently stung by this treatment to decide that he might as well be hanged for a sheep as for a lamb or whether his growing sense of intellectual power simply made him ready to emerge from tutelage and anonymity, he very soon seized an opportunity offered him to move from minor irritant to major scandal. In May 1841 Parker was invited to deliver the sermon at the ordination of Charles C. Shackford at the Hawes Place Church in South Boston. Thirty-two years earlier Channing had made the ordination of Jared Sparks the occasion to define "Unitarian Christianity." Now Parker would use the opportunity provided by Shackford's ordination to redefine Christian truth in his own way. As a recent scholar has pointed out, the title of Parker's sermon, "A Discourse of the Transient and Permanent in Christianity," translates the title of an article by Strauss — though few people besides Parker himself were learned enough to get the complicated point of the allusion. In 1838 Strauss had replied to wholesale lament about the destructiveness of *Das Leben Jesu* by offering a rare "positive" appreciation of Jesus, whom Strauss praises as the greatest genius in history, devoted not to outward works but to the creation of a perfect soul. Strauss called his article "Uber Vergängliches und Bleibendes in Christentum" and reprinted it in a volume called *Zwei friedlich Briefe* (Two peaceable letters).

Parker's division of Christianity is not quite the same as the one Strauss proposed in his article; rather, it returns to the distinction suggested in *Das Leben Jesu* between the granulary discourses of Jesus and the stream of myth and oral tradition in which they are embedded. But Parker's conscious intentions are peaceable. He simply wishes to rescue Christ's Word from his churches. He begins his discourse with fervent and glowing praise of the preaching of Jesus. He praises Jesus' words as simple, lucid, and self-explanatory. In the opening paragraphs he describes their miraculous survival in a world of constant change, where empires rise and fall:

The philosophy of the wise, the art of the accomplished, the song of the poet, the ritual of the priest, though honored as divine in their day, have gone down a prey to oblivion. Silence has closed over them; only their spectres now haunt the earth. But through all this the words of Christianity have come down to us from the lips of that Hebrew youth, gentle and beautiful as the light of a star, not spent by their journey through time and through space.

Nothing is more "fixed and certain" than this "real Christianity," the religion Jesus taught. "The old heavens and the old earth are indeed passed away, but the Word stands."

Yet Parker soon turns from the "permanent" element in Christianity to attack the "transient," and here the havoc wreaked by his critical faculty upon theological history must have left his audience gasping. For in the remainder of his relentlessly argued discourse Parker focuses the whole force of his richly stocked mind toward demonstrating that *no* doctrine advanced or ritual celebrated by any Christian sect can proclaim itself free of inherited error or local prejudice. An honest study of the history of religions forces us to confess that the Unitarians, with their two modest sacraments and their tiny collection of dogmas (that Jesus was divinely commissioned, as his miracles show; that after his death he rose again and ascended into heaven), are no more safe from critical analysis than the *Summa Theologica* or the Byzantine church.

Any one who traces the history of what is called Christianity, will see that nothing changes more from age to age than the doctrines taught as Christian, and insisted on as essential to Christianity and personal salvation. What is falsehood in one province passes for truth in another. The heresy of one age is the orthodox belief and "only infallible rule" of the next.

We now smile at the obsolete systems of the past, but how can we know that "our Christianity" will not share the same fate? "Many tenets that pass current in our theology seem to be the refuse of idol temples, the off-scourings of Jewish and heathen cities, rather than the sands of virgin gold which the stream of Christianity has worn off from the rock of ages." The Bible itself has suffered a loss of its authority, its texts unraveled by critics, its sacred canon revealed to be the product of "caprice or accident." With unfeigned delight Parker slyly enlists Andrews Norton on his side. "One writer, not a sceptic, but a Christian of unquestioned piety, sweeps off the beginning of Matthew; another, of a different church and equally religious, the end of John. Numerous critics strike off several epistles. The Apocalypse itself is not spared, notwithstanding its concluding curse."

How then can we be sure the Apostles themselves "were not sometimes mistaken in historical, as well as in doctrinal matters"? What then? Christianity does not stand or fall with the doctrine of the infallible inspiration of "a few Jewish fishermen, who have writ their names in characters of light all over the world." The truth of Jesus' Word is not dependent upon the infallibility of the document in which they are preserved, nor on the personal authority of Jesus, any more than the axioms of geometry are dependent upon the personal authority of Euclid.

So if it could be proved — as it cannot — in opposition to the greatest amount of historical evidence ever collected on any similar point, that the Gospels were the fabrication of designing and artful men, that Jesus of Nazareth had never lived, still Christianity would stand firm, and fear no evil. None of the doctrines of the religion would fall to the ground; for, if true, they stand by themselves.

And, in case any members of the audience balked at this willingness to jettison the founder of Christianity in the name of Christian truth, Parker proclaims boldly, "Christ set up no Pillars of Hercules, beyond which men must not sail the sea in quest of truth." Real Christianity is the source of life. "It makes us outgrow any form or any system of doctrines we have devised, and approach still closer to the truth."

In his South Boston sermon Parker manages to combine those two qualities he said he admired most in theologians like de Wette and Schleiermacher – criticism that is "bold, unsparing, and remorseless" with a spirit of "profound piety." Parker's sermon is as radiant with the love of Jesus as it is scornful of the narrowness of the theologians who have sought to define him. "If ever I wrote anything with an *Xn* zeal," Parker wrote after the storm of protest had broken, "it was that very discourse" (Parker to Ezra Stiles Gannett, June 17, 1841). In this respect Parker's sermon is strikingly different from the Divinity School Address, where Emerson's attitude toward Jesus fluctuates between strained expressions of admiration and outbursts of unmistakable resentment.

The piety that informs Parker's South Boston sermon might have protected it if three outraged Trinitarian ministers who attended the ordination had not published a two-page precis of its argument in the orthodox *New England Puritan* with an accompanying challenge to Unitarians to comment on it. Although the Unitarian clergy who replied directly to this challenge hewed to the position that Unitarians recognized no creed or covenant that interfered with individual liberty, Unitarian publications – the *Christian Register, Monthly Miscellany,* and *Christian Examiner* – published attacks upon the South Boston sermon. Parker replied to their charges in a series of five lectures at the Old Masonic Temple in the winter of 1841–2. Unfortunately, the habit Parker had of branding his opponents with the most opprobrious of epithets only increased their alienation from him, and they began to refuse pulpit exchanges.

Parker was hurt that so few of his friends were willing to stand by him; by 1842 only eight ministers would still exchange with him. The remainder doubtless felt with Frederic Henry Hedge that progressive Christian minds must be *in* the church and not out of it. Hedge wrote to Convers Francis in 1843 to express his worry that "if the principle of dissent from existing institutions & belief continues to spread at the rate it has done for the last two years, the entire *Clerus,* professional and parochial, will be ousted in ten years" (Hedge to Francis, February 14, 1843).

When Parker compounded the offense of the South Boston sermon by publishing the Masonic Temple lectures as *A Discourse of Matters Pertaining to Religion,* his colleagues in the Boston Association of Ministers invited him to a "tea" in January 1842 to inform him that many felt they could no longer bear the "vehemently deistical" tendencies of his writing and preaching. A minister named Chandler Robbins tried to convince Parker that "since the feeling in respect to him is so general," it was his "duty" to withdraw from the association, an argument seconded by others.

It cannot have been easy for a thirty-one-year-old man to stand up to the collective disapproval of his senior colleagues, but Parker refused to withdraw from the association, saying that what was at issue was the right of free inquiry. Then one of Parker's friends spoke up in defense of his sincerity; others (including some of his original attackers) hastened to join in that sentiment; and Parker broke into tears and left the room. Afterwards Robbins wrote to say that he "felt most deeply the delicacy and hard trial of your situation" and that he thought that Parker had acquitted himself nobly. But, he added, "It would have been unjust to you to have been less frank than we were" (Robbins to Parker, January 24, 1843).

In the end, Parker refused to be silenced or ousted from the church. He finally published his massive edition of de Wette's *Introduction to the Old Testament* in 1843 and then left for a tour of Europe made necessary by the cumulative exhaustion of the preceding years. Before departing he preached a sermon to his West Roxbury congregation thanking them for their fidelity to him in his time of trial. "Fear in the churches, like fire in the woods, runs fast and far, leaving few spots not burned," he told them. "I thought you would do what others did; others had promised more but fled at the first fire."

This sense — of what it takes to stand fast in the time of trouble — may be the most enduring personal legacy of Transcendentalism's period of challenge. Alcott and Emerson and Parker survived public immolations, but the same lesson was learned by those whose circumstances were necessarily more obscure. From her exile in West Newton, where Elizabeth Peabody had gone after the publication of *Conversations with Children on the Gospels* had ended her teaching career, Elizabeth wrote to her sister Sophia to explain what she meant by the "new light" she had attained by her experience at the Temple School.

I feel as I never felt before that to be true to one's self is the first thing — that to sacrifice the perfect culture of my mind to social duties is not the thing — that what we call disinterestedness of action is often disobedience to one's *daimon* — that one's inward instinct is one's best guide — that selfdenial may encroach on the region of the spiritual.

Her biggest mistake in Boston lay in not insisting upon a room of her own. "Something must be allowed to one's self for the infirmities of nature & it is better to be called selfish and oldmaidish than to lose one's own soul" (Elizabeth Peabody to Sophia Peabody, July 31, 1838).

6

LETTERS AND SOCIAL AIMS

T RANSCENDENTALISM WAS from the beginning a literary movement as well as a religious and philosophical one. The Transcendentalists kept journals and wrote poetry; they wrote long letters about
literature to one another; they tried their hand at prose sketches and Oriental
fables; they delivered lyceum lectures and commencement speeches; they
held "conversations" on topics like Beauty and Mythology; they reviewed
books for the *Christian Examiner* and the *North American Review.* But few of
the Transcendentalist texts that managed to find their way into print before
the 1840s could be classified strictly as belles lettres. Perhaps only Emerson's
Nature could really qualify as polite literature, a "prose poem" — though its
review by Francis Bowen in the *Christian Examiner* in 1837 suggests that even
Nature in its home territory was read more as a part of the philosophical
skirmishing going on between the Lockeans and the spiritualists than as a
work of the imagination.

There were many reasons for this state of affairs. The strong New England
prejudice against fiction made writing novels or short stories out of the
question for most of the Trancendentalists, even supposing that they had any
talent for plot or dialogue or any interest in the social complexities novelists
thrive on. Emerson ridiculed Jane Austen for her "vulgar boardinghouse
imagination," and Thoreau devoted a good part of the chapter "Reading" in
Walden to abusing those readers who read with saucer eyes and digest with
unwearied gizzards the latest romance about the Middle Ages. Poetry was
considered more respectable, but the kind of Wordsworthian Romanticism
practiced by William Cullen Bryant and the senior Richard Henry Dana
seemed too derivative to appeal to the fiercely independent Transcendentalists, and the vogue for Byronic imitations that had marked the 1820s in
America had died away without leaving much in its wake.

Some of the liveliest writing in the period was unpublished — the letters of
Emerson, Margaret Fuller, James Freeman Clarke, and Elizabeth Peabody;
the journals of Emerson and Thoreau. To think of these writings as really
"private" is not quite accurate, because both letters and journals were regularly passed around among the circle of friends — in fact, at one point Emer-

son had to borrow back one of his own letters from Margaret Fuller so that he could extract from it a passage for the essay he was writing, "Friendship." In these intimate reflections and exchanges the Transcendentalists could write with an exuberance their sense of decorum kept out of their published works; in letters particularly they could be witty, malicious, and seductive as well as high-minded and devoted to truth. Shortly after Emerson had completed his "Human Life" lecture series at the Concord Lyceum in 1839 the Reverend Barzillai Frost wrote to inform him that some Concord gentlemen who wanted to express their thanks for the lectures had gathered contributions to buy books for his library – the works of Sir Thomas Browne, Victor Cousin's twelve-volume translation of Plato, and the letters of Horace Walpole. Emerson enjoyed the Walpole as much as he did the Plato and Browne; to Margaret Fuller he boasted that Walpole had effected a change in his own style: "If I were in earnest to write you a letter, you would be forced to shade your eyes from my glitter."

Other Transcendentalists found in George Ripley's series, *Specimens of Foreign Standard Literature,* opportunities to translate works that had meant much to them. The spirit that moved these enterprises is best summed up in the words from John Milton's *History of Britain* that Margaret Fuller used as the epigraph to her 1839 translation of Johann Peter Eckerman's *Conversations with Goethe:* "As wine and oil are imported to us from abroad, so must ripe understanding, and many civil virtues, be imported into our minds from foreign writings; – we shall else miscarry still, and come short in the attempts of any great enterprise."

Periodicals remained, however, the most tempting form of publication for the Transcendentalists in the 1830s and 1840s. Magazines and reviews offered beginning authors the pleasure of seeing something quickly in print; they also offered the stimulus of deadlines and the excitement of working with a group of like-minded contributors. (Getting contributors to submit manuscripts and printers to print issues on time or subscribers to pay for the numbers they had received was another matter, as most editors soon discovered.) When the young James Freeman Clarke wrote to Margaret Fuller in the early 1830s declaring his confidence that she will found a "New School" of American literature in which he plans to enroll himself, he thinks of her as the editor of a magazine, a "Maga" that will "make the North Americans and American Quarterlies" fly like chaff before an angry wind.

In the early 1830s many of the Transcendentalists published their position papers in the form of reviews for the *Christian Examiner,* but as the group began to acquire a distinct identity the notion of publishing a magazine of its own naturally arose. As early as 1835, Frederic Henry Hedge and George Ripley were planning a "journal of spiritual philosophy" in which they hoped to enlist the aid of "all the Germano-philosophico-literary talent in the country." Emerson even tried to persuade Thomas Carlyle himself to come to America and assume the editorship, an offer Carlyle declined.

At the same time, a group of Unitarian clergy who had emigrated to cities in the Ohio Valley were determining to publish a magazine of their own, partly to disseminate Unitarian theology, partly to serve as a forum for discussion of western issues and a showcase for western literary talent. Ephraim Peabody, the Cincinnati editor who was responsible for putting together the first issues of their magazine, the *Western Messenger,* wanted to make the journal a forthright defense of Unitarian doctrine in a region dominated by varieties of Calvinism; he was wary of material too obviously recondite. But Clarke, now pastor of a congregation in Louisville, Kentucky, clearly hoped to find room in the *Messenger*'s pages for the works of his eastern friends as well, for he was soon pleading with Fuller to send him anything she had written to help fill the magazine, whose first issue appeared in May 1835.

Peabody was reluctant to publish Fuller's pieces, reminding Clarke that other magazines had perished from trying to satisfy tastes they had not yet created. For his part Clarke was furious that the pieces he had solicited had been treated cavalierly. He wrote to Peabody to demand that at least ten or twelve pages of each issue be given to him to do with as he wished. In those pages, at least, he could feel himself *"unlimited & absolute."* His appetite for dominion was soon to be satisfied, for by the end of 1835 ill health and family tragedy had forced Peabody to offer Clarke the sole editorship of the *Messenger.*

Clarke quickly discovered that the life of an editor is no despotism of unlimited and absolute power but a trial by petty miseries, particularly when a magazine's editors and subscribers alike are scattered over a vast territory and its finances are always approaching ruin. Still, the pleasure of being able to shape the journal at least partly as he pleased was considerable. By the spring of 1836 Clarke was publishing defenses of Goethe and Schiller, reviews of Wordsworth and Tennyson, and selections from the journals of John Keats, whose brother George had emigrated to Louisville, where Clarke met him and became his close friend.

One persistent source of disappointment for Clarke lay in the failure of the eastern church to contribute to the support of his magazine or even to buy subscriptions to it. He angrily accused his eastern brethren of indifference, yet in September 1836 he was forced to appeal to their charity to keep the *Messenger* alive. The trip he made back to Boston, where he preached at Dr. Channing's Federal Street Church, was successful in raising donations, and it had an unexpected benefit as well for the chronically homesick Clarke. He was on hand for the first two meetings of the Transcendental Club and was in

Cambridge to discuss the books that were published that season by the club's members.

How much this might have meant to Clarke can be guessed from the letters he sent Margaret Fuller from the very beginning of his Louisville ministry. His decision to move to the West had resulted in part from his sense that the atmosphere of Boston and Cambridge Unitarianism was stultifying and oppressive. In the West he had indeed found freedom, but it was a freedom so capacious that it devalued everything he had to say. "Intellectually speaking I am at present dead," he complained to Fuller in a long letter written in December 1834.

You know why I came West. I thought that here was real freedom of thought and opinion, and that it was therefore a more favourable scene for the development of a mind which wished to have the power to express individual convictions. I have so found it. We are free to speak here whatever we think – there is no doubt of it. Public opinion is not an intolerant despotism, for there is no such thing as Public Opinion. The most opposite and contradictory principles, notions, opinions, are proclaimed every day. Every variety of human thought here finds its representative. All is incongruous, shifting, amorphous. No spirit of order broods over this Chaos. (Clarke to Fuller, February 24, 1834)

Rebellion needs something rigid to overthrow, Clarke was discovering, and if he could not find it in Louisville he could enlist in the wars back home. Returning to Louisville in November 1836 he eagerly declared his allegiance to the New School by publishing largely favorable reviews of Furness's *Remarks on the Four Gospels* (in December 1836), Emerson's *Nature* (in January 1837), Brownson's *New Views of Christianity, Society and the Church* and Alcott's *Conversations with Children on the Gospels* (both in March 1837), and Ripley's *Discourses on the Philosophy of Religion* (in April 1837). Clarke did not write all of these reviews himself, but he did write the defense of Alcott, and in April he began writing letters to Boston periodicals protesting the savagery of Alcott's treatment by the press there. Alcott was grateful that anyone had the courage to praise him and noted in his journal that the young men of the Boston area "grow sturdy and free as soon as they leave the enervating influences of this region of shackle & authority."

The summer of 1837 proved to be a depressing one for Clarke. He had lost eastern subscribers not only for his championing of the New School but also for some of his tactless remarks about the lassitude of the American Unitarian Association. His own congregation, he thought, cared little for the ideas he was trying to import from the East, whereas Cambridge conservatives fumed at the way he had taken over a respectable Unitarian publication and used it to puff the works of the Transcendentalists. Moreover, the sense of isolation that Clarke had complained about in his letters to Fuller ever since his arrival at Louisville was particularly hard to bear when so much seemed to be happening back home.

Still, Clarke's distance from the "region of shackle & authority" would soon prove useful. His "Letter on the State of Unitarianism at the East," which appeared in the June 1838 number of the *Western Messenger* and announced the "death" of Unitarianism through its own coldness and indifference, happened to reach subscribers shortly before Emerson delivered his Divinity School Address. Clarke had published the letter anonymously but as editor of the magazine he could hardly avoid taking responsibility for it, and he now found himself permanently linked with the "New School" in the public mind.

If he were a young minister in Boston who had expressed himself with this degree of freedom he might have expected the same treatment that Emerson or Theodore Parker received — threats of social ostracism, denial of Christian fellowship, even accusations of blasphemy. Mild as these forms of persecution were, Emerson and Parker were distressed (though not silenced) by them at the time. But Clarke's distance from Boston rendered him immune from such pressures. His fellow editors at the *Messenger* were mostly young liberals like himself, and the members of his congregation cared little about what the Harvard Divinity School or the Boston Association of Ministers thought of Clarke or the *Messenger,* though they did resent the amount of time he spent visiting the East and writing about the theological battles there.

Clarke's frustrating distance from the intellectual life of Boston turned out to give him a freedom of expression no Bostonian could enjoy — a perfect example of what Emerson would come to call the Law of Compensation. Clarke was quick to take advantage of his freedom. When Andrews Norton, nine days after the Divinity School Address, published his intemperate attack "The New School in Literature and Religion" in the *Boston Daily Advertiser* and included the *Messenger* in his general condemnation as a "professedly religious work" that nonetheless declined to condemn "the atheist Shelley," Clarke treated the diatribe with insouciance. To Fuller he wrote, "What a lot of twaddle they have uttered about Mr. Emerson! I think of writing something in the next *Messenger* about his oration, and the New School. I am seized with an industrious qualm since I got well, and write much" (Clarke to Margaret Fuller, September 30, 1838). And in the next letter to Fuller he was able to announce, "I shall have an article in the next *Messenger* about Mr. R[alph] W[aldo] E[merson], and the New School. Why not? As well as the professor" (Clarke to Fuller, October 7, 1838).

This tone of insouciance surfaces in the published articles Clarke wrote as well. "R. W. Emerson and the New School," which appeared in the November 1838 issue of the *Messenger,* professes to be surprised that anyone could find Emerson's Divinity School Address dangerous.

Parts seemed somewhat obscure, and for that we were sorry – in places we felt hurt by the phraseology, but we bounded carelessly over these rocks of offence and pit-falls, enjoying the beauty, sincerity, and magnanimity of the general current of the Address. As critics, we confess our fault. We should have been more on the watch, more ready to suspect our author when he left the broad road-way of commonplace, and instantly snap him up when he stated any idea new to us, or differing from our pre-conceived opinions.

Clarke denies the existence of the kind of cabal Norton fears. What holds the members of the New School together is their dissatisfaction with the current state of affairs in literature, philosophy, the church, and the professions. "The common principle which binds them together and makes them if you choose a school, is a desire for more of LIFE, soul, energy, originality in these great departments of thought."

In his own way Clarke had tried to foster these qualities in the *Messenger,* publishing essays and sketches by Margaret Fuller, poetry by Emerson, Jones Very's mystical sonnets, and (in serial installments that threatened to extend to infinity) Clarke's own translation of W. M. L. de Wette's *Theodore; or, The Skeptic's Conversion,* a religious novel tracing the passage of a young man from doubt to intuitive faith. But Clarke had grown weary of the demands of the editorship and frustrated by his congregation's refusal to offer him a perma-nent call. His homesickness for Boston had never left him, and when his Cincinnati coeditors suggested transferring the magazine back to its original home he eagerly accepted. He had recently married Anna Huidekoper, the daughter of a wealthy western Pennsylvania landowner who had been one of the earliest patrons of the *Western Messenger,* The allowance of one thousand dollars a year given to the couple by her father made it possible for Clarke to contemplate leaving his position in Louisville without having a firm offer of another post elsewhere.

The role money played in underwriting Transcendentalist experimentation is considerable. Emerson, for instance, had a legacy from his first wife's estate when he resigned the ministry at the Second Church. He was certainly aware of (and bothered by) the possibility that his brave defiance of convention might be founded more on security than on courage. After returning from one lecture in which he had preached the gospel of self-reliance to young men he worried in his journal that it might be his twelve hundred dollars a year speaking and not him. In a similar way, the wealth of the Huidekoper family made possible James Freeman Clarke's break from a situation he had long found frustrating.

Both men still needed to find additional sources of income, but at least they could not be frightened into submission or compromise.

The Transcendentalists' endless obsession with issues of "manliness" is usually read by modern students as the expression of anxieties about gender — loss of masculinity or failure to attain it. But in its own time such language was easily recognizable as a part of a code that had more to do with livelihood than with manhood — or rather with the relationship between livelihood and manhood. The opposite of "manliness" in this code is not "effeminacy" but "servility." To be dependent on another person for one's livelihood places the strongest possible check on freedom of thought or speech. Transcendentalist ministers felt this check with particular irritation, because they were beholden both to the members of their own churches and to the ministerial organizations that might declare them heretical enough to be unworthy of sharing in pulpit exchanges.

Orestes Brownson would later explain in his own periodical, the *Boston Quarterly Review,* why New England ministers were likely to feel the temptation to compromise their principles. Very few congregations could support a minister if the three or four richest pew owners withheld their subscriptions or pew tax; hence these three or four individuals — who were always conservatives — dictated to the clergyman what doctrines he should preach.

If they are distillers, he must not speak of the sin of manufacturing and vending ardent spirits; if they are factory owners, the iniquities of the present factory system he must not point out; if they are merchants, he must not censure the unchristian spirit of trade which the mercantile world fosters; if slaveholders, he must labor to prove that slavery is sanctioned by all laws human and divine . . . ("The Laboring Classes" [Part 2] October 1840)

Leaving the religious for the secular pulpit, as Emerson did, is a partial solution, but many of the same dilemmas remain. An orator is before all else *a man who prays,* and a professional orator is obliged to confront his own tendencies toward complaisance in ways that producers of more tangible commodities need think about only on market day. To reach an audience at all one must please them enough to hold them, for — as Chaucer's Harry Bailly long ago pointed out to the tedious Monk, "Whereas a man may have noon audience / Noght helpeth it to tellen his sentence." Yet to please an audience too much is to do it no good, for only by awakening it to a sense of its own danger can it be saved.

Emerson remembered a clerical ancestor who liked to castigate his parishioners freely from the pulpit; when they rose, offended, to leave the church, he would cry out after them, "Come back, you graceless sinner, come back!" But Transcendentalist ministers had renounced claims to an authority like that, and Transcendentalist writers had not yet discovered how to acquire its equivalent in print — hence their sometimes uneasy veerings between flattery and excoriation.

To speak the truth and go on speaking it is no easy matter, and the man or woman who plans to speak truth habitually needs not only a tough soul but also a steady income. Increasingly, the Transcendentalists, as they left established posts in the church or had careers closed to them (as Alcott and Peabody were driven out of teaching by the furor following publication of *Conversations with Children on the Gospels*), had to find new ways of making a living. Alcott became a day laborer and conductor of "conversations," Emerson a lecturer, Thoreau a surveyor, Peabody the owner of a bookshop, Ripley the organizer of a communal organization, Brownson the writer and editor of a quarterly review. Even those who stayed in the church, like Clarke and Parker, felt the need to create new forms of church organization that would free them from financial dependence upon church members whose allegiance to the congregation depended upon their ownership of a pew in the church building rather than upon spiritual agreement with the minister and the rest of the congregation.

Clarke would eventually found such a church in Boston when he returned there — the Church of the Disciples, organized in 1841 and made up of spiritual seekers from all over the city who had found no sustenance in the established churches. But for now Clarke and his wife rested on the Huidekoper estate in Pennsylvania while Clarke preached at the local Unitarian church and tried to decide what to do about his future. Meanwhile, the magazine he had edited for three years was about to founder through its determination to discuss the growing problems of the urban poor.

The new editors of the *Western Messenger* in Cincinnati were William Henry Channing (a nephew of the Unitarian leader, who had arrived in Cincinnati in 1839 to become pastor of its First Unitarian Church) and James Perkins, both of whom were more concerned with problems of social reform than Clarke had been. Perkins in particular had become convinced that the human tragedies he witnessed in his ministry-at-large to Cincinnati's poor came not from individual failure but from the failure of social institutions. In October 1839 one of the magazine's nominal coeditors, a Cincinnati lawyer named John Vaughan, published in the *Messenger* an article, "Chartism," on the British movement for working-class rights, in which he hailed Chartism as a "glorious sight" and maintained that economic inequalities were in themselves sufficient justifications for revolution.

Needless to say, prosperous and conservative Unitarians like Clarke's father-in-law, Harm Jan Huidekoper, angrily denounced Vaughan's article. Huidekoper called it "Jacobinical" and expressed his regret that Clarke was no longer the *Messenger's* editor. He prepared his own rebuttal of the idea that the sins of the rich are responsible for the miseries of the poor, which the *Messenger* published in the summer of 1840. Its title — "The Right and Duty of Accumulation" — might serve as the motto for the kind of conservative Unitarianism that frequently bankrolled Transcendentalist enterprises and endured Transcendentalist scorn. Huidekoper argued that wealth represents the power to do good and that the desire to accumulate it is the parent of industry among the poor.

The *Messenger,* however, was not repentant, and when Carlyle's 1839 pamphlet *Chartism,* with its savage attack on the ineptitude of the British governing classes, was published in America by Emerson in 1840, Vaughan reviewed it in a three-part article that praised Carlyle's love of liberty and refused to criticize his proposals for reform. At the same time, back in Boston, a far more famous review of the same pamphlet was being published in the *Boston Quarterly Review* — Brownson's manifesto "The Laboring Classes." Brownson's prediction of imminent class warfare and his call for the outlawing of inherited property provoked a torrent of abuse not only from the Whigs but also from the Democrats whose cause he had embraced and who were now desperate to disown him.

The *Western Messenger* was willing to come to Brownson's defense. In October 1840 one of the editors published a review of "The Laboring Classes" that derided the "howling and shrieking of Conservative men and women" against Brownson and compared it to "the uproar by which the Peruvians tried to stop the moon's eclipse." Though the *Messenger* strongly disagreed with Brownson's proposals for eliminating inequality, deeming them unchristian in spirit and unwise in thought, it nonetheless declared its belief that the man himself was "as honest as Luther, as fearless as Knox, and as capable, either for good or evil, as any writer of our day."

If the *Messenger's* editors hoped to arouse sympathy for Brownson by likening him to the heroes of the Reformation they failed, for angry subscribers deluged them with letters protesting their support of Brownson. Huidekoper wrote to protest that the radicals rarely subjected their own ideas or the ideas of their friends to the same kind of "severe scrutiny" that they turned on conservative doctrines. "Either from the love of novelty, from the fear of appearing to be behind the age, or from a blind partiality for the innovator, these new opinions are often treated with a criminal indulgence."

The *Messenger* refused to back down. W. H. Channing, who had just returned from a visit to Boston, reported with heavy irony in the December 1840 issue that he had visited the "cave of this Cyclops" (Brownson) and had found no human bones. If he had offended his readers he could only repeat his determination to offend them again. "We became editors of this periodical, supposing ourselves to be freemen, and the Western Messenger an organ of Freedom; and, so long as we continue editors, we shall assuredly act on this supposition." Channing did not have long to act, for the magazine soon expired; the April 1841 number was the last.

Many lessons could be drawn from the *Messenger*'s demise. Subscribers to any periodical are likely to resent bewildering changes of editorial direction and to punish editors for ideological shifts by cancelling their subscriptions. Liberals will tolerate radicalism only so long as it does not interfere with the property relations from which they derive their income; it is one thing to assent to the doctrine that the evidences of Christianity are inward and spiritual, quite another to contemplate allowing the state to seize and redistribute one's estate in the interests of greater social equality. The writer who would speak his opinions on all subjects with perfect fearlessness and with scorn for consistency must either give up periodical publication altogether or vow to publish a periodical alone.

"Men like to make an effort," Orestes Brownson asserted in one of his early essays for the *Christian Examiner*. The proposition may not be true of the human race as a whole, but it certainly is true of the man who advanced it. Brownson's biographer calculates that he wrote nearly 150,000 words a year during the first two years of the *Boston Quarterly Review*'s existence, when he was filling the magazine he had started with every imaginable kind of material – long disquisitions on the theory of democracy, reviews of everything from the latest works of Carlyle and the novels of Bulwer Lytton to a series of cookbooks by a vegetarian (a cousin of Alcott's) who thought that roast beef was the Devil and who aimed to fight him with a diet of mush, apples, cold boiled potatoes, and desserts of parched corn.

The task of putting together four times a year a review each of whose issues was well over a hundred pages in length (one issue is 228 pages long) would have flattened most men, but the impression the early volumes of the *Boston Quarterly Review* make on anyone willing to read them straight through is one not of the founding editor's exhaustion but of his exuberance. Brownson does not so much review books as devour them and convert them to power. He is the only American who sounds like the *Edinburgh* reviewers – like Jeffrey, Brougham, and Hazlitt. His prose has the kind of aggressiveness and relentless logic that can make watching him conduct an argument a source of pleasure. It is a pity that Hazlitt did not live to read him, for Brownson has the quality of intellectual fearlessness that Hazlitt had found sadly lacking in William Ellery Channing's essays when he reviewed them in 1829.

Brownson's achievement is all the more impressive when one remembers that he had only the shortest contact with formal schooling, a brief stint at a country academy when he was fourteen. For the rest, he was self-taught and learned the journalist's trade by editing or contributing to a variety of religious and political journals whose titles chart his turbulent course through various denominations, cities, and political movements – from the Universalist *Gospel Advocate and Impartial Investigator* of Auburn, New York, through the New York *Free Enquirer* of Frances Wright and Robert Dale Owen, to the Genesee, New York, *Republican and Herald of Reform.* When Brownson had left in turn both the Universalist ministry and the Workingmen's party and declared himself a Unitarian, he signaled his change of heart by starting yet another journal, the short-lived Ithaca, New York, *Philanthropist.*

By the summer of 1832 Brownson had become a Unitarian minister in Walpole, New Hampshire. He soon began sending articles to the leading Unitarian journals in Boston. George Ripley, the editor of the *Christian Register,* struck up a friendship with him and tried to persuade him to come to Boston. Eventually Brownson's powerful articles began appearing in the prestigious *Christian Examiner* where others besides Ripley took notice of them. Emerson learned a great deal from Brownson's early pieces. In Brownson's 1834 review of Benjamin Constant's history of religion, for instance, there is a distinction between the religious sentiment and the succession of forms it inhabits that sounds like an early draft of Emerson's essay "Circles," with its evocation of the endless proliferation and decay of the spirit's various incarnations.

By July 1836 Brownson had moved to Chelsea and had become the editor of yet another journal, the *Boston Reformer.* William Ellery Channing, whom Brownson revered (hearing a friend read Channing's famous sermon "Likeness to God" had converted Brownson to Unitarianism), hoped that Brownson's experience preaching to working-class congregations might help him bring the Unitarian doctrine of salvation through self-culture to groups usually reached only by the fiercer consolations of evangelicalism on the one side or the anticlerical radicalism of Abner Kneeland on the other.

Still, Brownson longed to have a magazine free from the entanglements of denominational allegiance. He wanted to escape the kinds of compromises forced on writers by the expectations of editors; he was equally determined to avoid the miseries faced by editors whose contributors were dilatory or otherwise unreliable. And it seems clear that he nursed the ambition of providing an American alternative to the British reviews that had played such an important role in the self-education of his whole generation. Finally, he felt a prophet's sense of urgency to speak out on "the problem of the Destiny of Man and of Society," as he declares to his readers in the "Introductory Remarks" to the first issue of the *Boston Quarterly Review.* "I must and will speak. What I say may be worth something, or it may be worth nothing, yet say it I will. But in order to be able to do this, I must have an organ of utterance at my own command, through which I may speak when I what I please. Hence, the Boston Review." A farewell note at the bottom of the last page of the first number is similarly uncompromising. Brownson sends his magazine forth to make its own fortune. "If the public like it and want it, they will support it, and if they do not, – then of course they will not."

This blunt self-reliance was as far as possible from the gentility of Cambridge, and Brownson (whose rough manners and contentiousness grated on the Transcendentalists quite as much as it did on traditional Unitarians) lost no opportunity to flaunt his independence from every group that might think it could claim his allegiance. The longest piece in the first number of the magazine is the address that Brownson had delievered in September 1837 to the Democratic State Convention at Worcester, Massachusetts. Brownson had used the occasion not so much to glory in his new political allegiance as to lecture his fellow party members about their too-facile equation of "democracy" with "the sovereignty of the people."

Tocqueville himself could not have attacked the "tyranny of the majority" more ferociously. "Are the people the highest?" Brownson demands.

Are they ultimate? And are we bound in conscience to obey whatever it may be their good pleasure to ordain? If so, where is individual liberty? If so, the people, taken collectively, are the absolute master of every man taken individually. Every man, as a man, then, is an absolute slave. Whatever the people, in their collective capacity, may demand of him, he must feel himself bound in conscience to give.

The real object of democracy is not to replace the sovereignty of the privi leged classes with the sovereignty of the people but to restore to individuals their natural rights and to teach them to "perform those duties, and those duties only, which everlasting and immutable Justice imposes."

Yet if Whigs were gladdened by the severe lesson Brownson preached to the Democrats at Worcester they were likely to be brought up short by his scathing attack upon Francis Bowen, the young philosophy tutor at Harvard whose review of Emerson's *Nature* had turned into a denunciation of the Transcendentalist movement. Brownson treats Bowen as too muddled to be worthy of refutation, but the aristocratic pretensions of Harvard come in for a pounding. Followers of Locke, like Bowen and the Harvard school, see the mind as a *tabula rasa* capable of being inscribed only from without, and they very naturally imagine themselves the only trustworthy inscribers. "But in point of fact, the masses are not so poor and destitute as all this supposes. They are not so dependent on *us,* the enlightened few, as we sometimes think them." Brownson is most passionate when (as here) he speaks in anger to the class that has temporarily adopted him about the class from which he rose;

nothing infuriates him as much as the condescension of the educated classes toward the poor and ignorant. "Philosophy is not needed by the masses: they who separate themselves from the masses, and who believe that the masses are entirely dependent on them for truth and virtue, need it, in order to bring them back, and bind them again to universal Humanity."

Brownson's literary criticism is quite as vigorous and prickly as his political and philosophical theorizing. Even the Transcendentalists he had defended against Bowen's strictures had no particular reason to rejoice when it was their turn to come under Brownson's scrutiny. Emerson's utter disregard of logic exasperated Brownson, who valued logical consistency over life itself. And this attitude was shared by the young reforming minister to whom Brownson gave the task of reviewing "The American Scholar." William Henry Channing's review appeared in the January 1838 number of the *Boston Quarterly Review,* a year before Channing left for Cincinnati and his short-lived stint as editor of the *Western Messenger.* But he lamented that Emerson's conclusions are only "hinted, without the progressive reasonings through which he was led to them."

Brownson sounded a similar note when he reviewed the commencement day oration Emerson had delivered to the combined literary societies at Dartmouth College on July 24, 1838, shortly after the Divinity School Address. "Literary Ethics," like the Divinity School Address itself, had been published as a pamphlet in 1838, and Brownson attempted to review it in the January number of the 1839 volume. He tries at first to give a synopsis of Emerson's meandering oration, but the piece quickly turns into parody, and finally Brownson breaks off in exasperation:

But we give it up. We cannot analyze one of Mr. Emerson's discourses. He hardly ever has a leading thought, to which all the parts of his discourse are subordinate, which is clearly stated, systematically drawn out, and logically enforced. He is a poet rather than a philosopher – and not always true even to the laws of poetry.

Brownson rejects Emerson's contention that Americans are imitative rather than creative; the Patent Office furnishes proof enough to the contrary. As for the ritual laments about American acquisitiveness, Brownson dismisses them with the exuberance and largeness of sympathy that make the *Boston Quarterly Review* delightful: "It is said, that the whole nation has been absorbed in the pursuit of wealth. We admit it, and rejoice that it has been so. It is a proof of the unity of our national life." And he adds, more seriously: "The very intensity with which we pursue wealth is full of hope. It proves that the pursuit of wealth can be only a temporary pursuit, that we must soon satisfy our material wants, and be ready to engage with similar intenseness in providing for the wants of the soul."

Brownson reviewed the Divinity School Address in October 1838. There he had more serious charges to bring against Emerson than illogicality. The address strikes him as dangerous. Emerson, he says, tells us to obey our instincts and scorn to imitate even Jesus. But which instincts are we to obey? "How shall we determine which are our higher instincts and which our lower instincts? We do not perceive that he gives us any instructions on this point. . . . We are to act out ourselves. Now, why is not the sensualist as moral as the spiritualist, providing he acts out himself?" Worse still, Emerson appears to recognize no higher good in the universe than the perfection of the individual soul. Such "transcendental selfishness" provokes Brownson to genuine anger. "Are all things in the universe to be held subordinate to the individual soul? Shall a man take himself as the centre of the universe, and say all things are for his use, and count them of value only as they contribute something to his growth or well-being?" According to this system "I am everything; all else is nothing, at least nothing except what it derives from the fact that it is something to me."

This tendency to "pure egotism" Emerson shares with his masters Carlyle and Goethe. "The highest good they recognise is an individual good, the realization of order in their own individual souls." Can a person who adopts this moral rule really be called moral? "Does not morality always propose to us an end separate from our own, above our own, and to which our own good is subordinate?" It is indeed necessary to achieve harmony within the individual soul, but this is only a preliminary step. "Above the good of the individual, and paramount to it, is the good of the universe, the realization of good of creation, absolute good." The man who forgets himself is "infinitely superior to the man who merely uses others as the means of promoting his own intellectual and spiritual growth."

Emerson encourages us to recognize ourselves as God, but in doing so he is unwittingly destroying the religious sentiment he professes to venerate, because that sentiment springs from our sense of our own dependence and of God's infinite power. If Emerson is right in seeing God only in the soul, present in potentiality as the oak is in the acorn, who is there to depend on? "Is there really and actually a God? Is there any God but the God Osiris, torn into pieces and scattered up and down through all the earth, which pieces, scattered parts, the weeping Isis must go forth seeking everywhere, and find not without labor and difficulty?"

Brownson cannot believe that we are justified in dispensing not only with "historical Christianity" and the use of miracles as evidence for faith but even with Jesus himself. Nor can he really believe that the Gospel records are of no further use in the church, that they have become merely a "let and a hindrance." We need more faith than our own. "We want that record, which is to us as the testimony of the race, to corroborate the witness within us. One witness is not enough." If the church has recently erred in giving us only the historical Christ, "let us not now err by preaching only a psychological Christ."

Brownson's criticisms of the Divinity School Address were all the more telling because they proceeded neither from a desire to defend Lockean epistemology and the rickety structures of historical evidence nor from a fear of the murderous instincts of the lower classes who needed to be kept under control by a system of threats. And Brownson's questions must have hurt doubly because they came close enough to some of Emerson's own recent self-reproaches to sound like confirmation of his worst suspicions. Yet for Emerson, unlike for Brownson, one witness to spiritual truth *was* enough, and its radiance made all external aids superfluous.

Yet if Brownson did not hesitate to attack Emerson when he thought Emerson was wrong he was willing to retract his whole attack on the Divinity School Address half a year later – not because he had changed his mind about its shortcomings but because the abuse heaped on Emerson by other critics awakened his sympathies. In an article in the April 1839 number defending Bulwer Lytton (whose novels Brownson loved) from the usual charges of immorality Brownson suddenly speaks of a quarrel closer home:

Let the odds be against a man, and he may call us his friend, and count upon our taking up the cudgels in his behalf. Since the world has turned against our friend Emerson . . . we heartily repent of having appeared among his opponents. We were as much out of our place as Saul was among the prophets. Heavens! only think of the Boston Quarterly Review joining with grave doctors and learned professors to write down a man who has the boldness to speak from his own convictions, from his own free soul! It was a great mistake on our part, and one which, alas! we perceived not till it was too late. Honor to every man who speaks from his own mind, whatever be his word. He is an Iconoclast, a servant of the true God, even though it be a left-handed one.

Brownson was himself soon to discover what it felt like to be an iconoclast needing support from friends. Like the editors of the *Western Messenger* Brownson was deeply affected by Carlyle's *Chartism* with its indictment of the laissez-faire economic philosophy that first created and then justified the sufferings of the working class. "Is the condition of the English working people wrong; so wrong that rational working men cannot, will not, and even should not rest quiet under it?" Carlyle asks and proceeds to heap page after page of evidence to show how very wrong it is. With bitter urgency he tries to make his complacent readers understand that the condition of the laboring poor has become so intolerable and so degrading that unless some government capable of relieving their miseries and answering their demand for simple justice can be found to replace the "No-government" (the law of the marketplace, the economics of supply and demand) that presently ruled England, the working class will necessarily be moved to seize the government for itself in an upheaval as violent as the French Revolution.

Carlyle's indictments of the English government and the capitalist system were devastating, but the practical remedies he proposed to alleviate misery – education and emigration – were worse than useless, Brownson thought. Brownson reviewed Emerson's 1840 American edition of *Chartism* for the *Boston Quarterly Review* in July 1840. Carlyle is "good as a demolisher, but pitiable enough as a builder. No man sees more clearly that the present is defective and unworthy to be retained . . . but when the question comes up concerning what ought to be, what should take the place of what is, we regret to say, he affords us no essential aid, scarcely a useful hint."

Brownson in fact confesses that he always rises from reading Carlyle so disheartened and exhausted that he almosts dreads to encounter a new Carlyle text. But the example of *Chartism* helped precipitate Brownson's translating into literary form his growing dissatisfaction with the Unitarian response to the suffering of the poor in the United States. To preach self-culture or self-improvement in such circumstances is complacent to the brink of cruelty. Brownson turned his review of Carlyle, entitled "The Laboring Classes," into the occasion for his own version of *Chartism*, his own analysis of the class struggle.

First, Brownson laughs at Carlyle's fear that the English working class is close to revolution. The plight of the working class in England is the worst in Europe precisely because in England the middle class is more numerous and powerful than anywhere else on earth. "The middle class is always a firm champion of equality, when it concerns humbling a class above it; but it is its inveterate foe, when it concerns elevating a class below it." Brownson despairs for the workers of England because their enemies are impossible to escape. "Their only real enemy is their employer."

To prescribe education as a cure for the condition of men and women who work twelve to sixteen hours a day is also laughable, and emigration can afford only temporary relief, "for the colony will soon become an empire, and reproduce all the injustice and wretchedness of the mother country." Besides, the problem in Europe is not overpopulation but maldistribution of property. Workers now labor for the benefit of their employers, and Brownson offers a new economic principle, Brownson's Law: "Men are rewarded in an inverse ratio to the amount of actual service they perform."

Few laborers in modern factories can ever hope to achieve more than subsistence wages. Individuals born poor do sometimes become rich, but if they attain wealth it is not by accumulating wages. A rich man is a man who has "contrived to tax for his benefit the labor of others." Southern planters confess that it would be cheaper to abolish slavery and hire laborers by the hour; what greater proof is there of the injustice of the current wage structure?

As for Dr. Channing's self-culture, it is a very good thing, but "it cannot abolish inequality, nor restore men to their rights." It may restore to laborers their sense of dignity and hence give them the courage to contend for those rights, but as a "remedy for the vices of the social state" it is powerless. Self-culture is for the Abbott Lawrences who own the cotton mills, not for the girls who tend the spindles until their health breaks and then go home to their villages to die. The priestly class represented by Channing is in fact the historical oppressor of mankind, and mankind can never be liberated until it abolishes religion as a profession. "What are the priests of Christendom as they now are? Miserable panders to the prejudices of the age, loud in condemning sins nobody is guilty of, but silent as the grave when it concerns the crying sin of the times. . . . As a body they never preach a truth till there is none whom it will indict."

The only way to establish the kingdom of God on earth is to do away with all monopolies that keep the laboring classes poor. The government must be wrested from the control of the banks, for the banks represent the interests of the employers. But the reforms must be even more radical than that. All hereditary descent of property must be abolished, for it represents "the privilege which some have of being born rich while others are born poor." Brownson realizes that this measure will never be carried without "the strong arm of physical force." The war in which this transformation will be effected will be "the like of which the world as yet has never witnessed, and from which . . . the heart of Humanity recoils with horror."

"The Laboring Classes" is one of the most powerful and disturbing documents produced by the Transcendentalist movement. Its vision of the inevitability of class struggle and the murderous war of class interests is a far cry from the woolly benevolence that usually passes for Transcendentalist social thought. But with Brownson's attack on Channing, the man he had called his "spiritual father," and on the bankruptcy of Channing's "self-culture" as a way of erasing class differences, some deep personal bitterness suddenly seems to propel Brownson back to the working-class anticlerical radicalism of his days with Frances Wright and Robert Owen's *Free Enquirer*.

As for Brownson's curious vision of the kingdom of God on earth, it resembles a strange kind of casino where the management would collect all the winnings at the end of each evening and redistribute them anew for the next day's gaming, not the kingdom of love and mutual solace described in the New Testament. It is significant that Brownson never stopped to ask himself what would happen to a man's wife and children if his property were confiscated by the state at his death — a flaw in his argument, as he admitted in his later "defense" of the article, and one which led him to champion (briefly) the cause of property rights for women.

Brownson's real desire is not for a social state at all. At one point in his analysis he speaks of the "savage state" from which civilization emerged and commends it for its lack of inequality. "The individual system obtains there. Each man is his own centre, and is a whole in himself. There is no community, there are no members of society, for society is not." If it were possible to combine this state with "the highest possible moral and intellectual cultivation" it would be "the perfection of man's earthly condition." But human beings must take a long detour through history before they can reach again the perfect isolation of the self-centered individual.

Without realizing it Brownson has revealed his kinship with the Emerson of the Divinity School Address, the Emerson he had abused. Brownson, too, places the individual above all else, and "The Laboring Classes" finally leaves an impression not of class solidarity but of personal isolation. Brownson's ideal men, all born equal, some rising to great wealth but yielding that wealth back to the state at their death, seem an incarnation of Tocqueville's worst fears about Americans — cut off from ancestors, cut off from descendents, isolated forever within the solitude of their own hearts.

Loneliness, of course, was not what Brownson's critics feared as the worst result of his polemic. He was denounced on all sides as a Jacobin, a socialist, a hater of religion and a destroyer of society. The Whigs eagerly reprinted "The Laboring Classes" as campaign propaganda designed to show what the Democrats would do if they won the presidency; the Democrats quickly disowned him. Contributors to Brownson's magazine stopped sending their articles (the journalistic equivalent of a refusal of pulpit exchanges). Brownson replied to some of their objections in a later article with the same title ("The Laboring Classes," October 1840), but by then the election was almost upon the country, and the Democratic party went down to crushing defeat.

Almost the only sympathy expressed for Brownson in his home territory during the contentious summer of 1840 came from his closest friend among the Transcendentalists, George Ripley. Ripley had prepared an article on Brownson and the *Boston Quarterly Review* for *The Dial,* the magazine that the members of the Transcendental Club had long been planning. *The Dial*'s first number appeared in July 1840, the same month as "The Laboring Classes." This coincidence linked the two magazines in the public mind much more closely than the facts of the case warranted, for *The Dial* was as different from the *Boston Quarterly Review* as could be imagined. (Brownson put his finger on the most obvious difference when he reviewed the first volume of *The Dial* in the January 1841 number of the *Boston Quarterly Review*. "The Dialists belong to the genus *culottic,* and have no fellowship with your vulgar *sans-culottes,"* he wrote, quite well aware that most of the people who wrote for *The Dial* did not share his sympathy for the laboring classes – or, for that matter, for him.)

The Transcendentalists' plan to have a journal of their own, first broached in the mid-1830s, was revived again in earnest after the Divinity School Address and the controversy surrounding it, when established journals like the *Christian Examiner* were closed to the group. At the May 1839 meeting of the Transcendental Club, Alcott complained about the poor quality of contemporary journals, which seemed to him to be empty and lifeless. Again, in September 1839, club members discussed the possibility of starting a journal that should be "the organ of views more in accordance with the soul." Alcott suggested the title, which was meant to suggest both the magazine's openness to the light and its ability to mark the passage of current events.

An aim at once so lofty and so vague might seem an unpropitious one for a magazine, but *The Dial*'s planners could take heart from the flourishing state of the periodical press in the United States at the time. Periodicals of all kinds sold well – religious magazines, political journals, critical reviews, and ladies' magazines that mixed fiction and poetry with engraved fashion plates. The historian of the *The Dial*'s rise and fall points out that by 1842 nearly three million numbers of various periodicals were produced every year. Surely in a country so hungry for magazines there was room for one that aimed to look at life in a way more in accordance with the soul.

The connection with the Transcendental Club seemed to promise a healthy list of contributors, but finding an editor for *The Dial* was not easy. Emerson, who was engaged in the laborious process of reworking material from his lectures and journals to make up a volume of essays, flatly refused the post. He wrote to Margaret Fuller on October 16, 1839, to promise his assistance as a contributor but to decline any editorial position. "I should heartily greet any such Journal as would fitly print these Journals of yours, & will gladly contribute of my own ink to fill it up. But unless Mr. Ripley would like to undertake it himself, or unless you would, I see not that we are nearer to such an issue than we have been these two years past."

Emerson's willingness to suggest to Fuller that she herself consider the position may have come from his enthusiastic response to her translation of Eckermann's *Conversations with Goethe,* recently published as Volume 4 of Ripley's *Specimens of Foreign Standard Literature.* In the "Translator's Preface" Fuller spoke with an authority and simplicity that seemed to mark her coming of age as a writer. Emerson, to whom she had sent a copy of the book, wrote back in June 1839 to thank her and praise her "decision and intelligence." He told her that her translation was "a beneficent action for which America will long thank you," and the preface he praised as a "brilliant statement" that filled him with "great contentment & thanks" (Emerson to Fuller, June 7, 1839). When Ripley proved to be both too deeply embroiled in his pamphlet war over miracles with Andrews Norton and too occupied with his work as editor of the *Specimens of Foreign Standard Literature* series to consider editing *The Dial* as well, Emerson persuaded Fuller to take on the task, promising that Ripley would serve as coeditor to help with the business details.

For Fuller the editorship meant many things: a move from her role as occasional guest at Transcendental Club meetings to a position of authority; a chance to see her own work published and to invite contributions from her friends; a chance to work out her own aesthetic theories and explain them to the world. She had, it is true, long carried on correspondences with Hedge and Clarke and finally with Emerson that had allowed her to display her brilliance and exercise her peculiar powers of intrusion and caress. (In a letter of June 3, 1839, she had urged Emerson to visit her at her temporary residence in the Boston suburb of Jamaica Plain: "If you will come this week I will crown you with something prettier than willow, or any sallow. Wild geranium stars all the banks and rock clefts, the hawthorn every hedge. You can have a garland of what fashion you will Do but come.")

The learned Hedge treated her with respect; Clarke, from his exile in Louisville, adored her and tried desperately to amuse her; and Emerson, though he was startled by the impertinence of her first letter to him, soon found himself seduced by the way she invaded his reticences and demanded his responses. But her early "public" prose was disappointing even to her closest friends. Clarke could hardly conceal his surprise and dismay at the first pieces she sent him in response to his request for material to fill the *Western Messenger.* They were very unlike her letters; the style was Latinate and heavily mannered and the tone seemed alternately arch and patronizing.

All the Transcendentalists had problems with tone: their attempt to speak from the Reason rather than the Understanding led them to strain after effects that lent themselves to ridicule (one thinks of Norton's pardonable exasperation at being told by Emerson in the Divinity School Address that the religious sentiment is "myrrh, and storax, and chlorine, and rosemary"). But most of the male Transcendentalists had professions that obliged them to try their productions out on live audiences, those chastening critics of style. Clarke reported to Fuller in humiliating detail the disastrous reception of his first sermons in Louisville; still, he was getting an education in practical oratory no classroom could provide. Fuller knew all this and felt frustrated by her inexperience. If women's minds, as men complained, lacked precision and focus, it was partly because their "accomplishments" were meant for show rather than for use. In a world that denied them higher education, most kinds of employment, and entrance into the professions, women had little experience of the sharpening or toughening that takes place in the to-and-fro of public debate.

In the summer of 1839, Fuller consulted Bronson Alcott about how to hold a series of "Conversations" for women in Boston that might help bring women out of their habitual reticence. Fuller needed the money she could earn from the "Conversations" to help pay the rent on her family's house and to send two of her brothers to Harvard, and she wanted to avoid having to return to schoolteaching, which exhausted her and left her little time for writing. But she also wanted to oblige women to think for themselves, to examine their ideas as they discussed topics like "mythology" and "the fine arts" and to learn to revise, qualify, and defend what they had said. Notes taken by Elizabeth Peabody show how the process worked. To one young woman who had offered a definition of "life," Fuller replied, "Good, but not grave enough. Come, what is life? I know what I think; I want you to find out what you think." Such pedagogy hardly strikes anyone as revolutionary now, but to women who had scarcely ever been asked to do anything except repeat by rote, it seemed electrifying.

Fuller held a series of "Conversations" each winter between 1839 and 1844. The two-hour meetings were held at Elizabeth Peabody's house in Boston. Each of the twenty-five to thirty women who attended the meetings paid ten dollars for the thirteen-week session, enough to net Fuller almost five hundred dollars per year. The women who attended the "Conversations" came from different groups: Fuller's close friends, young women who were married to Transcendentalists or social reformers, and women who were themselves social activists, as well as older women from Boston's traditional Unitarian elite. (Men were invited to join during the second year, but they tended to dominate the conversation, and Fuller dropped the experiment after one attempt.) The women who paid to attend came to listen to Fuller's brilliant opening monologues, then to be coaxed out of their reticence by Fuller's kind yet insistent questioning. The way their stumbling replies were transfigured in her generous rephrasing made them feel transfigured as well. Ednah Dow Cheney (1824–1909), a young woman who attended the "Conversations," gave the best account of the way the love she felt for Fuller during the "Conversations" flowed back into confidence in herself.

I found myself in a new world of thought; a flood of light irradiated all that I had seen in nature, observed in life, or read in books. Whatever she spoke of revealed a hidden meaning, and everything seemed to be put into the true relation. Perhaps I could best express it by saying that I was no longer the limitation of myself, but I felt that the whole wealth of the universe was open to me. (*Reminiscences of Ednah Dow Cheney*, 1902)

Fuller's experience as editor of *The Dial,* on the other hand, involved her from the outset in a tangle of frustrations. She wrote to her old friend Frederic Hedge asking him to contribute something to the magazine's first number, but after a series of evasions he confessed that he now feared to associate himself in print with the Transcendentalists, whose recent wars with the Unitarian establishment during the miracles controversy had made his Bangor congregation uneasy. Fuller wondered whether her own contributions were "pertinent to the place or time." The material she had so far gathered – two of her own essays, extracts Emerson had made from the papers of his dead brothers Edward and Charles, an article on the Roman satirist Persius by Thoreau (taken at Emerson's insistence) – hardly seemed earth shaking, and she feared that those who looked to *The Dial* for the "gospel of transcendentalism" would be badly disappointed and would begin to blame her for what they could not find in the journal.

Her anxieties and the reactions they generated must have been intense, for the "Introduction" to *The Dial* that she drafted and sent to Emerson in April struck him as both arrogant and defensive. He volunteered an introduction of his own, which Fuller accepted. The correspondence between them makes clear that Emerson felt embarrassed by his need to intervene; it seemed to take away the authority he had urged her to assume. In fact Fuller's introduction, however callow or ill-judged it might have been, could not possibly have drawn as much ridicule down upon *The Dial* as another of Emerson's editorial suggestions did.

For several years Emerson had served, unhappily, as Bronson Alcott's chief manuscript critic and rejecting editor – telling him, for instance, that the manuscript of "Psyche" (Alcott's account of his daughters' childhood education) was simply not publishable even after three massive revisions, or sending back with similar discouragement a collection of "Orphic Sayings" Alcott had tried to pattern after Goethe's. Nothing is more irritating than a hopeless writer who dutifully revises what no amount of revision can save, but Alcott was incapable of taking hints, and by late April 1840 he had given his revised "Orphic Sayings" to Emerson in hopes of seeing them in *The Dial.* What made it worse was that Alcott had just moved with his family to Concord.

Emerson can be pardoned for wanting to get Alcott off his back, but the letter he sent to Fuller telling her that the revised "Orphic Sayings," though still bad, were not as bad as he had expected and might "pass muster & even pass for just & great" (Emerson to Fuller, April 24, 1840) shows how desperate he had become to find something of Alcott's he could publish. *The Dial* had been planning to publish pieces without identifying authors, but Emerson suggested that Alcott's name be printed over the "Orphic Sayings,"

because at least to people who knew Alcott they might then have a "majesti-
cal sound" (Emerson to Fuller, May 8, 1840).

Emerson of all people should have known that the *ethos* of the speaker in a
printed text can be constructed only from the text. For the readers and reviewers who encountered *The Dial* without any prior reverence for Alcott, the
"Orphic Sayings" quickly became not only famous but hilarious. Transcendentalist writing was always in danger of either rising unballasted into the clouds
in its pursuit of the Ideal or descending into obscurities in its drive to solve the
mysteries of existence. Alcott's "Orphic Sayings" does both at once.

"The poles of things are not integrated," Alcott complains in an Orphic
Saying entitled "Genesis." "Yet in the true genesis, nature is globed in the
material, souls orbed in the spiritual firmament. Love globes, wisdom orbs,
all things. As the magnet the steel, so spirit attracts matter, which trembles
to traverse the poles of diversity, and rests in the bosom of unity." The
popular press could hardly resist the temptation to deflate such pretentious-
ness. The New York *Knickerbocker* published in its November 1840 number a
selection of "Gastric Sayings": "The poles of potatoes are integrated; eggs
globed and orbed. . . . As the magnet the steel, so the palate abstracts
matter, which trembles to traverse the mouths of diversity, and rest in the
bowels of unity." A writer to the *Boston Post* compared the "Orphic Sayings"
to "a train of fifteen railroad cars with one passenger."

Alcott gave *The Dial* a reputation for silliness and unintelligibility it
found difficult to live down, particularly when Fuller, reluctant to hurt
Alcott's feelings, took another batch of "Orphic Sayings" for the January
1841 number. But a more serious charge than obscurity began to be leveled
at *The Dial* even by its friends. The magazine was too dreamy, too aesthetic,
too unreal; it lacked a backbone; its verse was saccharine or vaporous; it
ignored the real world. Orestes Brownson reviewed *The Dial* and found it
"vague, evanescent, aerial." Emerson himself, though he had chosen or suggested a good deal of the material for the first number of *The Dial,* began to
look enviously at the notoriety Brownson's journal was achieving. Shortly
after the first *Dial* had appeared Emerson tried (unsuccessfully, as it turned
out) to interest Fuller in printing a tract by Edward Palmer, the reformer
who argued against the use of money. Emerson even offered to act as "godfather" to the tract and introduce it himself. "O queen of the American
Parnassus," he pleaded, "I hope our Dial will get to be a little *bad*. This first
number is not enough to scare the tenderest bantling of Conformity" (Emerson to Fuller, July 21, 1840).

Emerson returned to this theme in subsequent letters. A week later he was
pestering Fuller to allow a friend named George Bradford to write on "the
Abolition question" for the magazine. "He is the properest person to write on

that topic, as he knows the facts, has a heart, & is a little of a Whig & altogether a gentleman" (Emerson to Fuller, July 27 and 28, 1840). In early August he confessed that he was beginning to wish for a different kind of *Dial* from the one he had first imagined. "I would not have it too purely literary. I wish we might make a Journal so broad & great in its survey that it should lead the opinion of this generation on every great interest & read the law on property, government, education, as well as on art, letters, & religion." He himself was trying to work on a paper that would treat the great subject of Reform. "And the best conceivable paper on such a topic would of course be a sort of fruitful Cybele, mother of a hundred gods and godlike papers. That papyrus reed should become a fatal arrow" (Emerson to Fuller, August 4, 1840).

The androgynous image Emerson conjured up to symbolize his ideal *Dial* essay — a Great Mother armed with a fatal arrow — may have been an attempt to appeal to Fuller, but it also suggests the difficulty he had deciding what kind of journal he wanted *The Dial* to be. Like others in the Transcendental Club Emerson feared that there was something "effeminate" about American art. It is not always clear whether Emerson thought American art lacked manliness because it was imitative or whether he feared that all art lacked manliness. But his anxieties ran deep. At the very first meeting of the group back in 1836 he had voiced his fear that the best talents of the day — Washington Allston, Horatio Greenough, William Cullen Bryant, William Ellery Channing — had a "*feminine* or receptive" cast rather than a "masculine or creative" one, and the idea troubled him repeatedly throughout the late 1830s when he was preoccupied with the problem of America's cultural dependence. Any journal of American *belles lettres,* then, was in danger of seeming effeminate, and *The Dial* particularly so because Emerson and Ripley had given the task of editing it to a woman.

Certainly Theodore Parker saw *The Dial* in this way. Parker, who disliked Fuller, wrote a letter to Convers Francis after the first two numbers of *The Dial* had come out complaining that *The Dial* bore about the same relation to the *Boston Quarterly Review* that "Antimachus does to Hercules, Alcott to Brownson, or a band of men & maidens, daintily arrayed in finery . . . to a body of stout men, in blue frocks, with great arms, & hard hands & legs — like the pillars of Hercules." Parker imagines an allegorical conflict in which the men and maidens of *The Dial,* bearing a banner with a cradle and pap spoon, confront the stout men in blue, led by Brownson "dressed like David; with Goliath's sword in one hand, & that giant's head in the other" (Parker to Francis, December 18, 1840).

If Fuller lacked something that Brownson and his hard-legged men obviously had, she also had something he lacked, as Emerson's comment about

George Bradford's projected article on abolitionism makes clear. Emerson wanted articles about reform, but most reformers were not gentlemen, and abolitionists were worst of all. To genteel ex-Unitarians, whose notions of self-culture necessarily included great stress upon personal refinement, offenses against taste were almost as serious as offenses against the spirit. When Emerson read "The Laboring Classes" he was surprised and delighted by its vigor. Brownson "wields a sturdy pen which I am very glad to see. I had judged him from some old things & did not know he was such a Cobbett of a scribe." But the catty remark he immediately adds says much about the impassible gulf between the culottic and sans culottic: "Let him wash himself & he shall write for the immortal Dial" (Emerson to Fuller, December 21, 1840).

Fuller's hopes for the new journal differed from Emerson's in significant ways. The prospectus printed on the back cover of the first number made it clear that under her editorship *The Dial* would aim at "the discussion of principles, rather than the promotion of measures" and that it would try to promote "the constant evolution of truth, not the petrifaction of opinion." At the same time she wanted to redefine literary receptivity in a way that removed it from the self-defeating terms in which Emerson had cast it. If all provincial or peripheral cultures must begin by importing their ripe understandings from foreign writings before they can attempt any great enterprise, as Milton had argued, then to be receptive is to be invigorated rather than emasculated.

In her manifesto in the first number of *The Dial,* the "Short Essay on Critics," Fuller describes the critical process in terms that make it seem anything but passive. Only the bad or "subjective" critic, who simply gives his impressions as laws, is feminine or receptive in Emerson's sense. The two good kinds of critics – the *apprehensive* critics, who "can go out of themselves and enter into a foreign existence," and even better the *comprehensive,* who actually "enter into the nature of another being and judge his work by its own law" – have learned how to turn receptivity into domination. As the Latin root of both words suggests – *prehendere,* "to seize" – both apprehensive critics and comprehensive critics are aggressive even when they are most sympathetic; they begin as emigrants but end as lawgivers at home in their own courts.

Fuller had every intention of remaining the lawgiver for *The Dial;* she insisted on making the magazine a reflection of her own interests and tastes, rejecting manuscripts Emerson had solicited, sometimes to his considerable exasperation. She looked with benevolence on the products of her own pen, publishing critical essays such as her forty-one-page survey of Goethe's life and works (July 1841); a "Dialogue" between Poet and Critic (April 1841); romantic fables like "Meta" and "The Magnolia of Lake Pontchartrain" (January 1841); and a good deal of her own poetry. And she gave generous amounts of room to the poetry of her girlhood friend Caroline Sturgis. But she also published some of Thoreau's essays and poems (though she rejected others), and she accepted as much material as she could from Parker, Emerson, Clarke, and Clarke's charming friend, Christopher Pearse Cranch (a poet and translator now perhaps best remembered for his cartoon of Emerson's Transparent Eyeball).

Fuller edited *The Dial* for two years. In April 1842 she announced her intention to resign. Her health, always poor, had suffered from the responsibilities of the job, and the salary she had been promised at the outset (two hundred dollars a year) had never materialized. Ripley, her coeditor, had become deeply involved with planning his community at Brook Farm and had announced in October 1841 that he was withdrawing from *The Dial*. Fuller needed to support her fatherless family, and *The Dial* could scarcely support itself.

After a few days deliberation Emerson decided to assume the editorship. The financial success of his recent lecture series, "The Times," meant that he could contemplate taking on a time-consuming job without pay. Under his editorship, many features of the magazine remained the same, and Emerson continued to solicit a good deal of material from Fuller (whose first article for him he hastened to praise as "manly"). Her most famous submission to *The Dial* after she had left the editorship was also her most militant. For the July 1843 *Dial* she sent Emerson a passionate article into which she distilled her pride and her anger. "The Great Lawsuit" speaks for the multitudes of women who were now, as never before, "considering within themselves what they need that they have not, and what they can have, if they find they need it." What they want is nothing less than "the intelligent freedom of the universe." What a woman wants is not the power to rule but the freedom "as a nature to grow, as an intellect to discern, as a soul to live freely, and unimpeded to unfold such powers as were given her."

Fuller has no wish to blot out difference between the sexes, so prominent in the mythologies she studies and loved. It may be true that "male and female represent two sides of the great radical dualism." But mythology seems to teach that these opposites are endlessly passing into one another: "Man partakes of the feminine in the Apollo, woman of the masculine as Minerva." It is therefore folly to set bounds to the limits of either sex. As for the argument that the highest bliss lies in the union of the two sexes, Fuller tartly replies: "Union is only possible to those who are units." Love to be strong must come "from the fulness, not the poverty of being." Fuller scornfully rejects Byron's arrogant belief that love is woman's whole existence. "Woman, self-centered, would never be absorbed by any relation; it would be only an experience to her as to man. It is a vulgar error that love, *a* love to woman is her whole existence; she also is born for Truth and Love in their universal energy."

As editor Emerson did more than offer Fuller a platform for the expression of her ideas. He began to bend *The Dial* in the direction he thought it should grow. He printed more poetry and solicited articles about social reform. He printed some selections from a Hindu text that had interested him the previous summer, *The Heetopades of Veeshnoo-Sarma;* in later numbers of the magazine he made selections from the holy books of other nations a regular feature entitled "Ethnical Scriptures," thus helping to encourage that religious syncretism that marks Transcendentalism's second phase.

Although Emerson still hated anything that looked like personal controversy he finally accepted for the October 1842 number an article by Theodore Parker entitled "The Hollis Street Council," so called after a recent meeting of the Boston Unitarian Association. The association's members had supported the dismissal of a minister who had angered his congregation by pointing out the contradiction between their pious condemnation of drinking and their willingness to profit from the liquor trade. Parker accused the association of hypocrisy and interference with freedom of conscience.

Emerson complained to Parker that his article was on a "most unpoetic unspiritual & un Dialled" subject (Emerson to Parker, September 8, 1842), but he accepted the piece as a way of honoring Parker, whose "Discourse on the Transient and Permanent in Christianity," delivered the previous winter, had brought down the wrath of the Unitarian establishment upon his head. Emerson could not bring himself to read Parker's manuscript completely through or to read proof for it. He instructed the printers to set it in type and send the proofs to Parker directly. This curious behavior says much about Emerson and his view of *The Dial;* he thinks of controversy as something that defiles the magazine's pages yet is unwilling to reject an author like Parker when the rest of the world is attacking him.

Emerson contributed a good many of his own poems and essays to *The Dial:* poems like "The Sphinx," which became almost as famous as the "Orphic Sayings" as an emblem for Transcendentalist unintelligibility; several of his lectures from the recent series "The Times"; an essay called "Transcendentalism" and one on modern literature; "The Chardon Street Convention," a wickedly funny account of a recent Boston convention of reformers and come-outers; an essay on Walter Savage Landor, woven out of journal passages from Emerson's 1833 visit to Landor in Italy, which drew an angry response from Landor himself. But Emerson had already published one complete book of essays when he began editing *The Dial* and was completing a second; he did not need the magazine to make his writings known. What he wanted to do with *The Dial* was to give space in it to talented young writers who needed encouragement and shepherding. Some of his enthusiasms are difficult to share. The verse of William Ellery Channing (Dr. Channing's nephew and Margaret Fuller's brother-in-law) is mostly weak and derivative, and the first installment of the murky allegory "The Two Dolons," by Charles King Newcomb, left no one but Emerson longing for the second (which never arrived). But Thoreau actually had the talent that Emerson ascribed to him, and in *The Dial* we can witness him becoming a major writer.

Henry David Thoreau (1817–62) was a Concord native, descended on his father's side from French Huguenots who had settled on the Isle of Jersey. Like Emerson, Thoreau had attended Harvard and like Emerson he had failed to distinguish himself there, graduating nineteenth in a class of forty-five. During his college years (1833–7) he nevertheless managed to acquire a rich education in Transcendentalism. He met and boarded with Orestes Brownson during a summer in Canton; he was tutored in Greek by Jones Very; he eagerly read Emerson's *Nature* and Emerson's edition of *Sartor Resartus;* and he was in the graduating class in 1837 for which Emerson delivered "The American Scholar" at commencement.

Some of the battles the first generation of Transcendentalists had waged seemed already won by 1837, and the battle they were about to wage over biblical miracles probably meant little to a young man whose first act upon returning to Concord was to *sign off* of the local parish. But the problem of finding work appropriate to the spirit – or any work at all – was acute in an economy made hostile by the recent financial panic, with its resultant deflation and mass unemployment. A job as a schoolteacher in the Concord public schools ended after two weeks. After that Thoreau applied unsuccessfully for teaching positions in a number of New England towns, then opened a small private academy in Concord, which soon grew large enough to need a second teacher. Thoreau asked his brother John to join him. He lived at home.

Emerson had come briefly into contact with Thoreau as early as 1835, when he examined a group of college students on rhetoric. But the two did not become friendly until the autumn of 1837, when Emerson's famous question to the twenty-year-old graduate – "Do you keep a journal?" – set Thoreau off on a literary project that would last almost as long as his life. Throughout the following years their friendship intensified. Acquaintances began to notice that Thoreau was imitating Emerson's style, his manner of speaking and gesturing, his handwriting – even (so one observer alleged) his nose. For his part, Emerson valued Thoreau's simplicity and directness, his union of intellectual brilliance with physical grace and strength, and his natural and instinctive nonconformity.

Thoreau served as curator of the Concord Lyceum from 1838 to 1840. He had delivered his first lecture there in 1838 on the subject of society. (The lecture, "Society," no longer survives, but the notes for it in Thoreau's journal suggest that it contained a lament over the insincerity of ordinary society and a plea for a better state that would foster ideal friendships.) Emerson may have realized that Thoreau would never make a successful platform lecturer; in any case he was eager to see Thoreau publish. When *The Dial* began, Emerson lobbied Fuller shamelessly (and not always successfully) to accept Thoreau's essays and poems. When Emerson took over he began accepting Thoreau's work in quantity.

To watch Thoreau develop from the first of his essays in *The Dial* ("Aulus Persius Flaccus") to the last ("Homer. Ossian. Chaucer.") is exciting, because it allows us to witness something that provincial literary magazines exist to foster and rarely do – the development of an immature writer into a powerful and confident one. Thoreau did a great deal of writing during the four years of *The Dial*'s existence, and only a portion of that was submitted to the magazine. Still, the experience of being accepted by (and rejected by) *The Dial* helped Thoreau understand what it meant to adopt letters as a profession and how that decision could shape prose.

"Aulus Persius Flaccus," the essay Thoreau gave to Emerson in the early months of 1840 and that Emerson finally badgered Margaret Fuller into accepting for the magazine's first number, starts out by sounding like hardly more than a college exercise, like the brief essays "The Greek Classic Poets" or "T. Pomponius Atticus" that Thoreau wrote at Harvard. In the "Thursday" section of *A Week on the Concord and Merrimack Rivers* Thoreau calls the essay (which he reprints there) "almost the last regular service which I performed in the cause of literature," and he would have us believe that he took Persius with him on that 1839 trip because "some hard and dry book in a dead language, which you have found impossible to read at home, but for which you still have a lingering regard, is the best to carry with you on a journey."

This affected indifference explains why Thoreau might have taken Persius to read in a country inn but hardly why he should have chosen to write about the experience; indeed, he begins the essay by lamenting that Persius seems "a sad descent" from the Greek poets and ends it by saying that there are scarcely twenty lines worth remembering from Persius's six extant satires. In what sense is this a service either to Persius or to the cause of literature? No wonder Fuller wanted to squelch the essay by pocket veto; it is hardly the sort of apprehensive or comprehensive criticism she was advocating in her "Short Essay on Critics." Instead, it seems a throwback to the kind of neoclassical essay in which gentlemen wandered through the classics pointing out beauties and faults.

Yet Emerson was right to see more in "Aulus Persius Flaccus" than that, for many passages give a startling glimpse into the future. So Thoreau, after blaming satire in general and Persius in particular for his "unmusical bickering," suddenly breaks out into a plea for true music in poetry whose paradoxes might fit neatly into *Walden:*

When the Muse arrives, we wait for her to remould language, and impart to it her own rhythm. Hitherto the verse groans and labors by the way. The best ode . . . has a poor and trivial sound, like a man stepping on the rungs of a ladder. Homer, and Shakespeare, and Milton, and Marvell, and Wordsworth, are but the rustling of leaves and crackling of twigs in the forest, and not yet the sound of any bird. The Muse has never lifted up her voice to sing.

There are also passages of Thoreau's familiar wit, as when he points out that the satirist always ends by arousing our suspicions. "We can never have much sympathy with the complainer; for after searching nature through, we conclude that he must be both plaintiff and defendant too, and so had best come to a settlement without a hearing." And in the final section of the essay Thoreau turns Persius's sneer at the sluggard who lives from moment to moment (*ex tempore*) into a matter for praise with a bilingual pun. "The life of a wise man is most of all extemporaneous, for he lives out of an eternity that includes all time."

If the Persius essay manages to mine wisdom and poetry from unpromising materials, Thoreau's next piece, "The Service," takes a subject very dear to Thoreau's heart — bravery — and makes a muddle of it. Like many young people of his generation, Thoreau had been moved by Emerson's writings about the possibility of military valor in civilian life, and "The Service," with its three portentously titled subsections ("Qualities of the Recruit," "What Music Shall We Have," and "Not How Many But Where the Enemy Are"), is meant to sketch the contours of the possible hero. But Thoreau had been reading too much Alcott and too much Emerson, and the result was a disaster. Some of Thoreau's sentences seem to call out for illustration by Edward Lear: "Mankind, like the earth, revolve mainly from west to east, and so are flattened at the poles."

Margaret Fuller rejected the essay in a letter of December 1, 1840. Writing rejection letters to a young man who is the protégé of one's own mentor is never easy, and under the circumstances Fuller tried to be diplomatic, casting her response in the military terms Thoreau had employed in the essay. She told Thoreau that she agreed with Emerson that essays not to be compared with Thoreau's had already been published in *The Dial;* but she added that she thought that his essay was "so rugged that it ought to be commanding." Although she offered to look at it again, Thoreau never resubmitted it or tried to publish it elsewhere.

Thoreau continued to publish poems in *The Dial,* but the next original prose composition he wrote did not find room there until Emerson assumed the editorship in 1842. By then much had changed in Thoreau's life. He had moved into Emerson's house in 1841 to serve as what one of his biographers calls a "transcendental handy man, combining manual and intellectual skills." He worked in the garden and tried to teach Emerson to graft apples; he managed *The Dial* when Emerson was away on lecturing tours; he became the close friend of Emerson's wife and children. Though Emerson never became the ideal friend Thoreau sought – one who would be "like wax in the rays that fall from our own hearts" and who could confer benefits without expecting gratitude in return – at least he gave Thoreau time to write and the patronage of an editor who was also his host.

Thoreau's happiness at finding a home and an environment suited for work was soon interrupted by tragedy. On the first day of 1842 Thoreau's beloved brother John cut himself while stropping a razor. Nine days later he developed the first symptoms of lockjaw, and, after suffering spasms and agonizing pain, died in Thoreau's arms shortly thereafter. Thoreau himself developed symptoms that mimicked his brother's a few days later, but he recovered quickly. His native stoicism helped him pull out of the worst period of grief, and by the middle of March he speaks in his journal of a sudden access of "superfluous energy." The pattern is eerily reminiscent of Emerson's response to the death of his brother Charles in May 1836, when a period of numbness suddenly gave way to a burst of creative energy that produced the apocalyptic closing chapters of *Nature.*

Emerson helped find an outlet for Thoreau's renewed energy when he returned from Boston with a collection of wildlife reports commissioned by the Massachusetts state legislature and asked Thoreau to review them for *The Dial.* On the face of it, the task Emerson set Thoreau looked as unpromising as Lady Austen's suggestion to William Cowper that he write a poem about a sofa, but the very dryness of T. W. Harris's *A Report on the Insects,* C. Dewey's *Report on the Herbaceous Flowering Plants,* D. H. Storer's *Reports on the Fishes, Reptiles and Birds,* A. A. Gould's *Report on the Invertebrata,* and E. Emmons's *A Report on the Quadrupeds* liberated something in Thoreau's imagination that his attempts to write conventional literary reviews and essays had failed to do. "The Natural History of Massachusetts," published in *The Dial* for July 1842, is the first of Thoreau's works to reveal his gift for evoking natural scenes in luminous, precise language.

In an opening section Thoreau praises the cheering effects of reading books of natural history, particularly in the winter, when their "reminiscences of luxuriant nature" restore health to the soul. He recommends keeping such books as "a sort of elixir, the reading of which should restore the tone of the system." With a high good humor Thoreau dismisses the whole of the practical and political world and even pokes fun at "the trumpeted valor of the warrior," preferring to it the complacency of Linnaeus setting out for botanical expeditions in Lapland with his leather breeches and gnat-proof gauze cap. He has discovered a new kind of heroism. "Science is always brave; for to know is to know good; doubt and danger quail before her eye."

Then comes one of those passages that show how far Thoreau had already advanced beyond the creakily scholastic notion of "correspondences" that had guided Emerson's quizzing of nature. Thoreau writes:

Entomology extends the limits of being in a new direction, so that I walk in nature with a sense of greater space and freedom. It suggests besides, that the universe is not rough-hewn, but perfect in details. Nature will bear the closest inspection; she invites us to lay our eye level with the smallest leaf, and take an insect view of its plain. She has no interstices; every part is full of life.

The remainder of the review alternates between a quiet recital of statistics ("Of fishes, seventy-five general and one hundred and seven species are described in the Report") and long cadenzas made from Thoreau's own observations of animals, insects, birds, and fishes. These observations convey a sense of sheer delight at the energy and grace displayed by the state's creatures, such as the fox, whose pace is a sort of "leopard canter" and whose course is "a series of graceful curves," conforming to the shape of the land's surface. Even when Thoreau pursues it the fox maintains its self-possession. "Notwithstanding his fright, he will take no step which is not beautiful."

Such regard for beauty permeates the whole kingdom of nature. "In the most stupendous scenes you will see delicate and fragile features, as slight wreaths of vapor, dew-lines, feathery sprays, which suggest a high refinement, a noble blood and breeding." Even man, who had seemed so corrupt when viewed in his "political aspect," turns into a graceful enchanter when he sets his nets to catch fish.

The small seines of flax stretched across the shallow and transparent parts of our river are not more intrusion than the cobweb in the sun. I stay my boat in mid-current, and look down in the sunny water to see the civil meshes of his nets, and wonder how the blustering people of the town could have done this elvish work. The twine looks like a new river-weed, and is to the river as a beautiful memento of man's presence in nature, discovered as silently and delicately as a footprint in the sand.

Two mottoes that sum up the rest of Thoreau's writing can be mined from "The Natural History of Massachusetts." The first and better known, which comes from the opening pages of the essay, is "Surely joy is the condition of life." But the second is just as characteristic. Admitting that the publications he has reviewed might seem dry to the general reader, Thoreau cautions: "Let us not underrate the value of a fact. It will one day flower into a truth."

Throughout 1842 and 1843 Thoreau continued his high rate of productivity, writing in his journal, working on translations from the Greek (his translation of "Prometheus Bound" appeared in *The Dial* for January 1843, and later numbers carried translations from Anacreon and Pindar), and helping to excerpt material from translated Hindu, Confucian, and Buddhist texts for the "Ethnical Scriptures" department of the magazine. But he also experimented with a new form, the "excursion," a kind of small-scale travel literature recording impressions and thoughts during a trip on foot or by boat.

"A Walk to Wachusett," the first of these excursions, was not published in *The Dial* but in the *Boston Miscellany of Literature* for 1843. It records Thoreau's thoughts and perceptions as he goes on an expedition with Richard Fuller (Margaret's brother) to climb a mountain that was visible from Concord. "A Walk to Wachusett" blends autobiographical detail, observations of nature, and literary rumination in a style that would find its fullest expression in *A Week on the Concord and Merrimack Rivers*. When, as Thoreau reports, he reached the summit of Mount Wachusett, he read Virgil and Wordsworth in his tent, and wondered (like a nineteenth-century version of the "rising glory" poets of the early Republic) whether "this hill may one day be a Helvellyn, or even a Parnassus, and the Muses haunt here, and other Homers frequent the neighboring plains?"

"A Winter Walk," Thoreau's next attempt to blend observation and thought, was published in the October 1843 number of *The Dial*. Here no distant peak serves as the destination; the essay records instead the strangeness and beauty of a day's walking in the neighborhood of Concord, from the sky's first lightening before dawn, when Thoreau unlatches his door to face the cutting air, till the winter evening when "the thoughts of the indwellers travel abroad" and the farmer, secure in the warmth his providence has insured, looks out with satisfaction at the glittering landscape around and the glittering stars above. As we accompany Thoreau in his stroll through the woods, and his examination of a glade in which a covering of snow is "deposited in such infinite and luxurious forms as by their very variety atone for the absence of color," or glide on ice skates deep into a frozen marsh that summer's heat will make inaccessible, or listen to the "faint, stertorous, rumbling sound" the rivers make beneath their surfaces of ice, we are invited to enjoy the exhilarations of winter.

Thoreau is mostly content to leave his countryside unmoralised, though in his praise of the "sort of sturdy innocence, a Puritan toughness," that he finds in all "cold and bleak places," like the tops of mountains, we find a constitutional attraction to a landscape that the painter Washington Allston would have called the objective correlative of Thoreau's stoicism. Such places, according to Thoreau, strike us as belonging to the original frame of the universe, "and of such valor as God himself."

In the next-to-last number of *The Dial* Emerson printed a lecture Thoreau had given at the Concord Lyceum the preceding November. "Homer. Ossian. Chaucer." attempts to consider poets who lie "in the east of literature," at once the earliest and latest products of the mind. Thoreau's Homer and Ossian are primitive bards, whose portrayal of the "simple, fibrous life" of warlike heroes makes our civilized history appear "the chronicle of debility, of fashion, of the arts of luxury." They speak "a gigantic and universal language." (The editors of Thoreau's translations remind us that classical education at Harvard in Thoreau's day gave the student "a distinctly romantic view of classical antiquity" and was based on European scholarship "openly primitivist in orientation.")

In the "Homer" and "Ossian" sections of his lecture, Thoreau scarcely departs from the Romantic commonplaces he shared with his contemporaries. But the "Chaucer" section — by far the longest part of the piece — is a surprise: Not only is it a shrewd and sympathetic appreciation of the beauty of Chaucer's poetry and of the deeper appeal of his humanity, but it is also a thoughtful meditation on the nature of literary history. Thoreau had studied both ancient and modern languages assiduously at Harvard, adding Italian, French, German, and Spanish to the required four years of Latin and Greek. He read Chaucer with Dr. Channing and studied literary history with George Ticknor, the historian of Spanish literature; he attended Henry Wadsworth Longfellow's lectures on northern European literature, Anglo-Saxon literature, and English medieval poetry.

Thoreau had a far wider knowledge of European literature and a far more sophisticated understanding of literary history than most of the other Transcendentalists, whose learning, although sometimes impressive, tended to favor philosophical or hermeneutical texts. In the fall of 1841 he seems to have been toying with the idea of compiling an anthology of earlier English poetry; he was reading every poetic text and anthology he could find in the Harvard library — ballads, romances, metrical tales, saints' lives. Though Thoreau never completed the anthology project, the effort of reading through a great deal of English and Scottish poetry of the Middle Ages gave him an understanding of Chaucer's peculiar excellences that few of his contemporaries shared.

Even though Chaucer, in Thoreau's view, is not a heroic bard like Homer or Ossian, he is still, in many respects, "the Homer of English poets" in being the wellspring of English literature, the most original of its origins. "Perhaps he is the youthfullest of them all." Modern poetry is mournful and reflective, but in Chaucer we still find "the poetry of youth and life, rather than of thought; and though the moral vein is obvious and constant, it has not banished the sun and daylight from his verse." Anyone who reads Chaucer can appreciate his humor, his perception of character, his "rare common sense and proverbial wisdom," but only someone who had approached him "through the meagre pastures of Saxon and ante-Chaucerian poetry," as Thoreau had just done, could understand how great Chaucer's contribution to the creation of literary language in England really was.

Chaucer, in fact, "rendered a similar service to his country to that which Dante rendered to Italy," for "a great philosophical and moral poet gives permanence to the language he uses, by making the best sound convey the best sense." And this was true even though Chaucer sought no part in the turbulent political strife of his century. He was a literary man and a scholar, not a man of action. "There were never any times so stirring, that there were not to be found some sedentary still." If we read him without criticism, it is because in his fidelity to his craft he has "that greatness of trust and reliance which compels popularity." And is that fidelity not a kind of heroism? The true poet is "a Cincinnatus in literature," weaving into his verse both "the planet and the stubble."

The nearly ten years spanned by the main Transcendentalist periodicals – the *Western Messenger* (1835–41), the *Boston Quarterly Review* (1838–44), and *The Dial* (1841–4) – were the formative and maturing years of the movement itself. Most of the contributors are now forgotten, and the thought of the time and energy spent in publishing such ephemera makes one want to exclaim (as Thoreau did of ante-Chaucerian poetry) that "it is astonishing to how few thoughts so many sincere efforts give utterance." Yet the work the periodicals did was important. They gave their editors and major contributors a sense of what the profession of letters was like; they provided a forum for the free expression of ideas; they let beginning writers like Thoreau experiment with forms and ideas. Their editors insisted on the right of free expression, even when they found one another's ideas distressing or repellent.

Most of all these periodicals cooperated in the great work of making midcentury American prose as flexible an instrument as the neoclassical prose of the Founding Fathers had been. Clarke's generous enthusiasm, Brownson's fierce logic, Fuller's critical sophistication and her feminist scorn, Parker's indignation, Thoreau's precision, Emerson's alternations between oracular statement and dry wit, and even Alcott's vaporous apothegms and the parodies they generated all helped to turn the language into something very different from the Unitarian prose of the 1820s and 1830s – made it sharper, tougher, more powerful; polished it for use and kept it ready to hand.

7

THE HOPE OF REFORM

R ELIGIOUS CONTROVERSY and the publishing of periodicals absorbed much of the Transcendentalists' energy during the early 1840s. But larger movements caught their attention as well. The various reform movements sweeping the country seemed to offer support to the theory that a new age was indeed at hand, an age when the mountainous obstructions of inherited evil would be forced to yield to the pure force of spirit. Life would learn to conform itself to the idea in the mind; a new church and state would flow outward from the wellsprings of regenerate souls. In an 1839 lecture, "Literature" (from a series entitled "The Present Age"), Emerson had predicted that the genius of the time would soon "write the annals of a changed world and record the descent of principles into practice, of love into Government, of love into Trade. It will describe the new heroic life of man, the now unbelieved possibility of simple living, and of clean and noble relations with men."

The sense that great things were taking place or were about to take place in the world often made Emerson at once hopeful and chagrined. He wrote to his young friend Caroline Sturgis in October 1840 that he felt that he and his friends were "the pets & cossets of the gracious Heaven, have never known a rough duty, have never wrestled with a rude doubt, never once been called to anything that deserved the name of an action. . . . I am daily getting ashamed of my life."

Yet the antislavery and temperance crusaders, the organizers of the factory workers, and the defenders of the poor, the imprisoned, the insane, were not likely to make many recruits among disciples of the newness, as Emerson himself acknowledged in a lecture entitled "The Transcendentalist," delivered in December 1841. "The philanthropists inquire whether Transcendentalism does not mean sloth. They had as lief hear that their friend was dead as that he was a Transcendentalist; for then he is paralyzed, and can never do anything for humanity."

The causes of this paralysis were several. At the heart is the old split between the life of the Understanding and the life of the Reason, which makes action seem either ineffectual or supererogatory: "One prevails now, all buzz and din; and the other prevails then, all infinitude and paradise; and, with the progress of life, the two discover no greater disposition to reconcile themselves." But less metaphysical causes were at work too. A patrician dislike of reformers — who were often evangelical in religion, crude in expression, peremptory in their demands for commitment — often crops up in Emerson's public and private writings from the period, and not only in Emerson's. When Fuller, who had migrated to New York in 1843 to take up a job reviewing books for Horace Greeley's *Tribune,* was called upon to review *The Narrative of the Life of Frederick Douglass,* she rebuked William Lloyd Garrison for the strident preface he had written for the book:

We look upon him with high respect; but he has indulged in violent invective and denunciation till he has spoiled the temper of his mind. Like a man who has been in the habit of screaming himself hoarse to make the deaf hear, he can no longer pitch his voice in a key agreeable to common ears.

To this Garrison might have replied that he was indeed screaming to make the deaf hear, and that Emerson and Fuller were the sort of deaf people he was particularly desirous of reaching.

A more serious obstacle in the way of their embracing any particular reform movement grew from the Transcendentalists' intense dislike of all forms of association. Any group of people gathered together to work toward good or to eradicate evil will find themselves obliged either to suppress dissent in the interests of solidarity or to endure endless ideological squabbling. Both of these alternatives were hateful to the Transcendentalists, who had just emerged from the old hypocrisy of Unitarian civility and had no wish to exchange it for a reformer's bullying or a reformer's cant. In his introductory lecture to the series entitled "Lectures on the Times," delivered in December 1841, Emerson asserts that the reformers of his own day are indeed "the right successors of Luther, Knox, Robinson, Fox, Penn, Wesley, and Whitfield. They have the same virtues and vices; the same noble impulse, and the same bigotry." The denouncing abolitionist who castigates the reluctant Northerner is himself a slaveholder in his habits and thoughts. "He is the state of Georgia, or Alabama, with their sanguinary slave-laws walking here on our north-eastern shores."

Yet in another mood Emerson could identify the various reform movements of the day as upwellings of the eternal life force. In a lecture entitled "Man the Reformer," delivered in January 1841, he asks:

What is man born for but to be a Reformer, a Re-maker of what man has made; a renouncer of lies; a restorer of truth and good, imitating that great Nature which embosoms us all, and which sleeps no moment on an old past, but every hour repairs herself, yielding us every morning a new day, and with every pulsation a new life?

Boston bankers who sneer at the idea of a juster world only show how corrosive is the national skepticism. "The Americans have many virtues, but they have not Faith and Hope."

How might a juster world be brought into being? Without coercion, without violating "the sacredness of private Integrity"? As he states in the lecture "Reforms" from which that phrase is taken, Emerson thought he glimpsed an answer.

Our doctrine is that the labor of society ought to be shared by all and in a community where labor was the point of honor the vain and the idle would labor. What a mountain of chagrins, inconveniences, diseases, and sins would sink into the sea with the uprise of this one docrine of labor. Domestic hired service would go over the dam. Slavery would fall into the pit. Shoals of maladies would be exterminated, and the Saturnian age revive.

The mixture of hyperbole and worldliness in this passage is a clue that Emerson was not taking this prescription for universal reform with entire seriousness, though he was probably not the only Massachusetts burgher to dream occasionally of returning to an agrarian simplicity, when a New Englander did not need to worry about either servants or slaves. In any case, a life devoted to labor would at least be *genuine,* not a tissue of conventions and hypocrisies. Would you live the heroic life? "Write your poem, brave man, first in the earth with a plough and eat the bread of your own spade."

At the end of this lecture Emerson carefully distances himself from the recruiters for any particular reform. "Though I sympathize with your sentiment and abhor the crime you assail yet I shall persist in wearing this robe, all loose and unbecoming as it is, of inaction, this wise passiveness until my hour comes when I can see how to act with truth as well as to refuse." Yet Jesus allowed himself to be persuaded to that first miracle at Cana, and hopeful reformers could hardly be blamed if they took Emerson's reluctance as an implicit invitation. Ellen, Emerson's elder daughter, remembered that about this time "all sorts of visitors with new ideas began to come to house, the men who thought money was the root of all evil, the vegetarians, the sons of nature who did not believe in razors nor tailors, the philosophers, and all sorts of come-outers." Feeding this menagerie was no easy task; her mother's recipes began with instructions like "take 3 pts. of sour milk" or "beat 2 doz. eggs." At the dinner table the vegetarians tended to bolt their squash and potatoes and glare at the slower meat eaters, eager for the pudding to come. One guest responded to an offer of tea with an exclamation of astonished outrage. "Tea! I!!!" When butter was offered to him a moment later his response was the same. "Butter! I!!!"

Understandably Emerson's patience sometimes wore thin, and on one occasion desperation pushed him into an unlikely feat. A certain "new light" had come to visit him in the morning, announcing that he planned to leave on the afternoon stage for Boston. When the stage drew near and the guest showed no signs of leaving, Emerson said, "Here comes the stage. I'll stop it for you," and he took off in a run after the departing coach while his amused wife looked on from the balcony. "My running," he said after the guest was safely dispatched, "was like the running of Ahimaaz the son of Zadok."

In the fall of 1840, however, Emerson received a visit from a reformer he could not so lightly dismiss. George Ripley had gradually come to believe that the Unitarian ministry could no longer serve as a platform from which to preach spiritual perfection or social reform. His battles during the miracles controversy with the conservatives in his own denomination had disheartened him, because they seemed to reveal a growing rigidity and intolerance in what had once been the most liberal of denominations. His continued preaching on social issues had wearied some members of his congregation. On October 4, 1840, he wrote a letter of resignation in which he vigorously castigated all his opponents but expressed renewed hope that a practical Christianity would eliminate suffering throughout society.

However tiresome they had sometimes found his preoccupation with issues of reform, Ripley's parishioners were finally reluctant to let him go. They prevailed upon him to stay through the beginning of the next year, but he remained determined to leave. On March 28, 1841, he preached his farewell sermon, reaffirming his faith in the obligation of all Christians to work toward establishing the kingdom of righteousness on earth.

Liberation from a pulpit where he had never felt truly competent as a preacher or comfortable as a would-be reformer gave Ripley an exhilaration that made this normally sober man look as if he were "fermenting and effervescing" (as James Freeman Clarke put it) with plans for the reformation of the world. Nor was he alone. Emerson wrote to Carlyle that there was not a man in New England but had the plan for a new social order in his pocket. The despair caused by the economic depression during the late 1830s had not succeeded in extinguishing the millennial zeal of the earliest days of the Transcendentalist movement; hope merely took a new form. Instead of assuming (as Emerson had in the closing sentences of *Nature*) that the redemption of the soul will cause the kingdom of God to organize itself around the beholder's sight, individuals like Ripley became convinced that only a reorganization of existing social structures could nurture the regeneration of the soul.

In recent years Ripley had felt himself drawn more and more strongly toward practical reform. He visited several English and German pietist communities and attended several conferences sponsored by "The Friends of Universal Reform" where he heard Christian socialists speak. In Albert Brisbane's *The Social Destiny of Man* (1840), an American exposition of the doctrines of the French social theorist Charles Fourier, Ripley came across the idea that a single perfectly organized community could by its example convert the whole society. The idea sounded enough like the old Puritan doctrine that the redeemed community should be a "city on a hill" to appeal to a man who had begun life as an orthodox Congregationalist, yet Fourier made it seem modern, scientific, secular. Fourier's plans for his ideal community wedded the prestige of French social science to the visionary arithmetic of the Book of Revelations. His carefully plotted phalanxes of 1,620 souls would rid the world of hunger and class hatred and would put an end to the ennui of the intellectual and the brutalization of the manual laborer.

Ripley could hardly hope to assemble a full phalanx, much less build the huge edifice that Fourier insisted was necessary to house it. For now his plan was simpler and more American. A corporation would be formed. Shares would be sold at five hundred dollars apiece, shareholders to be promised dividends of 5 percent from the profits of the enterprise. Land would be bought for farming. A school would be established to provide cash income. The shareholders and their students would live in buildings on the farm and take their meals together. The duties of running the farm, of feeding and washing for the inhabitants, and of caring for the residences would be shared, as far as possible, by everyone equally. All labor – teaching Latin, boiling vats of laundry, or cleaning out stalls – would be recompensed out of the expected profits of the enterprise at the same hourly rate.

As one of Ripley's early biographers puts it, however unlikely it seemed that a bookish parson should choose to exchange dignity, leisure, and elegance for toil and rudeness, and the works of Kant, Schelling, and Cousin for muck manuals, Ripley had come to think of it as the only possible solution to the alienation of the intellectuals and the misery of the poor. The Boston intellectuals' heads had become as distant from their own bodies as the whole scholarly class had become from the suffering workers. To labor in conditions of social equality would restore health to the body and the body politic at once. It would demonstrate to the world that the kingdom of heaven *was* possible on earth.

This sense that the planned community must be exemplary as well as functional explains why Ripley tried so hard to persuade Emerson to join. Ripley had brought up the idea of the community that would become Brook Farm at a meeting of the Transcendental Club in October 1840, where it was earnestly discussed. But no one was willing to enlist. Ripley visited Emerson again later in the month, this time accompanied by his wife, Sophia, and by Margaret Fuller. The famously ill-tempered judgment Emerson recorded in his journal after that visit, alleging that Ripley's planned community would be "not the cave of persecution which is the palace of spiritual power, but only a room in the Astor House hired for the Transcendentalists," reflects Emerson's lifelong distaste for using material means to produce spiritual ends. Its vehemence also suggests that he was chagrined at being challenged to live up to his recent call for an honest life, in which a true man will eat the bread of his own spade. Ripley's earnest request for aid continued to trouble Emerson; as late as December 2 he was still toying with the possibility of joining the community, as a letter he wrote to his brother then makes clear.

When he finally declined Ripley's invitation in a carefully drafted letter of December 15, 1840, Emerson gave his reasons in terms that recall his objections to the Lord's Supper many years before. What chiefly weighs with him is "the conviction that the Community is not good for me" (Emerson to Ripley, December 15, 1840). Ripley sent Emerson several more earnest letters, but in the end the small group of people who followed the Ripleys to West Roxbury had to begin life without either Emerson's presence or his financial support.

Their spirits nevertheless were high as they set out in April 1841 and remained so even through years of increasing discouragement and privation. The sandy ground beneath the picturesque meadows that Ripley had purchased proved stubbornly difficult to farm, and the community's small craft shops and greenhouse proved to be more drains upon their treasury than sources of profit to it. Indeed, whoever studies the accounts of the Brook Farm Association marvels that it managed to survive its natural and self-created difficulties for as long as it did – from the spring of 1841 until the autumn of 1847.

Yet an account of Brook Farm that told only of its financial difficulties would find it difficult to explain why the letters written by Brook Farmers during their years at the farm (even during the grimmer late years, when the various "retrenchments" had reduced the fare at table severely) and the reminiscences that many wrote later rarely complain of deprivation. They speak instead of joy – in the beauty of nature, in the exuberance of the young resident scholars coasting the snow-covered hills or going out before breakfast to gather spring wildflowers for the tables, in the constant flow of jokes and nicknames and execrable puns that enlivened their dinner-table conversations, in the dances and tableaux they staged in the evenings, in the feelings of robust health they got from working, in the cameraderie that freed them from isolation, and in the sense of purpose that freed them from aimlessness and despair.

To read these testimonies to the power of Brook Farm to create joy in its inhabitants is to understand why its residents continued to believe that they had found the remedy for all social evils – for poverty, hunger, ignorance, ill health, boredom, class hatred, sexual inequality (at Brook Farm the women voted and received the same pay as the men, and the men wiped dishes and shelled peas). They looked forward to the day when the land would be dotted with Brook Farms modeled on their own. In the autumn of 1842 Georgiana Bruce, a young resident at Brook Farm, wrote a glowing letter to a friend and concluded by saying that she thought that if their grandchildren collected the letters written from Brook Farm they would be able to "trace the history of the *first community.*"

John Codman, a Brook Farmer who arrived in 1843 at the age of twenty-seven, remembered how intoxicating the collective prospect seemed. "It was for the meanest a life above humdrum, and for the greatest something far, infinitely far beyond. They looked into the gates of life and saw beyond charming visions, and hopes springing up for all." In the memoir he wrote fifty years later he tried desperately to communicate some sense of the time when it was bliss to be alive:

Imagine, indifferent reader of my story, the state of mind you would be in if you could feel that you were placed in a position of positive harmony with all your race; that you carried with you a balm that could heal every earthly wound; an earthly gospel, even as the church thinks it has a heavenly gospel – a remedy for poverty, crime, outrage and over-taxed, hand, heart, and brain.

Is it any wonder that the Brook Farmers seemed a little giddy with joy? "And, after sound sleep, waking in the rosy morning, with the fresh air from balmy field blowing into your window, penetrated still with the afflatus of last night's thoughts and reveries, wouldn't you be cheerful? Wouldn't the unity of all things come to you, and wouldn't you chirrup like a bird, and buzz like a bee . . . ?"

Individual joy was valuable only insofar as it could be patented and distributed. The life the Brook Farmers led – milking the cows, haying the meadow, teaching in the school, laboring in the laundry or kitchen, cleaning the rooms – and the pleasantly Bohemian attire they adopted, with beards and belted tunics with Byron collars for the men, flowing tresses and broad-brimmed hats for the women, were obviously improvements over the dreary life of the "civilizees" (as the Brook Farmers contemptuously called them). But Ripley and his band of devoted associates thought of themselves as social reformers, not merely escapers from reality; they continued to insist that their community was a pattern upon which a new social reality could be built. Egalitarian, courteous, cultured, healthy, respectful of individuality yet suffused with the spirit of love, Brook Farm would show the way to a culture at once democratic and refined, where young men and women could hoe melons or scrub floors in the morning, study Greek at midday, and join the glee club in the evening to sing masses by Haydn and Mozart.

How far did the ideal correspond to the reality? Already during the first six months of operation Brook Farm had created its most famous critic. Nathaniel Hawthorne, fresh from his job at Salem's custom house, had joined the first settlers in hopes of finding a way to live cheaply and get time for writing. His letters to his fiancée, Sophia Peabody, during the spring of 1841 were at first full of enthusiasm. "I am transformed into a complete farmer," he boasts in a letter of May 3, 1841. "The whole fraternity eat together; and such a delectable way of life has never been seen on earth, since the days of the early Christians. We get up at half-past four, breakfast at half-past six, dine at half-past twelve, and go to bed at nine."

A month later, however, he is apologizing for not writing and complaining that "this present life of mine gives me an antipathy to pen and ink, even more than my Custom House experience did" (Hawthorne to Peabody, June 1, 1841). Though he tries to amuse Sophia with descriptions of the eloquence of the Brook Farm pigs, by August of 1841 he had already decided that the dream of *combining* labor and thought was a vain one.

Even my Custom House experience was not such a thraldom and weariness; my mind and heart were freer. Oh, belovedest, labor is the curse of this world, and nobody can meddle with it, without becoming proportionably brutified. Dost thou think it a praiseworthy matter, that I spend five golden months in providing food for cows and horses? Dearest, it is not so. (Hawthorne to Peabody, August 12, 1841)

By November Hawthorne had left the community.

In *The Blithedale Romance* (1852), the novel he set in a community modeled loosely on Brook Farm, Hawthorne's narrator and alter ego Miles Coverdale lodges a more serious charge against the practices of the community. Behind the boasted egalitarianism of Brook Farm – members of the finest Boston families working and eating side by side with mechanics and servants – lay an unquestioning snobbery, which took it for granted that the manners of the lower classes would be refined and softened by such contact. Many of the Brook Farmers testified to the sense of excitement they got from crossing class boundaries, though only Hawthorne subjected the emotion to later analysis. Here is how he describes the first supper at Blithedale, as the members of his imaginary community join the local couple they have hired to teach them how to farm.

We all sat down – grisly Silas Foster, his rotund helpmate, and the two bouncing handmaidens, included – and looked at one another in a friendly, but rather awkward way. It was the first practical trial of our theories of equal brotherhood and sisterhood; and we people of superior cultivation and refinement (for as such, I presume, we unhesitatingly reckoned ourselves) felt as if something were already accomplished towards the millennium of love. The truth is, however, that the laboring oar was with our unpolished companions; it being far easier to condescend, than to accept of condescension.

Indeed, the "equanimity" with which the aristocratic Blithedalers bore "the hardship and humiliations of a life of toil" owed much to their knowledge that they could choose at any time to leave their humble surroundings and return to lives of comfort. Coverdale concludes: "If ever I did deserve to be soundly cuffed by a fellow-mortal, for secretly putting weight upon some imaginary social advantage, it must have been while I was striving to prove myself ostentatiously his equal, and no more."

If the real Brook Farmers occasionally did show signs of the kind of condescension Coverdale blushes to remember – one elderly lady who had been a student at Brook Farm during its early days remarked that "the noble, sweet simplicity of the life there" and its lessons in the unimportance of worldly distinction helped her later to treat her servants "as if they were really equals" – it would be a mistake to dismiss the whole enterprise because of it. The Brook Farmers took seriously their mission to replace the greed and cruelty of the "civilized" economic system with a society founded upon the principles of generosity and love. A visitor to Brook Farm in the first summer of its existence gave this rendering of the motives that actuated the residents:

How *dare* I be a drone when others are drudges? How dare I sacrifice not only my own, but others' health, in sequestering myself from my share of bodily labour, or neglecting a due mental cultivation? How dare I have superfluities, when others are in want? How dare I oppose the unfolding of the spiritual progress of my whole race, by all the force of my personal selfishness and indolence? In short, is it not the sin against the Holy Ghost, with this new-found insight, to hesitate to enter immediately upon the immortal life?

The writer of this letter goes on to point out that the Brook Farm community has achieved "in the most peaceable manner in the world" the very "rectification of things which Mr. Brownson, in his Article on the Laboring Classes, is understood to declare will require a bloody revolution."

Surprisingly, Orestes Brownson (who sent one of his sons to the Brook Farm school) agreed. A long article he published in the *U.S. Magazine and Democratic Review* in November 1842 surveys all the current proposals for ending social misery and disposes of them all briskly. Only Ripley's attempt to found a community on love wins Brownson's approval. Brownson thought Ripley had succeeded where other communitarians like Robert Owen and Charles Fourier had failed, because he had avoided elaborate theorizing and organized Brook Farm around "the simple wants of his soul as a man and a Christian." The rule of that community is

the Gospel LAW OF LOVE and the rule to be honored is HONOR ALL MEN, and treat each man as a brother, whatever his occupation. In other words, the community is an attempt to realize the Christian Ideal, and to do this by establishing truly Christian relations between the members and the community and between member and member.

Emerson, too, followed the goings-on at Brook Farm with interest and amusement. But his own life was moving in a different direction, toward a vocation more literary, less local. A few weeks before Ripley's band departed for Brook Farm in the spring of 1841, Emerson published in Boston a book of twelve essays: "History," "Self-Reliance," "Compensation," "Spiritual Laws," "Love," "Friendship," "Prudence," "Heroism," "The Over-Soul," "Circles," "Intellect," and "Art." Each of these essays consisted of passages from Emerson's store of unpublished writings – his journals, letters, sermons, and lectures – that had been worked and reworked to increase their concision, vividness, and power.

We know from the letters Emerson wrote to friends when he was working on this book that he found the processes of revision and assembly painful. If his daily work for many years had been a labor of joy – reading, thinking, writing in his journal – the task of selecting and concatenating journal passages to make up lectures and essays forced him to play the role of editor to his own inspirations and be cold hearted and critical where he had once been excited and inspired. He often felt despondent as he tried to cobble his passages together into something larger than the one- or two-paragraph shape his thought seemed naturally to take in the journals, particularly because he was aware that the associative rather than strictly logical patterns of his discourses left many in his audience bewildered, as if they found themselves (to use his own comparison) in a house without stairs.

By the time Emerson had begun to work seriously at compiling a book of essays for publication he had already been writing professionally for thirteen years – first as a minister, then as a lyceum lecturer, and finally as an independent entrepreneur producing courses of ten or eleven lectures almost every year for the winter season. And he had learned that his unorthodox method of text making *worked,* at least in the opinion of his audiences. If it made his lectures elliptical, it also made them strangely stimulating. If his transitions were abrupt and his imagery startling, he managed to exhilarate as much as he puzzled. James Russell Lowell remembered what it was like to be part of that audience, to walk in from the country to the Masonic Temple on a crisp winter night to enjoy lectures whose "power of strangely subtle association" startled the mind into an attention almost painful, relieved only by "flashes of mutual understanding between speaker and hearer" that reminded Lowell of sheet lightning.

In the summer of 1839 Emerson set about revising material from these lectures to make the book of essays he had long hoped to publish. Work went slowly, partly because he had to write a new series of winter lectures for the 1839–40 season to pay the publishing costs for a collection of Carlyle's essays and reviews (four volumes of which Emerson edited and published between 1838 and 1840), partly because he found himself obliged to help Margaret Fuller as an unofficial coeditor of the fledgling *Dial*. But by the spring of 1840 he could look forward to an autumn of uninterrupted work. He wrote to a friend: "My chapter on 'Circles' begins to prosper and when it is October I shall write like a Latin Father" (Emerson to Elizabeth Hoar, September 12, 1840).

The pruning and revising that Emerson's journal passages underwent to become lectures became still more severe. Emerson understood very well that compression in a written text must create the intensity a lecturer can supply with his voice. He set out to prune empty repetitions, tighten syntax, sharpen images; he tore down bridges between ideas to leave gorges leapable only by the reader's wild surmise.

The resulting volume surprised even those who thought they knew Emerson well. Orestes Brownson, who had mocked or attacked Emerson for nearly everything else he had written, found that the *Essays* moved him not just to admiration but to reverence. In a brief notice written for the April 1841 number of the *Boston Quarterly Review* Brownson praised the book's transforming power. "He who reads it will find, that he is no longer what he was. A new and higher life has quickened in him, and he can never again feel, that he is merely a child of time and space, but that he is transcendent and immortal."

What kind of essays were these, that they were able to please even the ferocious Brownson? Some of them ("Prudence"; "Compensation") offer solid wisdom about the world of the senses, while others ("Intellect"; "The Over-Soul") rise insistently beyond it. Some essays celebrate personal courage ("Heroism"; "Self-Reliance"), while others urge a wise passivity and an entire trust in the self-executing laws of the universe ("Spiritual Laws"). Some examine the records of human civilization and human achievement ("History"; "Art"), while at least one ("Circles") celebrates time's power to swallow all traces of civilization and achievement alike as it ceaselessly generates new forms and new men. Against this energy individual men and women can oppose only the difficult love that binds strangers into fluctuating societies of affection ("Friendship") or the even more mysterious intoxication that begins with the erotic binding of one man to one woman and ends by connecting them both to society and to the race ("Love").

The essays are arranged for maximum contrast: a meditation on the collective experience of the race ("History") is followed by an intense focus upon the individual ("Self-Reliance"); a look at the hard economic balance of the universe ("Compensation") is followed by a hymn to the endless expansiveness of the soul ("Spiritual Laws"); and advice for achieving worldly success ("Prudence") is followed by exhortations to despise it completely ("Heroism").

Yet the effect of such juxtapositions is anything but self-canceling. On the contrary, what Emerson urges on every page is that we grasp the underlying principle of unity that binds together both the eternal laws and the phenomena that manifest them. "Let a man keep the law, – any law, – and his way will be strown with satisfactions," he says in "Prudence." Even the hard Law of Compensation – that nothing is got for nothing; that in nature nothing is given but everything is sold – had attracted him since boyhood, he says, because he thought a discourse on the subject might show human beings "a ray of divinity, the present action of the soul of this world, clean from all vestige of tradition" and so would bathe their hearts in "an inundation of eternal love."

So great is the force of love that its effects are visible in evil and disorder as well as in harmony and virtue. "Truth has not single victories; all things are its organs – not only dust and stones, but errors and lies," Emerson says in "Spiritual Laws." In the same essay he suddenly breaks out into an apostrophe that would startle if it did not stem from a real sense of the unbelief that Emerson detected beneath the conventions of society and the rituals of religion. "O my brothers, God exists. There is a soul at the centre of nature, and over the will of every man, so that none of us can wrong the universe."

It sounds strange to reassure readers that they cannot wrong the universe; but Emerson realized that guilt, like unbelief, was an enemy to the kind of radical self-culture his *Essays* promoted. He announces the project in the book's first essay, "History": "The world exists for the education of each man." As historians refuse to be condemned to ignorance by the pastness of the past but strive to "replace the preposterous There or Then and introduce in its place the Here and the Now" by reflecting that all history was made by the same mind that is now trying to read it, so every reader must approach the imposing richness of tradition as merely a portrait gallery "in which he finds the lineaments he is forming. The silent and the eloquent praise him, and accost him, and he is stimulated wherever he moves as by personal allusions."

Yet Emerson points out that the muse of history will never utter oracles to those who do not respect themselves and that the obstacles to self-respect in the Boston of 1841 are many and formidable. "Self-Reliance," the second essay in the book, is an assault upon those obstacles, the greatest of which is fear of opinion — fear of appearing foolish or selfish or insignificant or inconsistent. As Emerson says toward the close of the essay, "The sinew and heart of man seem to be drawn out, and we are become timorous desponding whimperers. We are afraid of truth, afraid of fortune, afraid of death, and afraid of each other." Against this primary disease Emerson fights back with epigrams designed to stiffen the backs of those poor, obscure young men he always thought of as his primary audience. "Trust thyself: every heart vibrates to that iron string." "Whoso would be a man must be a nonconformist." "A foolish consistency is the hobgoblin of little minds, adored by little statesmen and philosophers and divines." "The centuries are conspirators against the sanity and authority of the soul." "Check this lying hospitality and lying affection." "Insist on yourself: never imitate." "Nothing can bring you peace but yourself. Nothing can bring you peace but the triumph of principles."

Emerson's insistence upon self-assertion even to the point of rudeness has an unpleasant ring in the present day, when boorishness flourishes and self-forgiveness is an article of faith. Not surprisingly, a chorus of moralists has recently arisen to blame Emerson for all the woes of modern society — narcissism, infantilism, self-indulgence, the breakdown of marriage, the withdrawal from political life. It may be true that the pendulum has swung so far in the direction of the self that we almost long for a return to deference and repression — though one wonders how long these critics (urban intellectuals, most of them) could actually bear the stifling atmosphere of small-town intrusiveness that was Emerson's target in "Self-Reliance." Such critics should be encouraged to remember the fate of the Parisian in Stendahl's *The Red and the Black* who yearned to be the proprietor of a country estate, only to discover that rural life was a "hell of hypocrisy and petty vexations." Chastened, he returned to seek solitude and rustic tranquillity in "the only place where they exist in France — in a fourth-floor flat overlooking the Champs Elysées." (When Emerson visited Paris in 1848 he understood immediately why every young man from the provinces wanted to move there — to be *free from observation.*)

In fact, Emerson does not wish to leave the self in sterile isolation, endlessly contemplating its own magnificence. The essay "Love" opens with an unqualified hymn to Eros, builder of cities. Emerson praises love because it is a divine rage that

seizes on man at one period, and works a revolution in his mind and body; unites him to his race, pledges him to the domestic and civic responsibilities, carries him with new sympathy into nature, enhances the power of the senses, opens the imagination, adds to his character heroic and sacred attributes, establishes marriage, and gives permanence to human society.

But union is only possible to those who are units. And most men in Emerson's society are not units, only fragments and pieces of men; not sturdy oaks but "leaning willows."

Transforming willows into oaks will take more than exhortation. You cannot urge someone to absolute self-reliance without addressing the question of the self's constitution, for if the self is evil then absolute self-reliance is absolute death. Emerson's refusal to answer this question at first, except by saying "If I am the Devil's child, I will live then from the Devil," recalls in its irritation at being badgered some of Jesus' retorts to the Pharisees, but the question refuses to go away, and Emerson finally addresses it in a passage that rises up in the middle of the essay like a great mountain.

The magnetism which all original action exerts is explained when we inquire the reason of self-trust. Who is the Trustee? What is the aboriginal Self on which a universal reliance may be grounded? What is the nature and power of that science-baffling star, without parallax, without calculable elements, which shoots a ray of beauty even into trivial and impure actions, if the least mark of independence appear?

A star without parallax or calculable elements would defy astronomists and chemists alike in their attempts to analyze or place it, would be something irreducible to the terms of any known system.

That irreducible something Emerson calls, rather oddly, "Spontaneity or Instinct" – an *intuition* rather than a *tuition*. "Spontaneity" suggests activity and "instinct" passion, yet Emerson clearly is thinking of something quite different from both, for he goes on to describe a surprisingly passive primal self, a "sense of being" rising in our calm hours assuring us of our unity with things. "We lie in the lap of immense intelligence, which makes us receivers of its truth and organs of its activity." At its source, self-reliance turns into its opposite, self-abnegation. "When we discern justice, when we discern truth, we do nothing of ourselves, but allow a passage to its beams."

In this hour of vision we feel neither gratitude nor joy, but only a sense that "all things go well." From this height Emerson can even confess the inadequacy of the title of his essay. "Why then do we prate of self-reliance?" The word "reliance" is "a poor external way of speaking," focusing attention upon the dilapidations of the empirical self instead of upon the power that shoots through it in those precious moments of spontaneity or instinct. "Speak rather of that which relies, because it works and is."

If "Self-Reliance" is an attempt to look at truth from the perspective of the empirical self striving to attain it, "Spiritual Laws" looks at truth from truth itself, an effort that leads Emerson to write proverbs of the pure Reason, mysterious statements that are meant to sound like fragments of Eastern wisdom. "The soul's emphasis is always right." A man "may see what he maketh." He "may have that allowance he takes." "He may read what he writes." "He shall have his own society."

These odd little bits of gnomic wisdom are as far as possible from the militant exhortations of "Self-Reliance." Instead of telling us what to do they tell us that no doing is necessary. Emerson quotes an exclamation of Confucius — "How can a man be concealed!" — to point out the fruitlessness of sham. But he also points out the needlessness of worry, for the universe of "Spiritual Laws" is that lap of immense intelligence we only glimpsed in "Self-Reliance." "Place yourself in the middle of the stream of power and wisdom which animates all whom it floats, and you are without effort impelled to truth, to right, and a perfect contentment."

Do not choose is Emerson's advice to us now, as long as we realize that the puny activity of the conscious will is insignificant beside the perpetual choosing represented by our lives.

A man is a method, a progressive arrangement; a selecting principle, gathering his like to him, wherever he goes. He takes only his own, out of the multiplicity that sweeps and circles round him. He is like one of those booms which are set out from the shore on rivers to catch driftwood, or like the loadstone amongst splinters of steel.

For this reason we cannot go astray so long as we trust our fascinations. "What your heart thinks great, is great. The soul's emphasis is always right."

And this is so because, as Emerson finally asserts openly in "The Over-Soul," the book's ninth essay, "There is no bar or wall in the soul where man, the effect, ceases, and God, the cause, begins." The individual soul is distinct enough from the universal soul that it feels a "shudder of awe and delight" when they blend together, yet united enough that Emerson can quietly redefine "Revelation" as "the disclosure of the soul," without bothering to say whose soul is being disclosed. "Man is a stream whose source is hidden. Our being is descending into us from we know not whence." If there is something terribly frightening about Emerson's description of union with the divine — "The soul gives itself alone, original, and pure, to the Lonely, Original, and Pure" — at least the soul, like Moses, returns at last to other men. "More and more the surges of everlasting nature enter into me, and I become public and human in my regards and actions. So I come to live in thoughts, and act with energies which are immortal."

Such energies are necessary, because the world we live in is still a fallen one, however brilliantly its defects illustrate the workings of the moral law. Prudence is needed to manage the world of the senses, heroism to endure its cruelties, and a firm sense of the Law of Compensation to reassure us that the universe, though fatally flawed, is still thoroughly moral in its workings. It is a pity that the tough and often funny essays that treat these virtues are so rarely anthologized for modern students, because they show Emerson as the brilliant practitioner of a tradition of wisdom literature that includes both the book of Proverbs and the maxims of Epictetus.

Perhaps the most deeply felt of all the advice Emerson offers in these essays comes in "Prudence," where he warns against the folly of engaging in religious controversy. "If they set out to contend, Saint Paul will lie, and Saint John will hate. What low, poor, paltry, hypocritical people, an argument on religion will make of the pure and chosen souls!" Instead of arguing, Emerson urges a more generous (and more devious) tactic. "Though your views are in straight antagonism to theirs, assume an identity of sentiment, assume that you are saying precisely that which all think, and in the flow of wit and love, roll out your paradoxes in solid column, with not the infirmity of doubt." Does not the Bible tell us that by doing good to our enemy we shall heap his head with coals of fire?

Avoiding controversy has a deeper value as well. In "Intellect" Emerson explains why. "God offers to every mind its choice between truth and repose. Take which you please, – you can never have both." The man who loves repose will accept whatever creed he inherits, but the man who loves truth will "abstain from dogmatism, and recognize all the opposite negations between which, as walls, his being is swung." Dogmatizing forces us to defend some momentary apprehension of truth until it becomes falsehood and "incipient insanity."

Why should truth be so elusive? If we can lie in the lap of an immense intelligence, why cannot we repose on the bosom of an unchanging truth? In "Circles," the shortest essay in the book as well as one of the latest to be written, Emerson tries to answer this question. Alone of all the *Essays* "Circles" has no source in an earlier lecture, and it moves with a logical directness rare in Emerson. It is, as one critic has said, an attempt to measure the depth of the universe by the rapidity with which it swallows up institutions. "Our culture is the predominance of an idea which draws after it this train of cities and institutions. Let us rise into another idea; they will disappear."

If this instability were merely chaotic one might have cause for despair, but Emerson sees each culture's attempt to draw a new circle around the old one it inherited as a symbol of "the moral fact of the Unattainable, the flying Perfect, around which the hands of man can never meet, at once the inspirer and the condemner of every success." In every effort we strive to reach, or to represent, the Oversoul, and the detritus left by our failures is what we know as civilization.

Yet the dominant tone of the essay is anything but bitter or despairing. On the contrary, Emerson's standpoint within the eternal gives him a giddying look down at the universe below, vibrant with life and energy. "The life of man is a self-evolving circle, which, from a ring imperceptibly small, rushes on all sides outwards to new and larger circles, and that without end." For if each circle we form naturally tends to solidify into "an empire, rules of an art, a local usage, a religious rite," still the soul is strong and bursts over the boundary it has just formed. "Step by step we scale this mysterious ladder; the steps are actions; the new prospect is power."

The reason we can bear this endless self-overcoming is that, like God, we are circles whose circumference is everywhere and whose center is nowhere. If our empirical selves are ceaselessly tossed in the flux, our transcendental selves abide in the center. "Whilst the eternal generation of circles proceeds, the eternal generator abides. That central life is somewhat superior to creation, superior to knowledge and thought, and contains all its circles." All efforts at self-culture are inspired by this central life, laboring to create "a life and thought as large and excellent as itself, suggesting to our thought a certain development."

Still, the products of that thought can never be as valuable as the energy that throws them off. "Nothing is secure but life, transition, the energizing spirit. No love can be bound by oath or covenant to secure it against a higher love. No truth so sublime but it may be trivial tomorrow in the light of new thoughts." And then, in a final joke directed against all poor youths who hunger after a permanent position, Emerson sums up the wisdom he has learned so far. "People wish to be settled; only as far as they are unsettled, is there any hope for them."

Essays is still unsettling to read, and not merely in those passages where Emerson speaks as "the Devil's child." Yet the overwhelming impression the essays make is of faith and hope and if not quite of charity, at least of incandescent desire. Because God exists, nothing can be lost that matters to the soul, and everything should be jettisoned that hinders it. Or, as Emerson says in the final paragraph of "Circles": "The way of life is wonderful; it is by abandonment."

As if to prove that he meant what he said, Emerson tried to make some alterations in his own way of living — inviting the Alcott family (once again in financial trouble) to move into the house, acquiring habits of regular manual labor, and abolishing domestic service or at least abolishing the invidious class distinctions domestic service created. But his efforts to make the Emerson house into a little Brook Farm were mostly doomed to failure. Mrs. Alcott, foreseeing what might happen if two such transcendental egos as her husband and Emerson occupied the same house, turned down Emerson's offer of help. Emerson's wife and mother refused to do without domestic servants. And the cook and housemaid firmly declined to eat at the Emerson family table.

Anxious to salvage at least one plank in his reform platform, Emerson turned to Thoreau. "Henry Thoreau is coming to live with me & work with me in the garden & teach me to graft apples," he informed Margaret Fuller in April 1841. By the first of June he was writing to his brother William to say that the arrangement seemed to be working:

He is thus far a great benefactor & physician to me for he is an indefatigable & a very skilful laborer & I work with him as I should not without him. and expect now to be suddenly well & strong though I have been a skeleton all the spring until I am ashamed. Thoreau is a scholar & a poet & as full of buds of promise as a young apple tree.

The contrast between youthful energy and skeletal age would come to dominate the new lecture series that Emerson planned for the winter of 1841–42 in Boston, the last complete series he would manage himself. Called "Lectures on the Times," the series represents Emerson's clearest attempt to address the problem of reform directly. "These Reforms are our contemporaries; they are ourselves; our own light, and sight and conscience; they only name the relation which subsists between us and the vicious institutions which they go to rectify," he said in the introductory lecture of the series. Yet he is careful to give conservatism its due. In "The Conservative" he lets an imaginary defender of the established order rebuke the visionary. "The existing world is not a dream, and cannot with impunity be treated as a dream; neither is it disease; but it is the ground on which you stand, it is the mother of whom you were born." Reform deals in possibilities, "but here is sacred fact."

To this a reformer replies (in a lecture entitled "The Transcendentalist"): "You think me the child of my circumstances; I make my circumstance." What is mere fact before the dissolving power of consciousness? "I – this thought which is called I, – is the mold into which the world is poured like melted wax." In a radiant final lecture that bears the same title as the last chapter of *Nature*, "Prospects," Emerson leaves little doubt where his heart lies. "I hate the builders of dungeons in the air," he says. "We were made for another office, professors of the Joyous Science, detectors and delineators of occult symmetries and unpublished beauties, heralds of civility, nobility, learning, and wisdom, affirmers of the One Law." How can the conservative dispirit us with his facts? "The last fact is still astonishment, mute, bottomless, boundless Wonder."

There is nothing at last but God only. "All perishes except the Creator, the

Creator who needs no companion, who fills the world with his fulness, and instantly and forevermore reproduces Nature and what we call the world of men, as the sea its waves." The man who has learned to regard all his possessions and relations as mutable has put himself out of the reach of skepticism. "All its arrows fall far short of the eternal towers of his faith." We must be content to watch whatever spectacle the great spirit sends us, "to see it, and hold our tongues. Who asked you for an opinion?"

If this indeed was Emerson's mature faith it was about to be put to a severe test. He returned home to Concord to find Henry Thoreau suddenly ill with hysterical symptoms of lockjaw, the disease that had killed his brother a week earlier. Emerson was frightened until Thoreau's symptoms gradually abated. But a worse trial yet was in store. Emerson's five-and-one-half-year-old son, Waldo, came down with scarlet fever on Monday, January 24. By Thursday he was delirious. When his mother Lidian asked the attending doctor when she could expect her son to get better, the doctor could only reply, "I had hoped to be spared this." Waldo died shortly after eight o'clock that evening.

Grief left Emerson with a numbness he found more terrible than agony, but he hardly had time to reflect upon his sensations. The receipts for the Boston lecture series had been disappointing, and Emerson's bank had failed to pay its usual dividend. He calculated that he needed to earn another two hundred dollars by lecturing to meet his family's expenses. And he was still trying to find some way to help Alcott, whose move to Concord had brought him neither prosperity nor peace. Emerson thought that a trip to England, where Alcott's writings had acquired for him a band of enthusiastic disciples among reformers interested in education, might lift Alcott's spirits and improve his health; but his efforts to raise money for this "Alcott-Voyage-fund" among the wealthy citizens of Boston were unsuccessful.

Emerson had better luck in Providence, Rhode Island; a liberal friend of Alcott's gave money toward the voyage. But his own lecture audiences in Providence were so small that he sometimes earned as little as nine dollars for a lecture. Reluctantly, he decided he had to take the series to New York. Fortunately, audiences there were larger and his profits greater. (He was reviewed in New York by a young reporter for the Brooklyn *Aurora,* Walter Whitman.) By the time Emerson returned to New England in mid-March he had earned enough money both to cover his family's needs and to contribute to Alcott's voyage.

But that voyage, like almost everything else that involved the man Emerson had once, in an exasperated mood, called "Plato Skimpole," ended badly. It set in motion forces that would give rise to the shortest lived of all the reform efforts and would end by depositing Alcott and his family once again on Emerson's doorstep. Alcott sailed from Boston on May 8, 1842. In

London he was greeted by two admirers, Charles Lane and Henry Wright, who took him immediately outside of London to a school named after him, Alcott House. Lane and Wright were communitarians; they wanted to establish what they called a "New Eden." Like Brook Farm, it would invite laborers who would live on and work the land, both to provide subsistence for themselves and to achieve harmony between body and spirit. A society of people with chaste minds in healthy bodies would be able to achieve the perfection once thought lost by the Fall; strict vegetarian diets, cold baths, and exercise would undo the corruption and decay Alcott saw everywhere around him in England.

Alcott returned to America on October 21, 1842, bringing with him Wright, Lane, and Lane's nine-year-old son, who moved in with the Alcott family. By January 1843 Wright's enthusiasm for the New Eden had evaporated under the fanatical regimen of diet and cold bathing that the tyrannical Lane imposed on everybody; Wright took ship for England again. Lane and Alcott continued to proselytize and to look for a suitable farm to purchase.

Finally, in May 1843, Lane found a ninety-acre farm he liked in the Massachusetts village of Harvard. Only eleven of the farm's acres were arable, and these promised to be difficult to cultivate without the use of animal labor and animal manure, both of which Alcott and Lane scorned as exploitative or unclean. But the prospect from the farm, with woods behind and mountains in the distance, was lovely, and when "the consociate family," as they called themselves, set out on the first of June for Fruitlands (as they had decided to name their community, though ten ancient apple trees were all the orchard they had), their spirits were high. In the July issue of *The Dial* Alcott and Lane proudly announced their escape from the bondage of the cash nexus. "We have made an arrangement with the proprietor of an estate of about a hundred acres, which liberates this tract from human ownership."

Most of the people they had tried to persuade to join them had declined to come. The group they did attract was a motley one. There were two discontented Brook Farmers, a cooper who had once been imprisoned in a madhouse, a former nudist from England, and a mild revolutionary who had endured a year in the Worcester jail rather than pay the small tax then levied on men who wore full beards. Only one woman joined the group to help Abby, Bronson's long-suffering wife, with the cooking and domestic chores. This woman, Ann Page, deserves to be remembered, if only for the acerbic comment she made about all such reform efforts. A woman may live a whole life of self-sacrifice and die saying meekly, "Behold a woman," whereas a man who passes a few years in experiments of self-denial says "Behold a *god*."

Louisa May Alcott, who was ten when her family moved to Fruitlands, later wrote a brief account of her experience there; it was published in 1873 as

Transcendental Wild Oats. She gives a good idea of what life in this fantastic commune was like:

Such farming probably was never seen before since Adam delved. The band of brothers began by spading garden and field; but a few days of it lessened their ardor amazingly. Blistered hands and aching backs suggested the expediency of permitting the use of cattle till the workers were better fitted for noble toil by a summer of the new life.

But in other areas their determination to purge their lives of evil dictated severe measures:

Unleavened bread, porridge, and water for breakfast; bread, fruit, vegetables, and water for dinner; bread, fruit, and water for supper was the bill of fair ordained by the elders. No teapot profaned that sacred stove, no gory steak cried aloud for vengeance from her chaste gridiron; and only a brave woman's taste, time, and temper were sacrificed on that domestic altar.

Clothing was similarly ascetic. "Cotton, silk, and wool were forbidden as the product of slave-labor, worm-slaughter, and sheep-robbery. Tunics and trowsers of brown linen were the only wear."

Alcott and Lane proved fonder of talking about farming than of actually farming; during the harvest season they were off on a pilgrimage through New York and New England trying to enlist more members for Fruitlands, without success. Abby, three of her daughters, and Lane's son were the only crew on hand when an October thunderstorm menaced the grain stacks; they managed to get the crop in using clothes baskets and sheets, but the harvest was meager at best.

By the end of October 1843 Fruitlanders were drifting away, and tensions began to rise between Lane and Alcott. Lane, who had put up the money for the enterprise, believed that he had been misled by Alcott's optimistic assurance that America would yield cohorts of recruits for the consociate family. In early January 1844 Lane (who had long-standing objections to the nuclear family as a hotbed of selfishness and an obstacle to true association) left with his son to join a nearby Shaker community. Alcott, exhausted by work and hunger, moved his family to board with a nearby farmer. Deeply depressed, he refused to eat for several days, and only the presence by his bedside of his wife and daughters finally persuaded him to take food again. Louisa remembered that he emerged from his sickroom a "wan shadow of a man, leaning on the arm that never failed him." But the crisis had passed, though the few possessions they still had left had to be sold to pay Fruitlands debts.

Emerson had tried to prevent the Fruitlands debacle by writing to Alcott's English admirers warning them that Alcott was not to be trusted in practical matters (a letter he sent in care of Alcott himself, who dutifully showed it to the intended recipients). During the long months in America when Alcott and Lane were trying to gather a flock Emerson was impatient with them. In November 1842 he had written in his journal: "This fatal fault in the logic of our friends still appears: Their whole doctrine is spiritual, but they always end with saying, Give us much land and money." He was half-inclined to say, as the world would, "Let them drink their own error to saturation, and this will be the best hellebore." But now that Alcott was thoroughly saturated with his error Emerson felt pity at Alcott's despair. Alcott was, after all, being true to his principles, and if they led him to ruin in the world it was the world's fault. When Alcott moved back to Concord, Emerson joined with the trustee who managed Abby May Alcott's estate in buying a farm for the Alcotts in Concord. This time they made sure that the property would be held in trust, safe from Alcott.

Not all of Emerson's time during this busy period was taken up with caring for Alcott, lecturing to earn income, or editing *The Dial*. Slowly during the summer and fall of 1843 Emerson began to return to the literary project he had long planned – putting together a second volume of essays for the press. He found it difficult to find time to work. To Margaret Fuller he complained in a letter of December 17, 1843, that "the felon Dial, the felon lectures, friend, wife, child, house, woodpile, each in turn is the guilty cause why life is postponed." The tales he heard of the feats of the German scholars who studied eleven and twelve hours a day filled him with envy. He could scarcely manage five hours (Emerson to Fuller, November 5, 1843). Yet when the new year came he could at least rejoice that one source of distraction was ending. On April 1, 1844, he wrote to his brother William that proof sheets for the last *Dial,* that "perpetual impediment" to his new book, had been sent to the printer. Three chapters of the new book were almost ready for the printer. Work on the remaining five chapters and the concluding lecture took up the rest of the summer, and it was not until October 4 that he could write to William that he had been "released at last from months of weary tending on the printers devil!" In a moment of giddiness he agreed to buy eleven acres of land (at $8.10 an acre) on the shore of Walden Pond from some men who accosted him there on one of his solitary walks; he then bought a few more acres of neighboring pine grove. He was now "landlord & waterlord of 14 acres, more or less," and could raise his own blackberries. (A mention of Alcott later in the same letter made William fire back a warning against pouring any more money down that "Orphic sieve.") *Essays, Second Series* was published on October 19, 1844.

Like the first series of essays, the book was loosely arranged in groups of contrasting essays. The godlike power of discernment celebrated in "The

Poet" is followed by the bewilderment of "Experience"; an investigation of daimonic power in "Character" yields to studies of social relations in "Manners" and "Gifts." "Nature" shows the world as it appears to the solitary contemplator, whereas "Politics" studies men as they behave in senates and caucuses. The final essay in the book, "Nominalist and Realist," does not so much seek to reconcile all these opposites as to make them spin too rapidly to be distinguishable. The last piece in the book, included because Emerson's publisher had told him the book was too short, is a lecture Emerson had delivered in March 1844 entitled "New England Reformers," a witty survey of the various reform movements Emerson had witnessed with varying proportions of amusement and respect.

That Emerson chose to place "The Poet" first suggests how willing he had become to accept a merely symbolic transformation of his world. *Nature* had predicted the actual renovation of the world through the influx of spirit; the Divinity School Address had looked forward to a Teacher who could bring glad tidings of a gospel proclaiming the identity of science and law. "The Poet" celebrates the intoxications of perception itself. The poet stands nearer to that spot "where Being passes into Appearance, and Unity into Variety"; he "sees the flowing or metamorphosis; perceives that thought is multiform; that within the form of every creature is a force impelling it to ascend into a higher form; and, following with his eyes the life, uses the forms which expresses that life, and so his speech flows with the flowing of nature." This power to mimic by a flux of tropes the flux of nature "has a certain power of emancipation and exhilaration for all men. . . . We are like persons who come out of a cave or cellar into the open air." Emerson's theft of a famous image from Plato is no accident, for he means to insist upon the centrality of true poets to his ideal republic. "Poets are thus liberating gods." Unlike the mere men of talent, who imitate the contours of the phenomenal, or the mystics, who stop the free play of symbols by a premature quest for meaning, true poets give us the "cheerful hint of the immortality of our essence" by their refusal to be pinned down.

That "fugacity," which seems in a moment of joy the gift of an expansive universe, can seem in another mood a sign of the universe's mockery and retreat. In "Experience," now regarded as one of the greatest of his essays, Emerson attempts to describe what it feels like to live in a universe not merely in flux but in flight from the perceiving self. The essay begins by evoking a nightmare world of endless staircases and a speaker who feels drugged. It might almost be the beginning of a story by Edgar Allan Poe, except that the horror Emerson seeks to describe is simply everyday life as it is experienced by ordinary men and women as they try to gain wisdom and love in a world where the very condition of subjectivity seems to preclude both. We do not know where we are or where we are going; our temperament shuts us in a prison of glass we cannot see; the stream of moods is so powerful that we cannot long anchor in any affection or belief; and grief itself can only teach us how shallow it is. "That, like all the rest, plays about the surface, and never introduces me into the reality, for contact with which we should even pay the costly price of sons and lovers."

The numbness Emerson felt after the death of his son now seems a synecdoche for a greater impenetrability. "The Indian who was laid under a curse, that the wind should not blow on him, nor water flow to him, nor fire burn him, is a type of us all. The dearest events are summer-rain, and we the Para coats that shed every drop." It is difficult to avoid the doubt that begins to surface toward the end of the essay. "Perhaps these subject-lenses have a creative power; perhaps there are no objects." Yet the perceiving subject is not allowed even the comfort of a consistent skepticism, because at any moment the reality that has eluded us will manifest itself once again and make it clear that it had never really vanished. "Underneath the inharmonious and trivial particulars, is a musical perfection, the Ideal journeying always with us, the heaven without rent or seam." In the end, our journey must continue with a hope that we can neither fulfill nor relinquish – that victory will follow justice, that genius will be transformed into practical power.

In "Character" Emerson suggests that one means of achieving this transformation might be through the kind of daimonic power manifested in oratory, the "river of command" that flows from stronger natures into weaker ones. "Manners" concerns itself with that combination of manhood and gentleness the man of character will use toward his fellow human beings. The composure and self-content that are his trademarks are what might be called the social manifestation of self-reliance, and his motto is "Let us not be too much acquainted." Suddenly, toward the close of the essay, Emerson considers the very different manners he wishes to see in women. The whole passage is remarkable as a concealed tribute to the two women whose assaults upon the fortress of his shyness had precipitated him into such delicious confusion in the half-decade just past – Margaret Fuller and Caroline Sturgis. Margaret Fuller is clearly the woman whose generosity "raises her at all times into heroical and godlike regions, and verifies the pictures of Minerva, Juno, or Polymnia." Sturgis, on the other hand, fills Emerson's vase with wine and roses and breaches his walls of habitual reserve until his tongue is unloosed and he says things he otherwise never would have thought to say – though this seduction (in which Emerson seems to be playing the feminine role) finally ends in regression to asexual innocence: "We were children playing with children in a wild field of flowers."

"Gifts" contains no passages so revealing, though it does have some very funny maxims about the dangers of being a benefactor, a role Emerson had played at one time or another to most of his friends. "It is a very onerous business, this of being served, and the debtor naturally wishes to give you a slap." What makes the essay engaging is Emerson's complete sympathy with the indignation of the beneficiary. "It is not the office of a man to receive gifts. How dare you give them? We wish to be self-sustained. We do not quite forgive a giver. The hand that feeds us is in some danger of being bitten."

"Nature" turns back from the world we make to the world we inhabit. The first half of the essay concerns itself with the beauty of phenomena, *natura naturata,* the second with the "efficient nature," *natura naturans,* "the quick cause, before which all forms flee as the driven snows." Throughout the essay Emerson sees nature as an evolutionary process, shaping species slowly through the vast stretches of geologic time, equipping them to occupy particular ecological niches and, at the same time, equipping enemies to destroy them. Yet the essay is still closer in spirit to Genesis than it is to *The Origin of Species,* for this vast panoply still centers on us. "By fault of our dulness and selfishness, we are looking up to nature, but when we are convalescent, nature will look up to us." "The world is mind precipitated, and the volatile essence is forever escaping again into the state of free thought."

"Politics," though it is suffused with nostalgia for the old Federalist idea that property should make the law for property and people for people, at least admits that there is something injurious, something "deteriorating and de grading" in the influence property has on people. Although Emerson says that he refusess to despair of the republic, he finds little comfort in the current political scene, with radicals who are "destructive and aimless" and conservatives who are "timid, and merely defensive of property."

"Nominalist and Realist," the final essay in the book, attempts to find some virtue in polarities. "Jesus would absorb the race; but Tom Paine or the coarsest blasphemer helps humanity by resisting this exuberance of power." Even the scurrilousness of political campaigners opposes flaws in their opponents that would otherwise remain hidden; hence Emerson gives perhaps the best defense of the two-party system ever mounted: "Since we are all so stupid, what a benefit that there should be two stupidities!"

Our awkwardness in this life comes from the fact that we are weaponed for two elements, the particular and the universal. "We must reconcile the contradictions as we can, but their discord and their concord introduce wild absurdities in our speech." Nor are our psyches any less riven. We no sooner state a proposition than we wish to turn and rend it; no sooner expound a doctrine than we recant, saying, "I thought I was right, but I was not." Like the Zimri of John Dryden's *Absalom and Achitophel,* we are everything by starts, and nothing long. Emerson had said something similar in "Experience," but here the tone of the assertion is not elegiac or despairing. Instead it is indulgent, amused, even Augustan. Inconsistency is part of the human condition; indeed, it *is* the human condition; and it guards us against the fanaticism of bigots whose very single-mindedness is the best sign of their insanity.

The final piece in the book is not listed as one of the essays, but instead is presented with its original title: "New England Reformers: A Lecture Read before the Society in Amory Hall, on Sunday, 3 March, 1844." The Amory Hall Society was a very radical group indeed, organized when an eloquent Philadelphia antislavery editor named Charles Augustus Burleigh gave three lectures on social reform in Boston during January 1844. His auditors were unwilling to let the inspiration of the moment pass; they formed a society on the spot and deputized a committee to hire speakers to address them on similar topics for the next twelve Sundays. William Lloyd Garrison spoke there; so did Charles Lane and Adin Ballou, cofounder with Garrison of the New England Non-Resistance Society. There was even an address by a Jewish immigrant freethinker named Ernestine Rose, a convert to the communitarian ideals of Robert Owen.

Both Emerson and Thoreau delivered lectures in this series, although both dissented strongly from the principles of association most of the other lecturers espoused. Emerson begins his lecture with an amused survey of the schismatic frenzy that has taken over New England in the last twenty-five years. There are societies for the reform of everything. "In these movements, nothing was more remarkable than the discontent they begot in the movers." The "spirit of protest and of detachment" drives the members of the movements away from established institutions, then away from the conventions called to protest these institutions, and then from their colleagues in protest. "The country is full of rebellion; the country is full of kings. Hands off! let there be no control and no interference in the administration of the affairs of this kingdom of me!" What these "solitary nullifiers" often forget is that the would-be renovators must themselves be renovated before they can regenerate the world around them.

Those who hope to cure evils too big for single men and women to attack by joining together in associations will find that they are diminished, not expanded, by proximity to one another. Associations and rules will never liberate us. "We wish to escape from subjection, and a sense of inferiority, – and we make self-denying ordinances, we drink water, we eat grass, we refuse the laws, we go to jail; it is all in vain." Only when we obey our genius freely does an angel arise before us and lead us by the hand out of all the wards of the prison. "The union is only perfect, when all the uniters are isolated."

It is one of the ironies of history that Emerson made this familiar plea for the centrality of the individual at the time when his old friend George Ripley was attempting to lead his community in precisely the opposite direction. Even though Brook Farm to all outward appearances was happy and thriving in 1843, with a student population of thirty in a larger community of seventy, a study of its books in November of that year revealed a deficit of $1,160.84. Brook Farm was not a commune but a joint-stock company; those who wished to become full-fledged Associates needed to purchase at least one five-hundred-dollar share in the Brook Farm Association, which promised to pay a yearly dividend of 5 percent. Not enough new members with sufficient capital to buy the five-hundred-dollar shares in the Brook Farm Association were applying for admission (though Ripley was deluged with applications from people with no money, in poor health, and with large families). The task of bringing previously uncultivated soil into agricultural production proved to be far more difficult than Ripley had anticipated, and though he and his associates worked heroically, they were able to produce few marketable commodities besides milk and hay. They were not able to supply all of their own needs from the gardens, no matter how many luxuries they agreed to do without. The school itself was profitable, attracting students from as far away as Cuba and the Philippines; and the thousands of visitors who yearly descended upon Brook Farm became a modest source of income when the governing council finally decided to charge fees for entertaining them. But real self-sufficiency eluded them, and without real self-sufficiency how could they hope to regenerate the world?

At just the point when the Brook Farmers were longing to attract more members so that they could become truly self-sufficient, they were visited by proselytes for a new scheme of social regeneration. Albert Brisbane (1809–90), a well-to-do young New Yorker who had become a convert of the doctrines of the French social visionary Charles Fourier (1772–1837) during a six-year tour of European intellectual centers, had returned to America in 1834 determined to win converts to his master's doctrines. In the fall of 1840 he published *The Social Destiny of Man,* his own summary and exposition of Fourier's doctrines; it was one of the books Ripley had read when he was planning the Brook Farm Community. Brisbane also attracted the attention of New York publisher Horace Greeley (1811–72), who allowed him, for a fee of five hundred dollars, to write a front-page column in the New York *Tribune.* Brisbane's column, which ran from March of 1842 to September of 1843 and was titled "Association: or, Principles of a True Organization of Society," tried to suggest how Fourier's theories could be applied to American circumstances.

Fourier's voluminous writings aimed to explain how the economic misery of contemporary societies could be eliminated by reorganizing human living and working conditions completely. Instead of living in isolated houses and engaging in cutthroat economic competition that is as inefficient as it is cruel, people should be organized into "phalanxes" of 1,620 members. They would occupy a vast building called a "phalanstery," shaped like Versailles, which would contain everything necessary for human life. There carefully organized groups of laborers would raise food, manufacture needed objects, educate children, and provide arts and entertainment. Since Fourier believed that labor is made hateful through tedium, he argued that tasks should be broken down into shifts lasting no more than two or three hours, at which groups of laborers would never have to work until they were weary.

Such "attractive industry," where group replaced group in ordered succession, would provide material support for residents of phalansteries and would at the same time afford ample scope for the exercise of their passions, which Fourier tabulated with French precision: five "sensitive," four "affective," three "distibuting and directing." Because our passional attractions participate in a divine order, they therefore predict their own ultimate satisfaction; even apparent social disharmonies exist only to be resolved into a larger harmony. Indeed, Fourier was so strongly convinced of the correspondence between microcosm and macrocosm that he insisted that workers should form groups only in "harmonic" numbers – three, five, seven, or twelve. He believed that his discovery of the harmony of the passions deserved to be ranked with Newton's laws, and he expressed its fundamental law in the formula *Les attractions sont proportionelle aux destinées* (the attractions are proportional to the destinies). Life in the harmonious phalansteries would be so blissful that those outside would clamor to build phalansteries of their own, and soon the earth would be covered with a network of over two million interlocking and interconnected phalansteries, and a sixty thousand year period of creativity and happiness would commence.

It may seem odd that a doctrine so baroque in its complications and foreign in its terminology should ever have appealed to people in the United States. But Brisbane's proselytizing coincided with a period of severe economic stress and psychic dislocation. Many artisans were being displaced by the factory system, the economy seemed unable to recover from the disastrous crash of 1837, and recent immigrants to the cities often suffered from nostalgia for the more intimate world of the village and farm. Fourier claimed that his precise calculations were based upon social laws as immutable as the law of gravity. Suppose he were right? As many as thirty-five small phalanxes were formed in the United States during the 1840s.

Brisbane and Greeley visited Brook Farm during 1842 and 1843, urging

Ripley and others among the Brook Farmers to convert their community into a phalanx. By doing so Brook Farm could at once make itself more successful economically, attract members from a wider range of social classes, and offer hope to potential phalansterians still imprisoned within "civilization." The arguments sounded persuasive to the Brook Farmers, whose experiments so far had been mostly agricultural or educational rather than commercial, and who tended to underestimate the difficulties involved in the production of goods. Anna Russell, a well-traveled woman from a distinguished Boston family who had joined the association around 1843 and remained with it almost until the end, thought that the conversion to Fourierism was directly connected to naïveté about trade among the governing members: "Unused to commercial pursuits, the slow process so often needed to establish and successfully prosecute a business was to them a mystery; and I really believe that some of us thought that to place men in a workshop was sufficient to make our fortune."

The surviving documents from the Fourierist period that began roughly when Ripley and two associates drew up a new constitution for Brook Farm in 1844 make clear that far more was at stake than attracting more artisans in hopes of making a profit. Fourier's ambitions had been cosmic, and those of his American disciples were no less so. "Association" was meant to heal a wound in consciousness, even a wound in nature; Brisbane aimed (as one scholar put it) at nothing less than "the rehabilitation of the universe." In February 1844 John Sullivan Dwight, a Brook Farmer and former Unitarian minister, gave a lecture entitled "Association in Its Connection with Education" to the New England Fourierist Society. His lecture begins with an exposition of Fourierist theory and ends with an anguished cry from the heart, whose cadences Emerson himself would one day imitate.

We are harmonies; every man is a microcosm, or world in miniature, reflecting all the laws of all things; and each mortal child is as indispensable to the balance and completeness of the world into which he comes so small an atom, as is each planet in the system of our sun, or each sun in the celestial sphere, or each note in the great music of God. How comes it, then, that we clash? that our noblest aspirations prove our keenest misery? that we cannot put forth our hands to accept the promises of life without stealing food and joy from our neighbor? that we cannot seek our neighbor's good without being trampled under foot ourselves?"

If Fourier should be right, then these miseries will vanish when our children are gathered into phalanxes, laboring for one another's benefit rather than for one another's harm. Nor do we need to wait for these New Jerusalems to descend to us from heaven; we can start to build them now, and hasten that final consummation we so earnestly desire. Is it any wonder that Fourier displaced Kant and Schiller as the subject of Ripley's evening lectures? The Brook Farmers began to celebrate Fourier's birthday with festivities in which a bust of Fourier, flanked by azure tablets inscribed with "UNIVERSAL UNITY" and the motto *Les attractions sont proportionelle aux destinées,* presided over a room that also contained an inscription from the New Testament suggesting that the blessed Comforter would confirm the hopes of those who believe that association would bring down upon earth the kingdom of heaven. Someone even proposed the toast, "Fourier, the second coming of Christ."

Needless to say, this strange pasteboard-and-filigree religion did not appeal to everyone, nor did an exegesis of the works of Fourier much satisfy those who had preferred Kant and Schiller. Many of the original settlers did not choose to follow Ripley into the promised land of association, and some of the new working-class men and women who replaced them were markedly less willing to be gentrified than their predecessors had been. One student remembered that a group of "discontented mechanics" used to shout "Aristocrats!" as the Education Group passed by; things reached such a point of tension in January 1846 that Ripley had to threaten some residents with expulsion unless they stopped trying to create class conflict. For Anna Russell, such measures were fruitless as soon as they were thought necessary, for they proved that the old unity of heart was gone forever.

Still the exuberance of the old "Transcendental days," as the Brook Farmers themselves referred to the pre-phalanx association, did not wholly disappear. Fourier's frankly stated belief in pleasure as the end of human existence, though it gave rise among the "civilizees" to rumors of sexual license that damaged the school's ability to attract pupils, was friendly to the spirit of play that continued to enliven Brook Farm. And new members continued to fall in love with the joys of associated life.

A remarkable series of letters written during the later years of Brook Farm shows how much delight it still could generate. In 1844 a young woman named Marianne Dwight came to Brook Farm and began sending letters to Boston describing her experiences there back to her friend Anna Parsons and to her brother Frank. Marianne was the sister of John Sullivan Dwight, one of the original Brook Farmers and its teacher of music. Their parents and another sister were also Brook Farmers – Dr. John Dwight, the father, served as the group's doctor. It was natural that Marianne should feel a strong commitment to an enterprise in which her entire family was so deeply involved. Her sense of gratitude to Brook Farm produced a loyalty to it that never wavered throughout the darkest months of its existence, and her determination to record its life produced the only record we have of events written as they were happening during those last tumultuous years.

Women had more to gain from Brook Farm that anyone else, as John Codman argued in his own memoir.

It is often stated that the home circle is the sphere of women, but at times it is a very narrow circle — a very narrowing circle to its occupants. There are thousands who enter it as brilliant young ladies, and come from it at the end of a few years morbid, harassed, depressed; sunk in all the graces and powers that make a woman's life beautiful and distinct from a man's. The circle in many cases is so narrow that there is no room for growth.

At Brook Farm, in contrast, women were encouraged to expand and aspire, and they improved the opportunity. They were released from the isolation of the home; their labor was valued; there was even a Nursery Group designed to free women with small children for work elsewhere, or simply to give them temporary relief from the demands of child rearing. And women responded with devotion. Codman repeatedly praises the faithfulness of the Brook Farm women, their sacrifices and love of principle.

Marianne Dwight certainly proved herself capable of sacrifice and devotion. But she makes it clear that Brook Farm offered women something else — a sense of their own power. Marianne had been a teacher before coming to Brook Farm, but the association's chronic need for money prompted her to join with other women there in a "fancy group" devoted to making "elegant and tasteful caps, capes, collars, undersleeves, etc., etc." for sale in Boston shops. The experience of making money on her own triggered a frank and delightful explosion of feminism in her, along with a shrewd insight into the way liberation must be achieved.

In a letter to her friend Anna dated August 30, 1844, Marianne writes with amusement:

And now I must interest you in our fancy group, for which and from which I hope great things, — nothing less than the elevation of women to independence, and an acknowledged equality with man. Many thoughts on this subject have been struggling in my mind ever since I came to Brook Farm, and now, I think I see how it will all be accomplished. Women must become producers of marketable articles; women must make money and earn their support independently of man.

She sees what must be done: borrow some capital; purchase materials; turn out high-quality articles — the Boston distributors have already agreed to take all she can produce. When funds accumulate they may start other branches of business, but all proceeds (she swears) must be "applied to the elevation of women forever." She urges her friend to "take a spiritual view of the matter. Raise woman to be the equal of man, and what intellectual developments may we not expect? How the whole aspect of society will be changed! And this is the great work, is it not, that Association in its present early stage has to do?"

In fact Marianne did become a significant earner of capital for the association – her delicate watercolors of flowers and birds, painted onto lampshades and fans, sold so well that she was often painting eight hours a day. But Brook Farm proved to be a greedy consumer of all the capital she could generate, and the liberation of women had to be postponed (not for the last time in history) to the common good. Still, she was happy to have escaped women's ordinary lot among the "civilizees." To her brother she wrote, "For myself, I would not exchange this life for any I have ever led. I could not feel content with the life of isolated houses, and the conventions of civilization" (September 19, 1844).

Like Codman, Marianne Dwight is constantly entranced by the beauty all around her. The sight of the landscape after an ice storm makes her exclaim to Anna,

Oh, this day and yesterday! Was ever earth clad in such beauty? Would you were here to slide and coast over our hills of glistening white marble, – to admire the glitter-ing coral branches that border our paths, and the trees of crystal, of silver and of diamonds, that make magnificent this fairy palace. Have I seen such beauty in a former existence, – or is it the realization of some dream or fancy – that it continu-ally *reminds* me of something, I know not what?

Quite as fiercely as Emerson she scorns the notion that salvation must be achieved in a grim struggle with temptation; strength comes through happiness.

Look into your inner life. Did you ever feel that sorrow in itself gives you strength? Wasn't it rather an obstacle, an enemy, that, from some higher and happier source, some *hope* or *faith* or *joy* that was in you, you must draw strength to conquer? Have you not sometimes felt almost omnipotent from the impulse of some *joyful* emotion? (January 19, 1845)

The strength she got through hope Marianne wanted to devote to the cause of association, which was quite as holy an idea to her as it was to her brother John. In May 1845 she tells Anna:

The great doctrines of Association fire my soul every day more and more. I am awed at the vastness of the schemes it unfolds, I am filled with wonder and ecstasy. . . . A deep, solemn joy has taken possession of my soul, from the con-sciousness that there is something worth living for. In the hopes and views that the associative life has disclosed to me, I feel that I have a treasure that nothing can deprive me of. (May 19, 1845)

Nevertheless, conditions at Brook Farm were worsening. "Retrenchments" at the dinner table were called for so often that little was left to sacrifice. A kind neighbor had to supply the Thanksgiving turkeys; coffee and cakes put out for someone's wedding party seemed like unimaginable luxuries to the hungry Brook Farmers who clustered around the table. Throughout the grim autumn of 1845 and the outbreak of smallpox that affected twenty-six of the Brook Farmers in November (no one died, but two were severely scarred) Marianne tried to keep her hopes up. But by December 7 she is beginning to come to the same conclusion that Anna Russell had reached. Cautioning her friend to keep what she writes confidential, Marianne admits that Brook Farm has reached its severest crisis. "We are perplexed by debts, by want of capital to carry on any business, — by want of our Phalanstery or the means to finish it." The new building, started the preceding summer, was supposed to provide accommodations for fourteen families as well as for single people, but the construction costs were saddling the already strapped association with heavy debts, and the building was still less than half-finished when work had to stop for the winter. "I think here lies the difficulty, — we have not had business men to conduct our affairs — we have had *no* strictly business transaction from the beginning, and those among us who have some business talents, see this error, and feel that we cannot go on as we have done." A sad article by her brother John Sullivan Dwight in the November 1846 *Harbinger,* an associationist journal published at Brook Farm, imploring readers not to consider Brook Farm a failure "because in one point of view it has failed," already sounds like an epitaph.

Still, after a bleak winter things seemed to be looking up in the early spring of 1846. Sympathetic Fourierists were helping to raise money to complete the Phalanstery; work on it had begun again after the winter break. On the evening of March 1, 1846, most of the Brook Farmers decided to celebrate this renewal of hope with a dance. Suddenly someone broke in and shouted that fire had broken out in the Phalanstery. People seized buckets and ran in the direction of the fire, but the whole building was consumed in flames; they had all they could do to keep the surrounding buildings from going up in flames as well.

"Would I could convey to you an idea of it," Marianne wrote to her friend Anna three days after the fire. "I was glorious beyond description. . . . An immense, clear blue flame mingled for a while with the others and rose high in the air, — like liquid turquoise and topaz. It came from the melting glass. Rockets, too, rose in the sky, and fell in glittering gems of rainbow hue." All the onlookers were awed by the sublimity of the scene.

There was one moment, whilst the whole frame yet stood, that surpassed all else. It was fire throughout. It seemed like a magnificent temple of molten gold, or a crystallized fire. . . . The smoke as it settled off the horizon, gave the effect of sublime mountain scenery; and during the burning, the trees, the woods shone magically to their minutest twigs, in lead, silver, and gold. (March 4, 1846)

When John Codman ran to fetch buckets of water from the greenhouse where flowers were raised for the Boston trade he found the flowers there "lighted up with a heavenly glow of color, and so startlingly beautiful that in spite of my haste I lingered a moment to look on them. Roses and camellias, heaths and azaleas — whatever flowers there were in bloom looked superbly glorified in the transcendent light, and I uttered an exclamation of surprise at the lovely display." The fire lit up the sky for miles around. Crowds gathered from nearby towns, for the huge blaze was visible as far away as Boston. The Brook Farmers somehow contrived to feed two hundred of them on bread and cheese. Ripley even managed a few gallant jokes as he thanked the firemen who had driven out from Boston only to discover that their engines were useless.

No one wished to admit that the Phalanstery fire spelled the end of Brook Farm. But the financial loss had been severe — seven thousand dollars had been invested in the building, which was not insured. Though Ripley and his loyal supporters tried to keep the farm going through another summer and another winter, most people realized that the cause was lost. Brook Farmers began to drift away, so slowly that when Codman tried to remember it in later life the closing months of Brook Farm seemed "dreamy and unreal," like a skein of wool unraveling, or apple petals falling softly to the ground. In the spring of 1847 Ripley let the farm grounds for a year, and later on he and Sophia left Brook Farm for a furnished room in Flatbush, Brooklyn, where he tried to eke out a living by teaching school and by writing book reviews for Horace Greeley's *Tribune*. Sophia, seeking a firmer faith than association, converted to Roman Catholicism. Though Ripley eventually worked his way out of poverty, paid off the remaining Brook Farm debts, and became an influential literary critic in post-Civil War New York, he remained silent about his Brook Farm experiences — telling a friend who pressed him that he had not yet reached his "years of indiscretion." When Ripley reviewed *The Blithedale Romance* he contented himself with remarking that only the funny parts of the book would seem recognizable as portraits of the real Brook Farm to those who had actually been there.

For Marianne Dwight the sorrow of Brook Farm's end was tempered by private joy. On December 26, 1846, she had married John Orvis, a Brook Farmer who had been a tireless worker on the farm and a lecturer for association — a cause to which, in various forms, he devoted the rest of his life. That she and her husband were leaving together made her feel confident that the love of humanity she had learned at Brook Farm would continue strong in them, and neither feared poverty or hard work. Still, it saddened her to leave the place where she had been so happy. In her last letter from Brook Farm in March 1847 she writes that she hates to think of the greenhouse plants being sold off, and then, the Eve of this small Eden, gives way to momentary grief:

Oh! I love every tree and wood haunt – every nook and path, and hill and meadow. I fear the birds can never sing so sweetly to me elsewhere, – the flowers can never greet me so smilingly. I can hardly imagine that the same sky will look down upon me in any other spot, and where, where in the wide world shall I ever find warm hearts all around me again? Oh! you must feel with me that none but a Brook Farmer can know how chilling is the cordiality of the world.

Almost half a century later, Codman would remember his experience at Brook Farm with gratitude for the variety of his satisfactions there. "I had tasted of actual farm work. I had planted beans, potatoes, and melons. I had hoed corn, and on my knees weeded, in the broiling sun, the young onions. I had driven horse to plough, and side by side with others, trying to hoe my row with them, disputed, discussed social questions and ideas . . ." Had he been happy? "I loved the daily round of life. All were kind to me. I was well mentally and physically. I was in the bud of youth. I was like the pink rhodoras in spring, callow of leaf or fruit but brightly covered with promising blossoms. There remained one thing for me – to know I was happy. Did I know it? Yes, I did."

What lessons could be drawn from the collapse of Fruitlands and Brook Farm? For Emerson, the defeat of so much hope testified to the irreconcilability of the world of desire and the world of actuality. In the essay "Montaigne" he writes Brook Farm's epitaph: "Charles Fourier announced that 'the attractions of man are proportioned to his destinies;' in other words, that every desire predicts its own satisfaction. Yet all experience exhibits the reverse of this; the incompetency of power is the universal grief of young and ardent minds." Every man was born with a raging hunger, an appetite that could eat the solar system like a cake, yet as soon as he tried his strength, his senses gave way and refused to serve him. "He was an emperor deserted by his states, and left to whistle by himself, or thrust into a mob of emperors, all whistling, and still the sirens sang, 'The attractions are proportioned to the destinies.' "

A younger person, however, might draw a different conclusion. Although Thoreau's own (still unpublished) Amory Hall lecture in 1844 had been quite as passionate as Emerson's in rejecting collective solutions to the problem of reform, his aim was not so much to reject the project of reform as to transform it into a personal quest. In the lecture Thoreau scorned most reforms as death presuming to give laws to life, and suggested that the sun, who does most of his reforming in the spring, was the kind of reformer we ought to emulate. The trouble with Fourier was that he wanted more civilization; Thoreau wants less. Only in Nature is there hope and freedom, and only when we are rooted in her soil can we spring again refreshed.

The cabin Thoreau built on Emerson's new property at Walden Pond in the spring of 1845 and the life he lived there for the next two years sought to combine the best features of the two communities Thoreau was most familiar with while avoiding the mistakes that destroyed them. Like the Fruitlanders, he was a vegetarian and devoted to cold-water bathing. (He was also celibate, something John Lane believed in but never persuaded Alcott to agree to.) Like the Brook Farmers, Thoreau believed in the principle of "attractive industry," in the healthful alternation of mental and physical labor, in joyous recreation, even in obsessive punning. He was free of the personal and ideological squabbling that had split Fruitlands, free of the class tensions that had marred Brook Farm. Thoreau built the only successful phalanx in America: a phalanx for one. What would he later say he had learned?

I learned this, at least, by my experiment; that if one advances confidently in the direction of his dreams, and endeavors to live the life which he has imagined, he will meet with a success unexpected in common hours. He will put some things behind, will pass an invisible boundary; new, universal, and more liberal laws will begin to establish themselves around and within him. . . . In proportion as he simplifies his life, the laws of the universe will appear less complex, and solitude will not be solitude, nor poverty poverty, nor weakness weakness. If you have built castles in the air, your work need not be lost; that is where they should be. Now put the foundations under them. (*Walden,* "Conclusion")

8

DIASPORA

THE 1840S WITNESSED the slow fragmentation of the Transcendentalist movement and the departure of its members upon paths of their
own. The last meeting of the Transcendental Club was probably the
meeting held in September 1840. *The Dial* ceased publication in 1844. The
members of the group continued to meet and talk with one another, to write
letters to one another, to attend one another's lectures, and to read one
another's books; but they had begun to break into smaller groups defined by
interest, personal affection, or ideology and to regard one another with
friendly curiosity rather than with feelings of solidarity. Some of them returned to the Boston area after years of exile; others departed from it on long
journeys. Some remained within the Unitarian church (two even become
professors at the Harvard Divinity School); some left it for other religions or
for a "church of the future" they hoped would materialize. Most found
themselves being drawn into one of the practical reform movements of the
day – association, prison reform, opposition to the Mexican War, antislavery. Two witnessed the European revolutions of 1848, for Emerson crossed
the channel from England to witness the celebrations on the Champ de Mars
during the French uprising, and Margaret Fuller ran a hospital during the
siege of Rome.

Convers Francis slid gently from his position as the elder statesman among
the Transcendentalists (he was five years older than Alcott, eight years older
than Emerson) to a Harvard professorship. Francis had been ordained as
minister to a congregation at Watertown in 1819 and remained in that post
until he was invited to become professor of pulpit eloquence and pastoral care
at the Divinity School in 1842. Although he was one of the charter members
of the Transcendental Club, serving as its moderator when he was in attendance, and was a friend and mentor of Theodore Parker, he had no desire to
leave the Unitarian church, but rather sought to accentuate its historic
preference for the moral over the dogmatic, for internal principles rather than
for rituals or forms. When the club met in early September 1840 to discuss
"the organization of a new church," Francis joined Frederic Henry Hedge and
another member in supporting the existing Unitarian Association, despite

Theodore Parker's complaint that they were wedded to the past and Emerson's stronger charge that such distrust of the divine soul amounted to atheism.

If Francis could not follow Emerson in all of his flights, he still remained one of Emerson's sincerest admirers. In his journals he left a vivid account of the exhilaration he felt at Emerson's lectures, where the speaker seemed less a speaker than like the place from which truth radiated. If he had any criticism to make, it was that Emerson's lectures contained such a "succession of the best things in condensed sentences, that we can scarcely *remember* any of them" (January 9, 1839). Or, as Francis complained elsewhere, "I find that his best things are *slippery,* and will not stay in my mind" (February 16, 1837).

Francis attended the Divinity School Address and heard not a blasphemous tract but a discourse "full of divine life." Its accuracy and even its humor in portraying the "downfallen state of the church" Francis appreciated, and though he did not agree with everything Emerson said in the discourse he did not think that Emerson valued Jesus less than other people did, merely that he valued humanity more (Francis to Frederic Henry Hedge, August 10, 1838). The subsequent outbreak of wrath after that address he attributed to the long-smoldering jealousy felt by the *dii majores* of the pulpits and Divinity School against Emerson because of his popularity among the "brightest young people" (Francis to Frederic Henry Hedge, November 12, 1838).

Another first-generation Transcendentalist was blunter than Francis at expressing dismay about the direction the movement was taking in the 1840s. Hedge's 1833 article on Coleridge had been one of the early manifestos of Transcendentalism, and his June 1836 letter to Emerson had been instrumental in getting the Transcendental Club started. But he had never been as enthusiastic a believer in the newness as some of his fellow club members, and his constitutional tendency to value old institutions and traditional practices set him apart from those who, as he later remembered, "saw in every case of dissent, and in every new dissentient, the harbinger of the New Jerusalem." "My historical conscience, then as since, balanced my neology, and kept me ecclesiastically conservative, though intellectually radical" ("The Destinies of Ecclesiastical Religion," 1867). At one of the last meetings of the Transcendental Club in September 1840 he stoutly defended the American Unitarian Association against attacks by Parker, Ripley, Fuller, and Emerson.

Hedge's congregation in Bangor, Maine (where he was pastor from 1835–50), was a difficult team to drive, containing as it did both "*ultra* liberal" and "*ultra* conservative" factions, and at one point he offered to resign his position there because he was aware that some conservatives, doubting his orthodoxy, were trying to unseat him. At the same time, he was alarmed by what seemed to him the real skepticism underlying Transcendentalist radicalism. In a letter to his good friend Convers Francis in 1843 he complained that Emerson and Parker were publicly advancing doctrines that had been considered infamous a few years ago when associated with names like Fanny Wright or Tom Paine. Worse still were the social radicals, "that numerous class of persons, with large ideas & small faculty, who have not obtained what they covet from existing institutions & who think they shall find their account in a general overturn." Radicals trying to escape human evil reminded him of dogs with tin pots tied to their tails.

When Margaret Fuller wrote to Hedge in 1840 urging him to submit something to *The Dial,* he refused politely. When she pressed him, he admitted that he did not wish to be publicly identified with the Transcendentalists lest he be considered "an atheist in disguise." The same anxiety wells up in a letter he wrote to Convers Francis in February 1843. Francis had recently resigned his Watertown pastorate to accept a position at the Harvard Divinity School, a move Hedge encouraged. But Hedge feared that their friendship would suffer, as Francis would no longer feel free to enjoy genial "pernoctations and confumations" with someone who had "incurred the stigma of transcendental & heretical tendencies. . . . There is a rigid, cautious, circumspect, conservative *tang* in the air of Cambridge which no one, who had resided there for any considerable time can escape."

Yet Hedge was certainly not a conservative in other respects. He reacted with derision when he learned that Andrews Norton had recently stormed out of a sermon advocating religious liberty. "What stronger proof could he give of being pricked in his conscience? . . . The professor actually grows antic as the new age advances. 'And wroth to see his Kingdom fail / Swinges the scaly horror of his folded tail' " (Hedge to Convers Francis, January 26, 1842). Hedge remained true to what he thought were the central doctrines of Transcendentalism – the belief that human beings could perceive truth intuitively, and the hope that every genuine reform is "a step in that progressive incarnation of divine attributes in humankind, which illustrates and fulfills the prophetic prayer of Christ, 'that they all may be one in us.' "

Hedge's opinions on social questions were similarly complex. He considered himself a conservative, and condemned socialism as amoral, irreligious, and "grovelling." But he joined the Cambridge Anti-Slavery Society as early as 1834 and delivered an address the next year on emancipation in the British West Indies (nine years before Emerson did). After the passage of the Fugitive Slave Law in 1850, Hedge fully endorsed the use of force to rescue fugitive slaves from southern slavehunters who had tracked them down, arguing that a mob was better than the enforcement of an unjust law. He advocated women's suffrage and women's right to pursue at least certain careers outside the home. (He thought women might be doctors, for instance, so long as they treated only their own sex.) In 1866 he delivered an important address at Harvard urging replacement of the hated recitation system with an elective system in which the student's choice of material to study would be "self-determined."

He remained on friendly terms with his old associates and even relented about writing for *The Dial,* though most of his contributions were translations. He wrote a discerning review of Emerson's second book of essays (*Essays, Second Series*) for the *Christian Examiner* in 1845, objecting to Emerson's theology but praising the essay "Experience" as the best piece in the book and likening it to Ecclesiastes in its movement from doubt to affirmation. (He also spoke admiringly of "New England Reformers," probably because Emerson's skepticism about reform movements in that address matched his own.)

In 1858 Hedge joined the faculty of the Harvard Divinity School as a professor of ecclesiastical history; in the same year, he became the editor of the *Christian Examiner,* a position he held for three years. In 1859 he began a four-year term as president of the American Unitarian Association. *Reason in Religion,* his major theological work, which one scholar has called "the definitive statement of mainstream or moderate Transcendentalism," appeared in 1865.

Like Francis and Hedge, Theodore Parker and James Freeman Clarke chose to remain within the Unitarian church. But Parker and Hedge insisted upon trying to transform it radically. Parker's innovations were forced upon him by the reaction within his own denomination to the furor aroused by both "The Discourse of the Transient and Permanent in Christianity" and the ambitious *Discourse of Matters Pertaining to Religion* (1842). Although his own small congregation in West Roxbury had remained loyal to him throughout the controversy, most of his fellow Unitarian ministers refused to exchange pulpits with him — some out of a genuine belief that what Parker was preaching could no longer be considered Christianity and others because they feared the obloquy they would suffer if they allowed him in their pulpits. Even Convers Francis, who had been his friend and mentor, withdrew from a scheduled pulpit exchange on the advice of a colleague at the Divinity School, though he later mustered enough courage to supply Parker's Roxbury pulpit when Parker was in Europe.

The cost of befriending Parker could be severe. In December 1845, when a young minister named John T. Sargent invited Parker to preach at his Suffolk Street Chapel, a Unitarian "mission" chapel overseen by the Benevolent Fraternity of Churches, the officers of the Benevolent Fraternity rebuked Sargent so sternly that he felt obliged to resign his position. In January of the next year when James Freeman Clarke invited Parker to exchange pulpits, fifteen of the wealthiest and most prominent members of Clarke's congregation left his society.

Parker could glory in abuse heaped upon himself, but watching his few courageous supporters suffer for their allegiance to him was another matter. If he were to continue to preach outside of Roxbury it would have to be by other means than pulpit exchanges. Accordingly, in January 1845 a group of Parker's admirers met to pass a single resolution: "That the Rev. Theodore Parker have a chance to be heard in Boston." They engaged to rent space for him in a building quite as unorthodox as his preaching. The Boston Melodeon was a dirty theatrical hall, freezing cold in winter, roasting in summer, redolent with the scents of the variety acts that played there during the week — dancing monkeys, minstrel shows, acrobats. Parker noted in his farewell sermon there in 1852 that he often had looked down when he was preaching upon the spangles left by opera dancers who had performed on the stage the previous night.

But the society was open to all. There were no pews to purchase, no weekly collection (the expenses of the society, including Parker's own salary, were paid by subscriptions). Parker was a powerful and effective preacher, and he now felt free to let out all the length of his reins — to denounce, to uplift, to venerate, or to beseech, just as the spirit moved him. Before long he was drawing a congregation not only from all parts of the city but also from the surrounding suburban towns. By November 1845 there were enough members in Parker's church to organize themselves as the Twenty-Eighth Congregational Society of Boston; eventually his parish register contained seven *thousand* names (the largest congregation in Boston, possibly even in the United States). William Lloyd Garrison and Samuel May were members of the Twenty-Eighth, for Parker became increasingly vocal as a critic of slavery. In 1852 the growth of the congregation necessitated a move to the Boston Music Hall, an ample space illuminated from above by a row of gas jets in a way that reminded one visitor of Milton's Pandemonium.

James Freeman Clarke, though younger than Parker, was far more conservative theologically: He believed in miracles, in Christ's supernatural character and mediatorial role, and in the depravity of humanity and the consequent need for a Redeemer. In fact, when Parker's *Discourse of Matters Pertaining to Religion* had appeared in 1842, Clarke published a review denouncing it as "the new gospel of shallow naturalism." Nonetheless, Clarke refused to cancel pulpit exchanges with Parker even though some members of his congregation were upset with his decision, and he spoke out vigorously against the growing tendency among Unitarians to deny the free speech that they had so long regarded as sacred. When he persisted in his determination to exchange with Parker in 1845, the church members held a meeting at which they tried to persuade Clarke to cancel. Clarke remained unmoved. He stated that he was now determined to exchange with Parker even if *Parker* refused. The attempt to crush heresies had destroyed the Roman church and was now paralyzing the Protestant one. Free discussion was the only principle of union that could save it. "I think in this question is involved the question whether hereafter there shall be any Church of Christ on earth."

Clarke's bravery is all the more commendable because he, too, was experimenting with an unorthodox form of church organization. He had come back from Louisville in 1840 dismayed by the bitter rifts within Unitarianism but even more by the lifelessness that seemed to pervade church services. The spiritual distress of the congregants, who looked up like hungry sheep but were not fed, made Clarke determined to found a new kind of church, one in which the members would be bound together by the desire to grow in spiritual perfection rather than by common ownership of a meetinghouse, one in which anyone who wished to could take communion, and one in which the congregation would take an active part in the life of the church — by singing hymns and reading aloud devotional psalms during the Sunday services, by meeting in evening discussion groups or in Bible study groups, and by performing charitable work among the Boston poor. He thought that there were enough discontented worshippers in Boston to form this new church, and in early 1841 he rented a chapel for three evenings in order to preach three sermons that would set forth his own ideas of religion and attract potential worshippers.

Clarke's plan succeeded. By mid-February Clarke had met with a group willing to form a new church. They rented Amory Hall for the Sunday services and began to organize the evening discussion groups. By 1845 there were over two hundred active members in Clarke's Church of the Disciples, enough to force a move to larger quarters in the Masonic Temple. Weekly attendance could run as high as seven hundred. Even the crisis caused by Clarke's refusal to cancel his exchange with Theodore Parker, though it weakened his church financially for a time, failed to stop its growth or damage Clarke's reputation. In May 1845 he was elected to the Executive Board of the American Unitarian Association.

Yet if Francis, Hedge, and Clarke were becoming more firmly entrenched in Unitarianism and Parker was remaining as a kind of spectacular gadfly buzzing around it, another onetime member of the Transcendental Club was about to leave both Unitarianism and Transcendentalism behind. Throughout the early 1840s Orestes Brownson had become increasingly troubled with the view of the world he had worked out in the previous decade. The Transcendentalists had angered him by their misty refusals to face the reality of social injustice. But in 1840 the laboring classes whose interests he had tried to defend in his *Boston Quarterly Review* essays abandoned him to vote for (and elect) the Whig candidate for president, William Henry Harrison, whereas the Democratic party that he had embraced treated him as an embarrassment. As Brownson's biographer points out, such folly and ingratitude made it more and more difficult for him to believe that "the People" were the incarnation of God's spirit. "They could not be close to Him; they must therefore be divorced from Him; they could not be basically virtuous, they must therefore be basically corrupt." And if they were corrupt, the old Unitarian and Transcendentalist project of self-culture was a doomed enterprise, as impossible as a man's trying to lift himself up by his own waistband.

The world could be redeemed only through an infusion of grace. Logically, this conclusion might have pushed Brownson back in the direction of Edwardsean Calvinism, but he had grown increasingly distrustful of the egotism and isolation he thought Protestantism fostered, and Jonathan Edwards's eventual rejection by his own church in Northampton showed the danger of trying to channel grace through the fractiousness of the Congregational parish. Even as far back as his 1836 tract *New Views of Christianity, Society and the Church* Brownson had expressed a theory of history that identified spirituality with the medieval Catholic church and materialism with Protestantism. At that time he had seen Unitarianism as the reconciling term. Now, with Unitarianism found wanting in his eyes, Brownson began to be drawn toward the one church that could claim an unbroken line of succession from the time of the Apostles.

By the spring of 1843 friends began to hear rumors that Brownson was considering conversion to Catholicism, rumors that seemed to be confirmed when he had a brief interview with the Roman Catholic bishop of Boston. For a while Brownson resisted taking the final step. But by July 1844 he believed he had no legitimate reasons for delay. "Our logic allows us no alternative between Catholicism and Come-outerism," he announced, "and we have tried Come-outerism." He began taking instruction, and on October 20, 1843, he formally embraced the Roman Catholic faith. He began a new version of his old quarterly review (which had ceased publication in 1842). The new review was called *Brownson's Quarterly Review,* and Brownson used it to lambaste his former friends in the Transcendentalist movement, threatening them with eternal damnation unless they followed him into the Roman church immediately. They took it calmly enough. James Freeman Clarke merely observed: "No man has ever equalled Mr. Brownson in the ability with which he has refuted his own arguments."

Brownson's chief convert among the Transcendentalists was Sophia Dana Ripley, George Ripley's wife. Sophia had supported her husband throughout years of controversy and disappointment in his ministry; she had been a tireless worker at Brook Farm, even nursing one of the Filipino students through a gruesome attack of leprosy until her own health almost broke down. Emerson said after a visit to Brook Farm that he had never seen her so much to advantage. But she was unable to share her husband's enthusiasm for the conversion of Brook Farm to a Fourierist phalanx; the cause of association, which had filled Marianne Dwight with such joy, left Sophia Ripley unsatisfied and filled with doubts. When Brownson began coming out to Brook Farm to talk to the small community of Catholics there Sophia joined the group, and she soon began going into Boston for Catholic services. In 1846 she became a convert to Catholicism. After Brook Farm had collapsed and the Ripleys had moved to New York she lived a life of intense Catholic piety, devoting much of her time to prayer and to charitable works and concerning herself particularly with New York's large population of prostitutes. She helped raise the money to build a shelter, the Convent of the Good Shepherd, and served on its board of trustees. But George, though he occasionally accompanied his wife to Catholic services, never joined her in her new faith.

If Emerson paid much attention to the controversies in which his former associates were embroiled during the early 1840s, he must have believed that the wisdom of his own decision in the preceding decade to cut all ties with institutions had been amply confirmed. Hedge's unbecoming timidity, Francis's temporary lapse from moral courage, Parker's bitterness and disillusionment, Clarke's battles with his congregation over pulpit exchanges, Brownson's noisy proselytizing – all of these irritants Emerson had escaped by his decision to leave the church, join no party, and form no alliance more binding than any one he might make when he agreed to deliver a lecture series at this hall or that lyceum. Because he never asked his friends for their support he could not be hurt by their defections; because he claimed no authority for his statements except the authority his hearers or readers were willing to concede to them he need not worry whether he was shocking or offending people. They were at liberty to walk out of the lecture hall or throw his books in the fire the minute they were displeased; and in their freedom he found his own.

Emerson's horror of association has brought him into disfavor with modern readers, and he later came to repent that his shrinking from organized reform had kept him out of the antislavery movement far longer than he should have allowed it to. But he had all around him proofs of the vexatiousness of attempting to achieve anything through institutions. Brook Farm, Fruitlands, and the Unitarian squabbles of the 1840s were object lessons in the folly of attempting to reform the world by changing the behavior of people. If Emerson (and Thoreau) kept insisting on the need for *self*-emancipation, even to the point of arguing that evils as recalcitrant as slavery would somehow melt away before the righteousness of a few redeemed souls, it should be remembered also how few examples of success from associated action they had actually witnessed.

At the end of the essay "Experience" Emerson says that he had not found much that was gained by "manipular attempts to realize the world of thought." The people who try it "acquire democratic manners, they foam at the mouth, they hate and deny. Worse, I observe, that, in the history of mankind, there is never a solitary example of success, — taking their own tests of success." In the book *Poems,* which he published on Christmas Day 1846, Emerson included "Ode," inscribed to W. H. Channing, the unofficial Brook Farm chaplain and an enthusiast for most kinds of organized reform. The poem begins with a compliment to Channing and an apologia for Emerson's refusal to connect himself with any movement, ecclesiastical or political. "Though loath to grieve / The evil time's sole patriot / I cannot leave / My honied thought / For the priest's cant, / Or the Statesman's rant." No amount of reforming activity — not even joining in Garrison's famous cry "No Union with Slaveholders" and rending the northern states from the south — would make the commonwealth virtuous as long as it remained devoted to the protection of property (as all commonwealths are). "Boston Bay and Bunker Hill / Would serve things still; / Things are of the snake."

This mood of bitterness, brought on partly by the spectacle of the war President James K. Polk had recently declared on Mexico, surfaces in Emerson whenever he considers the increasingly squalid political situation in the United States. But bitterness is not his dominant mood. Indeed, while many of his former colleagues were embroiled in controversy or entangled in collapsing utopian schemes, Emerson was radiating a new sense of confidence. Although his "calling" of itinerant lecturer, journal editor, and mentor to the young might have seemed eccentric to a Boston banker, it *was* a calling and not merely a condition of alienation from society. He deposited his thoughts in his "savings bank," as he called his journals, and withdrew the interest in the form of lectures and essays. As for the banker, was not he too bought and sold? He built his countinghouse on Quincy granite, but the web of credit and speculation that supported him was no less a creation of the human imagination than the *Orlando Furioso,* and he himself was as subject to ecstasies, panics, and despairs as was any heroine of romance.

When it came time to consider possible lecture topics for the 1845–6 season, then, Emerson turned to a more inclusive look at the human condition. Unitarian humanism had always delighted to contemplate in Jesus the perfect man, though Emerson, in his youth, had refused to concur in the estimation. Now he begins to fill his journal with praises of an imagined being he calls "the central man," a Jesus without local or historical limitations, as the Oversoul is a Jehovah without personality and without wrath (though inaccessible and silent as the Sphinx). Emerson imagines the "varying play of his features" as the central man's face dissolves into a series of faces famous for either genius or sanctity – Socrates, Shakespeare, Raphael, Michaelangelo, Dante, Jesus.

There are limitations, however, to the attractions of a composite Redeemer. Instead, Emerson is drawn toward another model of human perfection, one he had adumbrated in "Nominalist and Realist" when he had said that Jesus would absorb the race unless Tom Paine or some other coarse blasphemer "helps humanity by resisting this exuberance of power." Here the model is not religious (as in the different incarnations of Vishnu) but federal, a question of checks and balances. "The sanity of society is a balance of a thousand insanities." This model evokes another one, possibly suggested to Emerson by a treatise he had read at Harvard on the marvelous construction of the human hand, considered as evidence of the Creator's wisdom. In March 1845 Emerson wrote in his journal: "I have found a new subject, *On the uses of great men.*" A book written on this subject should begin with "a chapter *on the distribution of the hand into fingers,* or on the great value of these individuals as counterweights, checks on each other." Great men *incarnate* various attributes of divinity; their differences *protect* us from excessive reverence for any one variety of incarnation; together they help us *grasp* some aspect of reality otherwise unreachable.

When Emerson received an invitation from the Boston Lyceum in August 1845 to deliver a course of lectures the next winter he hesitated; he liked being an independent lecturer, beholden to no one. But the prospect of being freed from the labor of hiring the hall and selling the tickets was tempting, and Emerson accepted the offer. The course of seven lectures known as "Representative Men" that he began in Boston on December 11, 1845, and repeated in many places during the next three years were revised into a book that was finally published on January 1, 1850.

The opening essay in the book, "The Uses of Great Men," sets the volume's tone. Some sentences from "Nominalist and Realist" might serve as its motto: "We want the great genius only for joy: for one more star in our constellation, for one more tree in our grove." Emerson opens by reminding us that all mythology begins with demigods, and then he explains why this should be so. Demigods, heroes, and great men "satisfy expectation"; they answer the questions we have not the skill to put. Then too, they are representative; they "serve us in the intellect" by embodying particular ideas. In their varying lives we find imaginative compensation for the poverty of our single existence; we are "multiplied by our proxies." For great men represent us not only as symbols represent ideas, but also as congressmen represent constituencies, with an authority that derives from the multitudes, not from the skies. We need great men to redress our imperfections and inspire our efforts, but as we grow we discard hero after hero. "Once they were angels of knowledge, and their figures touched the sky. Then we drew near, saw their means, culture, and limits; they yielded their place to other geniuses." Eventually we will cease to search for greatness in particular men at all, seeing heroes only as "exponents of a vaster mind and will."

Plato, Emerson's first representative man, is the easiest to praise, for he himself tried to dissolve existence back into essence at every turn. He was exactly poised between the world of eternal unity and the world of order and discriminations, in love both with vastness and with limit. Best of all, he brought the good news that these worlds are linked, corresponding to one another in a way that makes reality knowable. Emerson imagines him as saying,

I give you joy, O sons of men! that truth is altogether wholesome; that we have hope to search out what might be the self of everything. The misery of man is to be baulked of the sight of essence and stuffed with conjectures; but the supreme good is reality, the supreme beauty is reality; and all virtue and knowledge depend upon this science of the real.

If Plato has a defect, it is merely that his writings are of excessively literary or intellectual character and hence lack the authority that the Arab and Jewish prophets possess. But all our philosophies are "drift boulders" that have rolled down from his primeval mountain.

From this high tableland of praise we descend into a valley of abuse. "Swedenborg, or the Mystic" presents a figure whom Emerson had once considered an angel of knowledge but who now is discredited. Swedenborg was an eighteenth-century natural scientist of vast ambition who experienced in midlife a mystical illumination that revealed to him the heavens and the hells and suggested to him a method for unlocking the meaning of the Scripture through symbolical interpretation. Emerson still praises Swedenborg as a natural scientist, particularly for his grand unifying vision that tries to tie together the smallest phenomena of nature with the greatest, as when he revealed that the globule of blood gyrates around its own axis exactly like the planet in the sky. "His varied and solid knowledge of the world makes his style lustrous with points and shooting spicula of thought, and resembling one of those winter mornings when the air sparkles with crystals."

Swedenborg's theological works are another matter. Written in language borrowed from the foreign mythology of the ancient Hebrew religion, Swedenborg's books turn the "warm many-weathered passionate-peopled world" into a gloomy "grammar of hieroglyphs or an emblematic free-mason's procession." His hells are nightmares of filth and corruption, vindictive as Dante's but without imagination. His heaven is frivolous – "a *fête champêtre*, an evangelical picnic, or French distribution of prizes to virtuous peasants." Even the beloved doctrine of "correspondence," which to the young Emerson had seemed a possible key to the meaning of nature, is now dismissed with contempt as unworthy of serious consideration: "A horse signifies carnal understanding; a tree, perception; the moon, faith; a cat means this; an ostrich that; an artichoke, this other."

After the airless universe of the Swedenborg essay, it is a relief to emerge once again into the generosity and urbanity of "Montaigne, or the Skeptic." Montaigne, whom Emerson had loved since his young manhood, stands on the boundary between the world of sensation and the world of morals, but he attempts neither to link them in a scale of knowables (in the manner of Plato) nor to translate one into the other through a dictionary of correspondences (in the manner of Swedenborg). Instead he is there to consider, to weigh; his coat of arms is the balance, his motto "Que sçais je?"; his method an abstention from dogmatizing: "There is much to say on all sides." What prevents this openness from becoming confused with vacillation is Montaigne's own unquestioned probity and hatred of pretense. He enjoys with gusto and writes with utter frankness, and he is the representative of that midworld Emerson had praised in "Experience" and was increasingly coming to value as he reached his own middle age.

Yet even the good sense of Montaigne is finally found wanting in the face of the terrible ferocity of human desire. The end of "Montaigne, or the Skeptic" contains the best description of that desire to be found anywhere in Emerson's writings; that it occurs toward the close of an essay devoted to the joys of temperance suggests why even that venerable solution is helpless to satisfy:

The incompetency of power is the universal grief of young and ardent minds. They accuse the divine Providence of a certain parsimony. It has shown the heaven and earth to every child, and filled him with a desire for the whole; a desire raging, infinite, a hunger as of space to be filled with planets; a cry of famine as of devils for souls.

Art might assuage the hunger for perfection that experience leaves unsatisfied, but neither of the artists Emerson surveys in *Representative Men* quite escapes from his inherited distrust of art as frivolous. Shakespeare, for instance, gets a considerable praise for being the first poet in the world to have mastered the trick of "perfect representation": "Things were mirrored in his poetry without loss or blur; he could paint the fine with precision, the great with compass; the tragic and the comic indifferently, and without any distortion or favour" ("Shakespeare, or the Poet"). Like Daguerre, whose invention for fixing visible images had been announced to the world only six years before Emerson gave his lectures, Shakespeare had learned to make images with absolute fidelity, "and now let the world of figures sit for their portraits." But in the end this miraculous power is used for entertainment alone. With a power of illustration and an understanding of human character that might have done honor to a Hebrew prophet, Shakespeare was content to be a successful actor and playwright only, "master of the revels to mankind."

Goethe, the only modern writer with anything like Shakespeare's comprehensiveness, leaves Emerson even less satisfied. Emerson had never really caught Margaret Fuller's passionate love of Goethe, even though he cribbed many points from her brilliant two-part article on him in *The Dial* for his own essay, "Goethe, or the Writer." Although he praises Goethe for introducing to "Old England" and New England a novel idea – "that a man exists for Culture; not for what he can accomplish, but for what can be accomplished in him" – Emerson ultimately finds this idea wanting. "Goethe can never be dear to men. His is not even devotion to pure truth, but to truth for the sake of culture." This charge resembles Orestes Brownson's complaint about Goethe, Carlyle, *and* Emerson in his review of the Divinity School Address – that all three make "self" the highest aim, that "the highest good they recognize is the realization of order in their own individual souls" – resembles it so closely, in fact, that we must assume the accusation still rankled.

Still, Brownson's insistences that the individual must work to realize universal order, not just order in his or her soul, hit Emerson at what was always his most sensitive spot. He was not laboring in the Unitarian vineyard, like Francis, Hedge, and Clarke, nor proselytizing among the masses, like Parker; he was not constructing a phalanstery, like Ripley, nor even a cabin by a pond, like Thoreau. His 1844 address on emancipation in the British West Indies, however warmly it had been welcomed in Concord, was hardly likely to bring the slave power to its knees. What would it be like to possess power and to wield it effectively?

"Napoleon, or the Man of the World" is Emerson's longest sustained meditation on this topic. Though it is placed second-to-last in both the lecture series and the book, it was the first to be written; Emerson was delivering it as a separate lecture as early as April 1845. Emerson's Napoleon is neither the titanic hero of Romantic mythology nor the demon of Federalist propaganda, but a man whose spontaneity has all the characteristics of genius except its intimate relation to the moral law. Napoleon is an example of "the powers of intellect without conscience" and as such is – sad to say – the most truly representative hero of the book, "the agent or attorney of the Middle Class of modern society," that energetic, industrious, unscrupulous class that runs America as it ran France.

Napoleon had brilliance, courage, tenacity, and freedom from cant, and when we read of his victories we feel encouraged and liberated. Yet the absence of any moral principle in his aims or acts rendered him at last as forgettable as the vapid hereditary monarchs he dispossessed. "All passed away, like the smoke of his artillery, and left no trace. He left France smaller, poorer, feebler than he found it." And in his defeat we can read our own future fate. "As long as our civilization is essentially one of property, of fences, of exclusiveness, it will be mocked by delusions. Our riches will leave us sick, there will be bitterness in our laughter, and our wine will burn our mouth."

The lecture series "Representative Men" was a success, at least if contemporary accounts can be trusted. Convers Francis wrote to Frederic Henry Hedge on January 12, 1846, to report that Emerson was lecturing "with all his usual charm & power." But Emerson himself felt tired at the end of the course. He needed new sources of inspiration, and when a letter arrived from an old acquaintance named Alexander Ireland inviting him to lecture in England he considered the invitation seriously. He was worried that his fame was not sufficiently great to attract an audience that would make the trip worthwhile to him, and he dreaded having his English friends trying to collect an audience for him by "puffing & coaxing" (Emerson to Ireland, February 28, 1847). But Ireland persisted, and Emerson finally agreed to make the British tour. Lidian asked Henry Thoreau to live in the house again while Emerson was away, and he accepted, though the move put an end to his two-year residence at Walden Pond.

On October 5, 1847, Emerson set sail from Boston to Liverpool on the packet ship *Washington Irving*, auspiciously named after the first nineteenth-century American author to win wide popularity in England. At first Emerson's lecturing was limited to Manchester and Liverpool, but he soon expanded it to Nottingham, Derby, and a dozen other towns in the manufacturing regions of England. (Most of the lectures were from the recent series "Representative Men," though he found time to write new ones as well.) Emerson was fascinated by the wealth of the island, by the beefy, self-confident air of the people; but he also noticed the pollution caused by industry and the desperate poverty of an underclass shut out from the wealth that encircled it.

To his surprise and amusement, Emerson found himself a social lion courted by the fashionable and famous, despite the fact that he still considered himself a "parlor Erebus" and dreaded evening parties. In Edinburgh, where he had traveled in February 1848, he met Lord Jeffrey, whose *Edinburgh Review* had filled him with such delight twenty years earlier; Robert

Chambers, whose treatise on evolution, *Vestiges of Creation,* excited him with its proposed solution to the mystery of human origins; and the seventy-year-old Thomas De Quincey, who walked the ten miles from his cottage through a rainstorm to have dinner with him. Emerson then went west to the Lake District, where he called upon Wordsworth once again and went horseback riding with Harriet Martineau. When he reached London he enjoyed the meetings Carlyle had arranged for him with people such as the historian Thomas Macaulay and the geologist Charles Lyell. He met and charmed Crabb Robinson and visited Oxford as the guest of a young admirer named Arthur Hugh Clough.

Emerson's round of brilliant socializing was taking place against a backdrop of revolutionary unrest in England and on the Continent. In France the corrupt, inefficient regime of Louis Philippe, which had planted itself firmly on the side of material interests and had opposed every kind of reform, collapsed in the face of a popular insurrection on February 24, 1848. Louis Philippe abdicated and fled to London; the poet Lamartine proclaimed the restoration of the Republic, and a provisional government dominated by moderate republicans was established. But a group of radicals remained unconvinced that the restoration of civil liberties favored by the bourgeoisie would do anything to alleviate the misery of the poorest citizens. They demanded "national workshops" to guarantee work for the millions of unemployed, as well as universal suffrage to give them political power. They formed a rival government powerful enough to force the provisional government to compromise with them and set up the national workshops.

The apparent success of the revolutionaries in Paris stimulated similar activity all over Europe and awakened fear in the ruling classes – who, as Emerson remarked, were beginning to wonder if their own days were also numbered, and if the "splendid privileges" of their rich houses were not "in too dreadful contrast to the famine and ignorance at the door" (Emerson to Lidian Emerson, March 23 and 24, 1848). They had reason to be fearful. The workers'-rights movement known as Chartism was given new energy by the events in France. Emerson was naturally interested in Chartism, because Carlyle's pamphlet on the movement and Brownson's famous review of it had had such noisy repercussions in America. He attended a March 7 meeting of the Chartists in National Hall and heard the crowd sing the "Marseillaise" in solidarity with the new French government; he listened to revolutionary mutterings among the people there, who hoped that their example might cause the English soldiers to join their cause if an uprising occurred. There were disturbances in Glasgow and smaller outbreaks in Manchester and Edinburgh. Plans for a mass demonstration and march on the houses of Parliament to present Chartist petitions frightened the authorities sufficiently that they called out the military under the Duke of Wellington to prevent the march.

In the event only fifty thousand Chartists assembled on the appointed day, April 10, instead of the half million that had been expected, and the proposed march never took place. But people still feared that revolution was imminent. Emerson scoffed at the idea in the privacy of his journal. There might be a scramble for money, but as long as both sides wanted the same thing — material prosperity — no real *revolution* was possible. The old system would survive, though it might have a new set of masters.

Still, the radicals of Paris were proposing something far more sweeping than the peaceable six-point reform program the British Chartists had wanted to present to Parliament; the Parisians demanded nothing less, Emerson thought, than the "confiscation of France." Though Tennyson warned him he might be risking his life, Emerson decided to cross the Channel and get a closer look at the revolution. He arrived in Paris on May 7, just as events were reaching a crisis. The leaders of the radical clubs of Paris were unwilling to accept the results of the general election that had returned a constituent assembly dominated by moderates. They opened the National Guard in Paris to the workers of the "national workshops" and supplied them with arms. On May 15 a mob assisted by this proletarian militia attempted to invade the National Assembly. They were repelled after a struggle of several hours but not wholly defeated, and the capital still seethed with revolutionary fervor.

Emerson enjoyed himself thoroughly in this scene of passion and rage. He fell in love with Paris, "a place of the largest liberty that is I suppose in the civilized world," as he wrote his wife (Emerson to Lidian Emerson, May 24 and 25, 1848). In the company of another American he visited some of the radical clubs, including those of the revolutionary leaders Armand Barbès and Louis Auguste Blanqui. He admired the "terrible earnest" and "deep sincerity" of the clubs' speakers, who were "studying how to secure a fair share of bread to every man, and to get the God's justice done through the land." And he was fascinated by the "fire & fury of the people, when they are interrupted or thwarted," so unlike anything he had seen in New England even at the most passionate meetings. Every man in the street seemed to be wearing some kind of uniform; they were bearded like goats and lions; they wore red sashes, swords, and brass helmets. "I saw the street full of bayonets, and the furious driving of the horses dragging cannon towards the National Assembly," he boasted to his wife in a letter written two days later (Emerson to Lidian Emerson, May 17, 1848). But he was relieved when the army of shopkeepers who formed that part of the National Guard loyal to the National Assembly drove back the mob and jailed its leaders. In his journal he sternly warned all revolutionaries that they must not contemplate any reforms that would take away the incentive to labor.

After slightly more than three weeks in Paris, Emerson returned to London, where he delivered more lectures and prepared for his return to the United States. He agreed to take a brief trip with Carlyle. Their meetings during this visit had not been happy. Carlyle, deeply in Emerson's debt and too proud not to resent it, had been contentious and on one occasion insulting; after that Emerson had mostly tried to avoid meeting him in private and had taken a small vindictive pleasure in recording other people's cutting remarks about Carlyle in his journals. But he agreed to go with Carlyle to Stonehenge, where they wandered among the giant stones and listened to explanations of their astronomical function from a local antiquary. After a final week of meetings with famous people, including Marian Evans (George Eliot), with whom he was happy to discover a mutual fascination with Jean-Jacques Rousseau's *Confessions,* Emerson sailed for Boston, where he arrived July 27, 1848.

While he was still in London or Paris Emerson had received a half-teasing, half-truculent letter from Thoreau, which apparently amused him; in a letter to his wife he wrote: "Thank Henry for his letter. He is always *absolutely* right, and *particularly* perverse" (Emerson to Lidian Emerson, June 8, 1848). But some of Thoreau's jokes might have warned Emerson about problems to come. Emerson may have suggested to Thoreau in an earlier letter that he consider a trip to Europe; if so, Thoreau firmly rejected the idea.

Who has any desire to split himself any further by straddling the Atlantic? We are extremities enough already. There is danger of one's straddling so far that he can never recover an upright position. There are certain men in Old & New England who aspire to the renown of the Colossus of Rhodes, and to have ships sail under them. (Thoreau to Emerson, May 21, 1848)

Thoreau had in fact been traveling inward during the last half-decade, as he liked to remind his friends. The period had begun miserably enough. Emerson, who had tried to act as his patron and friend, was beginning to doubt that he would ever become a successful writer. In late March 1843, when Thoreau was about to end his nearly two-year stay with Emerson's family and move to Staten Island to take up the tutorial job Emerson had arranged there for him, Emerson recorded in his journal Elizabeth Hoar's comment: "I love H., but do not like him." He then added, in a passage he would incorporate into the essay "Experience": "Young men like H. T. owe us a new world & they have not acquitted the debt: for the most part, such die young, & so dodge the fulfillment."

Not all of Emerson's disappointment was literary. Nathaniel Hawthorne, to whom Emerson confided similar feelings in a conversation the next day, defended Thoreau but noted: "Mr. Emerson appeared to have suffered some inconveniency from his experience of Mr. Thoreau as an inmate. It may well be that such a sturdy and uncompromising person is fitter to meet occasionally in the open air, than to have as a permanent guest at table or fireside." Instead of a disciple to graft his apples, Emerson had — or at least felt that he had — a wolf by the ears. Thoreau was as truculent as he was devoted; indeed, his truculence and his devotion were never easy to tell apart. He demanded perfect and unwavering sympathy yet reserved the right to look with frank contempt upon the middle-class respectability Emerson was traveling to country lyceums and drafty big-city lecture halls to support. There was a time earlier in their relationship when Emerson found this youthful scorn a tonic, but by 1843 the signs of strain are evident.

When Thoreau moved back to Concord he did not return to the Emerson house, but lived with his family and worked in his father's pencil-making business. New York publishers had given him little encouragement, and his hopes of supporting himself by selling his writings now appeared dim. When *The Dial* ceased publication in 1844 he lost the only certain outlet he had ever had for his essays and poems. Thoreau stopped lecturing; he stopped writing regular entries in his journal for a year and a half.

Nor was this all. On April 30, 1844, Thoreau and a younger friend decided to explore the Sudbury River in a rowboat. They stopped for lunch. Foolishly, they built a fire inside of a decaying stump in order to cook their lunch, probably hoping to keep their nascent flame out of the wind long enough to kindle a blaze. But the stump itself caught fire and the fire quickly spread to the surrounding woods, menacing the town of Concord. Thoreau ran to the town and gave the alarm, but by the time the fire had been put out it had destroyed over three hundred acres. Six years passed before Thoreau could even bring himself to mention the incident in his journal.

Still, he had not entirely stopped writing. He was working steadily at attempting to transform his sketchy notes on a boating trip he had taken with his brother John on the Concord and Merrimack rivers in the late summer of 1839 into the kind of "excursion" he had already had success with in two earlier published essays — "A Walk to Wachusett" and "A Winter Walk." The idea of using the tour as literary material was an old one with him; references to it crop up in lists of potential lecture or essay topics as early as 1840, though the brief "Memoirs of a Tour" he began that summer were then abandoned for work on another project. The next year he again listed the tour as a possible subject for compositions.

His brother John's death in January 1842 suddenly made the 1839 journey take on a new significance for Thoreau. By the fall of 1844, when Thoreau appears to have revived his idea for a literary work based on the 1839 trip, he also had begun experimenting with a more ambitious method of composition, one that would allow room for memory to expand outward into meditation. At about this time he acquired a new blank book, larger than his usual journals, to hold transcriptions from his earlier journals. He would copy a passage from an old journal into this new book (which he called the "long book"), then leave a large blank space for future expansions.

Thoreau was more than ever determined to show Emerson that his earlier confidence in him had not been misplaced – that he was capable of producing a major literary work. (The fact that so many of the Transcendentalists were publishing books in 1843–4 only made Thoreau's determination stronger. Parker's *Discourses* came out in 1843, as did Ellery Channing's *Poems.* Emerson's second collection entitled *Essays* and Fuller's account of her western trip, *Summer on the Lakes,* came out in 1844.) Finally Ellery Channing suggested to Thoreau that the only solution to his perennial problem – how to support himself and still find time to write – would be to build himself a cabin on Emerson's newly acquired land at Walden Pond. In March 1845 Channing reminded Thoreau of a field near the pond he had named "Briars" and commanded: "Go out upon that, build yourself a hut, & there begin the grand process of devouring yourself alive. I see no other alternative, no other hope for you." Thoreau proposed to Emerson that he be allowed to live on the land if he would clear it and plant pines on it, and Emerson was happy to agree.

The cabin Thoreau began to build in March 1845 and moved into on the Fourth of July proved to be at just the right distance from Emerson – still on his property, no longer in his house. And the two years spent there were both the happiest and most productive of Thoreau's life. While there he finished two drafts of the book growing out of his 1839 river tour with his brother John, *A Week on the Concord and Merrimack Rivers,* as well as a first draft of *Walden* itself; he also found time to write a long critical piece on Carlyle, an account of his climb up Maine's Mount Katahdin, and a lecture prompted by his one-night's imprisonment in the Concord jail for nonpayment of his poll tax, later published as "Resistance to Civil Government."

The pace of Thoreau's maturation as a writer was equally swift. The prose of the first draft of *A Week on the Concord and Merrimack Rivers* has a limpid, delicate beauty that recalls the best passages of "The Natural History of Massachusetts," allowed now to flower into pure aestheticism (and diffuse eroticism). The Carlyle article exists at the opposite stylistic and intellectual extreme; it is public utterance, hugely self-confident even in the act of paying tribute. Thoreau is fascinated by Carlyle's own boisterous prose style and generous in his estimation of Carlyle's continuing influence on young writers. The story of Thoreau's ascent of Mount Katahdin resembles his accounts of earlier expeditions into nature only in its general subject matter; its tough, polished sentences are far closer to the prose of *Walden* than to that of *A Week,* and it is as bleak in its view of natural power as the earlier text was tender in its cataloguing of natural beauties. Finally, the lecture later called "Resistance to Civil Government" shows a disciplining of anger by logic that would make Thoreau one of the most powerful political writers in the nineteenth century.

The first of these projects to be completed was the first draft of the book that would one day be published under the title *A Week on the Concord and Merrimack Rivers.* At this point, however, Thoreau called it "Excursion on Concord and Merrimack Rivers." Scholars who have studied the relationship between the journals, the long book, and this first draft of the book itself have been able to show that Thoreau reworked and polished his original paragraphs considerably at each stage in the process – shortening them, refining them, pruning out abstractions and concentrating on significant sensory detail. In "Excursion on Concord and Merrimack Rivers," which he completed sometime in the fall of 1845, each water-borne "day" of the original two-week trip serves as a receptacle for these small masterpieces of sensation and reflection.

As the brothers row their homemade green boat with its blue stripe up the lazy Concord to Billerica, then cut via the Middlesex Canal over to the Merrimack River, and then row or sail up the Merrimack into New Hampshire as far as there are locks to take them around waterfalls and rapids, Thoreau notes the things they see, the people they pass, and the thoughts the trip gives rise to. The week-long land journey by stagecoach and on foot that the brothers actually took in 1839 up through the Franconia Notch to the distant northern rivers, together with their climb up Mount Washington, is summarized in a single paragraph; this is meant to be strictly a river book. Land days do not count. We skip from "Thurs. Sept. 5th" (when the brothers left their boat moored in the Merrimack) to "Thurs. Sept. 12th" (when they pick it up again for the rapid trip home).

The narrative thread is slender enough – a passage through a canal as one brother pulls a towrope and the other keeps the boat off the sides of the canal with a pole, an encounter with a young worker, a rise past rapids or falls in an old lock, a mooring at noon for dinner or at night for sleep. Yet on the trip are strung such exquisite moments of perception that the eddies in the narrative are as welcome as the forward pulls. Their silence of the tent at night is punctuated by foxes stepping about over the dead leaves and by "the startling throttled cry of an owl." They know there are pigeons in the woods by "the slight wiry winnowing sound of their wings." The asters of late summer have a "dry ripe scent," and the angular stem of the witch hazel bears "petals like Furies' hair, or small ribbon streamers." Seed vessels of the poppy look "like small goblets filled with the waters of Lethe." Logs rolled down the mountain by lumberers come with a rumbling sound that reverberates on the opposite shore like the roar of artillery. "Dense flocks of bobolinks russet and rustling as if they were the seeds of the meadow grass floating on the wind, rise before us in our walk — like ripe grain threshed out by the wind."

The book is full of remembered joy. "I have passed down the river before sunrise on a summer morning, between fields of lilies still shut in sleep, and when at length the flakes of sun light from over the bank fell upon the surface of the water, whole fields of white blossoms seemed to flash open before me as I sailed along, like the unfolding of a banner." Even the fog and the "genial drenching rain" that surrounds them again and again only increase their "boyancy" (as Thoreau spells it). "On foot indeed we continued up along the banks — feeling our way with a stick through the showery and foggy day. . . . & cheered by the tones of invisible waterfalls — scenting the fragrance of the pines and the wet clay under our feet — with visions of toads and wandering frogs — and festoons of moss hanging from the spruce trees — and thrushes flitting silent under the leaves — The road still holding together through that wettest weather like faith — "

Other men in this river world are also objects of affection as diffuse but intense as Whitman's. A sympathetic lock tender lets the brothers into the Middlesex locks on Sunday against his rules. In another set of locks Thoreau admires a "brawny N. Hampshire man — leaning upon his pole — bareheaded and in simple shirt and trowsers — a rude apollo of a man." The rhythmical poling motions of the boatman must, Thoreau thinks, communicate stateliness to his character until he feels the "slow irresistible motion under him" as if it were his own energy. The sight of the rough country boys coming to the Concord Cattle Show fills Thoreau with love for "these sons of earth," so much better prizes than the best specimens of their cattle. Reading Indian lore makes him long for such a friendship as existed in the days of Wawatam and Henry the fur trader, when the Indian, having dreamed of friendship between them, went to Henry's tent and adopted him henceforth.

The many long passages about friendship gathered in the "Wednesday, Sept. 4" section express an intense yearning for personal love. The love of friend for friend is the only thing worth living for, the center from which the rays of the universe radiate. "Our life without love is like coke and ashes." John Thoreau, the brother and companion on the original trip, always present in the book's "we" but never named or described, was one such friend, "flesh of my flesh bone of my bone." Nostalgia for that perfect union blends seamlessly into longing for an ideal friend who is to come, who will not insult with kindnesses but will trust without reservation and understand completely. "Our whole life is in some sense addressed to that one among men whom we most esteem — and who is most able to interpret it." He must treat us with reverence, give all and demand nothing. "Let him not think he can please me by any behavior, or even treat me well enough."

The imperiousness of that final sentence masks a terrible loneliness. Thoreau says he has heard rumors that the earth is inhabited but has at yet seen no footprint on the shore. "I walk in nature still alone / And know no one. / Discern no lineament nor feature / Of any creature." He cannot bear being discarded, ignored. "Use me, for I am useful in my way, and stand as one of many petitioners from toadstool and henbane up to Dahlia and violet supplicating to be put to my use, if by any means ye may find me serviceable." Batter my heart. "Strike boldly at the head or heart or any vital part — so you may possibly hit. . . . Depend upon it the timber is well seasoned and tough, and will bear rough usage." Nature is not enough. "Though all the firmament / Is oer me bent / Yet still I miss the grace / Of an intelligent and kindred face." In nature I seek the friend who blends with nature: "Who is the person in her mask, / He is the man I ask."

There is much more in "Excursion on Concord and Merrimack Rivers" — the local history Thoreau assiduously weaves in, with its recollections of American Indian life and the colonial past; meditations on the wisdom of the Hindu scriptures; and the allusiveness that links the shores of the Merrimack to Ostia and the Concord Cattle Show to festivals of Bacchus. All of this material would become even more significant in the hugely expanded version of the book that Thoreau finally published in 1849. Yet the confession of longing that occurs at the midpoint of the first draft is a clue to its liberating power for Thoreau himself, because the tenderness it displaces onto perception turns representation into an act of love.

By the fall of 1845 Thoreau is filling his journal with joyous descriptions of his new life, of hoeing the beans he had planted, of studying, and of writing. He appears to have finished "Excursion on Concord and Merrimack Rivers" in the fall of the year. He then turned to another project, one refreshingly external and "objective" after the intense retrospection of his book manuscript. In December 1845 a copy of Thomas Carlyle's edition (with commentary and "elucidations") of *Oliver Cromwell's Letters and Speeches* arrived in Concord. Thoreau now set about writing a lecture for the Concord Lyceum that would be an extended review of Carlyle's writings and an analysis of his remarkable style. The lecture Thoreau delivered at the lyceum on February 4, 1846, was an impressive piece. He hoped to publish it for profit and asked his friend Horace Greeley to help him place it with a magazine. Greeley did persuade his friend George R. Graham of Philadel-

phia to accept the manuscript for publication, though Graham proved to be
dilatory about publishing the piece (and even more dilatory about paying for
it). But in March and April of 1847 the two-part article "Thomas Carlyle and
His Works" finally made its appearance in *Graham's Magazine*. Emerson
quickly forwarded both numbers to Carlyle, who read them with satisfaction
and told a friend, "I have got an American review of me."

Carlyle could not have asked for a more generous admirer. Thoreau writes
as if his love of Carlyle marks him as one of the elect. "Only he who has had
the good fortune to read them in the nick of time, in the most perceptive and
recipient season of life, can give any adequate account of them." Conventional literary men are put off by Carlyle's mannerisms, frightened by his
raving. "We hardly know an old man to whom these volumes are not hopelessly sealed." To the young, on the other hand, the very wildness and
indecorum of Carlyle's speech come like an April thaw. "He has broken the
ice, and streams freely forth like a spring torrent." His style "has the rhythms
and cadences of conversation endlessly repeated. It resounds with emphatic,
natural, lively, stirring tones, muttering, rattling, exploding, like shells and
shot, and with like execution." He resembles an advancing army as he crashes
through "the host of weak, half-formed, *dilettante* opinions, honest and dishonest ways of thinking" and tramples them into the dust. His humor is
"rich, deep, and variegated, in direct communication with the back bone and
risible muscles of the globe." Even his invective can be bracing. If he falls
short of the highest wisdom, if his spleen becomes wearisome, at least he has
one sovereign merit: "Carlyle does not oblige us to think; we have thought
enough for him already, but he compels us to act."

Thoreau's desire to replace thought with action would soon be given assistance from an unexpected quarter. One day in late July 1846 when Thoreau
was walking into the village to pick up a mended shoe, he was arrested for
nonpayment of his poll tax by Sam Staples, the Concord constable and, from
1842–5, collector of taxes, whose contract entitled him to one and one-half
cents for every dollar of tax money he succeeded in collecting. The tax (not
more than $1.50 per year) was levied on every male inhabitant over the age of
twenty, but nonpayment was fairly common and was a continuing problem for
the Commonwealth, particularly because communities like Concord seem to
have been reluctant to jail people for evading the tax.

Staples, however, had already shown himself willing to jail evaders. Bronson Alcott had stopped paying the tax in 1842 to announce his refusal to take
part in the oppressive machinery of the state. No one bothered him the first
year, but on January 17, 1843, Staples came to his cottage with a warrant
and took him to the Concord jail. Unfortunately, the jailer was nowhere in
sight. Staples went off to look for him while Alcott waited peacefully at the

jail. In the meantime a friend, Judge Samuel Hoar, paid the tax and the fine for him. Thoreau described this anticlimactic martyrdom shortly after it happened in a high-spirited letter to Emerson, who was then off lecturing in New York. Thoreau announced that he and Charles Lane had been planning to "agitate the State" while Alcott "lay in durance," but their zeal fizzled when Alcott was released, "and the State was safe as far as I was concerned." One detail of the incident particularly amused Thoreau. Staples was used to collaring deadbeats, but Alcott's motives for nonpayment astonished him. Here was a man willing to go to jail, as he said, for "nothing but principle."

Thoreau apparently joined Alcott in his refusal to pay taxes, at least if his statement in the published version of "Resistance to Civil Government" (1849) is correct; there he says he has paid no tax for "six or seven years." Staples took no action against either of them in 1844 or 1845. Because the loss to the tax collector for any particular malefactor was only a cent and a half per year he was sometimes willing to let delinquents go unpunished for several years. But in 1846 Staples apparently decided to try to collect the overdue taxes from the previous years. He warned Alcott in April or May that he would advertise Alcott's land for sale if the tax was not paid, and he took out a warrant for Thoreau's arrest. Fifty years later, Staples told an interviewer that he had just gotten home from locking up Thoreau with the rest of the inmates and had taken off his boots when word was brought to him that a veiled woman had appeared at the jail with "Mr. Thoreau's tax" in an envelope. Unwilling to go to the trouble of unlocking the prisoners he had just locked up, Staples waited till morning to release Thoreau – who, he remembered, "was mad as the devil when I turned him loose." Thoreau's anger is understandable. Having a female relative shamed into paying his taxes was hardly his idea of heroic sacrifice.

What made it worse was that Emerson had no sympathy for either Alcott or Thoreau in this matter. He characterized Thoreau's behavior to Alcott as "mean and skulking and in bad taste." The first two adjectives seem a strange choice, because Thoreau had been perfectly frank about his refusal to pay taxes and had accepted his incarceration uncomplainingly. The last phrase is more revealing and suggests the real source of Emerson's anger. He had always recoiled from the ramping egotism of Garrison and the rest of the antislavery "martyrs" who treated themselves as exemplary sufferers. They were vulgar; they were self-advertising; they were *not our sort*. A gentleman may suffer, but he does not suffer over trifles like a poll tax, nor does he oblige a lady to muffle herself in veils while she ransoms him out of the town jail. Alcott's holy foolishness Emerson had long ago resigned himself to, but to see Thoreau indulging in the same sort of behavior exasperated him.

However much it may have hurt Thoreau to discover this conventionality in his mentor's soul, Emerson's charges drew from him an apologia that has become one of the classic documents of American political thought. In January and February of 1848 (when Emerson was in England) Thoreau read before the Concord Lyceum a lecture he entitled "The Rights and Duties of the Individual in Relation to Government," a lecture he published the next year in Elizabeth Peabody's short-lived periodical *Aesthetic Papers* under the title "Resistance to Civil Government." In the piece he argues that the individual has not only a right but often a duty to resist the government under which he lives, if his conscience tells him that compliance with the will of that government is morally wrong. Such behavior is neither skulking nor tasteless; it is in the original sense of the word, *decorous*. "How does it become a man to behave toward this American government to-day?" Thoreau asks near the beginning of his treatise. "I answer that he cannot without disgrace be associated with it."

Thoreau had witnessed in Wendell Phillips, the abolitionist leader, one example of the kind of conduct he could admire wholeheartedly. Phillips had spoken three times before the Concord Lyceum on the subject of slavery, the last time on March 11, 1845. On March 28 Thoreau published an admiring account of the last speech entitled "Wendell Phillips Before Concord Lyceum" in Garrison's abolitionist newspaper the *Liberator*. Phillips was a Boston aristocrat who had been converted to the cause of "immediate abolition" by Garrison and who shared Garrison's insistence that the individual must consider himself accountable for the monstrous injustice of slavery and must dissociate himself from governments that tolerate and foster it. According to Thoreau, the aim of Phillips's lecture had been to show what the state and church had to do with Texas and slavery, "and how much, on the other hand, the individual should have to do with church and state."

Phillips's willingness to defy the Constitution and say, of the Founding Fathers, "I am wiser than they," endeared him to Thoreau, as did his refusal to let his aims in life be reduced to a single objective. He was not, he said, born to abolish slavery, but to do right. With "soldier-like steadiness" and natural skill at oratory he combined "a sort of moral principle and integrity." His insistence that the individual must withdraw immediately from connection with the state won an admiring tribute from Thoreau. "He at least is not responsible for slavery, nor for American Independence; for the hypocrisy and superstition of the church, nor the timidity and selfishness of the state; nor for the indifference and willing ignorance of any." Phillips is the Red-cross knight, "one of the most conspicuous champions of a true church and state now in the field," and at the end of the review Thoreau mockingly wonders if any paynim champion will brave him in the lists.

Phillips's example – to dissociate yourself from the unjust church and state immediately — provided one important strand of Thoreau's argument in "Resistance to Civil Government." "It is not a man's duty, as a matter of course, to devote himself to the eradication of any, even the most enormous wrong; he may still properly have other concerns to engage him; but it is his duty, at least, to wash his hands of it, and, if he gives it no thought longer, not to give it practically his support." Some abolitionists are petitioning the state to dissolve the Union. "Why do they not dissolve it themselves, — the union between themselves and the State, — and refuse to pay their quota into its treasury?" As Carlyle said, it is no good thinking about things endlessly; we have already thought too much. It is time to act. "Action from principle, — the perception and the performance of right, — changes things and relations; it is essentially revolutionary, and does not consist wholly with any thing that was. It not only divides states and churches, it divides families; aye, it divides the *individual,* separating the diabolical in him from the divine."

This secular conversion experience is the fruit of Thoreau's ridiculous stay in the Concord jail. He tells the story of that night in an inset tale full of tenderness and humor: how the prisoners lounged chatting in the doorway until the jailer told them it was time to lock up for the night; how he found himself in a whitewashed room with an amiable companion who gave him the oral history of their cell; how rectangular tin trays of bread and chocolate were shoved under the door for breakfast; how his roommate, leaving to go to his usual morning job of haying, bid farewell to him, expecting him (correctly, as it turned out) to be gone before lunch.

Yet the sudden illumination caused by the night in jail is anything but funny. The constable's willingness to threaten his neighbor Alcott and jail Thoreau went far toward explaining how Massachusetts could support a war it thought unjust and a slave system it claimed to find abhorrent. The view from the deep, grated window of the jail gives Thoreau a new perspective on his town. "I was fairly inside of it. I had never seen its institutions before." He has a new view of the town's residents as well; he understands for the first time what they are about. "I saw yet more distinctly the State in which I lived" — both the state of Massachusetts and the state of man.

The sudden grasp of the interconnectedness of cruelty turns resistance from a right of private conscience into an obligation of citizenship. If William Paley (1743–1805), the English philosopher whose *Moral and Political Philosophy* Thoreau studied at Harvard, had devoted a chapter to explaining the "Duty of Submission to Civil Government," then Thoreau will now devote a chapter to explaining the duties of resistance. "When a sixth of the population of a nation which has undertaken to be the refuge of liberty are slaves, and a whole country is unjustly overrun and conquered by a foreign army, and subjected to military law, I think that it is not too soon for honest men to rebel and revolutionize." If the state has become a machine to hold slaves and invade Mexico, then you must let your life become a "counter friction" to stop the machine. Whenever you are obliged to be "the agent of injustice to another, then, I say, break the law."

The state – particularly a democratic state – has no defense against its own tendency to pass unjust laws except the willingness of individual citizens peacefully to resist them. To resist the state when the state is wrong is therefore to save it. "If the alternative is to keep all just men in prison, or give up war and slavery, the State will not hesitate which to choose." The political power of the individual is therefore potentially huge. "A minority is powerless when it conforms to the majority," Thoreau points out, "but it is irresistible when it clogs by its whole weight." Like an Abraham bargaining with the Lord to spare Sodom, Thoreau argues that "if one thousand, if one hundred, if ten men whom I could name," or even "*one* HONEST man" would withdraw from the state-imposed copartnership in slaveowning and let himself be locked up in the county jail "it would be the abolition of slavery in America."

Transcendentalism had always had trouble imagining how to bridge the gap between principle and action largely because it tended to think of action as a kind of sullying – a frustrating and degrading attempt to force pure ideas into a world of corruption and compromise. What Thoreau learned from people like Garrison and Phillips was that if you acted purely from principle to *withdraw* your allegiance from the world of corruption, the world would soon come to you. You would find yourself acting on it and in it as vigorously as Napoleon had and without having to compromise your integrity.

About a month after his night in the Concord jail in 1846 Thoreau left his cabin at the pond for a two-week excursion into the Maine woods with a cousin and two other men. They traveled up the Penobscot River to North Twin Lake, then hiked to the base of Mount Katahdin, at 5,268 feet Maine's highest mountain. The mountain's naked rocks jutted abruptly up, looking like a "blue barrier" formed as one of the ancient boundaries of the earth. While his companions set up camp in the late afternoon light, Thoreau decided to explore the mountain alone through the pathless wilderness, an ascent of such difficulty that it keeps reminding him of Satan's voyage through chaos in *Paradise Lost*. Here the only flocks are the gray silent rocks, "chewing a rocky cud at sunset," regarding Thoreau quietly without a bleat or a low.

The next day his companions join him in the climb. The scenery is quite literally Titanic, reminding him of the rock where Prometheus was bound.

"Some part of the beholder, even some vital part, seems to escape through the loose grating of his ribs as he ascends. He is more lone than you can imagine." The experience is startling, even for Thoreau. He realizes that he has always thought of nature as a place inhabited by humans. Now, descending the desolate side of a mountain burned bare by lightning, he sees nature as "something savage and awful, though beautiful. . . . This was that Earth of which we have heard, made out of Chaos and Old Night."

This sudden encounter with the material sublime triggers a passage of horrified self-awareness, as Thoreau suddenly realizes a kinship between the pure matter of Katahdin's rocks and the equally inhuman matter of which his flesh is made. "I stand in awe of my body, this matter to which I am bound." Each of us is Prometheus, bound to this rock. What is stranger or more mysterious than matter? "Talk of mysteries! – think of our life in nature, – daily to be shown matter, to come in contact with it, – rocks, trees, wind on our cheeks!" Everything we take for granted – "the *solid* earth! the *actual* world! the *common sense*!" – is as mysterious as the inhuman landscape of Katahdin. "*Contact! Contact! Who* are we? *Where* are we?" The things we take for granted are precisely the problems we should pose.

Thoreau quickly turned his notes on the Katahdin trip into a hundred-page manuscript that he would later publish. Horace Greeley helped place "Ktaadn: The Maine Woods" with the *Union Magazine of Literature and Art,* where it appeared in five installments between July and November 1848. But "Ktaadn" was only one of Thoreau's projects. In the next year he would begin work on "Resistance to Civil Government" and write a first draft of *Walden.* He also would write a second complete draft of the book he now called *A Week on the Concord and Merrimack Rivers,* condensing the two weeks' voyage into one week and adding long digressions on a variety of subjects to the seven "days." Earlier, he had delivered a lecture entitled "History of Myself" to the Concord Lyceum, helping to satisfy his neighbors' curiosity about his life at Walden Pond and had seen his long article on Carlyle in print, having the satisfaction of knowing that it was read by the master himself with approval.

By the time Thoreau left the cabin at Walden Pond to move back into the Emerson house (at Lidian's request) to look after things while Emerson was in England, he could feel that his experiment in living and writing was an admirable success. Temporarily freed from concerns about earning a living, living in a house he had built with his own hands, he had proven he could write rapidly and brilliantly. But Emerson had so far been unsuccessful at interesting a publisher in *A Week on the Concord and Merrimack Rivers,* and when Thoreau wrote him in England on November 14, 1847, he had to report that the book had been turned down by still more publishers. "The world is a cow that is hard to milk — life does not come so easily," he noted ruefully, "and oh, how thinly it is watered ere we get it!"

Thoreau's response to such discouragement was to expand the book again. He added to the "Sunday" chapter passages learnedly discoursing on "the Christian fable" and frankly avowing his preference for the Greek mythology over the Christian one (a position that raised the hackles of reviewers when the book was finally published) and expanded the dissertation on friendship in "Wednesday." And he completed two more drafts of *Walden*. He submitted both manuscripts to the Boston publishers Ticknor and Company early in 1849 and found to his chagrin that they were willing to publish *Walden* but not *A Week*. Finally James Munroe, Emerson's publisher, agreed to publish the book so long as Thoreau promised to pay the full costs of its publication if it did not sell. The book was published on May 30, 1849.

The publication of *A Week on the Concord and Merrimack Rivers* apparently precipitated a crisis in Thoreau's relationship with Emerson. Emerson had encouraged Thoreau to risk publishing the book, though he had criticized particular chapters of it. Some time in the half-year following the publication of *A Week*, Thoreau wrote an entry in a notebook complaining that because Emerson had become "estranged" from him he was now willing to shoot "fatal truth" at him on a "poisoned arrow," a criticism he had concealed while the two men were still friends. He notes bitterly that before the book was published Emerson had given him only praise for what was good in it; now he points out all its faults and blames Thoreau for them. This "difference" between the two friends left Emerson feeling wounded too; Thoreau complains in another notebook passage that Emerson had accused him of "coldness and disingenuousness" and in so doing had inflicted a wound too deep to be healed. "I had tenderly cherished the flower of our friendship till one day my friend treated it as a weed." It could not sustain the shock, but "drooped & withered from that hour."

It is difficult to read this last sentence without wincing. Many of Thoreau's earlier journal passages about Emerson contain expressions of longing and reverence so intense that they fill one with foreboding: The young man who wrote them seems headed for terrible unhappiness. And in the summer of 1849 Thoreau was more than usually vulnerable. His sister Helen had died after a long struggle with tuberculosis, and he had just published a book whose failure (should it fail) would plunge him deeply into debt for years. He had been working at high speed for four years but had gotten little recognition to show for it — a few invitations to lecture, a few acceptances by magazines. True, Emerson had praised "Ktaadn" as one of the few pamphlets worthy to save and bind in the last ten years, but what was "Ktaadn" beside *A Week on the Concord and Merrimack Rivers?*

It did not help matters that Emerson was now at the height of his fame, returning from an English tour where he had been flattered and caressed. He had published two books of essays and was about to publish a third, *Representative Men;* he had published a book of poems; and he was in the process of collecting and revising his early writings for publication by the same Boston publisher who refused to print Thoreau's *Week* without a guarantee. (Emerson's *Nature, Addresses and Lectures* appeared on September 7, 1849.) Thoreau complained in his journal that Emerson had become worldly and patronizing. That may have been true, but even if Emerson had remained a model of humility and tact it is difficult to see how fortunes so unequal could have failed to cause strain.

Meanwhile, the book Thoreau had spent ten years writing was proving to be — at least as far as sales were concerned — a disastrous flop. Though some reviewers had praise for parts of it they found its strange combination of narrative, meditation, and learned disquisition frustrating. James Russell Lowell complained in a review that he did not like to be invited to a river party and then preached at. Even Carlyle, to whom Emerson sent a copy of the book, could not get through it, though he had carried it with him all over Ireland. "Tell him so, please," Carlyle wrote brusquely in a letter of August 28, 1849. To his wife, Jane, he wrote that it was "a very fantastic yet not quite worthless book."

The problem with the final version of *A Week on the Concord and Merrimack Rivers* is not that its original charms have been lost in revision or that the material added to it is uninteresting. It is simply that the narrative frame keeps arousing expectations of movement and development that the lengthy meditative passages frustrate at every turn. Reading the book for the second time is much easier than reading it for the first time. But very few of Thoreau's early readers were willing to attempt a second reading, or even to complete the first.

The unbound sheets of Alcott's *Conversations with Children on the Gospels* had eventually been sold to a trunk maker as wastepaper. Thoreau was spared that humiliation, but only because having contracted to pay the publication costs (a two-hundred-ninety-dollar debt it took him four years to pay off) he was now the owner of the edition. In 1853 the publisher asked Thoreau what he wanted done with the unsold copies of his book. He had them sent to him at Concord. In his journal he noted, "I now have a library of nearly nine hundred volumes, over seven hundred of which I wrote myself. Is it not well that the author should behold the fruits of his labor? My works are piled up on one side of my chamber half as high as my head, my *opera omnia.*"

Discouragement did not stop Thoreau from writing. In the fall of 1849 he took a trip with Ellery Channing to Cape Cod. They had planned to take the steamer from Boston to Provincetown, but a violent storm kept the steamer in Provincetown. Handbills in the streets of Boston announced a terrible wreck off the shore at Cohasset. They decided to take the train south to Cohasset and thence to the western end of the Cape. From there they could travel by stagecoach out along its southern arm before heading north on foot to Provincetown. At Cohasset they saw the mangled bodies of Irish immigrants still being washed up on shore from the wreck two days earlier. Crowds were streaming to the beach, either to see the sights or to identify bodies and cart them away. The waves, still cracking the largest timbers of the wreck into pieces, showed how untameable a force was in nature. "I saw that no material could withstand the power of the waves; that iron must go to pieces in such a case, and an iron vessel would be cracked like an egg-shell on the rocks." Yet alongside this scene of tragedy two local residents, an old man and a boy, were gathering kelp and seaweed to use as manure, as if nothing out of the ordinary had happened.

Such contrasts – between the force of the wind and ocean and the obliviousness of the inhabitants – runs through the rest of Thoreau's description of the trip, which is marked by a kind of tough Yankee wit he had never exhibited before in such quantity. The descriptions of the eccentric inhabitants and of their stunted apple orchards and treeless towns, and the unintentional humor of the old histories that record the doings of their ministers, amused the audience at the Concord Lyceum when Thoreau delivered two lectures drawn from his notes of the Cape Cod trip on January 23 and 30, 1850. But the sea itself and the world it generated, the sounds and sights of the ocean and grasses – plover and gull, kelp and poverty grass, sea jellies and clams, crashing breakers and receding foam – are the real theme of the chapters Thoreau was slowly working up for publication. As he stands on the "Backside," the Atlantic side of the northern arm of the Cape, he suddenly realizes he has reached the edge of his continent, the place where America ends. "There was nothing but that savage ocean between us and Europe."

Margaret Fuller, who in 1850 was on the other side of that savage ocean, was preparing to return to America after a voyage of discovery that had taken her farther from her Massachusetts roots than any of the other Transcendentalists had cared to go. The life she lived after leaving Boston and Cambridge for New York and then Europe is so full of incident that any chronicler runs the risk of forgetting what Henry James said about reconstructing someone's past: "To live over people's lives is nothing unless we live over their perceptions, live over their growth, the change, the varying intensity of the same – since it was *by* these things they themselves lived." During the last eight years of her life Fuller grew from a strictly cultural reformer, who had worked out what one scholar has called her own brand of "elite-minded, countercultural proselytiz-ing" but who had found practical reformers like the abolitionists distasteful, into a foreign correspondent, whose firsthand experience with revolutionary upheavals in Europe convinced her that some kind of democratic socialism was the only way of ending the cycle of exploitation and rebellion in which most nations seemed trapped.

Fuller's writings reflect the changes in her ideas; indeed, the activity of writing often brings those changes about, as when a desire to know more about the lives of women for *Woman in the Nineteenth Century* leads Fuller to read journals written by imprisoned prostitutes, and that in turn leads her to rethink the whole relationship between chastity and economic privilege. Such interchange between living and thinking was a Transcendentalist ideal, as it had been a Unitarian one, but Fuller carried it to lengths that would have startled William Ellery Channing, her earliest mentor: writing about prison conditions and insane asylums for a New York newspaper; calling in Paris to pay her respects to that flouter of all conventions, George Sand; becoming the friend of prominent exiled revolutionaries in England and France; getting swept up in the Roman revolution; taking an Italian lover and bearing a child.

Emerson commented on the rapidity with which Fuller always seemed to grow, and certainly many aspects of her life even while she lived in Boston and Cambridge might have helped one predict the sudden eruption of force that took place when she left. Many of the participants in her celebrated "Conversations," those late-morning classes that aimed to liberate women by forcing them to systematize their thoughts and make them public in an atmosphere of mutual sympathy and love, have testified to the power of Fuller's "personal magnetism" and the liberating force of her talk:

Perhaps I can best give you an idea of what she was to me by an answer which I made to her. One day when she was alone with me . . . she said, "Is life rich to you?" and I re-plied, "It is since I have known you." Such was the response of many a youthful heart to her, and herein was her wonderful influence. (*Reminiscences of Ednah Dow Cheney*, 1902)

No less significant for the shape her development later took was her frankness with herself about the nature of her own sexuality, which was capacious. Most male Transcendentalists tended to be squeamish, saccharine, or icily remote about human desire, even when they were writing in their journals. Fuller was strikingly candid. In a fragmentary journal passage for 1842 she recalls seeing an engraving of the beautiful Madame de Récamier. "I have so often thought over the intimacy between her and Me de Stael," Fuller wrote. "It is so true that a woman may be in love with a woman and a man with a man." This kind of love, she adds, is "regulated by the same law as that of love between persons of different sexes, only it is purely intellectual and spiritual, . . . its law is the desire of the spirit to realize a whole which makes it seek in another being for what it finds not in itself." The love of Socrates for Alcibiades, of Madame de Staël for Récamier, like Fuller's own love for the New Orleans beauty Anna Barker Ward, strikes her as perfectly "natural."

Remembering her own passion for Anna Ward, she muses,

I loved Anna for a time I think with as much passion as I was then strong enough to feel – Her face was always gleaming before me, her voice was echoing in my ear, all poetic thoughts clustered round the dear image. This love was a key which unlocked for me many a treasure which I still possess.

When Anna's husband, Samuel Gray Ward (with whom Fuller had also been in love), was absent on business, Fuller took his place in Anna's bed, though she found it "exquisitely painful" to realize that the "strange mystic thrill" she once felt in Anna's embrace was dwindled into a "sort of pallid, tender romance." With libertine bravado she analyzes her sensations. "I do not love her now with passion, for I have exhausted her idea, and she does not stimulate my fancy, she does not represent the Beautiful to me now, she is only one beautiful object."

Even if Fuller is borrowing her language here from the rakes of eighteenth-century fiction, she makes it clear why she could hardly have stayed in New England even if *The Dial* had ever made enough money to pay her a living wage. Fuller's appetites were continually frustrated in a culture so repressed that a visit to the theater to see the Austrian dancer Fanny Ellsler was considered daring (Fuller went with Emerson, who seemed quite pleased with himself for doing something scandalous). Women responded easily to Fuller's appeal; Elizabeth Peabody once remarked that if Fuller had been a man any one of the fine girls who attended the Conversations would have married her. But the men who surrounded her in Boston and Cambridge could think of nothing better to do with a poor, brilliant, ambitious, high-strung, granite-faced woman than to treat her as a confidante or a prophetess.

Fuller tried to oblige them, but the role of confidante, though she accepted it with apparent relish, was finally a source of pain to her; and the role of otherworldly vestal never really suited someone who was as passionate as a heroine of tragedy and as hungry for experience as a hero of romance. In a famous letter of 1841 to W. H. Channing she described herself as a kind of volcano; she could feel "all Italy glowing beneath the Saxon crust." And she added, "I shall burn to ashes if all this smoulders here much longer. I must die if I do not burst forth in genius or heroism" (Fuller to Channing, February 19, 1841). She sought solace, as she always had, in the imaginative

identifications offered by literature. When Tennyson's new two-volume edition of poems came out in 1842 she was impressed with its calm nobility and
"still, deep sweetness, so different from the intoxicating, sensuous melody of
his earlier cadence!" One of Tennyson's themes, the last expedition of Ulysses, had long been a favorite of hers – "and his, like mine, is the Ulysses of
the Odyssey, with his deep romance of wisdom, and not the worldling of the
Iliad." (Fuller to W. H. Channing [?], August 1842).

Reading about questers is different from becoming one, however, and
though Fuller continued her literary work during the winter of 1842–3,
reviewing books for *The Dial,* giving another series of "Conversations" (this
time on the subject of education), and preparing her manifesto "The Great
Lawsuit" for the July 1843 number of *The Dial,* she began to long for an
opportunity to travel. When her old friend and correspondent James Freeman
Clarke invited her to join him and his sister Sarah on a journey to the West,
she happily accepted. As usual, Fuller had to depend on the generosity of
friends to make the trip possible; Clarke supplied some of the money himself.
He accompanied the two women to Niagara Falls, where they stayed for a
week, and then to Buffalo, where he put them on the steamboat for Chicago.
They were met there by another of Sarah's brothers, William, who took them
on a tour of the Illinois prairie in an open wagon. After they returned to
Chicago they went on to Milwaukee and the surrounding area. Then Fuller,
curious to see the annual gathering of the Ottowa and Chippewa tribes to
receive their yearly payment from the U. S. government, visited Mackinac
Island in the straits separating Lake Michigan from Lake Huron, where she
spent nine days alone, watching the Indians and mingling with them as they
camped on the beach in front of her hotel. She then rejoined Sarah in Chicago
for the voyage back to Buffalo, made a visit to New York, and finally
returned to Boston by September 1843.

Partly at Emerson's urging Fuller began to think of turning the journal
notes and the letters she had written during the trip into what she called "a
little book," though she cautions him not to expect much from it. "I cant
bear to be thus disappointing you all the time" (Fuller to Emerson, November 12, 1843). She was disappointed that her materials seemed so scanty;
exhaustion during the trip had often prevented her from writing down her
impressions as fully as she had wished. Memory helped, but she also sought
to make her account of the journey richer and more accurate by consulting
reference works dealing with the region – books of travels, accounts of Indian lore and Indian life – a project for which she sought and won the right
to use the library of Harvard College (the first woman to do so). The work
went slowly, and Fuller availed herself of the travel writer's privilege of
filling out the book with sketches and tales – the autobiographical tale of

Mariana; the story of a German clairvoyant known as the Seeress of Prevorst. She finished the book in May 1844; Emerson helped her find a publisher; and by June *Summer on the Lakes* was out, exposing Fuller for the first time in her life to the thing she feared, "that staring, sneering Pit critic, the Public at large" (Fuller to Emerson, May 9, 1844).

Fuller's reception was generally friendly, though the book was criticized for its rambling, episodic structure and the apparent irrelevance of some of its embedded tales and poems. Fuller herself claimed no great formal coherence for her book; she seems to have been more concerned to present her impressions freshly to a public already jaded by repeated descriptions of western grandeurs. In that she certainly succeeds. The book begins with Niagara Falls, but Fuller scrupulously avoids any attempt to paint the sounding cataract. Instead, she tells us how much eight days in its company have depressed her. "My nerves, too much braced up by such an atmosphere, do not well bear the continual stress of sight and sound. For here there is no escape from the weight of a perpetual creation." That sound finally inspires in Fuller such dread that she looks nervously over her shoulder, haunted by irrational fears of "naked savages stealing behind me with uplifted tomahawks." One day, as she is seated upon Table Rock, the better to enjoy this sublime spectacle, she sees a man coming to take his first look. "He walked up close to the fall, and, after looking at it a moment, with an air as if thinking how he could best appropriate it to his own use, he spat into it."

The contrast between the continent's sublimities and the vulgar acquisitiveness of the men who are gradually colonizing it continues to trouble Fuller throughout her western tour. There are many things she likes about the West; she admits that she enjoys escaping from the "petty intellectualities, cant, and bloodless theory" of Boston. But if Boston is all thought and no life, the West seems to her all life and no thought. Its men seem blind to the loveliness all around them, preoccupied only with how much wealth they can extract from the earth (Fuller to Emerson, August 17, 1843).

Fuller is naturally sensitive to two groups of people who have suffered most from the acquisitive habits of the men. The women who accompany their husbands out to the West are ill prepared for the hard labor and isolation their frontier existence imposes on them; they do not even have the masculine diversions of hunting and fishing to provide a break from the unrelenting drudgery of the home. The Northern European women used to heavy farm work – Germans, Scandinavians, Dutch – fare better on the whole than the women from the eastern United States, but they too could be left helpless by the illness or death of their husbands.

Even sorrier is the condition of the various Indian tribes Fuller sees on her journey – pushed from their ancestral lands, degraded with rum, and, finally, treated with contempt by the whites who regard them with the natural aversion people feel toward those whom they have injured. Worst of all is the plight of Indian women, bent down from their burdens and walking with a peculiarly awkward gait. The "soft and wild but melancholy expression of their eye" make Fuller think of the Paraguayan tribe she has read about whose women kill their infant daughters wherever possible to save them from the anguish and weariness of their lives. Yet the Indian women Fuller meets are not coarsened by their lot; on the contrary, she is amazed by their courtesy and natural delicacy. "They used to crowd round me, to inspect little things I had to show them, but never press near; on the contrary would reprove and keep off the children. Anything they took from my hand, was held with care, then shut or folded, and returned with an air of lady-like precision."

These descriptions make *Summer on the Lakes* a sad book, as Orestes Brownson said in his review of it in 1844. But it also contains passages of pure happiness, as when Fuller enjoys the prospect of the "limitless horizon" on the prairie. At first the absence of mountains or valleys disturbs her, but soon she learns to appreciate the exhilaration of unobstructed space.

I would ascend the roof of the house where we lived, and pass many hours, needing no sight but the moon reigning in the heavens, or starlight falling upon the lake, till all the lights were out in the island grove of men beneath my feet, and felt nearer heaven that there was nothing but this lovely, still reception on the earth; no towering mountains, deep tree-shadows, nothing but plain earth and water bathed in light.

On a sunny drive around the shores of Lake Michigan, stimulated by the blue sky and the gold and crimson of the flowers, she felt a kind of "fairyland exaltation" that would recur often as she traveled with her party through the rich landscape. Even raw Chicago, built for nothing but trade, fascinated her when she thought of it as a great valve through which the products of the West made their way to the eastern seaboard and admitted the tide of new immigrants coming from East to West.

Summer on the Lakes did not make Fuller any money, but at least it did not leave her saddled with debt; the publisher had been willing to assume the costs of publication. And the book won the admiration of Horace Greeley, the editor of the New York *Tribune,* who saw in its observations and impressions "an un-American ripeness of culture, and a sympathetic enjoyment of Nature in her untamed luxuriance." Greeley (a frequent visitor at Brook Farm) was already an admirer of Fuller, who impressed him as the "best instructed woman in America." In April 1844, shortly before *Summer on the Lakes* was due to appear, Fuller visited New York, where she spoke with Greeley and may have discussed then with him the possibility of expanding her 1843 *Dial* piece, "The Great Lawsuit," into a book. Prompted by his wife, who had spent much time in the Boston area and had become an admirer of Fuller and a participant in the "Conversations," Greeley invited Fuller to live with them in New York and become a writer for the *Tribune.*

The offer promised an escape from New England and a way of earning a living more stimulating than the drudgery of schoolteaching, but the step was a radical one. Bostonians looked down on New York as raw, vulgar, and vice ridden; and newspaper reporting was not a respectable profession even for a man. Fuller struggled with her decision all summer, even as she was working to revise and expand "The Great Lawsuit." Family troubles continued to plague her, and Emerson was not at all encouraging.

By September, however, Fuller had accepted Greeley's offer to work for the *Tribune* and had left Boston with her friend Caroline Sturgis for a long vacation in Fishkill, New York. She continued to work on her book, now entitled *Woman in the Nineteenth Century,* and to try to widen her understanding of the injustices inflicted upon women of all social classes. Georgiana Bruce, a lively young Englishwoman who had resided for a while at Brook Farm, was now working as an assistant matron in the women's prison at Sing Sing, aiding in an effort to reform what had been a brutal and violent prison. She had encouraged the women inmates (most of them in prison for prostitution) to keep journals, and in the summer of 1844 she had sent some examples to Fuller, who was fascinated by them. "Nothing could aid me so much as the facts you are witnessing[.] For these women in their degradation express most powerfully the present wants of the sex at large" (Fuller to Bruce, August 15, 1844).

The writings of two black women named Satira and Eliza seemed particularly powerful. Fuller was touched by the way Satira managed to maintain an idealized image of herself despite the debasement to which she had been subjected. Eliza gave an account of her "strong instinctive development" that Fuller judged "as clear and racy as Gil Blas." It seemed to her that few white women could have spoken with as much spirit and freedom. The discussion of sexuality among white women was still limited to murmurs and whispers, but Fuller was sure that the sentiments expressed by the black women would find an echo in the boudoirs of the richest mansions.

This thought led Fuller to another question. Bruce had told her that few of the women in Sing Sing had any feeling about chastity. This information made her curious. "Do they see any reality in it; or look on it merely as a circumstance of condition, like the possession of fine clothes?" (Fuller to Bruce, October 20, 1844). Bruce did in fact question the prisoners on this point; they told her that they did not feel "ruined" in the least, whether their sexual experience had been freely chosen or brutally imposed. Even a woman who had been forced into prostitution in a brothel said that she considered the word "ruin" ridiculous as long as the spirit could aspire and the body function. (Bruce decided that the word "ruined" was nothing but "a human, masculine verdict, pronounced by man to further the gratification of his grosser instincts.")

In the fall, Fuller visited Sing Sing with her companion Caroline Sturgis and her friend W. H. Channing. Channing preached a Sunday sermon to the men, and Fuller was allowed to talk with some of the women, whom she found decorous and frank. "All passed much as in one of my Boston Classes" (Fuller to Elizabeth Hoar, October 20 [28?], 1844). She told prisoners that she was writing a book about women and wanted to hear their experiences; they replied with candor, though some asked for a private interview in which they could say things they could not bear to talk about in front of one another. Fuller helped Bruce in her project of improving the dreary prison library (which at that time contained mostly religious tracts) by appealing to her women friends in Boston to send good books. She promised the prisoners she would return and did so, spending Christmas of 1844 at the prison.

These widening sympathies are reflected in the "never-sufficiently-to-be-talked-of pamphlet" that Fuller happily announced she had finished by mid-November 1844 (Fuller to Emerson, November 17, 1844). For once, her usual frustration when trying to put thoughts on paper gave way to fluency. She described to Channing how she had finished the book.

The last day it kept spinning out beneath my hand. After taking a long walk early on one of the most noble exhilarating sort of mornings I sat down to write and did not put the last stroke till near nine in the evening. Then I felt a delightful glow as if I had put a good deal of my true life in it, as if, I suppose I went away now, the measure of my foot-print would be left in the earth. (Fuller to W. H. Channing, November 17, 1844)

The firm of Greeley and McElrath brought out *Woman in the Nineteenth Century* in the spring of 1845. The whole edition was sold off to the booksellers in a week, and a delighted Fuller could report to her brother that she had earned eighty-five dollars from the sale. The book is indeed both the expression of Fuller's true life and the work that won her fame. It has been remarked that *Woman in the Nineteenth Century* represents both the grand summary of the Unitarian belief in self-culture and its widening to include the project of social reform. It is also Fuller's most extensive answer to the brutal reasoning of the passage from Spinoza's *Tractatus Politicus* that she prints in an appendix to the book. There Spinoza considers the question of whether man's supremacy over women is attributable to nature (in which case it is just to exclude women from a share in government) or to custom (in which case such exclusion is unjust). Observing that women nowhere share rule with men but are everywhere dominated by them, Spinoza concludes that women are naturally inferior to men and must be subordinate to them. He adds that because the love men feel toward women is "seldom any thing but lust and impulse, and much less a reverence for the qualities of soul than an admiration of physical beauty," and because physical beauty arouses male jealousy, allowing women a share in government would be destructive of peace and harmony.

Fuller ransacks the entire canon of Western literature and mythology to show that Spinoza's logic is faulty and his view of the relationship between the sexes vulgar and destructive — destructive not only to the happiness of women but also to the happiness of men. As long as women are raised to be frivolous, dependent, weak, and sentimental, men will have contempt for them; as long as women are raised to be wholly ignorant of their own sexuality, men will find themselves faced with the choice between wives whose erotic lives never rise beyond resentful compliance and prostitutes whose greater willingness means only that they have been bought. Greeley remarked that he had never met anyone as gifted at eliciting confidences as Margaret Fuller; people who had just been introduced to her suddenly found themselves pouring out their life stories into her sympathetic ear. The tales of misery she heard from "respectable" women in Boston seemed to her an expression of the same anger she heard in the blasphemies of Sing Sing's prisoners, "for society beats with one great heart" (Fuller to Bruce, August 15, 1844).

Woman in the Nineteenth Century is finally not as much a book of protest as it is a book of hope, of a hope that one scholar has rightly called "millennial." In "The Over-Soul" Emerson had taught Fuller how to reject all arguments (like Spinoza's) drawn from history. "We give up the past to the objector, and yet we hope. He must explain this hope." To say that women have never played a part in government does not prove that they cannot hope to in the future, for the United States itself exists as a giant challenge to the idea that "the people" are too ignorant to govern themselves.

Besides, even the art and literature created by men bears witness that women have always held a higher place in the reverence of men than political tracts suggest. As Fuller says, "no age was left entirely without a witness of the equality of the sexes in function, duty, and hope." Even in societies where women's social position was low, as in ancient Greece, literature abounds with portraits of female courage and nobility — "Cassandra, Iphigenia, Antigone, Macaria." And mythology everywhere is full of goddesses who radiate mystery and control mighty forces. In another appendix to the book Fuller prints a long passage from Apuleius's *Metamorphoses* (*The Golden Ass*) in which the goddess Isis appears to the hero in a dream, rising from the sea. She wears a crown bearing a shining orb like the moon, a crown wreathed in vipers and studded with ears of grain.

Fuller's effort to develop what one scholar has called a body of female archetypes upon which women can draw imaginatively is made in hopes of reclaiming for women the sense of power that Christian culture has largely denied them. Would you rather be a powerful and even terrifying goddess — Isis, Demeter, Minerva, Artemis, Cybele? Or a meek and Christian wife — "the useful drudge of all men, the Martha, much sought, little prized"?

In the same spirit Fuller urges women to retreat into themselves, to break the habits of dependence and find their strength within. She is even willing to hail as a sign of greater self-reliance the growth of that class contemptuously called "old maids." (No greater proof of Fuller's courage could exist than her willingness to make that claim in print.) Only by being driven back upon herself can a woman hope to be worthy of the salutation with which the unfallen Adam greeted the unfallen Eve: "Daughter of God and man, *accomplished* Eve." And it takes an accomplished woman to join in the only kind of relationship worthy of immortal souls. "Two persons love in one another the future good which they aid one another to unfold."

The writing of *Woman in the Nineteenth Century* brought to a close a period of unusual self-confidence for Fuller. When she had completed her last series of "Conversations" in Boston in the spring of 1844 she looked back with pride upon her six years of "noble relations" with a variety of women's minds and decided, rather to her surprise, that life for once seemed worth living. In a letter to Emerson that summer she was gracious about the dissatisfactions she had always felt with their relationship, realizing that she had been asking him for what was not in his nature to give. But her leave-taking was almost a slap: "Farewell, O Grecian Sage, though not my Oedipus" (Fuller to Emerson, July 13, 1844). Now, at the close of *Woman in the Nineteenth Century,* she feels the fullness of her powers: "I stand in the sunny noon of life. Objects no longer glitter in the dews of morning, neither are yet softened by the shadows of evening. Every spot is seen, every chasm revealed." Yet such realism is perfectly congruent with hope. "Always the soul says to us all, Cherish your best hopes as a faith, and abide by them in action. Such shall be the effectual fervent means to their fulfillment."

This mood of confidence and reconciliation with reality made it difficult for Fuller to read with patience the very first book she reviewed for the *Tribune* — Emerson's *Essays, Second Series.* The preceding summer she had read some of the book in manuscript. At that time she was abashed at the difference between the "rude" piece of her own writing she was sending Emerson (probably a reprint of chapters from *Summer on the Lakes*) and his "great results, sculptured out into such clear beauty" (Fuller to Emerson, July 13, 1844). But by December, with Boston and Sing Sing and *Woman in the Nineteenth Century* behind her, she found she could scarcely bear to read Emerson's book through. The paralyzing sense of unreality described in essays like "Experience," with its emphasis on the isolation of the self and its skepticism about the possibility of reform, grated on her, and the best she could say to Emerson in her thank-you letter to him for the copy of the book he had sent her was that "in expression it seems far more adequate than the former volume, has more glow, more fusion" (Fuller to Emerson, November 17, 1844).

The review Fuller published in the *Tribune* on December 7, 1844, was both a gesture of filial piety toward and a declaration of independence from Emerson. Fuller pays tribute to Emerson as a man of unquestioned sincerity, who worships one god only, the god of Truth. She gives a vivid portrait of Emerson as a public speaker and remarks that the lectures that thrilled the youth of New England "seemed not so much lectures as grave didactic poems, theogonies, perhaps, adorned by odes" and delivered by a speaker who brought to mind the poets and legislators of ancient Greece – "men who taught their fellows to plow and avoid moral evil, sing hymns to the gods and watch the metamorphoses of nature." And she pays him this fine tribute: "History will inscribe his name as a father of the country, for he is one who pleads her cause against herself."

Nevertheless, Fuller also registers disappointment with the lack of cohesion in all of Emerson's essays. Though the second series of essays is better than the first in this respect, "yet in no one essay is the main stress so obvious as to produce on the mind the harmonious effect of a noble river or a tree in full leaf." Worse still is Emerson's neglect of the affections, the glow which is given to a body "by free circulation of the heart's blood from the hour of birth." The ideal region in which he dwells is pure and holy, but it leaves him like an Antaeus cut off from the sources of his strength. "We could wish he might be thrown by conflicts on the lap of mother earth, to see if he would not rise again with added powers."

Anyone who looks at the best of the almost two hundred and fifty columns that Fuller wrote for the *Tribune* in her twenty months of residence in New York might conclude that there was some special magic in the city's soil, for Fuller seemed to acquire added powers almost as soon as she set foot there. To Samuel Gray Ward she wrote that she liked her new position: "It is so central, and affords a far more various view of life than any I ever before was in." Far from feeling overwhelmed by her new duties, she hopes her pen will be "a vigorous and purifying implement" (Fuller to Ward, December 29, 1844). To W. H. Channing, who would serve as her escort through the slums and public institutions of the city, she was even more confident. "I feel as if something new, and *good* was growing" (Fuller to Channing, December 29, 1844).

The effect on Fuller's prose style was striking. As one scholar has pointed out, the contract to write three columns a week forced her to write rapidly and freed her from the paralyzing sense that she should be doing something great every time she wrote. Then too, New York's constantly changing panorama never ceased to interest her. Did she miss Boston? No, she told a friend, "I find I don't dislike wickedness and wretchedness more than pettiness and coldness" (Fuller to Sarah Shaw, February 25, 1845). Best of all was her liberation from the coterie atmosphere of *The Dial* and the inbred literary society of Boston and Cambridge. Fuller quickly realized that it was exhilarating to know that her columns might be read by fifty thousand people. Best of all, they were *anonymous* people. In a long essay on American literature that she wrote for inclusion in a volume of her collected essays in 1846, Fuller explained the chief advantage of writing for newspapers: "We address, not our neighbor, who forces us to remember his limitations and prejudices, but the ideal presence of human nature as we feel it ought to be and trust it will be. We address America rather than Americans."

The prejudices of Fuller's Boston and Cambridge friends about what kind of writing a woman ought to do had affected her adversely. She had tried to be either oracular or intuitively sympathetic and as a result had too often written prose that sounds inflated or cloying. Only in her "Introduction" to her translation of Eckermann's *Conversations with Goethe* had she spoken with the straightforwardness that her *Tribune* articles show. In both places she was sustained by a sense of mission – to bring European literary culture to America – and by the knowledge that she was better qualified to accomplish this mission than almost anyone else in the country.

Fuller quickly embraced her new role. Greeley gave her a free hand to discuss anything she thought significant (his only complaint was that she did not write fast enough). She delighted to rescue authors whom she considered unjustly neglected, like Charles Brockden Brown, a novelist she once called "by far our first in point of genius and instruction as to the soul of things." An 1846 reprinting of Brown's novels *Wieland* (1798) and *Ormond* (1799) gave her a chance to recommend a writer who had become almost inaccessible to the public, though he was far superior in "the higher qualities of the mind" to novelists currently on sale in every shop. Fuller argues that Brown's special genius lies in showing "the self-sustaining force of which a lonely mind is capable." (Fuller naturally likes Brown's decision to make women characters the narrators of several of his books. Brown's willingness to put a "thinking royal mind" in a woman's body makes him the "prophet of a better era.")

If Brown has been unjustly neglected, a poet such as Henry Wadsworth

Longfellow has been praised and glorified all out of proportion to his talent or his achievement. Fuller's notorious and devastating review of Longfellow's *Poems* of 1845 shows how fearless, how merciless, she had become after a year's pursuit of critical truth. She begins her December 1845 review of America's most popular poet by making some discriminations. Between the creators of true poetry and the grinders out of the wretched metrical trash that daily issues from American presses there is a "middle class," composed of persons of little original poetic power but with taste and sensibility, whose function in the realm of the spirit is to develop those faculties in others. Longfellow is such a middle-class poet, "a man of cultivated taste, delicate though not deep feeling, and some, though not much, poetic force." Right now the poetic bouquets he offers us contain "the flowers of all climes, and wild flowers of none." Fuller is sure that Longfellow himself *must* be aware of his relative rank in the kingdom of poetry. But his admirers, by hailing him as a genius, make his poetry usurp the place of better poems, and so prevent the development of that poetic taste that was his only real contribution to the culture of his native land.

Aesthetic issues are impossible for Fuller to separate from moral ones, and some of her most interesting reviews in the *Tribune* are of works that raise moral questions with particular vividness. The publication in 1845 of Carlyle's edition (with commentary) of Oliver Cromwell's speeches and letters allowed her to comment upon Carlyle's descent from a celebrator of spiritual freedom into an admirer of brutality and autocratic rule. Though she praises Carlyle's editorial work, she refuses to admire Cromwell's massacres in Ireland or to find Cromwell's religious holdings forth other than repulsive:

We stick to the received notions of Old Noll, with his great, red nose, hard heart, long head, and crafty ambiguities. Nobody ever doubted his great abilities and force of will. . . . But as to looking on him through Mr. Carlyle's glasses, we shall not be sneered or stormed into it, unless he has other proof to offer than is shown yet. And we resent the violence he offers both to our prejudices and our perceptions.

In some ways the most complex and subtle of Fuller's reviews concerned the religious controversies still agitating the New England she had left behind. On January 26, 1845, Theodore Parker preached a sermon, "The Excellence of True Goodness," in James Freeman Clarke's Boston Church of the Disciples – the pulpit exchange that caused such an uproar and occasioned the defection of fifteen of Clarke's church members. The sermon was printed, and a month after it had been delivered Fuller reviewed it for the *Tribune*. She does not spend much time discussing the sermon itself. Parker avoids controversy in it, and it contains none of his peculiar doctrines. But she has a great deal to say about the controversy within the Boston Association of Ministers and its attempt to freeze Parker out of Boston. Fuller derides the effort of those who call themselves "Liberal Christians" to do away with that sacred tenet of Protestant belief, the right of private judgment. Their failure is part of a larger failure of Protestantism in this country, where "after so many years of political tolerance, there exists very little notion, far less practice, of spiritual tolerance."

The Unitarians promised themselves that they would refrain from such persecution, and as long as the Reverend Channing was alive, they had a leader "who had confidence in the vital energy of Truth, and was not afraid to trust others with the same privileges he had vindicated for himself, even if they made use of them in a different manner." But his followers lack the moral courage of Channing. They were afraid not so much just of Parker himself but of the comments made by other sects about Parker, and "they had not confidence enough in those principles which had been the animating soul of their body" to rise above their fear. Fuller concedes that a minister may exclude from exchanges people with whom he disagrees – though she thinks such exclusion is ill-judged, because it leads to mental petrifaction. But the attempts that were made to coerce Clarke and Sargent into canceling their exchanges with Parker she finds absolutely contemptible. She takes a fierce delight in the failure of the Boston ministers' plots. Denied the church, Parker took to the lecture room, and the congregations followed. "The flock ran out of the fold to seek the wolf."

Fuller necessarily wrote a good many reviews that fall below the standards set by her best ones. She could sound spiteful, and she was not above puffing the negligible poetry of her brother-in-law, Ellery Channing (probably less out of cynicism than out of desperation, for Channing proved as helpless at earning a living as Bronson Alcott had been). But Thomas Wentworth Higginson said of her work for the *Tribune,* "In that epoch of strife which I so well remember . . . she held the critical sway of the most powerful American journal with unimpaired dignity and courage."

Fuller's productivity is all the more remarkable because her personal life during this period was anything but calm. Early in 1845 she met a German-Jewish businessman named James Nathan and began a flirtation that quickly turned (on her side, at least) into love. She showered Nathan with letters and affection; they went on walks together, attended concerts, shared books, left notes for each other. For a while Fuller was blissfully happy. But a crisis soon developed. (Its stages must be reconstructed from Fuller's letters alone because Nathan's do not survive.) Fuller apparently heard through a woman who ran a lodging house that Nathan was visiting a young woman there. She confronted him with the rumor. He almost made a confession, telling her his conscience was suffering, then lost his nerve and told her that the young woman was an "injured woman" whom he was trying to help.

It is a measure of Fuller's innocence and her desperation that she accepted Nathan's story, even telling him she found his conduct "honorable nay heroic." She confessed that she too had done things society would blame her for if she were judged by conventional rules (Fuller to Nathan, April 6, 1845). Fuller may have been thinking of her unconventional passion for Anna Barker Ward, but one can hardly blame Nathan for reading this confession as an invitation to make more explicit advances. He seems to have asked her if he might "hope" for something beyond their present relationship. The word "hope" made her believe at first that he was proposing marriage. When he told her that he could nevery marry her, Fuller was both shocked and insulted. What was most galling was the feeling that she had brought this humiliation upon herself. They patched up the quarrel, and in the late spring of 1845 they returned to some semblance of their old relationship. But Nathan was clearly puzzled and increasingly bored by a relationship that had all the trappings of passion but none of the usual rewards. He made plans to return to Europe, though he told Fuller only that he planned to travel abroad for a time.

Nathan left in June with his parting gift from Fuller, a copy of Shelley's poems. Before he left she had given him back his letters and asked for her own in return. He refused to give them back, despite her distress and repeated requests by letter after he had left the country. Nathan may have kept the letters because he wanted to ensure Fuller's continued willingness to perform services for him. He may have hoped to use them to extract money either from Fuller herself or from someone interested in her life (his heirs eventually sold them for one hundred and ten dollars). Or he may simply have been flattered to have been the object of such eloquent adoration by a celebrated American woman.

Of course, the immortality Nathan purchased by his refusal to return Fuller's letters turns out to be a dubious one. If her willingness to subject herself to him in these letters is humiliating, his calculating selfishness is repellent. Still, this surviving half of correspondence at least makes clear why Fuller fell in love with him. He may have been a cad, but he was *her* cad (or at least so she thought). By appearing to return her desire, Nathan gave her the chance to move from the periphery to the center of erotic life, if only in imagination. The torrent of generosity, adoration, and forgiveness Fuller unlooses upon him resembles the floods of divine grace poured out upon the unworthy sinner in Puritan theology. No wonder (as Perry Miller said) Nathan fled for his life.

After Nathan left New York, Fuller moved from the Greeleys' place on Turtle Bay into town, where she began to attend parties and gatherings of other literary people. She continued to write for the *Tribune* and began to collect some of her *Dial* and *Tribune* essays for publication in book form (*Papers on Literature and Art*). She composed a long and thoughtful survey of American literature for the book as well. But she was restless and eager for a change. When a wealthy couple, Marcus and Rebecca Spring, Quaker philanthropists who had become friendly with her in New York, suggested that she accompany them to Europe as companion to Rebecca and tutor to their son, she accepted. She reached an agreement with Greeley to continue her writing for the *Tribune;* he would pay her ten dollars for every column she sent back from abroad. Before she left she visited Cambridge to say goodbye to her family and receive from Emerson a letter of introduction to Carlyle.

On August 1, 1846, Fuller sailed with the Springs from New York aboard the steamer *Cambria,* which made the crossing to Liverpool in a new record time of ten days and sixteen hours. After touring the grimy industrial cities of Liverpool and Manchester and making a walking excursion to Chester they set off to visit the Lake District, where they saw a good deal of Harriet Martineau and called on Wordsworth. Then they went on to Carlisle in Scotland, made romantic by its association with Mary, Queen of Scots; next to Edinburgh (where Fuller was shocked to receive a letter from James Nathan informing her of his forthcoming marriage to a woman in Hamburg). Two weeks in the highlands came next, during which Fuller spent a frightening night alone on Ben Lomond, having gotten separated from her companion when both lost their way down the mountain. After Fuller recovered from this incident, the party descended to Glasgow, where the slums were, if anything, more wretched than the ones they had seen in Liverpool and Manchester.

Back in England, the party visited the cathedral at York; saw Walter Scott's home and Warwick Castle; stopped at Birmingham, Sheffield, and Newcastle (where they descended into a coal mine); and finally arrived in London. Fuller met many people in London literary society during the several weeks her party stayed there. *Woman in the Nineteenth Century* and her new book of essays had made her name well known, and she was invited many places. But the two men who meant most to her were Carlyle – whom to her surprise she liked – and Carlyle's close friend, Giuseppe Mazzini (1805–72), the leader in exile of the Italian Republican movement, who continued to try through his writings to agitate for overthrow of despotic regimes and the establishment of republican government in a united Italy.

In November 1846 the Springs left London with Fuller for Paris, where Fuller attended the debates in the raucous Chamber of Deputies, went to the theater, and tried to enter the lecture hall of the Sorbonne to hear a lecture on astronomy, only to be told that women were not allowed in, even when the hall was empty. She was perpetually frustrated by her difficulties with spoken French but managed all the same to meet artists and literary people, including George Sand, Frederic Chopin, and the exiled Polish poet Adam Mickiewicz (1798–1855). Mickiewicz was an admirer of Emerson and quickly became one of Fuller's closest friends.

Late in February the party left Paris for Italy, passing through Lyons and Avignon (where Fuller visited the tomb of Petrarch's Laura) to board a steamer to Genoa at Marseilles. A tour of Italy followed: Leghorn, Pisa, Naples, and then at last Rome, where they took lodgings on the Via del Corso. Then came an extensive tour of northern Italy, including Florence, Bologna, and Venice. An illness forced Fuller to rest in Venice, where she separated from the Springs, who had decided to return home by way of Germany. When she was well she resumed the tour alone through Vicenza, Verona, Brescia, and Milan (where she met the Italian novelist Alessandro Manzoni, author of *I Promessi Sposi* [*The Betrothed*]). For a while she crossed over into Switzerland, then returned to Italy for two weeks at Lake Como with a new companion, the Marchioness Visconti, another friend of Italian unity recently returned from twenty-six years of exile.

By the middle of October 1847, Fuller was back in Rome. During her previous stay there with the Springs during Holy Week, she had become separated from them while visiting Saint Peter's Church. A young Italian man, fashionably dressed and polite, seeing her anxiety, had offered his assistance. When it proved impossible to locate her companions or to find a carriage, he walked her all the way back to her lodgings. He introduced himself as Giovanni Angelo Ossoli, the son of the Marchese Filippo Ossoli, who held a high position in the papal court.

During the rest of her stay in Rome they became better acquainted. His mother had died when he was a child; his father was ill; his brothers were hostile to him, the last child in the family; he was sad and felt lonely. Fuller's warmly sympathetic nature appealed to him. Ossoli was not the only man in whom Fuller was interested at the time; there is a bold letter from her to the American painter Thomas Hicks in which she invites him to visit her because she is suffering from want of congenial companionship (Hicks politely declined, though he remained her friend and later painted her portrait). But Ossoli was persistent. When she left Rome with the Springs he predicted she would return to him.

Fuller kept the existence of Ossoli a secret from her Boston friends but confided her uncertainties by letter to Mickiewicz, who replied with some blunt advice. In a letter of August 3, 1847, he tells her that he is worried about her tendency to romantic reveries which could exhaust her imagination. He reminds her of what he had said to her in Paris: "I tried to make you understand that you should not confine your life to books and reveries. You have pleaded the liberty of woman in a masculine and frank style. Live and act, as you write." Later he reminded her, "Literature is not the whole of life" (Mickiewicz to Fuller, September 16, 1847). Apparently this was the advice she wanted, for by the middle of October she had returned to Rome, moved into a small apartment on the Corso, and taken Ossoli for a lover.

For a while she was very happy. But her discovery early in 1848 that she was pregnant filled her with despair. Ossoli could not marry a Protestant without a papal dispensation, which required the consent of his family, and his family would hardly consent to his marriage to a poor American woman over ten years his senior who was a Republican sympathizer to boot. Fuller had little money and Ossoli was no richer; in order to survive she had to keep writing for the *Tribune,* though she knew that if any word of her true condition leaked back to New York even the broad-minded Greeley would have to drop her from the paper.

What made her situation more difficult was that Fuller had arrived for her second stay in Rome in the middle of profound political changes. Pope Pius IX had begun his reign in 1846 with a series of reforms that won him the gratitude of the people. In May 1847 Fuller had witnessed a torchlight procession down the Corso celebrating the pope's promise to the people of a representative council; further reforms designed to transfer power in the Papal States from the clergy to the laity followed throughout the year. In February 1848 the pope published a written constitution allowing for secular government of the Papal States. But his reforms never had a chance to take effect, for more radical revolutions suddenly broke out all over Europe. In Sicily the people rose against their king, the hated Ferdinand II; riots broke out in Naples; mobs in Paris forced the abdication of King Louis Philippe; the Milanese rose against the Austrians and drove them from the city. The Venetians had driven out the Austrians as well and proclaimed themselves a republic, followed by Parma and Modena. It seemed a season of hope and joy, but the pope increasingly drew back from a popular revolution he could not control.

At the end of May, Fuller, whose pregnancy could no longer be concealed, left for the country where she remained until her son was born on September 5, 1848. Ossoli stayed in Rome where he was a member of the civil guard. He wrote to her frequently and managed to obtain leave to be with her when the child was born. Because Fuller needed to be in Rome to write her *Tribune* dispatches and the child could hardly be concealed there, they left him with a nurse in the village of Rieti and returned to Rome. There they found the political situation tense. The pope's appointed minister, the Count de Rossi, was assassinated as he tried to open the Chambers, and a mob forced the pope to agree to the formation of a democratic ministry. On the night of November 24, 1848, dressed as a common priest, the pope with the help of his supporters escaped from the palace and fled to Gaeta in the kingdom of Naples.

The pope's flight opened the way to the declaration of a Roman Republic, which the Constituent Assembly decreed on February 9, 1849. But ominous forces were ranged against the new republic. The Austrians had already retaken some of the northern cities; King Ferdinand had suppressed the revolt in the south. The exiled pope appealed to various European powers to help him regain his throne, and the new president of the French Republic, Louis Napoleon, sent French troops under General Oudinot to besiege Rome. Ossoli fought with the civil guard during the siege; Fuller was appointed *regolatrice* (supervisor) of a hospital devoted to tending the wounded. The first assault upon the city on April 24 was repulsed by the Italian patriot Garibaldi and his legions, but the bombardment to which the city was then subjected and the overwhelming numerical superiority of the attacking army finally breached Rome's defenses and forced its surrender. On the Fourth of July, 1849, the French army entered to occupy Rome. With the siege broken Fuller and Ossoli were finally able to reach Rieti, only to find their son Angelino malnourished and dangerously ill. Because it was too dangerous for a former Republican to live in Rome, where harsh repressive measures had been adopted by the authorities, the three of them left for Florence when the child had recovered.

Even the barest summary of Fuller's life story between the time she landed at Liverpool in 1846 and the collapse of the Roman Republic in 1849 sounds impossibly romantic, like a fantasy invented by Fuller when she was a young woman exiled to the boredom of her father's unprofitable farm in Groton. English slums, mist-clad Scottish mountains, coal mines, London literary lions, sensitive exiled revolutionaries, George Sand, Chopin, Italian aristocrats, love, motherhood, political revolution, triumph, siege, resistance, defeat. Even if Fuller had done no more than *live* the life sketched here it would have qualified as a major imaginative achievement. Some sense of what Fuller's life meant to her own generation can be gleaned from a comment made by one of her Boston friends after her death. She said that Fuller had "the most successful woman-life of the nineteenth century." It seems a curious remark, given the amount of suffering and sheer bad luck that dogged Fuller from beginning to end, unless you think of what kind of hope the trajectory of her life offered to the women she had left behind.

Fuller drew upon her experiences to write thirty-seven lengthy dispatches to the *Tribune,* and these dispatches (which run to more than two-hundred-and-eighty pages in the modern edition recently published) form one of the most absorbing, brilliant, and far-ranging of all texts written by the Transcendentalists. The first twelve of the dispatches deal with Fuller's experiences before she got to Italy; the remaining twenty-five with Italy itself. The first twelve belong recognizably to the category of travel writing, but even a cursory reading will suggest how different they are from *Summer on the Lakes.* The excessive subjectivity of the earlier book has been replaced by a speaker whose sense of self, though strong, is not the focus of attention; instead, it is a lens through which events can be clearly seen. Fuller's *Tribune* experience in New York had taught her how to write for an audience, rather than for herself, a discipline that gives her dispatches pace and urgency. And her need for Greeley's ten-dollar payments kept her writing even when she felt desperate or depressed.

This professionalism means that Fuller reports with intelligent curiosity whatever comes into her field of observation: the slums and gin palaces of Glasgow or the "squalid, agonizing, ruffianly" misery of the London poor; boatmen in Walter Scott country singing on beautiful Loch Katrine; the aged Wordsworth, repeating with much expression some lines written by his sister Dorothy and asking Fuller to admire his long avenue of prized hollyhocks; the skeleton of Jeremy Bentham, dressed as in life and equipped with a wax portrait mask, seated companionably in the study of his good friend Dr. Southwood Smith.

Yet Fuller's passages of observation, good as they are, are not as good as her character sketches. The best is that of Carlyle. Fuller wanted to meet Carlyle, as she wanted to meet everyone, but she had not gone to England expecting to like him. She had complained that ever since *Chartism* his works could be reduced to a simple message: "Everything is very bad. You are fools and hypocrites, or you would make it better" (Fuller to R. W. Emerson, June 1, 1843). Her exposure to social conditions in England and Scotland, however, had given her a better understanding of his rage. Now she was simply overwhelmed by his conversation.

"Accustomed to the infinite wit and exuberant richness of his writings, his talk is still an amazement and a splendor scarcely to be faced with steady eyes," she wrote, even though she readily admitted: "He does not converse – only harangues." Carlyle was indeed arrogant and overbearing, with "the heroic arrogance of some old Scandinavian conqueror." But she found herself liking him anyway. His talk seemed like singing, or poetry. "He pours on you a kind of satirical, heroical, critical poem, with regular cadences, and generally catching up near the beginning some singular epithet, which serves as a *refrain* when his song is full." Lonely as the desert, readier than anyone to ridicule all attempts to remedy the evils he deplored, he seemed to Fuller an original, and therefore a source of the most hearty refreshment.

When Fuller moves through France we can see a widening of sensibilities and a growing complexity in her thought about social issues. But the dispatches she sent from Italy show her transforming the genre into something quite different. As her relationship to the revolutionary movements in Italy shifts from sympathetic spectatorship to active partisanship, as the revolutions breaking out all over Italy flower into early successes and then collapse more or less swiftly back into defeats, she begins to add to her descriptive powers political commentary that shows an impressive command of information, understanding of character, and grasp of strategic fact.

This aspect of the dispatches is the one most difficult to convey, because the passages describing the movements of regiments or speculating about the possible motives of dukes or petty kings do not lend themselves easily to summary or quotation. Yet the cumulative impression they make is of a mind both ironic and tough — just as passages about the goals of the revolution and the larger direction of history suggest capacities for passionate indignation and moral absolutism.

Italy's sufferings give Fuller an appreciation for America's amazing luck. As she watched the Romans try to throw off centuries of corruption, brutality, poverty, and ignorance to declare their republic in a world of wolves — tyrannical Austria to the north, the murderous King Ferdinand to the south, the menacing French to the west — the United States seemed more than ever fortunate in the circumstances of its nativity. The infant American Republic was protected by a vast ocean on one side and a wilderness on the other, led by men like Washington and Adams, free of priestcraft, blessedly empty of aristocrats on the one hand and ignorant peasants on the other. It managed to expel the British without becoming the prey of another great power, whereas the poor Roman Republic was menaced from all sides before its independence had even been formally declared.

What angers Fuller is that her native land should have fallen so far from the ideals it espoused at its founding — refusing to do anything about the "cancer of slavery," behaving toward Mexico like the Austrian occupiers of Italy, tolerating a growing gap between the rich and poor that already had begun to reproduce in the New World all the vice and misery of the Old. Her growing awareness of the connection between concentrated wealth and political oppression makes her long for a "reform" that will be more radical than "revolution." Even Mazzini, when he arrives in Rome after his seventeen-year exile, is not radical enough for Fuller; he aims only at "political emancipation" and not at that greater social and economic emancipation of which Fourierism is only a crude prophecy.

The story Fuller tells in her dispatches is a tragedy, and it affects the reader like one. Reading about the celebrations that attend the coming of Roman independence, watching the ominous clouds on the political horizon, hoping against hope that the French will sympathize with the spirit of their own revolutions instead of aid tyrants in crushing one, realizing with fury that the promises of the French General Oudinot are lies, watching the destruction of art and beauty in the city of Rome as the bombardment begins, looking at the mangled limbs of beautiful young men who are brought to Fuller's hospital for treatment, watching the departure of Garibaldi's forces a few steps ahead of the invading French, watching with rage and contempt as the French army enters the city on (a cruel irony) July 4, 1849, Fuller manages to make us feel that we are living through the scenes she describes. By the final dispatch we feel something like that pity and fear tragedy promises to arouse and purge.

Yet the dispatches are not melancholy, as *Summer on the Lakes* was. Fuller's faith in the ultimate direction of the historical process sustains her even during the last awful days of the bombardment of Rome and the collapse of the Republic. She predicts confidently that the age of reaction will be short; by the next century all of Europe will be under democratic governments. The old powers may have triumphed temporarily, but their thrones will either topple or crumble away, and the people will finally claim those rights so long denied them.

From Florence (where she had gone with Ossoli and Angelino after the fall of Rome) Fuller writes of her attempt to recover her spirits and her hope. "I take long walks into the country, I gaze on the beauty of nature, and seek thus to strengthen myself in the faith that the Power who delighted in these creations will not suffer his highest, ardent, aspiring, loving men, to live and die in vain." She breaks off the dispatch (the next-to-last) because she suddenly is offered an opportunity to send it, but not before she concludes with a final rebellious prayer to that other power who inspires revolutions and topples thrones: "O Lucifer, son of the morning, fall not this time from thy chariot, but herald in at last the long looked for, wept for, bled and starved for day of Peace and Good Will to men."

Fuller did not want to return to America. She knew she would be subjected to a "social inquisition" far more daunting than anything she faced in Florence, where her friends accepted (or appear to accept) her story of a secret marriage to Ossoli before Angelino's birth. But she had little choice. Her only marketable commodity was a history of the Italian revolution she had been working on while she was writing the *Tribune* dispatches. Unable to afford steamship fare, the family booked passage on the merchantman *Eliza-*

beth, due to sail from Leghorn under the command of a captain with the reassuring New England name of Seth Hasty.

They set sail on May 17, 1850. But Captain Hasty came down with smallpox shortly after they left Leghorn and died when the ship was off Gibraltar. (Angelino came down with the same disease but managed to recover.) The first mate took over the ship and managed to sail as far as the coast of New Jersey by July 18. He told the passengers to expect arrival in New York the next day. During the night a hurricane arose. Desperate to reach the harbor, the first mate continued to steer for what he thought was the mouth of the harbor. But the wind had driven the *Elizabeth* north and east. At four o'clock in the morning the ship ran aground on a sandbar a few hundred yards off Fire Island. The next wave slammed the ship sideways against the sandbar, and her cargo of Italian marble (including – of all things – a statue of John Calhoun made by an American sculptor in Florence) broke through the hold.

In the morning people were visible on the beach, which was only a few hundred yards away, but the force of the storm prevented lifeboats from being launched or rescue lines from being fired to the ship. During the lull as the eye of the storm passed over the vessel several crew members and a few passengers grabbed planks, jumped overboard, and managed to reach shore. Fuller refused to try unless she, Ossoli, and her child could all be rescued together. At about three o'clock in the afternoon the steward of the boat grabbed Angelino and tried to make it ashore; their bodies were washed up on shore a few minutes later. The incoming tide made the waves larger, and first Ossoli, then Fuller, were washed off the deck of the wrecked ship. Their bodies were never found.

Emerson heard the news of Fuller's death three days later. He dispatched Thoreau to the site of the wreck, hoping to rescue at least the manuscript history of the Italian revolution that Fuller had brought with her. But by the time Thoreau reached Long Island, five days had passssed since the wreck, and by then the huge crowd of wreck pickers who had appeared to scavenge the beach for the *Elizabeth*'s cargo had cleaned the beach thoroughly; no manuscript was found.

9

THE ANTISLAVERY YEARS

I
N ITALY MARGARET FULLER had discovered what it felt like to be caught up in historical processes larger than those any individual could control – to be unable to refuse participation, to be forced to watch helplessly the outcome of events. In the winter and spring of 1850 events in the United States Congress would give the other Transcendentalists a similar experience. By the terms of the Treaty of Guadelupe Hidalgo in 1848 Mexico had ceded huge tracts of western land to the United States. The question immediately arose: would slavery be permitted in the new territory? Mexico had abolished slavery, but settlers from the southern United States were determined to reintroduce it, less because they thought slavery likely to flourish there (the arid climate was unsuitable for the crops that needed slave labor) than because they feared they would be encircled by new free states formed from the Mexican Cession, which would upset the balance of power they had up to then maintained in the Senate.

Two years earlier, a freshman Democratic congressman from Pennsylvania named David Wilmot had startled his colleagues in the House of Representatives, which was then debating the possibility of purchasing territory from Mexico, by offering an amendment to the appropriations bill that made it "an express and fundamental condition" to the acquisition of territory from Mexico that "neither slavery nor involuntary servitude shall ever exist in any part of said territory." This famous Wilmot Proviso was never adopted, but under its threat Congress quickly divided – not along party lines (Whig against Democrat) but along sectional ones (North against South) – in a way that seemed ominous for the future of the Union.

By 1848 fortune appeared to favor the South again on the subject of territorial expansion for slavery. The Democratic candidate for preseident, Lewis Cass, was pledged to uphold slavery, and the Whig candidate, Zachary Taylor, was a major slave owner himself. But when Taylor won he quickly disappointed his southern supporters by choosing an antislavery Northerner as his chief adviser and by seeking ways to keep the new territory free. Congress was deadlocked on the subject of whether it had the power to regulate slavery *in the territories;* Taylor encouraged California, suddenly rich in settlers drawn by the Gold Rush of 1848 and badly in need of central government, to apply to the Congress for admission *as a state*. Congress might wrangle endlessly about who had power to regulate slavery in the territories, but no one could deny a state the power to write its own constitution and forbid slavery if it chose to do so. California held a convention in the fall of 1849, wrote a constitution, and sought admission to the Union as a free state.

Southerners were infuriated by Taylor's maneuvers and determined to prevent the admission of California to the Union; young southern radicals called for a convention in Nashville, Tennessee, to be held in the summer of 1850 to discuss secession. Taylor was adamant. He upheld California's right to be admitted and vowed to defend the Union against anyone who would menace it. But Taylor, a war hero drafted by the Whigs because they correctly guessed that his popularity would win the election of 1848, was politically inexperienced and had few ties to the congressional leaders of either party. With talk of secession growing daily louder in the South, Henry Clay, the venerable Whig senator from Kentucky, attempted to devise a series of compromise resolutions that would stave off secession by laying to rest southern fears and threats to the slave system while mollifying the free states by granting them important concessions, including the admission of California.

Most historians agree that the package of eight resolutions put together by Clay had more material benefits in it for the North than for the South. But one of the resolutions in what came to be known as the Compromise of 1850 was a frank concession to the South. A law had been on the books since 1793 stipulating that fugitive slaves who escaped from one state to another must be returned to their owners. But the law was rarely enforced in the North; indeed, some northern states had laws forbidding state officers to assist in capturing or returning fugitive slaves. Now Clay called for a new Fugitive Slave Law, one that provided for federal rather than state administration of the procedures taken to recapture escaped slaves and return them to their owners.

Clay enlisted the help of Daniel Webster, the Whig senator from Massachusetts, in support of his resolutions. Webster had opposed the Mexican War and supported the Wilmot Proviso, but he feared disunion as much as Clay did, and he agreed with Clay that the proposed legislation offered a chance to save the Union from division. On March 7, 1850, Webster delivered one of his most famous speeches in the Senate, "Constitution and Union," throwing his support behind Clay's compromise, including its most obnoxious provision, the Fugitive Slave Law, in the interests of preserving a Union he described as eminently worth the sacrifice of particular sectional interests. Webster was severely criticized in the North by antislavery leaders who regarded his speech of conciliation as a betrayal (Whittier wrote a famous poem portraying Webster as a fallen angel), but there were many among Boston's merchant and professional classes who hailed him as the courageous preserver of the Union. Toward the end of the month they presented him with a letter of praise signed by nearly a thousand prominent citizens.

Four days after Webster's Seventh of March speech Taylor's closest adviser had a chance to reply. William Henry Seward (1801–72) had been governor of New York State and was now its senator. He was a firm opponent of slavery who while he was governor had obtained the passage of laws prohibiting state officials from assisting in the capture of fugitive slaves and guaranteeing the right to a jury trial for fugitive slaves captured by someone else. On March 11 Seward delivered a speech in the Senate opposing Clay's compromise on both Constitutional and moral grounds. It was the second kind of argument that gave the speech the name by which it was popularly known. Seward argued that the moral law established by the Creator was a higher law than the Constitution and that the moral law was working everywhere in the civilized world toward the extirpation, not the extension, of slavery. Though Webster mocked the "higher law" speech, it was popular in the North, where over a hundred thousand copies of it were soon in circulation.

Clay and Webster were unable to secure passage of the compromise during the spring and summer of 1850. Then, suddenly, on the Fourth of July, President Taylor became ill with gastroenteritis; he died five days later. With their strongest opponent out of the way Southerners who were hostile to the terms of Clay's compromise managed to defeat most of its provisions, and by July 31 the compromise appeared dead and Clay defeated. But Stephen A. Douglas of Illinois realized that the Compromise could still be saved by judicious coalition building, and he felt sure that the new president, Millard Fillmore, would sign the measures into law. Douglas succeeded so well that by September 17 he had gotten passage of bills covering most items in the compromise Clay had tried to push through earlier, including two of the most contentious issues. California was admitted to the Union as a free state; and fugitive slaves would have to be captured wherever they fled and rendered back to their owners.

To Emerson the debate seemed at first merely another symptom of the "badness of the times" that was "making death attractive." That his former hero Daniel Webster would throw his weight behind the squalid compromise was bad enough, though by this time Emerson was more or less used to seeing Webster sacrifice principle for expedience. "It seem 'tis now settled that men in Congress have no Opinions; that they may be had for any opinion, any purpose," he wrote glumly in a journal entry headed "D Webster." The rush of Boston's mercantile elite to support Webster, on the other hand, elicited an outburst of contempt. "I think there was never an event half so painful occurred in Boston as the letter with 800 signatures to Webster. The siege of Boston was a day of glory. This was a day of petticoats, a day of imbecilities, the day of the old women." But Webster's mockery of Seward was the unforgivable sin. "The worst symptom I have noticed in our politics lately is the attempt to make a gibe out of Seward's appeal to a higher law than the Constitution, & Webster has taken part in it. I have seen him snubbed as *Higher-Law*-Seward." In "Montaigne," published in January 1850, Emerson had just argued that moral law was the only compass human beings had to steer them through seas of conflicting interests. Webster's ridicule of moral law threatened the one principle in human beings Emerson believed to be divine, and accordingly he called such mockery "atheism" — a term hurled often enough at Emerson during the miracles controversy, but one he almost never used himself.

When the Fugitive Slave Law finally went into effect on September 18, 1850, the abolitionists expressed their determination to oppose it. In October there was a meeting in Boston's Faneuil Hall to express indignation at the law; Theodore Parker and Wendell Phillips were speakers. For a time it seemed as if the new law might be as successfully defied as the old one had been. In the fall of 1850 the members of the Boston Vigilance Committee, which existed to protect black residents of the city from slave catchers and to assist fugitive slaves, got word that two fugitives, Ellen and William Craft, were being menaced by some men from Georgia. Parker called upon the Georgians and managed to persuade them that they themselves were not safe in Boston. Next he married the Crafts at their boardinghouse and then dispatched them to England and the protection of James Martineau.

The next case came closer to catastrophe. On February 18, 1851, Fred Wilkins (nicknamed "Shadrach"), a black waiter in a Boston coffeehouse, was arrested as a fugitive slave. He was being held prisoner in the federal courthouse when a black member of the Vigilance Committee and about twenty associates forced their way into the courthouse, swept Shadrach up into their midst, and got him away. They hid him first in Concord, and then moved him north through Vermont to Canada. Though the liberation of Shadrach looked like another victory, the apparent willingness of Chief Justice Lemuel Shaw of the state supreme court of Massachusetts to enforce the statute was a shock to those who had publicly boasted (as Theodore Parker did a year earlier) that no power on earth could force Bostonians to perpetuate slavery.

Finally disaster arrived. On April 3, 1851, a seventeen-year-old boy named Thomas Sims was captured in Boston and held in the federal courthouse, which was guarded heavily this time to prevent any attempts at rescue. Sims's lawyers tried every argument to persuade Justice Shaw (who was Herman Melville's father-in-law) to free Sims, but in vain. At four o'clock in the morning three hundred soldiers escorted Sims through a jeering crowd who cried "Shame!" at the soldiers but could not block their progress toward the docks, where Sims was put on a ship for Georgia. (As if to drive home the humiliation of Massachusetts, Sims's owner had him publicly whipped in Savannah on the anniversary of the Battle of Lexington and Concord.)

In April 1851 Emerson had formally declared his opposition to the Fugitive Slave Law by sending a letter to the annual meeting of the Middlesex Anti-slavery Society. Emerson apologized for not being able to attend the meeting in person (he was off on a lecture tour), but he declared his determination to oppose the "detestable statute" passed by Congress. He urged everyone to defend fugitive slaves against their owners. The tone of the letter, which was written in mid-March, is one of calm determination rather than anger. Although fugitive slaves had been caught and delivered up to their owners in other states, Emerson may have believed that greater devotion to liberty in Massachusetts would continue to drive the slave catchers out of the state empty-handed. Unfortunately, the day of the Middlesex meeting (April 3) was also the day Thomas Sims was captured in Boston.

The rendition of Sims moved Emerson from controlled anger to white-hot fury. The editors of his journals point out that he filled eighty-six manuscript pages of his 1851 journal with entries devoted to Webster, the Fugitive Slave Law, and the shame both were bringing upon the state that was the birthplace of American liberty. "Boston, of whose fame for spirit & character we have all been so proud. . . . Boston, which figures so proudly in Adams's diary, which we all have been reading: Boston, through the personal influence of this New Hampshire man, must bow its proud spirit in the dust, & make us irretrievably ashamed."

Emerson now had a full-blown case of what John Jay Chapman calls "the disease of antislavery" and felt obliged to take some kind of direct personal action. When the townspeople of Concord approached him on April 26, 1851, requesting that he speak to them on the subject of the Fugitive Slave Law, he agreed. On May 3 he delivered the first of his addresses on the law. The address, which was one of the strongest of his career, draws upon the diatribes with which Emerson had been filling his journals; its reiterated themes are the corruption of the land by the law and the cowardice of the citizens who allowed the law into the land. City and country are "involved in one hot haste of terror," journals are paralyzed with panic, and "one cannot open a newspaper without being disgusted by new records of shame." The irony of all these attempts to protect property, as Emerson points out, is the loss of its value. The Fugitive Slave Law has caused a collapse in land values all over the nation. "The very convenience of property, the house and land we occupy, have lost their best value, and a man looks gloomily at his children, and thinks, 'What have I done that you should begin life in dishonor?' "

Nevertheless, there is one great benefit to be derived from the recent disgraces. "The crisis had the illuminating power of a sheet of lightning at midnight. It showed truth." All of the protestations of love and the odes to liberty are revealed to be shams, and the poor black boy who has heard of the fame of Boston as he hides in his southern swamp finds out when he gets to the city that "the famous town of Boston is his master's hound" and that he has "taken the risk of being shot, or burned alive, or cast into the sea, or starved to death, or suffocated in a wooden box, to get away from his driver" only to be hunted by the men of Massachusetts and sent back to the dog hutch he had fled.

Yet the loss of state honor pales before the greater skepticism Emerson says has been induced by the law. In a sudden transition to sadness he lists all of the beliefs that the Fugitive Slave Law has caused him to give up, the first being the belief that passage of the law would instantly arouse "all moral beings" to resist it. But if Massachusetts has so far failed to rise up against the law, Webster has been no more successful in using the compromise to silence the debate about slavery. "Mr. Webster's measure was, he told us, final. . . . Does it look final now? His final settlement has dislocated the foundations. The state-house shakes like a tent." In fact, the law has "been like a university to the entire people. It has turned every dinner-table into a debating-club, and made every citizen a student of natural law."

What lessons are taught in this university? First of all, that the Fugitive Slave Law must be resisted. "It must be abrogated and wiped out of the statute-book; but whilst it stands there, it must be disobeyed." As for the larger question, Emerson argues only that slavery should be kept out of the territories; after that, the free states should help the slave states to make a peaceful end to slavery — if necessary, by buying the slaves, as the British nation bought the slaves of the West Indian planters. "Was there ever any contribution that was so enthusiastically paid as this will be? . . . A thousand millions were cheap." The thought of Massachusetts leading the drive to "dig away this accursed mountain of sorrow once and forever out of the world" revives Emerson's spirits, and the address ends on a note of hope. "We must make a small state great, by making every man in it true."

In a sign of the way that the struggle against slavery was overcoming old antagonisms, Emerson was asked to repeat his Concord address as a stump speech for John Gorham Palfrey, who had been dean of the Harvard Divinity

School at the time of the Divinity School Address and who was now seeking election to Congress on the Free Soil ticket. Emerson agreed, repeating his Fugitive Slave Law address at various places during the spring of 1851. At Cambridge toward the end of May he was hooted and hissed at by Harvard students who shouted the praises of Webster and Edward Everett; he maintained his composure, simply continuing with the next word in his speech when the hubbub died down. Though Palfrey lost the election Emerson found the experience of speaking out against the law in public exhilarating. In a letter to Theodore Parker thanking him for a printed Fast-Day Sermon ("The Chief Sins of the People") attacking the Fugitive Slave Law, Emerson mentions having read five similar speeches and says, "It half exculpates the State, that the protest of the minority is so amply & admirably uttered in the very place & hour of the crime" (Emerson to Parker, April 18, 1851).

The next summer held a bittersweet confirmation of Emerson's belief in the inerrancy of the moral law when Daniel Webster's final try at securing the 1852 Whig nomination for president went down to humiliating defeat. Webster had come to believe that obeying the law was a "Christian duty"; he had encouraged the marshals to arrest fugitive slaves and had accused their rescuers of treason; he had expressed his approval of the rendition of Sims. Now it appeared that Webster's support for the Fugitive Slave Law had been for nothing. Passage of the law had not stopped the agitation of the slavery question in the North, and it had not won the loyalty of the Southerners in his own party. In the Baltimore convention in June 1852 Webster received only 21 out of the 294 Whig votes; the rest of the votes were divided between Millard Fillmore and General Winfield Scott (who finally won the nomination on the fifty-third ballot). Emerson summed up the sad end of Webster's once-glorious career: "To please the South he betrayed the North, and was thrown out by both."

Webster did not long outlive his rejection by the Whigs. He died in October 1852. Emerson marked the event by writing in his journal some passages of admiration for the man who had once been his hero. But no tenderness for the dead kept Emerson from cursing Webster for bringing an evil law upon the land. When Emerson was invited in 1854 to deliver an address in New York to mark the fourth anniversary of Webster's Seventh of March speech, he carefully sketched out for his audience the reasons for Webster's previous greatness as a speaker – his manners, his carriage, the simplicity and wisdom of his rhetoric, and the power of his character, which could make his wrath the wrath of the cause he stood for. Yet in the hour of decision Webster had thrown his whole weight on the side of slavery and made the speech that corrupted the country. Its goodness or badness as a piece of logic or rhetoric was not in question. "Nobody doubts that Daniel

Webster could make a good speech. Nobody doubts that there were good and plausible things to be said on the part of the South. But this is not a question of ingenuity, not a question of syllogisms, but of sides. *How came he there?"*

The need for choosing sides would soon be on everyone's mind again. After the rendition of Sims in 1851 there were no more fugitive slave cases in Massachusetts for several years, and the intense anger aroused by that case gradually dissipated or sought an outlet in more conventional political activity. But on Thursday, May 25, 1854, an escaped Virginia slave named Anthony Burns was seized in Boston, where he had been working in a store. Like Shadrach and Thomas Sims before him, Burns was held prisoner in the federal courthouse in Boston, where he was to be tried on Saturday morning. Antislavery activists planned to hold a protest meeting in Faneuil Hall on Friday night. Members of the Boston Vigilance Committee held a meeting on Friday morning to try to plot some kind of rescue.

Vigilance Committee meetings, however, involved an unruly collection of individualists, completely untrained for revolutionary action and accustomed to follow their own consciences alone in schemes of reform. Thomas Wentworth Higginson (1823–1911), a Unitarian minister who would go on to become the literary mentor chosen by Emily Dickinson and the colonel of the first regiment of black soldiers in the Union army, remembered the Vigilance Committee meetings as "disorderly conventions, each man having his own plan or theory, perhaps stopping even for anecdote or disquisition, when the occasion required the utmost promptness of decision and the most unflinching unity in action." The Faneuil Hall meeting on Friday morning was as unruly as usual, and Higginson despaired of Burns's rescue. The United States marshals guarding Burns would certainly be prepared for a mob assault on the courthouse building after this meeting. Then a Vigilance Committee member named Martin Stowell suggested a plan that contained an element of surprise:

Could there not be an attack at the very height of the meeting, brought about in this way? Let all be in readiness; let a picked body be distributed near the Court House and Square; then send some loud-voiced speaker, who should appear in the gallery of Faneuil Hall and announce that there was a mob of negroes already attacking the Court-House; let a speaker, previously warned . . . accept the opportunity promptly, and send the whole meeting pell-mell to the Courthouse Square, ready to fall in behind the leaders and bring out the slave.

Higginson prepared a box of axes for an assault on the courthouse doors and joined in picking a small band of white and black men to lead the assault. But the plot failed. The Faneuil Hall meeting was so much larger than the Vigilance Committee had expected, filling the galleries, the floors, the stairways, that the chosen messenger could not get into the gallery to shout the prearranged signal. Higginson waited with the other men in Court House Square for a mob that never arrived. Then, just as Higginson had given up hope of rescuing Burns, Stowell appeared and whispered that he and some men were bringing a wooden beam up to the west side of the building and would attempt to hammer down the courthouse door.

At the time of the Sims case Higginson had noted in his journal how difficult it was "to educate the mind to the attitude of revolution. It is so strange to find one's self outside of established institutions . . . to see law and order, police and military, on the wrong side, and find good citizenship a sin and bad citizenship a duty, that it takes time to prepare one to act coolly and wisely, as well as courageously, in such an emergency." Now, three years later, he found himself at the head of a battering party, facing a muscular black man across a wooden beam they were using to try to smash in the doors of the Boston courthouse.

Eventually the door gave way and swung open wide enough for one man to pass through the opening. The black man jumped in; Higginson followed. The six or eight police officers who had been attempting to keep the door shut from within began clubbing them savagely, and one of the marshal's deputies inside the building fell dead – either stabbed by Higginson's black companion or shot by someone in the battering party still outside. Gradually both attackers were forced back across the threshold, where they discovered that their supporters had fallen back to the bottom of the courthouse steps. Though the chances looked slim Higginson still waited near the threshold hoping for reinforcements. Just at that moment Amos Bronson Alcott came forth from the crowd below. "Ascending the lighted steps alone, he said tranquilly, turning to me and pointing forward, 'Why are we not within?' " Higginson answered impatiently that the rest of the people would not stand by them. "He said not a word, but calmly walked up the steps, – he and his familiar cane. He paused again at the top, the centre of all eyes, within and without; a revolver sounded from within, but hit nobody; and finding himself wholly unsupported, he turned and retreated, but without hastening a step."

Alcott's serenity on this occasion seemed to Higginson worthy of Plato or Pythagoras. But if Alcott's trust in absolute spirit represented the driving force behind the antislavery movement, the murder of the marshal's deputy was a better predictor of what was to come. "In all the long procession of events which led the nation through the Kansas struggle, past the John Brown foray, and up to the Emanciption Proclamation, the killing of Batchelder was the first act of violence. It was, like the firing on Fort Sumter, a proof that war had really begun."

Warned by the magnitude of the disturbance, the federal government sent in troops – two companies of artillery and two of marines – to escort Burns back to the ship that took him south on June 2. The sense of outrage and violation now seemed complete. The black residents of Massachusetts were helpless before slave catchers; the white residents who tried to protect or rescue fugitive slaves saw themselves invaded by their own government as if they were a captured nation. The sense of humiliation was intensified when Massachusetts residents learned that the hated Kansas–Nebraska bill had finally passed Congress the day after Burns's arrest. Introduced by Senator Stephen A. Douglas in January, the bill opened the territory west of Missouri to settlement by slave owners and thus repealed the Missouri Compromise of 1820, which had prohibited slavery north of 36°30' in the territory acquired in the Louisiana Purchase. This repeal violated an agreement the North had come to regard as sacred and raised fears that, as Massachusetts senator Charles Sumner wrote to Emerson, "new outrages are at hand, in the concatenation by which the Despotism of Slavery is to be fastened upon the National Govt." (Sumner to Emerson, June 12, 1854).

When the customary celebrations of the nation's birthday came in 1854 they seemed a mockery. Ellen, the Emerson's daughter, remembered that her mother, Lidian,

considered our country wholly lost to any sense of righteousness, and hearing that there was to be some celebration of the Day, and seeing flags go up, she asked Father's leave to cover our gates with a pall. Father smiled and consented. So she got a quantity of black cambric, and made a great show of it on our front gate and gate-posts.

Henry Thoreau, too, was celebrating an unconventional Fourth of July at an antislavery rally in Framingham, where he read parts of an address entitled "Slavery in Massachusetts." Garrison, who had also spoken at the Framingham rally, printed the whole text of Thoreau's address in the *Liberator* for July 21; it was reprinted again by Greeley in the *Tribune* on August 2 and partially reprinted in the *National Anti-Slavery Standard* on August 12.

"Slavery in Massachusetts" grows directly out of Thoreau's journal passages written during the Burns affair. But Thoreau also used journal passages he had written about the rendition of Thomas Sims three years earlier. The "moral earthquake" in both cases had taken place without awakening the slightest resistance from the elected officials of Massachusetts, who sat tamely by while southern planters transformed them into slave catchers. "The whole military force of the State is at the service of a Mr. Suttle, a slaveholder from Virginia, to enable him to catch a man whom he calls his property; but not a soldier is offered to save a citizen of Massachusetts from being kidnapped!" The trial of Burns (like that of Sims before him) is really a trial of Massachusetts. "Every moment that she hesitated to set this man free – every moment that he now hesitates to atone for her crime, she is convicted."

Where is a slave to turn for comfort? To the courts? They regard him as property. To the governor of Massachusetts? The worst that can be said of him is that in the midst of the crisis nobody bothered to inquire after him or noticed his absence. "The law will never make men free; it is men who have got to make the law free. They are the lovers of law and order, who observe the law when the government breaks it." And again: "Whoever has discerned truth, has received his commission from a higher source than the chiefest justice in the world, who can discern only law. He finds himself constituted judge of the judge."

What should concern the state of Massachusetts is not the Kansas–Nebraska bill but her own "slaveholding and servility." People who think that government exists to protect property should remember that the value of life itself is diminished in a state that has lost its liberties. "I have lived for the last month," Thoreau says, "with the sense of having suffered a vast and indefinite loss. I did not know at first what ailed me. At last it occurred to me that what I had lost was a country."

That sense of collective loss makes "Slavery in Massachusetts" differ markedly from "Resistance to Civil Government," even when the 1854 address borrows arguments and imagery from the earlier essay. Though Thoreau now says that his thoughts "are murder to the State, and involuntarily go plotting against her," his protest is no longer an individual one. He speaks at a rally, not at a country lyceum, and gives his address to the newspapers, not to a fledgling journal of aesthetics that lasted for only one issue and attracted only fifty subscribers. The affectation of indifference to public life cultivated in "Resistance to Civil Government" is gone. Thoreau now speaks as a citizen to citizens, and with a sense of urgency. "We have used up all our inherited freedom. If we would save our lives, we must fight for them."

Yet dark as the times seemed, there were signs of hope. Charles Sumner had been chosen senator by the Massachusetts Legislature after nearly four months of political wrangling in 1851, and though Sumner lacked Webster's genius and Webster's influence he had been a committed opponent of the Fugitive Slave Law since its passage, several times attempting (without success) to move its repeal. In the spring of 1854 he turned his fury upon the Kansas–Nebraska bill. As one of only three Free Soil party members in the Senate he could do little to prevent the passage of the bill, but he could speak against it in lengthy orations that were quickly telegraphed back to his native state.

Sumner found more sympathy even among conservative Whigs than anyone could have predicted six months earlier. The Kansas–Nebraska bill seemed to most people a betrayal of the agreement Webster had persuaded them to accept in 1850. Worse still, it threatened to open to slaveholders northern territories bordering on free states – territories that people in the North believed had been secured permanently for freedom by the terms of the Missouri Compromise of 1820. On May 24, 1854, the day the Senate met to give its final approval to the Kansas–Nebraska bill, Sumner rose to denounce it as the worst bill ever enacted by Congress. But he also praised it as the best – because it "annuls all past compromises with Slavery, and makes all future compromises impossible. Thus it puts Freedom and Slavery face to face, and bids them grapple. Who can doubt the result?" That the reports of Sumner's speech reached Boston the day after the failed attempt to rescue Anthony Burns only gave it more point.

Political parties were thrown into disarray by the outrage over the Kansas–Nebraska bill. Democrats suffered defections because the bill was a Democratic piece of legislation; Whigs, because their dissension had rendered them too weak to prevent the bill's passage. New political parties sprouted all over the country, hoping to gain converts among disgruntled Democrats and Whigs. In Massachusetts the biggest gainers were not the Free-Soilers, as one might have expected, but the antiimmigrant, anti-Catholic party popularly called the Know-Nothings, which had been organized in response to the massive influx of immigrants during the late 1840s and 1850s. In the November 1854 elections the Massachusetts Know-Nothings got 63 percent of the vote; the voters returned a state legislature consisting of 1 Whig, 1 Democrat, and 377 Know-Nothings. That the long Whig dominance of the legislature should have been broken might have been hailed as a cause for celebration by progressives, but that it should have been broken by a collection of disreputable rabble-rousers like the Know-Nothings was dispiriting in the extreme. Rufus Choate, a Whig of the old school, remarked after the election: "Any thing more low, obscene, feculent, the manifold heavings of history have not cast up."

Emerson was inclined to agree, though he thought the inglorious way the two traditional parties had been turned out of office deserved rather to be called an "immense frolic," a mad joke that had gone too far. In a new lecture, "American Slavery," which he first delivered in Boston on January 26, 1855 (and repeated seven times in succeeding months), Emerson tries to make some sense of the moral and political upheavals of the preceding half decade. Many of the themes are familiar. Emerson manifests contempt for the elected northern officials who truckled to the South – "They ate dirt, and saw not the sneer of the bullies who duped them with an alleged state-necessity; and all because they had no burning splendor of law in their own minds." He professes a familiar faith in the "sound healthy universe" that can "rid itself at last of every crime," as a snake casts its skin by spasms. And he still finds the only trustworthy moral compass in the faith of "private men who have brave hearts & great minds." Indeed, "this is the compensation of bad governments, the field it affords for illustrious men."

Yet there is a new note in the lecture, which tries to take the longest possible view of the question of slavery. "But whilst I insist on the doctrine of the independence & the inspiration of the individual, I do not cripple but exalt the social action," Emerson asserts. Society, it turns out, is more than the joint-stock company he had contemptuously termed it in "Self-Reliance." Now he argues that the state is a reality, and "God is certain that societies of men, a race, a people, have a public function, a part to play in the history of humanity." And what is America's part? "The theory of our Government is Liberty." Liberty is not a fact or a private opinion; it is "a gradual & irresistible growth of the human mind."

It is for this reason that every American is justified, where there is a collision in statutes, to decide in favor of liberty. If the law is unjust, we must be willing to "put the Tea overboard in the Harbor, & hunt the slave hunter, — destroy the law before the principle." For if it is true that "heaven too has a hand in these events, and will surely give the last shape to these ends which we hew very roughly," it is also true that "our will and obedience is one of its means." In this collective effort even the scholar has a part to play, despite his unfitness for political strife. The curse of America is that its "immense industrial energy" has not been accompanied by "a great imaginative soul, a broad cosmopolitan mind." Hence the frivolity of its politics, the cruelty of its institutions, the superficiality of its culture. In this hubbub of conflicting voices, the scholar alone can recall his fellow citizens to a sense of the ideals they have abandoned, for "God instructs men through the Imagination."

This faith had animated the Transcendentalists from the beginning. In the heady days of the miracles controversy, when public discussion in New England for a time was focused on disputes within the Unitarian church, the Transcendentalists had been the "movement party," full of all the confidence revolutionary zeal generates in its possessors. But the stresses of the 1840s had been hard on them. If like Orestes Brownson they proposed schemes of radical social reform, they were blasted by angry responses clear into reaction and authoritarianism. If like George Ripley they tried to move from theory directly into social practice, they came to grief over the stinginess of nature, the recalcitrance of human beings, and the brusque laws of the marketplace. If like Theodore Parker they remained within the church and tried to reform it, they found the ice of entrenched conservatism depressingly resistant to the flame of zeal.

Refusing to enlist in any of these causes and insisting upon the integrity and authenticity of the individual self, as Emerson and Thoreau largely did, protected both men from this kind of disillusionment. But that carried its own costs: self-reproach, feelings of impotence and sometimes of unreality, and awareness that the proud refusal to be contaminated by inauthenticity could easily look like cowardice or petulance. Even Emerson never really understood what Thoreau was driving at by his night in the Concord jail or his move to the cabin at Walden, and Thoreau was contemptuous of the web of accommodations that allowed Emerson to turn out militant lectures and books in his study while leading a comfortable life in his Concord house.

The political indignities of the early 1850s, however, degrading as they were, confirmed Emerson and Thoreau in their sense that they had been right to insist on private integrity before all else – only in private integrity was there any defense against the stupidity of government or the immorality of law. The health of any democratic government depends upon the virtue of the individual citizen, for when the government has become corrupt only the rectitude of the citizens can restore what it has lost or abandoned. "When the public fails in its duty, private men take its place," Emerson said in "American Slavery." Emerson had not understood in 1846 what Thoreau had hoped to accomplish by his lonely protest against the Mexican War. Now, in 1855, after the Sims and Burns cases, after the Kansas–Nebraska bill, Emerson understands that "we have a great debt to the brave & faithful men who in the hour & place of the evil act, make their protest for themselves & their countrymen, by word & deed." Far from being eccentrics, such men are "the genius & future of the tribe."

Emerson thought well enough of "American Slavery" to write to his old friend William Henry Furness that he was willing to deliver it in Philadelphia. "I have a pretty good lecture this time, – good enough for me, or good 'considering' " (Emerson to Furness, January 26, 1855). But even this minimal confidence slowly evaporated. Though Emerson gave the speech seven more times he refused to write another when Furness asked him for one the next fall. "I believe I make the worst Antislavery discourses that are made in this country. They are only less bad than Slavery itself. I incline this winter to promise none" (Emerson to Furness, October 1, 1855).

Events though drew Emerson out of retirement. In 1856 open warfare had broken out in Kansas between groups of "border ruffians" from Missouri, determined to organize the new territory as a slave state, and emigrants from the free states, who wanted to keep the territory free. New Englanders raised money to send aid and weapons to the settlers. The struggle was at once depressing and portentous. A letter from Furness to Emerson written in the fall of 1856 expresses the contradictory feelings perfectly. Furness laments the current state of affairs in the United States. "What a mess the country is & how the elements spit & sputter." Yet he also says: "The struggle is tremendous. It is the world's battle. The regeneration of Europe is to be decided here. How grand it is to see the cause of God & man making its way against the passions, the interests the will of man!" (Furness to Emerson, October 18, 1856).

On May 19, 1856, Senator Charles Sumner began delivering a lengthy speech in the Senate against the "border ruffians" who were ravaging Kansas and the slave powers that supported them. "The Crime Against Kansas" was full of tasteless invective, some of it directed against the dignified elderly senator from South Carolina, Andrew P. Butler, and the state he represented. Sumner finished his speech on the next day. Butler had been absent from the Senate when Sumner spoke, but a young cousin of his, Representative Preston Brooks of South Carolina, had come over to the Senate to hear the speech and was outraged by it. Determined to avenge the insults to both kinsman and state, he waited for an opportunity to give Sumner a thrashing and finally found it when, on May 22, he saw Sumner seated alone at his desk after the Senate had adjourned, franking printed copies of "The Crime Against Kansas" (112 pages long). Brooks began beating Sumner savagely over the head with a cane, giving him about thirty blows during the time it took him to get out from beneath his heavy Senate desk and try to flee. The bleeding Sumner finally tore the desk from the floor as he rose, staggered a few feet, and collapsed. Brooks was still raining down blows when two other representatives intervened to pull him away.

Brooks quickly became a hero to fire-eating Southerners (his constituents voted to give him one gold-headed cane, and the students at the University of Virginia collected money for another). With the same speed Charles Sumner became a martyr to the North, where tens of thousands of copies of his "Crime Against Kansas" speech were distributed. Anger in Massachusetts was intense, particularly because the news of the assault upon Sumner reached the state just as news of a proslavery raid upon the free-state town of Lawrence, Kansas, arrived. Border thuggery and Brooks's cowardly attack upon a defenseless man were denounced together in the protest rallies held in large cities and small towns all over the North.

Emerson spoke at the Concord meeting, held on May 26, 1856. "The Assault upon Mr. Sumner" opens with an admission that the hopes for peaceful reconciliation with which "American Slavery" closed have been dashed by the ugliness of recent events. The time for compromise has ended. "I do not see how a barbarous community and a civilized community can constitute one state. I think we must get rid of slavery, or we must get rid of freedom." Sumner had endeared himself to Emerson as much by his refusals as by his deeds: by his refusal to seek votes during the long months when his first election to the Senate was pending, by his refusal to be hurried by the importunities of his abolitionist friends into speaking on the subject of slavery before he was ready. If he had been hesitant at first on the Senate floor, he has now gone beyond expectation, and "every friend of freedom thinks of him as the friend of freedom."

Kansas claimed Emerson's attention too. He attended meetings of the Kansas Aid Society in Concord, and on September 10, 1856, he delivered his "Speech on Affairs in Kansas." The beginning sounds like propaganda; Emerson writes of "the screams of hunted wives and children answered by the howls of the butchers." But he quickly moves beyond cliché as he contemplates the single lesson history now seems to teach:

> I do not know any story so gloomy as the politics of this country for the last twenty years, centralizing ever more manifestly round one spring, and that a vast crime, and ever more plainly, until it is notorious that all promotion, power, and policy are dictated from one source — illustrating the fatal effects of a false position to demoralize legislation and put the best people always at a disadvantage; — one crime always present, always to be varnished over, to find fine names for; and we free statesmen, as accomplices to the guilt, ever in the power of the offender.

The power of crime to imprison the country is matched by its power to deface language. If wise men pierce rotten diction and fasten words to things, vicious men dislocate innocent words from their referents and paper over cruelty with euphemism. "Language has lost its meaning in the universal cant. *Representative Government* is really misrepresentative; . . . *the adding of Cuba and Central America* to the slave marts is *enlarging the area of Freedom.*" Quietly, firmly, Emerson restores an abused word — *anarchy* — to its root when he says, "I am glad to see that the terror at disunion and anarchy is disappearing. Massachusetts, in its heroic day, had no government — was an anarchy. Every man stood on his own feet, was his own governor; and there was no breach of peace from Cape Cod to Mount Hoosac." The real danger is not that the social bonds are too weak but that they are too strong: "Vast property, gigantic interests, family connections, webs of party, cover the land with a network that immensely multiplies the dangers of war." If the defenders of freedom will not make a stand soon, they will find themselves, like the exiles who sought America in 1848, forced "to gather up their clothes and depart to some land where freedom exists."

What Emerson did not know when he gave his "Speech on Affairs in Kansas" was that recent events in that territory were to involve him once again in political action, this time on the side not of the victim but of the aggressor. On the night of May 24, 1856, a Kansas emigrant named John Brown, angered by proslavery raiders who harassed free-state settlements like

Lawrence and driven to fury by the news of the assault on Charles Sumner in the Senate Chamber, led seven men from a volunteer free-state militia known as the Pottawatomie Rifle Company to attack men associated with the proslavery forces (one of them a member of the territorial legislature). During their rampage, at each place Brown and his men stopped they shot or hacked to death with broadswords unarmed men. At one cabin they killed a father and two sons; at another they hacked to death a husband in front of his wife. They killed five people in all before rejoining their unit.

Regarding this act of terror, Thomas Wentworth Higginson (who was then in Kansas directing parties of free-state emigrants) claimed he had heard no one among the free-state men who did not approve of its beneficial effects in giving an "immediate check to the armed aggressions of the Missourians." But in fact many free-state residents of Kansas were horrified by Brown's deed, which helped fan what had been disorganized skirmishing into full-scale civil war.

Accurate news from Kansas traveled with difficulty. When Brown appeared in the East early in 1857 to raise money to continue the fight against the proslavery forces in Kansas, the Transcendentalists who heard him speak either did not know of the "Pottawatomie massacre" or chose to believe the antislavery press accounts of it, accounts that tried to place the blame on the proslavery forces themselves. To sympathizers in New England, Brown seemed like a Covenanter imagined by Sir Walter Scott, a man of zeal whose military bearing promised an end to the North's years of humiliation and victimization – in the bungled rescue of Burns, in the beating of Sumner, and in the threat of slave-power expansion in the Midwest and Southwest. In February 1857 Brown came to Concord to speak at the Town Hall about the war in Kansas and to ask for aid. He had lunch with the Thoreaus and there met Emerson, who invited him to stay his second night in town with the Emersons and later wrote approvingly of Brown's speech in his journal.

For the next two years Brown alternated between fund-raising in the East and fighting in Kansas and Missouri, where his band killed a slave owner and led eleven slaves to freedom. But his plans were growing grander. He told the "Secret Six" (a group of northern sympathizers that included Parker and Higginson) of his plans to send armed men into Virginia to set up mountain camps or settlements to which slaves could escape. Here they could either live in freedom or be forwarded along the underground railroad to Canada. To the general public Brown continued to appeal for money to fight slavery in Kansas. Emerson gave fifty dollars, Thoreau a smaller sum.

Even members of the Secret Six were startled when they heard of Brown's seizure of the federal arsenal at Harper's Ferry, Virginia, on the night of October 16, 1859. If (as his prosecutors later alleged) he was hoping to start a slave insurrection and then arm the slave with the weapons from the arsenal, his conduct was bizarre: he picked a site impossible to defend, attacked it with only eighteen men (carrying no rations), and made no effort to alert the slaves he planned to free of his presence or of his intentions. Though Brown's men did hold the arsenal for thirty-six hours, a detachment of U.S. marines commanded by Colonel Robert E. Lee easily retook it, killing ten of Brown's men and wounding him. More than one person wondered if Brown were mad, but he appeared lucid and self-possessed during the week-long trial that followed quickly upon his capture. Indeed, his calmness during his imprisonment under sentence of death impressed even Governor Wise of Virginia, who called him "cool, collected, and indomitable."

Brown had been sentenced to death on November 1. His hanging was set for December 2. In the weeks leading up to the execution both Emerson and Thoreau praised his heroism and pleaded publicly for his life. But many people in the North were shocked by Brown's suicidal raid and frightened by the evidence that he hoped to start a slave insurrection. It was partly to counter such a reaction that Thoreau announced on October 30 (the day before the sentence was handed down) that he would deliver "A Plea for Captain John Brown" in Concord, ringing the town bell himself. On November 1 he repeated the lecture at the Tremont Temple in Boston (filling in for Frederick Douglass) and gave it again on November 3 in Worcester. On November 8 Emerson delivered a lecture entitled "Courage" to Theodore Parker's society at the Boston Music Hall, praising Brown, just as his 1838 lecture "Heroism" had praised Elijah Lovejoy. (Parker himself had been driven by his worsening tuberculosis to leave Boston for Europe in quest of better health in February 1859, long before Harper's Ferry.) On November 18 Emerson spoke at the Tremont Temple in Boston at a meeting to raise funds for John Brown's family. When Brown was executed on December 2, Thoreau helped arrange a memorial service in Concord at which he read selections about heroism drawn from his commonplace books, and Emerson read Brown's last speech. In Boston, James Freeman Clarke preached a funeral sermon for Brown to his Church of the Disciples. Emerson delivered a new speech entitled "John Brown" at Salem on January 6, 1860. Finally, Thoreau wrote "The Last Days of John Brown," to be read at a Fourth-of-July "John Brown Celebration" held in North Elba, New York, where Brown was buried and where his widow still resided.

One of the objections to David Friedrich Strauss's hypothesis that the gospels were mythical was that not enough time had elapsed between the death of Jesus and the writing of the gospels for the mythical imagination to transfigure history. In these Transcendentalist orations about John Brown the shaping of history into myth begins while Brown is still alive. Brown is not merely a hero, he is an "Angel of Light" – saintly as a Puritan, courageous as the defenders of Lexington and Concord, powerful as Cromwell, romantic as a figure out of Scott, self-sacrificing as the Redeemer who by his suffering and death bought again mankind.

What Brown's deed offered to the people of the North was an escape from the degradation of the last ten years, when every blow, every jeer, every insult came from the South, and Northerners could do no more than weakly protest and shamefully concede. "The politics of Massachusetts are cowardly," Emerson said. "We want will that advances and dictates." Thoreau put it even more strongly: "We aspire to be something more than stupid and timid chattels, pretending to read history and our bibles, but desecrating every house and every day we breathe in."

The best proof of Brown's Messiahship, in fact, is the tendency of worshippers to see their own features in Brown's character. To Thoreau, Brown is the perfect soldier, tough, self-reliant, and ascetic, who can live in swamps and learn the lore of Indians, and who is full of contempt for the opulent tables of the rich and for the warriors who believe they can win victories with words. To Emerson, Brown is the man of courage whose character converts enemies into admirers and whose radiance sheds grace on circumstances, even the most ignominious, making the gallows as glorious as the cross. But both Emerson and Thoreau agree on the quickening power of Brown's practical demonstration of manhood. "Let us say then frankly that the education of the will is the object of our existence," Emerson says in "Courage." And Brown is will incarnate, will confronting the impossible and refusing to quail before it. Such courage exhilarates and puts a new face on everything. "Everything feels the new breath except the old doting nigh-dead politicians, whose heart the trumpet of resurrection could not wake," Emerson says, and Thoreau remarks that some men who were thinking of committing suicide have now changed their minds. Brown finally comes in these orations to take on the characteristics of the Transcendentalist Reason. To Emerson he is "transparent," a "pure idealist, with no by-ends of his own." To Thoreau he is "a transcendentalist above all." He is "pure spirit himself, and his sword is pure spirit." Even the brevity of his conquest adds to its glory. "His life was meteor-like, flashing through the darkness in which we live."

For Northerners, the 1850s began in humiliation, proceeded through shame, and ended in a desire for revenge, a desire that John Brown both made conscious and symbolized. But the same decade also saw the publication of Emerson's *English Traits* and *The Conduct of Life* and Thoreau's *A Yankee in Canada* and *Walden,* together with parts of his *Cape Cod* and *The Maine Woods,* and the expansion of Thoreau's journals into a massive project of observation and representation that contains some of his most brilliant writing. Though the gloom of the political situation sometimes causes these texts to plummet into misanthropy or nihilism, the new conviction of authority that the crisis of the times gave to Transcendentalists as moral philosophers more than compensated for the despair. During the 1840s Transcendentalists had often felt as if they were outside the main streams of human activity, either defiantly or plangently proclaiming their desire to be left alone. Even "Resistance to Civil Government," the most famous political document the movement produced, is full of the imagery of secession; its central statement is probably Thoreau's declaration that he would like to sign off of all societies he had never signed on to, if only he knew where to find a complete list.

For now, however, dragged from the study or the wood to protest the rendition of escaped slaves, the war in Kansas, the assault upon Sumner, or the execution of Brown, the Transcendentalists find that their old gospel – the primacy of the moral law, the innocence of nature, the centrality of intuition – is newly needed in a society corrupted by a deadly combination of material prosperity and moral bankruptcy. If God instructs through the imagination then artists are his prophets. They speak with authority and not as the scribes.

The effects of this transformation are evident in the two books Emerson published during the decade that ended in 1860, *English Traits* and *The Conduct of Life*. Both volumes take up familiar themes – the necessity of self-reliance, the war between impulse and limitation, the saving insanity of egotism, and the adequacy of the moral sentiment as a stay and anchor in a world bereft of the old religions. But both are also shaped by Emerson's need to incorporate into his writing the inevitable changes that time and experience had brought to him as he traveled from a New England giddy with experiments to renovate the world to an England solid with the complacency of achieved empire and to a France agitated by revolution – only to return to a homeland humiliated and debased by its compromises with slavery.

Had Emerson been a younger man he might have called for the overthrow of institutions, but he was forty-six when the decade began, already (as he would put it) "ripened beyond the prospect of sincere radicalism," and his respect for institutions had grown along with his success. Yet it had not grown so great that it pushed him into mere reaction – the immediate revulsion Emerson felt at the Fugitive Slave Law proved that the moral perfection he had followed in his youth was still the only deity worthy of his worship. Indeed, the derelictions of government made every stick of property in the commonwealth worth less, and so prudence and idealism at last pointed the same way.

The Conduct of Life was not published until 1860, but the book grew out of a series of lectures Emerson delivered first in the troubled winter of 1850–1. The book announces itself on its first page as a guide to conduct, as an answer to the question "How Shall I Live?" Several of its chapters – "Wealth," "Culture," "Behavior," "Beauty," and "Considerations by the Way" – offer advice to an audience eager to achieve refinement but not sure how to go about acquiring it in a country with rudimentary notions of civility and scarcely any idea of culture. Emerson refuses to give up his old belief in the principle of compensation, but he now extends its sway beyond the boundaries of the individual life. Thus he notes that the monomaniacs of trade are responsible for netting America with railroads and dotting it with factories, and he points out that the selfish capitalist does more for the welfare of the race than do benefactors like Florence Nightingale. "This *speculative* genius is the madness of a few for the gain of the world." But he also points out that temporary advantages prove in the long run illusory, just as the inflated prices that American traders charged the European nations during the Napoleonic wars serve only to create a glittering prosperity that drew to American shores millions of the European poor who then demanded to be fed and educated.

On a higher plane than behavior is religion. But the essay "Worship," is concerned not with religion itself but with the plight of nineteenth-century men and women facing the collapse of institutional Christianity. "The stern old faiths have all pulverized," Emerson notes, leaving behind "a whole population of gentlemen and ladies out in search of religions." Nearly thirteen years after the Divinity School Address Emerson realizes with amusement and chagrin that the trumpet he had set to his lips to bring down Jericho had been unnecessary; Jericho would have tumbled anyway. The "churches that once sucked the roots of right and wrong . . . now have perished away till they are a speck of whitewash on the wall." A French journal's brief explanation for rejecting an article entitled "Dieu" – "*La question de Dieu manque d'actualité*" – is more devastating than anything in Strauss.

Still, worship was never religion, and religion is in no danger of collapse merely because the old forms of worship are passing away. If the moral crisis of 1850 showed anything, it was that "the moral sense reappears to-day with the same morning newness that has been from of old the fountain of beauty and strength." The spirit that created the old forms will someday create new ones spontaneously, for the moral sense is at once the essence of all religion and "the basis of the human mind." In the meantime, individuals need only concern themselves with their own conduct. "Souls are not saved in bundles."

The individual is aided in the reformation of conduct by the fact that nature no less than mind is saturated with law. "In us it is inspiration; out there in nature we see its fatal strength." Essays like "Power" and "Fate" (the final lecture in the original series, though the first essay in the published book) trace the behavior of law in the mind and in nature, showing how the same brutal necessity that lies upon our hopes like a mountain of obstruction in "Fate" turns in the perceiving mind into power, the opposite of fate. "Thought dissolves the material universe by carrying the mind up into a sphere where all is plastic," Emerson says in "Fate." The famous catalogue of natural disasters near the beginning of the essay — earthquakes, epidemics, wild beasts, ocean storms — leads up to the insight that disarms them. What we call fate is at last "a name for facts not yet passed under the fire of thought; for causes which are unpenetrated." The man or woman who sees the ineluctable web of cause and effect everywhere in nature is no longer a helpless victim of the laws but a sharer in their power. "Thought takes man out of servitude into freedom." Now "we are as lawgivers; we speak for Nature; we prophesy and divine."

"Fate" was initially delivered in December 1851, after Emerson's first lecture against the Fugitive Slave Law; some sentences that sound very much as though they came from this lecture made their way into stray leaves from the manuscript of "Courage," the lecture that Emerson delivered shortly after John Brown's raid on Harper's Ferry: "The statistics show you the whole world under the dominion of the fate or circumstance or brute laws of chemistry. . . . Thought resists and commands Nature by a higher truth, and gives Nature a master." If "Fate" had its genesis in the struggle against slavery, it is hardly surprising that Emerson chose to place it first in the volume he published in November 1860. To take its place at the end of *The Conduct of Life* he now added an essay he had first published in the *Atlantic Monthly* in 1857, "Illusions." A strange intaglio of "Fate," "Illusions" does not so much dissolve fate into thought as reveal that all solidities are illusory to begin with. "Life is as sweet as nitrous oxide." The magazine version of the essay ends with a bit of Persian advice to "be the fool of virtue, not of vice," for folly is inevitable. But for the book Emerson added an Oriental fable that returns the text to the only subject he ever cared about deeply — the nakedness of the soul before God. The young mortal enters the temple where he sees the gods beckon but is instantly distracted by "snow-storms of illusions." He is confused, he is distracted. But when for an instant the clouds lift, "there are the gods still sitting around him on their thrones, — they alone with him alone."

With *English Traits* (1856), the book Emerson based on his two trips to England — the first in 1833, the second in 1847–8 — we are in another universe altogether, where the senses rule. The book is a shrewd but admiring portrait of a land and people superficially so different from Emerson's own that the filial relationship is sometimes difficult to believe, yet the two countries are also united by such deep similarities that Emerson secretly delights in the foreign greatness that dwarfs him — delights because as Britain now is, so shall America someday be.

English Traits opens with an account of the European tour Emerson made as a young provincial just out of the ministry, naively hoping to find in the Old World the personified forms of the books whose genius had so enraptured him. He was courteously received by everyone, but he was disappointed to meet instead of the giants of his imagination, ordinary men: a Landor hospitable but worldly; a Coleridge old, ill, and full of harangues against the Unitarians; a Wordsworth admirable for his "simple adherence to truth" but confined within "the hard limits of his mind." Only Carlyle at Craigenputtock, loosing the floodgates of his talk and boisterous laughter, was the man he had come to find.

Now, in 1847, Emerson is no longer the otherworldly young cleric so devoted to things of the spirit that he sees nothing else. His first view of the land shows the sharpness of his new attention to detail. "Under an ash-colored sky, the fields have been combed and rolled until they appear to have been finished with a pencil instead of a plough." The high finish and artificiality of life fascinates him; "facticious" is a word that recurs constantly in his descriptions. Is British capacity to subdue and manicure these unpromising islands in the cold northern ocean the result of extraordinary racial vigor or were the savage Norsemen who peopled the islands broken into civility by the harshness of the climate and the stubborn resistance of the soil? "The enchantments of barren shingle and rough weather transformed every adventurer into a laborer." However it happened, race and environment worked upon one another to produce a nation beefy, ruddy, valorous, truth-loving, opinionated, prosaic, passionately logical, tenacious of liberty and even more tenacious of property, chilly in company and sentimental in private life, tolerant of eccentricity in behavior and intolerant of it in thought. The contrast between these broad-chested self-confident specimens of Anglo-Saxon humanity and their cautious, spindly, deferential American cousins is so great that it provides an undercurrent of humor throughout the book even though Emerson does not often make the comparison explicit.

For someone who had been preaching against conformity all his life England was almost paradise. "They require you to be of your own opinion," Emerson remarks, and adds: "Everyone does everything without reference to the bystanders, consults only his own convenience, as much as a solitary pioneer in Wisconsin." Even British phlegm comes in for praise. "A saving stupidity masks and protects their perception, as the curtain of the eagle's eye."

Still, these virtues are purchased at the cost of adamantine limitations. The

Englishman is shut in by a horizon of brass the diameter of his umbrella. His universities are somnolent; his church is a doll, whose gospel is "By taste ye are saved." The English church in 1848 is not a persecuting church, but neither is it a believing one. It is "not inquisitorial; it is not even inquisitive." The spirit that animated the theologians, architects, and sacred poets of the seventeenth century has wholly departed, leaving behind only a worship of wealth. And though England is the richest and most powerful nation in the world, Emerson suspects that it has reached its apogee. He cannot help thinking that America, with its unlimited natural resources, in the long run can play the game with immense advantage, and that England must one day be content to be strong only in her children.

Wandering with Carlyle among the buttercups, daisies, nettles, and wild thyme growing around the stones at Stonehenge, "the old egg" out of which all the history and ecclesiastical structures of the British race had proceeded, Emerson thinks back to the continent to which he is returning. "There, in that great sloven continent, in high Allegheny pastures, in the sea-wide, sky-skirted prairie, still sleeps and murmurs and hides the great mother, long since driven away from the trim hedge-rows and over-cultivated garden of England."

By the time Emerson published these words in 1856, his greatest disciple was already more than halfway through a decade of unparalleled literary productivity taking the wildness of that "sloven continent" as one of its central themes. Emerson's failure to acknowledge Thoreau's achievement during these years has always seemed unpardonable to admirers of Thoreau; and certainly Emerson's willingness to puff Ellery Channing's poems while ignoring *Walden* is hard to forgive, even if one takes into account the deep rifts in the relationship between the two men that widened after Emerson's return from England.

Of course, Thoreau himself made it difficult to gauge the magnitude of his labors, because the main work on which he was embarked during the decade – the massive *Journal* – was wholly private until his death, and two other books whose serial publication in journals was begun – *A Yankee in Canada* and *Cape Cod* – were withdrawn by Thoreau before publication was complete in protest against editorial tampering with his text. As for *Walden*, it was in places so savage a denunciation of the kind of life Emerson had chosen to live (and about which the two men had been arguing in private and in print since the early 1840s) that Emerson's silence on the subject of its literary merits is perhaps not really surprising.

The weekly burden of sermon writing and, later, the economic pressures of maintaining a home and family had disciplined Emerson into a rhythm of literary production that lasted most of his life. First the daily work on the journals, thinking and writing; then the culling of passages from the journals for lectures to take on tour; finally the revisions of lectures into a book, negotiations with booksellers, and publication. Emerson was not a particularly canny businessman, and his daughter's memoir of her mother's life reveals how threadbare the household sometimes was. But he wrote steadily enough to keep the family afloat, and his family's demands kept him writing despite his frequent complaints of dessication or dullness.

Thoreau from the beginning had more difficulty finding a steady rhythm of production. He had revised and revised his first manuscript and then (on Emerson's advice) risked publishing it entirely at his own expense, a procedure that gave his publisher little incentive to advertise or sell it, having already recouped the cost of production. In 1850 Thoreau was faced with the fact that his first book had failed to find an audience and had left him with a debt he did not pay off till 1853; that he was forced to turn to surveying, odd jobbing, or helping in the family pencil business to earn money; and that he had no literary role or reputation, other than as an imitator of Emerson and a second-string lyceum lecturer. Yet his response to all this discouragement was not to abandon his literary vocation but to declare it with renewed force.

The first part of Thoreau's literary life to undergo metamorphosis were the journals that he had been keeping (probably at Emerson's suggestion) since 1837. Students of the journals have noticed several distinct phases in Thoreau's practice of journal keeping. Initially his journals are a place to hive transcripts of other writings; then they become more like Emerson's journals, individual meditations with more or less integrity, sometimes used in the published works. But in May 1850 Thoreau begins to write with increasing frequency in his journal, and by June of the next year he has established the habit he will follow until six months before his death: Notes taken down during his daily long walks are worked up into highly polished journal entries in which Thoreau repeatedly attempts the feat of translating natural appearance into language that is both strikingly metaphorical and mathematically precise. Some of these passages find their way into the books and lectures Thoreau writes during the decade, but the sheer bulk of these daily writings (some two million words in all, most written during the last decade of Thoreau's life) suggests that they must have been meant as something more than a source of immediately marketable material.

Whatever prompted Thoreau to begin his new experiment in journal writing — the reading of Wordsworth's recently published *Prelude,* which recorded the mind's relationship to natural phenomena with a fidelity new in English poetry; the need to find a literary work that would keep him constantly practicing his craft; the need to pin down experience that seemed to be vanishing; or even the need to find some source of sanity and health amid America's growing political squalor – by 1851 he has reached the point where *The Prelude* began. "I feel myself uncommonly prepared for *some* literary work, but I can select no work" (September 7, 1851). Gradually it occurs to Thoreau that the journal might be published as it stands rather than plundered for material to make essays of. In early 1852 he writes, "I do not know but thoughts written down thus in a journal might be printed in the same form with greater advantage – than if the related ones were brought together into separate essays. They are now allied to life – & are seen by the reader not to be far fetched" (January 27, 1852). And by July 1852 he is ready to define a journal as "a book that shall contain a record of all your joy – your ecstasy" (July 13, 1852).

Nature in Thoreau's journal is endlessly investigated, followed and recorded in all her seasonal changes. Unlike Emerson, who wanted to decode natural phenomena to release the human meaning hidden within, Thoreau does not ask for human significance in nature and in fact effaces himself as much as possible, except as observer and scribe of a beauty and order not his own. This vocation does not preclude other, more humanly accessible ones; Thoreau was still eager to find an audience in his own time and place, to see his works in print. But the "journal of no very wide circulation" (as he jokes about it in *Walden*) was a secret source of power and assurance for Thoreau that made all kinds of writing easier. The journal was at once a steadying discipline, an act of love, a source of authority, and a secret bid for posthumous fame.

The first half of the decade was a period of extraordinary creativity for Thoreau. In addition to the journal and the antislavery lectures, he wrote the lectures "Walking, or the Wild" and "Life without Principle", the four chapters of *Cape Cod;* all five chapters of *A Yankee in Canada;* the longest chapter of *The Maine Woods;* and the fourth, fifth, sixth, and final drafts of *Walden*. Of all these texts only *Walden* was published in its entirety during Thoreau's lifetime. (The books we know as *The Maine Woods, A Yankee in Canada,* and *Cape Cod* were published only after Thoreau's death.) Thoreau's willingness to accept Horace Greeley's offer of help in placing his pieces with periodicals hardly suggests a desire to remain unknown, though his determination to withdraw material when it was tampered with shows that he was not willing to accept an editor's decision about what he should be permitted to say.

A Yankee in Canada was the first of Thoreau's excursions to reach publication. Based on a trip Thoreau took to Montreal and Quebec with Ellery Channing during the autumn of 1850, *A Yankee in Canada* describes a round-trip journey by rail through Vermont to Canada, then by boat from Montreal to Quebec and back. The trip was made on a special excursion ticket good for only ten days, so Thoreau's acquaintance with French Canada is ridiculously brief. Moreover, his rudimentary French scarcely allows him to understand most of the residents, much less probe deeply into their thoughts. Still, the contrast between the feudal society of French Canada (its peasant Catholicism overlain by a veneer of British imperialism) and the Yankee democracy he has just left is sharp enough to make him meditate on many matters. And the spectacular valley of the St. Lawrence (particularly as seen from the citadel overlooking Quebec) impresses him with its beauty, while the thought of the country only a little way beyond it, uninhabited by any European, sweeps over him like an "irresistible tide."

The first sight Thoreau visits when he has crossed the river to Montreal is the church of Notre Dame, the largest in North America (it seats ten thousand). The gloom, the solitude, the huge space impress him favorably; it seems "a great cave in the midst of a city," and its altars and candles seem as innocent as stalactites. If only the priest could be omitted from the religion Thoreau concedes that he might visit such a church "*on a Monday*" – though fortunately he does not need to, because the Concord woods make a church "far grander and more sacred."

From Notre Dame Thoreau proceeds to the Champ de Mars, where he watches the British regiments drill, fascinated by the appearance of harmony that made the men look like "one vast centipede," depressed that such cooperation should only exist in the service of "an imperfect and tyrannical government." If free men could only put their hearts and hands together their harmony would in itself constitute "the very end and success for which government now exists in vain."

Yet finally none of the sights of Montreal affects Thoreau as much as the name of a point on the island it partly occupies, the Point aux Trembles, so called from the aspens that once grew there.

There is all the poetry in the world in a name. . . . I want nothing better than a good word. The name of the thing might easily be more than the thing to itself to me. Inexpressibly beautiful appears the recognition by man of the least natural fact, and the allying [of] his life to it. All the world reiterating this slender truth, that aspens once grew here; and the swift inference is, that men were there to see them.

This fascination with the poetry of French names, indeed with the sounds of the French language, grows even stronger as Thoreau leaves Montreal for Quebec. The saint's names on every village fill him with the "intoxication of poetry" and make him dream of Provence and troubadours and think wistfully that if English had only "a few more liquids and vowels" its speakers might "locate their ideals at once." We owe our word "prairie" to the French explorers. Nay, "their very *rivière* meanders more than our river."

The beauty of the St. Lawrence and its tributaries, with their thousand waterfalls, wins Thoreau's admiration, as does the "steel-like and flashing air" of Quebec, garlanded with its late autumnal flowers. And his readings in Canadian history lead him to praise the treatment accorded the Indian nations by the French, who respect their sovereignty and regard them as neighbors and allies, unlike the contemptuous English. But the poverty of the present-day French Canadians, ground between the priesthood and the British soldiery, makes Thoreau long for home, where "it is the most natural thing in the world for a government that does not understand you to let you alone."

The pointless cruelty of the British government, which sets sentinels to guard a wall in a country at peace and then changes them every hour (or even sooner) because of the intense cold, strikes Thoreau as the symbol of military folly everywhere. "What a troublesome thing a wall is! I thought it was to defend me, and not I it. Of course, if they had no wall they would not need to have any sentinel." Far more admirable is the soldier's cat he sees walking back into a high loophole in the wall "with a gracefully waving motion of her tail as if her ways were ways of pleasantness and all her paths were peace." The prosperity of an ordinary white farmhouse he sees on his return through Vermont suddenly shines out as testimony to the health of a country whose greatest blessing (at least for "lucky white men") is that it neither enlists them nor defends them.

Thoreau delivered chapters of his Canada manuscript as lectures during the 1851–2 season; in 1852 he sent them to Horace Greeley, who had asked him if he ever swapped his "wood-notes wild" for cash. Most magazines Greeley tried rejected the manuscript as too long, but Thoreau succeeded in getting his old friend George William Curtis (a handsome boarding student at Brook Farm) to accept it for the new *Putnam's Magazine*. Chapters titled "An Excursion to Canada" began appearing anonymously beginning in January 1853. But Thoreau stopped publication after the third (or March) installment and withdrew the manuscript when he discovered that Curtis felt free to censor his "heresies" without consulting him. (Curtis did pay him seventy-nine dollars for the three episodes he printed.) In 1866 the complete five-chapter manuscript was given the title *A Yankee in Canada* and printed together with Thoreau's antislavery and reform papers.

Another manuscript accepted by Curtis for *Putnam's* was also cut off after several installments, though this time Curtis appears to have been the one responsible for the decision to stop publication. Thoreau had sent Curtis some lectures based upon his Cape Cod journeys of 1849 and 1850 when he sent his Canadian manuscript in 1852. Though he had withdrawn both manuscripts from *Putnam's* in 1853 he remained on good enough terms with Curtis to resume negotiations for the publication of the Cape Cod material in

April 1855. Chapters began appearing in the June 1855 issue. But by August Curtis had wearied of arguing with Thoreau about the wording of objectionable passages, particularly because the piece seemed to be arousing resentment on Cape Cod itself. Thoreau asked for the return of his manuscript. He continued to work on the manuscript at intervals until the time of his final illness, though he made no more attempts to publish it. *Cape Cod* was finally published in 1865.

On the first page of *Cape Cod* Thoreau tells us that he has made three journeys to the Cape. But the narrative in the book follows rather closely the path of the earliest trip (1849), when Thoreau and Ellery Channing rode the Cape Cod railroad to its end at Sandwich at the beginning of the Cape. From there they followed the "bared and bended arm of Massachusetts," at first in a stagecoach and then on foot, until they reached the end of the Cape at Provincetown. The Cape's peculiar world of sand and drying cod and stunted vegetation, where apple trees look like plants in flower pots and orchards are small enough to leap over, seems like something from a fairy tale about elves or trolls. Many of its inhabitants in Thoreau's book are grotesques, like the Nauset woman whose jaws of iron looked as if they could bite board nails in two, or the old Wellfleet oysterman – petulant, complaining that he was "a poor good-for-nothing crittur," yet able to hold the two travelers spellbound with memories stretching back to the battle of Bunker Hill, whose cannon he had heard booming across the Bay when he was sixteen. They stayed the night with him, and in the morning he invited them to a Cape Cod breakfast: eels, buttermilk cake, cold bread, donuts, and tea.

The inhabitants' houses and gardens are equally strange. There are octagonal windmills affixed to cart wheels that can be turned to face the ever-changing wind, vats for drying salt from seawater, garden plots where vegetables thrive in pure sand, crops reckoned not only in bushels of corn but barrels of clams, and backyards filled with drying cod. Sand is everywhere, pitting surfaces so fiercely that one minister reported having to have a new pane of glass set every week if he wanted to see out of his house. Even the name of the ubiquitous beach-grass, *Psamma Arenaria,* combines the Greek word for "sand" with the Latin for "sandy": sandy sand.

Despite the absence of anything like the woods or streams Thoreau loved in Concord and admired in Canada, the spit of sand has patches of startling beauty, where shrub oak, bayberry, beach plum, and wild roses are overrun by woodbine. "When the roses were in bloom, these patches in the midst of the sand displayed such a profusion of blossoms, mingled with the aroma of bayberry, that no Italian or other artificial rose-garden could equal them. They were perfectly Elysian, and realized my idea of an oasis in the desert." Just outside of Provincetown they come upon a patch of bushes and shrubs so startling in their fall colors that they seem like a rich tapestry thrown over the white sand.

For Cape Cod the real source of beauty and terror is, of course, the sea itself. They see evidence of its ferocity before they ever get to the Cape. News of a terrible shipwreck in Cohasset prompts them to take that route to the Cape. When they arrive they find that a brig, the *St. John,* laden with Irish emigrants, had been wrecked on the savage rocks during a storm whose waves were still breaking violently on the shore. One hundred forty-five people have died, and the corpses are being laid out for identification and placed in coffins. When someone lifts a cover from a corpse Thoreau sees a "livid, swollen, and mangled body" of a girl, with bloodless gashes and staring, lusterless eyes. At the close of this first chapter, "The Shipwreck," Thoreau discovers that the humans are not the only victims sacrificed to the power of the sea; he sees a good-sized lake separated from the ocean by only a thin beach and is told that the sea had tossed the water over in a storm and that the fish who swam into the lake were now stranded by the gradual drying up of the water and were dying by the thousands.

The sea wrecks ships, topples lighthouses, and eats away the beaches of Cape Cod; it traps and drowns incautious walkers along the Atlantic beach of the Cape and pulls the strongest swimmers in its undertow or feeds them to sharks. In the ninth chapter, "The Sea and the Desert," Thoreau looks at the seashore — "a wild, rank place, and there is no flattery in it" — as a vast morgue where the carcasses of people and beasts lie rotting, turned by the tide that tucks fresh sand under their bodies. "There is naked Nature, — inhumanly sincere, wasting no thought on man, nibbling at the cliffy shore where gulls wheel amid the spray."

Yet the sea also possesses indescribable beauty and grace, glittering in the sun, rocking delicate sea jellies in its waves, nourishing fantastic shapes of kelp — oar-weed, tangle, devil's-apron, sole-leather, ribbon-weed — "a fit invention for Neptune to adorn his car with, or a freak of Proteus." Indeed, when Thoreau has his first sight of the Atlantic Ocean from the high bluff along the eastern shore of the Cape and then descends to the beach itself, the breakers look to him "like droves of a thousand wild horses of Neptune, rushing to the shore, with their white manes streaming far behind."

He watches the day break over the sea as if it came out of its bosom; on the other side of the Cape he sees the sun set into the Bay, and it makes him think of Homer: "The shining torch of the sun fell into the ocean." *Cape Cod* is full of Greek quotations, not only because the storms and sunrises naturally remind Thoreau of Homer but because Greek has convenient words for things like "the sound of many waves, dashing at once" (*polyphloisboios*). The ocean is still wild and untamed and therefore invigorating. Watching the

Atlantic breakers dash themselves against the high bank on a clear cold day in a gale Thoreau sees a primitive force as dangerous to the schooners anchored off Provincetown as it was to the ships of Odysseus or Aeneas. In the casual daily courage of the mackerel-boat fishermen and lighthouse keepers Thoreau finds ancient virtue surfacing off the shores of America.

The idea that the heroic ages are still accessible in the wild regions of the American continent inspires the happiest of Thoreau's "excursions" from the early 1850s, the lecture "Walking, or the Wild." In this lecture – published after Thoreau's death under the title "Walking" – Thoreau communicates his sudden understanding (brought on by looking at a panorama of the Mississippi) that *this was the heroic age itself, though we know it not.*" The wildness and vigor of the earliest ages have not vanished; an afternoon's walk will bring Thoreau into solitary forests and primeval swamps. "I enter a swamp as a sacred place, a *sanctum sanctorum.*"

Not every stroller can make the journey back to innocence. The clerks and shopkeepers who walk for a half hour to get exercise, the preoccupied thinkers who bring their worries with them into the woods, are not true walkers at all, nor will they ever know that deep "recreation" that contact with wildness brings. "If you would get exercise, go in search of the springs of life." And if you would join the ancient and honorable order of walkers you must be willing to leave father and mother, brother and sister, wife and child. "We should go forth on the shortest walk, perchance, in the spirit of undying adventure, never to return, – prepared to send back our embalmed hearts only as relics to our desolate kingdoms." For "every walk is a sort of crusade, preached by some Peter the Hermit in us, to go forth and reconquer this Holy Land from the hands of the Infidels."

Thoreau says that he walks for at least four hours a day and seeks out those places least touched by cultivation. "My spirits infallibility rise in proportion to the outward dreariness." Bogs attract him; given a choice between the best garden and the Dismal Swamp he would always choose the swamp. And he values the same rankness and undisciplined vigor in books and people. "In literature it is only the wild that attracts us. Dullness is but another name for tameness." We delight in "the uncivilized free and wild thinking" in all the scriptures and mythologies, just as we prefer the "awful ferity" of good men and lovers to the polite cultivation that leads in men as in ploughed land to exhaustion of the soil. Do New Englanders complain that the pigeons in the woods grow scarcer every year? "So it would seem, fewer and fewer thoughts visit each growing man from year to year, for the grove in our minds is laid waste, – sold to feed unnecessary fires of ambition, or sent to mill, – and there is scarcely a twig left for them to perch on."

The crowing of the cock reminds us to improve the present moment, to celebrate this instant of time. "Where he lives no fugitive slave laws are passed." If the cock's crowing reminds us how many times we have betrayed our master since we last heard his note, its freedom from all plaintiveness awakens in us a "pure morning joy" that reminds us what innocence is in nature. On a cold November day the sun breaking through the clouds at the horizon gilded an empty meadow — a marsh, a black stream, and a decaying stump — with so pure and bright a light that the place seemed like Elysium, "and the sun on our backs seemed like a gentle herdsman driving us home at evening." "Walking" was one of four essays Thoreau revised during the last months of his life to send to James Fields, the editor of the *Atlantic Monthly,* who had solicited contributions from him. It was published in 1862.

Thoreau's main work of these years, however, was the revision and publication of the long manuscript about his life at Walden Pond whose first draft he had probably completed even before he left his cabin in September 1847. The book, published by the Boston firm of Ticknor and Fields on August 9, 1854, as *Walden, or Life in the Woods* (Thoreau later dropped the subtitle), had been through seven revisions since the first version was completed, revisions that doubled its length and radically changed its structure and tone. Because Thoreau used different kinds of paper each time he revised, a modern scholar is able to reconstruct nearly all of the earliest version from the jumble of almost twelve hundred manuscript pages of work sheets left among Thoreau's papers and to trace the process of growth and alteration that led to the published book.

The story of *Walden*'s composition is nearly as remarkable as *Walden* itself. Few of the Transcendentalists cared much for revision; the forms they favored — the journal, the lecture, the essay, the sermon — emphasized spontaneity and pardoned haste. Even Emerson's lectures, though they often consisted of passages considerably polished and altered from their source in his journals, usually reached their permanent form quickly and there stopped — even when Emerson withheld them from publication for several years. Nothing quite like the wholesale dismantling, reshuffling, expanding, and reconstructing to which Thoreau subjected his original manuscript can be found among the literary works Transcendentalism produced.

Thoreau seems to have written the first version of *Walden* in response to questions from his fellow residents of Concord, who were curious to know why he was living at the pond and how he managed to survive there all alone. He probably began writing it sometime during his second winter there, late in 1846. The draft he wrote then is in many ways like the Brook Farm letters of Marianne Dwight or the reminiscences of John Codman: lyrical, full of wonder and discovery, suffused with a sense of joy. Many of the mocking passages of the later *Walden* are already there in full: the comparison of the ordinary inhabitants of Concord to the Brahmins who do penance in "a thousand curious ways," the suggestion that the worst form of slavery is experienced by the man who is the slave driver of himself. But (like the Brook Farmers who looked with pity upon the civilizees outside) Thoreau seems more eager to convert than to excoriate, and he is careful to include himself in the vices he laments. When he blames Concord's townspeople for their frivolous reading he notes that the Dialogues of Plato lie unread on his own shelf, too. And he underscores the point: "I describe my own case here." A title page he drew up for the second (1848) version of *Walden* addresses the book "To My Townsmen," a gesture in which there seems as much affection as reproach.

Thoreau had begun lecturing on his life at Walden Pond even before he left his cabin there, and he was negotiating as early as 1849 for the publication of *Walden* itself, still a single long essay with no chapter divisions. Ticknor and Company (later, Ticknor and Fields) expressed their willingness to publish *Walden* at their expense but refused to take Thoreau's first book, *A Week on the Concord and Merrimack Rivers,* and he refused to publish the second book first, despite his eagerness to get a book in print.

The disappointment of Thoreau's hopes after the failure of *A Week* and the burden of debt the book left him with coincided with other tests of his faith. His relationship with Emerson was badly strained; he was obliged to earn his living once again by trades like surveying, which always left him feeling vaguely sullied. The willingness to sacrifice principle to profit that led landowners to suggest to Thoreau that he survey their properties to give them the greatest amount of land led on the level of national politics to such abominations as the Compromise of 1850 and Sims and Burns cases.

There were also hopeful signs during these years. Thoreau's determination to make his journal his major literary project meant that he had a steady discipline as well as a rich source of new material to draw upon. His journeys to Canada and Cape Cod had shown him cultures, manners, and scenery different enough to challenge all his powers of representation; his excursions in the neighborhood of Concord had shown him that wildness was accessible within the radius of an afternoon walk.

When he returned to the *Walden* manuscript in full force in 1852 he worked with a new confidence and urgency. Greeley helped him place two pieces of the manuscript with *Sartain's Magazine,* which published them in July 1852 (though with Thoreau's usual luck, the magazine promptly collapsed before it paid him). By 1853 he was experimenting with a new principle of organization, dividing up the manuscript into chapters and adding material to the "winter" chapters to complete the cycle of the seasons hinted at in the first version of the book. After several more revisions Thoreau made a final copy of the manuscript for James Fields of the firm now called Ticknor and Fields, with whom he signed a contract on March 16, 1854. By the end of March 1854 Thoreau was correcting the first batch of partial proofs. He probably finished reading proof sometime in May, the same month in which the escaped slave Anthony Burns was captured and returned to slavery. The angry journal passages Thoreau wrote about that event formed the nucleus of the address "Slavery in Massachusetts," which he delivered on July 4. *Walden* itself was published a little more than a month later, on August 9.

The interleaving of Thoreau's final work on the proofs of *Walden* with the composition of his major political address between "Resistance to Civil Government" and the John Brown speeches is significant. Even though the Burns case came too late to influence the text of *Walden,* the attitudes that permitted Burns's rendition had long been visible in the surrounding culture. To trace the connection between individual folly and social corruption thus becomes one of *Walden*'s main burdens, the source of its frequent rages. This bitterness does not obliterate the memories of pure happiness enjoyed at the pond nor the beauty of the precise observations of nature drawn from the journal of the 1850s. Instead it lashes us in the direction we should go, pointing out the promised land we have stupidly forsaken and reminding us of the paradise still to be had for the asking. And it interrogates the world it describes. Why should nature serve as therapy for a mind diseased? If we crave only reality, what is the reality we crave?

The opening chapter of *Walden,* "Economy," begins by announcing that it will satisfy the curiosity of Thoreau's neighbors about his life at the pond. But before turning to his own life, Thoreau turns upon his neighbors to consider their condition – endlessly contorting themselves into agonies in pursuit of the things they foolishly deem "necessities." They labor under a mistake, and the mistake is costly. "The mass of men lead lives of quiet desperation."

A real survey of the "necessaries of life" will yield only a few, and these cheaply acquirable: food, shelter, clothing, and fuel. The simplest food, inexpensive but sturdy clothes, a cabin one can build for less than thirty dollars (less than the annual rent for a room at college), a few sticks of furniture scrounged from the endless stores in other people's garrets, six weeks of labor a year – Thoreau's formula for successful life involves him in vigorous exercise, endows him with leisure for contemplation, and keeps him in touch with the natural world. Unlike the "saints," whose "hymn-books resound with a melodious cursing of God and enduring Him forever," or the miserable farmers enslaved to the acres they till, Thoreau aims to take up life into his pores and banish dejection.

In the next chapter, "Where I Lived, and What I Lived For," he moves both outward and downward: outward into the world of the pond itself, throwing off its nightly clothing of mist until it became a "lower heaven" full of light and reflections. In such surroundings every morning becomes a "cheerful invitation" to make his life of equal simplicity and innocence with Nature herself. But the invitation to renewal has its heroic aspects as well. In a central passage Thoreau declares his reasons for the move to Walden Pond. "I went to the woods because I wished to live deliberately, to front only the essential facts of life, and see if I could not learn what it had to teach, and not, when I came to die, discover that I had not lived." The key to living deliberately is a single commandment: "Simplify, simplify." Instead of three meals eat one; instead of dusting your tabletop decorations throw them out of the window.

Yet the simplified person need not live in poverty. The richness of classical literature and the wisdom hived in the scriptures of the nations are there for anyone willing to read them. In "Reading" Thoreau mocks the romance readers and patrons of circulating libraries who seek escape instead of illumination. They remain imprisoned all their lives in the infantile mother tongue and never subject themselves to the severe discipline of the father tongues, the languages of classical antiquity. Unlike Emerson, Thoreau prefers the written to the spoken word, Latin and Greek to the vernacular. Yet he cherishes the country lyceum and hopes to see it patronize learning and the arts as the nobles of the Old World once did. "To act collectively is according to the spirit of our institutions," he says, and reminds his fellow townspeople how rich they really are. "New England can hire all the wise men in the world to come and teach her."

Below and behind the classical tongues is another language "which all things and events speak without metaphor, which alone is copious and standard." In "Sounds" Thoreau transcribes as many of the dialects of this language as he can — the tantivy of wild pigeons, the whistle of the locomotive, the scream of the hawk, the distant hum of the Sunday bells, the lowing of the cattle, the gelatinous gurgling of the screech owls, and the waterlogged ejaculations of the bullfrogs, who sound like drunken aldermen singing catches in the Stygian lake.

To live in nature this way makes the whole body "one sense," and Thoreau imbibes delight through every pore. In the next chapter, "Solitude," Thoreau answers with grand nonchalance the townspeople who wonder how he can live alone, especially on rainy or snowy nights. "Why should I feel lonely? Is not our planet in the Milky Way?" And anyway, is it really space that separates us? "I have found that no exertion of the legs can bring two minds much nearer to one another." Still, in "Visitors" Thoreau declares that he loves society as much as most people do, and entertains visitors either in his cabin or in the most elegant of *withdrawing rooms,* the pine wood behind his house. Chief among the welcome visitors is a certain French-Canadian woodchopper, a natural man whose humility and contentment seem a gift of Nature, whose glimmerings of original thought are all the more valuable because they so rarely find expression. Girls and boys, children come a-berrying, Sunday morning walkers in clean shirts, occasional runaway slaves, all will find welcome — all but the hopeless invalids and bores, who do not know when their visit has ended.

When the visitors have departed, Thoreau returns to his labors — the writing of his books and the hoeing of his beans. These two activities have much in common. In "The Bean-Field" he describes the "small Herculean labor" involved in making the yellow soil express itself in beans rather than in weeds, "making the earth say beans instead of grass." Pacing back and forth barefoot down the seven miles of bean rows, "filling up the trenches with the weedy dead," he engages in an activity at once heroic and philosophical: "I was determined to know beans." Yet the aggressivity of this declaration is misleading; the happiest moments in "The Bean-Field" describe not a burrowing past appearance to reality but a release from self-consciousness that calls into question the very division between subjects and objects. Listening to his hoe tinkle against the stones and the nighthawk swoop and scream, Thoreau harvests an "instant and immeasurable crop. It was no longer beans that I hoed, nor I that hoed beans; and I remembered with as much pity as pride, if I remembered at all, my acquaintances who had gone to the city to attend the oratorios."

Another sound sometimes penetrates the Walden woods, the "faint *tintinnabulum*" of the trainers readying recruits for the Mexican War. This noise proceeds from Concord, that distant civilization Thoreau visits every few days to hear the news, pay a call, or buy a sack of meal. "The Village" begins humorously enough, with an account of the gossip mongers who remind Thoreau of prairie dogs, each sitting at the mouth of its burrow. He admits that he too finds the gossip as refreshing as the rustle of leaves and the cheeping of frogs, so long as it is taken in small doses, like homeopathic medicine. And the adventures he creates for himself as he sets sail at night from a parlor or lecture room to try to find his cabin again in the pitch-dark woods makes him appreciate anew "the vastness and strangeness of Nature."

Yet the village is also where he was seized because he refused to pay his tax to a state that buys and sells human beings like cattle. He had not set out to run amok against the state. "I had gone down to the woods for other purposes. But, wherever a man goes, men will pursue and paw him with their dirty institutions." Since his release he has lived in peace again, leaving his cabin unbolted and open to any stranger who cares to rest there. If all people lived with equal simplicity robbery would be unknown and fear unnecessary. "I was never molested by any person but those who represented the state."

The village and its institutions represent uncleanness; ponds represent innocence and purity. In "The Ponds" Thoreau gives an account of Walden Pond – a pond of such "crystalline purity" that its bottom may be discerned at twenty-five or thirty feet, with waves of a "vitreous greenish blue," walled in by smooth white rounded stones, dropping off steeply from the shore to a sandy bottom. Without discernible inlet or outlet, pure as a well, it stays cold even in the summer because of its great depth. "It is like molten glass cooled but not congealed, and the few motes in it are pure and beautiful like the imperfections in glass." Its surface reports every motion of insect or fish in circling dimples, lines of beauty, inviting the beholder to days of idleness. A boat on its surface affords the best prospect of the surrounding woods and sky. The area around Walden and its neighboring ponds – Flint's Pond, with its ugly name, sandy waters, and shallow bottom; the little Goose Pond; Fair-Haven, a wide spot in the Concord River; and the distant White Pond, pure as Walden itself – forms Thoreau's own "lake country," of which Walden and White are the chief jewels, more noble than the diamond of Kohinoor and fortunately "secured to us and our successors forever."

Or so Thoreau once hoped. But Walden Pond's purity has been "profaned" not only by Thoreau himself but by the "devilish Iron Horse" who has by now browsed off all the woods on Walden shore and littered it with the sties of Irish workers. In "Baker Farm" Thoreau tells of his visit to one of these shanties, the home of a laborer named John Field who works at bogging a nearby meadow with a hoe. Thoreau tells us he means to help the luckless immigrants with his experience; but his revulsion from the dirty shanty with its "wrinkled, sybil-like, cone-headed infant" sitting upon its father's knee, the "round, greasy face and bare breast" of Mrs. Field, and the chickens wandering freely and pecking at his shoes keeps overpowering him and turning what seems intended as jocularity into something much less pleasant. As he sits lecturing the immigrants on how to save money by cutting out luxuries like meat, tea, and butter, Thoreau sounds priggish and condescending rather than helpful and companionable. Fortunately, the Fields appear to be more tolerant of their guest than he was of them.

The next chapter, "Higher Laws," suggests that Thoreau's disgust at the Irish may stem partly from deeper ambivalences in his attitude toward the body itself and its involvement in materiality. Although Thoreau begins the chapter by declaring that he reverences in himself both an instinct toward a higher or spiritual life and another toward a "primitive rank and savage one," primitivism yields very quickly to asceticism as the chapter proceeds. Eating is slimy and beastly, ebriosity enervating to men and to nations. The "generative energy" dissipates and makes unclean — unless we manage to stay "continent," in which case it "invigorates and inspires us." Without chastity we are like fauns and satyrs, the divine allied to beasts, and "our very life is our disgrace."

It may be, as some scholars have suggested, that Thoreau had been influenced by the writings of "reformers" like Sylvester Graham and William Alcott, who had advocated a severe vegetarianism and warned of the dire consequences of sexual activity, particularly for consumptives; it may be that "Higher Laws," for all its deference to Eastern scriptures, represents an outcropping of the old Puritan rock beneath the Transcendental sediment. In any case the chapter oscillates uncomfortably between an acceptance of nature, including the appetites that inflame it, and a rigorous rejection of these appetites in favor of a spirituality with which they are perpetually at war.

It is a relief to pass from the condescension of "Baker Farm" and the harshness of "Higher Laws" to the renewed tenderness for nature manifested in the next chapter, "Brute Neighbors." Thoreau happily lets a wild mouse run down his sleeve and eat cheese from his fingers, after which it wipes its face with its paws like a fly. He remarks that the "remarkably adult yet innocent expression" of the eyes of young partridges suggests both "the purity of infancy" and "a wisdom clarified by experience." Two armies of warring ants, small red against large black, fascinate by their savagery and reckless courage. But best of all is the solitary loon who taunts Thoreau as he tries to row close to it one evening on the pond. The loon dives deep; Thoreau tries repeatedly to guess where he will surface, only to hear the demoniac laughter of the loon behind him, holding him in derision — the only satirist more indefatigable than he is.

Thoreau had first taken up residence at Walden on July 4, 1845, and over half of the book seems to refer to a season that might be summer or early fall. But with the chapter "House-Warming" he reminds us of the calendar again. It is October, when the lowering temperatures force him to stop up the chinks in his board shanty with plaster and finish his chimney. The pond is now skimmed over with hard, dark, transparent ice, on which he can lie at full length and observe the pond bottom as if through a pane of glass. Night after night great flocks of Canada geese come, "lumbering in the dark with a clangor and a whistling of wings," bound for Mexico. Thoreau moves inside for good, making a study of different kinds of wood suited for burning, contemplating his woodpile with affection.

Alone in the whirling snowstorms of winter, Thoreau conjures up for company the shades of Concordians past in "Former Inhabitants and Winter Visitors" — slaves like Cato Ingraham, whose carefully planted walnuts survive him; the hospitable Fenda, round and black, who told fortunes; Breed the rum seller; and a loquacious Irish colonel reputed to have fought at Waterloo, with a face red as carmine and a perpetual tremor. They are all dead now, their houses dents in the earth, overrun with weeds, the wells sealed with a stone. But Thoreau is not lonely while a visiting poet (Ellery Channing) makes his house ring with laughter, or a serene philosopher (Bronson Alcott) helps him with endlessly expansive talk building castles in the air "for which the earth offered no foundation."

"Winter Animals" gives affectionate portraits of the companions Thoreau has even in the coldest months – hares, partridges, red squirrels, foxes, thievish jays, and chickadees who make "faint flitting lisping notes, like the tinkling of icicles in the grass." The next chapter, "The Pond in Winter," begins with Thoreau's expedition with ax and pail to harvest his morning's bucket of water through the foot-thick ice on the pond, pauses to pay tribute to the fabulous beauty of the gold and emerald pickerel native to it, then records the results of a series of soundings made by Thoreau through holes in the frozen pond with a cod line and stone to see whether or not the pond was really bottomless, as local superstition had it. The pond proved to be remarkably deep at its deepest point (102 feet) but nowhere bottomless. Thoreau includes in the chapter a map of the pond carefully recording his soundings. He is nevertheless tender to the superstition he explodes. "While men believe in the infinite some ponds will be thought to be bottomless."

At the end of "The Pond in Winter" Thoreau describes the January ice harvesting, when a hundred Irishmen with Yankee overseers came to plough and furrow the ice and take it away in cakes. They build these cakes into a vast blue fort or Valhalla, finally covering it with hay and boards. The thought of where these great emeralds of Walden ice might go leads Thoreau to contemplate trade with an altered eye. It may be that the "sweltering inhabitants of Charleston and New Orleans, or Madras and Bombay and Calcutta" will drink of the water that melts from these cakes. Accustomed to bathing his intellect "in the stupendous and cosmogonal philosophy of the Bhagvat Geeta," Thoreau is pleased to imagine the Walden water mingling with the sacred water of the Ganges, returning purity for purity at last.

Winter at Walden Pond has been full of life, but the joy recorded in "Spring" still seems like a resurrection. First the ice on the pond cracks and booms, then gets honeycombed with bubbles, then (in the last week of March or the first of April) melts in a warm rain. Thawing sand mixed with clay from a deep railroad cut bursts out in streams like lava, flowing down in interlacing streams that look like leaves, or vines, or bowels, or excrements, affecting Thoreau with a peculiar sense that he is standing in the laboratory of the Artist who made the world. Withered wild grasses revealed by the melting snow "are suggestive of an inexpressible tenderness and a fragile delicacy." Faint silvery warblings are heard over the bare fields. The river valley and woods are bathed in "so pure and bright a light as would have waked the dead, if they had been slumbering," and a slight and graceful hawk rises like a ripple and tumbles down again with a strange chuckle, over and over. "And so the seasons went rolling on into summer, as one rambles into higher and higher grass."

The first version of *Walden* ended here, with the year brought full circle. But the final version has a "Conclusion" in which Thoreau tries to tell something not only about what the two years at Walden Pond meant but what they still mean seven years later. "I learned this, at least, by my experiment; that if one advances confidently in the direction of his dreams, and endeavors to live the life which he has imagined, he will meet with a success unexpected in common hours." Living at Walden taught him that much. Working on *Walden* throughout seven long and discouraging years has taught him something else: "Drive a nail home and clinch it so faithfully that you can wake up in the night and think of your work with satisfaction, — a work at which you would not be ashamed to invoke the Muse." And who can ever set bounds to the possibility for regeneration or say that the hopes of youth were wrong? "There is more day to dawn. The sun is but a morning star."

Of course no summary of *Walden* can convey much that is worth knowing about the book. *Walden* is a cascade of wit, Yankee humor, erudition, invective, outrage, exhortation, philosophical rigor, precise observation, lyrical praise, longing, overweening arrogance, disarming candor, and disinterested curiosity. Thoreau once said that the highest goal was not knowledge but sympathy with intelligence, and sympathy with intelligence is what *Walden* best communicates.

Working to complete *Walden* and then "Slavery in Massachusetts" in the spring and summer of 1854 had been exhilarating for Thoreau. But shortly after his birthday on July 12 he seems to have sunk into an irritability made worse by the blistering heat and drought. He was now thirty-seven years old; his second book, upon which he had labored seven years, was about to be published, leaving him both adrift and bereft. He should improve the nick of time, but how? The sound of a thresher's flail late in August made him wonder whether he had spent his time as wisely as the farmer. If the journal was the field he had cultivated assiduously for the last four years, then it was now time to harvest passages from it: thresh them, winnow them, and grind them into something marketable. "The lecturer must commence his threshing as early as August, that his fine flour may be ready for his winter customers."

It was natural that Thoreau (who received his specimen copy of *Walden* from the publishers as early as August 2) should begin to think of the winter lecture season and imagine that the publication of *Walden* might lead to a flurry of lecture invitations for him. Emerson had lectured extensively in New England and New York before his books were published, but the fame of his books had been responsible for the steadily widening scope of his lecture tours. After *Representative Men* came out in 1850 Emerson found himself in demand everywhere. In 1850 he had gone as far as Kentucky and Michigan; in 1851 he toured upstate New York, Maine, and ended in Montreal (where he was wildly popular); in 1852–3 he had gone on the most extensive lecture tour of his career, a trip that had taken him down the Ohio to St. Louis and back up the river to Alton, Illinois, where he boarded a train to Springfield. Illinois seemed to him a "big bog," with mud so deep wagons sank helplessly in it over the wheels, and the stout Illinoians disconcerted him at first by getting up and walking out of his lectures whenever they were bored. But Emerson earned a good deal of money and learned things from his exposure to the crude energy of the West that Concord could hardly have taught him. On the train trip to Springfield an Illinois state senator and a congressman invited him to the baggage car to share brandy, buffalo tongue, and soda biscuit.

Emerson's lecture tours in the early 1850s were grueling feats of endurance; the traveling conditions and lodgings he had to put up with were so primitive that even a man of Thoreau's rigor could look upon them as enviable adventures. In the fall of 1854 Thoreau set about planning a course of lectures that he might take on the road, hoping to put together a tour that would take him West in December and January of 1854–5. His lecture barrel was not very full; he had been devoting most of his time in recent years to *Walden* or to travel lectures (*A Yankee in Canada, Cape Cod*). He had the "Walking, or the Wild" lecture, which could be split in two and the two parts then fleshed out with new journal passages to make two new hour-long lectures. He had a lecture, "Moosehunting," which recounted his adventures on a second journey to Maine in 1853 (it would eventually form part of the book *The Maine Woods*). And he had a rich harvest of passages recently gleaned from the journal on a subject largely ignored in *Walden:* nighttime, the dark, the moon.

When an old Harvard friend named Marston Watson wrote to him in mid-September to invite him to read a lecture in Plymouth to a "private party – social gathering – almost 'sewing circle,' " Thoreau agreed, though the prospect of suddenly embarking on the career of winter lecturer in the Emersonian mold worried him. He realized how much he had enjoyed his life of obscurity and poverty, experiencing the seasons "as if I had nothing else to do but *live* them, and imbibe whatever nutriment they had for me." Such carefree joy was likely to disappear, he believed, if the public started to expect as much of him "as there is danger now that they will." Initial sales of *Walden* had been promising. When Watson wrote again to inquire whether he wished to give one lecture or two, Thoreau responded that he was determined to read only once. "That is as large a taste of my present self as I dare offer you in one visit."

The lecture he titled "Moonlight (Introduction to an Intended Course of Lectures)" and read in Plymouth on October 8, 1854, no longer exists in its original form, though pieces of it are scattered in two later published texts. After Thoreau's death his publisher James Fields put out a volume of his essays and lectures entitled *Excursions* (1863). Fields apparently needed material to fill out a partially empty final "gathering" in the published book; someone (probably Thoreau's sister Sophia, who had custody of Thoreau's manuscripts) selected sheets from the lecture manuscript and assembled them into a brief piece entitled "Night and Moonlight," the final entry in *Excursions.* Some of the remaining lecture sheets and the journal transcripts not used in the lecture eventually found their way into the hands of an editor at Houghton Mifflin, who simply transcribed and published them in a small book titled *The Moon* (1927).

From this desperate jumble it is impossible to be sure about the order of the paragraphs in the "Moonlight" lecture. But the themes of that lecture are discernible even if its shape is not. Thoreau celebrates the strangeness and beauty of the landscape seen or sensed in moonlight. "Instead of singing birds, the half-throttled note of a cuckoo flying over, the croaking of frogs, the intenser dream of crickets." In this strange world shadows are more conspicuous than the objects that cast them. "The smallest recesses in the rocks are dim and cavernous; the ferns in the wood appear of tropical size. The sweet-fern and indigo in overgrown wood-paths wet you with dew. . . . The woods are heavy and dark. Nature slumbers." The sense of sight, so tyrannical by day, yields to the senses of hearing and smell in the darkened landscape. "Every plant in the field and forest emits its odor now, swamp-pink in the meadow and tansy in the road; and there is the peculiar dry scent of corn which has begun to show its tassels."

The night is mystery, the source of the Nile, Central Africa. Why should we not explore it? "Who knows what fertility and beauty, moral and natural, are there to found?" There is something "primal and creative" in the dewy mist that suggests an "infinite fertility. I seem to be nearer to the origin of things." The stalks of the rye fields in the moonlight form an impenetrable phalanx. "The earth labors not in vain; it is bearing its burden. How rankly it has grown! How it tastes to maturity! I discover that there is such a goddess as Ceres."

Above all reigns the moon, Selene, lover of Endymion and of every man who listens to her "weird teachings." The sun is universal, impersonal, but the moon is a "divine creature freighted with hints for me." Watching the moon alternately obscured by a cloud then triumphantly emerging again turns into a game between a queen who conquers and a lover who watches. "The traveler all alone, the moon all alone, except for his sympathy, overcoming with incessant victory whole squadrons of clouds about the forests and lakes and hills."

Erotic, sensual, fascinated by fecundity, worshipful toward goddesses, drawn toward a primitivism not of Indians or French-Canadian woodchoppers but of Central Africa and the Black Nile, "Moonlight" is Thoreau's attempt to write a night hymn to answer the dawn song he had just completed. After delivering his lecture in Plymouth to an appreciative audience that included Bronson Alcott and spending a few days surveying Watson's estate, Thoreau returned to Cambridge to continue work on the "Intended Course of Lectures" to which "Moonlight" was the introduction.

On October 18 a lecture invitation of a different sort arrived from Rhode Island, asking Thoreau if he would participate in a course of "reform lectures" scheduled to begin in November. Thoreau accepted, though he had not much time to write a new lecture on top of the two revised and expanded lectures that he was hoping to get out of his old "Walking, or the Wild" manuscript for a scheduled appearance in Philadelphia. But a search through the journal suddenly turned up a passage that could serve as the nucleus for the lecture he had promised Providence. Dated September 7, 1851, the passage concerned what might be regarded as the subject Thoreau had addressed in all of his works — the art of life. "Was there ever anything memorable written upon it?" Has anyone ever written about the art of getting not a living but a life? All around us are books telling us how to save time, but they are not what we want. "I do not so much wish to know how to economize time as how to spend it, by what means to grow rich, that the day may not have been in vain."

Until December 6, 1855, when he was scheduled to deliver the lecture he called "What Shall It Profit?" at Railroad Hall in Providence, Thoreau worked furiously on the manuscript, copying out passages from the journal to make a working draft, expanding it, revising it, rejecting passages and replacing them with others, carefully placing the rejected passages in a file. This lecture — Thoreau's most frequently delivered — was revised in 1859–60 and given a new title, "Life Misspent." It was revised one final time in the spring of 1862, during Thoreau's final illness, when he responded to an offer from Ticknor and Fields to publish his essays in the *Atlantic Monthly* by sending them the late lecture "Autumnal Tints" and promising to follow it with a piece he now wanted to call "The Higher Law." They objected to the title, possibly (as Thoreau's editor suggests) because it recalled the decade-old controversy surrounding the Fugitive Slave Law; Thoreau was willing to change but said he could think of nothing better than "Life without Principle," the title the published version now bears.

This strange shifting of titles is significant in itself and says something about the complex of emotions the text manifests. "Life Misspent" and "Life without Principle" suggest in different words the pity or contempt Thoreau feels for the majority of his neighbors, employed as they were in ways that degraded them and the country together: scheming, conniving, running to California to dig gold or (even more repulsively) to the Isthmus of Darien to rob graves, solemnly legislating in Congress to *regulate* the trade in slaves and tobacco, risking their lives on the seas to bring home cargoes of rags, juniper berries, and bitter almonds (things Thoreau had found washed up on the shore when he went to look for Margaret Fuller's body). Men who spend their lives in such "business" are accounted "industrious and hardworking"; men who walk in the woods for love of them are called idlers. It is difficult to buy a blank book in the stores to record one's thoughts; most are ruled for dollars and cents. To such mean wisdom Thoreau opposes his own, a Poor Richard's proverb for Richards willing to stay poor. "There is no more fatal blunderer than he who consumes the greater part of his life getting his own living."

So far "Life without Principle" is an angrier version of the "Economy" chapter in *Walden*. But the original lecture title, "What Shall It Profit?," with its explicit allusion to the Gospel of Mark, suggests that Thoreau had another audience in mind besides the burghers whose greed he mocks. Jesus has just predicted his death and resurrection for the first time to his disciples; the shocked Peter rebukes him for saying it. Jesus turns on Peter and rebukes him in turn, saying, "Get thee behind me, Satan; for thou savorest not the things that be of God, but the things that be of men" (Mark 8:33). A few moments later, when he has called the people together, Jesus asks the famous question: "For what shall it profit a man, if he shall gain the whole world, and lose his own soul?" (Mark 8:36)

We know that Thoreau had both of these chapters in mind when he wrote the original lecture, for he makes the former the subject of a joke about greed and the Gold Rush. "Satan, from one of his elevations, showed mankind the kingdom of California, and instead of the cry 'Get thee behind me, Satan,' they shouted, 'Go ahead!' and he had to exert himself to get there first." He dropped this passage from the final text of "Life without Principle," for by 1862 the Gold Rush was no longer news. But the portrait of a different tempter remains. "It is remarkable that among all the preachers there are so few moral teachers. The prophets are employed in excusing the ways of men. Most reverend seniors, the *illuminati* of the age, tell me, with a gracious, reminiscent smile, betwixt an aspiration and a shudder, not to be too tender about these things" – *these things* being the compromises everyone has to make to make a living, the laws of the world. Angrily Thoreau rejects all such advice. "A man had better starve at once than lose his innocence in the process of getting his bread."

It is hard not to see in this passage a portrait of Emerson, whose "Conduct of Life" series included the lectures "Power" and "Wealth" and whose *English Traits* (then being readied for publication) praised the power, wealth, aristocracy, manners – even the complacency – of the British race. Emerson's worship of all things English contains a chapter heaping praise upon the London *Times,* which Emerson credits with stamping out sympathy for the French Republic of 1848 and causing the Chartist rebellion to fizzle. Thoreau demolishes such admiration with a significant pun. "Read not the Times. Read the Eternities." To ignore the center for superficies (as Emerson now seemed to be doing) strikes Thoreau as a betrayal of genius, as a betrayal of truth. "Is there any such thing as wisdom not applied to life?"

Emerson, who was off on a lecture tour in upstate New York when Thoreau delivered "What Shall It Profit?" at the Concord Lyceum on February 14, 1855, would have agreed with that question, at least. Where he differed from Thoreau was not in his diagnosis of the problem – that the world of the senses was fatally severed from the world of the soul – but in his solution to the problem: prudence for the sensible world and spontaneity or instinct for the spiritual one. Thoreau insisted on bringing senses and soul into alignment in every act of his life, whether surveying or writing.

Thoreau's hopes of uniting vocation and avocation by turning his journal passages into lectures had already gone down to defeat. Lecture invitations from the Midwest and Canada had been so sparse that his fees would not have paid for his trip. Even within New England responses to "What Shall It Profit?" had ranged from puzzlement to disbelief (except on Nantucket, whose hardy residents had liked his truculent gospel). After the first reading in Providence, Thoreau believed he had failed to get "even the attention of the mass." Lecturing, he decided, was as violent as was fattening geese by cramming – and in this case the geese refused to get fatter. He had wasted an entire winter writing lectures for audiences that did not want to hear them; he had neglected his journal to turn out work until he felt like a spindle in a factory. He concluded that he would much rather write books.

Thoreau did not give up lecturing after 1855, but he gave up thinking that he might make a living from lecturing. A debilitating bout of illness he suffered in the spring of 1855 suggested that in any case he could hardly hope to stand the rigors of winter lecture tours over a half-savage country as well as Emerson did, though Emerson was fourteen years his senior. Instead he began sending out old manuscripts for publication. But the integrity too prickly for audiences proved too prickly for publishers as well, and the publication of *Cape Cod* that had begun in the June issue of *Putnam's* was ended by August when Thoreau refused to consider eliminating material his editor thought offensive.

Thoreau continued to work on his journal, taking now a more purely scientific interest in subjects like the propagation of plants by seeds or the apparently paradoxical fact that many groves of trees were more hospitable to the seedlings of alien species than they were to their own. A visit to New York in 1856 to see Alcott and Greeley led to a ferry trip across the East River to inspect one of Emerson's new enthusiasms – Walt Whitman. Though the contrast between Whitman's small clutch of mythological engravings (Bacchus, Hercules, a satyr) and the shabby bedroom he shared with his brother was sad, Whitman was then at the high tide of his poetic confidence. Emerson had hailed the first edition of *Leaves of Grass,* and though it sold considerably fewer copies than *A Week on the Concord and Merrimack Rivers* had, Whitman issued a second edition and was convinced that demand for his works would soon be great. Both men were guarded during the meeting, but Thoreau soon began displaying his copy of *Leaves of Grass* in Concord; Whitman later said he admired Thoreau's blazing capacity for dissent.

In 1857 Thoreau took the last of his three trips to Maine. In 1846 he had visited Maine with a group of friends and had climbed Mount Katahdin, a harrowing excursion he described first in a lecture and then in an essay entitled "Ktaadn," published in John Sartain's *Union Magazine of Literature and Art* in 1848. In 1853 he had taken a second trip to Maine's Moosehead and Chesuncook lakes with his cousin, who wanted to go moose hunting, and their Indian guide, the logger Joe Aitteon. When he returned he worked up a lecture for the Concord Lyceum about his experiences and repeated this "Moosehunting" lecture several times over the next few years. In January 1858 he offered an essay derived from his lecture but now called "Chesuncook" to James Russell Lowell, the editor of the new *Atlantic Monthly* magazine, who had asked him for something about his Maine trips. Publication of installments began in June 1858 but was marred by now-predictable quarrels. Thoreau resented editorial tampering with his text and became furious when Lowell deleted a sentence despite Thoreau's insistence that it be printed. When Thoreau discovered the omission in the July number of the magazine he fired off a letter to Lowell so angry and insulting that Lowell never forgave him. (Lowell got his revenge in 1865 with a merciless review of Thoreau's career in the *North American Review;* its famous opening paragraphs rank with Emerson's brief essay on the Chardon Street Convention as the best comic portraits of an era in which self-assertion and lunacy were difficult to tell apart.)

Thoreau's 1857 trip by canoe had taken him up the West Branch of the Penobscot River, then overland to the headwaters of the East Branch for an exhilarating return trip down a swift river corrugated by rapids and waterfalls. The trip furnished material for yet another essay, eventually titled "The Allegash and East Branch," by far the longest of the three Maine pieces. "The Allegash and East Branch" was never printed during Thoreau's lifetime, though he continued to work on it up until the time of his death. (Ellery Channing, who was with Thoreau when he died, said that his last audible words were "moose" and "Indian.") The three essays were published together with an "Appendix" as *The Maine Woods* in 1864. The Appendix contains lists of Maine plants, birds, and animals; two lists of words in the Abenaki language; and advice about how to outfit oneself for expeditions.

"Ktaadn" had recorded Thoreau's startled discovery that the bare rocks of the mountain's top are frightening because they remind us of the materiality of the universe, its alien "thingness," or solidity, a quality shared by the commonest objects and by our own bodies to which we are chained all our lives like Prometheus to his rock. The remaining two chapters in *The Maine Woods* examine forms of otherness less menacing but no less uncanny – the moose, the pine tree, and the Indian.

The last of these is the most important to Thoreau, who confesses in "Chesuncook" that he decided to employ an Indian guide "mainly that I might have an opportunity to study his ways." Joe Aitteon is a twenty-four-year-old Penobscot Indian, a son of the governor, with a broad face and reddish complexion, short and stout, dressed like a logger in a red flannel shirt and black Kossuth hat. Joe takes the stagecoach (with his canoe) from Bangor to Moosehead Lake sixty miles to the northwest; Thoreau and his cousin follow after in an open wagon. They take the steamer up Moosehead Lake – a "wild-looking sheet of water, sprinkled with wild, low islands," rougher than the ocean itself. At the head of the lake they must disembark and carry their canoe and belongings through the forest to the Penobscot River, but lumbermen have made the "carry" a broad straight swath several rods wide through the forest, where the spruce and fir trees "crowded to the track on each side to welcome us" and the wildflowers bloom in profusion.

This happy relationship to nature ends abruptly when they reach the Penobscot, where Thoreau's cousin intends to go moose hunting. Thoreau admits that he feels some compunction about tagging along on the hunt, but tells himself that he wants to see a moose near at hand and see how an Indian kills one. He will go as a "reporter or chaplain to the hunters," not as a hunter himself.

Yet like other reporters and chaplains he discovers that his own detachment ends when the killing is at hand. When at last they surprise a pair of moose in a tributary of the Penobscot, Thoreau finds himself staring at something very different from the majestic bull moose of the hunter's imagination. He sees a cow and her yearling calf peering round the alders at them. "They made me think of great frightened rabbits, with their long ears and half-inquisitive, half-frightened looks." His cousin fires at the larger moose, then at the calf; both animals flee, making no sound on the damp moss that carpets the forest floor. Half an hour later upstream they find the cow dead in the shallow stream, still warm. Thoreau grabs the animal's ears and helps Joe drag it to shore; he measures it carefully and notes the contrast between its "grotesque and awkward" shape and "the delicacy and tenderness of its hoofs."

Then the skinning commences. Whatever appetite Thoreau had to watch native skill with a knife evaporates as he watches the ghastly red carcass emerge from beneath the skin, the warm milk streaming from the rent udder. Though his cousin proudly keeps the ball with which he shot the moose to show his grandchildren, Thoreau feels that "the afternoon's tragedy, and my share in it" has destroyed the innocence and pleasure of his adventure and makes nature look sternly upon him.

Can humans think of no better use for animals than killing them, no better use of pine trees but to turn them into boards? "A pine cut down, a dead pine, is no more a pine than a dead human carcass is a man." Why do so few people ever come to the woods to see how the pine "lives and grows and spires, lifting its evergreen arms to the light – to see its perfect success"? The "higher law" we obey demands reverence for the pine as well as for moose and human beings. "It is as immortal as I am, and perchance will go to as high a heaven, there to tower above me still." (This last is the sentence Lowell found heterodox enough to expunge.)

Throughout the rest of his trip down the Penobscot to Chesuncook Lake and on the return trip to Bangor, Thoreau enjoys the wildness of a landscape still largely untouched by human hands, just as he enjoys the "purely wild and primitive American sound" of the Abenaki language Aitteon speaks with other Indians – something that takes him by surprise and finally convinces him that "the Indian was not the invention of historians and poets." He fills "Chesuncook" with transcriptions of Indian words and pesters Joe endlessly for translations (*kecunnilessu*, the chickadee; *skuscumonsuck*, the kingfisher). These form a vigorous native counterpoint to the flurry of the Linnaean binomials that Thoreau himself habitually uses to identify things (*Parus atricapillus,* the chickadee; *Alcedo alcyon,* the kingfisher).

Though Thoreau admires the woods he does not want to live there, and he confesses that he is relieved at the end of his trip to return to the "smooth but still varied landscape" of Massachusetts, more hospitable to poets than the barren wilderness of Maine. That seems valuable to him as a "resource and a background, the raw material of our civilization." If kings and nobles have their parks why cannot a free people have its "national preserves" where the bear and panther may rove freely and the trees be defended from the logger's saw? Or shall we "like the villains, grub them all up, poaching on our own national domains?"

The last chapter in *The Maine Woods,* "The Allegash and East Branch," records Thoreau's final journey to Maine in June 1857 with his old Concord friend Ed Hoar. They head for the Penobscot village at Oldtown, up the Penobscot River from Bangor, in hopes of finding an Indian to be their guide. The first man they see is an Indian named Joe Polis, who is prosperous (his two-story house looks as neat as one on a New England village street) and a member of the tribal aristocracy. They ask him if he knows of any Indian willing to guide them on their planned circular journey up to Moosehead Lake and across to the east branch of the Penobscot. He answers "from that strange remoteness in which the Indian ever dwells to the white man," that he wants to go himself to get some moose.

Thoreau is fascinated by Polis's remoteness, admiring his refusal to indulge in the "conventional palaver and smartness of the white man." Polis ignores attempts to make conversation, or else replies in grunts; such answers as he does give to questions are "vague and indistinct." One morning he is asked, rhetorically, "You did not stretch your moose-hide, did you, Mr. Polis?" Polis responds with irritation at the silliness of the question. "What you ask me that question for? Suppose I stretch 'em, you see 'em. May be your way talking, may be all right, no Indian way." Yet at other moments Polis loves to expatiate upon the history of his tribe or its exploits in battle. When the day's work is done he exhibits "the *bonhomie* of a Frenchman, and we would fall asleep before he got through his periods."

Polis is as hardy and skilled in woodcraft as any wilderness traveler could wish, and he endures without complaint the persecution by flies and mosquitoes that keep the white men swathed in veils and slathered with repellent lotions by night. Yet some of his attitudes surprise Thoreau. Polis has represented his tribe at the state capital in Augusta and once in Washington (where Daniel Webster was rude to him). He liked Boston, New York, and Philadelphia and would even like to live in one of the cities – though he realizes that in New York he would probably be "the poorest hunter" in the place. He has an enormous appetite for sugar. He loves to challenge Thoreau to contests of speed in carrying or paddling, and, when he wins, admits, "Oh, me love to play sometimes." And he probably understands very well how proud he makes Thoreau when he tells him near the end of the journey that Thoreau paddles "just like anybody."

And the landscape is as beautiful as Thoreau remembers it from his earlier journeys. One morning they drift down one of the many lakes in their path. "The morning was a bright one, and perfectly still and serene, the lake as smooth as glass, we making the only ripple as we paddled into it. The dark mountains about it were seen through a glaucous mist, and the brilliant white stems of canoe birches mingled with the other woods around it." Thoreau hears the wood thrush, then the laugh of some loons, whose echo is strangely magnified by the curving bay in which they ride.

Representing nature in prose so limpid that nothing seems to stand between the reader and the scene represented had been one of Thoreau's great gifts ever since "The Natural History of Massachusetts." The excursions and travel books are full of such passages; many chapters of *Walden* consist of nothing else. But in all these forms the egotism of the organizing fiction is at odds with the perfect self-effacement that representation implies. The speaker must tell us that *he* went on a walk or a river trip, that *he* traveled to Maine or Canada or Cape Cod, that *he* built a cabin and lived by a pond. In the journal such reminders are unnecessary, and that may be one of the reasons Thoreau found the journal an exercise of joy. At once pure enthusiast and pure craftsman, he can record what he perceives without needing to route his language through the petty concerns of the empirical self.

In the early 1850s, when Thoreau's journal expanded into the major literary project of his life, he had expressed frustration that he could not offer the reader his journal passages as they were, without transcription and rearrangement. As the decade wore on he conceived of an even more radical project – letting Nature speak for herself. One kind of work could use as its organizing principle the rhythms of flowering and decay by which trees and plants move in harmony with the seasons. Another could track the curious, prodigal, stochastic ways in which the trees and plants themselves are propagated.

The journal, with its years and years of patiently gathered observations of phenomena, could furnish data for both; the various works of natural history and natural science that Thoreau began reading with voracious intensity in the later 1850s could suggest a method and a stance. These twin projects were left unfinished at the time of Thoreau's death, but the two large bundles of manuscript ("Wild Fruits" and "The Dispersion of Seeds") came to almost a thousand pages. Parts of these longer manuscripts consisted of lectures he had delivered or apparently planned to deliver; along with the John Brown lectures they were the last lectures of his career.

"Autumnal Tints" was the first of these natural history lectures to be delivered. Thoreau had apparently begun working on it in 1857 but first delivered it in 1859, when he read it at Worcester, at the Concord Lyceum, and at Lynn. "Autumnal Tints" begins with Thoreau's confession that he had really dreamed of compiling a book about leaves in which language was unnecessary. He might trace the leaves of each "tree, shrub, and herbaceous plant" at just the moment when it had reached its brightest color as it changed from green to brown, then "copy its color exactly, with paint, in a book." If he could "preserve the leaves themselves, unfaded, it would be better still."

Yet this childlike "memento" of October would still be only a memento – and Thoreau would have the single copy. Description in language is distant from what it describes, but on the other hand, it is easily stereotyped; besides, what Thoreau discovers as he goes along is that the color of the single leaf, however brilliant, means little without the context that makes it beautiful. The earliest tree to redden (the red maple) stands out like a burning bush against the rest of the forest, making the green ones greener; whereas the last great red rose among the deciduous trees (the scarlet oak) depends upon the surrounding evergreens for half its intensity.

But "Autumnal Tints" is more than a series of still pictures. Thoreau wants to convey the excitement of seasonal change itself, as the year moves from late August – when the purple grasses bloom, the pokes redden into great "upright branching casks of purple wine," and the lowly beard grasses on their sterile and neglected soil suddenly amaze the walker with their beauty – through every variety of blaze and flame among the deciduous trees: the red maple, the elm, the sugar maple, and finally the scarlet oak, whose leaves are cut with such precision that a heap of them looks like scrap tin.

What is the purpose of this annual sacrifice? The fallen leaves suggest mortality and self-sacrifice, of course: "They teach us how to die." But a different lesson is taught by the leaves still on the trees. "Did not all these suggest that man's spirits should rise as high as Nature's, – should hang out their flag, and the routine of his life be interrupted by an analagous expression of joy and hilarity?" Trees are as important to villages as town clocks are. Elms form "great yellow canopies or parasols held over our heads and houses by the mile together, making the village all one and compact." Villages without trees fall prey to "melancholy and superstition" – indeed, they soon become the resort of "bigoted religionists and desperate drinkers."

Thoreau is only half-joking here. His growing sense of urgency about the need to preserve wild spaces extended not only to true wildernesses like the Maine woods but also to those humbler wild spaces that used to surround every township but were disappearing as fast as the white pine forests themselves. Fenced off, chopped down, ransacked for profit, the wild fields and forests were disappearing, and with them went the last possibility for a simple and wholesome relationship to nature. In another part of the "Wild Fruits" project Thoreau remarks bitterly that few people care much for Nature and would happily sell their share in all her beauty for a fairly small sum. And he adds, "It is for the very reason that some do not care for these things that we need to combine to protect all from the vandalism of a few." If people can give money to Harvard College, why can they not present a forest or a huckleberry field to the town of Concord? The true wealth of a town lies in its beauty and in the health it creates.

The final lesson "Autumnal Tints" teaches is that beauty is itself a kind of self-transcendence. The lesson that Milton's Raphael gives Adam about how bodies can work up to spirit is also preached by Thoreau's scarlet oaks. "Lifted higher and higher, and sublimated more and more . . . they have at length the least possible amount of earthy matter, and the greatest spread and grasp of skyey influences." Dancing arm and arm with light, the slender leaves with their glossy surfaces trip it so fantastically that "you can hardly tell what in the dance is leaf and what is light."

"Autumnal Tints" is the most beautiful of Thoreau's late natural history essays, and it was also one of the most popular. Ellen Emerson informed her sister that when the lecture was delivered in Concord "there were constant spontaneous bursts of laughter and Mr. Thoreau was applauded" (Ellen Emerson to Edith Emerson, March 2, 1859). Another lecture from the "Wild Fruits" manuscript was also popular. In "Wild Apples" (delivered first at the Concord Lyceum on February 8, 1860, and repeated six days later in New Bedford), Thoreau praises another long-time resident of the New England landscape, the wild apple tree. "Almost all wild apples are handsome. They cannot be too gnarly and crabbed and rusty to look at." The ancestors of all American wild apples are European, but the trees have been in this landscape so long as to seem indigenous – thorny, crabbed, growing fruits "brindled with deep red streaks like a cow, or with hundreds of fine blood-red rays running from stem-dimple to the blossom end, like meridional lines, on a straw-colored ground."

Wild apples are so spicy or tart that only a brisk walk in the November air can make them seem palatable. But Thoreau loves these "wild flavors of the Muse, vivacious and inspiriting" and deplores the vapid grafted varieties that are gradually displacing them, apples with neither *tang* nor *smack*. The temperance reformers have done their best to extirpate the wild apple; Thoreau tells of an orchard owner who cut down his unusually prolific trees for fear the apples would be made into cider. And people who plant grafted apples "collect them in a plat by their houses, and fence them in." Greed and sanctimony alike doom the wild apple to extinction. Thoreau ends with verses (1:5–7, 12) from the prophet Joel (strikingly appropriate, as it turns out, for a land infested with temperance men and women):

Awake ye drunkards, and weep; and howl, all ye drinkers of wine, because of the new wine; for it is cut off from your mouth. For a nation is come up upon my land, strong, and without number, whose teeth are the teeth of a lion. . . . He hath laid my vine waste, and barked my fig tree. . . . The vine is dried up, and the fig tree languisheth; the pomegranate tree, the palm tree also, and the apple tree, even all the trees of the field, are withered: because joy is withered away from the sons of men.

Such denunciation of the greedy and the sanctimonious found ready acceptance in Concord; the records of the lyceum note that there was "loud and continued applause" at the end of the lecture. Alcott noted in his journal that he had listened to it with "uninterrupted interest and delight." As with "Autumnal Tints," the audience seems to have enjoyed the blend of humor, precise description of familiar scenes, and concern for preserving the natural landscape in at least some of its wildness. A concern for preservation and a resolve to understand the mechanisms by which Nature ensures her own survival is even more strongly marked in Thoreau's final lecture in Concord, "The Succession of Forest Trees," which he delivered before the Middlesex Agricultural Society in the Concord Town Hall on September 20, 1860.

In the mid-1850s Thoreau had been struck by the observation made by a neighbor that whenever a pine wood was cut down an oak one would spring up, and vice versa. The folk belief (endorsed even by some naturalists) held that such trees sprang up "spontaneously," but Thoreau knew that trees sprang only from seeds. He began studying the various ways trees and shrubs and plants of all kinds propagated themselves – dispersed to the wind, floated on water, stuck to passing animals or eaten by them, carried by birds, buried by squirrels. This study led to the beginning of his second large unfinished manuscript in natural history, "The Dispersion of Seeds," of which "The Succession of Forest Trees" forms part.

Thoreau explains that when an oak wood is adjacent to a pine one the acorns will be carried into the pine wood by squirrels and other animals every year. A few will take root and spring up into seedlings, which will normally die after a few years. But if the pine wood is suddenly cut down so that light and air reach the oldest oak seedlings they seem to sprout up suddenly into trees. Pines (as the English planters discovered) are the best nurses for oaks, and oak seedlings planted among pines grow more vigorously than oaks planted alone, even though the pines must be pulled out for the oaks to reach maturity. But the greedy American farmer, unaware that he has an oak nursery in his pine wood, cuts the pines down and plows the land under, thinking to sow a crop or two of rye before he turns the land back to woodlot. Of course he kills the healthy oak seedlings ready to shoot into trees; afterwards puzzled that his woodlot remains barren, he complains that his land is "pine-sick."

To cultivate Nature successfully we must adopt the methods she has perfected. "There is a patent office at the seat of government of the universe, whose managers are as much interested in the dispersion of seed as anybody at Washington can be, and their operations are infinitely more extensive and regular." Those operations it is the task of the longer manuscript, "The Dispersion of Seeds," to chronicle. There Thoreau considers the dispersion of seed from every kind of tree, shrub, and plant, all the way from the giant sequoia of the California forests to the lowly thistle, whose ugly head conceals a "hedge of imbricated, thin, and narrow leaflets" enclosing the "delicate downy parachutes of the seed, — like a silk-lined cradle in which the prince is rocked." Everywhere there is immense waste, immense care, immense trust. The slender and brittle black willow shed cotton from its catkins until it forms a thick white scum on the pond; the minute brown seeds in the cotton float downstream to anchor in new mud and begin new life. Touch-me-not seed vessels explode and shoot their seed like shot. The pod of the milkweed contains in a "little oblong chest" around two hundred little pear-shaped seeds packed in layers like scales, seeds launched by the wind to fly over hill and dale. "Who could believe in prophecies of Daniel or Miller that the world would end this summer, while one milkweed with faith matured its seeds?"

Throughout the autumn and winter of 1860 Thoreau pursued his botanical studies, examining the growth patterns of trees by studying tree rings. After one such expedition on December 3 he came down with a severe cold, which he had probably caught from Bronson Alcott a few days earlier. He forced himself to keep an engagement to read "Autumnal Tints" to an audience in Waterbury, but his cold — now bronchitis — made him read in a monotone and the evening was not a success. It was in fact his last lecture. He returned to Concord exhausted and seriously ill. The tuberculosis that had killed his sister in 1849 and his father a decade later now involved him in a long, slow decline that a trip to Minnesota in the spring of 1861 did nothing to arrest.

He worked as long as he could, employing his sister Sophia as amanuensis when he could no longer write. When James Fields took over the editorship of the *Atlantic Monthly* he asked Thoreau to submit essays, and Thoreau worked to get "Autumnal Tints," "Wild Apples," "Life without Principle," and "Walking" ready for the printer. He persuaded Fields to buy from him the unsold copies of *A Week on the Concord and Merrimack Rivers*. He talked or whispered to the friends who came by to see him — Alcott, Emerson, Channing, Sam Staples (his old Concord jailer, now Emerson's neighbor). Thoreau was touched by the affectionate concern of his townspeople, but he resisted any attempts by the conventionally religious to catechize him on the state of his soul, telling one old friend who wanted to know how he stood with Christ that a snowstorm was more to him than Christ and retorting to an aunt who wanted him to make his peace with God that he did not know that he and God had ever quarreled.

Thoreau died on the morning of May 6, 1862. He was forty-four years old. Emerson insisted that the funeral be held from the First Parish Church, despite Thoreau's well-known antipathy to institutional Christianity. Alcott was in charge of planning the service, which was to consist of a hymn written by Ellery Channing, an address by Emerson, and selections from Thoreau's works read by Alcott. Louisa May Alcott reported to a friend that she thought Emerson's address "good in itself but not appropriate to the time and place." Far better, in her opinion, were the "wise & pious thoughts" from Thoreau read by her father, or the funeral procession to the churchyard where Thoreau's father and brother lay. "It was a lovely day clear, & calm, & spring like, & as we all walked after Henry's coffin with its fall of flowers, carried by six of his townsmen who had grown up with him, it seemed as if Nature wore her most benignant aspect to welcome her dutiful & loving son to his long sleep in her arms" (Louisa May Alcott to Sophia Foord, May 11, 1862).

What may have seemed inappropriate to Louisa in Emerson's address was its frankness, a frankness even more evident in the revised and expanded version of the address that Emerson published in the August 1862 number of the *Atlantic Monthly*. The anger that had divided the two men a decade earlier had long ago given way to peace — the two men spent long afternoons together in a rowboat Emerson bought; Thoreau larded his late natural history lectures with affectionate allusions to Emerson's works; Emerson hired Thoreau to survey his land and plant pines for him on the Walden lot. But looking through his old journals for passages about Thoreau made Emerson relive again the unhappiness of their long relationship:

There was something military in his nature not to be subdued, always manly and able, but rarely tender, as if he did not feel himself except in opposition. He wanted a fallacy to expose, a blunder to pillory. . . . It seemed as if his first instinct upon hearing a proposition was to controvert it, so impatient was he of the limitations of our daily thought.

Such militancy meant that "no equal companion stood in affectionate relations with one so pure and guileless."

Emerson's surviving manuscript of the *Atlantic* essay reflects the confict of emotions Thoreau still aroused in him. His first draft includes many passages from his journals recording Thoreau's truculence or conceit, along with passages praising his vigor, integrity, and purity of heart. The cancellations and revisions Emerson made when he readied the manuscript for the printer softened his criticism but did not wholly remove it. The effect made by the essay is of affection laced with bitterness, admiration mingled with anger, love ending in pain. Thoreau, in Emerson's view, was the one Transcendentalist who had practical skill to match his intelligence and moral power. If he would not have commanded an army, he might at least have built its bridges. Yet instead of "engineering for America" Thoreau had been content to be "the captain of a huckleberry party."

Emerson's frustration with what he saw as Thoreau's lack of ambition was an old subject, but his sense of disappointment was given a keener edge when he surveyed the state of the Union in 1862. Its armies, unprepared for war and incompetently led, had suffered humiliating defeats on the battlefield; its president, Abraham Lincoln, could not seem to make up his mind to emancipate the slaves. In January 1862 Emerson had traveled to Washington to give a talk entitled "American Civilization" to the Smithsonian Association. He addressed himself to any officials of the Lincoln administration who might be listening. "The evil you contend with has taken alarming proportions, and you still content yourself with parrying the blows it aims, but, as if enchanted, abstain from striking at the cause." Now the person Emerson called his closest friend was dead, and the Union itself seemed to be no closer to the one act that could justify its existence.

Then, a little over a month after Emerson's "Thoreau" appeared in the *Atlantic Monthly,* President Lincoln issued the Preliminary Emancipation Proclamation, declaring that the slaves would be freed by January 1, 1863. Emerson spoke at an abolitionist rally in Boston a few days later. "The Emancipation Proclamation" is full of the imagery of pestilence removed and shame expiated. "With this blot removed from our national honor, this heavy load lifted off the national heart, we shall not fear henceforward to show our faces among mankind. We shall cease to be hypocrites and pretenders, but what we have styled our free institutions shall be such." "Happy are the young, who find the pestilence cleansed out of the earth. Happy the old, who see nature purified before they depart."

At the end of the nineteenth century, the surviving Transcendentalists could look back on the movement they had participated in with a wonder reserved for the fortunate. Born in a period of innocence and hope and grown to maturity in a time of wild experimentation, they were defended from the excesses that plague most Romantic movements by the very rigidities of New England habit they sought to escape. Their minds were free to speculate (as Emerson said) because they were sure of a return. Though they lived through a period of national humiliation, when every year brought new shame, they never lost faith in the ultimate triumph of the moral law; and history, which so often shatters the hopes of idealists, in this case proved them right. The renovation they had first imagined thirty years earlier had not come about as they had imagined it, in peace and joy, but it had come nevertheless, and it proved what they had always believed – that the universe could be trusted. As Emerson had written in the essay "Nature": "Every moment instructs, and every object, for wisdom is infused into every form. It has been poured into us as blood; it convulsed us as pain; it slid into us as pleasure; it enveloped us in dull, melancholy days, or in days of cheerful labor; we did not guess its essence until after a long time."

NARRATIVE FORMS

Jonathan Arac

ESTABLISHING NATIONAL NARRATIVE

O F THE AMERICAN WRITERS from the mid-nineteenth century whose names are still recognized today, the majority are writers of prose narrative, such as Cooper, Poe, Hawthorne, Melville, and Stowe. Beyond these better-known writers, others will also appear in these pages, for the canon changes, and some writers who have never before, or not recently, played a significant part in American literary histories now seem important, such as the historians George Bancroft and Francis Parkman and the abolitionist Frederick Douglass. From the 1820s through the 1860s American prose narrative was produced and distributed within an increasingly established, yet conflict-ridden, publishing business, as Michael Bell shows in this volume. Narratives arose from, responded to, and contributed to continental and overseas expansion, racial struggles, and political debates, and elsewhere in this volume Eric Sundquist has detailed this complex process. But the production of narratives in a culture may be seen not only as a function of other institutions and structures but also as an institution that has a history and structure of its own, relatively independent of these others. Such a relatively internal history, in which the fundamental organizing terms are drawn from literary analysis rather than from economic or social analysis, is the work of this section. For in this period writers of prose narratives helped to form a definition of literature that still exerts power now.

The central event in the literary history of mid-nineteenth-century American prose narrative is the emergence, around 1850, of works, preeminently *The Scarlet Letter* and *Moby-Dick,* that still count as "literature" for many readers of the late twentieth century. Yet other valuable prose narratives of the time often trouble today's readers because there is no clear conceptual category into which the works fit. To understand this emergence requires acknowledging the problem of "genre," that is, the problem of defining different kinds of writing. In the discussion of narrative forms that follows, Chapter 4 addresses the newly emerging genre of literary narrative; Chapters 1 through 3 define the competing, earlier generic types in relation to which the specificity of literary narrative may be understood; and Chapter 5 sketches the fate of literary narrative in the period of its first emergence.

Although literary narrative dominates late-twentieth-century views of this period, the works that are now valued did not immediately establish themselves, and the very genre of literary narrative itself almost disappeared in the intense national crisis of the Civil War.

In the late eighteenth century, "literature" meant all culturally valued writing, including what would now be distinguished as "nonfiction," such as history, travel, philosophy, and science. By the late twentieth century, however, the most widely accepted meaning of "literature" is fiction that does not fit any defined marketing genre (science fiction, western, crime, romance, and so on). In the United States, mid-nineteenth-century prose narrative was a crucial place for this change in meaning. As a result of this change, it is now expected that literary culture and national culture will stand at a tense distance from each other. This historically limited conception often makes it difficult to understand the value of works that are based on a different relation to the national.

The dominant narrative type that preceded literary narrative, and that continued to flourish even after literary narrative had appeared, I call "national narrative." From the standpoint of America's present existence as an independent union, national narrative told the story of the nation's colonial beginnings and looked forward to its future as a model for the world. This story, which still has much force in the United States, began to take on its fully articulated form around the presidency of Andrew Jackson (1828–36). It could be told with equal power through fiction, especially in the work of James Fenimore Cooper, beginning in the 1820s, and through history, especially in the work of George Bancroft, beginning in the 1830s. When it first took shape, there was no fully operative national culture. National narrative was part of the process by which the nation was forming itself and not merely a reflection of an accomplished fact, yet it defined the ground against which the other major narrative types would stand out.

Within the imaginative space opened by the articulation of national narrative, two important smaller types of narrative flourished and competed with the national. First, in the 1830s, came what I call "local narratives." These were more resticted than was national narrative, either in the geographical area they encompassed or in the scale of the human experience with which they dealt. Following the example of Washington Irving's New York sketches, local narratives include stories by the "southwestern humorists" of Georgia, Alabama, Mississippi, and Tennessee; the northeastern tales of Nathaniel Hawthorne; and the works in which Edgar Allan Poe began to define the city as a new American locale. In the 1840s what I call "personal narratives" became prominent. Rather than express the collectivity of the nation, these works place in the foreground a single first-person narrator. Yet, contrary to both Puritan tradition and twentieth-century expectation, this "I" is a rather extroverted reporter, bringing news from the margins of the dominant culture rather than exploring spiritual or psychological inwardness. This narrative form includes works by travelers, such as Herman Melville, Richard Henry Dana (*Two Years before the Mast*), and Francis Parkman (*The Oregon Trail*), and also narratives by escaped slaves, such as Frederick Douglass.

Literary narrative emerged in 1850 together with a political crisis over slavery, which threatened the nation's existence and produced a compromise intended to subdue the controversy. At this moment, Melville and Hawthorne emphasized certain elements present in their own earlier writings and in those of Poe and set their work apart from national narrative. The "Custom-House" introduction to Hawthorne's *Scarlet Letter* illustrates this distancing from national concerns. In contrast not only to national narrative but also to local and personal narratives, which both addressed and reflected the concerns of everyday public life, the literary narrative of *The Scarlet Letter* turns away to develop a freely imaginative space. Whether through the hyperbole of Poe, the allegory of Melville, or the irony of Hawthorne, works of literary narrative not only differed from but seemed also to transcend and, implicitly, to criticize the world of common life. Yet their critical authority depended on their being limited to elite audiences, esoteric subjects, and indirect means. The possible glory of forming a "world elsewhere" through writing often was experienced by the authors themselves as deadeningly repetitive, solitary labor. This moment in which the "literary" writer was redefined as an "artist" marks a crisis in the relation of narrative to its public, for the work of the artist was understood to draw its primary value from its private relation to the writer's self.

This turn of American literary narrative was not unique. Since the later eighteenth century, Romantic writers in England and Germany had elaborated a new understanding of the place occupied by highly skilled writing within a culture. Conceptions such as "originality," "genius," and "imagination" defined literature as independent from the public world rather than interrelated with it, and notions of "psychology" and "development" defined new areas of attention and new techniques. Therefore, in analyzing American prose narrative in the mid-nineteenth century it is necessary also to discuss the transatlantic writers who were important as examples and resources. Especially significant were the English poets and critics William Wordsworth and Samuel Taylor Coleridge, for, paradoxically, they provided in theory and in practice models of writing newly democratic in spirit yet also newly difficult for readers to grasp and to enjoy.

JAMES FENIMORE COOPER

The power of national narrative codified by George Bancroft and James Fenimore Cooper continues to be felt in the United States. It circulates through media that are not understood as literary. Bancroft's conceptions of America are still common in the civic discourse of political education and debate. Cooper's images of America still prevail in the mass-cultural forms of movies and television. Bancroft's story tells of an America where freedom is established through the self-government of ever-larger communal groups, from Puritan congregations to revolutionary town meetings to the joining of states in a union. Cooper's story depends upon a version of Bancroft's. From the first, however, Cooper's readers have found his power to be less compelling in treating groups than solitary individuals; less in treating settlements than wilderness; less in treating government than the margins of the law. His most powerful figure is the solitary woodsman Natty Bumppo. Both Bancroft and Cooper enjoyed wide sales and acclaim, and both explicitly identified themselves with the side of "the people" in politics. The twentieth-century genre that has most fully integrated the modes of Bancroft and Cooper into a single narrative frame is the Hollywood western, which typically focuses on a solitary male figure who furthers the causes of civilization and the people, even if he cannot live in the town he has saved.

Cooper's work troubles modern readers because it is not realistic in its technique, but it is emphatically referential in its substance. More familiar and honored now are those works that are scrupulously precise in registering a world that stands at a fictional distance from specific national issues. Yet Cooper was the first author of what was accepted without question in the United States and abroad as truly "American" writing. Moreover, his importance is not merely historical, for his work, both in its ideas and in its technique, instances many problems that continue to cause concern in the culture of the United States.

Although Cooper wrote national narrative, to understand him requires an international context. American literary history thus resembles American economic history, which also, in a seeming paradox, requires international context. In Cooper's time, Americans liked to believe that the economy of the United States depended on self-sufficient farming. In reality, American involvement in export production and merchant shipping was so great that the international system was the primary generator of the nation's internal economic growth. Cooper's international dimension was recognized from his first successful novel onward. (For full accounts of Cooper's career, see Gilmore in volume 1 and Bell in this volume.) With the publication of *The Spy* in 1821, Cooper forever after was either praised or condemned as the "American Scott" (referring to the Scottish novelist Sir Walter Scott). A difference between history and literary history here emerges. Although it may be possible to place America within world history only to show, like George Bancroft, how America has transcended that history, no one has claimed that Cooper actually manifested the high point of the history of world literature, only that he was significantly different from, say, Scott.

The very process of establishing Cooper's American difference from Scott relies upon similarities that give the comparison its point. Starting with *Waverley* (1814), Scott wrote a series of historical romances set in periods ranging from the not-so-distant past (" 'tis sixty years since" is the subtitle of *Waverley*) all the way back to the Middle Ages. Writing as a Scot, whose nation had been united for more than a century with England, Scott especially focused on the border country between Scotland and England, historically a zone of conflict. This terrain clearly prefigures the "neutral ground" between revolutionary and Loyalist forces on which Cooper set *The Spy*. Moreover, although the recurrent pattern of captivity among the Indians in Cooper's Leatherstocking novels looks back to colonial American captivity narratives, it also echoes the misadventures of Scott's passive heroes, whom the author typically placed in the power of those threatening, but ultimately defeated, forces that opposed the course of history.

Cooper and Scott shared a broad cultural–historical understanding of the course of civilization, derived from the theorists of the Scottish Enlightenment. In Scott, the Romantic energies of the Highland clan system (*Rob Roy*, 1817) or the passionate enthusiasm of radical religious dissent seeking to remake the polity (*Old Mortality*, 1816) must yield to a more humdrum yet more progressive and beneficent way of life, which is associated with the lowland Scots, the union of Scotland with England, and the triumph of the Established church. So in Cooper the qualities of his most noble Indians, and of Natty Bumppo himself, must yield to the common day of civilization. In the works of both writers, glamorized, yet firmly derogated, "primitive" figures are the center of attention for most of the book, and banal, yet positively presented, figures are the ones given the future, as those who will carry on life through marriage.

Both Cooper and Scott thought about and were involved with the issues of their time and nations. Nevertheless, in the works by which they are still known, they meditate only obliquely on the concerns of their own time, projecting the issues into the past and subjecting them to plot devices that insure their safe containment. For example, social divisions troubling to 1820s Americans could be negotiated through the plot in *The Spy*. The title figure first appears disguised as a peddler, haggling and seductively oriented toward consumption. Yet this character proves to be fundamental to the national well-being. He is the trusted secret agent of Harper (General Washington in disguise), a figure who passes through the novel as its iconic promise that all will turn out well. The birth of the new nation as depicted here is not only martial but also marital: witness the respective fates of the two daughters of the British-leaning Wharton family. Sarah, the elder, is betrayed by her false, aristocratic beau from the British forces, while her sister Frances is united with the less socially elevated American revolutionary officer.

Similarly, in Cooper's *The Pioneers* (1823) the marriage of Judge Temple's daughter Elizabeth to Oliver Edwards, companion of Natty Bumppo and Indian John, provides a way to reconcile social differences. Not only does the marriage link an apparently contrasting couple – high social status to low, settled life to still-woodsy – but, through revelations of the mystery plot, it also links the now-American Temple family with the Loyalist Effingham family, spiritual adoptees of the Indians and the first white possessors of the lands that Temple now holds. Loyalist and revolutionary, white and red, high and low are symbolically integrated in the novel.

Not all of the parties are so integrated, however. Drunken Indian John – whose people bestowed the land – is burned to death, and Natty Bumppo – whose woodcraft made Effingham's success possible – sets out for the wilderness. *The Pioneers*, then, as opposed to *The Spy*, diverges importantly from Scott. In *Ivanhoe* (1819) Scott went back to the Middle Ages to tell his story of the making of the English through joining the Norman king Richard with the Saxon Ivanhoe; meanwhile, the evil Norman leader dies. Both Scott's fable and *The Spy* proceed by incorporation of the oppositional element (Norman or Loyalist) into the united, progressive, national whole (although the opposition leaders must die). The plot of *The Pioneers*, in contrast, operates by exclusion. Cooper does not depict the Indians and woodsmen as part of the future in *The Pioneers*, even though they are central to the Leatherstocking novels that follow. In *The Last of the Mohicans* (1826) the exclusion of the Indians is fully elaborated and rationalized. Thus the "good" Indians, the Mohicans, are already dying out. Their "last" hope, Uncas, dies tragically, and the good chief Tanemund is grotesquely superannuated. Only the "bad" Indians survive as a group, and they must be exterminated, as is their heroic, passionate, but villainous leader, Magua.

The Pioneers imaginatively works through the confrontation of two ways of life, the residual forest life of Natty Bumppo and the recently emergent and now dominant settlement life of Judge Temple. In *The Last of the Mohicans* the confrontation is more abstract. "Nature," represented by the heroic and unspoiled good Indians, is set against "civilization," represented by the

British. Civilization triumphs as Major Duncan Heyward marries Alice, the daughter of Colonel Munro. Nature is defeated as Uncas dies, along with Munro's other daughter, Cora, with whom he might have been united (Cora's West Indian, racially mixed origins having made her an inappropriate wife for a white man). This battle between the white British and the red Indians for possession of North America is not, however, the explicit conflict of the book. Instead, the natural Indians and the civilized British are shown united against their negative counterparts. The unnatural French are corrupted into weakness by the failure of their civilization (their great leader Montcalm cannot prevent the slaughter of British prisoners by Indians). Allied with the French are the savage Mingoes, the bad Indians of the story. The villain of the book is the Mingo leader Magua, who has lived among whites. He combines the worst of the uncivil and the unnatural, the savage and the corrupt. The hero of the book is Natty Bumppo. A white man "without a cross" of Indian ancestry, Natty nonetheless combines "natural" Indian skills with a mastery of the weapon of civilization, the long rifle.

The Last of the Mohicans also offers a phantom possibility of another ideal figure. Cora Munro is a woman with the spirit of a man, as opposed to her weak, blond sister. Cora combines the natural energies attributed to her parent of African ancestry with the civilization attributed to her father's people, and therefore her union with Uncas would unite the three most prominent racial groups of North America in the strongest couple that the book imagines. But that imagination is contained as purely optative, contrary to fact. America is defined in this founding national narrative as the land of pureblooded whites and male domination, not a land of interracial, multicultural equality of the sexes. Moreover, as shown in The Pioneers, Natty himself is not in the long run the victor. By the irony of history, none of the participants in The Last of the Mohicans is the hero so much as are Cooper's chosen readers, the Americans who are the actual possessors of the continent for which the British, French, and Indians believed themselves to be struggling.

The Prairie (1827) again sets "good" Indian against "bad" Indian. The machinery of plot resembles that in The Last of the Mohicans, but Cooper's concerns are quite different. The Last of the Mohicans went back in time to treat the forest life seen as vanishing in The Pioneers. The Prairie moves forward in time to treat the problem of law posed in The Pioneers by the confrontation of Natty with the hunting regulations established by Judge Temple. In The Prairie the conflict that in The Last of the Mohicans set civilization against nature here sets civilization against freedom. The lack of freedom in The Prairie is imagined as settlement – entirely absent from the represented world of the novel, though implicit in its frame of reference and that of its readers. The lack of civilization is imagined as a condition of lawlessness, an anarchy that may be either the exercise of arbitrary power or the absence of power.

This conflict is elaborated through the relations among the white characters; the Indians do no more than provide occasions for the various contrasting and conflicted relations among the whites. Ishmael Bush, the squatter patriarch, by combining the negative terms of anarchy and settlement, functions as the book's villain. Although Natty Bumppo is idealized in this work, his values nonetheless are set in a carefully qualified context, and if he embodies most fully the positive good of freedom, he also partakes like Bush of the dangers of anarchy. At the other extreme from Natty is the bee hunter Paul Hover. From the beginning, Paul is associated with civilization because the honeybee, as an import from Europe, was widely understood to live only within a certain proximity to settlements and thus to prefigure the frontier, where settlement encroaches on wilderness. By the book's end, Paul is ready to give up bee hunting and settle down. The closest the book comes to offering an ideal combination of the two conflicting positive values, freedom and civilization, is in the figure of the young soldier Duncan Middleton, whose middle name is Uncas because he is a descendant of Major Duncan Heyward from *The Last of the Mohicans*. Yet this genealogy, and Middleton's cross-cultural love for Doña Inez de Certevallos, give Middleton only an abstract association with the value of freedom, and readers have not experienced his as an ideal combination. Middleton is Cooper's unsuccessful attempt to place his imaginative emphasis where he placed his intellectual and political commitment.

This partial failure illustrates a crucial historical feature. Cooper's fictions operate as strategies of containment, that is, as imaginary techniques for negotiating the complexities of the life that both he and his readers were living. Yet the containments do not hold perfectly; the myth does not stand wholly free from the reality. Cooper never developed formal techniques wholly adequate to what he was trying to accomplish. Reviewers observed, or complained, that his works did not really have plots in the sense of an Aristotelian close meshing in which each element leads seamlessly to the next. He certainly did, however, have plots in the sense that by the end of the works a change in affairs has occurred from the initial state. But to achieve these changes, he called upon devices that seemed arbitrary and thus drew attention to the role of wish rather than necessity in what he was representing.

Moreover, while it is perfectly clear what kind, or genre, of work Cooper was producing — historical romance — the ground rules for that genre were not well established. Was it more like comedy or tragedy? *The Last of the Mohicans* sounds an elegiac note of loss beginning with its title, yet thirteen of its thirty-three chapters bear epigraphs from Shakespearean comedies, including five from *A Midsummer Night's Dream*. One reviewer protested passionately that readers were not prepared for the deaths of Cora and Uncas, that the book had been giving quite contrary signals heralding a happy union of the two. Echoing closely a famous essay by Charles Lamb, this reviewer complained that readers had been as badly served by Cooper as they had been by the Nahum Tate version of *King Lear*, which transforms the tragedy by allowing Lear and Cordelia to survive. In other words, to this reader the aesthetic satisfactions of generic coherence were much more important than the national issues. National narrative did not permit an alternative history of America in which the most heroic of Indians and the most passionate of mulattoes founded a new line. Yet this reviewer found that the logic of romance demanded such a deviation from national narrative. At issue here, then, are the concerns that led the "literary" to emerge as an independent realm, answerable only to the requirements of its own coherent fantasy rather than engaged in concerned dialogue with the life of the times.

If Cooper's large-scale management of his materials was open to criticism and question even from admiring readers (the comparison to *King Lear* is hardly unflattering), objections were also raised to his management of the local details of language. Mark Twain's 1895 essay on Cooper's literary offenses codifies these objections most tellingly, but it is worth trying to understand what Cooper has done, even if it is less the result of mastery than of struggle. In presenting characters whose language marks them as a radically incoherent set of attributes rather than as a psychologically plausible whole, Cooper is struggling with complex social issues.

Natty Bumppo is uneducated and culturally limited, and he often speaks a language that marks these social limitations. On the other hand, he embodies a way of life that is immensely different from that lived by anyone who reads about him. This way of life Cooper found immensely attractive, and he wished his readers to feel its value. At times, therefore, Cooper gave Natty a much grander syntax and diction than he otherwise possessed. The problem this causes is familiar from British Romanticism. Some twenty years before Cooper wrote, Wordsworth had argued, in his preface to *Lyrical Ballads*, that uneducated people leading a life close to nature are capable of intensely vivid figurative language when they are moved by passion. Cooper clearly shares Wordsworth's view. And just as Cooper was criticized, Wordsworth had been accused of inconsistencies in the relation of character to language.

Twain's criticism of Cooper resumed this line of attack. Cooper, however, took his Indians and Natty more seriously than Twain would take his own historically marginalized characters. For all of Twain's boasting about the accurate dialect in *Huckleberry Finn* (1884), none of the characters whose

language he so precisely registered has anything to say that effectively challenges the values of Huck and Jim. Readers never waver in their allegiance to
the two historically progressive forces in Twain's book, the boy breaking
through to an intuitive recognition of racial equality, and the slave winning
his freedom. In other words, Twain devised a technique to bring to life his
"positive" characters, the structural equivalents to Cooper's Major Heyward
and Middleton.

This accomplishment of Twain's is aesthetically powerful, and it has also
been held to promote democratic values, but in placing readers' sympathies
so entirely with the progressive characters, Twain excludes the losers of
history from serious attention. Even though Twain, like Bancroft and unlike
Cooper, found the cutting edge of progress in "plebeian" characters, his
work, like Cooper's, expresses a hierarchy of social values.

This difference between Cooper and Twain resembles also the difference
between Cooper and Parkman. Parkman testified that several of Cooper's
novels had so deeply influenced his life that "I sometimes find it difficult to
separate them distinctly from the recollections of my own past experiences,"
and his massive history of the French, English, and Indians in the American
wilderness aims to substantiate the reality that *The Last of the Mohicans* had
only suggested. Yet the overwhelming coherence of Parkman's vision and
prose produces much greater restriction than is found in Cooper. In his
overview of Cooper's career, Parkman wholly rejects Uncas, instead finding
in Magua the essential truth of all Indians, and he underwrites this judgment
in his history. New standards of realistic technique in fiction and in history
did not ensure writing that would embrace more of humanity than was
embraced by the world roughly shared between Cooper's fictions and the
reality of his times.

Cooper's challenge to the attempt to isolate "literature" as a separate sphere
can be marked in Poe's review of *Wyandotté*. According to Poe, Cooper won
readers by relying on the appeal of things of the world: of life in the forest, or
of life on the ocean. In contrast, Poe argues, a "man of genius" would have
eschewed such "hackneyed" themes. Poe distinguishes "two great classes of
fictions." One is "popular and widely circulated." It is read with "pleasure"
but without "admiration" and, above all, without thinking of "the author."
The other class, less popular, provides, "at every paragraph," pleasure "springing from our perception and appreciation of the skill employed, of the genius
evinced in the composition." Here, readers think of "the author," not merely
of "the book." The popularity of the first class is in contrast to the "fame"
open to the second: if popular books "sometimes live," nonetheless, their
"authors usually die"; but, in the case of genius, "even when the works
perish, the man survives." Poe places in the class of genius Charles Brockden

Brown and Hawthorne and in the popular class, Cooper. History, however, suggests that Cooper too was a genius, for his books now hardly survive. Yet his work made possible the dime novels and movies by which the American frontier has fixed itself in the world's shared cultural imagination; his sea novels were acknowledged as examples by writers such as Herman Melville and Joseph Conrad. Thus, the "man survives," and the problems he poses for meditation are immensely challenging.

Cooper succeeded, moreover, in surprising ways. His younger French contemporary Honoré de Balzac (1799–1850) found in Cooper's wilderness the inspiration for a certain mode of sensitivity to the city. Balzac had responded to Cooper from the beginning. In 1829 Balzac published the first of the novels that formed his massive *Human Comedy,* a historical novel about the French Revolution in Brittany called, after the Mohicans, *The Last Chouan.* A few years later, in his first great novel of Paris, *Old Goriot* (1834), Balzac's most powerful figure Vautrin asserts that Paris "is like a forest in the New World, where a score of savage tribes . . . struggle for existence." And in the next decade, *Splendors and Miseries of Courtesans* presents a character harassed by "invisible enemies" and searching for an abducted woman. The narrator observes,

Thus, that poetry of terror which the strategems of enemy tribes at war spread in the heart of the forests of America, and of which Cooper has made such good use, was attached to the smallest details of Parisian life. The passers-by, the shops, the hackney carriages, a person standing at a window . . . everything presented the ominous interest that in Cooper's novels resides in a tree-trunk, a beaver-lodge, a rock, a buffalo skin, a motionless canoe, a branch even with the water.

The "poetry of terror" in Cooper's wilderness enriched the resources of urban realism. This intensity of attention had been fostered by the historical romance, for the form asserted that in the past even apparently commonplace individuals had been involved in a process of great significance, the making of world history. Natty Bumppo's "hawk-eye" functioned in the wilderness of New York during the Seven Years' War, and it helped to make possible, through the British defeat of the French, the eventual American defeat of the British. The same "hawk-eye" functioned also to validate for Balzac a history of the present in fiction, in which even the most trivial and socially discredited elements of life played a role and thus demanded attention. In politics Balzac was a royalist, but as a novelist he learned from Cooper to be a democrat.

ALEXIS DE TOCQUEVILLE

Not Balzac, but Alexis de Tocqueville (1805–59) was the French writer who had the most famous encounter with American democracy. Tocqueville came to the United States in 1831 with Gustave de Beaumont (1802–66). These two youthful, liberal noblemen had been commissioned by the French Ministry of Justice to study the country's penal system, which had attracted international attention for its innovative techniques for moral reform. For nearly a year after their arrival in New York, the two traveled all over the nation, as far north as Boston (and even into Canada), as far west as the still scarcely settled Wisconsin territory, and as far south as New Orleans. Their report, *On the Penitentiary System in the United States and Its Application in France,* was immediately translated and published in the United States (1833).

The report contains a remarkable thumbnail analysis of a characteristically American type of reformer, which looks forward to Hollingsworth in Hawthorne's *Blithedale Romance* (1852). For this type, prisons become "the subject to which all the labours of their life bear reference. Philanthropy has become for them a kind of profession; and they have caught the *monomanie* of the penitentiary system, which to them seems the remedy for all the evils of society." "*Monomanie*" remains in French because "monomania" had not yet fully entered the English language. This concept, which is so crucial for understanding many characters in Poe and Hawthorne and, above all, for thinking about Captain Ahab in Melville's *Moby-Dick,* began to circulate widely in the United States only with Isaac Ray's *Treatise on the Medical Jurisprudence of Insanity* (1838). Even in their government report, Tocqueville and Beaumont showed that they were in touch with the emerging crucial concerns for Americans of their time, and Beaumont wrote a novel on the effects of slavery, *Marie,* published in France in 1835. Tocqueville wrote on his own the far more ambitious work *Democracy in America* (Volume 1, 1835; Volume 2, 1840), which from its first American translation by Henry Reeve in 1838 to the present has remained an essential resource for Americans in thinking about themselves. Although written by a Frenchman, Tocqueville's work has become part of the American national narrative.

The second volume of *Democracy in America* contains a chapter on "the Sources of Poetry among the Americans" in which Tocqueville has grasped a duality that helps to define also the particular perspective of Cooper's work discussed earlier. According to Tocqueville, the fundamental equality of all citizens in the United States means that there is no poetic inspiration to be received from great single individuals. Instead, "the nation itself" awakens imagination. Although Europeans "talk a great deal of the wilds of America," Tocqueville has learned that "the Americans themselves never think about them." Americans do not "perceive the mighty forests that surround them till they fall beneath the hatchet."

Tocqueville's analysis helps to make clear that Cooper's Natty Bumppo is the retrospective construction of an age in which the "hatchet" of settlement has already leveled enough American forest so that the historical loss of all wilderness begins to become conceivable. Natty prophetically mourns this loss in *The Pioneers;* nevertheless, the last sentence of the book places Natty not as a solitary mourner, but amidst what Tocqueville called "the nation itself." Natty has left for the frontier, and so, "He had gone far towards the setting sun, – the foremost in that band of Pioneers, who are opening the way for the march of the nation across the continent." Tocqueville finds that precisely "this magnificent image of themselves" is always present "before the mind" of Americans, so as to "haunt every one of them in his least as well as in his most important actions." Tocqueville registers this image in language much like Cooper's: "the American people views its own march across these wilds, draining swamps, turning the course of rivers, peopling solitudes, and subduing nature."

Tocqueville's primary goal is to understand a worldwide process that he calls the "democratic revolution." This revolution first occurs in the United States, and the United States therefore holds lessons for the future of Europe and the rest of the world. In using the notion of "equality" as the key concept for his analysis, Tocqueville is self-consciously participating in the democratic spirit, which, he argues, prefers abstractions and generalizations to the concrete, often personalized, specificity that marked aristocratic societies. Tocqueville's abstract conception of the democratic destiny of the United States echoes closely, as will be seen, the abstractions with which George Bancroft organizes his history of the United States.

Much of what Tocqueville shares with Bancroft has become common American self-understanding, even though it will not hold up to rigorous historiographic analysis. Tocqueville states in the introduction to his first volume of *Democracy in America* that "the gradual development of the principle of equality . . . is a providential fact," because "it is universal, it is lasting, it constantly eludes all human interference; and all events as well as all men contribute to its progress." Consequently, in studying democracy and equality in the United States, Tocqueville has been impressed with a "religious awe" from the force of "that irresistible revolution." The United States has a special historical role because America from its beginning has most fully embodied the principle that is providentially transforming the world: "the emigrants who colonized the shores of America in the seventeenth century somehow separated the democratic principle from all the principles that it had to contend with in the old communities of Europe, and transplanted it alone to the New World."

Tocqueville's national narrative begins in New England and spreads throughout the rest of America: "The principles of New England spread at first to the neighboring states; they then passed successively to the more distant ones; and at last, if I may so speak, they *interpenetrated* the whole confederation. They now extend their influence beyond its limits, over the whole American world." In a biblical figure that links American political discourse from John Winthrop's "Model of Christian Charity" (1630) to Ronald Reagan, Tocqueville sees this civilization as "a beacon lit on a hill." Tocqueville emphasizes the organic principle by which the democratic-egalitarian structure of America has developed. It has not, he argues, worked on the aristocratic principle of organization from the top down by central authority. Instead, "in America . . . the township was organized before the county, the county before the state, and the state before the union." In principle, therefore, no tension can arise between the nation as a whole and any of its local components, because they are what have made it.

Tocqueville's democratic abstractions take on the power of myth. His work gains credibility from its empirical detail, yet these details vanish into a national narrative. Indians are erased by the argument that they "occupied" the land without "possessing" it. Despite his knowledge that Virginia was colonized before New England, Tocqueville's definition of American "national character" does not take into account that there were numerous initial settlements, and so he does not recognize any contradiction between his claim for the priority of New England and his theory of harmonious national development. He writes as if there were only one single "origin of the Americans," which assures the continued favorable development of the nation: "their forefathers imported that equality of condition and of intellect into the country whence the democratic republic has very naturally taken its rise." Therefore, Tocqueville claims to see "the destiny of America embodied in the first Puritan who landed on these shores, just as the whole human race was represented by the first man."

Yet Tocqueville also at moments acknowledged that the United States could not wholly be explained by the national narrative of equality and the myth of New England. America was a land not only of freedom but also of slavery. Slavery depended on a principle of brutal inequality, which threatened the United States: "If ever America undergoes great revolutions, they will be brought about by the presence of the black race on the soil of the United States; that is to say, they will owe their origin, not to the equality, but to the inequality of condition." Tocqueville saw another potential for destabilizing inequality in the urbanization of America. An extraordinary footnote in Tocqueville's first volume warned that the growing size and heterogeneous population of "certain American cities" made them a "real danger" for the "future security of the democratic republics of the New World." He imagined that it would require a national armed force, "independent of the town population," in order to "repress its excesses." Tocqueville's critical capacity to conceive the problems, and not only the power and success, of American democracy has made his work the version of American national narrative from this period that is now still read.

GEORGE BANCROFT

Like Tocqueville, who came to the United States on a mission for the French government and who returned home to play a significant political role, George Bancroft compels interest as an example of the relations between writing and political power. He shaped the story of America both through his national narrative and through his service to the state. Born in 1800, the son of a clergyman in Worcester, Massachusetts, he graduated from Harvard in 1817, where his diligence and capacity won him special favor. Like the scholar George Ticknor before him and the poet Henry Wadsworth Longfellow after him, Bancroft was sent to Germany with the idea that his studies there would fit him for leadership on the Harvard faculty. But his studies at Göttingen and Berlin, and his further travels in France and Spain, apparently unfitted him for Harvard and Harvard for him. Within a year after his return, he had left Cambridge to collaborate in an experimental, progressive school at Northampton, Massachusetts, which he conducted with considerable success from 1823 to 1831. During these years Bancroft published verse, translations from the German, and essays on recent German literature and thought, much as his older contemporary the Scot Thomas Carlyle was doing before Carlyle found his vocation as historian and social critic.

Bancroft's personal connections marked him as a conservative New Englander and a likely Federalist. He married into the Dwight family of Springfield, Massachusetts, who were prominent in banking and in midwestern land speculation; his brother-in-law, "Honest John" Davis, became Whig governor of the state. Bancroft himself, however, developed in quite different directions. His German education opened to him the body of ideas in philosophy, theology, and history that also inspired the transcendentalist movement in New England at this time; and his first public appearances on political matters pointed in a popular, Jeffersonian direction. By the early 1830s, as he was leaving schoolteaching, Bancroft moved into his major activities in both scholarship and politics. He formed the plan for his *History of the United States* that was finally fulfilled in 1874, after ten volumes, with the settlement of the revolutionary war. He also formed a lifelong allegiance to the Jacksonian, Democratic party. His commitments to "the Democracy," as the Democratic party was known, and to his history seemed to arise together and to sustain each other.

Published to great acclaim and large sales, the first volume of Bancroft's

History appeared in 1834, carrying the story of America from Columbus through the English Civil War and Restoration (1660). The second volume (1837) progressed through the English Glorious Revolution and its immediate colonial consequences (1689). In 1838, when the Democrats, almost always the opposition party in those days in Massachusetts, won a state election, Bancroft moved to Boston to become collector of the Port of Boston, the major patronage position in the state. As Democratic boss of Massachusetts, he appointed Nathaniel Hawthorne the weigher and gauger at Boston Custom House, the first of the three patronage positions that Hawthorne held. Bancroft's political activity did not prevent his completing the third volume of the *History* (1840), bringing the story up to the mid-eighteenth century.

For the next decade, politics, on an increasingly larger scale, took the main share of Bancroft's time. In 1844, the same year in which he ran unsuccessfully for the governorship of Massachusetts, his support at the national convention was decisive for James K. Polk's presidential nomination, and he was rewarded with a cabinet position when Polk was elected president. As secretary of the navy, Bancroft was instrumental in establishing the U.S. Naval Academy, and during the Mexican War he was also in de facto charge of the Army Department. This was a difficult position for him, because New England opinion from the Whig right to the transcendental left solidly opposed the war. He was rewarded with the greatest prize in the federal government's patronage system, the position of ambassador to the Court of St. James. In London from 1846 until 1849, he used his position to gain access to a wealth of English and French documentation on the revolutionary period that had never been studied before. When he returned to writing his history, he held incomparable authority, through both his public position and his research. From 1852 through 1860, on the verge of the Civil War, volumes 4 through 8 appeared, at last bringing the story to July 4, 1776, the first actual moment in the history of those United States upon which he had already lavished some four thousand pages.

In the crisis of the Civil War, Bancroft stood with the Union, offering advice to Lincoln and even drafting the first message to Congress by Andrew Johnson after Lincoln's death. Although he still identified himself as a Democrat, he was invited to present the official Lincoln memorial oration to Congress in 1866, the same year in which volume 9 appeared. He was appointed ambassador to Berlin, where he served from 1867 through 1874. During these years, which encompassed the Franco-Prussian War, Bancroft associated closely not only with Otto von Bismarck and other leaders of the German military and political establishment but also with the great senior historians of what was then considered the world's leading center for the study of history. When he returned from Berlin to the United States in 1874, he published the last volume of the *History*. Bancroft lived until 1891, an honored figure in the political, diplomatic, and cultural life of Washington D.C., and he put the *History* through two sets of revisions. First he reduced the ten volumes to six for the 1876 Centennial; next he produced, in 1882, the *History of the Formation of the Federal Constitution;* and finally he integrated the two sets into the "author's Final" six volumes in 1886.

It is one indication of Bancroft's accomplishment in writing his *History* that over the forty years in which it was produced, years that saw so much change in the history of the United States, it was not necessary for him to alter his tone or standpoint. The revisions of the 1870s and 1880s trimmed what had come to seem antiquated rhetorical flourishes, but for all this, in the originally published ten volumes, no more than one single word at the end of the last sentence of the preface to the ninth volume (1866) was required to register awareness of the Civil War: "This contribution to the history of the country I lay reverently on the altar of freedom and union." As early as the end of the second volume Bancroft had declared that the two volumes thus far completed "show why we are a free people" and that the volumes to come would show "why we are a united people." In other words, the key terms of value around which the Civil War was fought by the North were already firmly in place in Bancroft's discourse.

Bancroft did not think of himself as an inventor. He conceived his task to resemble that of a primitive bard. He wanted to articulate what his people already knew and believed and had been telling each other, but to give it a shape and scope that would include as much of the story as possible, more than could be directly known by any single person or local tradition, and that would thus make possible the continuation of the people, their knowledge, and their story. Yet this nation-building narrative was something new. In giving formal expression to the inchoate ideas of the American people, Bancroft was performing what is etymologically the basic act of "ideo-logy," and by making this expression not in the form of analysis, but as a coherent narrative shape, he was providing an American "myth" in the sense that Aristotle uses the term in the *Poetics*. Twentieth-century readers are likely to notice the optimism and nationalism that make Bancroft's national myth seem untrue and dangerous and the racial categories that make the ideology seem a false consciousness.

Bancroft's position, however, has a centrality that will not allow it simply to be dismissed. It is instructive to compare Bancroft with another important political voice of his time, Nathaniel Hawthorne's friend John L. O'Sullivan (1813–95). In 1837 O'Sullivan founded and edited the *United States Magazine and Democratic Review* and was closely allied with Bancroft. In the *Democratic Review* the notion of America's "manifest destiny" to expand across and to rule the North American continent began to figure as early as 1845, in close conjunction with the Mexican War in which Bancroft played so prominent a role. Within a few years, though, O'Sullivan had discredited himself with adventurist schemes to conquer Cuba for the United States. He long lived abroad, during the Civil War trying to mobilize British support for recognizing the Confederacy.

As early as in the lead editorial of the first issue of the *Democratic Review,* the limitations of O'Sullivan's position were clear. In the editorial O'Sullivan analyzed the recent nullification controversy involving South Carolina, arguing that its crux was "the relative rights of majorities and minorities." The substance of O'Sullivan's argument shows that in American political discourse at this time "minorities" was a code word for the South and not, as it is now, a term for racial or ethnic groups that are vulnerable to discrimination. O'Sullivan was deeply involved in social reform of the sort that had brought Tocqueville to the United States. In 1841 he wrote a notable report urging the state of New York to abolish capital punishment. Yet in an exemplary 1840 article, "Democracy," O'Sullivan wrote about "human rights" in political theory and American practice, without any attention to the fact of slavery in the nation.

Bancroft, on the other hand, was unequivocal in his notion of human rights, and he took political heat for his position. In 1845 his record had to be vetted by a southern senator before he could be nominated to the Cabinet, and, after the Civil War, Wendell Phillips could express the judgment that Bancroft had "remodelled his chapters" in order to negotiate the issue of slavery. Nonetheless, Bancroft opposed the racism of his time. Unlike those who welcomed theories of the multiple origins of humanity, theories that claimed to demonstrate scientifically that races other than the white were not fully human, Bancroft insisted, "All are men. When we know the Hottentot better, we shall despise him less." Unlike O'Sullivan, Bancroft saw the southern arguments in the nullification controversy as "recklessly insulting the free labor of the North." The southern arguments did not, for Bancroft, represent the fundamental concerns of American democracy. Rather, they were "subversive of liberty" and tended toward "treason and disunion."

Yet if Bancroft could differ so significantly from his closest political associates, it was also the case that those on the other side of party lines could find almost nothing to object to in his works. William Hickling Prescott, best known today for his account of Cortés's triumph over the Aztecs in his *History of the Conquest of Mexico* (1843), was a largely apolitical, deeply conservative member of the prosperous Boston Whig establishment — the group to which Bancroft "should" have aspired. Prescott opposed the annexation of Texas and the Mexican War, which Bancroft supported. Nonetheless, appearing in the solidly traditional *North American Review,* Prescott's 1841 review of Bancroft's third volume demonstrates how much actually was shared across the party spectrum. This in turn explains why Bancroft and most other northern Democrats could later join the Republicans on the Union side in the Civil War.

In his review, Prescott uses as his own the progressive, democratic language that modern readers might wrongly assume to be the polemical, "Jacksonian," portion of Bancroft. Like Bancroft, Prescott sees in the history of America the "progress of freedom" based on concern for "the natural rights of humanity." Prescott connects this progress to the "contest between light and darkness" that is at issue in the democratic strivings of Europe in the 1840s. Like Bancroft and Tocqueville, Prescott sees American freedom as divinely planned. America was discovered and settled only after the "glorious Reformation" had assured that the right, Protestant principles would predominate among the settlers. For Prescott, this fact was no accident: it was not merely "fortunate," it was "providential."

The United States were not ready for a full-scale history immediately after independence, Prescott argues, but only for "local narratives, personal biographies, political discussions," and the like. But now that the country has acquired some history of its own, the time has come for national narrative. It can be seen that a "tendency" to self-government "connects" colonial history to the history of the modern union and gives a "true point of view" from which colonial history might be narrated. The great task that Prescott envisions for the historian of colonial America is to find some principle of "unity." Prescott's own work found unity in its biographical focus, as in his *History of the Reign of Ferdinand and Isabella* (1838) and in his concentration on Cortés in the *Conquest of Mexico.* But Bancroft's scope is too vast both geographically and chronologically for a single figure, or even for a string of biographies, to organize it fully. To achieve a "central point of interest among so many petty states," to find "an animating principle of his narrative," Bancroft needs to tell the story of freedom. His work is a history of ideas and of institutions, of principles more than of persons, even though it is always conducted in the name of the "people." This is the abstraction that Tocqueville connected with democracy.

In its narrative organization, Bancroft's history depends on two principles that are in considerable tension with each other: the figure of prolepsis and the trope of development. Prolepsis is not mere anachronistic error. It is the figure of anticipation, of placing something earlier than it would usually be expected. So, by prolepsis, Bancroft begins the history of the United States in the seventeenth century, thereby identifying the later political entity with the already existing, quasi-eternal, land itself. In the first volume, after the initial chapter, "Early Voyages. French Settlements," and a second chapter on the Spaniards, the third chapter is entitled "England Takes Possession of the United States." Centuries before the Declaration of Independence, the "United States" is made to live in Bancroft's pages. But if the United States are there already, what is the point of the history? Bancroft is always in the position of having to tell how something that is already present would nonetheless fully accomplish, realize, and manifest itself over time. Often his figure for this process is organic, modeled on the life of an individual. He asserts, like Tocqueville, that the first period of American history "contains the germ of our institutions" and that "the maturity of a nation is but a continuation of its youth."

Equally fundamental to Bancroft is the metaphor of light. Seventeenth-century Virginia witnessed "the happy dawn of legislative liberty in America." Before Darwin, the problem of change obscured the perspicuity of developmental metaphors. Light was clearer. No one can doubt that at dawn light is present and yet that a day will follow in which this light undergoes variations over time that may aptly figure history. So the light of freedom is present from the beginning: "As the Pilgrims landed, their institutions were already perfected. Democratic liberty and independent Christian worship at once existed in America." And yet noon is more glorious than dawn; a climax remains. Just as the first three chapters in the first volume of Bancroft's *History* move climactically from France to Spain to England so in this volume as a whole the story of New England occupies the last three chapters (of ten) but almost half the total pages; and in the overall construction of the *History,* three volumes get the story to the mid-eighteenth century, but seven more are required for the next thirty years.

It is also possible, moreover, that noon has not yet been reached. The conservative Tory looks to the past, and the Whig grasps the present, but democracy rules the future. Democracy is "the party of progress and reform" – the best is yet to be. Bancroft, in the middle of the first volume, summarizes his theme:

The enfranchisement of the mind from religious despotism led directly to inquiries into the nature of civil government; and the doctrines of popular liberty, which sheltered their infancy in the wildernesses of the newly-discovered continent, within the short space of two centuries, have infused themselves into the life-blood of every rising state from Labrador to Chili, have erected outposts on the Oregon and in Liberia, and . . . have distributed all the ancient governments of Europe . . . from the shores of Portugal to the palaces of the Czars.

Bancroft's narrative structure and his historical analysis both depend on dialectical procedures. His story moves by a principle of supersession. Institutions that at one historical moment are progressive, at a later moment cease to be so. This tension between immutable principles and transitory institutions produces considerable complexity. For example, in the later seventeenth century (Volume 3),

A revolution in opinion was impending. The reformation has rested truth on the Bible, as the Catholic church had rested it on tradition; and a slavish interpretation of the Bible had led to a blind idolatry of the book. But true religion has no alliance with bondage; and, as the spirit of the reformation, which was but a less perfect form of freedom of mind, was advancing, reason was summoned to interpret the records of the past, and to separate time-hallowed errors from truths of the deepest moment.

This increase in the scientific spirit was to change religion, making Calvinist forms outmoded, and Bancroft saw the Salem witchcraft trials as arising out of a politically retrograde attempt by ministers to reclaim their eroding power.

If even the Calvinists, dear to Bancroft for their gifts to freedom in Massachusetts, were to be transcended, so might the larger religious movement to which they belonged: "Protestantism is not humanity; its name implies a party struggling to throw off some burdens of the past and ceasing to be a renovating principle when its protest shall have succeeded. It was now [in the Seven Years' War] for the last time, as a political element, summoned to appear upon the theatre of the nations" (Volume 4). In turn, the "last war" of Protestantism proved to be "first in a new series of the great wars of revolution that founded for the world of mankind the power of the people." The American Revolution marked the moment when "the idea of freedom . . . for the first time . . . found a region and a race, where it could be professed with the earnestness of an indwelling conviction and be defended with the enthusiasm that had hitherto marked no wars but those for religion" (Volume 7). In the sphere of power politics, similar reversals and transformations may occur. By the eighteenth century, the "great European colonial system had united the world" (Volume 3). This united world formed a theater in which the American struggle for liberty could achieve the greatest resonance and be insured of a future as universal on earth as it was in spirit. By the time of Volume 5 (1852), Bancroft himself, now living in New York City, could find that the American principle of free trade had so effectually united the world in freedom that the multitude of races, cultures, and languages of New York made it "the representative city of all Europe."

This vision of an America that contained the world, by containing the principle that was reshaping and bettering the world, was an American ideology that was most fully articulated in Bancroft's national narrative and that was played out, in the years he was writing, by the national expansion that brought the United States all the way to the Pacific coast and that threatened to go further into Central America and the Caribbean. This national narrative emerged in the 1820s and 1830s, together with the strong presidency of Andrew Jackson, but it was not yet dominant. Space remained for local narratives that offered alternative emphases. The actual differences among the regions of the United States meant that the story of America was not the only story.

2

LOCAL NARRATIVES

In *The Sketch Book of Geoffrey Crayon, Gent.* (1819) Washington Irving established for decades the norms defining American local narratives, that is, small-scale pieces with regional subject matter. The basic modes of writing in Irving's work, as in the English periodicals of his time and in American periodicals for decades, were the sketch and the tale. The sketch, as its name suggests, is like a picture. Nothing happens in the sketch, except for the verbal action of displaying to the reader something that the narrating voice considers of interest. In the tale something does happen, often something rather remarkable. The sketch highlights the first-person narrative, as of the "Crayon" figure; the tale, in contrast, presents a third-person narration or else gives the narrative to another voice than that of the sponsoring narrator. Irving's voice echoed British tradition in periodical writing, and much of his subject matter resembled the colorful regionalism in Walter Scott's full-length romances. A sketch was, in effect, a descriptive chapter torn from its narrative context. By the same process, during the 1830s and 1840s, while George Bancroft and James Fenimore Cooper continued their writing, national narrative was being fragmented into local scenes by periodical writers following Irving.

Irving's most famous tales from *The Sketch Book* display a problematic relation between local and national. "Rip Van Winkle" notoriously passes over the founding American national events during Rip's protracted slumber, and the tale itself is attributed to Diedrich Knickerbocker, Irving's fictional antiquarian historian of Dutch New York. It is said to derive, moreover, from "legendary lore," which is available not from books and records — the materials of such a national history as Bancroft's — but only from men and women long at home in their locale. "The Legend of Sleepy Hollow" shows the resentment of the local community in the early days of the nation (like Cooper's *The Pioneers*, the story is set in the 1790s) against a Yankee intruder. The ghost, whose legend is mobilized to terrorize Ichabod Crane, comes from a dead Hessian officer, so that, in the overall structure of the tale, the conflict between two regions, Dutch New York and Yankee Connecticut, also comes to represent an old, quiet, and even colonial way of life set against a graceless, grasping yet inept, new national life. Schoolmaster, psalm singer, and would-be go-getter, Crane immortalized one American type, as did his rival Brom Bones, a horse racer, cock fighter, humorist, and village Hercules "always ready for either a fight or a frolic." These two regional varieties would appear in many other places and guises long after Irving himself had turned his attention to work on a national scale, from his life of Columbus, to his history of John Jacob Astor's fur-trading empire, to his life of Washington. (For full accounts of Irving's career, see Gilmore in Volume 1 and Bell in this volume.)

SOUTHWESTERN HUMOR

Starting in the 1830s, a group of writers followed Irving in writing regionally based sketches and tales. They did not deal with the long-settled regions of New York, as he had, or with New England, as Hawthorne was. Instead, they took on the newly settled areas of the frontier in the South reaching from Georgia into Tennessee, Alabama, Mississippi, and Arkansas, known at the time as the "South-West." Their work typically first appeared in the local newspapers where the writers might happen to live, but it soon was being published in regional newspapers, such as the St. Louis *Reveille* and the New Orleans *Picayune,* and in the journal, based in New York, that became the flagship for southwestern-humor writing, the *Spirit of the Times.* This intricate hierarchy of journals exemplifies the complex participation of southwestern humor in levels of cultural activity including the local, the regional, and the national.

Founded in 1831, the *Spirit of the Times* aimed at a national readership interested in horse racing, and the single greatest readership with that interest was southern planters. William Porter, the Vermont-born editor, defined his journal as "designed to promote the views and interests of but an infinitesimal division of those classes of society composing the great mass. . . . We are addressing ourselves to gentlemen of standing, wealth, and intelligence – the very corinthian pillars of the community." "Corinthian" pillars suggest the luxurious efflorescence of ornament that wealth allows and also echo the British slang term "Corinthian" used for wealthy amateur sportsmen or genteel profligates, as in Pierce Egan's *Life in London* (1824) about the adventures of young Jerry and his friend "Corinthian Tom." (Transformed into cat and mouse, "Tom and Jerry" would remain a comic pair in twentieth-century American cartoon art.) Porter's journal, which would become identified with a distinctively American subject matter, began from (and maintained) imaginative relations with British culture, and a metropolitan model stood behind its appeal to the far-flung corners of American leisure activity. After the Panic of 1837 damaged the financial base for horse racing, the journal shifted its emphasis away from news of the turf. Porter filled his pages from two main sources: he combed newpapers from all over the South and Southwest looking for items to reprint, and he invited readers of the journal to submit material of their own. Such writers' gentlemanly standing was emphasized by the fact that Porter did not pay contributors, although he boasted in 1856 a circulation of forty thousand.

The typical writer of the sketches and tales in the *Spirit of the Times* was a person of considerable cultural authority: white, male, a practitioner of a highly literate profession such as journalism or the law, and politically active. For example, Porter's contributor who called himself "Turkey Runner" was James McNutt, two-term governor of Mississippi (1838–42). McNutt was in favor of hard money and temperance, but his tales focused on backwoods hunters like "Chunkey," who liked easy credit and hard liquor.

In their social and political conservatism, these writers were typically associated with the Whig party. The rise of the southwestern "school" of writing coincided remarkably closely with the emergence of the Whigs as a focus of multiregional resistance to the presidency of Andrew Jackson. Although himself a slaveholder from Tennessee, Jackson as president proved to be more radically, autocratically, national than seemed right to many southerners who had been Democrats. When South Carolina declared its right as a state to "nullify" the federal tariffs of 1828 and 1832, Jackson threatened to use federal troops to enforce central political authority. Yet Jackson also held back from using federal economic power to further the "internal improvements" of roads and canals that appealed to many westerners. Finally, Jackson was repugnant to many northerners, both for his popular, democratic style and for his attack on the central Bank of the United States.

Thus, in the years from 1832 to 1834, the Whig party came into existence, uniting Daniel Webster of the North, Henry Clay of the West, and John Calhoun of the South. This was the moment not only of the nullification crisis but also of other distinct developments that changed the nation by changing the status of slavery in the South. A boom in cotton prices fueled the settlement of new lands on the southwestern frontier and dramatically enhanced the value of the slaves owned in the Old South. Meanwhile, in 1831 Nat Turner led the nation's most important slave rebellion in Southampton, Virginia, and opposition to slavery entered a new, passionate phase, as William Lloyd Garrison began publishing the *Liberator*. (For fuller accounts of these developments, see Sundquist in this volume.)

The Whig opposition to Jackson immediately produced local narratives that attempted to seize the imaginative initiative on Jackson's own terrain. *The Narrative of the Life of David Crockett* (1834), along with associated works written about and often purporting to be written by Davy Crockett, marks the attempt by the Whigs to exploit the backwoods prowess and jokes of an ambitious Tennessee politician who had broken with Jackson and who still lives in American popular memory. Almanacs continued to spin yarns about him even after his 1836 death. In their long afterlife, the Crockett narratives ceased to count as local. By the time Walt Disney took them up into massively circulated television, film, and song materials in the 1950s, they had become integrated into national narrative, standing no longer for a part or a party but for the whole of America.

The kind of writing these southwestern figures produced was known as "humor," but the term covered a wide variety of stances and practices. Along the frontier, for instance, there flourished a well-established oral practice of exaggerated self-display, which was reported back to civilization by travelers along the Ohio and Mississippi rivers. As early as 1808, two rivermen were heard arguing at Natchez, Mississippi: "One said, 'I am a man; I am a horse; I am a team. I can whip any man *in all Kentucky,* by G-d.' The other replied, 'I am an alligator, half man, half horse; can whip any man on the *Mississippi,* by G-d,' " and after several more verbal exchanges, a great fight followed. The primary sense, however, in which this whole body of work is "humor" is because it displays the eccentricities of people of lower social standing than that of its writers and presumed readers. As far back as Aristotle, the difference between tragedy and comedy had been defined not as pertaining to happy or sad endings, but rather in relation to the standing — in principle moral, but in practice social — of the characters portrayed.

Even though cultural developments as old as Christianity and as recent as the Romantic movement and democratic politics offered alternatives to this view, and, by the twentieth century, had largely changed it, it was still an established perspective, especially among the cultural conservatives who practiced southwestern writing. Although in their attention to life among the lower social strata and in their detail and frequent grotesquerie, the southwestern writers prefigure what is called realism and regionalist writing, in general they do not grant their characters the moral seriousness usual in these later movements. Nonetheless, this body of writing has taken on increasing importance over the last fifty years because modern readers recognize that southwestern "humor" was a major resource for writers now valued highly, such as Herman Melville, Mark Twain, and William Faulkner. These writers do grant their characters moral seriousness, but like the humorists they often provoke laughter and exceed the decorum of realistic verisimilitude.

The inaugural figure in the literature of southwestern humor is Augustus

Baldwin Longstreet (1790–1870). Born in Augusta, Georgia, and educated in South Carolina and at Yale, Longstreet returned to his native state to practice law. His career encapsulates almost every form of professional standing that his society offered: Longstreet won elections to the Georgia General Assembly and as judge of the state superior court (1822); in 1829 he was licensed as a Methodist minister; from 1834 to 1836, he edited the Augusta *State Rights' Sentinel;* and he went on to a career as a college and university president and a polemicist on behalf of the South (for example, he wrote *The Connections of Apostolical Christianity with Slavery* [1845]). In 1833 Longstreet started publishing his sketches and tales in the Milledgeville *Southern Recorder,* and he continued their publication in his own paper. Finally, he collected and published them himself (anonymously) in Augusta as *Georgia Scenes, Characters, Incidents, &c. in the first Half Century of the Republic: By a Native Georgian* (1835). The success of *Georgia Scenes* was great and enduring. Poe hailed it in the *Southern Literary Messenger,* and Longstreet boasted of selling thousands of copies without going north of the Mason-Dixon line. By 1840 Longstreet's collection was taken up nationally by Harper and Brothers in New York, and by 1897 it had gone through eleven editions.

Longstreet's collection includes such pieces as "A Sage Conversation," in which the narrator overhears several old women chatting desultorily through the night, trying to piece together a sexual scandal; "The Shooting-Match," where the narrator falls in among the "boys" of Upper Hogthief and by luck wins a prize; "The Turf," with "men, women, children, whites and blacks, all betting" at a horse race, but where the five-hundred-dollar prize proves to be no more than forty-eight dollars plus promissory notes; "The Gander-Pulling"; "The Turn-Out," a rebellion of students against their schoolmaster; "The Fight," where the clay-eating dwarf Ransy Sniffle tricks two handsome friends into mutilating each other, no holds barred; and "The Horse-Swap." In each of these pieces, the scene is set among dirty, uneducated people, and the polite, gentlemanly narrator's voice is contrasted to or at moments supplanted by, a character's racy, colloquial vernacular speech. Yet this speech, so welcome to modern readers, signals a social level and way of life that Longstreet keeps in close check. His own morality is not only decent, but "improving." He aims to record odd features of a way of life that he is happy to announce is passing. Here, as in many other ways, he resembles Twain rather than Cooper.

The opening sketch of the collection, "Georgia Theatrics," begins by warning readers that its account is not now "characteristic of the county in which it occurred." But, back in 1809, "The Dark Corner" of Lincoln County was known for its "moral darkness." Longstreet continues, "Since that time, however (all humor aside) . . . could I venture to mingle the solemn with the ludicrous, even for the purpose of honorable contrast, I could adduce from this county instances of the most numerous and wonderful transitions from vice and folly to virtue and holiness."

Longstreet is sincere in the sanctimony of this moral and cultural– historical stance, but he must shift away from it to energize his narrative. For after denying that he would "mingle the solemn with the ludicrous," Long- street immediately sets against his solemn narrative voice the voices that he hears, "loud, profane, and boisterous," over the way and out of sight: "You kin, kin you?" "Yes, I kin, and am able to do it! Boo-oo-oo! Oh, wake snakes, and walk your chalks!" Further boasting prepares the way for a big fight, which the narrator continues to overhear, right up to the climax, as he comes upon the scene: "I saw the uppermost one (for I could not see the other) make a heavy plunge with both his thumbs, and at the same instant I heard a cry in the accent of keenest torture, 'Enough! My eye's out!' " "Horror-struck," the narrator "stood transfixed." But he discovers that the whole thing had been a "rehearsal," in which a single teenager "had played all the parts of all the characters in a court-house fight."

This case offers humor in a usual and welcome sense. The trick is on the narrator who recounts it and on the reader who has been expecting terrible, sensational events. The vernacular character has the chance of retort, "You needn't kick before you're spurr'd. There a'n't nobody there, nor ha'n't been nother. I was jist seein' how I could 'a' fout." The comedy arises from the mingling of the voices and from readers' relief that the mutilation was only play. Nonetheless, the boy has not been granted any moral authority to match the narrator's. He remains part of a culture so savage that children play at eye gouging. The sketch closes with images that testify to fierce energies uncontrolled in the terrifying absence of civilization: "I went to the ground from which he had risen, and there were the prints of his two thumbs, plunged up to the balls in the mellow earth, about the distance of a man's eyes apart; and the ground around was broken up as if two stags had been engaged upon it."

In the process that made southwestern-humor writing a nationally circu- lated form, probably no author was more important than Thomas Bangs Thorpe (1815–75). Born in Massachusetts and raised in New York, Thorpe went to Louisiana in 1837, where he remained, for the most part, until 1854. In 1839 he published his first sketch, "Tom Owen, the Bee Hunter," "By a New Yorker in Louisiana." Rejected by a local paper, it was printed in the *Spirit of the Times,* where it proved immensely popular. A short piece with an Irvingesque narrator, the sketch has little appeal today, but it was re- printed in Rufus Griswold's *The Prose Writers of America* (1847) and along with "Georgia Theatrics" was the only piece of southwestern humor in the

Duyckinck brothers' massive *Cyclopedia of American Literature* (1855). In 1841 the *Spirit* published Thorpe's other important piece, "The Big Bear of Arkansas," which gave its title to the first anthology of southwestern humor. Published by Carey and Lea of Philadelphia in 1845 (under the editorship of Porter from the *Spirit*), *The Big Bear of Arkansas and Other Sketches, Illustrative of Characters and Incidents in the South and South-West* sparked a considerable publishing boom of southwestern humor. After this success, Thorpe went off to the Mexican War, accompanying Zachary Taylor, and his reports back from the war were among the major sources not only of news but also for early histories of the war. Thorpe's long involvement with Whig politics in Louisiana ended in frustration, and he returned to New York in 1854, serving with the Union in the Civil War, one of the few southwestern humorists not to side with the Confederacy.

Thorpe's "Big Bear" narrates an encounter between hunter and bear that rests on persuasive local detail but moves into the mysterious and the mythical, while featuring an unconventional narrative voice. This model obviously influenced William Faulkner's "The Bear" (1942), and it has resonance from *Moby-Dick* through much of Ernest Hemingway and on to Norman Mailer's *Why Are We in Vietnam?* (1967). As in Longstreet, a sketch narrator sets a frame within which vernacular voices appear, but in this case the vernacular voice is allowed to take over the bulk of the piece, and unlike in Longstreet, there is no moral dimension to the framing. The vernacular speaker, himself the "Big Bar of Arkansaw" after whom the story is named, appears not on his home ground, but on a Mississippi steamboat. He personally represents his locale, but the scene represents "every State in the Union":

Here may be seen jostling together the wealthy Southern planter, and the pedlar of tin-ware from New England – the Northern merchant and the Southern jockey – a venerable bishop and a desperate gambler – the land speculator, and the honest farmer . . . Wolvereens, Suckers, Hoosiers, Buckeyes, and Corncrackers, beside a "plentiful sprinkling" of the half-horse and half-alligator species of men, who are peculiar to "old Mississippi."

The narrator, aboard such a boat, behaves like a gentleman. He sits, "critically" reading, amidst the "heterogeneous" crowd, when all are interrupted by the arrival of the "Big Bar," who quickly charms them despite his rough manner. The "Bar" explains to the genteel hunters that animals are not "game" in Arkansas. In Arkansas, the main "game" is poker, but if you are hunting, "that's *meat*." When "twenty voices" cry out in astonishment at his mention of a wild turkey weighing forty pounds, he answers, "Yes, strangers, and wasn't it a whopper?" Thorpe shows the "Bar" playing humorously with his interlocutors, asserting the whopping size of his native fauna, while at the same time acknowledging that his narrative is itself somewhat a whopper. His Arkansas is "the creation State," and its bears, "feeding as they do upon the *spontenacious* productions of the sile," are fat all year round. After his protracted boast of the qualities of Arkansas, the "Bar" then tells at length the story of one particular hunt, quite unlike the usual hunt that may be "told in two sentences — a bar is started, and he is killed." (One short chapter of Crockett's *Autobiography* describes a season in which he killed one hundred and five bears.)

The hunter discovers traces of the largest bear he has ever seen or heard of; the bear mocks him by repeatedly marauding his pigs; and the hunter is consumed with anger, while feeling that the bear has reversed roles and is hunting him. Glimpsing the bear on a hunt, the "Bar" is awed by his beauty and "loved him like a brother"; nonetheless, he pursues the hunt, to an extended, frustrating, and unsuccessful conclusion. Finally, his pride at stake, he tries once more, and to his amazement, before he has even set out in the morning, the bear appears: "he loomed up like a *black mist,* he seemed so large, and he . . . *walked through the fence* like a falling tree would through a cobweb." Before the hunter has any chance to kill him, the bear has died, for he *"was an unhuntable bar, and died when his time come."* Thorpe's "creation bar" proved one of the great creations of this body of writing, the primary icon that the southwestern humorists fixed in national tradition.

The publishing opportunities opened by the success of *The Big Bear of Arkansas* were quickly exploited by Johnson Jones Hooper (1815–62). Born in North Carolina, Hooper by 1835 was learning law in his brother's office in Alabama. In 1842 he became editor of the *East Alabamian,* where he published his first sketch, "Taking the Census in Alabama." Hooper's subject too is a focus for the tension between local and national. Only as an employee of the federal government, performing a task so resented and feared by the local population that it was considered dangerous, did Hooper come into contact with the common people whose oddities became the stuff of his humor. His piece was a hit, taken up by Porter for the *Spirit of the Times.* Encouraged by Porter, Hooper produced a book that made him famous.

Published by Carey in 1845, Hooper's *Some Adventures of Captain Simon Suggs, Late of the Tallapoosa Volunteers; Together with "Taking the Census" and Other Alabama Sketches* enjoyed eleven editions in the next decade. Although occupying only part of the book, the story of Suggs was Hooper's great contribution. To the end of his days he had to endure being himself called by the name of his creation, much to his dismay and embarrassment. *Some Adventures of Simon Suggs,* dedicated to Porter, is a mock campaign biography, with a supposedly infatuated narrator recounting the qualities of his hero in a way that allows readers to laugh at the objects of the hero's roguery while

feeling superior to hero and narrator alike. The mode looks back to Henry
Fielding's satire on Sir Robert Walpole's political "greatness" in *Jonathan
Wild* (1743), and its tone often resembles that of William Makepeace Thackeray in *Catherine* (1839) and *Barry Lyndon* (1844), which ironically represent
the vogue for crime literature. Following his slogan "It is good to be shifty in
a new country," Suggs moves from playing tricks on his father into land
speculation, card playing, and his corrupt, incompetent leadership of the
militia, the "Tallapoosa Volunteers."

Probably the most memorable of the chapters in *Some Adventures of Simon
Suggs* is "The Captain Attends a Camp-Meeting," which is echoed in Mark
Twain's *Huckleberry Finn,* when "The King Turns Parson." Low on cash,
Suggs attends a revival meeting, where he is recognized as a notorious sinner,
preached at, and apparently undergoes a remarkable conversion, allowing
him to raise money from the assembled group and make off with it. As Suggs
relates his supposed "experience" of grace, in edifying "discourse" for all to
hear, Hooper looks over the crowd to note their reactions and lights upon a
Mrs. Dobbs:

"Dear soul alive! *don't* he talk sweet!" cried an old lady in black silk — "Whar's John
Dobbs? You Sukey!" screaming at a negro woman on the other side of the square —
"ef you don't hunt up your mass John in a minute and have him here to listen to this
'sperience, I'll tuck you up when I git home and give you a hundred and fifty lashes,
madam! — see ef I don't! Blessed Lord!" — referring again to the Captain's relation —
"ain't it a *precious* 'scource!"

Full pleasure in the narrative requires readers to share Hooper's assumptions that revival meetings are a bad business in themselves and that enthusiastic religion is not only degrading but even dangerous: morally dangerous
because it fosters hypocrisy, socially dangerous because it mixes whites and
blacks under the heat of passion, and politically dangerous because it is itself
a form of demagogy and conducive to that vice in the polity at large. To this
day in the United States, religious revival remains an important part of the
national life, and almost the same suspicions remain, except now it is generally the political left that holds the views that Hooper held from the right.

Even the southwestern humor that might seem most purely high-spirited
local color has a distinct relation to the politics of the decades from the 1830s
through the 1850s. In *The Flush Times of Alabama and Mississippi: A Series of
Sketches* (1853), Joseph G. Baldwin makes the connection unmistakable.
Baldwin (1815–64) was born in the Shenandoah Valley of Virginia, of an old
Connecticut family that had come south to run textile mills; in his teens, he
left for Mississippi, to practice law where there was less competition. In 1837
he moved to Alabama, where he was active among the Whigs, serving in the

state legislature and running unsuccessfully for Congress. He left Alabama for California after the publication of his book. Baldwin began publishing sketches in the *Southern Literary Messenger* – a much more conventionally polite periodical than usual for southwestern humor – and collected them with new pieces in *Flush Times,* which was published in New York and reprinted six times within six months.

"The Flush Times" of the title were "that halcyon period, ranging from the year of Grace 1835, to 1837; that golden era, when shinplasters were the sole currency; when bank-bills were 'as thick as Autumn leaves in Vallambrosa.' " The quoted phrase from Milton's *Paradise Lost* and the mythological reference mark Baldwin as the most belletristic of the southwest-humor writers. At the same time, fidelity to his subject required him to use "shinplasters," the Americanism for a small-denomination bill issued by a wildcat bank – the easy-credit fruits sought by those who supported Jackson's campaign against the Bank of the United States. As a Whig, Baldwin writes a mock-encomium to Democratic easy credit, although a modest nostalgia for the days when he was young ensures a greater equability of tone than in Hooper. The play of inflections within Baldwin's own narrative rather than extensive quotation from vernacular characters on display provides the great majority of the book's humor, but there is one remarkable exception, where a character is given extensive voice.

Baldwin's Alabama lawyer, "Samuel Hele, esq.," speaks with such satirical "directness" that "he tore the feathers off a subject, as a wholesale cook at a restaurant does the plumage off a fowl, when the crowds are clamorously bawling for meat." But Sam is displayed only in one shocking and anachronistic scene. A "strong-minded" Yankee schoolmistress has come to town, and people persuade Sam to help encourage her to leave town. What he does is give voice in grotesque hyperbole to all the worst fantasies that anyone might ever have entertained about the system of slavery and the degradation of life and character in the South. The teacher flees, accidentally leaving behind a letter to "Mrs. Harriet S----" on slavery in the South, "which I should never have thought of again had I not seen something like [its details] in a very popular fiction, or rather book of fictions, in which the slaveholders are handled with something less than feminine delicacy and something more than masculine unfairness." Baldwin has inserted into his reminiscences of the middle 1830s a response to Harriet Beecher Stowe's *Uncle Tom's Cabin.*

Baldwin's use of Hele suggests that the South of gothic fantasy was just big talk to scare Yankees, but the greatest of the southwestern humorists, George Washington Harris, made grotesque violence the essence of his South, embodied in a character named "Sut," to echo his region. Born near Pittsburgh, Harris (1815–69) lived primarily in East Tennessee, where he worked in a variety of trades and enterprises mostly connected to the world of current technology: he was for several years a steamboat pilot; he worked in, and owned, a metal working shop; he managed a sawmill and a copper mine; and he was involved with railroads. From the 1840s he occasionally contributed to the *Spirit of the Times,* but his major work appeared in the later 1850s, almost exclusively in Tennessee papers, including the fire-eating Democratic Nashville *Union.* As the Civil War approached, Harris contributed some remarkably savage political satires, such as a series mocking Abraham Lincoln en route to his inaugural in Washington, or another so antinorthern as to wish the *Mayflower* settlers had been massacred by the Indians. Nonetheless, after the war it was in New York that Harris's one book was published, *Sut Lovingood: Yarns Spun by a "Nat'ral Born Durn'd Fool"* (1867) — testimony to how thoroughly the North had won the conflict and to how harmless it therefore must have considered even something so fiercely unreconstructed as Sut's South.

Sut's yarns are almost always introduced by a gentlemanly narrator known only as George. Sut's powerfully eccentric and idiomatic backcountry language enters only through this initial mediation, but once entered, his is overwhelmingly the prevalent voice. Moreover, Harris goes farther to emphasize the linguistic eccentricity of his character than had any of the other southwestern writers. Sut's speech is rendered in elaborate phonetic reproduction, both to convey the character of his sounds and to emphasize that this is an illiterate we are reading. Himself a strict Presbyterian, Harris nonetheless gave Sut Lovingood the capacity to stand free of his author morally as he stands free from his narrator linguistically. Hooper's narrator would break into Suggs's discourse frequently to summarize or to point out metaphors, but Sut's language is almost uninterrupted, and, when Sut is interrupted, it is often only so that he can retort sharply upon his interlocutor. At one point, Sut digresses to inquire,

"How is it that bricks fits so clost enyhow? Rocks won't ni du hit."
"Becaze they'se all ove a size," ventured a man with a wen over his eye.
"The devil yu say, ho'ney-head! Haint reapin-mersheens ove a size? I'd like tu see two ove em fit clost. Yu wait ontil yu sprouts tuther ho'n, afore yu venters to 'splain mix'd questions."

The appeal to the reaping machine, a product of heavy industry, is perfectly characteristic of Sut's world. It may be the backwoods or a backwater, but the reach of modern technology extended even that far — just as American frontier tales involved prowess with rifles, and the steamboat framed "The Big Bear of Arkansas."

At times Sut appears in surroundings of more precisely rendered physical detail than even the low-life conventions of southwestern humor had seen before. A Sunday morning idyll sets the young Sut "ontu the fence a-shavin seed-ticks ofen my laigs wif a barlow knife." Even more striking is the intimacy of social detail. Sut's powerful emotions include fear and shame, and the stories reveal the social inequalities, the structures of hierarchy, that produce such feelings among the lower orders. The characters in this hierarchy include the financially gouging squire, who is deeply involved in the church and so seems to Sut to be "Secon enjineer ove a mersheen . . . fur the mindin giner'lly ove everybody else's bisness." The second such character, the sheriff, provoked Sut's first big scare when he was a child and has ever since figured as the object of his planned revenges: " '*The sheriff!*' his'd mam in a keen trimblin whisper; hit sounded to me like the skreech ove a hen when she sez 'hawk,' tu her little roun-sturn'd, fuzzy, bead-eyed, stripid-backs." The preacher is the third hierarchical character. Parson John Bullen tells her parents that their daughter has kissed Sut, and, in revenge, Sut plays on him a painful and humiliating prank.

Sut's realistic environment and feelings sprout into fantastic highjinks that typically involve considerable preparation and then, as if of their own volition, explode into frantic, destructive noise and movement. At one moment Sut himself speaks of his "skeer makin mersheen." In general, he seeks devices that need only the smallest incitement to go, while he can "stan clar ove danger, an watch things happen"; or again, "Jis' pullin a string wer my hole sheer in all that ar cumbustifikashun, hurtin, an' trubbil." The mechanical ingenuity of some of Sut's devices, and the machine metaphors in which the results are often described, make Harris's work seem as if they could be scripts for the animated cartoons of the 1930s and 1940s: "I sot these yere laigs a-gwine onder three hunder' pound preshure ove pure skeer. Long es they is, they went apast each uther as fas' as the spokes ove two spinnin wheels a runnin contrary ways."

As also in the cartoons, in Sut's yarns the rapidity, complexity, and intensity of motion produce heroic messes: "Pickil crocks, perserves jars, vinegar jugs, seed bags, yarb bunches, paragorick bottles, aig baskits, an' delft war — all mix'd dam permiskusly, an' not worth the sortin, by a duller an' a 'alf." The subject matter is not worth sorting out, but the prose sets it in rhythmic order. The sentence is hinged around the dash, with almost an equal number of words before and after, subdivided into eight shorter units in the first half, three almost equal longer units in the second half. Despite its everyday vocabulary and energetic stresses, Harris organizes his material with the elaborate syntactical constructions of formal rhetoric: "taters, cabbige, meat, soup, beans, sop, dumplins, an' the truck what yu wallers 'em in; milk, plates, pies, puddins, an' every durn fixin yu cud think ove in a week, wer

thar, mix'd an' mashed, like it had been thru a thrashin-meesheen." From the
beginning of the grammatical subject ("taters") to the beginning of the
predicate ("wer thar") almost two lines intervene, a dozen single-word items
punctuated by two echoing relative clauses ("what yu wallers" and "yu cud
think ove"). Harris is equally effective with more straightforwardly repetitive
structures: "The street wer white wif milk an' aigshells; hit wer red wif
cherrys; hit wer black wif blackberrys, an' hit were green wif gardin truck."

Unlike Hooper, who resisted identification with his shifty rogue Suggs,
Harris was widely called after his plebeian troublemaker, even though his
naming the polite narrator "George" might seem to suggest a different
leaning. Taking his own stand with the Democrats, Harris followed through
the logic of the Whig political mythology that linked the Democrats with
the people and the people with trouble. Bancroft's national theme was the
self-governing powers of the people, the capacity of Americans to achieve
order without either government or hierarchy. Harris's smaller scale displayed, apparently without regret, a poetry of destruction – what the people's energies might cost someone like himself, a skilled technical craftsman
who required a significant degree of inviolate space and calm. In a ruckus
that Sut witnesses, a drunken, tall-talking white man kicks a young Negro.
At once the young boy is dehumanized into a projectile: "Away hit flew,
spread like ontu a flyin squirrel, smash thru a watch-tinker's winder, totin in
broken sash, an' glass, an' bull's-eye watches, an' sasser watches, an' spoons,
an' doll heads, an' clay pipes, an' fishin reels, an' sum noise." As the watch-
maker sat "a-peepin intu an ole watch, arter spiders, wif a thing like a big
black wart kiverin one eye," the next thing he knew, "he wer flat ove his
back, wif a small, pow'fully skeer'd ash-culler'd nigger, a-straddil his naik,
littil brass wheels spinnin on the floor, an' watches singin like rattil-snakes
all roun." East Tennessee was not slaveholding country, and there is little
place for African Americans in Sut's world, but this scene suggests the
animus some southerners felt toward a social system that they believed
doomed the region to technological and economic backwardness. Harris's
image of the "nigger," surrounded by the chaos he has proximately caused
and astraddle the craftsman's neck, constructs a scene that blames the victim.
The initiating kick is out of the picture, which makes the slave appear
responsible for the destruction that seems to foreshadow what finally came
with the Civil War.

NATHANIEL HAWTHORNE

In 1830, just a few years before Augustus Longstreet began publishing his
anonymous scenes from the early days of Georgia in the Milledgeville *South-*

ern Recorder, Nathaniel Hawthorne (1804–64) published anonymously in the Salem *Gazette* five biographical sketches and tales from the early days of Massachusetts. The subjects included "Mrs. Hutchinson," the antinomian leader of the 1630s to whom he would later compare Hester Prynne, and "The Hollow of the Three Hills," a tale of shame and of the violation of privacy – a theme that Hawthorne would make obsessively his own. Perhaps already by the time he left Bowdoin College in 1825 Hawthorne had planned and written much of a projected book of "Seven Tales of My Native Land." No less than that of the southwestern writers, Hawthorne's initial identity as a writer was intensely local. But despite his location in a more culturally developed part of the nation, Hawthorne experienced much greater difficulties in his path to publication than did the southwestern writers. The response to his projected "Tales of My Native Land" was so discouraging that it is not certain whether Hawthorne actually preserved anything from that undertaking, although it seems likely that the fictional pieces in the *Gazette* derived from it.

Returning after college to live with his widowed mother and two sisters in his native city of Salem, Hawthorne began an intensive program of reading in the library of the Salem Athenaeum. For some dozen years he wrote in isolation. By 1829 he had a new book project, "Provincial Tales," and had presented it to a Boston publisher, who would not risk the book but offered to publish pieces in *The Token,* an annual gift book. In *The Token* for 1831, Hawthorne published an anonymous sketch, "Sights from a Steeple." For the next half-dozen years, some of his sketches and tales were published as "By the Author of 'Sights from a Steeple.'" That sketch remains memorable for its fantasy that "The most desirable mode of existence might be that of a spiritualized Paul Pry, hovering invisible around man and woman, witnessing their deeds, searching into their hearts." Such unseen observation was a crucial feature of nineteenth-century culture. It figured fundamentally in defining the stance of the narrator in realistic fiction; it was no less important as the stance of the emerging social sciences; and it comprised an actual practice both in social welfare reform (prisons, poorhouses) and in industrial organization. In this figure of the sensitive spectator, who is also an inquisitor, Hawthorne shows the marks of his age, even in works that have no evident social content.

In *The Token* of 1832, Hawthorne published several pieces from "Provincial Tales." Still only in his late twenties, he had already produced some of the works on which his reputation would rest. "The Gentle Boy," like "Sights from a Steeple," became a signature piece for his subsequent anonymous works; "Roger Malvin's Burial" and "My Kinsman, Major Molineux" ("By the Author of 'Sights from a Steeple'") are two of the works that since the end of the second world war have figured most frequently in anthology selections and critical discussions of Hawthorne. In the years up to 1838, Hawthorne published some score more of tales and sketches in *The Token,* including "The May-Pole of Merry Mount" ("By the Author of 'The Gentle Boy' ") and "The Minister's Black Veil" ("By the Author of 'Sights from a Steeple' "), both in 1836.

While parceling out his "Provincial Tales" to *The Token,* Hawthorne conceived yet another project for a book of local character. "The Story-Teller" would be a frame narrative that dramatized its teller and set the pieces in relation to the history and geography of the places encountered on a trip through New England up to Niagara. Once again, Hawthorne's project came to nothing, except for fragments that appeared in periodicals. In 1834 *New-England Magazine* published two portions from "The Story-Teller," and over the next year some fifteen further pieces by Hawthorne followed in that journal, including "Wakefield" and "Young Goodman Brown." By 1837 he had published nearly fifty pieces; yet, when he was looking back in the 1851 preface to the third edition of *Twice-told Tales,* Hawthorne judged that at this point he had been "the obscurest man of letters in America."

For the gentlemen who wrote the southwestern tales and sketches, obscurity was not troubling as it was for Hawthorne. They might even seek obscurity in order to stand clear of the lower-class associations of their subject matter. Hawthorne's case was quite different. Although his paternal ancestors, as Hawthorne learned through his intensive reading of local history in the later 1820s, had included several distinguished figures in earlier colonial times, his own family, especially after his father's premature death, was financially dependent. Hawthorne went to college with considerable reluctance, not wanting to be "living upon Uncle Robert for four years longer." In a letter to his mother from college, he rejected the professions of law, medicine, and divinity, and then exclaimed, "Oh that I was rich enough to live without a profession." He then immediately went on to ask his mother, "What do you think of my becoming an Author, and relying for support upon my pen?" The emotional logic of this sequence suggests that Hawthorne considered writing a profession that was not quite a profession. It offered him greater freedom, but, economically, the pen was a weak "support."

Hawthorne left Salem for Boston in 1836 to become editor of the *American Magazine of Useful and Entertaining Knowledge,* but the promised five-hundred-dollar salary yielded him no more than twenty dollars in the six months that he stuck out the work before the publisher went bankrupt. He and his sister Maria Louisa then worked together as hacks for *Peter Parley's Universal History, on the Basis of Geography.* For one hundred dollars they put together a work that is said to have sold over a million copies. By 1837,

Hawthorne's financial situation was worsening, for the family stagecoach business, linking Boston and Salem, was about to be ruined by the construction of the first railroad between the cities. It became necessary for Hawthorne to "scribble for a living," to become a "scribbler by profession." This exigency drove him to produce four more history books for children: *Grandfather's Chair, Famous Old People,* and *Liberty Tree* (all 1841) and *Biographical Stories for Children* (1842).

To earn a decent living by writing, Hawthorne needed to earn a name for himself. Achieving an identity as a known writer of quality was all that stood between Hawthorne and endless drudging hack work; it made the difference between the "author" Hawthorne had dreamed of becoming and the "scribbler" that he had become. Yet not only was Hawthorne's work appearing without his name, it was even appearing under different rubrics. Such a strategy served the publisher of *The Token,* who did not want it known that a single writer was responsible for eight pieces in the 1837 annual, but it was not in Hawthorne's interest. Hawthorne's friend Horatio Bridge argued, "You scatter your strength by fighting under various banners." Hawthorne's writings were admired by a readership to whom his name was unknown. Bridge therefore urged Hawthorne, "Put your name upon the title-page" of a book. With Bridge's secret financial guarantee, *Twice-told Tales* appeared in 1837, collecting nineteen of the pieces Hawthorne had published up to that point. Although sales began well, with six to seven hundred copies sold in the first months, the Panic of 1837 and the ensuing depression chilled sales and bankrupted the publisher. Yet as Hawthorne reflected in the preface to the reissued edition in 1851, it had served to "open up an intercourse with the world."

From this point, Hawthorne's career was strikingly worldly; like the amateur writers of the southwest, he did not make writing his primary concern. In the twenty years from the publication of *Twice-told Tales,* Hawthorne devoted himself primarily to writing for less than half the time: 1838, when he wrote some dozen pieces that would help make up a second volume of *Twice-told Tales* (1842); the three-and-a half years at the "Old Manse" in Concord, where he lived with his wife Sophia immediately after their marriage and wrote most of the materials for *Mosses from an Old Manse* (1846); and the years from mid-1849 through 1852, in which he wrote full-length romances (*The Scarlet Letter* [1850], *The House of the Seven Gables* [1851], *The Blithedale Romance* [1852]), more stories, collected in *The Snow-Image* (1851), along with more children's books (*True Stories from History and Biography* [1851], *A Wonder-Book* [1852], and *Tanglewood Tales* [1853]), and finally the campaign biography of Franklin Pierce, his old college friend who became president of the United States in 1853. (On Hawthorne's romances, see Chapter 4.)

The intervals between writing were spent primarily in political office. From the mid-1830s through the mid-1850s, each time a Democratic president came into office, Hawthorne received a patronage appointment: in the Boston Custom House, 1839–41; in the Salem Custom House, 1846–9; and as consul in Liverpool and Manchester, England 1853–7. The one other interval was spent in an experiment in a different kind of politics, at the Brook Farm utopian community in 1841. When Hawthorne completed his service as consul in 1857, he published only one more romance, *The Marble Faun* (1860), and a collection of essays reflecting on England, *Our Old Home* (1863). Along with his journals, the bulk of his writing in the years before his death in 1864 (discussed in Chapter 5) remained unpublished until his family found in them a continuing financial resource. As a famous author, Hawthorne could continue to earn from beyond the grave.

Once Hawthorne had set his name to the title page of a book, an extraordinary process of construction became possible. His college friend Henry Wadsworth Longfellow reviewed *Twice-told Tales* in the weightiest American cultural organ, the *North American Review.* Longfellow undertook to define the "point of view" from which the tales and sketches were produced – that is, he began to make a rich, complex, and integral figure out of what had been a fragmented assortment of writings. Meanwhile, Elizabeth Peabody, the sister of Hawthorne's future wife, Sophia Peabody, used her connections to bring him to the attention of George Bancroft. Bancroft not only came through with patronage employment, he also connected Hawthorne with an important journal. From its very first issue, Hawthorne appeared in John O'Sullivan's *Democratic Review,* and from 1837 through 1845, he published some two-dozen pieces there, about half of his total output for the period.

Now that he was appearing in a national journal, Hawthorne could be taken up in yet further reaches of cultural politics. The strongest advocate for an American national literature, understood as significantly different from British or any other foreign literature, was Evert Duyckinck of New York, and in 1841 he published in the first volume of his new journal *Arcturus* a powerful appreciation of Hawthorne's work. Duyckinck had admired Hawthorne for as long as there had been an identity to be known. In 1838 he and a friend called on Hawthorne in Salem; Hawthorne later recollected this as the first attention ever paid him in his character as "literary man." In the *Arcturus* essay, Duyckinck figured Hawthorne's literary character in the terms that Romanticism had made exemplary for literature itself. Hawthorne was a "Hamlet," whose "consciousness" and "imagination" were immense, but whose "will" lagged behind. He was conceived as a figure whose inwardness was the chief locus of value, and for whom action would be quite secondary, if not impossible.

A few years later, Duyckinck again wrote about Hawthorne, this time in the *Democratic Review,* with which he too had associated himself. James K. Polk had already been elected, and Hawthorne was looking forward to a patronage position. O'Sullivan was playing the angles. He wrote to Hawthorne, "For the purpose of presenting you more advantageously, I have got Duyckinck to write an article about you in the April Democratic, . . . and I want you to consent to sit for a daguerrotype. By manufacturing you thus into a personage, I want to raise your mark higher in Polk's appreciation." In this essay, Duyckinck compared Hawthorne's moral passion to that of King Lear — a comparison that would stick in the mind of Duyckinck's protégé Herman Melville when in 1850 he wrote "Hawthorne and His Mosses" for the *Literary World,* edited by Duyckinck and his brother George. Duyckinck himself in fact was responsible for the publication of *Mosses* in the Library of American Books series he was editing for Wiley and Putnam.

The southwestern writers were Whigs; Hawthorne was a Democrat, like Cooper and Bancroft. Yet Hawthorne was not a popular writer like his fellow Democrats, nor did he follow the Whig humorists in vernacular writing. From the beginning, those who most memorably supported Hawthorne were those most associated with the development in America of the separate, high aesthetic sphere of "literature": Longfellow, Duyckinck, Poe. In 1842, just the year before his critique of Cooper's popularity, Poe had hailed Hawthorne for the "creation," "originality," and "genius" — all key terms of the new Romantic aesthetic — that placed his work in "the highest region of Art." Throughout his career, Hawthorne was praised as a cultivated stylist, who like Irving avoided the Romantic eccentricities of Charles Lamb and followed the eighteenth-century norm of Joseph Addison. Nonetheless, his work was considered difficult.

Hawthorne was a Massachusetts local writer not by virtue of his employing Yankee vernacular diction, but by his historical resurrection of the colonial past. This was not merely a choice of subject matter. It involved his use of a larger strategy that had had greater influence in New England than in any other part of the United States. Hawthorne was notorious for his use of allegory, a mode that looked back to the practices of the early Puritans, as well as to Edmund Spenser and John Bunyan in England, and one that he directly echoed in "The Celestial Railroad." Thus the wife of Young Goodman Brown is named "Faith," and the alluring young woman in "scarlet petticoat," who invites Robin in, rather than helping him to his kinsman Molineux, recognizably echoes the apocalyptic scarlet woman, the "whore of Babylon" in Puritan anti-

Catholic propaganda. In the work of the Old Manse period, allegory persists, and the mise-en-scène is less particularized. Hawthorne's abstraction reflects the preference of his transcendentalist neighbors. Aylmer in "The Birth-mark" finds human fleshly imperfection emblematized in his wife's slight blemish, and "Rappaccini's Daughter" bears the name Beatrice from Dante's allegorical *Divine Comedy*.

Yet even if he employs a literary mode associated with his New England ancestors, Hawthorne takes a distance from their positions. The destruction of the maypole of Merry Mount figures the triumph of Puritanic "gloom" over "jollity" in American cultural life, and there is nothing in the description of the Puritans, who take their pleasure in the whipping post, to suggest that Hawthorne was nostalgic for their rule. Hawthorne's allegory is displayed for criticism, even as it is employed for construction. Moreover, established allegorical practice distinguished between conventional allegory and esoteric allegory. Esoteric allegory is farfetched and self-consciously more difficult in order to achieve a "deeper," or more socially suspect, meaning than conventional allegory. For example, the action of "Roger Malvin's Burial" begins and ends at a massive granite rock; nearby is an oak, unexpected in the landscape, which by the end is strangely withered. The heavy emphasis given to these features provokes speculation. Might the blasted oak echo the famous Charter Oak of Connecticut, and the great rock allude to Plymouth Rock? If so, the meaning of the story as a reflection on American patriotic mythology becomes much deeper, but there is no way to establish that such meanings were in fact intended.

A contemporary reviewer faulted "Young Goodman Brown" for its "obscurity of execution," which made its "lesson" incomprehensible to "nine out of ten intelligent readers." It was "an illustration, that needs to be illustrated," an "allegory with crutches." Like Bancroft, Hawthorne recognized in the Puritans the ancestors of still-current ways of living and of understanding life, but he also acknowledged that the political basis of democracy in the nineteenth century was fundamentally different from the religious basis of the seventeenth century.

Hawthorne's difficulty stemmed from another feature of his stylistic practice, his tendency to ellipsis – to saying less than a situation might warrant. "The Gentle Boy" is the longest of Hawthorne's tales except for "Rappaccini's Daughter," and part of its length comes from its dwelling in some detail on the fireside values of domesticity that have no similarly large place in Hawthorne's other tales, although they are frequent in his sketches – and letters. Such domestic values may well be implicit in those other tales too, but they are no more than hinted, and this leaves the tales open to alternative interpretations, especially by modern readers who no longer value domesticity in fiction. Frequently what Hawthorne has left out is precisely the judgment that would allow his readers to be certain which of several alternatives is correct – if indeed correct decision rather than hovering suspension is the goal of his work.

To the extent that Hawthorne's stories provide an emotional impact without a definable meaning, they partake of the aesthetic realm of literature that Poe was struggling to define. Then, too, the thematic resemblances among stories of quite different emotional power suggest that Hawthorne was more concerned to offer a distanced examination of alternatives than either serious moral teaching or deep psychological obsessions. For example, both "Wakefield" and "Young Goodman Brown" take as their action a man's leaving home. He lingers on the threshold as he leaves, and when he returns – after an abortive reunion with his wife amidst a crowd – things have changed for the worse. Wakefield has been too little affected by the intervening years, and the story's tone is satirically externalized. Brown, in contrast, has been too much affected by a single night, and the story is feelingly internalized.

Like Poe's, Hawthorne's work before 1850 is in short forms – another elliptical choice, for a long work usually establishes authorial values more securely than can an unconventional short work. To this day, short prose fictions typically fall into two classes, the highly conventionalized (whether science fiction, crime, western, or "New Yorker") and the radically innovative. Bancroft's extensive narrative with its well-defined shape and its repeated narrative guidance to the reader was clearly coherent with his commitment to the party of the people. In contrast, Hawthorne broke up the national narrative into minutely examined local units, not necessarily of any preestablished significance, and this technique conflicted with his Democratic allegiance. If he resisted the arrogance of the Puritan religious elect, how could he participate in a secular cultural elite?

The primary mark of Hawthorne's political difference from the Whig humorists and his solidarity with Bancroft shows in the seriousness with which Hawthorne treats people of no special social distinction in various everyday situations. The strongest works of the southwestern writers display their social animus, preeminently in George Harris. Hawthorne's most powerful works also convey political implications. These stories are not only somber in moral coloring, but their somber tones are not reserved for the highest social orders. At the same time that Hawthorne and Bancroft were writing, Ralph Waldo Emerson in "The American Scholar" (1837) emphasized the value of "the familiar, the low . . . the meal in the firkin; the milk in the pan; the ballad in the street." To illustrate this concern, he praised the "genius" of such Romantic writers as Wordsworth. Modern readers of Wordsworth, however, more readily admire the "egotistical sublime" of "Tintern

Abbey," the Immortality Ode, and above all *The Prelude,* and it takes historical recovery to appreciate Wordsworth's more radically democratic attempts like "Michael," which present the "literature of the poor," the "meaning of household life" that Emerson praised. In the case of Hawthorne, however, the culturally and socially secure first-person narrator of the sketches now compels far less attention than his third-person tales of what Bancroft, or Hawthorne himself in his occasional political writings, would call "the people."

The equal and opposite fanaticisms of Puritans and Quakers in "The Gentle Boy" could make for bleak comedy in the hands of someone like Simon Sugg's Hooper, but Hawthorne treated them respectfully, even while not identifying himself with, or urging readers to side with, either. Not only for modern readers but also for Duyckinck and Melville, "Young Goodman Brown" represented a high point of Hawthorne's accomplishment, which they compared to *King Lear,* although Brown was very much a commoner. So, too, did the kind of popular, mass political activity satirized in southwestern writing become the partially humorous, but finally painfully moving, experience of "My Kinsman, Major Molineux." And when Hawthorne treated the subject of Indian fighting and the frontier in "Roger Malvin's Burial," there is none of the energy of tall talk and high spirits that mark the Davy Crockett kind of writing. Hawthorne's story begins after the fight is over and the Indians – for several years at least – are out of the picture; the action returns to the frontier only for a scene of somnambulistic violence between the members of the pioneer family.

In their treatment of common life the southwestern writers reduced the actions they related to superficiality by their externalized comic renderings and lack of concern for consequences. Hawthorne, in contrast, reduced the actions he treated to feelings by his internalized psychological rendering and obsessive concern for individual consequences. Thus Hawthorne resembles Cooper and Bancroft in acknowledging the dignity of everyday life, in the forests or settlements rather than in the courts or capitals. But he does not resemble them in finding any active ideal in the everyday, either as a heroic individual like Cooper's Leatherstocking or as a political community such as those with which Bancroft populated his American history.

The characteristic situation toward which many of Hawthorne's most effective stories move involves an isolated figure and a crowd. Robin Molineux searches for his kinsman while everyone he meets is involved in a conspiracy against the major, unknown to him until the punitive procession at the end. Young Goodman Brown sneaks off for a meeting in the woods and discovers everyone of high or low repute from Salem to be there. Wakefield goes around the corner from his home and hides for twenty years concealed by the crowd of London. If the crowds are not treated dismissively as mobs, neither are they hailed as the will of the people incarnate. They are powerful and frightening, whether as the community of evil into which Brown refuses induction or as the Puritan vigilantes that the Lord and Lady of May are left to face after their maypole has been cut down.

The problem of crowds, mobs, and riots came to sharp attention in the American 1830s. At the time that Hawthorne had drafted "Provincial Tales," in which his strongest crowd scenes occur, the public issue had not yet arisen, but from 1834 through 1837, there was a tremendous increase in the number of crowd disturbances becoming known through news, and much concern about its significance. The single greatest provocation for these mob activities was abolitionism, and those who participated in group actions against abolitionists were typically respectable people, "gentlemen of property and standing." Hawthorne's meditations on the Puritan crowd as the basis for American politics form a sober counterpoint to the controversies in the popular press.

Antiabolition mobs often self-consciously modeled themselves on the group actions of revolutionary America. In Philadelphia in 1835 and Cincinnati in 1836 mobs specifically invoked the example of the Boston Tea Party, an illegal but righteous action. The only way many Americans of the 1830s could understand abolitionism was as a British conspiracy against the American way of life. Thus in 1837, after the concerted mob action in Alton, Illinois, against Elijah Lovejoy, the abolitionist editor, culminating in his murder, the attorney general of Massachusetts told the multitude at Faneuil Hall that the Alton rioters were following the example of Samuel Adams, Charles Warren, and James Otis. This context does much to explain why Hawthorne might have preferred to forget about "My Kinsman, Major Molineux," which he did not reprint until *The Snow-Image* (1851). He even resisted Duyckinck's suggestion to include "Young Goodman Brown" in *Mosses,* although he finally yielded. Stories of mobs had become highly topical. What might originally have been a historically appropriate, complex, and sober attitude toward prerevolutionary mob activity could scarcely avoid being transformed into apparent approval of either abolitionism or antiabolitionism – neither of which Hawthorne supported.

The characteristic situation of heightened individual subjectivity set against the crowd bears an obvious and important resemblance to certain aspects of Hawthorne's personal situation. The case of Young Goodman Brown may illustrate this resemblance. The story shows what it might have been like for an individual who held the Puritan theological beliefs, in the third generation of the Massachusetts colony, that led to the witchcraft persecutions. As opposed to Bancroft's suggestion that the clergy led the persecution as a means to negotiate a difficult political and ideological moment, Hawthorne locates the problem in the holier-than-thou psychology of a perfectly ordinary member of the community. Young "Brown," wedded to "Faith," seems intended as a generic, typical figure. Yet he proves capable of believing (he is not and need not be certain) — even heroically capable, insofar as the belief greatly pains and shocks him — that everyone except himself is secretly in league with the devil. The last paragraph of the story, however, in depicting the dreary end to which such suspicions doom Brown, makes an eccentric out of him. No longer typical, he is an isolated individual.

The very methods of Hawthorne's art are intensely individualizing and, in this respect, alienating. Popular historiography had made Cotton Mather the villain of the witchcraft scandal. Hawthorne, in contrast, has fixed critical attention on someone who did not wield great power. Mather could have been responsible for leading communal action; Brown could not have been. So Hawthorne's attempt to show the psychological basis for a historical event makes it increasingly difficult to imagine how any event at all could have occurred; the very technique of closely analyzing a single person cuts that person off from any community. Hawthorne dreaded the power to isolate of Calvinist theology in the New England Puritan past and of idealist philosophy in the transcendentalist present, and yet his own mode of writing, like his own situation as a writer, seems to insist upon an isolation that contradicts his commitment to the communally shared world of everyday. Hawthorne's writing reenacts the contradiction of Jacksonianism, which honored the common people but also promised every white, male, native-born Protestant the chance to make of himself something better and special, something no longer common.

EDGAR ALLAN POE

Unlike Hawthorne and the southwestern humorists, Edgar Allan Poe did not have a well-established regional residence, nor do his writings draw upon local history, lore, and customs. Yet the controversies surrounding his life and reputation testified to the continued absence of any national literary culture. Poe strove to make his art a world of its own, a place beyond locality or even nationality, but his success began only after his death. While he lived, his problems exemplified the fragmentation of cultural life in the United States. As James Russell Lowell explained in a favorable review of Poe in 1845,

The situation of American literature is anomalous. It has no center. . . . It is divided into many systems, each revolving round its several suns, and often presenting to the rest only the faint glimmer of a milk-and-watery way. Our capital city, unlike London or Paris, is not a great central heart. . . . Boston, New York, Philadelphia, each has its literature almost more distinct than those of the different dialects of Germany.

Poe's life is a tale of five cities: Boston, Richmond, Baltimore, Philadelphia, and New York. He was born in Boston in 1809 and raised in Richmond, Virginia (except for five years spent in London) until 1826, when he entered the newly founded University of Virginia. Leaving the university because of gambling debts, he enlisted in the army under a pseudonym, serving in Boston, where he privately published his first book, *Tamerlane and Other Poems,* "by a Bostonian" (1827). While seeking entry to West Point, he lived in Baltimore and published there a second volume of poems, *Al Aaraaf, Tamerlane and Minor Poems* (1829). After a brief period at West Point, he paused in New York to publish *Poems: Second Edition* (1831) and then returned to Baltimore. From 1831 through 1834 Poe tried to make a place for himself in the world of periodical writing. He submitted stories to prize competitions for the Philadelphia *Sunday Courier* and Baltimore *Saturday Visiter,* leading to publication and a prize in 1833 for "MS. Found in a Bottle."

In 1835, with the recommendation of John Pendleton Kennedy, a Baltimore man of letters, Poe began writing for the *Southern Literary Messenger,* founded in Richmond the year before. His first story in this journal was "Berenice," and soon he went to Richmond to serve as the *Messenger's* editorial assistant and principal reviewer. Over the next year and a half, Poe published more than eighty reviews in the *Messenger,* notable for their early appreciation of Charles Dickens and of Longstreet's *Georgia Scenes,* as well as for their advocacy of Samuel Taylor Coleridge and Percy Bysshe Shelley, still little known in the United States. He increased the journal's circulation but won notoriety for the "tomahawk" he swung in his savage reviews of many current American productions. For example, reviewing *Paul Ulric: Or the Adventures of an Enthusiast* (1835), by Morris Mattson, Poe began,

When we called Norman Leslie the silliest book in the world [2 months earlier] we had certainly never seen Paul Ulric. . . . In itself, the book before us is too purely imbecile to merit an extended critique – but as a portion of our daily literary food – as an American work published by the Harpers – as one of a class of absurdities with an inundation of which our country is grievously threatened – we shall have no hesitation, and shall spare no pains, in exposing fully before the public eye its four hundred and forty-three pages of utter folly, bombast, and inanity.

Meanwhile Poe had himself compiled some sixteen tales framed by "The Folio Club," a set of comic characters each of whom in turn tells one of the tales, and he sent them to the same Harper that had published *Paul Ulric.*

Harper's letter of rejection says much about the condition of American publishing. The publisher cited as problems the previous appearance of the tales in magazines; the general public's feeling against collections (readers preferred one "single and connected story" to fill "the whole volume, or number of volumes"); and the particular character of the tales, which were "too learned and mystical": "They would be understood and relished only by a very few." As a southerner trying to publish in New York, Poe encountered discouragement similar to that met by Hawthorne in New England when he was attempting to publish his first planned books. Poe, however, took immediate steps to follow Harper's advice. Having left Richmond and the *Messenger* and settled in New York in early 1837, he completed a volume-length pseudofactual sea story, *The Narrative of Arthur Gordon Pym* (see Chapter 3). By the time Harper published this work, with Poe listed as its editor rather than its author, in July 1838, his possibilities in New York seemed exhausted, and he moved to Philadelphia.

From 1838 into 1844 Poe remained in Philadelphia. Here he succeeded in publishing, with Lea and Blanchard, his two-volume *Tales of the Grotesque and Arabesque* (1839), which included all twenty-five of the pieces he had already published in periodicals. Included in this collection, among many pieces that even Poe's greatest admirers do not much care for, are "William Wilson" and "The Fall of the House of Usher," both reprinted from the *Gentleman's Magazine*, where from 1839 Poe had editorial responsibilities. When in 1840 *Graham's Magazine* incorporated the *Gentleman's*, Poe went along, publishing "The Man of the Crowd" in December, and in April 1841 he became the magazine's editor. Sales of *Graham's* flourished, spurred by Poe's invention of the detective story in "The Murders in the Rue Morgue" and by his powerful reviewing, including his famous piece on Hawthorne's *Twice-told Tales*. Conflicts with the owner, however, led Poe to resign in 1842. In 1843, Poe won a cash prize for "The Gold Bug," which was widely reprinted and began to make him famous enough for a publisher to venture a pamphlet series, reissuing *The Prose Romances of Edgar A. Poe* – but only one number appeared.

Poe's troubles with owners and editors at the *Southern Literary Messenger* and the *Gentleman's Magazine* had already led him by 1840 to plan a journal under his own control, the *Penn Magazine*. After his further frustrations with *Graham's*, he renewed his plans for a journal, to be called *The Stylus*, the earlier name being "somewhat too local in its suggestions." Poe imagined that he might reach the intellectually most worthy audience if he produced a journal in "mechanical appearance . . . typography, paper and binding" superior to anything produced in the United States. The so-called "*cheap* literature" of the day was to be combated by something at once valuable and costly. The connection of the economic and the spiritual was further under-

lined in Poe's insistence that he required "proprietary right," an "interest . . . not merely editorial," in the magazine, if he were to "stamp" on the
journal that *individuality* that only a "single mind" can give. A proper
journal must be his sole property, with no split between ownership and
editorship; intellectual integrity required no division of labor (a logic that
would dictate Poe's writing the entire contents). On this basis, as a proprietor supported by subscribers, Poe could bring the work into "the Republic
of Letters" and "insist upon regarding the world at large as the sole proper
audience for the author," bending to the whims of neither readers nor owner
by pursuing "a criticism self-sustained; guiding itself only by the purest rules
of Art."

This plan never succeeded, and when Poe came to New York in 1844, he
found himself once more enmeshed in local turbulences. He joined the staff
of the *Evening Mirror,* for which he wrote on the literary scene, and he also
published a series of reflective "Marginalia" in the *Democratic Review,* the
nationalist organ. Evert Duyckinck, as he had with Hawthorne, recruited
Poe for the Library of American Books of Wiley and Putnam. In justifying
his republication of periodical pieces, Duyckinck explained (not wholly accurately) that they had "hitherto been scattered over the newspapers and magazines of the country, chiefly of the South, and have been scarcely, if at all,
known to Northern and Eastern readers." Selected by Duyckinck, *Tales* was
published in 1845 and did well enough to encourage the publication of *The
Raven and Other Poems* a few months later. Finally, in July 1845, Poe got
control of a paper of his own, the *Broadway Journal,* but beyond publishing
revised versions of most of his earlier poems and tales he did little distinctive
in the months before he had to abandon the project. In 1846 he published a
series of pieces on the "Literati of New York" in *Godey's Lady's Book,* and in
1848 he resumed reviewing for the *Southern Literary Messenger,* while also
publishing *Eureka: A Prose Poem,* a cosmogonical–aesthetic speculation. The
last year of Poe's life resumed the threads of his whole entangled career.
While still living in New York, Poe was writing for the Boston weekly *Flag
of Our Union* and still hoping to realize *The Stylus.* To raise money for his
project, he traveled to Richmond, on the way stopping with friends in
Philadelphia. After a happy late summer in Virginia, he traveled north
again, but he died, delirious and in mysterious circumstances, in Baltimore,
in October 1849.

Poe's successor as editor of *Graham's,* Rufus Griswold, became his literary
executor. Griswold published versions of Poe's life that made Poe anathema
to respectable literary culture, until modern scholarship restored the facts.
Although many who had known Poe protested, Griswold's version still
captures much of the feeling that his memory has provoked:

He walked the streets, in madness or melancholy, with lips moving in indistinct curses, or with eyes upturned in passionate prayers (never for himself, for he felt, or professed to feel, that he was already damned), but for their happiness who at that moment were objects of his idolatry; or with his glance introverted to a heart gnawed with anguish, and with a face shrouded in gloom, he would brave the wildest storms; and all night, with drenched garments and arms wildly beating the wind and rain, he would speak as if to spirits.

This shabby-genteel, urban successor to the aristocratic, Byronic hero alone with the wild elements helped define the *poète maudit* for his younger French contemporary, and posthumous admirer, Charles Baudelaire, through whose translations Poe has powerfully affected European literature. Within the culture of the United States, Poe served as an early exemplar of what has become a commonplace. As Duyckinck put it, "Our most neglected and best [*sic*] abused authors, are generally our best authors." This was not obviously true in the England of Dickens, Macaulay, and Tennyson, but it had powerful relevance for the America of Poe, Hawthorne, Emerson, and Whitman.

In his own time, and for readers since, Poe's work has posed above all problems of tone. It has never been certain quite how to take any piece written by him. In an anonymous review of the 1845 *Tales,* largely written by Poe himself, his style is praised as "strictly . . . earnest," but this earnestness need not actually derive from the writer's "belief in his statements"; rather it comes from a "power of simulation" that allows "high genius" to produce its chosen effects. Was this pseudoearnestness the narrator's self-delusion, the author's wish to delude the reader, or play in which all parties shared? Readers were confident in laughing at southwestern humor, and Hawthorne's complex ironies only emphasized his thoughtfulness, but Poe's work provoked fundamental uncertainty in response. Was he serious? Should his readers be serious? The problem is one of genre: What kind of work is this?

As early as 1835, Poe faced this problem in a letter to the editor of the *Southern Literary Messenger,* where he had just published "Berenice." In this tale, the eccentric first-person narrator explains his obsession with the teeth of his cousin Berenice, which he endows with spiritual value: "tous ses dents etaient des idées" ("all her teeth were ideas," a neoplatonic figure known in the English metaphysical poetry of the seventeenth century, as in John Donne's famous phrase "her body thought"). Poe's story turns on the narrator's drive to possess the teeth after his cousin's death, a possibly comic reduction of the ideal to its material base. He removes them from her entombed corpse; but she had been buried alive, which turns the bizarre into torture.

Poe's editor complained that the story was "by far too horrible," and Poe replied that he had written the story against a friend's "bet" that it would be impossible to write anything "effective" on a "subject so singular" if treated "seriously." Against the claims of purest art, Poe went on to insist that "the history of all Magazines" shows that just this kind of story is the basis of their success, and then he defined the kind: "the ludicrous heightened into the grotesque: the fearful coloured into the horrible: the witty exaggerated into the burlesque: the singular wrought out into the strange and mystical." Poe denied that such excess was a matter of "bad taste," for such stories, far more than "simplicity," were what was actually "*read*." Nor were these stories easy to write: they required both "originality" and also "much labour spent in their composition." Although Poe invoked British magazines, the work of Coleridge, and Thomas De Quincey's *Confessions of an English Opium-Eater,* (1822), the aesthetic principles he set out were known as those of German Romanticism (discussed more fully in Chapter 4) – so much so that in his preface to *Tales of the Grotesque and Arabesque,* he felt compelled to insist that "terror is not of Germany, it is of the soul." These Romantic premises held that the traditional generic categories and divisions between high and low, serious and comic modes, no longer pertained, and through the mixture of these levels, or tones, the strongest, and most appropriately modern, effects could be achieved.

Many contemporary reviews, however, did not find Poe Romantic. For them his writing was of quite a different kind. They compared him to a lawyer, a type widely recognized as characteristic and important in America. Both Edmund Burke, in warning Britain to seek reconciliation with the colonies, and Alexis de Tocqueville, in his study of American democracy, had emphasized that lawyers gave a distinctive tone to American culture. The lawyer addresses a case professionally rather than from any personal commitment to the issues or individuals involved; both nature and custom yield to analytic power. The lawyer is public, formal, cold, and insincere, even though also often inventive and mystifying. Thus Poe was criticized for shunning the "homely," with its familiar sentiments and comfort. (The "most wild, yet most homely narrative" of "The Black Cat" evidently did not count.) The legal profession seemed to many readers to be the cultural source of the pseudoearnestness so striking in Poe. And legal skills were associated with self-promotion, which, in contrast to the obscurity Hawthorne feared, offered the publicity Poe sought.

The lawyer was the first great American model of the professional, and Poe strove to develop two further models, which might or might not prove reconcilable: the professional writer and the "artist." He had defended "Berenice" as highly skilled magazine writing, and as late as 1844, he proclaimed that he was "essentially a magazinist." On the other hand, in discussing with Duyckinck the selection of tales for the 1845 collection, Poe

expressed a wish for something *"representing* my mind in its various phases."
He claimed that even though he had written the pieces for specific occasions
over many years, he had, nonetheless, kept "the book-unity always in mind"
and that each piece was to serve "as part of a *whole.*" For this reason, Poe
always sought the greatest possible *"diversity and variety,"* not only of "subject" and "thought" but also of *"tone."* His stories offered "a vast variety of
kinds," with the kinds varying in their value, but "each tale is equally good *of
its kind."* Poe claimed in effect that Duyckinck's "Library of American Books"
was too partial, compared to the "Republic of Letters." Yet a contradiction
remained. Having proclaimed the unity of mind that his works revealed, Poe
then explained that this unity was achieved only at the level of craft. The
professional model prevailed over the wholeness that art promised, the local
occasion over the world at large. Poe may have been more honest than those
who held that literature could achieve a unity that overcame the social and
economic conditions of modern life.

Poe's career depended on a primary fact of modern American life: the
growth of cities. New York, Philadelphia, and Baltimore were the nation's
three largest cities, and from 1820 to 1860 their population increased some
sixfold. In the United States only 6 percent of the population lived in cities in
1810 and 1820, but by 1860, nearly 20 percent did. Urban population
increased over 90 percent in the 1840s, growing almost three times as fast as
total population. Cities were still less industrial than they were commercial,
places of exchange and transfer more than of primary production. This period
also saw the growth of office work, as the economic functions of cities became
separated from people's residences, and the split between men's and women's
"spheres" became a marked fact of social, economic, and cultural life. In
Hawthorne's fiction the split between a male world of science and a female
world of spirit could figure directly in a story like "The Birth-mark." In Poe's
work, however, such social effects were displaced and transformed. In this
respect, Poe's work may be related to an important tendency in English
Romanticism.

When in 1800 William Wordsworth wrote his preface to *Lyrical Ballads,*
England had already begun to live through the transformations that would
come later to the United States. In defining the social significance of his
poetic experiments, Wordsworth emphasized that "a multitude of causes,
unknown to former times, are now acting with a combined force" to change
the character of the human mind. He included the democratic excitements
provoked by the French Revolution and the "increasing accumulation of men
in cities." As opposed to the seasonal variation of labor in the country, the
"uniformity of their occupations" provokes city dwellers to a "craving for
extraordinary incident," which the new mass journalism of the day "hourly

gratifies." Wordsworth thus wrote against his age; his poetry set in the country depends upon an analysis and a rejection of his experience of London. Wordsworth hoped to oppose the "gross and violent stimulants" offered, in differing ways, by gothic fiction and by the news.

Poe, in contrast to Wordsworth, allied himself with the powers of journalism. He achieved several successful new hoaxes (notably, stories of a transatlantic balloon journey in 1844), and his fiction relies upon the gothic trappings that Wordsworth found degrading. Wordsworth offered a poetic memory that stabilized and harmonized experience; Poe's characteristic first-person narrators are focuses of disturbance and overstimulation. Yet reviewers noted less the sensational elements of Poe's work than its coldness. "The Fall of the House of Usher" was judged to be like "a finely sculptured statue, beautiful to the eye, but without an immortal spirit" and, by another reviewer, to lack "any link of feeling or sympathy." Poe's writing made the reader feel that it came from a lawyer's office, not from a home (even when it was dealing with a "House"). Readers placed Poe's work in the masculine "sphere," while the delicacy that Wordsworth had sought was placed with "female," sentimental writing.

Poe's cunningly elaborate prose sought to awaken powerful emotions through reorienting his readers' perception of such sensational topics as murder, entombment, and decay. He explained that the effect of "The Fall of the House of Usher" was to derive from "discovering that for a long period of time we have been mistaking sounds of agony, for those of mirth or indifference." This formulation perfectly echoed the journalism of urban social exposé: the poor were starving, they were not happy wastrels. Wordsworth found in the country the opposite of the city, and sentimental writing turned from the streets to the hearth, but Poe reversed them. He transposed the elements of urban experience into the imagined unrealities of his artistic world elsewhere. Yet his earnestness involved such mastery of detail that reviewers frequently compared him to Daniel Defoe rather than to the Romantics.

Poe is obviously a city writer in the London of "The Man of the Crowd," which fully matches the urban sketches of Dickens's London and Gogol's St. Petersburg, which were also written in the 1830s. Poe's imagined Paris in "The Murders in the Rue Morgue" and "The Purloined Letter" defines the genre of urban crime writing more sharply than Balzac in *Splendors and Miseries of Courtesans*. Even where the setting is not urban, however, the models of city life prevail. "The Fall of the House of Usher," despite its backcountry setting, shows the power of an "environment" to determine physical and spiritual characteristics alike. This same concern with environment organizes much of Balzac's most characteristic and powerful writing about Paris, as in the evocation of the Pension Vauquer at the opening of *Old Goriot*.

In America as abroad, new conditions of life produced new forms of experience. The pressure of urban crowds and the split between home and work both helped to establish a heightened sense of personal interiority and a need to define and cherish particularity. Shared, public circumstances produced a new form of privacy and offered new media through which to communicate privacy – whether privacy that one owned as a "self," in personal sketch writing, or privacy that one owned as another's, in news and fiction. Poe established a characteristic form of writing. A person defined by a great trauma confesses the event. His first-person narrative is as precise in its homely details as Defoe and yet Romantically strange in its feelings, which it coldly analyzes. This combination defines a moment in the making of the modern individual.

A comparison with Wordsworth may make this point clear. In *The Prelude,* published only in 1850 and therefore unknown to Poe, Wordsworth writes of the "spots of time" that stand as "memorials" permitting the "restoration" of "our minds" when they are "depressed." The power of these moments comes from their revelation that "The mind is lord and master – outward sense / The obedient servant of her will." One such moment for Wordsworth was in his childhood when, lost in the hills, he came upon

> A naked pool that lay beneath the hills,
> The beacon on the summit, and, more near,
> A girl who bore a pitcher on her head,
> And seemed with difficult steps to force her way
> Against the blowing wind.

This "ordinary sight" took on a power of "visionary dreariness" that the poem conveys by a differentiated verbal repetition, which, in turn, models the recurrence-with-change of the scene in his memory and later life. So, in the next lines, the "naked pool" that first had headed the scene is recombined with its different elements, the "moorland waste and naked pool" and "the naked pool and dreary crags."

"The Fall of the House of Usher" hinges on questions of self-identity and the powers of the mind for restoration, but Poe is much less hopeful than Wordsworth. Roderick Usher believes that his ancestral dwelling has developed an "atmosphere" that gives it a "terrible influence" that has long "moulded the destinies of his family." The narrator sees here only madness that "need[s] no comment"; not only does the ending of the tale, however, support Roderick's belief – the whole edifice collapsing as Madeline and Roderick die together – but the narrator has himself expressed similar beliefs in the opening paragraph. His first sight of the House fills him with "insufferable gloom," a "dreariness" that "no goading of the imagination could torture into aught of the sublime." (In German Romantic theory, the sublime derived precisely from the power of the mind over nature.) This "utter depression" allows no sense of the "visionary" in dreariness that so powerfully moved Wordsworth, for "combinations of very simple natural objects . . . have the power of thus affecting us," although we cannot analyze the reasons. Having thus taken in "the bleak walls . . . the vacant eye-like windows . . . a few rank sedges . . . a few white trunks of decayed trees," the narrator tries to assert mastery by imposing a "different arrangement of the . . . details," but when he looks in the lake, he is even more chilled by "the remodelled and inverted images of the gray sedge, and the ghastly tree-stems, and the vacant and eye-like windows." In this story the pattern of differentiated repetition shows the power of things, the consciousness of urban fragmentation against which Wordsworth was writing, but from within which Poe writes.

It makes no more sense to judge Poe's work from the standpoint of a socially and historically different sense of the self than it does to judge the organization of political and cultural life in the United States during Poe's lifetime by the standards that came to reign after the Civil War and that largely prevail in the United States now. Despite the establishment of national narrative by Cooper and Bancroft, the Union was still not wholly integrated as a nation. During the period from 1830 to 1850, sectional and local differences increased at least as much as they were overcome through the proliferation of new means of communication and transportation. Only after the Civil War could the South properly be called repressed, and only in relation to the monstrous new energies of nation building that the Secession had provoked and the Civil War had channeled. Split between his five cities, Poe shared neither in a national culture nor in the Republic of Letters; he was an engineer of sensations, his craft neither the "purest art" to which it aspired nor the "literature" against which modern readers judge it.

3

PERSONAL NARRATIVES

L OCAL NARRATIVES partake of place; personal narratives arise from and depend on displacement: Pacific voyages, overland journeys to the frontier, slaves' escapes, or even a displacement as small as Thoreau's within Concord. This displacement is physical, but it also defines the fundamental rhetorical situation of the narratives: their intelligibility and force depend on the difference between the world that the reader knows, and reads within, and the world that the narrator has experienced. Etymologically, the Latin word from which "narrative" derives is closely related to the adjective *gnarus*, "knowing." The relation of narrative to individual life-knowledge is sharper in this kind of narrative than in any of the others studied here. In the terminology of classical oratory, the "narration" was the plain and manifest setting forth of the facts of the case. Such an emphasis on plainness and focus on externals typify these narratives. They pay much less attention to the shifting nuances of personal, and especially interpersonal, feeling, than would be expected in a novel.

As reports of activity on the margins of national life, these personal narratives are more like the genre of captivity narrative stemming from Mary Rowlandson's account of her life among the Indians (1682) than they resemble the narratives of inner religious experience, which Jonathan Edwards's "personal narrative," dating from around 1740, exemplifies. For the more privileged white authors, personal narratives characteristically have the circular shape of descent and return – a touching of ground, even a humiliation before the return to the elevation of ordinary civilized life; for slave narrators, the more usual pattern is that of an ascent to freedom. A generic appeal of personal narratives in their time and since is their registration of what seems a more archaic way of life, a virtual past achieved by travel in space rather than in time, but from the perspective of a narrator who is, like the readership, part of a modern world, making contact with that "other" world and transforming it while integrating it. Personal narratives may act thereby to colonize places and kinds of experience, which are then appropriated into national narrative.

TWO YEARS BEFORE THE MAST

Published by Harper Brothers in 1840, *Two Years before the Mast: A Personal Narrative of Life at Sea,* by Richard Henry Dana, Jr., made for its publishers some ten thousand dollars (at forty-five cents a copy) in its first two years. Dana came from a distinguished family of Cambridge, Massachusetts (his father had founded the important quarterly, the *North American Review*), but there were money troubles by the time he was at Harvard, and when his studies were interrupted by eye troubles in 1834, he decided to relieve his family's financial burden by going to work. His choice to sail as a common sailor was unusual. He joined a ship that carried cowhides from California to Boston, where it helped make possible the booming Massachusetts shoe industry. Much of Dana's trip, and much of the book, involved his work on land in California, treating and loading the hides. When California became part of the United States in 1848 and a center of world attention with the 1849 Gold Rush, Dana's was one of the very few books that could give any information about it, and the book received an immense second wind of popularity. By the turn of the century Dana's narrative had become a classic of a bygone age, before steamers had replaced sailing ships. It was so widely admired for the clarity and simplicity of its prose that oculists used passages for their eye charts.

Dana wrote against the predominant literature of the sea, derived from Lord Byron and from James Fenimore Cooper's maritime romances. He asserted that there was "no romance" in the "every-day life" of sailing, but "plain, matter of fact drudgery and hardship." Yet Dana also shared a major concern of Romanticism, associated more with William Wordsworth than with Byron – the attempt to purify written language by putting it back in touch with the speech and experiences of people in simpler conditions of life. Dana sought to present "as it really is" the perspective of the "common" sailor, even if this meant using language that would be judged "coarse": for example, "To work hard, live hard, die hard, and to go to hell after all, would be hard indeed!" Equally rooted in the temporal rhythms of work, but more poetic, is another sailors' saying, "In coming home from round Cape Horn, and the Cape of Good Hope, the north star is the first land you make." Dana judged that the sailors' "hard" life exacted emotional costs: "An over-strained sense of manliness is the characteristic of seafaring men." To give "sympathy" even to a sick shipmate would seem "sisterly," and the men's relations with each other are therefore "cruel": "Whatever your feelings may be, you must make a joke of everything at sea" – especially of a close brush with death. The result makes of sea-life a "frigid routine."

This routine was in the first instance physical rather than moral or psychological. Dana devoted pages to establishing the routine of "a day's work" and emphasizing that the whole voyage is marked by the "unvarying repetition of these duties," which include not only the strenuous athletics and fine technical detail of work among the sails and the endless chores of cleaning and carpentry upkeep but also the ceaseless production out of "old junk" of the various fabrics used for innumerable functions aboard ship. Once California is reached and the new routines of work begin, Dana narrates "the whole history of a hide," from its being taken off the bullock to its being taken on to Boston. By 1840 much work was becoming increasingly specialized. The development of factory labor was much noticed. More people, however, were affected by the integration of farms into national market-patterns that encouraged farmers to raise specialized crops for sale and to buy their necessities rather than practice subsistence farming and domestic production. In this context, sailors were interesting because their work still required them to perform many different tasks. The forecastle "looked like the workshop of what a sailor is, – a Jack at all trades." Even the sailors' songs were closely integrated into the work process. When several new members join the crew, their new songs are a great "windfall," because the old ones "had got nearly worn out by six weeks' constant use," and this "timely reinforcement of songs" helped work get finished several days faster.

Its variety, and its movement to vocal rather than mechanical rhythms, made sailors' work, however strenuous, seem an image of residual fullness, but their work also partook of the newly emerging patterns of "discipline and system." Thus "three minutes and a half" were allowed for dressing in the morning, and similar precision ruled every other duty. Over history, prisons and factories have been closely linked, and, in the nineteenth century, techniques of human organization were often tried out in prisons before being generalized to the management of labor. The practice of work on board a ship carried this process to its peak: "In no state prison are the convicts more regularly set to work, and more closely watched. No conversation is allowed among the men at their duty."

The sailors are held to their rigorous routine by the ship's officers, among whom the captain is "lord paramount," source of all power. The extreme stratifications of life on board echoes the sailors' views of class divisions on shore: "Sailors call every man rich who does not work with his hands, and wears a long coat and cravat." There is no easy gradation between the more and the less well off, as in imagined American equality, but a stark division between rich and poor. The captain's authority extends to the power of administering corporal punishment without appeal, and one of the strongest sequences in Dana's book details the flogging of one hapless crew member, and then of the most respected of the sailors, who had questioned the reason for the flogging. Dana is horrified to see "a man . . . whom I had lived with and eaten with for months, and knew almost as well as a brother . . . a man – a human being, made in God's likeness – fastened up and flogged like a beast!" By asserting his human dignity, the victim had provoked the captain's determination to flog him:

> "I'm no negro slave," said Sam.
> "Then I'll make you one," said the captain. . . . "Seize him up! Make a spread eagle of him! I'll teach you all who is master aboard!"

The captain concludes by threatening all of the men, "I'll see who'll tell me he isn't a negro slave." ("Who ain't a slave?" Ishmael asks, more metaphysically, in *Moby-Dick*.) Dana went on to devote his career to maritime law, with special concern for the rights of sailors, and in 1848 he was one of the first from his social group to ally himself with the Free Soil party.

The experience of shipboard life intensely focused the meaning of life in the United States, and it did not show it in the best light. Dana's narrative demonstrates a licensed tyranny that produces frustrations in the politics of daily life that are assuaged only pseudopolitically. When shore leave is finally granted him, Dana will "never forget the delightful sensation . . . of being once more in my life, though only for a day, my own master." Despite his patriotic upbringing, only at this moment "for the first time, I may truly say, in my whole life" did Dana feel "the meaning of a term which I had often heard – the sweets of liberty." He and a shipmate on leave discuss "the times past, when we were free and in midst of friends, in America, and of the prospect of our return." Yet the book registers no consciousness that it is the laws of the United States that empower the captain and permit slavery. "America" stands as the alternative to the lack of liberty that it in fact legitimates. What most recalls to Dana his lost America is the chance to read a copy of the *Boston Daily Advertiser:* "Nothing carries you so entirely to a place, and makes you feel so perfectly at home, as a newspaper." Such a passage at once makes the mundanity of home dearer to all who read it and defuses completely the sense that any changes are needed there.

Dana himself shared the work ethic that subjected the sailors to their regretted toughness. From his first impression through to the end of the book, he reiterates the judgment that "there are no people to whom the newly-invented Yankee word of 'loafer' [this is the earliest *Oxford English Dictionary* citation] is more applicable than to the Spanish Americans." Of California, he speculates, "In the hands of an enterprising people, what a country this might be!" Yet he also fears that the Spanish cultural model will ruin even the children of "Americans (as those from the United States are called) and Englishmen" who might be born there. Dana himself remained the "son of a gentleman," one of the "rich," and recognized that to the sailors he could never seem entirely "one of them."

This ambiguity in Dana's social position affects some of the most significant moments in the shaping of his book. In thinking about a lost opportunity to find out the life story of a suddenly departed shipmate, Dana reflects,

We must come down from our heights, and leave our straight paths, for the byways and low places of life, if we would learn truths by strong contrasts; and in hovels, forecastles, and among our own outcasts in foreign lands, see what has been wrought upon our fellow-creatures by accident, hardship, or vice.

This movement of descent, a chastening humiliation, resonated powerfully with American democratic ideals, and yet it rests only upon an improved power to "see." There is no hint offered of more intimate involvement, of actual solidarity. In this respect, Dana does not prove a clear alternative to the overview offered in British novels of social exploration by Charles Dickens. Dickens called for the imaginative power to rise above the city and "take the house-tops off," to reveal to his readers the unknown vice and poverty they live amidst. He believed that the knowledge gained from this vision would lead people to "apply themselves, like creatures of one common origin . . . tending to one common end, to make the world a better place!" Dana has actually been among the sailors; nonetheless, Dickens offers the more activist stance in his writing.

A less programmatic passage in Dana acknowledges the distance that might be needed for seeing, or understanding, a large whole and, at the same time, acknowledges that even being there with a common sailor does not mean that a gentleman sees things the same way. The passage begins in the mode of anti-Romantic deflation: "Notwithstanding all that has been said about the beauty of a ship under full sail, there are very few who have ever seen a ship, literally, under all her sail." For those who see a ship only near shore, "a ship coming in or going out of port, with her ordinary sails, and perhaps two or three studding-sails, is commonly said to be under full sail." Only far from shore, however, does a ship ever have up all her sail, "when she has a light, steady breeze, very nearly, but not quite dead aft, and so regular that it can be trusted." Then indeed, "she is the most glorious moving object in the world." Even among sailors, however, this sight is rare: "Such a sight, very few . . . have ever beheld." The reason for this apparent paradox is that "from the deck of your own vessel you cannot see her, as you would a separate object." But one night, on duty "out to the end of the flying jib-boom," upon turning around Dana realized that he was distant enough to "look at the ship, as at a separate vessel" and see "a pyramid of canvass, spreading far out beyond the hull, and towering up almost, as it seemed in the indistinct night air, to the clouds." The perfectly quiet sea and steady breeze filled the sails so continuously that "if these sails had been sculptured marble, they could not have been more motionless."

All through his rapt contemplation of this spectacle, Dana has forgotten that there was another man out with him — a "rough old man-of-war's man" — who has also been looking. Dana closes the scene with the words of his fellow sailor, which are poetic enough to dignify him and yet different enough from Dana's to mark their divergent perspectives, the gentleman's aesthetic contemplation against the laborer's assessment: "How quietly they do their work!"

NARRATIVE OF FREDERICK DOUGLASS

Dana's earnest exposure of the brutalities of maritime labor was read nostalgically within a few decades of its writing: sailing ships and Spanish California were irrevocably distanced by the mechanization of seafaring and the Americanization of California. No less strange has been the history of the *Narrative of the Life of Frederick Douglass, an American Slave, Written by Himself.* When it originally appeared in Boston under the imprint of the Anti-Slavery Office (1845), the narrative made a powerful impact, fostered by the reputation Douglass had achieved as an abolitionist speaker. Within five years, it had sold over thirty thousand copies. When Douglass revised and expanded his life story in *My Bondage and My Freedom* (1855) (see Chapter 5), the introduction by James McCune Smith hailed Douglass as "a Representative American man — a type of his countrymen." During the Civil War, Douglass advised President Lincoln, and he held many prominent public positions before writing *Life and Times of Frederick Douglass* (final version, 1892). Yet in the first *Cambridge History of American Literature* (1917), Douglass merits one half of one line, and in the *Literary History of the United States* (1948) he is not mentioned at all. Since the Civil Rights movement of the 1960s, Douglass has regained a place in American consciousness, and the *Narrative* in particular has become more widely read than it was even in its first days of currency.

Douglass's work and career, like those of his fellow escaped slaves and abolition workers, pose deep questions about the meaning of "America" for freedom and equality. Solomon Northrup, a free black of upstate New York, was kidnapped, drugged, and spent *Twelve Years a Slave* (1853). From the slave quarters where he was sold in Washington D.C., he caught his first glimpse of the Capitol. The *Narrative* (1847) of William Wells Brown emphasized the irony of terrified slaves fleeing the United States, the "land of whips, chains, and Bibles," in order to reach, in the words of one slave song,

"Victoria's Domain," British Canada, where they would be free and safe from seizure and extradition. The same North Star that meant America and home to Dana's mariners was the beacon leading out of America for the slaves, and it gave a title to Douglass's abolition newspaper, published from Rochester, New York, after his freedom had been bought, and he was no longer vulnerable to capture and reenslavement. The searing experience of witnessing a whipping – for Dana the climax of his voyage out, marking the farthest point of his removal from the freedoms enjoyed by a white American – was for Douglass the "blood-stained gate" through which he entered the "hell of slavery." The first knowledge of the world Douglass recalls is the screaming of his aunt while she was flogged.

Douglass's *Narrative* now figures as a culturally valued work of writing, but it stands at some distance from what usually counts as "literature." For even so marginal a literary genre as autobiography, it has seemed aberrant, because Douglass's most valued experiences were not those of the self, as would be expected in autobiography, but rather were moments of social solidarity. When he was about sixteen, Douglass secretly ran a Sunday school in which he taught fellow slaves how to read:

I look back to those Sundays with an amount of pleasure not to be expressed. They were great days to my soul. The work of instructing my dear fellow-slaves was the sweetest engagement with which I ever was blessed. We loved each other. . . . Every moment they spent in that school, they were liable to be taken up and given thirty-nine lashes. They came because they wished to learn. . . . I taught them, because it was the delight of my soul to be doing something that looked like bettering the condition of my race. . . . We were linked and interlinked with each other. I loved them with a love stronger than any thing I have experienced since.

Thus Douglass's strongest love – and in the *Narrative* he also mentions his marriage – arose from this collective activity of resistance. We may understand this in part because of the condition of deprivation from which he started. His individual identity was restricted by the ignorance that was part of being a slave. Like all the other slaves of his acquaintance, he had "no accurate knowledge" of his age, knowing as little of it "as horses do." The passage of a slave's life was marked by collective approximation: "planting-time, harvest-time, cherry-time." The "means of knowing" the identity of his father, widely believed to be a white man, "was withheld from me." Although he knew his mother's name, "I never saw my mother, to know her as such, more than four or five times in my life." Douglass could not "recollect of ever seeing my mother by the light of day," for she could visit him only by travelling twelve miles from the plantation where she had already put in a day's work.

Yet if Douglass was incapacitated from forming what is considered a normal individual identity, such as an autobiography recounts, and instead formed deeply meaningful group ties, he nonetheless left his fellow slaves and escaped north to freedom. It was the masters, however, who destroyed the Sunday-school community, "with sticks and stones," preferring to see their slaves spend Sundays in "boxing and drinking" rather than in learning to "read the will of God." And, later, it was Douglass's owner who brought him to Baltimore to work in the shipyards, at the risk of his life amidst racist whites rather than amidst other slaves. And every such wrenching from his community brought Douglass closer to freedom. Even so, the point of Douglass's escape deeply challenges the usual standards for "literature." Douglass refused to rest with the spiritual, but sought instead the material. It was not enough for him to be free internally; he must possess his freedom also really, physically, in the world.

In Douglass's account, "a slave was made a man" by his protracted physical resistance in a fight with the man entrusted with breaking the slave's spirit. Douglass's success in this fight marked for him "a glorious resurrection, from the tomb of slavery, to the heaven of freedom," based on the demonstration that any white man who might expect to flog Douglass "must also succeed in killing" him. This "freedom," at once existential in its wager with death and Christian in its sense of "resurrection," would be enough in any number of twentieth-century first-person narratives; nevertheless, Douglass insists on escape north. Having escaped, however, Douglass then breaches the usual contract between writer and reader by refusing to narrate his actual escape. His reason is soundly practical, but hardly literary: the same route might well be used again by others, who would be imperiled if anything about it were revealed. In *My Bondage and My Freedom,* Douglass specifically criticized fugitive slave narratives that detailed techniques of escape. Yet Douglass also violates literary expectations at a more local level. In an allegorical story, it would be no surprise to encounter an overseer who is strict named "Severe" or one named "Gore" who is famous for shooting out the brains of a stubborn slave; but historical documents show that these were the names of actual people.

The final problem that Douglass's *Narrative* poses for "literature" is in its language. Instead of a personalized shaping of experience, Douglass's language is rather conventional. In evoking the sufferings of his grandmother, whom he believes was abandoned by her owners to die in a hut, after decades in which she had served and cared for them, Douglass quotes a stanza from John Greenleaf Whittier's abolitionist verse. Rather than speak for himself, he turns to a Yankee. Or again, while serving with the slave breaker, Douglass has moments by Chesapeake Bay, where he sees sailboats moving freely, and moving toward freedom, and he contrasts their state with his own:

I would pour out my soul's complaint, in my rude way, with an apostrophe to the moving multitude of ships: — "You are loosed from your moorings, and are free; I am fast in my chains, and am a slave! . . . You are freedom's swift-winged angels, that fly round the world; I am confined in bands of iron! O that I were free! . . . Alas! betwixt me and you, the turbid waters roll.

This is self-conscious, traditional rhetoric, an avowed "apostrophe," highly antithetical and exclamatory, with time-worn epithets. In his preface to the *Narrative,* the abolitionist leader William Lloyd Garrison singled out this passage for special praise, as the book's most "thrilling," irresistible in its "sublimity": "Compressed into it is a whole Alexandrian library of thought, feeling, and sentiment." By twentieth-century American standards of litera-ture, such antiquarian bookishness no longer works, yet Garrison rightly recognized Douglass's "Alexandrian" learning. Douglass had studied the traditional forms of oratory. When he was about twelve, Douglass had "got hold of a book entitled *The Columbian Orator,*" first published in 1797 by Caleb Bingham of Massachusetts and almost as inevitable in American educa-tion as *Webster's Speller* was and McGuffey's *Eclectic Readers* later would be.

In *The Columbian Orator,* a work of republican education, Douglass found arguments against slavery and arguments, in the words of the Anglo-Irish Richard Brinsley Sheridan, for emancipation (of Catholics). Through this work, "the silver trump of freedom had roused my soul to eternal wakeful-ness." Thus, the slave writes and speaks in the language of American Fourth of July speeches. Such oratory had become conventional by this time, reinforc-ing but not directing American politics and values. Yet Douglass's work was not even in this sense literary, for it had a precise practical purpose. It meant to explain how he came to be so capable an abolitionist spokesperson — at once to authenticate his own experience as a slave and to explain why he did not talk the way a slave was expected to.

Douglass's goal, which he shared with his fellow writers of slave narra-tives, was much less to recover the language and experience of slavery than to end them. Scarcely a word of direct speech by slaves appears in his narrative; the only extended sequence of vernacular registers the chaotically competing voices of white workers calling for Douglass while he worked as an assistant in the shipyards. Early in the narrative, Douglass recalls the slaves' "wild songs," of which he quotes only a chorus, "I am going away to the Great House Farm! / O, yea! O, yea! O!" The words of the songs, he explains, "to many would seem unmeaning jargon" but to the slaves "were full of mean-ing." Douglass expresses his belief that "the mere hearing of those songs would do more to impress some minds with the horrible character of slavery, than the reading of whole volumes of philosophy on the subject could do." Yet he confesses that "I did not, when a slave, understand the deep meaning of those rude and apparently incoherent songs," for he was himself "within the circle." Even though all along the songs have the emotional power to move him to tears, only through the distance of his own freedom can he grasp their rational sense. Against any northern misconceptions, he must insist that slave songs are no evidence of contentment, any more than might be "the singing of a man cast away up on a desolate island." Nevertheless, this extended meditation on the meaning of the songs makes no attempt to put them on the page. Douglass's goal is to rescue the castaways, not immortalize the products of their exile.

In one significant respect, however, Douglass's *Narrative* is as self-consciously "literary" as any work could be, for its guiding thread is the story of how it came to be written, that is, the story of how Douglass gained the intellectual and moral power that fit him for his work as an abolitionist orator and thus made it necessary for him to explain his origins. The "new and special revelation" that guided Douglass's life dated from the moment his master instructed his mistress to stop teaching Frederick how to read, on the grounds that this knowledge could have no result except to make the slave disobedient. From this admonition, Douglass "understood what had been . . . a most perplexing difficulty – to wit, the white man's power to enslave the black man," and he determined to gain this power for himself. What he had valued as part of the "kindly aid" of his mistress, he now valued even more because of the "bitter opposition" of his master, to whom he opposed himself. Echoing the Satan of Milton's *Paradise Lost,* who declared, "Evil, be thou my good," Douglass decided that what to his master "was a great evil" would be to him "a great good."

In later learning to write, Douglass devised means of tricking his white playmates into instructing him, and finally he perfected his skills by working over the abandoned copybooks with which his young master had learned his letters. The result was that by the time he had learned to write, it was with the hand of Master Thomas (even as earlier he had learned to speak like young Master Daniel, as he explained in *Life and Times*). The role of *The Columbian Orator* has already been noted, but there is one more extraordinary function of established white culture in the making of Frederick Douglass. Born Frederick Bailey (his mother's name) in Maryland, he took as a fugitive an alias – Johnson – to help prevent his detection, but he discovered that there were so many by this name that it was confusing, so he needed a new name. This name he took at the suggestion of a friend from a book that the friend was reading, the poetic romance *The Lady of the Lake* by Walter Scott (in its Gaelic etymology, "douglas" connotes blackness). Thus Douglass's narrative tells of taking on the powers of white culture in order to oppose that culture, of learning the republican arguments of freedom in order to extend that freedom beyond the limits the United States had set for it.

The same double-sidedness marks many features of slaves' experiences as recounted in other narratives. Christianity was used hegemonically to teach slaves that God meant them to serve their masters, although it was also taken up by slaves as a tool of resistance, as in Douglass's Sunday school. The technical and bureaucratic means by which white society extended its power, thus promoting the exchanges of messages and goods on which the expansion of the slave economy depended, also provided slaves the means to escape. After years on a cotton plantation in Louisiana, Solomon Northrup finally gained writing materials and found a white man he could trust to mail a letter for him, back home to those who knew him. The national postal service did its work, and friends came South to release him. As Douglass revealed in his *Life and Times,* he himself had escaped by the recently opened railroad that linked Baltimore with Philadelphia. Its bustle and crowds let him board the train unnoticed; a borrowed sailor's documentation certified his right to travel; and the train's speed meant that before he was even expected home from his workday in the shipyards, he had already reached freedom.

THE OREGON TRAIL

Neither Richard Henry Dana's displacement from land to sea nor Frederick Douglass's displacement from south to north was the major direction of American history in the 1840s. By 1845 the "manifest destiny" of the United States to spread over the whole continent had been proclaimed by John O'Sullivan in the *Democratic Review,* and in that same year Texas was annexed to the United States. In 1846, the Mexican War began, which allowed the acquisition of almost all of what is now the southwestern United States. Likewise in 1846, its dispute with Great Britain over the Oregon Territory resolved, the United States reached its present boundary in the northwest. Meanwhile, the "Bear Flag" rebellion in California began the process that made California a state in 1850. By 1840, overland migration to the west coast had begun along the Oregon Trail; and in 1846 nearly three thousand emigrants took that route.

This context gave timeliness to a series of pieces by Francis Parkman that was published in New York's genteel *Knickerbocker Magazine* from 1847 into 1849 entitled "The Oregon Trail. Or a Summer's Journey out of Bounds. By a Bostonian." With revision and addition, the work appeared as a book from G. P. Putnam and Company in 1849: *The California and Oregon Trail: Being Sketches of Prairie and Rocky Mountain Life.* Parkman was already launched on the large project of historical writing that would run from *The Conspiracy of Pontiac* (1851) through the seven volumes of *France and England in North America* that appeared after the Civil War (see Chapter 5), yet *The Oregon Trail* is not directly a national narrative. Parkman recognized in the movement of transcontinental migration a force like the one that had "impelled" the barbarians "from the German forests," the "ancestors" of those now on the move, "to inundate Europe, and break to pieces the Roman empire." That is, he saw a modern version of the theme that had moved his great historiographic model Edward Gibbon. But this is not Parkman's topic, even as he momentarily poses a tableau in which the "slow, heavy procession" of the settlers' wagon train passes an encampment of Indians, "whom they and their descendants, in the space of a century, are to sweep from the face of the earth."

Parkman undertook his trip on the Oregon Trail as part of his historical research. Born in 1823 of a long-established and financially comfortable Boston family, Parkman became in his early teens "enamored of the woods." While studying at Harvard, he took long, arduous journeys into the wilderness that still existed in New England. These became the field trips that he carried over into upstate New York and then the Ohio Valley and Great Lakes for his chosen project. At first he planned to write the history of "the Old French War" (the Seven Years, or French and Indian, War) but soon he was aiming to go back to the beginnings of that conflict and take in the whole "history of the American forest" (by which he meant, its history from the first arrival of Europeans). Parkman was "haunted with wilderness images day and night." He determined to rely as little as possible on books and as much as possible on "personal experience" as the basis from which he would write. The goal of his western travels in 1846 was to gain an "inside view of Indian life," to study "the manners and characters of Indians in their primitive state."

Along with most of his contemporaries, Parkman believed that in studying currently existing Indian communities on the Great Plains or on the edges of the Rocky Mountains he was encountering the past, for it was the essence of primitives to be, and to remain, at an earlier stage of cultural development than that of "civilized" white Europeans and Americans. Thus, although himself located on the cutting edge of contemporary history as he encountered individuals and groups, both private and military, that played key roles in the events of 1846 and in the history of the westward expansion of the United States, Parkman preferred to devote his attention to the living past, to which he brought himself with great pains and extraordinary will. For several weeks he lived in a settlement of Oglala Sioux, and from this experience he believed that he knew "the Indian" – in particular, the forest-dwellers of the seventeenth and eighteenth centuries.

Parkman had long been fascinated by Indians, but he was frustrated by his reading on the subject, and so he "resolved to have recourse to observation." To accomplish this purpose, "it was necessary to live in the midst of them, and become, as it were, one of them." As with Dana among sailors, but to a much greater degree, Parkman shows in his book the impossibility of becoming "one of them," and yet he does not acknowledge any consequence of this failure. He does not puzzle over the tension between knowledge through observation and knowledge through the experience of living "in the midst," which Dana noted in discussing the image of a ship "under full sail," and which so disturbed Douglass as he thought about the meaning of slave songs. Having been "domesticated for several weeks among one of the wildest of the wild hordes that roam over the remote prairies," Parkman is certain that "these men were thorough savages," wholly unmodified by contact with white civilization. All that they do has come down "from immemorial time." The fruit of Parkman's hard-won experience is the same basic understanding that his culture already held. Himself a historian and engaged in historical research, Parkman is so thrilled at reaching this long-sought living archive that he does not reckon with the changes that history has worked there too. For example, the horses that are so crucial in the lives of these Sioux were introduced to the Americas by the Spaniards, and thus the way of life that Parkman observes results from the interaction of cultures, not from aboriginality.

Parkman asserts that there are almost no "points of sympathy" between the "nature" of a "civilized white man" and "that of an Indian": an "impassable gulf lies between." To the extent that the desired inward knowledge thus is not available, the Indians come to seem so "alien" that one "begins to look upon them as a troublesome and dangerous species of wild beast, and if expedient, he could shoot them with as little compunction as they themselves would experience after performing the same office upon him." (Presumably, this is one of the few "points of sympathy.") For Parkman, the act of shooting has a special relation to the movements of the mind. In an expository set piece describing the "easiest and laziest" method of killing buffalo, he describes the climax, "Quick as thought the spiteful crack of the rifle responds to his slight touch, and instantly in the bare spot appears a small red dot." As opposed to the Indians' arrows, the rifle shot is as invisible and instantaneous as thought; civilization proceeds by such spiritualization.

Parkman's narrative repeatedly charts the movement from observation to revulsion to aggression: " 'You are too ugly to live,' thought I; and aiming at the ugliest, I shot three of them in succession." This time it is buffaloes, but the language and feeling are much the same as those that he had expressed toward Indians. Moreover, so intimately linked is the life of the Plains Indians with the buffaloes that "when the buffalo are extinct, [the Indians] too must dwindle away." Buffalo bulls are so "ugly and ferocious" that "at first sight . . . every feeling of sympathy vanishes." This may shock our pieties, but every person who has "experienced it" knows "with what keen relish one inflicts his death wound, with what profound contentment of mind [one] beholds him fall." Observing an old Indian with "hard, emaciated face and gaunt ribs," Parkman thinks,

He would have made a capital shot. A rifle bullet, skilfully planted, would have brought him tumbling to the ground. Surely, I thought, there could be no more harm in shooting such a hideous old villain, to see how ugly he would look when he was dead, than in shooting the detestable vulture which he resembled.

In John Keats's "Hyperion," the dispossessed Titans speculate that it is only right that they be replaced by the Olympian gods, "for 'tis the eternal law / That first in beauty should be first in might." In Parkman this aesthetic ideology means that to call others ugly gives one rights over their lives. Yet in Parkman's narrative, even beauty is no defense. Having first mistaken an antelope for a wolf, he prepares to shoot it, and does so even after realizing his error. When he examines the kill: "The antelope turned his expiring eye upward. It was like a beautiful woman's, dark and rich. 'Fortunate that I am in a hurry,' thought I; 'I might be troubled with remorse, if I had time for it.'" This moment is characteristic of Parkman's effects. His remorse is registered but only under negation; he gives us the very words with which to specify our discomfort. Yet there is no remorse, because Parkman is absolutely confident that he can do no real wrong. Later, when he sees an antelope "like some lovely young girl" coming close to some buffaloes like "bearded pirates," which, therefore, look "uglier than ever," he draws a bead on them as if buffaloes were the killers of antelope. Any remorse has turned into aggression.

At one moment Parkman exercises greater modesty than elsewhere. Encountering an Indian "immovable as a statue, among the rocks and trees," his eyes "turned upward," Parkman surmises that he is communing with a pine tree that is "swaying to and fro in the wind . . . as if the tree had life." (Parkman's sense of his difference from the Indian is so powerful as to obscure for him the fact that trees do have life.) Parkman "long[s] to penetrate his thoughts" but recognizes that he can "do nothing more than conjecture and speculate": "Among those mountains not a wild beast was prowling, a bird singing, or a leaf fluttering, that might not tend to direct his destiny, or give warning of what was in store for him." Having reached this sense of the intensely aware participation in the world that another person, from another culture, might experience, Parkman has the "delicacy" not to disturb the Indian. As he leaves the scene, he sees a peak, which "something impelled me to climb." After a long, arduous ascent, he reaches "the very summit" and, seated "on its extreme point," looks over the prairie "stretching to the farthest horizon." Parkman's momentary, respectful self-restraint fuels an action that overgoes the Indian's contemplation. The Indian, in the midst of the scene, looks up; Parkman, from his extremity, looks down. Parkman believes that everything that the Indian sees carries meaning for him, but for Parkman himself, only the fact of the apparently endless expanse, and no particular of the scene, carries meaning.

In this overreaching, this drive for mastery, this movement from observation to revulsion to aggression, Parkman was living out the energies that were winning the West. However much he might look down on the overland emigrants and even though his social peers in Boston did not support the Mexican War, he was joining in the emigrants' expansionism and ethnic chauvinism. The knowledge Parkman gained of what Indians were really like empowered him to begin his massive history. This work rested on the claim that the Indians of North America had been doomed by the triumph of the British – committed to establishing settlements and thus to civilization – over the French, who merely exploited the products of the wilderness, while letting the Indians live. Thus, according to Parkman, the whole history of crimes against Indians by the United States need cause no remorse, for the Indians were for all practical purposes already dead long ago. From the "cannibal warfare" of little fishes, eating each other in a pool in the Rockies, Parkman had learned that although "soft-hearted philanthropists . . . may sigh long for their peaceful millennium," nonetheless, "from minnows up to men, life is an incessant battle."

NARRATIVE OF ARTHUR GORDON PYM

The encounter with savagism that motivated Parkman's journey figures climactically in Edgar Allan Poe's *Narrative of Arthur Gordon Pym of Nantucket,* published in 1838, roughly a decade earlier. For the verisimilitude of this fictional narrative, Poe drew upon the large body of writings about disaster at sea and upon reports of exploration in the South Seas (immediately before the first sections of *Pym* appeared in the *Southern Literary Messenger,* Poe wrote articles on the grand plans of J. N. Reynolds for a South Seas expedition). In presentation, *Pym* takes its form from the procedures of personal narratives like those discussed in this chapter, and it also joins a tradition of fiction that includes Daniel Defoe's *Robinson Crusoe* (1719) and Jonathan Swift's *Gulliver's*

Travels (1726). Yet Defoe, in adapting the conventions of religious narrative, helped establish conventions for creating fictional character, and Swift's increasingly complex satirical allegories obviously related to life in the England of his time. Poe's narrative neither establishes a complex interior history for its protagonist nor presents fictional worlds that offer lessons for the contemporary world of its readers. Within this particular imitation of personal narrative, Poe begins to fashion a world of his own, an imaginative space of writing to stand apart from the space of the nation.

Pym's elaborate subtitle gives some feel for its contents:

Comprising the details of a mutiny and atrocious butchery on board the American brig *Grampus,* on her way to the South Seas, in the month of June, 1827[;] with an account of the recapture of the vessel by the survivers; their shipwreck and subsequent horrible sufferings from famine; their deliverance by means of the British schooner *Jane Guy;* the brief cruise of this latter vessel in the Antarctic Ocean; her capture and the massacre of her crew among a group of islands in the *EIGHTY-FOURTH PARALLEL OF SOUTHERN LATITUDE; together with the incredible adventures and discoveries* STILL FARTHER SOUTH to which that distressing calamity gave rise.

And there is much more than this: Pym's delirium and near-starvation while he is hidden in a chest within a ship's hold; his nearly being eaten alive by his own maddened Labrador dog; cannibalism among the famine-struck "survivers"; and life among black "savages," whose "apparent kindness" concealed for a time their "most barbarous, subtle, and bloodthirsty" nature.

The reader is propelled with Pym from one catastrophe to the next, but there is neither any rationalized speaker to figure as a fictional character in the usual sense nor any organized plot. In the earlier pages of the work, Pym refers to events that fall between those being narrated and the later time of writing, but by the book's end, nothing has come of these hints. They even prove misleading, suggesting, for instance, that Pym and his initial companion – who dies of starvation halfway through the story – discussed the narrated events years later. Pym himself as good as dies in the opening pages of the book. A high-spirited boat trip turns into a nightmare after Pym's little vessel is run over in the stormy night by a much larger ship. According to accounts of the ship's crew, "The body of a man was seen to be affixed" to the ship's bottom and was finally rescued, "although life seemed to be totally extinct." Pym explains, "The body proved to be my own," which had been "fastened" to the bottom of the ship by a protruding bolt that "made its way through the back part of my neck, forcing itself out between two sinews and just below the right ear."

Returned to life, Pym thrills to visions "of shipwreck and famine; of death or captivity among barbarian hordes," and he acknowledges that such "visions" actually "amounted to desires." If the narrative thus functions as wish fulfillment, responsibility for those wishes has been displaced from Poe to his protagonist. From this situational basis, however, no further interrelation is established between character and action; the episodes that follow present a disconnected array of dreadful sensations, of "anticipative horror," like the "longing to fall" that overwhelms Pym while he is trying to descend a cliff. Like Poe's briefer local narratives (discussed in Chapter 2) *Pym* may register the shock of city experience, and it projects that shock from its metropolitan origin onto the far-flung oceanic periphery upon which urban economic growth depends.

As the narrative ends, Pym and a companion, having escaped from the savages, float southward in a canoe amidst the increasingly warm and milky waters of the Antarctic Ocean, until finally they

rushed into the embraces of the cataract, where a chasm threw itself open to receive us. But there arose in our pathway a shrouded human figure, very far larger in its proportions than any dweller among men. And the hue of the skin of the figure was of the perfect whiteness of the snow.

This cliff-hanging conclusion is justified by a final note, explaining that Pym had died before he finished writing. Thus the completion of his life substitutes for the completion of his narrative. This fractured and truncated form partakes of what Aristotle would have judged the randomness of biography rather than the shaping of plot, and it stands as rhetorical evidence that the account is truth rather than fiction. Pym's companion may supposedly be found in Illinois.

This concluding note resumes the concerns of the preface, in which the book represents itself as an exercise in the rhetoric of verisimilitude. The preface begins with Pym's fear that he cannot write effectively enough to give his narrative "the *appearance* of that truth it would really possess." Pym's imperfect memory combined with the "marvellous" character of the events; the result made his narrative seem "merely an impudent and ingenious fiction." Pym explains that "Mr. Poe," then of the *Southern Literary Messenger,* encouraged him to trust to the "shrewdness and common sense of the public," for any "uncouthness" in the narrative would only enhance its credibility. Pym, however, still swayed by "distrust in my own abilities as a writer," does not act until Poe offers to present the narrative in his journal "*under the garb of fiction.*" This extraordinary twist accounts for the appearance of the first chapters of Pym's narrative as Poe's "pretended fiction," and Pym professes himself sufficiently heartened by readers' responses to conclude that "the facts of my narrative would prove of such a nature as to carry with them sufficient evidence of their own authenticity." Finally he can offer them to the public himself, and as the truth that they are.

The preface and final note, which frame the book, suggest that its narrative may be interpreted in relation to conditions of writing as well as to the social or political conditions of American life. The journey southward that leads to a fantastic interplay of white and black, not only in human conflict but also in the very fauna and landscape, may have as much to do with black ink and white pages as with slavery or ethnology. When Poe claimed that "terror is not of Germany, but of the soul," he defined his intricate, "arabesque" works as effectively structured stimulants. Through the chaotic sequence of sensations in *Pym,* Poe manipulates the form of personal narrative to produce feelings rather than to communicate experience. Despite its emphatic claim to truth, the book's character as a fictional production was clear to its reviewers. Nonetheless, through the 1840s, Harper and Brothers still advertised the Pym narrative among its works of travel. So important did the claim to truth remain as a criterion for personal narrative, that when in 1845 Harper was offered a sailor's narrative of four months among the cannibals of the Marquesas Islands, an editorial "council" decided that "it was impossible that it could be true and therefore was without real value" and so rejected the manuscript for *Typee.*

HERMAN MELVILLE

Although suspicious that this sailor's manuscript by Herman Melville was the work of a "practised writer," John Murray of London nonetheless published in his nonfictional Home and Colonial Library series the *Narrative of a Four Months' Residence among the Natives of a Valley of the Marquesas Islands; or, A Peep at Polynesian Life.* Then, with the endorsement of Washington Irving, it was picked up by Wiley and Putnam in New York for their Library of American Books series and published in 1846 under its author's preferred title, *Typee* (with the Murray subtitle). Poe could only claim an authenticating companion for Pym's narrative, but Melville's companion, known as "Toby," actually came to light to vouch for the book after reading about it, and Toby's narrative appeared as a supplement to the book's second edition. Even with this good luck, however, and even with the example of Dana, invoked by several of the first reviewers, it remained especially hard for English readers to credit that *Typee* was really written by a "poor outcast working seaman," rather than by an "educated literary man."

The opening chapter of *Typee,* the pages by which Herman Melville first became known to the reading public, immediately show an impressive power in evoking "Six months at sea!" There is no fresh food, salt water around is matched by salt fare aboard. Ordinary, middle-class "state-room sailors" complain even of a brief transatlantic voyage. Melville's more extreme experience contrasts the privileged leisure of tourists to sailors' exploited labor. The book takes its stand on the democratic, and the extraordinary, side. Against the sensory deprivation of maritime routine rise "strange visions," conjured by the very name of the Marquesas: "Naked houris – cannibal banquets – groves of cocoa-nut – coral reefs – tatooed chiefs – . . . *heathenish rites and human sacrifices.*" These purely conventional images come to life through the play of assonance and rhythm. Each phrase begins with a stressed syllable, and the sequence of items without conjunctions enforces a higher level of stress than is usual in prose, yet without the metronomic regularity that would sound merely like poetry. Likewise, the rhyme of "reefs" and "chiefs" prepares for the more distant echo between "rites" and "sacrifices."

Melville's evocation introduces expository background about the islands; the chapter ends with a vivid personal anecdote, drawn from a second Marquesan visit several years later. France had taken possession of the islands, and the French navy was presenting the king and queen of the islands to an American commodore. The queen was fascinated by the tattooing of an old seaman, much to the embarrassment of her French sponsors, and

all at once the royal lady, eager to display the hieroglyphics on her own sweet form, bent forward for a moment, and turning sharply round, threw up the skirts of her mantle, and revealed a sight from which the aghast Frenchmen retreated precipitately, and tumbling into their boat, fled the scene of so shocking a catastrophe.

Like much satire, the passage risks racism and misogyny in order to attack those in power. The Shakespearean wordplay, by which the emphasized second syllable of "catastrophe" signals an unmentionable physical part, shows the "freedom" that reviewers always found, for better or worse, in Melville's work, and the anecdote takes a further freedom in stripping from French imperialism its pretensions to a civilizing mission.

From its very beginning, *Typee* stood as an impressively, and suspiciously, powerful piece of writing; yet it was true enough. Herman Melville had actually lived among the Typee. He had arrived among them in just the way the book describes: he jumped ship with a companion, and they made their way through the surprisingly difficult island terrain until they reached the wrong valley, for the Typee were believed to be fierce cannibals, unlike the Happars, who dwelt in the neighboring valley. Melville's sojourn lasted only four weeks, rather than the four months he claimed, and he required the aid of other books of travel and exploration to supplement his memories, but the force of this personal narrative rests on experience. The high cultural skills shown by a sailor, so unsettling to some readers, have a simple explanation: the notorious social mobility of the nineteenth century allowed Americans to fall in life as well as to rise.

Melville was born in 1819 into great financial comfort, with parents whose fathers were both revolutionary heroes. At first the family lived in New York, away from his father's Boston family; in 1830, when the father's business began to fail, they moved to Albany, his mother's base, and in 1832 the family's ruin was sealed by Melville's father's death. For the next dozen years, Melville was adrift, working as a clerk, a farmer, and a teacher before his first experiment as a sailor, a trip to Liverpool in 1839. After an unsuccessful search for work in the Mississippi Valley in 1840, he sailed with the whaler *Acushnet* from New Bedford, Massachusetts, in 1841. This was the ship he abandoned in the Marquesas. After escaping from the Typee, he signed on with an Australian whaler, which he soon left in Tahiti under nearly mutinous circumstances. Another American whaler brought him to Hawaii, and after several months of various jobs there, he returned home as a sailor on an American naval vessel, the *United States*.

Almost at once upon his return, Melville began writing up the stories of his travels, stories with which he had fascinated his family, and the success of *Typee* encouraged a sequel. *Omoo: A Narrative of Adventures in the South Seas*, centers on Melville's time in Tahiti (expanding two weeks into two months). *Omoo* (a Polynesian word for "wanderer") confirmed the reputation won by the author with *Typee*. Melville was again praised for his vigorous, skillful narrative, and his social standing still seemed anomalous. One British journal found "Herman Melville" obviously like "the harmonious and carefully selected appellation of an imaginary hero of romance." Moreover, aspects of Melville's work provoked not just social suspicion, but moral disapproval. Already in *Typee*, Melville's commentary on missionaries caused so much discomfort that he removed nearly thirty pages from the second American edition, and even so, he had to change publishers for *Omoo*, this time successfully persuading Harpers.

An evangelical, abolitionist journal had complained of *Typee* that it was written "not for Americans," but for the London circles familiar with "theaters, opera-dancers, and voluptuous prints," and a reviewer of *Omoo* found himself driven in "recoil" from the book's "reckless spirit," its "cool, sneering wit," and "perfect want of *heart*." These exaggerated responses register that *Omoo* is more comic than earnest (it portrays vagabondage rather than a movement to settle down) but, above all, they show that Melville continued to offend the interests of missionary piety. In recounting the dreadful depopulation of Tahiti through the transmission of European diseases, Melville quotes the cry of the islanders to the missionaries, "Lies, lies! you tell us of salvation; and, behold, we are dying. We want no other salvation than to live in this world."

What a reviewer called *Typee*'s "paradisiacal barbarism" powerfully suggests, in the form of credible personal experience, that there might actually exist in the South Seas a heaven on earth. Unlike Parkman and Dana, but like Douglass, Melville drew on his time outside what was considered the normal life of the United States in order to challenge the values of that life. Yet Melville could not fully commit himself to this position, and therefore *Typee* is at once fascinating and incoherent. Despite its biographical basis, no more than in *Pym* can a narrative identity be firmly defined for Melville's pseudonymous "Tommo." The large narrative cycle of entry into and exit from the valley of the Typee contains not only smaller cycles of daily rhythms but also an oscillation of feelings — from bliss to revulsion — that seems governed by no law beyond that of change.

In *Typee,* drawing on his life in the South Seas as well as on his reading, Melville works through a series of commonplaces, each of which becomes vivid through rhetorical elaboration. Melville's distrust of what may lie "beneath the . . . fair appearances" of native hospitality is no different from Pym's concern with the horrors beneath the "apparent kindness" of the "savages." Melville's experience is at every moment qualified by the sense that he is among "after all, nothing better than a set of cannibals," just as Parkman diminishes an "Apollo"-like Sioux brave with the reflection, "after all, he was but an Indian." Yet Melville can also reflect that the term "savage" is improperly applied to the islanders, when one considers the "civilized barbarity" of western culture — which reveals "white civilized man as the most ferocious animal on the face of the earth" — without adding the approval that Parkman's survivalist ethic would dictate. Among the Typee, Melville observed, and to some degree himself enjoyed, not only a negative freedom from all the "thousand sources of irritation that the ingenuity of civilized man has created to mar his own felicity" but also a positive "happiness" arising from an "all-pervading sensation" described by Jean-Jacques Rousseau as "the mere buoyant sense of a healthful physical existence."

As his reference to Rousseau suggests, Melville most powerfully responded to elements of Typee life that matched subordinated or repressed elements within his own culture. His most acute registration of real difference comes in his description of the Typee way of making fire, a lengthy and exhausting, almost orgasmic, process that is in contrast to both the ascetic sobriety of the Romans, who preserved a sacred flame with the Vestal virgins, and the casual comfort of modern America, where a match can be struck in an instant. This contrast suggests relations among temporality, sexuality, and economics that set Typee apart from Western models of simplicity and complexity alike. Yet despite his criticisms and explorations, Melville bears the marks of his culture so deeply that he chooses to return, making an escape from the Typee against considerable resistance. He explains his wish to escape by invoking his fears of either of two fates: tattooing or cannibalism. These clichés of Polynesia represent alternative forms of total incorporation into an alien way of life, necessitating that his body be worked over either by human teeth or by the shark teeth used as tattooing needles. At one point, the narrative explains that even if cannibalism does exist among the Typee – as it does also among the supposedly more civilized Happar – it is not the indiscriminate eating of humans but a part of a very specific ritual. Yet Tommo's departure is shadowed by his increasing anxiety lest he be eaten. Likewise, his reflections show the innumerable ways in which American life disfigures those who live it, and yet, for no reason that is rationally explained, he dreads tattooing as irremediably separating him from his life back home. The American sailor whose tattoos provoked the rivalry of the Typee queen is forgotten.

After *Omoo,* Melville married and settled in Manhattan as a professional author. His next book, *Mardi* (1849; to be discussed in Chapter 4), went further than Poe's *Pym* in trying to stake a claim beyond that of personal experience, but its disastrous reception brought his work back to this safer narrative form. In five months of 1849, Melville wrote both *Redburn: His First Voyage* and *White-Jacket; or, The World in a Man-of-War. Redburn* approaches the socially and personally explosive materials of Melville's own adolescence, the family's financial fall and the author's consequent sea voyage to Liverpool. It does so, however, in a more overtly fictionalized form than does either *Typee* or *Omoo,* even though *Redburn's* subtitle, "Being the Sailor-Boy Confessions and Reminiscences of the Son-of-a-Gentleman, in the Merchant Service," works to neutralize the problems of credibility provoked by those earlier works.

By locating the book's experiences in a "boy" several crucial years younger than he himself had been, Melville gains both intensity and distance, for, by convention, youthful perception and feeling are more acute and less reliable than those of adults. No matter how powerful, then, they need not be fully credited. Melville asserts this distance through the use of formal, third-person chapter titles, which show the control of the narrative persona (an older Redburn) over the youthful protagonist (e.g., the first chapter, "How Wellingborough Redburn's Taste for the Sea Was Born and Bred in Him"). The boy's perspective at once suggests, selects, and controls the topics that can emerge. The effect is not so complex as that of Dickens's *Great Expectations* (1861) or even of his *David Copperfield* (1848–50), but it does make possible Melville's first direct approach to the materials of contemporary American life, especially poverty and social conflict.

Even before he gets to sea, Redburn appears as a social victim, who is aggressive against those more fortunate or less sensitive than himself. Traveling down the Hudson from his family home to New York City, Redburn feels marked by the "scent and savor of poverty." He is excluded from the other passengers' sociability, and when he discovers that the fare has been raised so that he lacks the funds, he makes a surly scene, which leaves "every eye fastened" upon him. Staring back proves insufficient retaliation, and finally he levels his gun at one "gazer"; after this action has provoked a stir, Redburn spends the rest of the trip cold and wet on the deck in the rain. The chapter concludes, "Such is boyhood." This deflation does not put the problem to rest. In New York, Redburn's poverty marks him like Cain: while waiting to board a ship, he rests in "a mean liquor shop"; lacking the right clothes and "not looking very gentlemanly," he feared that from "any better place," he would be "driven out."

This social animus allows Melville to bring to life on shipboard the problem that Dana for himself had defined only as his not being "one of them." The insistent hard manliness of sailors that Dana described means that no special concern is shown for a young newcomer, and Redburn, because he is also a "gentleman with white hands," becomes a special butt. Yet he is no innocent victim either, for his own priggish condescension to the other sailors provokes them. He believes he feels "compassion" for their "sad conditions as amiable outcasts," deep in "ignorance" and lacking "proper views of religion," but when he tries to share his proper views, the sailors turn against him with abusive laughter. The chapter's ending again acts to control and to defuse the situation: "my being so angry prevented me from feeling foolish, which is very lucky for people in a passion." The anger is not denied, but it is placed as youthful folly rather than explored as part of a constellation in which habit, expectation, and upbringing had distanced Redburn from the social role that his economic condition requires him to fill. This distance leads Redburn to feel himself an "Ishmael," "without a single friend or companion." A fearful "hatred . . . against the whole crew" is growing up in him.

Redburn's complicated and bitter social comedy culminates with a chapter in which Redburn "contemplates making a social call on the captain in his cabin." The chapter strikes a norm of democratic sociability against which the captain, Redburn, and the crew are all found wanting. The sailors mock Redburn as they see him doing his best to put together a decently clean outfit for his proposed visit. Discovering that his hands are stained yellow from a morning's work tarring, and lacking the kid gloves dictated by social decorum, Redburn "slipped on a pair of woolen mittens" knit by his mother. To the reader too, Redburn looks quite a clown. Obstructed by the mate from making his call, Redburn tries the next day to address the captain, who flies into a rage against him. This provokes a series of reflections by Redburn that conclude, "Yes, Captain Riga, thought I, you are no gentleman, and you know it!" For Redburn can imagine no reason, whatever the customs of rank at sea, for a captain to be so intemperate in response to a sailor's attempt at civility, however ignorant and misguided. Resentment and justice could hardly be more perfectly mixed. This painful episode of greenhorn humor was the only excerpt from Melville's works included in the massive *Cyclopedia of American Literature* (1855), compiled by George and Evert Duyckinck, who had in the late 1840s been among Melville's closest associates.

Redburn is beset by high and low alike for his violations of the ship's social code, but he is not himself even a quixotic version of the golden mean between high and low. He snobbishly trusts that the captain "could not fail to appreciate the difference between me and the rude sailors among whom I was thrown." If he disavows solidarity with the crew, why should the captain avow fraternity with him? Yet to judge these transactions requires that readers learn to stand apart from the positions of all the characters represented in the book. That is, in training readers to make democratic judgments, the book exercises a troubling exclusiveness.

Redburn's shipboard experience of social displacement unsettling social norms is reenacted when he lands: his father's guidebook proves useless for finding his way around Liverpool. This old English city has been so transformed that it is effectively no older than New York. In England, Redburn encounters poverty and misery far more desperate than his own, and the book's mode shifts to emphasize other characters more prominently than Redburn himself. Redburn meets the improbably handsome Harry Bolton, who has lost his money gambling and is going to sea. In a glamorized style that reviewers found "melodramatic," Harry echoes Redburn's own condition, and Melville further hints at this link by Harry's choice to go whaling after landing with Redburn in New York. This good angel is set against the "diabolic" sailor Jackson, whose wasting disease makes him look "seamed and blasted by lightning," a premonition of Ahab. Their deaths are the major interests of the book's ending, leaving Redburn alone in a world that has been shorn of its extremes.

The relatively limited focus of *Redburn* opens up to an astonishingly ambitious scope in *White-Jacket,* subtitled "The World in a Man-of-War." Its most obvious relation is to Dana's narrative, and in fact Dana, who had become an acquaintance through his family's connection with that of Melville's wife, had helped encourage Melville to work up his naval experiences. The book is powerfully disciplined in restricting itself to life aboard ship; even when the ship is in harbor, any time on shore is rigorously excluded. Thus in Melville's book the life on board functions quite differently from the way it does in Dana. In Dana life before the mast is contrasted to the shore life of a free American, but in Melville the emphasis is on their similarities — at times allegorically precise, at others symbolically suggestive. Yet in fictionalizing his own service aboard the *United States* – and entrusting the narrative to a semifictional sailor known by his strange white jacket – Melville changes the name of the ship itself to the *Neversink* and thereby further generalizes his procedure.

It is emphatically not the United States that is being microcosmically represented by the ship and its life, but the "world." Thus American values can still offer a new world that opposes the way of the world aboard the ship. The "world" of the *Neversink,* moreover, is that of men without women, of men at work; this world utterly excludes the domestic life of home relations and feminine values, as if that sphere were wholly otherworldly. These alternative values appear almost uniquely in a moment that also echoes Dana, but with a difference: "To be efficacious, Virtue must come down from aloft, even as our blessed Redeemer came down to redeem our whole man-of-war world; to that end, mixing with its sailors and sinners as equals." Against the distanced knowledge of "seeing" that Dana sought, the goal here is a full "mixing," which carries with it the pain of intimacy and even possibly death.

As opposed to such a humanistic hope, however, the world of *White-Jacket* is strenuously modern. The *Neversink* is not a knowable community, but an endlessly subdivided society. The men who work among the "water-tanks, casks, and cables" in the hold below decks are scarcely ever seen, and "after a three years' voyage . . . still remain a stranger to you." Living on board ship "is like living in a market," in its lack of privacy and constant crowding. At the rare moments of leisure, when sailors can walk freely on deck, the effect is like that of promenaders "on Broadway." And like a large city, the ship has street crime; when a *"gang"* learns that a shipmate has three or four gold pieces in a bag hidden under his shirt, they will lie in wait for him, knock him down, and carry off the cash. The result is a perverse primitive communism, as a constant series of robberies establishes a rough equality of poverty among all the sailors.

The ship is thus highly disordered, but it is no less highly ordered. In its regimentation, it is "like life in a large manufactory": "the bell strikes to dinner, and hungry or not, you must dine." The figure of speech by which a worker's hands are made to stand for his whole person, so familiar in the dehumanizing industrial discourse of the nineteenth century, had already in the seventeenth century begun to dominate the way in which sailors were spoken of, and to. Unlike the specialization of a factory worker, each sailor has so many different functions to perform, under various circumstances both regular and extraordinary, that the routines can only be known by numbers: "White-Jacket was given the *number of his mess;* then, his *ship's number,* or the number to which he must answer when the watch-roll is called; then the number of his hammock; then, the number of the gun to which he was assigned." These numbers must be memorized by a sailor immediately upon his coming on board, and severe penalties follow if they should be forgotten. The minute, arithmetical detail that organizes the man-of-war annihilates all previous maritime experience a sailor may have accumulated: "Well-nigh useless to him now, all previous circumnavigations of this terraqueous globe . . . his gales off Beachy Head, or his dismastings off Hatteras. He must begin anew; he knows nothing; Greek and Hebrew could not help him, for the language he must learn has neither grammar nor lexicon," but only a disconnected sequence of numerals.

The modern social arrangements of this world contrast with its archaic politics. Life on board is a "despotism," extending from the captain down through his chain of command: "The captain's word is law; he never speaks but in the imperative mood." He is even "lord and master of the sun," for when the functionary responsible for the solar observation at noon has done his work, it is reported to the captain, who orders, "*Make* it so." Only then is the bell struck, "and twelve o'clock it is." Against this system, Melville invokes "the common dignity of manhood," which the sailors possess despite all their other failings. The common seamen are known to the officers as "*the people*," and the democratic political suggestions of this term are important to Melville's overall shaping of the book.

The officers exercise such total control that they can even order carnival. When the ship is becalmed in frigid weather off Cape Horn and it is necessary to stir the men's blood, the order comes down, "*all hands skylark!*" At once there erupts "a Babel here, a Bedlam there, and a Pandemonium everywhere." This scene from Breughel, however, soon produces ugly consequences; a fight breaks out, and its instigator is flogged the next day, while the officers look on with imperial impassivity. As Melville observes of a similar incident later, "Of all insults, the temporary condescension of a master to a slave is the most outrageous and galling." Like masters and slaves, the people and their officers form two "essentially antagonist classes," with wholly different interests. The officers' glory, pay, and promotion may depend on the "slaughtering of their fellow-men," and they can rise only "over the buried heads of killed comrades and mess-mates." Yet the officer class is "immeasurably the stronger" and enforces its will; therefore, "tyranny" must prevail as the political norm.

In some respects, Melville's portraits of modern society and archaic governance run in parallel in *White-Jacket*, but they are sharply connected in his consideration of flogging, an even more essential feature of shipboard discipline in the military than in the merchant service in Dana's book. In a little over a year on the *United States*, Melville was required to witness the flogging of some one hundred and sixty-three of his shipmates, about one-third of the crew. In questioning the justice of flogging, Melville recalls St. Paul's claim of privilege as a Roman citizen. Eighteen hundred years later, Melville asks, "Is it lawful for you, my countrymen, to scourge a man that is an American?" Even if on the ships of some nations flogging may "conform to the spirit of the political institutions of the country," America is different, and, therefore, its navy should not "convert into slaves" any of its citizens. In the current state of affairs, for an American sailor "our Revolution was in vain; to him our Declaration of Independence is a lie."

One of Frederick Douglass's most famous speeches, entitled "What to the Slave is the Fourth of July?" (1852), explored a similar contradiction. Douglass charged that the Fourth of July "reveals to [the slave], more than all other days of the year, the gross injustice and cruelty to which he is the constant victim." And Douglass added that the appropriate rhetorical decorum for dealing with such facts was not "argument," but "scorching irony." Thus Melville, in seeking his different goal of "abolition," notes the fact that naval laws and customs combine to assure that officers "are exempted from a law" that terrorizes the people; officers are never punished for the sort of minor violations that lead to sailors being flogged. He then asks, "What would landsmen think, were the State of New York to pass a law against some offence, affixing a fine as a penalty, and then add to that law a section restricting its penal operation to mechanics and day laborers, exempting all gentlemen with an income of one thousand dollars?" The political inequality on board ship is brought back home to the social inequalities of the modern city. Melville's ironic question first provokes outrage at the contrast of sea to land: in New York the laws make no allowance for social rank. But then the question provokes a second thought: on land economic inequality does affect one's relation to the law. (The law impartially forbids rich and poor alike to spend the night on park benches, but only the poor are likely to do so.)

Melville's main argument against flogging relies on the American political rhetoric of equal rights. Such rhetoric is not merely a past heritage for White-Jacket; it is also a future force for change. Even if flogging has always been considered necessary, it must be so no longer: "The world has arrived at a period which renders it the part of Wisdom to pay homage to the prospective precedents of the Future in preference to those of the Past. . . . The Past is the text-book of tyrants; the Future the Bible of the Free." Even while calling on America to march in the "advance-guard" of nations, freed from the "lumbering baggage-wagons of old precedents," Melville invokes as precedent the biblical Exodus that had inspired so much Puritan rhetoric and been refashioned as a model for the nation by George Bancroft: "we Americans are the peculiar chosen people – the Israel of our time; we bear the ark of the liberties of the world." Therefore, because "the political Messiah . . . has come in *us*," American "national selfishness is unbounded philanthropy . . . to the world."

This panegyric echoes the political rhetoric of manifest destiny that had justified the Mexican War, which had ended only the year before, and it resonates as well with the claims of American literary nationalism that were prevalent in the Duyckincks' circle in New York, which Melville frequented. Moreover, it precedes the debates that led to the Compromise of 1850. These debates strove to cool the apocalyptic strain of American national self-conception on the grounds that such liberationist rhetoric threatened the Union, which was resanctified as a stabilizing rather than a transformative power. As a result, the compromise sickened many Americans who loved the values of freedom and loathed the Fugitive Slave Law, which subordinated freedom to national unity. The fervors of White-Jacket are themselves nonviolent. They serve a rhetorical strategy that aims to persuade America to overcome a national flaw – the arbitrary flogging of free men – and their author makes clear his contempt for martial glory. Melville makes the language employed by the bloody jingoist War Hawks against Mexico work instead in the cause of a modest, liberal reform. The problem is to decide whether such a strategy does more for the good cause, or for a morally dubious nationalism.

Melville's treatment of flogging does not depend wholly on such rhetorical utopianism, for the book's climax comes in a powerful moment of fictional utopia. White-Jacket is himself about to be flogged. He had never been assigned one of the necessary numbers when he joined the ship, and, by relying on his merchant-sailor's experience, he is consequently out of place at a key moment, for which he must be punished. His assertion that he had never been told the number means nothing against the officer's assertion that he must have received it. The book focuses closely on the mind of White-Jacket as he prepares for the flogging. Even though he feels his "soul's manhood so bottomless" that nothing the captain could do would reach and degrade it, he yields to an "instinct diffused through all animated nature . . . that prompts even a worm to turn under the heel." He will seize the occasion to "rush" the captain and "pitch him headforemost into the ocean," even though he would drown as well. Nature has given him "the privilege, inborn and inalienable, that every man has, of dying himself and inflicting death upon another." Here the social bond is powerfully reduced to its minimal elements of pure, conflicting individualities.

No less powerful, however, is the imagination that recalls White-Jacket to the world. The corporal of marines and the best of the sailors join in vouching for White-Jacket's character, and he is spared by the captain. Both archaic political authority and modern, rationalized details of labor organization are overcome through the human respect that the captain suddenly feels for the calm judgment of his subordinates, and the sense of justice that moves them to speak out, at risk to themselves (as Dana shows) and with no individual interests to serve. At the very moment that the "world" threatens to dissolve into warring, individual atoms, it is socially redeemed. This hope is quite different from that of the American apocalypse, but it is no less present, even in the world's current state, and perhaps it is both more possible and more worthy of realization.

White-Jacket was widely and warmly reviewed, but one reviewer complained that the book had been discussed "in a literary light only." Readers had praised the "power and vividness of its descriptions, of its wit, its humor, its character-painting," as if it were simply another "new novel." This critic, however, judged that "the literary feature" of the book was trivial beside its "didactic" concerns. For the book was no "romance of fiction" but aimed instead at "great practical subjects," like the Articles of War and flogging. Here, however, the reviewer found the book severely flawed, for a successful literary writer, however gifted with "theories, fancies and enthusiasm," lacks the necessary "character, wisdom and experience" to discuss serious matters. In criticizing the navy, Melville repeats the errors of the cobbler in the story, who successfully criticized "the foot" of a new statue but made a fool of himself when he presumed to judge any of the higher parts.

The reviewer draws the lesson that "the mind as well as the body is subject to the 'Division of Labor.' " In drawing this lesson, he was himself helping bring about a very important division of labor. This review is quite an early use of the term "literary" in the limited, modern sense that confines it to fiction, romance, and novels. The relation of Melville's work to the category of the "literary" would prove crucial, and explosive, in his next two works, *Moby-Dick* (1851) and *Pierre* (1852) (see Chapters 4 and 5). The marketing problems of these "literary" narratives drove Melville to writing periodical fiction (republished in book form, *Israel Potter* [1855] and *Piazza Tales* [1856]) before trying literary narrative again in *The Confidence-Man* (1857). After the failure of this work, Melville published no further prose, but at his death in 1891 he left nearly completed a long story, "Billy Budd," published in 1924 as part of the revival of Melville's reputation as a "literary" figure.

The defense of "poetry" (which included fiction and drama) from Sidney in the Renaissance to Shelley in the earlier nineteenth century had emphasized the capacity of poets to address the weightiest issues of their times. Poets might guide statesmen more effectively than could historians or philosophers. By the middle of the nineteenth century, however, it seemed common sense to confine the power and vividness of "literature" to a realm of fiction that has no impact on the governance of life. Like the cobbler, the literary writer was unquestioned in a delimited realm and was out of place anywhere else.

WALDEN

No more than Melville could Henry David Thoreau embrace such a division of literature from life. Both writers were literary in the sense of their aiming for a wide range of impressive stylistic effects as well as in their fabricating shapes that gave unity to their works; yet both also were writing from their own experiences and with the wish to change the experiences and actions of their readers. No one could be more "local" than Thoreau, the man of Concord, who carried out his most notable exploration within the limits of his native town. It was also Thoreau's goal to define what the "only true America" might be, that is, to provide an alternative national narrative. Moreover, there is an immense, a comic, gap between what the titles promise in Dana's *Two Years before the Mast* and Thoreau's *A Week on the Concord and Merrimack Rivers* (1849). Nonetheless, Thoreau, both in *A Week,* his first book, and in *Walden, or Life in the Woods* (1854), set the genre of personal narrative as the norm from which he was departing. (For a comprehensive account of Thoreau, see Packer in this volume.)

    Walden begins by striking the note of personal narrative. Thoreau explains that any egotism of the prose merely acknowledges that "it is always the first person speaking," and he states as his aim to offer a "simple and sincere account" of his experiences. In the opening chapter, a key articulation hinges on the simple narrative sentence which begins, "Near the end of March, 1845, I borrowed an axe and went down to the woods by Walden Pond." Likewise in the second chapter, "When first I took up my abode in the woods, that is, began to spend my nights as well as days there, which, by accident, was on Independence Day, or the Fourth of July, 1845, my house was not finished for winter." In the Conclusion, Thoreau defines what he has done as going "before the mast and on the deck of the world"; that is, like Dana and Melville, Thoreau claims to be learning from and reporting about work that he has done with his own hands, contrary to society's conventional expectations of polite writers. If one were really to go west, he argues, one better have something to do there (a reader might think of Cooper's Natty Bumppo). Hunters or trappers have better reason than any touristic traveler for paying serious attention to what they might encounter in the wild. The hunter, therefore, despite slaughtering animals, may provide more "true *humanity*" than the conventionally humane tourist, for what Thoreau means by "humanity" is "account of human experience."

    Yet in placing himself in the woods, "out of bounds," Thoreau works very differently from Parkman. Having lived wild, he seeks a writing to match: "*Extra vagance!* it depends on how you are yarded. The migrating buffalo, which seeks new pastures in another latitude, is not extravagant like the cow which kicks over the pail, leaps the cow-yard fence, and runs after her calf, in milking time." Thoreau wishes his discourse likewise to be homely, comic, and passionately surprising: "I desire to speak somewhere *without* bounds; like a man in a waking moment, to men in their waking moments." At his very moment of extremity, Thoreau catches and bridles himself: he echoes one of the most important formulations of nineteenth-century poetic theory, Wordsworth's definition of the poet as a "man speaking to men." Like Wordsworth, Thoreau works with the tension between the model of direct orality and the actual condition of writing, in which he fears that the "volatile truth" of words will always escape from their "residual statement."

Like White-Jacket on the *Neversink,* Thoreau recognizes the modernity of his world. He pitilessly insists that "the old have no very important advice to give the young, their own experience has been so partial," and any "experience which I think valuable" proves to be something about which the elders were silent. The railroad has disciplined Americans to live like William Tell's son, fearlessly indifferent to the metal bolts of death that shoot by. In order to write his book, Thoreau must share his bookkeeping. His "account" proves to be that of an accountant, as he fills pages with the petty arithmetic of dollars and cents for boards and nails and beans, as many numbers as those White-Jacket had to learn. To triumph over life, Thoreau explains, one must "rout it in detail."

In this world, accounts need pondering, and the difficult labor of reading is more important than the effortless skill of hearing. The language that is "spoken" and "heard" is learned "unconsciously," but the language of writing and reading comes from "maturity and experience," which require being "born again." Formal oratory and racy vernacular and intimate conversation all fall short of this power: "If we would enjoy the most intimate society . . . we must not only be silent, but commonly so far apart that we cannot possibly hear each other's voice in any case." Thomas Carlyle had praised Shakespeare in "The Hero as Poet" by proclaiming, "Speech is great; but Silence is greater." In the early twentieth century Joyce summarized the literary vocation as "silence, exile, and cunning." Thoreau shares in this history.

Thoreau complained of modern life, "Where is this division of labor to end? and what object does it finally serve?" Yet he himself depended on such divisions. The opposition of conscious writing to unconscious speech, Thoreau's constant search for the inner meaning, participate in the social separation of the sphere of literature. The exhortation to be "a Columbus to whole new continents and worlds within you, opening new channels, not of trade, but of thought" takes its point and value only in a world that has devalued outer action and set a privilege upon the spiritual, with which literature is allied. This privilege drives Thoreau to reverse the values he most typically avows. Instead, he urges that "we should oftener look over the tafferel of our craft, like curious passengers, and not make the voyage like stupid sailors picking oakum." The mind and eye pull away from the hands, as personal narrative becomes literary narrative.

4

LITERARY NARRATIVE

ROMANCE, ROMANTICISM, AND THE LITERARY

In his extended works from *The Scarlet Letter* (1850) through *The House of the Seven Gables* (1851), *The Blithedale Romance* (1852), and *The Marble Faun* (1860), Nathaniel Hawthorne was the writer of prose narrative most important in establishing the kind of writing now recognized as "literary." Spurred by the success of *The Scarlet Letter,* Hawthorne's publishers moved to consolidate his position by reissuing *Twice-told Tales* (1851), collecting several of his recent sketches and tales along with some dozen previously unrepublished pieces in *The Snow-Image* (1851), and commissioning from him a book of mythological narratives for children, *A Wonder-Book for Girls and Boys* (1851–2, followed by *Tanglewood Tales* in 1853). The first year in which Hawthorne's writing provided enough income for his family to live on was 1851. Nevertheless, the gap in his career as a writer of fiction – seven years to *The Marble Faun* after only three years of high activity – indicates that even Hawthorne was not fully or clearly established in the role of a professional writer. His *Life of Franklin Pierce* (1852), written for the successful presidential campaign of his college friend, gave him access to a lucrative patronage position as American consul in Liverpool (1853–7), and with the financial security he earned from this position Hawthorne spent further years in France and Italy. These biographical facts emphasize the fragility of the newly emergent literary narrative.

Along with his college acquaintance and friend Henry Wadsworth Longfellow, Hawthorne was the figure around whom the recognition of "literature" was established in the United States. Hawthorne best combines recognition in his own time wth recognition in later discussions of American national literature, but Edgar Allan Poe did more to put into place the theories and perspectives that have formed the twentieth-century notion of literature. I have noted that a review of Melville's *White-Jacket* sharply distinguished between the work's "literary" and "didactic" qualities. Poe vigorously promoted this newly specialized sense of the word "literary." In his "Literati of New York" series, for example, he observed of Catharine Maria Sedgwick (whose *Hope Leslie* [1827]

had been a notable predecessor of Hawthorne in the fiction of colonial Massachusetts), "As the author of many *books* − of several absolutely bound volumes
in the ordinary 'novel' form of auld lang syne, Miss Sedgwick has a certain
adventitious hold upon the attention of the public, a species of tenure that has
nothing to do with literature proper."

By appealing to "literature proper," Poe was establishing a distinction
between the mere fact of book publication and higher values that are essential
rather than "adventitious." These values depend on spiritual facts rather than
just on physical appearance in a familiar format. In fact, the familiar, "ordinary . . . form of auld lang syne" is suspect. Literature proper apparently
will be innovative, recognizable by its difference from, rather than its resemblance to, what has gone before. Yet there will necessarily be some problem
with new work. It may require special talents to acknowledge it, to understand that the work in question is not a failed example of an old form but
rather a uniquely innovative accomplishment. In his major review of the
second edition (1842) of Hawthorne's *Twice-told Tales,* Poe emphasized, therefore, that Hawthorne was the "example, par excellence, of the privately-
admired and publicly unappreciated man of genius." Even though his work
represented the "highest regions of Art," indeed, precisely for that reason,
Hawthorne did not attract the public that Poe (as noted in Chapter 1) found
Cooper to have won with his predictably popular thematic material.

I use the term "literary narrative" to characterize the work of which
Hawthorne is the great exemplar, because "literature" and the "literary" are
words still in use and because they begin to achieve their present meanings in
Hawthorne's time. The term most closely associated with this body of fiction
in its own time, however, was not "literature" (despite Poe's advocacy) but
"romance." This is especially the case because in the prefaces he wrote to his
long fictional works, Hawthorne himself made extensive and significant use
of this term, and through his usage the term became important again in mid-
twentieth-century claims for a tradition of fiction that might be specifically
American.

The term "romance" takes its meaning both positively and negatively.
Negatively, the main idea of romance is as a contrast to everyday life. Thus in
the preface to *The Marble Faun,* Hawthorne explains his choice of Italy "as the
site of his Romance," because it offered "a poetic or fairy precinct, whose
actualities would not be so terribly insisted upon as they are, and must needs
be, in America." He gave much the same explanation in the preface to *The
Blithedale Romance,* in which he explains that his concern with a "socialist
community" related to Brook Farm (where he had a decade earlier involved
himself) was "merely to establish a theatre, a little removed from the highway of ordinary travel," in order to avoid "exposing" his work to "too close a

comparision with the actual events of real lives." This language of terrible insistence and of exposure sounds a note of defensiveness that is a major feature of Hawthorne's prefaces. More important than any consistent theory may be Hawthorne's attempt to escape the hostility of those in his native Salem who resented the critiques of named or recognizable local personalities in *The Scarlet Letter* and *The House of the Seven Gables*. Even in these earlier works, Hawthorne had already tried to mark his distance from the local. In the "Custom-House" sketch introducing *The Scarlet Letter*, he defined "neutral territory" as the proper ground for the "romance-writer." In "appropriating" for *The House of the Seven Gables* a "lot of land which had no visible owner," Hawthorne sought a space secure from "inflexible" and "dangerous" criticism, insisting that his romance had "a great deal more to do with the clouds overhead" than with "the actual soil" of his home county.

The second major negative sense of "romance" functions not as part of a distinction between writing and life, but within the realm of writing. "Romance" as a kind of fiction is distinguished from the "novel." Hawthorne begins his preface to *The House of the Seven Gables*, subtitled "A Romance": "When a writer calls his work a Romance, it need hardly be observed that he wishes to claim a certain latitude, both as to its fashion and material, which he would not have felt himself entitled to assume had he professed to be writing a Novel." The novel seeks "a very minute fidelity . . . to the probable and ordinary course of man's experience," whereas the choice of "circumstances" for the romance is much more greatly "of the writer's own choosing or creation."

Hawthorne was adapting a distinction that had had some currency in the eighteenth century and more recent support from Walter Scott, yet Hawthorne's distinction was not uniformly observed, even by those readers and writers closely linked to him in their taste and character. In reviewing *The Scarlet Letter*, Evert Duyckinck proclaimed it a "psychological romance": "the veriest Mrs. Malaprop would never venture to call it a novel." The review by Edwin Percy Whipple, however, quite calmly and without any second thought did call it a novel. Whipple was himself deeply involved in the Boston literary society that Hawthorne had joined with the publication of this book, and he became one of Hawthorne's closest literary advisers, so he can hardly be considered inept. In *The House of the Seven Gables* Hawthorne himself blurs any distinction between "novel" and "romance." He writes that "a romance on the plan of Gil Blas, adapted to American society and manners, would cease to be a romance." "Romance" here has the sense of "fiction," for the French work *Gil Blas* (1715) by Alain-René Lesage is a prototypical picaresque novel of wanderings across the whole range of society. Hawthorne's point is that such great social movement could not really hap-

pen in the Old World, but in America it is "the experience of many individuals among us." American social mobility makes possible for some an "ultimate success" that "may be incomparably higher than any that a novelist
would imagine for his hero." America is too improbable for a novel, and too
true for a romance, and Hawthorne's generic distinctions are occasional tools
used for polemical contrasts.

When used less as a contrastive term and more positively, "romance" continues to have much the same range. Its primary meaning is not much different
from "fiction." As Herman Melville was at work on his third book, *Mardi,* he
found that he wanted to make it different from *Typee* and *Omoo.* In these first
two books he had (as noted in Chapter 3) taken some liberties with literal truth
and had relied on travel writing to supplement gaps in his own knowledge or
memory, but *Typee* and *Omoo* could still safely appear as nonfiction. In the
months that he was working on *Mardi* and meditating a change of direction,
Melville also changed the tenor of his reading. No longer were the books that
he bought so heavily oriented toward travel narrative. His reading included
Shakespeare, Montaigne, and the *Biographia Literaria* (1817) of Samuel Taylor
Coleridge, the most important critical book of English Romanticism and
crucial for the emergence of "literature" in that national culture.

In the winter months of 1848, Melville had decided, as he wrote to his
publisher John Murray, to "change" his mode of writing to "Romance,"
"downright and out," "real" romance as opposed to the relative factuality of
his earlier books. He explained that *Mardi* "opens like a true narrative," but
from there "the romance and poetry" would "grow." By this departure from
personal narrative, Melville hoped to gain a greater play of "freedom and
invention" and to achieve a work that was "original." The result would be
"better" and "so essentially different" from *Typee* and *Omoo* as a "literary
acheivement [*sic*]." Murray shared the scorn of "fiction" that may, paradoxically, be found also in the new best-selling novels of the 1850s. Ellen, the
heroine of Susan Warner's *The Wide Wide World* (1850), is warned by her
mentor, "Read no novels," and she must regretfully put away issues of
Blackwood's that had inadvertently come into her hands. Ellen's values are
those of middle-class evangelicals, but Melville associates his choice of fiction, romance, and the literary with social elevation. He insisted to Murray
that an "American" could be a "gentleman," who had read the Waverley
novels, even "though every digit may have been in the tar-bucket." As in
Poe's claim for "literature proper," the claim for romance is a claim for social
status.

In his preface to *Eureka,* which he subtitled a "Prose Poem," Poe addresses
himself "to the few" who love and understand him; to them he offers the
book for its "Beauty," even while also insisting on its "Truth." For these elite

readers – his chosen audience for whom he is their chosen writer – he asks that the book be considered not as a work of scientific truth but rather "as an Art-Product alone," "let us say as a Romance" or even as a "Poem." In "The Philosophy of Composition," where he discusses the principles that he claims to have applied in his writing of "The Raven," Poe defines "unity of effect or impression" as the necessary goal of a poem, the same goal he claimed for the tale in his earlier review of Hawthorne. *Eureka* raises this goal to its highest pitch. In *Eureka,* Poe offers the reader the possibility of "an individual impression" of the universe. From the top of a mountain, he points out, the "*extent* and *diversity*" of the scene are more impressive than its oneness. Only by the improbable, somewhat comic, expedient of "rapid[ly] whirling on his heel" could a viewer grasp "the panorama in the sublimity of its *oneness.*" To tell the story of the universe in an analytic narrative that has a hypothesized beginning, a middle in which we live, and an imagined end, Poe uses a mixed form that combines the intensity of a poem with the commitment to truth of prose.

In calling such a work "a romance," Poe recalls the debates over the "romantic" in German literary theory around 1800, where the mixture of modes, the breakdown of "classical" genres helped to define the modern, "Romantic" product of verbal art. The "novel" (*Roman* in German, *roman* in French) was the name given to this genre to end genre. The novel was the epic of the modern world, but it was not in verse, and as prose it could include both the disorienting clownery of spinning round on one's heels and the sublime mysticism of the secret of the universe. The emphasis on "romance" and the rise of the literary in mid-nineteenth-century America also connect in other ways to the Romanticism of earlier generations in Germany and Britain. In both of these cultures, the basis for what is now understood as "literature" was laid through the sharp sense of an absent public sphere. The French Revolution seemed to promise free speech among equals, but the promise failed, and in England, Wordsworth and Coleridge turned from public life. *The Prelude,* Wordsworth's great poem of vocation, demands epic scale and length, only to recount "the growth of a poet's mind." Deprived of an acceptable world of political exchange and no longer in a position to enjoy patronage, the Romantic writers had to develop their work in relation to market concerns. The relation they chose was opposition.

Wordsworth and Coleridge expressed their democratic hopes in a sturdy commitment to the idea of writing for "the people," but they found no actual audience to which they would give that honored name, only a degraded "public" – like those eager for the "gross and violent stimulants" discussed in Chapter 2. In *White-Jacket,* Melville catches this tension in an exchange about the poems written by one of the men on board. The poet denounces the "public," and his shipmate objects that, after all, he is himself part of the public. The poet replies that the shipmate is a member of "the people" (the name, recall, also given to the sailors on the ship), and the two agree to maintain a sharp distinction between the public and the people, always to "hate the one [the public] and cleave to the other [the people]."

Shakespeare was above all others the writer of the past to whom the English and German Romantics turned to explore the concerns they felt most strongly. In the political frustrations of Hamlet, who was forced into dissimulation and soliloquy by the constraints of the deadly court in which he lived, the Romantics found a model for the interiorization that they both suffered and valued. They recognized, too, in Shakespeare a writer who had had to deal with a market system. In his sonnets – first beginning to be widely appreciated and discussed only in the Romantic period – Shakespeare shows strong self-pride together with a pained awareness of his low position in the social scale. In England, the theory of "literature" can hardly be separated from the attempt to pry Shakespeare from the theater and make his existence most vivid in books. Charles Lamb's essay "On the Tragedies of Shakespeare" (1811) determined that these plays could be appreciated only in the study, not on the stage. In the next generation, Thomas Carlyle, in *On Heroes, Hero-worship, and the Heroic in History* (1841), treated Shakespeare as an example of "The Hero as Poet." Carlyle lamented Shakespeare's subjugation to "cramping circumstances," which had forced him to dilute his tremendous insights into passable crowd-pleasers that showed their greatness only in "bursts of radiance." Melville's "Hawthorne and His Mosses" (1850) almost echoes Carlyle. Melville deprecates the "popularizing noise and show" of "Richard-the-Third humps and Macbeth daggers." Shakespeare's greatness, he proclaims, comes in "occasional flashings-forth," in "short, quick probings at the very axis of reality," through his mad characters such as Timon and Lear. The plot of the drama becomes a sop to the audience, and the characters become the test of greatness, characters known through their soliloquies and tirades rather than through their actions and dialogue.

In the 1790s, Wordsworth's engagement with the French Revolution – his disillusion with both the French course of terror and the British refusal to democratize – fueled his neo-Shakespearean drama, *The Borderers,* which was not published until 1842 but was quoted by Coleridge in his 1813 Bristol lecture on Hamlet. The most powerful lines in the play are spoken by the villain, but this did not diminish their influence:

> Action is transitory – a step, a blow –
> The motion of a muscle this way or that.
> 'Tis done, and in the after-vacancy

> We wonder at ourselves like men betrayed.
> Suffering is permanent, obscure, and dark,
> And shares the nature of infinity.

Character no longer reveals itself in action but forms a mute, dark concretion to be known. This Romantic turn to the inner world served some of Hawthorne's best and most sympathetic critics in characterizing his work. In reviewing *The Scarlet Letter* as a psychological romance, Duyckinck (a devoted reader of Coleridge) quoted a tag from these lines, and in his review of *The Marble Faun,* looking back in summary of the whole of Hawthorne's career, Whipple quoted the full passage that I have just cited.

In the United States, as in England, "literature" emerged in relation to the market. The moment at which "literature" took shape was the very same moment in which the "best-seller" also arose. Eighteen fifty, the year of *The Scarlet Letter,* was also the year in which Susan Warner's *The Wide Wide World* established sales figures that two years later were topped by Harriet Beecher Stowe's *Uncle Tom's Cabin* but by few other books of the nineteenth century. The very moment Hawthorne reached a substantial public was the moment in which his rivalry began with what he called the "damned mob of scribbling women," who reached a much larger public. Having a potential readership greater than that in any European nation because of its high literacy rates, the United States, by 1850, had become available as a national market because of both the improved transportation that railroads permitted and the new steps in the technical organization of publishing and bookselling that made this audience actual.

After the Panic of 1837 (which had damaged Hawthorne's career by stopping sales of *Twice-told Tales*), from 1843 into the middle 1850s, economic expansion was uninterrupted in the United States. James Fields, a partner in the Boston publishers Ticknor and Fields, had worked for years to establish New England literature in a national market, and, at this point, his efforts started to reap their reward. Under Ticknor's imprint, Hawthorne's *Scarlet Letter* began to establish the basis for the cultural leadership that was exercised through the *Atlantic Monthly* (founded in 1857, taken over by Ticknor and Fields in 1859, and edited by Fields from 1861 to 1871, when William Dean Howells took over) and that made Boston for several generations a publishing center of greater cultural weight than New York. Part of the process at work here was a stratification of audiences, so that by 1851 Hawthorne could make a living through publishing his kind of fiction, while publishers could do well financially with the work of more popular authors like Warner.

This market situation illuminates the complexities of a letter that Melville wrote to his father-in-law, Lemuel Shaw (chief justice of the Massachusetts Supreme Court), in October 1849, just after publication of *Redburn* and shortly before he went abroad to negotiate the sale of *White-Jacket*. Having just spent the summer writing these two books after *Mardi*, published in March, had met a hostile reception, he wrote:

For Redburn I anticipate no particular reception of any kind. It may be deemed a book of tolerable entertainment; – & may be accounted dull. – As for the other book [*White-Jacket*], it will be sure to be attacked in some quarters. But no reputation that is gratifying to me, can possibly be achieved by either of these books. They are two *jobs*, which I have done for money – being forced to it, as other men are to sawing wood. And while I have felt obliged to refrain from writing the kind of book I would wish to; yet, in writing these two books, I have not repressed myself much – so far as *they* are concerned; but have spoken pretty much as I feel. – Being books, then, written in this way, my only desire for their "success" (as it is called) springs from my pocket, & not from my heart. So far as I am individually concerned, & independent of my pocket, it is my earnest desire to write those sort of books which are said to "fail." – Pardon this egotism.

Here the literary is set firmly against the economic: only one kind of writing is done for "money"; it is a "job." A double scale registers success and failure in a way that uses the same words to mean totally opposed things. For many nineteenth-century writers at moments of risk, whether Douglass determining to gain the powers of literacy or Melville reckoning the costs of the literary, the model for this doubleness was Satan's "Evil, be thou my good." Melville, accordingly, defines failure as success. Against the mere "desire" that stems from the "pocket," there is the "earnest desire" that comes from the "heart": an inner "individual" essence against the adventitious garb of society. Melville needed money to support his wife and child, but his necessary "egotism" as a writer ambitious of literary fame dictated his prose. Even writing to his father-in-law, Melville does not name as motives his wife, Shaw's daughter, or his eight-month-old son, Shaw's grandson. To the "individually concerned" writer, these intimate others are reduced to his pocket, from which he wishes he were "independent." The writer's activity is set in counterpoint to the obscured agency of the marketplace world, in which things may be "deemed," "accounted," "attacked," "called," or "said" without the apparent intervention of people. Even the writer is "forced" and "obliged," barely able to assert that he is not wholly "repressed."

Throughout the history of Western vernacular writing of high ambition, almost all of its practitioners either had lived on patronage, or had been persons of independent means, or had been members of the learned professions in positions of some comfort. Melville had no profession, no means, and no patronage. Only the existence of a market for his writing had drawn

Melville into authorship in the first place, but he found that, once it had been entered, the world of literature opened horizons that he could not reach. Having drawn him in by its positive attractions, it protracted his relation in a negative way, in experiments to see how much he could speak "as I feel" and still make a living, experiments to see how much failure he could survive.

In describing transatlantic Romanticism, I mentioned the political problems of public speech in England and Germany. The United States should have posed no such problems. Its founding allowed the possibility of, and seemed to demand, public speech of a sort that was impossible elsewhere. Just at the moment he received a large advance payment on *Mardi,* in March 1849, Melville wrote to Duyckinck: "I would to God Shakespeare had lived later, & promenaded in Broadway." Then he would have been free of "the muzzle" imposed by Elizabethan restrictions. Even if no one can be "a frank man to the uttermost" in his writing, still, Melville believed, "the Declaration of Independence makes a difference." Shakespeare on Broadway soon proved more explosive than Melville imagined.

In May 1849, two rival actors were in New York playing Macbeth: the English tragedian William Macready at the Astor Place Opera House and the popular American actor Edwin Forrest at the Broadway Theatre. The tensions between a more fashionable audience at the Astor and a more popular audience at the Broadway, exacerbated by nationalist rivalries, led to a mob's closing down Macready's performance. Cultivated public opinion, including Melville, petitioned Macready to perform again, promising him protection. Hundreds of police and militia tried to control the protesters without success, and the militia fired directly into the crowd. Twenty-two people were killed. The shocking outcome of the Astor Place Riot cast doubt on the difference the Declaration of Independence had made. Over the years, from the founding of the United States until the middle of the nineteenth century, changes occurred in the nation's political culture that provoked the emergence of a literature surprisingly like that which elsewhere had grown from the frustration of democratic hopes.

By 1850, the United States was at once more intensely national and more intensely sectional than it had been when Cooper began to write. The expansion to the Pacific, the Mexican War, the whole apparatus of manifest destiny, sealed by the astonishing growth of overland railroad connections, strengthened the nation as a whole and brought it to a new level of power. Yet the tensions that developed over the future of slavery tremendously enhanced both solidarity within sections and antagonism between sections. The Old South and the new Southwest fused into the "South" that soon became the Confederacy, while New England, New York, Pennsylvania, and the Old Northwest were fusing into the "North" that became the "Union" of the newly formed Republican party. Moreover, the demands of entrepreneurs in the new industrial system that was becoming increasingly important in national economic life required a thorough transformation of the grounding of American law. The law shifted from its basis in English common law into elaborate codifications that required a much higher level of professional expertise than before. Economic issues that once would have been matters for public debate and legislative activity were channeled into the courts, and political questions of the utmost consequence were shunted away from the forums of debate, on the grounds that they threatened the sacred Union.

Politics was displaced into two different venues. In the courts, issues that seemed to be too difficult or explosively dangerous to debate publicly could be resolved ad hoc, as individual cases, through an adversarial but nonpartisan proceeding. In the characters of separate individuals, matters could be resolved silently and privately. Emerson wrote in "Politics" that the "antidote" to the "abuse of formal government" is "the influence of private character, the growth of the Individual." In *Mardi* an enigmatic document is discovered that reproaches the nationalistic oratory of a figure who transposes the rhetoric of "Young America" into this South Sea fiction. The document powerfully claims that "freedom is more social than political." Freedom's "real felicity is not to be shared," but is rather of "a man's own individual getting and holding." Standing against the republican principles of the American Revolution, this claim rehearses the analysis Tocqueville had made of American "individualism."

"Individualism," Tocqueville had argued, was a new word for a new thing; it was not merely selfishness, which is a passion, but a "mature and calm feeling, which disposes each member of the community to sever himself from the mass of his fellows." Selfishness corrupts all virtue, but individualism, at least at first, "only saps the virtues of public life." Yet the solitary powers of the literary writer, the romancer, were very much individual. Looking back to Shakespeare's great individualist Coriolanus, who turned against the republican freedoms of his native Rome to find a "world elsewhere," the English critic William Hazlitt worried that the "power" of the greatest writing might be at one with the "power" of autocratic politics. For "the imagination is an exaggerating and exclusive faculty," a thoroughly "anti-levelling principle." As the imagination formed its elite among those who hoped to make a career in literature, the more intensely specialized legal profession generated its own elite; both opposed everyday plain thought, speech, and sense. The new systems of courts and character both required education as a prerequisite and then a process of interpretation in order to make the system work.

By midcentury, national narratives like that of George Bancroft came to seem sectional in their necessary emphasis on one side or another of issues that were increasingly contested; local narratives, like those of the southwestern humorists, could seem increasingly divisive in a nation that feared splitting apart into antagonistic sectional cultures; and even "personal" narratives – not just that of Frederick Douglass – proved intensely ideological. In this situation, "literature" could fill a special function that had not had a place before. It offered an internalized psychology that had not been part of "personal" narrative, and it took place in a "neutral territory" that was neither here nor there, neither national nor local, with regard to the intensely debated political issues of the day. It proposed eternal questions of "the human heart," rather than discuss more immediate and controversial issues.

The great speeches of political oratory, for which such senators as Henry Clay, John Calhoun, and Daniel Webster were known throughout the United States, became a less important form than they had been. The "Compromise" of 1850, which occupied Congress for almost the entire year, was meant to end once and for all the debate over the issues surrounding slavery, and in their speeches Clay, Webster, and Calhoun had all emphasized that political oratory was itself a divisive mode, creating problems where none would exist if one only would trust to the loyalty of the American people.

The case of Webster was the most crucial for the figures who became associated with literature, for they were northerners, like Webster, while Clay represented the West and Calhoun the South. To accept Webster's position in his famous speech of March 7, 1850, was to opt for silence (as against dangerously divisive debate); while to reject his position could well mean to reject both oratory and politics as the corrupt means by which Webster had compromised morality in order to preserve the Union. In his speaking tour of the southern states in 1847, part of his continuing presidential ambitions, Webster had already begun to lay the basis for this position. He had explained there, "I desire to see an attachment to the Union existing among the people, not as a deduction of political economy, nor as a result of philosophical reasoning, but cherished as a heartfelt sentiment."

The opposition of heart to head that was to be so crucial in Hawthorne's romances is in Webster's statement presented as a formula for political harmony, and the heart's sentiments are seen as the stable ground on which political tranquillity may be established. In his moralizing, exemplary biography of George Washington, Parson Weems had maintained that "Private Life is always *real* life," and Hawthorne's romances emphasize the private as the reality that public life either mocks or conceals. In the "Custom-House" preface to *The Scarlet Letter,* the documents about Hester Prynne left by Surveyor Pue are available for Hawthorne's imaginative use because they were "not official, but of a private nature." Only the popular female writers of the time are now known as "sentimental" novelists, but Hawthorne's fiction is no less committed to sentiment. The hearth replaced the great natural landscapes of James Fenimore Cooper as the locus of a "natural" moral virtue on which the preservation of America depended. This was the tendency of Hawthorne's fiction as much as it was that of the women writers. Despite his fascination with the protracted agonies of moral guilt, Hawthorne's positive position was no different from that of Edmund Burke. It was a position that became increasingly important for mid-nineteenth-century American culture: the "normal instincts of mankind" are valuable because they make up the "conservative principle of society." In 1856 the American critic Henry T. Tuckerman wrote, concerning George Washington, that "sentiment is the great conservative principle of society." Tuckerman had earlier argued in a review of *The Scarlet Letter* that Hawthorne's "psychological" writings served to rectify the nation's sentiments. Hawthorne thanked Tuckerman for this "beautiful" review, which "understood what I meant."

Webster, in emphasizing the importance of unreflective loyalty and commitment, had already contributed to a reinterpretation of the American Revolution in line with Burke. In his speech at the completion of the Bunker Hill Monument (1843), Webster explained that the American Revolution had not been a violent innovation, but a development from the previous two centuries of American life. Bancroft also believed in the developmental character of the Revolution, but he did not deny, as Webster's claim for sentiment tended to, that logic, analysis, and argument had gone into justifying, motivating, and waging the Revolution.

The week after Webster's speech on compromise, *The Scarlet Letter* appeared, on March 16, 1850, and its sales were surprisingly strong, requiring a second edition within weeks. The book obviously could not have been directly influenced by the compromise debates, but it was written out of the same national situation. In ending the Missouri Compromise of 1820, which had established a specific geographical boundary north of which slavery would not be permitted in federal territories, the Compromise of 1850 replaced something that had been clear-cut, arbitrary, and arithmetical with a set of possibilities that left much open for interpretation. Hawthorne's concern with interpretation, his fiction of the possible and the potential, was not new at this time. As early as the *Twice-told Tales,* a review in the *Church Examiner* contrasted Hawthorne's stories to more highly mimetic fictions, which "usurp the realm of real fact" and thereby "disturb and displace the fabric of things as they are." As an example of "higher fiction," Hawthorne's work, like "true poetry," "leaves things as they are." Yet this preservative function enhances what is left in place, for it "breathes into them a vital glow."

When the Union had to be cherished and fostered rather than shaken up and tampered with, Hawthorne's long-standing mode of writing became newly relevant. The essence of its relevance, however, lay in its not being recognized as relevant. It provided a welcome alternative to politics, but it also kept in play, in displaced form, certain elements of the political scene. The long period of relative tranquillity over the slavery issue had been based upon a principle of strict segregation: slavery was uniquely a matter for state decision and not for national discussion. But the sudden accession of new national land forced the question of slavery out into the territories and made it a matter at once of fantasy – might there be slaves there? – and of principle – should there be slaves there? – rather than of fact: there were actually almost no slaves there.

Hawthorne's "neutral territory" for the romance writer's imagination had a strange relation to the imaginative spaces of the West that were being peopled with slaves or free farmers in the minds of ideologists. Purist logic held, as Lincoln would remark, that the nation must be either all slave or all free. The corollary was usually unspoken, except by Garrisonian abolitionists and, increasingly, by southern "fire-eaters," namely, that if Americans remained divided by slavery there would no longer be a Union. The "moderate" position tried to reconcile the claims of slavery (or freedom) and union. Such reconciliation of opposites was the specific task of the imagination, as Coleridge had defined it in the *Biographia Literaria,* and the imaginary resolution of these real problems was one of the means by which romance in Hawthorne's hands helped to negotiate the moment of political crisis in the middle of the nineteenth century. Nevertheless, in "The Custom-House" Hawthorne explained his spiritual dejection by claiming that "imagination" was incompatible with receiving "public gold." Thus he established his own literary authority on grounds that discredited the speeches of Senator Webster and the history of Ambassador Bancroft, both of which for the previous two decades had been more widely sold, read, and admired than the fictional oeuvre of any author. To the question, in 1850, what was the greatest American literature? Bancroft's *History* and Webster's speeches might have proven likely answers; less than a century later, they had been wholly displaced, not merely by a shift in taste or evaluation, but by a radical and thoroughgoing redefinition of literature.

That the imagination was held to make possible creativity, the primary feature of the new idea of literature, was clearly seen in the claims made by mid-nineteenth century writers for "romance." The power of originating from nothing, which had been God's, was now available to humans. The first English usage of "original" had been in the theological phrase "Original Sin," but Adam's, or Eve's, assertion of freedom was now revalued. The imagination achieved its creative capacity through a process of growth and development. The romance of Hawthorne's that most explicitly focuses on the issue of development is *The House of the Seven Gables,* in which the artist-figure is a photographer. In the 1840s the sense of "development" as a biological process of transformation became prominent — when Charles Darwin published *Origin of Species* in 1859, what is now called evolution was usually referred to as the "development hypothesis" — at the same time that the word began to be applied to the processing of photographs (the term still used now). Also at this moment, the English clergyman John Henry Newman published his *Essay on the Development of Christian Doctrine* (1845) and became a convert to the Roman Catholic church. Newman's *Essay on Development,* as it was called, made available a sense of development as the process by which truth is revealed gradually through history.

Because the process occurs over time, it will necessarily be imperfect at earlier points in a writer's career. Thus Poe explained in his review of Hawthorne that those most capable of judging, that is, those using these new criteria, the "few," judge differently from "the public." Maintaining the older criteria of literary criticism as a judgment of the skills of craft shown in the performance of a composition, the public judges a writer on the basis of action, "by what he does"; but the new standards emphasize character instead, "what he evinces the capability of doing." Melville made the same point in "Hawthorne and His Mosses," writing of Shakespeare: "The immediate products of a great mind are not so great, as that undeveloped, (and sometimes undevelopable) yet dimly-discernable greatness, to which these immediate products are but the infallible indices." The criterion is not achievement but potential, "indices" to be interpreted. This distinction illuminates a crucial difference between two notions of "character" in the narratives of the mid-nineteenth century. In the most popular narratives, such as *The Wide Wide World,* the character of the heroine is shown as produced by the didactic ministrations of those who love her, and her character is judged from her actions. Character in Hawthorne is instead a given, not to be formed but to be found out, as if a natural fact that the writer explored rather than produced.

The result of successful imaginative activity is the literary creation of a world that stands free from the world of everyday life as an independent whole. In Melville's *Mardi* (1849), the "romance" that takes over from the narrative of shipwreck and sailing adventure is initiated through the chapter title as the voyagers come upon the new islands of Mardi: "World Ho!" A crew of European and South Sea sailors yields to a new group of characters. Conversations among a half-divine king, a philosopher, a historian, and a poet allow Melville to launch into both speculative and satirical reflections on his world through the shape of this new world. This voyage not only narrates fictional discoveries; it also enacts the writer's discoveries in the resources of fiction as a high mode of literary ambition.

In Chapter 169, the writer addresses the reader: if he has "chartless voyaged," it has been in order to reach a "new world," the "world of mind." Melville's language in this chapter seems attuned to that of John Keats's poetry. In his "Ode to Psyche" (1819), Keats had charted a similar internalization, in honoring the heroine of a fiction of late antiquity, Psyche, the "soul": "Yes, I will be thy priest, and build a fane / in some untrodden region of my mind."

Mardi includes within its fiction a chapter on the literature of the fictional world of Mardi. The great author "Lombardo" supposedly emulates the old blind bard who, it is said, proclaimed, "I will build another world." The bard's model for Lombardo proves identical to one marked out by the models of Romanticism, such as Keats's formulation, "That which is creative must create itself." As Lombardo works on his poem, he goes "deeper and deeper into himself," working through a fearsome interior landscape, until he emerges into a pastoral pleasance, at which point he can rejoice, "I have created the creative." Here the inner struggle of the author to transform his own soul into a beautiful, productive world provides the basis from which it may be reproduced in the world of the imaginative poem.

This interiority where imagination works and growth develops, where character is known and formed, is the privileged space of the literary, both in authors and in their characters. In the great Shakespearean prototype, Hamlet has "that within which passes show." Yet this creative originality was not supposed to diverge utterly from common life. Hawthorne, in the preface to *The House of the Seven Gables,* had emphasized that the romancer – even while freed from ordinary probabilities – remained bound to observe "the truth of the human heart." William Hazlitt had defined "originality" as "seeing nature differently from others, and yet as it is in itself"; that is, "originality" had not only the now usual sense of uniqueness, but it also maintained an etymological connection with "origins." The "original" is more in touch with the primary source of things – for Hawthorne, precisely the human heart.

The effect of such work, Poe observed in reviewing Hawthorne, was "totality." This term had been put into current usage by Coleridge in his lectures on Shakespeare. Addressing the old "unities" of neoclassical dramatic criticism, Coleridge suggested a change: "instead of unity of action, I should greatly prefer the more appropriate, though scholastic and uncouth words, homogeneity, proportionateness, and totality of interest." These new terms, Coleridge believed, involve the "essential difference" between the "shaping skill of mechanical talent," a lower form of accomplishment, and "the creative, productive life-power of inspired genius." The "harmony that strikes us" in even the "wildest natural landscapes" is effected by a "single energy modified *ab intra* [from within] in each component part." This energy is the "particular excellence" of Shakespeare's plays and gives them their unique power of harmony. Reviewing Coleridge's work in 1836, Poe had praised his "gigantic mind" and recommended that the *Biographia Literaria* be published in the United States, which had much to learn from its "psychological science."

The harmonious, interactive power that Coleridge admired in natural landscape and found in Shakespeare, Poe in *Eureka* calls "mutuality of adaptation," and from it he argues an aesthetic point comparable to Coleridge's: "The pleasure which we derive from any display of human ingenuity is in the ratio of *the approach* to this species of reciprocity." In a crucial difference from Coleridge, Poe does not so readily assume that even Shakespeare actually achieved the level of full integration; and Poe resists Coleridge's distinction between the merely mechanical skill of craft and the purely organic growth of genius. Nonetheless, he continues,

In the construction of plot, for example, in fictitious literature, we should aim at so arranging the incidents that we shall not be able to determine, of any one of them, whether it depends from any one other or upholds it. In this sense, of course, *perfection* of plot is really, or practically, unattainable − but only because it is a finite intelligence that constructs.

In contrast, however, "the plots of God are perfect."

Poe then reverses the usual direction of comparison between human and divine. He takes a term from aesthetics and transposes it into cosmotheology: "The Universe is a plot of God." The purpose of *Eureka* is to analyze, and narrate, that plot: "Oneness is a principle abundantly sufficient to account for the constitution, the existing phaenomena, and the plainly inevitable annihilation of at least the material Universe." The "arms and the man" of this modern epic will then be, "*In the Original Unity of the first Thing lies the Secondary Cause of All Things, with the Germ of their Inevitable Annihilation.*" In using the principles of literary criticism to understand the universe, Poe relies on the convertibility of truth and beauty. The world he has created through his argument, he asserts, must be identical to the world that God has created, for otherwise the universe would be less perfect than this critical construction.

HAWTHORNE'S ROMANCES

However perfect the universe as a whole might be, it was clear to the romance writers of the middle nineteenth century that their daily experience was flawed and fragmentary. This split is acknowledged in Melville's letter to Lemuel Shaw or in Hawthorne's contrast between the deadness of his work in the customhouse and the liveness of imagination that he sought. This experience had been with Hawthorne for a long time. As early as his first patronage work, the place Bancroft had gotten him in the Boston Custom House from 1839 to 1841, Hawthorne's letters to his fiancée, later his wife, emphasize his sense of there being two distinct worlds, one of which is "the" world and is much inferior to the world of the hearth, love, and imagination. So he wrote from work to Sophia,

My Dove is at home . . . in the midst of true affections; and she can live a spiritual life, spiritual and intellectual. Now, my intellect, and my heart and soul, have no share in my present mode of life — they find neither labor nor food in it; every thing that I do here might be better done by a machine. I *am* a machine, and am surrounded by hundreds of similar machines; — or, rather, all of the business people are so many wheels of one great machine — and we have no more love or sympathy for one another than if we were made of wood, brass, or iron, like the wheels of other pieces of complicated machinery.

The "home" and the "spiritual" are set against the "machinery" of "business." Although the United States was indeed becoming a more industrial economy at this point, Hawthorne's "mechanical" does not stigmatize the industrial so much as the bureaucratic and commercial, the middle-class male sphere. Hawthorne's terms of analysis were widely shared, even beyond the use in Coleridge that has already been noted. In his great essay of 1829, Thomas Carlyle had read the "Signs of the Times" and proclaimed this age "not an Heroical, Devotional, Philosophical, or Moral Age, but, above all others, the Mechanical Age . . . in every outward and inward sense of that word."

The problems that afflict Hawthorne reach out to Sophia. Because he finds in Sophia's leisured home life the values that he misses, he joins that life to his to serve a compensatory function. In another letter he explains that Sophia "must listen to the notes of the birds," because "the rumbling of wheels will be always in my ears." Yet this demand transforms Sophia's life from one of leisure to one of responsibility. He enjoins her: "thy spirit must enjoy a double share of freedom, because thy husband is doomed to be a captive." Sophia's "enjoyment" becomes part of an arithmetical, ledger-keeping process in which it is her "office" to register "the additions" to "our common stock." This quantification of enjoyment is part of what Carlyle meant by "Mechanical."

Carlyle referred in his essay not only to the literal machinery of industrialism but also to the spiritual machinery of commercial organization, which, he argued (like Wordsworth condemning "gross and violent stimulants") had affected even the writing and reading of poetry. When Hawthorne has escaped from the machinery of the city and party patronage, to join in the socialist experiment of Brook Farm, he finds not an integration of his being, but only another split, this time between his true self – the sensitive writer – and the physical demands of agricultural labor. To work in nature is not automatically to achieve an "organic" escape from the mechanical.

To Hawthorne the experience of Brook Farm was "unreal": "The real Me was never an associate of the community; there has been a spectral Appearance there, sounding the horn at day-break, or milking the cows, and hoeing potatoes, and raking hay, toiling and sweating in the sun." He evokes a situation that echoes the world of "Young Goodman Brown," a world in which it was believed that the Devil had power to display "spectres" of those he controlled. The putatively ennobling activities of the farm become demonic. Hawthorne finally discounts as joking his claim that "this Spectre was not thy husband," but Coverdale's narrative of *The Blithedale Romance* depends upon a similar distance from shared communal life, a split between poetic sensibility and daily activity that is a further part of what Carlyle meant by mechanization. The problem is the same at Brook Farm as it was in the customhouse, where Hawthorne wrote to Sophia that a journal of his "whole external life" would be "dry" and "dull," in contrast to what he could also write, a "journal of my inward life throughout the self-same day." The gap between the accounts would challenge belief: "Nobody would think that the same man could live two such different lives simultaneously."

Imagination asserts a wholeness that may be purely imaginary, a fictive compensation for the real fractures that provoke it. The question remains, Is it the same person, or is there no integral identity, only a dispersion among roles that define a self through their relations of difference rather than of similarity? The search in literature for "character" is one response to this problem. So in *The House of the Seven Gables* the daguerrotypist Holgrave, the "artist," has by the age of twenty-two been a country schoolmaster, a salesman in a country store, the political editor of a country newspaper, a peddler, a dentist among factory workers, a supernumerary on a merchant ship, a Fourierist, and a mesmerist. Yet through all these roles, each "taken up with the careless alacrity of an adventurer" and then "thrown aside as carelessly," Holgrave, Hawthorne asserts, "had never lost his identity," and he possesses "his law," which is different from what governs other characters. As opposed to the pain of Hawthorne's split between inner and outer, Holgrave represents a pure triumph of the spiritual, of inner essence over external accident.

If the character Holgrave is a contrast to Hawthorne, Hawthorne's own experience is exacerbated in *The Scarlet Letter,* where Dimmesdale leads a "life of ghastly emptiness" because he has become wholly caught in a split between his "official" role as spiritual leader in the Boston community and the private facts of his responsibility for Hester's adultery. He is unaware of Chillingworth's true relation to him, as the wronged husband of Hester exercising a long, terrible vengeance in the role of physician to Dimmesdale's sick body and soul, and his concealment has been so rigid that he does not know that Hester may still love him, as he discovers he loves her. A community that represses the emotional bases of life by allowing them to be known only within its "iron framework" of law nonetheless responds with excitement and yearning to Dimmesdale's election sermon, which he has achieved through his emotional reintegration. Yet his prophecy of America's future is belied by the customhouse from which Hawthorne begins the book. Once again – in the actual nineteenth century as in the imagined seventeenth century – American politics have disconnected real feeling from public life; the "sentiment" that Webster had summoned to preserve the Union must remain in the heart rather than fuel public debate. *The Scarlet Letter* carries out this agenda by transposing its "psychological romance" into a faraway time, fulfilling the political commandment not to speak of politics. The separate, and better, world of romance helps to support the fragmented world of everyday life, as it also depends on it. This might have been the plot of God to preserve the Union, but it proved otherwise.

This interdependence of romance and everyday marks the relation of "The Custom-House" to "The Scarlet Letter," that is, of the introductory sketch of modern life to the long tale of the seventeenth century with which it shares a book. Because the phrase "the scarlet letter" names both the whole book and one of its parts, "The Custom-House" occupies a space that in its absence would not be recognized as vacant. It adds something that was not required and so complicates the tale that follows. For example, it offers to prove the "authenticity" of the narrative, but it does so by invoking "literary propriety," an appeal to convention rather than a warrant of authenticity. By taking possession through "The Custom-House" of the (physical) scarlet letter as his property, the author of "The Custom-House" personalizes the narrative.

There are many correspondences between the authorial figure of "The Custom-House" and the characters of "The Scarlet Letter." Both Hester in the tale's opening and Hawthorne in the sketch are subjected to disapproval by an imagined crowd of Puritan authorities. Both Dimmesdale in the tale and Hawthorne in the sketch are split by a passionate inner life that is wholly at odds with their "official" public position. Both Chillingworth in the tale and Hawthorne in the sketch display prowess as critical analysts of character. These and other resemblances allow readers to justify the presence of "The Custom-House" by integrating it thematically with "The Scarlet Letter." Such resemblances, however, also undermine the self-sufficiency of "The

Scarlet Letter," making the tale an allegory of the writer's situation in 1850. "The Custom-House" concludes that the public figure of the "decapitated surveyor" — Hawthorne in the newspapers — is only "figurative" and that Hawthorne's "real human being" is a "literary man." By the same logic, the public life of Hester — in the tale — is also only figurative, and its reality is Hawthorne's literary life.

A recurrent mood of "The Custom-House," emphatic near its end, is harried dejection, which leads Hawthorne to welcome his "execution" in the change of political administrations that costs him his patronage job. It is as if, he explains, a man planning suicide had "the good hap to be murdered." From this mood issues forth "The Scarlet Letter," only to end where it began, in the mood of the questions the heartsick women of Massachusetts ask Hester: "why they were so wretched and what the remedy." From the man alone in 1850 to the women alone in the seventeenth century, there is no action that will bring happiness. With luck one will be decapitated, or else, as Hester envisions, "the angel and apostle of the coming revelation" will appear. The only remedy is patient trust in the future. "The Scarlet Letter" does, however, propose a specific source for the misery: Hester's past action, which both found her a child and lost her its father. Action lies only in the past, feeling in the present, and hope in the future.

Here *The Scarlet Letter* shows its consonance with the politics of sentiment that Webster and others proposed as the means to negotiate the threat of disunion over the issue of slavery. Politics is internalized and personalized, and issues are removed from consideration in the public world in which Hawthorne wrote just as they are in the private world that he wrote about. Hawthorne's critique of the emptiness of life under the eagle of "Uncle Sam" in the customhouse is accurate. "Official" politics have been cut off from anything that might seem real.

Consider a major rhetorical motif of "The Custom-House," the insistence that the gloom of "The Scarlet Letter" stems in part from an act of revolutionary victimization. Hawthorne's loss of his political appointment has "decapitated" him and he now writes as a "politically dead man." This joke hinges on a common hyperbole of the age, that of likening patronage dismissals to acts of French revolutionary terror. Even Franklin Pierce, a man of no linguistic originality, had used the figure in a speech of 1841 that Hawthorne quotes in his *Life*. What makes the phrase jocular is that patronage changes are not "revolution," but carry out the etymologically related action of "rotation" in office: revolutionary principle becomes rotatory patronage. Whether one is in office or out, one is as good as politically dead, for the officeholder, Hawthorne argues, "does not share in the united effort of mankind." Paradoxically then, public office is private. In a polity that allows for no significant action, politics can be only the corrupting hunt for spoils or else a noble, inert, and silent love for the Union.

As mid-nineteenth-century politics became merely office holding and patronage brokering, articulated, speculative passionate intelligence withdrew from the ranks of the Democrats and Whigs. The sketches of "official" character that occupy Hawthorne in the avowedly antipolitical literary practice of "The Custom-House" correspond to his occupation during his maximal political involvement, when after Pierce's election he devoted great energy to helping Pierce assign patronage positions. In the *Life of Pierce,* Hawthorne's claim to authority is his knowledge of "the individual," his capacity to read Pierce's "character" and judge his "motives." This emphasis on character is not the idiosyncrasy of a "literary man." The Whigs on their side ran exactly the same kind of campaign. The 1852 election allowed no issue between the major parties, only personality, although the marginalized Free Soil candidate, John P. Hale, had in fact strongly acted on principle. In 1845, while serving as a Democratic member of Congress from New Hampshire, Hale wrote that he had been "decapitated" when the regular party establishment, led by Pierce, denied him renomination because he opposed the extension of slavery into Texas.

The 1850s proved a turning point in American political history: the Whig party disappeared; the long time Democratic majority, begun by Andrew Jackson, became a sectionalized and ethnicized minority; the Republicans emerged and ruled for three generations. The Union would shortly split and be reunited by bloody conquest. Slavery was crucial in this transformation, but such changes were unthinkable for the still-dominant established parties, especially during the period between the Compromise of 1850 and the renewal of trouble over the Kansas–Nebraska Act in 1854. This interlude of paralytic calm was the moment of Hawthorne's greatest commitment to writing.

Consensus reigned between the two major parties. The *Life of Pierce* declared that no "great and radical principles are at present in dispute" between the Democrats and the Whigs, but both are "united in one common purpose," that of "preserving our sacred Union." In the politics of the early 1850s, character offered a ground for choice when there were no issues at stake, for Pierce did not undertake to do anything if elected. Hawthorne recognized slavery as potentially divisive: he did not favor slavery; he urged only that nothing be done about it. In the *Life of Pierce* he explained that slavery was

one of those evils which divine Providence does not leave to be remedied by human contrivances, but which, in its own good time, by some means impossible to be anticipated, but of the simplest and easiest operation, when all its uses shall have been fulfilled, it causes to vanish like a dream.

Such a fantasy of evanescence recalls the extinction of Chillingworth after Dimmesdale has escaped him in *The Scarlet Letter,* but it comes even closer to the death of the villain Jaffrey Pyncheon in *The House of the Seven Gables,* like a "defunct nightmare." The key to redemption in *The House of the Seven Gables* is the replacing of all human action, which is guilt ridden, with the beneficent process of nature — in particular, a nature that has been domesticated, in keeping with the book's intense household focus. The dreadful pattern of stasis in the house and repetition in the crimes of its inhabitants is undone by the natural development of Phoebe at her moment of transition from girl to woman.

The point of the plot in *The House of the Seven Gables,* in a drastic transformation of Aristotle, is to erase and undo all action. Just as Holgrave is about to repeat his ancestor's mesmeric possession of a Pyncheon woman, he holds back; instead, he will be united with Phoebe through the natural course of love. So too, the apparent murder of Jaffrey proves to be death by natural causes, and so likewise the death thirty years earlier for which Clifford had been imprisoned. In both cases "a terrible event has, indeed, happened . . . but not through any agency." Even Jaffrey, we learn, had not actively committed any crime in allowing Clifford to be convicted. The long-standing class conflict between owners and workers, Pyncheons and Maules, is mediated through modest marriage. The daughter of the Pyncheons, Phoebe, is herself a housewife rather than a lady waited on by servants; the son of the Maules, Holgrave, is both a radical and an entrepreneur. Together they embody a nation where a small business can lose five dollars or gain a million — all without government interference, social motion regulated by Providence alone. Hawthorne envisaged this logic of romance for America in politics as well. As late as 1863, he wrote to his sister-in-law Elizabeth Peabody that the Civil War would achieve only "by a horrible convulsion" what might otherwise have come by "a gradual and peaceful change," and Sophia Hawthorne echoed her husband's judgment in a letter to a Union general, agreeing with his conviction that "God's law" would surely have removed slavery "without this dreadful convulsive action."

Action is intolerable; character takes its place in the Romantic internalization that moved Shakespeare off the stage and into the book. No longer the traditional Aristotelian one who acts, nor, as in many great novels, one who speaks, a character becomes one who is known. Following the technique he developed in writing his tales, Hawthorne, in his longer works, maintains an extremely high proportion of narration to dialogue, while at the same time abandoning most of the materials — that is, the actions — of traditional narration. In certain ways his fiction technically anticipates that of Gustave Flaubert and Henry James in its emphasis on its characters, as narrated.

Such narrative inquisition takes place within those great changes of the nineteenth century that produced vast new amounts of knowledge about individuals in the social sciences and that exercised vast new powers over individuals in their roles as soldiers and workers. Nevertheless, when the narrative is not social science, but literature, its special concern is to represent as personalized what in fact depended on impersonality. In *The Scarlet Letter* the reader does not penetrate the "interior" of Dimmesdale's "heart" until Chillingworth has led the way there. The relation between the two men more closely anticipates psychoanalysis than it corresponds to any actual medical practice in either the 1850s or the 1640s, and it allows Hawthorne to achieve a powerfully ambivalent fantasy of being perfectly known: the dream of therapeutic intimacy and the nightmare of analytic violation.

Such extremes are no greater than those in "The Custom-House." There Hawthorne's wish to reach "some true relation with his audience" through literature found its demonic counterpart in official life — the stenciled and black-painted name "Hawthorne" that circulates the world on "all kinds of dutiable merchandise." The characters of the name are known and effective, but through no action of Hawthorne's. Yet even as a writer, Hawthorne's signature in the periodical press was valuable to his party, and his appearing in the Democratic-controlled *Salem Advertiser* converted book reviews into political capital. Hawthorne's name circulated in a complex system of exchange that made it worth the party's while to provide him a livelihood and that gave him the character of a Democrat without requiring any act on his part.

Hawthorne's own contradictory situation here may be compared with that of his party, which, in the 1850s, wished to go ahead into the future yet feared losing control over what had already been established. (In contrast to the Democrats' temporal anxiety, the Whigs feared the spatial extension into new territories as a threat to the established Union.) This tension between motion and regulation operates in both *The Life of Pierce* and *The Scarlet Letter*. In the *Life* this tension determines the contradiction between progress and stability that Hawthorne's fiction must resolve. In *The Scarlet Letter* the turn from action to character means that the terms of contradiction emerge in Hawthorne's analysis of what prevents a character from acting — as when Hester tempts Dimmesdale in the forest. Hester's "intellect and heart had their home . . . in desert places, where they roamed as freely as the wild Indian." In contrast, Dimmesdale "had never gone through an experience calculated to lead him beyond the scope of generally received laws," although "in a single instance" he had transgressed one. Hawthorne elaborates, "But this had been a sin of passion, not of principle, nor even purpose." Dimmesdale, "at the head of the social system . . . was only the more trammeled by its regulations, its principles, and even its prejudices." Therefore, "the framework of his order inevitably hemmed him in." Dimmesdale's emotional wavering is structured like Pierce's political trimming: the tension of regulation versus motion that determined the contradiction between stability and the future in the *Life of Pierce* here determines the contradiction between "principle" and "passion" ("e-motion").

The interrelations of principle and passion define a set of possibilities that give meaning to the characters of *The Scarlet Letter* in a way that readers usually expect to be done by the plot. Dimmesdale himself, as noted earlier, is defined by passion without principle; opposed to him is the "iron framework" of Puritanism, principle without passion. Lacking both passion and principle is Chillingworth: he "violated, in cold blood, the sanctity of a human heart" – violation negating principle and cold blood negating passion. At times, however, the text marks Chillingworth with "dark passion," making him a double of Dimmesdale (for they are the two men with claims on Hester). Finally, the combination of passion and principle can be found in the ideal Hester. Readers may construct this figure but then must confront Hawthorne's failure to actualize her in his text, for in most of the book Hester buries her passion and is dominated by ascetic principle, making her a double of the Puritan establishment's "iron framework."

The *Life of Pierce,* in contrast, does not hesitate to offer Pierce as the imaginary mediating figure who combines the future with stability. Pierce's Whig opponent General Winfield Scott shares the value of stability, but he has already done his work; he does not belong to the future. Slavery negates stability, for it threatens the Union, and because slavery is also providentially doomed, the slave South combines the two negatives: instability and no future. Free Soilers and abolitionists point toward a future without slavery, but no less than the slavery they oppose, they too threaten stability.

The organization of (in)action in both romance and biography works through a structure of conflicting values related to the political impasse of the 1850s. The famous ambiguity of Hester's scarlet letter may also be related to the fundamental problems in the 1850s over the meanings of such documents of American life as the Declaration of Independence and the Constitution. The turn to the courts to adjudicate constitutional issues made these documents no less subject to interpretation than was Hester's letter. Recall particularly that "adulterer" or "adultery" is nowhere spelled out in Hawthorne's text, just as the word "slavery" is nowhere present in the Declaration or in the Constitution. Just as it became necessary for these documents to take on new meanings, and for theories to be developed to justify these meanings, so, as the letter leaves its original context, it takes on new meanings: "Many people refused to interpret the scarlet A by its original significance." Hester plans never to abandon the letter, for while it endures,

it will be "transformed into something that should speak a different purport." The letter enters into a career of indeterminacy that allows it to
combine the celebratory communal hopes of *A* for "angel" in the sky after
Winthrop's death and the anguished solitary pain of Dimmesdale's *A* in his
flesh. The identification of Pearl with the letter further emphasizes that its
meaning must be understood through experience, growth, and development.

Taken back into politics, such an emphasis would follow the developmental conservatism of Edmund Burke and protect the Constitution against
abolitionists just as Newman had sought to protect Christianity from Protestantism. (Such protection has been a more partisan activity than its authors
have intended. Hawthorne himself believed that Protestantism was fundamentally Christian, and good cases have been made that the Constitution is
fundamentally antislavery.) It denies the need for any tampering innovation
and denies also the value of any reductive fixation on the original meaning or
intention. The established position during the 1850s was to want things
both ways. The Constitution was a document appropriate to guiding America to a better future, for it did not mention slavery; yet in the bad present of
the 1850s one had also to recognize the original constitutional "guarantees"
of slavery. This double vision preempted action, and in refusing to open itself
to the new issues of the day, the system, shared by Jackson and Webster,
became a dead letter, even as Hawthorne made it the basis for a new cultural
form in the shimmering life of the scarlet *A*.

Hawthorne was aware that his chosen romance writing was a fragile and
unreliable mode. Echoing a figure that Coleridge had used in the *Biographia
Literaria* to characterize the effect he and Wordsworth had sought in *Lyrical
Ballads,* Hawthorne defined the special "medium" of the romance writer as
"moonlight, in a familiar room," thus domesticating the emphasis on external nature in Coleridge's "moonlight or sunset diffused over a known and
familiar landscape." Yet if his primary tool is the uncanny atmospheric
effect — the ordinary made strange by moonshine — nonetheless, the claims
for his art are high. I have argued for the attempt to link safely together the
present and the future in the *Life of Pierce.* In *The House of Seven Gables,* the
task of romance is defined in equally grand and specific terms as "the attempt
to connect a bygone time with the very present that is flitting away from us."
The persistence of the past and the evanescence of the present teach a lesson
that Hawthorne offers while shying away from any too emphatic a "moral"
claim. Too obtrusive a moral, like an "iron rod" or a "pin through a butter-
fly," causes a story to "stiffen in an ungainly and unnatural attitude." Thus
between the mobile present of the "novel" and the totally static "moral," the
romance again mediates.

These metaphors for his accomplishments and his concerns help to explain some of the major tensions in Hawthorne's long fictions. He focuses on temporal processes: Hester's long penance in *The Scarlet Letter;* the working out over centuries of Maule's curse in *The House of the Seven Gables;* the consequences of bringing together old Moodie's previously separated daughters in *The Blithedale Romance;* the emergence of modern consciousness and conscience in Donatello in *The Marble Faun.* Yet his technique is also strongly oriented to optical presentation, whether of hovering atmospheric, picturesque effects or of allegorical fixities. Hawthorne's temporal concerns emphasize persistence with development. Their effect is not change (although *The Transformation* was the title of the English edition of *The Marble Faun*); rather, it is the unfolding of an essence, in accord with the laws of the human heart. Hawthorne tends to place the decisive moment of origination offstage, away from the main narrative, which itself presents an aftermath. He prefers to stage a "theater," in which things may be contemplated, rather than a drama, in which people do things.

The key figure in Hawthorne's long narratives, in keeping with his theatricality, is the "sensitive spectator," the descendant of his "spiritualized Paul Pry." At times this role is embodied in one of the fictional characters, but more frequently the role names an achievement that the author is implicitly claiming for himself and challenging the reader to match. The "sensitive spectator" is another of the bridging devices by which Hawthorne's romances function. The notion of "sensitive," as referring to sensibility rather than to the physical senses, dates only from the early nineteenth century, with Walter Scott and Washington Irving among the first to use it in this way. By long tradition within its usage, the term had suggested a contrast to the "intellectual" or rational features of humankind. With a force like that of the physical, a force that can leave one "shocked" by some form of powerful "impression" as it acts directly on the "nerves," the psychological aspects of a situation strike the sensitive spectator and provoke response, just as, in a usage beginning in the 1840s, a "sensitive" photographic plate, one that has been properly "prepared," traces the action of something as impalpable as light.

Cooper's Hawkeye looked on a scene to act; in the extreme but exemplary case, for him to see is to kill, by means of his rifle. In the historical panoramas that Bancroft offered in overview of centuries, the act of vision empowers a discriminating judgment that separates the most laudable from the lesser forms of human action. In Douglass's *Narrative,* the vista of boats in the Chesapeake exacerbates the pain of enslavement and further motivates the quest for freedom; and in *The Oregon Trail,* Parkman's acquisitive vision dominates the Indian's mystical vision. Dana and Melville criticized the position of overview in favor of that of the involved participant. Closest to Hawthorne's "sensitive spectator" are the narrators of local sketches and tales, who offer a norm that is shared with the reader and set against the poor, weak, comic, or provincial "others" that so typically are the objects of narration. In Hawthorne's romances, he maintains the sketch's distance from the narrated characters and its closeness to the reader, while the social level of the scene rises somewhat, and the tightly focused vision of the sketch is generalized by its extension over a full-length narrative.

In *The Scarlet Letter* the sensitive spectator is invoked importantly early and late in the book to guide readers' responses to Hester. Within a page of Hester's first appearance in the tale, the narrator describes her and her effect on the assembled viewers as she emerges from prison with her baby and her letter. Those who "had expected to behold her dimmed and obscured by a disastrous cloud" were instead "astonished" by "how her beauty shone out, and made a halo of the misfortune and ignominy in which she was enveloped." Against this outer view, however, "to a sensitive observer, there was something exquisitely painful in it." The sensitive observer grasps the essence of inner experience, unlike the crowd that remains spiritually hostile to Hester even if awed by her beauty and the splendor of her embroidery.

In contrast to the splendor, with its hidden pain, of this opening scene, in the final sequence of the narrative Hester appears "familiar" to the crowd, her coarse gray clothing "making her fade personally out of sight and outline." Her face resembles a "mask," or "the frozen calmness of a dead woman's features," because Hester no longer has any "claim of sympathy" on her world. Against the crowd, a "spiritual seer" might find in Hester the resolve to "convert what had so long been agony into a kind of triumph," as she plans to escape with Dimmesdale. Having "first read the heart," this "preternaturally gifted observer" could then afterwards have "sought a corresponding development in the countenance and mien" and thereby have "detected" in her expression something "unseen before." In an Emersonian movement of compensation, the sensitive spectator responds to the absent and contrary features of a face or context, feeling the pain in bravery and the triumph in humility that together make Hester a reconciliation of opposites, embodying the power Coleridge had attributed to the imagination.

In *The House of the Seven Gables* a similar complexity is established through play on the figure of the sensitive spectator with regard to the House itself. After the long easterly storm, during which Jaffrey Pyncheon has died in the House, the weather finally dawns bright and beautiful. In presenting the House in this new light, Hawthorne first invokes the figure of "any passerby," who might wrongly surmise from the "external appearance" that the history of the House must be "decorous and happy." Even a "person of imaginative temperament," who would give a second look and become "conscious of something deeper than he saw" might still imagine that the House bore an ancestral "blessing," rather than the curse around which the book revolves. One feature in particular would "take root in the imaginative observer's memory" – the great "tuft of flowers" called "Alice's Posies," which "only a week ago" would have seemed "weeds." This image of beneficent natural process suggests that perhaps there is indeed a more positive heritage from the past than the apparently unrelieved evil on which the book has dwelt.

The "common observer," who watches an Italian street organist playing outside the House, expects only an "amusing" scene when the door opens; but "to us," that is, the reader and the narrator, "who know the inner heart of the Seven Gables" as well as its "exterior face," there is a "ghastly effect" in the contrast between the frivolity outside and the corpse within. Yet even stronger than "our" knowledge is the power of imaginative observation, which has perceived the beauty of Alice's Posies and recognized, even in the history of crime, the utopian potential that motivates the book's end.

The Blithedale Romance highlights the complexities of spectatorship in its narrative structure. Departing from his usual technique, Hawthorne experiments with a first-person narrator. The materials of the narrative are also unusually close to Hawthorne's own life, for "Blithedale" is transparently a version of Brook Farm, and Miles Coverdale, the narrator, is a literary artist. Consequently, some readers have been fascinated by the possible autobiographical dimensions of the work, while others have been eager to argue that the apparent events of the work instead reflect Coverdale's distorted perceptions. The book itself invites this line of analysis, because it delays until its very last words "Miles Coverdale's Confession." Coverdale reveals a secret that puts into a new light all that has gone on and that he has recounted. He has been in love with Priscilla, the mysterious young seamstress. Because the action of the book has involved Priscilla's love for the obsessive philanthropist Hollingsworth and Hollingsworth's rejection of the passionate feminist intellectual Zenobia, who commits suicide, the revelation calls into question all that has gone on before. The "confession" also explains the bitterly ironic tone that at times inflects the narrative, for Coverdale seeks to distance himself from the pain of lost love, which has made his later years increasingly barren and frustrated.

Miles Coverdale himself is the primary sensitive spectator in *The Blithedale Romance.* (Priscilla's special sensitivities are not combined with the spectator's distance but are rather part of a more complex vulnerability.) Coverdale offers contradictory descriptions of his role. At one point he criticizes himself for "making my prey of other people's individualities," which would make him hardly any different from the more assertively egotistic Hollingsworth. But only a few pages earlier, Coverdale observed that he would have done something only "had I been as hard-hearted as I sometimes thought." His spectatorship compromises his relation to the community at Blithedale. He often retreats to his "observatory," a hidden nook up in a tree. Its isolation and secrecy, he thought, "symbolized my individuality." From its aerial distance, however, everything going on at Blithedale "looks ridiculous." Yet his spectatorship also implicates him in the affairs of the others. Returned from Blithedale to Boston, Coverdale finds a post of observation in the third-floor back room of a hotel. Days of watching the "backside of the universe" lead him to reflect that "realities keep in the rear," and soon he sees Zenobia and Priscilla, on the brink of a crucial decision in which he tries to intervene.

Coverdale gives an intricate summary of his position. He reflects that Zenobia

should have been able to appreciate that quality of the intellect and the heart which impelled me (often against my own will, and to the detriment of my own comfort) to live in other lives, and to endeavor – by generous sympathies, by delicate intuitions, by taking note of things too slight for record, and by bringing my human spirit into manifold accordance with the companions whom God assigned me – to learn the secret which was hidden even from themselves.

In its union of mind and heart, its scrupulous attentiveness, and its quest for the unrevealed, even the unconscious, this self-image presents an ideal of what Hawthorne's narrative and his readers might seek. Yet in *The Blithedale Romance,* this ideal is compromised by its location in a flawed character. Even in this passage, Coverdale's case is obviously exaggerated by the force of defensiveness and desire alike.

Nor in the earlier romances was the "sensitive spectator" a simple matter. In *The Scarlet Letter* Chillingworth is the character who most fully carries out the agenda of penetration into the secrets of others through intimate knowledge, fueled by intuition as much as by science. Still, Chillingworth, however wronged and suffering, is the villain. The covert and malicious, yet institutionally legitimated, surveillance that he carries out on Dimmesdale is echoed, more coarsely, in *The House of Seven Gables,* where Jaffrey Pyncheon searches into "the secrets of your interior" to threaten Clifford with incarceration for lunacy. Although Holgrave is a descendant of the Maules and is implicated in the history of the House, he presents himself only as a "privileged and meet spectator," whose task is to "look on" and "to analyze." Phoebe, however, is distressed that he speaks "as if this old house were a theatre," because "the play costs the performers too much, and the audience is too cold-hearted."

Sensitivity is susceptibility, and such openness may not be part of any warmth. Even "sympathy" may be "nervous," more physiological than spiri-

tual. It does not necessarily convey concern for others, but testifies only to
one's capacity to be affected by others' feelings. So Coverdale reflects that his
"cold tendency, between instinct and intellect, which made me pry with a
speculative interest into people's passions and impulses, appeared to have
gone far towards unhumanizing my heart." He fears that "with the power to
act in the place of destiny" to help his friends, he has, instead, "resigned
them to their fate," as mere "figures on my mental stage."

The power to harm by distance, the uncaring irresponsibility that refuses to
act on knowledge, may be distinguished from another dangerous power, what,
in *The House of Seven Gables,* Hawthorne calls the power of the "sadly gifted eye"
of a "seer." Faced with the "tall and stately edifice" of character presented to the
outside world by a hypocrite like Jaffrey, this seer's power of vision causes the
"whole structure" to melt "into thin air," until all that remains is the evidence
of the original, hidden crime: "the hidden nook, the bolted closet . . . or the
deadly hole under the pavement, and the decaying corpse within." Reminiscent of the archeological metaphors so dear to Freud in his theory of unconscious repression, this figurative language also echoes that of the household of
the Union so common in the political rhetoric of the 1850s. It seems an
extraordinary instance of Hawthorne's own motivated unconsciousness that he
never registers an awareness that slavery might be a founding crime that
vitiates the glories of the national structure built upon it.

Hawthorne's fiction does not challenge the political order, yet there are
respects in which it stands against its age. The power of his hesitant stylistic
effects to undo the reality of what they describe, as the seer unsees the reality
of the edifice, provoked one reviewer to complain, "We want the result, and
not the process. . . . We want *things*." Because a book is a marketable
commodity, and therefore itself a thing, are readers entitled to demand that
it also contain things? Hawthorne resisted such a demand. Even while he
himself was operating within the market system and the whole machinery of
business that made half his life seem like no life at all, Hawthorne tried to
find a space for freedom in his romances. By highlighting a process of
creation that had not yet solidified into things, Hawthorne tried to distinguish imagination from commodity.

The Marble Faun is the book in which these issues are most elaborately
turned over, for with three artists among the four main characters, the
question of vision and its relation to life is crucial. The mysterious, dark,
Miriam displays in a suite of her drawings a "beautiful imagination" that
reaches out with "sympathies" of such "force and variety" that she can make
art out of the common experiences of womanhood that have, exceptionally,
been denied to her. But her sympathetic receptivity is joined with an intimidating acquisitiveness. Faced with the famous painting of Beatrice Cenci

(who had been sexually abused by her father and then in retaliation caused his death), Miriam exclaims, "If I only could get within her consciousness!"

The young American Hilda is not an original artist, but a copyist. Nonetheless, the "depth of sympathy" by which Hilda operates allows her to achieve "what the great master had conceived in his imagination" but had failed thoroughly to execute. Other copyists "work . . . entirely from the outside" and "only reproduce the surface." They leave out "that indefinable nothing, that inestimable something, that constitutes the life and soul through which the picture gets its immortality." Hilda, in contrast, is "no such machine." She intuits her way into "following precisely the same process . . . through which the original painter had trodden to the development of his idea."

Fully equal in sensitivity to the artist is the Italian naïf Donatello, whose roots in the countryside link him to both cultural antiquity and natural vitality. He loves Miriam and he hates her persecutor, the mysterious Capuchin; when the Capuchin menaces her, Donatello hurls him off the Tarpeian Rock. He explains, "I did what your eyes bade me do, when I asked them with mine." This dialogue of the eyes proves the true love between the couple, yet it is proved in a surge of hatred and its criminal response. The sensitive spectator, when not an artist but a person of no reflective consciousness, may prove a dangerous agent, as Hawthorne shows in this terrifying fantasia on a cliché of ordinary social exchange, the scornful woman's "killing glance." Hilda accidentally comes upon the scene just as it occurs, and "that look" from Miriam to Donatello, like "a flash of lightning," fixes itself in her memory and shatters her moral repose. The look is not only deadly but also contagious, when it is seen with responsive sympathy.

Finally the whole action of *The Marble Faun* and the fates of its characters are controlled by a system of politically regulated surveillance, a vision more powerful in its effects than even the artists' and lovers' exchanges of glances. The secret police of the Roman government have Miriam under control: "Free and self-controlled as she appeared, her every movement was watched and investigated far more thoroughly by the priestly rulers than by her dearest friends." The artists' exchanges of vision are one figure within the book for the artistic power of the author's imaginative sympathy, but the figure of state control offers an alternative. It acknowledges the writer's total command in shaping form and inventing incident, even while he tries to give the form and the event the spontaneity of nature.

There is a further force at play in this sequence, still another coercive spectator. Hawthorne's "Postscript" explaining the police plot was added to the second English printing of the book, after reviewers had complained about the lack of resolution in the original ending. Hawthorne had hoped to justify his procedure by arguing that narrative is itself a dubious and tenuous enterprise. Narratives require beginnings, ends, causes, and connections; in contrast, "the actual experience of even the most ordinary life is full of events that never explain themselves, either as regards their origin or their tendency." Hawthorne does not deny that things happen ("events"), but they are inexplicable, and therefore "any narrative of human action and adventures — whether we call it history or romance — is certain to be a fragile handiwork." Readers did not accept this excuse. As he acknowledged, "everybody" was dissatisified, and so he made the change, invoking the quasi-historical narrative of state agency to provide origin and tendency. Yet he also asserted, "For my own part, however, I should prefer the book as it now stands." The romance enacts a compromise. Hawthorne may give the appearance of being "free and self-controlled" as an artist, but his conceptions are under surveillance by a powerful readership whose demands he must meet. Hawthorne's revision attributes to politics (the secret police) responsibility for what is actually a matter of economics (his audience), but elsewhere in the book he does focus attention on the economic conditions of artistic production.

Hawthorne explains that "a sculptor in these days has very little to do" with the "process of actually chiselling the marble," for there are Italian artisans who can take any object placed "before their eyes" and reproduce it in marble with consummate "mechanical skill." If the artist but gives them the model, at the appointed time, "without the necessity of his touching the work with his own finger," he will discover the statue from which his fame will spring: "His creative power has wrought it with a word." Hawthorne becomes sarcastic about the sculptor's fortune in avoiding "the drudgery of actual performance." The sculptor's apparently magical potency actually unmakes him, for his works are "not his work," when they derive from "some nameless machine in human shape."

The Romantic theory of art, by its emphasis on the spiritual, the "creative," has itself become another crippling split, reminiscent of Hawthorne's need for Sophia to double her investments in pleasure while he worked. The image of artistic wholeness does not wholly cover the division of labor on which it depends as a business. The establishment of literary narrative made possible the dream of an autonomous world of art and pleasure, which proved however to depend on economic and political conditions that produced misery at the personal, local, and national levels. Hawthorne's romances powerfully proclaim the separation of art from life and also show that such separation is impossible. Even as it was becoming established as a relatively autonomous practice and institution, literature was at once more powerful than it feared and more responsible than it wished.

MOBY-DICK

In dedicating *Moby-Dick* to Nathaniel Hawthorne, "in token of my admiration for his genius," Herman Melville announced that after the failure of *Mardi* and the successes of *Redburn* and *White-Jacket* he was again writing literary narrative. The special power of this particular literary narrative is its voracious capacity to swallow many other forms and kinds, beginning with the learned "Etymology" and "Extracts" that launch the book from the library and place it in a world history stretching back to Genesis. The generic basis of *Moby-Dick* is personal narrative, like so much of Melville's earlier work, but Melville pushed beyond its limits. In a letter to his English publisher, Bentley, Melville boasted of "the author's own personal experience of two years and more as a harpooneer," but he had never been one. In *Moby-Dick,* as he had done in his earlier personal narratives, Melville freely supplemented his own experience with relevant books, both of whaling and about whales.

As the narrative begins, the most immediate signals are those of local sketch writing. Since 1830, with the "Jack Downing" sketches by Seba Smith, "Down East" humor about Yankees had paralleled the popularity of southwestern humor. One frequent mark of these Yankee characters was an outlandish biblical name. "Call me Ishmael" becomes richly suggestive, but it begins as the name of a grimly comic, self-mocking narrator who introduces the reader to odd happenings in the life of the shoreside whaling community. The "damp drizzly November" in Ishmael's soul joins him to a line of hypochondriac periodical writers. The basic form of *Moby-Dick* follows that of Thorpe's "Big Bear of Arkansas." Each frames a story about the most astonishing hunter of the most amazing animal. Yet the immensely greater size of *Moby-Dick* breaks the generic mold, and its resemblance to two different kinds of local narrative suggests that it can properly belong to neither.

National narrative was the established large form of the time, and it often demonstrated its national scope by taking in the characteristic narratives of various locales, as Prescott suggested that Bancroft did. Melville, in *Moby-Dick,* as he had earlier in *White-Jacket,* strikes key notes from the prevailing rhetoric of America. The claim for human equality helps to justify treating the mates and harpooneers of the whaler the *Pequod* as characters capable of tragedy, even though they are workers, not nobles. The narrative calls upon the "great democratic God," who granted literary immortality to Cervantes the pauper and Bunyan the convict and who placed "Andrew Jackson . . . higher than a throne!" As with Bancroft and Tocqueville, national narrative extends to the global. Playing "Advocate" for the glory of whaling, Ishmael boasts of "the whaleman who first broke through the jealous policy of the Spanish crown" concerning the Pacific colonies of South America. He explains that "from those whalemen at last eventuated the liberation of Peru, Chili, and Bolivia from the yoke of Old Spain," which made possible "the establishment of the eternal democracy."

Without Ahab, *Moby-Dick* would not be a literary narrative. Ahab hijacks national narrative by leading the *Pequod,* which in many ways has been made representative of America, into disaster, disrupting the genre's triumphalism. As a tragic hero, modeled on Shakespeare's, Ahab fulfills the Romantic program for the literary. Yet without Ishmael, Ahab could not achieve his tragic stature. The dramatically styled speeches of Ahab require the narrative contextualization and speculative interpretation provided by Ishmael as sensitive spectator. This suggests a combination of Shakespeare and Hawthorne, which Melville first sketched in "Hawthorne and His Mosses," written in early August 1850, just after he met Hawthorne. By October, Melville had moved from New York to the Berkshires, where he could frequently visit Hawthorne while working on *Moby-Dick.*

The slim documentary evidence indicates that Melville had begun *Moby-Dick* in early 1850, after returning in February from some months abroad. By May he wrote to Dana that he was half done with "the whaling voyage," and in early August, Evert Duyckinck, who was with Melville in the Berkshires, wrote back to New York that the work was "mostly done." Yet *Moby-Dick* was not actually completed for another year. It seems that the experience of meeting Hawthorne provoked Melville to imagine a new level of ambition. He articulated this ambition in "Hawthorne and His Mosses," and he then determined to revise his romance-in-progress to try to reach the goal of matching Shakespeare's tragic power with an American work.

The encounter with Hawthorne may have catalyzed Melville's aspirations, but already in the letter to Dana he anticipated that he was writing "a strange sort of a book." He vowed that he would include not only the "truth" of whaling but also the "poetry." *Truth and Poetry* was the title of Goethe's autobiography, which was one of a cluster of important works of Romantic literature that Melville had bought and read during his trip abroad. It appears that before he met Hawthorne, Melville had been trying to create through his reading an imagined literary community that did not exist in the America of his time. His purchases in England form a catalogue of important Romantic writers and the works that the Romantics admired. Besides the Goethe book, he acquired the works of Charles Lamb, *Confessions of an English Opium Eater* (1822), by Thomas De Quincey, and Mary Shelley's *Frankenstein* (1818), as well as volumes of Renaissance drama (which Lamb particularly had highlighted), and he read with great excitement Laurence Sterne's strange, innovative *Tristram Shandy* (1760–7). Moreover, on that trip he participated in many intense conversations on "metaphysics," on "Hegel, Schlegel, Kant & c," with George Adler, the German-born philologist, whose philosophy Melville described as "Coleridgean," as he might have recognized from reading the previous year in his then newly acquired copy of the *Biographia Literaria*.

By importing the techniques of Shakespeare into a novel, Melville echoes the ambition and encounters the problems of Goethe's *Wilhelm Meister's Apprenticeship* (1796) which he borrowed while he was writing *Moby-Dick*. Goethe's novel inaugurated the tradition of the *Bildungsroman*, which focuses on the formation of a character. The action that shapes Wilhelm revolves around his aspiration to bring *Hamlet* to the German stage. Goethe deepens the way character figures in the novel by drawing on the play of Shakespeare that had most impressed readers with the mysterious depth of its central character. Within *Wilhelm Meister*, Goethe put forward important speculations about the novel as a genre in contrast to drama. In drama, the emphasis falls on the "deeds" of "characters"; in novels, "it is chiefly sentiments and events that are exhibited." The hero of drama actively presses forward to hasten the end, but "the novel hero must be suffering," or at least "retarding": by whatever means, "the sentiments of the hero . . . must restrain the tendency of the whole to unfold itself and to conclude." This theory justifies Goethe's choice of *Hamlet*, because it makes *Hamlet* seem a novelistic drama. *Moby-Dick*, however, is a dramatically inflected novel. While Ahab actively presses forward, Ishmael's sentiments and reflections keep the book from ending too fast.

Friedrich Schlegel's "Letter on the Novel" (1799) builds from Goethe's work to a somewhat different end. For Schlegel, the difference between drama and novel depends on the place that the work occupies in its social setting: plays are meant to be "viewed," and novels are "for reading." In contrast, then, to Shakespeare's plays, Schelegel defines a novel (in German, *Roman*) as "a romantic book." The key term "romance," discussed earlier, takes some of its force from this context. For Schlegel, a novel gains unity not from its plot, but through a central focus on thematic or conceptual materials. This "higher unity" allows a novel to be formally a "mixture," incorporating "storytelling, song, and other forms." The novel has the privilege that Schlegel in his most famous critical statement reserves to "Romantic poetry" (*romantische Poesie*, which might also be translated "novelistic poesis"): to "mix and fuse" all divergent types so as to become the only "kind of poetry . . . that is more than a kind."

Moby-Dick, as a work of literary narrative that incorporates national, local, and personal generic elements under this dominance, as a "romantic book," is a novel (*Roman*), and, as a novel, it is liable to problems concerning the status of action in its hero. Ishmael goes to sea to evade suicide by submitting himself to a regimen that frees him from the need for self-regulation. Rich and various as are the activities that engross him throughout the book, they all are therapy rather than action. Ishmael is repeatedly healed or purged. Queequeg cures him of misanthropy; the "Mast-Head" chapter warns against his speculative excess; the "Try-Works" teaches him the danger of gloomy obsession; and at the end of the book, "tossed" overboard, "dropped" astern, and "buoyed" by Queequeg's coffin, he is "picked up." Only insofar as he acts as the book's writer, and insofar as the action of the novel is that it is being written, does Ishmael perform an action. This literary action, however, has precisely the force of its differentiation from all other kinds of action available in the culture. Thomas Carlyle, whose pages on Shakespeare were echoed by Melville in "Hawthorne and His Mosses," had lamented in *Heroes and Hero-Worship* that the modern writer has "importance" only for the book trade. Otherwise, "He is an accident in society. He wanders like a wild Ishmaelite."

In contrast to Ishmael, Ahab is modeled on tragic heroes, and the passionate power of his quest seems an obvious source of action, providing direction rather than wandering. Yet his revenge is really a reaction. "I will dismember my dismemberer," Ahab proclaims. The overall movement of the book seriously compromises the status of his action. In its broadest structure, the plot is a satire on human impotence: St. George comes up to the dragon, and it does him in; there is really no contest. Melville emphasizes this pattern in many ways in the climactic chase sequence. Ahab is presented as the greatest of all whale-hunters; he actually finds the whale by "snuffing" like a dog, rather than requiring all the elaborate paraphernalia of technology that he has ostentatiously stripped away. As the chase begins, in his eagerness to locate the whale that he has already sensed, Ahab cries out after it, "flattening his face to the sky." This image of intensity and eagerness is cast down into humiliation after the whale, without even being harpooned, has caught Ahab's whaleboat by surprise and held it between his jaws, while Ahab, trying to get free, "fell flat-faced upon the sea."

The same reversal of intended agency into passivity occurs between the description of Ahab's initial approach to the whale and the conclusion of the whale's toying with the whaleboat. First, the boats approached the whale, and the "breathless hunter [that is, Ahab] came so nigh his seemingly unsuspecting prey, that his entire dazzling hump was distinctly visible." (Note the transfer that carries "his" over from Ahab to the whale.) But then, after the whale has caught the boat by surprise, "Ripplingly withdrawing from his prey, Moby Dick now lay at a little distance." The same phrase, "his . . . prey," has reversed its direction. Ahab is the whale's prey.

Melville's writing in *Moby-Dick* produces extraordinary entanglements for action, not only on the large scale of genre but also in the local procedure of particular passages. After Ahab first appears to the crew on "The Quarter-Deck" and exhorts them to join his mission of revenge, there follows a series of chapters that in their formal variety and complexity register Ahab's disruptive effect within the texture of the book. "Sunset" trumpets the model of Shakespeare. Its prose is metered to imitate blank verse, and it represents the speech of Ahab to himself alone, a soliloquy. This explodes the personal narrative. How could Ishmael report what Ahab says to himself? The next two chapters play off soliloquies by the mates, earnest Starbuck and jolly Stubb. "Midnight, Forecastle" is written as a stage scene involving all the crew in drunken talk and revelry. It looks back to the "Walpurgisnacht" of Goethe's *Faust* and forward to "night town" in Joyce's *Ulysses*. Following this chaos, Ishmael broods reflectively for two chapters, explaining to the reader what Moby Dick meant to Ahab and then what "The Whiteness of the Whale" meant to Ishmael himself.

"The Chart" follows these chapters. Ahab is poring over the technical charts whale-hunters used to predict where and when to find whales, but the chapter shows that something in Ahab cannot so rationally be accounted for. Ahab's will is a force that breaks apart his individuality, and therefore it is very difficult to determine who, or what, is responsible for things that happen. One extraordinary sentence charts both Ahab's "spiritual" struggle and Ishmael's struggle to grasp what is going on:

Often, when forced from his hammock by exhausting and intolerably vivid dreams of the night, which, resuming his own intense thoughts through the day, carried them on amid a clashing of phrensies, and whirled them round and round in his blazing brain, till the very throbbing of his life-spot became insufferable anguish; and when, as was sometimes the case, these spiritual throes in him heaved his being up from its base, and a chasm seemed opening in him, from which forked flames and lightnings shot up, and accursed fiends beckoned him to leap down among them; when this hell in himself yawned beneath him, a wild cry would be heard through the ship; and with glaring eyes Ahab would burst from his state room, as though escaping from a bed that was on fire.

Carrying "hell in himself" like Satan in Milton's *Paradise Lost,* Ahab's interior is a broken landscape. He does not securely possess himself; he is "forced" by "dreams of the night," which usurp his "own intense thoughts." He proves even more complex, as Ishmael elaborates on the mode of agency that may have produced this spectacle of Ahab bursting into sight. "Crazy Ahab" the "steadfast hunter," this "Ahab that had gone to his hammock" was "not the agent that so caused him to burst from it in horror again." Ahab has split into two parts, an active "agent" and an acted-upon "him."

Ishmael explains that the "agent" is the "principle or soul." In sleep it is freed from the "characterizing mind," which otherwise "employed it for its outer vehicle or agent." This instrumental sense of "agent" opposes the motivating force that is being described, so that, it seems, the soul is now free to act as agent because it is not forced to serve as agent. Ishmael's metaphysical fantasia speculates further: "The tormented spirit that glared out of bodily eyes when what seemed Ahab rushed from his room, was for the time but a vacated thing." Ahab is not Ahab, for the "thing" if still frantic is now "vacated." The individual has been further divided. The self-created being is "formless," because if the soul has fled, the mind no longer has an "object" to shape through its "characterizing" power. Moreover, the being has no consciousness; it is "somnambulistic," because sleep is required for the psychic fissioning that in turn creates new elements. Ahab's pure will is a "blankness" like the horrifying "Whiteness of the Whale" that Ishmael had just analyzed and like the "blank" spaces on the chart that Ahab himself is painstakingly filling in at the beginning of this chapter.

To summarize Ishmael's analysis: when Ahab burst out "as though escaping from a bed that was on fire," he is not the agent. Instead, his soul is the agent, for its "escape from the scorching contiguity" of the mind has triggered the process by which pure will flares up, from which the body tries vainly to flee, thus projecting into visibility the simulacrum of Ahab. The "outer vehicle" of the body transports the "tormented spirit"; nonetheless, the body is not agent of the spirit, for in carrying the will out of the stateroom, it is not carrying out the will's will.

These involuted paradoxes of agency bring fully into literature a major theme from Romantic philosophy, particularly from Coleridge's *Biographia Literaria*. In "The Whiteness of the Whale," Coleridge is specifically mentioned, and the chapter is concerned with the need for "imagination," which is the major topic of the *Biographia*. In this chapter, whiteness is twice characterized as an "agent." Once whiteness is designated as "prime agent," the phrase Coleridge had reserved in the *Biographia* for his fundamental definition of the "primary imagination." In the second reference, whiteness is called an "intensifying agent." The word "intensifying" was a coinage of the *Biographia,* as Coleridge boasted in a footnote. It occurs in a sentence about the will, following a paragraph about the imagination, in a chapter that asserts the need for an active theory of mind against the passive mechanism that Coleridge found in eighteenth-century psychological theory. Coleridge criticizes this theory because it leaves no room for the soul as a "real separate being." Any effects that might be attributed to the soul are instead "produced by an agency independent and alien." Coleridge fears the alienation of agency, that is, the dispossession of a proper identity with the dispersal of soul, will, and self.

Melville does not share Coleridge's confidence in the relations between the soul and the will. Instead he works out a case – which "The Chart" lays out in its microscopic form – in which the real separability of the soul does not do as much good as Coleridge hoped and in which the independent, alien agency is constructed in considerable elaboration. To mock the mechanical theory, Coleridge proposed a hyperbolic reduction of the act of writing, in which "the whole universe co-operates to produce the minutest stroke of every letter, save only that I myself, and I alone, have nothing to do with it . . . for it is the mere motion of my muscles and nerves." Coleridge hoped his readers would reject such a conception, but Ahab cries out with full feeling, "Is Ahab, Ahab? Is it I, God, or who, that lifts this arm?"

Moby Dick, the whale itself, at every moment reminds readers that agency cannot be confined to human form or to human control. *Moby-Dick* explores the uncertain borders of agency. Things happen, but it remains a question how. Hawthorne argued in *The Marble Faun* that events might fall within ordinary human experience and yet not be explicable in relation to their origins or tendencies. The whale may be partially predictable as to time and place, but it is not known where it comes from or where it is going. To write a book that centered on the whale, rather than on its hunters, would go far beyond human powers of narrative, and yet even a narrative that merely includes Moby Dick shows that human individuality cannot account for the way the world works. In *Moby-Dick,* individuality is neither a goal nor a premise. At best, it is a puzzling possibility.

Issues of action, agent, and responsibility are first highlighted in "The Quarter-Deck." Behind the "pasteboard masks" of all "visible objects," Ahab seeks a subject, "some unknown but still reasoning thing" that may be surmised through its effects in "each event – in the living act, the undoubted deed." This "inscrutable thing," hidden behind the "wall" of the "whale," yet, to Ahab's sight, "sinewing it" with "malice," he seeks to reach, but his only access is through the whale. Therefore, "be the white whale agent, or be the white whale principal, I will wreak that hate upon him." Ahab denies the possibility of blasphemy, which Starbuck has warned against, because he denies hierarchy: "Who's over me?"

Ahab's stance points in two directions to the America in which Melville was writing. His pseudoutopian democratic promise – there is none above him, and he is not ruling the crew, but they are "one and all with" him in the enterprise – engages the political theory of John Calhoun. Calhoun argued that the southern states were made up not of "individuals," but of "communities": "Every plantation is a little community, with the master at its head, who concentrates in himself the united interests of capital and labor, of which he is the common representative." This organic model echoes the key term of

Romantic aesthetics: all interests will be "harmonized." Yet "labor" here meant slaves, so Starbuck's critique of Ahab takes on even more force: "a democrat to all above; look, how he lords it over all below!"

Ahab's interpretation of agency as equality — his willingness to take the subordinate, the "agent," as responsible in place of the "principal," the master or owner — was not unique. It was shared by the American culture then reshaping itself to mobilize resources for the enormous industrial expansion that had followed the depression of 1837. In Ahab, coexisting with the residual political position of Calhoun, is an emergent legal position that began from railroad cases around 1840 and dominated the later nineteenth century. Ahab's multiple figurations are not all archaic: he is also cast in the language of modernity. In his "Sunset" soliloquy, Ahab identifies himself with the railroad: "the path to my fixed purpose is laid with iron rails." This figure of titanic will may seem to fit with Calhoun's "master," but there is another side to the railroad. Railroads were a notably impersonal system of employment. No American occupation had more employees who were less likely to have direct acquaintance, even by sight, with their employer. And the railroad image suits the whale as well as it does Ahab. The regularity of the whale's rate of travel resembles that of "the mighty iron Leviathan of the modern railway." This nonhuman force reduces humans to equality and shatters the system of representation that structured the relations of master to servant, principal to agent.

A whole new area of law, the law of torts, grew up to deal with railroad injuries, and, later, with factory injuries. For industrial expansion brought industrial accidents, and railroads were the scene and means of tremendous human damage. In common-law tradition, a "principal" was responsible for any damages done or caused by that principal's agent, slave, servant or other member of the household, or employee. In the new law, this "rule of agency" did not apply. Instead, a doctrine known as the "fellow-servant rule" held that an employee (servant, agent) could not sue the employer (master, principal) for injuries suffered through the negligence of another employee (a fellow servant), or "co-agent." The net effect of this was to protect corporations for decades from liability for much of the immense misery they caused. The judge who wrote the key decision (1842) in this area was Chief Justice Lemuel Shaw of Massachusetts, Melville's father-in-law.

The emergence of the American literature that readers still recognize today, the novel or the romance (*Roman*) as practiced by Hawthorne and Melville, is connected with the political crisis of the mid-nineteenth century, a situation of which Emerson could write, "Men live on the defensive, and go through life without an action, without one overt act, one initiated action." As argued earlier, the Compromise of 1850 defined political responsibility as regulation — preserving the Union — rather than as motion — extending free-dom to the disadvantaged within the Union. Urgent questions of how best to share newly produced goods as well as new obligations were displaced from the electoral arena to the legal system, and the courts ultimately defined economic responsibility as motion — extending enterprise — rather than as regulation — preserving common-law protections.

Politics thus centered on the fiction of identity of the Union, but econom-ics undid the "fiction of identity" (as Oliver Wendell Holmes later called it) that had subordinated agents to principals. The new law multiplied the number of individuals who had no relations with each other other than those of contractual equality. These newly emergent individuals had little scope for action, however; they were "free agents" in a most restricted sense. The national consensus held that there was nothing to be done politically, and one's responsibility was to be silent; whatever was done economically was understood simply to have happened, and one's responsibility was to be patient, that is, to not take action, for injuries were not actionable. This consensus was not total. The movement against slavery stood emphatically outside it. *Uncle Tom's Cabin,* like *Moby-Dick,* drew on national, local, and personal narrative materials; and it emphasized not political change, but moral transformation. Nevertheless, it did not define itself as literary narra-tive, for it clearly engaged the shared world of its readers and did not make action a problem. *Uncle Tom's Cabin* was a polemically alternative national narrative (see Chapter 5).

Literary narrative offered a place to be heard separate from politics and only partially subordinated to the economy, but this privilege came at the cost of acknowledging literature as fiction, that is, as saying nothing that bore on the shared public world in the way that national, local, and personal narra-tives had done. To be thus outside partisan politics is to give ground in hope of finding a transcendent alternative. That is, the literary work acts as a one-way valve, drawing the materials of the world into its own world, from which they do not return. This is the effect of Ishmael's complex literary mediation. This literary compromise, a diminishment in the scope of the writer's action, may be seen also in the book itself, as Ahab's failure to achieve individual agency. In this particular American form of the generic problem of action in the novel, what marks and mars Ahab is also what places *Moby-Dick* in its moment.

In contrast to Hawthorne's romances, which hew closely to a conservative line of political quietism and thus shift attention from action to the "sensitive spectator," *Moby-Dick* more closely approaches the transformative energies of the economy and therefore places action as a problem in the foreground. Ahab most strongly asserts his individuality precisely at the moments that he is challenged by the impersonal structures of the economy. Rhetorically, he seizes that impersonality as freedom from hierarchy. When on "The Quarter-Deck" Starbuck challenges Ahab, "How many barrels will thy vengeance yield thee? . . . it will not fetch thee much in our Nantucket market," Ahab's response is to cut free from the question of "agent" or "principal," to proclaim that there is no power over himself, not even the invisible hand of the market: "But not my master, man, is even that fair play." In cutting off the "superior," the "principal," the "master," or the owner from responsibility for the injury caused one agent by another, courts transformed "servants," "agents," workers into individuals, even as they were also becoming "hands." Ahab offers a heroic fantasy — both nostalgic and critical — of such individuality. When Starbuck later challenges Ahab for the second time on economic grounds, he invokes the absent owners. Ahab rises to the challenge by applying an argument from John Locke that had once helped to make the American Revolution, "The only real owner of anything is its commander." This individuality has often impressed readers as the book's accomplishment.

Yet the complexity of *Moby-Dick* demonstrates, both in its overall shape and through the particular language of meditative moments, that such individuality cannot be sustained. As the nineteenth century went on, however, an ever more intense rhetoric of individuality paralleled the unprecedented growth of corporations. Ahab dies asserting that "Ahab is for ever Ahab," but Ishmael has, for example in "The Chart," speculatively shown what Ahab does not know, the complex, alien causality that produces "what seemed Ahab." Or, as Ishmael also puts it, "That before living agent, now became the living instrument." Ahab's individual agency keeps collapsing into instrumentality or impotence because things happen on a scale — intrapsychic fission, cetacean power, an absent and irresponsible hierarchy of ownership — that is not commensurate with human individuality.

The writer's isolation as individual artist, cut off from the collectivity of local and national, and even personal, narratives, made possible the achievement of literary narrative in creating an alternative world. However, the political and economic pressures that limited the power of literary narrative to imagine action produced formal tensions that puzzled most readers, who were not fully content with the supplemental interpretive energy of the sensitive spectator. Amidst the political and economic crises from the mid-1850s into the Civil War and Reconstruction, readers and writers alike began to doubt the experiment of literary narrative, and national narrative returned to the fore.

5

CRISIS OF LITERARY NARRATIVE AND CONSOLIDATION OF NATIONAL NARRATIVE

The Compromise of 1850 had displaced politics and opened a possibility for the literary narratives of Hawthorne and Melville, but in the years before the Civil War, American national narrative still flourished. Volumes 4 through 7 of Bancroft's *History of the United States* appeared from 1852 through 1860, and in 1851 *Moby-Dick* made far less of an impact than did two works that had adapted national narrative to establish careers for their authors which would outshine Melville's through the rest of the century: Harriet Beecher Stowe began serial publication of *Uncle Tom's Cabin* in the Washington abolitionist journal the *National Era,* and Francis Parkman published *The History of the Conspiracy of Pontiac.* Like *Moby-Dick,* both these works are on a large scale. They range broadly over the geography of North America, and they encompass a wide range of human experience, including shocking extremities of horror. Like *Moby-Dick,* too, they present problems that arise from the multiracial character of the United States, from its colonial past into the present. Their commitment to national narrative, as opposed to the subordination of national to literary narrative in *Moby-Dick,* may be gauged most readily through their narrative technique. They establish no fictional intermediary like Ishmael; rather, they encourage readers to identify the narrating presence with the author, who in each case holds a clear ideological position on issues of major national consequence.

In a letter to Hawthorne commenting on *The House of the Seven Gables,* which Hawthorne had just given him, Melville strikingly images the autonomy both he and Hawthorne asociated with what I have been calling literary narrative. Hawthorne has caught a "certain tragic phase of humanity," which may be found in "human thought in its own unbiassed, native, and profounder workings." This "intense" exploration of the "mind" reveals what Melville calls "visible truth": "the apprehension of the absolute condition of present things as they strike the eye of the man who fears them not, though they do their worst to him." Such a man enjoys radical independence: "like Russia or the British Empire," he "declares himself a sovereign nature (in himself), amid the powers of heaven, hell, and earth." More solidly individ-ual than anything Ahab achieved, this fearless, masculine vision makes possi-ble the "grand truth about Nathaniel Hawthorne": "He says NO! in thunder; but the Devil himself cannot make him say *yes.*" The brave truth tellers who say no are "unincumbered," traveling through life with only their "Ego," but "all men who say *yes, lie.*"

As American national narratives, *Uncle Tom's Cabin* and *The Conspiracy of Pontiac* would seem to Melville bound to a fundamental affirmation that compromises their power, even though each also exercises a powerful nega-tion. Stowe redefined national narrative to oppose the compromised Ameri-can consensus of 1850 that the Union required silence about slavery. Park-man challenged what he considered the idealization of Indians fostered by Cooper's national narrative. Even though the lives of Pontiac and Uncle Tom end terribly and might therefore be understood in Melville's terms as "tragic," neither work emphasizes the workings of "thought" or focuses intensely on the "mind." Parkman's elaborate renderings of settings, strate-gies, and events and Stowe's close attention to the details of regional speech and the fluxes of feeling might both seem external and conventional com-pared to the original, internalized profundity Melville found in Shakespeare and Hawthorne and sought to achieve for himself.

Different as they both are from *Moby-Dick*, *Uncle Tom's Cabin* and *The Conspiracy of Pontiac* also differ from each other. Their divergences demon-strate, in the same way as had William Hickling Prescott's approval of Bancroft (see Chapter 1), that national narrative covered a very broad ground, which made it hard for Hawthorne or Melville to maintain a place apart. Both Parkman and Stowe were children of New England ministers, but Lyman Beecher came from working-class, rural Connecticut, while Francis Parkman, Sr., was born to Boston wealth. Furthermore, Beecher was a fiercely orthodox Calvinist and Parkman one of the first for whom Unitarian-ism was already an established option. Each child turned away from the parent's direction – Stowe from fear of predestination to hope of universal love, and Parkman from bland optimism to severe struggle. The chosen sites for their narrations were the camp fire for Parkman and the home fire for Stowe. Parkman helped to form a national elite audience that prided itself on its tough, masculine strength. In his last years, he received the dedication of Theodore Roosevelt's *The Winning of the West* (1889–96). Stowe reached beyond the United States, and beyond the mass audience of women that were the base of her readership, so that in *What Is Art?* (1898) the great Russian novelist Leo Tolstoy could prefer *Uncle Tom's Cabin* to *King Lear*, opposing the century-long tendency to value the "literary."

The Conspiracy of Pontiac was the first fruit of the huge historical project that Parkman had formed in his youth and that had motivated his encounters with Indians narrated in *The Oregon Trail* (see Chapter 3). On his return from his trip west, Parkman suffered a physical collapse that all but totally incapacitated him for the next eighteen years. Nonetheless, after dictating *The Oregon Trail,* he began work on his history, employing the method perfected by Prescott, who was almost blind. Documents were read aloud to him, and by means of a mechanical device to guide his hands, Parkman wrote drafts in a darkened room without using his eyes. Parkman's theme of heroic struggle against natural obstacles strangely echoed his own situation of work, and his earlier periods of intense out-of-doors activity energized his representations of what others had done that he could do no longer.

Although Parkman was not yet thirty years old when *The Conspiracy of Pontiac* was published, the work, from its opening words, achieves the tone of authority, as it declares the meaning for North America of the British triumph over France in the Seven Years' War (French and Indian War, 1754–60):

The conquest of Canada was an event of momentous consequence in American history. It changed the political aspect of the continent, prepared a way for the independence of the British colonies, rescued the vast tracts of the interior from the rule of military despotism, and gave them, eventually, to the keeping of an ordered democracy. Yet to the red natives of the soil its results were wholly disastrous.

Parkman details several resources for his authority – his research in archival materials, his first-hand knowledge of Indian life, and his personal investigation of "the sites of all the principal events recorded in the narrative." Moreover, his dedication of the volumes to President Jared Sparks of Harvard signals not only his authoritative institutional connections but also his command of the documentary and antiquarian basis for American historical research that Sparks had notably helped to establish.

Parkman's greatest authority is unacknowledged, however. The knowledge Parkman draws on in his opening, and which focuses his whole narrative through the seven further books that completed his history over the rest of the century, comes neither from the past nor from his personal experience: it is knowledge of the future. As part of the teleology of American "independence" and "democracy," he "aims to portray the American forest and the American Indian at the period when both received their final doom." In contrast to his knowledge, the Indians' "ignorance" leads them to their "desperate effort" to struggle against "the doom of the race," which "no human power could avert." Although Indians and forest survive, unacknowledged, at the time Parkman is writing, his prophetic frame of understanding is the American destiny to rule and civilize the continent. Parkman drew inspiration from Cooper and Bancroft (discussed in Chapter 1), although he found each insufficiently severe within the outlines of the national narrative that all three shared.

Parkman takes on a pious responsibility toward the doomed peoples and landscape of the past. Pontiac (c. 1720–69) was chief of the Ottawa; his "conspiracy" was an attempt in 1760 to coordinate Indian resistance to British rule, uniting Indian groups across the whole western frontier. This "great and daring champion" led the Indians in their last possible moment of conceivably successful resistance, yet the story of this "heroism and endurance" lies "buried." Parkman seeks to "rescue it from oblivion." He must not only recover the story, however, but also improve it; his task is not only conservative but also progressive. Once encountered, the historical material takes on the shape of a savage landscape, "uncultured and unreclaimed." In order to "build" his book, Parkman must carry out "labour . . . like that of the border settler, who . . . must fell the forest-trees, burn the undergrowth, clear the ground, and hew the fallen trunks to due proportion." Parkman's labor of writing repeats the work of the settler, but this means that with every stroke of his pen he reenacts the doom of the forest at the same time that he is restoring it to knowledge. This paradox derives from Parkman's understanding of his social and cultural position. As a white American, he stands as the opposite to the Indian: "there is nothing progressive in the rigid, inflexible nature of an Indian. He will not open his mind to the idea of improvement." A white American is sufficiently flexible to respond to the Indian way of life, but the Indian is too pure to make use of what Cooper called white "gifts."

The Conspiracy of Pontiac draws strength and interest from the opportunity its subject presented: an event of world-historical significance, still recent enough to permit the gathering of oral traditions and radically different in character from the subjects of British and European historiography. The New World renewed its subject: "In America war assumed a new and striking aspect." Parkman was freed from the "old battle-ground of Europe," where "the same familiar features of violence and horror" were repeated from "former generations." Unlike the more pacific Bancroft, but much like Cooper, Parkman found in America not freedom from violence and horror, but a stirring freshness in horrors. The "western paradise" of America "is not free from the curse of Adam"; rather, its "wilderness" forms a "sublime arena," where "army met army under the shadows of primeval woods."

The setting, the "land thus prodigal of good and evil," figures more constantly in the narrative than any single character, for this warfare was widely dispersed over the frontier. Moreover, there was not really adequate documentation to allow Pontiac consistently to play the central role of "savage hero of this dark forest tragedy," the "Satan of this forest paradise," that

Parkman at times rhetorically announces. This structural inconsistency points also to an inconsistency in the organization of the book's values. To imagine Pontiac as satanic corrupter is both to grant a purity to the wilderness and to enforce a distinction between the Indian and the wilderness that at other moments is denied. For the land is "not free from the curse of Adam," and the Indian is one with the land. At the climax of his first chapter, a long introduction to Indian life and character, Parkman defines the Indian as inseparable from the forest, the "irreclaimable son of the wilderness, the child who will not be weaned from the breast of his rugged mother."

Parkman never overcomes his triumphal, civilized contempt for Indians, and he never overcomes his fascination with the lost wildness they embody. His imagery is not stable; it shifts from one side to the other of the opposed forces. It is part of the Indians' doom, for example, that they are not flexible: "the Indian is hewn out of a rock"; yet they are doomed precisely because their futile ignorant revolt opposes "the rock-like strength of the Anglo-Saxon." At one point the massacre of a schoolmaster and nine pupils by Indians is proclaimed "an outrage . . . unmatched, in its fiend-like atrocity, through all the annals of the war." Yet it turns out that the savages are not unmatched. A white man named Owens, who has lived and married among the Indians, returns to civilization, after slaughtering his wife and children and several other Indian companions, to be rewarded with the bounty offered for each Indian scalp. Parkman finds this "one of many" cases in which "the worst acts of Indian ferocity have been thrown into shade by the enormities of white barbarians."

Both for such atrocities and for the large theme of the Indians' doom, Parkman's history is more "tragic" than Bancroft's, and Parkman disparages the "sentimental philanthropy" that might imagine a better or different outcome. Parkman relies fully as much as does Bancroft on the American narrative of destiny, but he is less happy with it, less able to soften past horrors by reference to present or future glories. Civilization, for Parkman, is the fate of American whites no less than it is of American Indians. At the end of Parkman's work, Pontiac, after the author has resurrected him, is again buried (on the site of present-day St. Louis, Missouri). The contrast between 1769 when Pontiac was murdered and 1851 rings with irony: "Neither mound nor tablet marked the burial-place of Pontiac. For a mausoleum, a city has risen above the forest hero; and the race whom he hated with such burning rancour trample with unceasing footsteps over his forgotten grave."

Against the ironic closure that ends *The Conspiracy of Pontiac*, *Uncle Tom's Cabin* reaches out into an open future. Pontiac lies forgotten and dishonored, but the cabin in Kentucky from which Tom is sold early in the book stands at the very end as a memorial. The emancipationist son of the slaveowner who has sold Tom exhorts the freed blacks who had known and loved Tom: "Think of your freedom, every time you see UNCLE TOM'S CABIN." This last chapter of the fictional narration is entitled "The Liberator," echoing the title of William Lloyd Garrison's abolitionist journal, founded over twenty years earlier. The chapter title joins under a single description both the master who frees the slaves and Tom, the slave whose example of love and resistance frees that master from the system that supports slavery. Christ as the liberator of souls stands in turn as the model for Tom's actions.

As a theory of history, Christianity is often understood to be closed, because it anticipates the end of time in the apocalypse, and the social-scientific beliefs that support Parkman's version of national narrative are understood to be open, because the progress of civilization has no definite term. *The Conspiracy of Pontiac,* however, is more "closed" than *Uncle Tom's Cabin.* Parkman's national assurances about the relations of race and civilization place the Indians' doom beyond the reach of human alteration. In some senses the past is always beyond alteration, but for Parkman there was never a chance that Pontiac might have succeeded. Stowe, however, looks toward the future, and she understands that future as being formed through present human choice and action. She renews the radical potential within Christianity.

Stowe's "Concluding Remarks" turn from her completed fiction to the ongoing historical existence of the Union. Her last words warn of "the wrath of Almighty God," but her message is that it is not too late for "this Union to be saved" through "repentance, justice and mercy." The last chapter of *Uncle Tom's Cabin,* as already noted, ends by repeating the words of the title. In this respect Stowe comes close to Hawthorne, for the titular domicile of *The House of the Seven Gables* serves as the last words of Hawthorne's romance. Stowe, however, does not rest content with the aesthetic closure of literary narrative, by which, in thinking of the edifice, readers think too of the book that invented it and bears its name. The last chapter done, Stowe begins the supplementary "Concluding Remarks" with the issue that Hawthorne's preface was meant to disarm. She says many correspondents have written to inquire "whether this narrative is a true one." No less than Parkman's history, Stowe's novel claims the authority of truth, not of imagination. Different as they are, both speak to the nation of its destiny.

In order to achieve her national address, Stowe had an exceptionally difficult rhetorical task, for she began by writing in a partisan journal on the most explosively divisive issue of the day, one that had been barred from discussion within the national consensus (see Chapter 4). Once it had been published as a book, *Uncle Tom's Cabin* set a new standard for the sale of fiction, and it is especially notable that its popularity flourished also in the

South, despite attempts to ban it there. The fascinating and powerful Civil War diary of Mary Boykin Chesnut from the South Carolina plantation aristocracy contains many references to *Uncle Tom's Cabin* as a provocation for thought about the realities of life with slaves. Stowe's act of cultural daring proved that there was more room in the national consensus than the established political parties allowed, and her example helped in the renewal of free-soil agitation and in the formation of the Republican party, which set the terms of national narrative for the rest of the century. Yet Stowe herself followed a resolutely antipolitical strategy. In reaching out as she did to address "Farmers of Massachusetts," "men of New York," "ye of the wide prairie states," "noble-minded men and women, of the South," Stowe built on the fundamental connection that she had established with her readership, not as legislators or even as voters, but as "mothers of America." Women's exclusion from politics made it possible to address, through them, the politically forbidden issue in a nonpolitical way.

In the segregation of activities and values by gender in the nineteenth century, the male specializations of economic and political life were distinguished from the woman's "sphere" of the home, where the values of the "human" resided. Stowe's chapter that most focuses the technique of the book as a whole is entitled "In Which It Appears that a Senator Is but a Man." This title could appear in a satirical work, showing a high-talking political idealist taking a bribe ("man" connoting human weakness) or even taking sexual advantage ("man" connoting the simultaneous moral vulnerability and social power of the masculine gender). Stowe's reduction of "Senator" to "man," however, is not destructive but, it appears, improving. Face-to-face, caring responsibility replaces abstract legalism, as the Ohio state senator, who has participated in legislation forbidding assistance to fugitive slaves, nonetheless assists Eliza and her baby in their escape. As a politician, he had criticized the "sentimental weakness" of those who would threaten the Union for a few wretched fugitives, but "the magic of the real presence of distress" converts him — as, Stowe adds, it has also led many southerners themselves to assist runaways, "in Kentucky, as in Mississippi."

This transformation of political man to common humanity takes place through the power, called "influence," of women. The senator's wife, already disposed to sympathy, is fully won over when Eliza asks her, "Ma'am . . . have you ever lost a child?" Death here, unlike in Parkman's wilderness, opens connections, between present and past and between person and person. Across barriers of class, race, and gender, we "feel but one sorrow." This powerful theme and technique of "Union" distinguishes *Uncle Tom's Cabin* from Garrisonian abolitionism, which judged the Constitution an unholy compromise with slavery.

Stowe's revision of politics into humanity also affects the story of George Harris, whose conventionally masculine escape and armed resistance are contrasted to Tom's conventionally feminine Christian quietism, even in resistance. The American revolutionary value of liberty energizes George. He begins by throwing in the face of southern whites their "Fourth-of-July speeches" that proclaim values belied by his condition as a slave, and he himself abandons America to seek liberty. Stowe meditates on his situation: "Liberty — electric word! . . . Is there anything more in it than a name — a rhetorical flourish? . . . To your fathers, freedom was the right of a nation to be a nation. To [George Harris] it is the right of a man to be a man." She rephrases the collective political rights as individual human rights.

As part of her national narrative strategy, Stowe takes special care not to give undue privilege to New England. Simon Legree, the villain who has Tom beaten to death on his plantation on the Red River frontier, comes from New England. Even more important for establishing Stowe's position, however, is Miss Ophelia from Vermont, who is cousin to St. Clare, Tom's good master in New Orleans. Miss Ophelia is ideologically an abolitionist, but at first she lacks human understanding and warmth. Neither being a Yankee nor being a woman makes her immediately able to do what for Stowe is the one thing needed for ending slavery: to *"feel right."*

Miss Ophelia does not speak for Stowe in an early conversation with her cousin, when she declares, "This is perfectly horrible! you ought to be ashamed of yourselves." Her pharisaical righteousness is compromised by an earlier exchange in which she reveals that she could not imagine any white person, let alone herself, kissing a black person. As she undertakes the care of Topsy, she thinks that her "prejudice against Negroes" can remain hidden, even though she "could never bear to have that child touch" her. Only the death of little Eva breaks through to Miss Ophelia's feelings sufficiently to make it possible for her to love Topsy, and her commitment to that love takes a shocking form. In order to save Topsy from slavery, Ophelia must first become her owner, so as then to take her north and free her. To learn what real abolitionism might be like, as opposed to the well-meaning complacencies of even liberal New England, Ophelia must experience not only personal, emotional relations to blacks, but also legal, institutional relations to slavery.

Miss Ophelia insists on having the papers for Topsy at once, "because now is the only time there ever is to do a thing in." As a result, after St. Clare's shocking, sudden accidental death, Topsy is the only slave to escape the breaking up of his household, in which Tom is sold to Legree. Despite his good intentions, St. Clare "hated the present tense of action." In St. Clare's ironic wit, anguished sensibility, and paralyzed self-contempt, Stowe severely yet sympathetically criticizes the sensitive spectator so fundamental to

Hawthorne's literary narrative. "Instead of being actor and regenerator," St. Clare has deepened his interiority. In his inner self, he is a nay-sayer, but the cost of his autonomy is that he is a "natural spectator" in the life of his society. The course of events terribly bears out Miss Ophelia's conviction that "it is impossible for a person who does no good not to do harm."

Stowe's work stands in a long tradition of activist sentimentality. Commenting on a fictionalized version of Nat Turner in *Dred* (1856), Stowe observes that "under all systems of despotism," the Bible "always" has been "prolific of insurrectionary movements." From the first days of Christianity, the claim for valuable human feeling and spiritual dignity among the wretched of the earth had been felt as a challenge to the powers that ruled, even when as in Stowe, following Jesus' teachings, care was taken to indicate a political disengagement. In the generation after Stowe, Friedrich Nietzsche's analysis of "ascetic ideals" in his *Genealogy of Morals* (1887) traces the story, to him distasteful, of how "slave" morality from the time of St. Paul had achieved a reversal of hierarchy, so that first in the later days of the Roman Empire, and then again in the history of the modern West, "master" morality was marginalized, and in its place reigned democratic humanitarianism. Somehow the weak had triumphed over the strong. Feelings were not the only tactic, but they had played their part.

In the eighteenth century the rise of sentimental fiction and drama was understood by both sides as a challenge posed by newly emergent social groups against the values and position of the traditional elite. The greatest international success was Samuel Richardson's epistolary novel *Clarissa* (1748), in which Lovelace, a landed aristocrat, rapes Clarissa, a gentlewoman of commercial family, whom he might have married. The outcome is disastrous for him, but a tragic, yet exemplary, moral triumph for her. In the *Key* (1853), published to document her portrayal of slavery in *Uncle Tom's Cabin*, Stowe refers to Laurence Sterne and Charles Dickens, significant English predecessors in the practice of sentimental writing that its readers understood to have social consequences. The effect she ascribes to Dickens is one that she sought to achieve with her own writing of "Life among the Lowly," as *Uncle Tom's Cabin* was subtitled: "the writings of Dickens awoke in noble and aristocratic bosoms the sense of a common humanity with the lowly." In contrast, the falsely sentimental Marie St. Clare demands that her own feelings as woman and mother be respected but cannot believe the same applies to her slave: "Mammy couldn't have the feelings that I should."

In the nineteenth century the groups that had earlier polemicized from feeling, having gained many of their goals, began to harden themselves. Malthusian demographics, laissez-faire economics, and what became known as Social Darwinism but which already appears in Parkman, all required resisting the appeals of what Parkman called "sentimental philanthropy." If *to feel* may seem weak, however, *not to feel* may seem brutal, and feeling was not utterly abandoned by the new ruling class. Feeling was segregated to the domestic sphere. Stowe's tactic was to bring this honored, but marginalized, value more powerfully into play, keeping alive a notion of "humanity" that included women as well as people of all classes and races.

In its original periodical publication, the subtitle for *Uncle Tom's Cabin* had been "The Man Who Was a Thing." Just as the "Lowly" in the final subtitle signals that the book is sentimental, this first version signals the systematic dimension of Stowe's analysis. Stowe's national rhetorical appeal emphasizes that southerners are as individuals no worse than northerners. As the problem with Miss Ophelia suggests, white southerners may even be more humane than northern whites in personal relations with blacks. The other side of this individual exculpation is national guilt: slavery exists as it does because it is part of a whole structure of commerce, law, and religion that defines the Union as it is. The religious subordination of slave to master, the legal denial of rights, and the commerce in bodies combine to make people "living property." By this process an institution that, if it were truly "patriarchal," might be tolerable is opened to the worst of abuses, which are held in check only by the decency of individuals. The existing system offers no protection against such a man as Legree; even public opinion cannot reach the owner of an isolated plantation. Although Legree is a spiritually haunted villain, it is essential to Stowe's design that he speak the language of market rationality: "I don't go for saving niggers. Use up, and buy more . . . makes you less trouble, and I'm quite sure it comes cheaper in the end."

When Tom is brutally beaten, he is thrown among economic refuse: "pieces of broken machinery, piles of damaged cotton." The closer the system approaches optimal market rationality in the economic understanding of the times, the more brutal it will become: "no tie, no duty, no relation, however sacred," can hold when "compared with money." This is the power of the "cash-nexus," which Thomas Carlyle had decried in *Past and Present* (1843) and which Karl Marx and Friedrich Engels analyzed in the *Communist Manifesto* (1848). In the very opening pages of *Uncle Tom's Cabin,* as Tom's master first discusses selling him, he explains to the slave trader his reluctance in terms that powerfully evoke the tension between an organic and an economic sense of relation: "I don't like parting with any of my hands." As a worker, a person is a hand, but readers may also register the sense of hand as member of the body, and the sentence then images a dreadful self-mutilation. Through membership in the body of Christ, Stowe wishes to restore this sense.

Stowe's radical Christianity is also at issue in the twentieth-century African-American response to her novel. "Uncle Tom" has become the derogatory term for a submissively loyal or servile black. The term is first recorded in 1922, used by the African American labor activist A. Philip Randolph, who is contrasting it to the "New Negro," and there can be no doubt that the model of George's secular liberation may be more appealing. Yet current usages degrade the "Uncle Tom" far more than Stowe ever did. Stowe's Uncle Tom does not shuffle, clown, pull his forelock, or otherwise try to ingratiate himself, as do those now called Uncle Toms. He repeatedly refuses to escape, but always in order to benefit other black people, and his death culminates a protracted struggle to resist Legree. This is how Stowe defines it in the *Key* and how the book shows it. Stowe's hypothesis of nonviolent resistance stands with that of her contemporary Henry David Thoreau and with the twentieth-century attempts to carry out such a strategy, from Gandhi to Martin Luther King, Jr.

UNCLE TOM'S ECHOES

Uncle Tom's Cabin helped to establish the audience and conventions for the best-selling sentimental fiction discussed by Michael Bell, and it also acted powerfully on the local, personal, and literary narratives that continued to be produced in the decade after its publication. The path-breaking local narrative "Life in the Iron Mills" (1861) by Rebecca Harding Davis; the major woman's personal narrative of slavery, *Incidents in the Life of a Slave Girl, Written by Herself* (1861), by Harriet A. Jacobs; many of the revisions Frederick Douglass made in the 1855 edition of his narrative, *My Bondage and My Freedom;* and even Herman Melville's literary narrative *Pierre* (1852), all bear traces of their authors' engagement with Stowe's work.

"Life in the Iron Mills," the extraordinarily successful first publication of its thirty-year-old author, appeared in the *Atlantic Monthly* just as the Civil War was beginning in April 1861. The unnamed locale of the story is modeled on Davis's home, Wheeling, Virginia (now West Virginia), but Davis displaced attention from slavery, which existed there, to what was becoming widely understood as wage slavery, as, for example, in George Fitzhugh's pro-southern polemic *Cannibals All! or Slaves Without Masters* (1857). Davis renewed the local narrative sketch through the resources of the social-problem writing on "life among the lowly" that Stowe had pioneered but which had also been much practiced in England. In *Mary Barton* (1848), set among the textile mill workers of Manchester, the English writer Elizabeth Gaskell had preceded Stowe in developing the stance of earnest Christian sympathy that a concerned middle-class woman would feel for fellow human souls, whose miseries the existing political structure had no will to remedy. Not only in her attention to urban industrial workers but also in a crucial structural respect, Davis is closer to Gaskell than to Stowe: both *Mary*

Barton and "Life in the Iron Mills" organize their plots around the legal process provoked by a worker's crime against an economic superior.

The work of an ambitious young writer often particularly illuminates the ethos of a literary institution. Founded in 1857 and edited from 1859 by Hawthorne's publisher James Fields, the *Atlantic Monthly* had serialized Stowe's New England historical fiction *The Minister's Wooing* (1859), while in these years the most consistent presence in its pages was Dr. Oliver Wendell Holmes, professor of medicine, essayist, and novelist. Davis's story appeals to a reader concerned with both art and social problems, at once urbane like Holmes, speculative like Hawthorne, and earnest like Stowe. It is a difficult feat, and it is hard to imagine Davis's accomplishing it without the model of "George Eliot" (Mary Ann Evans), whose works, themselves influenced by Stowe, had begun to appear in Britain in 1858. Eliot's novel *The Mill on the Floss* (1860) exemplified a narrative capaciousness that could range over high culture, reach out in human sympathy toward lives warped by "the emphasis of need," and sensuously render evocative details of remembered scenes. Like Eliot, but unlike Stowe and Gaskell, Davis mellows her narrative by setting the main action thirty years in the past, even though its interest was still urgent.

The *Atlantic Monthly* reader was more sophisticated than the reader of the *National Era*. Davis addresses her readers not collectively as "mothers" or "farmers," but individually as "amateur psychologist" (the Holmsian culti-vated scientist) or as a more transcendentalist, "Egoist, or Pantheist, or Arminian." Although biblical references are as important for Davis as they are for Gaskell and Stowe, considerable further learning is assumed or im-puted for her readers, as it is for Eliot's. Davis's story contains phrases in French and Latin and references to Dante, Goethe, and German philoso-phers. When the machinery is described at work, "the engines sob and shriek like 'gods in pain.' " This perfect line of iambic pentameter ironically alludes to John Keats's erotic medieval romance "The Eve of St. Agnes" (1819): "The music, yearning like a god in pain."

Echoing Richard Henry Dana from *Two Years before the Mast,* the narrator summons the reader: "I want you to hide your disgust, take no heed to your clean clothes, and come right down with me." Yet the narrator remains at a meditative distance, not actively involved like "personal" narrators or, in her different way, like Stowe. The narrator's attitude to the working characters fluctuates between aesthetic and scientific and is never so fundamentally passional as in Stowe. They are a "figure," a "type," presenting a "symptom" to be "read." Above all, Davis demands that readers "judge" the worker-artist-criminal on whom the story centrally focuses: "Be just — not like man's law, which seizes on one isolated fact, but like God's judging angel." Stowe would say, rather, "judge not, lest ye be judged"; the divine mission is to love. Religion in "Life in the Iron Mills" plays a much less active and potentially transformative role than is claimed for it in *Mary Barton* or *Uncle Tom's Cabin*. As in Stowe, there is an idealized Quaker woman, but in Davis she appears only at the end, to help the working woman expiate her crime, which has cost her the man she loved. The story ends with God's "promise of the Dawn," but there seems no possibility of change in this world. Before James Fields, as editor, named the story, Davis had suggested entitling it "Beyond," clearly differentiating her from Stowe's or Gaskell's belief that religion operates here and now.

Like religion, art also can offer a "beyond." Davis's alternative story title was "The Korl-Woman," after the sculpture that the worker Hugh Wolfe has made from korl, a "refuse" material. When a group of privileged visitors comes through the mills, it encounters this "nude woman's form, muscular, grown coarse with labor, the powerful limbs instinct with some one poignant longing," what the narrator later calls "desperate need." Between the "gentleman" Mitchell and the "artist sense" of Hugh an inarticulate understanding arises, but neither can make anything of it. Mitchell insists that "reform is born of need, not pity," and that therefore it must come from the oppressed themselves, not from above. Nothing in the story directly questions this circumscription of the notion of need or suggests that Wolfe may offer something that Mitchell, and the story's readers, need. Such an ironical reading is possible, but only against the story's grain.

During the group's discussion around the sculpture, Deborah ("Deb"), a deformed worker who hopelessly loves Hugh, has stolen Mitchell's wallet, and later she gives it to Hugh, to allow him the freedom his poverty has denied him. This is "the crisis" of Hugh's life, and the story asserts that in choosing to keep the money, he "lost the victory." Hugh, we are told, "did not deceive himself"; he acknowledges, "Theft! That was it"; yet he hopes that good can come of it. Instead he is apprehended, sentenced to nineteen years in prison, and commits suicide. The story's power depends on the power of the ruling classes. Only the system of law enforcement allows this work its chosen tragedy. The speculative aesthete Mitchell had in conversation kept aloof from the mill owner's praise for the "American system," but Mitchell in practice adheres to that system by bringing legal charges against Hugh. Although the story is silent on the precise legal proceeding, the structure of the story requires the absolute inevitability of punishment after crime.

No less than Mitchell does, the worker-artist Hugh takes part in the system that has devastated his life. To Mitchell's disgust, the conversation on the "American system" had allowed "money" to appear as "the cure for all the world's diseases." Deb's hearing this has helped impel her to theft, and Hugh's "consciousness of power" from the money tempts him to dream of being "Free!" Art, it seems, can express the "need" for a beyond, and religion can fulfill that need for isolated individuals, but the "American system" is impervious to change. For Stowe, a decade earlier, there was no fictional need to punish people for breaking laws that supported an immoral system; for Horatio Alger, later in the 1860s, Deb's theft would have provided Hugh the chance to get a new start in life by returning the wallet and being rewarded by Mitchell's patronage. Unable to accept either popular agitation or popular fantasy as a solution, Davis, in her dense, complex, and powerful story, precociously sketches an impasse that would preoccupy many of the most serious, self-consciously elite, writers for the rest of the century.

The "crisis" that Harriet Jacobs recounted in her *Incidents in the Life of a Slave Girl* differs greatly from that which Davis posed for Hugh. Jacobs's choice involved both morality and tactics, but not the law. For her, as for all her fellow fugitives, the absolute condition of freedom was to break the law, usually requiring also the implication of others in crime. The legal protections for slaveholders' property were "the regulations of robbers, who had no rights that I was bound to respect." The long-term happiness of herself and her children would depend on a struggle between two qualitatively different forces: "My master had power and law on his side; I had a determined will. There is might in each." Because she had lived without benefit of law, however, she greatly valued law when it was on her side. While visiting England as a nursemaid, she found even the "poorest poor" agricultural laborers to be better off than "the most favored slaves in America" because there was "no law forbidding them to learn to read and write" and their "very humble" homes were "protected by law." Therefore, sickening as it was to need to buy one's freedom, Jacobs acknowledges that she and her children will never be secure without "all due formalities of law." Her story ends "not in the usual way, with marriage," but instead "with freedom." In order for this to occur, however, Jacobs must first learn news that "struck [her] like a blow," even though it was good news: "So I was *sold* at last!"

Writing as a mother, Jacobs wishes to "arouse the women of the North" to realize the conditions of "two millions" of slave women in the South, still suffering as Jacobs had. Jacobs's personal narrative of testimony occupies the space opened by Stowe's sympathetic report on the vulnerability of parental love under the "patriarchal" institution. Jacobs's story does not end in marriage because she never married, and her shame over her social standing as an unmarried mother was one reason she chose to present her narrative displaced into the fictional identity of "Linda Brent." Despite her being what would conventionally, brutally, have been called a "loose" woman, her narrative shows that the ties of family love were the dominant feature in her life. The most astonishing feature of her story forms a real-life, yet grotesque, perfection of the woman's domestic role, within her own separate sphere. For seven years, while she was thought to have run away to freedom, Jacobs lay hidden in her hometown in the small attic of the house of her grandmother (known as "Aunt Martha"). This terrible confinement was the prerequisite of her liberty.

Jacobs's grandmother was a free black property owner who commanded respect in the small town of Edenton, North Carolina. (Symbolically as the name rings, it is not part of Jacobs's narrative and has only been discovered by modern research.) At a crucial stage in the escape, a white woman who had known the grandmother all her life came forward to hide Jacobs – just as Stowe had surmised that even in the South relations of sisterhood would prevail. Jacobs enjoyed a strong, positive sense of the Edenton community, while she also experienced the vulnerabilities and abuses of slavery. Even in the days of white vigilante terrorism after Nat Turner's rebellion of 1831, Jacobs's household was rightly confident that "we were in the midst of white families who would protect us." Stories were told that the grandmother had once "chased a white gentleman with a pistol, because he had insulted one of her daughters." The grandmother's expectations of sexual propriety offered protection when, from age twelve, Jacobs was subject to sexual harassment from the master of the household in which she lived. Despite her rejecting him and, further, his wife's jealousy, public opinion held him back from the whip: "how often did I rejoice that I lived in a town where all the inhabitants knew each other! If I had been on a remote plantation, or lost among the multitude of a crowded city, I should not be a living woman at this day."

The "crisis" was provoked when "Linda" was fifteen and the doctor set about building a "lonely cottage" where she would live isolated from the eyes and ears of the town and would therefore be helpless against him. The worst of it, according to Linda, was that the doctor was notorious for selling off his "victims," even with "his babies at the breast." At the same time, a sympathetic white gentleman, "educated and eloquent," was paying her attention. Although Linda recognized his interest in her as sexual, she also felt "something akin to freedom in having a lover who has no control over you, except that which he gains by kindness and attachment." This same attachment made it likely that she could "ask to have [their] children well supported." "With these thoughts revolving in [her] mind," Linda chose seduction over rape and "made a headlong plunge." Unlike the "drifting circumstance" by which Davis characterizes Hugh's step into crime, and unlike Hugh's crime itself, which is not so much a transgression as the failure to take restorative action, Linda here makes her choice and goes forward, although painfully.

She appeals to the "virtuous reader" for pity and confesses that the "humiliating memory will haunt me to my dying day." Yet she has also achieved an independent standpoint: "Still, in looking back, calmly, on the events of my life, I feel that the slave woman ought not to be judged on the same standard as others."

In *My Bondage and My Freedom,* Frederick Douglass also argues that slave morality demands a different standard. Living under a master who fails to provide sufficient food, Douglass must steal to survive. This bare fact was recorded in the 1845 narrative, but in the 1855 revision, several pages of moral reasoning are added, which conclude, "The morality of *free* society can have no application to *slave* society." If a slave steals, he only "takes his own," and in killing his master, he would "imitate the heroes of the revolution." The reason for Douglass's claim is that "freedom of choice is the essence of all accountability," and therefore by enslaving a person, "you rob him of moral responsibility." This argument does not do justice to what any reader finds to be Douglass's own powers of choice, even in slavery, and to the moral admiration he wins, but as part of an ongoing struggle, it is an important polemical claim. In Stowe's terms, this is more George Harris than Uncle Tom, and in her *Key* she cites Douglass's 1845 narrative to demonstrate that George's heroism has a basis in reality.

In several important respects Douglass's changes to the work in 1855 brought his narrative much closer to the world of Stowe than his 1845 version had been. In the decade between the versions, he had ceased to be a Garrisonian. He no longer understood the Constitution as a compromise with slavery, but rather as "in its letter and spirit, an anti-slavery instrument." Therefore, he no longer looked to a dissolution of the Union but committed himself to America. No longer prefaced by William Lloyd Garrison and Wendell Phillips, the 1855 narrative is introduced by James McCune Smith, a Scottish-educated black physician. Smith presents Douglass's life story as "an American book, for Americans, in the fullest sense of the idea." Douglass's 1855 work is more unequivocally national than the 1845, and it is also more strongly Christian. Although both versions severely criticize the complicity of American Christianity in slavery, only in 1855 does Douglass speak of his own conversion at age thirteen.

My Bondage and My Freedom resonates with *Uncle Tom's Cabin* in its increased concern with domestic and family issues. The whipping of Douglass's Aunt Esther concludes the first chapter of 1845, some five pages into the work; in 1855 the incident concludes the fifth chapter, over fifty pages on. The tremendous expansion of Douglass's experiences and reflections around his early childhood makes the single largest structural difference between the two versions. In 1845 he merely reports that at first he had "lived with his

grandmother." In 1855 the expansion takes on a detail and emotional intensity that may owe as much literarily to Dickens's *David Copperfield* (1850) as
it does ideologically to Stowe:

The old cabin, with its rail floor and rail bedsteads up stairs, and its clay floor down
stairs . . . and the hole curiously dug in front of the fire-place, beneath which
grandmammy placed the sweet potatoes to keep them from the frost, was MY
HOME – the only home I ever had; and I loved it, and all connected with it.

In his early youth, before he becomes economically useful, the slave is free to
be that emergent icon of America, "a genuine boy." In contrast to 1845, in
which the whipping of Aunt Esther marks Douglass's "entrance to the hell of
slavery," in 1855 it is his pain at separation from his grandmother, when she
leaves him off at the house of "the old master," that becomes his "first
introduction to the realities of slavery."

For Douglass in 1855, as for Stowe, the overwhelming reality of slavery
was its destruction of the family, its failure in any way to fulfill its "patriarchal" self-presentation. Separating children from their mothers was part of
the overall strategy of slavery "to reduce man to a level with the brute."
Douglass asserts that slavery succeeds in "obliterating from the mind and
heart of the slave, all just ideas of the sacredness of the *family,* as an institution." Only when he was first brought to the old master's house did he meet
his brothers and sisters, but he does not understand or feel his relation to
them: "I heard the words brother and sister and knew they must mean
something, but slavery had robbed these terms of their true meaning." The
system of slavery meant that Douglass's "poor mother . . . had *many children,*
but NO FAMILY!" In his experience of slavery, there was no "domestic
hearth, with its holy lessons and precious endearments."

Yet this cannot be exactly true, based on what he has just reported of life
with his grandmother. A contradiction exists between the tremendous, real
damage inflicted by systematic oppression and the astonishing resourceful-
ness that resisted by building relationship and love. This is a textual problem
in Douglass and Stowe that is a living, historical problem in contemporary
African-American life. By legally prohibiting marriage between slaves, the
system, Douglass argues, "does away with fathers as it does away with
families." Then he complicates his statement: "When they *do* exist, they are
not the outgrowths of slavery, but are antagonistic to that system." That
creative antagonism against all odds remains an example to provoke readers'
thought and action.

My Bondage and My Freedom shares Stowe's intense concern with the social
bases of affective experience and the structural possibilities for moral education, but Douglass's experience does not support her hopes for the transforma-

tive power of face-to-face encounter between human suffering and human decency, at least when both parties are male. As if directly reflecting on Stowe's scene between the Ohio senator and the fugitive Eliza, Douglass revises a crucial episode in his own life. Before the decisive fight, after the slave breaker Covey had brutalized him for the first time, Douglass runs away to appeal to his master. In both versions, the master refuses to intervene despite Douglass's pitiable appearance: "From the crown of my head to my feet, I was covered with blood. My hair was all clotted with dust and blood; my shift was stiff with blood. My legs and feet were torn in sundry places with briers and thorns, and were also covered with blood." The 1855 version of the exchange begins with Stowe's premise: "It was impossible – as I stood before him at the first – for him to seem indifferent." The breakthrough by which a "master" would become a "man" seems imminent: "I distinctly saw his human nature asserting its conviction against the slave system, which made cases like mine *possible*." What happens then, however, is that "humanity fell before the systematic tyranny of slavery." The master's initial "agitation" is calmed when he gets "*his* turn to talk," and by reiterating the commonplaces of the master class "he soon repressed his feelings and became cold as iron." Douglass implicitly takes issue with Stowe, even as he reshapes his work to make it at once, like *Uncle Tom's Cabin,* national, domestic, and sentimental. He follows with greater success a strategy also tried by Herman Melville.

Published less than a year after *Moby-Dick, Pierre: or, The Ambiguities* (1852) stands apart from Melville's earlier work in its mode of presentation and in the character and setting of its action. *Pierre* is not a personal narrative, even so much as *Mardi* or *Moby-Dick.* It is a third-person narrative primarily concerned with the moral and psychological development of the young man it is named after. It refers to and shapes itself in relation to *Hamlet,* in the literary-narrative mode opened by Goethe's *Wilhelm Meister,* the founding example of the *Bildungsroman.* Melville's first six books had largely exhausted his direct maritime experience, and unlike them, *Pierre* is set at home rather than abroad. It is doubly domestic, for within its American locales, its action springs from and remains within the network of family relations. Like *Uncle Tom's Cabin,* it begins with an apparently happy family that is then put to trials and brought to misery. In its domestic, familial focus, it seems aimed to engage the wider, "feminine" audience that had become defined since the middle forties, when Melville had begun writing, but it failed to satisfy this or any other audience.

Pierre lives in an idealized version of the Berkshire (Massachusetts) countryside, where Melville had moved during the writing of *Moby-Dick.* Pierre's situation draws on elements of the wealthy, civically outstanding families from which Melville was descended on both sides. A national framework is established by references to Indian land conveyances and revolutionary hero- ism, but these concerns are eclipsed by questions of Pierre's "interior develop- ment." Pierre's inheritance is "patriarchal": his grandfather, "grand old Pierre," was "loved" by his "stable slaves" just as "his shepherds loved old Abraham" in the Bible. As in *Hamlet,* but also in *Uncle Tom's Cabin,* the book's action springs from a crisis in patriarchy. Pierre's deceased, revered father, it appears, had fathered a daughter, Isabel, before he was married. The stern, heroic image of old Hamlet and the smiling, lecherous Claudius are suddenly combined. Isabel is now living, unacknowledged, in poverty nearby.

Pierre must decide whether to acknowledge his "dark" sister, whose hand is "hard" with "lonely labor." The color-coding evokes the narratives of slavery, and the social gap between siblings recalls *The Blithedale Romance,* also published this same year, in which Zenobia enjoys luxury while the hands of her sister Priscilla are hardened by labor as a seamstress. The question for Pierre is posed in the language of sentiment. Will he be "cold and selfish" and yield to the "dreary heart-vacancies of the conventional life," or will he choose "God's anointed," "the heart"? Despite her wild curls, Isabel is no "Gorgon." The Gorgon turned people to stone, but Isabel's face could "turn white marble into mother's milk," from conventionally mascu- line, cold hardness to conventionally feminine, flowing warmth. Pierre chooses the heart, and "thus, in the Enthusiast to Duty, the heaven-begotten Christ is born."

Roughly the first third of the book brings things to this point. Then a different approach to psychology begins to predominate, changing the book's focus, emphasis, and tone. For example, the narrator had earlier acknowl- edged that Pierre's decision to stand by Isabel was made easier because of her extraordinary, fascinating beauty, but the narrator disclaims any "censorious" intent. Later, however, a sharp distinction is emphasized between the thoughts presented "as Pierre's" and those of the narrator "concerning him." The narrative becomes more analytic and more ironically distanced, no longer claiming to be "magnanimous."

The further Pierre is subjected to individualizing scrutiny, the more am- biguous he becomes. As Pierre begins to glimpse his father's hidden life, he thinks of "two mutually absorbing shapes" that alternate from snake to human in Dante's *Inferno.* Later, at the culmination of an interview between Pierre and Isabel, he kisses her with a passion hardly fraternal: "Then they changed; they coiled together, and entangledly stood mute." Their transfor- mation into joined serpentine coils identifies them with their morally com- promised father. A strange speculative pamphlet no sooner read, near the book's middle, than lost, holds out a formula for the resolution of ambiguities, "by their very contradictions they are made to correspond," but its purport remains obscure.

Just like his father, Pierre hides a sexual secret. As he meditates his course of action, he is pained and frightened by the uncharitable rigor his mother reveals in discussing the illegitimate child of a neighboring farm girl. Both for this reason, and also to protect his mother's image of her husband, he determines not to confront her with what he understands to be the facts about Isabel. Moreover, the pointedly named clergyman Falsgrave shows a weak prudence, subservient to social authority, and so offers no alternative moral resource. Nor is the evidence of Isabel's birth sufficient to prove a legal case. In order to grant Isabel full familial honor and equality, Pierre therefore determines to present her to the world as his wife, but this has the effect not so much of raising her as of destroying his social position, as well as devastating his mother and his pale blond fiancée.

The first movement of *Pierre* criticizes the conventional social order, much in the mode of Stowe's radical sentimentality. In the second movement Pierre's "enthusiasm," the gush of spirit that shatters convention, is criticized by the narrator as "infatuated." Without the institutions of family, church, or state to guide and support action, the heart proves weak and dangerous. Pierre acts "without being consciously" aware of the upshot of what he is doing; his actions are oriented by feelings that spring from sources of which he is "unconscious." As in Freud's theory of the unconscious, Melville presents both a dynamic emphasis – the unconscious as an agency, a process of displacement by which things happen – and a topographic emphasis, in which the unconscious can be spatially figured as a place. Gothic figures, such as Poe's favorite topic of premature burial, turn into psychological theory: "as sometimes men are coffined in a trance, being thereby mistaken for dead; so it is possible to bury a tranced grief in the soul, erroneously supposing that it hath no more vitality of suffering"; but the feeling actually survives.

In the worldly psychological perspective associated with Machiavelli or La Rochefoucauld, a debunking analysis of idealism and self-sacrifice, like that enacted in this portion of *Pierre,* contributes to speculation on the dynamics of human life in social and political communities. This tradition accounts in part for Tocqueville's analysis of America. Although Melville also knew and valued such work, Pierre, in contrast, heads into isolation, and the novel offers a topographic play of figures rather than actions. In one of the most significant figures of the topographic unconscious, what a child ignorantly witnesses and overhears remains preserved in memory until certain adult experiences trigger understanding. Once the "key of the cipher" is provided, "how wonderfully, he reads all the obscurest and most obliterate inscriptions he finds in his memory; yea, and rummages himself all over, for still hidden writings to read."

This textualization of the unconscious points to literary narrative as the possible ground for bringing contradictions into correspondence. In the book's third and final movement, Pierre is revealed not only as a reader but also as a writer. He leaves his ancestral Saddle Meadows to start a new life with Isabel, as a writer in New York. Perhaps from Melville's bitterness at the reception of *Moby-Dick,* the New York literary world he had shared with the Duyckincks is severely satirized as "Young America in Literature." After the narrator's attitude toward Pierre has shifted in the second movement, the book's relation to the audience also changes, with a declaration of independence: "I write precisely as I please." In trying to follow the shifting "phases" of Pierre, readers must not hope for the guidance of any "canting showman" of a narrator: "Catch his phases as your insight may." The reader too is granted freedom. Declaring himself sovereign in his intense, tragic exploration of mind, Melville has broken the bonds of the institutions of reading and writing in his time just as Pierre breaks the institutional bonds of his home.

In trying to support himself as a writer, however, Pierre runs athwart of conventions that are just as firm as those at home had been, and even more crippling, because he is more vulnerable and needy. His publishers write, "Sir: — You are a swindler. Upon the pretense of writing a popular novel for us, you have been receiving cash advances from us, while passing through our press the sheets of a blasphemous rhapsody." Something like this was also the situation of Melville, who considered Ahab's diabolic baptism the "motto," but the "secret one," of *Moby-Dick.* "Dollars damn me," he wrote to Hawthorne while composing *Moby-Dick:* "What I feel most moved to write, that is banned, — it will not pay. Yet, altogether, write the *other* way I cannot. So the product is a final hash, and all my books are botches." As the brother and sister coiled together, entangled like lovers, so the satirical analyst and the object of his criticism, the author and character, threaten to merge in the last portion of *Pierre.* The deluded author Pierre, who has "directly plagiarized from his own experiences" in constructing his "apparent author-hero Vivia," becomes an object of pity to his author Melville, even as the plot leads to the final absurdities of murder and suicide.

During this last phase of *Pierre,* Pierre's "ever-present self," the individuality on which nineteenth-century psychology is based, proves unstable, for no thought or action "solely originates" in a single "defined identity." Such instability also challenges the "originality" on which literary narrative depends. The "creative mind" may promise a "latent infiniteness," but as surfaces are peeled away, influences foresworn, the final, central point may be "appallingly vacant." It seems improbable that critics will ever achieve a

satisfactory definition of the central meaning of *Pierre* because to its own
time, as to modern readers, the book stands as a failure, though now increasingly fascinating. Its central vacancy, it seems clear, was produced through
the interaction of conflicting impulses and intentions that exercised their
effects at different stages in the largely undocumented process of composition. Nonetheless, the power of literary narrative makes form even out of
such absences.

The contradictions are brought into correspondence when Pierre sees a
painting. This painting resembles a portrait of his father that had played a
key role in making the case for Isabel's parentage, but there is no reason to
think that this painting was drawn from his father. It may not even be a
portrait at all, but a "pure fancy piece," that is, a work of pure imagination.
If there is "no original" here, then Pierre has probably been wrong in trusting
Isabel's story on which he has staked their lives, just as he has been wrong to
trust in his literary originality. The combination of these two devastating
errors prepares him for the final debacle. Ironically, however – and this irony
is essential to the book's literary form – because "original" in this usage
means "model," its absence would be the strongest testimony to the power of
unaided artistic inspiration. Rather than a double loss, then, Pierre has been
offered a chance to renew his confidence, but he proves incapable of taking
the chance, and because he does not take it, it remains untried, unconsumed
by the book's criticism. It betokens the alternative by which Melville as
author of the work stands free of his character Pierre, building literary work
from fictional disaster.

In reviews and sales, however, *Pierre* was a thorough disaster. Reviewers
recognized that Melville was writing more like "Poe and Hawthorne" than he
had in his earlier books, and they saw that *Pierre* was a "prose poem," based
on a "new theory of art." But the result was judged a "perversion of talent."
Like the "abuses" of the "German school," Melville's literary narrative ignored the "ordinary novel reader." The "supersensuousness" of *Pierre* provoked moral outrage, and it was a "dead failure."

DEAD ENDS FOR LITERARY NARRATIVE

The severe setback posed by *Pierre* to Melville's career was especially disturbing because he needed income from his writing. Faced with this failure, after
the election of Franklin Pierce, Melville's family and friends, including
Hawthorne, worked, finally without success, to gain him a patronage position like that awarded Hawthorne. By the spring of 1853, Melville seems to
have produced a new manuscript (never published and now lost), which
Harper was not ready to take on so soon after *Pierre*. At the beginning of

December, however, the publisher offered Melville an advance for a novel-in-progress on "tortoise-hunting." On December 10, 1853, a devastating fire destroyed Harper's stock of bound books and unbound sheets, including copies of Melville's earlier works that would have brought him about a thousand dollars when sold. For the same reason that Melville would have felt special need of money, Harper felt pinched; they were in no position to go ahead on the project, and Melville never completed it.

By late 1853, Melville was already launched on a new phase of his existence as a writer, as a magazinist. From late 1853 into 1856, when he traveled abroad for eight months, he published fourteen tales and sketches plus a serialized novel in the pages of *Harper's New Monthly Magazine* and *Putnam's Monthly Magazine of American Literature, Science, and Art*. *Harper's* had been founded in 1850 and immediately achieved great popularity by reprinting the most interesting current works of English writers. In contrast, *Putnam's*, founded in 1853, aimed to bring American writers to the fore, as in the previous decade Putnam's American Books series had. Evert Duyckinck was no longer involved in this Putnam American project, however. The editorial group of the new magazine included Charles Briggs, George William Curtis (a friend of Hawthorne's), Parke Godwin, and Frederick Law Olmsted.

Both magazines offered Melville a rate of five dollars per published page, the top rate they paid. Seven short pieces appeared in *Harper's*. *Putnam's* published the novel *Israel Potter*, in nine installments, and seven other pieces, three of which themselves appeared in more than one part: "Bartleby, The Scrivener," "The Encantadas," and "Benito Cereno." Melville thus appeared twenty-one times in the thirty-five monthly issues running from his first contribution to the magazine's termination in the financial crises of 1857. Immediately after its serialization, *Israel Potter* was published by Putnam as a book, and in 1856 Dix and Edwards, successors to Putnam as sponsors of the magazine, published *The Piazza Tales*, which collected the five pieces that had appeared in the magazine to that point. Both *Israel Potter* and *The Piazza Tales* were well reviewed, recouping for Melville the loss of esteem he had suffered after *Pierre*, even if not restoring the prominence he had held by the completion of *White-Jacket*.

After his initial success as a writer of personal narrative, and after his experiments with literary narrative in *Moby-Dick* and *Pierre*, Melville now worked in local narrative, and reviewers recognized his standing with Washington Irving, Edgar Allan Poe, and Nathaniel Hawthorne, who then as now marked the American norm for this kind of writing. Melville used established types: sketches of city characters ("Bartleby, "Jimmy Rose," "The Fiddler"), sketches of country characters ("Cock-A-Doodle-Doodle-Doo!," "The Lightning-Rod Man," "The Happy Failure"), travel sketches ("The

Encantadas"), domestic sketches ("The Piazza," "I and My Chimney," "The Apple-Tree Table"), and tales ("The Bell-Tower," "Benito Cereno").

Melville also tried out a new way to achieve the effects of contrast so often essential in sketches. Three pieces are built from the doubled pairing of England and the United States, rich and poor. "Poor Man's Pudding and Rich Man's Crumbs" contrasts the mixed shame and dignity of a poor country family in the United States, neglected by the complacently well-off, with the terrifying energy of a starving London crowd, maddened by the ostentatiously contemptuous charity of the rich. "The Two Temples" contrasts the stultifying hot air of a fancy society church in New York with the hot breath of life at a popular theater in London. This piece was rejected by *Putnam's* for fear of offending the New York objects of its satire. "The Paradise of Bachelors and the Tartarus of Maids" contrasts the blissful comfort of a London lawyers' club with the dreadful misery of American factory "girls" in a mountainside paper mill.

A similar technique of contrast gave a principle for constructing a volume. The six pieces that make up *Piazza Tales* show off Melville's command of varied modes and locales. As Hawthorne had introduced his *Mosses from an Old Manse* with a sketch of life in the Concord Manse, so "The Piazza" (previously unpublished) opens the volume in a setting like that of Melville's Pittsfield home. This rustic domesticity is in contrast to the urban homelessness in the sketch that follows, "Bartleby, The Scrivener," but "The Piazza" had already sounded notes of pathos that "Bartleby" deepens and complicates. "Benito Cereno" comes next, a tale rather than a sketch, emphasizing terror more than pity, and set at sea several generations earlier. Between this long piece and the lengthy "Encantadas" (ten linked sketches of the Galapagos Islands) is placed "The Lightning-Rod Man," the shortest and lightest piece in the volume, which returns to the contemporary Berkshire countryside. "The Encantadas" are meditative rather than touristic. These bleak volcanic islands, like "cinders" on the "vacant lot" of the sea, testify to a "world" that is "fallen." The volume concludes with "The Bell-Tower," a short tale of far away and long ago, vaguely set in Renaissance Italy, that speculates on technology and death with somewhat the feel of Hawthorne's "Ethan Brand."

"Bartleby, The Scrivener," as first published in *Putnam's,* had been subtitled "A Story of Wall-Street." Part of the special force of the story, its narrator thinks, comes from its setting in a "solitary office," in a "building entirely unhallowed by humanizing domestic associations." The office building – a structure devoted exclusively to commerce with no residential units – was a relatively new development in American urban life, and it added a third space to a world previously divided between "public street" and "private residence." This encounter of a narrator with the opacity of city misery plays a variation on Hawthorne's "Wakefield" – concerned especially with private residence – and Poe's "The Man of the Crowd" – concerned especially with the public street. Bartleby moves the narrator by his "solitude," the sense he conveys of being "absolutely alone," like Wakefield, who became the "outcast of the universe," and Poe's character, who "refuses to be alone" physically, presumably because of his terrifying inner state.

Each of these three characters fascinates the story's narrator, who struggles to penetrate the character's mystery. Melville, however, differs from Hawthorne and Poe by dramatizing the narrator, making him a character who speaks to the object of mystery rather than simply speculating, as in Hawthorne, or observing, as in Poe. The story thus becomes less metaphysical and more ethical. The narrator asks himself, "What shall I do?" The problem is to find a space for human action between the absurd, pseudopaternalistic claim of the next tenant in the office vacated by the narrator that "you are responsible for the man you left there" and the narrator's equally absurd legalistic response that he is "nothing to me – he is no relation or apprentice of mine." Despite the narrator's character as a "*safe*," prudent lawyer, he is moved by Bartleby. The problem is that Bartleby is immovable. Among all the other things he "would prefer not to," Bartleby is unresponsive to the narrator's attempts to assist him. His passive aggression puts Stowe's sentimental structure in a new light. What if not the rich and powerful but the objects of sympathy, the poor and needy themselves, are like stone? This may be the self-serving fantasy of those who find it easier to do nothing, or it may be a powerful claim that the poor too have the privilege of stoicism.

Putnam's was based in New York, and much that it published, like "Bartleby," had a New York flavor, but its ambitions were national. *Israel Potter: His Fifty Years of Exile* began serialization with the subtitle "A Fourth of July Story." Potter was a New England farm boy who became a revolutionary soldier, fought at Bunker Hill, served as a secret courier for Benjamin Franklin, and was stranded in London after the Revolution, only returning to the United States in advanced old age. In adapting Potter's story, Melville made different use of a technique he had developed for his first-person narratives. From *Typee* through *Moby-Dick,* he had freely supplemented his own experience with materials drawn from travel books and others' personal narratives. For *Israel Potter,* Melville made a third-person account out of an existing personal narrative, which had evidently preoccupied him. As early as 1849, he had bought an old map of London "in case I serve up the Revolutionary narrative of the beggar."

In the early decades of the nineteenth century, some two hundred personal narratives of the Revolution were in print. *The Life and Remarkable Adventures*

of Israel R. Potter (1824) was published in an inexpensive pamphlet, the year
of Potter's return to America, by a Providence, Rhode Island, printer whose
publications included such other popular personal narratives as a version of
Daniel Boone's and *Life and Adventures of Robert, the Hermit of Massachusetts,* an
escaped slave. Despite Melville's claim to offer "almost a reprint" of the
Potter narrative, save for "change in the grammatical person," he made very
substantial changes. Perhaps because he and Potter shared the birthdate of
August 1 and had both served on whalers, Melville shifted Potter's birthplace
from Rhode Island to the Berkshire region, where Melville was then living.
The first six chapters of *Israel Potter* otherwise correspond fairly closely to the
first half of the 1824 narrative, and Melville's last four chapters follow,
although drastically abridging, the last half.

   In between these opening and closing chapters, Melville has sixteen chapters that extensively add to and elaborate the 1824 work. They nationalize
the personal narrative by devoting several chapters to Benjamin Franklin and
some fifty pages to John Paul Jones, the great naval hero of the Revolution,
who did not at all figure in the original. Israel's adventures culminate in
Jones's naval battle between the British *Serapis* and the revolutionary *Bon-
homme Richard.* As the two ships grapple, the bloody horrors of this great
victory become a figure of civil war: "It was a partnership and joint-stock
combustion company of both ships; yet divided, even in participation. The
two vessels were as two houses, through whose party-walls doors have been
cut." Appalled witticism turns the language of commercial enterprise to
destruction and cooperation to "combustion"; the door joining two houses
opens only to let death enter. Jones himself had been earlier revealed as
tattooed, like Queequeg in *Moby-Dick,* in a way "only seen on thorough-bred
savages – deep blue, elaborate, labyrinthine, cabalistic."

   After the battle, the narrator asks whether civilization is indeed "a thing
distinct," or "is it an advanced stage of barbarism?" Through this reflection on
a founding deed of the nation, the categories that grounded American national
narrative in Parkman, Bancroft, and Cooper come under severe questioning.
This narrative of the wanderings and exile of "Israel" resonates suggestively
because, ever since the seventeenth century, America had been understood as
what in *White-Jacket* is called the "Israel of our time." Melville, therefore, is
licensed to find in the story of Israel Potter "a type, a parallel, and a prophecy"
for America. America may prove to be "the Paul Jones of nations" because like
him it is "intrepid, unprincipled, reckless, predatory, with boundless ambitions, civilized in externals but a savage at heart." One review found notable
political virtue in this passage, contrasting its directness to the "fine phrases"
of current American expansionist political discourse.

   After the election of Pierce, the problems of slavery, supposedly settled by the Compromise of 1850, reemerged over the organization of the Kansas and Nebraska territories, which soon escalated into guerrilla civil warfare, and with the "filibuster" activity of Americans determined to bring the Caribbean into American hands as slave territory. In October 1854, Pierce's ambassadors to Spain, France, and Great Britain (James Buchanan, who would succeed Pierce as president) signed a memorandum known as the Ostend Manifesto, which proclaimed that Cuba was "necessary to the North American republic," and that if the United States determined to possess it and Spain refused to sell it, then "by every law, human and divine, we shall be justified in wresting it from Spain." Appalled that this "scheme of spoliation" made high-flown appeals to "conscious rectitude" and to the "approbation of nations," the reviewer found that Melville's speculation, in contrast, "comes to the point." By drawing on popular traditions of personal narrative to gain a purchase on national narrative, *Israel Potter* succeeded in pleasing readers and provoking thought on important contemporary issues.

A similar strategy directs "Benito Cereno," which Melville had originally intended to be the title and lead piece in the volume of *Putnam's* pieces that became *Piazza Tales.* Without acknowledging his source, Melville takes his action from *A Narrative of Voyages and Travels* by Captain Amasa Delano (1817). Going on board a Spanish ship in trouble off the coast of South America, Delano is unaware that the ship is actually controlled not by its captain, Don Benito Cereno, but by the blacks on board, whom Delano believes to be slaves and who act the part, but who have previously mutinied and taken charge; nonetheless, he finally learns the truth, and his ship recaptures the blacks. Even the technical peculiarities in Melville's piece, what he calls the "nature of this narrative," the "intricacies" of materials "retrospectively" or "irregularly" ordered, have precedent in Delano's account, which begins with a summary of the events from the ship's log and ends with a dossier of court records, placing Delano's own first-person version in the middle. By removing the preliminary logbook record and shifting from Delano's retrospective first-person to a third-person narration closely tied to Delano's flawed perception and fluctuating thoughts, Melville gains the potential for both the suspense of a good magazine tale and the ironies of literary reflection.

In transforming the personal narrative into a tale, Melville uses the rhetoric of gothic fiction, which combines the glamor of ruinous dilapidation with the danger arising from moral weakness. The ship is like a "strange house," perhaps "haunted." The "influence" of its atmosphere produces "heightened" impressions, "enchantments" such as might be felt by the "prisoner in some deserted chateau." The courtly reserve, the sudden coldnesses, and the agitated gnawing of his fingers by Benito Cereno recall Poe's Roderick Usher.

The climax of Poe's tale figures here as a simile; the final revelation is like a "vault whose door has been flung back." Gothicism is not just decor. In "Benito Cereno," no less than in William Faulkner's *Absalom, Absalom!* (1936), gothicism is a technique for historical tragedy, representing the continuing power of the past in the present as the consequence of ancestral crime.

By changing the name of Cereno's ship from the *Tryal* to the *San Dominick*, Melville serves his gothic motif while directly engaging a history living on into the present. The saint's name enhances the gothic aura of Spanish Catholicism, fearsomely strange to antebellum America. More crucially, however, it names a place. This place, first called Hispaniola, was the Caribbean island where Columbus had landed, and Melville invents a figurehead for the ship, "the image of Christopher Colon, the discoverer of the New World." After the extermination of its native Indian population, this island received the first African slaves brought to the New World. In a historical irony already noted by Bancroft, this was also where the largest and most important uprising in the history of African-American slavery occurred, in the days of the French Revolution, establishing the independent, black-governed state of Haiti as the second free nation in the western hemisphere.

The Haitian revolution immediately affected the United States because many thousands of the island's slaveholding class emigrated to the United States. It further affected the United States, as Henry Adams first recognized and W. E. B. Du Bois emphasized, because once France no longer held the "pearl of the Antilles," its Louisiana holdings lost their point. Napoleon's sale of the Louisiana territory and the chance for the United States to expand westward followed from the revolution. Most importantly, Haiti's revolution stood as archetype of the terror that some imagined inevitably would follow any slackening of white control over slaves. As late as the 1860 election, Chief Justice Roger Taney of the U.S. Supreme Court wrote in fear of race war if Lincoln were elected, "I am old enough to remember the horrors of St. Domingo." Taney's fearful memory played some role in his judgment in the Dred Scott case of 1857. In determining that black people had no rights that the United States was constitutionally obligated to honor, Taney, while hoping to assuage southern concerns, further exacerbated sectional antagonism.

Delano, too, has fearful memories, of things heard "as stories" of pirates, and he worried lest "the San Dominick, like a slumbering volcano, suddenly let loose energies now hid." No figure was more used by the nineteenth century for revolutionary violence than that of the volcano, yet it is fundamental to the ironic form of "Benito Cereno" that Delano be capable of every fear about his circumstances except the right one. His racist underestimation of the powers of blacks is so entrenched that even the ship's name does not bring to his mind the "horrors of St. Domingo." After Nat Turner's rebellion, a series of shipboard uprisings, such as on the *Amistad* (1839) and on the *Creole* (1841), were the most notable instances of mass black resistance. Frederick Douglass devoted his one attempt at fiction to "The Heroic Slave," a version of the life of Madison Washington, who led the *Creole* slaves. Delano's incapacity to imagine black revolutionary agency is ironically repeated by Melville's scrupulous refusal to enter the mind of Babo, the leader of the uprising. Even Douglass, after having established the character of Madison Washington, leaves the narrative of the uprising to be recounted externally and retrospectively by a white survivor. Only in Stowe's *Dred* (1856) and in *Blake; or The Huts of America* (1859), by the black activist Martin R. Delany, is there any attempt to represent large-scale slave rebellion from the inside.

Delano's misdirected fears might recall the polite squeamishness of *Putnam's*, which had rejected "The Two Temples" in 1854 for fear of "offending the religious sensibilities of the public," as was explained to Melville in separate letters from the editor Charles Briggs and the publisher George Palmer Putnam. But as times changed, the journal proved not at all timid. In May 1856 the most outspoken congressional voice against slavery, Senator Charles Sumner of Massachusetts, was assaulted, while seated in the Senate, by a South Carolina congressman, and beaten unconscious; that June the Republican party nominated its first presidential candidate. An 1856 advertisement by *Putnam's* new publisher, Dix and Edwards, stated that the journal's work "cannot always be done without offense." While establishing a standard of quality that led the great English novelist William Makepeace Thackeray to call it "much the best Mag. in the world," the editors of *Putnam's* were responding to the challenges of American politics. Frederick Law Olmsted was publishing controversial travel books with Dix and Edwards, beginning with *A Journey in the Seaboard Slave States* (1856). George William Curtis, the journal's literary editor and author of five volumes of minor sketches, underwent a political conversion. Soon after his 1856 Wesleyan University oration on "The Duty of the American Scholar to Politics and the Times," published by Dix and Edwards as a pamphlet, he became primarily a political publicist, imitating the "sublime scholarship of John Milton," which "began in literature and ended in life."

Parke Godwin collected his pieces from *Putnam's* as *Political Essays* (1856), also from Dix and Edwards, and dedicated the volume to Sumner. In "The Vestiges of Despotism" (1854), Godwin attacked the stifling of fundamental debate by the combined efforts of the churches, the party system, and the slave interest. He also defended the legitimacy of his own kind of writing appearing in a magazine of "American literature, science, and art": "Literature is the full and free expression of the nation's mind, not in *belles-lettres* alone, nor in art alone, nor in science alone, but in all of these, combined with politics and religion." Writers, as the "cultivated men," the "literary men of the nation," must be "free to utter their wisest thoughts" wherever they saw the need, on "every subject which concerns the interests, the sensibilities, and the hopes of our humanity." In such a magazine, which preserved an older sense of "literature" and resisted the specialization to belles lettres characteristic of Poe and Hawthorne, and at times Melville, "Benito Cereno" might seem part of a new moment in the formation of national consciousness.

In *The Confidence-Man: His Masquerade* (1857) Melville draws on more recent popular narrative materials than he used in *Israel Potter* or "Benito Cereno." The term "confidence man" was coined in 1849, to describe a particular New York shyster named William Thompson. The key to his criminal technique was a direct appeal to a stranger to trust him. The term was immediately recognized as suggestive for thinking about many aspects of American life. The Duyckincks' *Literary World,* in reprinting some paragraphs that characterize "the young confidence man of politics" and the middle-aged "confidence man of merchandise," reflected that "it is not the worst thing that can be said of a country that it gives birth to a confidence man." Melville nationalizes his scene by removing the confidence man from the urban East to the American heartland, setting the action on a Mississippi steamer going south from Saint Louis, like Thomas Bangs Thorpe in "The Big Bear of Arkansas." Thorpe had localized his tale by focusing on the hunter's narrative, but Melville stays with the diversely representative characters gathered on board.

The tall talkers of southwestern local narratives, as well as the specific tricks of a rogue like Simon Suggs, stand behind Melville's procedure. *The Confidence-Man* focuses on a series of appeals to trust, made both to groups and in one-on-one conversations, by a variety of figures – among them a crippled black man, a mourning widower, an agent for Indian charities, an official of the "Black Rapids Coal company," an herb doctor, and a "Cosmopolitan" – all of whom may be a "masquerade" by the single titular figure. The "Wall Street spirit" pervading contemporary America is tested through the various traditional perspectives that the characters offer, such as "this ship of fools" and "All the world's a stage." Most notably, on this steamer named *Fidèle,* the first scene shows a deaf and mute man writing out St. Paul's words on "charity," including that "charity believeth all things," and the last chapter includes discussion of what belief should be granted the Apocrypha, the "uncanonical" part of the Bible.

The work's diverting incidents seem intended to provoke thought on ultimate matters, but how seriously? St. Paul spoke earnestly of charity, but

The Confidence-Man presents a "game of charity." In a time and place very different from Melville's America, the street theater of medieval mystery plays provided a ritually institutionalized space that integrated play and devotion into communal life. The *Fidèle,* however, can only contain such disparities as a problem. One character complains to another, "You pun with ideas as another man may with words." The book dwells on paradoxes, such as the "genial misanthrope," and in the midst of this complexly satiric work, a character exclaims, "God defend me from Irony, and Satire." This book's repeated staging of its incommensurability with itself is a virtuoso performance of literary narrative that reveals how marginal and improvisatory that literary narrative remained.

As the various speakers make their appeals, they tell stories to and elicit stories from their interlocutors. The variety of voices is notable. At moments the narrator and some characters use a disingenuous gentility: "the merchant, though not used to be very indiscreet, yet, being not entirely inhumane, remained not entirely unmoved." Other characters burst out in vernacular freedom, "Look you, nature! I don't deny but your clover is sweet, and your dandelions don't roar, but whose hailstones smashed my windows?" Structurally the work is a frame narrative, confined within the hours from sunrise to midnight on the thematically apt April Fools' Day. In mentioning "Chaucer's Canterbury pilgrims," Melville signals a traditional affiliation that, however, had not easily been available for earlier American use. Hawthorne in "The Storyteller" and Poe in "The Folio Club" both had wished to make books out of their local narratives by establishing a social context to frame, motivate, and complicate the narratives as Chaucer had done, but they had found no support from publishers.

In the speculative intellectual perspectives and complex techniques of construction through which Melville raises his contemporary American life into exemplary shapes of human possibility, he returns again to literary narrative. He comments on his own procedures in three chapters that reflect on the art of fiction. These chapters address the topic of character, with regard to consistency, realism, and originality. In the 1850s claims had begun to be made that certain "psychological novelists," such as Thackeray, gave positive knowledge of the motives for their characters' otherwise incomprehensible actions. Deprecating any claims to scientifically "fixed principles," Melville still allies himself with the search to reveal "the heart of man." The "nature" that readers seek in fiction must be "exhilarated" and "transformed." Fiction may provide even "more reality, than real life itself can show." Fiction serves the same function as religion: "it should present another world, and yet one to which we feel the tie." The power required to produce a character "original in the sense that Hamlet is, or Don Quixote, or

Milton's Satan" is as great and rare as that of a "new law-giver" or "the founder of a new religion."

One sentence extraordinarily exemplifies the interplay between the world and the writer's power that Melville is concerned to elucidate. The truly original character is "like a revolving Drummond light, raying away from itself all round it – everything is lit by it, everything starts up to it." Named after the British engineer who invented it in the 1820s, the Drummond light, now most familiar as the limelight, provided by far the most brilliant artificial illumination known in its time. It had aroused a tremendous sensation when first introduced to New York in the 1840s by P. T. Barnum to advertise his American Museum (as recounted in his personal narrative, *The Life of P. T. Barnum, Written by Himself*, 1855). This technical device, then, was associated with the man who epitomized fame and fortune through hoax and humbug. Melville lifts the Drummond light from the world of technology and shady commerce, and he makes it a figure for the highest moments in the psychology of creation. The light's brilliance is like the "effect" produced when "certain minds" receive "the adequate conception" of a truly original character. In turn, the psychology of artistic creation is joined to the first and highest creation. It is "akin to that which in Genesis attends upon the beginning of things." The divine "Let there be light" is echoed in the flash of literary genius but also in the glare of advertising practices. In these chapters of reflection, Melville went beyond Poe in developing the theory of literary narrative, a form that Melville was about to abandon.

For Hawthorne and Poe, the failure to publish their frame narratives defined the beginnings of their careers as professional writers; for Melville the failure of his frame narrative's publisher marked the end of his career. *The Confidence-Man* was published by Dix and Edwards on April 1, 1857, and before the end of the month the publisher was bankrupt. By September, so were its successor firms, and the stereotype plates of their books were auctioned off. No one was willing to bid on Melville's works; he could not raise funds to purchase them himself; and he authorized their sale for scrap. He had realized no income from either *The Piazza Tales* or *The Confidence-Man*. *Putnam's*, too, was sold off and merged into another magazine. Melville had another chance, however; in August 1857 he was invited to contribute to the projected *Atlantic Monthly*. He agreed to be listed as a contributor, but he had nothing ready nor any date at which he expected to. In fact, he did not publish prose again in his lifetime. From 1857 into 1860, he earned money lecturing; after the Civil War he finally received a position in the New York customhouse. Although he produced a good deal after 1857, he chose to write only poetry (see volume 4) until the last years of his life, when he began work on "Billy Budd," which remained incomplete at his death (see later discussion).

During the years that Melville's career came to its end, Hawthorne was American consul in Liverpool. Anticipating their use for fiction at a later point, Hawthorne kept voluminous notebooks while he was in England, bulking larger in four years there than those he had kept for decades in the United States, and he continued his notes after leaving the consulship and taking up residence in Italy from 1858 into 1860. Yet before his death in 1864, Hawthorne published only two more books, *The Marble Faun* (1860) (discussed in Chapter 4) and *Our Old Home* (1863), sketches of England that had appeared in the *Atlantic Monthly* from 1860. Beginning in 1858, he also worked on some six different drafts of romances, which his modern editors have grouped as the "American Claimant" manuscripts (including "The Ancestral Footstep," "Etherege," and "Grimshawe") and the "Elixir of Life" manuscripts (including "Septimius Felton," "Septimius Norton," and "The Dolliver Romance"). After *The Marble Faun,* with Melville not writing and Hawthorne not publishing, it would be some twenty years before American literary narrative was resumed, by Henry James, under new circumstances. Meanwhile, Hawthorne's heirs gradually released the materials he had left in manuscript at his death: *Passages from the American Note-Books* (1868), *Passages from the English Note-Books* (1870), *Passages from the French and Italian Note-Books* (1871), *Septimius Felton; or the Elixir of Life* (1872), *The Dolliver Romance and Other Pieces* (1876); *Dr. Grimshawe's Secret* (1883), and *The Ancestral Footstep* (1883). These seven posthumous volumes helped preserve the idea of literary narrative in America.

Although Melville did not directly participate in the political engagements of his editors at *Putnam's,* he successfully wrote in consonance with them, until the economic crisis of 1857 destroyed the institutional basis that had allowed him to earn a living. Hawthorne was more directly affected by the political crises of secession and civil war. He was not converted to a militant antislavery position, nor even to hearty unionism, and he felt himself wholly out of touch with the enthusiastic feelings around him. The best he could imagine was an independent New England. Hawthorne registered his extreme discomfort in "Chiefly about War Matters" (*Atlantic,* 1862), which ironically supplements its text with footnotes written by a straightforward unionist "Editor." Ostentatiously placing friendship over politics, Hawthorne dedicated *Our Old Home* to Franklin Pierce, who was in extremely bad repute because of his concessions to the South while he was president, but whose patronage had made the book possible by allowing Hawthorne to live in England. The Compromise of 1850 had defined a moment of political suspension, in which Hawthorne's speculative uncertainties about action could be meditatively elaborated, but during the decisive action of the war, Hawthorne pushed his distrust of action so far that he could no longer imagine a plot for romance. The plot of *The Marble Faun* had scarcely animated the massive descriptive passages that distract the reader and, it seems, comfort the writer by burying the action. The new work showed a further erosion in Hawthorne's commitment to reaching any audience.

The "American Claimant" project stemmed from a paragraph in the notebooks of 1855, sketching an English emigrant to America who bears a family secret that could ruin the family. He passes on the secret until, "at last, the hero of the romance comes to England, and finds that . . . he still has it in his power to procure the downfall of the family." Originally named "Middleton," the protagonist is a man in the middle, isolated between America and England and hoping to mediate between them. He seeks "links" or a "connection," but anything that will join him to England will sever him from America, and the project gets stuck in this dilemma. Although Middleton is "sensitive," he has led an active political life, which, however, he has recently abandoned in "disgust." It is a significant innovation for Hawthorne to make his central figure someone who is in between actions. This figure is only temporarily a spectator; unlike major characters in Hawthorne's earlier romances, he is not a photographer, poet, or sculptor. Hawthorne cannot carry this plan through. The protagonist's possible action is swallowed up by his antagonists (representing the current possessors of his English inheritance) and his helpers (figures from his American childhood). Yet even with these characters, Hawthorne struggles at an impasse.

In fascinating notes to himself that interrupt the incomplete manuscripts, Hawthorne wrote, "Still there is something wanting to make an action for the story." Frustrated, he notes, "The story must not be founded at all on remorse or secret guilt – all that I've worn out." Struggling to devise a motivation for the Italianate villain, he tries and discards many possibilities: is his peculiarity "a leprosy? – a eunuch? – a cork leg? – a golden touch? – a dead hand? – a false nose? – a glass eye?" Turning to the tutor of the protagonist, he decides to make this old man the "real hero," but as a "martyr," in contrast to the "young American politican" and all other "self-seekers." The legendary "bloody footstep" shall be the track "not of guilt, but of persecution," because the old man and all his family have always exemplified "the weakness of too much conscience," its "indecision" and "incapacity for action." In his "inability for anything but suffering," the old man raises Hamletism to the pitch of Uncle Tom. Against the grain of his own narrative intention, Hawthorne notes that conscience is incomparably "disorganizing": it is "certain to overthrow everything earthly." Where he wants a motive, he can find none, and where he expects weakness he finds strength. This was no way to organize a romance, but it does suggest Hawthorne's struggle to grasp the dynamics of southern secession and the northern response.

In the "Elixir of Life" project, the first two versions focus on Septimius, a theology student in Concord at the outbreak of the revolutionary war, whose identity is defined by his killing of a British soldier and by his quest for physical immortality. Hawthorne acknowledges the excitement of the revolutionary moment as something "we" know "now," as the Civil War carries off young men, yet despite killing the soldier, Septimius stands aloof. Hawthorne intends "dealing as little as possible with outward events," because "our story is an internal one." Like everything else "outside of Septimius's brains," the "great historic incident" figures in the narrative only to help "develop and illustrate what went on within" him. Yet Septimius is criticized because his "characteristic egotism" makes him think that "the war would hardly have a more important result than the vivifying of his thought" by the secret learned from the dying Englishman. Hawthorne's own narrative technique, however, has prescribed that self-centeredness, and it is hard for this criticism of Septimius to work without also working against the romance.

Hawthorne directly relates the character's psychology to his own experience as a "Romance writer." Septimius's disappointment with his elixir is a disillusion with which a romancer can "sympathize." For a romancer suffers equal pain when the world of fiction is confronted by the ordinary world. Outside the "magic influence" of romance, "destruction, disturbance, incongruity" ruin the "nicely adjusted relations" that had established a "truer world" than everyday, with a "fitness of events" otherwise unavailable. Hawthorne could no longer extend faith to his literary narrative. By comparing his character to himself, he attempts to buttress the fiction with fact, seeking to draw stability from the world of chaotic confusion. Hawthorne failed to separate himself from his hero even to the extent that Melville had achieved in *Pierre,* and he could not complete the work.

In "The Dolliver Romance," Hawthorne no longer tries to command such challenging materials as the revolutionary war or a politician in temporary exile. The romance springs from a simple, sketchlike domestic setting, yet even in his notes for this extremely truncated manuscript, Hawthorne struggles to structure and motivate action. Given a magical potion that makes an old person gradually younger, Hawthorne tries to determine why someone would want to "live back" in this way. Perhaps he wants to "confer a material benefit on the world," to "get rid of poverty, or slavery, or war." The point of the story would be that his "toil," which threatens to "disturb . . . the order of nature" and "destroy . . . the whole economy of the world," had no effect. On the contrary, "without any agency of his," the goal would be accomplished by "the real tendency and progress of mankind." Faced with the "convulsive action" of the Civil War, however, Hawthorne could no longer effectively commit himself to this faith in romance as progress without agency, which had made possible the independent worlds of his literary narratives.

EPILOGUE: POSTWAR NATIONAL NARRATIVE

The Civil War debilitated Hawthorne and inhibited literary narrative, but it did not prevent all new narratives. The greatest talent to emerge during the war was Mark Twain. His first books clearly link him to the traditions of local and personal narratives: *The Celebrated Jumping Frog of Calaveras County and Other Sketches* (1867), *The Innocents Abroad* (1869), and *Roughing It* (1872), which the preface characterizes as "merely a personal narrative." During the war, Francis Parkman recovered from his nearly two decades of debility and renewed his national narrative. Dedicated to three of his relatives who had fallen in the Civil War, Parkman's *Pioneers of France in the New World* appeared in 1865; after twenty-three reprintings it was revised in 1885 to take account of research in Florida that Parkman had been unable to accomplish during the war. Over the last decades of the century, until his death in 1893, he completed his series on "France and England in North America," to which *The Conspiracy of Pontiac* had formed a proleptic coda: *The Jesuits in North America* (1867); *The Discovery of the Great West* (1869; revised and enlarged as *La Salle and the Discovery of the Great West*, 1879); *The Old Regime in Canada* (1874; revised and enlarged, 1893); *Count Frontenac and New France under Louis XIV* (1877); *Montcalm and Wolfe* (1884); and *A Half-Century of Conflict* (1892).

In the "Introduction" which from the first edition stood at the front of *Pioneers of France,* Parkman set out the conceptual terms and antithetical oppositions that govern the whole history as he wrote it over the next thirty years. His work lays bare the "springs of American civilization," for "France in America" is subsumed within American national narrative. It was France that "conquered for Civilization" the land of America, but the United States is fulfilling the course of civilization. In Parkman's allegory of historical principles, his series recovers "the attempt of Feudalism, Monarchy, and Rome to master a continent where, at this hour," as Parkman writes during the Civil War, "half a million of bayonets are vindicating the ascendancy of a regulated freedom." France in America was "all head." Pope and king stood for the principle of "Centralization," which infantilized the French by denying them their independence, just as savagery had made Indians remain children. The principle of "steadfast growth" was to be found in New En-

gland's "body without a head." (Parkman shows no awareness of the gro-
tesquery.) New England was "fruitful" and offered "hope" because it was
based on "Liberty"; New France was "barren" and doomed to "despair" because it was the "representative" of "Absolutism."

British "blood and muscle" made New England "pre-eminently the land of
material progress." In contrast, however, the aristocratic, archaic, and savage
qualities of the French and Indians made New France rich in "striking and
salient forms of character." The greatest effort of Parkman's thousands of
pages goes to recovering the "contrast" — grave priests and naked Indians,
sober merchants and bushrangers "tricked out with savage finery" — that
made the "whole course of French Canadian history" so "picturesque." Because the further course of events has "dwarfed" the French period and
reduced it "to an episode," it now must be evoked as a "memory of the past"
that rises in "strange, romantic" shape: "A boundless vision grows upon us;
an untamed continent; vast wastes of forest verdure," in which "plumed
helmets gleamed." All this Parkman undertakes to represent with "photographic clearness and truth," employing the best documentary methods of
scientific historical technique in the service of recovering glamor.

The heroic figures of Champlain and La Salle among the explorers, Mar-
quette and Jogues among the Jesuits, Frontenac and Montcalm among the
governing aristocrats, organize the narrative for large stretches, but as in *The
Conspiracy of Pontiac,* the land itself provides the largest continuity. Parkman
notes at times his own recent visits to the scenes about which he writes.
Sometimes they had remained wilderness; sometimes they were more casually
accessible, and the "tourist," the "sportsman," the "wandering artist" might
take leisure where Indians once had lived in deadly earnest. Some wilderness
had been painfully lost. A great rock, once covered with Indian religious
images visible from afar, now advertises "Plantation Bitters." The "great
natural beauty" at the Falls of St. Anthony has been "utterly spoiled" by the
new city of Minneapolis. Other wilderness has been gained for progress. The
"yellow . . . ripened wheat" of a "hardy and valiant yeomanry" has "strangely
transformed" the "rolling sea of dull green prairie," once "boundless pasture of
the buffalo."

The interplay of science and glamor, the use of photographic precision to
allegoric effect, may be seen in a notable passage from Parkman's last years.
To introduce "Queen Anne's War," Parkman begins with the "unbroken
forest" of Maine, a "waste of savage vegetation," which, he notes, "survives,
in some part, to this day." Its "prodigality of vital force" in "the struggle for
existence," however, does not distinguish it, but only makes visible the
"same" process at work in "all organized beings, from men to mushrooms."
The forest scene carries implications beyond itself:

Young seedlings in millions spring every summer from the black mould, rich with the decay of those that had preceded them, crowding, choking, and killing each other, perishing by their very abundance; all but a scattered few, stronger than the rest, or more fortunate in position, which survive by blighting those about them. They in turn, as they grow, interlock their boughs, and repeat in a season or two the same process of mutual suffocation. The forest is full of lean saplings dead or dying with vainly stretching towards the light. Not one infant tree in a thousand lives to maturity; yet these survivors form an innumerable host, pressed together in struggling confusion, squeezed out of symmetry and robbed of normal development, as men are said to be in the level sameness of democratic society.

In such a passage Parkman's intense feeling for the "universal tragedy of nature" is in contrast to his progressive national narrative framework. Checked only by the irony of "said to be," it threatens to reduce the course of history to the mere "revolution" (in the astronomical sense) that marked Indian life: "mutable as the wind" in power relations, but "hopelessly unchanging" in cultural "development." It was a "gloomy and meaningless history . . . of extermination, absorption, or expatriation."

For the United States, however, the experience of the Civil War gave a powerful new shape to national narrative. By virtue of the war and of Lincoln's death, understood as martyrdom, the state itself (in the sense of the sovereign power, not in the sense of the united "states") became sanctified, taking on the prestige that had previously been reserved for the "Union" and the "People." This new American reverence for earthly power made possible Melville's final work of prose fiction, "Billy Budd," on which he worked for the last several years of his life and left near completion at his death in 1891.

"Billy Budd" is the most wholly fictional of Melville's works. It is not drawn at all directly from his experience, nor does it rework specific documents. It is set in 1797 on a British warship, and Billy is not even an American. America is no longer so unique that major work by an American writer must treat an American subject (or one with obvious bearing on the United States, such as Prescott's *Conquest of Mexico*). Parkman's history even praises the continuing spread of British colonialism in the nineteenth century, rather than treating empire as superseded by democracy. A Britain threatened by revolutionary France might begin to seem a congenial figure for the United States. After the Civil War, slavery was ended, but other forms of social inequality increased until farmers' populism and industrial workers' agitation to unionize threatened the existing order.

Although "Billy Budd" is fiction, Melville's rhetoric is antifictional. Subtitled "An Inside Narrative," "Billy Budd" repeatedly appeals to the documentary expectations of narrative. Readers should understand that this is "no romance," and it must, therefore, lack "the symmetry of form attainable in pure fiction." Using a term not yet in the language when he began his career,

Melville defends his procedures as "realism." As an "inside" narrative, the work corrects the news account (itself part of the fiction) of the events it recounts. In 1851, Melville had been happy to encounter a newspaper report that confirmed *Moby-Dick* by reporting a whale's sinking a ship, but now he reenacts a fundamental gesture of self-consciously innovative high culture, from William Wordsworth in the preface to *Lyrical Ballads* (1800) to Joseph Conrad in *The Secret Agent* (1907): defining the truth of one's writing by the falsity of newspapers. As "romance" had been in the 1850s, "realism" in the 1880s was the password for literary narrative.

"Billy Budd" performs an extraordinary historical reconstruction. It defines a limited fictional action within the "juncture" of important public events. These events are not just the revolutionary wars, but, specifically, the mutinies of 1797 within the British navy, and, yet more precisely, the constraints of commanding a ship detached from the fleet. Its "inside narrative" does not function like the "internal story" of *Septimius Felton* to displace attention from history to psychology. Two paragraphs from the manuscript that served as the work's preface from its first publication in 1924 until the scholarly edition of 1962 greatly enrich the complexity of historical thought by arguing that "not the wisest could have foreseen" at the time that the revolutionary excesses, or the sailors' mutiny, would eventually lead to "political advance" and "important reforms." It seems that only because they were opposed by the wisest have these movements succeeded; progress requires resistance.

Combined with the complex realism of its historical narrative, "Billy Budd" equally gains power through allegorical simplification. Billy Budd, the natural child of an unknown lord, an illiterate "upright barbarian," is like "Adam." Claggart, the master-at-arms, serves the ship as its corrupt "chief of police"; his eyes exercise "serpent fascination," and he satanically lies in accusing Billy of treason. Tongue-tied by a natural speech defect, Billy tries to speak in self-defense, but he "could only say it with a blow," and he strikes Claggart dead. Captain Vere, a hero in action yet a meditative reader of "unconventional" books, is the "troubled patriarch" who must resolve the situation, which he summarizes, "Struck dead by an angel of God! Yet the angel must hang!"

The "jugglery of circumstances" means that Billy's righteousness counts as mutiny. In explaining the case to the drumhead court-martial he has summoned, Vere emphasizes the need to "strive against scruples that may tend to enervate decision." At whatever pain, he avoids Hamletism. Hawthorne's "American Claimant" had similarly argued on behalf of "efficient actors," those "who mould the world." But the claimant's life in "politics" had taught him that such efficiency required an ugly "something else" to be "developed more strongly than conscience," and upon reflection, his argument pains him with its "ugliness and indefensibleness." Vere shows that power may have conscience, and even moral beauty. Feeling still the "primeval" in "our formalized humanity," he takes Billy Budd to his bosom like Abraham when he is about to sacrifice Isaac.

When Melville in *Typee* first challenged his readers as "state-room sailors," it was on behalf of the crew. "Billy Budd," however, invokes "snug card players in the cabin" to set them against the lonely, agonized responsibility of "the sleepless man on the bridge" who guides the craft. Billy himself, condemned by Vere for his deed, cries out before being hanged, "God bless Captain Vere!" The narrator concludes that "the condemned one suffered less" than his judge did, for Billy's consciousness is like that of "children," but Vere is a mature adult.

The Civil War, fought for the Union and against slavery, had brought the state an imaginative moral legitimacy unavailable in the 1850s. Nothing admirable stood behind Legree as Vere stands behind Claggart. After the Civil War, the "conservative" position no longer had to be also progressive – as was Judge Temple in Cooper's *Pioneers* – in order to be right. Billy Budd and Uncle Tom are both innocent martyrs, but the feelings Tom provokes reach out to the reader; those of Billy are contained by Vere. In Melville's pre-war "Benito Cereno," the revolutionary slave Babo remains opaque to Cereno, to Delano, and to the reader. This is far different from the moral and intellectual comprehensiveness that allows Vere to sympathize with Billy and still judge him. Vere has incorporated Stowe's lesson of feeling, and his power to give himself pain by his own judgment enhances his authority.

To the extent that readers accept Vere, "Billy Budd" reconciles force with principle. Parkman had emphasized the dominance of principle. Only at moments in Parkman did the predominance of force over principle produce a complicating undercurrent, but this imbalance becomes the primary irony in Henry Adams's *History of the United States During the Administrations of Thomas Jefferson and James Madison* (9 volumes, 1889–91). Adams aims for thoughtful, "scientific," rather than spectacular, "dramatic," history. For Adams human agents may no longer be "heroes" but only "types" that are illustrative rather than in themselves "sources of power." He transforms the narrative of America from prophetic to analytic. Parkman's concluding paragraph looks forward from the end of the Seven Years' War to anticipate the present nation: "the disunited colonies became the United States. The string of discordant colonies along the Atlantic coast has grown to a mighty people, joined in a union which the earthquake of civil war served only to compact and consolidate." Adams looks back within the history of the United States and places the consolidation much earlier than the Civil War; his unstated premise is that the nation must have been consolidated already for the North to have had the will and capacity to defeat the South's secession.

Parkman took his analytic topic of "centralization" from Tocqueville, who had broached in *Democracy in America* and developed in *The Old Regime and the French Revolution* (1856) the thesis that it was not the French Revolution that had introduced centralization to French government (even though the term itself was a revolutionary neologism). Rather, Tocqueville argued, the process had begun in the Middle Ages and developed with unparalleled rapidity and complexity from the Age of Louis XIV. This argument concerning centralization helped Parkman explain what was wrong with New France: "the government, and not the individual, acted always the foremost part." Adams, who during the Civil War had made Tocqueville's life and work "the Gospel of my private religion," does not simply appropriate Tocqueville's argument. He reverses Parkman's evaluation by treating centralization as strength, and he transposes Tocqueville's analysis from old France to new America. Centralization of the government of the United States had not occurred during the Civil War, as usually understood, but had begun much earlier, in fact, during the administration of Thomas Jefferson, the president most associated with the anticentralist principles of strict construction and states' rights.

Implicitly rebuking the theoretical grounds offered for southern secession, Adams proposes an ironic thesis: "The Constitution was violated more frequently by its friends than by its enemies, and often the extent of such violations measured the increasing strength of the Union." From the moment of his first presidential message to Congress in 1801, Jefferson did not try to block up "loopholes for the admission of European sovereignty into the citadel of American liberty." Instead, he "stretched out his hand to seize the powers he had denounced" before becoming president. The debate over Jefferson's purchase of Louisiana from Napoleon came down to the particulars of whether it should be a state, colony, or territory, rather than the basic question of whether the Constitution permitted such an acquisition. Adams draws the moral: "for the first time in the national history all parties agreed in admitting that the government could govern." Reduced to a tautological triviality, the fundamental debate of the first decades after the Declaration of Independence no longer counted and should have had no force when resuscitated in midcentury.

Centralization occurred not only in mute practice but also in public opinion. Adams notes that the Constitution never mentions the "nation" but only the "Union" in order to characterize the American collectivity, and he argues that only through the War of 1812 did the Union became a nation (which in turn could be mobilized to preserve the "Union" in the Civil War). Adams identifies June 1807 as the moment when "for the first time in their history the people of the United States learned . . . the feeling of a true national emotion." The British had humiliated the U.S. frigate *Chesapeake*, and the outrage "seethed and hissed like the glowing olive-stake of Ulysses in the Cyclops' eye, until the whole American people, like Cyclops, roared with pain, and stood frantic on the shore, hurling abuse at their enemy, who taunted them from his safe ships." This crucial phase in American consciousness becomes mock-epic. The new-found national unity is figured in the single, centralized, but blinded eye of the Cyclops: great force but little understanding or control.

Adams fixes the moment when "the rhetorical marks" of antebellum political discourse were established. In February 1810, the young Henry Clay spoke for a new generation that "for fifty years" would prevail through its "devotion to ideas of nationality and union." The key figures of this discourse were the Union itself and the Founding Fathers. This national rhetoric was powerful because it belonged "to no party." It was available "with equal advantage" to "orators of every section." This new political language was formed to serve a counsel of war. Idealizing as the Fathers and the Union may seem, they were part of the "War Hawk" movement. Led by Clay and John Calhoun, the War Hawks sought to end in practice America's exceptional status among nations, even while sanctifying it figuratively. Adams sees their goal as granting the government "the attributes of old-world sovereignty under pretext of the war power." Moving into the war, "America began slowly to struggle, under the consciousness of pain, toward a conviction that she must bear the common burdens of humanity, and fight with the weapons of other races in the same bloody arena."

Adams sets at the beginning of the national period a loss of America's uniqueness, a transition from innocence to force. "Billy Budd" shows a comparable transition at about the same time. A major difference between 1800 and 1815, Adams explains, was that "the Rights of Man occupied public thoughts less, and the price of cotton more." This shift was not just from idealism to worldliness, but from an age of liberation to an age in which slavery would seem more and more indispensable. Melville seems to allegorize this change. The action of his story begins with the "handsome sailor," the Adamic Billy Budd, forced to leave the merchant ship *Rights of Man* in order to serve the king on the battleship *Bellipotent*.

Many of Adams's generation, however, preferred to date this shift from the Civil War. In his study of Hawthorne (1879), Henry James claims that Hawthorne's contemporaries, "that generation which grew up with the century," held a "superstitious faith in the grandeur of the country." Because they thought a "special Providence" protected America (as we have seen in Bancroft's *History*), they were free to enjoy "simple and uncritical" faith and "genial optimism." But since the Civil War, the "good American," Hawthorne's equivalent in sensibility and seriousness, "has eaten of the tree of knowledge." James claims experience against Hawthorne's innocence, but Adams finds even such knowingness still caught in American innocence of history, as James's residual biblical myth might suggest. James claims to know better than the national narrative of Hawthorne's time, with its optimistic providentialism, but Adams shows how little James knows of the cyclopean fires of war and pain that forged the supposedly innocent tools of American national narrative. James claims that "good" Americans are now beyond the seductive powers of national narrative. Adams's ironic genealogy must discount James's claim as a wish, yet by showing a beginning, Adams's account may make possible an end.

In the first chapter, I suggested that American national narrative is now much more recognizable in movies, television, and political rhetoric than in the culturally honored realm of "literature." Adams's *History* may stand for the point at which national narrative became an object of study for American high culture rather than, as in Bancroft or Webster, being the very substance of that culture. In the fifty years after Adams's *History,* modernism brought literary narrative a far higher authority and prestige than it had ever won in its first decades, the time of this study. In its own time, however, literary narrative could not maintain its separate realm against the crises that from *Uncle Tom's Cabin* through the end of Reconstruction again brought to the fore national narrative. Hawthorne and Melville incorporated in their literary narratives the emphasis on experience of personal narratives and the keen observation and complex tonal modulations of local narratives; in *The Scarlet Letter* and *Moby-Dick* they also subdued national narrative to their purposes. They produced a kind of narrative that was new to the United States and that is now known through much of the world and valued as a living heritage.

CHRONOLOGY
1820–1865

Cyrus R. K. Patell

	American Texts	American Events	Other Events and Texts
1820	**Channing, William Ellery** (1780–1842), *The Moral Argument against Calvinism* (essay)	Missouri Compromise outlaws slavery in lands of the Louisiana Purchase north of latitude 36°30'.	George IV crowned king of England.
	Cooper, James Fenimore (1789–1851), *Precaution* (novel)	Maine admitted to the Union as the twenty-third state.	Keats, *Lamia and Other Poems*
	Eastburn, James W. (1797–1819), *Yamoyden, A Tale of the Wars of King Philip* (poem)	President Monroe reelected.	Malthus, *Principles of Political Economy*
	Irving, Washington (1783–1859), *The Sketch Book of Geoffrey Crayon, Gent.* (fiction and nonfiction; first installment 1819)	Susan B. Anthony born (dies 1906).	Shelley, *Prometheus Unbound*
	Noah, Mordecai M. (1785–1851), *The Siege of Tripoli* (drama)		
	Symmes, John [Adam Seaborn] (1780–1829), *Symzonia: Voyage of Discovery* (novel)		
	Five volumes of new prose fiction by native authors published in the United States.		
1821	**Adams, John Quincy** (1767–1848), *Report on Weights and Measures* (nonfiction)	Henry Clay effects "Second Missouri Compromise."	Mexican Revolution.
	Bryant, William Cullen (1794–1878), *Poems*	Missouri admitted to the Union as the twenty-fourth state.	John Keats dies (born 1795).
	Channing, William Ellery (1780–1842), "The Evidences of Revealed Religion" (tract)	Andrew Jackson becomes military governor of Florida.	Constable, "Hay Wain" (painting) Hegel, *The Philosophy of Right*

Chase, Owen (?), *Narrative of the Most Extraordinary and Distressing Shipwreck of the Whale-Ship Essex* (nonfiction)

Cooper, James Fenimore (1789–1851), *The Spy* (novel)

Schoolcraft, Henry Rowe (1793–1864), *Narrative Journal of Travels through the Northwestern Regions of the United States* (nonfiction)

Saturday Evening Post founded in Philadelphia.

Santa Fe Trail for commercial travel between Independence, Missouri, and Santa Fe, New Mexico, is mapped by William Bicknell.

First public high school established in Boston.

Junius Brutus Booth, English actor and father of John Wilkes Booth, makes his American debut in *Richard III* in Richmond, Virginia.

Population of the United States reaches 9.6 million.

James Mill, *Elements of Political Economy*

Southey, *A Vision of Judgment*

1822 Irving, Washington (1783–1859), *Bracebridge Hall* (fiction and nonfiction)

McHenry, James (1785–1845), *The Pleasures of Friendship* (verse)

Morse, Jedidiah (1761–1826), *Report to the Secretary of War . . . on Indian Affairs* (nonfiction)

Neal, John (1793–1876), *Logan* (novel)

Paulding, James Kirke (1778–1860), *A Sketch of Old England, by a New England Man* (nonfiction)

Sedgwick, Catharine Maria (1789–1867), *A New England Tale* (novel)

American colony of Liberia established.

Florida organized as a territory.

Planned slave rebellion led by Denmark Vesey in Charleston, South Carolina, is prevented; Vesey and 30 others are executed.

Stephen F. Austin establishes first Anglo-American colony in Texas.

Henry Ashley advertises in a St. Louis newspaper for "Enterprising Young Men" to spend several years developing routes to the Pacific.

Greeks proclaim independence; war between Turkey and Greece.

Percy Bysshe Shelley dies (born 1792).

Matthew Arnold born (dies 1888).

Byron, *The Vision of Judgment*

De Quincey, *Confessions of an English Opium-Eater*

Schubert, Symphony No. 8 in B minor ("Unfinished")

	American Texts	American Events	Other Events and Texts
1823	Sigourney, Lydia (1791–1865), *Traits of the Aborigines of America* (epic poem) Bold, Edward (?), *The Merchant's and Mariner's African Guide* (nonfiction) Cooper, James Fenimore (1789–1851), *The Pioneers* (novel); *Tales for Fifteen* (stories); *The Pilot* (novel) Doddridge, Joseph (1769–1826), *Logan: The Last of the Race of Shikellemus, Chief of the Cayuga Nation* (play) Hunter, John Dunn (1798?–1827), *Manners and Customs of Several Indian Tribes Located West of the Mississippi* (nonfiction) James, Edwin (1797–1861), *Account of an Expedition from Pittsburgh to the Rocky Mountains* (nonfiction) McHenry, James (1785–1845), *The Wilderness; or, Braddock's Times* (novel); *The Spectre of the Forest* (novel) Neal, John (1793–1876), *Errata; or, The Works of Will. Adams* (novel); *Randolph* (novel); *Seventy-Six* (novel) Paulding, James Kirke (1778–1860), *Koningsmarke* (novel)	Francis Parkman born (dies 1893). Monroe Doctrine in the president's Annual Message to Congress.	Mexico becomes a republic. John Stuart Mill founds Utilitarian Society (1823–6). William Wilberforce forms antislavery society in England.

Payne, John Howard (1791–1852), *Clari; or the Maid of Milan* (musical; contains song "Home, Sweet Home")

Smith, Ethan (1762–1849), *Views of the Hebrews* (nonfiction)

The New York Mirror (1823–60).

1824 Child, Lydia Maria (1802–80), *Hobomok* (novel)

Cushing, Eliza (1794–?), *Saratoga* (novel)

Everett, Edward (1794–1865), "The Circumstances Favorable to the Progress of Literature in America" (essay)

Hunter, John Dunn (1798?–1827), *Memoirs of a Captivity Among the Indians of North America* (nonfiction)

Irving, Washington (1783–1859), *Tales of a Traveller, by Geoffrey Crayon, Gent.*; with John Howard Payne, (1791–1852), *Charles the Second* (drama)

Potter, Israel R. (?), *The Life and Remarkable Adventures of Israel R. Potter* (nonfiction)

Say, Thomas (1787–1834), *American Entomology* (nonfiction, 1824–8)

Seaver, James E. (1787–1827), *A Narrative of the Life of Mary Jemison* (nonfiction)

Sedgwick, Catharine Maria (1789–1867), *Redwood* (novel)

Texas is incorporated into the Mexican Federal Republic.

James Bridger, fur trader and guide, discovers the Great Salt Lake.

First college of science and engineering founded (now Rensselaer Polytechnic Institute).

783

American Texts	American Events	Other Events and Texts

Tucker, George (1775–1861), *The Valley of the Shenandoah* (novel)		
Bryant, William Cullen (1794–1878), "A Forest Hymn"; "The Death of the Flowers" (verse)	John Quincy Adams elected by the House of Representatives as sixth president of the United States after failure of any candidate to win an electoral majority.	Portugal recognizes Brazilian independence.
Child, Lydia Maria (1802–80), *The Rebels* (novel)	American Unitarian Association founded.	Bolivia becomes independent of Peru, Uruguay of Brazil.
Cooper, James Fenimore (1789–1851), *Lionel Lincoln* (novel)		Czar Nicholas I quells Decembrist uprising.
Ellis, William (1794–1872), *A Journal of a Tour Around Hawaii* (nonfiction)	Texas opened to American colonization by Mexican law.	Jacques Louis David dies (born 1748).
Hentz, Nicholas (1797–1856), *Tadeuskind, the King of the Lenape* (novel)	Completion of Erie Canal.	Johann Strauss, Jr., born (dies 1899).
Neal, John (1793–1876), *Brother Jonathan* (novel)	U.S. government adopts removal policy that provides for transfer of eastern Indians to areas west of the Mississippi River.	
Paulding, James Kirke (1778–1860), *John Bull in America* (nonfiction)	Robert Dale Owen, an Englishman, establishes Utopian community at New Harmony, Indiana.	Coleridge, *Aids to Reflection*
Schoolcraft, Henry Rowe (1793–1864), *Travels in the Central Portions of the Mississippi Valley* (nonfiction)		Pepys, *Diary* (posth., ed. Lord Braybrook)
Winthrop, John (1588–1649), *The History of New England from 1630–1649* (nonfiction, 1825–6)		
Woodworth, Samuel (1785–1842), *The Forest Rose* (play); *The Widow's Son* (play)		
Eighteen volumes of new prose fiction by native authors published in the United States.		

1825

1826

Boudinot, Elias (Jr.) (1804–39), "An Address to the Whites" (pamphlet)

Channing, William Ellery (1780–1842), "Unitarian Christianity Most Favorable to Piety" (pamphlet) "Remarks on the Character and Writing of John Milton" (essay)

Cooper, James Fenimore (1789–1851), *The Last of the Mohicans* (novel)

Flint, Timothy (1780–1840), *Recollections of the Last Ten Years, Passed in Occasional Residences and Journeyings in the Valley of Mississippi* (travel writing); *Francis Berrian, or the Mexican Patriot* (novel)

Irving, Washington (1783–1859) and **John Howard Payne** (1791–1852), *Richelieu* (drama)

Kent, James (1763–1847), *Commentaries on American Law* (nonfiction, 1826–30)

Rankin, John (1793–1886), *Letters on Slavery* (nonfiction)

Reed, Sampson (1800–80), *The Growth of the Mind* (nonfiction)

The Casket: Flowers of Literature, Wit and Sentiment launched by Samuel C. Atkinson and Charles Alexander in Philadelphia.

US mission to Panama Congress fails.

Thomas Jefferson and John Adams die within hours of each other on the fiftieth anniversary of the Declaration of Independence.

Russia declares war on Persia.

E. B. Browning, *Essay on Mind, with Other Poems*
Disraeli, *Vivian Grey* (1826–7)
Mary Shelley, *The Last Man*

	American Texts	American Events	Other Events and Texts
1827	**Audubon, John James** (1785–1851), *The Birds of America* from Original Drawings (nonfiction, folio ed., 1827–38)	North and South split over revival of tariff question.	Peru secedes from Colombia.
	Cooper, James Fenimore (1789–1851), *The Prairie* (novel); *The Red Rover* (novel)	United States and Britain share occupation of the Oregon Territory.	Ludwig van Beethoven dies (born 1770).
	Custis, George Washington (1781–1857), *Pocahontas; or, The Settlers of Virginia* (play)	Thurslow Weed takes up the cause of anti-Masonry.	William Blake dies (born 1757).
	Dana, Richard Henry, Sr. (1787–1879), *Poems*	First passenger railroad line incorporated (Baltimore and Ohio).	Schubert, "Die Winterreise," song cycle to words by Wilhelm Müller.
	Hale, Sarah Josepha (1788–1879), *Northwood: A Tale of New England* (novel)		
	McKenney, Thomas (1785–1859), *Sketches of a Tour to the Lakes* (travel)		
	Poe, Edgar Allan (1809–49), *Tamerlane and Other Poems*		
	Sedgwick, Catharine Maria (1789–1867), *Hope Leslie* (novel)		
	Tuscarora [David Cusick] (?–1840?), *Sketches of Ancient History of the Six Nations* (nonfiction)		
	Cherokee Phoenix, bilingual newspaper (1827–32).		
	Western Monthly Review (Cincinnati, 1827–30).		
1828	**Calhoun, John** (1782–1850), *South Carolina Exposition and Protest* (pub. anonymously, nonfiction)	Democratic party formed by Jackson-Calhoun faction.	Duke of Wellington becomes prime minister of Great Britain.

Carey, Matthew (1760–1839), *Letters on the Coloniza- tion Society* (nonfiction)

Cooper, James Fenimore (1789–1851), *Notions of the Americans: Picked up by a Travelling Bachelor* (nonfiction)

Flint, Timothy (1780–1840), *The Life and Adventures of Arthur Clenning* (novel); *A Condensed Geography and History of the Western States* (expanded 1832 as *The History and Geography of the Mississippi Valley*)

Hall, James (1793–1868), *Letters from the West* (nonfiction)

Irving, Washington (1783–1859), *The History of the Life and Voyages of Christopher Columbus; A Chronicle of the Conquest of Granada* (1828–9, written under pseudonym Fray Antonio Agapida)

Neal, John (1793–1876), *Rachel Dyer: A North Ameri- can Story* (novel)

Stewart, C[harles] S[amuel] (1795–1870), *A Resi- dence in the Sandwich Islands* (nonfiction)

Walker, David (1785?–1830), *Appeal . . . to the Col- oured Citizens of the World* (pamphlet)

Webster, Noah (1758–1843), *An American Dictionary of the English Language*

Ladies' Magazine (Boston, 1828–36).

Congress passes "Tariff of Abominations."

Andrew Jackson elected seventh president in victory for new Democratic party.

Thomas Rice introduces minstrel character "Jim Crow" in Louis- ville, Kentucky.

Liberal revolt in Mexico; Vicente Guerrero becomes president.

Francisco José de Goya y Lucentes dies (born 1746).

Franz Schubert dies (born 1797), having finished his Symphony No. 9 ("The Great").

1829	President Jackson's "Kitchen Cabinet" and "spoils system." William Cullen Bryant assumes ownership and editorship of the *New York Evening Post* (until his death in 1878).	Slavery abolished in Mexico. Mariano Vallejo leads Mexican troops against Indians at Mission San José. Balzac, *Le dernier Chouan* (beginning of *La comedie humaine*) Carlyle, "Signs of the Times" Rossini, *Guillaume Tell* (opera)

Apess, William (1798–1839), *A Son of the Forest. The Experience of William Apes, a Native of the Forest* (autobiography)

Austin, Stephen Fuller (1793–1836), *Establishing Austin's Colony* (nonfiction)

Cooper, James Fenimore (1789–1851), *The Wept of Wish-ton-Wish* (novel); *The Water-Witch* (novel)

Flint, Timothy (1780–1840), *George Mason, the Young Backwoodsman* (novel)

Hale, Sarah Josepha (1788–1879), *Sketches of American Character* (nonfiction)

Horton, George M. (1798?–1880), *The Hope of Liberty* (poetry)

Kettell, Samuel (1800–55), ed., *Specimens of American Poetry, with Critical and Biographical Notices*

Knapp, Samuel Lorenzo (1783–1838), *Lectures on American Literature* (nonfiction)

Marsh, James (1794–1842) [ed.], *Aids to Reflection* (Coleridge, American edition)

Poe, Edgar Allan (1809–49), *Al Aaraaf, Tamerlane and Minor Poems*

Sealsfield, Charles [Karl Postle] (1793–1864), *Tokeah; or, The White Rose* (novel)

Stone, John Augustus (1800–34), *Metamora, or The Last of the Wampanoags* (play)

Young, Robert Alexander (?), *Ethiopian Manifesto Issued in Defense of the Black Man's Rights in the Scale of Universal Freedom* (nonfiction)

1830 **Bird, Robert Montgomery** (1806–54), *Pelopidas, or the Fall of the Polemarchs* (published 1919; play)

Child, Lydia Maria (1802–80), *The Frugal Housewife* (nonfiction)

Flint, Timothy (1780–1840), *The Shoshonee Valley* (novel)

Hawthorne, Nathaniel (1804–64), "Mrs. Hutchinson" (essay); "The Hollow of the Three Hills" (story)

Neal, John (1793–1876), *Authorship: A Tale* (novel)

Paulding, James Kirke (1778–1860), *Chronicles of the City of Gotham from the Papers of a Retired Common Councilman* (fiction); *The Lion of the West* (play)

Schoolcraft, Henry Rowe (1793–1864), *The Rise of the West* (poem)

Sedgwick, Catharine Maria (1789–1867), *Clarence* (novel)

Smith, Joseph (1805–44), *The Book of Mormon*

Jackson vetoes Maysville Road bill. Webster-Hayne Debate over states' rights.

Anti-Masonic party holds first national party convention.

Joseph Smith founds Church of Jesus Christ of Latter-Day Saints (Mormons).

Emily Dickinson born (dies 1886).

William IV crowned king of England.

Charles X forced to abdicate throne of France; Louis Philippe becomes king.

Camille Pissarro born (dies 1903).

Delacroix, "Liberty Leading the People" (painting)

Lyell, *Principles of Geology* (1830–3)

Tennyson, *Poems, Chiefly Lyrical*

American Texts	American Events	Other Events and Texts
Tanner, John (1780?–1847), *A Narrative of the Captivity and Adventures of John Tanner* (edited by Edwin James)		Alexis de Tocqueville and Gustave de Beaumont sent by French government to study the American prison system.
Twenty-six volumes of new prose fiction by native authors published in the United States.		The great cholera pandemic, which started in India in 1826, now spreads into Central Europe, reaches Scotland in 1832.
Godey's Lady's Book (New York, 1830–39; Philadelphia, 1840–98).		Charles Darwin's voyage on *HMS Beagle* (1831–6)

1831

American Texts	American Events	Other Events and Texts
Bird, Robert Montgomery (1806–54), *The Gladiator* (published 1919; play)	President Jackson breaks with Calhoun.	Hugo, *The Hunchback of Notre Dame*
Child, Lydia Maria (1802–80), *The Mother's Book* (nonfiction)	Peggy Eaton affair forces reorganization of Cabinet.	Pushkin, *Boris Godunov*
Cooper, James Fenimore (1789–1851), *The Bravo* (novel)	Nat Turner's slave insurrection. Anti-Masonic party meets (first American "third party").	Stendhal, *The Red and the Black*
Hawthorne, Nathaniel (1804–64), "Sights from a Steeple" (story, published anonymously)	*Cherokee Nation v. Georgia*	
Irving, Washington (1783–1859), *The Voyages and Discoveries of the Companions of Columbus* (nonfiction)	Population of the United States is 12.8 million; Great Britain 13.9 million.	
Kelley, Hall J. (1790–1874), "A General Circular to All Persons of Good Character Who Wish to Emigrate to the Oregon Territory" (pamphlet)		
Marsh, James (1794–1842) [ed.], *The Friend* (Coleridge)		

Pattie, James Ohio (1804?–50?), *Personal Narrative* (nonfiction, ed. Timothy Flint)

Paulding, James Kirke (1778–1860), *The Dutchman's Fireside* (novel); *The Lion of the West* (play)

Poe, Edgar Allan (1809–49), *Poems: Second Edition*

Snelling, William (1804–48), *The Polar Regions* (nonfiction)

Stewart, C[harles] S[amuel] (1795–1870), *A Visit to the South Seas* (nonfiction)

Turner, Nat (1800–31), *The Confessions of Nat Turner* (recorded by attorney Thomas Gray)

Wayland, Francis (1796–1865), *Discourse on the Philosophy of Analogy* (nonfiction)

Whittier, John Greenleaf (1807–92), *Legends of New-England in Prose and Verse*

Zavala, Lorenzo de (?), *Ensayos históricos de las revoluciones de México* (nonfiction)

The Liberator founded by William Lloyd Garrison (ceases publication 1865)

Spirit of the Times founded in New York by William Porter (ceases publication 1861).

1832   Barreiro, Antonio (?), *Ojeada sobre Nuevo-México* (nonfiction)

Jackson vetoes Bank bill in beginning of "war" against the Second Bank of the United States.

Reform Bill redistributes seats in British Parliament.

American Texts	American Events	Other Events and Texts
Bird, Robert Montgomery (1806–54), *Oralloossa, Son of the Incas* (published 1919; play)	Special convention in South Carolina nullifies new protective tariff.	Giuseppe Mazzini seeks unification of Italy.
Boscana, Fray Geronima (?), *Chinigchinich*	*Worcester v. Georgia* gives federal government jurisdiction over Indian territories; unenforced by Jackson.	Johann Wolfgang von Goethe dies; his *Faust, Part II* published. Edouard Manet born (dies 1883). Sir Walter Scott dies (born 1771).
Cooper, James Fenimore (1789–1851), *The Heidenmauer* (novel)		
Dew, Thomas R. (1802–46), "Abolition of Negro Slavery" (essay, expanded as *Review of the Debate in the Virginia Legislature of 1831–2*)	Black Hawk War in Illinois and Wisconsin.	Berlioz, "Symphonie Fantastique" (revised version)
Drake, Samuel (1798–1875), *Biography and History of the Indians of North America* (nonfiction)	President Jackson reelected. First horse-drawn streetcars, in New York City.	Donizetti, *L'Elisir d'Amore* (opera) Harriet Martineau, *Illustrations of Political Economy* (1832–4)
Dunlap, William (1766–1839), *The History of the American Theatre* (nonfiction)		Frances Trollope, *Domestic Manners of the Americans*
Fay, Theodore Sedgwick (1807–98), *Dreams and Reveries of a Quiet Man* (nonfiction)	Philip Freneau dies (born 1752). Louisa May Alcott born (dies 1888). Horatio Alger born (dies 1899).	
Flint, Timothy (1780–1840), *The History and Geography of the Mississippi Valley* (nonfiction)		
Garrison, William Lloyd (1805–79), *Thoughts on African Colonization* (nonfiction)		
Hall, James (1793–1868), *Legends of the West* (fiction)		
Hawthorne, Nathaniel (1804–64), "Roger Malvin's Burial," "My Kinsman, Major Molineux," "The Gentle Boy" (stories)		

1833

Irving, Washington (1783–1859), *The Alhambra* (fiction and nonfiction)

Kennedy, John Pendleton (1795–1870), *Swallow Barn* (sketches of Virginia life)

Paulding, James Kirke (1778–1860), *Westward Ho!* (novel)

Peabody, Elizabeth (1804–94), *Key to History* (three-part textbook, 1832–3)

Simms, William Gilmore (1806–70), *Atalantis: A Story of the Sea* (verse)

Thatcher, Benjamin Bussey (1809–40), *Indian Biography* (nonfiction)

Apess, William (1798–1839), *Indian Nullification of the Unconstitutional Laws of Massachusetts Relative to the Marshpee Tribe* (nonfiction); *Experience of Five Christian Indians of the Pequot Tribes* (nonfiction)

Black Hawk (1767–1838), *Autobiography* (also pub. as *Life of Ma-Ka-Tai-Me-She-Kia-Kiak*)

Boudinot, Elias (Jr.) (1804–39), *Poor Sarah; or, The Indian Woman* (fiction)

Child, Lydia Maria (1802–80), *An Appeal in Favor of that Class of Americans Called Africans* (nonfiction)

Jackson vs. Bank of the United States over public fund deposits.

Congress provides for a gradual lowering of tariffs but passes the Force Bill authorizing Jackson to enforce federal law in South Carolina.

Convention of Texas settlers at San Felipe votes to separate from Mexico.

General Antonio López de Santa Anna becomes president of Mexico.

Start of the Oxford Movement (begins with John Keble's sermon "On National Apostasy").

Johannes Brahms born (dies 1897).

Carlyle, *Sartor Resartus* (1833–4).
Chopin, Twelve Etudes Op. 10

American Texts	American Events	Other Events and Texts
Cooper, James Fenimore (1789–1851), *The Headsman* (novel)	American Anti-Slavery Society founded.	Mendelssohn, "Italian" Symphony
Fanning, Edmund (1769–1841), *Voyages to the South Seas* (nonfiction)	Oberlin College founded by the revivalist Charles Grandison Finney; it admits men and women.	Puskin, *Eugene Onegin*
Flint, Timothy (1780–1840), *Biographical Memoir of Daniel Boone, The First Settler of Kentucky* (also pub. as *Life and Adventures of Colonel Daniel Boone*); *Indian Wars of the West* (nonfiction)		Sand, *Lélia*
Hall, James (1793–1868), *The Harpe's Head, A Legend of Kentucky* (novel)		
Holley, Mary Austin (1784–1846), *Texas: Observations, Historical, Geographical, and Descriptive* (nonfiction)		
Leslie, Eliza (1787–1858), *Pencil Sketches; or, Outlines of Characters and Manners* (fiction, 1833, 1835, 1837)		
Longfellow, Henry Wadsworth (1807–82), *Outre-Mer* (travel sketches)		
Marsh, James (1794–1842) [trans.], *Spirit of Hebrew Poetry* (Herder)		
Neal, John (1793–1876), *The Down-Easters* (novel)		
Owen, W. F. W. (1774–1857), *Narrative of Voyages to Explore the Shores of Africa, Arabia, and Madagascar* (nonfiction)		

Peabody, Elizabeth (1804–94), *The Hebrews*; *The Greeks* (textbooks)

Simms, William Gilmore (1806–70), *Martin Faber: The Story of a Criminal* (novel)

Smith, Seba (1792–1868), *The Life and Writings of Major Jack Downing of Downingville* (humor)

Tocqueville, Alexis de (1805–59) and Gustave de Beaumont, *On the Penitentiary System in the United States and Its Application in France* (U.S. trans.)

Whittier, John Greenleaf (1807–92), *Justice and Expediency* (pamphlet)

1834
Bancroft, George (1800–91), *A History of the United States, from the Discovery of the American Continent*, Vol. I (ten volumes, 1834–74)

Bird, Robert Montgomery (1806–54), *The Broker of Bogota* (published 1917, play); *Calavar; or, The Knight of the Conquest* (novel)

Caruthers, William Alexander (1802–46), *The Kentuckian in New York* (novel)

Cooper, James Fenimore (1789–1851), *A Letter to His Countrymen* (nonfiction)

Crockett, Davy (1786–1836), *Narrative of the Life of David Crockett* (nonfiction, attrib.)

First use of federal troops to resolve labor dispute (Chesapeake and Ohio Canal riots).

Whig party succeeds the New Republicans as the anti-Jackson party.

Antiabolition riots in New York and Philadelphia.

Seminole Indians forced out of Florida.

Abraham Lincoln (age 25) becomes assemblyman in Illinois legislature.

Aleksandr Borodin born (dies 1887).

Samuel Taylor Coleridge dies (born 1772).

Edgar Degas born (dies 1917).

Charles Lamb dies (born 1775).

Balzac, *Père Goriot*

Bulwer-Lytton, *The Last Days of Pompeii*

	American Texts	American Events	Other Events and Texts
1835	Gilman, Caroline Howard (1794–1888), *Recollections of a Housekeeper* (nonfiction) Hall, James (1793–1868), *Sketches of History, Life, and Manners in the West* (nonfiction) Hart, Joseph (1798–1855), *Miriam Coffin* (novel) Pike, Albert (1809–91), *Prose Sketches and Poems* Schoolcraft, Henry Rowe (1793–1864), *Narrative of an Expedition through the Upper Mississippi* (nonfiction) Simms, William Gilmore (1806–70), *Guy Rivers: A Tale of Georgia* (novel) Zavala, Lorenzo de (?), *Viaje a los Estados Unidos del Norte de America* (nonfiction) *Southern Literary Messenger* (Richmond, Va., 1834–64). Anonymous, *Lionel Granby* (novel) Beecher, Lyman (1775–1863), *A Plea for the West* (nonfiction) Bird, Robert Montgomery (1806–54), *The Infidel; or, The Fall of Mexico* (novel); *The Hawks of Hawk-Hollow* (novel) Bolokitten, Oliver (?), *A Sojourn in the City of Amalgamation* (novel)	Attempted assassination of President Jackson. Second Seminole Indian War (1835–42). Armed fighting between Mexico and Texas. 1,098 miles of railroad are in use in the United States.	Vincenzo Bellini dies (born 1801). Camille Saint-Saëns born (dies 1921). Andersen, *Fairy Tales* (1835–72) Gustave de Beaumont, *Marie, or Slavery in the United States* Alexis de Tocqueville, *Democracy in America*, Vol. I (U.S. trans. 1838)

Samuel Langhorne Clemens ("Mark Twain") born (dies 1910).

Caruthers, William Alexander (1802–46), *The Cavaliers of Virginia* (novel)

Channing, William Ellery (1780–1842), *Slavery* (nonfiction)

Cooper, James Fenimore (1789–1851), *The Monikins* (novel)

Fay, Theodore Sedgwick (1807–98), *Norman Leslie: A Tale of the Present Times* (novel)

Gurley, Ralph R. (1797–1872), *Life of Jehudi Ashmun* (nonfiction)

Hall, James (1793–1868), *Tales of the Border* (fiction)

Hawthorne, Nathaniel (1804–64), "Wakefield," "Young Goodman Brown" (stories)

Herbert, Henry William (1807–58), *The Brothers, a Tale of the Fronde* (fiction)

Hoffman, Charles Fenno (1806–84), *A Winter in the West* (nonfiction)

Irving, Washington (1783–1859), *The Crayon Miscellany* (nonfiction)

Jay, William (1789–1858), *Inquiry into the Character and Tendency of the American Colonization Society* (nonfiction)

Kennedy, John Pendleton (1795–1870), *Horse-Shoe Robinson* (novel)

American Texts	American Events	Other Events and Texts
Longstreet, Augustus Baldwin (1790–1870), *Georgia Scenes, Characters, Incidents, &c., in the first Half Century of the Republic* (published anonymously)		
Newcomb, Harvey (1803–63), *The North American Indians* (nonfiction)		
Parker, Theodore (1810–1860), "Report on German Theology" (nonfiction)		
Paulding, James Kirke (1778–1860), *Letters from the South* (rev. ed.)		
Peabody, Elizabeth (1804–94), *Record of a School* (nonfiction)		
Poe, Edgar Allan (1809–49), "Berenice" (story)		
Reynolds, Jeremiah N. (1799?–1858), *Voyage of the U. S. Frigate Potomac* (nonfiction)		
Sedgwick, Catharine Maria (1789–1867), *The Linwoods* (novel); *Home* (novel)		
Simms, William Gilmore (1806–70), *The Yemassee: A Romance of Carolina* (novel); *The Partisan: A Tale of the Revolution* (novel)		
Stewart, Maria (?), *Productions of Mrs. Maria W. Stewart* (nonfiction)		
Tuckerman, Henry T. (1813–71), *Italian Sketch Book* (nonfiction)		

798

Wallace, William R. (1819–81), *The Battle of Tippecanoe* (nonfiction)

Fifty-four volumes of new prose fiction by native authors published in the United States.

1836 Alcott, Bronson (1799–1888), *The Doctrine and Discipline of Human Culture* (nonfiction); *Conversations with Children on the Gospels* (nonfiction, 1836–7)

Apess, William (1798–1839), *Eulogy on King Philip* (nonfiction)

Ball, Charles (?), *Slavery in the United States: A Narrative of the Life and Adventures of Charles Ball, a Black Man* (composed by Isaac Fisher)

Brownson, Orestes (1803–76), *New Views of Christianity, Society and the Church* (nonfiction)

Child, Lydia Maria (1802–80), *Philothea* (novel)

Emerson, Ralph Waldo (1803–82), *Nature* (nonfiction)

Emmons, Richard (1788–?), *Tecumseh; or, The Battle of the Thames* (play)

Field, Joseph (1802–82), *Three Years in Texas* (nonfiction)

Francis, Convers (1795–1863), *Christianity as a Purely Internal Principle* (pamphlet)

Arkansas admitted to the Union. (nonfiction)

Creation of Wisconsin Territory.

Jackson's "specie circular."

Siege of the Alamo.

Battle of San Jacinto.

Sam Houston elected president of the Republic of Texas.

Harvard University celebrates bicentennial; first meeting of "Hedge's club" (Transcendental Club)

Martin van Buren elected president.

Winslow Homer born (dies 1910).

Carlyle's *Sartor Resartus* published in Boston.

Chartists in Britain demand universal suffrage and vote by ballot.

William Godwin dies (born 1756).

Dickens, *Sketches by "Boz."*

Gogol, *The Inspector General*

James Martineau, *Rationale of Religious Inquiry*

American Texts	American Events	Other Events and Texts
Freeman, Frederick (1799–1883), *Yaradee; A Plea for Africa* (nonfiction)		
French, James S. (1807–86), *Elkswatawa; or, The Prophet of the West* (novel)		
Furness, William Henry (1802–96), *Remarks on the Four Gospels* (nonfiction)		
Gallatin, Albert (1761–1849), *Map of the Indian Tribes of North America* (nonfiction)		
Grimké, Angelina (1805–79), *Appeal to the Christian Women of the South* (nonfiction)		
Hawthorne, Nathaniel (1804–64), "The May-Pole of Merry Mount," "The Minister's Black Veil" (stories)		
Hildreth, Richard (1807–65), *The Slave; or, Memoirs of Archy Moore* (novel)		
Irving, Washington (1783–1859), *Astoria; or, Anecdotes of an Enterprise Beyond the Rocky Mountains* (nonfiction)		
McKenney, Thomas (1785–1859), *History of Indian Tribes of North America* (published 1836–44, with James Hall, nonfiction)		
Paulding, James Kirke (1778–1860), *Slavery in the United States* (nonfiction)		

Priest, Josiah (1788–1851), *Stories of the Revolution* (nonfiction)

Ripley, George (1802–80), *Discourses on the Philosophy of Religion Addressed to Doubters Who Wish to Believe* (nonfiction)

Sedgwick, Catharine Maria (1789–1867), *The Poor Rich Man and the Rich Poor Man* (novel)

Simms, William Gilmore (1806–70), *Mellichampe: A Legend of the Santee* (novel)

Tucker, Nathaniel Beverly (1784–1851), *George Balcombe* (novel); *The Partisan Leader: A Tale of the Future* (novel)

Very, Jones (1813–80), "What Reasons There Are for Not Expecting Another Great Epic Poem" (essay)

Willis, Nathaniel Parker (1806–67), *Inklings of Adventure* (nonfiction)

1837   Bancroft, George (1800–91), *A History of the United States, from the Discovery of the American Continent*, Vol. II (ten volumes, 1834–74)

Beecher, Catharine (1800–78), *Essay on Slavery and Abolitionism* (nonfiction)

Bird, Robert Montgomery (1806–54), *Nick of the Woods; or, The Jibbenainosay. A Tale of Kentucky* (novel)

Martin van Buren inaugurated as eighth president of the United States.

Michigan admitted to the Union. Financial panic causes bank failures and suspension of specie payment.

Death of William IV; Victoria crowned Queen of England.

John Constable dies (born 1776).

Carlyle, *The French Revolution*
Dickens, *Pickwick Papers*

American Texts	American Events	Other Events and Texts
Boudinot, Elias (Jr.) (1804–39), "Letters and Other Papers Relating to Cherokee Affairs" (pamphlet)	Speaking tour by Angelina and Sarah Grimké.	Harriet Martineau, *Society in America*
Emerson, Ralph Waldo (1803–82). "Philosophy of History" (lecture series); "Address on Education"; "The American Scholar" (address)	William Dean Howells born (dies 1920).	James Mill, *The Principles of Toleration*
Hawthorne, Nathaniel (1804–64), *Twice-told Tales* (fiction)		Pushkin, *The Bronze Horseman*
Irving, John T. (1812–1906), *The Hawk Chief* (novel)		
Irving, Washington (1783–1859), *The Adventures of Captain Bonneville in the Rocky Mountains and the Far West* (nonfiction)		
Lee, Hannah Farnham (1780–1865), *Three Experiments in Living* (novel)		
Norton, Andrews (1786–1853), *The Evidences of the Genuineness of the Gospels* (tract, 1837–44)		
Sedgwick, Catharine Maria (1789–1867), *Live and Let Live* (novel)		
Tucker, George (1775–1861), *Life of Thomas Jefferson* (nonfiction)		
Ladies' Magazine absorbed by *Godey's Lady's Book* (Philadelphia), edited by Sarah Josepha Hale until 1877. *United States Magazine and Democratic Review* founded by John L. O'Sullivan (ceases publication 1859).		

1838

Beecher, Edward (1803–95), *Narrative of Riots at Alton* [Illinois] (nonfiction)

Cooper, James Fenimore (1789–1851), *The American Democrat* (nonfiction); *Homeward Bound* (novel); *Home as Found* (novel); *The Chronicles of Cooperstown* (nonfiction)

Drake, Benjamin (1794–1841), *The Life and Adventures of Black Hawk* (nonfiction)

Embury, Emma Catharine (1806–63), *Constance Latimer; or, the Blind Girl, With Other Tales* (fiction)

Emerson, Ralph Waldo (1803–82), "Divinity School Address" (lecture)

Flagg, Edmund (1815–90), *The Far West: Or, A Tour Beyond the Rocky Mountains* (nonfiction)

Ganilh, Anthony (?), *Mexico Versus Texas* (nonfiction)

Gilman, Caroline (1794–1888), *Recollections of a Southern Matron* (novel)

Grimké, Angelina (1805–79), *Letters to Catharine E. Beecher* (nonfiction)

Grimké, Sarah (1792–1873), *Letters on the Condition of Women and the Equality of the Sexes, Appeal to the Christian Women of the South* (nonfiction)

Harper, William (1790–1847), *Memoir on Slavery* (nonfiction)

Creation of the Iowa Territory.

Beginning of the Underground Railroad (to aid escaped slaves).

Samuel Morse introduces his telegraphic code.

Army Corps of Topographical Engineers becomes a separate branch of the military under the command of Colonel John James Albert.

Henry Adams born (dies 1918).

Hawthorne appointed to Boston Custom House (1839–41).

Georges Bizet born (dies 1875).

Max Bruch born (dies 1920).

Dickens, *Oliver Twist*

American Texts

Kennedy, John Pendleton (1795–1870), *Rob of the Bowl* (novel)

Macomb, Alexander (1782–1841), *Pontiac; or, The Siege of Detroit* (play)

O'Sullivan, John L. (1813–95), "The Great Nation of Futurity" (nonfiction)

Owen, Robert Dale (1801–77), *Pocabontas* (play)

Poe, Edgar Allan (1809–49), *The Narrative of Arthur Gordon Pym of Nantucket*, "Ligeia" (nonfiction)

Prescott, William Hickling (1796–1859), *History of the Reign of Ferdinand and Isabella* (nonfiction)

Ransom, James B. (?), *Osceola: A Tale of the Seminole Wars* (novel)

Simms, William Gilmore (1806–70), *Slavery in America* (pamphlet); *Richard Hurdis; or, The Avenger of Blood* (novel)

Tocqueville, Alexis de (1805–59), *Democracy in America*, Vol. I (U.S. trans.)

Whittier, John Greenleaf (1807–92), *Narrative of James Williams* (fiction)

Boston Quarterly Review founded by Orestes Brownson (1838–42).

| 1839 | Briggs, Charles Frederick (1804–77), *The Adventures of Harry Franco: A Tale of the Great Panic* (fiction)

Channing, William Ellery (1780–1842), *Remarks on the Slavery Question* (nonfiction)

Cooper, James Fenimore (1789–1851), *The History of the Navy of the United States of America* (nonfiction)

Drake, Samuel (1798–1875), *Indian Captivities* (nonfiction)

Emerson, Ralph Waldo (1803–82), "Human Life" (lecture series)

Forbes, Alexander (1778–1862), *California* (travel)

Kirkland, Caroline (1801–64), *A New Home – Who'll Follow? Or Glimpses of Western Life* (travel)

Leonard, Zenas (1809–57), *Narrative of the Adventures of Zenas Leonard, Fur Trader* (nonfiction)

Matthews, Cornelius (1817–89), *Behemoth: A Legend of the Mound-Builders* (novel)

Montgomery, George Washington (1804–41), *Narrative of a Journey to Guatemala* (travel)

Morton, Samuel (1799–1851), *Crania Americana* (treatise)

Motley, John Lothrop (1814–77), *Morton's Hope* (fiction) | Major depression begins, causing widespread bankruptcies and default by several states.

Liberty party (antislavery) formed.

Charles Goodyear accidentally vulcanizes rubber.

Elias Boudinot (Jr.), John Ridge, and Major Ridge executed by Cherokee nation. | Chartist riots in Great Britain.

First Opium War between Great Britain and China.

Paul Cezanne born (dies 1906).

Modest Mussorgsky born (dies 1881).

Alfred Sisley born (dies 1899).

Dickens, *Nicholas Nickleby*

Stendhal, *The Charterhouse of Parma*

Thackeray, *Catherine* |

807

Weld, Theodore Dwight (1803–95), *American Slavery As It Is: Testimony of a Thousand Witnesses* (nonfiction, published anonymously)

1840 Audubon, John James (1785–1851), *The Birds of America from Drawings Made in the United States and Their Territories* (nonfiction, octavo ed., 1840–4)

Bancroft, George (1800–91), *A History of the United States, from the Discovery of the American Continent,* Vol. III (ten volumes, 1834–74)

Channing, William Ellery (1780–1842), "Emancipation" (nonfiction)

Cooper, James Fenimore (1789–1851), *The Pathfinder* (novel); *Mercedes of Castille* (novel)

Dana, Richard Henry (1815–82), *Two Years Before the Mast* (nonfiction)

Frost, John (1800–59), *Indian Wars of the United States* (nonfiction)

Gilman, Caroline Howard (1794–1888), *Love's Progress* (novel)

Hildreth, Richard (1807–65), *Despotism in America; or, An Inquiry into the Nature and Results of the Slave-Holding System in America* (nonfiction)

Independent Treasury Act establishes federal depositories.

World Anti-Slavery Convention refuses to admit women delegates from the United States.

William Henry Harrison elected president; Whigs in power.

2,815 miles of railroad in operation in the United States.

Thomas Nast, cartoonist, born (dies 1902).

Marriage of Queen Victoria and Prince Albert.

Great Britain annexes New Zealand.

Samuel Cunard founds transatlantic steamship line.

Penny Post established throughout Great Britain.

Caspar David Friedrich dies (born 1774).

Thomas Hardy born (dies 1928).

Claude Monet born (dies 1926).

Nicolo Paganini dies (born 1782).

Pierre Auguste Renoir born (dies 1919).

Auguste Renoir born (dies 1917).

Peter Ilich Tchaikovsky born (dies 1893).

Emile Zola born (dies 1902).

Darwin, *Zoology of the Voyage of the Beagle*

	American Texts	American Events	Other Events and Texts
	Hoffman, Charles Fenno (1806–84), *Greyslaer: A Romance of the Mohawk* (novel)		Harriet Martineau, *The Martyr Age in the United States*
	Kennedy, John Pendleton (1795–1870), *Quodlibet* (political satire)		Tocqueville, *Democracy in America*, Vol. II (U.S. trans. 1841)
	Poe, Edgar Allan (1809–49), *Tales of the Grotesque and Arabesque*; "The Man of the Crowd"; "The Journal of Julius Rodman, Being an Account of the First Passage Across the Rocky Mountains of North America Ever Achieved by Civilized Man" (fiction)		
	Willis, Nathaniel Parker (1806–67), *American Scenery* (nonfiction); *Loiterings of Travel* (nonfiction)		
	Wislizenus, F. A. (1810–89), *Journey to the Rocky Mountains in the Year 1839* (nonfiction)		
	Arcturus founded in New York by Evert Duyckinck (1840–2).		
	The Dial (1840–4)		
	Graham's Magazine (Philadelphia, 1840–58) formed through merger of *The Casket* and *Burton's Gentleman's Magazine*.		
	Emerson publishes Carlyle's *Chartism* (1839).		
1841	**Beecher, Catharine** (1800–78), *Treatise on Domestic Economy* (nonfiction)	President William Henry Harrison dies one month after his inaugura-	Anton Dvorak born (dies 1904).

Catlin, George (1796–1872), Letters and Notes on the Manners, Customs, and Condition of the North American Indians (nonfiction)

Cooper, James Fenimore (1789–1851), The Deerslayer (novel)

Dana, Richard Henry (1815–82), The Seaman's Friend (nonfiction)

Drake, Benjamin (1794–1841), Life of Tecumseh (nonfiction)

Drake, Samuel (1798–1875), Tragedies in the Wilderness (nonfiction)

Emerson, Ralph Waldo (1803–82), Essays, First Series, "Lectures on the Times" (series); "The Transcendentalist" (essay)

Farnham, Thomas Jefferson (1804–48), Travels in the Great Western Prairies (nonfiction)

Hawthorne, Nathaniel (1804–64), Grandfather's Chair; Famous Old People; Liberty Tree (children's books)

Ingraham, Joseph Holt (1809–60), The Quadroone; or, St. Michael's Day (fiction)

Olmsted, Francis A. (1819–44), Incidents of a Whaling Voyage (nonfiction)

tion; John Tyler becomes president.
Repeal of Independent Treasury Act.
Brook Farm, cooperative community, founded in West Roxbury, Massachusetts.
Preemption Act.
Population of the United States reaches 17 million.

Carlyle, On Heroes, Hero-worship, and the Heroic in History
Frances Trollope, Jonathan Jefferson Whitlaw (fictional slave narrative)

Parker, Theodore (1810–60), "A Discourse of the Transient and Permanent in Christianity" (nonfiction)

Pennington, James W. C. (?), *A Text Book of the Origin and History of the Colored People* (children's book)

Poe, Edgar Allan (1809–49), "A Descent into the Maelstrom," "The Murders in the Rue Morgue," (stories)

Priest, Josiah (1788–1851), *A History of the Early Adventures of Washington Among the Indians of the West* (nonfiction)

Simms, William Gilmore (1806–70), *The Kinsmen; or, The Black Riders of Congaree* (novel; later renamed *The Scout*); *Confession; or, The Blind Heart* (novel)

Stephens, John Lloyd (1805–52), *Incidents of Travel in Central America, Chiapas, and Yucatan* (nonfiction)

Stringfellow, Thornton (1788–1869), *A Brief Examination of Scripture Testimony on the Institution of Slavery* (nonfiction)

Thorpe, Thomas Bangs (1815–75), "The Big Bear of Arkansas" (story)

1842

Tocqueville, Alexis de (1805–59), *Democracy in America*, Vol. II (U.S. trans.)

Poe becomes editor of *Graham's Magazine*.

Channing, William Ellery (1780–1842), *Duty of the Free States* (nonfiction)

Colton, George H. (1818–47), *Tecumseh; or The West Thirty Years Since* (poem)

Cooper, James Fenimore (1789–1851), *The Two Admirals* (novel); *The Wing-and-Wing* (novel)

Hawthorne, Nathaniel (1804–64), *Twice-told Tales* (second volume)

Hooper, Johnson Jones (1815–62), "Taking the Census in Alabama" (story)

Kennedy, John Pendleton (1795–1870), *A Defense of the Whigs* (nonfiction)

Kirkland, Caroline (1801–64), *Forest Life* (nonfiction)

Lane, Lunsford (?), *Narrative of Lunsford Lane* (nonfiction)

Longfellow, Henry Wadsworth (1807–82), *Poems on Slavery*

Matthews, Cornelius (1817–89), *The Career of Puffer Hopkins* (novel)

Dorr Rebellion against Rhode Island constitution.

Webster-Ashburton Treaty establishes U.S.-Canadian border.

P. T. Barnum opens his American Museum in New York City.

Albert Gallatin founds Bureau of American Ethnology.

William Ellery Channing dies (born 1780).

Treaty of Nanking (China cedes Hong Kong to Great Britain).

Dickens, *American Notes*

Sue, *Mysteries of Paris* (1842–3)

American Texts	American Events	Other Events and Texts
Parker, Theodore (1810–60), *A Discourse of Matters Pertaining to Religion* (nonfiction)		William Wordsworth named poet laureate of England.
Poe, Edgar Allan (1809–49), "Eleonora"; "The Masque of the Red Death"; "The Mystery of Marie Roget" (stories)		Edward Grieg born (dies 1907).
Savage, Timothy (?), *The Amazonian Republic* (fiction)		Carlyle, *Past and Present*
Snelling, Anna (?), *Kabaosa* (novel)		Dickens, *A Christmas Carol*
		John Stuart Mill, *A System of Logic*
Peterson's Lady's Magazine (Philadelphia, 1842–92). Emerson becomes editor of the *Dial*.		
Edgar Allan Poe resigns as editor of *Graham's Magazine*, succeeded by Rufus Griswold.		
1843 **Bidwell, John** (1819–1900). *A Journey to California* (nonfiction)	Settlers move westward over the Oregon Trail.	
Briggs, Charles Frederick (1804–77), *The Haunted Merchant* (fiction)	Debates over the potential annexation of Texas.	
Channing, William Ellery (1780–1842), *Poems*	Washington Allston dies (born 1779).	
Child, Lydia Maria (1802–80), *Letters from New York: First Series* (nonfiction)	Henry James born (dies 1916).	
Cooper, James Fenimore (1789–1851), *Wyandotté* (novel); *Ned Myers, or A Life Before the Mast* (novel); *The Autobiography of a Pocket-Handkerchief* (novel)		

Frémont, John (1813–90), *A Report on an Exploration of the Country Lying Between the Missouri River and the Rocky Mountains* (nonfiction)

Fuller, Margaret (1810–50), "The Great Lawsuit" (essay)

Goodrich, Samuel (1793–1860), *Lives of Celebrated American Indians* (nonfiction)

Hall, Bayard Rush (1798–1863), *The New Purchase; or, Seven and a Half Years in the Far West* (novel, written under the pseudonym Robert Carlton)

Hawthorne, Nathaniel (1804–64), "The Birthmark," "The Celestial Railroad" (stories)

Poe, Edgar Allan (1809–49), "The Black Cat", "The Gold Bug", "The Pit and the Pendulum", "The Tell-Tale Heart" (stories); "Notes on English Verse" (republished as "The Rationale of Verse," 1848)

Prescott, William Hickling (1796–1859), *History of the Conquest of Mexico* (nonfiction, 3 vols.)

Stephens, John Lloyd (1805–52), *Incidents of Travel in the Yucatan* (nonfiction)

Stowe, Harriet Beecher (1811–96), *The Mayflower; or, Sketches of Scenes and Characters Among the Descendants of the Pilgrims* (fiction)

Sumner, Charles (1811–74), *White Slavery in the Barbary States* (nonfiction)

American Texts	American Events	Other Events and Texts
Thompson, William Tappan (1812–82), *Major Jones's Courtship* (fiction, expanded version 1844)		Gerard Manley Hopkins born (dies 1889).
Thorpe, Thomas Bangs (1815–75), *The Mysteries of the Backwoods* (sketches)		Friedrich Nietzsche born (dies 1900).
Seventy-seven volumes of new prose fiction by native authors published in the United States.		
	Annexation of Texas.	Dickens, *Martin Chuzzlewit*
Andrews, Charles W. (1807–75), *Memoir of Mrs. Anne R. Page* (nonfiction)	Dispute with Great Britain over Oregon boundary.	Dumas père, *The Count of Monte Cristo; The Three Musketeers*
Beecher, Henry Ward (1813–87), *Seven Lectures to Young Men* (nonfiction)	James Polk elected president.	
Briggs, Charles Frederick (1804–77), *Working a Passage; or, Life in a Liner* (novel)	Bronson Alcott founds Fruitlands, a cooperative community, at Harvard, Massachusetts.	
Cooper, James Fenimore (1789–1851), *Afloat and Ashore* (novel); *Adventures of Miles Wallingford* (novel)	George Bancroft runs unsuccessfully for governorship of Massachusetts; he becomes secretary of the navy.	
Emerson, Ralph Waldo (1803–82), *Essays, Second Series;* "Emancipation in the British West Indies" (address)		
Farnham, Thomas Jefferson (1804–48), *Life and Adventures in California* (nonfiction)		
Fuller, Margaret (1810–50), *Summer on the Lakes* (travel)		

1844

Goodloe, Daniel Reeves (1814–1902), *Inquiry into the Causes Which Have Retarded the Accumulation of Wealth and Increase of Population in the Southern States* (nonfiction)

Grandy, Moses (?), *Narrative of Moses Grandy* (nonfiction)

Gregg, Josiah (1806–50), *Commerce of the Prairies; or, The Journal of a Santa Fé Trader* (nonfiction)

Hawthorne, Nathaniel (1804–64), "Rappaccini's Daughter" (story)

Hodgson, William B. (?), *Notes on Northern Africa, the Sahara, and the Soudan* (nonfiction)

Jarves, James (1818–88), *Scenes and Scenery in the Sandwich Islands and a Trip Through Central America* (travel)

Kendall, George Wilkins (1809–67), *Narrative of the Texan Santa Fe Expedition* (nonfiction)

Lippard, George (1822–54), *Quaker City; or, The Monks of Monk Hall* (novel)

Morton, Samuel (1799–1851), *Crania Aegyptiaca* (treatise)

Nott, Josiah (1804–73), *Two Lectures on the Natural History of the Caucasian and Negro Races* (nonfiction)

Poe, Edgar Allan (1809–49), "The Raven" (poem)

	American Texts	American Events	Other Events and Texts
	Postle, Karl (1793–1864), *The Cabin Book; or, Sketches of Life in Texas* (nonfiction); *Life in the New World* (nonfiction) Smith, W. H. (1808–72), *The Drunkard, or The Fallen Saved* (play) Thompson, William Tappan (1812–82), *Major Jones's Courtship* (fiction, expanded version) Tucker, Nathaniel Beverley (1784–1851), *Gertrude* (novel, serialized 1844–5) 102 volumes of new prose fiction by native authors published in the United States.		The Great Famine in Ireland. Anti-Corn Laws agitation in England. John Henry Newman converts to Catholicism.
1845	Bradbury, Osgood (1795?–1886), *Lucelle; or, The Young Iroquois* (novel) Bridge, Horatio (1806–93), *Journal of an African Cruiser* (nonfiction) Caruthers, William Alexander (1802–46), *The Knights of the Horseshoe* (novel) Child, Lydia Maria (1802–80), *Letters from New York: Second Series* (nonfiction) Cooper, James Fenimore (1789–1851), *Satanstoe; or, The Littlepage Manuscripts* (novel); *The Chainbearer; or, The Littlepage Manuscripts* (novel)	James K. Polk inaugurated as eleventh president of the United States. John L. O'Sullivan uses term "manifest destiny" to justify national expansion. Texas and Florida admitted to the Union. John Frémont leads "Bear Flag Revolt" culminating in capture of northern California for the United States.	Disraeli, *Sybil* Engels, *The Condition of the Working Class in England* Richard Wagner, *Tannhäuser* (opera)

Knickerbocker Baseball Club codifies rules of baseball.

Dallam, James W. (?), *The Lone Star* (novel)

Douglass, Frederick (1817–95), *Narrative of the Life of Frederick Douglass, An American Slave, Written by Himself* (nonfiction)

Frémont, John (1813–90), *Report of the Exploring Expedition to the Rocky Mountains in the Year 1842, and to Oregon and North California in the Years 1843–'44* (nonfiction)

Fuller, Margaret (1810–50), *Woman in the Nineteenth Century* (nonfiction)

Hastings, Lansford (1818?–68), *The Emigrant's Guide to Oregon and California* (nonfiction)

Hooper, Johnson Jones (1815–62), *Some Adventures of Captain Simon Suggs, Late of the Tallapoosa Volunteers; Together with "Taking the Census" and Other Alabama Sketches* (fiction)

Ingraham, Joseph Holt (1809–60), *Montezuma, the Serf* (fiction)

Jones, Justin (?), *The Rival Chieftains* (fiction)

Kirkland, Caroline (1801–64), *Western Clearings* (novel)

Matthews, Cornelius (1817–89), *Big Abel and the Little Manhattan* (novel)

Maturin, Edward (1812–81), *Montezuma: The Last of the Aztecs* (fiction)

Mowatt, Anna Cora (1819–70), *Fashion* (play)

Poe, Edgar Allan (1809–49), *Tales; The Raven and Other Poems*

Porter, William (1809–58), *The Big Bear of Arkansas and Other Sketches, Illustrative of Characters and Incidents in the South and South-West* (editor)

Simms, William Gilmore (1806–70), "The First Hunter of Kentucky" (essay on Daniel Boone); "Literature and Art Among the American Aborigines" (review of Schoolcraft); *Views and Review in American Literature, History, and Fiction* (nonfiction)

Thompson, William Tappan (1812–82), *Chronicles of Pineville* (fiction, republished as *Scenes in Georgia*, 1858)

Tucker, Nathaniel Beverly (1784–1851), *Series of Lectures on the Science of Government* (nonfiction)

Wilkes, Charles (1798–1877), *Narrative of the United States Exploring Expedition* (nonfiction)

Willis, Nathaniel Parker (1806–67), *Dashes at Life with a Free Pencil* (nonfiction)

Broadway Journal founded by Charles Frederick Briggs.

158 volumes of new prose fiction by native authors published in the United States.

1846

Bradbury, Osgood (1795?–1886), *Larooka: The Belle of the Penobscots* (novel)

Child, Lydia Maria (1802–80), *Fact and Fiction* (includes the story "The Quadroons")

Cooper, James Fenimore (1789–1851), *Lives of Distinguished American Naval Officers* (nonfiction); *The Redskins; or, Indian and Injin: Being the Conclusion of the Littlepage Manuscripts* (novel)

Farnham, Eliza (1815–64), *Life in the Prairie Land* (nonfiction)

Hall, Bayard Rush (1798–1863), *Something for Everybody* (novel)

Hawthorne, Nathaniel (1804–64), *Mosses from an Old Manse* (fiction)

James, Thomas (1782–1847), *Three Years Among the Indians and Mexicans* (nonfiction)

Johnson, Overton (?), *Route Across the Rocky Mountains* (nonfiction)

Jones, Justin (?), *Inez, the Beautiful: Or, Love on the Rio Grande* (novel)

McCarty, William (?), *National Songs, Ballads, and Other Patriotic Poetry, Chiefly Relating to the War of 1846*

Iowa admitted to the Union.

Oregon Treaty with Great Britain divides United States and Canada at the Forty-ninth Parallel.

Mexican War (1846–8).

Wilmot Proviso banning slavery in lands acquired from Mexico fails to pass.

Walker Tariff, adopted for revenue only, eliminates the principle of protection.

Donner Party (California migration).

James Renwick designs the Smithsonian Institution.

George Bancroft becomes Ambassador to the Court of Saint James (1846–9).

Hawthorne appointed to Salem Custom House (1846–9).

Great Britain repeals Corn Laws.

Berlioz, *Damnation of Faust* (dramatic cantata)

Lear, *A Book of Nonsense*

Mérimée, *Carmen*

American Texts	American Events	Other Events and Texts
McKenney, Thomas (1785–1859), *On the Wrongs and Rights of Indians* (nonfiction); *Memoirs* (nonfiction)		Liberia proclaimed an independent republic.
Melville, Herman (1819–91), *Typee: A Peep at Polynesian Life* (nonfiction)		Felix Mendelssohn dies (born 1809).
Paulding, James Kirke (1778–1860), *The Old Continental* (novel)		
Robinson, Alfred (?), *Life in California* (nonfiction)		Charlotte Brontë, *Jane Eyre*
Sage, Rufus B. (?), *Scenes in the Rocky Mountains* (nonfiction)		Emily Brontë, *Wuthering Heights*
Thompson, Waddy (?), *Recollections of Mexico* (nonfiction)		Ann Brontë, *Agnes Grey*
Thorpe, Thomas Bangs (1815–75), *The Mysteries of the Back Woods* (fiction); *Our Army on the Rio Grande* (nonfiction)		

1847

American Texts	American Events	Other Events and Texts
Averill, Charles (?), *The Mexican Ranchero; Or the Maid of the Chapparal* (novel)	American troops occupy Mexico City; Santa Anna renounces Mexican presidency.	
Bingham, Rev. Hiram (1789–1869), *A Residence of Twenty-One Years in the Sandwich Islands* (nonfiction)	Peace talks with Mexico begin. Brigham Young establishes a new colony at Salt Lake, Utah.	
Briggs, Charles Frederick (1804–77), *The Trippings of Tom Pepper* (novel, 2 volumes, 1847–50)	Frederick Douglass founds antislavery newspaper *North Star* (re-	
Brougham, John (1810–80), *Metamora; or, The Last of the Pollywogs* (drama)		

820

Disraeli, *Tancred*
Marryat, *The Children of the New Forest*

named *Frederick Douglass's Paper* in 1851.

Brown, William Wells (1816–84), *Narrative of William W. Brown, a Fugitive Slave* (nonfiction)

Channing, William Ellery (1780–1842), *Poems, Second Series*

Cooper, James Fenimore (1789–1851), *The Crater* (novel)

Copway, George (1818–69), *The Life, History, and Travels of Ka-ge-ga-gah-bowh* (nonfiction)

Coyner, David (?), *The Lost Trappers* (fiction)

Curtis, Newton (?), *The Hunted Chief; or, The Female Ranchero* (novel)

Emerson, Ralph Waldo (1803–82), *Poems*

Greeley, Robert (?), *Arthur Woodleigh: A Romance of the Battle Field of Mexico* (novel)

Griswold, Rufus Wilmot (1815–57), ed., *The Prose Writers of America* (nonfiction)

Halleck, Fitz-Greene (1790–1867), *The Poetical Works of Fitz-Greene Halleck*

Howard, H. R. (?), *The Life and Adventures of John A. Murrell, the Great Western Land Pirate* (novel)

Jarves, James (1818–88), *History of the Hawaiian Islands* (nonfiction)

Jones, Justin (?), *The Volunteer: Or, the Maid of Monterey* (novel)

Lippard, George (1822–54), *Washington and His Generals* (nonfiction); *Legends of Mexico* (fiction)

Longfellow, Henry Wadsworth (1807–82), *Evangeline: A Tale of Acadie* (verse)

Melville, Herman (1819–91), *Omoo: A Narrative of Adventures in the South Seas* (novel)

Morgan, Lewis Henry (1818–81), "Letters on the Iroquois" (nonfiction)

Palmer, Joel (1810–81). *Journal of Travels Over the Rocky Mountains* (nonfiction)

Parker, Theodore (1810–60), "A Letter on Slavery" (nonfiction)

Prescott, William Hickling (1796–1859), *History of the Conquest of Peru* (nonfiction)

Robb, John S. (?), *Kaam; or Daylight . . . A Tale of the Rocky Mountains* (fiction)

Ruxton, George Frederick (1820–48), *Adventures in Mexico and the Rocky Mountains* (nonfiction)

Taylor, Benjamin (1819–87), *Short Ravelings from a Long Yarn* (fiction)

Thorpe, Thomas Bangs (1815–75), *Our Army at Monterey* (nonfiction)

1848

Young, Samuel (?), *Tom Hanson, the Avenger* (novel)

Anonymous, *A Sketch of the Life of Okah Tubbee* (nonfiction)

Alcaraz, Ramon (?), *Apuntes para la historia de la guerra entre México y los Estados-Unidos* (nonfiction, trans. 1850 as *The Other Side*)

Averill, Charles (?), *The Secret Service Ship* (novel)

Bennett, Emerson (1822–1905), *Kate Clarendon; or, Necromancy in the Wilderness* (novel); *The Renegade* (novel)

Bradbury, Osgood (1795?–1886), *Pontiac; or, The Last Battle of the Ottawa Chief* (novel)

Brown, William Wells (1816?–84), *The Anti-Slavery Harp* (poems)

Bryant, Edwin (1805–69), *What I Saw in California* (nonfiction)

Burlend, Rebecca (1793–1872), *A True Picture of Emigration* (nonfiction)

Conner, Charlotte Barnes (?), *Forest Princess* (play)

Cooper, James Fenimore (1789–1851), *Jack Tier* (novel); *The Oak Openings* (novel)

Garnet, Henry Highland (1815–82), *Address to the Slaves* (lecture); *The Past and the Present Condition, and the Destiny, of the Colored Race* (nonfiction)

Wisconsin admitted to the Union. Mexico cedes territory that will become California, New Mexico, and parts of Arizona and Nevada to the United States for $15 million.

Seneca Falls Convention on women's rights.

Free-Soil party (antislavery) formed; Van Buren runs for president on its ticket and receives 10 percent of the vote.

Zachary Taylor elected president. Oneida Community founded (1848–79).

Revolutions in Denmark, France, Italy, Germany, and Hungary.

Dickens, *Dombey and Son*

Gaskell, *Mary Barton*

Marx and Engels, *The Communist Manifesto*

John Stuart Mill, *Principles of Political Economy*

Thackeray, *Vanity Fair*

American Texts	American Events	Other Events and Texts
Halyard, Harry (?), *The Chieftain of the Churubusco, or, the Spectre of the Cathedral* (novel)		
Leslie, Eliza (1787–1858), *Amelia; or, A Young Lady's Vicissitudes* (novel)		
Lippard, George (1822–54), *'Bel of Prairie Eden: A Romance of Mexico* (novel)		
Lowell, James Russell (1819–91), *Poems: Second Series*; *A Fable for Critics*; The Biglow Papers (first series); *The Vision of Sir Launfal* (verse)		
Luff, Lorry (?), *Antonita, The Female Contrabandista* (novel)		
Poe, Edgar Allan (1809–49), *Eureka: A Prose Poem*; "The Rationale of Verse" (nonfiction); "The Poetic Principle" (nonfiction published 1850)		
Simpson, Henry (?), *Three Weeks in the Gold Mines* (travel sketches)		
Smith, Elbert (?), *Ma-Ka-Tai-Me-She-Kia-Kiak; or, Black Hawk and Scenes in the West: A National Poem*		
Thompson, William Tappan (1812–82), *Major Jones's Sketches of Travel* (fiction)		
Webber, Charles (1819–56), *Old Hicks the Guide* (fiction)		

824

	American events	World events
Wislizenus, F. A. (1810–89), *Memoir of a Tour to Northern Mexico*		Rome proclaimed a republic under Giuseppe Mazzini.
1849 Anonymous, *Amelia Sherwood; or, Bloody Scenes at the California Gold Mines* (fiction)	Zachary Taylor inaugurated as twelfth president of the United States.	
Averill, Charles (?), *Kit Carson, The Prince of the Gold Hunters* (fiction); *Life in California; or, The Treasure Seeker's Expedition* (fiction); *Aztec Revelations* (fiction)	The Astor Place Riot. California Gold Rush begins. Creation of Minnesota Territory.	Fredric Chopin dies (born 1810). Johann Strauss, Sr., dies (born 1804).
Bennett, Emerson (1822–1905), *The Prairie Flower; or, Adventures in the Far West* (novel)	U.S. Department of the Interior established. Slavery debated in California and New Mexico.	Charlotte Brontë, *Shirley* Macaulay, *The History of England from the Accession of James II* (1849–61)
Bibb, Henry (1815–?), *Narrative of the Life and Adventures of Henry Bibb* (nonfiction)	Edgar Allan Poe dies.	Ruskin, *The Seven Lamps of Architecture*
Cooper, James Fenimore (1789–1851), *The Sea Lions* (novel)		
Eastman, Seth (1808–75) and **Mary** (1818–90), *Dahcotah; or, Life and Legends of the Sioux* (nonfiction)		
Eliot, Samuel A. (1780–1883), *Life of Josiah Henson* (nonfiction)		
Escudero, José Augustín de (1801–62), *Noticias históricas y estadísticas de la antigua provincia del Nuevo-México* (nonfiction)		
Kennedy, John Pendleton (1795–1870), *Memoirs of the Life of William Wirt* (nonfiction)		

American Texts	American Events	Other Events and Texts
Melville, Herman (1819–91), *Mardi: And a Voyage Thither* (novel); *Redburn: His First Voyage* (novel)		
Motley, John Lothrop (1814–77), *Merry-Mount* (novel)		
Parkman, Francis (1823–93), *The California and Oregon Trail: Being Sketches of Prairie and Rocky Mountain Life* (nonfiction)		
Paulding, James Kirke (1778–1860), *The Puritan and His Daughter* (novel)		
Pennington, James W. C. (?), *The Fugitive Blacksmith* (personal narrative)		
Thompson, George (?), *City Crimes; or, Life in New York and Boston; Venus in Boston: A Romance of City Life* (novel)		
Thoreau, Henry David (1817–62), *A Week on the Concord and Merrimack Rivers* (nonfiction); "Resistance to Civil Government" (nonfiction, republished as "Civil Disobedience," 1894).		
Thornton, J. Quinn (1810–88), *Oregon and California in 1848* (nonfiction)		
The New Mexican (bilingual newspaper) founded.		

1850

Abbey, James (?), *California, A Trip Across the Plains* (nonfiction)

Armstrong, Arthur (?), *The Mariner of the Mines; Or, the Maid of the Monastery* (novel)

Bennett, Emerson (1822–1905), *The Forest Rose; A Tale of the Frontier* (novel)

Briggs, Charles Frederick (1804–77), *The Trippings of Tom Pepper* (novel, volume 2)

Colton, Rev. Walter (1797–1851), *The Land of Gold; or, Three Years in California* (nonfiction)

Cooper, James Fenimore (1789–1851), *The Ways of the Hour* (novel)

Copway, George (1818–69), *Traditional History and Characteristic Sketches of the Ojibway Nation* (nonfiction); *The Ojibway Conquest* (poem)

Emerson, Ralph Waldo (1803–82), *Representative Men* (essays)

Foley, Fanny (?), *Romance of the Ocean: A Narrative of the Voyage of the Wildfire to California* (fiction)

Garrard, Lewis (1829–87), *Wah-To-Yah, and the Taos Trail; or, Prairie Travel and Scalp Dances, with a Look at Los Rancheros from Muleback and the Rocky Mountain Campfire* (nonfiction)

President Taylor dies sixteen months after taking office; Millard Fillmore inaugurated as thirteenth president of the United States.

Compromise of 1850: California admitted as a free state; New Mexico and Utah organized as territories; passage of the Fugitive Slave Act.

Clayton-Bulwer Treaty with Great Britain assures neutrality of Panama Canal project.

Jenny Lind tours United States, managed by P. T. Barnum.

Population of United States is 23 million (includes 3.2 million black slaves).

Margaret Fuller dies (born 1810).

Tennyson becomes poet laureate of England.

Balzac dies (born 1799).

Wordsworth dies (born 1770).

Dickens, *David Copperfield*

Tennyson, *In Memoriam*

Wordsworth, *The Prelude*

American Texts	American Events	Other Events and Texts
Gilbert, Olive (?), *Narrative of Sojourner Truth* (nonfiction)		
Grayson, William J. (1788–1863), *Letter to Governor Seabrook* (nonfiction)		
Hawthorne, Nathaniel (1804–64), *The Scarlet Letter* (novel)		
Hodges, M. C. (?), *The Mestico; or, The Warpath and Its Incidents* (novel)		
Hollister, Gideon (1817–81), *Mount Hope; or, Philip, King of the Wampanoags* (novel)		
Judson, E. C. [Ned Buntline] (1822 or 23–86), *Norwood; or, Life on the Prairie* (fiction)		
Kip, Leonard (1826–1906), *California Sketches with Recollections of the Gold Mines* (nonfiction)		
Lugenbeel, James (1819?–1857), *Sketches of Liberia* (nonfiction)		
Melville, Herman (1819–91), "Hawthorne and His Mosses"; *White-Jacket; or, The World in a Man-of-War* (novel)		
Mitchell, Donald Grant ["Ik Marvel"] (1822–1908), *Reveries of a Bachelor* (fiction)		
Robinson, John H. (1825–?), *Kosato; The Blackfoot Renegade* (novel)		

Sawyer, Lorenzo (1820–91), *Way Sketches, Containing Incidents of Travel Across the Plains from St. Joseph to California* (nonfiction)

Taylor, Bayard (1825–78), *Eldorado; or, Adventures in the Path of Empire* (fiction)

Warner, Susan Bogert (1819–85), *The Wide, Wide World* (novel)

Webster, Daniel (1782–1852), "Constitution and Union" (speech)

Harper's New Monthly Magazine founded in New York.

1851 Billings, Eliza Ann (1826–?), *The Female Volunteer* (novel)

Brown, Henry (?), *Narrative of Henry "Box" Brown* (nonfiction)

Calhoun, John (1782–1850), *Disquisition on Government* (nonfiction); *Discussion on the Constitution and Government of the United States* (nonfiction)

Emerson, Ralph Waldo (1803–82), "The Fugitive Slave Law" (address, first version)

Grayson, William J. (1788–1863), *Letters of Curtius* (proslavery nonfiction)

Hanson, Samuel B. (?), *Tom Quick, the Indian Slayer* (novel)

General Narciso Lopez undertakes expedition to free Cuba from Spanish rule.

Sojourner Truth speaks at a women's rights convention in Ohio.

Isaac Singer patents the sewing machine.

James Fenimore Cooper dies.

Coup d'état in France by Louis Napoleon.

Thomas Cook's first guided tour from England to the Continent.

Ruskin, *The Stones of Venice* (1851–3)

Verdi, *Rigoletto* (opera)

Hawthorne, Nathaniel (1804–64), *The House of the Seven Gables* (novel); *The Snow-Image and Other Twice-told Tales* (stories); *True Stories from History and Biography* (children's book)

Melville, Herman (1819–91), *Moby-Dick* (novel)

Morgan, Lewis Henry (1818–81), *League of the Ho-de-no-sau-ne, or Iroquois* (nonfiction)

Parkman, Francis (1823–93), *The Conspiracy of Pontiac and the Indian War after the Conquest of Canada* (nonfiction)

Pierson, Emily C. (?), *Jamie Parker, A Fugitive* (novel)

Richardson, John (1796–1852), *Wacousta; or, The Prophecy* (novel)

Schoolcraft, Henry Rowe (1793–1864), *Historical and Statistical Information Respecting the History, Condition, and Prospects of the Indian Tribes of the United States* (nonfiction, published 1851–7)

Shaw, William (?), *Golden Dreams and Waking Realities: Being the Adventures of a Gold-Seeker in California and the Pacific Islands* (nonfiction)

Shepherd, J. S. (?), *Journal of Travel Across the Plains to California and Guide to the Future Emigrant* (nonfiction)

Simms, William Gilmore (1806–70), *Katharine Walton* (novel)

Stowe, Harriet Beecher (1811–96), *Uncle Tom's Cabin* (novel, serialized 1851–2 in the *National Era*)

The New York Times founded.

1852 Aiken, George L. (1830–76), *Uncle Tom's Cabin* (play, adapted from Stowe's novel)

Bancroft, George (1800–91), *A History of the United States, from the Discovery of the American Continent,* Vol. IV (ten volumes 1834–74)

Beecher, Lyman (1775–1863), *Works* (nonfiction)

Carnes, J. A. (?), *Journal of a Voyage from Boston to the West Coast of Africa* (nonfiction)

Cary, Alice (1820–71), *Clovernook* (prose sketches)

Child, Andrew (?), *Overland Route to California* (nonfiction)

Clarke, Asa B. (?), *Travels in Mexico and California* (nonfiction)

Criswell, Robert (?), *Uncle Tom's Cabin Contrasted with Buckingham Hall* (novel)

Delany, Martin (1812–85), *The Condition, Elevation, Emigration, and Destiny of the Colored People of the United States* (nonfiction)

New postal regulations reduce rates for magazines and allow publishers to pay postage.

Daniel Webster dies (born 1782).

French president Louis Napoleon proclaims himself Emperor Napoleon III.

Douglass, Frederick (1817–95), "What to the Slave is the Fourth of July" (speech)

Eastman, Mary H. (1818–90), *Aunt Phillis's Cabin; or, Southern Life as It Is* (novel)

Ellet, Elizabeth Fries (?), *Pioneer Women of the West* (nonfiction)

Elliott, E. N. (?), ed., *The Pro-Slavery Argument* (anthology)

Goodell, William (?), *Slavery and Anti-Slavery* (nonfiction)

Hale, Sarah Josepha (1788–1879), *Northwood; or, Life North and South* (novel)

Hall, Bayard Rush (1798–1863), *Frank Freeman's Barbershop* (novel)

Hawthorne, Nathaniel (1804–64), *The Blithedale Romance* (novel); *A Wonder-Book for Girls and Boys*; *The Life of Franklin Pierce* (campaign biography)

Kelley, William (?), *A Stroll through the Diggings of California* (travel sketches)

Melville, Herman (1819–91), *Pierre* (novel)

Peterson, Charles ["J. Thornton Randolph"] (1819–87), *Cabin and Parlor, or Slaves and Masters* (novel)

Rush, Caroline (?), *North and South; or, Slavery and Its Contrasts* (novel)

Simms, William Gilmore (1806–70), *The Sword and the Distaff* (novel, republished as *Woodcraft*, 1854)

Smith, W. L. G. (?), *Life at the South; or, "Uncle Tom's Cabin" As It Is* (novel)

Southworth, E.D.E.N. (1819–99), *The Curse of Clifton* (novel)

Stansbury, J. Howard (?), *An Expedition to the Valley of the Great Salt Lake of Utah* (nonfiction)

Warner, Anna (1824–1915), *Dollars and Cents* (fiction)

Warner, Susan Bogert (1819–85), *Queechy* (novel)

1853   Baldwin, Joseph Glover (1815–64), *The Flush Times of Alabama and Mississippi* (sketches)

Brown, William Wells (1816?–84), *Clotel: Or, the President's Daughter* (novel)

Douglass, Frederick (1817–95), "The Heroic Slave" (story)

Eastman, Seth (1808–75) and Mary (1818–90), *The Romance of Indian Life* (nonfiction); *The American Aboriginal Portfolio* (nonfiction)

Fabens, Joseph W. (1821–75), *A Story of Life on the Isthmus* (travel)

Franklin Pierce inaugurated as fourteenth president of the United States.

Creation of the Washington Territory.

Rise of the Know-Nothings and political nativism.

Gadsden Purchase from Mexico completes present borders.

Commodore Perry and the American fleet arrive in Tokyo Bay.

Horatio Greenough's sculpture *Rescue Group* erected at the Capitol.

Crimean War between Turkey and Russia, 1853–6.

Arnold, "Sohrab and Rustum" (poem)

Charlotte Brontë, *Villette*

Dickens, *Bleak House*

Gaskell, *Cranford*

Verdi, *Il Trovatore* and *La Traviata* (operas)

Wagner completes text of *Der Ring des Nibelungen*

American Texts	American Events	Other Events and Texts
Goodell, William (1792–1894), *The American Slave Code* (nonfiction)	Nathaniel Hawthorne serves as consul in Liverpool and Manchester (1853–7).	
Hale, Sarah Josepha (1788–1879), *Liberia; or, Mr. Peyton's Experiment* (novel)		
Hawthorne, Nathaniel (1804–64), *Tanglewood Tales for Girls and Boys* (fiction)		
Maury, Matthew (1806–73), *The Amazon and the Atlantic Slopes of South America* (nonfiction)		
Northup, Solomon, *Twelve Years a Slave* (nonfiction)		
Page, John W. (1786–1861), *Uncle Robin, in His Cabin in Virginia, and Tom without One in Boston* (fiction)		
Payson, George (1824–93), *Golden Dreams and Leaden Realities* (fiction)		
Pearson, Emily C. (?), *Cousin Franck's Household* (fiction)		
Phillips, Wendell (1811–84), *The Philosophy of the Abolition Movement* (nonfiction)		
Ruffin, Edmund (1794–1865), *Political Economy of Slavery* (nonfiction)		
Stowe, Harriet Beecher (1811–96), *A Key to Uncle Tom's Cabin* (nonfiction)		

Warren, William (1825–53), *History of the Ojibways* (nonfiction, published 1885)

Whitfield, James M. (?), *America and Other Poems*

Willis, Sara Payson ["Fanny Fern"] (1811–72), *Fern Leaves from Fanny's Portfolio* (sketches); *Little Ferns for Fanny's Little Friends* (sketches)

Putnam's Monthly Magazine founded (ceases publication 1857).

1854 Adams, Nehemiah (?), *A South-Side View of Slavery* (essays)

Arthur, Timothy Shay (1809–85), *Ten Nights in a Barroom* (fiction)

Belisle, David (?), *The American Family Robinson . . . Lost in the Great Desert of the West* (fiction)

Clappe, Louise Amelia Knapp Smith (1819–1906), *Dame Shirley Letters* (sketches published in *Pioneer Magazine*, collected 1922)

Conneau, Theophilus ["Theodore Canot"] (?), *Captain Canot; or, Twenty Years of an African Slaver* (nonfiction)

Cooke, John Esten (1830–86), *Leather Stocking and Silk* (novel); *The Virginia Comedians* (novel)

Know-Nothings score election victories.

Collapse of Whig party; emergence of new Republican party.

Kansas-Nebraska Act repeals Missouri Compromise and revives sectional conflict over slavery.

Ostend Manifesto on Cuba.

Britain and France conclude alliance with Turkey and declare war on Russia; battle of Balaclava; siege of Sevastopol.

Florence Nightingale nurses British soldiers in Turkey.

Pope Pius IX declares doctrine of Immaculate Conception.

American Texts	American Events	Other Events and Texts
Cummins, Maria Susanna (1827–66), *The Lamplighter* (novel)	Treaty of Kanagawa opens Japan to American trade.	Oscar Wilde born (dies 1900).
Delano, Alonzo (1802?–74), *Life on the Plains and Among the Diggings* (geological study)		Dickens, *Hard Times*
Delany, Martin (1812–85), *Political Destiny of the Colored Race on the American Continent* (nonfiction)		Tennyson, "The Charge of the Light Brigade"
Dewees, Jacob (?), *The Great Future of America and Africa* (nonfiction)		
Fitzhugh, George (1806–81), *Sociology for the South; or, The Failure of a Free Society* (nonfiction)		
Foote, Andrew Hull (?), *Africa and the American Flag* (nonfiction)		
Frost, John (?), *Heroic Women of the West* (nonfiction)		
Godwin, Parke (1816–1904) "The Vestiges of Despotism" (nonfiction)		
Harper, Frances Ellen Watkins (1825–1911), *Poems*		
Hentz, Caroline Lee (1800–56), *The Planter's Northern Bride* (novel)		
Herndon, William Louis (?), *Exploration of the Valley of the Amazon* (nonfiction)		
Hughes, Henry (?), *Treatise on Sociology* (nonfiction)		

Kane, Elisha (1820–57), *The U.S. Grinnell Expedition in Search of Sir John Franklin* (nonfiction)

Nott, Josiah (1804–73), *Types of Mankind* (George R. Glidden coauthor, nonfiction)

Parker, Theodore (1810–60), "The Nebraska Question" (speech)

Perkins, Edward T. (?), *Na Motu: Or, Reef-Rovings in the South Seas* (nonfiction)

Pike, Mary Hayden [Langdon] (1824–1908), *Ida May* (novel)

Ridge, John Rollin ["Yellow Bird"] (1827–67), *The Life and Adventures of Joaquin Murieta* (novel)

Simms, William Gilmore (1806–70), *Woodcraft* (novel)

Stowe, Harriet Beecher (1811–96), *Sunny Memories of Foreign Lands* (nonfiction)

Thoreau, Henry David (1817–62), *Walden, or Life in the Woods* (nonfiction); "Slavery in Massachusetts" (nonfiction)

Thorpe, Thomas Bangs (1815–75), *The Hive and the Hunter* (sketches); *The Master's House, A Tale of Southern Life* (fiction)

Victor, Metta Victoria (1831–86), *Mormon Wives* (fiction)

	American Texts	American Events	Other Events and Texts
1855	Willis, Sara Payson ["Fanny Fern"] (1811–72), *Fern Leaves* (sketches, second series)	"Kansas Question" on slavery. William Walker's expeditions to Nicaragua. First U.S. Court of Claims established.	Alexander II becomes czar of Russia. Ferdinand de Lesseps granted concession by France to build the Suez Canal.
	Barnum, P[hineas] T[aylor] (1810–91), *The Life of P. T. Barnum, Written by Himself* (nonfiction)		Charlotte Brontë dies (born 1816).
	Beecher, Henry Ward (1813–87), *Star Papers* (nonfiction)		Charles Kingsley, *Westward, Ho!* Tennyson, *Maud and Other Poems* Anthony Trollope, *The Warden*
	Brougham, John (1810–80), *Po-Ca-Hon-Tas; or, The Gentle Savage* (play)		
	Brown, John (1800–59), *Slave Life in Georgia* (nonfiction)		
	Brown, William Wells (1816?–84), "St. Domingo: Its Revolutions and Its Patriots" (lecture)		
	Christy, David (?), *Cotton Is King* (nonfiction)		
	Douglass, Frederick (1817–95), *My Bondage and My Freedom* (nonfiction)		
	Duyckinck, Evert Augustus (1816–78) and George Long (1823–63), editors, *Cyclopedia of American Literature* (nonfiction)		
	Emerson, Ralph Waldo (1803–82), "American Slavery" (address)		
	Grimes, William (?), *Life of William Grimes, Runaway Slave* (nonfiction)		
	Helper, Hinton Rowan (1829–1909), *Land of Gold; Reality Versus Fiction* (nonfiction)		

Irving, Washington (1783–1859), *The Life of George Washington* (5 volumes, 1855–9); *Wolfert's Roost and Other Papers* (nonfiction)

Lester, Charles Edwards (1815–90), *Life of Sam Houston* (nonfiction)

Linforth, James (?), *Route from Liverpool to Great Salt Lake Valley* (nonfiction)

Longfellow, Henry Wadsworth (1807–82), *The Song of Hiawatha* (verse)

Melville, Herman (1819–91), *Israel Potter: His Fifty Years of Exile* (novel)

Parsons, C. G. (?), *Inside View of Slavery; or, A Tour Among the Planters* (travel)

Roe, Elizabeth (?), *Aunt Leanna* (novel)

Simms, William Gilmore (1806–70), *The Forayers* (novel)

Taylor, Bayard (1825–78), *A Visit to India, China, and Japan in 1853* (nonfiction)

Thomas, Charles W. (?), *Adventures and Observations on the West Coast of Africa* (nonfiction)

Thoreau, Henry David (1817–62), "What Shall It Profit" (lecture, revised and published in 1863 as "Life without Principle")

Ward, Maria (?), *Female Life Among the Mormons* (fiction)

	American Texts	American Events	Other Events and Texts
	Ward, Samuel **Ringgold** (?), *Autobiography of a Fugitive Negro* (nonfiction)		
	Whitman, **Walt** (1819–92), *Leaves of Grass*, (verse, first edition; final edition, 1891–2)		
	Willis, **Sara Payson** ["Fanny Fern"] (1811–72), *Ruth Hall* (novel)		
1856	Beckwourth, **James P.** (1798–1867?), *The Life and Adventures of James P. Beckwourth, Mountaineer, Scout, and Pioneer and Chief of the Crow Nation of Indians* (nonfiction)	"Bleeding Kansas" (five-year border war). John Brown's raid at Pottawatomie Creek.	Congress of Paris; end of Crimean War.
	Cary, **Alice** (1820–71), *Married, Not Mated* (nonfiction)	James Buchanan elected president. Charles Sumner delivers speech ("The Crime Against Kansas") and is assaulted on the Senate floor by Preston Brooks.	Sigmund Freud born (dies 1939). Heinrich Heine dies (born 1797). Robert Schumann dies (born 1810). George Bernard Shaw born (dies 1950).
	Colton, **Joseph** (?), *Colton's Traveler and Tourist's Guide-Book Through the Western States and Territories* (nonfiction)		Tocqueville, *The Old Regime and the French Revolution*
	Curtis, **George William** (1824–92), "The Duty of the American Scholar to Politics and the Times" (oration)		
	Dana, **Charles** (1819–97), *The Garden of the World; Or, the Great West* (nonfiction)		
	Drew, **Benjamin** (1812–1903), *Northside View of Slavery* (nonfiction)		
	Emerson, **Ralph Waldo** (1803–82), *English Traits* (essays)		

Farnham, Eliza (1815–64), *California, In-doors and Out* (nonfiction)

de Gobineau, Joseph Arthur (1816–82), *The Moral and Intellectual Diversity of Races* (nonfiction, U.S. edition)

Godwin, Parke (1816–1904), *Political Essays* (nonfiction)

Grayson, William J. (1788–1863), *The Hireling and the Slave* (poem)

Hawks, Francis (1798–1866), *Narrative of the Expedition of an American Squadron to the China Seas and Japan* (nonfiction)

Kane, Elisha (1820–57), *Arctic Explorations* (nonfiction)

Melville, Herman (1819–91), *The Piazza Tales* (fiction, includes "Bartleby, The Scrivener," "Benito Cereno," and "The Encantadas")

Motley, John Lothrop (1814–77), *The Rise of the Dutch Republic* (nonfiction)

Olmsted, Frederick Law (1822–1903), *A Journey in the Seaboard Slave States* (nonfiction)

Payson, George (1824–93), *The New Age of Gold* (nonfiction)

Postle, Karl (1793–1864), *Frontier Life* (nonfiction)

American Texts	American Events	Other Events and Texts
Reid, Mayne (1818–83), *The Quadroon* (novel)		
Schoolcraft, Henry Rowe (1793–1864), *The Myth of Hiawatha* (nonfiction)		
Simms, William Gilmore (1806–70), *Eutaw* (novel)		
Squier, E. G. (1821–88), *Nicaragua* (nonfiction)		
Stowe, Harriet Beecher (1811–96), *Dred: A Tale of the Great Dismal Swamp* (novel)		
Stringfellow, Thornton (1788–1869), *Scriptural and Statistical Views in Favor of Slavery* (nonfiction)		
Thompson, John (?), *Life of John Thompson, A Fugitive Slave* (nonfiction)		
Tucker, George (1775–1861), *History of the United States* (nonfiction, 4 volumes, 1856–7)		
Willis, Sara Payson ['Fanny Fern'] (1811–72), *Rose Clark* (novel)		
Wilson, Robert A. (1812–72), *Mexico: Its Peasants and Priests* (nonfiction)		
1857 Borthwick, John D. (?), *Three Years in California* (nonfiction)	James Buchanan inaugurated as fifteenth president of the United States. Dred Scott decision.	Great Mutiny in India. Transatlantic cable laid (through 1866).
Bowen, Thomas Jefferson (1814–75), *Central Africa: Adventures and Missionary Labours in Several*		

842

Countries in the Interior of Africa from 1849 to 1856 (nonfiction)

Christy, David (1802–?), Ethiopia: Her Gloom and Glory (nonfiction)

Cummins, Maria Susanna (1827–66), Mabel Vaughan (novel)

Davis, William W. H. (1820–1910), El Gringo; or, New Mexico and Her People (nonfiction)

Denslow, Van Buren (1834–1902), Owned and Disowned; or, The Chattel Child (fiction)

Fitzhugh, George (1806–81), Cannibals All! or Slaves Without Masters (nonfiction)

Griffith, Mattie (?–1906), Autobiography of a Female Slave (nonfiction)

Helper, Hinton Rowan (1829–1909), The Impending Crisis of the South: How to Meet It (nonfiction)

Henson, Josiah (1789–1883), Truth Stranger than Fiction: Father Henson's Story of His Own Life (nonfiction)

Holly, James T. (1829–1911), A Vindication of the Capacity of the Negro Race for Self-Government and Civilized Progress, as Demonstrated by Historical Events of the Haytian Revolution (nonfiction)

Hopkins, Eliza (?), Ella Lincoln; or, Western Prairie Life (fiction)

Proslavery Lecompton constitution ratified in Kansas when free-state men refuse to vote.
Financial panic.
Frederick Law Olmsted and Calvert Vaux design Central Park.

Joseph Conrad born (dies 1924).
Edward Elgar born (dies 1934).

Baudelaire's Les Fleurs du mal published; Baudelaire fined for offending public morals, and six poems are banned from subsequent editions.
Dickens, Little Dorrit
Flaubert's Madame Bovary published; Flaubert, his publisher, and his printer are tried for obscenity, but acquitted.
Hughes, Tom Brown's Schooldays
Anthony Trollope, Barchester Towers

American Texts	American Events	Other Events and Texts
Jacobs, Peter (?), *Journal of the Reverend Peter Jacobs* (nonfiction)		End of Mogul Empire in India.
Jarves, James (1818–88), *Kiana: A Tradition of Hawaii* (fiction)		Robert Owen dies (born 1771).
Melville, Herman (1819–91), *The Confidence-Man: His Masquerade* (fiction)		Giacomo Puccini born (dies 1924).
Olmsted, Frederick Law (1822–1903), *A Journey Through Texas* (nonfiction)		
Sedgwick, Catharine Maria (1789–1867), *Married or Single?* (novel)		
Steward, Austin (1794–1860), *Twenty-Two Years a Slave, and Forty Years a Freeman* (nonfiction)		
Stratton, Royal (?–1875), *The Captivity of the Oatman Girls* (nonfiction)		
Webb, Frank J. (?), *The Garies and Their Friends* (novel)		
The *Atlantic Monthly* founded in Boston.		

1858

American Texts	American Events	Other Events and Texts
Henson, Josiah (1789–1883), *Truth is Stranger than Fiction: Father Henson's Story of his Own Life* (nonfiction)	Minnesota admitted to the Union.	
	Lincoln-Douglas debates.	
Peters, DeWitt C. (?–1876), *Life and Adventures of Kit Carson* (nonfiction)	Lincoln's "House Divided" speech.	
	William Henry Seward's "Irrepressible Conflict" speech.	

1859

Squier, E. G. (1821–88), *The States of Central America* (nonfiction)

Tidball, William L. (?), *The Mexican Bride; Or, the Ranger's Revenge* (novel)

Boucicault, Dion (1820–90), *The Octoroon* (play)

Cooke, John Esten (1830–86), *Henry St. John, Gentleman* (novel)

Davis, Noah (1803 or 4–?), *Narrative of the Life of Reverend Noah Davis* (nonfiction)

Delany, Martin (1812–85), *Blake; or, The Huts of America* (novel)

Southworth, E. D. E. N. (1819–99), *The Hidden Hand* (novel)

Stowe, Harriet Beecher (1811–96), *The Minister's Wooing* (novel)

Thoreau, Henry David (1817–62), "A Plea for Captain John Brown" (nonfiction)

Tucker, George (1775–1861), *Political Economy for the People* (nonfiction)

Wilson, Augusta Evans (1835–1909), *Beulah* (novel)

Wilson, Harriet E. (1808–c. 1870), *Our Nig; or, Sketches from the Life of a Free Black* (novel)

1860

Craft, William (?) and Ellen (?), *Running a Thousand Miles for Freedom* (nonfiction)

Thomas McKenney's "Indian Gallery" becomes part of the Smithsonian Institution (largely destroyed in 1865 fire).

Oregon admitted to the Union.

John Brown's raid on Harper's Ferry, his trial, and execution.

Comstock Lode (discovery of silver deposits in Nevada).

First Indian head penny minted.

Washington Irving dies.

William Hickling Prescott dies.

Democratic party is deadlocked at Charleston Convention and

George Eliot, *Scenes of Clerical Life*

Morris, *The Defence of Guenevere*

War of Italian Liberation.

Thomas de Quincey dies (born 1785).

Lord Macaulay dies (born 1800).

Alexis de Tocqueville dies.

Darwin, *On the Origin of Species*

Dickens, *A Tale of Two Cities*

George Eliot, *Adam Bede*

Marx, *Critique of Political Economy*

John Stuart Mill, *On Liberty*

Tennyson, *Idylls of the King* (1859–85)

Thackeray, *The Virginians*

Florence Nightingale founds first nursing school, in England.

American Texts	American Events	Other Events and Texts
	splits along sectional lines at Baltimore.	Anton Chekhov born (dies 1904).
Cummins, Maria Susanna (1827–66), *El Fureidis* (novel)	Lincoln elected president; delivers Cooper Union speech on the problem of slavery and the Constitution.	Gustav Mahler born (dies 1911).
De Bow, James D. B. (?), *The Interest in Slavery of the Southern Non-Slaveholder* (nonfiction)	Crittenden Compromise; South Carolina secedes from the Union.	Burckhardt, *The Civilization of the Renaissance in Italy*
Elliot, E. N. (?), ed., *Cotton is King and Pro-Slavery Arguments* (anthology)	Pony Express (1860–1).	Collins, *The Woman in White*
Ellis, Edward S. (1840–1916), *Seth Jones; or, The Captive of the Frontier* (dime novel)	U.S. Secret Service established.	George Eliot, *The Mill on the Floss*
Emerson, Ralph Waldo (1802–82), *The Conduct of Life* (essays)	Theodore Parker dies (born 1810).	
Flanders, Mrs. G. M. (?), *The Ebony Idol* (novel)		
Garrison, William Lloyd (1805–79), *The New "Reign of Terror" in the Slaveholding States* (anthology)		
Gilpin, William (1813–94), *The Central Gold Region. The Grain, Pastoral and Gold Regions of North America* (nonfiction, republished as *The Mission of the North American People*, 1873)		
Hawthorne, Nathaniel (1804–64), *The Marble Faun* (novel)		
Hosmer, Hezekiah (?), *Adela, the Octoroon* (novel)		
Olmsted, Frederick Law (1822–1903), *A Journey in the Back Country* (nonfiction)		

Schoolcraft, Mrs. Henry Rowe (?), *The Black Gauntlet* (novel)

Stringfellow, Thornton (1788–1869), *Slavery: Its Origin, Nature, and History* (nonfiction)

Thompson, Daniel Pierce (1795–1868), *The Doomed Chief* (novel)

Victor, Metta Victoria (1831–86), *Alice Wilde, the Raftsman's Daughter* (dime novel); *The Backwoods Bride* (dime novel)

Walker, William (1824–60), *The War in Nicaragua* (nonfiction)

First Beadle dime novel published.

1861

Adams, Nehemiah (?), *The Sable Cloud* (novel)

Conway, Moncure D[aniel] (1832–1907), *The Rejected Stone* (novel)

Crummell, Alexander (1819–98), "The Relation and Duties of Free Colored Men in America to Africa" (nonfiction)

Davis, Rebecca [Blaine] Harding (1831–1910), "Life in the Iron Mills" (fiction)

Jacobs, Harriet [Linda Brent] (1813–97), *Incidents in the Life of a Slave Girl, Written by Herself* (nonfiction)

Kansas admitted to the Union.
Mississippi, Florida, Alabama, Georgia, Louisiana, Texas, Virginia, Arkansas, Tennessee, and North Carolina secede.
Jefferson Davis elected president of the Confederate States of America.
Fort Sumter bombarded.
First Battle of Bull Run.
Richmond becomes capitol of the Confederacy.

Emancipation of Russian serfs.

Elizabeth Barrett Browning dies (born 1806).
Dickens, *Great Expectations*
Dostoevsky, *Memoirs from the House of the Dead* (1861–2)
George Eliot, *Silas Marner*
Palgrave, *The Golden Treasury of Songs and Lyrics*

	American Texts	American Events	Other Events and Texts
	Jones, Peter (?), *History of the Ojibway Indians* (nonfiction)	Creation of the Colorado, Dakota, and Nevada territories.	Bismarck becomes Prussian prime minister.
	Olmsted, Frederick Law (1822–1903), *The Cotton Kingdom* (travel)	First federal income tax.	Sarah Bernhardt debuts in Paris.
	Pollard, Edward A[lfred] (1831–72), *Black Diamonds Gathered in the Darkey Homes of the South* (nonfiction)	Mathew Brady begins photographing the Civil War.	
	Stedman, Edmund Clarence (1833–1908), "The Battle of Bull Run" (verse)	Population of the United States is 32 million.	Meredith, *Modern Love*
	Van Evrie, John H. (?), *Negroes and Negro "Slavery"* (nonfiction, reissued 1868 as *White Supremacy and Negro Subordination*)		Ruskin, *Unto This Last*
1862	Burdett, Charles (1815–?), *Life of Kit Carson: The Great Western Hunter and Guide* (nonfiction)	Second battle of Bull Run.	Spencer, *A System of Synthetic Philosophy* (10 volumes, 1862–96)
		Lee's invasion of the North stopped at Antietam.	Anthony Trollope, *North America*
	Crummell, Alexander (1819–98), *The Future of Africa* (nonfiction)	Siege of Vicksburg (1861–2).	
	Emerson, Ralph Waldo (1803–82), "Thoreau" (eulogy); "American Civilization" (lecture); "The Emancipation Proclamation" (lecture)	Homestead Act encourages westward migration.	
		Union Pacific railroad chartered.	
	Hawthorne, Nathaniel (1804–64), "Chiefly about War Matters" (essay)	Henry David Thoreau dies.	
		Edith Wharton born (dies 1937).	

Howe, Julia Ward (1819–1910); "The Battle Hymn of the Republic" (verse)

Stowe, Harriet Beecher (1811–96), Agnes of Sorrento (novel); The Pearl of Orr's Island (novel)

Thoreau, Henry David (1817–62), "Walking"; "Autumnal Tints" (nonfiction)

1863 Alcott, Louisa May (1832–88), Hospital Sketches (nonfiction)

Brown, William Wells (1816?–84), The Black Man: His Antecedents, His Genius, and His Achievements (nonfiction)

Cooke, John Esten (1830–86), The Life of Stonewall Jackson (nonfiction)

Hawthorne, Nathaniel (1804–64), Our Old Home (nonfiction)

Kennedy, John Pendleton (1795–1870), Mr. Ambrose's Letters on the Rebellion (nonfiction)

Soule, Caroline (?), Little Alice; or, The Pet of the Settlement (novel)

Stowe, Harriet Beecher (1811–96), A Reply . . . in Behalf of the Women of America (nonfiction)

Thoreau, Henry David (1817–62), Excursions; "Life without Principle" (nonfiction)

Winthrop, Theodore (1828–61), Isthmiana (travel)

Arizona and Idaho organized as U.S. territories.

West Virginia admitted to the Union.

Emancipation Proclamation.

Lincoln's Gettysburg Address.

Thanksgiving Day proclaimed national holiday.

George Santayana born (dies 1952).

Thackeray dies (born 1811).

Fanny Kemble, Journal of a Residence on a Georgia Plantation, 1838–39

Lyell, Geological Evidence of the Antiquity of Man

John Stuart Mill, Utilitarianism

American Texts	American Events	Other Events and Texts
1864		
Cummins, Maria Susanna (1827–66), *Haunted Hearts* (novel)	Ulysses Grant named commander of the Union armies.	Archduke Maximilian of Austria and his wife Carlotta become emperor and empress of Mexico.
Hall, Charles Francis (?), *Arctic Researches; Life with the Esquimaux* (nonfiction)	Sherman's march to the sea. Nevada admitted to the Union. Creation of the Montana Territory.	Richard Strauss born (dies 1949).
Mars, James (?), *The Life of James Mars* (nonfiction)	"In God We Trust" first appears on U.S. coins.	
Thoreau, Henry David (1817–62), *The Maine Woods* (nonfiction)	Nathaniel Hawthorne dies.	Dostoevsky, *Notes from Underground* Verne, *Journey to the Center of the Earth*
1865		
Parkman, Francis (1823–93), *Pioneers of France in the New World* (nonfiction)	General Lee surrenders at Appomattox.	Jean Sibelius born (dies 1957).
	President Lincoln assassinated.	Arnold, *Essays in Criticism*
	13th Amendment (abolishing slavery) ratified.	Carroll, *Alice's Adventures in Wonderland*
	Freedman's Bureau (1865–9) created to assist freed blacks.	Dickens, *Our Mutual Friend*
	Ku Klux Klan organized.	Swinburne, *Atalanta in Calydon*
	Opening of Union stockyards, in Chicago.	Tolstoy, *War and Peace*
		Wagner, *Tristan and Isolde* (opera)
	Edward Everett dies (born 1794).	

BIBLIOGRAPHY

This selected bibliography is drawn from lists provided by the contributors to this volume. It represents works that they have found to be especially influential or significant. The bibliography does not include dissertations, articles, or studies of individual authors. We have also excluded primary sources, with the exception of certain collections that present materials that have been generally unknown or inaccessible to students and scholars.

Aaron, Daniel. *The Unwritten War: American Writers and the Civil War.* New York: Oxford University Press, 1973.

Allen, Paula Gunn. *The Sacred Hoop: Recovering the Feminine in American Indian Traditions.* Boston: Beacon, 1986.

Anaya, Rudolfo A., and Francisco Lomeli, eds. *Aztlán: Essays on the Chicano Homeland.* Albuquerque, N. M.: El Norte Publications, 1989.

Anderson, Benedict. *Imagined Communities: Reflections on the Origin and Spread of Nationalism.* London: Verso, 1983.

Anderson, Quentin. *The Imperial Self: An Essay in American Literary and Cultural History.* New York: Knopf, 1971.

Andrews, William L. *To Tell a Free Story: The First Century of Afro-American Autobiography, 1760–1865.* Urbana: University of Illinois Press, 1988.

Arac, Jonathan. *Commissioned Spirits: The Shaping of Social Motion in Dickens, Carlyle, Melville, and Hawthorne.* 1979. New York: Columbia University Press, 1989.

Baker, Houston A., Jr. *Blues, Ideology, and Afro-American Literature: A Vernacular Theory.* Chicago: University of Chicago Press, 1984.

The Journey Back: Issues in Black Literature and Criticism. Chicago: University of Chicago Press, 1980.

ed. *Three American Literatures: Essays in Chicano, Native-American, and Asian-American Literature.* New York: Modern Language Association, 1982.

Banta, Martha. *Imaging American Women: Idea and Ideals in Cultural History.* New York: Columbia University Press, 1987.

Baym, Nina. *Novels, Readers, and Reviewers: Responses to Fiction in Antebellum America.* Ithaca, N. Y.: Cornell University Press, 1984.

Women's Fiction: A Guide to Novels by and About Women. Ithaca, N. Y.: Cornell University Press, 1978.

Bell, Michael Davitt. *The Development of American Romance: The Sacrifice of Relation.* Chicago: University of Chicago Press, 1980.

Bender, Thomas. *New York Intellect: A History of Intellectual Life in New York City, from 1750 to the Beginnings of Our Own Time.* New York: Knopf-Random House, 1987.

Bercovitch, Sacvan. *The American Jeremiad.* Madison: University of Wisconsin Press, 1978.

   The Puritan Origins of the American Self. New Haven, Conn.: Yale University Press, 1975.

   The Rites of Assent: Transformations in the Symbolic Construction of America. New York: Routledge, 1993.

   ed. *Reconstructing American Literary History.* Harvard English Studies 13. Cambridge, Mass.: Harvard University Press, 1986.

Bercovitch, Sacvan, and Myra Jehlen, eds. *Ideology and Classic American Literature.* Cambridge University Press, 1986.

Bewley, Marius. *The Eccentric Design: Form in the Classic American Novel.* New York: Columbia University Press, 1959.

Bierhorst, John, ed. *In the Trail of the Wind: American Indian Poems and Ritual Orations.* New York: Farrar, Straus, & Giroux, 1971.

Blassingame, John. *The Slave Community: Plantation Life in the Antebellum South.* Rev. ed. New York: Oxford University Press, 1979.

Botkin, B. A., ed. *Lay My Burden Down: A Folk History of Slavery.* Chicago: University of Chicago Press, 1945.

Brandon, William, ed. *The Magic World: American Indian Songs and Poems.* New York: Morrow, 1971.

Bridgman, Richard. *The Colloquial Style in America.* New York: Oxford University Press, 1966.

Brodhead, Richard. *The School of Hawthorne.* New York: Oxford University Press, 1986.

Brooks, Van Wyck. *The Flowering of New England, 1815–1865.* New York: E. P. Dutton, 1936.

   The Times of Melville and Whitman. New York: Dutton, 1947.

   The World of Washington Irving. New York: Dutton, 1944.

Brown, Gillian. *Domestic Individualism: Imagining Self in Nineteenth-Century America.* Berkeley and Los Angeles: University of California Press, 1990.

Brown, Herbert Ross. *The Sentimental Novel in America, 1789–1860.* Durham, N. C.: Duke University Press, 1940.

Brown, Jerry Wayne. *The Rise of Biblical Criticism in America, 1800–1870: The New England Scholars.* Middletown, Conn.: Wesleyan University Press, 1969.

Buell, Lawrence. *Literary Transcendentalism: Style and Vision in the American Renaissance.* Ithaca, N. Y.: Cornell University Press, 1973.

   New England Literary Culture: From Revolution Through Renaissance. Cambridge University Press, 1986.

Chapman, Abraham, ed. *Literature of the American Indians: Views and Interpretations.* New York: New American Library, 1975.

Charvat, William. *Literary Publishing in America, 1790–1850.* Philadelphia: University of Pennsylvania Press, 1959.

The Profession of Authorship in America, 1790–1850. New York: Columbia University Press, 1992.

Chase, Richard. *The American Novel and Its Tradition.* 1957. Baltimore: Johns Hopkins University Press, 1979.

Chevigny, Bell Gale. *The Woman and the Myth: Margaret Fuller's Life and Writings.* Old Westbury, N. Y.: Feminist Press, 1976.

Cheyfitz, Eric. *The Poetics of Imperialism: Translation and Colonization from the Tempest to Tarzan.* New York: Oxford University Press, 1991.

Clarke, James Freeman. *Autobiography, Diary, and Correspondence.* Edited by Edward Everett Hale. 1891. New York: Negro Universities Press, 1968.

Colacurcio, Michael. *The Province of Piety: Moral History in Hawthorne's Early Tales.* Cambridge, Mass.: Harvard University Press, 1984.

Cott, Nancy. *The Bonds of Womanhood: "Woman's Sphere" in New England, 1780–1835.* New Haven, Conn.: Yale University Press, 1977.

Davis, Charles T., and Henry Louis Gates, Jr., eds. *The Slave's Narrative.* New York: Oxford University Press, 1985.

Diehl, Carl. *Americans and German Scholarship, 1770–1870.* New Haven, Conn.: Yale University Press, 1978.

Douglas, Ann. *The Feminization of American Culture.* New York: Knopf, 1977.

Drinnon, Richard. *Facing West: The Metaphysics of Indian-Hating and Empire Building.* Minneapolis: University of Minnesota Press, 1980.

Dundes, Alan. *Mother Wit from the Laughing Barrel.* Englewood Cliffs, N.J.: Prentice Hall, 1973.

Ellison, Julie. *Delicate Subjects: Romanticism, Gender, and the Ethics of Understanding.* Ithaca, N. Y.: Cornell University Press, 1990.

Epstein, Dena. *Sinful Tunes and Spirituals.* Urbana: University of Illinois Press, 1977.

Feidelson, Charles, Jr. *Symbolism and American Literature.* Chicago: University of Chicago Press, 1953.

Ferguson, Robert. *Law and Letters in American Culture.* Cambridge, Mass.: Harvard University Press, 1984.

Fiedler, Leslie A. *Love and Death in the American Novel.* 1960. Rev. ed. New York: Stein & Day, 1982.

The Return of the Vanishing American. New York: Stein & Day, 1968.

Fisher, Dexter, and Robert B. Stepto. *Afro-American Literature: The Reconstruction of Instruction.* New York: Modern Language Association, 1979.

Fisher, Philip. *Hard Facts: Form and Setting in the American Novel.* New York: Oxford University Press, 1985.

Forgie, George. *Patricide in the House Divided: A Psychological Interpretation of Lincoln and His Age.* New York: Norton, 1979.

Forguson, Lynd. *Common Sense.* London: Routledge, 1989.

Foster, Frances Smith. *Witnessing Slavery: The Development of Antebellum Slave Narratives.* Westport, Conn.: Greenwood, 1979.

Fox-Genovese, Elizabeth. *Within the Plantation Household: Black and White Women of the Old South*. Chapel Hill: University of North Carolina Press, 1988.

Franklin, H. Bruce. *Future Perfect: American Science Fiction of the Nineteenth Century*. New York: Oxford University Press, 1966.

Frederickson, George M. *The Black Image in the White Mind: The Debate on Afro-American Character and Destiny, 1817–1914*. New York: Harper & Row, 1971.

Frei, Hans W. *The Eclipse of Biblical Narrative: A Study in Eighteenth and Nineteenth Century Hermeneutics*. New Haven, Conn.: Yale University Press, 1974.

Fussell, Edwin. *Frontier: American Literature and the American West*. Princeton, N. J.: Princeton University Press, 1965.

Gates, Henry Louis, Jr. *Figures in Black: Words, Signs, and the "Racial Self."* New York: Oxford University Press, 1987.

    The Signifying Monkey. New York: Oxford University Press, 1988.

Genovese, Eugene D. *Roll, Jordan, Roll: The World the Slaves Made*. New York: Pantheon, 1974.

Gilbert, Sandra, and Susan Gubar. *The Madwoman in the Attic: The Woman Writer and the Nineteenth-Century Literary Imagination*. New Haven, Conn.: Yale University Press, 1979.

Gilmore, Michael T. *American Romanticism and the Marketplace*. Chicago: University of Chicago Press. 1985.

Goetzmann, William H. *Exploration and Empire: The Explorer and the Scientist in the Winning of the American West*. New York: Vintage, 1966.

Gonzales-Berry, Erlinda, ed. *Pasó por Aquí: Critical Essays on the New Mexican Literary Tradition, 1542–1988*. Albuquerque: University of New Mexico Press, 1989.

Green, Martin. *The Problem of Boston: Some Readings in Cultural History*. New York: Norton, 1966.

Grimsted, David. *Melodrama Unveiled: American Theater and Culture, 1800–1850*. Chicago: University of Chicago Press, 1968.

Grusin, Richard. *Transcendentalist Hermeneutics: Institutional Authority and the Higher Criticism of the Bible*. Durham, N. C.: Duke University Press, 1991.

Guarneri, Carl J. *The Utopian Alternative: Fourierism in Nineteenth-Century America*. Ithaca, N. Y.: Cornell University Press, 1991.

Harding, Brian. *American Literature in Context (1830–1865)*. London: Methuen, 1982.

Harding, Vincent. *There Is a River: The Black Struggle for Freedom in America*. New York: Harcourt, Brace, Jovanovich, 1981.

Harris, Neil. *Humbug: The Art of P. T. Barnum*. Boston: Little, Brown, 1973.

Hart, James D. *The Popular Book: A History of America's Literary Taste*. Berkeley and Los Angeles: University of California Press, 1961.

Herbst, Jürgen. *The German Historical School in American Scholarship: A Study in the Transfer of Culture*. Ithaca, N. Y.: Cornell University Press, 1965.

Hoffman, Daniel. *Form and Fable in American Fiction*. New York: Oxford University Press, 1965.

Horsman, Reginald. *Race and Manifest Destiny: The Origins of American Racial Anglo-Saxonism*. Cambridge, Mass.: Harvard University Press, 1981.

Horwitz, Howard. *By the Law of Nature: Form and Value in Nineteenth-Century America*. New York: Oxford University Press, 1991.

Horwitz, Morton J. *The Transformation of American Law, 1780–1860*. Cambridge, Mass.: Harvard University Press, 1977.

Howe, Daniel Walker. *The Unitarian Conscience: Harvard Moral Philosophy, 1805–1861*. 2nd ed. Middletown, Conn.: Wesleyan University Press, 1988.

Hubbell, Jay B. *The South in American Literature, 1607–1900*. Durham, N. C.: Duke University Press, 1954.

Hutchison, William R. *The Transcendentalist Ministers: Church Reform in the New England Renaissance*. New Haven, Conn.: Yale University Press, 1959.

Irwin, John T. *American Hieroglyphics: The Symbol of the Egyptian Hieroglyphics in the American Renaissance*. New Haven, Conn.: Yale University Press, 1980.

Jackson, Bruce, ed. *The Negro and His Folklore in Nineteenth-Century Periodicals*. Austin: University of Texas Press, 1967.

Johannsen, Robert W. *To the Halls of the Montezumas: The Mexican War in the American Imagination*. New York: Oxford University Press, 1985.

Kasson, John F. *Civilizing the Machine: Technology and Republican Values in America, 1776–1900*. New York: Grossman, 1976.

Kelley, Mary. *Private Woman, Public Stage: Literary Domesticity in Nineteenth-Century America*. New York: Oxford University Press, 1984.

Kerber, Linda K. *Federalists in Dissent: Imagery and Ideology in Jeffersonian America*. Ithaca, N. Y.: Cornell University Press, 1970.

Kolodny, Annette. *The Land Before Her: Fantasy and Experience of the American Frontiers, 1630–1860*. Chapel Hill: University of North Carolina Press, 1984.

The Lay of the Land: Metaphor as Experience and History in American Life and Letters. Chapel Hill: University of North Carolina Press, 1975.

Kroeber, Karl, ed. *Traditional Native American Literatures*. Lincoln: University of Nebraska Press, 1981.

Krupat, Arnold. *For Those Who Come After: A Study of Native American Autobiography*. Berkeley and Los Angeles: University of California Press, 1985.

The Voice in the Margin: Native American Literature and the Canon. Berkeley and Los Angeles: University of California Press, 1989.

Lawrence, D. H. *Studies in Classic American Literature*. 1923. Garden City, N. Y.: Doubleday, 1951.

Lehmann-Haupt, Helmut. *The Book in America: A History of the Making, the Selling, and the Collecting of Books in the United States*. New York: Bowker, 1939.

Leverenz, David. *Manhood and the American Renaissance*. Ithaca, N. Y.: Cornell University Press, 1989.

Levin, David. *History as Romantic Art: Bancroft, Prescott, Motley and Parkman*. New York: Harcourt, Brace, & World, 1963.

Levin, Harry. *The Power of Blackness: Hawthorne, Poe, Melville*. New York: Knopf, 1958.

Levine, Lawrence W. *Black Culture and Black Consciousness: Afro-American Folk Thought from Slavery to Freedom.* New York: Oxford University Press, 1977.

Lewis, R. W. B. *The American Adam: Innocence, Tragedy, and Tradition in the Nineteenth Century.* Chicago: University of Chicago Press, 1959.

Limon, John. *The Place of Fiction in the Time of Science: A Disciplinary History of American Writing.* Cambridge University Press, 1990.

Lincoln, Kenneth. *Native American Renaissance.* Berkeley and Los Angeles: University of California Press, 1983.

Lovell, John, Jr. *Black Song: The Forge and the Flame.* New York: Macmillan, 1974.

Lynn, Kenneth. *Mark Twain and Southwestern Humor.* 1959. Westport, Conn.: Greenwood, 1972.

Maddox, Lucy. *Removals: Nineteenth-Century American Literature and the Politics of Indian Affairs.* New York: Oxford University Press, 1991.

Martin, Terence. *The Instructed Vision: Scottish Common Sense Philosophy and the Origins of American Fiction.* Bloomington: University of Indiana Press, 1961.

Marx, Leo. *The Machine in the Garden: Technology and the Pastoral Ideal in America.* New York: Oxford University Press, 1964.

Matthiessen, F. O. *American Renaissance: Art and Expression in the Age of Emerson and Whitman.* New York: Oxford University Press, 1941.

McDowell, Deborah, and Arnold Rampersad, eds. *Slavery and the Literary Imagination.* Baltimore: Johns Hopkins University Press, 1989.

McKinsey, Elizabeth R. *The Western Experiment: New England Transcendentalists in the Ohio Valley.* Cambridge, Mass.: Harvard University Press, 1973.

Merk, Frederick. *Manifest Destiny and Mission in American History.* New York: Knopf, 1963.

Michaels, Walter Benn, and Donald Pease, eds. *The American Renaissance Reconsidered.* Baltimore: Johns Hopkins University Press, 1985.

Miller, Perry. *The Life of the Mind in America: From the Revolution to the Civil War.* New York: Harcourt, Brace, 1965.

Nature's Nation. Cambridge, Mass.: Harvard University Press, 1967.

The Raven and the Whale: The War of Words and Wits in the Era of Poe and Melville. New York: Harcourt, Brace, 1956.

Mitchell, Lee Clark. *Witnesses to a Vanishing America: The Nineteenth-Century Response.* Princeton, N. J.: Princeton University Press, 1981.

Moers, Ellen. *Literary Women.* 1977. New York: Oxford University Press, 1985.

Moses, Wilson J. *The Golden Age of Black Nationalism, 1850–1925.* Camden, Conn.: Archon, 1978.

Mott, Frank Luther. *Golden Multitudes: The Story of Best Sellers in the United States.* New York: Macmillan, 1947.

A History of American Magazines, 1741–1850. New York: Appleton, 1930. Republished as Vol. 1 of *A History of American Magazines,* 5 vols., Cambridge, Mass.: Harvard University Press, 1938–68.

Murray, David. *Forked Tongues: Speech, Writing, and Representation in North American Indian Texts.* London: Pinter, 1991.

Myerson, Joel. *The New England Transcendentalists and the "Dial": A History of the*

Magazine and its Contributors. Rutherford, N. J.: Fairleigh Dickinson University Press, 1980.

Nichols, Charles H. *Many Thousands Gone: The Ex-Slaves' Account of Their Bondage and Freedom.* Leiden: Brill, 1963.

Papashvily, Helen. *All the Happy Endings: A Study of the Domestic Novel in America, the Women Who Wrote It, the Women Who Read It, in the Nineteenth Century.* New York: Harper, 1956.

Parrington, Vernon L. *Main Currents in American Thought. Vol. 2, 1800–1860, The Romantic Revolution in America.* New York: Harcourt, Brace, 1927.

Pattee, Fred. *The Feminine Fifties.* New York: Appleton-Century, 1940.

Pearce, Roy Harvey. *Savagism and Civilization.* Baltimore: Johns Hopkins University Press, 1965.

Pease, Donald E. *Visionary Compacts: American Renaissance Writings in Cultural Context.* Madison: University of Wisconsin Press, 1987.

Perry, Lewis. *Radical Abolitionism: Anarchy and the Government of God in Antislavery Thought.* Ithaca, N. Y.: Cornell University Press, 1973.

Pessen, Edward. *Jacksonian America: Society, Personality, and Politics.* 1978. Urbana: University of Illinois Press, 1985.

Porte, Joel. *The Romance in America: Studies in Cooper, Poe, Hawthorne, Melville, and James.* Middletown, Conn.: Wesleyan University Press, 1969.

Potter, David. *The Impending Crisis, 1848–1861.* Edited by Don E. Fehrenbacher. New York: Harper & Row, 1976.

Pryse, Marjorie, and Hortense J. Spillers, eds. *Conjuring: Black Women, Fiction, and Literary Tradition.* Bloomington: Indiana University Press, 1985.

Quinn, Arthur Hobson. *A History of American Drama from the Beginning to the Civil War.* Rev. ed. New York: F. S. Crofts, 1943.

Rawick, George. *From Sundown to Sunup: The Making of the Black Community.* Westport, Conn.: Greenwood, 1972.

Reynolds, David S. *Beneath the American Renaissance: The Subversive Imagination in the Age of Emerson and Melville.* New York: Knopf, 1988.

Reynolds, Larry J. *European Revolutions and the American Literary Renaissance.* New Haven, Conn.: Yale University Press, 1988.

Rogin, Michael Paul. *Fathers and Children: Andrew Jackson and the Subjugation of the American Indian.* New York: Knopf, 1975.

Rourke, Constance. *American Humor: A Study of the National Character.* New York: Harcourt, Brace, 1931.

Rowe, John Carlos. *Through the Custom-House: Nineteenth-Century American Fiction and Modern Theory.* Baltimore: Johns Hopkins University Press, 1982.

Rudolph, Frederick. *Curriculum: A History of the American Undergraduate Course of Study Since 1636.* San Francisco: Jossey-Bass, 1989.

Saldívar, Ramón. *Chicano Narrative: The Dialectics of Difference.* Madison: University of Wisconsin Press, 1990.

Schmitz, Neil. *Of Huck and Alice: Humorous Writing in American Literature.* Minneapolis: University of Minnesota Press, 1983.

Sekora, John, and Darwin T. Turner, eds. *The Art of the Slave Narrative: Original*

Essays in Criticism and Theory. Macomb: Western Illinois University Press, 1982.

Sheehan, Bernard. *Seeds of Extinction: Jeffersonian Philanthropy and the American Indian*. New York: Norton, 1974.

Simpson, David. *The Politics of American English, 1776–1850*. New York: Oxford University Press, 1986.

Slotkin, Richard. *The Fatal Environment: The Myth of the Frontier in the Age of Industrialization, 1800–1890*. New York: Atheneum, 1985.

Regeneration through Violence: The Mythology of the American Frontier, 1600–1860. Middletown, Conn.: Wesleyan University Press, 1974.

Smith, Henry Nash. *Democracy and the Novel: Popular Resistance to Classic American Writers*. Oxford: Oxford University Press, 1978.

Virgin Land: The American West as Symbol and Myth, 1950. Reissued with a new preface, Cambridge, Mass.: Harvard University Press, 1970.

Sollors, Werner. *Beyond Ethnicity: Consent and Descent in American Culture*. New York: Oxford University Press, 1986.

Southern, Eileen. *The Music of Black Americans*. New York: Norton, 1971.

Spencer, Benjamin T. *The Quest for Nationality: An American Literary Campaign*. Syracuse, N. Y.: Syracuse University Press, 1957.

Starling, Marion. *The Slave Narrative: Its Place in American History*. 2nd ed. Boston: G. K. Hall, 1988.

Steele, Jeffrey. *The Representation of the Self in the American Renaissance*. Chapel Hill: University of North Carolina Press, 1987.

Stepto, Robert B. *From Behind the Veil: A Study of Afro-American Narrative*. Urbana: University of Illinois Press, 1979.

Stuckey, Sterling. *Slave Culture: Nationalist Theory and the Foundations of Black America*. New York: Oxford University Press, 1987.

Sundquist, Eric J. *To Wake the Nations: Race in the Making of American Literature*. Cambridge, Mass.: Harvard University Press, 1993.

Swann, Brian, ed. *Smoothing the Ground: Essays on Native American Oral Literature*. Berkeley and Los Angeles: University of California Press, 1983.

Takaki, Ronald T. *Iron Cages: Race and Culture in Nineteenth-Century America*. New York: Oxford University Press, 1979.

Tatum, Charles. *Chicano Literature*. Boston: Twayne, 1982.

Taylor, William R. *Cavalier and Yankee: The Old South and the American National Character*. New York: Doubleday, 1963.

Tebbel, John. *Between Covers: The Rise and Transformation of Book Publishing in America*. New York: Oxford University Press, 1987.

A History of Book Publishing in the United States: Vol. 1, The Creation of an Industry, 1630–1865. New York: Bowker, 1972.

Thomas, Brook. *Cross-Examinations of Law and Literature: Cooper, Hawthorne, Stowe, and Melville*. New York: Oxford University Press, 1987.

Toll, Robert. *Blacking Up: The Minstrel Show in Nineteenth-Century America*. New York: Oxford University Press, 1974.

Tompkins, Jane. *Sensational Designs: The Cultural Work of American Fiction, 1790–1860*. New York: Oxford University Press, 1985.

Tuveson, Ernest. *Redeemer Nation: The Idea of America's Millennial Role*. Chicago: University of Chicago Press, 1971.

Van DeBurg, William L. *Slavery and Race in American Popular Culture*. Madison: University of Wisconsin Press, 1984.

Wall, Cheryl, ed. *Changing Our Own Words: Essays on Criticism, Theory, and Writing by Black Women*. New Brunswick, N. J.: Rutgers University Press, 1989.

Walters, Ronald G. *The Antislavery Appeal: American Abolitionism after 1830*. Baltimore: Johns Hopkins University Press, 1976.

Washburn, Wilcomb. *The Indian in America*. New York: Harper, 1975.

Weisbuch, Robert. *Atlantic Double-Cross: American Literature and British Influence in the Age of Emerson*. Chicago: University of Chicago Press, 1986.

Wellek, René. *Confrontations: Studies in the Intellectual and Literary Relations between Germany, England, and the United States during the Nineteenth Century*. Princeton, N. J.: Princeton University Press, 1965.

Wells, Ronald Vale. *Three Christian Transcendentalists: James Marsh, Caleb Sprague Henry, Frederic Henry Hedge*. 1943. New York: Octagon Books, 1972.

Welter, Rush. *The Mind of America, 1820–1860*. New York: Columbia University Press, 1975.

Wicke, Jennifer. *Advertising Fictions: Literature, Advertisement, and Social Reading*. New York: Columbia University Press, 1988.

Wilson, Edmund. *Patriotic Gore: Studies in the Literature of the Civil War*. New York: Oxford University Press, 1962.

Winters, Yvor. *Maule's Curse: Seven Studies in the History of American Obscurantism: Hawthorne, Cooper, Melville, Poe, Emerson, Jones Very, Emily Dickinson, Henry James*. Norfolk, Conn.: New Directions, 1938.

Wolf, Bryan Jay. *Romantic Re-Vision: Culture and Consciousness in Nineteenth-Century American Painting and Literature*. Chicago: University of Chicago Press, 1982.

Wright, Conrad. *The Beginnings of Unitarianism in America*. Boston: Beacon, 1957.
  The Liberal Christians: Essays on American Unitarian History. Boston: Beacon, 1970.
  ed. *American Unitarianism, 1805–1865*. Boston: Massachusetts Historical Society and Northeastern University Press, 1989.

Yates, Norris Wilson. *William S. Porter and the "Spirit of the Times."* Baton Rouge: Louisiana State University Press, 1957.

Ziff, Larzer. *Literary Democracy: The Declaration of Cultural Independence in America*. New York: Viking, 1981.

INDEX